D0857660

High Treason

High Treason

Essays on the History of the Red Army, 1918–1938 by Vitaly Rapoport and Yuri Alexeev

Vladimir G. Treml, Editor

Bruce Adams, Co-Editor and Translator

Duke University Press   Durham 1985

355
R219

Treason is the most serious crime against the people.
—Constitution of the USSR, 1977, Article 62

Memory, however bitter, be a notch through ages.
—Tvardovsky

Naked truth breeds hatred.—Trediakovsky

Can we not praise the Fatherland without inventing miracles in its honor?
—Anonymous publicist from Orel, eighteenth century

It is vain in years of chaos
To seek a good end.
Some will kill and repent,
Others will end at Golgotha.
—Pasternak

Contents

Author's Preface

A number of people deserve credit for making the publication of this book possible.

I should start by recognizing the special role played by the editor, Professor Vladimir G. Treml. On the long road to the publication of this book his strong support and encouragement were decisive, and I can say without exaggeration that it was primarily due to his efforts that the manuscript reached the printing press.

Professor Bruce F. Adams, coeditor and translator, has done an excellent job of organizing the authors' often disjointed language. I watched his labors with admiration and can only hope that the travail of this book will not discourage him from other translations of Russian works.

It is difficult to find the proper words to express my warmest feeling of gratitude to two courageous and modest women—one American and one Russian—who undertook the risk of taking the manuscript out of the USSR. Regrettably, they must remain unnamed here.

There is another group of people, also to remain unnamed, who have left an important imprint on this book. These are the people who generously provided us with information and sources, often unique, about the events discussed in this book. Our deepest gratitude is extended to them.

And last but not least I must recognize the support and encouragement given me by the National Council for Soviet and East European Research and the Center for Planning and Research and their executive officers, respectively, Vladimir Toumanoff and Richard Laurino.

This preface is written by me alone, for the simple reason that my coauthor, Yuri Alexeev, is in the USSR. Because of the distance and other factors he could not join me in writing this, but, I am certain, he shares the sentiments expressed.

Vitaly Rapoport
New York
January 30, 1985

Editor's Introduction

The phenomenon and the term samizdat are by now well known to the Western reading public. Facing archaic and oppressive censorship, Soviet authors have circulated their manuscripts in typewritten form throughout the country. Since the late 1950s, these manuscripts have made their way to Western publishers in ever-increasing numbers. However, by far the largest share of samizdat smuggled out of the USSR and published in the West consists of belles lettres, memoirs, and a genre of eyewitness stories. Unfortunately, little of substance has appeared of scholarly or scientific literature. This is not too surprising. Novelists, poets, memoir writers—even under oppressive Soviet conditions—can write in relative safety in the privacy of their homes. Historians, philosophers, economists, and sociologists find themselves in a much more restricted situation as they seek access to libraries, laboratories, special data banks, archives, and the like, where the very nature of their interest or topic, and the absence of an official imprimatur, make access difficult if not impossible.

There are, of course, some exceptions, particularly in a broadly defined genre of social commentary and in historical writing; but unfortunately there are very few.

The Rapoport–Alexeev book is one such exception: A set of carefully researched and documented essays on the history of the Red Army. The book is not an eyewitness account of clashes between the military and the Party, or of purges of Red Army commanders, nor is it a memoir, as neither of the authors was directly involved in the described events.

Vitaly Rapoport was born in Dnepropetrovsk in the Ukraine in 1937. As a young boy he survived the German invasion and the ravages of his homeland. His father was fortunate to survive, so his family was not destroyed by the war as were so many others. But, as were many others in the generation that survived the war, Vitaly Rapoport was haunted by persistent questions raised by the early defeats of the Red Army, by the country's devastating losses. Although trained in engineering and management, Rapoport continued to pursue his true interest—history. In the early 1970s he met a person with a similar and equally strong interest, Alexeev. Since Alexeev—a pseudonym —is still living in the USSR, we cannot say much about him, except to indicate that he is somewhat older than Rapoport.

The two men collaborated in research and study and wrote the book, which was completed in 1977. In the late 1970s the manuscript was smuggled out of the Soviet Union by a young American student who, although known to the editor, must remain unnamed. But both authors acknowledge with gratitude this person's courageous help.

Rapoport came to the United States in 1980 and now lives in New York with his family.

How does one write a history book exploring issues the government would not want explored, discussing personalities that libraries would not want to admit existed?

As the reader will see, the authors went meticulously through available historical and periodical literature. The authors also availed themselves of samizdat manuscripts circulating in the country—see, for example, the story of Mironov. One way or another they also got hold of some historical works published in the West, but these were clearly not among their major sources. Some events described in the book —for instance, the kidnapping of General Kutepov in Paris—are obviously based on such Western sources and, as obviously, suffer because the authors could not find more comprehensive and more scholarly works. The authors were fortunate to be able to talk to many contemporaries of described events, and in some instances to relatives of some of the military personnel depicted in the book, and to read the notes and incomplete memoirs of some others. They also had opportunities to examine documents in restricted archives. For easily understood reasons these interviews and archival documents cannot be fully footnoted and referenced.

Western experts must make their own judgments as to the authenticity of this book based largely on its contents. Obviously, the authors know a great deal about Soviet military history. It is quite possible that some of the events that we learn from this book did not happen quite that way. Perhaps we shall never know, but the evidence presented here is as good as we are likely to obtain in the foreseeable future. After a careful reading of the original Russian-language text, after consultation with Western authorities on Soviet military history and discussions with the author Rapoport, I am convinced of this document's authenticity and of its importance to scholars.

The book carries the reader through the formation of the "Red Army of Workers and Peasants," the Civil War, the growing role of the Communist Party in matters not only of ideology but of military doctrine and strategy, the modernization of the early 1930s to the devastating purges of the end of the decade and their tragic consequences in the early part of the war.

Western readers are familiar with many events and developments described in the book, but the reliability of original sources of historical writing in the West on this subject matter is not uniform. Some events have been well researched, documented, and analyzed while others have been only roughly sketched out in sources of varying reliability and in different monographs. In particular, no single history of the early days of the Red Army has been published in the West. In this respect, the Rapoport and Alexeev book is invaluable, as it brings together the early history in a single, well-integrated narrative. The book also brings to light new facts and offers new interpretations of known developments, such as Stalin's role in the Polish campaign, early purges of Soviet military academicians and theoreticians, and the role played by Stalin's cronies from Civil War days.

The book also offers numerous fascinating anecdotes—most of them unverifiable but credible. We find described here such events as an abortive attempt by security forces to arrest Stalin's Civil War crony Budenny, details of the elimination of the security head Ezhov, Voroshilov's endless blunders, the story of the absence of Blucher from the bench of judges in the first major trial of top military commanders. Parenthetically, we should note that most Western historians concluded that there was no trial and that the accused, including Marshal Tukhachevsky, were shot immediately after the arrest. Rapoport and Alexeev offer conclusive evidence that the trial did indeed take place, although the defendants were judged guilty and the sentences determined prior to the trial.

The book differs from most dissident literature by focusing on the damage inflicted by Stalin on the Red Army. The many historical sketches of military leaders of the period and the detailed discussions of military strategy indicate that the authors are directing their book to an audience of professional military people and others with an interest in military history. The book is very sympathetic to the Red Army military professionals and hostile to the political party and the political generals of the period. Professional military leaders making contributions to the strategy, operations, organizations, and training of the Red Army are generally treated as heroes and patriots. The complicity of many of these officers in repressive measures of the Party against the people is generally passed over without comment (as in the case of Tukhachevsky). However, high-ranking officers close to Stalin are generally treated with disdain. The authors leave no doubt about their belief that the Army leaders of the period could have and should have taken action to resist Stalin's purge of the officer corps.

The authors somewhat exaggerate the capabilities of the Army of this period. They characterize the Army as "strong enough to face any enemy. It is impossible to imagine that the [Red Army] would have surrendered half the country to Hitler" in the absence of the purge of the officer corps. While the purge undoubtedly weakened the Red Army, many experts would be skeptical of these claims about the Red Army's capabilities, since the relatively inexperienced Red Army would still have had to face a battle-tested German army that had the initial advantages of timing and other conditions in the attack.

On the other hand, the Red Army had considerable strengths, including outstanding theorists, before the Stalinist purges. But a more detached historian would have at least raised the possibility that the poor performance and morale of the troops could also be explained by the fact that the majority of soldiers in 1941 and 1942 were young peasants with vivid memories of the brutality and harshness of forced collectivization. Of course, the collectivization was directed by Stalin and the Party, but the leaders of the Red Army—Tukhachevsky, Yakir, Blucher, and others—carry some of the responsibility.

The authors attempt to answer perhaps the most significant question relating to these events: Why did the accused leaders (both political and military) not resist more effectively the repressions of Stalin? For the political leaders, the authors suggest that they were so closely identified with the Bolshevik Party and its bloody rule after the Civil War that they basically "had no path back to the people."

The Army leaders were in a stronger position. They had command of the military forces; and as the authors suggest, the Army could win any conflict with the police forces. Yet they made no effort at rebellion against the Party. In addition to a failure of moral courage, the authors contend that there were other factors. They suggest that Yakir was a true idealist and believer in the revolutionary cause. He could not attack Stalin without attacking the Party and the cause, which were dearer to him than his safety. They suggest another set of motives for Tukhachevsky. He was supposedly very egocentric. Since all his honors and position flowed from the Party and the system, he could not attack them without destroying the things he loved most.

The authors provide many chapters describing the historical development of the Red Army and clearly indicate what they consider to be good and bad in the officer corps. In keeping with recent Soviet scholarship about the Civil War, the authors give primacy to the Red Army (RKKA) activities on the Eastern Front over the more publicized activities on the Western Front. The Eastern Front "was the furnace in which the RKKA was forged." It was here that the commanders who formed the real professional core of the RKKA in the postwar period were developed. These included I. I. Vatsetis and S. S. Kamenev, both commanders-in-chief during the Civil War, and emerging leaders, such as M. V. Frunze and M. N. Tukhachevsky.

In contrast, the authors denigrate the reputation of some commanders and units that emerged during the Civil War. Their greatest disdain is reserved for the leadership of the First Horse Army—a unit "sacrosanct in Soviet military history." In popular memory "only the [exploits] of the 30,000-strong Horse Army have been preserved." The authors indicate that in the 1920s and 1930s the officers of this unit "dominated the leadership of the armed forces" to the detriment of both strategic concepts and readiness for war. During the period between the end of the Civil War and the beginning of the "Fatherland War" cavalry leaders running the Red Army included K. E. Voroshilov (1925–40), S. K. Timoshenko (1940–41), and A. A. Grechko. Marshal Grechko was minister of defense from 1967 to 1976. Others reaching deputy ministerial rank included S. M. Budenny, G. I. Kulik, and others who ultimately proved inadequate: "Only when actual combat began [Fatherland War] was the unfitness of [these leaders] revealed."

The major debunking of Stalin's military reputation concerns his behavior immediately before and during the Fatherland War. In addition to having almost fatally weakened the Army through the purge of the military leadership, Stalin is pictured as not being alert to the imminence of a German attack in 1941 and exhibiting a lack of understanding of the proper strategy for meeting such an assault.

The authors cite evidence that Soviet intelligence first obtained information about preparations to attack the USSR "only a few days after the German general staff began to work on it." Throughout the period of about a year during which preparations were being made, information continued to flow in from many sources, including Richard Zorge, the Soviet master spy. This information was not acted upon, primarily because a "fear of war paralyzed Stalin." The authors are convinced that he "feared war, primarily because he felt his own incapacity as a leader. He also understood that the real military leaders had been destroyed at his personal orders." Statements attributed to Khrushchev in *Khrushchev Remembers* tend to confirm this view. Stalin knew as a result of the Finnish War that the Army was not ready to fight a first-class adversary.

Having revealed the crimes of Stalin and his henchmen, the authors reflect on the fact that the guilt must be shared by everyone in the Soviet Union. They indicate that "there is something not quite right with ourselves . . . . It is toleration of evil and submissiveness to unjust authority." In a chapter entitled "Personality and History" the authors reject the notion that Stalin was the critical determinant of Soviet post-revolutionary development. "The system gave birth to Stalin. Not otherwise." Lenin had concentrated power at the center and had allowed the development of a powerful *Apparat* that under Stalin would crush the Party. The people's willingness to accept strong leadership together with "insignificant development of legal consciousness, service docility . . . greatly increased the chances that such a personality would emerge."

The authors believe it was unlikely that other leaders could have acted much differently from Stalin and still retained power. However, the authors make a call for greatness in each individual: "Even if we accept the existence of historical predestination, still every statesman, every man in general, has the choice to be a weapon of the inevitable or not." The authors see hope only in purging the past by telling the full truth. "The spiritual rebirth of the country is impossible while evil remains hidden away, unjudged, while the triumphant lie paralyzes our will, devours our soul, and lulls our conscience."

In this manner, the authors end their history of the Red Army. They have provided a document that could have an impact both in the Soviet Union and in the West. In particular, the document illuminates political–military relationships of the past and provides important insights into the future.

The polemical style of the text may bother some readers who are used to a more detached and balanced narrative. But here lies one of the fascinating aspects of the book, and the constant presence of the emotional dimension of the unfolding tragic events has a cumulative impact upon the reader.

A Western scholar also will find some weaknesses and shortcomings in the book—both in style and substance.

The treatment of some events and the analysis of some developments, particularly of a political and economic nature, is oversimplified and somewhat naive. For example, modernization of the Red Army and creation of the modern defense industry in the early 1930s is discussed against the background of rapid industrialization launched by the first Five-Year Plan and forced collectivization. The cost of collectivization was enormous: ten million human lives by Stalin's own admission as well as huge losses of livestock. However, Western readers will probably find the authors' description and analysis of collectivization simplistic, naive, and somewhat exaggerated. Both Western and Soviet scholarship today offer a somewhat more balanced view.

The most significant aspect of this powerful and angry book is that it was fully researched, documented, and written in the USSR* and thus offers us a picture of the attitudes, knowledge, and understanding of history by a segment of the Soviet public. Among other things, it shows that the omnipotent Soviet censor has not been particularly successful in suppressing or distorting events in history.

High Treason is not a definitive history of the Red Army and the Party and Stalin's role in its development. Such a definitive book cannot and will not be written for a long time. But it offers us an important new and comprehensive picture of this history, and it offers us invaluable insights into the understanding and knowledge of this history by the Soviet public.

Vladimir G. Treml
Duke University
April 1985

---

*It must be stressed that except for a few corrections and the addition of some editorial explanatory notes, the text is as it was when carried out of the USSR. The translator has deliberately not edited out the non-English-speaker style of the Russian authors.

Prologue

On the Eve of Catastrophe

This is what they said before their execution.

Army Commander Ion Yakir: "Long live Stalin!"

Marshall Mikhail Tukhachevsky: "You are shooting not us, but the Red Army."

Both proved to be prophets. Stalin reigned another decade and a half, and in the year or two after Tukhachevsky's death the high command of the Red Army was destroyed almost to a man, losses unthinkable in the heaviest military campaign. Men who had created the Red Army, who had led it to victory in the Civil War and had turned it into the best army in Europe, fell victim to this Bartholomew's Night.

A short while later, German tanks roared to the outskirts to Moscow, while Stalin, "the most brilliant commander of all times and all nations," feverishly considered plans to save himself.

Almost twenty years had to pass before the destruction of our Army was recognized as a crime. And no one was ever punished. The greater part of the facts and details have not been publicized, nor has anything been said to this day about how it could have happened.

To remain silent about the destruction of the Red Army is to abuse the memory of the innocent dead. To be silent is to betray the interests of the Motherland. Without the publication of such tragic events — without a merciless analysis of them — it is impossible to reach conclusions vital to us, to our children, and to our grandchildren. Without such an analysis, there is no reason to study history.

Our aim is not to call for revenge or retribution. It is not yet in our power to give an exhaustive historical analysis. That will be the task of our descendants who will have the necessary documents. This is a history of what is already known, although not known with absolute certainty.

This book is awkward and confused, with many gaps and much vagueness; it does not claim to be academic. It can be only a reminder of a great tragedy. It is a small stone at the foundation of a future memorial to the Army that was shot in the back.

1 Assembly on Nikolskaia

Nikolskaia Street is especially rich in historical monuments.

—A Moscow tour guide, 1903[1]

The incident with which we begin our story occurred on Nikolskaia Street, the oldest street in the Kremlin settlement, Kitaigorod. It was along this street, already seven centuries old, that the roads to Vladimir, Suzdal, and Rostov Veliky (the Great) once led from the Nikolskie Gates of the Kremlin.

The air here is filled with Russian history. Moscow's oldest monastery was built on Nikolskaia in the thirteenth century; Russia's first book was printed there in the sixteenth century; it was along Nikolskaia that Prince Pozharsky pushed the retreating Poles back to the Kremlin; some seventy years later Russia's first institution of higher learning opened on Nikolskaia.

From ancient times Nikolskaia had been a center for monasteries and cathedrals, for bookish wisdom and bustling commerce. In the middle of the last century it was one of the main business streets of the city. "Home after home, door after door, window after window, everything from top to bottom was hung with signs, covered with signs as if with wallpaper," wrote Kokorev in his memoirs.[2] At the turn of the century it was filled with expensive commercial buildings. It was the first street in Moscow to be paved with asphalt.

In the days of the October Revolution the street saw battles between the Reds and cadets. Under War Communism it fell briefly quiet, but with the advent of the New Economic Policy (NEP) it once again hummed with trade and commerce. As before, it teemed with warehouses, stores, and offices. But a change in its fate was already creeping upon it, standing in the wings. The Slaviansky Bazaar had already been given into the care of various Soviet organizations headed by *Osoaviakhim*.[3] A famous hotel, in whose restaurant Russian composers had feted Dvořák, closed its doors. Stanislavsky had sat there with Nemirovich over wine and hors d'oeuvres for more than a day discussing the founding of the Khudozhestvenny (Art) Theater. The upper rows of shops, more than a quarter of a kilometer long, glass-roofed, built in the old Russian style, was turned into GUM, the State Universal Store. Tsentroarkhiv was moved into the Holy Synod's Press, Chizhovsky Court became quarters for the Revolutionary Military Council. But these were just minor changes.

The year 1932 brought the reconstruction of Moscow, which struck Nikolskaia no less forcefully or painfully than earlier fires. Its former name was lost; it became 25 October Street. At the same time many of its remarkable buildings were razed. The Kazan Cathedral with its miraculous icon of the Kazan Mother of God disappeared. In place of the cathedral, which had been erected by Prince Pozharsky to mark the end of the Polish invasion, there is now a lawn and a public toilet. Practically nothing remains of the Zaikonospassky monastery, in which Simeon Polotsky had founded the first higher ecclesiastic school in 1682, the Greek-Slavic-Latin Academy. The great Lomonosov, the mathematician Magnitsky, the poets Kantemir and Trediakovsky, the geographer Krasheninnikov had all studied there. The founder of the Academy had been buried in the sacristy amid the magnificent church valuables.

The ancient buildings of the Nikolsky Greek monastery with its two churches and the chapel that held the miraculous icon of St. Nicholas the Miracle-worker also disappeared. The monastery had been founded by Ivan the Terrible. Kantemir was buried in its walls.

The Bogoiavlensky monastery, founded in 1276 under Prince Danil, was destroyed. Of its five temples only one, the Bogoiavlensky cathedral, survived. It became home for some shops and now stands without its cupola, chipped and peeling, deteriorating before one's eyes. In the 1920s a Soviet guidebook called it "one of the finest creations of Moscow baroque. Its stone fretwork is so light and delicate that it gives the impression of lacework. Within the cathedral there are sculpted images ('the coronation of the Mother of God'), which are a great rarity in Moscow's Orthodox churches." Not a trace remained of the Lower Kazan church of the monastery, which had enclosed the burial vault of the Golitsyn princes, "a whole museum, beautifully representing the whole development of Russian sculpture of the eighteenth century."[4]

The walls of Kitai-gorod with the Vladimir gates and the nearby cathedral of the Vladimir Mother of God were destroyed. Now the way was clear from the Kremlin to the Lubianka (Dzerzhinsky Square), from the location of the Soviet government to the home of its main organ, the organ of security.

But the historical role of Nikolskaia had not ended. At its far end on the left side, facing away from the Kremlin and beyond the Ferrein pharmacy, there remained an unimposing three-story building, that of the Central Military Procuracy. Built in 1830, it was famous only for the fact that Stankevich had lived there a long while and Belinsky had been a frequent visitor. On the morning of May 11, 1937, a meeting began in that building. The ranks and responsibilities of the men who met there suggest that this was a meeting of the highest military leaders of the country: Deputy People's Commissars of Defense, the Chief of the General Staff, military district (*okrug*) commanders, department chiefs of the People's Commissariat, four of the five Marshals of the Soviet Union, all four Army Commanders First-Class, a Flag Officer of the Fleet First-Class, four Army Commanders Second-Class, and others.

If a few details are added, the picture changes. A meeting was going on, but it was the sort of meeting that military officers have only rarely to attend. One group, in full dress uniform, was seated at a long table. The second group, in military uniforms from which all decorations and medals had been torn, sat behind a barrier.

It seems natural now that Military Jurist of the Army First-Class V. V. Ulrikh, Chairman of the Military College of the Supreme Court of the USSR, sat at the head of the table. He is a famous man: in the 1920s he had chaired the trial of Savinkov; just recently, in August 1936 and January 1937, he had conducted the infamous "Moscow trials" with Vyshinsky.[5] His colleagues at this meeting were: Army Commander Second-Class Ia I. Alksnis, Deputy People's Commissar and Commander of the Air Force (vvs); Marshal V. K. Blucher, Commander of the Separate Far Eastern Army of the Order of the Red Banner; Marshal S. M. Budenny, Deputy People's Commissar and Inspector of the Cavalry; Division Commander E. I. Goriachev, Commander of the Sixth Cossack Cavalry Corps named for Comrade Stalin; Army Commander Second-Class P. I. Dybenko, commanding the Leningrad Military District; Army Commander Second-Class N. D. Kashirin, commanding the North Caucasus Military District; Army Commander First-Class B. M. Shaposhnikov, Deputy People's Commissar and Chief of the General Staff. Of the eight military judges, seven, unlike Ulrikh, were new in their roles and uncomfortable, possibly from lack of experience. All of them were illustrious commanders of the Red Army and among its distinguished organizers.

The same is true to an even greater degree of those on trial. One has only to leaf through any history of the Civil War published before 1937 or after 1956 to find their names, usually linked with the most complimentary epithets. There were eight of them also: A. I. Kork, Army Commander Second-Class, Superintendent of the Frunze Academy; Corps Commander V. M. Primakov, deputy commander of the Leningrad Military District; Corps Commander V. K. Putna, military attaché in England; Marshal M. N. Tukhachevsky, until May 11, 1937, the First Deputy People's Commissar and Chief of Combat Preparedness of the Red Army (RKKA), and until May 26, commander of the Volga Military District; Army Commander First-Class I. P. Uborevich, commander of the Belorussian Military District; Corps Commander B. M. Feldman, chief of the Central Administration (*Glavnoe upravlenie*) of the RKKA; Corps Commander R. P. Eideman, chairman of *Osoaviakhim*; Army Commander First-Class I. E. Yakir, commander of the Kiev Military District.

Except for the People's Commissar, Marshal K. E. Voroshilov, the whole high command of the Red Army was present. Several observers were as highly ranked as the others present: Marshal A. I. Egorov, Deputy People's Commissar, who was responsible for maintaining order in the court; Flag Officer of the Fleet First-Class V. M. Orlov, Deputy People's Commissar and Commander of the Navy; Division Commander M. F. Lukin, Military Commandant of the City of Moscow.

Despite the similarity of titles and service records of the judges and the defendants there was an important difference between them, one that had been noted long before. Those on trial were the cream of the Army intelligentsia, authors of fundamental scholarly works, pathbreakers of new ways to organize the Army, and pioneers of new methods of armed combat. The others, with the exception of Shaposhnikov and Alksnis, were intrepid warriors and swashbucklers, strangers to theoretical research, reactionaries and careerists. Although they were all exceptionally brave men, their intellectual levels were clearly unequal, and their views on the majority of military questions were diametrically opposed. We will show below that the composition of the two groups was not accidental and that it was not only disagreements about the future development of the Army that led them to this hall.

June 11, 1937. Some of the leaders judged, others were judged. In a relatively short time most of the judges lost their lives in similar circumstances. For some this happened in just a few months, for others in a year or two. It is possible that some of them sensed what would happen. But we had better not jump ahead.

Why were the honored commanders being tried? It is still hard for us four decades later to answer that question. Contemporaries were in an even more difficult position. The following announcement appeared in the papers that day:

> IN THE PROCURACY OF THE USSR
>
> The case of those arrested at various times by the NKVD [there followed the names of those now familiar to us]. . . . They are accused of violating their military oaths, of treason against the Motherland, of treason against the peoples of the USSR, of treason against the RKKA.
>
> Investigative materials have established the participation of the accused, and also of Ia. B. Gamarnik, now deceased by suicide, in antigovernment associations with leading military circles of a foreign state, which conducts an unfriendly policy toward the USSR. In the service of the military intelligence of that state, the accused systematically provided military circles with information about the condition of the Red Army, carried out acts of sabotage to weaken the strength of the Red Army, attempted to ensure the defeat of the Red Army in case of a military attack on the USSR, and had as their goal the reestablishment of the power of landlords and capitalists in the USSR.
>
> All of the accused admitted their full guilt to charges against them.
>
> The case will be heard today in a closed session of the Special Court of the Military College of the Supreme Court of the USSR: [there followed the composition of the court].
>
> The case will be heard in accordance with the law of December 1, 1934.

That was all Soviet citizens could learn from the papers. This was the only announcement to appear about the trial.

We will refrain for the time being from an analysis of the document, but we note the obvious roughness of the style, which permits us to surmise that it was hastily written. We will summarize briefly the main points. The accused were agents of foreign intelligence (espionage and subversive activity). They conspired to cause the defeat of the country in war and the overthrow of the government (treason against the state). The sentence, in all probability, would be passed that very day; the phrase, "the case will be heard today," suggests this. Otherwise it would have read "will begin." The reference to the law of December 1, which provided for accelerated procedure for trials of enemies of the people, supports this interpretation.

And that is how it was. The sentences were passed on June 11 and carried out that day and the next. The trial was not covered in the press—not then, not later. Therefore the public, and inner party circles as well, remained ignorant of it. In this way in just a few hours the flower of the command of our Army was condemned without appeal.

Let us try to reconstruct the trial. The information we will use is fragmentary and exists only in accounts transmitted by word of mouth. Not all can be verified. Although sometimes we will have to deal with myths, we will not scorn them. Our people are necessarily great creators of myths, because much of our history is concealed from us. Myths are not arbitrary fabrications: their foundations are real; and in this case, more often than not they are bloody.

The trial began at 10:00 A.M. The charges were as imprecise as in the newspaper, although more involved. No documents or other material evidence was introduced at the trial.

The charges against three of the accused are well known. Tukhachevsky: organization of a revolution to overthrow the government, association with German intelligence, and moral degradation (this is what a weakness for the fair sex is usually called in official papers).

Yakir was also accused of attempting to overthrow Soviet power and of associating with Germans. In his case there were specific details, but they were not entirely clear. Yakir was incriminated by association with his subordinate D. A. Shmidt, who had been arrested in 1936. Shmidt had been commander of what was then the only heavy tank brigade in the RKKA. According to one story, Yakir ordered Shmidt to keep the brigade prepared to move against Moscow. In another version he ordered Shmidt to destroy his equipment or to render it useless. It is unclear which of these accusations was brought against the Army Commander. All that is known is that Shmidt, according to the People's Commissar of the NKVD, made both statements, or rather signed them.

Uborevich was accused, in part, of intentionally having left breaches in the border defenses of Belorussia, the construction of which he had overseen, to make it easier for the enemy to break through. It is true that there were breaks in the line, but these were related to local conditions. In the area of Pinsk, for example, defensive works, moved back behind impenetrable swamps, were of course strengthened. When Shaposhnikov, a member of the court, asked Uborevich why the defenses had been moved, however, Chairman Ulrikh disallowed it as a leading question.

So far as we know, the other defendants were charged with working for German intelligence and deliberately weakening the combat strength of the Red Army.

All eight pleaded not guilty to all charges. In the surviving typed report of the trial their "noes" were changed in ink to "yeses." An exception was made only for Tukhachevsky, who refused to answer any further questions. The other seven continued to deny everything during the interrogation. Toward the end of the session Yakir, who was known for his unparalleled bravery and self-control, could not restrain himself. He shouted at his former comrades-in-arms, "Look me in the eyes! Can you really not understand that this is all lies?" Primakov, who was sitting beside him, tried to restrain him, "Give it up, Ion. Don't you see who we are dealing with here?" Yakir asked nonetheless for paper and wrote letters to Stalin and Voroshilov.

Several members of the court became unwell during the proceedings. Shaposhnikov, who tried with his question to give Uborevich a chance to acquit himself, clearly felt uncomfortable. Blucher claimed to be indisposed and left the hall. He was absent for most of the interrogations but returned before sentence was passed.

Budenny, on the other hand, was unrelenting. In the course of the session he sent a report to People's Commissar Voroshilov, in which he called the defendants "all swine" and "enemies" and complained that none had confessed. This report has been preserved.

By two o'clock it was all over. The sentence, which could not be appealed, was the same for all: capital punishment. The convicts were led away to Lubianka.

Army Commander Yakir was shot that day. The others were shot at dawn on June 12. Their bodies were taken to Khodynka to a place where construction work was going on. In an area cordoned off by soldiers of the Red Army they were dumped into a trench, covered by quicklime, and buried.[6]

A quarter century earlier the field camp of the Aleksandrovsky Cadet Academy, at which Tukhachevsky had studied, was located at Khodynka.

2 Discord in the Face of Danger

In 1936 Mikhail Tukhachevsky reached the peak of his service career. On April 4 he was appointed First Deputy People's Commissar of Defense and Chief of Combat Preparedness of the RKKA. Events preceding these promotions testify to the steady rise of Tukhachevsky's official position and of his influence. In the summer of 1931 he had become Deputy People's Commissar and Chairman of the Revolutionary Military Council, and Chief of Ordinance of the RKKA. On February 21, 1933, he was awarded the Order of Lenin, and on November 7 it was he who reviewed the parade of troops on Red Square—a rare distinction, as that was usually done by the People's Commissar. At the Seventeenth Congress of the Communist Party in 1934 Tukhachevsky delivered a speech and was elected candidate member of the Central Committee. In November 1935, when personal military ranks were reintroduced, Tukhachevsky was among the first five to receive the highest rank, Marshal of the Soviet Union. He traveled to England in February 1936 to attend the funeral of King George V and successfully carried out his mission, which went beyond simply representing the Soviet Union. The forty-year-old marshal and the film he presented on massive airborne landing impressed the English. Even skeptics like General Bell acknowledged they were impressed by Tukhachevsky's pet forces, the airborne troops. On his return trip Tukhachevsky stopped in Paris for talks with General M. G. Gamelin, the chief of the French general staff. Soon after his return he was appointed to another high post, which had been created especially for him.

All was well, it would seem. But behind the scenes, where so much that is important in Russian affairs takes place, things were not so rosy. The problem was that Stalin had never particularly liked Tukhachevsky. During the struggle for power he had forced Tukhachevsky to accept a demotion from his post as chief-of-staff of the RKKA to command the Leningrad Military District. When he had consolidated his power, Stalin permitted Tukhachevsky to return to the central apparatus of the People's Commissariat and even to move higher. We cannot know with absolute certainty what Stalin's logic or motives may have been; but we can make educated suppositions, which the reader will find in the third part of the book.

In 1931 Tukhachevsky was brought back from his three-year exile in Leningrad. In his new role he quickly became exceptionally and productively active. He initiated, defended, and supported the development of new weapons that later became the basis of the Red Army's strength. The most modern airplanes; the T-34, which turned out to be the best tank in the Second World War; airborne troops; unique research and pioneering work in radar, rocketry, and jet-propelled weaponry, all were among the fruits of this work. We are omitting details because all of this is elaborated in memoirs and other historical literature. What is important for us is that Tukhachevsky worked in this field not because he was enchanted by the technology, but because the technical equipment of the army was a necessary condition for the military doctrine he preached. Tukhachevsky had propounded the theory of deep battle and operations in the early 1920s. Over the following decade the theory had been developed and worked out in detail by a group of his young colleagues. The greatest credit for the final formulation of the doctrine belongs to V. K. Triandafillov and his colleagues in the First (operational) Directorate of the RKKA General Staff, among whom G. S. Isserson stands out.

In just a few years Tukhachevsky had achieved a great deal. At the Seventeenth Party Congress the fiery People's Commissar Voroshilov had proclaimed, "The basic tasks of reconstructing our army have now been accomplished." In 1933 for every Red Army infantryman there were 7.74 horsepower. This figure was higher than that for the French, American, or even the English army, which was the most mechanized of that time. Of course we ought not rely too heavily on statistics from ceremonial speeches. In the same speech Voroshilov, sagaciously looking back sixteen years, spoke in favor of the horse, since at the end of the First World War there had been over a million of them in the French army, about 880,000 in the German, and in the tsarist army 1,142,000!

While Voroshilov was showing off, firing his pistol from the rostrum for effect, Tukhachevsky and colleagues were creating a new army. In two of the most important military districts, the Ukraine and Belorussia, Yakir and Uborevich boldly introduced new principles for training troops and worked out totally new forms of coordination of land and air units. The Ukrainian maneuvers of 1935, and especially of 1936, provoked unconcealed admiration among foreign military observers and shook up military thinking in all of Europe, setting it off in a new direction. At the same time a strong fortified line was being constructed along the western and southern borders of the USSR.

Whatever other military problems Tukhachevsky may have set his mind to, he always remained principally a strategist. Problems of strategic and operational arts were always his favorite food for thought. In the eyes of western specialists Tukhachevsky was first of all a strategist. His turning maneuver around Warsaw in 1920 was highly regarded, despite the failure of the operation as a whole. Even in 1936, while he was hurriedly preparing the field manual of the RKKA, Tukhachevsky also prepared a new edition of his *New Questions of War*, which had first been published in 1932.[1] That manuscript is apparently buried in the bowels of the NKVD.

According to G. S. Isserson, "in strategic matters Tukhachevsky stood head and shoulders above many representatives of the higher command of the Red Army." But in the mid-1930s he "did not have direct access to the plan for the strategic deployment of our armed forces, which was worked out in the General Staff." The cadres decided everything. That is why at the head of the General Staff Stalin had put Marshal Egorov, whom he knew from the time of the Civil War to be obedient and loyal. Egorov also had a skeleton in his closet, which Stalin might use. Tukhachevsky did not have this merit and therefore could not be admitted.

From the time the fascists came to power Tukhachevsky intently followed developments in Germany. In his work, *Military Plans of Contemporary Germany*,[2] he pointed out that the accelerated militarization of the country seriously imperiled peace on the continent. Time was on Hitler's side. His first aim would be to conquer France, but he also posed a major threat to the USSR. In 1935, with the Wehrmacht's strength grown to 849,000, Tukhachevsky warned that the USSR, with a population two-and-a-half times as large as Germany's, had an army of only 940,000.

Tukhachevsky's strategy was always offensive—"smashing" (*sokrushenie*). Now he had urgently to rethink how he could change his strategy to employ it effectively against an enemy that itself tore into battle. That Hitler would attack he had no doubt. Moreover, the attack would come suddenly. Norbert Wiener once noted that in peacetime it is impossible to determine the fitness of generals for the next war.

Today those who were successful in the most recent war seem good, while those who had successfully led in the previous war are considered obsolete.[3] Tukhachevsky was a very ambitious man, but he did not delude himself about his powers. He did not hope to divine the course—or even the character—of the coming war. Only the opening phases of a war could be predicted, as they were largely determined by the features and factors of peacetime. In his article "The Nature of Border Fighting," Tukhachevsky repudiated the generally accepted idea of "concentrating massed armies at the borders by railroad" because of the vulnerability of railroads to air attack.[4] For the same reason he had to discard the old schemes of mobilization and concentration of armies.

Not long before, Tukhachevsky had refuted the idea of A. A. Svechin, the outstanding military writer, that it would be advantageous to fight a strategic defense ("exhaustion"—*izmor*). Events in Europe suggest that Svechin was right.

New views require verification. But how can new concepts of warfare be checked out short of going to war? There is a way, however imperfect it might be: war games, or as it is more commonly called now, simulation, reproducing the conditions of war. Toward the end of 1935 Tukhachevsky proposed that the General Staff conduct war games. His idea was accepted, and the games took place in November 1936. They have been mentioned in print only twice. The first article was by G. S. Isserson, whom we have already mentioned, then a brigade commander and actual director of the Operation Directorate of the General Staff, as well as head of the operations faculty of the General Staff Academy. Isserson worked up the assignments for the games. The second article came from the pen of A. I. Todorsky, who in 1936 was superintendent of the Air Force Academy.[5] Corps Commander Todorsky commanded an air group (*aviasoedinenie*) for the "German" side in the games.

The western front of the "Red" forces was comanded by Uborevich, the "German" forces by Tukhachevsky, the "Poles" by Yakir. In setting the conditions of the games the General Staff tried to base them on the current military-political situation in Europe without trying to peer into the future. The German forces were estimated on the basis of the mobilization formula of 3:1, the existence of thirty-six divisions in the Wehrmacht, inexact information about the formation of three tank divisions, and an air force that had at its disposal four to five thousand planes. (When the real war began, Germany was able to put one hundred divisions under arms and sent fifty to fifty-five against the USSR in the regions where the games were conducted. The Poles contributed another twenty.) The Kremlin strategists had learned their political lessons well and understood that the capitalists, imperialists, and fascists were one gang. If they weren't for us, they must be against us. The Poles therefore had no choice but to cooperate with the Germans and to attack the USSR together.[6]

Even an intelligent and subtle writer like Isserson defended this prognosis eighteen years after the Second World War, when he wrote, "In 1936 there was no reason to suppose that Germany would first swallow Poland whole and end her existence as an independent country. This deprived Germany of the support of a well-organized and trained army that could mobilize more than fifty divisions."[7] Of course the General Staff could not know as they planned the war games that the deal between Hitler and Stalin would lead to the division of Poland. They should have noted, however, that the organization of the Polish army was outdated and their arms obsolescent.

Tukhachevsky objected most of all to the accepted disposition of forces for the simulated exercises. If Germany could put ninety-two divisions in the field at the beginning of the First World War, now they could count on two hundred; otherwise the once-beaten Germans would not start a fight. Therefore, Tukhachevsky insisted there would be at least eighty German divisions to the north of the Poles. He apparently did not think much of the Poles. In actuality, in 1941, plan "Barbarossa" threw seventy-nine German divisions against the Soviet Union in the "Center" and "Northern" groups. Altogether on the Eastern Front they had 152 divisions.

Tukhachevsky further insisted that the grouping of German forces between the Narev River and the mouth of the Neman was only a preliminary concentration after crossing over by railroad. He demanded to be permitted, before the operational part of the games began, to deploy his "German" forces to prevent the concentration of the "Reds." He also demanded that he be permitted to strike first. Tukhachevsky believed that German propaganda about the blitzkrieg was not empty boasting. Germany did not have the resources to conduct a long war. Tukhachevsky took seriously the factor of surprise.

Tukhachevsky's thoughts on the course of the early part of the war, as conducted in the games, are also known, although the memoirists don't write about them. Because of the unexpectedness of their attack, the Germans would enjoy tremendous success in the first months, moving 100 to 250 kilometers into Soviet territory. The "Reds" would not be able to carry out a full mobilization of the Army or to replace the losses of this initial period. For eight to twelve months they would be forced to fight defensive battles before going over to a decisive counterattack. Tukhachevsky did not expect that in real conditions an attack could come entirely as a surprise. Intelligence and reconnaissance would insure against that. Stalin fully disproved that theory in 1941.

The conditions proposed for the games were exceptionally difficult. They were not derived directly from contemporary assessments of the enemy's strength, but for educational purposes they were justified. As we know, reality was much crueler.

Marshal A. I. Egorov, who by nature was more a clerk than a military commander, was in charge of the games. He had always been a compliant executor of orders from above. In 1905 he dispersed a demonstration in Tiblisi; during the Civil War he obediently followed the ignorant command of Stalin, who was then a member of the Military Revolutionary Council of the front; finally on June 11, 1937, also on orders from Stalin, he maintained order at the trial of his comrades. Above all Egorov wanted to display the work of his office in the best light, in this case to show that the plans developed by the General Staff for deployment in case of war were the best plans, the correct and only possible plans. Therefore, with full assurance that the Master would be on his side, he discarded Tukhachevsky's sagacious suggestions. Egorov did not want to adopt the methods of Suvorov, who, it had been established, had operated on a "feudal" basis. Nor did he wish to burden himself by learning anything new. The enemy's troops received no strategic advantages: they would have to approach the border after the main Soviet troops had been deployed. Isserson wrote:

> In the final analysis what happened was that the two sides began the games evenly matched. The main forces of the Red side were deployed along the border. The possibility that we might be able to prevent the concentration of the enemy's forces or that we might strike the first blow were not considered. The factor of surprise and suddenness, to which the Germans attached such great importance and which in their open discussions in the press comprised the main feature of their strategic doctrine, found no expression in

the games. In these circumstances, which deprived the games of fundamental strategic meaning, the course of events led to a frontal clash like the border engagements of 1914 and ended with no decisive outcome.[8]

The circle tightened. The Red Army was ordered to fight according to plans that were twenty-five years old and tragically useless. Todorsky's description of the games agrees completely with Isserson's. A few important details, which have not been previously published, complete the picture.

Before the games began, Tukhachevsky traveled in the border districts to update his information on the German forces. At the same time the games' other participants gathered in Moscow: all of the commanders of military districts, chiefs of district headquarters or their assistants, corps commanders, many division commanders. A day before "hostilities" commenced, they met in house number 2 of the People's Commissariat of Defense at the intersection of Kuibyshev Street (formerly Ilinka) and Red Square. That evening an important message came: the games were being transferred to the Kremlin. Members of the Politburo wanted to participate in them. The next morning all except Tukhachevsky were in the Kremlin. For several hours they waited. When Stalin arrived, he asked what had caused the delay. He was told that because Tukhachevsky was absent, they did not have complete information on the "blue" side, the enemy. Stalin very reasonably noted that we had a General Staff who could supply the missing information. Egorov and his colleagues worked all night. When the participants gathered again the next morning, Egorov announced his findings.

Germany and Poland would declare their mobilization of ninety and twenty divisions, respectively, and take the offensive. Nor would we be caught napping. We would immediately put sixty mobilized divisions on the border, and within two weeks another forty. A little after that we would advance twenty to twenty-five more from interior districts. The aggressor would attempt to break through our lines of defense for two or three weeks but would have no success. The Red Army would launch a crushing counteroffensive and carry the war into Poland. Revolts would break out against the fascist regimes in Germany and Poland. It was all like in a song or a report: if tomorrow we're at war, if tomorrow we're on the march . . . with a little blood in a foreign land. . . . Stalin nodded approvingly. The commanders received their assignments and set to work with their staffs.

Tukhachevsky finally showed up. All the participants were rounded up again. Stalin asked Tukhachevsky to familiarize himself with Egorov's arrangements and to express his opinion of them. Tukhachevsky replied that his information was different from Egorov's. Germany would mobilize 150 to 200 divisions and would attack the Soviet Union without declaring war. Because of the suddenness of the attack and the numerical superiority of the enemy, we would have to fight a long defensive war on our own territory before we could possibly go over to a counteroffensive.

Stalin reacted curtly, "What are you trying to do, frighten Soviet authority?" The games were conducted according to Egorov's plan.

"Tukhachevsky was clearly disenchanted," wrote Isserson[9] with magnificent understatement. Tukhachevsky understood—he could not help but understand—that on the eve of unavoidable world carnage the defense of the country, its fate, lay in the hands of vain, shortsighted, and ignorant men. We will begin by taking a giant step backward in an attempt to find the causes of the catastrophe that struck the Red Army. The Civil War stamped an ineradicable mark on the future development of the new Army. In this unusual war, a fratricidal war in which the enemies were not foreign invaders but countrymen, the RKKA was not only born but came of age. It was then that the traditions, the doctrines, and the relationship between the young Army and the new political authority took root.

From this eventful period we will take just a few incidents. They have been selected for the light they shed on the personalities of the men who later played decisive roles in shaping the Army. We will also touch on negative aspects that have heretofore been deliberately ignored or distorted. By this we do not mean to dishonor the Red Army or add glory to its enemies. Who will take it upon himself to be a judge in the tragic internecine war? If we must say something not entirely praiseworthy about some of the leaders of the Red Army, that is not our fault. For too long official Soviet historiography has lied or simply been silent about this. More than enough has already been written about the deeds of their opponents.

I

The Civil War: A Few Pages

Brothers, let us celebrate liberty's twilight . . .
—Mandelshtam

3 1918: The Birth of the RKKA

The decree establishing the volunteer Workers-Peasants' Red Army was signed by Lenin on January 28, 1918. Four months passed before regular units were formed. Beginning in 1922, however, the anniversary of the creation of the Red Army was marked on February 23.

The history of how this date came to be chosen deserves a moment's notice. For a long while, the official version explained that on that day the young Red units received their baptism of fire by stopping the attacking German troops near Narva and Pskov. In the mid-1960s this version was refuted in the press; since then February 23 has been marked as the day of national opposition to the enemy, and the pre-1938 explanation has once again been adopted.

Let us briefly explore the events of that period. On February 10, 1918, negotiations at Brest-Litovsk were broken off. The situation for the young republic was desperate. Soviet authorities could do nothing but wait for the German reaction, and on the eighteenth the Germans attacked. Because they did not commit many troops to the offensive, and most of these were militia (*Landwehr*), the offensive developed slowly. The units of the old Russian army that still occupied the front did not put up an active defense and were easily driven eastward. The Red Army did not really exist yet. On February 18 the Central Committee of the Communist Party met and after two stormy sessions accepted Lenin's ultimatum on the immediate conclusion of peace on any terms. The Germans were informed.

While the Germans continued their attack and Soviet authorities sued for peace, the formation of Red Guard militia detachments continued. On February 21 Lenin appealed to everyone capable of bearing arms with the slogan, "The Fatherland is in peril." For the next ten days the factory sirens and whistles of Petrograd sounded the alarm. Practically all the men of the city took up arms. Together with the militia units that had already been formed—the soldiers of the Petrograd garrison and the sailors of the Baltic fleet—they marched off to meet the Germans. They could not, however, mount effective resistance.

The German command, whose major concerns were now in the West, were not seeking to reopen a war with Russia. They hoped only for some easy loot. On the evening of February 22, the Germans occupied Pskov. All was then quiet from the twenty-third through the twenty-seventh. During the next week a few minor clashes occurred, and on March 3, P. E. Dybenko surrendered Narva. That same month he was tried by a military tribunal and removed from his post as People's Commissar for Naval Affairs.

In February 1919 a group of women workers from Petrograd wrote to Lenin to suggest commemorating those memorable ten days with a holiday in honor of the "birth of the Red Army." Lenin agreed although he did not evince any particular enthusiasm. In view of the difficult circumstances in which the country still found itself, the holiday was fixed on a Sunday, which that year happened to fall on the twenty-third. So, the choice of the date was to a large extent accidental.

The holiday was not marked in 1920 or 1921. Perhaps little importance was yet attached to it. In 1922 it was entered in the official calendar of saints. It seemed more appropriate to celebrate this rather accidentally born holiday after the victory in the Civil War.

One way or another a Red Army Day was necessary. Ideology, however, would not permit that it be celebrated as an anniversary of any, even the most glorious, victory in the internecine war. The Red Army had to have been born in battle with an external enemy. Starting from this ideological basis, the Entente was declared the chief enemy, and Kolchak, Denikin, Yudenich, and Wrangel its agents. Somewhat later, Stalinist historiography took that thesis to its logical extreme: the entire Civil War was turned into a repulsing of foreign aggression in the form of three separate campaigns of the Entente. In this way the war lost its internecine character and became a defensive struggle; but the common name—the Civil War—was retained, possibly through inadvertence. That is why the holiday was kept on February 23. At the dawn of Soviet power there was no other episode associated with the attack of a foreign enemy.

In World War II the story of the holiday was improved. The story about the defeat of German aggressors near Pskov and Narva surfaced in 1938, and in 1942 Stalin spoke of "the destruction of elite German corps and divisions." It was not mentioned, of course, that on February 23 Pskov was already in German hands or that the Germans were still three hundred kilometers from Narva. It is more interesting that Stalin never tried to attach Red Army Day to his own participation in the Civil War, for example with the defense of Tsaritsyn.

The Red Army was born. The circumstances surrounding the registration of the birth did not foretell an easy fate.

4 1918: Tsaritsyn

Stalin made his first appearance on the Civil War battlefields in the spring of 1918. In May near Tsaritsyn, when echelons of the retreating 5th Ukrainian Army under Vovoshilov were crossing the Don, Stalin arrived as an extraordinary commissar of supply for South Russia. Later, obliging historians transformed the Tsaritsyn sector into the decisive front of the Civil War and proclaimed Stalin the chief organizer of the Red Army. At the time even Stalin did not know his destiny. He wrote Lenin on July 7, 1918, "I am driving and berating everyone who needs it. I hope we will soon reestablish [rail communication with the center]. You may be assured that we will spare no one, not ourselves, not others, but somehow we will supply the grain."

At Tsaritsyn Stalin joined the staff of the Military Revolutionary Council of the North Caucasus Military District. Using his high position as a member of the government (he was still People's Commissar for Nationality Affairs), he immediately began to interfere in purely military matters, which, because of ignorance and inexperience, he did not understand. Stalin himself, of course, thought differently. From that same note to Lenin: "If our miliary 'specialists' (cobblers!) weren't sleeping or doing nothing, the [railroad] line would not have been cut. If the line is reestablished, it won't be because of the specialists, but despite them."[1] It is immediately apparent that Stalin, himself the son of a real cobbler, had no use for military specialists, or that in any case he meant to put himself above them.

On May 2 Andrei Evgenevich Snesarev, an ex-lieutenant general of the tsarist army, who had joined the Red Army voluntarily, was appointed commander of the North Caucasus Military District. Snesarev was an experienced commander and an outstanding Orientalist. At the end of May he arrived at Tsaritsyn with a mandate from the Council of People's Commissars, signed by Lenin. In a region where partisan operations, and Soviet and Party work were all poorly organized, according to a report by Commissar K. Ia. Zedin,[2] Snesarev was to undertake the establishment of regular military units.

Snesarev stepped on a lot of toes. Most important, he clashed with a group of Party workers, headed by K. E. Voroshilov and S. K. Minin, who did not understand the need for a regular army. Free-spirited guerrilla units, meetings, and the free election of commanders seemed to them the only true methods of revolutionary struggle. The establishment of military discipline looked like a return to "tsarist" ways. The commanders of the numerous partisan detachments held the same view. The leaders of small units of two hundred or so men, who liked to call themselves commanders or commanders-in-chief, were mostly soldiers and noncommissioned officers of the old army. They were jealous of the almost unlimited power they had gained over other men, and intuitively they felt that in a regular army they would not retain their command positions. Leaders in a regular army would have to be literate and to have at least an elementary military education, which many of them lacked. History would show that these fears were exaggerated. Old Bolsheviks like Voroshilov and Minin, who had fallen into military work, thought little about careers and felt a class distrust of former tsarist officers.

Stalin momentarily considered the circumstances and supported the partisans. Like a true revolutionary he earned his popularity with the masses. Moreover, he was always repelled by men like Snesarev who stood on a higher intellectual level.

Under these conditions the constructive work of Snesarev and his staff went slowly. When General Krasnov's Cossack units attacked Tsaritsyn, it required a tremendous effort by Snesarev's units to drive them off and to reestablish communication with the center. Then, in the middle of July, Stalin—with the help of Voroshilov and Minin —arrested almost all of Snesarev's staff officers and incarcerated them on a prison ship. Soon Snesarev was also put under guard on an unfounded charge of sabotage that the local Cheka did not confirm. But already in 1918 Stalin realized that actual guilt was not the most important element. It was necessary to declare enemies those who had to be removed for other reasons.

The repression affected not only staff officers. This is how Voroshilov reported that Stalin reacted to the news that a monarchistic organization had been discovered: "Stalin's resolution was terse, 'Shoot.' Engineer Alekseev, two of his sons, and together with them a considerable number of officers, some of whom belonged to the organization, and some of whom were only suspected of sympathy with it, were seized by the Cheka and immediately, without a trial, shot."[3] Voroshilov took this quotation from the journal *Don Wave*. We might not have believed a White Guard organ, but Voroshilov used this very piece to describe Stalin's style of revolutionary work.

Moscow did not believe Stalin's accusations and sent a commission from the Supreme Military Inspectorate to investigate. It was headed by A. I. Okulov. When he learned they were coming, Stalin gave the order to kill the arrested officers. The barge was towed to a deep channel in the Volga and sunk. Several days later Okulov and his commission arrived and quickly established that the charges against Snesarev were groundless. He was freed and transferred to a different front. The drowned officers were written off as losses in the Civil War. As was normal for those times, no one was brought to account for the "mistake."

Strategically Stalin's activity also bore fruit. In the spring of 1918 the Soviets faced two main enemies in the south: the Don Cossacks, and the voluntary officer detachments of Generals L. G. Kornilov and M. A. Alekseev, both of which had retreated into the Caucasus.

The Cossacks were tired of war and did not wish to fight with anyone, including the Soviets. They reacted unenthusiastically in April when the newly elected ataman Krasnov proclaimed an independent Don state in which he included not only the traditional Cossack territories but also the Taganrog, Tsaritsyn, and Voronezh districts. Krasnov himself recorded that the Cossacks were not up to fighting for new land.[4] But the Bolsheviks' grain-requisitioning policies, put into effect in the spring of 1918, forced the Cossacks to take up arms.

The Volunteers turned out to be natural allies of the Cossacks. Kornilov and Alekseev planned to lead their officers out of Russia through the Caucasus to save them for a future army. However, the Volunteers, like Krasnov's troops, were very weak. In May Krasnov had 17,000 fighters, many of whom were not reliable, and twenty-one guns. He was opposed by much larger Red forces: the Southern Screen (*Zavesa*) with 19,820 infantry and cavalry and 38 guns, and the 10th Army with 39,465 infantry and cavalry and 240 guns. The Volunteer forces had numbered only 3,500 in February, almost one hundred of them sick or wounded. They rested until March in the southern *stanitsas* (large Cossack villages) under the protection of the Cossacks. To carry out their plan they had to cross the Kuban peninsula, where their way was blocked by significant Red Forces: Kalnin's group with 30,000, the Taman Army with another 30,000, and the 11th Army with 80,000 to 100,000. The Red Army's superiority was overwhelming. All of these troups were subordinate to the North Caucasus Military District, whose headquarters had been moved from Rostov to Tsaritsyn because of the Cossack threat.

In April the Volunteers made a desperate attempt to break out. On April 13, during the storming of Ekaterinodar, General Kornilov perished. The Whites under General Denikin retreated to the Don. It seemed that the Reds could very quickly defeat the enemy. They were hindered, however, by the absence of full authority in the hands of the district commander and by the super-revolutionary activity of the district Revolutionary Military Council headed by the recently arrived Stalin. We have already described his actions; it remains to explain the results.

While Stalin and his comrades were battling the headquarters staff of their army, Krasnov and Denikin were gathering forces. Although relations between them were tense and there was a struggle for supreme command, nonetheless in the summer of 1918 the enemies of the Soviet government achieved considerable success. By August Krasnov's army consisted of 40,000 reliable soldiers, and his authority stretched across the whole Don Cossack Territory. In May the Volunteer Army, still made up of officer units, included 5,000 infantry and cavalry. Denikin destroyed Kalnin's group, occupied the villages of Torgovaia and Velikokniazheskaia in June, and took Tikhoretskaia on July 13. The strategic position of the Soviet forces in the North Caucasus became critical. Now the Volunteer Army represented a more serious threat. It had 20,000 fighters and was continually attracting more officers, mainly from the south.

The successes of the Don and Volunteer armies occurred during Stalin's usurpation of military leadership in Tsaritsyn and to a significant extent because of it. Stalin commanded the North Caucasus Military District on his own for two months after Snesarev's removal in the middle of July. It was during this period that Denikin began his successful offensive and his army suddenly began to grow. He seized Ekaterinodar on August 16. By the end of September there were 40,000 soldiers under the White flag.

Having freed himself of Snesarev, Stalin arbitrarily altered the plans for the defense of Tsaritsyn. By autumn these changes seriously endangered the city and almost destroyed the cooperation of Red forces in the south. Stalin clashed again with the military leadership, this time with former General P. P. Sytin, who had been appointed commander of the Southern Front.

This was a difficult time for the Soviet republic. Lenin lay wounded in his apartment in the Kremlin while Sverdlov and Tsiurupa directed the government. On September 2 a new military organ was created, the Revolutionary Military Council of the Republic, with L. D. Trotsky at its head. I. I. Vatsetis was appointed Commander-in-Chief. Merciless Red terror was proclaimed throughout the country; defensive measures took on new forms; new fronts and armies were established. The Central Committee and the Council of People's Commissars confirmed appointments, but it was the Revolutionary Council that ordered the appointment of front commanders. Sytin was made commander of the Southern Front, which had been formed from the old North Caucasus Military District; but Stalin did not obey Moscow's directive. He sabotaged the order to move the administration of the front to Kozlov, and then by an order of the Revolutionary Military Council of the front he dismissed Sytin as a former tsarist general and replaced him with Voroshilov. Most likely it was not Sytin's past that disturbed Stalin but the power he exercised as troop commander. Stalin always took questions of power seriously. Conditions near Tsaritsyn and throughout the Northern Caucasus became so perilous at this time that Moscow finally had to intervene. On October 6, Sverdlov and Stalin exchanged angry telegrams, after which the Central Committee recalled Stalin from the Southern Front and reorganized the Revolutionary Military Council. Voroshilov and Minin were removed, replaced by K. A. Mekhonoshin, B. V. Legran, and P. E. Lazimir.

The new front command set about to clean up the mess Stalin had made. When the Cossacks approached Kamyshin, the Soviet command transferred some of its forces from the Eastern Front to save Tsaritsyn. Sytin successfully defended Tsaritsyn; but he was not able to save anything in the Northern Caucasus, where the front collapsed. Inspired by the example of the Revolutionary Military Council, lower-ranking commanders began to behave in the same independent fashion. Matveev, Commander of the Taman Army, refused to subordinate himself to the orders of the Kuban–Black Sea Central Executive Committee and was therefore shot by the local Commander-in-Chief Sorokin. In his turn, Sorokin sabotaged the formation of regular units of the 11th Army and arrested and shot members of the Kuban–

Black Sea government. Declared an outlaw, he fled but was captured by one of Matveev's comrades, who avenged his commander. Brigade Commander Kochubei, surrounded by Denikin's troops, went over to the enemy with part of his forces. He was, however, hanged on the orders of General Lukomsky.

The whole Northern Caucasus fell into the hands of the Volunteer Army, and Denikin became an enemy to be reckoned with for another two years.

However important were the events at Tsaritsyn, in the spring of 1918 the main front for the Soviet republic was in the East. It continued to be so until the summer of 1919 when Kolchak was decisively defeated in the battle for the Urals. Nonetheless, until recently the importance of this front has been intentionally depreciated, because Stalin, Voroshilov, and other comrades-in-arms of the Great Leader participated very little or not at all on the Eastern Front. According to the official historiographical concept of the war, Stalin was always sent to the decisive sectors of the Civil War.

Now, however reluctantly, the truth has been reestablished. The primacy of the Eastern Front is recognized even by writers who in the 1930s, 1940s, and 1950s made their scholarly reputations by praising the activity of Stalin in the fateful Tsaritsyn sector.

It is not enough to say that for a year and a half the question of the existence of Soviet power was being decided in the East. The Eastern Front, besides, was the furnace in which the RKKA was forged. The first regular units were created there; the leadership qualities of many, if not most, of the leaders of the Red Army were first displayed there. Here is a list, far from complete, of commanders who gained their experience in the East: both Commanders-in-Chief during the Civil War, I. I. Vatsetis and S. S. Kamenev; Front Commander, and later People's Commissar for Navy and Chairman of the Revolutionary Military Council of the USSR, M. V. Frunze; Front Commanders M. N. Tukhachevsky, N. D. Kashirin, M. M. Lashevich, S. A. Mezheninov, I. P. Uborevich, R. P. Eideman; prominent political workers L. N. Aronshtam, A. S. Bulin, I. M. Vareikis, V. V. Kuibyshev, I. N. Smirnov; commanders of lesser ranks who later occupied higher posts, I. P. Belov, M. D. Velikanov, N. V. Kuibyshev, K. K. Rokossovsky, V. D. Sokolovsky, V. I. Chuikov; and legendary divisional commanders V. M. Azin and V. I. Chapaev.

The troops from the Eastern Front, who were thrown into the southern and western sectors after the defeat of Kolchak, turned the tide of battle there also. The leaders of the Eastern Front played important roles in the victory in the Civil War. Practically none of them survived the repression of 1937–38.

The Eastern Front was opened in May 1918 as a result of the mutiny of the 50,000 men of the Czechoslovak Legion. Under the protection of the Czechoslovaks, White governments were established in the East with their center at Omsk. By August the Omsk government had at its disposal 40,000 to 50,000 troops. These units were only being formed and brought up to strength, however. The front was held by 40,000 Czechoslovaks. Another 12,000 Czechoslovaks had gone over to the Reds at the time of the mutiny. The Red Army under Vatsetis comprised 80,000 to 90,000 men. Moscow had by that time recognized its mistake in underestimating the danger in the East. At first the Czech Legion dominated the whole Volga region. At Kazan the gold reserves of Russia fell into their hands. In the middle of August the Soviet forces went on the offensive and crushed the White Czechs; they took Kazan, Simbirsk, and Samara. The Czechs quit the fight and began their long retreat to the Far East. The Russian White Guards under General V. G. Boldyrev retreated into the Orenburg steppe.

It was clear to Boldyrev that his only salvation lay in a breakthrough toward Perm and Kotlas so that he could link up with the government of Chaikovsky and Miller and the Anglo-American troops in the north. Only in that way could the White Guards find the arms and other military supplies they needed. On December 25 the Whites seized Perm. By itself this event does not stand out among the many similar episodes of the Civil War, but official historians have inflated its importance because the Central Committee sent a commission composed of Stalin and Dzerzhinsky to investigate its fall. The sonorous term "the Perm catastrophe" was invented to lend importance to Stalin's acts.

Reality was more prosaic. The 3rd Army defending Perm surrendered the city because they did not have enough men to hold it. The Army commanders who replaced one another there—M. M. Lashevich, P. I. Berzin, S. A. Mezheninov—repeatedly asked for reinforcements, which they did not receive.

At that time the surrender of any city without the order of central authority was investigated by a special commission, and the guilty parties were turned over to a military tribunal. After the surrender of Narva, Dybenko was tried in this way; after the fall of Kharkov, Voroshilov. The commission investigating the surrender of Perm affirmed the conclusions of the 3rd Army command. No one was tried. The Army sent reinforcements and the enemy offensive was halted. That was basically all that happened. The appearance of Stalin on the Eastern Front is significant in that it was the only occasion in the history of the Civil War in which he appeared in a theater of military operations without causing harm to the Red Army.

The major events of the Eastern Front occurred two months after Stalin's departure in the battle with Kolchak. Vice-Admiral Aleksandr Vasilevich Kolchak, former commander of the Black Sea Fleet, was one of the most able and best-educated officers of the Russian Navy. After graduating from the Naval Academy (*Morskoi korpus*) he served several years in the Navy; then, as a hydrologist and oceanographer, he participated in several northern and far eastern expeditions sponsored by the Academy of Sciences. Kolchak was a first-rate scientist, who at one time had worked with F. Nansen.

After fleeing from Sevastopol and traveling most of the way around the world, Kolchak wound up in Omsk as Minister of War of the White government. On November 18, 1918, he carried out a coup and proclaimed himself Supreme Commander-in-Chief and Supreme Ruler of Russia. His army represented a serious threat to the Soviets, for a while a mortal danger. The Red Army was still quite small and recruitment was difficult. The policy of requisitioning grain from the peasants had caused a large part of the peasantry to reject Soviet authority. Many of them fled to areas held by Kolchak, but his government strove to resurrect the landlords' power, especially along the Volga. The peasants, who had seized the landlords' land, were punished with terrible cruelty. There were mass executions and whippings.

Lenin, on the other hand, having assessed the extent of the danger, changed his tactics toward the peasants. The committees of poor peasants were disbanded, and the seizure of grain was halted until spring. As a result, Kolchak lost his major source of recruits and the Red Army gained them.

At its largest, Kolchak's army had 150,000 cavalry and infantry, while the Red Army grew to almost 200,000 and continued to grow. In Siberia, in the Whites' rear, a peasant partisan movement also grew in numbers. The fate of Kolchak's army was decided.

6 1919–21: The First Horse Army

The First Horse Army is sacrosanct in Soviet military history. So far as the average Soviet citizen knows, the First Horse was the Red Army of the time of the Civil War, the unconquerable force that defended the workers-peasants' republic from the assaults of fourteen enemy powers, from Denikin, Kolchak, Yudenich, and Shkuro. On the Red side in the Civil War there were seventeen field and two cavalry armies with a total enlistment of about 5 million men, but in popular memory only the 30,000-strong Horse Army has been preserved. Many books have been written about it, and songs have been composed in its honor. Its heroic battles have served as the theme for movies, plays, paintings, and monumental sculpture.

In the 1920s and 1930s cavalrymen dominated the leadership of the country's armed forces. In the fifty-eight years from 1918 to 1976 the country has had, under various titles, ten ministers of war. The three who had served in the Horse Army guided the defense of the country for twenty-five years. These were K. E. Voroshilov, 1925–40; S. K. Timoshenko, 1940–41; and A. A. Grechko, 1967–76. In the nineteen-year interval between the end of the Civil War and the beginning of the Fatherland War, it was only during the first three years that cavalrymen did not run the Red Army.

Service in the First Horse served as a pass to higher command responsibilities. The dictatorship of the cavalry, which is unique among the great powers of the twentieth century, was possible only because of the dictatorship of the country by the patron of the First Horse, Stalin, and because of the control of the armed forces by its political mentor Voroshilov. As Caligula had brought his horse into the senate, these two horse lovers packed the Army's command with cavalrymen. S. M. Budenny, G. I. Kulik, E. A. Shchadenko, A. A. Grechko, and K. S. Moskalenko were all deputy ministers or deputy people's commissars of defense. K. A. Meretskov was chief of the General Staff. When individual ranks were reintroduced in 1935, two of the five first marshals were cavalrymen; a third, Egorov, commanded the front on which the First Horse was created. It ought to be noted that neither of the two commanders-in-chief of the Army during the Civil War became marshals, nor did Yakir or Uborevich. Altogether eight marshals of the Soviet Union, nine generals of the Army and marshals of branches of the service, and a large number of other generals came from Budenny's First Horse.

Before the Second World War Budenny's men played an exceptional role in the Red Army. They are largely responsible for the catastrophe of 1937–38 and for the defeat in the first years of the war. Only when combat actually began was the unfitness of Voroshilov, Budenny, Timoshenko, Shchadenko, Tiulenev, Apanasenko, and Kulik revealed. Kulik was twice demoted for shameful behavior at the front; having begun as a marshal he became a major. Stalin would not, however, permit one of his chief advisors from before the war to be professionally destroyed; Kulik died a major general. In the mid-1960s he was posthumously returned the marshal's baton. To be fair, we ought also to note that several cavalrymen, who were little known before the war, showed themselves to be capable military leaders and achieved high rank on the field of combat; these included Eremenko, Rybalko, Katukov, and others.

All of this suggests we ought to look carefully at the First Horse Army. We do not intend to write its whole history but will try to reestablish the truth about a few incidents.

In Soviet literature it is considered unarguable that the First Horse Army was the first large unit (*ob'edinenie*) of strategic cavalry in the modern history of war. The matter is not so simple. It is true that horse armies did not exist previously. However, the idea of forming a strategic cavalry to carry out independent tasks separate from the main forces and deep in the rear of the enemy belongs to Anton Ivanovich Denikin. Not only did he introduce this bold idea, but in August 1919 he joined together two cavalry corps to form a larger unit. Later the cavalry corps under Shkuro was linked to this group, which was commanded by General Mamontov. This gave Denikin a strategic cavalry group equal in size to an army. Mamontov's group broke through the Red Army's Southern Front and for a month successfully operated in its rear, taking Tambov, Kozlov, and Voronezh. The Soviet counteroffensive was broken. Mamontov's successes permitted General Mai-Maevsky to move his army far to the north, where they took Kursk and Orel and directly threatened Tula with its arms factories and Moscow itself.

In the third volume of the *History of the Civil War* we read, "the importance of massed cavalry in the conditions of the civil war were correctly learned by the Red commanders from the example of Mamontov's raid. That raid made up their minds about the creation of massed cavalry in the Red Army. . . ."[1] This testimony about the priority of Denikin is all the more valuable because it comes from the highest leadership of the Red Army of that period. The editors of that volume were S. S. Kamenev, Bubnov, Tukhachevsky, and Eideman. Later Soviet historians tried to forget that admission.

The second and extremely complex question is, where did the First Army come from? For a long while we have been told that it arose from the cavalry corps of Budenny, which in turn had grown out of his 4th Cavalry Division. In the 1960s the screen of lies was temporarily lifted by the efforts of several honest historians, including T. A. Illeritskaia and V. D. Polikarpov. This called forth an extraordinarily sharp reaction from the Budenny camp, and further research was halted.

What caused the stormy anger of these aging but influential men? The commandant of the Frunze Military Academy, Army General A. T. Stuchenko, for example, turned up with his cavalry sword at the editorial office of *Nedelia*, the journal that had printed Polikarpov's article. They were disturbed, even insulted, by the attempt to reestablish the true circumstances of the demise of B. M. Dumenko, one of the participants of the Civil War. From the facts of his biography, which are presented below, it will become clear that the veterans were upset unnecessarily.

Don Cossack Boris Mokeevich Dumenko formed a cavalry detachment of the insurgents of Salsky and other districts in 1918. In July the detachment became the 1st Peasants' Socialist Punitive Cavalry Regiment. Dumenko commanded the regiment and Budenny soon became his assistant. Under Dumenko's leadership the regiment developed first into a cavalry brigade, then into a division, the same 4th Petrograd Cavalry Division from which the Budenny men say the First Horse was taken. Dumenko commanded the division until May 1919 and during that time was awarded an Order of the Red Banner. Then in connection with the organization of larger cavalry formations he was appointed head of the cavalry of the 10th Army. He had under him the 4th Cavalry Division, commanded by Budenny, and the 6th Cavalry Division under I. P. Apanasenko. Not long after, Dumenko was seriously wounded and put out of action until the fall. While he was recuperating, the First Horse Corps was formed from the 4th and 6th Divisions. Upon his return to duty Dumenko was made commander of the Combined Horse Corps, which was being formed. In January 1920 Dumenko's corps defeated Denikin's cavalry at Novocherkassk, making it easier for the First Horse and the 8th Army to take Rostov.

In February Dumenko was visited by two of Budenny's men: Divisional Commander S. K. Timoshenko, who had been temporarily suspended for drunkenness, and B. S. Gorbachev, commander of the Special Cavalry Brigade (the Horse Army's). They came to arrest Dumenko; but as they would not be able to do so in the presence of his men, they had to devise another plan. They persuaded Dumenko to have a drink. Since he had had part of his stomach surgically removed, he quickly became drunk. The plan worked. Timoshenko went under the table first, but Dumenko soon followed him. Gorbachev rolled Dumenko in a carpet and dragged him to his cart; then he lugged out the future marshal and people's commissar.

They delivered Dumenko to the headquarters of the First Horse, and from there took him and three of his subordinates to Rostov, where they were tried by a tribunal. The four were accused of organizing the murder of Mikeladze, a commissar of the Combined Horse Corps, who had died under mysterious circumstances. Although the tribunal had no evidence, Dumenko and his comrades were shot. More than forty years later, Deputy General Procurator of the USSR Blinov studied the materials of the case and had to ask, "If this is law, what then is scandalous illegality?"

Dumenko's name was erased from the History of the Red Army and Budenny attributed Dumenko's honors to himself. In 1920 Dumenko represented a serious threat to Budenny's claim to be the Red Army's leading cavalryman. There is reason to believe that Budenny and Voroshilov planned Dumenko's removal. The circumstances surrounding Dumenko's arrest support this supposition, as does the presence on the tribunal of E. A. Shchadenko, a First Horseman. The long-lasting malevolence toward Dumenko and Budenny's behavior toward another of his rivals, F. K. Mironov, about which we will have more to say, also lend credence to this supposition. It is worth noting as well that the commanders of the First Horse frequently proposed subordinating Dumenko's corps to themselves.

After Uborevich's group defeated the Volunteer Army at Orel, Budenny's unit became the trump card in the hand of the Red command.

In October 1919 his horse corps, reinforced by a cavalry division and an infantry brigade, dealt the fatal blow to the Whites' strategic cavalry in the Voronezh–Kastonaia operation. Budenny now had in effect a horse army under his command; it was formally constituted the First Horse in November. The result was seen not only in the defeat of Mamontov's group, which never recovered, but also in the colossal boost it gave to Red Army morale. From then on Denikin's rear remained constantly in danger.

The White front broke all along its length, and the Soviet Command hastened to pursue its strategic advantage. In January 1920 the First Horse took Rostov with a lightning-quick strike. The 8th Army secured the cavalry's success. As Denikin's troops retreated, they formed a line of defense on the left bank of the Don with a key position at Bataisk. The Reds' strategy, which the First Horse helped carry out, was devised by the command of the Caucasus Front under V. I. Shorin; they were to surround or seize Bataisk to prevent the main White force from reaching Novorossiisk. In that way they would prevent Denikin from crossing over to the Crimea where he could organize a new front.

History has shown that Shorin properly appraised the situation. Denikin had planned to retreat to the Crimea through Novorossiisk if he were unable to hold his position on the Don. But the Reds failed to break through the White front immediately. The First Horse and the 8th Army tried several times to take Bataisk, but they failed. The delay in the Red Army's offensive eventually proved costly. Denikin took advantage of it and crossed over to the Crimea with 40,000 men.

The "Bataisk Bottleneck" gave rise to very bitter arguments in the Red camp. Shorin accused Budenny and the commander of the 8th Army, G. Ia. Sokolnikov, of failing to take decisive action. Budenny complained about "the terrain that is entirely unsuitable for cavalry." Sokolnikov reproved the Horse Army for its display of "extraordinarily little combat hardiness." Without going into the details of the argument, let us note that it was at Bataisk that the inability of strategic cavalry to overcome solidly prepared defenses was first discovered. Undoubtedly the unfavorable conditions of the terrain also played a role: the water barrier of the Don and the swampiness of the left bank hampered the cavalry. But we cannot exclude the psychological factor. It was extremely difficult for Voroshilov and Budenny to drag their horsemen from the warmth and comfort of Rostov in the middle of winter.

In the spring of 1920 the First Horse was transferred in march

formation from the Caucasus to the Polish Front. On May 18 they
arrived at Elizavetgrad. The Poles had just taken Kiev and were going
on the defensive all along the front. Putting the Horse Army into action
turned things in the Soviets' favor. On June 5 they broke through the
enemy front at the village of Ozernaia and with all four divisions
advanced to the Polish rear. It was a huge operational success and the
culmination of the First Horse's fighting. It posed the threat of complete encirclement and destruction to the 3rd Polish Army of General
Rydz-Smigla. But operation "Kiev's Cannae" was not to be carried
out.[2] Yakir's and Golikov's groups were slow to complete their assignments; and the First Horse, in violation of its orders, did not strike
Rydz-Smigla's rear. Instead they bypassed fortified Kazatin and seized
Berdichev and Zhitomir with their rich warehouses. The success of the
Southwest Front was incomplete. The Poles lost all of the territory they
had seized in the Ukraine, but they managed to escape as an army.

During the Soviet offensive Commander-in-Chief Kamenev devised
a plan for the further conduct of the campaign, which received the
approval of the Politburo. It was projected that once all the Red forces
had reached the Brest–Southern Bug line, the administration of the
Southwest Front (Commander Egorov, and Revolutionary Military
Council members Stalin and Berzin) would turn over to Tukhachevsky
(as commander of the Western Front) the First Horse and the 12th and
14th Armies; and that they themselves would proceed against Wrangel,
who was advancing into northern Tavrida. Stalin was not at all pleased
with the prospect of not participating in the forthcoming capture of
Poland. Tukhachevsky later wrote that "the existence of the capitalist
world, not just of Poland, but of all Europe was wagered on that card."[3]
Stalin, the fiery revolutionary, wanted to attack world capitalism
personally.

By the middle of July 1920, Tukhachevsky's troops had overrun the
opposing front of General Szeptitski, had occupied Bobriusk, Minsk,
and Vilno, and had burst into Polish territory. The Poles' situation
became desperate. Warsaw was in danger and with it the young Polish
state. Western diplomacy rushed to help Jozef Pilsudski. On July
12, Curzon issued an ultimatum. The English minister of foreign
affairs demanded that military activity cease and that a so-called
ethnographic boundary be established between Poland and Soviet
Russia, approximately where the border is now. The ultimatum was
rejected, but after a direct appeal by the Poles, negotiations were

begun at Borisov. Meanwhile, the Red offensive continued on both fronts.

At the beginning of August Kamenev reached the decision about a concentric strike with all forces against Warsaw. In connection with this he gave the order to transfer to the command of the Western Front (to Tukhachevsky) the 12th and First Horse Armies at first, and later also the 14th. The Polish leader, Pilsudski, considered his situation at that moment to be catastrophic. He believed that Polish forces would not be able to hold back an attack from the east and south and asked the commandant of Lvov fortified region to draw in at least three Red divisions.

Suddenly Pilsudski was given reason for hope. The command of the Southwest Front stormed Lvov with the very armies that were to have been sent against Warsaw. The Red's original plan was destroyed, and the enemy received an unexpected chance to organize a counteroffensive. Part of the blame has to be laid on Kamenev because he was insufficiently firm in implementing his own directives and at the last moment became frightened of an imaginary Rumanian threat. But the greater responsibility must rest with Stalin, who so badly wanted the sensational success of taking Lvov. Spineless Egorov could not stand up to the future Great Leader. Lvov was well fortified, however, and the First Horse and the 12th Army were not up to taking it. Lenin categorically protested against striking "with five fingers spread wide" and insisted upon taking Warsaw. Stalin stood by his guns. For ten days a fruitless exchange of telegrams went on. Finally on August 13, under pressure from Lenin, Kamenev categorically demanded that his directive to transfer the three armies to Tukhachevsky be carried out. Stalin remained true to himself and did not sign the order prepared by Egorov. It should be remembered that in those years an order by a commander did not have legal force unless it was also signed by one of the members of the Revolutionary Council. Until then Stalin, as the senior member of the Revolutionary Military Council, had signed all of the operational orders of the commander. Another of the political commissars of the front, P. I. Berzin, tried to stay out of purely military matters and signed the order only after a direct command from Trotsky.

Stalin's willfulness stopped his military career for twenty years. He was about to send a telegram of resignation to Moscow, calculating that this threat would force acceptance of his plan of action. But the plenum of the Central Committee, which was then meeting, removed Stalin from the front and from all other military work as well. He was not reelected to the Revolutionary Military Council of the Republic.

The First Horse was transferred and assigned to the Warsaw offensive. But time had been wasted and the situation had drastically changed. The Poles took advantage of the breathing space and went over to the counteroffensive. The Polish command directed a strike between the Soviet fronts at the weak Mozyrsk group and further disrupted the campaign. Now the Poles' slight numerical superiority and better equipment complemented a solid operational advantage. The war had also aroused the Polish people's patriotic feeling. The hope of the Bolsheviks and their Polish colleagues (Dzerzhinsky, Markhlevsky, Unshlikht) that the Polish proletariat would support the Bolsheviks turned out to be a chimera.[4]

The Red Army retreated on both fronts, yielding to the Poles the western parts of the Ukraine and Belorussia. The First Horse drew back to Zamoste, barely escaping destruction. The Peace of Riga, in March 1921, established the border much farther east than the "Curzon line."

Tukhachevsky, whom Stalin's self-seeking actions had deprived of the chance to successfully complete the operation, never did try to identify those responsible for the defeat.[5] Stalin and his minions were not so delicate. Even before Tukhachevsky's arrest, they accused him of mistakes on the Polish Front. After the marshal's death all the textbooks and military works carried the standard formula that the traitors Trotsky and Tukhachevsky prevented the capture of Lvov and Warsaw.

The lessons of the Polish campaign permit a sober assessment of the strengths and weakness of the First Horse Army and also of the conception of a strategic cavalry in general. Massed cavalry were effective in breakthroughs, in raids into the enemy's rear, and in forays. The Civil War differed from the just-concluded World War in that the front lines were not continuous and the fire was not as dense. Each of the extremely long fronts had only 135 to 185 riflemen for each verst (0.66 mile), less than the corresponding ratio for outposts in the World War and not enough to prevent a breakthrough. Because of the absence of echeloned defenses, incursions into the rear of the enemy were often unopposed, and assaults on troop concentrations were frequently carried out with complete surprise. When the cavalry tried to overrun prepared defenses, however, it lost its advantage, suffering large losses and often failing. This happened at Bataisk and at Lvov, where repeated assaults were repulsed.

The cavalry was also badly suited to conduct defensive battles, where the close support of the infantry was needed. The strength of the cavalry, however, lay in its ability to carry out assignments independently of an army's main forces. A seemingly insoluble contradiction arose. Massed cavalry were needed only for a short period of the Civil War and were useful only in certain conditions. Voroshilov, Budenny, and Egorov found, however, that armed with the dialectic, Marxist military thought could solve the dilemma. They declared that all future wars would be exclusively mobile, and since the Red Army would only attack, it could not do without a powerful cavalry.

In all types of combat actions the First Horse was vulnerable from the air. Aerial attacks caused heavy losses at Lvov and later against Wrangel. Voroshilov complained to Frunze in November 1920, "We have nothing to counter aerial bombing by groups of airplanes against massed cavalry."[6]

Earlier, however, on its way to the front against Wrangel, the Horse Army suffered its worst experience. Having just tasted the bitterness of defeat, the battered First Horse began to come apart. The ill-assorted troops of Budenny's army never had sinned on the side of excessive discipline. The Revolutionary Military Council of the First Horse only with difficulty reined in the free-spirited horsemen. Also, because of the necessity of provisioning themselves, the Army often came into sharp conflict with the civilian population. The army command on several occasions had had to justify their conduct on this score to higher authorities, all the way up to Lenin and Trotsky. Voroshilov turned A. Ia. Parkhomenko, commandant of the city of Rostov, over to a tribunal for having organized a pogrom against the Jewish population. He was sentenced to death, and only the intervention of Stalin and Ordzhonikidze saved the life of this legendary divisional commander.

What happened when the First Horse was transferred from the Polish Front was even more serious. The cavalrymen's morals, which were honestly described by Babel, horrified many of his readers. On their way to the Crimea, the troops pillaged the civilians. Shepelev, commissar of the 6th Cavalry Division, was killed trying to stop them and Voroshilov had to act decisively. According to his biographer Orlovsky, himself a former secretary of the Horse Army's Military Revolutionary Council, Voroshilov believed that this outburst of "partisan behavior" could destroy the Army.[7] He put a whole division on trial, an event unprecedented in the Red Army, and had it disbanded. Under the muzzle of the "special forces" the troops surrendered their colors and arms and began to name the pillagers. Of the 150 taken, 101 were shot. With their blood the men of the division were given the chance to wash away their shame.

The First Horse traveled slowly to the front against Wrangel and arrived seriously weakened. Moreover, Voroshilov and Budenny did not want to fight in the Crimea except according to their own plans. Because they had gained special status, Frunze sent them into action only when victory was no longer in doubt.

The last major outbreak of "the partisan movement" occurred in 1921 in the Northern Caucasus. Because of opposition to the grain requisitioning, a brigade led by Maslakov broke off from the First Horse and became an anti-Soviet partisan detachment. Self-provisioning continued, with its unavoidable theft. The tribunals that followed did their work, and a substantial number of the Horse Army's troops were executed. The First Horse Army itself was soon disbanded.

7 Mironov

The battle for the Crimea, which developed in the fall of 1920, was full of tension and drama. The confrontation between Wrangel and Frunze ended in the complete victory of the latter. However, the history of the Crimean-Tavridian operation has long been misrepresented. Most attention has been paid to those personalities who are supposed to have played the leading roles in the Civil War, namely the First Horse Army, whose participation in that operation was minor and not particularly successful.[1]

The facts of the matter were considerably enlightened by the appearance of V. V. Dushenkin's book, *The Second Horse*.[2] It was impossible, however, to tell the whole truth about the fate of Army Commander Mironov in a censored publication. S. Starikov and R. Medvedev did that in their substantial—320 typed pages—historical essay "The Life and Death of Filipp Kuz'mich Mironov: Soviet Authority and the Don Cossacks 1917–1921." From that unpublished work, which contains numerous genuine documents of the time, we have taken the main facts for a brief biography of Mironov.[3]

Filipp Mironov was born into a poor Cossack family in 1872. He completed the local parish school and two years of high school in his native Ust-Medveditsky region (*okrug*). He completed high school by examination, without attending further classes. Mironov received his military education at a Cossack cadet school and at age thirty held the rank of cornet. In the Russo-Japanese War he earned four decorations and a promotion (to *podesaul*). In 1906 at the height of the Revolution, he spoke at his Cossack village meeting against the mobilization of the Cossacks for internal, that is, police duty. Because of that, soon after he returned to his regiment he was deprived of his officer status. Mironov returned to his native village and farmed. From 1910 to 1912 he served as head of the land department of the Don Territory (*oblast'*) administration, where he worked out projects for the equalization of land allotments for Cossacks of the upper and lower villages and for the allotting of land to non-Cossacks.

At the beginning of the World War, Mironov volunteered and went to the front. He was made an officer again and fought bravely for which he was awarded the Order of St. George's Sword, four other decorations, and two promotions to *esaul* and troop elder (the Cossack equivalent of lieutenant colonel).

Mironov was a Cossack *intelligent*, a rebel, and a defender of the people's rights. He put the ideals of freedom ahead of any party programs. The revolution gave great scope to his social temperament. Later, when he was on trial, his defender was quite right to call him "the lion of the Revolution."

In April 1917, after a run-in with his regimental commander, Mironov took leave and headed for the Don. In his native village he organized a local group of People's Socialist Workers. During the Kornilov revolt he spoke openly against Kaledin and made an unsuccessful attempt to arrest him.

In October Mironov returned to the front to his regiment. He greeted the Bolshevik Revolution, in his word, "unsympathetically." His political platform was "a democratic republic on a federative basis, the right of popular referendum, the right of popular initiative, etc." However, Mironov actively and successfully resisted the use of Cossack units to put down the Bolsheviks. He took the 32nd Regiment under his command and led it to the Don, where he arrived in January 1918.

By that time Mironov's sympathies were with the Bolsheviks. He was not, however, a thorough Bolshevik himself, and he never did become one. He immediately opposed the revolutionary committee of Mikhailovka village, which was shooting officers by the bunch just because they were officers. He succeeded in having the committee reelected, then he disbanded his regiment and went to Ust-Medveditsky to establish Soviet authority. Mironov became military commissar of the region and a member of the executive committee.

Kaledin committed suicide. By March 1918 the Soviets had taken over almost the whole Don, but they did not keep it long. General Krasnov organized a White Cossack army and invited the Germans to the Don. Detachments of officers made their way there. The Don Soviet Republic ceased to be, its Council of People's Commissars moved to Tsaritsyn. They held out longer in the north, in Ust-Medveditsky and Khopersky regions, where Mironov commanded the troops. He had very small forces, but he fought successfully. His popularity grew on both sides of the front. Krasnov is supposed to have said, "I have a lot of officers, but I don't have a single Mironov."

Mironov worked miracles to hold off the White Cossack armies storming Tsaritsyn. That, however, did not increase the political commissars' trust of him. Stalin wrote Lenin on August 4: "Cossack units that call themselves Soviet cannot but want to fight the Cossack counterrevolution; Cossacks have gone over to Mironov's side in whole regiments to get weapons, to learn the disposition of our troops on the spot and then lead away whole regiments to Krasnov's side; Mironov has been surrounded three times by Cossacks who knew everything about his sector and, naturally, destroyed him utterly."

Stalin, of course, did not pay particular attention to the facts and invented the threefold destruction of Mironov to justify the generally bad situation around Tsaritsyn, which had been caused by Stalin and Voroshilov's glaring stupidities and their destruction of the specialists. It was Stalin who, having killed the honest officers in the RKKA's ranks, overlooked the real traitor Nosovich and who, when Nosovich defected to the Whites, appointed Denikin's agent Kovalevsky as military instructor. There was no need for Mironov to carry out Nosovich's treacherous orders. Moscow tended to believe a TSK member rather than the Cossack lieutenant colonel, and Mironov did not receive the reinforcements he requested.

Mironov hung on despite all odds. Instead of reinforcements they gave him a decoration. His brigade continued to grow as deserters continued to leave Krasnov; it soon became a division, at first the 1st Ust-Medveditsky, later the 23rd. Mironov tried to maintain the honor of the revolutionary army. He struggled against pillaging, anti-Semitic agitation and pogroms. He did not shoot his prisoners, but permitted them to return to their homes.

During the Red offensive in early 1919 Mironov commanded a group of troops of the 9th Army. Once they had taken the northern part of Don territory from Krasnov, the Bolsheviks no longer fooled around with elected Soviets. Revolutionary committees were set up everywhere with power over the life, death, and property of the local inhabitants. It broke Mironov's heart to see how people were becoming heads of local revolutionary committees who "should not be permitted to run regional affairs because of the way they had behaved when the Revolution was in danger. Now, when the Revolution was strong, all of the slugs were crawling out in the sun and dirtying it."

Mironov protested energetically, but his quixotic outbursts were as useless as he knew they would be. Everyone knew that the commissars he complained of were good for nothing. Still they were left in place. Such things were going on at the Don that everyone needed his own men in place, however bad they might be. There was no room for Mironov. The first to ask for his removal was Chairman of the Donburo S. Syrtsov, later head of the Revolutionary Military Council of the Southern Front: "remove Mironov from his native villages, if necessary by promoting him." Trotsky ordered Mironov to come to the commander-in-chief's headquarters in Serpukhov. Despite all the efforts of Sokolnikov, who was a member of the RVS of the Southern Front and the TSK, and of Kniagnitsky, commander of the 9th Army, Mironov had to leave his units at the height of the offensive. On the surface Mironov's recall looked entirely regular. The RVSR awarded Mironov a gold watch and chain, and the 23rd Division was given the Red Banner.

If one thinks about it, the recall was a good, humanitarian act. It was just then, in early 1919, that at the Don and in other Cossack regions the Bolsheviks began something that Mironov, who was extremely sensitive to injustice, arbitrariness, and violence, could not have stood — "de-Cossackization."

Mironov, a Cossack who was still not a Party member, knew nothing of all this. During his enforced idleness at headquarters he sent a report to the RVSR, which read in part:

> So that the Cossack population remains sympathetic to the Soviet authorities, it is necessary:
>
> 1. To be concerned with the historical, traditional, and religious facets of their life. Time and capable political workers will dispel the darkness and the fanaticism of the Cossacks, inculcated by centuries of barracks upbringing. . . .
>
> 2. During the revolutionary period of the struggle with the bourgeoisie, until the counterrevolution is suppressed on the Don, circumstances require that the idea of communism be transmitted to the minds of the Cossack and peasant populations by means of lectures, conversations, brochures, etc., but in no circumstances forced upon them violently, as seems to be the case now in the acts of the "casual communists."
>
> 3. At the moment it is not necessary to make an inventory of livestock and dead stock. It would be better to announce firm

prices and demand delivery of products from the population . . .
in the course of which it is necessary to take their prosperity into
account. . . .

Of course, the capable political workers, just like the casual communists, took guidance from a circular (and secret) letter of the TSK
RKP(b) of January 29, 1919. Here is that startling document.

> It is necessary, considering the experience of the civil war with the
> Cossacks, to recognize that the only proper approach is a merci-
> less struggle against the *whole* Cossack leadership *to destroy them
> to the last man.*
>   1. Carry out *mass terror* [emphasis in the original] against
> wealthy Cossacks, and *having killed them all* conduct merciless
> mass terror against *all Cossacks* who take *any part, direct or
> indirect*, in the struggle with Soviet power. Take all *measures
> against the middle Cossacks* to guarantee there will be no efforts
> on their part to mount new demonstrations against Soviet power.

What sort of measures they had in mind was best explained by I.
Yakir, a member of the RVS of the 8th Army, which was then operating
at the Don. He wrote: "There will be rebellions in the rear of our
troops in the future unless *measures* are taken to nip in the bud even the
thought of such rebellions. These *measures*: the *complete annihilation
of all* who rebel, *execution* on the spot *of all* who possess weapons, and
even the *execution* of a certain *percentage* of the male population.
There must be *no negotiations* with rebels."

Thus, the complete annihilation of (a) the rich, (b) those who take
any part in rebellions, (c) those who possess weapons. It is interesting
to ask, what Cossack did not have a weapon? A percentage of the rest,
who happened not to fall into any of those categories, were to be killed
to teach the others not even to think of rebellion. And who would live
on this land purified by revolutionary justice? The answer is contained
in that same letter of the TSK to which we now return:

>   2. Confiscate grain [since it is not said *from whom*, it implies
> *from all*] and require that all *surplus* [an obvious logical redun-
> dancy, for what can be surplus after confiscation] be brought to
> specified places. This refers to grain as well as to *all other* agricul-
> tural products.
>   3. Take all measures to assist poor, newly arrived settlers;

organize resettlement where that is possible.

4. Equalize newly arrived non-Cossacks with the Cossacks in land holding and in all other relations [except apparently in mass executions].

5. Carry out full disarmament. Shoot *everyone* who possesses a weapon after the deadline for turning them in.

6. Distribute arms only to reliable elements among the *non-Cossacks*.

7. Maintain armed detachments in Cossack villages until complete order is established.

8. All commissars who are assigned to Cossack settlements are expected to be *absolutely firm* and to carry out these orders *unswervingly*. The Central Committee decrees that the obligation be passed to the People's Commissariat of Agriculture through the appropriate Soviet organs to work out as soon as possible the actual means for a *massive* resettlement of poor peasants to Cossacks lands. TSK RKP(b).

The Cossacks are a nationality, close to the Russians in language and religion, but with a wholly different way of life formed by centuries of history.[4] The TSK directive was a firm plan for genocide to be carried out in all eleven Cossack territories. It called also for organized colonization of the land thus freed by another ethnic group, chosen on the basis of property. This policy was applied all through the first half of 1919 and had particularly noticeable results in the Don and Ural River territories.

Proscriptions reached the scale of a natural disaster. Exact totals have not been made, but the toll reached the tens of thousands. Reliable non-Cossacks under the leadership of the commissars cut the Cossacks down right and left, brandishing the red banner as they did so. The thin shell of class struggle immediately fell to pieces, laying bare its animalistic essence. They killed the wealthy and the middling; nor did they spare the malcontents who let slip a harsh word. They just settled their accounts. If the Cossack men were not at home, they led out their wives, even their daughters, to be shot.

Not all of the executions were illegal. The Cheka and Army tribunals were hard at work. From the time of their arrival at the Don they were organized in every regiment. An order of the RVS of the Southern Front said, "Witnesses may be questioned if the tribunal finds it necessary."

The tribunals hardly ever availed themselves of that right, preferring to judge by lists. Usually the trial and sentencing (death by shooting) took only a few minutes. The 8th Army alone officially signed eight thousand people over to the hereafter. Other armies did not lag far behind, particularly the 10th. Worldly-wise Cossacks had to admit that the Bolsheviks were "pretty severe."

All this monstrous cruelty could not remain unanswered. On the night of March 11–12 a rebellion broke out in Kazanskaia and Veshenskaia *stanitsas*. A description of it can be found in the novel *And Quiet Flows the Don*,[5] although the picture given there is incomplete. Sholokhov, using Kriukov's manuscript, toned things down, as he admitted in a letter to Gorky, "I left out on purpose certain facts about the direct cause of the rebellion, such as the senseless shooting of sixty-two Cossack old men in Migulinskaia or the shootings in Kazanskaia and Shumilinskaia, where the number of Cossack victims exceeded 400 in the course of six days." From the novel one might think the revolutionary committees committed several abusive acts, which cost the lives of a few dozen people. Because of that the sixth part of *And Quiet Flows the Don* was withheld from the printers for a long time.

When their facile circular letter resulted in a desperate rebellion, which moreover had broken out dangerously close to Denikin, Moscow had to stop and think again. On March 16, in response to Sokolnikov's report, the TSK decided to halt the effort to destroy the Cossacks. That same day Ia. Sverdlov, who had been seriously ill and who had not attended the meeting, died. Because of that coincidence several historians have tried to place the blame on him alone. They claim that the directive of January 29 had been promulgated by the Orgburo, headed by Sverdlov, without the knowledge of the TSK or Lenin. The only evidence for this is that Sverdlov signed the covering letter sent with the circular letter. It is not possible to explain away, however, the fact that in carrying out the final part of the directive the Council of People's Commissars issued a directive in April (!) concerning the resettling of poor peasants on Cossack lands.

The people on the spot were reluctant to stop the genocide. The Donburo continued the former policy until June despite the protests of various Party workers.[6] The Southern Front revoked its orders about terror only at the end of April. The de-Cossackization was actually stopped by Denikin's offensive, which by the end of June occupied all the Don territory and seized Tsaritsyn.

We left Mironov at the moment that Trotsky's orders took him from the front. Mironov did not find the People's Commissar of Army and Navy at Serpukhov headquarters and had to go on to Moscow. It immediately became clear in his conversation with Trotsky that Trotsky did not have definite plans for using him. They agreed that Mironov would form a Cossack cavalry division of six regiments, which was confirmed by an order of the RVSR on March 15. Mironov went to Kozlov where the Southern Front command was located. There he was to receive 15 million rubles, mainly to purchase horses.

The behind-the-scenes maneuvering started again. The commissars of the Donburo and the Southern Front were determined not to allow Mironov to return, because he might serve as a rallying point for shattered Cossacks. They convinced Trotsky that Mironov was a threat to the Donburo, Soviet authority, and Trotsky himself. At Kozlov they refused to give him the money and forbade him to leave for the Don. They sent him to Serpukhov and put him at the service of Commander-in-Chief Vatsetis. Mironov was posted to Smolensk as assistant commander of the Belorussian-Lithuanian Army. He soon became commander, but still he felt as if he were in exile. Vague rumors of what was happening on the Don reached him, but of course he could not know what was really going on.

Meanwhile the bloody chaos in the Don territory was paving the way for the defeat of the Red forces. The rebels defeated Khvesin's expeditionary (punitive) corps, which was sent to pacify the Don. Three of Denikin's regiments broke through the front from the South and pushed as far as Kazanskaia. The northern Don territories were now threatened by the uprising.

Now was the time for Mironov to make his reappearance. At Sokolnikov's suggestion the RVSR appointed Mironov commander of the expeditionary corps, which was renamed a Special Corps. Mironov hurried to the Don, where in the northern regions, which were now in extreme danger, an emergency mobilization was in progress. Mironov agitated passionately at meetings urging the Cossacks to attack Denikin. His enormous personal authority got the job done.

Mironov and the newly appointed commissar, V. Trifonov, rode to take over the corps from Khvesin. The corps presented a sad spectacle. Whole Cossack squadrons had gone over to the enemy. Only eighty men were left in a regiment, 120 in the brigades. He would have to start from scratch and so informed the Southern Front command.

By this time Mironov knew the truth of de-Cossackization and the Veshenskaia uprising. Through all the turmoil of forming new units he was tormented by doubts. He cast about desperately for some way out of this bloody nightmare. He understood that he could not make common cause with Denikin and that the Reds, in the name of their sociological schemes, were prepared to tear the Cossack presence out by the roots. Mironov poured all of his troubled soul into an extremely long telegram to Trotsky, Lenin, and Kalinin, which he sent from Anna Station on June 24. One cannot read that document without emotion.

> I stood and I stand not for the cellular organization of national life along a narrow Party program, but for a public structure in which the people take an active part. I do not have the bourgeoisie and kulaks in mind here. Only this sort of structure will gain the sympathies of the peasant masses and parts of the honest intelligentsia.

Further on he described the condition of the corps:

> The special corps has about three thousand men to cover 145 versts of front. The units are strained and exhausted. Except for three classes all the cadets have proven to be beneath criticism and those pitiful tens and hundreds are all that are left of many thousands. The communist regiment has fled. There were men in it who did not know how to load a rifle. The special corps might serve as a screen. The situation of the special corps is saved now only by the fact that Cossacks mobilized from Khopersky region have been brought in. General Denikin's reliance on that region was not wholly justified. As soon as the White guards have corrected that deficiency, the special corps, as a screen, will be broken.

Without equivocation or evasions Mironov named the causes of the impending catastrophe:

> It is not only on the Don that the actions of some revolutionary committees, special detachments, tribunals, and some commissars [Mironov wrote "some" only because he did not know of the TSK directive] have caused a massive uprising. That uprising threatens to spill over in a broad wave through peasant villages across the face of the whole republic. To say that voices called out

openly in village meetings at Novaia Chigla, Verkho-Tishanka, and elsewhere, "Give us the tsar," sheds light on the mood of the peasant masses, which has resulted in such a high percentage of deserters and has created detachments of Greens. The uprising in Ilovatka on the Tersa River is contained for the time being, but serious unrest in most of the *uezds* of Saratov *guberniia* threatens to destroy the cause of socialist revolution. I am not a Party man, but I have spent too much of my strength and health in the struggle for socialist revolution, to watch unconcerned while General Denikin on his horse "Komuniia" tramples the red banner of labor.

Having analyzed the situation and come to the point, Mironov made his recommendations. The first concerned the Special Corps:

Looking thoughtfully into the future and seeing the death of the social revolution, for nothing disposes me to optimism and I am rarely a mistaken pessimist, I consider it necessary to recommend the following measures urgently: first, strengthen the special corps with fresh divisions; second, transfer to it the 23rd Division as the foundation for a future powerful new army, with which I and division commander Golikov will personally seize the initiative to set an example for other divisions and armies; or (third) appoint me commander of the 9th Army, where my combat authority stands high. . . .

Then came his political program:

Fourth, the political condition of the country urgently requires the calling of a popular representative body, and not just of one party, so as to cut the ground out from under the traitorous socialists, while continuing the struggle on the front and establishing the power of the Red Army.

This step will recapture the sympathy of the people, who will gladly take up arms to save their land and freedom. This representative body need not be called a *zemskii sobor* or a constituent assembly, *but it must be convened. The people are groaning.* I have sent many reports to the Southern Front *revvoensovet* among them this: a peasant of the 34th Department, now renamed Lenin Region. A family of twenty-one with four pairs of oxen. Their own commune. For refusal to enter a commune a commissar seized their oxen, and when the peasant protested, they killed him. I also transmitted a report from chairman Ermak of one of the tribunals, whose words were terrible to read. I repeat, the people are *ready* to fling themselves into the embrace of the land-lord cabal, in hopes that their suffering will not be so painful, so obvious as it is now.

His last suggestion concerned the holy of holies, the Bolshevik Party:

Fifth, the purge of the Party must be carried out on the following principle. All Communists (who joined the Party) after the October Revolution must be formed into companies and sent to the front. You will then see who are the real communists, who are the self-seekers, who are the provocateurs, and who have been polluting all the revolutionary committees and special detachments. The Morozovsky revolutionary committee, which killed sixty-seven people and then was itself shot, is a good example.
[Original signed by Special Corps Commander Citizen Mironov]

After so many years it makes no sense to judge which of Mironov's suggestions were realistic and to what degree. This was a cri de coeur of an honest and ardent warrior for the Revolution. His telegram was not answered.

Denikin continued to advance. The Reds lost the Don, Donbass, and Tsaritsyn. The Special Corps was no longer useful either as a punitive unit or as a screen. Mironov advanced the idea to create a Cossack Corps from men already mobilized and those who had fled from the Don region to attack Denikin's cavalry. This time the capital was not deaf. The corps commander was called to Moscow. On July 7 he appeared in the Cossack department of the vtsik and was made part of its staff. The next day he and Makarov, commissar of the department, visited Lenin. Lenin supported the creation of a corps of Cossacks, and after Mironov left he said to Makarov, "We need such men. We must use them well." They did indeed use men like Mironov—as long as they needed them.

With the authorities' blessing Mironov set off for Saransk to form his corps. But once again all expectations, promises, and hopes proved chimerical. They gave him nothing—no horses, no men, no ammunition, not even decent political workers. The so-called "Khopersk communists" had ensconced themselves in the RVS and the political department. Larin, Boldyrev, Rogachev, Zaitsev, who were splattered from head to foot with Cossack blood, felt no remorse for their victims, only fierce hatred. The Cossack department of the VTSIK warned that they "must not be allowed in the Don territory, because they have left there an awful memory. . . . in general they must not be trusted in any case. . . ." This warning was disregarded. The commissar of the Special Corps, V. Trifonov, refused to work with Mironov after it was decided to organize a Cossack corps. The old Party man felt at home in a punitive unit, but he considered Cossack units foolhardy.

The "Khopersk communists" waged a deadly campaign against the commander. Slanderous reports flew to Moscow demanding that the corps be dispersed or at least that Mironov be removed.

Mironov was squeezed from all sides. The Southern Front RVS and individual "commissar-Cossack eaters" held up the formation of the corps. Refugees from the Don told him new horror stories of violence against the Cossacks. Mironov decided to turn to Lenin, whom he now knew personally. The letter was sent on July 31.

Mironov began with an account of his telegram of June 24, after which he described the repressions on the Don and in Saratov *guberniia*. He wrote that news of mass executions did not surprise him,

> because I have already seen the main outlines of the Communists' policy toward the Cossacks, who are guilty only of ignorance and illiteracy; guilty of the fatal mistake of having been born of free Russian peasantry who at some time ran away from the yoke of the boyars and their truncheons to the free steppe of the Don; guilty because the Russian people during the reign of Peter I stifled their freedom at the cost of their blood; guilty because after enslaving them the tsarist authorities became more attentive to the Cossacks and by means of long disciplinary regime exterminated their humane feelings and turned them into the police guards of Russian thought, of Russian life; guilty because agents of Soviet power paid them even greater attention and instead of the word of love brought to the Don and the Ural—revenge, arson, and destruction. How can we justify what those villains did in Veshenskaia, the village which first understood their fatal mistake and in January 1919 abandoned the Kachaevo-Bogucharsky Front? That behavior caused the massive rebellion on the Don. If it was

not fatal, it was in any case an awful thing, fraught with endless consequences for the course of the whole revolution.

Again he offered examples of executions and pillaging. The 8th Army tribunals often shot Cossacks only for asking to be paid for horses and grain that were taken from them.

> It is impossible, there is not enough time and paper, Vladimir Ilich, to describe the horrors of "building communism" on the Don . . . . A certain D. Varov in Pravda, #136, in an article "On the Don" touched upon the events in Veshenskaia, but feared apparently to offend the Communists. For him these events were only "discomforting," and the Cossacks who rebelled against the violence and oppression became "White guard sympathizers."
> . . . Another Soviet correspondent, a certain A. V. poured all of the atrocities, violence, and horrors into the single phrase, "the not always tactful acts of the representatives of authority." The servile soul of the autocracy's scribblers has passed into the scribblers of the Soviet authorities. The people do not need their servants of the free word in servants' livery.

Mironov *did not believe* that Lenin knew what was going on:

> I cannot agree, I cannot accept that you have looked perfunctorily on all these horrors, and that it was done with your approval. I can no longer be silent, I have not the strength to bear the people's suffering in the name of an abstract, far-distant something or other.

Turning to the situation on the Southern Front, Mironov explained to Lenin:

> Only by successfully strengthening the rear might the fighting line of the front have been made invincible. To strengthen the rear it was necessary to understand its psychology, its peculiarities, its weak points, etc. Unfortunately, the political leaders of the Southern Front did not have that knowledge. . . . Our units marched forward in good order, causing no disturbances among the Cossacks, who had been told and written so much about the "atrocities" of the Bolsheviks. The impression, therefore, was most favorable. . . . When our units had passed, the Political Departments of the armies, divisions, and brigades set about their

organization, but unfortunately because of technical limitations and purely bureaucratic organization they were not able to carry out a single one of their grandiose plans. . . . The hastily put together *okrug* and *volost* revolutionary committees did not understand their functions, they looked on the Cossacks with the eyes of *suppressors*. And then the requisitions, confiscations, arrests, and so forth began. . . . The destruction of the Cossacks became an irrefutable fact, as soon as the Don became Soviet. . . . I do not believe that honest factory workers have accepted the elimination of honest people and the shooting of innocent village workers like themselves, even in the name of social justice. . . .

Mironov hurled the most serious accusation in Lenin's face: "What do we call these acts by the Reds? The whole activity of the Communist Party, led by you, is directed at the destruction of the Cossacks, at the destruction of mankind in general." He recalled:

In a telegram to you, Vladimir Ilich, I implored you to change the policy, to make a revolutionary concession, to ameliorate the suffering of the people and by that step to attract the people to the side of Soviet power, to the side of strengthening the revolution. . . . In these views, I repeat, I differ from the Communists. This is the root of the distrust of me. And the Communists are right. I will not support their policy of destruction of the Cossacks and then of the better-off peasants. . . . I will not participate in this madness, which has just become evident to me, and with all the strength that is in me I will fight against the destruction of the Cossacks and the middle peasantry. . . . I am in favor of leaving the peasants alone as far as their religion and traditions go and of leading them to a better life by *our example*, by demonstration, not by the fine, ringing phrases of half-baked Communists, whose lips are still wet with milk, the majority of whom cannot tell wheat from barley, although at meetings, with great aplomb they teach the peasants how to farm.

In this emotional and not particularly coherent letter he repeats frequently his appeal to stop the destruction of the Cossacks: "I demand in the name of the Revolution and on behalf of tortured Cossackdom a halt to the policy of their destruction. . . . If this continues, we will have to stop fighting Krasnov and fight the Communists." Nonetheless the independent Mironov announced: "I will go to the end with the Bolshevik Party—if they conduct a policy which does not diverge in word or deed—as I have done so far. . . ." At that point he produced his demands:

> The social life of the Russian people, to which [category] the Cossacks belong, must be constructed in accordance with its historical, cultural, and religious traditions and views, and the future must be left to time. . . . In carrying out the current struggle we had the opportunity to see . . . for Marxism the present is only the means, and the future is only a goal. And if that is so, I refuse to take part in such construction in which the whole people and everything they have earned is squandered on the goal of a distant, abstract future. Is contemporary man not a goal? Is he really so bereft of organs of sensation that we want to build the happiness of some far-off mankind at the cost of suffering? No it is time to stop the *experiments*. The almost two-year experiment in the people's suffering must have convinced the Communists that denying the human personality is madness.

The situation left Mironov deeply divided: "Because of my long-held revolutionary and social convictions, I do not want to ally myself with Denikin, Kolchak, Petliura, Grigor'ev, and the other counterrevolutionaries, but I look with equal repugnance upon the violence which false Communists have inflicted upon the laboring people, and because of that I cannot be their supporter either. . . ."

Mironov knew very well that his struggle with the evil, "caused by individual agents of authority," might cost him his life, but he was given strength by the certainty that his was not "an individual protest against this evil spread across the face of the republic, but a collective protest, a protest of tens of millions of people."

Mironov wanted to remain a soldier of the Revolution:

> Suffering with all my soul for the laboring people and the possible loss of revolutionary conquests, I feel that I can render important assistance at this critical moment of the struggle *under the following conditions*: that there be a clear and definite policy on the Cossack question and complete trust in me and my *independent* but vitally healthy views. Whether I deserve that trust, you can judge by this letter.

Since this letter reflects not [only] my personal view of the situation, but the view of millions of peasants and Cossacks, I have thought it necessary to send copies of this letter at the same time to my many loyal friends. Sincerely respectful of you and devoted to your ideas [I am] Commander of the Don Corps, Citizen, Cossack of Ust-Medveditskaia *stanitsa*, Mironov.

Mironov did not receive a reply to his confession, his desperate call, his cri de coeur. The same was true of his telegram from Anna Station. Lenin read Mironov's letter. That is evidenced by notes in his hand, "important," "very important," "very good," and so forth. It is said that he received the letter after a long delay—not until the autumn. That is possible, although very strange. But, really, what could he have written in reply?

Not having received a reply to his appeal, Mironov made one more attempt to improve relations with the Soviet authorities. On August 8 he submitted to the Politial Department a request "to register him as a member of the RKP" and to bring that to the attention of Kalinin, Trotsky, and Lenin. The "Khopersk communists" refused with great pleasure. The situation at the front was bad. The breakthrough of Mamontov's cavalry corps had put Tambov and Kozlov in the Whites' hands. Inactivity became unbearable. Mironov began to prepare the corps for an attack on Denikin, reports of which reached the RVS of the Republic. I. Smigla, a TSK and RVSR member, whom Mironov trusted, ordered him by direct-line telegraph "not to dispatch a single unit without permission." In reply to Mironov's objections Smigla invited him to come to Penza.

Mironov made ready for the trip, but the stationmaster refused him the cars for his escort of 150 men, to which Smigla had agreed. On August 18 it became known that the Political Department had officially ordered the disbanding of the Don Corps on the grounds that Mironov was a "Grigorevite." He could not travel without his escort. Mironov knew the commissars were set on violence. Mironov decided upon a demonstration. The denouement was approaching.

On August 22, Mironov issued his "Order-Proclamation." Having described the destruction of the Cossacks being carried out "by new Vandals, who have revived by their evil deeds the times of the Middle Ages and the inquisition," he declared:

There remains only one way to save the victories of the Revolution: overthrow the Communist Party. As soon as this news from the Southern Front reaches the Cossacks, they will stop and abandon the generals and landlords, whom they have followed only in the name of trampled truths.

Citizen Cossacks and soldiers of the Don Territory! We die on the front, spilling blood in unequal battle for land and for the true happiness of men, which only they themselves can fashion, not a bunch of people who do not know life. By its appearance the corps will lift the spirits of Red soldiers. Remember, you are not alone. The true spirit of the suffering people is with you. If you die in battle, you die for truth. Christ loved truth and died for it. Better to die in the open field than to lie on one's stove resenting the people's suffering.

That same day Mironov spoke at a meeting. The next day he informed the Southern Front, "I am setting out with the forces at my disposal to fight Denikin and the bourgeoisie."

On August 24, the day of the attack, he addressed a telegram to "Citizen member of the RVS of the Republic Smigla, copy to the Russian people." Mironov declared that he was not after the Communists' blood and would not shoot first. He offered to make an alliance against Denikin to save the Revolution, saying, "do not forget that the Paris Commune was killed by the common man. The Don Corps waits on your political wisdom and statesmanship in order to destroy Denikin with our common forces. . . ." He issued an appeal to the Russian people:

Weary Russian people, in view of your suffering and torment, and outrages upon yourself and your conscience—no honest citizen who loves the truth need bear this violence any more. Seize all the power, all the land, the factories and mills. And we, the true defenders of your interests, will fight your evil enemy General Denikin, believing deeply that you do not want the landlords and capitalists to return, and that you will try, however hard it may be, you will apply all your strength to save the revolutionary front, to save the victories of the revolution.

On the red banners of the Don revolutionary corps is written: all land to the peasants, all factories and mills to the workers, all power to the people through true councils of workers, peasants, and Cossacks' deputies, elected by the workers on the basis of free socialist agitation. Down with the autocracy of commissars, who have ruined the revolution.

I am not alone. The true spirit of the people, which has suffered for truth, is with me, which guarantees that the revolution will be saved.

ALL SO-CALLED DESERTERS join me and form that terrible force before which Denikin will quake and the Communists bow down. I call all who love truth and true freedom to the ranks of the corps.

The corps set off, planning to join up with the 23rd Division, which had been commanded by Mironov.

The hopes he had placed on the wisdom of the Communists were in vain. "People who do not know life" knew well, however, the taste of power, and they perceived in Mironov's acts only an encroachment upon their power. Smigla issued a statement in which Mironov was declared a traitor, a rebel, and an outlaw. The order to "deliver him alive or dead to the headquarters of Soviet forces," was made. In the next order Mironov was accused of being in league with Denikin. Lenin ordered Skliansky to have "Sokolnikov's godchild" caught.

The Russian people were deaf to the call of their Messiah. No one came to help him. Under the influence of Smigla's order most of his soldiers deserted the Corps. With a detachment of five hundred Mironov made his way through the forest paths, avoiding settlements. He tried to avoid fighting the Red units sent to capture him. There were only a few minor skirmishes in which ten men from both sides died. Finally on September 14 Mironov came across Budenny's cavalry corps and surrendered to him without a fight.

The non-Cossack Budenny planned to shoot the Cossack Mironov on the spot, but as bad luck would have it Trotsky was present and did not let him.

The RVSR chairman had his reasons. The political side of the matter interested him. Mironov and all of the men seized with him were sent to Balashov and handed over to a judicial investigative commission (troika) headed by D. Poluian, a Kuban Cossack. Three days later the commission was given the powers of a tribunal.

Trotsky thought that "the trial ought to have a significant educational meaning for the Cossacks." As his personal emissary to Balashov he appointed Smigla who oversaw the whole trial.

Trotsky was kept informed. Before Mironov had been caught, Trotsky had written an article, "Colonel Mironov," in the RVSR paper, *V puti*. His sharp revolutionary eye had discerned in Mironov "personal ambition, careerism, a desire to rise up on the backs of the laboring masses," even the intention to become the Don ataman. His next article, "Lessons of the Mironov Movement," appeared when the corps commander was already in the tribunal's hands. Trotsky interpreted even the fact that the corps had surrendered without a battle in a way that reflected badly on Mironov. But we ought not to judge Lev Davidovich too severely, because as his later behavior showed he did not believe what he wrote. To a fiery Party publicist like Trotsky propaganda was more important than the truth. Because of that, the unavoidable labels were applied to Mironov. He was declared the expression of the middle Cossacks' indecision; the Mironov movement was the embodiment of the partisan movement that would have to be crushed. We must, however, give Trotsky his due: he was not bloodthirsty. Had Stalin been in his place, Mironov would have been put against the wall without delay.

The judicial procedure lasted three days. The hearings were open. The objectivity of the indictment would surprise Soviet citizens of the next generation who became used to well-organized trials. It included Mironov's appeal and his conversation with Smigla, and described accurately his behavior after his rebellion. There was not a word about an association with Denikin. His acts were considered treasonous.

Mironov admitted his guilt, most of the accused denied it. The corps commander explained his motives in great detail and asked for mercy. At his request his letter to Lenin was admitted as evidence and a number of witnesses were questioned. The court also listened to the testimony of the "Khopersk communists."

Smigla acted as prosecutor. He exercised his rather informal eloquence at some length, apparently in imitation of his patron, Trotsky. He demanded that Mironov be shot, along with every tenth commander and one of every twenty of the remaining soldiers.

Mironov had a defender, Rybakov, who portrayed Mironov as a superlative military leader and the "lion of the Revolution." (Smigla called him a drake.) Rybakov laid out his military service in detail. Mironov's only guilt was that "as a warrior of the Red Army he was a

bad politician . . . and as a warrior he was direct in his actions."
Rybakov was not afraid to name the true causes of the rebellion: repres-
sion on the Don, indifference of the authorities to the fate of the
Cossacks, and the silence of Lenin. He compared Mironov's acts with
Trotsky's declaration "I cannot be silent!" The defender asked the
court to pardon Mironov.

In his final words Mironov dwelt on what had brought him to the
court. Without denying his guilt, he made reference to his political
ignorance (he had not read Marx) and begged indulgence. "I ask you
for probation, give me a chance to remain a revolutionary warrior and
prove that I can defend Soviet power. . . ."

The sentence ordered that Mironov and another ten men from among
the commanders and Communists be shot and the rest be imprisoned
for various terms, to be carried out at midnight.

Sentencing occurred on October 7. But that same day, before the
sentence could be carried out, the fate of the accused was determined
by Trotsky in a telegram to Smigla:

> The report on Mironov's trial leads me to think that we ought to
> provide a lenient sentence. In view of Mironov's behavior, I think
> that such a decision would be expedient. The slowness of our
> advance on the Don necessitates that we increase our political
> influence among the Cossacks with the purpose of causing a
> schism. For that mission we might, perhaps, be able to use
> Mironov, by bringing him to Moscow after sentencing, pardoning
> him through the TSIK with the obligation of working in the rear
> area to cause an uprising. . . .

All this, we hope, is clear. It was expedient to use Mironov to cause
a schism among the Cossacks. This was a high-stakes game involving
the fates of people, the country, the Revolution, and the court, which
like the VTSIK, are simply instruments in the game, like hockey sticks.

Smigla heeded his boss's wishes. The next day the court sent to
Moscow a petition to pardon the prisoners. They had already taken
from the prisoners their "word of honor to serve Soviet power and the
Revolution honestly in the future." The spectacle had turned out well.
The educational purpose had been achieved.

The long hours and days of waiting to be executed cost Mironov and
his comrades dearly. Mironov described this period two weeks later
when he was in Moscow. The convicts, at their request, were put

together in a single room where they sang, wrote letters, and talked: "death in battle is not frightening: one moment . . . and it is all over. But the consciousness of close, inevitable death is horrifying, when there is no hope, when you know that nothing can halt the approaching grave, when until the frightful moment there remains less and less time, and finally when they say to you, 'your pit is ready.' "

Even the hardy Communist Smigla, who did not recognize the existence of the soul, was touched by the appearance of Mironov. He wrote that "Mironov aged overnight. When I told him that I would petition about a pardon, the *old man* [The commander was forty-seven, Smigla was twenty years younger] broke down and sobbed. It was easier for the old soldier to part with life than to return to it." Did Smigla recall that while he was waiting to be shot in 1937?

The VTSIK's pardon was issued on October 8, but the prisoners were told of it four days later. Mironov wrote an application for Party membership.

On the tenth Trotsky devised a new plan by which the Cossacks would become "autonomous." He said: "The Cossacks are deserting Denikin altogether. Appropriate guarantees must be established that Denikin might be replaced by Mironov and his comrades, who will have to go to the heart of the Don." The plan did not find support —because of the "autonomy," which seemed excessive even in quotation marks.

Mironov and his men were sent to Moscow under guard, where a commission under Dzerzhinsky looked them over. The impression was favorable. On October 23 the Politburo ordered that they all be pardoned and sent to the Army. Mironov was treated separately. He was accepted into the Party on the standard basis and put on the staff of the Don Executive Committee. Opinions differed on how he was to be used. Lenin and Kamenev supported the idea of the Don Executive Committee, Krestinsky favored a command, Kalinin abstained. (Good old Mikhail Ivanovich wanted to avoid responsibility; he later refrained from helping Mironov in a time of mortal danger.) Because the majority was so small it was decided to get the opinion of Trotsky, who was absent. And what do you think? L. D. said that Colonel Mironov, the careerist, the Denikinist, and the Cossack ataman, should be sent to the Southwest Front in a command position. Nothing came of this, however, mainly because Mironov was at the limit of his strength.

He wrote an appeal to the Don Cossacks, which was approved by the

TSK; then he went to Nizhni Novgorod to see his wife. On the way he contracted typhus and was hospitalized. In early December he returned to Moscow, where he met with Lenin and Dzerzhinsky.

On the Don, Mironov found another policy pursued by the Soviet authorities. A sea of spilt blood and failures on the Denikin front had convinced Moscow that they could not fight their own population with impunity. It would be better to attract them to the Soviet side, especially the Cossacks, who were so valuable to the Army. In September 1919 Trotsky formulated "Guiding Principles of Current Policy on the Don," which was the basis of the TSK's thesis "On Work on the Don." Now—temporarily, of course—the approach to the Cossacks would be determined, not by class principles but by their relations with the Red Army. The troops and organs of power were instructed not to commit violence and to pay in time and in full for all items of supply.

Everything is better understood by comparison, even misfortune. After the shootings and requisitions of 1919 the "surplus appropriation system" of 1920, which was none too gentle, did not seem all that bad to the Cossacks.

Mironov became head of the land section of the Don Executive Committee. It was a familiar matter, but life in the rear oppressed him. All his thoughts were directed toward the front. Mironov wrote a few appeals to Cossacks serving with Wrangel.

In July 1920 the Second Horse Army was formed on the Wrangel Front under the command of Budenny's divisional commander O. I. Gorodovikov. In their first battles they experienced defeats. Then they remembered about that useful man Mironov. On August 30 the RVS of the Republic at the request of the Southwest Front (Egorov, Stalin) appointed F. K. Mironov commander of the Second Horse Army.

Mironov practically flew to Tavria, where he found the Army in rather bad condition: badly shrunken units, a half-literate command staff, only 2,760 horsemen, 130 machine guns, and 19 artillery pieces. Mironov worked nonstop. Along with reinforcements sent by the Army, numerous volunteers from the Don joined him. By the end of September he already had 6,228 horsemen.

An independent Southern Front, under the command of M. V. Frunze with RVS member S. I. Gusev, was formed on September 20 to fight Wrangel. Poluian, former chairman of the Balashov tribunal, was put on the Second Horse Army's RVS. Mironov took these Jesuitical insults badly. Frunze and Gusev sent a telegram of protest to Moscow, but they were unable to change anything. Apparently someone in the center had decided that Poluian would be a good watchdog and at the same time a live warning to the commander.

On October 8 Wrangel's shock units began the trans-Dnepr operation to consolidate their hold on the right bank. The Second Horse Army stood in their way. The Whites took Nikopol but were unable to get any farther. At the cost of huge losses the Second Horse destroyed some crack White units (Barbovich's corps, Markov's and Kornilov's divisions, and Babiev's cavalry) and drove them back across the Dnepr. The might of Wrangel's army was sapped, its spirit broken, its death agony begun. At the height of the battle Mironov himself led his cavalry in attack. His horse was shot out from under him.

Distrust of Mironov showed through occasionally nonetheless. During the battles in northern Tavria the commander-in-chief, and later Voroshilov and Budenny, tried to join the Second Horse Army to the First. Frunze put a stop to their attempts.

The success of the Second Horse Army undermined Voroshilov's and Budenny's dominance in the cavalry. Moreover, Frunze, who was one of the most authoritative and independent Red Army leaders, did not particularly like the commanders of the First Horse. When they received transfer orders from the Polish Front, Voroshilov and Budenny tried to have themselves subordinated to the commander-in-chief instead of to the front. Lenin and S. S. Kamenev rejected the attempt. Upon their arrival in Tavria, which was much delayed (we have discussed the reasons), the Horse Army RVS tried again to impose their conditions and put forward their own plan for taking the Crimea. The commander-in-chief did not bother to look it over. As a result, during the attack on the peninsula Frunze preferred to keep the First Horse in reserve and entered the fray only on the sixth day.

We refrain from describing the combat in the Crimea. That has been done well enough in Dushenkin's book. It is interesting to note, however, that Makhno's Insurgency Army, which fought against Wrangel on the side of the Reds, was also subordinated to Mironov. Mironov was not afraid to take the Guliai-Pole anarchists under his command. He used them brilliantly in the decisive battle on Litovsk peninsula when Frunze's forces, which had broken through onto the Crimea, were almost driven into the sea by the White's desperate counterattack. This is how Mironov described the events of November 11:

The 52nd and 15th Rifle Divisions were overrun by the Whites and retreated in disorder. General Barbovich's cavalry, and Drozdov's and Kornilov's cavalry units, which were mostly composed of crack officer units for whom there was nothing left to do but die, broke through to the north and threatened to break into the rear of the 6th Army. Hard after the retreating Red Armymen galloped the White cavalry with blades bared, sweeping the retreating Red Armymen from their path with wild yells and whistles. Head-on into the brutish band appeared the lava flow of the 16th and 2nd Cavalry Divisions; the correlation of forces was one to three. The lava flows neared one another. Cries of "hurrah" drowned out the machine-gun fire and the explosion of shells. Now only a thousand paces, seven hundred, five hundred. Sabers clashed. Suddenly the 2nd Horse units galloped aside, and 250 machine guns brought up on carts behind the Red cavalry opened up on the enemy a deadly automatic fire. Horses and men rolled on the ground. The first ranks were wiped out, the rear turned back and in their turn fell under the rifle and machine-gun fire of the 51st Rifle Division [Blokher's]. The enemy fled in panic.

On the machine-gun carts sat *Makhno's men*. The songwriters later always forgot that the *"tachanka"*—a light carriage with a machine gun—was first used by Nestor Makhno and was his main weapon.

The Whites raced into the depths of the Crimea. That same day Frunze offered Wrangel a truce, guaranteeing those who surrendered their lives and a chance to leave the country. The next day Lenin reprimanded the front commander for his liberalism, but more about that later.

On the evening of the eleventh, Mironov and Makhno finished off Barbovich and occupied Voinka Station. On the twelfth they were in Dzhankoi and a day later in Simferopol. The First Horse followed after, staying a day's march behind.

The campaign was over. Wrangel did not reply to Frunze's offer, but on November 13 he disbanded his army, leaving everyone to his own fate.

Mironov was at the zenith of military glory. The decisive contribution of the Second Horse Army to the conquest of the Crimea was acknowledged by all. Mironov was decorated with Honorary Revolutionary Arms (a sword with a gilt hilt and overlaid with an Order of the

Red Banner) and then, along with two hundred soldiers of the Second Horse, with an Order of the Red Banner. This was his first decoration; at Tsaritsyn he had only been recommended for one, but for some unknown reason the award had not been made.

The war ended, and the Second Horse Army was made into the 2nd Horse Corps. But the struggle continued. On November 23 Frunze gave an ultimatum to Makhno, who during the Crimean campaign had remained in Guliai-Pole with a large force, to disband all of his detachments. Makhno did not capitulate and was declared an enemy of Soviet power. Mironov was unwillingly thrown into the fray. These punitive functions were like a sharp knife in his heart. He read Frunze's orders to his men, but he also ordered them to avoid a clash. At the same time he requested that Moscow recall him: he did not want to fight against his recent comrade-in-arms. The center agreed that it would be best to transfer Mironov to other duties, but he was to remain in his position until a new commander arrived. The Horse Corps wandered about the southern Ukraine for more than a month, reluctantly pursuing the elusive Makhno. Finally they were transferred to the Caucasus Front (Likhaia Station). Only in January 1921 did Mironov receive his new appointment: as assistant commander-in-chief (chief inspector) of cavalry.

The last act of Mironov's tragedy had begun. Having turned his command over to N.D. Tomin, he left Usmanskaia Station for Moscow on January 30. The hero was given special accommodations: a Pullman car for himself, his wife, two orderlies, and a cook; and a heated car for two horses and a machine-gun cart. He traveled without a guard unit. What would he need the guards for when at practically every station he was met triumphantly by crowds, orchestras, official greetings?

After the festive ceremony at Rostov, Smigla visited Mironov's car. The conversation was friendly, and the frightful days of the Balashov trial could be recalled with humor. But Mironov may have forgiven and forgotten too soon. The Cheka, as is expected of it, was wide awake. The situation on the Don was not at all good. The "surplus appropriation system" was bleeding the Cossacks dry and turning them once again against the authorities. It was much the same throughout rural Russia. The politically unsophisticated muzhiks did not want to give away all of the grain they had raised for some ideal that they did not yet understand. The demobilized Red Armymen returned to their homes;

and when their grain was taken, they got no discount. Peasant riots and uprisings broke out all over the country. At first the Soviet authorities did not take them very seriously. It was early February, and the chairman of the VTSIK, Kalinin, was in the Kuban. A local worker complained to him, "It's bad, they take the appropriations from us at the point of a gun. They come, and they take everything. The old women beg them to at least leave something for the *children* or for the horses, but they only shout, 'Take it all.' And they really do take *everything*, they don't leave anything. . . ." Kalinin, the muzhik from Tver, replied:

> *Of all people* we must not offend the Cossacks. They are a warlike people, they will start an uprising, there will be disorder. But as much as it might like to, the government cannot do *anything differently*, because it would be criminal if in one part of the state the people had more than enough to eat while in another they were literally starving. The government must take the *last giblet* from the peasant who has and can give for those who are starving . . . [our emphasis].

Well, who would have thought, what an imp, excuse me, a dialectician. Of all people not to offend and take to the last giblet. Somewhere there is famine; therefore we will take everything from you. What those people would eat, all of whose grain was taken, Mikhail Ivanovich was not prepared to discuss at this historical stage.

The Cossacks for the umpteenth time found their treatment unreasonable and took to their guns. Vakulin, a former regimental commander of the 23rd "Mironov" division, rebelled in the northern Don Territory and in early February 1921 occupied Kamyshin. In his proclamations he promised the Cossacks the support of the Tambov leader Antonov, as well as of Mironov and Budenny. The 2nd Horse Corps, now without Mironov, was sent to put the rebellion down.

In these extremely tense circumstances Mironov decided to visit his native territory on his way from Rostov to Moscow. In a word: "In Europe it is cold, in Italy it is warm. Power is as repulsive as the hands of the barber." Mironov's visit was not welcomed by the Don Cheka and its head, Burov. Dispatches flew on ahead of the army commander with directions to redouble vigilance and to take measures.

Immediately upon his arrival at Ust-Medveditsky Mironov spoke at a large meeting that had been called by the revolutionary committee. He called upon the Cossacks to preserve the peace and promised to help

correct the mistakes of the local authorities. The village Party organization delegated him to a regional conference, which was to open in
Mikhailovka village where Vakulin—who, by the way, held an Order
of the Red Banner—had recently raised his rebellion. Mironov was in
a hurry to get to Moscow, but allowed himself to be persuaded by his
fellow villagers.

The next day a group of his comrades from the 23rd Division gathered around him. Among them was a certain Skobinenko, a "surplus"
appropriator, who was also a civilian informer for the Cheka. Skobinenko's assignment for the Cheka was to lead the discussion to abuses of
the local authorities. Mironov spoke candidly. In his opinion, the continuation of grain requisitioning would cause new rebellions by spring.
Before they broke up, the men present at the meeting agreed to send
coded messages to Mironov in Moscow to keep him informed of events
on the Don. The material on Mironov was ready; what came later
would only add to it.

At the conference Mironov attacked the local Cheka by speaking
openly of the disorders they had caused. He asked that they permit
private trade and that they replace expropriations by a direct tax, in a
word, put an end to "War Communism." These heretical demands
horrified the local commissars. They dispersed the conference and put
Mironov under arrest.

Similar heresies were being discussed at the time in the Politburo.
On February 16 they decided to publish an article for discussion on a
tax in kind. But what is permitted to Jupiter would land the bull in
Lubianka. Mironov's wife and several of the conference participants
were also arrested. Skliansky informed Lenin that Mironov was under
arrest by the local Cheka charged with attempting to incite rebellion.
That much is documented; Lenin's reaction is unknown.

The Kremlin leaders had all they could handle at the time: peasant
rebellions, the Kronshtadt mutiny, and in the Party the discussion on
trade unions and the Tenth Congress (March 8–16). After the sounds
of the Congress's debates had died away, after expropriation was
replaced by a tax in kind, and after the Kronshtadt sailors had been
suppressed, Mironov still sat in jail. True, he was not in the Lubianka,
but in the Butyrka.

We ought not to judge the All-Russian Cheka (VCheka) chairman
Dzerzhinsky too harshly. To his other difficult duties the Party had
added the post of People's Commissar of Transportation. Returning

from Kronshtadt, Feliks suddenly ordered that Mironov and his comrades be quickly brought to Moscow. In the complex Lubianka organization is was not easy to find a man.

March drew to a close, but still the Mironov matter was not settled. An unhurried investigation was under way. In the middle of the month he declared a hunger strike—in vain. Several times during walks he met his wife, who was also being held there. The regime, apparently, was not yet well established. They gave Mironov newspapers, even a pen and paper. Having lost hope, on March 30 he wrote a last confession:

> A Party letter. To Chairman of the VTSIK Citizen M. I. Kalinin.
> Copies: Chairman of the Council of People's Commissars V. I. Ulianov.
> Chairman of the RVS of the Republic L. D. Trotsky.
> Chairman of the TSK RKP L. B. Kamenev. . . .

It was a long letter. Mironov rejected the charges against him and discussed the provocation of the Don Cheka. He asked, Why am I in prison? Because I was ready to lead Red forces on Bucharest, Budapest, and so forth? Because I protested against the abuses and mistakes that the Party and its leaders have admitted, and demanded the establishment of a tax that has now been introduced by law?

> People in general, and I all the more, do not lie in the face of death, for I have not lost faith in my God, who is embodied in conscience. As I have always done all my life with friends and enemies alike. . . . I repeat, that is my God, and I have not and I will not cease to pray to him as long as there is a soul in my frail body. . . . And if you, Mikhail Ivanovich, remain deaf until April 15, 1921, I will die of starvation in prison. . . . I do not want to admit the thought that the Soviet authorities on the basis of false and unfounded denunciations would guillotine one of their best fighters, "the valiant commander of the 2nd Horse Army" (RVS order of 4/12/20). . . . Let there not be this shameful page to gladden Generals Krasnov and Wrangel, who were beaten by me. . . . I remain with deep faith in the truth. Former Army Commander of the 2nd Horse Army, Communist F. K. Mironov.

Mikhail Ivanovich remained deaf. Nor did the other chairmen raise their voices. But Mironov had hope. On the day he sent the letter he made plans to see his wife on April 2, thinking that by that time he would have an answer. But something else happened that day. All of the prisoners' walks were cancelled. Except Mironov's. He was led out to walk in the stone enclosure of the inner yard. The guard shot once. . . . That is how, many years later, one of the wardens of Butyrka tells it.

Once again we are told with regret that Mironov's letter did not reach the addressee. Or rather, not quite that way. Comrade Kalinin did read it, but it was too late. Recall that Lenin's telegram pardoning N. Gumilev also arrived late. "It is too late," said Lafayette to the king's messengers. "What can we do? We will believe . . . in good intentions."

The Mironov case with all its documents has survived. There is a card on which is written in pencil in an unknown hand, "Shot by a decision of the VCheka collegium 2 April 1921." The others arrested in connection with the Mironov case were held a while longer in prison and then released without trial. His wife was also freed. In 1922 Kalinin summoned her. Their conversation was long, but not a word was said about Mironov's death. The all-union elder had showed he had a heart; he gave orders to give her a pass to Mineralnye Vody spa in the Caucasus. In 1924 the People's Commissariat for Army and Navy established a personal pension for her.

After that it was as if Mironov had been forgotten. True, Smigla mentioned him not unkindly in his memoirs in the 1920s. Then silence fell. Mironov does not figure in the encyclopedias and books on the history of the Civil War. From 1937 on he became a traitor and rebel. Mironov's military accomplishments were transferred to Budenny, and partially to Gorodovikov.

We do not know who ordered Mironov killed. Possibly the authorities tired of bothering with the refractory Cossack, especially after the war was over. Maybe the Kronshtadt mutiny decided his fate: he could be seen as the center of future insurrections. It is also very likely that some personal scores were being settled—maybe by someone of those who would have served under the new inspector of cavalry. (Two years later Budenny was assigned to that post.)

It is more than likely that Kalinin read the letter in time. But it would not have been like him to intervene for a prisoner before the fearsome Cheka. Who has forgotten how after the pardon in 1919 he washed his hands of it in the Politburo?

In 1956, during the revelations and rehabilitations, in the torrent of crocodile tears for the millions of innocent victims, Mironov was remembered also. For four years the Military Collegium of the Supreme Court batted the case back and forth until they came to the portentous conclusion: "Abrogate the order of the Presidium of the VCheka of April 2, 1921, in regard to F. K. Mironov and dismiss the case for lack of criminality in his actions."

That was it. They abrogated an order that had not been. We therefore did not learn who was guilty of Mironov's death. However, those who had his death on their hands responded quickly. In 1961, twenty-five former commanders and political workers of the First Horse Army sent an angry letter to the TsK demanding that the Military Collegium's decision be laid aside. There was no answer.

The case of the most famous cavalryman was still not reconciled. In 1966 a display was erected at the Central Museum of the Soviet Army, dedicated to the Second Horse and Mironov. Budenny was invited to the opening. When he saw the photograph of Mironov, the marshal reddened and stamped his feet. Some feared for his health. The museum workers found a Solomonic solution. Mironov was replaced by Gorodovikov. Budenny gradually calmed down. After his departure the display was restored to its former appearance. But every time the marshal visited, Mironov's portrait had to be removed.

Mironov stands by himself among the great Red military leaders. The others, whatever their pasts might have been, were servants of the new authorities. Mironov, while a soldier, remained a revolutionary. He understood revolution as the free creativity of the people creating new ways of life for themselves.

For others the Revolution ended with the seizure of power and the formation of a new national leadership. For Mironov, on the other hand, that was only the beginning. It was his conviction that only the people could determine their future, determine it according to their own understanding and not at the instruction of people "distant from life." And they do it for themselves without sacrificing the living to Party dogma for the doubtful sake of future generations. Mironov wanted freedom and justice for the people in his own day. He firmly believed that they needed it as much as their descendants. Only the people were sovereign, not the commissars, the Cheka, the TsK or SNK.

Having come to power as a result of the October coup, the new state-political leadership usurped the governing powers of the Russian people. All decisions of the TsK came to be passed off as the will of the

Revolution. This form of government took the name dictatorship of the proletariat. Everyone understood, of course, that the dictatorship was run not by the working class, which was still laughably small—1.5 to 2 million in a population of 150 million—but by the Communist Party, or more precisely by the Party elite, who were actually beyond any other control and were irremovable.

The higher Red Army commanders were, with few exceptions, officers of the old Army.[7] Nicholas II's abdication freed them from their former oaths. They swore loyalty to the new authorities and served them faithfully. Any directive, any order from above was obligatory for them regardless of its purpose or content. Nor were the Communists in the best of positions. Their revolutionary consciousness was not free, but subordinate to the will of the TSK. Every decision of the Party leadership had to be carried out, or one ceased to be a member of the Party. It is hard to imagine that every Bolshevik, and they numbered in the hundreds of thousands, agreed with the destruction of the Cossacks; but practically all who were ordered to do so put the savage directive of January 29 into effect.

If the Communists were deprived of free will, what might be said of the officers over whom hung the damnation of unclean birth and past service? Only unquestioning obedience gave them any sort of guarantee for their lives; otherwise they risked being accused of treason and shot. This is not to speak of the officers who were killed for no reason at all, for example those who were drowned in the Volga at Stalin and Voroshilov's orders. They all weigh on the conscience regardless of their background. The former landlord and lieutenant Tukhachevsky skillfully commanded the suppression of the Kronshtadt mutiny, after which he was sent to suppress the Tambov peasants. Yakir, the school dropout from a poor Jewish family, not only directed mass executions but created a program of genocide that such masters of that sort of business as Hitler, Goebbels, and Rosenberg would have signed with both hands.[8]

Mironov cannot be cast in the role of suppressor. He fought according to the dictates of his conscience and wanted to fight only those whom he considered enemies of freedom. He was opposed to shooting peaceful villagers, prisoners, and even rebels. Because of that he fought passionately against de-Cossackization and the slaughter of peasants. He, therefore, did not want to fight Makhno's Insurgency Army. Mironov knew that he was being sent against Makhno, with whom he had recently fought on the same side, not because of pillaging, but because he would not submit to Moscow's will. To be sure, Makhno's boys liked to indulge themselves at others' expense, but such sins were more than sufficient on the Red Armymen's side.

Mironov was in some ways like Makhno and Antonov, who, whatever the official historians might say of them, were ideological fighters. These men believed that they had the right to their own understanding of freedom, not coordinated with the Kremlin, and they fought for that freedom.

A folk *intelligent*, a born commander, a true individual, a philanthropist, and truthseeker, Mironov was doomed, as was everyone who did not care to or could not become an industrious cog in the new governmental machine. It would not mean much to say that he would not have lived past 1937. We cannot imagine him commissar-obedient after war's end in either the Army or civil service. Mironov was killed by personal enemies, but had their attempt been unsuccessful some other conflict with the authorities would have awaited him. It would have come soon and undoubtedly would have been fatal.

It is deeply symbolic that during the Civil War Mironov was forgiven for independence and even rebellion, but that he was dealt with in the first days of victory. The new authorities, who called themselves revolutionary, needed a strong Army, which they called the defense of the Revolution. But for the lion of the Revolution, Mironov, and other real revolutionaries, as distinct from tame revolutionaries, there was no longer room—not in this Army, not in this life.

1921: Suppression

The Red Army's victory over Wrangel concluded the larger Civil War in European Russia. For two more years campaigns were waged in Central Asia and in the Far East, which resulted in the conquest of those outposts of the former empire. During that time the Army found a new occupation, which did not bring it martial glory, but which was vitally important for the new state. In this little Civil War the RKKA finished off the partisan movements, which for propaganda purposes were called bandit gangs; the leaders of the partisans included their recent ally Makhno, the Polish mercenary Tiutiunnik, and many others. In 1921 the mailed fist of the Army crushed two other popular uprisings: the soldiers and sailors at Kronshtadt, and the peasants at Tambov. These episodes of the Army's history deserve special attention for several reasons, not the least of which is that in both cases the Red forces were commanded by Mikhail Tukhachevsky.

On the basis of a false historical analogy one might assume that the victorious side in a civil war might display magnanimity—or at least mercy—to the defeated enemy. It would seem there could not be a better way to quickly heal the open wounds of the recent slaughter, to erase the bloody memories from the national memory, to douse the violent flames of hatred and brutality. As much as or more than its daily bread, the country needed a national reconciliation, which alone could ensure a peaceful future. The Americans took that path after their bitter Civil War, but in Russia things went differently.

In 1921, when most of the country was free of civil war, the regime became harsher. It was a direct result of the victory. The Bolshevik leaders felt that at last there was no power capable of quickly overthrowing them, either in the country nor beyond its borders. Therefore they began to consolidate their authority. It is not contradictory that the New Economic Policy was proclaimed that same year. NEP was only a tactical maneuver in the economic sphere, a forced retreat in the face of famine and growing popular dissatisfaction, mostly on the part of the peasants. Trotsky, by the way, had suggested ending the direct expropriation of grain from the peasantry as early as February 1920.

Political authority became openly totalitarian. Extraordinary powers that had earlier been justified by wartime conditions now became normal. The pervasive punitive apparatus and its product, the Gulag, grew stronger. The limitations on civil rights lost their temporary character and became more widespread and more severe. The last non-Bolshevik organs of the press were closed, and censorship was made stringent. The Orthodox Church, whose congregation had until recently comprised the majority of the Russian population, was dealt a mortal blow. Other religious sects did not fare better. All political parties except the Bolsheviks were utterly liquidated. The Communists thus achieved a monopoly on ideology and political activity.

In the Bolshevik Party itself an Arakcheevan[1] regime was more and more tightly imposed, rooting out the weak shoots of inner-party democracy in the form of factions and groups. Lenin's infamous resolution "On Party Unity" was enacted immediately after the Civil War. During the mortal struggle for the existence of the Party and its power it had been all right to dispute and to insist on one's own point of view, but when that battle had been won, such freedom became an unallowable luxury. One ought not take literally Lenin's argument that the more or less open debate about trade unions had made the Party vulnerable to criticism by the petite bourgeoisie and had brought the Party to the brink of catastrophe.[2] The leadership that realized its power over the country through the Party considered this a suitable moment to strengthen its dominant position. The clash of opinions expressed in bitter polemics and conflicting resolutions at annual conferences had undermined the authority of the top leaders and interfered with truly scientific leadership. Compulsory unity, reminiscent of the inviolability of church dogma, opened the way to the absolute power of the apparatus —and to the dictatorship of Stalin.

Total cruelty as a form of government policy was given clear expression in the fall of 1920. When it became clear that the Reds would win the Crimean campaign, Frunze gave in to unforgiveable weakness and attempted to avoid unnecessary bloodshed. On November 11 he addressed the commander of the White forces:

> In view of the uselessness of further resistance by your troops, which threatens only to shed superfluous streams of blood, I suggest you cease your resistance and surrender with all of the

forces of your army and navy, military reserves, supplies, arms, and all other military goods.

In the case that you accept this offer, the Revolutionary Military Council of the armies of the Southern Front—on the basis of the powers bestowed upon it by the central Soviet authority—guarantees the surrendering forces, including its highest commanders, full pardon for all their offenses connected with the Civil War. All of those who choose not to remain and work in socialist Russia will be given an opportunity to emigrate without hindrance on the condition that they promise to refrain from waging further war against workers'-peasants' Russia and Soviet authority. I expect a reply before 2400 hours on November 11.

Moral responsibility for all possible consequences of refusing this honorable offer lies on you. . . .

This appeal was broadcast by radio. At the same time the Revolutionary Military Council of the Southern Front (M. Frunze, I. Smigla, B. Kun, M. Vladimirov) addressed the following appeal, also by radio, "to the officers, soldiers, Cossacks, and sailors of Wrangel's army":

We do not seek revenge. All who lay down their arms will be given the chance to expiate their guilt before the people by honest labor. If Wrangel rejects our offer, you are obliged to lay down your arms against his will. . . .

At this same time we are issuing an order to Soviet troops about chivalrous behavior toward those who surrender and the merciless extermination of those who raise arms against the Red Army.

The next day Lenin dressed his commander down in a telegram, reminding him that he was "endowed with powers by the central Soviet authority": "I have just learned of your offer to Wrangel to surrender. I am extremely surprised by the excessive leniency of your conditions. If the enemy accepts them, you will have to expedite the seizure of the fleet to ensure that not one ship is permitted to escape; if the enemy does not accept these terms, you must not repeat them and must deal with the enemy mercilessly."[3]

Frunze's appeal went unanswered, which did not save him from having to do Party penance. Wrangel preferred flight to capitulation. He managed to escape by sea with 83,000 others, military personnel and refugees. Tens of thousands more remained on the Crimea—peaceful citizens from all over Russia and rear-guard units covering the flight of the White Army. Soviet sources say nothing about prisoners, as if there were none. Only in the unpublished memoirs of F. Mironov do we find that the Second Horse Army took 25,000 prisoners. Maiakovsky has the following lines in his poem "Khorosho" (1927):

"Wrangel is driven into the sea. No prisoners. An end—
for the time being. . . ."[4]

No prisoners. It is quite possible that the poet knew what that meant. P. I. Lavut, who organized his public readings, was an eyewitness to the events on the Crimea. That is mentioned in the poem.

Captured officers of Wrangel's army were shot. So were many other soldiers and refugees. Some who escaped captivity in mid-November fled to the mountains and joined the Green partisan units. They could not escape the Crimea. The entire shoreline and the narrow isthmus to the mainland were controlled by the Reds. After several months of pursuing them, the Soviet authorities in the Crimea called upon them to lay down their arms and save their lives. Many did surrender, and all of them were shot.

We know practically no details of this action. One eyewitness claimed that 80,000 were shot.[5] The fiery revolutionaries, Rozaliia Zemliachka and Bela Kun, members of the Revolutionary Military Council of the Southern Front, were in charge of the operation.[6] There is no information about Frunze's participation. The role of the leaders in Moscow is also unknown. Bela Kun was removed from the Crimea with a reprimand, but that happened in 1922.

If Wrangel was a strong military enemy, the Kronshtadt rebellion posed a different sort of danger—political. The sailors' slogan "Soviets without Bolsheviks" threatened to isolate the Bolsheviks from the population; it deprived them of their appropriated monopoly on revolutionary behavior. Lenin and his party could not discard the slogan "Power to the people." Without that they would be as superfluous as the Constituent Assembly, which they had disbanded. The Red Army men, most of them peasants, had fought not for the Bolsheviks but for the Soviets of Workers' Deputies, in which they saw their own power.[7] The destruction of the tender shoots of democracy, the suppression and liquidation of other political parties, occurred behind the back of the populace and without publicity. If all of Russia would draw the conclusions to which the Petrograd workers and Kronshtadt sailors had come, the Bolsheviks would not have been able to retain control of the Red Army—the shield and sword of Bolshevik power.

The conclusions drawn by the revolutionary class in the cradle of the Revolution were discomfiting for Lenin and his colleagues. The true proletariat decided to fight a third revolution against famine and the violence of the Cheka and the bureaucrats. In February 1921 Petrograd was paralyzed by strikes (those holding power preferred to call them slowdowns). A proclamation dated February 27 stated: "Workers and peasants need freedom. They do not wish to live by Bolshevik fiat. They want to determine their own fate. Comrades, preserve revolutionary order. Organize and insistently demand: the liberation of all arrested socialists and unaffiliated workers; the lifting of martial law, freedom of expression, of the press, and of association for all workers; free re-election of factory committees, professional unions and soviets."

The next day in the Nevsky region the following appeal was pasted to walls: "We know who fears the Constituent Assembly. It is those who will no longer be able to steal, who will have to answer to the national delegates for deceit, for theft, for all crimes."

The fall of Bolshevik authority in Kronshtadt occurred suspiciously easily. Only a third of the Communists opposed the rebellion, another third joined it, and the remaining third waited passively to see what would happen. The rebels published a new paper, *News (Izvestiia) of the provisional revolutionary committee of sailors, soldiers and workers*." Here are a few excerpts from it:

> What is happening now was caused by the Communists themselves, by their bloody, destructive work. Letters from the villages are full of complaints and damnation of the Communists. . . .
>
> The peasant was right who said at the Eighth Soviet Congress: "Everything is all right except . . . the land is ours, but the grain is yours; the water is ours, but the fish are yours; the forests are ours, but the wood is yours. . . ." They shout from the bloody stage, all land to the peasants, factories to the workers. The Communists . . . have sat on the neck of the poorest peasant more firmly than the landlords. . . .[8]

Words were not enough to answer such pronouncements. The answer was written with the bullets and bayonets of the Red Army. The Army marched to suppress peasants and workers, their class brothers, who wanted only a better, freer life. The majority of those storming Kronshtadt had exactly the same reasons for dissatisfaction as the rebels.

After the failure of the assault on March 8, the most powerful leaders of the Army were brought to Petrograd: Chairman of the Revolutionary Military Council Trotsky, Chairman of the Cheka Dzerzhinsky, Commander-in-Chief Kamenev, Commander of the Western Front Tukhachevsky. The latter was temporarily put in charge of the 7th Army, which was reinforced by elite battalions of Red cadets. The first assault was timed to coincide with the opening of the Tenth Party Congress. When it failed, a large detachment of political commissars was sent directly from the meeting. There were 300 delegates, 140 of whom had voting rights, including Voroshilov, Bubnov, Dybenko, and S. Uritsky.

Tukhachevsky approached his task according to all of the rules of military art. He directed the attack from where the besieged defenders would least expect it, from the side of the Finnish Gulf on which the ice had begun to melt. It was risky, but the assaulting troops even dragged artillery across the ice. On March 16 the Party Congress was closed ahead of schedule because of unrest in the provinces. On the seventeenth Soviet troops, in white camouflage cloaks, advanced across the shaky ice to Kronshtadt. They quickly broke into the fortress, and all resistance soon stopped. The ships of the Baltic Fleet also surrendered. The leaders of the rebellion, including the commandant of the fortress, former General Kozlovsky, and the chairman of the revolutionary committee, the sailor Petrechenko, escaped to Finland.

At this point Soviet authors usually end their work. In only one instance has anyone described the losses. S. Uritsky, in the first volume of the fundamental work, *The Civil War 1918–1921*, fixed the casualties as follows: The Reds lost 700 killed and 2,500 wounded and shocked; the Whites, that is the rebels, suffered 600 killed, 100 wounded.[9]

No one has anything to say about what happened to those who were captured. Moreover, in the academic and naturally objective research of S. Semanov there is an interesting note:

> While I was working on this monograph, I was able to converse with participants of the Kronshtadt mutiny. Altogether, I was able to find five. Several of them granted interviews but asked that I not use their *materials*. We will note only that *they* unanimously affirmed that *only* the *leaders* of the mutiny and *officers* who

actively participated in it suffered *repression*. Workers, peasants, and sailors, who surrendered in Kronshtadt were demobilized or transferred to other fleets and units.[10]

Thus, only five could be found, and not all of them (how many: two, one?) would speak with an honest historian. Not one would permit what he had said to be used, although they unanimously agreed that nothing untoward had happened. We will note only the following:

Breathing hard from the effort, poor Semanov contradicted both logic and Russian grammar in the preceding quotation, all to keep from saying too much. In another place in the same work, the thought he tried to hide shows through. On the one hand, there were no Bolshevik atrocities; on the other, had there been, Russian émigrés and western anti-Soviet writers would surely exaggerate them.

The matter is simple to explain. Those who fled were not able to see anything. Those who remained and lived knew something that even fifty years later they were reluctant to tell. Most of the rebels immediately lost the ability to speak.

Here is what I. Ts., a military engineer who commanded a battalion of cadets in the assault, had to say. After the surrender his battalion, comprised of three companies, was marching in formation along a narrow street in the fortress when all of a sudden the rear company was opened up on in cross fire at close range from basements. The company was almost wiped out. The maddened cadets surrounded the block and indiscriminately bayoneted all males "taller than the belt of an adult man." Revenge was not taken on the ambushers, according to I. Ts., because they apparently managed to escape (they had fired at the back of the last company). We will not trouble ourselves to judge who was more humane, or inhumane, the cadets or the mutineers firing from ambush.

Tukhachevsky was outraged. The battalion was declared a penal unit and deprived of the decorations that were given by the handful to the other assault troops — in Petrograd district alone 350 were awarded. Their punishment did not end there. Along with other soldiers who had looted and raped, the cadets were ordered to execute the captured sailors. They drove the sailors out onto the cracking ice of the Gulf and shot them. Thus 7,500 men died. The whole mutinous garrison had numbered 12,000. Several of the cadets went out of their minds lying behind their machine guns. March came, the ice soon melted, and the bodies of the sailors slipped beneath the water.

We do not know whether Tukhachevsky had anything to do with executions personally. Two months later, after a personal audience with Lenin, he was put in charge of special troops in Tambov province, detailed to suppress a peasant rebellion.

The Socialist Revolutionaries (SRS), who had much more support than the Bolsheviks among the peasants, had the upper hand in Tambov. The Bolsheviks held on there after October only by the force of arms. Late in 1917 the provincial Congress of Soviets had elected an all-SR executive committee; but now, for the good of the working people, it would have to be disbanded. Still many of the local workers considered themselves SRS. Evforitsky, the chairman of the provincial Soviet of People's Commissars was an SR; his comrade Bulatov headed the provincial militia.

At first the SRS refrained from active opposition to central Soviet authority. In 1918 they even supported the committees of poor peasants. That was probably an effect of their battle with the White Czechs and because pressure from the populace was weak. From the beginning, however, the SRS were their own men. For example, in Nakhatny Ugol they formed a model SR commune whose members worked the land and learned military skills. When grain requisitioning units came through the villages in 1920 after the Civil War had ended in the reigon, the peasants rose up in rebellion. Aleksander Antonov became their leader.

The son of a metal worker, Antonov had joined the SR Party in 1905, and before the February Revolution (1917) he had spent a long time in exile. His assistant, Ishin, had a similar biography. After October Antonov was sent from Tambov to Kirsanov as head of a county (*uezd*) militia, which he whipped into shape and armed well with weapons taken from the retreating Czechoslovakian Legion. During Mamontov's breakthrough, Antonov and his men became partisans. After the Whites were driven off, he did not return to regular service but declared himself a defender of the peasants, whom he considered oppressed by the Bolsheviks. The provincial Cheka could do nothing about this new detachment. Men loyal to Antonov, who served in local government organs and in the Cheka itself, always warned him in time.

The uprising began on August 20, 1920, and soon spread throughout the province. The driving force behind it was the peasants' dissatisfaction with grain requisitioning. In January 1921 the rebels controlled five counties: Tambov, Kirsanov, Borisoglebsk, Morshan, and Kozlov. They numbered 50,000 in two armies, which were organized in regiments, each attached to a particular territory. In many ways Antonov's armies copied the RKKA: they had commissars, political departments, and tribunals. An operational headquarters headed by Antonov directed all the rebel forces. The source of their fighting spirit was the consciousness of each soldier that he was defending his home and his land. Intelligence was well organized.

The rebels formed their own party, the Union of Working Peasants. A peasant from the village of Inokovok, Tokmakov, headed its Provincial Committee, which carried out agitation among Red Army men sent to subdue them. Often their propaganda was most amateurish. The following flyer, which we have reproduced with its original flavor serves as a good example:

> Mobolized friends it is time to wake up long enough we have listened to the arrogant communists porosites of the Whole working people. Down with the porosites of the Whole working people, down with the fratricidal war, mobolized friends throw down your weapons go home to defend your bread, earned by the sweat and blood of your civil rights. Remember mobolized brother know what you are doing, why are you defending these arrogant communists terrorists of the Whole working People. Down with Lenin's Jewish decrees and the foul soviet. Long live the committee of the constituent assembly.

The SRs' hand is obvious in other appeals:

> You will find your rights in struggle. Mobilized Red Army men. End your ignorance. Stop your ignoble acts against the peasants, especially against the rebels. It is time for you to come to yourself, to be aware of your worthless conduct. Fighting the peasant rebellions with the communists, you turn the people's anger against yourself. Aren't your fathers, brothers and families in the same circumstances as the rebellious peasants, squeezed on every side by the communists and soviets? Look around you: where are the freedoms of speech, press, unions, association, and faith, the inviolability of the individual. . . .

Soviet sources, especially those from the early twenties, acknowledged, had to acknowledge, the purely peasant, apolitical, and spontaneous nature of the uprising. Hot on the tracks of the events it is harder to distort the truth. One wrote:

> We cannot doubt, however, that the Antonov uprising, in which the leading active roles were taken by kulaks, deserters, the criminal element, and in part the "village intelligentsia," also was supported by a spontaneous, usually passive, dissatisfaction of the greater peasant mass with the requisitioning policy of the Soviet authorities. The villages, if they did not actively support the movement, did not hinder it, and where it came to guerrilla fighting showed similar support.[11]

A significant admission! On the one hand there were only kulaks, deserters, criminals, and the village intelligentsia, whom comrade Litovsky, unable to hide his revulsion, places in quotations marks. But there was also a small problem of another sort—grain *requisitions*—to which the peasant masses could not reconcile themselves. It is not surprising that the muzhiks did not hinder the rebels who were defending them from the thieves, the requisitioning detachments. It was more than that, the local peasants were the manpower of the uprising.

The tone of another book published at the height of the *Antonovshchina* was more vicious and abusive. What can you do? That is freedom of the press! In it the rebels were "*kulaks, vicious deserters* from the Red Army, inveterate *scoundrels* and *cutthroats*—lovers of easy gain by theft and murder. They are *old tsarist officers, intelligentsia*, priests. The *socialist-revolutionaries* lead them. *It was they who prepared the uprising and organized the bandit gangs.*"[12]

Things were bad, as we can see. What self-respecting peasant would want to wind up companion to the intelligentsia, officers, and scoundrels, especially under the leadership of socialist-revolutionaries? The same author, Vladimir Dokukin, offers an excerpt from a resolution passed at a conference of independent peasants of Tambov and Lebediansk counties, written, doubtless, by a Bolshevik: "Some of the Tambov peasants have surrendered to bourgeois deceit. . . . Soviet institutions are not working the way they should. They are filled with muddleheaded workers and *criminal hangers-on*."[13]

We might ask, why are the criminals on one side (with the muddleheaded workers) better than the scoundrels and cutthroats of the other? Our own always smells better.

There are more hints about the character of the Soviet authorities' relations with the peasantry in the anthology *Antonovshchina*: "Those who suffered most were the peasants who were not associated with the SR bandits. They fell under the blows of *the Reds* and *the Whites*. Frequent incidents of extreme repression from both sides were absolutely unavoidable."[14]

What have we here? The Whites, or rather the *Antonovtsy*, we can understand. They had the nature of wolves, of SRs, of bandits. But what about the Reds? Why were acts of extreme repression against peaceful peasants who had no relations with anyone absolutely unavoidable? Why should we think of the Reds as superior in this ugly business?

In truth, words can lead us astray, and not just the words of poets. Hail, comrades Evgenov, Litovsky, and Dokukin, who past the blinders of the Party bias brought us these crumbs of truth. Future, more watchful editors from the new intelligentsia (without quotation marks) removed the last hints of authenticity from written history.

The Kremlin was seriously alarmed by the large uprising in the very heart of Russia. At first, in the autumn of 1920, they thought they could handle it with central directives and local forces. A Plenipotentiary Commission of the All-Russian Central Executive Committee headed by Antonov-Ovseenko came to Tambov. They decided to pit two of theirs against the rebellious Antonov: another Antonov was appointed chairman of the provincial Cheka. It did not help.

They had to take more serious measures. On February 10, 1921, a month before the Tenth Party Congress and the cancellation of grain requisitioning throughout the country, requisitioning was abolished in Tambov, and all of the requisitioning squads were removed. Lenin received a delegation of Tambov peasants on February 14 and personally confirmed that decision. Still the uprising continued.

Such callous ingratitude called for stronger measures. Special Tambov province units were created, subordinated directly to the commander-in-chief. At first they were commanded by P. A. Pavlov, then from May 1921 by Tukhachevsky with N. E. Kakurin as chief of staff. The Tambov peasants could not stand up to the relentless onslaught of regular troops.[15] There was nowhere they could get supplies, no one to support them. They were constantly called upon to surrender with the promise of complete amnesty. Unfortunately we do not have any information about how this promise was honored.

The death agony of the uprising began in 1921. Here are the official statistics. From May 28 to July 26, 5,585 men turned themselves in voluntarily, 1,260 with weapons, 4,325 without; 5,285 were seized in roundups, 572 armed, and 4,713 unarmed; 985 others were captured; and 4,555 were killed in fighting. Altogether in these two months, the total was 16,370. Together with deserters (7,646) and those who had turned themselves in voluntarily before May 28 (12,903), the losses of the rebel forces numbered 36,919. The large number of rebels who were taken unarmed seems to suggest that as a group they were not heavily armed.

Remnants of the rebel bands resisted longer, until the end of 1922. On June 22, 1922, Aleksander Antonov and his brother Dmitri were surrounded in the remote village of Nizhny Shibriai in Borisolglebsk county by a detachment of two Chekists and six former rebels under M. Pokaliukhin. They were killed in an exchange of gunfire.

The Tambov uprising was not an isolated or exceptional episode. During 1921 and 1922 the Red Army was kept busy in the "little" Civil War against the muzhiks. Here is a list of the names of the SR-kulak (read peasant) uprisings for that period, which are given in official historiography:

Surgutsky	Oirotsky (Kaigorodovs' gang)
Zauralsky (Kurgan)	Ukrainsky (Makhno)
Irkutsky	Ekaterinburgsky
Ishimsko-Petropavlovsky	Severo-Kavkazsky
Vitebsky	Zavolzhsky (Sapozhkov)
Vernensky (Kazakhstan)	Karelsky
Iaroslavsky	Bashkirsky
Kostromskoi	

II

Those Turbulent Twenties

So let us try. A huge
And squeaky turn of rudder.
—Osip Mandelshtam

9 The Party: Battle of the Lines, or the Fight for Portfolios

All our political history, from the illness and death of Lenin to the expropriation of the peasantry, can be seen as a series of battles between Stalin and other leaders of the Russian Communist Party. Each brought Stalin closer to complete sovereignty in the Party.

In support of this point of view we can offer the following approximate periodization for the 1920s:

1923–24. Stalin in a bloc with Zinoviev and Kamenev against Trotsky. The secret deal with Bukharin and his group. Appointment of Rykov as Chairman of the Council of People's Commissars and of Frunze as Assistant Chairman of the Revolutionary Military Council of the USSR.

1925. Replacement of Trotsky by Frunze. The defeat of Zinoviev and Kamenev. Liquidation of Frunze. Appointment of Voroshilov People's Commissar of the Navy and Chairman of the Revolutionary Military Council.

1926. Struggle with the united Trotskyite-Zinovievite opposition. The death of Dzerzhinsky.

1927. The complete defeat of Zinoviev, Kamenev, Trotsky, and their supporters. Departure of Tukhachevsky from the Headquarters of the RKKA. Pogrom at Gosplan, the massive slaughter of engineers. Industrialization. Beginning of the campaign against the "Right."

1929. Political liquidation of Bukharin, Rykov, Tomsky. Collectivization. Voroshilov's article "Stalin and the Red Army."

Stalin showed himself to be an exceptional political strategist in those years. He employed his talent in behind-the-scenes machinations, intrigues, conspiracies, and provocations. Stalin preferred indirect action, at which he was an intuitive master. His favorite device was to demoralize his enemies so that when he actually struck, they were already significantly weakened. Stalin's rivals almost always disagreed with one another and were unable to act decisively. He artfully manipulated their discord to set them against one another. At the right moment he isolated the most dangerous, allied himself with the others, and removed the one.

In 1923 and 1924 Stalin was able to use Zinoviev and Kamenev to deliver several crushing blows to Trotsky, from which Trotsky never recovered. Remaining in the shadows, Stalin removed from his path to power a politician whose name from the moment of the October Revolution was invariably associated with Lenin's and who seemed to the majority of the population Lenin's rightful successor. Trotsky and other prominent men, who were independent in their views but were branded with the convenient common epithet Trotskyite, did not strive primarily to gain personal power, but rather to overcome a tendency they feared might destroy the Revolution: domination by the Party apparatus and a rebirth of bureaucratism. Zinoviev and Kamenev were so frightened of Trotsky's apparent Napoleonic pretensions, of which Stalin had warned them, that in the heat of battle they did not notice the weakening of their own positions. Kamenev, Stalin's friend and his recent protector, did not become head of the government in January 1924. He had performed that function for more than a year during Lenin's illness and was the primary candidate for the position. The ostensible reason was that because of the prejudice of the peasant masses, it would be politically harmful to have a Jew at the head of the government. The question of whether it would be useful to have a Georgian as the general secretary of the Party seems not to have been raised. A. I. Rykov became the chairman of the Council of People's Commissars. Kamenev had to be satisfied with the portfolio of chairman of the Council of Labor and Defense. Lenin had filled that post, too. Now the two posts were separated to give Kamenev a little something to sweeten the pill.

Rykov was part of a new, and for the time being secret, group of allies of Stalin, as were Bukharin and Tomsky. It is likely that the chief attraction of these new friends for Stalin was their purely Russian heritage, which contrasted very usefully with the Jewish domination of the Party's hierarchy, especially in the circles of Zinoviev, Kamenev, and Trotsky. Bukharin got to work zealously and attacked Trotsky with praiseworthy diligence. Not long before, at the Tenth Congress, he had aligned himself with Trotsky on the question of trade unions.

In 1925 Zinoviev and Kamenev felt Stalin's hand and hurried to put together their own faction based in Leningrad. But they were too late. At the Fourteenth Congress Stalin dealt them a severe blow. Bukharin's group and Stalin's faceless protégés, who now made up a majority of the party, attacked them savagely. Trotsky, already beaten and humiliated, chose not to interfere.

It would be a mistake to see Stalin's victory at the Congress as a result of behind-the-scenes maneuvering only. It was not that simple. The very openness of the struggle was its hallmark. The personal quarrels of the leaders surfaced publicly for the first time at the Fourteenth Congress. Previously there had occurred bitter conflicts of opinions, platforms, and positions, but never before had there been talk about organized repression of individuals—especially of the top leaders. In the first years of the Revolution Kamenev, Zinoviev, Bukharin, Nogin, and many others had broken with Lenin over basic questions of policy, had resigned from their posts, and had announced their departure from the Central Committee. But each time the problems had been worked out bloodlessly.

This was how Lenin conceived Party structure. Already at the turn of the century he saw the Party as a centralized organization welded together by iron discipline and headed by a stable, that is irremovable, collective leadership. In this way he hoped to secure the continuity of policy and inviolability of basic ideology.

Lenin's collective included Sverdlov (who died in 1919), Kamenev, Zinoviev, Stalin, Trotsky, Bukharin, Dzerzhinsky, Kalinin, and a number of others. It was assumed that these comrades would run the Party and the state. Disagreements on individual questions became public only with the permission of the Central Committee; and after a decision was reached, all would submit to it.[1] However bitter the verbal battles became, the blood of the minority was never demanded.

That is the way things went until Lenin's illness knocked him from the saddle. Enmity immediately flared up among his colleagues. We can say it another way: they discovered they could not work together collectively. It all began with the conspiracy against Trotsky. Zinoviev advanced the cunning plan, which was discussed by a narrow circle of conspirators in a grotto near Kislovodsk ("the cave meetings"). To strengthen the leadership during Lenin's illness, he proposed to replace the Politburo with a "politicized" Secretariat composed of Zinoviev, Stalin, and Trotsky. Kamenev would remain head of the Council of People's Commissars and the Council of Trade and Defense. That combination would make Trotsky a permanent minority; he would not be able to form blocs on various issues as he had done in the Politburo. But the plan was shelved by Stalin, who had extremely unfriendly relations with Trotsky, but who up to this time took care to clothe his animosity in official resolutions. He spoke about this in 1925:

In 1923 after the Twelfth Congress the men who gathered in the "Cave" [laughter] worked out the platform about the destruction of the Politburo and the politicization of the Secretariat, that is about turning the Secretariat into the leading political-organizational organ run by Zinoviev, Trotsky, and Stalin. What was the idea of that platform? What did it mean? It meant running the Party without Rykov, Kalinin, Tomsky, Molotov, and Bukharin. Nothing came of the platform and not only because it was unprincipled, but because without those comrades I have mentioned it was not possible to run the Party. To the question posed me in writing from the bowels of Kislovodsk, I answered in the negative, announcing that if the comrades insisted, I was ready to leave the place quietly, without discussions, open or secret, and without demanding guarantees of the rights of the minority [laughter].

Stalin for understandable reasons did not want to make public all the inner secrets of the Central Committee. He did not expose his personal motives in that affair. He evidently sensed immediately that he himself might turn out to be in the minority if the wind shifted. In any case, Stalin appeared to outsiders to be the preserver of Party solidarity and the enemy of intrigue.

After Lenin's death late in 1924 Zinoviev and Kamenev thought of an easier way to get rid of Trotsky. Again Stalin's words:

The Leningrad provincial committee passed a resolution to expel comrade Trotsky from the Party. We, that is the majority of the Central Committee, did not agree with that [Voices: "Right!"]. We had something of a fight with the Leningraders and convinced them to eliminate the point about exclusion from their resolution. A little while later when we had a meeting of the Plenum of the Central Committee, the Leningraders and comrade Kamenev demanded the immediate exclusion of comrade Trotsky from the Politburo. We disagreed with that proposal, won a majority in the Central Committee, and limited ourselves to removing comrade Trotsky from his post as People's Commissar of War.[2]

Immediately Stalin made a statement staggering for its candor and sagacity:

We did not agree with comrades Zinoviev and Kamenev because we knew that the policy of expulsion was fraught with serious dangers for the Party, that the method of expulsion, the method of letting blood—and they were demanding blood—was dangerous, infectious: today we cut one off, tomorrow another, the day after that a third. What would be left of the Party? [Applause.][3]

It hardly matters what Stalin thought when he objected to expulsion. What is more important is that he claimed to stand for unity and for the inviolability of the Leninist leadership, while his opponents preached a pogrom. This position made him more popular with the leadership and the rank and file of the Party; his authority grew enormously.

In the second half of 1925 Zinoviev and Kamenev split with the majority of the Central Committee, which was headed by Stalin, over the formulation of the general political line. Zinoviev and Kamenev suggested a contradictory and psychologically unacceptable course: on the one hand they wanted to put the squeeze on capitalistic elements, that is to continue the Civil War in peacetime; and on the other hand they would admit that socialism could not be built in Russia until the world revolution had come. Bukharin protested that there was no reason to start a war, that it would do them no good now they were in power. He insisted also that it would be foolish to touch the peasants, because they were supplying grain for now, and they would grow into socialism later. Stalin said, "We have had our socialist revolution, now let's build socialism. If there should be a world revolution, wonderful; if not, we will get along without it. We can't just mark time waiting for it; no one knows when it might come." Without going into the essence of the argument, it is enough to note that Stalin's position looked more logical and attractive.

On the eve of the Congress Zinoviev decided to strike through his Leningrad *oprichnina*[4] at Bukharin and took aim at his slogan "Get rich." (Stalin at that time apparently accepted the idea if not the formulation of it.) At the Congress, where they were in a clear minority (only the Leningrad delegation), the inseparable pair put on a noisy demonstration. Zinoviev delivered an extremely long supplementary report in which he said nothing except that socialism in one country was impossible. Kamenev, supported by Sokolnikov, openly demanded a shake-up of the organs of the Central Committee and the removal of Stalin from his post as general secretary.

Stalin, having made himself part of the overwhelming majority, limited himself to discrediting his opponents as unprincipled intriguers and bad Leninists; but he did not demand their blood. Both of them remained on the Politburo.

Zinoviev and Kamenev miscalculated badly. Striving for absolute power, they planned to use Stalin, the hard-working but rather dull organizer, to push Trotsky aside and trample the rest. On the way to this goal they encroached upon the organizational bases of the Party. They did not achieve what they were after, but they did clear Stalin's path to personal supremacy.

It is very likely that Stalin had dreamed of personal dictatorship before this but did not know how to go about getting it. Not having a glorious past of indisputable authority, the cautious mountain man did not want to take a premature risk. If he had grabbed for power and failed soon after Lenin's death, his removal would have caused little stir. Most people thought of him then only as a minor figure in the Central Committee, like Krestinsky or Molotov. (In January 1925 he put his enemies to a test. He offered his resignation, which they refused.) At the Fourteenth Congress he gained enormous political capital at one stroke. Besides that, the means by which he would reach power—the method of removal—was put on the agenda. The taboo against consuming the flesh of the leaders had not been lifted, but their halos had been tarnished. The careless acts of the next opposition strengthened Stalin even more.

By 1926 Zinoviev and his group realized their position was shaky and hurried to ally with their recent victims, first of all with Trotsky. But the leaders of this new bloc had already lost their key positions. In the eyes of the rank-and-file Party members, whose numbers had sharply increased after Lenin's draft of 1924, they appeared to be schismatics who had set themselves against the Party line and were now trying to regain their lost influence. Only the older Party intellectuals from before the Revolution were able to differentiate shades of opinion and regularly allowed themselves to make their own judgments. The dispute had made no sense to most people; they commonly explained it as a "fight for portfolios." In these circumstances the new Party members preferred to vote the way the local apparatchiks told them to. For them the Central Committee Secretariat, which was firmly controlled by Stalin, was as holy and sinless as the Pope in Rome. The Secretariat issued directives and orders, usually verbally and always secretly, which arbitrarily interrupted decisions of congresses and plenums to the advantage of Stalin's group. The opposition had no way to get their point of view to the local Party organizations. Their difficulties were greatest just before a congress or conference. Any attempt to address the Party directly qualified as an illegal act, a violation of the rules. To give the opposition the rostrum at a congress did not have much meaning. They had to address a select and hostile audience. By the time of the next congress the form of disagreement had changed, and all had to begin again.

The new "united" opposition was unable to present a coherent program. In the past Trotsky and Zinoviev had rarely held the same opinion. By character and by conviction they were exact opposites. Trotsky was by temperament revolutionary; he was decisive and adventuresome. Zinoviev, having spent many years as Lenin's literary secretary, was a tedious theoretician, an intriguer, and a coward. In October Trotsky had been the soul of the uprising (Lenin was its head); fearing historical responsibility, Zinoviev and Kamenev had deserted.

For the sake of unity the faction had to pile rather contradictory views into one eclectic heap. From the Trotskyites came the slogan about the struggle with bureaucratization and a Thermidorean reaction in the Party, and also superindustrialization at the expense of the peasants. From the Zinovites came the thesis about the impossibility of building socialism without help in the form of a world revolution. (The question arises, why hurry with the development of industry if we will nonetheless not be able to attain socialism on our own?) The opposition's hastily rigged program, together with their tactical impotence and organizational weakness, foreordained their defeat.

In 1926 Stalinists and other officials hostile in one way or another to the opposition held all the most important posts. The General Secretary of the Party was Stalin himself; Ordzhonikidze was chairman of the Central Control Commission; Rykov was chairman of the Council of People's Commissars; Bukharin was editor of *Pravda*; Tomsky was head of the Unions; Dzerzhinsky was head of OGPU, NKVD, and the VSNKh. While not a strong supporter of Stalin, Dzerzhinsky was an irreconcilable enemy of Zinoviev and Kamenev. In July 1926 he dropped dead at a meeting of the Central Committee, where he had spoken twice on secondary issues, polemicizing violently with Zinoviev and Piatakov, his assistant at VSNKh. His death greatly benefited Stalin. "Iron Feliks" had the reputation of a fervent and incorruptable fanatic, merciless to any enemy of the Party and socialism. Whether he actually was or was not is hard to say, but he had the reputation. However that

may be, Stalin could consider himself lost if Dzerzhinsky had suspected him of improper activities or intentions. And there was something to fear. Only very recently Frunze had died a very messy death.
The head of the punitive organs left the scene at a very opportune time.
We will have another occasion to speak of this affair.

The opposition appeared at that time to be in a much less imposing
position. Trotsky was chairman of the Concessions Committee;[5]
Kamenev was People's Commissar of Trade. Zinoviev after his removal
from the Executive Commitee of the Comintern was apparently nothing at all. The fact that they remained members of the Central Committee and the Politburo only weakened them further. According to Party
rules, members of the Politburo did not have the right to speak publicly
without the agreement of that body, and Stalin had power over the
majority. Besides, Bukharin blocked their access to the Party press.
The game was played mostly at one end of the field.

When the opposition lost patience and decided to ignore the rules,
they publicized their platform and even risked forming their own
procession at the tenth anniversary celebration of the October Revolution. But these were more than gestures done for effect. It was as if
Stalin had been waiting for something like that. An organized purge
began even before the Congress. On November 14, 1927, a joint
plenum of the Central Committee and the Central Control Commission
resolved to expel Trotsky and Zinoviev from the Party. Kamenev
remained for the time being. It was all done by Party rules. This was
the first application of the seventh point of the resolution "On Party
Unity," which had provoked such argument and doubts at the Tenth
Congress.[6]

A little more than a month later, at the Fifteenth Congress, the
Stalin–Bukharin coalition achieved the destruction of their enemy.
Trotsky's and Zinoviev's appeal to this lofty gathering availed them
nothing. They were trying to close the barn door after the horse had
escaped. The delegates had been carefully selected and thoroughly
instructed. This was the last Congress at which the opposition was
permitted to express their views. It was a sad spectacle: one after
another the few opposition speakers were driven from the rostrum by
the hoots of a well-rehearsed claque. Only Kamenev persevered to
complete his speech despite the diabolic noise.

The game of inner-Party democracy came to an end. A decision was
made to drive all opposition from the Party en masse and to permit

applications for readmission to be heard on an individual basis by the Central Committee, not the Congress. Part of the opposition, including its leaders, immediately surrendered and submitted a penitent statement to the Congress, but a fresh indignity awaited them. Their capitulation was refused, and the whole question was turned over to the Central Committee.[7] Trotsky was exiled to Verny (now Alma-Ata) and in 1929 was thrown out of the country. Hundreds of lesser Trotskyites went into Siberian exile. These were the first repressions by the Bolsheviks against members of their own Party.

Stalin was far from drunk with success. The victory was total but not final. There were groups left in the Party who recognized him as their leader and the instrument of the will of the majority, but not the God-given Great Leader. There were many such comrades, but with each passing month they were spread more thinly among the faceless mass of new recruits, the time-serving and self-serving people who flooded into the ruling Party. Yet these seemingly independent older members enjoyed popularity and influence among the masses because of their earlier activities, the years in the underground, the Revolution, the Civil War, and their literary fame. The time had not come to muzzle them all, so Stalin decided to strike at the more notable of them near the center of power. Politburo members Bukharin, Rykov, Tomsky, the leader of the Moscow Party organization Uglanov, and others associated with them were worthy objects of attack. They continued to believe in their own importance and to attempt to guide theory and practical affairs in their own way. Stalin had long perceived their defenselessness; moreover, he was indebted to many of them for their services in the battle with Trotsky and Zinoviev. The General Secretary did not like to feel obligated; he much preferred to pick the moment to repay his creditors. Finally, they were widely popular and deflected to themselves part of the people's attention and love, which by rights belonged to Stalin alone.

In 1928 and 1929 Stalin suddenly redirected his fire. While he was attempting to rid himself of the opposition, he had followed Bukharin's ideological lead, advocating civil peace and the opening of social and economic opportunities for the rural producers, that is, for the kulaks. But once the Zinovievites had been kicked out of the vanguard along with Trotsky, Stalin made a sharp turn to the left, much sharper than Zinoviev and Kamenev had wanted, and more decisively than Lev Davidovich himself would have done. At this sharp turn the Bukharinites skidded into the ditch; they were now called the Right. This was an even more impressive victory for Stalin, even though it was not so sensational. Bukharin, who stood for the peaceful development of socialism for all the peasantry, had a very wide following.

It could not have been otherwise in the land of the muzhik. The rural people craved a life of peace and plenty, whatever scholarly theoreticians might call it. Bukharin, however, disappointed the hopes and expectations of his simple supporters. When under the guise of collectivization Stalin declared the crusade against the muzhik, they put up an abstract, theoretical opposition; but they did not engage him openly. At the Sixteenth Congress in 1930 they offered a white flag: Rykov, Tomsky, and Uglanov confessed to errors they had not committed; Bukharin, pleading illness, did not appear at all. The Bukharinites' betrayal of other Party leaders came back to haunt them; they did not keep their hold on power.

It did not matter that Bukharin and Stalin were personal friends, that they visited each other at home and shared a dacha. In Party matters Josef Vissarionovich was able to put sentiment behind him. True, in destroying the Right, he long refrained from extreme measures. They (the Rightists) were only expelled from the Politburo and driven from the commanding heights. They remained members of the Central Committee and received lesser posts. It is possible that personal feelings played a certain role in this. When he battered his friends, Stalin did not work to the limit of his strength, although in his own way he kept his purposes in mind. He had to remember that Bukharchik was the darling of the Party.

Stalin would not have been Stalin had he given himself entirely to the fight with these pitiful opponents, either real or fancied. Comrade Stalin had studied Lenin well, he had certainly read Engels, and he knew something of Marx. He had assimilated what was most important, and that was that at the base of political power lay the mastery of the economy and of productive relations. And it was precisely in the economic area that things were not going well. The nationalized industry was barely functioning; the country was experiencing a shortage of consumer goods. The peasants carried on with their backward small-scale agriculture. They might at any time decide to withhold grain, and then the country would experience a real famine. True, the muzhiks were for the time being turning over their produce, but they were grumbling that there was nothing for them in the stores. Stalin, who had just yesterday declared the building of socialism in one country, in bast-sandal Russia, preferred satisfaction and universal gratitude to grumbling. He looked about for the means to his ends, and they immediately turned up.

This breadth of views was characteristic of Stalin. He did not hesitate to adopt a useful idea or a slogan that had originated with others. He selected what he could use, and when the time was right, he put it into action.

When the Trotskyites, fervid revolutionaries and impatient visionaries that they were, called for the accelerated development of industry (superindustrialization) and for harnessing the peasantry to achieve it (it looked a lot like robbery), Stalin, it would seem, opposed them. He unleashed upon them a pack of circumspect theoreticians headed by Bukharin, who were protective and indulgent of the muzhik. Bukharin was considered an economist in the Party—not the sort, God forbid, who busied himself with the vulgar economy, but who knew all about surplus value and the inescapable failure of world capitalism. In his leisure hours he liked to think about the village and dreamed up the slogan "Get rich!" to advocate the peaceful integration of the kulak into socialism. The peasants found this a satisfying contrast to the demands of the Trotskyites, those kikes and muzhik eaters. (Stalin never supported the slogan in public, and when the tactical necessity for it faded, he required Bukharin to renounce it. That was in 1925–26.) Stalin fought against the Trotskyites' ideas; but being a thrifty person, he filed them in his memory in case they should later prove useful. Although he could not accept these ideas directly from the hands of sworn enemies, he recognized the advantages of a cavalry approach to the economy, which paved the way for brutal centralization and the complete destruction of independent economic units.

Trotskyism had hardly ceased to be a real force when Stalin began to use its slogans. He only slightly altered the phraseology (the Five-Year Plan, collectivization) and neglected to cite his sources. Instantly the good-humored Bukharin and his comrades became Right deviationists and supporters of the kulaks.

From a safe distance, in exile abroad, Trotsky tried to defend his priority. He asserted that the idea to force all the peasants into collective farms belonged to him and his supporters. Stalin laughed. In the first place, for Marxists it is axiomatic that the role of the individual in history must not be exaggerated, especially of such individuals as

Trotsky. Second, what was important was the building of socialism. Quarrels about who said what first and who did not were minor. In the third place, all the circumstances of the moment must be taken into consideration. To propose a slogan prematurely was to run ahead of the masses, to alienate oneself from the masses as an ultraleftist. Fourth, and finally, if one were to ask those same masses, the workers, the collective farmers, they would tell it straight: it was Stalin's plan for collectivization, Stalin's Five-Year Plan. That's how it was with industrialization, the collectivization of agriculture, and the pretenses of Mr. Trotsky.

Stalin did not only borrow. His creative faculties were also wide awake. In 1928 he apparently devised the thesis "the cadres decide all"; and, keeping it to himself, decided to start by destroying the old engineer cadres. That year a zealous investigator from the town of Shakhty in Rostov province concocted a charge of sabotage against a group of mining specialists. R. Menzhinsky, the chairman of OGPU, saw the charges as provocation and threatened the investigator with a tribunal if he did not present real evidence of guilt. Stalin, on the other hand, saw the possibilities of the case, latched onto it, and gave it national importance. Such trials, trumped up for show, enabled him to create and sustain an atmosphere of uncertainty, suspicion, and fear in the country and greatly facilitated his rule. With the Russian aptitude for muddling and bungling, it was easy to pin charges of sabotage or wrecking on any worker or group. Victims for repression could be found at will. The Shakhty case helped develop the methods, the technology of the sort of trial that was to prove so useful in the future.

The trial was successful. True, at first Menzhinsky opposed him; but Stalin defeated him in the Politburo[8] and made him toe the line. Later on, the punitive organs did what they were told and even displayed some initiative.

The nascent personal dictatorship had found a suitable weapon. Stalin hurried to try out the relatively untested method on a larger scale. He struck at the technological intelligentsia.

It is worth pausing a moment at this point. In essence, Stalin's dictatorship was more than personal, for he already had behind him the Party bureaucracy, which was composed of old Bolshevik backbenchers and newcomer Party careerists. The dilution of the revolutionary party began immediately after the October Revolution. In the early 1920s it assumed threatening proportions. Merciless purges did not solve the problem. It was a labor of Sisyphus: the careerists and thieves were replaced by others, more numerous and more insistent. The monopoly on political power had an ugly reverse side. All the unscrupulous people, who in different circumstances would have been spread among many parties, flocked to the Bolsheviks.[9]

The new people, like all nouveaux riches and parvenus in history, were insolent, impatient, and unscrupulous. They joined the ruling party to rule and to get their hunk of the state pie; they did not care about implementing Marx's outline from "Critique of the Gotha Program," nor were they in accordance with "Anti-Dühring" to make the leap from the kingdom of necessity to the kingdom of freedom; certainly they did not join to enjoy philosophical and political-economic discussions. It must be acknowledged that they did have to learn a certain amount of the dogma from the Party catechism, but they viewed that as an "entry fee," an unavoidable evil. In the mid-1920s two groups blocked their way to power: the Party intelligentsia with their laurels of service to the Revolution, Marxist erudition, powerful pens, and ability to speak to the masses; and the technological intelligentsia, without whom, or so thought the first Soviet leaders, it would be impossible to advance economically and culturally. The newly converted Communists looked upon the intellectuals with hostility: organic, since they mostly came from the same middle class; and social, since they were privileged competitors.

Stalin had long ago perceived that force, and he understood that the future belonged to it. It was to this new Communist force that he addressed his sermons, in which the most complex problems were reduced to absurdity and, in his seminarian's way, were summed up in questions and answers. The bureaucratic mass quickly came to value Stalin. They were attracted by the clarity (which was more truly primitiveness) of his speeches, which contained no scholarly flourishes or painful contradictions. Most important, he always set them against the very things and people they themselves despised. First the oppositionists, who spoke with unintelligible cleverness, who kept the simple people from making their way, and who were practically all Jews anyway. (About that, it is true, no one spoke openly, but like it or not, the thought came to mind as one looked at those noses, those bulging eyes, that curly hair.) Then the specialists, who treated the newcomers so condescendingly, who strutted their knowledge and culture, and who in any case came from the class of former exploiters. (Questions like that it was all right to discuss.) By his intellectual development and his education Stalin was the same sort of superficial, half-educated person as this new generation of timeservers. He spouted the same prejudices.

When Stalin invented wrecking and generously shared his discovery with the rank and file of the Party, they were more than grateful. They understood: Stalin was the messiah of the new religion, the new living god and commander they had wanted since Lenin had died. The process by which Stalin and the Party bureaucrats found one another is fascinating, and it still awaits its researchers.

Hesitation, confusion, and disorientation were all unavoidable in the struggle with the oppositionists. Many of the young members of the Party were awed by their names and reputations: Trotsky, the great leader of the Red Army; Zinoviev, head of Comintern; and others. On the other hand, with the specialists everything was clear and easy. As A. Belinkov has correctly noted, the relations between the intelligentsia and the Revolution, that is Soviet authority, were no longer open to question.[10]

The destruction of the old engineering cadres was carried out quickly and without loss by the attackers. Some of the specialists were executed; others were imprisoned for obstinacy, to be used later in the projects of the Five-Year Plan and to meet quotas. The rest went into hiding and no longer dared to contradict any of the plans of the leadership. In 1937 they would be forced to publicly lick the boots of the NKVD, but that is another story, which will be told in its own place.

One of the most glaring examples was the pogrom of the experts —the Menshevik economists and the banking and industrial bigwigs at Gosplan and VSNKh. Now all of the conditions were in place for the first Stalinist Five-Year Plan, for truly Stalinist—that is purely paper —planning. Entirely unreachable goals were written into the plans, but nonetheless the Five-Year Plan was fulfilled in four years. Now Kuibyshev and Ordzhonikidze could furrow their brows and toss about billions of rubles and millions of tons of steel, and there was no one to think to refer them to Malinin and Burinin's *Arithmetic*.[11]

These were the circumstances in which Voroshilov's article "Stalin and the Red Army" appeared.[12]

10 The Trojan Horse and the Cavalryman

From the beginning of the 1920s serious changes occurred in the status of the Red Army. Maintaining a force of five million men became more of a burden than the Republic could bear. But demobilization was complicated by two factors: fear of disarming too soon, and the effort of the government to follow the letter of Party ideology. Red Armymen released from service were not permitted to go straight home: they were formed into labor armies, according to Marx's recipe, to resuscitate the economy. In fact, they became forced laborers. This undertaking proved fruitless, and after only a few months it was abandoned. In 1922 and 1923 the Army shrank precipitously, to 500,000 men.

Even after that, however, the character of the Army contradicted Marxist doctrine. The founders, and Lenin after them, considered a regular army an instrument of oppression and a major element in the plundering of a nation's wealth. A militia, the people armed on the example of Switzerland, was considered ideal. The workers could be given military training without being taken from productive work; in a time of danger they would rise to defend the homeland. Real service in peacetime was excluded or permitted only for short periods of training.

It is interesting to note Lenin's views on the Army. In 1903 in "On Village Poverty" he wrote:

> A standing army is not needed to defend the state from attack; a people's militia is sufficient for that. If every citizen of the state is armed, no enemy can frighten Russia. And the people would be free of the burden of militarism: *hundreds of millions of rubles a year* are spent on militarism. Taxes are raised so high to support it that it becomes harder and harder to live. Militarism strengthens the power of the police and bureaucrats over the people.[1]

In 1905 in "The Army and Revolution" Lenin wrote that it was necessary to destroy the standing army and replace it by arming all the people. "A standing army, everywhere, in all countries, serves not so much against external as against internal enemies," he stated. "Standing armies have everywhere become weapons of reaction . . . the executioner of people's freedom. . . . We will utterly destroy the standing army. . . . No force on earth will dare invade free Russia if the armed people, having destroyed the military caste, are the bulwark of freedom."[2] At the height of the imperialist war he maintained this position. "The contemporary national army remains a weapon in the hands of certain individuals, families, classes. . . . The army of the democratic collective of socialist society is nothing more than the armed people, since it consists of highly cultured people, freely working in collective shops and participating fully in all areas of the life of the state."[3]

On the eve of the February Revolution he wrote, "The Social Democrats want to destroy all armies . . . after the victorious socialist revolution."[4] After the fall of the autocracy he recalled, "The first decree of the Commune was the abolition of the standing army."[5]

If you were to show these quotations to a Soviet general today without naming the author, at best he would laugh. But even at the dawn of Soviet power this noble scheme could not have been realized. The Red Army was formed at first as a voluntary force, but very soon regular military units were being organized by compulsory conscription. After the Civil War, one more attempt was made to operate according to the Party program. That was the famous military reform of 1923–25. Its authors, particularly Frunze, worked out a compromise. The Red Army was given a dual structure in which regular units coexisted with territorial units that were more like a militia. However, this was only a formal concession to ideology. They took as their model the scheme employed by Field Marshal D. Milyutin in 1864–74.[6] They also borrowed Arakcheev's idea for military settlements in the border armies.[7] (The settlements in the Ukraine were liquidated quickly because of the Chuguevsk uprising of 1922, but they existed in the Far East until the end of the 1930s.)

We will describe Frunze's reforms only very briefly. We refer readers interested in greater detail to I. Berkhin's very thorough study.[8] From 1921 to 1925 the Army was reduced from 5,300,000 to 562,000 men. Military service became compulsory. Of the seventy-seven infantry divisions existing in 1925, only thirty-one, fewer than half, were regular Army. Militia units were assigned the task of giving the population a general military education in peacetime. They were also required to supply thirty divisions for the first weeks of war, while mobilization was being carried out. From the very beginning the Bolsheviks were apprehensive about giving weapons to the people. Berkhin complains that the territorial units were infected with "peasant" attitudes: demands were heard for the creation of a "farmer's union," which would defend the peasants' interests. Therefore the authorities bent their efforts in the 1920s and 1930s to increasing the strength and size of the regular Army. The significance of the militias continuously waned; they were assigned auxiliary functions (military education of the population, guarding military and industrial objects, etc.).

In the period we are describing the Army, or more precisely its top leadership, was drawn into a maelstrom of political passions. The struggle centered on one of the most colorful and most controversial figures of the Revolution, the head of the RKKA, Lev Trotsky. During the Civil War the epithet "great leader and founder of the Red Army" affixed itself to Trotsky. Ironically, it may have been Stalin who devised the formula; in any case it appears in one of his articles from 1919.

Trotsky can be characterized in a single word: he was a revolutionary. Revolution was the governing passion of his life. He quickly came to the fore during the Revolution of 1905 when he became the real leader of the Petersburg Soviet. In the period between the revolutions, when the movement flagged, he tried to reconcile the feuding factions; he wrote on questions of literature and art; but he remained in surprising isolation, still not having found an outlet for his turbulent energy. Trotsky was an internationalist and a foe of the imperialist war, but he did not become, as Lenin did, a defeatist. The revolutionary upheaval in February 1917 brought him back to Russia. In the period immediately after February he did not join with the Bolshevik organization, but he did agree with them on the largest question of the Revolution, the necessity of seizing power.

In the July days of 1917 Trotsky was exceptionally brave. At the entrance to the Tauride Palace he literally snatched Minister of Agriculture Chernov from the hands of sailors who were about to kill him. When the Provisional Government began its campaign against the Bolsheviks, Lenin and Zinoviev on the orders of the Central Committee went into hiding. Trotsky, on the contrary, turned himself in voluntarily and demanded a public trial. "I do not belong to the Bolshevik organization formally," he announced, "but I share their views, and I am prepared to share responsibility." Kerensky's government held him for two months in Kresty Prison but was then forced to release him. By that time he was extraordinarily popular, especially among the soldiers, who were drawn by his enormous energy and exceptional oratorical talent. When the Bolsheviks gained a majority in the Petrograd Soviet, Trotsky became its chairman. This gave Lenin and the Bolsheviks the ideal platform from which to launch the Revolution. Units of the Petrograd garrison would listen to no other organization. From then on Trotsky advanced hand in hand with Lenin in the debates about the immediate seizure of power. In these historic hours they did not have time to remember their earlier literary polemics in which Lenin had called Trotsky a "little Judas" and Trotsky had labeled Lenin the "exploiter of everything backward in the Russian workers' movement." As long as Lenin had to remain in hiding, Trotsky was without doubt the central figure in preparations for the October uprising. Even the moment of the convocation of the Second Congress of Soviets, which was timed to coincide with the Revolution, was not arbitrarily set: October 25 was Trotsky's birthday.

In Lenin's first cabinet Trotsky received the portfolio of People's Commissar of Foreign Affairs. His activities in the diplomatic sphere were, however, brief and highly unsuccessful. Trotsky was not suited for machinations and intrigue. His position in the negotiations with the Germans—"neither peace, nor war," combined with an appeal to the world proletariat—received Lenin's support, but led to disaster. The Germans attacked, and the Soviets did not have the strength to oppose them. They were forced to submit to the "obscene" Brest peace.

Trotsky was transferred to the post of People's Commissar for Military and Naval Affairs, where he was truly in his element. His frenzied energy and exceptional organizational abilities enabled him in a very short time to create the armed forces of the Soviet Republic, which saved the country in the Civil War. This was Trotsky's finest hour, when his personality unexpectedly blossomed. He saw himself as a doctrinaire Marxist, perhaps more orthodox than his spiritual fathers. But he had both a powerful mind and the ability—although not always, it is true—to put common sense ahead of ideological prejudices.

Party catechism required the establishment of a militia–army composed of the proletariat and the poorest peasantry, who would produce their own commander–revolutionaries on the field of battle. At first Lenin thought exactly along those lines. On November 24, 1918, he said, "Now, in building the new Army, we must take our commanders *only* from the people. Only Red officers will have authority among our soldiers and will be able to establish socialism in our Army."[9]

Trotsky understood that this could lead only to guerrilla bands and defeat. They could be saved only by a regular Army led by professionals. He boldly recruited unemployed officers of the tsarist army, who came to be called "military specialists." Half of the 300,000-man officer corps fought for the Reds. This solved another problem at the same time: if these officers had not been given the chance to serve the central authority in Moscow, most of them would have wound up fighting for the Whites.

The use of military specialists caused serious dissatisfaction in the Party. The doctrinaire theoreticians grumbled. The Army's Communists wailed heartrendingly; they did not want to carry out the orders of class enemies. But Trotsky, supported fully by the realist Lenin, stood firm and won.[10] The highest positions of command in the Red Army, not to mention headquarters posts, were given to former imperial officers: both commanders-in-chief, Vatsetis and S. Kamenev; all front commanders with the exception of Frunze; all Army commanders except Voroshilov, Sokolnikov, and Budenny. It was even truer of headquarters: former general P. Lebedev headed the Field Headquarters of the Revolutionary Military Council of Republic (RVSR). Even the staff of the First Horse Army, which was led by the specialist-baiters Voroshilov and Budenny, was manned by former officers.

Throughout the war Trotsky rushed about the fronts on his train inspiring enthusiasm and maintaining order with an iron hand. Everyone unreservedly recognized his decisive contribution to the victory of the Red Army—Lenin, Stalin, and many others. When the war ended, however, there was no suitable task for a man of his talents. A revolutionary has nothing to do in peacetime. For a time his acute mind found an outlet in devising bold schemes—he had proposed the idea of NEP a year before Lenin—but these were only episodes. Once again Party discipline began to stifle him. In 1922 from boredom he began to write a series of articles of literary criticism in which he first expressed the tenets of socialist realism.

Lenin's illness emphasized Trotsky's isolation. Hostilities found expression in office politics, intrigues, and alliances in which he did not wish, indeed was not able, to participate. In 1923 he spoke out against the Thermidorean reaction and the domination of the Party by apparatchiks. This was not a struggle for personal power as official historians try to present it. Quite the opposite, it was a protest against the real agony of the revolutionary spirit, against those who did seek a

personal dictatorship—Zinoviev, Stalin, Kamenev. Trotsky's denuncia-
tory pathos evokes the style of the Jewish prophets. The incorrigible
revolutionary damned his former comrades-in-arms as soft, gentrified,
and wrapped in red tape. But Trotsky cried in the wilderness. Only half
a hundred well-known Party activists spoke out with him (the platform
of the forty-six); only a few thousand shared his fears. The Party did not
understand him. Trotsky could ignite a crowd for immediate revolutionary action; but he could not conspire, bend with the fashionable
breezes, or win supporters with bribes, promises, or deceit. At the
Thirteenth Party conference he suffered total defeat.

It is not our purpose to compare the characters of Stalin and Trotsky,
and certainly not to idealize the latter. We mean only to describe
Trotsky's role in founding the Red Army and the consequences of his
removal from military leadership. In that context it is enough to note
that both of these famous Bolshevik revolutionaries were proponents of
extreme measures, but with an important difference. Trotsky represented a European radicalism that did not go beyond the bounds of
civilization. Stalin was a concentrated expression of Asiatic brutality,
which was crueler in him as it was mixed with limitless perfidy. Only
contemporary Stalinists, deprived of the chance to deify their idol, are
able to say that Trotsky, had he come to power, would have been as
ruthless as the Great Leader of the People. It cannot be denied that
Stalin consulted time and again the cookbook of Trotskyism; but as
Lenin said, his cuisine turned out unbearably spicy—and indigestible.

We have already said that the inviolability of Lenin's staff was
breached first not by Stalin but by the black-comedy team of Zinoviev
and Kamenev. Trotsky always despised them for cowardice and panic-
mongering. They in turn openly accused him of Bonapartism. There is
a saying that real misfortune is born of unnecessary fears. These two by
their intrigues against Trotsky untied Stalin's hands and brought about
their own destruction.

The undermining of Trotsky began with the weakening of his position in the Army. After the Civil War the Secretariat of the Central
Committee removed many of the political workers from the RKKA. In
part this was a natural process connected with demobilization, but it
was Trotsky's supporters who were first to be transferred. In 1923 the
intrigues against the People's Commissar of the Army and Navy came
out into the open. On June 2, a plenum of the Central Control
Commission passed a resolution on the investigation of the activities of

the military department (*vedomstvo*). A commission was formed under the chairmanship of V. V. Kuibyshev with N. M. Shvernik as his assistant; neither can be suspected of Trotskyite sympathies. In September, S. E. Gusev became the head of the Commission. He had once been dismissed from the post of Chief of Political Administration of the RKKA by Trotsky.

The Stalinist-Zinovievite apparatus took aim at the leader of the Red Army and hemmed him in from all sides. On October 30 Zinoviev's ally M. M. Lashevich and Stalin's creature K. E. Voroshilov were made members of the Revolutionary Military Council of the USSR; two years later they headed the supreme organ of defense. On January 12, 1924, A. S. Bubnov replaced V. A. Antonov-Ovseenko as chief of the Political Administration of the RKKA. Two days later a plenum of the Central Committee of the RKP(b) formed a commission to investigate the instability of the personnel and the condition of supplies in the armed forces. There is a provocative note in the way they phrased their task: it would not be difficult to find instability in an army that had just been reduced to one-tenth its former size. The commission was packed: it included Stalin and his people Voroshilov, Egorov, Ordzhonikidze, Shvernik, Andreev; Bubnov, who had just been forced upon the War Commissariat; the insulted Gusev; Frunze, who aspired to Trotsky's position; also Unshlikht and Skliansky. From the first day of the existence of the RVSR, Skliansky had been deputy chairman and had taken upon himself the whole burden of operational and chancellery work. Lenin regarded him highly and trusted him implicitly. He was included only for the sake of form, as he was intended to be the first victim.

The plenum met without Trotsky, who was seriously ill and had gone to the Caucasus to recover. The Central Committee's commission did not investigate the matter themselves but worked only with material that was presented to it by Gusev. How easy it would have been to predict that the conclusions would go against Trotsky: he had neglected his work in the military department, and his assistants, E. M. Skliansky and Chief of Staff P. P. Lebedev, had not provided competent leadership.

Lenin died on January 21, but the intrigues against Trotsky did not let up even in those tragic days. Stalin misinformed him about the date of Lenin's funeral, telling him it was a day or two earlier. The train on which Trotsky was traveling from Tblisi to Sukhumi would not be able to make it to Moscow in time. (The train along the Caucasus shore then traveled the roundabout way through Baku.) It was officially announced that the Central Committee had prescribed that comrade Trotsky remain where he was for the sake of his health, since he was so valuable to the Revolution. Therefore, at the moment of the passing of power Trotsky was far from Moscow and remained away until April.

On Feburary 2 the Central Executive Committee (TSIK) confirmed the composition of the new government headed by A. I. Rykov. Trotsky still kept his posts as People's Commissar of War and Chairman of the Revolutionary Military Council of the USSR. On the next day, however, Gusev read to a meeting of the Central Committee a report that was highly critical of the military department's work and portrayed the Red Army as unfit. Unshlikht, Lashevich, Frunze, Voroshilov, and Ord-zhonikidze supported Gusev; Tukhachevsky, Kashirin, and other military men had spoken in a similar way at previous commission meetings.

The general public was not aware of this behind-the-scenes maneuvering. Other songs were sung for show. The plenum of the Central Committee, which met March 31–April 2, did not agree with the commission and completely approved the work of the military department. Even before that, however, Stalin and Zinoviev had made further organizational changes. On March 21 Skliansky was removed from the Revolutionary Military Council of the USSR.[11] Frunze was made first deputy chairman, and Unshlikht, second.[12]

Frunze immediately concentrated enormous power in his hands. In April he was also appointed Chief-of-Staff of the RKKA, superintendent of all military academies, and commander of internal security forces. At the same time the position of commander-in-chief was eliminated. The point was obvious: to reduce Trotsky's influence in the military hierarchy to a minimum and to be able to show later that he was not needed there at all.

To all appearances Zinoviev was leading the beaters in this hunt. Stalin, who had much to gain by Trotsky's loss of power, did not interfere and remained in the shadows. By the time the Thirteenth Party Congress opened in May, Trotsky had been eased out of military affairs. He was opposed by a monolithic majority formally grouped around Zinoviev, who presented the Central Committee's political report. The report contained vicious attacks on Trotsky and Trotskyism, although not a single word was said specifically about the Army. Stalin emphasized statistics and inner-Party business in his organizational report. It drew very little criticism from the opposition. The General Secretary undoubtedly wanted to appear a businessman and an organizer, distant from the squabbles within the Party. The speakers who followed him helped. Kamenev in a well-constructed speech dissected Trotskyism bone by bone and branded it a petty bourgeois deviation. Bukharin, Uglanov, and Riutin continued angrily in the same vein. How were they to know that they would later be put up against the wall as Trotsky's accomplices?

Trotsky defended himself weakly at the Congress. Either he had not fully recovered from his illness, or he understood the hopelessness of his situation. He came to attention and eloquently testified that one must not be right before the Party; one must share all with the Party, including its mistakes and delusions.

As if he suddenly realized that he had been avoiding military matters, Zinoviev addressed them briefly in his concluding remarks:

> The reform carried out in the military . . . was devised at the initiative of the military men of the Central Committee with the full and enthusiastic support of the Central Committee, which discussed this extremely urgent reform many times in plenums and in the Politburo. The initiative belonged not so much to the military as to the Central Committee of the Party. We all believe that it has been properly carried out and that we will soon feel its results.

After his windy tirade with its veiled criticism of Trotsky, Zinoviev mentioned in passing personnel changes in the defense hierarchy: "I think we were right to appoint a number of Central Committee men, headed by comrade Frunze, to the Revolutionary Military Council. *They will help comrade Trotsky carry on his work there* and help the Revolutionary Council forge closer relations with the lower ranks of the Red Army."[13]

Frunze, who was a rather independent and popular figure, gravitated toward the Zinoviev camp. In any case he had no intention "to help comrade Trotsky carry on his work." Rather he tried with all his might to displace him. He was well placed to try. Behind him stood the anti-Trotsky majority of the Central Committee; Frunze himself became a candidate member of the Politburo. When Trotsky reopened debate in the Party in 1924, he was defeated again. In the fall the Zinovievites tried to show Trotsky the door, but Stalin prevented his ouster.[14]

Against the background of these repeated setbacks the retirement of the politically defeated Trotsky from the supreme military post seemed natural. On January 26, 1925, the Presidium of the Central Executive Committee approved the request of Trotsky, L. D., to be released from his duties as People's Commissar and Chairman of the Revolutionary Military Council; they appointed Frunze in his place. Trotsky's removal had already been decided for purely political reasons several days earlier at a plenum of the Central Committee.

Frunze's elevation was accompanied by a small purge of the officer corps. On February 24 V. I. Shorin, who had recently been deputy commander-in-chief, was retired with a pension, deep gratitude, and the honor of remaining on the roles of the RKKA for life (which did not save him from execution in 1937). The political motivation for his release shows through in the Revolutionary Military Council order: "retired because of the impossiblity of further usefulness."

By the beginning of 1925 the Stalin–Zinoviev coalition had severed its primary rival's ties with the military. But Stalin was more farsighted than his temporary allies. He provoked them into speaking carelessly at Leningrad while he prepared another purge at the Congress. At the same time, but in deep secrecy, a more important act was being planned.

The Army as a whole accepted Trotsky's retirement quietly, even with some relief. Their commissar was an arrogant man; he had loved to pose as a great leader. He was ill at ease in personal contacts with his subordinates and not infrequently injured their pride. He was unable to conceal his scorn for fools, an attitude that in Russia was at the very least dangerous. Frunze was a firm leader, but socially more graceful. In some eyes he was seen as a political overseer, but he also had a reputation as a military commander, the conqueror of Kolchak and Wrangel. Only the Trotskyites were dissatisfied with the removal of their idol, but they could do little more than sing a hurried chorus of the song "After Trotsky, Frunze is such a shame, such a shame. . . ." The Army still did not suspect what awaited it.

While Stalin artfully maneuvered in the battle with Zinoviev, planning to open the decisive campaign on the eve of the Congress in December, he maintained emphatically loyal relations with Frunze. Moreover, with the understandable aim of deflating memories of Trotsky, the Stalinists promoted Frunze as the incomparable great leader of the Red Army. But Frunze was unable to make use of Stalin's sympathies; he was more drawn to Zinoviev, and in any case he was not Stalin's type. Stalin permitted Frunze's promotion for two reasons. One was to weaken Trotsky; the other was to use the new People's Commissar as a Trojan horse under the cover of which he could put his own protégé at the helm of the RKKA. The plan was rather subtle, but its realization, as was usual with Stalin, was rather rough.

To try to dismiss Frunze by legal means would have been inexpedient and difficult; therefore sudden death was chosen. In July 1925 Frunze was in two automobile accidents. Voroshilov disclosed this in the press immediately after the commissar's death.[15] Since that did not work, Stalin resorted to medical murder, possibly for the first time in his career.

Frunze suffered from stomach ulcers. In the summer of 1925, he took a course of medication at Mukholatka in the Crimea, which gave him considerable relief. He felt so much better that he went hunting. Subsequent events are not difficult to reconstruct from Voroshilov's article, "The Memory of Our Dear Friend Mikhail Vasilievich Frunze." Trying to deflect suspicion from himself and his crew, Frunze's successor employed too many details from which the sinister truth can be guessed.

Stalin, Voroshilov, and Shkitriatov, a confirmed Stalinist and one of the prominent figures of the 1937 terror, vacationed with Frunze. They repeatedly told the People's Commissar that his life was in danger and that resolute measures must be taken. With this excuse Voroshilov refused to go hunting with him. Frunze's personal physician, military doctor Mandryka, was sent from the Crimea on some pretext and replaced by two doctors, Rozanov and Kasatkin, who were brought from Moscow with a large staff. They observed the patient for two weeks and under pressure from a concerned Stalin came to the conclusion that an operation was necessary.

On September 29, the whole group left for Moscow, the Stalinist trinity to the Central Committee plenum and Frunze to a hospital. Between October 7 and 10 Voroshilov and Bubnov visited him in the hospital and found him in good health. On one of those days they learned from a doctor Levin that seventeen prominent specialists were consulting on the case. Rozanov spoke in favor of the operation. Late that night Bubnov announced the doctors' unanimous decision to operate. Everyone accepted it calmly: "What was there to be concerned about when Rozanov and Kasatkin persuaded us, assured us, that there was no reason for alarm. I believed. I believed as we all believed, as our unforgettable, best of the glorious, friend and comrade

Mikhail Vasilievich calmly and confidently *went under the knife.*[16]

For understandable reasons Voroshilov eulogized the dead and winked a dirty wink toward medicine. As far as is known, none of the doctors was ever punished.

On October 31, upon his return from the Crimea, Voroshilov learned in a telegram from Stalin, "Frunze died today of a heart attack."[17]

Voroshilov lied. The Peoples Commissar did not go under the knife calmly, but with great reluctance. He expected to die and asked his friend I. Gamburg to see that he was buried at Ivanovo-Voznesensk. (He was not.) Frunze underwent the operation in obedience to a special decision of the Secretariat of the Central Committee, which relied on the conclusions of the medical experts. The medical opinion was obtained in a rather straightforward way. The medics, who were not Party men, were told beforehand that marked improvement in the health of the patient was expected of them immediately. The question of the operation was decided therefore even before the consultation. Nor is it certain that the decision was actually unanimous. What is certain is that when they did operate, the surgeons discovered that the operation was unnecessary—the ulcer had formed scar tissue and healed itself. But by that time another problem had come up. They had difficulty putting the patient under anesthesia and gave him an overdose of chloroform. His heart could not stand it.

There is an oral tradition about the operation that gives a different picture. On the evening of the day of the consultation, one of the doctors was seized by doubts about the expediency of the operation. He expressed these doubts to Stalin's technical secretary in the Kremlin. The latter immediately informed his superiors, after which the professor was thanked and sent home in a Kremlin car. On the Bolshoi Kamenny bridge—the old one that was lower than the one now standing—the car struck a railing and fell into the river. The driver managed to escape, but the unfortunate doctor died.

The circumstances and atmosphere of Frunze's medical murder were used by B. Pilnyak in his "Story of the Unextinguished Moon."[18] Army Commander Gavrilov, having been cured of stomach ulcers, returns from a resort to Moscow, where he learns from the newspapers that he is to undergo an emergency operation. He goes to an important official, whom he finds writing a book on political economy. The latter informs him, "You must, comrade Gavrilov, otherwise in a month you will be a corpse; your health is necessary for the Revolution." For form's sake, consultation is held with two Russian professors and a German. The latter categorically opposes the operation; so do the Russians, but they have no choice: they have read the papers. One of them says, "As I understand it, they want only one decision from us—to operate. He will have to have surgery." One surgeon says to the other, "I would not put my brother on the table in that condition." Gavrilov has a premonition about his death and writes a will, but he cannot violate revolutionary discipline. The operation discloses a well-healed ulcer, but the commander's heart stops under the influence of the anesthetic.

The most damning evidence was given by Stalin himself. In a speech delivered at Frunze's open grave he outlined with characteristic brevity the destruction of the revolutionary cadres: "Comrades: I am in no condition to speak long, my heart does not let me. . . . This year has been cursed. It has taken from us many of our leading comrades. But even that was not enough, and there had to be still another sacrifice. Maybe that was actually *necessary*, that *the old comrades* so *easily and simply* slipped into the grave."[19]

The Party did not suffer any particularly important losses in 1925, but Stalin's nervous condition is explicable: this was his first experience of this sort, and the risk was great. Later it became easier. This pronouncement by the murderer is worthy of the attention of the author of *Crime and Punishment*.

That Stalin already had, if only in rough outline, a program to make his way to personal dictatorship is tangentially confirmed in his speech at Dzerzhinsky's funeral in July 1926. It begins with the words "After Frunze, Dzerzhinsky. . . ."[20] It was as if Stalin were counting, and for the time being the fingers on one hand were sufficient. And what if what Trotsky said in 1939 was true, that Stalin had poisoned Lenin? Stalin said himself in 1924 that Ilich had been given poison.

Dzerzhinsky's death was certainly timely. The suspicious circumstances of Frunze's death had to sooner or later come under the scrutiny of the OGPU. Stalin might well have feared that Iron Feliks, who was in the last stages of consumption, might show mercy to no one should he untangle the thread.

The circumstances of Dzerzhinsky's death give food for thought. According to the published diagnosis, he died of a heart attack during a meeting of the Central Committee, at which he twice engaged Kamenev and Piatakov in angry debate. The text of those speeches surprises one by the insignificance of the subject matter discussed. It seems unlikely that a man so sick would find it necessary to speak out twice on such an ordinary matter. It is said that Stalin intentionally poured oil on the fire to drag out the meeting. Finally Dzerzhinsky collapsed before the eyes of his comrades, with some of whom he had managed to quarrel irreparably. Knowing Stalin's ways, one can surmise that medical aid was not given in time or not entirely properly.

Regardless of how Frunze died, in November 1925 the position at the head of the RKKA fell vacant. There was no obvious successor to the People's Commissar. Trotsky's return was politically impossible. Skliansky was dead. None of the purely military figures—S. Kamenev, Tukhachevsky, Egorov, or others—could be considered because of their pasts. By contemporary standards the head of the Red Army had to possess two qualities: a solid party background (a member or candidate member of the Politburo, or at the very least a member of the Central Committee) and military experience. That narrowed the choice drastically.

An additional limitation was placed by the two main factions within the Central Committee. They would not consider the appointment of any of Trotsky's former associates; N. I. Muralov, Antonov-Ovseenko, and I. N. Smirnov were eliminated by that consideration. The Stalinists and Zinovievites would have to agree to the appointment, as neither faction had the upper hand with the Congress.

Who might the Central Committee factions recommend? The first might nominate Stalin, Ordzhonikidze, and Voroshilov; the second Lashevich, and possibly G. Ia. Sokolnikov. From the military's point of view none of these was a first-class candidate; but they met the formal qualifications. The great majority of the Party leadership—the "swamp"—were perplexed. It got to the point that several members of the Central Committee and the Central Control Commission asked the military men gathered for Frunze's funeral whom they would like to see as People's Commissar? Tukhachevsky, for one, named Ordzhonikidze.[21] But such questions were not decided by referendum.

Finally Voroshilov's candidacy was advanced. We do not have reliable information on how that appointment was accomplished. There is an interesting legend, however, that is worth recording. At a special meeting of the leadership (it is unknown if this was a formal plenum of the Central Committee) the candidacies of Ordzhonikidze and Stalin were discussed first. The secretaries of the national Communist parties are said to have advanced Stalin's candidacy, hoping thereby to free themselves from his brilliant leadership and iron hand, which they had felt earlier than others. But Josef Vissarionovich's situation was not ideal. Emmanuil Kviring was slated to replace him as general secretary. Kviring was not an unimportant person: in 1914 he had been secretary of the Bolshevik faction in the state duma; after the Revolution he was one of the organizers of the Communist Party (Bolsheviks) in the Ukraine; and in 1923 he became its first secretary. The post of general secretary was then considered technical and organizational, but not political. It became political only after the Fourteenth Congress, which met a month later.

If it had been proposed to replace Stalin with one of the great leaders of the Party, then Stalin, through his underlings, might complain of intrigues. But with Kviring it was different. He was the same sort of bureaucratic figure as Stalin. To let the Party apparatus out of his hands was like death to Stalin, but he rose to the occasion. "Of course," he said about himself in the third person, "comrade Stalin will go where the Party needs him. But Kviring will make a bad General Secretary."[22] Ordzhonikidze was allegedly irreplaceable as executive secretary of the trans-Caucasus regional committee. (Beria was still very young, and Stalin did not have another of his own men at hand.) Then someone, probably one of the Stalinists, proposed Klim Voroshilov, an old Bolshevik (since 1903), an ex-metal worker from Lugansk, a hero of the Civil War, and currently a commander.

As usual, the fresh suggestion at a protracted meeting provided psychological relief and seemed therefore attractive. Zinoviev, who was preoccupied with the battle brewing within the Party, apparently did not raise serious objections. Avoiding Unshlikht, M. Lashevich was appointed Voroshilov's first deputy.

Voroshilov's appointment as Chairman of the Revolutionary Military Council and People's Commissar of Army and Navy was one of the great sensations of the time. Only twenty-one months after Lenin's death, while the Party leadership was seriously divided, and the country in serious economic difficulties (who knew then that they would become chronic?), responsibility for the defense of the country was laid upon a man whose abilities and past activities, it would seem, made him unsuitable for the role.

Let us try to examine Voroshilov's qualities calmly and objectively, from the standpoint of those times. On the one hand, he was enormously popular: an activist of the revolutionary underground, the first

Army commander to rise from the working class, political commissar of the victorious First Horse Army, and so forth. On the other hand, Voroshilov did not enjoy authority at the top either in the military or among the politicians. Lenin, by the way, did not think much of Voroshilov. And that is understandable. Only recently had he become a metal worker, and he had never studied. He had neither a general nor a military education. The Civil War had shown that he possessed personal bravery and revolutionary enthusiasm, but he had not risen higher than commissar–mass agitator. There were serious failures in his military career. We have mentioned the Tsaritsyn episode, but there were worse. After the unauthorized surrender of Kharkov in 1919, Voroshilov was turned over to a revolutionary tribunal. They did not consider his action treasonous, but they judged him incompetent and decided not to permit him to hold positions of command in the Army in the future.[23] Voroshilov became a political worker. Only Stalin's patronage and Voroshilov's personal participation in taking Kronshtadt helped him regain a troop command. In 1921 he was made head of the North Caucasus Military District and in May 1924 was transferred to the Moscow district. Voroshilov simply did not compare favorably with his predecessors, not with Frunze, even less with Trotsky. No underground songs were composed about him. But soon there were others, official and providing royalties.

We might be accused of prejudice or lack of objectivity. Fortunately we have a characterization of Voroshilov written by a man who stands ideologically above suspicion. This is what Lieutenant General A. I. Todorsky, a famous military figure and a participant in the Civil War, who worked with Voroshilov many years in the central apparatus of the People's Commissariat, wrote:

> Everyone knew that Voroshilov was Stalin's arms bearer, his spokesman and mouthpiece. Even Budenny and Egorov, Voroshilov's Army friends, greeted his appointment with no particular enthusiasm. For such military figures as Tukhachevsky, Voroshilov's appointment as People's Commissar marked the coming to military power of an openly unobjective Party leader, an apologist for the doctrine and mind-set of the former member of the Revolutionary Military Council of the South-West Front, Stalin. It was very revealing that in all the years he knew them, Voroshilov never could find a common language even with

Blucher and Dybenko, who were ex-workers like himself.

The People's Commissar zealously employed famous Stalinist aphorisms, like: "We do not want a foot of others' land, but we will not yield an inch of our own," "War only on enemy territory," et cetera. Of course, one could not base a whole military program upon these Stalinist expressions [to take measures to defend interior territory for example; or to work out plans for evacuation, etc.]. The Commissar's narrowly propagandistic views on the larger questions of defense were adopted with misplaced enthusiasm by such of his followers as E. A. Shchadenko, one of the most odious petty tyrants in our Army.

Voroshilov entered the postwar history of the Red Army as a good driver and marksman with a revolver. Undoubtedly these personal qualities were not sufficient for the leader of the Workers-Peasants' Army, especially in a country [then] in capitalist encirclement. However, Voroshilov became famous in the postwar period for turning the whole history of the Civil War into glorification of Stalin, in service to the cult of his personality. In 1929, to mark Stalin's fiftieth birthday, Voroshilov published his work, *Stalin and the Red Army*, which opened a new era in the study of our military history. More than that, Voroshilov besmirched his own reputation as a hero of the Civil War by his complicity in the liquidation of the old military specialists in 1930 and the destruction of the commanders and commissars in 1937–1938. . . .

The whole organism of the Red Army was like an ordinary apple tree to Stalin and Voroshilov. As long as it would produce new apples next year, they would shake it as hard as they liked.[24]

However you look at it, it becomes clear that in 1925 Voroshilov did not possess the personal qualities needed in a top military leader. This did not necessarily portend his failure in that role. Life can be likened to theater, but with an important reservation: life's actors do not have written roles, they must improvise, often in the most incredible situations.

At the age of forty-four Voroshilov could open in an unexpected new role. The Revolution for the time being had brought to the stage people who in the previous era had not been quoted on the political markets, who literally had no value. Who in 1915, 1916, or even 1917, could have foreseen in civilian Frunze, Lieutenant Tukhachevsky, or noncom Budenny the commanders who would lead huge masses of people into battle and for several decades determine the fate of the country? Even the Commanders-in-Chief Vatsetis and S. Kamenev, and Army Commanders Egorov and Shorin were only colonels in the World War without any real prospect of becoming generals or occupying top posts. Therefore his worker heritage and lack of education did not foreordain the failure of Voroshilov's career as leader of the armed forces of the Soviet Republic.

These considerations were and remain purely speculative. It was precisely in the battles of the Revolution that Voroshilov's worthlessness as a military leader was revealed. He was not swept to the top by the revolutionary wave, but by conspiracies carried out for narrowly selfish purposes.

Voroshilov's appointment was accompanied by numerous other changes in the apparatus of the People's Commissariat and in the commands of military districts. These rotations did not have the character of purges. Their goal was, first of all, to remove top commanders from posts they had long occupied and thus to disrupt relations among them and thereby avert possible resistance to the new leadership. Only a week after his appointment Voroshilov announced a major shake-up of commanders.[25] Egorov lost his post as commander of the Ukrainian region but remained a member of the Revolutionary Military Council. Yakir, who had been commandant of the Department of Military Academies (UVUZ), took his place. Putna replaced Yakir. The commander of the Turkestan Front, Levandovsky, was put in charge of the Caucasus Red Army, which Kork had just left to take over the Western district. The former commander of the Western district, Tukhachevsky, became chief-of-staff of the RKKA, a position until then occupied by Commander-in-Chief S. Kamenev, who became inspector of the Red Army.

Thanks to all these changes, Stalin could be assured during the battles of the December Congress that the Army was busy surviving the reshuffling of its commanders.[26] To a large extent this was done as a precaution. Zinoviev did not have many supporters in the Army and did not trust former officers. That intriguer and panicmonger slept badly nights, tortured by historical and foreign analogies. In 1926 he convinced himself that the Red Army of the NEP period would produce a Soviet Chiang Kai-shek.

Tukhachevsky was very young, only thirty-two, when he became head of the General Staff. Previously he had not had to do any headquarters work. His strategic concepts were still very immature. The main thrust of his activity at that time was an attempt to organize the technical rearmament of the Army. He was not able to accomplish much. True, in 1926 the secret Soviet-German agreement on military cooperation was concluded. In contravention of the confining articles of the Versailles Treaty the Reichswehr obtained testing grounds for its tanks and airfields in Soviet territory, in exchange for which Germans instructed Red commanders in military science. In 1928 and 1929 Yakir, Tukhachevsky, Blucher, Timoshenko, and many others attended courses at the German General Staff Academy.

There was nothing with which to arm the Red Army. There were various types of small arms, for which there were often no shells. The tanks, planes, and cars could be counted on fingers. To give the Army the technical equipment it needed, it would be necessary to construct a special defense industry as part of the general process of industrialization. Tukhachevsky wrote about all this in a memorandum in 1927, but Stalin and Voroshilov were too preoccupied to give it the attention it deserved. They were in the midst of the struggle with the opposition to see who would run the Party and the country. Stalin exclaimed, "Nonsense," when he read Tukhachevsky's report. In 1930 when Tukhachevsky repeated his appeal, the reaction was the same. Stalin told him, approximately, this would constitute militarization of the country; no Marxist in his right mind would embark on that course.

Early in 1928 Tukhachevsky wrote the Central Committee and the government: "Either I do not understand general political circumstances, or I am misunderstood by the political leadership. In either case I cannot remain at my post." It is possible that more than pride was at stake, that Tukhachevsky wanted to extricate himself from an awkward situation. His resignation was accepted. Tukhachevsky departed for Leningrad to take over command of the military district.

11 Scholarly Arguments

Between them everything was subject to controversy and debate.
—Pushkin

The Red Army, like every army, needed military science. In the first two years of its existence a fairly extensive system of study and preparation of commanders was organized along with its executive organs. Practically all the professors and instructors of the military educational institutions came from the old army. This did not mean that they brought with them the spirit and mood of the past. On the contrary, most of them had believed before the Revolution that the autocracy and its army could not guarantee the defense of the country. Now in the new conditions they had a chance to establish the theoretical basis for the RKKA.

The enormous disruption of the whole structure of life led inevitably to a reexamination of accepted views. Bitter disputes broke out in all spheres. In the Army they took the form of arguments about a unified military doctrine.

This problem had its history. It had arisen after the defeat in the war with the Japanese. Some of the generals (notably A. M. Zaionichkovsky and M. D. Bonch-Bruevich) feared that accepting such a doctrine might pattern and stagnate military thought. Others (such as A. A. Neznamov and A. Dmitrievsky) insisted on the fruitfulness of an orderly unity of views. The Emperor, Nicholas II, summed the matter up in 1912, when he announced to the commandant of the Military Academy, General Yanushkevich, "Military doctrine consists in fulfilling my orders. I ask you to tell Neznamov for me to address this question in the press no longer. . . ."

The discussion was reopened in 1918 in a speech by former Major General V. E. Borisov and was widely debated in 1920 and 1921. In the latter period most of the participants displayed quick tempers and a peremptory manner. The subject of the debate was never clearly defined.

A. A. Svechin's report, "The Foundations of Military Doctrine," and his article on that topic triggered the debate in 1920. According to

Svechin, military doctrine was "a point of view from which to understand military history, its experience, and lessons. . . . Military doctrine is military, and particularly, tactical philosophy; doctrine creates certainty, which is the soul of every action." He thought it necessary to unify views at a tactical level and through educational programs, regulations, and manuals to reach the "great mass of the Army." Svechin considered it useful to deal only with a required minimum of technical knowledge and did not infringe on creative freedom in strategy and politics.

Neznamov spoke out again to support the position he had earlier held. He believed that "military doctrine expresses the view of the people and the government on war, in accordance with which foreign policy is conducted and the armed forces are organized." Such convictions have the scent of militarism upon them, because they make the approach to war (military interests) the foundation of politics. After the formulation and adoption of a doctrine, it is reflected in military regulations. Various other military specialists to differing degrees supported Svechin or Neznamov. But the primary watershed of opinion lay elsewhere.

F. Trutko, a participant in the Civil War and a student at the Academy, posed the principal question of the discussion. He said there was no point in discussing whether a doctrine was needed; we needed our own, proletarian, communist, military doctrine; we had only to devise it. But that function could not be entrusted to the generals of the tsarist army. First of all, they had had more than enough time before the Revolution and had failed to produce a military doctrine. Most important, they did not understand the Marxist method.

After this reconnaissance in force, the heavy artillery was brought into play in the persons of Trotsky and Frunze. Strange as it may seem, these two Bolsheviks sharply disagreed. Frunze's position was (1) our military doctrine must be a *class* doctrine, i.e., proletarian, i.e., Marxist; (2) its basic tenets must be worked out, precisely formulated, and decreed. Frunze based his own ideas on the experience of the Civil War, to which he attached exceptional importance, often to the detriment of previous military history.[1]

Trotsky retorted to both of Frunze's points in his article "Military Doctrine or Pseudo-military Doctrinairism?"[2] Without denying the need for unity of view on military questions, he decisively rejected the possibility of fixing them as firmly as standard weights and measures.

Trotsky's view was that if there were not a pertinent paragraph, one must think; but if there existed a paragraph, then no one would bother to think. Trotsky spoke against making a fetish of the experience of the Red Army in the Civil War and called upon his countrymen to diligently study the military arts. He ridiculed the suggestion that there might be a particularly proletarian military science. In general, the People's Commissar did not highly regard the application of the Marxist method outside politics, as this rather famous dictum of his testifies: "Those who think we can arrange work in a candle factory with the help of Marxism, know very little about Marxism or about making candles."

The discussion was carried over to the Eleventh Party Congress, at which nothing was decided. At a special meeting of military delegates, Trotsky and Frunze made reports. Before that, Frunze spoke of the Congress in the lobby with Lenin, who gently but firmly supported Trotsky. Lenin disliked pseudo-Marxist blather. It would seem that that helped Frunze see the excessive dogmatism of his position. In any case, he announced at the meeting that on the question of military doctrine and science he had no disagreements with Trotsky. True, they still disagreed about the character of a future war, but we will discuss that later.

No official Soviet military doctrine was proclaimed. In the 1930s, however, the Army had foisted upon it three provisions by Stalin, which turned out to be more harmful than any decreed doctrine: (1) war could have few casualties and must be fought on foreign soil, (2) we need not a foot of foreign land, but we will not give up a single inch of our own, and (3) in the rear of any aggressor the Red Army will find support in the form of an uprising of workers and peasants.

The polemics surrounding military doctrine were not the only point of disagreement in the military. Therefore the inglorious end to the discussion did not lead to agreement and unity of views. A heated, uncompromising debate arose about an even more important subject, and many military commanders and scholarly authorities were drawn into the argument. Each had to answer the vital question, what will be the nature of future war, and what action will the Red Army and the Soviet government take in it.

It ought to be remembered that this discussion came hot on the heels of the Civil War, and that most of the participants in it had not yet cooled off from the heat of battle. It is entirely likely therefore that the experience of the Civil War served as the starting point for practically all the reasoning, assertions, and prophecies involved in it.

The subject of the debate has been well and thoroughly described by Svechin. There are two major forms of strategy—the strategy of "smashing" or "destruction" (*sokrushenie*) and the strategy of "attrition" (*izmor*). Svechin admitted that the terms themselves were not entirely adequate; but they have become established in military literature. Smashing assumes decisive action, unrestrained offense with the goal of total destruction of the living forces of the enemy, or at least of taking them out of action. Proponents of attrition see the more skillful use of resources—people, arms, economy, and territory—as the major factor in winning a war. Placing a primary emphasis on physical destruction or neutralization always costs dearly and as a rule leads to the aggressor's defeat: if we have enough strength when the enemy weakens, we will go on the offensive and defeat him, or he will not be in condition to continue the war and will capitulate.

That is how Svechin presented the problem. The younger commanders of the Red Army led by Frunze unanimously favored the strategy of destruction. Trotsky, without getting involved in the debate, supported thorough preparation for war and warned against neglecting defense. Frunze several times reappraised his position; but Tukhachevsky, Triandafillov, Varfolomeev, and others maintained their views for a long while. The logic of the "destroyers" was simple. War would be exclusively mobile. Success depended on mobility and firepower, for whch troops would have to be supplied to the utmost with tanks, automobiles, planes, artillery, and the chemicals of war. Defense was senseless, because there was no defense against such powerful offensive weaponry. It would be best to gather as much force as possible into a strike force and with a series of well-planned strikes destroy the enemy.

This was the strategy of blitzkrieg, which in Russia came from two sources. One was associated with ideology, and here the destructive conception continued the line of our particularly proletarian doctrine. This doctrine holds that: we are a young class, rising and aggressive and the moving forces of history are working for us. Torn by contradictions, the capitalist world will be forced to the defensive. Its destruction is inevitable, as was taught by the only truly scientific theory, Marxism. The capitalist countries cannot be strong in their rear areas. Without fail their proletariats will revolt and welcome the Red Army as liberators.

The other source of inspiration was the recent victory in the Civil War. In that war combat action was carried out most energetically. The larger campaigns were brief and ended decisively. Both sides preached the strategy of the destructive offense, despite the fact that the Bolsheviks, as a rule, not only turned back the offensives thrown at them (as witness Kolchak, Denikin, and Yudenich), but eventually effected the total defeat of their enemies. There was only one sad exception—the march on Warsaw—but the preferred explanation for that was to blame the mistakes of the front commanders.

Such arguments for the offensive strategy were entirely convincing for many, but not for all. Svechin and a number of other old generals considered the analysis of the Civil War incomplete and superficial, and the conclusions hasty. First of all, there was no certainty that later wars would resemble the Civil War. That war—like all other civil wars —was an exception from the point of view of strategic circumstances. Both sides had to understand that their enemies' victory meant not simply their own military defeat but also their physical destruction. Hence the extreme bitterness of the fight and the effort to decide its outcome by strategic means alone as soon as possible.

Along with this subjective factor, objective factors were at work that determined the offensive nature of the campaigns. Both the Whites and the Reds had to depend on unreliable rears: weak economies, disrupted communications, populations tired of war. Additionally, the rear areas frequently changed hands. The front was not continuous, and there were practically no prepared defenses. The density of fire was much less than in the World War.

In such conditions, a war of maneuvering and a preference for attack were natural. In the confrontation with Poland, which did have a relatively solid rear, such a strategy was not justified. The deeper the Red Army advanced into the enemy territory, the stiffer the resistance became; it did not weaken as the preferred theory said it should. As strange an aberration of their class view as it might have been, the proletariat of Poland did not view the Red Army as their liberators. At the same time it was being learned that the Entente's home fronts were sufficiently strong and reliable.

The most serious error was made in the assertion that the Red Army had gained victory over the Entente. This assertion ignored the fact that the notorious campaign of fourteen nations was only a propagandistic exaggeration. The author of that cliché was Winston Churchill, who proclaimed early in 1919 that he would send that number of states against Russia and take Petrograd by September. As is well known, the campaign of the united forces never happened; the troops of the major powers had been too exhausted in the World War. On January 16, 1920, the Supreme Council of the Entente resolved not to interfere directly in Russian affairs. Official Soviet historiography has refused even until now to recognize that fact.[3]

No enumeration of the fourteen nations, unfortunately, can be found in any Soviet publication. We have barely managed to compile such a list, which includes sixteen countries: England, France, Italy, Greece, Japan, Germany (the voluntary corps of Fon-der Golts), Czechoslovakia (the Czechoslovak Corps), Poland, Ukraine, Belorussia, Lithuania, Latvia, Estonia, Turkey, Finland, and the United States. It can even be expanded, since the independent trans-Caucasian republics are sometimes counted among the enemies of Soviet power.

Altogether the so-called interventionists numbered approximately 400,000,[4] including the armies of the national minorities on the borders of the Russian empire, which fought on their own territories. The major countries of the Entente were able to send only small expeditionary contingents with limited goals: England, 45,000; France (together with Greece), 20,000; the United States, 7,000; Japan, three infantry divisions (or by other data 70,000). The contribution of the West to the Civil War came down, basically, to material assistance to the Whites.

In analyzing the Civil War, the destroyers changed their accents. They did not understand that the Reds' victory had been gained not only and not mostly by military successes, but by superior policies —the decree on land, massive mobilization, more skillful propaganda and agitation, possession of the capitals, recruitment to their side of a significant part of the officer corps.

These errors, so obvious today, had an entirely reasonable explanation. Beaten armies examine past defeats to learn their errors, while victors tend to exaggerate the value of their actions. In any case, they are strongly tempted to adhere to the strategy that brought them victory yesterday. We must give Trotsky his due; several times he warned the Bolsheviks not to pride themselves too much on their military victories. He pointed out that these had been achieved not because of any great military skill, but because of the revolutionary enthusiasm of the masses, numerical superiority over the enemy, and other less-than-glorious reasons.

We have come now to the story of the military figure who already in the 1920s had rejected the destruction concept. He worked out a theory of the conduct of a future war that has turned out to be so perspicacious that half a century later we have little to add. That was Aleksander Andreevich Svechin. Soviet historiography to the present has not given him the attention he deserves, and in the few instances in which he is mentioned treats him prejudicially.[5]

Svechin was born on August 17, 1878, in Ekaterinoslav (now Dnepropetrovsk). Following the example of his father, a major general in the Russian army, Svechin embarked on a military career from boyhood: the cadet corps and Mikhailovsky military school. In line service from 1895, he later completed the Nikolaevsky Academy of the General Staff. Svechin displayed a profound interest in new weapons and in 1909 was sent to Germany to attend an aviation exhibition. He had earlier served through the whole far eastern campaign and survived the catastrophe of the Russian army. From the time of Mukden, in his words, he began a serious revision of his values, which for a man of his position was very painful. His conclusion was likewise discomfitting: the autocratic order did not guarantee the defense of the country.

Svechin spent most of the World War at the front. He was wounded. He advanced from regimental commander to chief-of-staff of the Army. He was decorated with all the military orders from St. Vladimir to St. George, with medals, and with St. George's Sword for bravery.

In 1918 Svechin voluntarily entered the service of the new-born RKKA. They immediately employed the experienced combat general in highly responsible positions: chief-of-staff of the Western sector of the Screen (*zavesa*), military instructor of the Smolensk region of the Screen, chief of the All Russian Main Staff (*Vserosglavshtab*), which was at first the general staff and from September 1918 the organ directing the organization of reserves.

In 1918 Svechin also began to teach at the Military Academy. At first this was just one of his duties, but he soon was doing it full time and not long after became the director of the history of military arts for all academies. Svechin was extremely strict with his students. He gave no one points for a proletarian background, military honors, or Marxist erudition. One has to think that even then Svechin had begun to be disenchanted with the Bolsheviks' methods. All the ideological blather, which had no place in military affairs, and the commissar-overseers, who were for the most part semiliterate but were nonetheless becoming intrusive busybodies, must have been especially annoying. But Svechin could not just stand aside and shirk responsibility. He saw his duty as a patriot and a soldier to contribute to the defense of Russia by thoroughly preparing its commanders.

His approach to teaching resulted in sharp confrontations with his students, among whom were numerous illustrious commanders of high rank. In these episodes Svechin did not stand on ceremony. He could ridicule and embarrass laggards, braggarts, and militant ignoramuses in the classroom.

Svechin was hated and feared, and respected. Even V. I. Chapaev, who left the Academy after a famous run-in with Svechin, apparently acknowledged that Svechin had been right. In his report to the higher command he explained his desire to leave the Academy as caused not by nagging or persecution, but by his own ignorance, and promised to complete his education after the war.[6]

Svechin was a great military writer, undoubtedly the most outstanding of the post-October period in Russia. An extraordinary number of works flowed from his pen,[7] including the famous *Strategy*, a unique and in its day vital book, which ought to have begun a new era in Russian and world literature. But in Russia only the old army intelligentsia recognized its worth, and to Western readers it remained largely unknown. The last publication of *Strategy* in its entirety was fifty years ago. Its author's fate was tragic, in the spirit of his country and his epoch.

Svechin was the first to note that the changing conditions and forms of war had made the traditional division of military arts into strategy and tactics unsatisfactory. "Clausewitz' strategy began to sink into obsolescence the moment cannons came into use, leaving the direction of the whole battle to tactics."[8] Contemporary battle (operation) is unbelievably extended in time and space; it no longer fits within the framework of the old tactics. Svechin detached the strategy of battle, which he called "operational art." The name has been adopted in Soviet military literature without reference to its author.

Svechin's primary interests lay in the field of strategy. He developed his concepts on the basis of a thorough study of military history combined with a sober analysis of international affairs. The conclusions he reached are free of political blinders and nationalistic prejudices. Svechin was among the first to understand that the total and prolonged character of a world war was not happenstance, nor a result of errors by military and state leaders. The next war would spread across the planet even more widely and demand of every warring country an extreme concentration of all their energies. All state and economic institutions, all the life of the nation would be subordinated to military interests.

In a total war, Svechin affirmed, the strategy of destruction was not only useless but suicidal. It had been suitable for the Napoleonic wars, but the strategy of attrition had replaced it. The foes of Germany had achieved victory in the World War by its application. Svechin is rarely written about in the Soviet Union; and when he is, invariably the stories are fabrications. Some say he invented the strategy of attrition, which is foreign to the spirit of the Soviet Army. Others assert he plagiarized from the works of Delbrück. All of this is intentional distortion of the facts, or at best just a superficial glance at his significance. Svechin did not need to invent his strategic principles, inasmuch as the laws of military art have been known from ancient times and, in general, are as invariable as the laws of logic on which they are founded. The forms of their application change depending on the scale and character of the wars, the development of weapons, and so forth. Strategies calculated to exhaust the enemy were widely used in the eighteenth century, and Delbrück did write a great deal about it; but familiarity with his work is in no way a reproach to Svechin. His great merit consists in having worked out a strategy of attrition for contemporary conditions. He furthermore showed that in a world war attrition is sensible and economic, and apparently the only way to achieve victory.

The dominant view of the time, that the Red Army must attack, Svechin rejected as groundless. In modern war a resolute assault ("an attack of the destructive style") consumes incalculable resources, and as a rule is not justified by the operational gains. Attacking troops always must face the threat that their lengthening lines of communication will be cut, or that they will be attacked on their flanks or from the rear. In other words, the risks in attacking are great, and the value of possible gains is doubtful. In the opening phase of war it is more expedient to keep on the strategic defensive. "A politically aggressive goal can be combined with strategic defense. The battle is conducted at the same time on economic and political fronts, and if time works in our favor, that is if the balance of pluses and minuses is favorable, then the armed front, even if it only marches in place, might gradually achieve a favorable change in the relationship of forces."[9]

Strategic defense might permit the loss of some territory and therefore cannot always be applied by small countries. For Russia, however, Svechin insisted, that method of conducting a war was the most suitable. The enemy would be forced to waste resources to conquer territory, to establish communications, to overcome intermediate defense lines, and so forth. Meanwhile we would preserve our forces until the advantage became ours. That goal must be held unwaveringly without giving in to the seductive temptation to give battle in unfavorable circumstances from considerations of prestige or historical memory: "A hurriedly deployed defense would act least economically by heaping up troops in front of the attackers or by occupying a series of lines in the path of the assault. Saddest are those defensive maneuvers which expend armed forces in large numbers in conditions for which the enemy has best prepared."[10]

It was precisely this wanton course that Stalin, Timoshenko, and Zhukov chose in the early period of the Fatherland War. Not only were they responsible for the country's entering the war unprepared, but they aggravated the extent of the catastrophe. With the country ravaged and perplexed internally, still they chose to demonstrate their iron resolve— in an attempt to save their foundering prestige. In the first months of the war, with dull persistence, they threw millions of Red Armymen under the wheels of Hitler's locomotive and still let the Germans reach the walls of Moscow. It is easy to cite examples of the ignorance of our command in elementary strategic questions, but we will not do so in this chapter. It is sufficient to note that Svechin predicted the principal aspects of the war with startling precision. It is easy to believe that neither Stalin nor his subordinate commanders had read Svechin. What is strange is that now official Soviet historiography, led by General Zhilin,[11] has to acknowledge the decisive role of the counteroffensive, which was prepared in the depths of a strategic defense. This is presented as a revelation during World War II, practically an invention of the Soviet command. References to Svechin are, as usual, absent. But surely the generals were aware of his work.

In examining the forms of offensive action, Svechin again demanded the test of expediency and that decisions be well-founded. "The forms of operations—operational encirclement, breakthrough, seizure, flank assault—are not chosen arbitrarily, but are dictated by the relationships of forces and means, the existing distribution of forces, the strength of various main lines of transportation, and the configuration of the theater of military action and its most important boundaries."[12]

Preparation for attack must meet the requirement of defense, that is, the security of one's forces. Operational deployment can only be successful when it is realized quickly and secretly. The offensive itself must unhesitatingly pursue its objectives, but it is important to recognize in time "the boundary where an offensive becomes an adventure" and presents the enemy a good target for counterattack. In general it is a mistake to assume an offensive formation when there is not about to be an offensive. In that formation the defensive options of the troops are necessarily weakened.

These and other provisions of his strategy sound like common truths. All the more do people who undertake to lead troops without having learned the rudiments of military science deserve no mercy. Svechin did not seek the laurels of a prophet: "Prophecy in strategy can only be charlatanry. Not even a genius has the power to foresee how a war will actually turn out." That he was able to foresee as much as he did adds to the greatness of this remarkable man.

The literature about Frunze is rather extensive, although not all of it is entirely veracious. We have already mentioned that interesting figure above. Here we will discuss only those aspects of the man and his work that are connected with the subject of this chapter.

Frunze was a true revolutionary who firmly believed in the justice of the Bolshevik cause. It is not surprising that he wholeheartedly supported the offensive school. "Between our proletarian state and the rest of the bourgeois world there can be only a state of war, long, obstinate, desperate war to the death."[13] Aggression was the inalienable right of the proletariat: "By the historical revolutionary process of life itself the working class will be forced to go on the offensive whenever favorable conditions arise."[14]

(Such pronouncements put those who varnish the truth about the history of Bolshevism in an awkward position, but a true picture of Frunze can be gained only from such honesty and candor.) The Red Army, the main weapon of the working class, must be prepared to carry out its aggressive mission in any sector of a future front: "The borders of that front are first of all *the whole continent of the Old World*."[15]

Starting from these political purposes, Frunze at first took an extreme "destructive" position. In the main, his views were indistinguishable from those of most of the commanders of the RKKA. Wars would be revolutionary, exclusively mobile, and consequently perfectly suited for an offensive strategy. "I recommend that except for the absolutely necessary we undertake no defensive work. It would be better to spend the money to repair barracks."[16]

That was in 1922. Soon, however, Frunze began to express other views in his speeches and articles. He was a man with a highly developed sense of responsibility. Pedantic dogma could not replace common sense for him. As he advanced through the ranks, Frunze's strategic views changed until they were unrecognizable. Familiarity with Svechin's book (1923) seems to have played an important role. Frunze was one of only a few Bolshevik military leaders who valued Svechin and protected him from attacks. He never spoke against Svechin, although the latter often expressed open disapproval of commissars, Marxism in military affairs, and other sacred relics.

By 1925 Frunze was ready to admit that the Red Army had not invented special proletarian power and decided to make use of the Army's bourgeois heritage. He maintained that the revolutionary destiny of the working class necessarily gave the RKKA primarily an offensive character, but there was little left to his former aggressiveness.

Frunze was getting more serious. He expressed concern that the bourgeois world would long retain its technical superiority. That would have to be opposed by greater maneuverability and "little" partisan wars. The latter was natural in the land of the muzhik, because "guerrilla warfare . . . is nothing more than the military expression of the psychological makeup of our peasantry.[17] Most important was his evaluation of a future war. He no longer spoke about the blitzkrieg and jaunty marches of liberation. "In the collision of two powerful enemies the outcome will not be decided with one blow. War will assume the character of a long and cruel contest, which will try all of the economic and political bases of the combatants. In the language of strategy, this marks the transition from the strategy of blitzkrieg to the strategy of attrition (*istoshchenie*)."[18]

On that most important point Frunze accepted Svechin's concept. Frunze continued to believe that the rear areas of the capitalist countries would be unreliable, but he did not attach much importance to it.

Having acknowledged the total character of future war and the strategy of exhaustion-attrition, Frunze did not fear to make the logical conclusion about the militarization of the country.

The task of preparing to defend the country in contemporary conditions was no longer within the current capabilities of the Army or of the military alone. This had to become the task of the whole country, of the whole Soviet apparatus.[19]

Of course, a highly developed country can prepare for war relatively quickly and does not need to undergo a long forced militarization. The United States is a good example. But Russia little resembles America, and Frunze knew that well. "We are not rich in good organizers. All of our work suffers from thousands of various shortcomings. Many of them are the result not of inability, but of simple disorder, slovenliness, and the absence of system. This explains why we have had so little success despite our colossal opportunities."[20]

Frunze sincerely feared that these national characteristics would harm the defense capabilities of the country. He was not at all inclined to think that everything would take care of itself because of some natural advantages of the socialist system. Today his words sound like an ominous prophecy: "It would be a scandalous crime if in the face of such opportunities we were not able to place the defense of the Soviet Union on a high level."[21]

If Svechin was the leading military scholar of the 1920s, and Frunze the main figure in the organization of military affairs, Tukhachevsky was for a long while the ideologue of the young wave and the prime opponent of Svechin. At first the argument had an academic flavor, but between 1930 and 1931 it lost that characteristic. We will discuss that later.

Tukhachevsky's early work reveals talent, powers of observation, and, unfortunately, the peremptoriness of a lieutenant. The level of his thought on strategy always lagged behind his grasp of operational-tactical matters. His 1920 essay "National and Class Strategy," despite its title, is essentially a combat manual. In it the 27-year-old front commander enlightened middle- and high-level commanders about changes in the methods of conducting combat operations, which distinguished the Civil War from the World War. Primarily, Tukhachevsky gave practical advice on how to quash various anti-Soviet uprisings, mainly peasant rebellions.

Already in this early work the author let slip many careless pronouncements that had pretenses of universality. For example: "War always has economic causes. Capitalist countries wage wars to obtain markets or natural riches."[22]

Such sententiousness belongs in political literacy lessons but not in a generalization about strategy. Further: "Civil war is waged by an oppressed class against the class of exploiters. . . ."[23]

Where then does the Civil War in the United States fit, or similar wars in Mexico, Bolivia, Argentina, or contemporary Africa? And where do you put peasant uprisings against Soviet power in this schema? His pronouncement that "the usefulness of strategic reserves has always been doubtful" needs no comment.[24]

His next four works on the nature of future war all had the same shortcoming.[25] We will try not to make unsubstantiated statements. Tukhachevsky wrote, "Getting the enemy to stand and give battle is advantageous for the attacker . . it is most advantageous to conduct an offensive operation against an enemy who is stationary."

The author's thought is understandable. It is certainly simpler to plan such an offensive operation. But that is all. To speak of advantages is at least rash since this line of thought does not take into consideration the nature and strength of the defense.

His effort to find an all-embracing formula took Tukhachevsky too far. He asserted, "The most useful destruction is achieved by capturing the enemy, since not only does it weaken the enemy, but the prisoners strengthen the captor's rear economically."[26] Tukhachevsky, who had been a German prisoner, clearly did not understand the economic side of keeping prisoners of war. Furthermore, he displayed ignorance of the applicable international conventions. More: "Strategy must make the tasks of tactics easy."[27] It has always been the task of strategy to win wars, not to make life easy on the tactical level. On the contrary, tactics are supposed to serve strategy, which places before it tasks that are needed but not necessarily easy. We could continue to extend the list of absurdities.

In the mid-1920s a group of military men who agreed with Tukhachevsky and wished to reconstruct the Army gathered around him. Among the most prominent of these were Assistant Chief-of-Staff of the RKKA V. K. Triandafillov; Inspector of the Armored Forces K. B. Kalinovsky; and young commanders of various ranks, N. E. Varfolomeev, S. M. Belitsky, A. M. Volpe, and G. S. Isserson. All were actively involved in the work of military science. All preferred decisive action using modern technical means, and it was precisely in this area that they achieved significant success. Thanks to their tireless work, which was fired by revolutionary enthusiasm, principles were worked out that laid the foundation for the greatest achievements of Soviet operational art in the next decade, the theory of deep operations.

There were other commanders who worked on the history and theory of combat operations. The old generals A. A. Brusilov, V. M. Klembovsky, and A. M. Suleiman emphasized historical research and published a series of excellent works. The former commander-in-chief, S. S. Kamenev, analyzed separate aspects of the experience of the Civil War. B. M. Shapashnikov worked out the theoretical bases for the operations of a general staff. I. I. Vatsetis, a former commander-in-chief, the prominent scholars A. E. Snesarev, A. I. Verkhovsky, who supported Svechin, and A. A. Neznamov, who opposed him, all made important contributions to theory.

By the end of this period an interesting tableau had formed. Intense scholarly work and active debates had brought the opposing points of view closer together. Everyone agreed that future war would be total, that it would become an exhausting contest of the warring sides. This view was adopted by the political leadership as well. But at the same time the old premise hung on: the Red Army must always attack.

12 Psychological Attack

On December 21, 1929, the fiftieth birthday of the General Secretary of the TSK VKP(b), Voroshilov's article "Stalin and the Red Army" appeared in *Pravda*. Kliment Efremovich, a simple man, employed no journalistic evasions but immediately took the bull by the horns: "For the last five or six years Stalin has been at the center of a large, contentious struggle. Only these circumstances can explain why the importance of comrade Stalin, one of the chief architects of victory in the Civil War, has been somewhat pushed to the background and he has not received the credit he is due."[1]

See how simple: his contribution has been overshadowed by the other struggle, the internal Party struggle, and only for that reason has not received its due credit; that is, of course, the highest credit.

Voroshilov did not pretend to elucidate the whole problem. He wanted only to "refresh the facts in the comrades' memories" and also "to publish several little-known documents, to show by the simple evidence of facts the truly exceptional role played by comrade Stalin at the tensest moments of the Civil War."

It turned out, although it had not been noticed earlier, that from 1918 to 1920 comrade Stalin was "the only man whom the Central Committee threw from one front to the other, choosing the places most dangerous, most threatening to the revolution."

Pay attention: Stalin was the TSK's last trump, its magic wand, the man who saved the Revolution when all else failed. It sounds convincing. Ten years had not passed since the end of the Civil War, and all the senior members of the TSK of that time, with the exceptions of Lenin and Dzerzhinsky were still alive. Consequently, they could confirm what Voroshilov wrote. The problem was that as a result of the "large and contentious struggle," by the end of 1929 the men who had been leaders of the Party in the first years of the Revolution had been expelled from political life and deprived of a forum within the country. Trotsky, Zinoviev, Kamenev, Krestinsky, Sokolnikov, Smigla, and many others were expelled from the Party before the Fifteenth Congress or at the Congress itself. Rykov, Bukharin, and Tomsky were destroyed as rightists shortly after the Congress. All of them could of course confirm or, God forbid, deny, but they preferred to keep silence. If they were to say anything, where could they say it and whom would it interest? If victors are not judged, the defeated are not believed. Neither could the political leaders of the Red Army raise their voices. Trotsky was banished, Frunze and Skliansky dead. There were still commanders of the Civil War, but we will discuss them later. The people, as they always have in Russia, hearkened to the voice of historical truth and kept silent.

Voroshilov could therefore boldly continue his research. From his article we learn that already at the dawn of Soviet power Stalin possessed those traits of omnipresence and omnipotence that became so easy to discover from the 1930s to his death. Where all was quiet and peaceful during the Civil War, "comrade Stalin was not to be found." But if things were bad, there "comrade Stalin appeared. He did not sleep nights [that was because he preferred to sleep days], he organized, he took leadership into his own strong hand [entirely true], he smashed mercilessly [there is no denying that], turned the tide, and made things right."[2]

That was the thesis of Voroshilov's article. Stalin ensured success in all decisive sectors. It did not matter that Stalin himself had once called Trotsky the architect of the Red Army's victory. Great events are meant to be reevaluated. Voroshilov went on to describe episodes of the Civil War in which Stalin's miracle-working powers were displayed. These episodes long remained landmarks of Soviet historiography. Only in them was the outcome of the war decided; all other events became secondary, insignificant.

Let us briefly trace Voroshilov's account. The reader ought to be sufficiently prepared for this by the chapters on the Civil War.

Tsaritsyn. Stalin arrived there in June 1918 with a detachment of Red soldiers and two armored cars "in the capacity of head of all provisioning in South Russia." Voroshilov, who participated directly in the event, described how Stalin immediately usurped military authority. As documentation, Voroshilov produced a telegram from the Revolutionary Military Council of the Republic, that is from Trotsky, with a note about Lenin's concurrence. True, the quotation marks in the citation opened after Stalin's name, which leaves the meaning of the text open to question. We read in Voroshilov's article: "On comrade Stalin is laid the task 'to establish order, to combine the detachments with regular units, to establish proper command, to expel all who will not submit.' " First Stalin set about establishing "proper command": "Headed by comrade Stalin the RVS is established [a good use of the impersonal form], which will undertake the organization of a regular Army." And of course: "The RVS headed by comrade Stalin will establish a special Cheka." Stalin criticized and persecuted everyone, especially Snesarev and his staff; but others were not left out. Voroshilov quoted the citation from the journal *Donskaia volna* (*Don Wave*), with which the reader is already familiar.

This ardent but amateur performance almost resulted in the loss of Tsaritsyn. The RVS of the Southern Front, of which Voroshilov had become a member, was reorganized and Stalin recalled, but Voroshilov chose not to mention that in his article, apparently out of respect for the birthday boy.

Perm. At the end of 1918 the 3rd Army surrendered Perm. To investigate the causes the TSK sent a commission composed of Dzerzhinsky and Stalin: "The TSK asks the commission to take all necessary measures to restore Party and Soviet work in the regions of the 3rd and 2nd Armies."[3] That would seem clear. The commission was given no military assignments. Dzerzhinsky soon returned to Moscow. As was his wont, Stalin very quickly became involved in military affairs. In particular, he requested that Lenin send three reliable regiments. Later in one of his reports he offered that as his own accomplishment: "1,200 reliable infantry and cavalry were sent to the front on 15 January." Voroshilov needed say no more. At that point he drew a conclusion that was neither logically nor factually supported by his evidence but was apparently politically necessary: "As a result of these measures not only was the enemy's advance halted, but in January 1919 the Eastern Front went over to the offensive. . . . Uralsk was taken."

That was how comrade Stalin understood his assignment "to investigate the causes of the catastrophe." We have already shown that there was no catastrophe, but without one the act does not possess the required glory. "I investigated, discovered the causes, and on the spot with my own forces removed them and turned the tables." Specifically: "on the spot . . . my own forces . . . turned the tables."

Petrograd. Spring 1919 saw the Yudenich offensive and mutinies at Fort Red Hill and Fort Gray Horse: "It was necessary to rescue the situation. The TSK again chose comrade Stalin for the job. In three weeks comrade Stalin was able to turn things around."

Even without that, everyone knew that Josef Vissarionovich was the greatest specialist in turning points. The same year that Voroshilov's article appeared, 1929, the great about-face in Russian agriculture, from which the country has never recovered, was begun at Stalin's initiative.

Whatever the truth of this episode, Stalin's role could not have been significant. He was sent on temporary duty to Petrograd as the plenipotentiary extraordinary of the TSK (decision of May 17) in connection with the possible attack by Rodzianko's corps and the Estonians. The attack, which began May 26, broke through the Soviet front and took Yamburg and Pskov. The defending 7th Petrograd Army was unable to repulse the attack immediately because of a shortage of men and the defection of a number of commanders—the mutiny of the forts on June 13. The mutiny was suppressed by the end of June, but no decisive action occurred on the front until the fall. Pskov was retaken from the Whites on September 8. Stalin had departed long before that. In May and June 1919, while Stalin was there, Petrograd experienced neither mortal danger nor a turning point.

In 1919 the then all-powerful member of the Politburo Zinoviev was also chairman of the Northern Commune. Petrograd was his eparchy, as Kamenev similarly ruled Moscow. Stalin could be sent to Petrograd as representative of the TSK, but only Zinoviev could establish order or display power.

The Southern Front. Voroshilov was under Stalin's command on the Southern Front; therefore he devotes a great deal of space to this period: "Spring 1919. Danger threatened Tula, danger hung over Moscow. The situation had to be saved [how many times!]. The TSK sent comrade Stalin to the Southern Front as a member of the RVS. There is no longer any need to conceal [that, undertaking his assignment, Stalin made three stipulations:] (1) Trotsky would not interfere in the affairs of the front, (2) officials not wanted by Stalin would be transferred, and (3) people he wanted would be sent to him." The conditions sound fantastic and they are not confirmed by documentation. Moreover, Voroshilov himself soon contradicted them. As for sending needed people, that was the natural right of every leader and was unlikely to have been specifically stipulated. Stalin tried to plant his own people everywhere. For example, he brought his friend from

Tsaritsyn, Voroshilov, to the Southern Front. The latter, after the unauthorized surrender of Kharkov, as we know, had been removed from the 14th Army and released from command altogether. He had been entrusted with the formation of the 61st Rifle Division but was unable to lead it after its creation. Stalin called him not as a commander but as a political worker.

According to Voroshilov, comrade Stalin began with the most important job—to change the strategic plan for Denikin's destruction. That story has long since been disproven. Even from the document presented by Voroshilov it is obvious that Stalin simply supported one of the two available plans, Vatsetis's plan. This did not bother Voroshilov: "Comrade Stalin's plan was accepted by the TSK. Lenin wrote in his own hand the order to the field headquarters to immediately change the obsolete directives."

In passing, Stalin created the First Horse Army. But it is strange that the independent Stalin (of the RVS of the Southern Front) wrote the RVS of the Republic, that is Trotsky, a humble report about the formation of the Horse Army, with the concluding line: "Please confirm the aforesaid." The document is dated November 11, 1919. Trotsky issued the order about the creation of the First Horse on November 17, and on November 19 the RVS of the Southern Front (Egorov and Stalin) duplicated the order. That last date is celebrated as the birthday of the First Horse.

After Denikin's defeat, Stalin, according to Voroshilov, became indispensable. The authorities hurried to transfer him to the Northern Caucasus. But the unfailing Stalin balked.

> In January 1920 as a result of serious errors by the front command [that is, Shorin] our offensive at Rostov was dangerously held up. . . . The TSK sent comrade Stalin a telegram: "In view of the necessity of establishing true unity of command on the Caucasus Front, supporting the authority of the front commander [the same Shorin; apparently the serious errors had not been discovered] and the army commander [Budenny], the Politburo considers it absolutely necessary that you immediately join the RVS of the Caucasus Front."[4]

This refers to the Bataisk Bottleneck.[5] Stalin understood perfectly well that Voroshilov and Budenny lacked the strength to drag their troops out of comfortable Rostov to storm Bataisk. Relations between the command of the First Horse and Shorin were utterly destroyed. Stalin was supposed to pacify his protégés. But such a role was not to his taste, and he resisted the assignment (1) on the condition of his health (as if there were a different climate at the Southern Front), and (2) because he feared that "all of these transfers will be incorrectly understood by local party organizations, which will tend to accuse me of frivolously skipping from one field of administration to another, because of their ignorance of TSK decisions."[6] How could Stalin know that ten years later this very skipping about would be proclaimed an enormous service?

The problem was settled by the nomination of Shorin's assistant Tukhachevsky.[7] Stalin was assigned to the battle against Wrangel, who was only of secondary importance at the time, but "illness [new?] freed him from that work."

The Polish Campaign. Illness did not prevent Stalin from becoming a member of the RVS of the Southwest Front, the command corps of which had been transferred as a unit from the Southern Front. Of course it was not a matter of his health. It was simply easier for Stalin to work with the colorless and tractable Egorov.

In describing the events of the Polish theater, Voroshilov suddenly became reserved and careful. That is understandable. Warsaw was not taken. To a large degree it was the fault of Stalin, who sabotaged the commander-in-chief's order to transfer the First Horse and other troops from Lvov to Tukhachevsky. For that, Stalin earned a reprimand from the TSK and was removed from military work.

Voroshilov summed up Stalin's merits with brief reference to "comrade Stalin's organization of the First Horse raid." The ticklish situation of insubordination he settled in two sentences: "The operations of the Southwest Front brought the Red troops right to Lvov. Only the failure of our troops at Warsaw ruined [the plans of] the Horse Army, which was preparing to attack Lvov and was situated ten kilometers from it."

So that's how it was. It turns out that it wasn't the delay of the Horse Army that ruined the storming of Warsaw, but vice versa. Having performed that logical somersault, Voroshilov hastened to change the subject. "However, the period is so eventful, to explain it would require such massive documentation and thorough analysis, that it takes us far beyond the bounds of this article." It is hard to believe that the dashing commissar has suddenly become the professor-analyst. And why was such carefulness applied only to this one period? Simple.

Voroshilov did not want to attach Stalin's name to an unsuccessful campaign.

Summing all of this up, Voroshilov offers a general, rather confused description of Stalin as a strategist, which concludes with the following pearl: "Comrade Stalin was always a proponent of the strictest military discipline and of centralization under the absolute but thoughtful and consistent administration of the highest military organs." In other words, the orders of the center must be carried out only when one agrees with them. It would be interesting to know if Stalin still agreed with that interpretation of military discipline later when he promoted himself to commander-in-chief.

Voroshilov's article was a heavy blow to the Red Army. The People's Commissar and the Politburo member clearly demonstrated to the soldiers that in the USSR heroes and leaders of men were made not on the fields of battle but in the stillness of Kremlin offices.

It was another warning: All your honors count for nothing. If we want, we will rewrite history. Whenever it is needed.

It was also a spit in the face. They were telling men who had participated directly in the Civil War—men who had been in the thick of the events—*how* those events had happened. Later this became history, the only acceptable account. They had to study the lesson and forget the way they had remembered things.

Stalin, as always, acted carefully, leaving himself an out. If the balloon were shot down, he could always step aside and dump it all on Voroshilov: look, hotheaded Klim got carried away with the birthday celebrations. And anyway, what is important for us Marxists is classes, not personalities. It was a victory of the proletariat. Stalin could do that.

He did not have to retreat or take evasive action. The soldiers wiped themselves, put their hands in their pockets, and gave him the bird. In the third volume of the fundamental work *Civil War, 1918–1921*, printed in 1930, the editors, S. Kamenev, Tukhachevsky, and Eideman, included the following footnote: "From the editors. This volume had gone to press when Voroshilov's article "Stalin and the Red Army" (GIZ, 1929) appeared. [The article] contains much new information about how the decision was made to direct the main attack against Denikin in the direction Kursk-Kharkov-Donbass. Realization of the plan, as is well known, led to the destruction of Denikin. . . ."[8] There followed long excerpts from Voroshilov's article.

Former commander of the Southern front Egorov wrote in the foreword to his book *The Defeat of Denikin* (1931): "The author would like to emphasize here that the appearance of K. E. Voroshilov's extraordinarily valuable historical essay . . . helped him clarify and supplement several parts of this work."[9]

Here and above we hear the insult, possibly involuntary. Egorov, Commander-in-Chief Kamenev, et al., needed Voroshilov's opus to understand how they had defeated Denikin. It is unfortunate that only a handful of specialists could read that in the phrase. We ought also to note that the military histories we have mentioned were published in runs of only a few thousand, while Voroshilov's article appeared in millions of copies of *Pravda* and was reprinted in huge editions.

In his first collision with the whole RKKA Stalin, thanks to artful maneuvering that was for the time being bloodless, gained an impressive moral victory.

The Great Turning Point

13 Personality in History: Role and Style

An apathetic society broken into small powerless elements, while it offers large opportunities for the development of a great power, at the same time creates many problems for that power by making difficult the establishment of state order without which such power is unstable.—Kliuchevsky

The question of the role of personality in history has not been sufficiently explained. It is hard to accept the viewpoint of total determinism, in which the role of personality is clearly secondary, in which it is wholly the obedient transmitter of inescapable historical laws and commands of the time. The opposite view, voluntarism, ascribing unlimited potential to a strong personality, is no more convincing. In particular it rejects the timeliness of the appearance of great figures and the rapidity of their advancement. How can we believe that people of that nature and with those talents did not appear earlier? It would seem that, like disease-causing organisms, they are always present in the social body but that favorable conditions for their manifestation are not. If the conditions are present, they become the creators of history; if not, they vegetate in anonymity or fail to achieve anything. At the same time there is no doubt that each great person makes an original contribution to his epoch, puts upon his time the mark of his individuality. One must also think that the success of a historical person must also depend to a certain degree upon the persistence of his pursuit of a goal—if he has one. Last: all of the above is insufficient if happenstance is not also taken into consideration.

In light of this amorphous and primitive conception, Stalin does not look like the guiding force of Russian history. It is impossible to believe that had he not been there the postrevolutionary development of the country would have taken an entirely different course. And if there had not been a Revolution, what could Stalin have hoped for: to become a prominent provocateur? Did he have the courage and style to be another Azef?

Stalin did not create his own system. That is uninspired mysticism.

The system gave birth to Stalin, not otherwise. When it comes to talking about the complete contempt of "formal" (and every other) democracy, the legitimization of terror against potential enemies,[1] not to mention real enemies; when the punitive organs take into their own hands immediate execution without trial or investigation; when the taking and shooting of hostages is considered normal; when with a flourish of the pen whole ethnic and social groups can be systematically destroyed, it is meaningless to shed crocodile tears over Stalin's so-called abuses of power. The spirit and the letter of the type of law that lay at the base of his power demanded people like Stalin. Such legal norms open limitless horizons to the most pathological aspects of a leader's personality.

Stalin? What was Stalin? He, for the most part, gave that power form. The road toward that type of power had already been taken.

The features of his personality and the circumstances of his career explain why it was specifically Stalin and not somebody else who became the all-Russian dictator, but they do not allow us to conclude that without him there would not have arisen just such a dictatorship.

After the October Revolution Stalin was in a very advantageous position. A representative of the national minorities, of which except for the Jews there were very few among the Bolsheviks, he was part of the small group that seized power. It is worth remembering that he did not become a member of the Bolshevik TSK for services rendered to the Revolution, for they were few. By displaying quick obedience, he managed to please Lenin, who coopted him into the Russian bureau of the TSK. For five years Stalin did not distinguish himself in any way, but he did manage to quarrel with Sverdlov, who had become powerful. In 1917, however, Stalin arrived in Petrograd earlier than Lenin and Sverdlov. Kamenev recruited him for work on *Pravda*. Ilich arrived and scolded Kamenev and his subordinates for appeasement. Stalin did not take offense. The whole time between the revolutions he lived in Petrograd legally and got along with everybody. It is little known that in the name of the Petrograd Soviet, which was then led by the Mensheviks and Socialist Revolutionaries, Stalin persuaded the Kronshtadt sailors, who had occupied the Peter and Paul fortress after the failure of the July days demonstration, to surrender their arms and leave the city. Stalin told them: "You shouted, 'All power to the Soviets!' Now carry out the Soviet's order." Stalin was not impatient for an armed uprising, and he rather skillfully defended Kamenev and Zinoviev from Lenin's wrath.

In the first Council of People's Commissars he received the post Ilich thought suitable, People's Commissar of Nationalities. It would have been impossible to fill the position with a Russian, and inexpedient to appoint a Jew—there were already too many of them. Besides that, although the Jews were an oppressed minority, they were not typical of the minorities in that they did not occupy a traditional territory. Stalin had written about that in his role as specialist on the nationalities question. His writing smacked of anti-Semitism, but its packaging was purely Marxist, and Lenin chose to pretend that all was in order; it was useful in his struggle with the Bund.

Stalin was fairly quiet, businesslike, and extremely energetic, although not all his energy was directed toward the business at hand. Lenin's trust for him grew. Stalin's military errors were not especially visible; all of the leading Bolsheviks made their share of mistakes at the front. Stalin understood earlier than most of the others that it paid to follow Lenin without bothering to consider where or why, because Lenin was the strongest of them. At the Eighth Congress he fell from grace but quickly recovered. He sided with the leaders of the "military opposition," who fought against the use of tsarist officers in the Red Army. As soon as he noticed Lenin's negative reaction, however, he immediately stepped aside, leaving his erstwhile compatriots to extricate themselves as best they could. At the stormy Tenth Congress he followed directly in the wake of Lenin's battleship. For that he was rewarded with another commissariatship: in the Workers and Peasants' Inspection. The stern and decisive Stalin gained the reputation of a capable organizer.

In this way he became General Secretary of the RKP in 1922. Of course, the post was then considered technical and clerical: someone had to keep the books and assign work to the Party cadres. It was not the work most revolutionaries cherished. While Lenin was in charge, the apparat did not have a powerful role. Lenin would make the decisions, or the Politburo, or rarely the TSK; and the apparat would follow orders. Lenin's illness changed things dramatically. His comrades-in-arms began to consciously measure the vacant purple. The combination of Zinoviev, Stalin, and Kamenev against Trotsky was born. For the time being the distribution of roles satisfied everyone: Kamenev ran the affairs of the government, Zinoviev had the political leadership, and the secretary of the TSK for organizational matters, Stalin, ran the apparat. It was in this role that Stalin participated in the first congress after Lenin's death. He worked hard making connections, putting his people everywhere. Imperceptibly the apparat crushed the Party. An active Lenin would not have allowed that. He was supersensitive to questions of power. Even sick he tried to oppose the evolution and raised the question of replacing Stalin. But Lenin was isolated from his Party by the very triumvirs and by Stalin—whom the TSK had empowered to protect him from visitors out of concern that he get well soon.

Now Stalin's position was most advantageous in comparison with the other great leaders. So what if their merits were greater, their names more famous. As the near future would show, that was just talk, empty sound. Stalin had real power, connections with thousands of people who controlled life in their various spheres.

Lenin concentrated unbelievable power in the center of the Party and reduced other organs, Soviet and administrative, to the position of simple executors and even powerless attendants. This made way for the future power of the apparat. It was not possible to run the country from the center without a huge bureaucratic machine. And this apparat inevitably turned into the all-powerful master of the country, unchecked by representative institutions, a legislative system, or public opinion. It replaced the former Russian bureaucracy and became even more arbitrary. The apparatchik in his office is omnipotent and all powerful as long as he enjoys the trust of the leadership and keeps his position. The right of appointment and dismissal was strictly centralized in the TSK; as a practical matter it was conducted by the Secretariat headed by Stalin.

The power of appointment placed the Party from top to bottom in the hands of the apparat. No local organization could express its opinion without the knowledge of the higher apparat. The apparatchiks, especially in the middle levels, depended entirely upon the Secretariat. They were concerned not to contradict it and thereby to lose their jobs.

For several more years the annual Party congresses continued to play a certain legislative role. But then the supreme apparatchik, Stalin, worked an important change in the composition of the congresses. Apparatchiks, who had not long before been appointed by him, became the significant majority of delegates. Some interesting documents have been preserved. Stalin wrote the secretaries of provincial committees notes that read approximately: "Kabakov, I ask your support at the congress. Stalin will not forget you." He did not forget. He had them shot.

The domination of the congresses by apparatchiks is well confirmed by official party statistics. The last published statistics about the distribution of delegates by occupation refer to the Thirteenth Congress in May 1924.[2] For following congresses only social origin was reported. Altogether at the Thirteenth Congress there were 748 deputies with voting rights. In the category "machine workers," that is *workers* by social *condition*, there were 54, or 7.2 percent of the total. Those occupied "wholly with Party work" numbered 488 or 65.3 percent. Within this group only 37 delegates, or 7.6 percent, were low-ranking Party workers. There were 90 representatives of Soviet institutions, 12 percent; 51 from unions, 6.8 percent, 8 of whom were simple workers; 44 from the Red Army, 5.9 percent; 20 from economic organs, 2.7 percent; and 1 from a cooperative, 0.1 percent. Bureaucrats of various stripes—Party, union, Soviets, economic—made up 86.0 percent. In the highest supposedly representative organ of the proletarian party there was one real worker for each twenty apparatchiks, who had the additional advantage of being better educated, learned, and more verbal. The question of who would make decisions at the Congress was not raised.

There was also the enormous material differentiation even within the Party. At that time when a worker's monthly income was the beggarly level of twenty-five to thirty rubles and often less, Communist executives received salaries in the hundreds of rubles. The Central Control Commission reported to the Congress that some Communist officials, bank administrators for example, received up to 1,200 rubles per month. The Congress found that unacceptable and set an upper limit of 360 rubles, which was, however, commonly violated.

At earlier congresses pliant voting majorities had taken shape more or less naturally under the influence of Lenin's unquestionable authority and the blindness of the Party masses. Now they were consciously organized. Democratic centralism had led Lenin and his closest comrades to military discipline combined with unrestrained centralization and the unrepresentative nature of the Party organs.

Unlike Stalin, his rivals held revolutionary ideals (this is a statement of fact, not praise) and were confirmed Marxists (which did not prevent them from carrying on a bitter fight about its correct interpretation).

They were intellectuals, which meant they were strongly influenced by impersonal, ideological motivations. All of them, with the exception of Trotsky, were intriguers and contrivers but at an amateur level. As intellectuals they were insufficiently pragmatic and were unhealthily impatient of others' ideas. This helped Stalin set them against each other.

This very briefly is the immediate political background in which Stalin operated. His success in the struggle for power was determined, however, by other, deeper historical factors. Stalin's dictatorship, which arose at the end of the 1920s, undoubtedly bears the stamp of his personality but in its basic characteristics is a natural continuation of the tendencies and intentions begun by Lenin at the dawn of Soviet power. Those characteristics are in their turn a result of the centuries-long development of the Russian state and of the spiritual and material life of the people.

Indisputably Lenin, with his younger partner Trotsky, took upon himself a gigantic task of state revolution and the succeeding struggle to hold power. This was his greatness as a revolutionary, as leader of the state and the Party. But there is no doubt that Lenin did not get the state or the social order he dreamed of but only that which could actually exist in Russian conditions.

Military-bureaucratic, obscurantist, barefoot, servile, downtrodden Russia, as it was on the day before the Revolution, could not be transformed overnight. The holders of power changed, some of the facades in the empire of facades were torn down, but the essence remained. People remained the same in their relations with one another, with work, with the legal order, and with freedom. The architects of the new life, although they did not notice it themselves, bore some of the burdens of the old psychology. There were more of the old-regime way of doing things in their behavior than might have been expected from revolutionaries, including those of the most extreme persuasion. Then in the 1930s, and even more so in the next decade, Stalin would rely on great-power chauvinism and copy the external forms of the former state structure right down to details, to the full dress uniforms and the ranks to go with them.

But from the very beginning Stalin relied on the fossilized traditions of national psychology. For the people the ideal of a leader had always been a dreadful power overlaid with justice. You beat us, but for our own good.

The people have always been ready to accept violence. That the severity, the cruelty usually left little room for justice seemed ordinary and acceptable. Russian social thought had not yet arrived at the understanding that the tsars' power retained its godly nature only so long as they ruled through laws and in the interests of their subjects. That concept first developed with Tsar Peter. It could happen then that emperors could be murdered by court janissaries but never executed by the people. Charles I of England and Louis XVI of France were immeasurably more humane than the most liberal of our autocrats.

From time immemorial the power of those in authority, the monarch's will, and tradition have all stood higher in the eyes of the people than justice, law, or even religion. Therefore the seizure of power and the possession of its attributes have been the deciding factor in any political, juridical, or even moral issue. Public opinion unhesitatingly justified the victor, the man at the summit of power. If rational or scholastic arguments did not suffice, there were the mysterious considerations known only to the one at the top.

All of this provided exceptionally fertile soil for the growth of a strong personality. The insignificant development of legal consciousness, servile docility, which barely permitted the thought of opposing authority with force, greatly increased the chances that such a personality would emerge. It was natural that such a man would be constrained by few ideological or moral limitations. After achieving power, other attributes accrued: the peoples' love, infallible wisdom, the force of history. The Russian people, who have never so much as smelled freedom, are not prone to resist tyrants. They tend rather to sympathize with strong personalities like Ivan IV and remember their evil deeds with masochistic admiration.

All the popular rebellions of Russian history were incited and led by free men on its borders or by aliens. The Cossacks were Russian only by language and religion, not by ethnicity or, most important, by psychology. Even so-called independent thought, such as that of the schismatics and other religious dissidents, was often stagnant. Oppression is the normal way of Russian life. The yoke of the hateful Mongols is usually said to have lasted three hundred years. It was really less, but still more than 150 years. More burdensome serfdom lasted about as long, from the end of the sixteenth to the middle of the enlightened nineteenth century. We will not try to judge if these phenomena were the cause or the result of Russians' compliance in the face of oppression.

The Russian people's tendency toward or preparation for democracy underwent a severe test in the months between February and October 1917. The old order had oppressed practically everybody, and they were glad to see it pass. Therefore it collapsed. There was no revolutionary conspiracy or organized movement. Powerless, obsolete, deprived of support, the old regime fell beneath the natural pressure of general dissatisfaction. The revolt was directed not so much against monarchism per se, as against particular parts of its structure, which the autocracy did not understand and was not able to change in time. Military defeat, as it often does, simply displayed the rottenness of the structure and sharpened the discontent. It was also important that the old order was unable to digest the rapid economic growth that continued even during the war. There was one other factor, which is frequently ignored. Tsarism had not only created its organs of power (read violence) but for centuries had been carrying on an exhausting battle with them. The bureaucracy, which had slowly evolved from the Varangian and Mongolian system of "feeding" into commonplace bribery, was not an inconsequential foe. "Russia is governed not by emperor, but by a department chief," Nicholas I once acknowledged.

The apparat, the bureaucracy, fought with tsarism in its own special interests, but it remained loyal to the form of government. In February 1917 the bureaucracy failed to defend the Romanovs; it had ceased to believe in the form. Tsarism fell.[3] The old bureaucracy lost its power and position. Its intuitive assurance that any succeeding regime would need it was not justified.

We know well from the experience of other countries that toppling a monarchy does not automatically and inescapably lead to the establishment of the people's power. We are aware also of model democracies flourishing under the aegis of royal authority. Lenin wrote that a revolution cannot only seize power. It must smash the old state machinery and replace it with its own, or the goals of the revolution will not be realized. Before the Russian supporters of democracy there arose a tormenting problem. Everyone understood that it was necessary to remove as quickly as possible those forces that had destroyed tsarism, the old forms of social life and the former structure of relationships. If they succeeded at that, if Russian democracy proved to be strong enough, decisive enough, capable of creative work, then the country at long last could live in a new order, more just and more humane.

Alas! Flesh of one flesh with the people, the democratic community languished for decades waiting for the change, wrote mountains of books, threw a few bombs, but did not manage to acquire any practical preparation for building a new life. The Provisional Government was created not only by the liberals but also by all of the socialists, including the Bolsheviks, all of whom at first feared the return of the autocracy. This organ of the Revolution chose a strange way to operate. Instead of meeting the real needs of the nation, it preferred to mark time for eight fateful months waiting for the Constituent Assembly, which was to perform the democratic miracles—that is, to take the burden of responsibility from Kerensky. Only very naive people could believe that the Constituent Assembly, which was to meet in conditions of growing hunger and continuing slaughter, could freely choose Russia's future path. The cities hungered for bread, the peasants for land, the soldiers for the end of war. Not many were deeply concerned with the form of government. If the Assembly did not give them what they wanted, they would follow someone who could satisfy their real needs, or who was at least willing to promise. Once the decisions of the Assembly of the Land were made, they would have to be carried out immediately.

It cannot be said that once they were in power the liberals, democrats, and socialists did not understand the needs of the time. But they were too used to saying lofty phrases; in the Russian tradition they did not know how to act with the necessary speed and were scared to death of the responsibility. The Provisional Government preferred to mark time. It failed to provide agrarian reform, food supplies, or peace—those basic conditions with which they might have begun to rebuild Russia. The people lost patience and their sympathies drifted left. The untended power was easily seized by the Bolsheviks, far left of democracy, who immediately established—in part contrary to their own expectations— an extreme right, a most despotic form of government.

The Bolsheviks solved two of the greatest problems at once: they gave the land to the peasants and proclaimed peace, thereby strengthening their position. This excellent political gambling won them the whole pot. True, bread soon disappeared entirely, and peace and order (for which even some of the monarchists had supported the Bolsheviks) turned into the bloody chaos of the Civil War. It must be admitted, however, that the land did remain the peasants', for all of twelve years.

Having pushed out the Provisional Government, the Bolsheviks sat in the old government's armchairs. Yesterday's revolutionaries soon forget that the people's existence determines consciousness—one of the few reliable tenets of their doctrine. The people were not disturbed that social harmony was achieved by executions and requisitions, that the beautiful building erected in the name of future generations was being raised on the bones of the current generation. Insensitive to their own suffering, the people set out with irrepressible determination to realize the dream of their foolish leaders of prosperity for all through obedience. In a short time they had trampled Russia and mangled it more thoroughly than their predecessors had ever dreamed of doing. In all this Stalin's contribution was entirely ordinary. It is hard even to distinguish him.

Later, after the Civil War was won, the Bolsheviks removed a few archaic obstacles, which sluggishness and laziness had kept the old regime from clearing from the path of economic development. This without a doubt helped rapid industrialization and the growth of military might. They introduced universal education and liquidated illiteracy, something tsarism had definitely not wanted to do.

Economic successes improved the life of the average citizen, but not nearly as much as might have been expected from such a rapid rate of growth. The omnipotent government gathered the lion's share of the new wealth to benefit its great power and imperialistic policies and to maintain the new, greedy ruling class.

Industrialization progressed one-sidedly. It was oriented toward military and prestige projects. The people's needs were at the bottom of the list. As a result, the level of life remained extremely modest, although it gradually improved. For weapons, the most expensive and up-to-date, there was always money. Countless millions and billions of rubles were wasted through theft, improvidence, and ignorant ventures on a huge scale. Finally, collectivization and the ensuing cruel experimentation in the spirit of Swift's learned men led to the collapse of agriculture.

It is time to return to the starting point. Just how much did Stalin's personality influence this history? It is very likely that Stalin's role is seen mostly in the coloration of specific events, in the appointment and removal (usually destruction) of individuals, however many there were. The general course of history after the October Revolution could hardly have taken a different course had there been a different person in his place.

All the same, the Bolsheviks would have had to muzzle and suppress the opposition with their natural multiplicity of opinions and interests. It was not Stalin who began to do that. A collision was unavoidable between the state, which had seized industry, and the peasantry, which did not want to give up its produce for the needs of industrialization in exchange for primarily immaterial goods. No one could have taken the peasants' land and property bloodlessly. Such repression in a peasant country would invariably produce anger, hatred, and restrained aggression. This was the psychological preparation for the terror of 1937 and 1938. Terror was the constant companion of power, its primary weapon in the battle with its own population from the very first day.

In his concern for personal power Stalin only gave form to this process, but he could not and he did not mean to change its direction. He did not do what he wanted, but what was necessary, and consequently what was possible.

In other words, only those of Stalin's undertakings succeeded that suited the spirit and level of development of our society, the concrete relations of social forces, the psychological expectations of the people, and their concepts of the personality and policies of a leader. We cannot ignore the fact that even today, after the cult of personality has been revealed, millions of the simplest people continue to feel deep sympathy for Stalin. In their memories he has remained the Great Leader, severe and merciless, but with marks of greatness and an inflexible will. A prime component of the nostalgia for Stalin's time is the motif of order. No one denies that that order was expressed not in harmony but in general terror and widespread, cruel violence. Nonetheless, in reminiscences about that time one hears notes of genuine regret. Explain after that the mysterious Russian soul.[4]

It would not be accurate to portray Stalin merely as a willful ogre. He was an unprincipled and monstrously amoral person, a wily and perfidious intriguer, a bloody and callous tyrant, ready to do anything for the sake of power. But as a statesman he was distinguished more by shortsightedness, indecisiveness, and inertia, which from time to time gave way to bursts of energy during the introduction of idiotic innovations, which were usually abandoned uncompleted.

Stalin certainly did not mean to destroy Russia, though he took it to the brink. He did what he did not from malice or insanity, but to keep his hold on power. Like every leader, he sincerely wished to see the country prosperous and powerful, the population flourishing. He worked at that too, although he achieved little because the system he headed was not suited to such purposes.

Historical fortune-telling is unreliable. It is hard to see how things would have been had Trotsky or Kamenev or Bukharin run the country. But it seems obvious that any of them would have had to act much as Stalin did. If they did not have the stomach for it, the system would have removed them and put the same tasks before their successors.

This is not to excuse Stalin. He was responsible, as are we all, for all he did. It is doubly useful, then, to separate out from the myriad accusations (historical but, unfortunately, not criminal) those that relate to Stalin personally and cannot be assigned to the faceless system.

Stalin did not invent terror and mass repression. Methods of terrorization, suppression, destruction, and expropriation of large groups of the population were known before he took power.

The Red Terror was declared after the attempt on Lenin's life in 1918. All of the members of the imperial family were murdered that year. Early in 1918 the Bolsheviks nationalized industry in the largest seizure of private property without compensation in Russian history.[5] At the same time they took the apartments and personal property (including libraries and art collections) of the nonproletarian elements.

In 1919 at the direction of the TSK a massive extermination of Cossacks was carried out. During the Civil War bourgeois and gentry hostages were routinely shot. Tens of thousands of Wrangel's officers and Greens, who had surrendered under the condition that their lives be spared, were killed in the Crimea in 1921. During the widespread famine of 1921 the government seized church valuables and frequently acted against the clergy. Also in 1921, numerous popular uprisings were brutally crushed, including those at Kronshtadt and in Tambov.

In the early 1920s thousands of members of outlawed political parties, bourgeois and socialist, were put in concentration camps and "political isolators." In 1922 the Cheka exiled from the country a large group of prominent intellectuals.

Repressions were already normal when Stalin came to power. Even depriving the peasants of land—collectivization—cannot be blamed entirely on him. The Bolsheviks had always wanted to socialize the land, which in practice meant state ownership. The decree on land had been forced on them by circumstances. It was a tactical measure to take the steam out of the SRs' political program, and it succeeded in attracting soldiers and peasants away from what had been the most influential party of the time. During the Civil War, without touching the land, which there was no one to work except the peasants, the Soviet authorities took most of its harvest (requisitioning). Only the threat of a national peasant uprising forced them to abandon that policy and to introduce NEP. During the 1920s they tolerated the peasants as the only producers of grain; but the contradiction, the incompatability, the "scissors" between state-owned industry and privately owned agriculture was always a problem waiting on the agenda. In a totalitarian state the situation was an anomaly that could not be permitted to go on forever.

When capital was needed for industrialization (primary accumulation), the peasantry was the only class of the population from whom it could be taken. The property of others had already been expropriated. The main result of collectivization was the transfer of land to the unshared ownership of the state. Collective farms were a screen, a palliative, an intermediate form, and they naturally were gradually abandoned. So what if grain production fell at first. What there was went directly to the state, which no longer had to depend on the vagaries of the market and could pay the farmers as little as it liked. Now the harvest could be employed for the highest purposes. Stalin proved to be more inventive than Lenin; he very sensibly figured that there was no need to rely on requisitions, which had always been accompanied by excesses and anxiety, if the state just once would seize the source. There was famine in the country, but the greater part of the wheat harvest was exported. Equipment for new construction was purchased with the hard-earned foreign currency.

It was not as important to join the peasants together for cooperative work, their land having been taken, as it was to turn them into laborers or serfs. Full legal enslavement was unnecessary, but something similar was done. Residents of most rural areas were deprived of their internal passports and thereby of the right to move. Having lost their land, the peasants were no longer economically independent.[6] In the name of these state purposes the most productive agriculturalists, that is, the kulaks, were removed (killed or exiled) just as ten years earlier the captains of industry were dispossessed and routed. Stalin later admitted to Churchill that collectivization had cost ten million lives.[7]

The naive younger generations have the right to ask, wasn't it possible to take the land without killing the kulaks? Unfortunately it was not possible. Stalin's report to the Seventeenth Party Congress contains figures that help us assess the scale of that historical necessity. In 1932 industry produced a total of 51,000 tractors. At that time there were 217,000 collective farms (kolkhozes). The next year there were

224,500 kolkhozes but only 204,000 actual tractors. The Machine Tractor Stations serving the kolkhozes had only 122,300 tractors or $122,300/224,500 = 0.54$ tractors per kolkhoz.

The slogan "to put the USSR in a car, and the peasant on a tractor" belonged to the future long after collectivization was carried out. Still the authorities had to be concerned for the material basis of the kolkhozes. Most of the stock and equipment for them was expropriated from the kulaks. The frightened middle rank peasants, weeping copiously, turned over their modest belongings, too; it would have been dangerously easy otherwise to be taken for a kulak. True, they slaughtered a significant part of their livestock in the process, to eat well one last time.

Soviet writers and artists have invariably depicted the kulak as a grizzly, brutal man with a sawed-off shotgun in one hand for killing kolkhoz activists and a torch for burning the kolkhoz buildings in the other. Probably collectivization could not have been accomplished without the violence. The kulaks fought not collectivization as a process, however, but the kolkhozes themselves, which were being established with their property.

The rural poor joined the kolkhozes without particular coercion, often quite willingly; but they brought to them only their hungry mouths and their inability and unwillingness to work. They were attracted to collectivization by the share, up to a third, they received of the property confiscated from the kulaks. By ascribing the well-to-do peasants to the kulak category, the basest social instincts were appealed to and enthusiasm for collectivization was fanned.

In his greatest acts affecting the national economy Stalin did nothing original. He simply carried existing policies to their logical conclusions. Having said that, it would be unjust to deprive him of author's rights for the innovations he really did devise and realize.

Stalin was the first to so widely apply political and judicial repression in the struggle for power within the Party. Millions of Bolsheviks, including practically all the old revolutionaries, became objects of repression. The bloody war among groups and individuals for control of the ruling Party led to the complete destruction of governmental and state institutions. Even the Army did not escape, although it stood outside the main battles and reliably supported the Party against the country.

The unrestrained violence that the Bolsheviks constantly directed against the population finally boomeranged. The nation's history had prepared the people for the violence, but still it was not entirely natural. It was carried out by people, various people, many people. Stalin was producer and director.

Even if we accept the existence of historical predestination, still every statesman, every man in general, has a choice (free will) to be a weapon of the inevitable or not. Every historical inevitability is the sum of many factors and processes, not the strict determinism characteristic of geological and physical phenomena. Acts are committed by people. The system, the political order, only creates the conditions and stimulations in which they act.

Stalin sooner and better than the other leaders of the 1920s recognized that in the current situation only power was valuable—not choosing the correct line in politics, or successfully pursuing it, just power. In a totalitarian dictatorship it is easy enough to present any results in a good light. The greater part of the population will not protest but will believe the proffered interpretation. A monopoly of the information media permits failure to be called unheard-of success; theft, incomparable charity; slavery, the highest form of freedom; mass murders and concentration camps, feats of a new, perfect humanism.

The hostile opposition of the ruling class to the people, combined with the customs of collective responsibility and mutual protection, made the whole structure of power permanently unstable. The personal struggle for positions of leadership within this instability from time to time resulted in large-scale dismissals. Stalin's greatness consisted precisely of this unleashing of enormous repressions, of the adaptation of the structure of the state and society, of the whole life of the country to this task. This was his historical role. This is his contribution to the art of state administration.

There were appreciable differences in the external staging of the repressions. The opposition were dismissed to the accompaniment of deafening propaganda. Stalinists were destroyed just as mercilessly, but silently and privately. Sometimes after their murder, either normal or medical, the victims' names remained in the calendar of saints: those such as Kirov, Ordzhonikidze, in all probability Kuibyshev, Gorky, Menzhinsky, Zhdanov, Scherbakov, in an earlier period Frunze and Dzerzhinsky. Others departed life quietly, condemned by secret courts, shot without a trial, or sent to languish in prison—and passed into official oblivion: including Postyshev, Kosior, Eikhe, Unshlikht, Ezhov,

Voznesensky, Kuznetsov. Members of the two groups were similar in their relative independence and their personal popularity. Whether or not they were later included in official histories often depended on the degree of their popularity.

A similar situation occurred in relation to figures of the Red Army. First, the most talented and independent thinkers among the commanders were executed and loudly defamed (in that order); their ranks included Yakir, Tukhachevsky, Uborevich, Feldman, Primakov, and others. Then the more backward and mediocre officers, who had been forced to become accessories and accomplices of the crime, quietly disappeared from the scene; these were Blucher, Dybenko, Kashirin, and many others.

Beginning with the Sixteenth Congress in 1930, the Party and the country experienced a new type of leadership. Previously there had been coalitions of groups. Now there was the Great Leader and his cohorts. For the most part these were people of the second water, the minor figures of the Revolution, who while Lenin was alive could not even dream of holding key positions. They were devoted to Stalin, energetic, unprincipled, and faceless. This last quality permitted gradation. Those who possessed stronger personalities than the others, the brightest of the colorless—Kirov, Ordzhonikidze—had the least chance of staying in the saddle. The exception was the colorful Kaganovich, who possessed boundless energy, an iron grip, and outstanding organizational talents, which unfortunately he used too often and not in the people's interests. Possibly Stalin kept him for his deep personal devotion, which was not shaken by the repression of his two brothers. For any of Stalin's cohort, suspicion of intellectualism was the worst insult.

All his life Stalin remained a professional conspirator. Therefore within the group of leaders he gathered, who were rather servile and fawning, there always operated a small, isolated nucleus. This nucleus not only controlled the planning of policy and of its execution, but its members also continuously conspired against the other leaders, and at the proper moment crushed them.

At first Molotov and Kaganovich made up this nucleus with Stalin; and the operational headquarters, that is, the Secretariat, was comprised of Malenkov, Ezhov, Poskrebyshev, Tovstukha, and Mekhlis. Most of these shady characters became very important men, except for Tovstukha who died young of tuberculosis. Voroshilov was close to this privy council, but he never became a member. And there were many others who always remained outside: important dignitaries like Ordzhonikidze, Postyshev, Rudzutak, Kirov, Kuibyshev, and Yagoda; powerless supernumeraries like Kalinin; and special envoys like Mikoyan. The nucleus gathered enormous power to itself. All the questions submitted to plenums and congresses were first discussed and decided at meetings of this narrow group. Malenkov, who was responsible for cadres, kept a card file on almost every member of the Party.

The composition of the nucleus changed with time. Ezhov, who worked overtime in the period of the repressions and came to embody them, became expendable and was replaced by Beria. Malenkov came to occupy a leading place. Zhdanov and Shcherbakov, the ideologist of anti-Semitism, became part of the group.

Within Stalin's staff there was another battle. From the beginning of the war Malenkov and Beria gained influence at the expense of "the old men." At the end of the 1940s this pair, with the cooperation or connivance of Stalin, got rid of Zhdanov and his supporters ("the Leningrad affair"). At the Nineteenth Congress Malenkov assumed significant power over the Party apparatus that had been Stalin's. Sick, and having suffered two insults, Stalin tried to regain the initiative by playing up the "doctors' plot." The whole Stalinist guard now came under attack. Stalin began to press them on all fronts, hoping to replace them with new people (by expanding the Presidium of the TSK).

But the old guard had studied too well under the master and knew his habits. In the face of a common threat they ceased their feuding and joined together. Beria and Malenkov worked with Molotov, Kaganovich, and Khrushchev, a protégé of Stalin and a member of the Politburo, but not a member of the nucleus.

Stalin died just in time. There is much to suggest that the conspirators poisoned the Father of the People in the best Stalinist style. In any case, on the day after his death they restructured all the organs of power, that is, they accomplished a coup d'état.

To better understand the nature and genesis of the Stalin phenomenon it is useful to draw an analogy with a Russian classic. It has long been noted that Dostoevsky's penetrating mind saw more in postreform nihilism—and its concrete expression the *Nechaevshchina*—than was yet there when he wrote *The Possessed*. That prophetic novel was a successful description of the future psychology of that particular environment in which the microbiological culture of twentieth century revolution grew.[8]

It does not require much imagination to say that Josef Vissarionovich Stalin strongly resembles Peter Stepanovich Verkhovensky[9] One can see similar psychological traits and value systems from which arose similar behavior.

The younger Verkhovensky needed nothing in life except power over people, and not just some power but absolute power. So it was with Stalin. The technical difference between them was that the literary character had to explain himself in monologues, or readers would not understand him, but Stalin had to be silent, otherwise he would be discovered. Neither of them had ideas about transforming the world as, for example, Zheliabov and Lenin had.

Their guiding idea was power. Other ideas and whole ideologies were only means to dominance. World dominance. Verkhovensky dreamt of subjugating the planet. His weapon was the gloomy, detailed, and alas attainable (we were convinced) utopian system of Shigalev ("He was a genius like Fourier, but bolder than Fourier, and stronger than Fourier").[10] The cover was the figure of the Roman pope. "All that is needed is that the International agree," he said and immediately added optimistically, "It will happen." Dzhugashvili, the expelled seminarian, chose as his weapon another but not very different utopia. The analogy stretches farther. To achieve domination of the planet, the great leader of the world proletariat was prepared to ally himself to the pope, not the Roman pope, true, but the fascist. On November 25, 1940, J. V. Stalin, a member of the Russian section of the Communist International, telegraphed Berlin his agreement to enter the tripartite (anti-Comintern) pact. It was not his fault that the deal did not last. Like his literary prototype he wanted it to.

Other traits coincide closely: cunning; perfidy; guile; inventiveness and indiscrimination in the selection of means, tendency to intrigue, purposefulness, and colossal energy. Neither was Stalin squeamish about murder, not to mention pseudojuridical executions. When it was useful, he employed criminals. He was like that as a youth; it would seem he was not expelled from the seminary for his politics. Criminals participated in the robbery of the Tiflis bank and in other of Stalin's expropriations. Their tracks are clear in the murder of V. M. Bekhterev. Later, when he had reached the pinnacle of power, criminals became superfluous. More powerful means were found.

Like Peter Stepanovich, Stalin highly regarded the utilitarian value of ideology and organization. This brings us to the *Shigalevshchina*.

Shigalev's social program grew from the discord between his personality and his environment. As a thoughtful but barely educated and impatient young man, he was offended by the disorderliness of Russia. Socialist literature offered him an ideal ordering of life on rational, scientific, and just grounds. But the more he juxtaposed his models to the loathsomeness of the real world, his sterling people of the future to his contemporaries, the better he understood the unfeasible, the chimerical nature of all those phalansteries, communes, and Cities of the Sun. As he wrote:

> Having devoted my energy to studying the question of the social organization of future society, which will replace this, I have reached the conclusion that all creators of social systems from ancient times to our 187– . . . were dreamers, fable tellers, and fools, who contradicted themselves, who understood nothing of natural science including that strange creature called man. But since a future social structure is needed right now, when we are all ready to act, so as not to meditate any longer I offer my own system. . . . I announce beforehand that my system is not complete. . . . I got lost in my facts, and my conclusion directly contradicts the ideas from which I began. Starting from unlimited freedom, I conclude with unlimited despotism. I will add, however, that there can be no other solution of the social formula than my own.[11]

At this point readers will be laughing, but in vain. Shigalev was not the worst dialectician. He was not the first thinker whose conclusions contradicted his first premises, or more precisely whose means denied the end he wished to reach. In Shigalev it happened in thought, for some others in practice.

Shigalev's system was comprehensive. In the novel he allotted ten nights for its explication. But the basic idea is clear: one tenth of mankind receives absolute authority over the rest, who "must lose their personality and become like a herd and through perfect obedience achieve rebirth of original innocence, as in primeval paradise; however, they will work."[12]

This ideal seems very familiar, although not in the same words: the dictatorship of the proletariat, in Russia a dictatorship by fewer than 2 million in a population of over 150 million. It is the classless society with true equality, socialist education of the masses, creation of the new man. And, of course, he who does not work does not eat.

The *Shigalevshchina* anticipated the actual temper of the Russian Bolshevik version of Marxism, which took almost as much from Blanc and Nechaev as from Marx and Engels. When they seized power, they were inspired by the strong and sincere conviction that a small socialist avant-garde (the Party) could in short order transform the life and psychology of the people and lead them to socialist paradise, which because of their backwardness they did not yet perceive. They put no limits on the means they would use to achieve their goal. In the words of the poet, Korzhavin,

Just a little pressure more
and to man's damnation an end.
The last skirmish, the last battle,
No pity for foe nor friend.[13]

We could continue the comparison, but there is something more interesting. With the coming of the Bolsheviks to power, a boundless horizon was opened to the impetuous proponents of Shigalev's ideas. With astonishing speed they created their own theories and schemes, clothed them in Marxist terminology, and with the support of the dictatorship set to work. The whole country, all aspects of life, became fair game for unthinking, fantastic experiments. We tend to remember the cultural and scientific madness, but there were other events and conditions even worse. Here are a few examples taken at random.

Immediately after the October Revolution socialism was declared with the confiscation of bourgeois property, and with equal pay (almost) for any work. A little later when there was nothing to eat, equality was replaced in one swoop with a fifteen-category hierarchy of rationing. As it turned out, the principles of privileged allocation of goods was tenacious. For a long time the calendar was tinkered with: there were five- and six-day weeks, years without weeks or months. In the schools, loose-leaf texts were used, students were taught in brigades, nature was transformed beyond recognition. There were endless campaigns, movements, initiatives.

The social sciences in the country suffered terribly. Soon there were neither sociologists nor economists in the normal professional sense. The same was true of historians. In literary studies vulgar socialist realism raged; in linguistics, Marr's theory of the labor origins of language. Enthusiasts of the new theater won a monopoly and closed such harmful establishments as the Bolshoi and the Mariinsky and other theaters as well. New artists and sculptors demanded the near abolition of other styles.

RAPP conducted a crusade to make literature an organized productive process, and not without success. Futurists, just like Turgenev's Bazarov, called for the destruction of the classical heritage, to free space for truly socialist literature. This was less successful, but there were some outstanding examples of vandalism. A certain tall poet, who could not yet have known that after his death Stalin would call him the most talented poet of the era, arrayed himself in a yellow jacket and led his compatriots in smearing Pushkin's statue with feces.[14] Enough examples.

Stalin took over the country at the height of its Shigalevian daring. He was a conservative man. Strict authority, inspired servility, and selfless obedience were his ideals. He was constitutionally unable to like the fevered and frenzied innovation. But as a clever, sober politician, he was wise enough not to resist the current. Stalin preferred to live and rule in a Shigalevian atmosphere; and it worked out all right for him. In the bedlam it was easier to grasp and expand power. Therefore, for the time being he remained outwardly tolerant of phenomena he could not help but regard with utter distaste.

Only when his position was unassailable did he begin to tame the cultural wilds, which were no longer needed. In every field an idol of indisputable authority was set up. Again it worked out all right. The frantic restlessness came to a full stop. This was especially apparent in the sciences that up to then had been allowed to operate independently: genetics, agrobiology, psychology, physiology, cybernetics. It would be superfluous to speak of literature and art again. From time to time, in accordance with the Shigalev blueprints, convulsions were arranged: the struggle with servility, the pogrom of geneticists, the revolution in language studies, etc.

The convulsion holds a special place in Shigalev's system. Stalin not only adopted that part of his teaching but developed it extensively. As Verkhovensky explained: "Slaves must have masters. Complete obedience, complete loss of personality. But every thirty years Shigalev allows a convulsion, and they all begin to eat one another, for the most part just to chase boredom. Boredom is an aristocratic sensation. In Shigalev's system there will be no desires. We can have desires and suffering. Slaves will have the *Shigalevshchina*."[15]

He could hardly help liking the general idea, but it needed elaboration. Boredom was an unimportant factor for Stalin, and he never felt a personal need for suffering. The convulsions were unleashed not as emotional prophylaxis for the workers and peasants, but rather as a regular means of strengthening the tyranny.

This was not a contradiction. The system created the conditions for millions of convulsions, but the Stalinists took it upon themselves to give them universal scope. Otherwise the little rumblings might have come to nothing or been vented in modest, useless explosions.

Here we end our comparison with Dostoevsky's famous novel, although we have not exhausted its possibilities. Our aim has not been so much to work out the analogy in detail, as to indicate the potential.

14 Attack on Headquarters

Having gained important strategic positions, Stalin and Voroshilov engaged in one more action to fortify their success. This time it was an open attack on the Red Army cadre. In 1930 the organs of the NKVD arrested a large group of prominent military specialists who had served in the old army. Among them were generals and colonels of the tsarist general staff, all of whom had participated in the Civil War on the Soviet side. At the time of their arrest most of the specialists were professors at higher military schools. A partial list includes A. A. Svechin and A. E. Snesarev, already known to us. Snesarev had been awarded a Hero of Labor medal at the tenth anniversary of the October Revolution. Others on the list were the former war minister of the Provisional Government A. I. Verkhovsky; former chief-of-staff of the Eastern Front Olderrogge; former chief-of-staff of the 4th Army and the Turkish Front Baltiisky; chief of engineers and hero of the Crimean crossing A. D. Malevsky; also the well-known military writers and teachers B. K. Verkhovsky, Bazarevsky, Besiadovsky, Vysotsky, Kolegov, A. G. Lignau, S. I. Lukirsky, Mikheev, Dolivo-Dobrovolsky, Golubin-tsev, Sapozhnikov, Seger, Rants, Sokolov, Suvorov, V. G. Sukhov, V. N. Egorev, and many, many others. All of them were honored, authoritative, respected, decorated.

The interrogations yielded little, as not everyone was yet ready to confess to things they had not done. But on the other hand, the NKVD had already learned that innocence was not grounds for discharge. They were sent to camps in the Leningrad region. In the spring of 1932 those who had survived the healthful lumbering were freed and returned to their former posts. A few were later permitted to teach at the new Academy of the General Staff. Among them were Svechin and A. Verkhovsky, for example. A few remained outside the army—Egorev, B. Verkhovsky, Snesarev. Despite their subsequent liberation, the blow to the Army was serious. A. I. Todorsky, in a review in the form of an historical essay, which we have already cited, wrote of the arrested professors:

these men were the real flower of the old army in the most positive sense, and I would say to a certain extent the flower of the Red Army. They became part of it, flesh and blood, and were as proud of it as of their own army. . . . By that time all the old generals and higher officers without exception had adjusted fully to Soviet conditions and justly considered themselves active participants in building the new world, inasmuch as they had all been in the civil war and served the RKKA, and service in the Red Army was in itself considered especially honorable.

We offer another quotation from Todorsky's work. It is especially valuable as it is the only written testimony of an eyewitness.

This glaring lawlessness expresses the traditional approach of Stalin and Voroshilov to military specialists, which was apparent from the beginning of the Civil War. I especially remember those tragic days of 1930 when the grief-stricken wives and children of the arrested men rushed for protection to People's Commissar Voroshilov, who without bothering to look into their petitions sent them to me as chief of UVUZ [Administration of Military Education Institutions]. What could I do, one of many chiefs of central administrations, when the arrests had been carried out at the orders of Stalin and with the sanction of Voroshilov? My appeals to the then assistant people's commissar of internal affairs, my good acquaintance comrade Messing did no good.[1]

This is how Todorsky, a Bolshevik from a poor peasant background, appraises the actions of Stalin's leadership. Strictly speaking, practically nothing was known about the charges against the men. It was whispered that these old men comprised a monarchist conspiracy. They hoped, we would have to assume, that they could find the strength to break the power of the Red Army and the NKVD.

Nonetheless, some came to believe in the generals' plot. For example, the former nobleman and lieutenant Mikhail Tukhachevsky not only accepted the Stalin-Voroshilov version, but gave it a military-scientific basis. Today at a historical distance it does not appear credible. We have gotten used to the fact that without exception in all the memoirs published since Tukhachevsky's posthumous rehabilitation he has been depicted as the embodiment of an angel.

Alas, one cannot take the words out of history any more than from songs. On April 25, 1931, at the Leningrad branch of the Communist Academy an open meeting of the plenum of the section for the study of problems of war took place. The stenographic notes of that scholarly meeting were published as a brochure.[2] Discussion is a normal part of scholarly life, but this one was given particular piquancy by the circumstance that it was conducted in the absence and against the will of a silent opponent. Svechin was called professor only from hypocritical convenience. He was at the time a common camp prisoner who with his academic colleagues was felling trees for the glory of the Five-Year Plan. As is usual in Soviet discussions, all the speakers held the same opinion. The first and main report was Tukhachevsky's "On the Strategic Views of Svechin." Tubs of hatred and lies were dumped on the defenseless opponent. Tukhachevsky proved himself an apt pupil of his great leader and his commissar in the art of misrepresenting others' views and falsifying facts. We will turn to the text of his report.

At first, Tukhachevsky noted, as Chief of the General Staff Svechin fought the Germans willingly, but, "from the beginning of the Civil War he actively participated in nothing. He worked at the Military Academy. . . . His articles, we see, are of an embittered nature and anti-Soviet content."[3] At the height of the Civil War there reigned such freedom in Soviet territory (in the city of Moscow and not much anyplace else) that a former tsarist general could with impunity severely criticize Soviet authority in print and still remain in its service. It took ten years of intensive Marxist analysis to divine the true purport of these articles. Tukhachevsky continues, "Svechin saw the commissars of the Red Army as a basic hindrance to the work of the commanders: . . . every efficient [commander] trying to concentrate on his work is besieged by a swarm of counselors, planners, delegates, committees, busybodies of every sort and rank, blocking his way, taking credit for his work, usurping his authority."

It is interesting that commissars are not mentioned in the quote. Maybe the word counselor (*sovetchik*) seemed politically suspicious to Tukhachevsky? To be serious again, Tukhachevsky found more and more negative characteristics in the old general: "Svechin regarded political work with scorn and hostility. . . . Svechin never was and never wanted to be a Marxist." That was foolish enough, but there was worse to come. In 1919 Svechin had been so bold as to announce: "White, gray, or red army—that is a matter of the taste of the organizers of the armed forces. A red militia, however, is as probable as red bread."

His thought was unorthodox, but it would seem that the old man was closer to the truth than his accuser. Why else explain that Tukhachevsky himself, a progressive from the time he was in diapers, heroically defended tsarism in the ranks of the old army for three years, shoulder to shoulder with millions of simple people who later transferred to the Red Army? Unquestioning subordination, without which no army exists, makes an obedient weapon of command. Was the Red Army used only for missions of liberation?

Tukhachevsky's wrath was aroused by Svechin's assertion that the strategy of both sides in the Civil War differed little because they shared "a common basis of starvation, poverty, destroyed transport, a peasantry tired of war and avoiding conscription." From this there came "a certain coincidence of the basic strategic line of the Reds and Whites. Denikin's march on Moscow in 1919 had its continuation in the Reds' march on Warsaw in 1920." This offended Tukhachevsky personally. He sought support in a quote from Lenin: "just a few more days of the Red Army's victorious offensive and not only would Warsaw have been taken (that would not have been so important), but the Versailles Treaty would have been destroyed. . . ." He does not mention, however, that even Lenin acknowledged that the assault on Warsaw was a political mistake. That scoundrel Svechin meanwhile had the nerve to write, "The Red Armies, as if ignoring the material forces of the Poles . . . went to battle with the Versailles Treaty. That is mysticism, especially in the conditions of [the strategy of] destruction." Svechin believed in the universality of military science, its independence from politics and ideology: "We investigate war with all its possibilities and do not try to narrow our theory to a sketch of a Red Soviet strategic doctrine." Therefore, Tukhachevsky logically concluded, "Svechin did not write his *Strategy* to prepare the victory of the Red Army. On the contrary, the essence of Svechin's *Strategy* is defeatist when applied to the USSR."

Tukhachevsky never did fully understand Svechin's main idea—about the decisive role of strategic defense in modern war. Only small or weak countries, which do not have sufficient resources but which want to or are forced to make war, need gamble on destruction. Five years earlier Svechin had predicted that blitzkrieg would have little success in a large war: "An assault of the destructive style places the attacking army in very unfavorable material conditions. It so weakens the defense of their flanks and rear, and demands such efforts at supply, that only by winning signal operational victories can eventual defeat be prevented."[4]

Surely Tukhachevsky experienced this in full measure during the Warsaw operation. Hitler's armies offered a more obvious illustration as they raced toward Moscow and the southeast.

In truth, he did not know what he was talking about. His general evaluation of Svechin's strategy sounds malicious and abusive; it was a political denunciation, slander: "Svechin's theory of 'attrition' as applied to the USSR becomes . . . a defense of imperialism against the offensive of the proletarian revolution."

Touching on economic questions in passing, Tukhachevsky found further cause to kick the disgraced professor, who was not particularly impressed by the wonders of the Five-Year Plan: "It would be a crude error, a cruel omission to forget the huge virgin spaces, in which Dneprostroi and the future Nizhnyi Novgorod automobile plant appear drops in the bucket."

Of course, the old general slightly oversalted his skepticism, but a good deal less than others exaggerated their dutiful optimism. It is not hard to see that he was only asking for care in evaluating our economic potential. Tukhachevsky was not up to his subtlety. The end of his report is surprising in its theoretical profundity: "In developing military theory it is of prime importance to be properly armed with the Marxist-Leninist method, and in light of this cleansing our military thought of all Svechinist effluvia is a question of paramount and immediate importance."

At the meeting Svechin was gouged and flayed from all sides. According to the many speakers he was a terrible military historian (K. Bocharov), his methodology was all wrong (I. Slutsky), his operational views were faulty (A. Sediakin). Svechin did not understand the nature of future war (P. Suslov), or the role of the navy (I. Duplitsky). His views on the mobilization of industry in wartime were pure treachery (V. Dunaevsky).[5] It was not possible to say anything positive about the man's politics (I. Fendel) or his relations with the Red Army (I. Gazukin).

Svechin did have a terrible defect. He did not take the trouble to camouflage his words. He did not conform and was careless enough to speak the naked truth. At the Academy he was unflinchingly strict with his students and did not tire of saying that the enemy would not bother to consult the *Alphabet of Communism*. Nor would he give preference to anyone for his proletarian heritage, political literacy, or progressive views. For this, the best Russian military theorist of the postrevolutionary period was thrown in a prison camp and publicly defamed.

It remains to make a few, but bitter, conclusions. The Revolution deprived Tukhachevsky not only of officer's rank (which had not yet been reintroduced in 1931), but also of the conception of military honor. It takes neither much intelligence nor a conscience to perceive the dishonor of slandering a man with a gag in his mouth and his hands tied behind his back. That was how, by degrees, a moral climate hospitable to terror was established in the Army. It is hardly surprising that not long after, commanders selected by a tyrant sent their comrades-in-arms to their deaths, although they did not believe in their guilt. And they themselves would go to the torture chambers followed by the taunts of their successors.

15 A Brief Flowering

Sudden, sharp turns at the helm of the ship of state are normal in Russian history. In 1930, for the second time, Stalin scornfully rejected Tukhachevsky's appeal to arm the Red Army with modern technology, which would require the creation of a defense industry. But in May 1931 Tukhachevsky was appointed Deputy People's Commissar and Chief of Armaments for the RKKA. This happened immediately after his shameful participation in the slandering of Svechin and as if to reward him for his devotion to the leadership. The reasons probably lie deeper. A new chapter opened in the history of the Red Army, and it was the most glorious in its twenty years of existence.

Signs of a major change were visible in the summer of 1930 at the Sixteenth Party Congress. Stalin, who was distracted by the attacks on the rightists and the report on kolkhoz construction, ignored questions of defense in his own report. On the other hand, Voroshilov's speech in the discussion that followed was notable for its unconcealed alarm. Of course, the Chairman of the RVS USSR approached his task like a true Bolshevik. He spoke in Aesopian language, but for the initiated his message came through rather eloquently.

Voroshilov began at a distance and in broad strokes painted a picture of the condition of the Western armies. The imperialists were intensifying the mechanization of their armed forces and increasing their firepower. The number of their tanks, planes, cars, and heavy guns was increasing with frightening speed. He attached special importance to the quality of military technology. Preparation for war was becoming total: "A country, its economy as a whole—industry, agriculture, and transport, its cultural institutions and its scientific forces—these are the elements being used to prepare for cruel future struggles."[1]

All of this was correct and intelligent; and others, in particular Tukhachevsky and Triandafillov, had said the same two or three years earlier.

Now it would have been natural to turn to internal matters and discuss the condition of the technical armaments of the Red Army. But such consistency and candor would not have been normal for a Stalinist politician. It was said by a delegate to the congress that "the armed forces of our Union are organizationally, militarily, and politically a reliable armed buttress of the dictatorship of the proletariat." As proof, Voroshilov produced figures on the social composition of the RKKA: workers and field laborers made up 33 percent, and peasants 58 percent. The officer corps was composed of 30 percent workers and 51 percent Party members. What of the old officers, that thorn in the side of the left opposition and a constant object of attack? They were practically all Party members, and they were only 10 percent of the command cadre. The main thing was that in the two years between the Fifteenth and Sixteenth Congresses the number of Communists in the Army had grown from 82,000 to 129,000.

All of this gave great hope and even confidence. But the commissar did not stop there. Mentioning that many military questions had passed through the TSK and the Politburo in the past two years, he suddenly let fall, "But decisions are one thing and acting on them is something completely different." He had no complaints about the TSK or the government, "but our military industry and industry as a whole, as far as supplying the military with everything it needs is concerned, falls down pretty seriously both in quantity and in quality."

The accusation was serious. Worse than that, despite the polite disclaimer, it was directed right at the higher leadership. As if he sensed the contradiction, the commissar promised, "I will speak to these problems in response to comrade Kuibyshev's report, and I will have some unpleasant words for our industry."

Kuibyshev's report was almost flippant. It was sprinkled with promises about growth and progress, the more important of which in coal and metals were not even half fulfilled. The needs of the Army were not mentioned.[2] Voroshilov did not respond to Kuibyshev as he said he would; at least no speech or even mention of a speech appears in the stenographic report. Yet everything was not just smoothed over.

The director of the shipbuilding industry, R. Muklevich, took up the cudgels. He began by saying that in Kuibyshev's speech the general tasks of industry "were outlined concretely, and reinforced by facts and figures." (There were more than enough figures, but as far as the facts were concerned, they were, as we say in our newspapers, unconfirmed. We will speak of that in the chapter on the Seventeenth Congress.) Unfortunately, Muklevich continued, "questions of defense, the importance of industry for defense are depicted with too large strokes. We must speak about these tasks because under the *screen of secrecy* in some places, in factories, and often *in higher institutions, nothing is being done*."[3]

So, that particular variety of native Soviet *tufta* flourished back then. The reproach that time was thrown right in the face of higher authority. It was little enough that Muklevich accused them of ignorance about military economy: "There is a conviction that the growth of industry will automatically strengthen the defense capabilities of the Army. That is not entirely true." He explained further that he did not only mean work to increase military reserves, but also the working out of a plan to quickly put industry on a war footing, and repeated, "The simple interchangeability of nonmilitary and war industry, which many people assume, does not exist."

Among the many who did not understand was Stalin, who did not fully appreciate this elementary truth until the war. Muklevich kept his speech exceptionally dry and businesslike. He had no use for praise and congratulations for the standard successes. Near the end of his speech he pushed Stalin's nose into the problem once more. "Attention to military problems in our industry is minimal. Necessary preparation for defense is not being carried out."

Kuibyshev did not accept Muklevich's challenge. In his concluding speech he left these serious accusations unanswered. Except for Budenny's stupid remarks,[4] the problem of defense was not raised again at the Sixteenth Congress.

It is evident from Voroshilov's sortie that even before the Congress someone was applying serious pressure on the Stalinist leadership to review the state of defense and the Army. It is difficult to identify all the people who were raising these questions, but some of them stand out clearly. The pressure was applied in two directions. The first was associated with the technical equipping of the Army and the creation of a defense industry. At the highest levels it was represented by Tukhachevsky, Triandafillov, Muklevich, Alksnis, Khalepsky.

The second group encouraged building a line of strategic fortifications along the western and southern borders, similar to those being erected in Germany, France, and Finland. We do not know precisely who was involved in this group, but most probably it included Yakir, who had returned from studying in Germany, Uborevich, Garmarnik, and several members of the TSK, who were then involved in civilian work but still had some influence in military affairs—particularly Khataevich.

These were two separate groups, although several years later they did join forces. Tangential evidence for that is Triandafillov's book *The Nature of Operations of Modern Armies*[5] (1929), which served as a manifesto for Tukhachevsky and his supporters. The book zealously defends the concept of a mechanized army and expounds the principles of sequential operations, from which the theory of "deep" offenses was derived. It did not say a single word about the advisability of erecting strategic fortifications. This is not surprising. Tukhachevsky's team at that time much preferred an offensive strategy.[6] They remained faithful to that idea later but in a somewhat milder form.

Stalin, Voroshilov, and their old pal Egorov, chief-of-staff of the RKKA, were not men to make subtle distinctions. Both groups' views were alien to them. They planned to fight simply, with saber and rifle. And of course to attack. Theoretical considerations of specialists could not convince them any more than other intellectuals' ramblings could. At that time Stalin was being proclaimed the greatest strategist of the Civil War, and the other two were his closest comrades-in-arms. Together with Budenny they thought themselves strong enough to conquer any enemy. Only changes in the military and political situation in Europe, the example of other countries' armies, and the growing influence of the fascists in Germany forced them to retreat.

Because the new course was taken unwillingly and under great pressure, it was not smoothly carried out. Side by side with the innovators in the command post sat dyed-in-the-wool conservatives who considered the changes superfluous, almost capricious in the way they reflected foreign practices. People's Commissar Voroshilov spun like a weather vane, attracted first to one and then to the other. Chief-of-Staff Egorov tended to conservatism. As before, the role of the major strike forces was given to the cavalry. Cavalrymen like Budenny and Gorodovikov enjoyed enormous influence. They did not tire of asserting that tanks could not replace horses, if only because Russia lacked roads. There were a number of zealous veterans who would sooner believe an old-regime sergeant major than any military professor. They had fought bravely in the Civil War. In peacetime they thought all a Red Armyman needed was a dashing appearance, knowledge of the manual of arms, and a precise marching step. In this spirit, musters and parades, so very dear to Blucher's heart, were held.

Nonetheless, the new course slowly but surely became a reality. New men little liked by Voroshilov and Stalin had to be admitted to the leadership ranks of the RKKA. Ia. B. Gamarnik, an independent and decisive man and a proponent of progressive views, became First Deputy People's Commissar and Chairman of the RVS USSR. He headed the Central Political Department (GLAVPUR). Tukhachevsky assumed the post of Second Deputy and Chief of Armaments. The only professional military man in the leading troika, he headed not only the technical but also the scientific rearming of the Army. Yakir, one of the most thoughtful and authoritative commanders, also became a member of the RVS USSR.

In the first half of the 1930s there developed a very strong leadership group for the military apparat, which was intent on improving the efficiency of the Army. The RVS remained the highest organ of the RKKA. Since the time of the Revolution it had increasingly become a formality of an office, rubber-stamping the decisions of the top four or five military leaders. However, it existed, and to a certain extent it tied Voroshilov's and Stalin's hands. In 1934, under the pretext of improving the military apparat, the RVS was abolished and the People's Commissariat of Military and Naval Affairs was renamed the People's Commissariat of Defense. The new commissariat became the sole commanding body of the RKKA and RKKF (Navy). It received the authority to make decisions without discussion; but Voroshilov, knowing well the extent of his incompetence, did not dare to make independent decisions of great importance.

The rearming of the Army went ahead full speed and well. Toward the end of the 1920s all institutions of higher learning of the technical branches had been foolishly combined into a single Military-Technical Academy. Now out of it were re-created the Military-Engineering, Electrotechnical, Chemical Defense, Mechanization and Motorization, and Aviation Engineering Academies of the RKKA. New Air Force and General Staff Academies also appeared. By the mid-1930s several graduating classes had qualitatively strengthened the Army's intelligentsia.

At Tukhachevsky's initiative a new office was established to develop and introduce new military technology. Outstanding engineers, such as L. V. Kurchevsky, V. I. Bekauri, N. E. Langemak, and P. I. Grakhovsky, worked in the Ostekhburo, the special technical bureau.

They were impressively successful at developing new military technology. The creative enthusiasm of the Five-Year Plan was probably more strongly evinced in constructing highly developed armaments than in any other field. Tupolev's planes set several new records that startled the rest of the world—including a flight across the North Pole to the American mainland. Soviet armored vehicle technology, which had barely existed in the 1920s, progressed very rapidly.[7] The crown of its development was the T-34 tank, which was unrivaled until the end of the Second World War. Work in such new fields as radar and jet weaponry also made pioneering achievements. Tukhachevsky, Alksnis, Khalepsky, and their coworkers were responsible in large part for these achievements. Not only did they value the research of the outstanding engineers, but they succeeded in creating for them favorable working conditions, a far from easy task. The best military engineers of the time worked under their protection: in aviation were Tupolev, Polikarpov, Iliushin; in small arms, Degtiarev and Tokarev; in tank construction, Kotov; in jet-propelled projectiles, the "katiusha" prototypes, Langemak and Pobedonostsev; in rockets, Tsander and Korolev.

The new technology was quickly put on-line. Todorsky remembered that "in 1932 the Kharkov factory completed two tanks with difficulty [that was in a full year], but in 1935 whole companies of the machines rolled off its conveyors daily." It is worth pointing out that the head of the Kharkov Tank Factory was the Ukrainian commander Yakir.

The troops began to assimilate the technical innovations. The Belorussian and especially the Ukrainian Military Districts were used as experimental proving grounds. It was in the Ukraine that the famous maneuvers of 1935 and 1936 were conducted in the presence of foreign observers. Besides the English, French, and Czechs, there were also Italians. The maneuvers had a two-fold purpose. First of all, they were an exercise in cooperation of the new tank, aviation, and airborne troops with the infantry. Yakir deserves the credit for coordinating their movements and instructing the units in these new skills. He was an outstanding practitioner of military organization but unfortunately left behind no written works. At this time he worked very closely with Tukhachevsky, the apostle of the mechanized army offensive. Yakir, while he agreed fully about the importance of technology, preferred strategic defense. Besides the line of fortifications in which he was involved, it was due to his efforts that a network of partisan bases was established in case of enemy occupation. This project died an early death before the start of the Second World War.

Yakir's defensive sympathies, in this case supported by Tukhachevsky, determined the character of the maneuvers of 1935, which were called "Battle for Kiev." The "Red" troops, fully armed with modern technology, skillfully defended the city from an enemy attack. Documentary films of the maneuvers became very popular.

The second purpose of the exercises was to demonstrate to the West the might of the RKKA. The foreign observers were startled. The world press buzzed with reports of Soviet strength.

Over the next several years powerful, permanent fortifications were constructed in the Ukrainian and Belorussian military districts. Uborevich and especially Yakir were closely involved with them. One can question the practical value of such fortifications in general, but as an example of the art these were not in any way inferior to the Maginot and Mannerheim lines. Unfortunately they were not tested in war. Stalin in his wisdom thought to disarm them before the war began.

Side by side with these changes, military theory developed rapidly and fruitfully. The most noticeable results were produced in the fields of tactics and operational skills. Here the Soviet school kept pace with all of Europe and in some cases outstripped the Europeans. The theory of "deep operations" crowned the thought of the period. Tukhachevsky, N. N. Movchin, N. E. Varfolomeev, V. K. Triandafillov, and B. K. Kalinovsky (the last two died in 1931 in a plane crash) had laid the ground for that work with their ideas of "sequential operations" in the 1920s. It was carried further by a group of able and energetic theoreticians led by G. S. Isserson.

Inasmuch as the offensive was considered the basic form of combat activity of the RKKA, the theory began with offensive operations. At this point we must make a brief digression. Although the forms of conducting war have undergone many radical changes in human history, the logical principles at its foundation were discovered long ago. This is particularly true of tactics, the art of organizing battle, direct armed conflict. Thus in the fourth century B.C. the Theban general Epaminondas applied a concentration of his forces against a vulnerable point in his foe's formation. Two-and-a-half thousand years ago Hannibal faced the formidable Romans at Cannae with (to use its modern name) an operational pocket. Both of these principles remain effective. When they were working out their theory of deep operations, the Soviet theoreticians made them applicable to modern weaponry.

The enemy's front, even if it is continuous, unavoidably has weak places, usually where the flanks of adjoining units meet. This determines the direction of the main strike, where troops must be concentrated to outman the enemy troops and weaponry by three to five times and must be disposed three or four echelons deep. The breakthrough of the tactical zone of defense begins with a massive artillery bombardment of the sector selected for attack. Then the infantry with its direct support tanks accomplishes the breakthrough and consolidates its hold to allow the second echelon, the sappers, to make the defense zone passable for the mobile units. Then mechanized and cavalry corps, which had not participated in the first wave, are thrown against the enemy's operational deep defenses. There should theoretically be several of these sectors along a front, one for every army or group. The theory postulated is that such operational breakthroughs by mobile units, supported by airborne landings, will lead to surrounding and destroying considerable forces of the enemy and finally to seriously weakening his combat potential.

For the time, this was an original theory of offense. It was worked out in the maneuvers of the 1930s with mechanized corps and large airborne formations, both of which branches of service were first established and tested in the RKKA. The young Soviet theoreticians became pioneers in solving some of the problems of attack in future war. It should be noted, however, that the theory they created was neither complete nor mature.

We give here only a condensed summary of the basic premises of deep operations, based on the writing of one of its creators, G. S. Isserson. Other interesting developments of the period, for example the ideas and principles of organizing and employing large units of mechanized forces, have too specialized a character to discuss here.[8]

Isserson very colorfully described the essence of deep operations: "from an exhausting, crawling, sequential overcoming of resistance by fire bit by bit, stage by stage, we have arrived at the simultaneous containment and suppression of the whole tactical depth of the enemy. With one simultaneous, completely overwhelming strike we will break and destroy opposing resistance. This solves the problem of overcoming the fire front in all its depth."[9] Such a radical approach was a reaction to the excruciating, muddy trench war of 1914–18, in which the main factors were powerful defense works, the spreading of the front to natural limits, and the insufficient striking power of attackers. It was thought that fronts would be as continuous in the next war and more deeply echeloned. To effectively use the increased strength—both striking and mechanized— of the offensive, it was decided to resort to deeply echeloned offensive formations: "Modern operations are operations in depth. They must be planned in their whole depth and prepared to overcome the whole depth [of the enemy] . . . a linear strategy of one wave of operational efforts cannot solve the problem of offense."[10]

The goal can no longer be reached by a single strike or battle. Operations will be complex. They will become a planned sequence of deep strikes. Extensive planning will precede every operation. That stage will be fully controlled; it is almost entirely in the hands of the commander. "The greatest pressure and crisis can be expected at the end." The character of battle: "It will be a solid sea of fire and battle, which spread widely across the front in the [First] World War, and which will spread through the whole depth in future war." He who at the moment of crisis in the slaughter proves stronger and better organized will win: "an offensive must become like a whole series of waves, which with increasing force beat against the shore, to wipe it away, to destroy it with ceaseless blows from the depths. A modern, complex, deep operation is not decided by one simultaneous blow of coinciding efforts. It requires the deep, operational layering of these efforts, which must become stronger as the moment of victory comes nearer."[11]

It is easy to see that this conception leaves no room for art, skill, or efforts to outfox the enemy and catch him off guard. "Reason lies at the foundation of military operations," Clausewitz once said. Here power, will, organization, and purposefulness are all. The goal is the physical suppression and literal destruction of the enemy. The method must be a programmed series of crushing frontal attacks. In this "sea of battle" the victor is he who possesses the stronger forehead and fist.

It would be a mistake, however, to see the theory of deep operations simply as mechanized violence. It accurately reflected, in a concentrated form, the tendency of military thought of the 1930s. The Germans employed it with great success in Poland and France. In 1943–45 Soviet troops frequently inflicted deeply echeloned strikes. The problem was that it was promoted as universal, as the only possible method of conducting combat operations. Moreover, it contained flaws, which its proponents tried not to see. In the absence of decisive superiority over the enemy, in the face of the skill and mobility of his defense over a large strategic area, the attacker would achieve victory, but would at the same time make himself extremely vulnerable. Every boxer knows that it is when he tries to deliver the knockout punch that he is himself most open. If the punch does not land, the opponent can move in easily with counterpunches. Svechin had already applied that analogy to strategy in the 1920s, but no one cared to listen to him. The creators of the deep operation only rarely, reluctantly, and in passing mentioned defense. And in those instances their colorful, energetic language suddenly became dull and lifeless. They were utterly silent about the cost of any offensive. We, however, will have to touch upon those dull subjects.

Even a fleeting acquaintance with the theory of deep operations suffices to isolate its principal traits. It is extremely aggressive and exclusively straightforward. It starts with an assumption of overwhelming superiority for the attacker and does not take losses into account. The reasons, of course, are not to be found in the bloodthirstiness of the theoreticians, but in their professed strategic ideology. He who believes in the strategy of destruction (blitzkrieg in German) cannot come to other conclusions about operations and tactics. The only acceptable act was to grind the enemy and his defenses to powder. What this frontal approach might cost in modern warfare did not interest the doctrine's creators. They had already proclaimed that flanking attacks would be rare, and frontal attacks the rule. There was nothing left but to beat one's head against the nearest defensive wall.

The Germans thought in the same way. Looking back over three decades, Isserson noted that Guderian had preached the same methods of breaking through prepared defenses with tanks in 1937 that Soviet theoreticians had introduced in 1932 and 1933. That is close to the truth, but what is more important than the priority of authorship is that the methods of deep operations were extensively applied in the Second World War. They yielded individual operational fruits, but their cost, as a rule, was extremely high. They were paid for by strategic exhaustion.

Tukhachevsky, Triandafillov, and Isserson heatedly refuted Svechin's conclusions about the advantages of mobile, strategic defense in a large war. Svechin was liquidated in 1938, but his conclusions were confirmed. Hitler and the Japanese did fine while they were fighting weak or unprepared countries. But then in total war, assaults in the blitzkrieg style failed, despite their stunning successes at the outset. German troops mastered Western Europe; invaded Africa; occupied the Balkans and Scandinavia; seized Poland, the Ukraine, Belorussia, the Baltic countries, and almost half of European Russia. They pushed almost to Moscow and Leningrad, broke through to the Volga, threatened Transcaucasia—and ended in unconditional surrender. The same fate awaited Japan, which at one time controlled enormous territory in East and Southeast Asia and almost all of the Pacific Ocean basin.

Even more strongly than these generally known facts, another circumstance supports Svechin's concept. Superaggressive Germany was forced in 1943 to change from deep operations to strategic defense; then the Germans held out for two years, fighting almost alone against the world. B. Liddell Hart, the most prominent military theoretician in the West, came to this conclusion at the end of the Second World War:

> When account is taken of the shrinkage of the German forces, and of their material resources, it appears almost a miracle that their resistance lasted as long as it did, when stretched over so wide a circumference . . . it was, above all, proof of the immense inherent strength of modern defense. On any orthodox military calculation the German forces were inadequate to resist for even a week the weight of attacking power which they withstood for many months. When they could hold frontages of reasonable proportion to their strength, they frequently beat off attacks delivered with a superiority of a force of over six to one, and sometimes over twelve to one. . . .
> If Germany's opponents had recognized that condition in advance, and had themselves prepared to meet aggression in a way suited to make the most of the defensive advantage, the world would have been saved immense trouble and tragedy. Long ago, that famous pugilist, Jem Mace, summed up all his experience of the ring in the maxim: "Let 'em come to ye, and they'll beat theirselves." The truth of Jem Mace's maxim became the outstanding tactical lesson of the battlefields in Africa, Russia, and Western Europe. With growing experience all skillful commanders sought to profit by the power of the defensive, even when on the offensive.[12]

We might be criticized in that it is easy to find fault in hindsight. But here Isserson can help us. This important military writer, who miraculously survived Stalin's purges, in the mid-1960s published a retrospective survey, which includes many bitter admissions.[13]

Most importantly he asserts that the theory of "deep operations" developed independently of strategy:

> The theory of deep operations reached the level of development it did in 1936, when it was no longer possible to exclude the strategic sphere of its application, and when only strategic scale and circumstances in the whole theater of military operations might give it intelligent meaning, purposeful and justified by conditions of the time. . . . In other words, to turn the scheme of deep operations into a real phenomenon, it was necessary to put it against a strategic background and breathe strategic content into it.

It should be said that the strategy of destruction, the spirit of which fills the theory of deep operations, was not worked out in the same sense as Svechin's doctrine but was merely proclaimed. We might object to Isserson, arguing that it would be more fruitful to first formulate and interpret strategic principles and then be guided by them in developing campaign tactics. That would be superfluous, however, as neither was done at the time.

In 1936 the operations department of the Frunze Academy was made into the Academy of the General Staff. But "this changed nothing in the system of our higher military education in relation to strategy." Why? Surely the Academy had been formed to prepare a higher—that is strategic—cadre. As for how that was done:

> the slightest hint that it was necessary in one form or another to introduce into the Academy a course on strategy as the basis of campaign tactics ran into objections from on high. When this question was raised at a meeting before the Academy was opened, the Chief of the General Staff, Marshal Egorov, directly questioned representatives of the Academy in an exasperated voice: "And what sort of strategy will you study? The plan of war? Strategic deployment? The conduct of war? No one is going to let you do that, because that is the business of the General Staff."
>
> When he put it that way, of course, no one was going to protest. . . .

If strategy in this manner was to be the personal property of Stalin, Voroshilov, and Egorov, then the blindness of campaign tactics was inevitable. Stalin and his stooges thought of war only as "a little blood on foreign territory" and did not care to hear about defense in any form. The higher commanders, carefully trained in their stupidity, relied exclusively on the deep destructive strike and ignored a multiplicity of aspects of combat conditions. This was true also of their beloved offensive:

> It was assumed that the initial strategic deployment would form a solid front, which would have to be broken through and necessarily by a frontal assault. From the point of view of the calculation of forces and the capacity of the theater that was generally true. But that did not take into consideration the new potentials of motorized-mechanized forces to broach the front before it has time to be organized and established.

Without doubt this refers to the German success of 1941. Questions of strategic deployment in the earlier phases of war and the action of invasion groups Egorov interpreted in the old way, in the spirit of the First World War. Tukhachevsky protested energetically but unsuccessfully against this approach. Observing rapidly arming Germany, which revealed itself in 1935, he began to understand that blitzkrieg alone would not be enough. They would have to concern themselves as quickly as possible with preparing strategic defense.[14]

Meanwhile, things were not going well with the methods of defense on either the strategic or the operational level.

> Throughout the history of the Frunze Military Academy and the Academy of the General Staff, the topic "The Army and Defense" was never thoroughly investigated. Our tactical defense was well worked out and occupied the place it should in all our field manuals. But it seemed almost to contradict our offensive doctrine and it was considered somehow indecent to discuss defense of the Army over a significant sector of a theater of military operations.

Only after most of the commanders had been liquidated was a timid attempt made to do something about defense. The Academy published *The Foundation of Defensive Operations* in 1938. No one dared go further, however. The work did not receive official approval and went for naught. No one so much as mentioned strategic defense.

The war came even closer, and the stagnation of military thought went on:

> Our campaign tactics were shut up in their own framework to a certain extent, and the strategic aspects of war remained, unfor-

tunately, uninvestigated in our military theory. Needed interest in the early phases of war was not stimulated, and the necessary theoretical conclusions applicable to our western theater of military operations were not made. This was certainly a gap in our military theory, and, of course, it showed at the beginning of the war in 1941.

That was not all. There was even an attempt to retreat from the positions we had gained. In the period of the purges Voroshilov, bathed in a sweat of fear, called the theory of "deep operations" the "theory of treason." For several years it was banned, which was understandable. Practically all of the authors of original works and texts had been repressed, and their books were withdrawn from circulation. The fists of the deep operation, the mechanized corps, were disbanded after the Polish campaign and the failure in Spain. At the same time the development of bombardment aviation was curtailed. Mechanized corps were reestablished in December 1940.

Uncertainty and fear for one's life became part of the Army environment. Nonetheless, the enemy was still scorned:

> Even the events in Poland in 1939 and in France in 1940 did not change the dominant official views, did not shake them. However, in the recesses of their minds the higher-ranking officers of the General Staff understood that the circumstances of the early period of a war might turn out completely differently. In several circles of the General Staff and the AGsh, men spoke rather concretely with the relevant calculations in hand. However, these conversations were conducted behind closed doors only and did not go beyond their offices.

It was with this theoretical baggage and in this temper that the Red Army went to war. If we are to be precise, this was no longer the Red Army but its successor, as yet not renamed. The RKKA ceased to exist in 1938 when its higher command staff was almost entirely wiped out along with more than half of its mid-level commanders.

Let us go back a few years. In spite of all the obstacles and difficulties, both real and invented by the Stalinist leadership, the RKKA of the mid 1930s, was a magnificent, first-class army, the best in the history of the country. It was the best army in Europe at the time, certainly the most intelligent. It was rich in talented people, having searched out and absorbed what was best among the people.

It was an army created by the Revolution. The politicians used the Army frequently, but still the RKKA more than any other state institution embodied the revolutionary spirit: liberation from the fetters of centuries of slavery, and from the shackles of backwardness and ignorance, striving for limitless improvement, and irrepressible optimism. As Liddell Hart said about the army of the French Revolution, this spirit "made pedantic regimentation impossible, and gave scope to the development of the talents and initiative of individuals."[15]

A new generation of military intellectuals grew up in the Army. They took on extremely difficult tasks and accomplished many of them brilliantly. From top to bottom it was an army willing to learn. Commanders of a new sort educated a new type of soldier, unknown to the imperial army. They succeeded extraordinarily well. They taught barely literate country boys not only the wisdom of cannon fodder but the skills of culture. They prepared them for life. It is unlikely that there was anywhere else an atmosphere more full of the reforms and hopes aroused by the Revolution.

The simple soldiery and gentlemen officers of the tsarist army were gone. In their place were comrades-in-arms—Red Armymen and commanders. Regimentation was replaced by study, brass polishing by combat training. The lower ranks did not stand to attention for the higher. There were no ranks until 1935, only responsibilities. Regular forms of address entailed only respect for human dignity. Acknowledgement of an order was a simple "yes." Having shot the RKKA, they instituted the servile form "I obey," "just exactly," and "in no way, no." They were ashamed to return to such barracks gems as "glad to try" and "extremely grateful," but the effect was the same.

Even the external appearance of the men of all ranks in the RKKA had something noble and severely romantic about it. The uniform was simple and exactly the same for everyone. To eradicate this hated spirit, the old uniform was done away with and the field uniform of the tsarist army was reintroduced. The epaulets alone provoked complex memories and emotions. At the same time the militia were decked out like tsarist policemen. What Stalin was thinking at the time is hard to say. Maybe he hoped that men dressed in greatcoats like that would feel less of a desire to think. Maybe he wanted to wipe out even the external reminders of the Revolution, an epoch that in his opinion had passed. It cannot be excluded that he wished to attract the sympathy of that part of the population who would prefer a simply Russian army to a revolutionary army.

God knows what it was, but a goal was reached. The image of the warrior—the soldier in his khakis and the officer in better cloth—drooped and paled. The senior officers and generals got the old-regime look they wanted. The former soldier's tunic did not suit most of them. The baggy jackets still hid the belly a little, that important organ that protruded a bit on most of the Soviet leadership of the time. Little operetta details, stripes and red linings for the generals, fur caps for the colonels, and other tinsel, could not make it right.

The best of times for the Red Army were hateful to Stalin. He was not an enemy of the Army in general. To the contrary. From the time of the Civil War he always dressed in a uniform of sorts, with boots. In 1929 he appointed himself the Great Leader of the Revolution. No, Stalin, who probably could not fieldstrip a rifle, loved to direct operations and command all the armed forces.

But the failed seminarian, having become the leading light of all other affairs, still could not impress the RKKA, where the revolutionary spirit that had already died in the Party and other bureaucracies was still strong. (The manual of garrison duty still read that all orders, except clearly counterrevolutionary orders, must be obeyed.) He especially disliked the higher command, which was composed mostly of young, intelligent men with independent ideas that he simply could not understand. It was not entirely without purpose that he killed them all, even those who danced to his tune.

After 1938 it was easier. Stalin appointed tamer men, who were without particular ideas and who, most important, were mute. But still for a long time they pursued and repressed everything that might remind them of the past. It did not end with changing uniforms. In 1941–42 many large units were written off the books as if they had perished in battle, or they were disbanded. In 1942, along with the reintroduction of shoulder straps, the idea of an officer corps was revived and officers were sharply separated from the soldiers. At the same time the institution of commissars was abolished. It had happened several times before, but this was the last. In 1944 they renamed the whole Army.

Along with the cadre, they destroyed what was best in the Red Army—the spirit, traditions, military culture. In the young, powerful organism of the RKKA even many of the shortcomings were continuations of strengths. With maturity these phenomena would have had to fade away; the dogmatism of conclusions and the excessively offensive temper would have to go. This was an army strong enough to face any enemy. It is impossible to imagine that the RKKA would have surrendered half the country to Hitler.

16 The Seventeenth Congress:
The Victors Dig Their Own Grave

Piously sure of the truth of classes / and not knowing other truths, / they themselves gave meat to smell / to the beasts that later ripped them.
—Korzhavin

When the Congress convened on January 26, 1934, the country was experiencing famine, but the bureaucrats' morale was high. Stalin showered the delegates with data, mostly expressed in percentages, which were meant to prove the unprovable—that everything was all right.

The word famine was, of course, unsuitable and was not used. Instead, difficulties that had been successfully overcome were mentioned. Grain supplies, for example, were sufficient. Table 16.1 gives the figures presented by the general secretary on the gross yield of grain in millions of metric centners (100 kg).[1]

According to Stalin's figures, there was a small decrease in the gross yield in the years of most active collectivization, 1931 and 1932. Compared with the figure for 1929, there was a decrease of 3 to 4 percent. The delegates must have scratched their heads. The loss was insignificant, but the famine was terrible. Even by the most conservative estimates, 5 million to 6 million peasants died of malnutrition in those years.

Where can we find a solution to this paradox? It might be suggested that certain officials improved the statistics just a trifle for the report. We are not able to test such an assertion, but we can run a different sort of check on the basis of official statistics.

Proclaiming collectivization, Stalin complained about the low marketability of products from individual peasant farms. The 1926 harvest almost equaled the last prewar harvest (95 percent), but marketable grain (in circulation outside the villages—in fact, given to the state) was only half the 1913 level. In 1927 and 1928 marketable grain reached only 37 percent of the 1913 level. Because of the draconian

Table 16.1   USSR Grain Yield, 1913–33*

1913	1927	1928	1929	1930	1931	1932	1933
735	725	725[1]	717	835	695	699	898

*Gross yield, in millions of metric centners.

measures employed in collecting grain in 1929, this figure jumped to 58 percent, and at the height of collectivization in 1930 to 73 percent. Stalin was modestly silent about subsequent years, but it is not hard to guess that marketable grain did not decrease because it was easier to collect grain from state farms than it was from individual peasant farms.

Turning to natural indexes (table 16.2) we can see how much grain was collected by the state and how much remained in the villages. For reference, marketable grain in 1913 amounted to 208 million centners.

We see that the decrease was not so modest after all. It turns out that in the years of artificial harvest shortfalls there was 25 percent less grain in the villages. One might think that this shortfall was not so terrible, but we have not finished our calculations.

We must not forget that in the early 1930s two-thirds of the peasants became collective farmers (kolkhozniki).[5] The first commandment in the kolkhoz was well known: GIVE GRAIN TO THE STATE! And they gave—no less than 30 percent.[6] As recently as 1927 the farmers had given only 9.5 percent. They poured another 20 percent at least into the state seed fund,[7] 15 to 20 percent was taken for the kolkhoz seed fund and for feed for the kolkhoz's cattle; at least another 10 percent was lost in harvesting, threshing, and storing—which the backward yeoman farmer would understandably not have permitted. Taken altogether, it appears that the peasant had only one-half or one-third of the grain for himself that he had had in 1927–28.[8]

A half or two-thirds less bread might not be so hard on us, just a little belt-tightening. But bread was the staple of the Russian peasants' diet, and losing one half to two-thirds of it meant famine. He had never had enough meat for most of the year, only in the fall after the annual butchering. Now there was no meat or milk to speak of. The peasants had butchered as much of their livestock as they were able on the way to the kolkhoz, and the kolkhoz's animals were not for him. In 1933 there remained these percentages of the levels of 1929: cattle, 56.6

Table 16.2   Disposition of Grain, 1927–32*

| | | Collected by the State | | | |
1927	1928	1929	1930	1931	1932
77	77	119	152	183^3	$205\text{-}210^3$
		Remaining in the villages			
658	648	598	683	512	494
Percentage					
100	98.5	91	108	77.5^4	75^4

*In millions of metric centners.

percent; sheep and goats, 34.5 percent; pigs, 58.1 percent; horses, 48.7 percent.

And how was it for the inhabitants of the nonblack-soil regions where even in good years there was not enough grain to last from one harvest to the next? Now, after collectivization, they could not buy supplementary grain on the free market because no grain was available. The peasants, like the workers and office workers, were not given rationing cards. They died of starvation, whole villages and *volosts*.[9] But the same horrors occurred in the fertile Ukraine.

The state received three times more grain for its own use, so collectivization seemed successful from its point of view. What did the state do with all the excess grain accumulated by doling out only limited amounts through rationing to the urban population? Surely Stalin and his courageous comrades-in-arms could not devour millions of centners of bread (and meat and butter)? They did not starve, of course. But most of the grain was exported to pay the huge expenses of industrialization.[10]

Stalin did not think of anything new. He followed Trotskyist recipes. One of their authors, Preobrazhensky, devised the theory of "primary socialist accumulation." According to the theory, the building of socialism in its first stage should be accomplished mainly by the maximum appropriation by the state of the surplus product produced in the "un-socialist sphere" by peasants, craftsmen, NEPmen. It sounded excessively candid, and the theory was criticized as destructive of the alliance with the peasantry. That did not stop Stalin from carrying it out with a zeal found in neither Preobrazhensky or Trotsky.

Molotov announced at the 1933 Congress that during the Five-Year Plan 1.5 billion rubles in gold were spent abroad to purchase industrial equipment. This is a huge figure. It is enough to glance at a list of the largest projects to see where the money went. Each project was equipped with foreign machinery, built according to plans made by foreign firms and in consultation with foreign specialists. Only the slave labor was native and cheap: prisoners, kulaks, and starving peasants from all over Russia who were willing to work for food alone.[11] In the five years of the plan the following enterprises were put into operation: in ferrous metals industries—Magnitka, Kuznetsk, Zaporozhstal, and the first part of Nizhny Tagil; several plants were also constructed—tractor factories in Kharkov, Stalingrad, and Cheliabinsk; automobile plants in Moscow and Nizhny Novgorod; Dneproges and Bereznikov chemical *combinat*. In addition, several enterprises in other fields were reconstructed, again using imported tools and machines.

Thus, much of the foundation for heavy industrialization was laid in the first Five-Year Plan. The people ought to have been told, however, at what cost this was achieved. It was not only the price of labor and sweat. The industrial cathedrals cost the lives of millions of Russians. To the 5 million who died of famine must be added another 10 million liquidated as a class.

The capital accumulated at the cost of human lives sank into the bottomless maw of the Five-Year Plan, and a good amount simply evaporated into thin air. There were many reasons: the unrestrained, grandiose fantasies of Kuibyshev, who crushed vsNKh and Gosplan, removing every specialist who might know a little something, so he could insert ridiculous figures into the plan; the absence of qualified workers because the old engineers were purged on the eve of construction in 1928–30; theft and slovenliness; the pomposity of the political overseers.

The first Five-Year Plan was catastrophically unfulfilled in metals production and coal mining. The story of the ferrous metals industry is especially instructive. In 1928 Kuibyshev's vsNKh submitted its own version of the Five-Year Plan—the so-called optimal or maximal plan —which exceeded Gosplan's goals by 150 to 200 percent. The Gosplan experts laughed and tried to explain that the tempo could not be sustained, that the figures were unrealistic: "The vsNKh's figures are beyond the bounds of the possible in this Five-Year Plan" (Professor Bogolepov). "I expect that Gosplan would evaluate the vsNKh Five-

Year Plan as possible in eight, if not ten, years" (Professor Kalinnikov).

Not likely! Comrade Kuibyshev did not graduate from universities; he had dropped out of high school; in everything he was guided by class consciousness. The muddleheaded wrecker-professors were cleared out—imprisoned or exiled.[12] Kuibyshev exulted. At the Sixteenth Congress, just warming to the battle, he said:

> do you remember when VSNKh proposed a figure of ten million tons of cast iron, when the alternatives were six, then seven, then eight million tons in Gosplan's original plan. At that time the smelting of ten million tons of iron seemed impossible. . . . Bourgeois economists who scoffed at us and called our plans fantasies had in mind first of all that figure—ten million tons of iron. Now that "fantasy" has been increased by seven million tons, and the increased plan of seventeen million tons will provoke even greater fury in the capitalistic world. When we fulfill that program, comrades, we will become the leading producer of iron in Europe (applause).[13]

It did not do Kuibyshev any good to fill everyone's ears with tales of 10 million to 17 million tons. The bourgeois economists had a right to laugh. The "fury of the capitalist world" was a figment; so was the metal.

A new Congress met in 1934. For some reason no one gave a specific report on the results of the first Five-Year Plan outlining how much of anything was projected and how much achieved. Stalin and all the others used only excerpted facts, only the most positive, and never side by side with the plan's targets. Instead there were two reports on the second Five-Year Plan by Molotov and Kuibyshev. The chairman of the Council of People's Commissars noted that in 1932 6.2 million tons of iron were produced. The favorite device of percentage gains was missing, but it is not hard to figure. If we take the minimal estimate of 10 million tons, the plan was 62 percent fulfilled. Recall that the experts had suggested 6 million, 7 million, then 8 million tons. In that case the percentage would have been lovely. But if we take Kuibyshev's last, triumphal cry, then the results are sad indeed, only 36.5 percent.

Ordzhonikidze let slip in a swaggering sort of speech how some of the newest, largest plants of the time managed to produce so little metal:

I remember that an engineer of the MacKee firm implored me not to put the blast furnace into operation that winter: "If there are no political considerations, please do not use it," said engineer Haven in 1931, "because it will collapse." He proved to be a prophet as far as the first blast furnace was concerned. We killed it. But we destroyed it because we mishandled it, while our young engineers operated the fourth blast furnace when it was 35 degrees below, and it works fine.[14]

They destroyed one, and the other worked fine. So said the director of all heavy industry. That is, the success rate was 50 percent.

Ordzhonikidze forgot to say that the foolish destruction of equipment was not the only problem. The Chairman of the TSKK added a little something. On July 1, 1933, said Rudzutak, almost 220 million rubles worth of equipment, almost entirely foreign, was found idle in metallurgical plants.[15] To evaluate just how large a loss this was, we have to know that in the previous three-and-a-half years 1 billion rubles worth of machines were imported for all heavy industry.

So what did Kuibyshev do? Was he embarrassed, did he acknowledge his error, set the professors free with an apology? Nothing of the sort. Without saying a word about his monstrous error, he projected a goal of 18 million tons of iron for the end of the second Five-Year Plan in 1937.

Apparently there were serious disagreements among those compiling the second Five-Year Plan. Ordzhonikidze opined that the tempo was just right, Leninist, Stalinist and "let's not overdo it." He recommended decreasing the plan's goals by 10 percent for the whole economy and by 6 percent for heavy industry. He did not forget iron: why say 18 million, he asked, 16 million would be fine. At this point Voroshilov, Vareikis, and Kirov shouted, "Right!" and Molotov expressed agreement. They did not want to have to cope with Kuibyshev's fantasy for another five years.

Things were bad with coal also. At first a goal of 75 million tons was set, but then in connection with the change of plans in metals that figure was raised to 125 million. Already in 1930 knowledgeable people were warning that coal was being taken at an accelerated pace only from existing mines. No new mines were being opened up, and the apparent rise in production could not be maintained. In the last year of the Five-Year Plan 64.2 million tons was mined, that is 85.6 percent and 51.5 percent of the original and final goals, respectively.

Failures in the metallurgical and mining industries were not exceptions. They stand out clearly because in these industries the production
of all enterprises is the same—iron, steel, rolled metals, coal—and
because it is all measured in tons. It is hard to play with the figures.

Machine-building is a more fruitful field for paper successes: the
results of production are displayed in rubles. Thanks to that, everything
came out the way Stalin and Kuibyshev wanted. In his unfortunate
speech at the previous congress Kuibyshev had said that 17 million
tons of iron would determine everything else, especially machine-
building. But marvelous are Your works, Lord! You did not give
Kuibyshev all the metal he asked for, only one-third of it, and still the
growth in machine-building was as expected, to the furious envy of the
capitalist world. Production of ferrous metals doubled, but production
of machines increased thirteen times! In 1928, 703 million rubles
worth of machinery was produced;[16] in 1932, 9,300 million rubles
worth.[17] It was a miracle wrought by a Bolshevik. One might also think
that there had been huge metal reserves hidden away somewhere. But
that was not the case. Before the Five-Year Plan the country had experienced a severe metals shortage.

The explanation is simple. Industrialization was accompanied by increasing specialization of separate factories, and this led to an increase of
double counting. Prices on metals and machines increased extraordinarily (which Voroshilov vaguely referred to), and of course figures were
also exaggerated. All of this produced extra machines on paper, but not
in reality since the necessary steel and iron for them did not exist.

Not everything was quite so sad. The one aspect of the Five-Year Plan
for which the figures were wholly accurate was capital investment. When
it came to wasting the people's money, everyone strove to do it more and
faster, caring little for the utility of what was bought. Investments for
the whole Five-Year Plan were said to be 13 billion rubles, but already
in the first three years they had managed to spend 11 billion instead of
the planned 6.86. Where the rest came from it is better not to ask.[18]

The reader must not think that the whole plan was a sham. A number
of huge factories were actually put into operation, most of which we
have already mentioned. The Soviet Union began to produce some of
its own machines, including tractors, combines, trucks, tanks, planes.
It is impossible to dispute the vital necessity of industrialization. But
we must question the need for such an hysterical race, in which

elementary technical and economic rules were consciously violated and that led, naturally, to huge losses. Why were things not run by the specialists instead of the untrained politicos? Why was it so unplanned (Kuibyshev's fantasies cannot be considered planning)? Why, finally, did we have to pay such an enormous price in human life, dooming millions of people to death or suffering?

All the fuss about tempos could only fool fools. Low starting points easily produce high percentage growth figures. If you add one new factory to the only other one in operation, you get growth of 100 percent. But still it is only one factory in a huge country. Even Stalin understood that.

The Bolsheviks preferred to forget that Russia had undergone very rapid economic growth beginning in the 1890s and continuing into the First World War. Economic dislocation increased rapidly in 1918. The major cause was not the Civil War, as is commonly thought. Neither the Reds nor the Whites bombed industrial enterprises in that war. The destruction was caused by the nationalization of industry, recklessly carried out by the Bolsheviks. Almost immediately the new masters were incapable of running the economy. There followed a decade of stagnation and regression, hypocritically called a period of "reconstruction." Had it not been for nationalization and other wonders, the plants and factories—like almost everywhere else in the world—would have gone on making a profit and accumulating capital. It would not have been necessary to rob and destroy the peasantry. Great leaps would not have been needed. To put it mildly, we stood around for ten years and then hurried to make up for it in just five years, which urgently became four years. If we compare the real tempo of the Five-Year Plan to the whole period from 1921 to 1932, it immediately becomes clear: Russia would probably have industrialized faster in normal economic conditions. Everything was done, however, to make conditions as abnormal as possible, and in the end there was not much to brag about. The Bolsheviks only partially filled the vacuum they had created.

We have bored the reader with statistics (and grown weary of them ourselves), but an economic picture drawn only with words looks pale and incomplete. Probably many of the participants at the Congress saw through the statistical lies of Stalin and Kuibyshev. Maybe they felt an icy draft from the millions of graves. Maybe they seethed with anger and indignation. Stalin, the instigator, organizer, and inspirer of the whole bloody deception, understood best of all the critical nature of his position. But just let them try to get to the bottom of it and there would be less than the proverbial damp spot left, not an ink spot. Everything hinged on the long-suffering people. Also on the ignorance, disorganization, sluggishness, indecisiveness, and cowardice of the Party masses. And of course Stalin's personal dexterity, purposefulness, and unscrupulousness were central.

As we see it, Stalin's plan was to avoid discussion of recent events at the Congress and to use the forum to deafen the delegates and their constituents with false propaganda, the noise of self-glorification, and theatrical effects. Later he would get around to breaking heads, which was more practical than trying to shut mouths or tie hands. The signal to begin mass terror within the Party was the murder of Kirov and that signal was given the year of the Congress.

It is said, and it can be believed although not with complete certainty, that many delegates were considering trying to remove Stalin from his post as leader of the Party. The tactic they adopted for the purpose would not be to criticize Stalin or, God forbid, to expose him in speeches at the Congress so that the Party might still appear monolithic abroad and at home. Rather, in elections to the TSK they would cast more votes against the Great Leader. Although Stalin would be reelected (they did not expect to be able to exclude him), it would be awkward for him to remain General Secretary. They expected that Kirov would take that position.

Nothing came of the efforts. Stalin kept his wits about him, had the protocols of the balloting commission (whose chairman was V. P. Zatonsky) changed, and later cruelly avenged himself on the delegates to the Congress. Almost 80 percent of them perished in the purges.

If these rumors are true, the conspirators fell to their own cowardly and fallacious tactic. It was much easier for Stalin to falsify the balloting because during the twenty-six meetings of the Congress not one critical comment, not a hint of one, was directed at him. In those circumstances even a single vote against his election to the TSK would have seemed out of place. Instead, there was inordinate praise in every speech and enthusiastic applause throughout the entire hall.

The tactic of silence was the greatest hypocrisy. It was treason. The people were tormented, starving, crushed. They craved a champion to speak aloud of their suffering, to provide words of comfort and hope; but they did not get them.

Stalin, on the other hand, was alreay looking far ahead. He succeeded in presenting the main figures of the coming repression in a properly unfavorable light at the Congress. By various machinations he managed to get his erstwhile critics and rivals to praise him from the rostrum, to breathlessly glorify Stalinist deeds and to praise Stalin himself as the "field marshal of proletarian forces" (Bukharin's phrase). At the same time they made a show of their own mistakes, blindness, stupidity, and insincerity. Their admission sounded much more convincing than the sycophantic speeches of Stalin's accomplices.

Having played their appointed roles, the former oppositionists immediately became the first objects of the terror. They truly brought it on themselves. In 1934 they still wrote their own speeches without the assistance of the NKVD, and they confessed to everything. They recognized the historical righteousness and wisdom of comrade Stalin; they confessed to the viciousness of their own policies, which would lead to the restoration of capitalism and to strengthening the kulak (Bukharin); they confessed to a passive link with determined counterrevolutionaries (Kamenev, Zinoviev, Tomsky). How can we be surprised that they would move from such nasty things to open conflict with proletarian authority, to planning the murders of Party leaders, to communicating with fascist intelligence. "A monstrous, but natural development," wrote one publicist. Only the grave cures hunchbacks. An argument like that was sufficiently convincing for the average man, Party member or not. It did not pretend to be more. Neither did Stalin.

These public confessions destroyed the victims', shall we say, moral right to oppose their accusers to the end. Many of them were dragged out in public trials. It is interesting that the other victims, who had not been previously put through the public penitence, were harder to break. They were usually killed secretly.

Seven members of former oppositions repudiated their past from the rostrum at the Congress: Bukharin, Zinoviev, Kamenev, Lominadze, Preobrazhensky, Rykov, and Tomsky.[19] The positions of these reformed heretics were various. The three from the right opposition remained in the TSK and held more or less responsible posts: Bukharin was editor of *Izvestiia*, Rykov was Peoples' Commissar of Communications, and Tomsky was a member of the VSNKh Presidium. Lomindaze had been ejected from the TSK in 1930 and sent to Magnitogorsk to atone for his sins.

Zinoviev and Kamenev had been expelled from the Party in 1927, but they were soon restored and given work. Kamenev was made head of the Scientific-Technical Department in VSNKh and in 1929 became chairman of the Main Concessions Committee. Zinoviev became a member of the Presidium of Tsentrosoiuz.[20] In 1932 they were expelled again and sent to Siberia because when they had become acquainted with Riutin's platform through Sten, they had not informed the TSK. In 1933 they suddenly showed up in Moscow and after talks with Stalin and Kaganovich were reinstated in the Party. The main condition was their confession at the Congress. Preobrazhensky's situation was similar. He had been expelled in 1927, admitted his error in 1929, was expelled two years later and readmitted in 1933.

The oppositionists' speeches were chock-full of hypocrisy and self-abasement. They all immoderately exalted Stalin. Bukharin, Zinoviev, and Kamenev were at their most repulsive.

Bukharin led the procession of penitents. He began by describing his complete political bankruptcy:

> the rights, to whom I belonged, had a different *political* line, a line against full-time socialist offensive, against a new attack on capitalist elements . . . it was in fact against the forced development of *industrialization* . . . against the extraordinary and bitter struggle with the *kulaks*, a struggle that was later exemplified by the slogan, "liquidation of the kulaks as a class". . . .
>
> It is clear that *precisely because* of this, that group inevitably became the center of gravity for all forces that fought against the socialist offensive. . . .[21]

We, Bukharin said, fought with the Party regime, with

> comrade Stalin as the supreme spokesman and inspirer of the Party line, Stalin who won the inner-Party struggle on the *profoundly principled basis of Leninist policy*, and specifically on that basis received the warm support of the overwhelming, the utterly overwhelming mass of the Party and the working class. . . .
>
> The decisive destruction of that [Bukharinist, rightist] opposition, just like the destruction of the Trotskyite and so-called Leningrad opposition, was a *necessary precondition* to the successful and victorious development of the socialist offensive.

Therefore

the duty of every member of the Party is to struggle with all anti-Party groups, actively and mercilessly struggle, regardless of whatever personal ties and relations there may be, to rally around the TSK, to rally around comrade Stalin as the personal embodiment of the mind and will of the Party, its leader, its theoretical and practical great leader.

Along the way Bukharin lashed out at all of the most recent groups that "ever faster and more consistently have slipped into counterrevolution," and disowned "my former pupils, who have received their just punishment." He had in mind first of all Slepkov, who was imprisoned with Riutin.

Having finished with his errors, self-flagellation, and treachery, Bukharin reminded his listeners that he was a prominent theoretician and was still an active member of the Academy of Sciences. With figures and citations in hand he spoke of the remarkable successes of the Soviet economy, especially of agriculture.

In the recent past Bukharin had also been an international figure, as leader of the Comintern. This had brought him into contact with the foreign policy of Stalin's government, which he owned to be magnificent. There followed a long denunciation with extensive excerpts from foreign sources of Hitler; of Spengler, the ideologue of fascism; of its poet Yost; and also of the Japanese militarists. Bukharin concluded:

> We are the only country that embodies the progressive forces of history. Our Party and comrade Stalin personally are powerful heralds not only of *economic*, but also of *technical* and *scientific* progress on our planet. We are going to battle for the fate of *mankind*. For that we need unity, unity, and more unity.
>
> Down with all disorganizers.
>
> Long live our Party, that great fighting fraternity, a fraternity of tempered warriors as hard as steel, of brave revolutionaries, who will win all victories under the leadership of the glorious field marshal of the proletarian forces, the best of the best—comrade Stalin (applause).

Zinoviev and Kamenev, the Dobchinsky and Bobchinsky[22] of the Bolshevik Revolution, were for some reason let loose during the discussion of the reports on the Five-Year Plan, although they did not mention that topic at all.

Zinoviev did not follow Bukharin's example. He did not even bother to pretend to make a report, but spoke only of his errors:

> I must, it would seem, and it's my own fault, entirely my fault, speak only of errors and illustrate them by my own example, to present myself as living illustration of those deviations, those infidelities, those errors and scandalous diversions from Leninism, in battle with which the Party has achieved those successes to which the whole world attentively turns a watchful eye.
>
> No one can say that I committed any one specific political error. That is half the trouble. I committed a chain of errors, a chain in which one link was unavoidably attached to another. I had the temerity to impose on the Party my own personal understanding of Leninism, my own particular understanding of "the philosophy of an epoch."[23]

He went on in the same vein, in the same long phrases, as if he were translating from bad German.

Appropriately and inappropriately, Zinoviev fervently and repeatedly bowed deeply to Stalin:

> Vladimir Ilich said of Engels that he belonged to the number of rare, extremely rare writers and thinkers, whose works you can reread many times, every time finding some new wealth of content. Comrade Stalin's work undoubtedly belongs to this class of works. All of you have done this long ago, done what I have only recently come to. I read and reread his fundamental works, which are the quintessence of Leninism in this epoch, which are the algebra of communist work in the course of all history. . . . Comrade Stalin's report, which entered the treasury of world communism at the moment it was delivered here . . . deserves to be called the second program of the Party.

Stalin, like an attentive mother, always tried to keep Zinoviev from misbehavior:

> after I was readmitted to the Party the first time. I once heard from the mouth of comrade Stalin the following comment. He told me: "You have been hurt and are being hurt in the eyes of the Party not so much by fundamental errors, as by your deviousness in relation to the Party over many years." (Many cries of "Right, properly

said!'') Absolutely right, comrades! That is how it was. And I hope that I have now thoroughly understood that comment.

Zinoviev confessed with gusto the sin of his failure to denounce:

> When Sten showed me the double-dyed, kulak, counterrevolutionary, rightist platform, instead of fulfilling the most elementary obligation of a member of the Bolshevik Party, instead of doing that, instead of demanding that Sten himself immediately inform the Central Committee of our Party of all that he knew, instead of that I kept Sten's secret, which in fact turned out to be the conspiracy of Riutin and company, of the whole group, which is not worth mentioning from this rostrum.
>
> Comrades, it would seem, I was punished by the Party a second time and entirely deservedly. And, comrades, I must speak of this entirely candidly, as I will speak always and everywhere, that this was my most serious mistake up till now.

Long-winded and inspired, the orator heaped filth on Trotsky. Nor did he spare himself. Again and again he praised Stalin. At the end he fell to his knees:

> I have entirely and finally understood that if it were not for that leadership, for those iron cadres, which have led the Party into battle against all oppositions, then the Party, the country, the working class, Lenin's plans and the Revolution itself would be threatened by greater dangers than they are. That leadership, which is revered by the people of our country and the working class, by all of the best people of our country and the working class of the whole world, saved us from that danger (applause).

(In his sycophantic zeal Zinoviev did not notice that he insulted the working class by excluding it from the ranks of the "best people of our country." Neither, incidentally, did his listeners.)

Kamenev, as in past years, followed Zinoviev's line: "I have the sad duty at this congress of victors to present a chronicle of defeats, a demonstration of that chain of efforts, delusions and crimes to which every group and every individual is doomed who separates himself from the great teachings of Marx-Engels, of Lenin-Stalin, from the collective life of the party, from the directives of its leading institutions."[24]

On the Riutin group: "the ideology of the Riutinists is as sawed-off as the shotguns the kulaks fired at the Communists carrying out collectivization. . . . Different, more material weapons of influence were needed here, and they were applied to the very members of that group, and to their accomplices and protectors, and entirely properly and justly they were applied to me."[25]

Kamenev recalled an episode of 1928 when Bukharin, that man of principle, having just worked so hard to expel the Trotskyite-Zinovievite opposition from the Party, appealed to him, defeated and powerless as he was, to form a bloc against Stalin. Kamenev, by the way, wasted no time informing the Central Committee and was quickly reinstated in the Party. Remembering that, he enjoyed covering the rightists with mud.

Kamenev did not spare repentance either, understanding that he would not be able to overdo it. He said, "Comrades, I have expressed my deep regret for the mistakes I have made (*Voice*: 'You must not only express yourself, but justify yourself in the matter!') I want to say from this rostrum that I consider the Kamenev, who from 1925 to 1933 fought with the Party and its leadership, a political corpse, and that I wish to go forward dragging behind myself in the biblical (excuse me) expression that old skin (laughter)." Toward the end came the obligatory hallelujah: "Long live our socialist country! Long live our, *our* great leader and commander comrade Stalin! (applause)."

The Congress listened attentively to the speeches of Bukharin, Kamenev, and Zinoviev (only Kamenev was cued once and reminded of the time limit). They left the rostrum to applause. It would seem that sentimental memories, remnants of their former fame, still clung to their names. It must be admitted that they spoke well and skillfully. But the content of the speeches was repugnant: the collapse of personality, denial of convictions, the ability to admit to errors that they had not made, the attempt to worm their way into the audience's good graces, to assume the tone of the collective psychosis, their desire to ignore facts were all thoroughly hypocritical and false.

Rykov and Tomsky were received differently. At the Fourteenth and Fifteenth Congresses Aleksei Ivanovich Rykov was met with prolonged applause and seen off with a thunderous ovation and the singing of the Party's anthem. Now the audience was cold and unfriendly. Twice he was interrupted to be reminded of regulations. Listeners yelled out rudely.

> By that member of the Party leadership [he said], who spoke out to defend that thesis of building socialism in one country. . . .

[Voice: That was comrade Stalin!] I meant to describe the role of comrade Stalin in the period immediately after Vladimir Ilich's death. [Voice from the hall: We know without your telling us!]

The comrades did not accept his repentence. Peters, the well-known Chekist, called out, "He has talked for an hour without saying anything!" Rykov did not wait for applause.

Neither was there applause for Tomsky, a recognized buffoon who has lost the wit he once had. He was received with extreme hostility. Peters twice demanded that he tell about Eismont and Smirnov, and Acting Chairman Postyshev cut Tomsky short, although he had not been speaking long: "Comrade Tomsky, it is time to finish." Obviously upset, Tomsky hastened to put distance between himself and his arrested friend: "The Party correctly judged my error, my closeness to Smirnov, which gave the counterrevolutionary Eismont-Smirnov group the opportunity and the basis to take refuge behind my name." Then he despondently descended from the rostrum.

Kirov spoke after Tomsky and offered a conclusion to the speeches of the rightists; he sneeringly compared the three former Politburo members to transport drivers.

> What is there left to do to all these people, who until today were on the train? (Applause, laughter.)
>
> It would seem, comrades, that they were trying to push their way into the general celebration, to get back into step with our music, to join in our enthusiasm. But no matter how they try, it doesn't come off. (Applause, laughter.)
>
> Take Bukharin, for example. In my opinion he sang as if from music, but his voice just wasn't the same. (Laughter, applause.) To say nothing of comrade Rykov and comrade Tomsky. . . .[26]

Kirov said there was no place for the penitents in the higher leadership: "And it seems to me, I do not wish to be a prophet, but it will be some time before this host of transport drivers joins our communist army (applause)."

Under the circumstances there was no need to prophesy. All had been already decided. The Rights were not returned to the general staff. Quite the opposite, they were demoted. At the Congress they were elected not members but candidate members of the TSK.

Kirov still could not foresee his fate. Only ten months later he would be murdered on Stalin's orders. But now he was trying as hard as he could to please the great leader. His speech was specially titled "The Report of Comrade Stalin—The Program of All Our Work." Kirov suggested that instead of approving, as usual, a detailed resolution on the political report of the тsк, the Congress approve Stalin's report in toto and accept its proposals to be carried out as Party law. In a joyous outburst the delegates jumped to their feet. Stalin came out on the platform only to decline, from modesty, a final word and to give the signal for a tremendous ovation, which turned into the singing of the "Internationale," at the end of which the ovation broke out with renewed vigor. When this collective demonstration quieted, Khrushchev formally repeated Kirov's suggestion on behalf of the Moscow, Leningrad, and Ukrainian delegations. It was approved enthusiastically and became a customary part of all later congresses.

Let us return briefly to the former oppositionists. The Congress listened politely to the insignificant Lominadze. He left to applause. They were harder on Preobrazhensky. He made a pitiful impression. Of the former polemicist and theoretician there remained only ruins. Although his theory of pitiless exploitation of the peasantry ("primary socialist accumulation") had become the foundation stone of official economic policy, it was impermissible to speak of it. All that remained for him was to cry into his vest, which had already gone out of Party style. Preobrazhensky tearfully repented. He smeared his Trotskyite past, Trotsky himself, and his past mistakes with the blackest paint. He concluded with a deliberately stupid passage calculated to arouse indulgence and a favorable response:

> at the present time, more than ever I feel, more than ever I recognize the truth of the worker who advised me: if you don't thoroughly understand something, go with the Party, vote with Ilich. So much more, comrades, now when I am reexamining everything, when I have sufficiently recognized all my mistakes, I repeat these words of the worker to myself in a different stage of the Revolution and say: vote with comrade Stalin, you won't be mistaken.[27]

The hall was silent. The trick did not work. Not long after, Kabakov, possibly with prompting, rebuked him from the rostrum:

> fundamentally wrong and inappropriate was the statement by Preobrazhensky, when he said that he had to act as had the worker

who apparently voted blindly for comrade Lenin's theses. It is untrue that the program put forth by Lenin and Stalin was ever accepted by workers who voted for those theses blindly. The workers voted for the theses of Lenin-Stalin then, as they do now, enthusiastically and with conviction. They accept enthusiastically the program presented at the Seventeenth Congress by comrade Stalin because it expresses the proletarian program, the hopes and aspirations of the working class of the whole world. When a man who pretends to have achieved a certain theoretical level comes out on this rostrum and says that he has to vote for these theses blindly, then let us say plainly that this expresses entirely and thoroughly the spinelessness of a rotten intellectual.[28]

The speeches of Stalin's broken opponents were but drops in the swollen stream. The overwhelming majority of the remaining orators delivered speeches cut from a single pattern. Each began with a description of the unbearable pride he experienced looking at the mighty successes and victories gained under the wise leadership. Then, coming back to earth, each spoke of particular problems, some of which appeared to be unprecedented disorders. This was especially true of speeches dealing with railroads and industry. Very sensitive agrarian themes were treated more gingerly. Interestingly, this was the last Congress at which the negative sides of reality were dealt with so openly. In conclusion, the speakers invariably soared to rarefied heights of pure optimism and exclaimed wishes for health and long life.

There were comic interludes in the great spectacle. One was played by the respected revolutionary Gleb Krzhizhanovsky. Having clambered up onto the platform, he began by saying he had been a member of the party for forty-two years.[29] Then, shaking with tender emotion, he revealed other astonishing things. There was no need to be distressed, he told his comrades, that we had not yet outdistanced everyone else in the world. Bolsheviks possessed their own arithmetic and physics. "Every kilowatt of our station is twice as strong as its foreign counterpart." That was guaranteed by the authority of the Academy of Sciences. And that was little enough. In our socialist conditions every tractor has "six times the useful strength of tractors used by, say, farmers in the North American United States." Therefore the 160,000 tractors enumerated at the end of the second Five-Year Plan were equal to one million of theirs.[30]

Tukhachevsky's speech did not stand out at the Congress, but we examine it because it helps clarify some subtleties of the Army's relationship with Stalin. Most of the speech was routine. He spoke of the needs of the Red Army and of pretensions about industrialization. But it began:

> The technical might of the Red Army grew in step with the construction of our industrial base. Comrade Voroshilov has reported on that with clarity and detail. . . .
>
> I want to add to that, that in the development of our technical might comrade Stalin not only played a general guiding role but also took a direct and daily part in selecting the necessary types of weapons and in putting them into production. Comrade Stalin not only outlined the general tasks, especially concerning equipping the Army with an air force, tanks, and long-range and rapid-firing artillery of the most modern sort, but he met with the organizers of production and worked out the practical and successful plans of production. . . . This work, this leadership created that technical might, which the Red Army possesses and which you will see again on parade.[31]

Amazingly, Tukhachevsky gave Stalin credit not only for setting out the general tasks, but also for personally creating the technical might of the RKKA. It was as if none of the rest had happened: the 1927 report on the necessity to technically rearm the Army, which was twice rejected and ridiculed by Stalin, did not exist. Nor did the retirements of 1928, nor the squabbles, insults, and intrigues that invariably accompanied any discussion of military questions with the General Secretary.[32]

Of course Tukhachevsky did not burn with love for Stalin. He, too, was a master strategist and tactician. Tukhachevsky accomplished a deep encircling movement and licked the Great Leader in an undefended sector. It is also possible that he was following the popular aphorism, "Military discipline is the ability to show the chief that you are stupider than he." Not only Stalin believed that.

The Congress was long and luxurious. The delegates were well entertained and not only in Moscow's theaters. On January 31 there was a mass meeting on Red Square, after which there passed before the delegates and guests of the Congress "a procession of workers from the plants and factories and the employees of the regions of Moscow, in which military units participated." There was a parade of the troops of the Moscow garrison at noon on February 9, and in the evening there were elections to the TSK. It is hard to decide whether the military was marched past the delegates on the eve of the elections to calm, to encourage, or to frighten.

All worked out according to Stalin's plan. One after another, people pretending to be masters of the country and the future masters of the world climbed onto the rostrum to proclaim boundless praise: Stalin did this . . . Stalin did that . . . Stalin indicated . . . Stalin taught . . . Long live Stalin.

They thought they were making history. Stalin declined to make concluding remarks and grinned in his mustache. For him they were already dead men. In his heart he had already buried them. He had reserved no place for them in the earthly utopia they were exalting.

IV

Conspiracy Against the RKKA

Up to now we have spoken of Caligula as a princeps.
It remains to discuss him as a monster.
—Suetonius

There is a commandment to forgive our enemies,
but there is no commandment to forgive our friends.
—L. Medici

Some comrades think that repression is the main thing in the
advance of socialism, and if repression does not increase,
there is no advance. Is that so? Of course it is not so.
—Stalin

Events after they have occurred become subjects of investigation. Historians want to know what caused Napoleon to lead the Grande Armée on its catastrophic march to Moscow. Defending their opinions they polemicize bitterly, suggest reasons, cite facts. Even if they, as is usually the case, do not find a single formula, still the general understanding of history is enriched with points of view and conceptions.

The destruction of the Red Army was, in its consequences for the nation, Stalin's most important act. To date it has been very little researched. In the preceding parts of this book we have tried to describe the path that led to this catastrophe. Now we will talk of the catastrophe itself.

Without access to the most important documents we will not be able to discuss the problems with the depth we would like. We will try to reestablish the course of events and suggest probable causes. That is all that can be done today.

17 The Political Background: Coup d'État

They unleashed it themselves
trying to lead, to master the country,
and 1937 came
not just misfortune but punishment.
— Korzhavin

After the Seventeenth Congress, nothing apparently threatened Stalin's position at the pinnacle of power. Rivals and enemies had been politically and organizationally destroyed. They had admitted their defeat and lost their influence. The cult of the Great Leader flowered profusely. References to his utterances and toasts in his honor became an obligatory part of every public speech on any topic. Collectivization was accomplished. Stalin's five-year plans were being fulfilled at top speed. The international position of the country was sufficiently secure. The reorganization had made the Red Army one of the best in Europe.

There were difficulties, however. True, as Stalin had said, "Our problems are such that they *themselves contain the possibility for overcoming them . . . they give us the basis for overcoming them.*"[1] Still the problems remained. Since 1929 the country had experienced a severe supply crisis. In 1935 the system of rationing cards was ended; but some products, particularly meat, were still in very short supply. The predominance of heavy industry and the demise of the private entrepreneur had led to deficits of consumer goods. The quality of goods was extremely poor. Industry was constantly short of metals and other materials, not to mention machinery. Plans were chronically underfilled in ferrous metals, energy, and machine construction. Available capital did not cover the demands of huge capital-intensive projects. The government resorted to printing money, which caused inflation.

In 1934 the problems of power became especially acute. Stalin could understand that, although he had achieved supreme power, it was by no means guaranteed. The economic failures of the first Five-Year Plan, the dissatisfaction of the population, the opposition's attacks of

1930–33, the fluctuation of moods at the Seventeenth Congress, all revealed the vulnerability of Stalin's position. Power, achieved at the cost of enormous efforts with the help of painstaking intrigue and risky provocations, could easily be lost in a day. If a rebellious plenum or a disobedient congress should suddenly refuse to accept black as white and should remove Stalin from his post, he would immediately turn into a pitiful oppositionist, a former great leader, a toothless lion, a general without an army.

The fact that the opposition's efforts, however feeble, continued between the Sixteenth and Seventeenth Congresses, after the victory over his most powerful opponents, Bukharin's group, must have put Stalin on his guard. As long as thoughts were still stirring in Party minds, he could not sleep soundly. There was little comfort in the apparent fact that the centers of opposition were weak and their methods resembled partisan warfare. Stalin could and did see in these desperate hit-and-run attacks the germs of more general dissatisfaction, nuclei around which that dissatisfaction could be consolidated. Therefore his reprisals came quickly and sharply, without discussions and organizational maneuverings. It is very likely that it was precisely these minor manifestations of insignificant opposition that finally set Stalin on the course of mass terror within the Party.

Three such little attacks are known. The first occurred in 1930. Shortly after the Congress, Syrtsov[2] and Lominadze, supported by the Komsomol leader Shatskin, spoke out at a plenum of the TSK against Stalin's economic policy, which they labeled "Potemkin industrialization." Stalin was able to take care of them immediately. On December 1, by a decision of the TSK and the TSKK, without a plenum, Syrtsov and Lominadze were declared a "right-leftist group," were expelled from the TSK, and removed from their posts. Syrtsov had been chairman of the Council of the National Economy of the RSFSR, where he had just replaced Rykov.

The second attack occurred two years later. The year 1932 was marked by the appearance of the Riutin-Slepkov group. These were apprentices to Bukharin and in their time had worked heroically to destroy various oppositions. Stalin had hardly begun to go after the rightists when Riutin began to regret the passing of inner-party democracy. An extensive program was worked out that called for a softening of the party regime, policy changes (including policy toward the peasantry), and the removal of Stalin. The program had hardly made its way into Party circles when leaders of the rightists, led by Bukharin, hastened to dissociate themselves from it. Stalin took the case to court, but he did not get Riutin's head. The majority of the Politburo members preferred not to execute their recent comrade. There are rumors that Kuibyshev, Ordzhonikidze, and Kirov offered active resistance and were supported by Kosior and Kalinin. Voroshilov, Andreev, and Molotov took a temporizing position, while Kaganovich alone remained loyal to Stalin. All three opponents of terror were themselves soon dispatched: Kirov on December 1, 1934, Kuibyshev on January 25, 1935, Ordzhonikidze slightly later, on February 18, 1937. Kosior also perished, but later and in connection with other, Ukrainian, matters. Kalinin quickly learned to behave, as did his vacillating comrades. Nonetheless, in 1932 the Riutinists got only ten-year sentences, which did not keep them from disappearing in the bowels of the NKVD. Until the Great Purge got under way, any connection with the Riutin group, real or imagined, was certain cause for reprisal. Having known of the Riutin program and not having denounced it was cause for expulsion from the Party at the very least.

The third incident concerned the Eismont–A. P. Smirnov–Tolmachev group, which had barely reared its head at the end of 1932. These men, too, were unhappy with Stalin's violence and desired a change. A joint plenum of the TSK and TSKK, meeting January 7–12, 1933, expelled them from the Party. It was not announced in the press. There followed, as usual, a secret trial, long sentences, and death.

As we have seen in this brief digression, there were real difficulties, which did, however, contain the means for their own liquidation. After the Seventeenth Congress Stalin could no longer be content merely to hold off the attacks of the disgruntled. He understood that the next Congress might be his last.

It was impossible in Soviet conditions to establish a mechanism for lifelong rule, that is, a monarchy or legalized dictatorship. Stalin was sufficiently practical not to try to copy Bonaparte's career.

Stalin deserves some sympathy. His way was much harder than that of Mussolini or Hitler. Their power was based on nationalism and unquestionable personal authority ("the word of the leader is the highest law"), which had a certain mystical quality. It is even easier for the leaders of the young states of the "Third World" today, who act in a historical and cultural vacuum. They need no camouflage. Comrade (or Mr.?) Mobutu Sese Seko Kuku Ngbendu Va Za Banga is called Chairman-Founder of the National Movement of Revolution. In a central African republic another joker, an ex-sergeant proclaimed himself emperor and his little country, with a population less than 2 million, an empire. It would be difficult even to imagine such escapades in the USSR. From the pre-Stalinist period there remained the heritage of centuries of history, three revolutions, official doctrine, and a ruling party. Traditions, people, books all interfered. They were all falsified, changed until they were unrecognizable, and destroyed. But it was impossible to carry this process to completion; something still remained.

There was another way. The political atmosphere could be changed in such a way as to remove all current pretenders to power, real and potential. More than that, conditions had to be created in which such people could not ever appear in the future. In such a case there would be no need to change the government structure, the national emblem, anthem, or flag. It was necessary only to widen the geography of terror, to include the Bolshevik Party within it, and to maximize centralization, concentrating in one man's hands all aspects of state-political life. Both these means had long been within the grasp of Soviet authorities. It is not surprising that Stalin resorted to them to pursue his personal goals.

The danger for the country was not that Stalin had such goals. Aspiration to power and megalomania greatly inflame the imagination, and people with such psychic constitutions are found in every society — in thousandth parts of a percent. Russia's tragedy was that this nightmare came true. The dreams of a paranoid maniac, rather than becoming a subject for psychiatric work, determined the life of the country for two decades. Everyone who is not indifferent to the fate of the Motherland should ask himself the heartrending question why it happened.

Until the mid-1930s the punitive functions of Soviet power were carried out within definite bounds. At the same time the continuity of repression was never disturbed. True, from the moment of the victory of the Stalin-Bukharin coalition at the Fifteenth Congress, the scale and tempo of arrests had steadily, although slowly at first, increased. Late in 1927 and early in 1928, hundreds of Trotskyites were sent into exile. In 1928, after the Shakhty affair, open season was declared on technical specialists and was carried out under the slogan of "struggle with wrecking." The trial of the Industrial Party (Prompartia), which took place in 1930, led to the sentencing of a number of prominent engineers. The next year important economists and finance experts were tried in the Menshevik trial. The hunt for technicians, whom the country vitally needed, continued, but now purposefully. The Belomor-Baltic Canal was being constructed, actually being dug by hand. Because of it a large contingent of highly qualified hydrotechnicians fell into the hands of the OGPU, which was in charge of the project. The absolutely useless canal was being dug with feverish haste in the most unfavorable and difficult conditions, and the project cost tens of thousands of lives. Work was done almost exclusively by prisoners under the direction of Chekists. This building of the Egyptian pyramids was passed off as the rehabilitation through labor of "socially close" criminals. Political prisoners, as socially distant and foreign, had to perish without the joyful prospect of rebirth. The building of the Moscow-Volga Canal was carried out in the same way.

From 1929 to 1933 the system of repression displayed monstrous energy. Under the pretext of "dekulakization" millions of peasants were deported or shot. Propagandists babbled about destroying the kulaks as a class, while what was actually going on was the intentional physical destruction of the most enterprising and industrious peasants. The number of victims cannot be known precisely. Together with those who died of the unprecedented famine that accompanied collectivization, they may have totalled more than 15 million.

The paradelike spectacle of the Seventeenth Congress signaled the end of that period. Further repression directly served the aims of the state revolution as conceived by Stalin. The signal was given on December 1, 1934, with the death of Kirov. On that day, or according to some sources on the preceding day, the TSIK passed a law that provided for an accelerated and simplified investigation and trial of enemies of the people. Sentences could be carried out within forty-eight hours of being passed. Appeal was not permitted. It should be noted that this occurred in peacetime and in the absence of any major social disturbances, such as mutinies or rebellions. Even during the Civil War people sentenced to death could ask for pardon.[3]

Not losing a minute, Stalin hastened to avenge himself on his recent rivals in the Politburo. Kamenev and Zinoviev, since the latter had extensive contacts in Leningrad, were named conspirators in the murder of Kirov. The imaginary terrorist organization was for some reason called the "Moscow center." I. Evdokimov and several others were also implicated. The trial was conducted behind closed doors, but it limped along uneventfully and ended unsuccessfully for its organizers. Zinoviev and Kamenev repented at length for their political errors, as they had a year earlier at the Congress; but they categorically denied having taken any part in the terror. The confusion was great, and the sentences were laughable. Zinoviev and Evdokimov got ten years' and Kamenev five years' imprisonment. Kamenev was subsequently tried again on July 27, 1935, and given a ten-year term. The charge was that while he was in prison he used his brother's wife, who worked in the Kremlin hospital, to organize an attempt on Stalin's life; the attempt was of course unsuccessful.

The absence of confessions weakened Stalin's position in the Politburo where Kuibyshev and Ordzhonikidze still opposed the use of extreme measures against Party leaders or even against former leaders. Stalin dealt with the first of them immediately. The sentencing of the Moscow center was made public on January 18. On January 25 Kuibyshev was officially mourned after his untimely demise. During the trial of Bukharin in 1938 the public learned that Kuibyshev had been medically murdered. Yagoda had ordered his death, Kuibyshev's secretary Maksimov-Dikovsky had organized it, and his doctors Levin and Pletnev had carried it out. In such cases it was usually Stalin who let the cat out of the bag, but others were accused of the crimes.[4] All telephone connections to the office of the seriously ill Kuibyshev had been severed. When his heart attack began, Maksimov could not call the medical department in the Kremlin. Nor could he decide to leave to get help, for there was no one nearby to stay with Kuibyshev. Finally he took Kuibyshev home.[5] Only an hour or so after the attack did Maksimov get medical help. Then they either administered the necessary medicine, or the delay had been sufficient. In any case he soon died. It is interesting that Maksimov's testimony at the trial largely corroborates this version. The misfire with Zinoviev and Kamenev held up the development of the campaign. Stalin had good reason to be upset with the NKVD and its chief G. Yagoda. The organs had everything needed in their hands, but they had not gotten the results.

The Great Leader of the world proletariat had to take care of things himself. Another trial was prepared. This time the fallen Bolshevik leaders were put on trial in the proper setting. Fourteen others were tried with them, including Evdokimov (a former secretary of the TsK) again and I. N. Smirnov (a former member of the TsK), a prominent associate of Trotsky. The political geography of the trial was broadened. This was advertised not as a trial of isolated conspirators but of a powerful, far-flung organization, the Trotskyite-Zinovievite terrorist center. They were not just former leaders who stopped at nothing, including political murders, to regain their commanding positions. Things were much more serious. These were agents in a bitter class war, former oppositionists, now enemies of the people, who had behind them the remnants of the exploiters and foreign patrons, the fascists.

This was the first in a series of show trials. Its success was carefully prepared for. First of all, the notion was rejected that the guilt of the accused had to be proven. The Procurator General A. Vyshinsky proclaimed that the presumption of innocence was a bourgeois prejudice, for which he was made a member of the Academy of Sciences. Now it was enough that during the preliminary investigation, while he was entirely in the power of the NKVD, a citizen confess to being an enemy of the people. (Other suspects sometimes did so also, but usually the confession and NKVD custody went together.) He would then automatically fall under the extraordinary law. After that he would be tried in an extrajudicial procedure (which was a widely used phrase in those years). Other evidence of guilt was not required; therefore no material evidence was presented at the trials.

Vyshinsky widely expanded the concept of criminal conspiracy and complicity. People who had not even known of one another's existence until the investigation or trial, but who had allegedly acted on orders from a single center, were now defined as accomplices. This made it possible to select a useful combination of victims.

The investigator had but one task—to extract from the prisoner a confession of guilt that had already been worked out by the NKVD. They could use any means to their ends, including torture. In response to a secret directive from Stalin the TSIK legalized physical torture in 1936. They managed, for example, to break I. N. Smirnov, a man of strong will and personal courage. They "refreshed" him with ice baths until he lost all interest in living. He acted detached and indifferent at the trial and shrugged off Vyshinsky's questioning: "You need a leader? I'll be your leader. . . ."

Self-slander was the main weapon of the prosecution, but not its only one. The accused were forced to slander one another as well. This cross-pollination yielded bountiful fruit. Entirely isolated from the outside world, a man soon learned that he had nowhere to go. If he insisted on his innocence, he would be convicted by the testimony of other prisoners; these might be old friends, comrades of the underground and fronts, or, often, complete strangers. The investigators persuaded him that such evidence was sufficiently damning for the court and that only candid repentance, that is, accepting the NKVD version, could ameliorate the sentence. All of that was of course combined with torture. Most such prisoners were unable to stay out of the devilish trap. To the very stubborn other pressures were brought to bear: the families of some were threatened; others were persuaded to give evidence as an act of Party discipline (strange as it may seem, this was from time to time effective).

All these crushing pressures proved nonetheless to be insufficient at first in the preparations for a new Zinoviev trial. It is said that Zinoviev and Kamenev resisted all pressures to accept the charge of organizing terror, because it supposedly contradicted their Marxist convictions. That put Stalin in a difficult position. He could not permit a second failure. But Josef Vissarionovich was not the sort to shrink from problems. It wasn't only coincidence that the song "who desires shall achieve, who seeks will always find . . ." was popular at the time. Stalin sought a way to win. He sent his friend Ordzhonikidze to see the stubborn men.[6] They would not have spoken with any of the other current members of the Politburo—Molotov, Kaganovich, Voroshilov, or Mikoyan. On Stalin's orders Sergo told them roughly the following: You have lost. Stalin's line is victorious on all fronts; you said so yourselves at the Congress. Now the Party desperately needs a dramatic political trial to help it in its struggle with hidden enemies. If you do not admit to terror, you will be liquidated without a trial, and your families will not be spared. If you confess, you will be given the mandatory sentence, execution by shooting, but your lives will be spared, and your families will not be harmed. I guarantee that on my word as a Bolshevik.

After long hesitation Zinoviev and Kamenev accepted the deal. They behaved loyally at the trial. All the accused were sentenced to be shot—and they were executed.

One other novelty was tried out during that trial. The accused named as accomplices people who were still at liberty, which served as an excuse to bring them to justice. Serebriakov and Preobrazhensky suffered that fate in August 1936. Cases were quickly worked up against them. A short while later Sokolnikov and others were linked with them. Allusions to the complicity of the rightists provoked anguished cries from the press. The same recurred in January 1937. The question of their prosecution was decided at the February-March plenum of the TSK.[7]

The long-winded confessions and mutual accusations gave the Moscow trials a certain degree of verisimilitude, especially in the eyes of Western observers sympathetic to the USSR. Even an old hand like Leon Feuchtwanger fell for the trap. To fortify the impression, regular provocateurs of the NKVD were included among the accused. They readily gave the needed testimony, and then they were executed with the rest.[8]

Participating in the rehearsals for the August show cost Ordzhonikidze his life. Fiery Bolshevik that Sergo was, he could not free himself of some bourgeois prejudices. When he gave the prisoners his word as a revolutionary, he was sincere and meant to keep it. In February 1937 he learned that Zinoviev and Kamenev had been killed nonetheless. He had an angry disagreement with Stalin. The Great Leader understood that his old comrade was a lost man, stubborn in his misconceptions. A week before the opening of a very important plenum of the TSK, of Feburary 18, Ordzhonikidze was shot by a Chekist in the office of his Kremlin apartment.[9] Stalin announced to members of the Politburo in top secret that Ordzhonikidze had cracked under the pressure of the struggle and had killed himself. To preserve his good Bolshevik name it was decided to announce to the nation that he had died unexpectedly of a heart attack.

The first trial achieved its goal. The atmosphere in the country became intense. Stalin considered the moment opportune to seize the punitive organs, all the more so since during his absence on vacation to the south there had been indecisive wavering in the Moscow leadership. Nikolai Ezhov, secretary of the TSK, who had accumulated his power in the bowels of the secret Stalin chancellery, was made head of the NKVD. The smooth success of the August trial did not save Yagoda. His replacement had been foreordained by a telegram from Stalin and Zhdanov.[10]

Ezhov was the ideal man for the task assigned him. In contrast to Menzhinsky and Yagoda he did not have a distinguished revolutionary past or corresponding ambitions. Raised by Stalin's hands, he viewed the world through Stalin's eyes. In bloodthirstiness and suspicion he surpassed even his patron.

The tempo of persecution accelerated. The trial of the parallel terrorist center (Piatakov, Sokolnikov, Serebriakov, and Radek) began in January 1937. The country was told that the enemy had a gigantic organization with many branches to carry on in case one should fail. Hints, which were first made in August, that military people had participated in the plots were repeated more strongly here. (We will speak of that in detail below.) The trials' techniques were improved. Lawyers were now permitted to participate. Sentences were varied; some defendants received prison sentences rather than being shot. A well-rehearsed public raged in the papers and at meetings. Western leftists applauded.

Now the offensive could be opened along the whole front. It remained only to get formal approval from the country's high court. It is said that the TSK turned Stalin down in September 1936. Apparently by spring the evidence presented was sufficient. After meeting for a week the Party priests gave Stalin carte blanche for a campaign of terror. The country was put under an unannounced state of emergency. Postyshev tried to protest, but Stalin leaned on him, and the others preferred to remain silent. Myopic, never able to think for themselves, overwhelmed by the roar of propaganda, they pronounced a death sentence for themselves and for millions of their countrymen.

After the February-March plenum all the semaphores on Stalin's way to absolute power had been raised. He had won in the center by demoralizing the Party leadership, taking control of the NKVD, and frightening the government. The state revolution was a fait accompli. The repression spread far and wide to force acceptance of the new order.

There was still one force in the country that Stalin could leave unsubdued only at risk of his own neck. That was the Army. Before we describe the circumstance of its destruction, we must first make a necessary digression.

It is very tempting to blame the terror of the 1930s on a single individual, Stalin. We would be wrong to do so, however. Frequent reference to his name was necessary only to make the telling of the story easier. There is too much that suggests that the regime established by Stalin was a natural stage in the development of Bolshevism.

The roots of the Stalin dictatorship, as it became in 1936–38 and remained until 1953, must be sought first of all (but not exclusively) in the human material from which the Bolshevik Party was composed. The Tolstoyans did not flock to the Bolsheviks; nor would they have been welcome. The Bolsheviks were always distinguished by their desire to solve all social problems by a single blow, by violence and terror. Therefore it was natural that the man who made terror a daily part of state policy and perfected hypocrisy as an ideology was able to keep himself at the pinnacle of power for so long. Violence in the name of future justice and dishonesty for the sake of narrow Party interest were from its first days the alpha and omega of the regime. Blaming it all on Stalin explains very little. Stalin was great because he relied only on these principles. He never tied his hands with collateral considerations or sentimental memories. He relied not on specific people but on the basic psychology of his Party.

His reliance was justified. The mass of the Party accepted and supported the terror. Even those who fell under the NKVD's wheels remained faithful to the Bolshevik ideal and Stalin's policy to the end. In the name of higher Party interests they gave false testimony, which proved fatal to themselves and others. They died with the Party's name on their lips. It is terrible to say, but they deserved their fate.

Stalin not only wrote the script and directed the terror. Knowing from the history of the French Revolution that instigators of slaughter usually lost their heads, he feared it as much as anyone else. It was a justified premonition. He was later destroyed and defamed by the same psychology, the same system of views, that had earlier raised him up. Stalin was not joking or being hypocritical when he told numerous supplicants that he himself feared the NKVD. Ezhov was personally devoted to Stalin and never thought to harm him even when he found himself on the brink of the abyss. Beria in a similar situation would have behaved more rationally.

Stalin was not an exception, not a pathological accident. He was an organic figure in a communist regime, just as were Rakosi, Gottwald, and Bierut. The last, by the way, worked as an investigator for the NKVD in the USSR under the assumed name Rutkovsky. The idealist Dubček held power for only a few months, while Gomulka, who came into power on a wave of national enthusiasm for freedom and justice, ended his days with anti-Semitic agitation and shooting workers' demonstrations.

It is unscientific and untrue to say that it was only the personal power of Stalin that grew stronger in the 1930s. Although the means used to achieve those ends may seem inhuman and insane, the power of the Party was consolidated as well.

We should not forget that already in the early 1930s Stalin personified the Party for all without exception, even for his enemies. Had

Maiakovsky lived until then, he could have quite correctly written, "We say the Party and mean Stalin, and vice versa."

Even Trotsky, who was by then exiled, damned, and slandered in his native land, held to that point of view. He wrote to his son, L. Sedov, that he could not use the slogan "Down with Stalin!" If anti-Soviet forces were ever to raise their heads in the USSR, then he, Trotsky, would have to at least temporarily come out in support of Stalin.

Many Party leaders saw the harm of Stalin's political line and opposed it, but they consciously avoided calling openly for the removal of the tyrant. They were more concerned for the authority of the Party than they were for its power. They clung to the Party-Stalin fetish right to the grave. In the name of Party discipline and solidarity they did willingly what Yagoda and Ezhov could not achieve with torture. They piled the most absurd slander on themselves and others when every letter of accusation became a mountain of corpses.

We are told that they believed in the Party; we should not doubt their faith. But we should ask why they thought only of the Party and forgot completely about the people to whom, supposedly, they had dedicated their lives? Why did they never look for support among the people?

The answer to that question screams the merciless, murderous truth. They were always strangers to their people. They always stood above their people, with an admonishing finger or a threatening sword. They considered only their Party comrades to be worthy of freedom, justice, well-being. The people were for them the masses, building material, clay, objects, guinea pigs for untried experiments. On the way to power they constantly proclaimed that the good of the people was the highest law, but once they had gained that longed-for power by the hands of the people, they sat on the people's necks and proudly announced that they would not be guided by the backward sentiments of the masses. From the first day they set about driving and herding the masses to the next abyss.

That is why they did not appeal to the people. For millions of their countrymen a Bolshevik was a stranger and an oppressor. In the terrible year of the destruction of the peasantry, Bolsheviks who did not agree with the policy preferred to hold their theoretical debates in Kremlin offices and the halls of the Communist Academy. The Bukharinites, focs of the forced collectivization, did not turn to the nation, did not extend their hand to the little brothers, against whom the NKVD carried out undisguised genocide. Trotsky greeted collectivization sympathetically. He tried only to defend his priority in the matter. He wrote angry philippics from abroad on the occasion of every imprisonment or removal of his proponents, but he did not say a word about the suffering or death of millions of muzhiks.

After the unprecedented violence the Bolsheviks had no way back to the people, whom they had betrayed and condemned to starvation and death. Instead there was a headlong rush to their own graves, under the Party banner, under the leadership of Stalin.

One had only to read Bukharin's political testament. "I am leaving life. I bow my head, not before the proletariat's ax which must be merciless but chaste . . ." and so on to the end . . . "earlier the revolutionary idea justified cruelty to our enemies [so it was all right to kill others]. . . . Storm clouds hung over the Party." Party solidarity was his only standard: "It has already been seven years since I have had even a shade of disagreement with the Party." (On the eve of the destruction of the peasantry Bukharin disagreed, but that disagreement had vanished? In 1937 he agreed with the Party when it preached terror? So long as it didn't get him?) The blinders of Party thought hindered his vision. Nothing else existed, not the Motherland, not close friends. In the face of death Bukharin could not find a single word of sorrow or of love. Only Party, struggle, blood. "I have never been a traitor. For the life of Lenin I would have given my own without hesitation. I loved Kirov. I did not plot against Stalin. . . . Know, comrades, that on that banner which you carry in the victorious march to communism, there is a drop of my blood." Period. Nothing more to be said.

If the Party were dearer to them than anything else on earth—the nation, justice, truth—and if Stalin were the personification of the Party, then everything that might benefit him would have to be met with hymns of welcome, not excluding even their own deaths. The mass destruction of Party members did not threaten the Party's power. On the contrary, the Party's power was fortified. It was historically progressive, at least until the process came under Stalin's aegis and was directed by his will. And even after that, however many necks they broke, the Party's primacy was preserved.

If all the squabbling and bloodshed had not gone beyond the pack of professional conspirators, the whole subject would interest only Party historians. To the misfortune of the people, however, there was an extremely powerful amplifier between the Party and the people; and for every Bolshevik who perished, there were five, ten, or more non-Party, simple citizens who had never read Marx, Trotsky, or Stalin and who could not see the differences among them. They were unable even to begin to understand why they were being sent to camps or killed.

And this wasn't the end of the country's grief, only its beginning. The merciless inner-Party conflict broke out at a time when the smell of powder was abroad in the world, but the ambitious politicians were too maddened to pay heed. On the threshold of war they dealt a fatal blow to the undefended rear of their own Army.

Preparing for the Harvest

Such acts as the destruction of a huge army do not happen suddenly or all by themselves. The undermining of the RKKA was begun along with the state revolution. For a long while there were no external marks to betray the progress of the work.

After the military-historical discoveries of 1929 and the bandit raid of 1930, Stalin's relations with the military leadership seemed unclouded. Tukhachevsky was brought back from his Leningrad exile and entrusted with an important post to take charge of rearming the Red Army as he had suggested. Military specialists were freed and returned to work. The reorganized army was filled with strength and worked hard. The generals were showered with favors and distinctions. The stern warriors in their turn found much to praise in their great leader. There was no end to the idyllic alliance, it seemed.

On May 4, 1935, Stalin spoke at a Kremlin banquet for the graduates of the Red Army Academy. It was in that speech he introduced the famous slogan "The cadres decide everything."[1]

The timing of the new policy should not be surprising. Stalin's explanation was that earlier, when we were so backward, technical matters had to be in first place. Then, when we moved out of our backward stage, when we advanced (very rapidly in just five or six years, but this did not surprise anyone), the main thing became the people, especially people with technical skills. Technical things themselves, what are they? We had a surplus of them in the Army (along with a million horses, which the speaker did not mention), and everywhere else. Therefore, he reasoned, armed to the teeth with first-class technical weapons, we replaced the old slogan with a new one.

That May 4 speech also contained hints that the opposition had threatened to use terror: "We chose the plan of attack [meaning accelerated industrialization] and went ahead on the Leninist path leaving behind those comrades who could see only as far as their noses who closed their eyes to the near future of our country, to the future of socialism."

But the matter had become much more serious. Those comrades

did not always limit themselves to criticism and passive resistance. They threatened us with rebellion in the Party against the Central Committee. More than that: they threatened some of us with bullets. Apparently they thought to frighten us and force us to turn away from the Leninist path. These people must have forgotten that we Bolsheviks are a special kind of people. They forgot that you do not frighten Bolsheviks with difficulties or threats. . . . Understandably, we never even thought to swerve from the Leninist way. More than that, having determined on that path we went more determinedly ahead, sweeping from the road all and every obstacle. True, along the way we had to thrash a few of those comrades. I must confess that I too had a hand in the matter. (Stormy applause, shouts of "hurrah.")

The interpretation of the facts did not seem overly logical. It is one thing when some *comrades* (without quotation marks) do not see farther than their own noses and close their eyes to the future of socialism. This is a sad defect of vision called myopia. But what were they doing threatening rebellion and bullets? An explanation was in order. No one noticed the contradiction. They were all saving their breath for the next hurrahs.

Stalin did not insert the passage just for eloquence. No one had threatened him with bullets, but he was busily preparing the way for the opposition's confessions of planning terror. He was just saying what was on his mind. Chronology will help us here. The speech was made on May 4. The first Zinoviev trial, which was heavily but unsuccessfully embroidered with accusations of plans to shoot the leaders, had taken place in January. Another case prepared that summer was not publicized: Kamenev was accused of planning while he was in prison to murder Stalin. Soon after the banquet, on July 27, a secret trial took place, and that time Kamenev, who admitted to nothing, escaped the firing squad.

Nearer the end of his long moralizing toast Stalin told a little story. In light of later events it reads like a masterpiece of hypocrisy:

I recall an incident from distant Siberia where I was once in exile. . . . About thirty men went to the river to gather wood that had been washed up by the huge, turbulent river. Toward evening they returned to the village but without one of their comrades. To the question about where the thirtieth man was they answered indifferently that the thirtieth had "stayed there." To my question "What do you mean, stayed there?" they replied with the same indifference, "What's to ask? He drowned." At that point one of them hurried off somewhere saying he had to go milk the cow. To my admonition that they cared more for the cattle than for people one of them answered to the general approval of the rest, "Why should we care for them, for people? We can always make people. But a cow . . . just try to make a cow."

The moral was even shorter than the story: "It seems to me that the indifferent attitude of some of our leaders to people, to cadres, and the inability to value people is a vestige of that strange relationship of people to people that was apparent in this episode in distant Siberia."

It would add little to comment on more such pearls. They should be learned by heart. The speech's finale was prophetic:

> If our Army will have real hardened cadres in sufficiency, it will be unbeatable. To your health, comrades! (Stormy applause throughout the hall. All rise and greet comrade Stalin with loud shouts of "Hurrah.")

The year 1935 passed and ended well for the Army. A resolution in November announced the introduction of personal military titles. Until then the RKKA had managed for seventeen years without them. There were Red Armymen, junior commanders, and commanders. The commanders wore distinguishing emblems on collar tabs: triangles, cubes, rectangles, and rhombuses, which corresponded to their duties. Personal titles demonstrated the concern of the Party, the government, and comrade Stalin personally for our armed forces, and more important they were a step on the way back to old-regime style. Most of the titles still reflected posts: brigade commander, division commander, corps commander, and army commander; but there were also lieutenants, captains, majors, colonels, and marshals. In 1939 lieutenant colonel was added, and in 1940, general. From there it was a small step to shoulder straps, that very feature by which the enemy was recognized in the Civil War.

Nothing was heard about repression of the military in 1935. With one exception. The Red commander Yakov Okhotnikov was arrested and shortly thereafter shot.

Stalin, as everyone who knew him has noted, was gifted with an exceptional memory. It was not difficult for him in 1935 to remember an event from 1927. Just before November 7, the tenth anniversary of the October Revolution, the struggle between the Stalinists and the Zinoviev-Trotsky faction reached a critical point. Oppositionist demonstrations were expected in Moscow and Leningrad, in connection with which special precautions were taken. Not only the Chekists but also students from the military academies were made to guard the invaluable lives of the leaders lined up on the speakers' platform at the mausoleum. On the day of the celebrations R. P. Eideman, head of the Frunze Academy, entrusted three of his pupils with special passes and ordered them to hurry to their assignment. Along with Okhotnikov (who, incidentally had been Yakir's adjutant during the Civil War), Vladimir Petenko, and Arkady Geller raced to Red Square. They got into the Kremlin without any trouble, but at the wooden gate to the tunnel leading to the speakers' stand they were detained. The guard, a Georgian, refused to let them pass. The hotheaded trio were not daunted by the insolence of the Chekist. They knocked him aside, breaking the gate in the process,[2] and hurried on. In seconds they were up behind those standing on the tribune. Guards jumped the newcomers, but Okhotnikov got loose and leaped to Stalin, whom he somehow considered responsible for the annoying confusion, and punched him in the head. At that moment Stalin's bodyguard drew a knife—it was forbidden to shoot—and wounded Okhotnikov in the hand. Officers present intervened and ended the scuffle. Okhotnikov was given first aid, and the three were let go. That night they were sent for. Okhotnikov had prudently spent the night away from home. Geller and Potenko were seized. Eideman managed to hush up the affair.

The night of November 7, Stalin suffered a serious attack of paranoia, for which Professor V. M. Bekhterev treated him. That visit, or more accurately that diagnosis, cost the famous psychiatrist his life. He was poisoned on Stalin's orders. Stalin did not try to make anything of the incident at the time; he was not in a position to do so. Eight years later he got even with the man who had insulted him. Petenko and Geller perished in 1937.

In 1936, when physical destruction of the opposition was begun, the Army was not forgotten. Military men were taken, not yet in large numbers and without special fuss, but with an eye to the future. Most of the early arrests were made in the provinces.[3] The NKVD worked especially hard in the Ukraine. On July 5 Division Commander Dmitri

Shmidt, commander of the only heavy tank brigade then in the RKKA, and Boris Kuzmichev, chief-of-staff of large air force units, were seized. Both were trusted associates of Yakir. Division Commander Yu. Sablin and others suffered the same fate.[4] They included another of Yakir's comrades from the time of the Civil War, N. Golubenko, then chairman of the Dnepropetrovsk provincial executive committee. It is said that he had spoken out against repression.

As the repression grew, Stalin began to pay back old debts. As he remembered Okhotnikov, he was bound to remember Shmidt. Shmidt, son of a Jewish cobbler, a projectionist from Priluki, joined the Party in 1915. He fought bravely on several fronts with a corps of Red Cossacks; after the war he commanded a Cossack division. In the 1920s he was an active Trotskyite. A former partisan and a man of desperate courage, Shmidt had little use for idols or authority. Trotsky's expulsion from the Party on the eve of the Fifteenth Congress enraged him. He drove to Moscow and found Stalin during a break between meetings. Wrapped in a long Circassian coat, with a tall sheepskin hat on his head, he strode up to the General Secretary. He swore at him and brandishing an imaginary sword threatened, "Watch out, Koba. I'll cut your ears off!"

Stalin had to swallow that offense. The time had not yet come to accuse the opposition of terror. They were still talking about illegal printing presses. In 1936 he of the long memory not only avenged himself on Shmidt but made political hay of it. At the August trial the first of the witnesses, Mrachkovsky, told of the existence of a "group of murderers" in the Army, led by Shmidt. Later Dreitser implicated Putna. I. N. Smirnov repudiated that testimony, but Pikel, Reingold, and Bakaev confirmed it. Several days later Procurator General Vyshinsky announced that a number of people mentioned in the testimony of the accused would be tried separately under the laws of special procedure. Among them were Shmidt and Kuzmichev.

Putna was not mentioned, but that is easily explained. At the time he was military attaché in London. Had legal proceedings been begun against him, he would likely not have returned. He was simply recalled to Moscow, and in September he was arrested. That is how the first of the eight to be tried in the June 1937 trial fell into the paws of the NKVD. Apparently, however, no definite plans had yet been worked out about what use to make of Putna.

The NKVD and the Procuracy concentrated on Shmidt in the fall of 1936. A military man and a Trotskyite, he would have to be the connecting link between the oppositionists and the conspirators in the Army.

There was a slight hitch in September in the mechanism of the widening repression. Someone in the TSK tried to oppose Stalin while he was away from Moscow on vacation. There was even talk about a secret plenum of the TSK where Stalin was still in a minority on the question of terror. This seems unlikely, if only because a plenum could not take place in Stalin's absence. Nonetheless, it was in September that signs of an anti-Stalinist movement appeared. An announcement was made on the tenth that the case against Rykov and Bukharin was being dropped. An open circular of the TSK that speaks of the necessity of stopping baseless repression is dated September 21. With it there was also a call to watchfulness and provision for the prosecution of real enemies, but nonetheless this was a slap at Stalin.

In this fateful hour Stalin reacted immediately and effectively. The famous telegram about replacing Yagoda was sent on the twenty-fifth; formalities occupied a few days, and by the thirtieth Nikolai Ivanovich Ezhov had taken over his job. He appointed two new assistants—Matvei Berman, former chief of Gulag, and Mikhail Frinovsky, former chief of border forces—and set to work.

The second show trial began on January 21, 1937, the anniversary of Ilich's death. Piatakov, Sokolnikov, Serebriakov, and Livshits freely gave testimony about their reserve (parallel) terroristic center, which had been established in case of the failure of the main center headed by Zinoviev and Kamenev. As the accused had spent many years in economic work, much time was devoted to describing their various heroic deeds of wrecking, most of which are indistinguishable from normal slovenliness and fraud.[5] Their attempts to kill the Party leaders, all of which had failed, of course, were not left out.

Among the accused was also Karl Radek, the gasbag, teller of jokes, and pen pusher, who in the early 1930s turned from an oppositionist into a Stalinist minion and informer.[6] According to the trial's scenario, Radek was not involved in terrorism or wrecking. His role was his connection with Trotsky. Radek betrayed Bukharin, he sang the NKVD's praises ("It wasn't the interrogators who tortured us, but we who tortured them"), and dropped most damaging hints about the participation of military men in the plots. At one of the morning sessions he testified: "Vitaly [correctly Vitovt] Putna met with me in 1935 to ask a favor from Tukhachevsky." Somehow Vyshinsky did not pick up on that fact and led the questioning off in a different direction.

The evening of that same day he returned to that theme. (This supports the likely supposition that Tukhachevsky hurried to explain the matter to Voroshilov and Stalin, after which Vyshinsky got orders to formally exonerate the marshal, which he did in a characteristically strange way. Vyshinsky asked Radek why Tukhachevsky had approached him. From the trial records:

> RADEK: Tukhachevsky had a government assignment for which he could not find necessary material. Only I had the material. He called to ask if I had that material. I had it, and Tukhachevsky sent Putna, with whom he was working on the assignment, to get the material from me. Tukhachevsky had no idea of Putna's role, nor of my criminal role.
>
> VYSHINSKY: And Putna?
>
> R: He was a member of the organization. He did not come on organization business, but I used his visit to have a needed conversation.
>
> V: And Tukhachevsky?
>
> R: Tukhachevsky was never associated with our cause. . . . I affirm that I never had and never could have had any association with Tukhachevsky along the lines of counterrevolutionary activity, because I knew that Tukhachevsky was a man absolutely devoted to the Party and the government.

Radek said the word "material" four times, but the procurator never asked about its contents. He was not even interested in what the conspirators Putna and Radek were talking about. For Vyshinsky the incident was closed, but for Tukhachevsky it would turn out badly. The association of his name with such company threw a long shadow. Further explanations only raised more suspicions. What does an honest man need with a flattering character witness from the known counter-revolutionary Radek? Even the form of Radek's announcement put one on guard. It could seem that in singing the marshal's praises and denying even the possibility of associating with him, he was trying to distract attention from a deeply implicated coconspirator. In 1937 that interpretation was considered sufficient proof.[7]

One of the eight, Putna was kept at the Lubianka. Tukhachevsky was publicly shamed. Yakir felt "like a beast in a pen." After all, Shmidt and Kuzmichev were accused of planning to kill the People's Commis-

sar in Yakir's office. Yakir must be given his due. He tried to break the
closing ring. He went to Stalin and told him he did not believe either
Shmidt or Kuzmichev guilty, and that in general he did not especially
trust Ezhov. Stalin, always sympathetic to Yakir, met him halfway. He
granted him an interview with Shmidt. The prisoner looked terrible; he
had the "look of a Martian." The meeting did not last long. Shmidt
did, however, have time to tell the commander that the charges were
lies and give him a note for Voroshilov.

Yakir visited the People's Commissar, gave him the note, and told
him he was convinced that the prisoners were innocent. Yakir had
barely returned to Kiev when Voroshilov called to say that under
requestioning Shmidt had confessed that he had gulled Yakir and
himself. He confirmed his earlier testimony. P. Yakir, the Army commander's son, writes: "In this same conversation Voroshilov informed
[my father] that Corps Commander Garkavy had been arrested. Father
sat down in an armchair and put his head in his hands. Ilia Ivanovich
Garkavy was my father's oldest friend from 1917. He was also a
relative, the husband of mother's sister."[8]

When did this happen? According to P. Yakir, his father was at the
Lubianka and with Voroshilov on the seventeenth or eighteenth, returned
to Kiev, spoke on the telephone with Voroshilov, and on the next day
returned to Moscow to be present at the trial that was to begin on the
twenty-first. Returning to Kiev for only a day or two seems strange.
Why would he waste more than a day on the road for only a day at
home? If we accept a date of April from other sources for Garkavy's
arrest, then this episode must have occurred at the end of April or the
beginning of May. This is more likely, as M. F. Lukin, a former
subordinate of Yakir and commandant of Moscow in 1937, recalls
accompanying Yakir from the city in May shortly before his arrest.[9]

Another of Yakir's old friends, Yakov Livshits, was tried at the
January trial. He was an old working-class Bolshevik from before the
Revolution who had long worked in the Cheka-OGPU. Most recently he
had been Deputy People's Commissar of Transportation. Livshits confessed to everything that was demanded of him, but just before he was
shot he cried out, "Why?" Yakir heard of it.

19 Harvest

In 1937 Tukhachevsky, Yakir, Uborevich, and other monsters were sentenced to be shot. Elections to the Supreme Soviet of the USSR took place after that. The elections gave Soviet authority 98.6 percent of the vote. . . . One asks where are the signs of "decay" here, and why was the "decay" evident in the elections?
—Stalin

Value the cadres as the gold reserve of the party and state, treasure them, respect them.
—Stalin

We will now describe what happened in the Army in 1937 and 1938. We cannot draw a complete picture of what happened. Therefore we will concentrate on a few episodes and aspects of the larger events.

Tukhachevsky. In early May 1937 the marshal's scheduled trip to the coronation ceremonies in London was suddenly cancelled, supposedly because of the planned assassination attempt in Warsaw. Flag-officer V. M. Orlov, Commander of Naval Forces (VMS), was sent instead. On May 11 Voroshilov summoned Tukhachevsky and informed him that he had been removed from his duties as first deputy people's commissar and appointed commander of the troops of the Volga Military District. The announcement was curt, completely official, and without explanation. Tukhachevsky was stunned; all the memoirists agree on that. He asked Stalin for an explanation. The story goes that Stalin reassured the marshal, explaining his removal by his close acquaintance with several of the accused in the recent trial. "But we trust you. It would be better for you to leave Moscow temporarily, and when the rumors die down, we will bring you back."

Tukhachevsky arrived in Samara (now Kuibyshev) on May 26 and set about taking over from his old friend P. E. Dybenko, but that very day he was arrested.

Yakir. On May 23 Yakir, a member of the TSK VKP(b) and the Politburo of the TSK(b) of the Ukraine, received an official secret paper, which informed him of Tukhachevsky's arrest and asked for his concurrence about initiating a criminal case. Yakir replied that he did not doubt for a second that Tukhachevsky was innocent, but he would not object to a trial seeing it as the best possible means for explaining all the circumstances of the case. On the twenty-ninth, or more likely the thirtieth, Voroshilov phoned the Army commander and ordered him to come to Moscow immediately for a meeting of the Military Council. There were no more trains that day for Moscow, and Yakir wanted to take a plane. Voroshilov did not permit that, however, and ordered him to use the personal train at his disposal as commander. Yakir set off about 1:00 A.M. on the thirty-first. During the night his car was uncoupled at Briansk. Agents of the central apparatus of the NKVD seized the sleepy Yakir and took him by car to the Lubianka.

Primakov. Also called to Moscow, Primakov set off in a personal train. When Chekists tried to arrest him along the way, he made use of his Red Cossack past and with the help of his personal guard put them to flight. He called Voroshilov. The People's Commissar answered, "There has been a misunderstanding. Some people are coming who will explain everything." Soon a reinforced detachment of NKVD arrived. Primakov surrendered his Mauser and went to the Lubianka.

Gamarnik. He was sick during the last days of May and lay at home. One of those days, probably the thirty-first, he was visited by his assistant, A. S. Bulin,[1] and Assistant Chief of the General Staff Smorodinov, who asked for the key to a safe that contained materials needed for a meeting of the Military Council. Gamarnik was depressed. He already knew of the arrest of Tukhachevsky and others. His visitors tried to calm him. Soon they left. About an hour later agents of the NKVD arrived. As his daughter opened the door to the new guests, two pistol shots rang out in his room. According to another version, Gamarnik shot himself immediately after Bulin and Smorodinov's visit, and they heard the shots as they departed.[2]

In an official communiqué Gamarnik was called an accomplice of those on trial. (Stalin referred to him at a Military Council meeting on June 4 as "Gamarnik who is absent from court.") There are two other possible explanations for his suicide: to avoid being a member of the Military College of the Supreme Court, or to avoid giving testimony against the others accused.

Uborevich. He was grabbed on May 29. It is hard to say exactly where that occurred. According to his daughter it was on the way from

Smolensk to Moscow. According to other sources, it happened on the station platform as he got off the train.

We have already mentioned Putna's arrest. Kork, Feldman, and Eideman worked in Moscow. They were arrested in the second half of May. If it is true that Feldman was relieved of his duties on May 28, that is probably the date of his arrest. It seems that Yakir already knew of it in Kiev. There are some indications that Eideman was arrested on the twenty-second, during the Moscow Party conference, for association with Kork, who had been seized a few days earlier.

Besides these, the NKVD arrested other prominent men: at the end of April the chief of the international department of the People's Commissariat of Defense, Corps Commander A. I. Gekker, and the commander of the Urals district, Corps Commander I. I. Garkavy, were seized (both were shot on July 1, 1937). Corps Commander A. Ia. Lapin, former chief-of-staff of the Special Far Eastern Red Banner Army, was arrested on May 11. Exact dates are not known, but in any case before the trial began, even before June 1, the chief of the Administration of Antiaircraft Defense, Commander of the Second Army A. I. Sediakin, Chief of the Academy of the General Staff Division Commander D. A. Kuchinsky, Chief of the Political Administration of the Leningrad Military District, Army Commissar Second Class I. E. Slavin, and professor of the Frunze Academy, Corps Commander G. D. Gai (Bzhishkian) were all arrested.

Gai had to be arrested twice. He was first arrested on the night of June 2–3, 1935, in Minsk. An NKVD special conference in Moscow gave him five years in prison. On the way to the political isolation prison in Iaroslavl, Gai managed to break a board out of the floor of the railroad car and jump out. He injured his leg but still had enough strength to reach the nearest field with haystacks. Despite his pain the old soldier covered his tracks well. He made a depression in the hay, climbed in, and fell asleep. A general alarm was soon raised throughout the district and hundreds of eager *komsomoltsy* (young communists) led by Chekists combed the fields and forests. They looked under every bush, poked bayonets into every haystack and stock of grain. All the komsomoltsy carried enlarged photographs of Gai, but they did not find him.[3]

Gai successfully slept through that ceremony in his honor. When he woke, he decided not to run any farther and to ask for help. His leg hurt tremendously, and he had nothing to eat. Reaching a village, he went to the nearest hut. The owner recognized Gai, as he had once served under him, and told him that he was being searched for. Several days later Gai decided to go to Moscow, but the peasant dissuaded him. "Come to the station," Gai told him. "Look. Are the pictures of Lenin and Stalin still hanging?" They were. "That means the Soviet authority still exists!" Gai walked out on the platform. He considered his arrest an arbitrary act of the NKVD. The stationmaster recognized him also and advised him to hide. Gai demanded to be connected with Moscow by telephone, and on a direct line he spoke with Voroshilov, who reassured him that some people were being sent for him who would explain everything. He did not have long to wait. In the Lubianka, Gai was put in the same cell with Putna. He still did not understand what had happened. "When they start to tear the skin from your back, you'll understand it all!" answered Putna.[4]

Blucher. The first repressions against the Army barely touched the Far East. All of 1937 and the first half of the next year passed relatively peacefully there. Only in the summer of 1938 did mass arrests begin in the OKDVA, the Separate Far Eastern Red Banner Army. L. S. Mekhlis, Chief of the Political Administration of the RKKA, and Deputy People's Commissar of Internal Affairs Frinovsky arrived there at the end of May on separate trains. Soon thereafter commanders were seized by the hundreds.

It cannot be said that the moment was well chosen. The situation along the border was extremely tense, thanks to Stalin. The great leader had gotten the idea that the Far East was a powder keg, that the Chinese and Koreans, living under the heel of Japan, were only waiting for a spark to set off the flame of wars of national liberation.

In June 1938 the OKDVA was reorganized as the Far Eastern Front comprised of the 1st and 2nd Separate Red Banner Armies. Blucher remained its commander. The NKVD, which had charge of all reconnaissance, continuously warned him that the Japanese were about to attack. The deployment of Soviet troops could not fail to put the Japanese on their guard.[5]

The punitive organs were assigned the task of striking the spark. There were sectors where the border was not demarcated; however, border patrols from both sides walked definite routes daily and no confrontations had taken place. Late in July Frinovsky and the Assistant Chief of Administration of the NKVD in the Far East Goglidze visited the border. They took with them fresh border troops not familiar with local conditions, and gave them new maps on which several sectors actually controlled by the Japanese were marked as Soviet. They warned them to be especially vigilant and to be alert to the possibility of Japanese provocation.

On July 29 an incident occurred near Lake Khasan in one of the improperly marked sectors. Soviet border guards brought back a captured Japanese officer as proof that the border had been violated. Zaozernaia and Bezymiannaia Heights, where the capture took place, were considered by tacit agreement to be no one's. The Japanese drove the Soviet units out of the area and reinforced their own. Large-scale military hostilities began.

The Soviet troops' situation was complicated by a foolish order from Stalin. They were to fight but were to make sure that not one bullet landed in Japanese territory. Because of that they tried to regain the heights almost solely on the strength of bayonet charges. Blucher was a brave warrior, but of the old school. He trained his troops without any of the newfangled ideas. He would use artillery, for example, only against a broad front, not against reconnoitered fire points. Such tactics were already outmoded for the Red Army. When Soviet units charged, the Japanese fire points opened up at full strength. Soviet losses were heavy.

Finally, at the cost of large sacrifices, Soviet troops took the disputed heights. Military action was halted on August 11. The border was clearly demarcated and confirmed in a peaceful agreement. Wars of national liberation did not break out.[6]

During the conflict Blucher was not mentioned once in the press and a week after the battles ended he was recalled to Moscow. Voroshilov gave him a magnificent snow job and ordered him to take a vacation until a new appointment for him was decided on.

Blucher left with his wife and brother, commander of a large air force unit, for the Crimea (by other accounts to Sochi). At his leisure the old warrior thought a lot about the recent failure and finally decided he understood the true cause. According to his wife, he wrote a letter to Stalin early in October. "All that happened was the result of provocation. . . . I was thoroughly misinformed. . . . My boys walked right into the Japanese machine guns. . . . Frinovsky and Goglidze should be removed from the Far East and punished. . . ." Blucher was soon ordered to Moscow, and on October 22 he was arrested.

They put the marshal in Lefortovo prison. The new Deputy People's

Commissar L. P. Beria took the first interrogation. The charges were serious: association with the Japanese since 1921, and intention to defect to them with the help of his brother, the pilot. Blucher denied everything.

His death occurred on November 9. By questioning witnesses the late V. V. Dushenkin, chief of the Central Archive of the Soviet Army, has established that Ezhov personally shot Blucher in his office. Sentence was pronounced over the body.

The examples offered above are only fragments of the gigantic effort to destroy the command staff of the RKKA. The information we have about dates of arrest—and even more of executions—are fragmentary and often contradictory. The total number of victims can only be guessed at. We will have to reconcile ourselves to describing the process only very incompletely.

The repression encompassed tens of thousands of officers (Red commanders). The distribution of victims by rank is included in the following chapter. Here we will try only to present the dynamics of personnel changes in higher positions: in the central apparatus of the Commissariat of Defense and in military district commands.

Massive arrests of military men were conducted from the spring of 1937 late into autumn 1938. The end of the arrests might be associated with the elimination of Blucher and the fall of Ezhov. In the following years although the repression of Red commanders did not entirely cease, it became individualized, isolated, one could even say insignificant in contrast to the bacchanalia of 1937–38.

The tables to be found in appendix IV show the devastation wrought in the leadership of the RKKA by the proletarian ax. We have not been able to fill in all the blanks, but the facts we have offered are reliable. Only those dates that have been checked against official sources have been included. None of those indicated as having perished in the repression died a natural death.

The following selective statistics give a particular picture of the quantitative side of the process. It concerns a small group of military men—deputy people's commissars and district commanders—but the dynamic picture of the repression in the Army as a whole was similar, only many times larger.

Before the June trial two deputy commissars and four commanders were killed; after the trial and before 1938, two and four more. In the first four months of 1938 the numbers were one and six; after that, one and three. Altogether six deputy commissars and seventeen commanders of military districts and fleets were victims of the repression.

On January 1, 1937, there were seventeen military districts and fleets. Until that date only one of the victims (Shtern) had not occupied one of those posts. The command of military districts was entirely liquidated in two years. Of all the men in those two categories only two survived: Shaposhnikov and Budenny.

Those who were removed were replaced quite arbitrarily with others chosen simply because they were handy. It did not make much difference because most of the newly appointed commanders soon perished as well. Stalin cared little for individuals, except of course for himself, and that only because the country needed him so. The various screws of the huge government mechanism were interchangeable, each one like the other. If every cook can run the state, why not entrust the command of army corps and districts to the first fool or ignoramus to come along.

A few examples will demonstrate just how intelligently the cadres were selected. In June 1937 three brigade commanders were recalled from Spain, promoted, and appointed: N. N. Voronov to chief of artillery of the RKKA, Ia. V. Smushkevich to assistant chief of the air force (he assumed Proskurov's post after the latter's arrest but was shot in 1941), D. G. Pavlov to assistant chief of the Armor of Tank Administration (he was arrested in the first months of the war while he was serving as commander of the Western Front and shot in October of 1941).

Colonel A. M. Vasilevsky, who had attended the first course of the General Staff Academy, was appointed head of the department of rear studies in August 1937. Two months later he took over the department of operational preparations of the higher command staff in the General Staff. Further promotions followed rapidly: in 1939 he became assistant chief of the operations department; in 1940, assistant chief of the operations administration; in July 1941, assistant chief of General Staff. Thus a man who had never commanded larger units, who had no experience in headquarters work, and who had little education came to head the country's major military organization. It was enough that his promptness, lack of personality, and industriousness pleased Stalin, who himself was an absolute ignoramus in military matters.

In 1939–40 we meet P. V. Rychagov and I. I Proskurov, both lieutenants in 1937, as lieutenants general serving as deputy commissars of aviation. Both were shot, Proskurov in 1940, and Rychagov in 1941.

There were more amazing flights. Captain Peresypkin from commander of a communications squadron two years later became People's Commissar of Communications of the USSR and from the first days of the war also chief of communications of the Red Army.

Vasilevsky's classmates N. F. Vatutin, M. V. Zakharov, and A. I. Antonov—none of whom had the education or experience for the jobs—became chiefs of staff of the most important regions in Kiev, Leningrad, and Moscow. Fortunately, unlike Vasilevsky, they were able, especially Zakharov and Antonov, to quickly achieve the level of competence demanded by their positions.

Not everyone succeeded. It was their misfortune and not their fault, but they often paid dearly for it, they and the country. The commander of the Western Special Military District D. G. Pavlov went in three peacetime years from a brigade commander to general of the Army. He was practically the only one of the commanders who literally obeyed the suicidal prewar orders of Stalin, Timoshenko, and Zhukov. Because of that the Western region proved the least well-defended when Germany attacked. Pavlov lost control of his troops in the first hours of the war and doomed them to almost complete destruction. He was simply unable to take any positive action. For that he was declared a traitor and shot.

Other commanders of border regions—F. I. Kuznetsov (Baltic), Ia. T. Cherevichenko (Odessa), M. M. Popov (Leningrad)—did not share Pavlov's fate, but neither did they achieve particular success. M. P. Kirponos, commander of the Kiev Special Region, is better known. In 1940 he had been commandant of the Kazan infantry school and had begged to be sent to the Finnish Front. The colonel got his wish and was given a division. During the war he became a major general. Kirponos's division was the first to get into Vyborg. A month later he was made lieutenant general and commander of the Leningrad Military District, and half a year later he was colonel general and commander of the Kiev district. Entering his office he drew his hand across his throat and said, "A division was as much I could handle." Kirponos was an honest and courageous soldier, but was not able to save his troops from defeat or his native Ukraine from capture. It is possible that his death in battle saved him from repression.

In Marshal S. S. Biriuzov's memoirs there is an interesting description that well illustrates the situation in the Army after the slaughter of the command staff. After he graduated from the Academy he was sent as chief of staff to the glorious 30th Irkutsk Rifle Division. When he arrived at his assignment, he went directly to headquarters. A senior lieutenant was sitting in the chief's office. Biriuzov assumed he was an adjutant and asked where the chief-of-staff was. The answer was, "I am the chief-of-staff." The young officer was very glad to see Biriuzov's orders. "Go see the division commander, comrade colonel, we are utterly exhausted here." In the division commander's office sat another senior lieutenant. It turned out that all the senior officers of the division had been arrested. Command according to combat orders had been taken by company commanders and heads of headquarters departments.

20 The Executioners: Modus Operandi

All these people were apparently immune and impervious to the simplest sense of compassion only because they served. They, as serving people, were impervious to the feeling of humanity as paved earth is to rain. . . . It may be that these governors, superintendents, policemen, are necessary, but it is terrible to see people deprived of their chief human quality, of love and pity for their fellow men. . . . Indeed, they are terrible people, more terrible than robbers. A robber may have pity, these never can; they are ensured against pity as these stones are against vegetation. — Lev Tolstoy, *Resurrection*

When people want to kill a dog, they say it is rabid. — Popular saying

It is naive to moralize to people who do not acknowledge human morality. — Stalin

Probably you don't shudder
killing a person.
Oh, martyrs of dogma,
You, too, are victims of the times.
— Pasternak

It is still hard today to determine with any precision what Stalin's and Ezhov's whole plan was for the destruction of the Army leadership. There is no doubt that there was such a plan. Who in the USSR works without a plan?

It would be easy to say that there were several plans, that they changed, became intertwined, and were coordinated; or on the other hand that they came into conflict. That is not so important. What is important is that from the summer of 1936 there was a widespread, deeply conspiratorial plot against the Red Army, against its leadership.

The Original Conception

The basic plan, which did not exclude variations held in reserve, lay in the mainstream of Stalinist policy. The enemies of the people had their own military organization or, worse still, close association with con-spirators in the Army. Such an assumption led logically to a show trial of military officers, most likely together with civilian oppositionists.

The plan was not so foolish, but it was destroyed when it came up against a powerful obstacle. For the trial to succeed it needed promi-nent military officers who would agree to take upon themselves the roles of traitors to their country, conspirators, and accomplices of ene-mies internal and foreign. As bad luck would have it, the NKVD, hard as they tried, could not find suitable candidates. In 1936 and 1937, as later, the officers—with very few exceptions—refused to cooperate with the prosecution.

Failure haunted the NKVD and the Procuracy from the very beginning. Dmitri Shmidt, who was chosen to get the process started, behaved miserably, unconscionably, not like a Bolshevik. At first glance he would seem to have been a good choice. His Trotskyite past permitted the prosecution to tie him in with the civilian enemies of the people, as they did in Mrachkovsky's testimony in August 1936.

It remained only to associate him with the criminal activities of the prominent commanders with whom he had been close since the Civil War. That made it possible to implicate, for example, Primakov, Eideman, Dubovoi, and less directly Yakir. If association with the opposition was easy to show—and here Shmidt was the object at whom others pointed their fingers—his relations with the military officers proved just the opposite. Shmidt was supposed to give testi-mony that would serve as the basis for bringing charges against his comrades-in-arms.

The NKVD investigators understood that it would be difficult to get an admission of guilt from Shmidt. Therefore they charged him at first only with the intention, together with Kuzmichev, to kill Voroshilov. Very likely Shmidt had little use for Voroshilov, who was a zealous Stalinist, and the investigator, playing on this hostility, implied the possibility of such intentions. Together with torture, similar psychologi-cal treatment often bore fruit. If they could get Shmidt to crack on that point, they would drag him further, force him to admit to a widespread conspiracy in the military. They would have suggested to him that once he had admitted to the one part, he would have to admit the rest. The intention to kill the People's Commissar was sufficient cause to sen-tence him to death, and he could lighten his penalty by naming his conspirators, the ringleaders, etc.

Nothing came of the NKVD's good idea. Tortured practically to death, Shmidt did not give in. If in moments of extreme torment he admitted to anything, when he came to himself he denied his testimony. But it probably wasn't even that. While Yakir was in the Lubianka, he was never shown copies of Shmidt's confessions, only told of them, just as Voroshilov only told of his subsequent retractions.

Shmidt stood firm. The plan for an open trial was destroyed. Putna was also in the Lubianka. There is some information that he was also tortured, but again unsuccessfully. They saved Putna for the June trial, which was carried out in secret. Shmidt apparently looked too bad to present him even at that closed spectacle for invited guests. He was shot almost on the eve of the trial, on May 20, 1937.

The scenario for an open trial still existed; at least it had been thoroughly worked out. Vyshinsky, the chief playwright, regretted the lost inspiration, and he determined to get something out of it. Large parts of the inspiration went into another show, the Bukharin trial of 1938. Two considerations support the idea that the "military episodes" were not written especially for the event but were taken from old plans: (1) the criminal association of Bukharin, Rykov, Iagoda, Krestinsky, and Grinko with the military added nothing to the criminal visage of the accused; they are completely absent from the prosecution's conclusion and are not at all used in the procurator's speech; (2) Yakir is barely mentioned in the inserted episodes (instead Gamarnik is active in the Ukraine), which is natural since he was added to the list at the last moment.

These are valuable to us as the only charges publicly laid against the Tukhachevsky group, if only after the fact. We include them here in their entirety, preserving the chronology of the trial session.[1]

Evening session, March 2; Examination of G. F. Grinko

GRINKO: First, the association with the right-Trotsky center. My association went along this line—Gamarnik, Piatakov, Rykov. I was connected with Gamarnik through Liubchenko, who was also associated with Yakir and Gamarnik. Through Gamarnik I had connections with Piatakov, and later with Rykov. I carried out foreign policy tasks because Piatakov and Gamarnik had told me that Trotsky had agreed to pay compensation at the expense of the Ukraine for military assistance in our struggle against Soviet authority. . . . My association with Gamarnik, Piatakov, and Rykov began approximately late in 1935. . . .

On the basis of a number of conversations and associations, and tasks assigned me by Rykov, Bukharin, Gamarnik, Rozengolts, Yakovlev, Antipov, Rudzutak, Yagoda, Vareikis, and a large number of other people, it became clear to me that the right-Trotskyite center was relying mainly at that time on military assistance from aggressors. . . . In addition to that the right-Trotskyite center had an alternative plan to seize the Kremlin . . . .

In that period terrorism was one of the main weapons in the common arsenal of the struggle against Soviet power.

VYSHINKSY: From whom did you learn this?
G: From Rykov, Yakovlev, Gamarnik, and Piatakov. . . .
V: Grinko, where did this terroristic line come from?
G: From Trotsky. I learned about that from Gamarnik . . . the question was also directly raised about the removal of Ezhov as a man especially dangerous for the conspirators.
V: What does removal mean?
G: Removal—that means murder. . . . I heard from Gamarnik that Yakir and Gamarnik ordered the Trotskyite Ozeriansky, who then worked in the People's Commissariat of Finance, to prepare a terrorist act against Ezhov. . . .[2]

A second fact that I know . . . was the preparation of a terrorist act against Stalin by Bergavinov from the Main Administration of the Northern Sea Route. I found that out also from Gamarnik. . . . I heard it also from Bergavinov himself, who told me he had accepted Gamarnik's assignment and was trying to carry it out.

There was nothing more to drag out of Grinko, so Vyshinksy plugged in Rykov:

V: Grinko just spoke of the group of military traitors—Tukhachevsky and others who in their turn were convicted by the Supreme Court. Do you corroborate that part of the testimony which concerns you?
RYKOV: I knew of Tukhachevsky's military group. . . . That military group was organized independently of the bloc or of any tinge of Trotskyite or Bukharinites. The military group had as its goal the violent elimination of the government of the Union, and in

particular participated in planning the Kremlin revolution. . . . I learned about that from Tomsky in 1934.

Evening session of March 3; Examination of N. N. Krestinsky[3]

VYSHINSKY: Accused Krestinsky, tell us, please, what do you know about the participation of the Tukhachevsky group in the "right-Trotskyite bloc?"

KRESTINSKY: About Tukhachevsky's participation I know the following. When I met with Trotsky at Meran in October 1933, he indicated to me that in planning a state revolution we must not rely solely on our Trotskyite forces, because they were insufficient for that, but must strike a deal with the rights and with the military group. He paid particular attention to Tukhachevsky as an adventurist, ambitious to hold the highest position in the Army,[4] who would likely be willing to risk much. He asked me to tell Piatakov about this and to discuss it with Tukhachevsky personally.

V: Did you talk with Tukhachevsky?

K: I talked with him early in 1934 after Piatakov had spoken with him. I told him of my conversation with Trotsky. Tukhachevsky said that in principle he agreed not only with the idea of joining forces but also with the goal before us. . . . I subsequently spoke with Tukhachevsky about these things several more times. That was in the second half of 1935, in 1936, and 1937. . . . During one of these conversations in 1935 he named several men on whom he relied. He named Yakir, Uborevich, Kork, and Eideman. Later in another conversation, a very important conversation, which took place at the Extraordinary Eighth Congress of Soviets, Tukhachevsky urged upon me the need to hasten the revolution. The problem was that we had associated the revolution with our defeatist orientation and had timed it to coincide with the beginning of war, with the attack by Germany on the Soviet Union. Inasmuch as the attack was delayed, so was the practical realization of the revolution. The gradual destruction of counterrevolutionary forces was beginning at the time. Piatakov and Radek had been arrested; the Trotskyites were beginning to be arrested; and Tukhachevsky began to fear that if things were put off they might fall through altogether. Therefore he posed the question of accelerating the counterrevolutioanry attack. . . .

V: Accused Rozengolts, do you corroborate this part of Krestinsky's testimony?

ROZENGOLTS: Yes, I corroborate it.

V: Did you speak with Tukhachevsky and with Krestinsky?

R: I had a talk with Krestinsky at the end of May 1937 about accelerating the organization of the revolution. . . .

Evening session of March 4; Examination of A. P. Rozengolts[5]

V: Did Rykov tell you that Tukhachevsky was promising to act, but did not act?

R: Yes.

V: Who else told you?

R: Krestinsky told me about it, and Sedov transmitted Trotsky's opinion. . . .

V: Accused Krestinsky, tell us, did you tell Rozengolts in 1936 that Tukhachevsky was procrastinating with the counterrevolutionary action? . . .

KRESTINSKY: Yes. Late in 1936 the question was raised at the same time by Trotsky from abroad in a letter to Rykov and by Tukhachevsky about hastening the revolution and not be timed to coincide with the outbreak of war. . . .

V: That means that Tukhachevsky was in a hurry?

K: By the end of 1936 Tukhachevsky began to hurry.

V: And at that time did you push him on?

K: I agreed with him. . . .

R: The point at which I stopped was the meeting which we had with Tukhachevsky.

V: Where was that meeting?

R: At my apartment.

V: You had a meeting, with whom?

R: With Tukhachevsky and Krestinsky. . . . That was in late March 1937. At that meeting Tukhachevsky informed us that he could count with certainty on the possibility of revolution and indicated the timing, that before May 15, in the first half of May, he could accomplish the military revolution.

V: Of what did that counterrevolutionary act consist?

R: Tukhachevsky had a number of alternatives. One of the alternatives, the one on which he counted most, was the chance for a group of his military supporters to gather at his apartment, to get into the Kremlin under pretext, seize the Kremlin telephone exchange and kill the leaders of the Party and government. . . .

K: We spoke with Rozengolts and Gamarnik about this. We discussed the necessity of terrorist acts against the leaders of the Party and government.

V: Against whom specifically?

K: We had Stalin, Molotov, and Kaganovich in mind. . . . Ever since November 1936 I was decidedly in favor of speeding up that revolution as much as possible. There was no need to push Tukhachevsky as he had the same feeling, and he himself put that question to us—the rights—to me, to Rozengolts and Rudzutak. . . . Our feelings on the question of revolution coincided. . . .

V: (to Rozengolts). What do you have to say about your meetings with Gamarnik?

R: I confirm the testimony I gave during the preliminary investigation.

V: What was that?

R: Concerning Gamarnik the most important point was that Gamarnik told us about his proposal, with which Tukhachevsky apparently concurred, about the possibility of seizing the building of the People's Commissariat of Internal Affairs during the military revolution. Gamarnik further assumed that this attack would be carried out by some military unit directly under his command, assuming that he had sufficient party and political prestige in the military units. He expected that several commanders, especially the most valiant, would help him. I recall that he mentioned Gorbachev's name.[6]

V: That means that not only did Tukhachevsky inform you of the plan of his criminal conspiracy, but Gamarnik also informed you of the plan?

R: Yes. . . .

Second examination of N. I. Krestinsky

KRESTINSKY: [Krestinsky narrated the contents of a conversation that allegedly took place between him and Trotsky on October 10, 1933] The first thing was an agreement with foreign governments. The second was the establishment in the Soviet Union of a combined force of Trotskyites, rights, and military conspirators. . . .

As far as the military men are concerned, when Trotsky spoke of them he mentioned only one name, that of Tukhachevsky, as a man like Bonaparte, an adventurer, an ambitious man who strove to play not only a military, but a politico-military role and who would undoubtedly cooperate with us. . . . He asked me to inform Piatakov about these policies and especially about the need to communicate with the Japanese. In addition he asked that I just not have Matakov speak with Tukhachevsky and Rudzutak, but that I meet with them as well. . . . When I returned I immediately informed Piatakov and Rozengolts of my talks. Piatakov spoke with Tukhachevsky and Rudzutak. . . .

In February 1934 I met with Tukhachevsky and with Rudzutak and told them of my conversation. I got from both confirmation in principle of their acceptance of the idea of cooperation with foreign governments, of their military assistance, the defeatist line, and the establishment of a united organization within the country. . . .

Concerning the timing of the act: From the time of my meeting in Meran it was considered indisputably decided that the act would coincide with the start of war, and that therefore we in the Union could not set the date for Tukhachevsky's action. . . . Late in November 1936 at the Extraordinary Eighth Congress of Soviets, Tukhachevsky spoke with me excitedly and in grave terms. He said things had begun to fall apart. It was obvious that there would be more repressions of Trotskyists and rights. . . . He drew the conclusions: we could not wait for interventionists; we would have to act ourselves. . . . Tukhachevsky spoke not only for himself, but also in the name of the counterrevolutionary military organization. . . . It turned out that Trotsky on his own initiative had decided the act should be moved up and sent an order to that effect in a letter to Rozengolts. . . . After receiving that reply, we began to make more concentrated preparations for the act. Approximately in the beginning of February [1937] Rozengolts and I were officially made members of the center. In November [1936] Rozengolts, Gamarnik, and I had to take over the leadership of the Trotskyites. Piatakov was already gone. So was Radek. . . . A date was set for the revolution—the second half of May. But at the very beginning of May it was learned that Tukhachevsky was not going to London. . . . He declared that he could accomplish the act in the first half of May.

Morning session of March 7; Examination of N. I. Bukharin

BUKHARIN: In that period [1929–30] we had already discussed the question of overthrowing the Soviet government by violent means with the help of a group of military participants in the conspiracy.

VYSHINSKY: Tukhachevsky, Primakov, and several others?

B: Exactly correct. . . . The forces of the conspiracy were the forces of Enukidze plus Yagoda. . . . At the time [1933–34] Enukidze had managed to recruit, as best I remember, the former military commandant of the Kremlin, Peterson, who by the way had been commandant of Trotsky's train. Then there was the military organization of conspirators: Tukhachevsky, Kork, and others.

That was all. The literary exercises of academician Vyshinsky need no comment. We are left only to marvel at how simply the frightening news of widespread treachery in the Army command was presented to the people.

The Red Folder

A myth about the destruction of the leadership of the RKKA begun by Khrushchev has taken root in Soviet propaganda: that it was the result of an evil plot by the Germans who slipped Stalin false documents about Tukhachevsky's association with the German general staff. That version saves face for Stalin and the system, but only people like Lev Nikulin[7] could possibly believe it.

The only truth to it is that there was a collection of documents, which is usually called "the red folder." It was prepared in Germany, and it did fall into Stalin's hands. The rest accords less well with the truth.

The essential question is, who fabricated the folder? All sources —and there are many—although they do not agree in all details, do agree on one thing: the papers were made to order for someone in Moscow. It was the NKVD acting, most probably, on orders from Stalin. That can be considered certain today. Remaining details give the matter entertainment value as a mystery, but they do not change its ominous significance.

The history of the "red folder" is in itself fascinating. We will try to summarize all that has become known. Everything is not clearly known; the details are not complete, which is natural when one has to speak of the activities of the secret services.

At the center of this story stands the Russian general Nikolai Vladimirovich Skoblin (1893–?). In November 1918 the twenty-five-year-old Captain Skoblin became commander of the illustrious Kornilov division of Whites and remained in that post in emigration. General Skoblin was a prominent figure in the White émigré military organization, the Russian All-Military Union (*Russkii Obshche-Voinskii Soiuz* —ROVS).

Skoblin's biography remains incomplete. He disappeared from Paris at dawn on September 23, 1937, only hours after the kidnapping of the head of ROVS, General Miller, by agents of the NKVD. Even then, however, it was clear that Skoblin played a central role in that act. As early as 1930 he had been involved in the kidnapping of the ROVS' first leader, General A. P. Kutepov.

Most likely Skoblin had been recruited by the NKVD through his wife, the famous Russian singer Nadezhda Plevitskaia.[8] Plevitskaia's superior in the NKVD was the legendary Naum Ettingon. Her contact and bagman was Ettingon's brother Mark.[9]

Although, as we have already said, recollections about the "red folder" are many, they can be divided into two finished versions. The first is told by Victor Aleksandrov,[10] the second by Robert Conquest.[11]

Strictly speaking, these two versions do not contradict each other in any important way. Aleksandrov's description is much longer, a whole book of almost two hundred pages, which reads like fiction. He tries to reconstruct long dialogues between the dramatis personae: Stalin with Radek, Stalin with Voroshilov, Radek with Nikolai, Feldman with Tukhachevsky, Skoblin with Heydrich, and many others. Conquest devoted all of four pages to this affair. His sources are far fewer, but they are perhaps more reliable.[12]

It should be said that both authors give only an incomplete picture and leave several important circumstances unclear.[13]

Aleksandrov's Version. Stalin sent K. Radek on a secret mission to establish contact with the Germans with the aim of further close cooperation. Radek met with Colonel Nikolai in the Polish Baltic town Oliwa near Sopot. After that Ezhov ordered Yagoda to arrest Radek on the grounds that he had had talks with Colonel Nikolai as an agent of the Trotskyite opposition.[14] This is the most difficult part of Aleksandrov's version to verify.[15]

After Ezhov replaced Yagoda he sent to Paris the deputy director of the foreign department of the NKVD, Aleksander Spigelglass and a certain Sarovsky.[16] This was part of Ezhov's plan to begin discrediting Tukhachevsky as a German agent. Spigelglass ordered Skoblin to inform the Czechs (through their resident in Geneva, Nemanov) that the Trotskyites had established contact with the Germans through Radek and Piatakov. Skoblin was to deliver to Nemanov Radek's statement that he (Radek) had agreed to organize a military coup d'état with Tukhachevsky and Putna. In exchange for that favor Skoblin was promised that the NKVD would remove General Miller, which would make it possible for him (Skoblin) to become head of the ROVS.

But Skoblin was not only a paid agent of the NKVD. He also hated the Soviet regime. He dreamed of its destruction and placed his main hope on Hitler. Skoblin worked on the Germans also: he had close ties to R. Heydrich, the head of the SD. Skoblin figured that he had to go further than the NKVD's instructions. If it were possible to prepare documents about Tukhachevsky's association with the Germans and make these available to Stalin, the latter would be sure to destroy the top leadership of the Red Army, and then Hitler would not be able to withstand the temptation to attack the weakened Soviet Union. Skoblin decided that this plan would find an ally in Heydrich, who was opposed to Nikolai's efforts to bring Berlin and Moscow closer, and who, more than that, knew that Tukhachevsky saw in Nazi Germany the main threat to the USSR.

Heydrich accepted Skoblin's idea to reinforce the information sent to Beneš with documentary proof.[17] He found support from his superior Himmler and from a specialist in Russian affairs, Rosenberg. It remained only to secure the approval of Hitler and Hess. The decisive meeting took place on Christmas Eve 1936 in Hitler's office. The matter was kept in strict secrecy even from the high military command. Besides Hitler, Rosenberg, Hess, and Heydrich, only a few high officials of the SD and the Gestapo, including V. Hoettl[18] and Herman Berens,[19] attended. Technical implementation of the operation was entrusted to Colonel Naujocks.[20]

Work went ahead full speed from the first days of 1937. Tukhachevsky was in Germany six times, not including his captivity. From all of these trips there remained authentic documents in his hand. They were used in preparing the forgeries. Citing SS General Schellenberg, Aleksandrov offers an interesting detail. Tukhachevsky's original letters had been gathered for the most part by military intelligence. Its head, Admiral Canaris, did not want to give them to Heydrich. At that point M. Borman, with the help of several professional thieves, organized a burglary of the Nachrichlendienst archives.

After that a special team of forgers set to work. It included a Russian émigré counterfeiter convicted of forging English pounds. Skoblin traveled periodically to Berlin. He was the chief expert in evaluating the finished documents.

Ezhov waited impatiently for the work on the dossier to be completed.[21] He promised Stalin that he would put proof of Tukhachevsky's conspiracy on his desk by the end of March 1937. When it became clear that the work would not be done by the appointed date, he sent an emissary to Skoblin to get something he could show to Stalin. Skoblin went to Berlin and got from the Germans a list of the documents making up the dossier.

Finally in mid-April all was ready. Ezhov's deputy Zakovsky arrived in Berlin. He offered to pay the Germans 200,000 marks (in rubles) for the dossier. Berens considered the sum far too high. Zakovsky insisted. He said that no one in the Politburo would believe that such important documents could be bought for less; besides that, he needed a formal receipt for the money. Finally the deal was consummated.[22]

Conquest's Version. This is shorter and drier. The NKVD informed Heydrich through Skoblin of Tukhachevsky's secret association with the German General Staff. The security services, understanding that the source of that information was in Moscow, decided nonetheless to make use of it, first of all to compromise the General Staff with whom the SD had strained relations. It soon became clear, however, that they had a good opportunity of another sort in their hands.

Rumors of Tukhachevsky's German ties were spread by way of Czech president Beneš in the last months of 1936. In March or April 1937 Heydrich and Berens ordered their subordinates to prepare "documentary evidence." That delicate work was carried out by an engraver, Franz Putzig, a specialist in counterfeit documents. The dossier comprised thirty-two pages. According to Colonel Naujocks, there was a "letter" in the dossier signed by Tukhachevsky and stamped "top secret." The letter mimicked Tukhachevsky's style. The marshal's signature was taken from the Soviet-German agreement of 1926 about technical cooperation in the field of aviation. Signatures of German generals on other letters were copied from their bank checks.

German security services transmitted these documents to the NKVD. The NKVD, it would seem, sneaked the dossier to the Czechs "to create the impression in Stalin (to whom Beneš sent them) that he, Stalin, received them from friendly foreign hands. . . ." One way or another, by the beginning of May the dossier was in Stalin's hands.

Such, in brief, is the history of the "red folder." Despite some disagreement about some details, we can consider as established fact: (1) the Germans fabricated documents slandering Tukhachevsky at the behest of Skoblin, who acted with the knowledge of or according to instructions from the NKVD; (2) when Ezhov got the documents in one way or another, he was aware they were forgeries.

Stalin's role remains incompletely explained. It is entirely possible that the initiative in the affair was not his, but the NKVD's. History knows of many instances of such institutions acting independently. The tsarist Okhrana, to pick a homegrown example, was involved in the murder of a Russian prime minister, Stolypin. Stalin might have been fooled for a while, but that does not diminish his responsibility. If his favorite child had fooled him, it had acted entirely in his spirit.

The June 11 Affair

In early May 1937 the "red folder" lay on Stalin's desk. It seemed to be just what he wanted. In May preparations for the trial were sped up. On the eleventh the shake-up of the generals was announced. Tukhachevsky resigned from his duties as Deputy People's Commissar and went off to command the remote Volga district. Yakir was transferred from the Kiev district, which he had headed for twelve years, to Leningrad. His responsibilities were almost the same, with the important difference that in moving to Leningrad he automatically lost his important position as a member of the Ukrainian Politburo. At the same time Egorov, while he remained Deputy People's Commissar, gave up his post as commander of the General Staff. He was replaced by Troop Commander of the Leningrad Military District Shaposhnikov. It was then that the restoration of the military commissars was announced.[23]

Two of the personnel changes were especially important: those of Tukhachevsky and Yakir. For some time, however, both stayed where they were. On May 23 Yakir even spoke at the Party conference of the

Kiev district. Tukhachevsky arrived in Samara only on May 26 and was arrested that same day in the regional Party committee building, where he had been summoned by P. P. Postyshev.

It is hard to explain why Stalin gave such a reprieve to the two main figures of the upcoming trial. All the more since Kork (May 11), Eideman (May 24), and Feldman (May 24 or 25) had been arrested before Tukhachevsky left Moscow.

Uborevich's turn came on May 30, and Yakir was seized on the thirty-first, the same day Gamarnik shot himself. The date of Primakov's arrest is still uncertain.[24]

The reestablishment of the commissars' power was a vital measure that betrayed the evil seriousness of Stalin's intentions. Since the Civil War, commissars had occupied key positions in the Army hierarchy. Without the commissar's signature (as a member of the RVS) none of the commanders' or commanding officers' orders had the force of law. This restriction was originally caused by the lack of trust of commanders, especially those in the highest ranks, who frequently did not have proletarian backgrounds.

Unity of command was established in the RKKA in 1934. The Revolutionary Military Council of the USSR (the board of the People's Commissariat of Army and Naval Affairs) was liquidated, as were the RVSS of districts, armies, fleets, etc. The military department received a new name, the People's Commissariat of Defense (NKO). From the statute on the NKO, which was confirmed by the Central Executive Committee and the Council of People's Commissars of the USSR on November 22, 1934, we read, in part: "1. At the head of the NKO stands the People's Commissar of Defense. He also stands at the head of the RKKA. . . . 6. Under the People's Commissar is the Military Council, which is a consultative body. . . ."

Commissars became assistants to the corresponding military commanders for politial affairs. There were no consultative organs at lower levels.

The decree of the TSIK and SNK of May 10, 1937, signified a sharp turn of the wheel. From regimental level on up, commissars were restored to their former powers. Despite the fact that the law on military commissars was to go into force only on August 15, on that very day, May 10, military councils that were executive rather than consultative were formed in regions, armies, and fleets. The Law on Regional Military Councils, confirmed May 16, 1937, read in part:

1. At the head of a Military District stands the Military Council comprised of the commander of troops and two members.

2. The commander chairs meetings of the Military Council.

3. The Military Council is the highest representative of military authority in the region. All military units and institutions located in the territory of the region are subordinate to the Military Council. . . .

. . . .

5. The Military Council is subordinated directly to the People's Commissar of Defense. . . .

. . . .

7. All orders for the region will be signed by the commander of troops, one of the members of the Military Council, and the chief-of-staff.

Regional commanders, who were about to be liquidated, were stripped of command of the troops entrusted to them. It was symptomatic that the new order did not affect the People's Commissar, Stalin's apprentice, Voroshilov. The Military Council under him retained its consultative status. It was as if a state of emergency had been declared in the Army.

Now, at least in theory, any commander could be held in check by assigning to him reliable members of the Military Council. True, the political workers were pretty well soiled by Gamarnik's hostile activities and they would soon suffer purges and shake-ups; but the Stalinists never were squeamish about that sort of work.

Stalin had just about everything he needed for the trial by this time, except the sanction of some higher organ. We are not, of course, talking about observing constitutional guarantees. It was simply that Stalin did not want to take upon himself sole responsibility for such a decision. He could without difficulty have gotten the approval of the powerless TSIK headed by kindly Kalinin. Molotov stood ready to arm the SNK's resolution. Tukhachevsky's arrest had been approved in a written interrogatory of the members of the TSK, including Yakir. All this was not enough for Stalin.

Calling a plenum of the TSK entailed a certain risk: the memory of the problem at the February meeting was still fresh. But that was not the only problem. The general Secretary could in the end force the Party to make the right decision. He could say to them, "Remember, I told you of the great damage done by a few spies ensconced somewhere in Army headquarters. Now these people have been unmasked and seized." That could leave an unpleasant aftertaste, however. "Someone could say," Stalin calculated, "that the Party had judged the Army. Is that correct from the political point of view? No, it is politically wrong." Stalin decided to let the military have the last word. LET THE ARMY JUDGE THE ARMY.

On June 1 the People's Commissar of Defense summoned the Military Council. That consultative organ included the top Army brass: the deputy people's commissar, department heads of the Commissariat, regional commanders-in-chief, commandants of academies; altogether eighty people. Official reports of that session of the council are very skimpy. It was only on June 14, after the trial was over and the executions carried out, that newspapers published Voroshilov's order: "From June 1 to 4 the Military Council of the People's Commissariat of Defense met in the presence of members of the Government. They heard my report on the discovery by the NKVD of a treacherous, counterrevolutionary, fascist organization. . . ." As a matter of fact, there was no more interesting information in the order, only name-calling and curses. It was not even said what decision had been taken or if one had been taken. Members of the council were almost all liquidated. One of those remaining alive has told us what happened at those historical meetings.

Those present were stunned; no, they were utterly dispirited. Voroshilov's speech, of course, convinced no one. There was a feeling of impending catastrophe. They waited for Stalin.

Before the Great Leader appeared, the audience was properly demoralized. Stalin hurled thunder and lightning. The guilt of the eight prisoners, and also of "Gamarnik, absent from the trial," was fully proven. They were monsters of the human race, traitors, accomplices of the fascists, spies. They were proven guilty also by the testimony of their accomplices: Army Commander Sediakin, Commandant of the Academy of the General Staff Kuchinsky, Chief of the Administration of Institutions of Higher Learning Slavin. No facts were presented, no documents were offered, but no one dared ask about those things.

Members of the council sat around a long table. Stalin walked around it. From time to time he stopped behind one of them, and that person would shrink into his chair and hang his head. It was shameful and frightening.

In the silence of the hall Stalin saw his victory. He tried to make more of it. Continuing to walk around the table, he suddenly hesitated and struck up a conversation. Here he met with a setback—minor and personal, but perceptible.

At first everything went well. Stalin turned to Blucher, "Tell me Blucher, Aronshtam[25] says that nothing interests you except what women have between their legs. . . ." The marshal, who had a reputation in the RKKA as a lady-killer, exploded, "The old goat. He maligns me just because he can't get it up any more." Blucher realized that he was easily provoked and said no more. Stalin, satisfied, moved on. Standing near Budenny he said, "Here sits Semen Mikhailovich, a real proletarian commander; and these turds say he can only handle a cavalry squadron." The flattered cavalier uttered a few choice curses at the "turds." Then it was the turn of Ivan Naumovich Dubovoi, an old friend and long-time comrade of Yakir: "Tell me, Dubovoi, is it true what your buddy Yakir says, that you are incompetent to command troops?" Dubovoi shot back, "I don't believe this. We still have to examine what Yakir is guilty of." "What, you don't believe this?" said Stalin, using the familiar form of address in his excitement. He had to give up trying to feel out the future judges. (There is some evidence that all three of the men questioned were already included in the Special Board of the Military College.) On his way out of the hall Dubovoi was arrested.

Nonetheless, Stalin had reason to be satisfied. The generals had not rebelled. They had not demanded real proof and had seemed satisfied with what had been said. The external decencies had been observed: the Red Army commanders would not be tried by civilians or the NKVD, but by their brothers—by the military.

Stalin did not flatter himself with what he had accomplished. Dubovoi's prank had shown that not everyone could be convinced, deceived, or frightened, that there were a few who still kept their own council, who would doubt, feel disgust, hate, and maybe eventually act. Above all else Stalin feared a counterconspiracy and retaliatory acts.

It can be assumed that Stalin and Ezhov did not find it easy to decide just how to destroy Tukhachevsky's group. Indeed, at first they rushed ahead, and then, suddenly, paused. On May 31 the last of the accused was arrested. The next day the Military Council met. Haste. But then for some reason it met for four days. And from there the situation got worse; a whole week passed before the trial. Such delay could certainly have fateful consequences.

If Stalin seriously feared a hostile reaction from some of the generals, the best thing to do would be to wrap up the whole affair quickly and all at once. Otherwise the displeasure aroused by the arrest of Tukhachevsky, Yakir, and others might ripen. That whole week the commanders-in-chief were not permitted out of Moscow to return to their troops. The purpose of the isolation is understandable. But another danger was lurking, not less dangerous than the first.

After all, all the leaders of the Red Army were together. However many spies there might be among them, they still had the chance to come to an agreement, to join together against their common enemy, the Stalin-Ezhov gang. They still had communications with the troops. With what could Stalin oppose the might of the million-man RKKA? Nothing. Of course, the NKVD was watching in Moscow and in the provinces, but the threat was great and real.

The week's delay is an historic fact. How can it be explained? Most likely, Stalin did not have a clearly thought-through plan. There were so many agonizing, fateful questions to be decided.

The first unanswered question was Hamlet's: would there be a trial at all? It was still not too late to turn back from an enterprise that entailed fatal risk. If they challenged him on this, he would not get away with quotations and theses about escalating the class war. Destruction of the leadership of the Army was clearly treason. Bridges were not yet burned; the press had not yet been notified. The arrest of the Red generals could easily be announced as the intrigues of the enemy, the bloody fool Ezhov could be offered as a scapegoat and the whole venture passed over without excessive publicity. There was no certainty that the Army would not act. If the Army bestirred itself, Stalin could hope for intercession only from God, who had been repealed, or from the blue-caps.[26] But the temptation and the need to remove the Army leadership were too great. Stalin risked it. He counted on the passivity and indecisiveness of the victims. It is sad, but such assumptions of tyrants are often justified.

To decide to go ahead with the trial still does not presuppose a precise program. One thing was clear from the start: an open court could not be used in this case. This was a great misfortune, but from the very beginning the illustrious commanders behaved badly. From the political point of view as well as from the educational, it was not possible to drag such inveterate miscreants before the public. There would be no openhearted repentance. These were lost, hopeless people, and comrades Stalin, Ezhov, and Vyshinsky had given up on them. They did not even bother to torture them in view of the uselessness and risk of such measures. After all Tukhachevsky and his comrades-in-arms had to be presented to the military judges if only at a closed session of the Special Board of the Military College of the Supreme Court of the USSR. Marks of torture or revelations about its use might anger the judges, sharpen their unavoidable moral dilemma. It might also have repercussions in military circles, which Stalin did not want.

All right, torture was unnecessary and Stalin would do without an open trial, but that was not yet the end of the disappointments. Of what, specifically, were these scoundrels, lowlifes, traitors, and double-dealers guilty? The question seems an idle one, but its answer determined the course pursued by the prosecution. Of course, as Kafka had one of his heroes say, guilt is always proven. Nonetheless, court procedure requires an indictment and proof—or their surrogates.

The reader would be right to wonder about our questions. Wasn't the "red folder" sufficient accusatory material? And why was such an effort made to obtain it? At this point the most telling, and outrageous, point of the whole matter surfaces. Stalin had nothing with which to charge the accused. It was a lot easier to invent the corpus delicti than to bring charges against them.

God knows we do not mean to seek out paradoxes. It is known for certain that the "red folder" did not appear in the Military Council or at the trial of June 11. That fact only initially seems to lead us into a blind alley, and knowing it makes the circumstances under which the "folder" was ordered seem meaningless and inessential. Whether Ezhov acted on his own or on Stalin's orders, once the Leader of the People had seen the SD's documents, he realized they were useless fakes. What could he do with a photograph of Trotsky and a group of German officials. Who could forget that it was he, Stalin, who had invented the intimate relations between the Jewish Trotsky and the Judophobe fascists. And what was Trotsky doing in the case at all? Trotsky had never been close with Tukhachevsky! Doubts about the marshal himself were even sharper. Who could believe that he, who had escaped German captivity five times in the World War, would be rubbing elbows with the Germans? Glory, medals, the highest military rank at age forty-two, the most important post in the Army—he had all that. What more could they offer him in Berlin? To be sure, such categories as love of country and fidelity to duty did not exist for Stalin, and he did not look for them in others. Stalin did not seriously believe in Tukhachevsky's Bonapartism. He destroyed Tukhachevsky because this was a man around whom others in the Army who were dissatisfied with his, Stalin's, usurpatious behavior *might* rally. But it wasn't possible to actually make such charges publicly.

That is not what we were speaking of, however. The decision to liquidate Tukhachevsky had already been made. It remained only to decide how to dress the act up before presenting it to the Army and the people. Thus, if Stalin did not initiate the fabrication of the "red folder," he knew it was a forgery from first glance. Any subsequent checking would only confirm that opinion.

However, the decision not to use the "red folder" was not dictated by doubts of its authenticity. In the end there were two more telling reasons.

The first was that, at the two previous, celebrated, trials and at most trials of less importance, only oral testimony had been presented, no documents. Presenting essential proofs, even fabricated, seriously threatened to diminish the speed of the Stalinist machine, if not to bring it to a standstill. It would be a most dangerous precedent. The public or their appointed representatives would in the future expect proof of guilt in some form they could touch, read, and study. The whole plan of the coup based on massive judicial slaughter was threatened. Stalin did not want to risk open slaughter. That would clearly signify seizure of the state, and the Stalinists feared that. They wanted their seizure to seem a defense against seizure by others. Their cruel protective measures took place under the cover of law, juridically doubtful, logically absurd, but nonetheless *law*, which, by the way, was enough for the Russian population who were used to anything. Documentary proof was repugnant to the spirit and idea of that upside-down law. The Stalinist machine was not capable of making up even approximately proper indictments for millions of people. It is enough to glance at the cases of the so-called "enemies of the people": five or six pages of cheap paper covered with the slovenly handwriting of the newly promoted investigator. Today, when our society still does not groan under the burden of excess legality, one must fill out tens of pages, almost a hundred pages, to bring a known and clearly guilty thief to court. In the end the thief will get—it is hard to say it—a year or so in prison.

The second reason Stalin did not use the "red folder" was that he feared the Germans might double-cross him. As long as the accusations against the military officers were unsubstantiated, the Germans could react to them only as to any other propaganda. But they could respond to the published documents or mention them much more harmfully. They could tell the history of the "folder." That would give Hitler a double victory. Not only would the Army leadership be weakened, but the political leadership of Russia would also be discredited. Stalin would be held up to universal ridicule.

Tempting as it was to use the documents in this critical trial—they would impart solidity and parry the potential counteraccusation of arbitrariness—the "red folder" had to be left aside. Stalin made no use of it. He not only showed it to nobody, but he never once so much as referred to it.

The Stalinist brain trust had something to think about in June. They had a week to worry and make a very difficult decision. In the end Stalin, who never was inclined to delicacy, preferred a coarse farce. The most primitive, coarsely malevolent accusations were presented at the secret trial: treason, weakening defense capabilities, the attempt to seize power. Proofs were absurd and unsubstantiated. Of the special board only Budenny might have believed them. Only one thing was demanded of the judges: to conduct themselves loyally and not to interfere with Ulrikh prosecuting the case to the desired outcome. And that is how it was.

The short announcement tossed to the people was knocked together carelessly. Everything in it contradicted logic and common sense, but maybe they were counting on that. Stalin was a greater master of the stunning propaganda lie than Goebbels. He was also counting on Russia's endless patience.

We return to the trial's starting point. Of the sixteen main participants belonging to the military only two died natural deaths. Why then on that June day were some participants executioners, or judges, and others their victims? We will try to evaluate several factors that might have played a role in selecting the two groups. To make it easier, table 20.1 presents the facts about the participants in the trial.

Nationality. The hand of the great expert of the nationalities' question is easy to see. We will not have much to say about this either now or later, but you can judge for yourself: two Latvians, two Jews, two Lithuanians, and only two Russians. All of their names sound strange to the Russian ear, except one, Primakov, and it seems he may have been a Jew. The average man of the people, contaminated by the remnants of the past, might think they were all "kikes." Lord save us, no one need tell him, but he might think it, he certainly might. How common it is to think that all traitors and spies are non-Russians.

The composition of the court, on the other hand, at least sounds entirely Orthodox: Belov, Kashirin, Shaposhnikov, Dybenko, Budenny. Alksnis does not fit, nor does Blucher seem to, but he is a Russian. His name was given to his serf grandfather by his master who was a great admirer of the Prussian field marshal.

There is no need any longer to prove that Stalin was an anti-Semite; and we have no particular interest in divining whether his anti-Semitism was pathological, religious, or political. He was using that weapon against the oppositionists already in the 1920s. The Bukharin group, which was primarily Russian, was counterposed to the Zinoviev-Trotsky faction, which was heavily Jewish. Russian party members from these groups were told directly that they did not belong. Stalin is said to have asked Preobrazhensky, "What are you doing in that Jewish company?"

In the 1930s Stalinist propaganda played up the oppositionist Jews' connections with the Gestapo. Strange as it may seem, that did not surprise the public. The Soviet press was usually silent about—or in any case did not emphasize—Hitler's Judophobia. After the signing of the Soviet-German pact in 1939, that became a firm rule. A consequence was to increase the number of victims among the Jewish population of occupied territory. The Soviet government did not try to evacuate Jews. Earlier, in 1939–40, the NKVD regularly turned in to the Gestapo German Communists of Jewish descent.

We cannot, of course, claim that the accused and judges were chosen exclusively because of the nationalities indicated by their names. But it was in 1934 that passports with a blank for "nationality" were introduced; there had already been carried out in Moscow two trials of terrible malefactors and traitors whose names for the most part were very inferior. Sow the good, the kind, the eternal! Something will remain and take root. If not now, then in 1947, 1949, 1953!

Origins and Party Membership. In this category the two groups A (accused) and J (judges) were almost equal. In the first, five were former tsarist officers; in the second, four. That small imbalance in the unproletarian character of group A was balanced by the greater representation of members of higher party organs: one member (Yakir), and two candidate members of the TSK (Tukhachevsky and Uborevich); in

Table 20.1   Characteristics of Participants in the June 11 Trial

Name of accused	Nationality	Former officer	Pre-1917 Party member
1. M. N. Tukhachevsky	Russian	X	
2. N. E. Yakir	Jew		X
3. I. P. Uborevich	Lithuanian	X	
4. V. M. Primakov	Russian?		X
5. B. M. Feldman	Jew		
6. A. I. Kork	Latvian	X	
7. R. P. Eideman	Latvian	X	
8. V. P. Putna	Lithuanian	X	
Total		5	2
Judges			
9. S. M. Budenny	Russian		
10. V. K. Blucher	Russian		X
11. P. E. Dybenko	Ukrainian		X
12. I. P. Belov	Russian	X	
13. N. D. Kashirin	Russian	X	
14. B. M. Shaposhnikov	Russian	X	
15. Ia. I. Alksnis	Latvian	X	
16. E. I. Goriachev	Russian		
Total		4	2

group J there were only two candidate members (Budenny and Blucher). The number of prerevolutionary Communists was the same in both groups.

Cavalrymen and Comrades-in-Arms of Stalin. Group J had the lead in these categories, 3:1 and 2:0, respectively.

Intelligentsia. Here group A unquestionably dominated, by a ratio of 7:2. Except for Primakov, they were the flower of the Army's intelligentsia; men of great military erudition and expansive, cultured outlook; authors of scholarly works; major innovators in military science. In group J only Shaposhnikov and Alksnis fit into that category. Blucher, although he had studied in the German Academy of the General Staff, was primarily a careerist.

Unity of the Groups. By this we mean the presence of service and personal associations among members of one group. From this point of

Studied in Germany	Cavalry	Fought with Stalin	Associations with members of other group	Military intelligentsia	Associations within the same group
X			3,7	X	2,5,7,8
X			2,3,5	X	1,4,5,7
X				X	1,2,5
	X				2
				X	1,2,6
				X	1,5,7,8
				X	1,2,6
				X	1,6
3	1	0		7	
	X	X			8
X			2		5
			1,2		
	X				2
				X	
			1	X	
	X	X			1
1	3	2		2	

view group A seems to have been almost monolithic, while group J seems to have comprised an artificial conglomeration. That had its pluses and minuses for Stalin. It was easy to present the cohesive group A as a conspiracy. On the other hand, it would be difficult to split such a collective; it would be hard to bend them to one's will and to keep them from presenting a unified front at the trial—which is what happened. The individuals of group J could more easily be worked on in isolation. They did not have a chance to agree among themselves on a course of action.

Intergroup Associations. The corresponding column of the table shows that there were few connections, and those that existed could serve a specific purpose—camouflage. Inasmuch as information about the trial was skimpy and came mainly from rumors, former personal relations between the accused and the judges created the appearance of objectivity. It was one thing for Tukhachevsky's confirmed enemies Budenny and Kashirin to condemn him, but quite another for his close friend Dybenko and long-time associate Alksnis to do so. The same could be said about Blucher, Dybenko, and Kashirin, friends and colleagues of Yakir. Apparently that was the role assigned Dubovoi.

Of course, the foregoing analysis has primarily an illustrative character. It is naive to suggest that Stalin, Ezhov, Voroshilov, and Vyshinsky used precisely these methods to select the two groups. But if only in part, these factors must have been considered by them. We will dare to assert that two of these factors played important, if not determining, roles in their decision: the opposition of Russians to non-Russians and the opposition of careerists to the intelligentsia.

Voroshilov was mentioned purposely in the previous paragraph. His name retains a sort of halo—a legendary hero with clean hands, a brave, but simplehearted warrior who did not involve himself in politics and was therefore not implicated in Stalin's acts. Alas, that is only another illusion maintained by ignorance of facts. During his career as leader of the RKKA, Voroshilov was more the politician than the military man. Although he did not occupy first place among them, Voroshilov was deeply involved in the affairs of the Stalinists.

Here are some facts: (1) In 1925 it was Voroshilov who publicly proclaimed the false version of Frunze's death to deflect from Stalin and himself the fully justified suspicions of responsibility for murdering him. (2) In 1930 he sanctioned the arrest of a large group of military specialists. (3) In 1937 he was an active and direct participant in the destruction of the command staff, not disdaining the role of provocateur. It is enough to recall his perfidious behavior in organizing the arrest of his friend and comrade-in-arms Yakir. A general picture of Voroshilov's behavior during that period only confirms this conclusion. There is not the slightest hint that Voroshilov protected anyone from repression, or even that he tried to. To the contrary, he signed everything, he sealed it all with his bloody hand. The People's Commissar jotted on a letter written by Yakir asking that he take care of his family, "I doubt the honor of a dishonorable man in general." That was all. Voroshilov preferred to wash his hands of the matter, knowing that shame and suffering awaited Yakir's wife and child.

This has nothing to do with bravery. In battle Voroshilov did not fear death; but Yakir, Tukhachevsky, Primakov, Shmidt, and many others were not less courageous. Voroshilov's courage evaporated in the presence of Stalin.[27]

It is said that in 1936 and early 1937 Voroshilov was opposed, in theory, to the massive destruction of the RKKA's officer corps. The reasons were most prosaic. Voroshilov could not help but understand that without capable commanders he would not be able to lead the People's Commissariat and could not guarantee the Army's combat readiness. The turning point occurred on the threshold of the February-March plenum. Stalin and comrades posed the commissar a question widely used at the time, "Whom are you with? Them or us?" Other considerations, including the defense of the country, had to be put aside. Saving his skin, Voroshilov joined the executioners, with whom, it is true, he had much more in common than with the military. The First Red Officer stopped tormenting himself with doubts and gave himself body and soul to the destruction of the RKKA. Even Tukhachevsky, who did all of the ongoing work at the Commissariat for him, he gave over entirely to the Chekists. Telling him of his dismissal as his first deputy, he found not a single word of justification or comfort.

The main burden of preparing and carrying out the June villainy lay on the valiant men of the NKVD. Stalin hastened to show them his gratitude. A decree on decorating the Chekists was published on June 22. That they were not listed in alphabetical order leads one to think that their place in the list reflects the importance of their work. All the more that first of the honored was L. M. Zakovsky, whose participation in the trial of June 11 is undoubted.[28] N. E. Shapiro-Daikhovsky, P. A. Korkin, and P. E. Karamyshev also received the Order of Lenin. Ten men were awarded the Order of the Red Star. Other high-ranking executioners were mentioned. After a decent interval an announcement was made that Ezhov had been awarded the Order of Lenin on July 17. There was a great fuss in the press. Vyshinksy received his commendation on the twentieth.

Proscription

The June trial turned out to be prologue to catastrophe. Repression against the high and middle command staff took on the character of general slaughter. It is not possible to explain why one or another commander perished. It makes more sense to ask why some survived.

There is a certain sad logic to the order in which the victims were

Table 20.2   Disposition of High Command Staff, by Rank[29]

Rank	Modern equivalent	Existed	Arrested	Returned	Perished
1. Marshal	Marshal	5	3	—	3
2. Army commissar I	General of the army	1	—	—	1*
3. Army commander I	General of the army	4	3	—	3
4. Fleet flag-officer	Admiral of the fleet	2	2	—	2
5. Army commander II	Colonel general	10	10	—	10
6. Fleet flag-officer II	Admiral	2	1	—	1
7. Army commissar II	Colonel general	15	15	—	15
8. Corps commander	Lieutenant general	55	49	1	48
9. Flag officer I	Vice admiral	6	5	—	5
10. Corps commissar	General lieutenant	28	25	2	23
11. Flag officer	Rear admiral	15	9	1	8
12. Division commander	Major general	199	136	11	125
13. Division commissar	Major general	97	79	10	69
14. Brigade commander	Major general or colonel**	397	221	21	200
15. Brigade commissar	Major general or colonel**	36	34	—	34
16. Corps engineer	Engineer Lieutenant general	2	2	1	1
17. Corps intendant	Lieutenant general	3	3	—	3
18. Corps doctor	Lieutenant general of medical services	2	2	—	2
19. Corps veterinarian	Lieutenant general of medical services	1	1	1	—
20. Division intendant	Major general	10	6	—	6
21. Division engineer	Engineer Major general	9	7	2	5
Totals		899	643	60	583

*Ya. B. Gamarnik shot himself to death on May 31, 1937, to avoid arrest.
**Rank dependent on responsibilities.

destroyed. First taken were those associated with the participants of the June 11 trial, then were those associated with the victims of the second group. A few were executed who dared to speak out even timidly against the terror (Kuibyshev, Fedko, Blucher), as were hundreds and thousands who said nothing. Finally the rulers of evil—the judges —were reached.

Losses in the high command staff can be delineated by the ranks of the victims, as seen in table 20.2. Lists published in 1935 and 1940 help in the task.

Of those of lieutenant general's rank or higher (lines 1–11, and 16–18 on the table) 93 percent died in the purge. For ranks corresponding to major general and colonel (lines 12–15, 20, 21) the figure is 58.5 percent. The names of those who perished are in the appendixes to this book.

Data on commanders of the rank of colonel and lower are not yet available. It is therefore impossible to say what the RKKA's losses were at those ranks in the Great Purge. There are few references to such losses in official sources; most are indirect and do not lend themselves to interpretation. The size of the loss is mentioned only once in a Soviet source and that in relative terms.[30] There it is said that 20 percent of all military officers died in the purge. In all of Soviet military literature, however, it is impossible to learn the absolute size of the officer corps at that time. The estimate we have made, which is necessarily rough, suggests that there were 100,000 to 130,000 officers on active duty in the Red Army in 1937 and 1938. That puts the loss at between 20,000 and 25,000. There is reason, however, to think that that significantly understates the loss.

In Yu. Petrov's book, *Building the Party in the Soviet Army and Fleet*,[31] it is said that the repression cut the number of Communists in the Army in half, from 250,000 to 125,000. We can assume that the NKVD's only targets in the military were commanders and political workers. All of the latter were Party members. Of the former, 80 to 85 percent were members. That figure climbs to 95 to 97 percent in the technical branches. Consequently, the losses in the Army's Party organization fell mainly on the officer corps. But if we recall that in those years expulsion from the Party automatically led to arrest, then we must also conclude that practically all of the commanders on active duty at the beginning of the purge were repressed. We must be very careful about such a conclusion.

We cannot definitively solve that problem without more information and that is not yet available. But we can make a few further observations. We have no reason to doubt Petrov's statistics. A Soviet author would not exaggerate the scale of the repression in an official publication; no one would let him. On the other hand, we cannot significantly increase our estimate of the size of the officer corps, recalling that early in 1937 a total of approximately 1,600,000 men were serving in the Red Army. We are forced therefore to think that the loss of cadre in two years of purge comprised approximately 100,000 men. This is not an overstatement, because we are assuming admission into the Party was closed for those two years. If there were new admissions, we would have to increase the figures of the loss. It may be assumed, however, that some people who served in the Army's Party organization, but who were not at the time military servicemen, became part of that statistic. This does not include wives of commanders or noncommissioned soldiers who were expelled from the Party. They probably fall into the group of 25,000 we subtracted from Petrov's figures. We are speaking here of men in *special services*. These men served in the Army's counterintelligence while attached to the NKVD, but they worked directly in military units and were registered there on Party registers. There were a great many special servicemen: there was such an overseer in every company; from the battalion on up there were special detachments. The special servicemen numbered between 20,000 and 30,000, and they were liquidated almost to a man as were other categories of Chekists. Subtracting these we can decrease the figure for the loss of cadre to 70,000 to 80,000. If we also consider Petrov's statement that the repression took no fewer than 20,000 political workers, then the loss of "pure" commanders (combat officers, technicians, staff officers, instructors) can be set at 50,000 to 60,000.

Any attempt to explain why the repression was so widespread in the Army runs into numerous difficulties. It is impossible to assume that Stalin intended from the beginning to exterminate almost the entire officer corps, but the fact is there.

The greater part of the explanation, it seems to us, must be found in the psychology of mass terror, in conformity with its spontaneous development. Stalin had no reason to liquidate everyone in the Army one after another. The armed forces had accepted the order resulting from the state revolution. Even if the dictator could still see potential opponents or rivals in Tukhachevsky or to a lesser extent in Yakir, as hard as he might try he could not have found men of such potential in all the other victims. We must assume other causes. Having set off an avalanche of hate, suspicion, and blood, Stalin found himself unable to stop it until it had exhausted itself, run out of momentum.

It does not necessarily follow that after the June trial the Most Brilliant Commander of All Times and Nations became a passive spectator in the destruction of the RKKA. He was not that sort of man. If the scale of the repression in the Army seemed to him excessive, and he found himself unable to curtail it, he would still take an active leading role in it.

In June 1937 at the TSK plenum Stalin called for a hardening of punitive policy, not excepting the Army. In January 1938 a sealed letter of the TSK, "On Shortcomings in Party-Political Work in the RKKA and Measures to Overcome Them," was distributed by his order. The document demanded the discovery of concealed enemies of the people. It also attacked "silent" people, who had no criminal associations, but who were "politically spineless" and therefore potential enemies. It must have been easier for the proverbial camel to pass through the eye of a needle than to remain an "honest Soviet man" in such conditions. Righteous anger against enemies, their public defamation, ceaseless denunciations—nothing guaranteed safety. It was always possible to claim that someone was not exposing enemies with sufficient enthusiasm, or was doing so as a provocateur, or only to advance his career.

Neither were Stalin's subordinates in the Army napping. Voroshilov, Mekhlis, and Shadenko ceaselessly demanded that the last-born offspring of Tukhachevsky-Yakir and the minions of the Gamarnik-Bulin gang be rooted out. Throughout the country, as in the Army, a psychological climate was created that made mass terror unavoidable.

The people everywhere correctly understood their leaders' call. They rushed to search out live carriers of evil within their field of vision. A flood of denunciations swept through the country. The NKVD gladly made use of them and, more than that, "organized material" on those as yet untouched by denunciations. The higher one was on the scale of ranks, the more visible he was and the greater the probability that someone would denounce him. The motives were varied: envy, revenge for old offenses, personal dislike, career ambition; but the result was always the same.

This is how the proscription lists for arrest and execution were drawn up. Thousands of these documents went up the chain of command and landed on Stalin's and Voroshilov's desks. The reaction of the People's Commissar, who was frightened to death, was consistent. He did not dare contradict Ezhov, fearing that tomorrow he might present materials on him to the Great Leader.

Stalin's position was hardly better. Even in the summer of 1938, when it became clear that the repression was growing at a geometric progression and threatened to seize the whole population, even then he could not stop the demonic machine at will. Stalin could not tell Ezhov, "That's enough imprisoning and shooting of innocent people!" He could not because it was he who had sired that bloody dwarf, because from the very beginning he had been part of the plot, because among the conspirators they could talk only of whom to take next and when. The word "guilt" was absent from their vocabulary as superfluous and harmful; otherwise they could not have begun the coup. And that is not all. At first the excesses of the repression suited Stalin's purposes inasmuch as it sucked into its whirlpool numerous informers, provocateurs, and executioners who had become expendable.[32] There came a moment, however, when it became absolutely necessary to give the order to stop. It was not easy for the Great Leader. He was afraid of the NKVD. He feared he would seem soft, kindly, and consequently weak. He feared a conspiracy against himself and his power that would accuse him of conniving with the enemy. He could not change the policy without changing people. To stop the repression he would have to behead the NKVD and then destroy it thoroughly.[33] And that would take time. For the time being he would have to accept the liquidation of people he would otherwise, perhaps, have left alive.

We will return directly to the Army. It is possible that Ezhov liquidated some of the commanders with Stalin's coerced sanction or entirely on his own. Of course, that is only a guess, but it might have been the case with Voroshilov's old friends Levandovsky and Gorbachev. When Goriachev, one of the eight judges in the June trial, learned of their arrest, he shot himself.

Fate did not spare the members of the Special Judicial Board, who sent their comrades-in-arms to their deaths.[34] Five died in the proscriptions of 1937–38. Only Shaposhnikov and Budenny died in their beds.

Stalin must have had mixed feelings about the judges. On the one hand, to leave them alive was extremely undesirable. Having done their dirty work, they were no longer valuable. On the contrary, they might expect something in return for their valuable service. Stalin must have known that most of them had pronounced sentence against their wills. When they recovered they might think of revenge. In any case, it would be hard to rely on their silence about what really happened at the trial. I. Erenburg has left witness; I. P. Belov, talking about the trial, shared his gloomy forebodings about his own and his colleagues' fate. Stalin had to take care of them.

At the same time there were arguments in favor of the opposite action. To remove the judges would inescapably throw a shadow over the whole trial and cause doubts about the justness of the sentence.

One way or another the judges had to follow the judged. Shaposhnikov's survival can be explained by the undoubted sympathy Stalin felt for him. Shaposhnikov was practically the only man whom the dictator called by first name and patronymic both to his face and in his absence. Budenny, who gladly signed the sentence, seems to have been saved by his closeness to the Great Leader, which went back to the Civil War. There is however, a story, almost legendary, that Budenny escaped arrest only by a miracle.[35] It is worth mentioning that his wife Mikhailova, a singer at the Bolshoi, was killed.

Egorov, also a Stalinist toady from the time of the Civil War, was less lucky. In May 1937 he was temporarily promoted to deputy people's commissar in place of Tukhachevsky, but he was later sent to the provinces and soon disappeared entirely.

Stalin took an important step toward ending the purge in July 1938, by which time the repression had exceeded all conceivable bounds. L. P. Beria was made Ezhov's first deputy. In the several months of his decline the bloody Stalinist dwarf managed to take many more victims from the Army's ranks. The most famous of them were Fedko and Blucher. If the story that Ezhov shot Blucher in his office without a trial is true, very likely that incident served Stalin as the formal reason for finally getting rid of his favorite. The coincidence of the dates supports this theory. Blucher was killed on November 9; Ezhov was removed from his post as People's Commissar of Internal Affairs on December 9, 1938.[36]

Whatever Stalin's original intentions were, by the end of 1938 all that was left of the Red Army was the name. The officer corps had been utterly destroyed. All the deputy people's commissars and almost all the leaders of the central apparatus had disappeared. All regional commanders-in-chief, all commandants of military academies, all corps commanders, the overwhelming majority of divisional commanders, and more than half the commanders of regiments were gone.[37]

For the second time in twenty years the country would have to rebuild its army.

The Victims: Motives of Inaction

To remember them means to regret that they are not.
—Kliuchevsky

"Do you really not see where this is leading? He will suffocate us all one by one like baby chicks. We must do something."

"What you are suggesting is a coup. I will not do that." That is how Marshal Tukhachevsky replied to his friend Corps Commander Feldman. The conversation took place at the end of 1936 or at the very beginning of 1937. Feldman did not stop there. He went to Kiev to another friend, Yakir.

The Army Commander had company at his dacha, among them the general secretary of the Ukrainian Party, S. Kosior. They drank, proposing toasts. Someone suggested, "Let's drink to Stalin, whom we follow to the end—with our eyes closed." The host objected, "Why closed? We follow Stalin, but with our eyes open."

When the guests had departed, Feldman told Yakir of his talk with Tukhachevsky. The reaction was the same. Yakir still believed in Stalin.

The above episode—and there is no doubt that it happened—is the only attempt to organize resistance to terror in the Army that we know took place.

We are too distant from that time, of course, to recapture its moods. Still the question keeps coming back, persistently and poignantly: why did these strong, brave men, who had so many troops under their command, give themselves up to be killed without a murmur? Why didn't they resist?

Of course, a lot was done to keep the officers from acting. Stalin had powerful forces on his side: the aura of power, the NKVD with its extensive network, and also millions of honest fools who would denounce others without a moment's hesitation.

But the officers were far from weak. Many of them were connected by wartime friendships; they trusted one another to the end. The authority of Yakir, Tukhachevsky, and Primakov in the Army was enormous. Many line commanders would have followed them with their regiments and divisions. They had only to call. But they didn't.

The enemy was powerful, but the officers were not lacking in bravery and resoluteness. Yakir had accomplished his legendary march in 1919 in less favorable conditions. And isn't it more honorable to die in battle than in a torture chamber?

Apparently the physical balance of forces did not play a role. These experienced warriors must have had some internal reasons, preventing them from defending themselves.

One simple explanation comes to mind immediately. Courage in war and courage in everyday life are not the same thing. Examples to illustrate this are familiar. The hero returning from war is helpless before the bureaucrat, the boor, the conman, and not infrequently before his wife. There at the front everything tells you to fight bravely: responsibility, discipline, comrades, and finally the enemy seeking to kill you. In peaceful conditions the threat is not usually so sharp, the enemy is almost invisible, the rules of the fight are different. Here you don't advance on the enemy en masse, and a different sort of courage is needed. You have to stand up alone against an authority behind whom stands the indifferent and servile masses. In war, bravery brings laurels; here, it threatens shame and humiliation.

These general observations are true enough, but in our case they are not sufficient. There is something else. We will try to explain what we have in mind, but the reader must not expect precise definitions, a clear picture, or rock-hard conclusions. The material we are discussing is very delicate and will not stand rough handling. We will base our account on several examples.

Yakir. The Revolution made him a military commander. A little past twenty and a student of chemistry, he proved to be not only a capable agitator and organizer, but also an outstanding commander, about whom legends were already growing during the Civil War. Yakir had a tenacious mind and a native intelligence. He could rally people and lead them in unequal battle. The human material the Revolution gave him was motley in the extreme: yesterday's underground revolutionary who did not know how to hold a rifle; green youth; Chinese volunteers; former tsarist officers; "the Red Robin Hood" Gregory Kotovsky; and Mishka Yaponchik, the Odessa bandit, with his boys.

Yakir was exceptionally brave. He threw himself into battle with the many various Whites. He was stirred to fight not only by revolutionary ideals but also by tragic memories. He grew up Jewish in Kishinev, where he saw the horrible pogrom of 1903 with his own eyes.

After the war the young Yakir's military and Party career advanced rapidly. In 1921 he became commander of the Kiev Military District; in 1923, assistant commander of troops in the Ukraine and Crimea under Frunze; in 1924 he was made head of the Main Administration of Military Schools of the RKKA. In November 1925 he became commander of the Ukraine Military District; in December 1925, a member of the TSK of the Communist Party (Bolsheviks) Ukraine; and in 1927, a member of the Ukrainian Politburo.

In 1928–29 Yakir, together with a group of the top-ranking commanders (Tukhachevsky, Blucher, Uborevich, Sediakin, and others), attended the German General Staff Academy. He earned highest distinction at graduation. Field Marshal Hindenburg, the aged president of Germany, gave Yakir Shleiffen's book *Cannae* and inscribed it very flatteringly, "To the best modern commander."

With Yakir's arrival the Ukrainian district became the primary training ground of the RKKA, where the newest methods of warfare were developed. Yakir was not a theoretician; he did not write books; but he may have understood the spirit of modern warfare better than all the other high-ranking commanders. The first paratroop units in the Red Army were created in his district, as was the first mechanized corps, the 45th under A. N. Borisenko. He worked hard to develop methods of cooperation between the branches of the military (land and sea forces, land and air forces) and imparted his style to his subordinates.

From the beginning Yakir attributed little importance to the strategy of destruction. He worked urgently at strategic defense and induced his commander colleagues to do so. The first systems of echelonned defenses were born in the Ukrainian Military District; partisan bases were first developed there in case of retreat. Tukhachevsky's conversion to strategic defense came about under the unobtrusive but firm influence of Yakir, despite the fact that Yakir was not only three years younger than Tukhachevsky but had not attended tsarist military academies or fought in the First World War.

Yakir's authority as a leader and teacher was uncontestable. It is no exaggeration to say he was idolized by his subordinates. He tirelessly fought martinets and swaggerers in the Army. With junior officers he was evenhanded, affable, and benevolent. He thought it more important to educate than to punish. The officer corps of the Ukrainian Military

District was always the best in the Army. Yakir knew almost all the commanders of the district, and from regimental commanders on up that relationship was so close that he was aware of their family problems. Yakir was distinguished by his genuine democratic spirit. He always resisted attempts to separate the officer corps from the soldiers, to turn it into a closed caste.

Our idyllic picture would not be complete if we did not mention another fact. Yakir was first and foremost a Bolshevik. His Bolshevism was not affected or forced as was many officers'. Yakir held Party ideals sacred. For him the Party's interests, the matter of building socialism, came first, before personal and professional considerations. Here is where Yakir's strength and greatness should be sought: in these high principles combined with altruism, absence of career ambitions, and profound decency. But precisely for those reasons in the decisive moments he was weak and helpless.

Yakir's deep conviction of the rightness of the cause he served at times made him act in ways hard to reconcile with this picture of his morality. In the chapter on Mironov we spoke of his attitude toward anti-Soviet rebellions while he was with the 8th Army. His beliefs were quite simple: (1) no negotiations, (2) the complete destruction of all rebels, (3) immediate execution of anyone caught with weapons, (4) in a number of cases the preventive execution of a certain percentage of the male population. The 8th Army left a bloody trail along the Don with thousands of executions. But Yakir was not an inveterate scoundrel or a bloodthirsty fanatic. On the contrary, his behavior after the war said otherwise.

Yakir was an important political figure. He alone among the military commanders was a full member of the TSK. (Gamarnik and Voroshilov were both commissars.) In that capacity Yakir had to deal with matters that were quite distant from military service. His role in building the Kharkov tractor factory is well known. He also took an active part in carrying out collectivization in the Ukraine. The results horrified him. The year 1933 was particularly terrible for Ukrainian villagers. Despite the drought Stalin's plan was carried out strictly by the book. It wasn't enough that millions of people in the villages died of starvation, but grain saved for seed was taken from the villages. Yakir and several other Ukrainian leaders suggested that the grain collection be halted and seed grain be returned to the farmers. Kosior, fearing Stalin, did not agree. Then Yakir, Dubovoi, and secretaries of the provincial committees Khataevich and Veger wrote to Moscow. Stalin grudgingly offered concessions, but he expressed his displeasure to Voroshilov: why couldn't military men mind their own business. It may be that his honesty cost Yakir promotion to marshal in 1935.

Earlier, in mid-1930, another more characteristic episode occurred. At the same time the former generals were being arrested in Moscow, the Ukrainian OGPU was cooking up a local affair. A large group of tsarist officers was accused of organizing a conspiracy with the aim of raising an anti-Soviet rebellion. Among other things, they were accused of planning to kill the top leaders of the Ukrainian Military District: Yakir, Dubovoi, and Khakhanian. Yakir strongly protested the provocation and did not hesitate to lock horns with the chief Ukrainian Chekist, Balitsky. The case went right to the top. On December 30 Yakir and Dubovoi were called to Moscow where they were received by Ordzhonikidze. They succeeded in defending the majority of the accused. Balitsky was transferred from the Ukraine. The reader may compare Yakir's and Tukhachevsky's behavior in the same situation.[1]

Yakir was neither weak nor cowardly. He did not fear the all-powerful GPU, but he was powerless before the Party. In 1937 Yakir tried to rescue Shmidt and Kuzmichev at the risk of running afoul of Ezhov. He asked Stalin to intervene when his good friend Garkavy was arrested. But he could not rebel against the policy of repression because the Party, his Party, stood behind it. The Party was everything for him; serving it gave his life content and meaning. It was impossible, unthinkable for him to change his convictions. This is the tragedy of the whole generation that made the Revolution. Yakir did not quail before any enemy, but to raise his hand against the Party—even the thought of such a thing was unnatural for him.

That is why he did not call out his crack regiments, which could have destroyed the NKVD. That is why in the face of death he cried, "Long live the Party! Long live Stalin!" Yes, Stalin, because for Yakir the Great Leader and the Party were the same.

Tukhachevsky. Although Tukhachevsky and Yakir spent many years in harness together and faced death together, they were entirely different people. Tukhachevsky was made of different clay from his colleague. This was not just a matter of class origins, but of personality. If for Yakir ideals that he served with religious fervor stood in first place, then Tukhachevsky's primary motivation was ambition. It was not Stalin's unrestrained striving after power, nor Voroshilov's careerism, that drove him to make any compromise with his conscience, but ambition, pride, hunger for excellence, glory, the desire to be first, the best. By itself ambition is not necessarily negative. On the contrary, lacking it, it would be hard to be a great commander.

Tukhachevsky's ambitions were serious and far-reaching. In that way he resembled the young Bonaparte, and the comparison was obvious to many. But in vain did detractors ascribe such ambitions to him. Tukhachevsky was not enticed by the role of political leader. If he were carried away in dreams, he saw himself crowned only with a commander's glory. He considered strategy his calling. That is apparent in his early written works.

A lieutenant just yesterday and not yet thirty, he wrote with enviable assurance. On every page one can find naive, immature, and basically wrong statements; but the tone was nonetheless certain, dry, didactic. The author had no doubts: he trusted his own conclusions more than the entire previous experience of mankind.

Tukhachevsky was gifted. Natural intelligence, decisiveness, independence of judgment, courage—all of these qualities distinguished him from the mass of revolutionary commanders. He was handsome, attractive to women, exceptionally strong,[2] and highly cultured. He especially loved music: he built violins, haunted the concert halls, and was among the first to notice and support the young Shostakovich.

However, it was not only his personal qualities that accounted for the success of Tukhachevsky's career. Two circumstances helped him greatly. First, he joined the Party early, in April 1918. For Yakir the Revolution was a desired and logical occurrence. Tukhachevsky saw it as unavoidable reality, a natural phenomenon or disaster. When he returned from captivity, he found the old army in its death agony. He went to the only organized power at the center, the Bolsheviks, to participate in building a new army. Joining the Party was not a result of enlightenment or ideological rebirth. It was an entry fee, a necessary condition for a military career. Tukhachevsky was not a timeserver. He simply decided that the Bolsheviks were here to stay. He did not imagine himself outside the military profession. In tsarist times it was almost impossible to get ahead if you were not a member of the Russian Orthodox Church. True faith was not demanded. Indeed, that was impossible. The military existed to break the commandment, "Thou shalt not kill." But external loyalty to the church was required. Now it was necessary to convert to a new state religion; that was all. Tukhachevsky's quick-ripening Bolshevism was and remained mainly for show.

As a young officer working in the military department of the All-Russian Central Executive Committee, Tukhachevsky was soon noticed and valued. He was sent to a high command post in the Army. His courageous behavior during Muraviev's Left-SR revolt was the second most important moment of his career. Now in the eyes of the central authorities and local commissars he was finally one of them, a real Red commander. He was given access to all information. Other commanders, who were thought of as military specialists, were not trusted in this way. As a rule they knew less than the Revolutionary Military Council members attached to them.

Tukhachevsky fought well. Successes on the Eastern Front brought him great glory. Stalin, who was slow to praise, called him "the demon of the Civil War." They transferred him to the Southern Front against Denikin, and again he displayed his best qualities. Tukhachevsky was a born operations commander. In the Civil War, operations pushed strategy to the background. Successive battles over a short period decided the fate of a campaign. Many, including Tukhachevsky, took that temporary, specific condition as an unalterable law for all future wars. It is in this conviction that the ideological foundation of the blitzkrieg and the strategy of destruction should be sought. Tukhachevsky became one of its foremost proponents for many years. Even the failure of the Polish campaign did not cool his enthusiasm. As he saw it, the defeat was the result of strategic miscalculation; large operational mistakes on the neighboring fronts were not fatal. Most important was the underestimation of the enemy's resources and his ability to strike back. But the "destructive" form of action had an irresistible attraction for Tukhachevsky. He hoped that the new military equipment would give this strategy the decisive trump. He expended a great deal of energy to establish the technical basis of the Red Army. Only toward the end of his life did he partly revise his strategic views.

We will not develop this topic further; it is treated in sufficient detail in the preceding chapters. Other things are much more important in describing Tukhachevsky's personality. During the Civil War he performed many valuable services for the Soviets, not only on the fronts against the Whites, but also in suppressing popular uprisings. The glory of the suppressor was not as great, but it was properly valued by the government. After his success at Kronshtadt, Tukhachevsky was immediately sent against Antonov. (It is interesting that the romantic adventurer G. Kotovsky, who was also active in suppressing the Tambovshchina, fulfilled his role in the punitive expedition with great reluctance.)

These episodes from 1921, which are morally suspect however you look at them, throw new light on Tukhachevsky's personality. They display his political immaturity and his social callousness. Characteristically he not only put the rebellion down, but not long before he wrote a manual on how to do it.[3] It would seem that had the little Civil War dragged on, Tukhachevsky might have become a regular suppressor.

If we keep this side of him in mind, his methods in the polemic with Svechin do not seem so surprising. From using political labels he logically moved on to persecuting his opponent, who was already in the NKVD's torture chamber: he assiduously played first violin in the Party's orchestra of political persecutors. Neither in 1930 nor in 1937 did Tukhachevsky intercede for anyone.

Tukhachevsky thought himself an integral part of the Soviet establishment. He had gotten everything from it—glory, decorations, high position. He would hardly have accepted the post of executioner, but the power he served and that rewarded him so generously was in his eyes God-given—itself and its bearers. Thus ambition came to contradict patriotism and paralyzed it, made it abstract, speculative.

Tukhachevsky was organically incapable of social protest, let alone action. He did not confront Stalin in 1936 when he saw that the dictator had taken the wrong course concerning the defense capabilities of the USSR, nor did he later when Stalin attacked the Army.

By a bitter irony of history Stalin destroyed Tukhachevsky, fearing he was another Bonaparte, while the marshal was wholly unsuited for the role. In his moment of truth he proved to have nothing inside the cover of his strong and purposeful personality. His pursuit of glory proved expensive. In the face of this mortal danger he felt loneliness, isolation, and spiritual weakness. He did not heed Feldman's warning a few months before the catastrophe. After he was removed from his duties on May 11, he no longer doubted he would be killed, but he did nothing to defend himself. His own life, the Red Army, which he had worked so hard to build, even the fate of his Motherland, suddenly meant nothing to him. Everything had been destroyed, it was all in vain, his life had lost its meaning, there was nothing to hope for in his last hour.[4] He could not, like Yakir, die for the Party idea, because he had never believed in it. "It seems to me as if all this were a dream," was all Tukhachevsky could say in court. He put his head in his hands and remained silent for the rest of the session.

The Military Council, June 1–4. Eighty of the highest-ranking military leaders of the country accepted, without a murmur, the Great Leader's brazen act that falsely slandered their comrades-in-arms. He forced them to pronounce the death sentence, and they complied. Except for Dubovoi, no one dared express doubts.

What made them do it? Obsequiousness, indifference to the fate of others, malicious joy at others' misfortune, fear? Possibly fear together with confusion played the major part. S. P. Uritsky said that after the meeting he, like all the rest, left the hall with the firm conviction that they would all soon be arrested.

It is easier to understand the behavior of Budenny and others like him who were openly glad to see the fall of the hated intellectuals. But they were the minority. Alksnis and Khalepsky, Tukhachevsky's closest associates, could not have thought that way, and they did not. Yakir's comrades Fedko, Krivoruchko, and Khakhanian did not think that way. The giant Krivoruchko, who commanded the 2nd Cavalry Corps after Kotovsky, was distinguished by his spontaneity and unrestrained morality. He worshipped Yakir, who treated his behavior very gently, like a father. In other circumstances Krivoruchko would have given his life for the Army commander without hesitation. Here he kept his peace. He kept his temper; he did not attack the offender, whom he could have crushed with a finger. Only later in prison did Krivoruchko's nature come through. He grabbed an investigator and throttled him and then using his body as a club beat back his guards—until they shot him.

Several dozen brave men, whose profession demanded they not lose their heads in the moment of danger, who led their men in battle, sat shamefully silent. Stalin spat in their faces and they just lowered their eyes, unable to swear or even to scream in helpless rage.

Four long days they sat together and were unable to come to an agreement. They had several alternatives: passive resistance, open protest, or even physical action against Stalin and Voroshilov.[5] They preferred servile approval. A year and a half later almost none of them were still alive.

Blucher. For several years he was the military dictator of the Far East. Conditions on the border, expectation of a clash with Japan, gave him unlimited power. Blucher's authority among his subordinates was unquestioned. Ten thousand versts from Moscow, linked only by the thread of the Trans-Siberian Railroad, he was well shielded from Stalin.

The few hundred private guards who accompanied Mekhlis and Frinovsky could not, of course, frighten him. One word from Blucher and they would cease to exist. What could Stalin do after that? Send the Red Army marching against the Far East? Hardly.

But Blucher did nothing, and the NKVD harvested his commanders. Then without a murmur he set off for Moscow, where he could not expect any help. The hero of Perekop had lost courage, laid down his arms. When he recovered his senses a few months later, it was too late.

The twofold treachery in June, accepting the role of executioner of his comrades, had deprived him of his courage and sharp wits. It had even blunted his instinct for survival. In the Far East the Red Army had its last chance to oppose Stalin.

The surprising passivity of the commanders of the Red Army in 1937 and 1938 will long fascinate psychologists and historians. Today we have too few facts to research the problem fully. However, we can draw one lamentable conclusion now. Yakir, Tukhachevsky, Blucher, and many other talented commanders, strong personalities, courageous warriors, did not withstand the ultimate test and proved unworthy sons of the Motherland. They did not just give their own lives to the tyrant, they put the whole Army at his feet.

No one is guilty because he is born a slave;
but the slave who not only does not strive to be free, but who justifies
and prettifies his slavery . . . such a slave is a groveler and cad who provokes a
natural feeling of indignation, scorn, and loathing. —Lenin

We will digress for a short while from the complex intrigues and gloomy secrets of the Moscow court. We will sip the invigorating atmosphere of those years. Let us see how the Soviet press and public reacted to these events.

We will begin a little before the beginning, in the summer of 1936. So as not to bore the reader, we will confine ourselves to material from one newspaper, the official organ *Izvestiia* (News) *of the Council of Workers' Deputies*.

The Soviet people had just been given (actually presented for discussion, but no one was about to take it back) a new constitution, the Stalin Constitution. It was undoubtedly a landmark in man's history. A distant precedent might be sought in 1215 in England when the Magna Carta was accepted, but the scale of the events was vastly different. Our people's joy and gratitude were unbounded.

Representative entries in *Izvestiia* between July 1936 and the end of June 1937 include the following:

July 6. The chief editor of *Izvestiia*, N. I. Bukharin, wrote in an article "The Paths of History": "If we were to seek one word to express these changes, we would certainly be right to say: unification or consolidation, . . . consolidation of the widest popular masses around the party, around Stalin."

July 11. A rhymed message from the Belorussian people to comrade Stalin contained these lines:

> We heard Kaganovich's word here
> In Gomel he helped our Party grow
> The workers of Vitebsk remember Ezhov,
> Who labored hard for the Party.

July 14. Through the joyous events shortcomings were not neglected. An article entitled "Why Are There No Gramaphone Records?" appeared.

July 16. A report by A. I. Mikoyan: "We will achieve an abundance of food products." It is appropriate to mention here an anecdote of those years, which, it is true, did not get into the papers: A delegation of workers came to the Academy of Sciences to ask that the letter "M" be excluded from the Russian Alphabet as useless. As they explained it there was no meat, no butter (*maslo*), no margarine, no macaroni, no soap (*mylo*). All that began with "M" that was available was the Commissar of Trade Mikoyan, but there wasn't much sense in keeping a special letter around just for him.

There was also an order of the TSIK USSR to relieve comrade G. Ia. Sokolnikov, from his duties as People's Commissar of Forestry and transfer him to local work in the commissariat.

July 20. On the tenth anniversary of the death of F. E. Dzerzhinsky, a photo was published of the Great Leader in the embrace of Iron Felix (summer 1925).

July 22. The nonstop flight of Chkalov, Baidukov, and Beliakov, from Moscow to Chita via Petropavlovsk was announced.

July 24. The life of the people became better, more prosperous. This advertisement appeared:

The PRAGUE Restaurant is open

Roof Garden

Meals prepared by experienced chefs

August 2. A speech by L. M. Kaganovich, "The Stalinist Year in Rail Transport," was reported.

August 10. The Soviet people read with pleasure an article by the well-known publicist Karl Radek, "How to Become Chkalov: If you want to be a Chkalov, heed the call of our great leader and teacher Stalin: study, study, and study to catch and surpass the capitalist world."

August 12. Professor E. Tarle in an article "Historical Parallels" compared the electoral systems in the USSR and in the West.

August 20. Pushkin wrote: "We do not have a parade, we have a war." As if to prove the poet's words, the lead article screamed "Trotskyite-Zinovievite Gang on Trial." The trial had just begun in open court, but the paper ran in its first column telegrams from workers: "NO MERCY! SHOOT THE FASCIST MURDERERS!" Below there followed an official statement about the beginning of the trial. The case of the Trotskyite-Zinovievite terrorist center was in court. The accused included Zinoviev, Kamenev, Evdokimov, I. N. Smirnov, and twelve others. (According to the Stalinist Constitution all nationalities of our country were completely equal. Therefore the list of accused included nine Jewish names plus Zinoviev (Radomyslsky), Kamenev (Rozenfeld), one Armenian, one Pole, and three Russians.)

The judges were: chairman V. V. Ulrikh, members I. O. Matulevich and V. G. Nikitchenko, alternate I. T. Golikov, secretary A. F. Kostiushko, state prosecutor A. Ia. Vyshinsky.

The accused admitted the charges against them, but it is not the trial itself that interests us here.

August 21. From the lead article "Fascist Monsters": "The stimulus of the underground is hunger for personal power." Headline on the first column: WORKERS OF THE SOVIET UNION UNANIMOUSLY DEMAND THAT PEACEFUL LABOR BE PROTECTED, SHOOT THE FASCIST GANG!

That, so to speak, was the official slogan. What of the real Soviet people? Maybe just a few of them were surprised, even perplexed, by the monstrous metamorphosis of their recent leaders? Not in the least! They immediately understood who was who and what was what. The interrogation of the accused was still under way, but the people were already expressing their firm and final opinion. A schoolgirl from Kadievka expressed it best of all. Here is the end of her poem, published on the second day of the trial:

Thrice scorned, loathsome creatures.

Whom did they dare threaten with death.

No! Expect no more mercy.

There's only one sentence for you: shoot them like dogs.

In truth, from the mouths of babes. . . .

There were ten other comments above that one all saying one thing: SHOOT!

The writers of Leningrad: A. Tolstoi, V. Shishkov, Iu. Libedinsky, N. Brykin, G. Belitsky spoke out. Together, unanimously: "This is the vilest treachery of all the treason known in the history of mankind."

The public's favorite, Karl Radek, was not left out. He wrote in an article, "The Trotskyite-Zinovievite Fascist Gang and Their Hetman Trotsky": "The accused do not have and never did have a political program. Only a desire for personal power." He had a few choice epithets for Trotsky: "fascist *ober*-bandit," "bloody bandit," "bloody jester." Radek was sure the proletarian court would bring in the verdict the "bloody killers deserve. . . . The chief organizer of the gang and its deeds, Trotsky, has already been nailed to his shameful post by history. He will not escape the sentence of the world proletariat."

Nor, comrade Radek, will you escape the sentence of the Military College of the Supreme Court, a later historian might say.

August 22. The lead article: "The Hour of Revenge Approaches."

New notes sound in friendly chorus: UNRAVEL THE CRIMINAL TANGLE TO THE END! DISENTANGLE THE THREADS LEADING TO TOMSKY, SOKOLNIKOV, THE LEADERS OF THE RIGHT OPPOSITION, RADEK, SEREBRIAKOV! How life hurries on: only yesterday they had run Radek's article.

The other of the two leaders of the right opposition, N. I. Bukharin (Tomsky was named), was as before the editor of *Izvestiia.* That edition came out under his signature.

The Moscow writers. V. Stavsky opened the meeting. V. Kirshon, V. Inber, E. Zozulia, M. Shaginian, the poets Lugovskoi, Lakhuti, and others spoke of their enormous scorn for the inveterate double-dealers and murderers, and demanded they be shot. They acknowledged the greetings of comrades Stalin, Voroshilov, and Yagoda.

We promised not to discuss the trial itself, but we cannot refrain from mentioning one episode:

Interrogation of I. N. Smirnov

> VYSHINSKY: When did you leave the center?
> SMIRNOV: I did not plan to leave it, there was nothing to leave.
> V: Did the center exist?
> S: What center are you talking about?

In turn the procurator asked several of the accused "Did the center exist?" and they willingly confirmed that it did.

A statement by General Procurator Vyshinsky. "Serebriakov and Sokolnikov have already been brought to trial. The matter of the others is under investigation."

There was no announcement in the papers that on that very day one of the leaders of the rights, M. P. Tomsky, shot himself at his dacha in Bolshevo. Soon thereafter the TSK condemned his act a weakness unworthy of a Bolshevik.

Comments from the provinces called him "A secret Trotskyite: Double-dealer excluded from the Party."

N. Izgoev, a former assistant on Miliukov's émigré paper, called them "Trotsky's dive-bombers."

August 23. Lead article: "Shoot the Rabid Dogs."

Headlines on the first column: UNRAVEL THE EVIL TANGLE TO THE END, EXPLAIN ALL TIES OF RYKOV, BUKHARIN, UGLANOV, RADEK, AND PIATAKOV WITH THE CENTER.

WE INDIGNANTLY NOTE THE LOW DOUBLE-DEALING OF THE RIGHTS. INVESTIGATE AND EXPLAIN TO THE END, demand the workers.

Bukharin signed that issue of the paper, too.

Speech of General Procurator Vyshinsky. The state prosecutor spoke for four hours and concluded with the very precise juridical formulation, "I demand you shoot the rabid dogs, every one of them."

An announcement of a new altitude record by pilot V. Kokkinaki appeared nearby.

From a poem by N. Sidorenko:

They will not save their slippery skins.
The sword of the proletarian dictatorship,
The sword that unerringly strikes
Can slice vile creatures.

From an article by V. Antonov-Ovseenko: "Kill them all." (This was still another prophet of his own fate.) Everyone speaking out in the paper agreed with the sentence.

A brief article on the discovery of terrorists in the People's Commissariat of Agriculture in Uzbekistan was titled "Trotskyite Offspring Uncovered."

People's artist from Georgia Ak. Vasadze wrote, "Destroy the villainous people of this villainous case."

August 26. The death of S. S. Kamenev, commander-in-chief during the Civil War was announced.

"There will be no mercy for you, traitors of the people!" wrote Sofia Bortman, pediatrician from the Bauman region. "THE COURTS VERDICT IS OUR VERDICT!"

August 29. Botvinnik and Kapablanka were victorious in a tournament in Nottingham.

August 30. The flight of V. Molokov was announced.

And thus, the first show trial was over. The protests fell silent, the people returned to their creative work. Stalin and the NKVD set about getting ready for the next trial. The experiences of August would be analyzed and learned from. In the future the noisy preparation would be noisier and more massive, the sentences more varied.

December 25. A speech by T. D. Lysenko, at a meeting of the All-Union Academy of Agricultural Science was quoted: "I do not understand how Vavilov can insist on his mistaken conclusions after a conclusive examination. That is not simply wrong now, but harmful."

N. I. Vavilov had second thoughts, and during the next trials carefully added his voice in support. That was historically progressive, but it did not save him from death in prison.

December 26. An all-union conference of the wives of the command and administrative staff of the RKKA was reported. The story also carried a photo of Stalin, Voroshilov, and Zhdanov among the commanders' wives. Stalin sat next to S. L. Yakir during the meeting. Talking with her affably, he said, "You take care of the commander. He is very valuable to us."

December 29. It was announced that an all-union census would be conducted on January 6. The census did take place as scheduled, but the results never saw the light of day, and those who conducted it were shot.

1937: THE FINAL YEAR OF THE SECOND FIVE-YEAR PLAN

January 3. Yesterday Stalin received the German writer Lion Feuchtwanger. Their conversation lasted three hours. Feuchtwanger was completely charmed and wrote everything Stalin wanted.

January 16. N. I. Bukharin signed for the last time as editor of *Izvestiia.* From then on it was signed by a faceless editorial board. That was easier.

January 21. THE DAY OF LENIN'S DEATH. Next to that article in the first column was a piece entitled DAMNED TRAITORS.

> The NKVD under the leadership of Ezhov has unmasked a parallel center: Piatakov, Radek, Sokolnikov, Serebriakov. . . .
>
> They were the most dangerous, most evil enemies of our people. These Trotskyite beasts, bloody and cynical, worse than Denikin, worse than Kolchak, worse than the worst White guards, soaked in the blood of workers and peasants. . . .

Radek, that cringing, hypocritical, fornicating scum, poisonous Trotskyite scum, concealing poisonous teeth behind his fawning smile. . . . and these evil enemies of Lenin, these villains dared call themselves Leninists. . . . Judge them with all the severity of the law, judge strictly and mercilessly. Destroy all the Trotskyite filth without mercy.

January 22. A session of the TSIK RSFSR: acceptance of the new constitution.

January 24. (The paper was not printed on Saturday the 23rd) A lead article, in three columns: "Traitors, Lackeys of Fascism, Base Restorers of Capitalism": "Crush the Trotskyite scum. That is the unanimous demand of all honest people who love their Motherland and freedom."

No telegrams and outraged protests from citizens appeared yet.

Bruno Yasensky's article, "The German boots of Mr. Trotsky" described "the professor of double-dealing, Radek. . . ." Now it was Radek's turn to wear the abusive epithets. Yasensky took his place as publicist. He would do his best at that trial, but the NKVD did not believe the articles.

There were official announcements about the trial of the anti-Soviet Trotskyite center. The accused included Piatakov, Radek, Sokolnikov, Serebriakov, Muralov, Livshits, Drobnis, and ten others. The court consisted of Ulrikh, Matulevich, N. M. Rychkov. The prosecutor was Vyshinsky. Defense attorneys were Braude (for accused Kniazev), Kommodov (Pushin), Kaznacheev (Arnold). The organizers of the trial thought it would look better to have some defense attorneys.

January 25. In the lead article, "Allies and Abettors of the Fascist Aggressors" we read, "Radek is a fornicating, thoroughly rotten double-dealer, a dishonorable political intriguer, an old scout of Trotskyism, an evil Jesuit, outdoing even Loyola, Talleyrand, and Fouche."

Radek must have been flattered to be put in such company! The article continued, "waves of popular anger, tumultuous and growing, sweep from all ends of our great country to the doors of the House of Unions. Thousands, tens of thousands of meetings are held night and day in factory shifts, in mines, at kolkhozes."

And in fact angry comments took up two whole columns, and the court report two more.

Decorated professor of medicine N. I. Burdenko wrote, "Punish the enemies of the people without mercy!" If memory does not fail, the Hippocratic oath does not contain such a phrase.

From an article "Word of a Mother": "I am a woman, I am a mother, I am a grandmother. But my hand would not shake for a second if they told me to carry out the merciless sentence, which the Supreme Court *must* pronounce on them all."

In all times, despite the large rewards, there has always been a shortage of executioners. But here was a volunteer executioner, a grandmother at that. Here is a heretofore unknown achievement of the Stalinist era! We almost forgot to mention who that courageous lady was. Remember, dear countrymen, Maria Mikhailovna Vasileva, a worker at the "Red Triangle" factory. People should know their executioners.

B. Yasensky wrote of "Professor double-dealer." It is not hard to guess that it was about Radek.

Lion Feuchtwanger wrote on the first day of the trial: "Already the first day of the court proceedings have *shown the desire*[1] to carry out this important trial peacefully, with dignity, and impressively. The guilt of the accused seems already mostly proven. However, in the interests of determining the truth once and for all I hope that in the course of the trial the motives for which the accused have made their detailed confessions will be made clear."

There is no argument that their guilt seemed proven. The problem was only that there was no proof, for example, documents. Everything was based on the testimony of the accused about themselves and others, that is, on slander and self-slander. Therefore Feuchtwanger made this reservation in the spirit of rotten Western liberalism. Never mind that, as later articles would show, the progressive German writer was satisfied with what was given. Possibly he remembered the Hegelian postulate "all that is real is reasonable." Apparently the Moscow air has some magical quality that deprives even those who have no use for it of reason.

K. Volsky's "The Scorned *Ober*-Traitor" was about Trotsky.

AN ANGRY WORD FROM THE WORKERS OF MOSCOW

Weaver Topchevskaia of the Trekhgorka factory: "For me Trotsky and his gang are worse than Hitler! Hitler at least discarded his mask! That scum Radek, how he fooled us, flattering, and worming his way. I'd like to kill him with my own hands!"

M. M. Vasilieva was not alone in her noble anger. Maybe we see the start of something new here, a national movement of women executioners.

Secretary of the Party committee Beliaeva wrote, "We've got to squeeze the Trotskyite-Fascist gang of traitors and the traitors led by Bukharin out of the rightist camp. Hatred boils in the hearts of the workers of Trekhgorka. We must become Chekists."

Yes, there were women in the Russian Party committees.

"Bukharin, Rykov, and everyone who was with them must be made to answer. It must be thoroughly investigated, what the degree of their involvement was in the crimes of the Trotskyite gang!" Such was the unanimous demand of the workers at the Voitovich factory.

It seemed that Nikolai Ivanovich was to be awarded highest honors, that is, capital punishment, for many years of faultless struggle with Trotskyism.

From Leningrad, the senior female worker of the Skorokhod factory Voronova, wrote: "We are sure that the organs of the NKVD will even more vigilantly guard the interests of our people and, most importantly, save our great leaders. And we will help them in this work however we can."

They used to say, "A woman's path is from stove to door." Now she has two other paths to choose: to be an executioner or a Chekist.

From workers in the Tbilisi locomotive repair shop: "Destroy every last scum."

Academician A. Palladin: "We demand the complete destruction of the whole gang."

From people's artist Yablochkina: "We must once and for all clear our land of these despised people."

An article by P. Lapinsky called it: "The monstrous but logical development."

January 26. The lead article, "Trotskyite Monsters, Stranglers of the People," proclaimed, "They will be wiped from the face of the earth."

A. Tolstoy's "Plan for World War Nipped in the Bud" was a professional analogy between Trotsky and . . . Stavrogin.

Yakub Kolas wrote: "They have no right to live." Let history not be confused. It was not Kolas who "called for mercy for the fallen." That was Pushkin.

Aleksei Stakhanov, Makar Mazai: "Wipe Piatakov, Radek, Sokolnikov, and the whole rotten gang from the face of the earth! We demand the vile roles of Bukharin and Rykov be investigated to the end. Mercy for no one!"

Professors of chemistry B. Klimov, A. N. Nesmeianov, V. I. Nikolaev, O. E. Zviagintsev condemned the traitors.

The opening of the Moscow Institute of Cosmetics was not neglected. About a hundred people visited the first day, it was reported.

From a poem by Aleksander Zharov:

Supreme Court!
Strike the filthy paws
Of monsters, sowing flames of war,
So the fornicating suckling of the Gestapo
Judas-Trotsky feels the blow.

January 27. The lead article was "Trotskyite Marauders— Scouts of the Intervention." Another headline read: WE WILL BEAT ENEMIES WITH STAKHANOVITE LABOR!

"We demand merciless revenge against the vile traitors of our great Motherland. We demand the destruction of the vile monsters." So wrote academicians V. Komarov, A. Bakh, B. Keller, A. Arkhangelsky, N. Vavilov, N. Gorbunov, I. Gubkin, G. Krzhizhanovsky, A. Terpigorev; honored scientists N. Obraztsov, E. Pavlovsky, A. Speransky; and professors V. Veger, V. Vysotsky.

"There is no room on earth for that gang!"—from the resolution of a meeting of Moscow composers and musicians.

January 28. Nikolai Ivanovich Ezhov was awarded the rank of General Commissar of State Security.

Ia. I. Alksnis was confirmed as Deputy People's Commissar of Defense and Commander of the Air Force; V. M. Orlov as Deputy People's Commissar and Commander of the Navy.

Academician Bogomolets: They must be destroyed.

A. Korneichuk: Shoot the scum!

An article by Vsev. Ivanov: "Monsters."

General Commissar of State Security G. G. Yagoda was transferred to the reserves.

"Rub out the traitors!" demanded the collective of the Arctic Institute and professors P. Samoilovich and V. Iu. Vize; doctor of geology N. N. Urvantsev; and others (altogether 170 signatures).

VILE SCUM

"Once and for all stamp out fascist vermin," and so forth. The signatures included: honored artists A. Gerasimov, S. Gerasimov, K. Iuon, D. Moor, E. Lansere, E. Katsman, I. Mashkov, I. Grabar, M. Cheremnykh, D. Shterenberg; artists Favorsky, Perelman, Sokolov-

Skalia, Ioganson, and others; and sculptors I. Shadr, B. Mukhina, S. Lebedeva, S. Merkurov, and others.

January 29. Popular rejoicing on the occasion of Ezhov's appointment. Congratulatory letters of collectives of workers.

Vyshinsky's speech: "I demand only death!"

Foreign information: "The Gestapo in disarray."

A Cossack Song

From the Don, Terek, and Ural
A single cry flies across the country
You can't just take a viper's sting
You must take a viper's head off!

From a poem by P. Markish, IN RETURN FOR EVERYTHING

We'd drive you to the slaughterhouse with ropes around your necks
So the eagle eye could watch you with scorn
of him who suffered in the trenches for the Motherland
of him who became the Motherland in the hearts of the people.

Not everything is clear here. Only Stalin could have become the Motherland in the hearts of the people. But he never did happen to be in the trenches. Could this be about two people? Then undoubtedly the second must have been Voroshilov. His trench exploits are, of course, unknown to us, but we can forgive the author some poetic license. All the more since the image of the Great Leader watching as the accused are led to the slaughterhouse sounds fresh and authentic. Maybe that is why they did not take Markish immediately, as they did Yasensky, but only ten years later. Or maybe poetry was more highly regarded in the Cheka than prose.

People's artist Moskvin: THE PEOPLE'S COURT

January 30. The long-awaited sentence: thirteen men to be executed; Sokolnikov, Radek, Arnold got ten years' imprisonment; Stroilov, eight years.

Try to figure the logic of the proletarian court! Radek, on whom so much spleen and ink had been spent, had his life spared, and other practically unknown people got the ax. To give this exercise a religious flavor: approve because it is absurd. They approved.

From Radek's last words:

The investigators did not torment us, we tormented them . . . I am guilty of one more thing. For a long while I did not denounce

Bukharin. I waited for him to give honest testimony to Soviet authority. I did not want to take him bound to the People's Commissariat of Internal Affairs . . . I refer to those who were associated with us. Go with the guilty . . . I want before I die to be of some use.

Someone else can comment on that.

From a poem by V. Lebedev-Kumach:

Thank You Proletarian Court

Shaking with indignation
the nation tolled as an alarm bell.
Thank you, warriors of the Commissariat,
Guardians of the great republic.

In the title there is gratitude to the court, but in the text to the NKVD. But then everyone knows they are one and the same thing.

HEROES OF THE SOVIET UNION A. Liapidevsky, V. Molokov, I. Doronin, M. Vodopianov: "They got what they deserved!"

People's actress Korchagina-Aleksandrovskaia: "I applaud the proletarian court."

Professors Speransky, Pavlovsky, and others: "Truly popular justice."

An obvious and instructive example of civic duty. These learned men were not too lazy to speak out for the second time in the course of this single trial.

L. Feuchtwanger, FIRST IMPRESSIONS OF THIS TRIAL: "We can say with satisfaction that the trial did shed light on the motivations of the accused to confess. Those who truly strive to determine the truth, will find it easier thereby to evaluate these confessions as evidence."

There was no evidence, but in their absence they got along with confessions. The honorable writer had not made a discovery. This is Vyshinsky's contribution to jurisprudence. As far as the motives behind the confessions are concerned, they should not be sought in the huge hall of the House of Unions, but in the comfortable offices of the Lubianka investigators. We need not doubt that had Feuchtwanger wound up there, he could have told the court anything they wanted, even to admit that he was Hitler's adoptive father.

February 1. Announcement of a meeting, which took place on January 30 on Red Square. Some 200,000 people attended and heard speeches by N. S. Khrushchev, N. M. Shvernik, Academician Komarov, and others.

Everyone, of course, approves and welcomes.

In Leningrad a meeting on Uritsky Square attended by 100,000.

V. Chizhevsky: THE FIRST SOVIET STRATOPLANE. The idea of taking people to the North Pole by stratoplane was mentioned.

An All-union census of cattle would take place February 1.

The country is slowly getting back to normal.

February 2. An order of the TSIK and SNK "On increasing the pensions of invalids of the Civil War." They took care of the enemies and took care of the people. The pensions were not extraordinary, however. Invalids of group I would receive 65 rubles per month. That would only buy 5-1/2 pounds of butter or ten bottles of vodka.

OUR REPLY TO THE ENEMIES: STAKHANOVITE LABOR

February 4. Lead article: "Soviet Statehood Is Strengthened."

February 5. N. Krylenko's article: "Enemy of the People Trotsky"

The last spontaneous response to the trial.

We beg the reader's pardon for dragging all this material in front of him. Without it, however, much of what happened is completely incomprehensible. We would contend that without this general support much of it would not have happened.

The two trials were undoubtedly important events in themselves. At the same time they were dress rehearsals for the main event of 1937, the trial of the officers, an event that had catastrophic consequences for the nation. For that reason we will describe the months that remained until the trial of Tukhachevsky and his comrades in the same fashion.

February 11. Pushkin celebrations in the Bolshoi theater were attended by Stalin and his disciples.

A. Svanidze: "On the question of Hittites and their kinship with Georgian tribes."

February 18. An order of the SNK about scholarly degrees and titles.

February 19. An official announcement: YESTERDAY AT 5:30 PM G. K. ORDZHONIKIDZE DIED UNEXPECTEDLY. A photo of the Great Leader at the grave. The paper carried a black border, and again on the twentieth and twenty-first. M. Tukhachevsky's article: "The Commander-in-Chief of Heavy Industry." Many other articles about the deceased.

They got rid of Ordzhonikidze, but unlike Stalin's other victims, he was buried with suitable pomp.

February 26. Mezhlauk appointed People's Commissar of Heavy Industry in place of Ordzhonikidze. Not a word about the TSK plenum beginning that day.

March 4. Major Spirin's NONSTOP FLIGHT AROUND THE WORLD

March 6. Information about the TSK plenum, which met February 26 to March 5. Its agenda: (1) on Party work in elections, (2) economic Party-building, (3) on the anti-Party activities of Bukharin and Rykov (expelled from the Party).

A resolution on Zhdanov's report on Party work.

March 11. Zhdanov's report of February 26 at the TSK plenum.

March 13. TWENTY YEARS FROM THE DAY OF THE FALL OF THE MONARCHY.

March 14. M. Moskalev, BUKHARIN AND RYKOV'S FIGHT AGAINST THE PARTY IN 1917: "These men . . . turned out to be agents of the fascist bourgeoisie."

March 17. A meeting of the Moscow Party activists. Khrushchev's report: "Some directors and even some commissars think that there was no wrecking." He reported Stalin's speech at the plenum.

March 18. People's commissariats' activists on the plenum.

March 20. L. Feuchtwanger: JEWS IN THE USSR AND IN FASCIST GERMANY. "I experience the greatest comfort and relief when one compares events in Germany with the fate of Jews in the USSR."

March 21. Party activists' meeting in Leningrad. Report by Zhdanov.

March 23. Moscow prepares to receive Volga water.

March 29. Stalin's speech at the plenum March 3. Yesterday the speech had been broadcast on the radio; today it would be repeated twice more.

April 1. Stalin's concluding remarks at the plenum March 5.

Now the people knew that terrorists and wreckers were not isolated individuals, monsters, and renegades, but a massive natural phenomenon.

Professor E. Tarle: "Espionage and diversion as a continuation of politics of the bourgeois state." Progressive scholars were always available.

April 2. Lead article: WE WILL MAKE THE PARTY SLOGAN LIVE. "The nature of Bolshevism abhors idleness just as physical nature abhors a vacuum."

Vl. Sorin: THE STRUGGLE OF BUKHARIN AND RYKOV AGAINST THE PARTY OF LENIN-STALIN (historical essay)

THE VICTORY OF THE SOVIET SCHOOL OF MUSIC: D. Oistrakh, E. Gilels, M. Kozolupova.

April 4. A report on the removal of People's Commissar of Communications G. G. Iagoda from his duties in connection with the discovery of malfeasance of a criminal nature. "The case has been turned over to the investigative authorities."

The post of Commissar of Communications truly was fatal. Rykov held it until he turned out to be anti-Party. Yagoda replaced him for a few months and got involved in a criminal case (later it turned out to be much worse). Ai-yai! Despite all those years he ran the OGPU and NKVD. Army Commander I. A. Khalepsky would be appointed, and it would cost him his head, but this time quietly.

April 11. A guilty plea: "Recently the criminal investigation department in Tbilisi rounded up more than one hundred recidivists. Many of them were employed. Juveniles were sent to children's colonies."

Such an idyll! By now they didn't bother with the criminals: they were "socially close" to the Kremlin's bosses. And why should they overburden the camps and prisons?

April 21. V. Molotov: OUR TASKS IN THE STRUGGLE WITH TROTSKYITES AND OTHER WRECKERS, DIVERSIONISTS, AND SPIES.

April 23. Stalin, Molotov, Voroshilov, Ezhov on the Moscow-Volga Canal.

April 29. On lowering the retail price of industrial goods

May 1. A. Vyshinsky TWO SYSTEMS—TWO DEMOCRACIES: "Proletarian democracy is *always higher* than bourgeois democracy, representing the next higher step in the development of democratism."

Precisely, *representing*. . . .

May 8. V. Antonov-Saratovsky: ON SEVERAL METHODS OF WRECKING ON THE JURIDICAL FRONT: "Workers in justice, called to struggle with the enemies of the people, . . . have overlooked enemies in their own field."

May 11. On this day MARSHAL TUKHACHEVSKY WAS RELEASED FROM HIS DUTIES AS FIRST DEPUTY PEOPLE'S COMMISSAR OF DEFENSE AND APPOINTED COMMANDER OF THE VOLGA MILITARY DISTRICT. No announcement was made.

May 17. Lead article: SOVIET LAW IS INVIOLABLE

May 22. ON MAY 21 ELEVEN BRAVE SONS OF THE SOCIALIST MOTHERLAND LANDED AT THE NORTH POLE. THE POLE IS TAKEN BY US!

M. Vodopianov: BOLSHEVIKS AT THE POLE

May 23. Lead article: BOLSHEVIK ROMANTICISM

Seven issues of the paper, May 22–29, were filled with the assault on the North Pole. Meanwhile, on May 26, Marshal Tukhachevsky was arrested; other military commanders were arrested in the same days.

Iakir, Uborevich, and Primakov were seized on May 30 and 31 on their way to Moscow for the meeting of the Military Council. The meeting of the Military Council took place at the Commissariat of Defense, June 1–4. Nothing was said in the newspapers.

June 3. Workers of the Bolshoi Theater decorated.

June 4. Decorations for Music teachers: Stoliarsky, Iampolsky, Tseitlin, Gnesina, and others. Laureates of musical competitions: David Oistrakh, Emil and Liza Gilels, Busia Goldshtein, Marina Kozolupova, Iakov Flier, Abram Diakov.

June 5. Lead article: POLITICAL AND MORAL RELIABILITY OF OUR CADRES. It told how Soviet citizens were recruited by foreign residents. The conclusion: "Bolsheviks cannot be frightened. Fighting fearlessly with the enemies of the people, Bolsheviks direct all the strength of the dictatorship of the proletariat to the destruction of double-dealers, spies, and diversionists, tearing out every last rootlet and seedling."

Plenum of the TSK KP/b/Ukraine: a new Politburo was elected, this time without Yakir.

Plenum of the Executive Committee of the Leningrad Soviet: "Expel Sveshnikov, *Primakov*, and Vasiliev from the Executive Committee as unmasked enemies of the people."

June 6. Moscow Provincial Party Conference. Khrushchev opened the meeting: The work of the Moscow city conference had just been completed, including elections to the city committee in which trusted, dedicated Bolsheviks were elected. However, one Trotskyite traitor also became a member of the city committee, the betrayer of the Motherland, the enemy of the people Gamarnik. This fact shows once more that the enemy evilly conceals himself.

Nikita Sergeevich put it very adroitly: trusted Bolsheviks were *elected*, but the enemy of the people Gamarnik *became* a member of the city committee.

June 8. Lead article: GUARD STATE SECRETS AT SACRED MOSCOW PARTY CONFERENCE. S. M. Budenny told "of the foul work of spies and diversionists among the Trotskyites and rightists."

June 9. IN THE COUNCIL OF PEOPLE'S COMMISSARS OF THE USSR: on criminal responsibility for shortage of THREAD.

The government is always thinking of the needs of the people!

The MOSCOW CONFERENCE: Member of the Moscow Military District Council Troyanker informed "on attempts by spies and traitors to weaken the might of the country. . . . The vile double-dealer *Gamarnik* carried on wrecking work. . . ."

June 10. Lead article: BOLSHEVIK UNITY AND SOLIDARITY

Dm. Kutuzov: AGAINST THE FALSIFICATION OF HISTORY. Radek and Tarle's views on Napoleon.

Medical Society held in shame the rapist and sadist Pletnev. In 1938 Pletnev would be a defendant in the Bukharin-Rykov trial.

June 11. Lead article: METALLURGY ON THE OFFENSIVE

In the second column, IN THE PROCURACY OF THE USSR: "The case of those arrested at various times by the organs of the NKVD: Tukhachevsky, Yakir, Uborevich, Kork, Eideman, Feldman, Primakov, and Putna." (We include the full text of the announcement in the chapter, "Assembly of Nikolskaia Street.")

The editors objected that Tarle was associated with Radek and called a falsifier. Tarle was no Marxist, but his book was good.

Apparently Stalin called. He liked the book, and Napoleon even more.

The Basque soccer team came to Moscow.

June 12. Lead article: A DESTRUCTIVE BLOW TO FASCIST RECONNAISSANCE

"We certainly *do not plan* to lose battles in the war, into which fascism with all its strength and means is trying to draw us. To the contrary, the enemy who attacks us will be beaten on *his* territory to complete destruction."

THE COURT'S SENTENCE—AN ACT OF HUMANITY. Announcement of the sentence: ALL TO BE EXECUTED

WORKERS OF MOSCOW'S PLANTS AND FACTORIES UNANIMOUSLY APPROVE

The ball-bearing plant: LET FASCISM'S SCOUTS TREMBLE

The Kuibyshev electric plants: THERE COULD BE NO OTHER SENTENCE

The Lepse factory: THE SENTENCE TESTIFIES TO OUR MIGHT AND TO YOUR MADNESS AND INHUMANITY!

"Dynamo": PUNISHMENT DESERVED

"Kalibr": AND IN THE FUTURE MERCILESSLY DESTROY ENEMIES OF THE PEOPLE; THE INTELLIGENTSIA WILL NOT LAG BEHIND THE AUTHORITIES

People's artist L. M. Leonidov: SHOOTING IS THE ONLY WAY TO DEAL WITH SPIES

Architect N. Ia. Kolli: a just sentence
Presidium of the Academy of Sciences of the USSR (V. Komarov, N. Gorbunov): GIVE THEM A SHAMEFUL DEATH

Calm down, old men. They are already dead, your defenders. Writers: WE DEMAND SPIES BE SHOT! TOGETHER WITH THE PEOPLE IN ONE ANGRY VOICE WE SAY—DO NOT LET ENEMIES OF THE SOVIET UNION LIVE

Stavsky, Lakhuti, Vs. Ivanov, Vyshnevsky, Fadeev, Leonov, Malyshkin, Panferov, Novikov-Priboi, Fedin, Pavlenko, Sholokhov, A. Tolstoy, Tikhonov, Pogodin, D. Bedny, Gladkov, Bakhmetev, Trenev, Surkov, Bezymensky, Ilienkov, Iudin, Kirpotin, Mikitenko, Serafimovich, Kirilenko, Lugovsky, Selvinsky, Golodny, Pasternak, Shaginian, Karavaeva, Makarenko, Gidash, Bekher, Vainer, Volf, Slonimsky, Lavrenev, Prokofev, N. Aseev, and others.

Passionate greetings to Soviet writers—valiant Chekists of the pen! Russians, forget none of those who speak and write in your name! Academician S. Vavilov expressed the unanimous opinion of the collective of the Optical Institute: "Having demanded merciless revenge. . . ." A meeting of the workers of the Second Clinical Hospital of the First Medical Institute: TREMBLE YOU SCUM!

June 14. Lead article: OUR LAND IS SACRED AND INVIOLABLE

"Defeat is not our lot; we can only expect victory. . . . The bloody Marlboroughs of fascism cannot set one foot on Soviet soil."

ORDER OF PEOPLE'S COMMISSAR VOROSHILOV:

> June 1–4 the Military Council of the People's Commissariat of Defense met in the presence of members of the government. My report of the discovery by the NKVD of a traitorous, counterrevolutionary, fascist organization was heard. . . . The final goal of that gang was to liquidate by any means the Soviet order in our country, to destroy Soviet authority, to overthrow the workers-peasants' government and reestablish in the USSR the yoke of landlords and industrialists. . . .

Logical and therefore convincing: first liquidate the order, then destroy the authority, after which there is nothing left to do but to reestablish the yoke. . . .

M. I. Ulianova died
K. Volsky: Black Friday for Fascist Intelligence
"ALL THE PEOPLES OF THE UNION CURSE THEM," wrote

young women from the *kolkhoz* sanatorium in Gurzuf.

Academician I. Orbeli: THEIR DESTRUCTION IS OUR SACRED DUTY. This was a man of enormous culture, director of the Hermitage Museum.

Academician S. Vavilov: HISTORY CANNOT BE TURNED BACK

Sergei Ivanovich, you are better at optics, but all the same . . . be president of the Academy.

A. Tolstoy: TO THE MOTHERLAND: Vigilance, vigilance! "Stavrogin was a potential Trotskyite. . . . As if every citizen who did not love the Motherland were a Trotskyite, diversionist, and spy. Yes, it is like that. Such is the form of our revolution. . . ."

Yes, Count, such is the form of *your* revolution. After it, every citizen becomes a diversionist and a spy. No need for participal constructions. And concerning Stavrogin, you have made an error. On January 26 of this year you were gracious enough to say that Trotsky was Stavrogin. By the way, the government values your services. You will be needed for the investigation of the murder of Polish officers in Katyn forest.

Academician N. I. Vavilov (among others): HONOR AND PRAISE TO THE GLORIOUS WORKERS OF THE NKVD!

You lick their heels in vain, Nikolai Ivanovich, all the same they will kill you.

N. Tikhonov: IF THE EIGHT SPIES HAD NOT BEEN KILLED, HOW MANY VICTIMS WOULD THEY HAVE TAKEN FROM THE RANKS OF THE DEFENDERS OF FREEDOM.

Obviuosly the poet Tikhonov holds to that view to this time. In any case he has not found an opportunity to publicly repudiate his words.

P. Markish: HENCEFORTH WE SHALL BE LORDS OF BATTLE:

> We yoked mountain peaks to mountain peaks.
> We stretched our power to the clouds, to the winds.
> Where needed, valleys stretch.
> Where needed, peaks tower to the skies.
> Translated (from Yiddish into Russian) by D. Brodsky

Our people remember only too well what happened when Markish's masters became the lords of battle in place of Tukhachevsky and Yakir. But the flight of fantasy concerning the government's leadership of nature is splendid. Even Aleksander Khristoforovich Benkendorf would have envied that.

THE ARTISTS AND SCULPTORS OF MOSCOW JOIN THEIR ANGER TO
THE ANGER OF MILLIONS OF WORKERS OF THE SOVIET UNION
People's artist Khmelev: ETERNAL SHAME AND DAMNATION TO
THEM.
People's artist Tarasova: DESERVED PUNISHMENT BEFELL THE
TRAITORS OF THE MOTHERLAND
June 20. THE FLIGHT OF CHKALOV-BAIDUKOV-BELIAKOV FROM
MOSCOW TO AMERICA VIA THE NORTH POLE HAS BEGUN
June 21. THE FLIGHT SUCCESSFULLY COMPLETED
June 28. PARTICIPANTS OF NORTH POLE EXPEDITION DECORATED

This ends our show. In the prologue and epilogue feats of aviation
were effectively employed—to the North Pole and across it. The audience departed to go about their daily routines. But the seeds of hate and
violence implanted in their souls bore superabundant fruit. Denunciations, attacks, sentences, executions, camps, and most of all fear
became part of their daily lives—withering, all-consuming fear, leading to madness, to loss of humanity. What had earlier been the thoroughly camouflaged domain of separate groups and classes splashed
over and flowed to all ends of the Soviet land, became the very flesh of
the nation's being. In a short time by the efforts of the domestic devil
and his cohorts both active and passive, the country was bled dry and
demoralized. Deprived of its best defenders, it became a tantalizing
object for a foreign conquerer. He did not wait long.

From these newspaper excerpts it is obvious that Stalin did not act
alone but with numerous supporters, or more accurately, accomplices.
These were not only the direct accomplices (executors) from the
punitive, Party, and other organs, but also those who are usually called
"society": the more active scientists, workers, peasants, artists. In the
USSR this public replaces the people in most social processes; they
willingly and garrulously speak on behalf of the people and instead of
them. Stalin, like any other dictator, could propose all sorts of far-
reaching plans, but without the broad support of society he would not
have been able to carry out a hundredth part of them.
Because of special Russian conditions our society has an elitist
nature. Not all the people are interested in politics and actively engaged
in it. In the Soviet Union it is those people who have achieved visible
success or influence in their various professions who make up society:

scientists with international reputations, famous actors and writers, highly skilled workers, decorated flyers, heroes of the war, etc. We leave aside the question of the authenticity of their merits; it is enough that they have distinguished themselves from their colleagues.

The role of Russian society is different from that of the West. Ours cannot actively influence government policy. It is meant solely to publicly approve the acts of the state, certainly not to criticize them. But even in this role they have a powerful weapon. A man who is permitted only to clap can, without breaking any rules, do nothing at all; he can remain silent even if he has no possibility of protesting. This form of disapproval is allowed by the Soviet regime. It remains to be explained why society during the period under discussion did not use it. We will examine this behavior not from the heights of general human morality but by taking into account the opportunities and characteristics of the environment in which this society had to operate.

Despotic powers try to remove from their subjects the opportunity to express personal opinions and, alas, they succeed too often at it. They want even more, of course, to have every act of the authorities approved by the population and their representatives. In this undertaking the situation of the leaders is less secure and their success less complete than they would like.

This is not surprising. To keep those who disagree from speaking out, they are suppressed: deprived of forums, fired from their jobs, put in prison, shot. To convert the unbelievers—or at least to get their public approval—the authorities must resort to persuasion, to agitation. It could be no other way.

Of course, the methods of persuasion can be extremely rough and aggressive, or they might be dominated by threats. However, most of the time it is not necessary to actually carry out the threats, and this is only natural. In Russia the people have always been silent. In other words, the overwhelming majority prefer not to discover what their relations are to the acts of the authorities or to the authorities themselves. There is nothing to be done about that. The leaders have always been content with this secretiveness, silence, and insufficient awareness. It is impossible to prosecute every citizen who says nothing or who yells "hurrah" too quietly. It is physically impossible to find enough oppressors, persecutors, and punishers.

There is another way to control: try to influence the representatives of the people and put their opinions forth as the voice of the whole people. That is how it is done in Russia. And it is mainly done by persuasion, suggestion, bribery, deceit, and flattery—not violence. We do not need to mention any of the above; it is enough to point out that there is no evidence of consistent coercion to make public denunciations. Who would have dared, without dissembling, to say that he was forced at the point of a pistol or the threat of imprisonment to write a letter to the paper approving the execution of Tukhachevsky and Yakir? On the contrary, instances are known, they are common enough, when respected citizens sweated and toiled to praise Stalin's acts—and did not lose their heads.

The writers Leonid Leonov and Konstantin Fedin, together with other brothers of the pen, approved the execution of the military leaders, while Mikhail Prishvin and Konstantin Paustovsky found the strength to say nothing—and remained free and ended their lives with clean consciences and reputations. Names dear to our hearts, like Mikhail Bulgakov, Osip Mandelshtam and Andrei Platonov are also absent from the list of the bloodthirsty.

The writer Bruno Yasensky wrote a series of articles filled with explanations for the executions. He soon died of starvation in the camps. Poet Perets Markish wrote verses, which can only be called cannibalistic, but a dozen years later he was shot down by Stalin's police. Servility to the executioners did not guarantee personal safety.

The motives for cooperation were various. Some were carried along by the herd of maddened rhinoceroses, the timid gave in to fear, too many were simply afraid to think. Only a few maintained their humanity and, even if they stumbled from time to time, did not fall entirely.

How many souls are sickened to find among the pack of literary scum the name of the great Pasternak. In the 1950s the poet claimed that his signature had been printed in the paper without his permission.[2] It was then that he published his novel, which has become the most valuable testimony of the epoch. Aleksander Tvardovsky, after he and others had unleashed the smear campaign against Pasternak, felt deep remorse at his death and did a great deal to help Russian literature. He gave Solzhenitsyn to his readers and bravely defended him until he (Tvardovsky) lost his editorship.

There were others, like Bulgakov and Platonov, who continued to create great literature in anonymity and poverty, unenticed by sinecures and publication. Their fate and their behavior remain a strong reproach to those who sold themselves—a denial of their shameless lie. And then there were those who, like Mandelshtam and Pilniak, died for the right to express the truth.

What we have said about the writers could be said of other groups in society. Nor is it possible to ignore the role and the behavior of the Western intelligentsia. We cannot forget that their representatives, the most progressive, liberal, thinking, sensitive, famous, and conscientious of them, approved Stalin's crimes, regarded them with "understanding," and often welcomed them. More than that, they viciously attacked anyone in the West who tried to expose the Soviet terror.

We will not spare the room to name all the Stalinist apologists among the Western intelligentsia. There were Romain Rolland, Bernard Shaw, J. P. Sartre, Lion Feuchtwanger, Henri Barbuse, Bertolt Brecht, Theodore Dreiser, John Pritt, Pierre Daix,[3] but this is far from a complete list; it includes only some of the most famous names. We have neither the time nor the desire to try to completely explain their shameful behavior. We do not believe that they could not have known the truth. If Andre Gide could renounce the cause, if Koestler and Orwell could understand, then so could the others. The greatest Russian philosopher of the twentieth century, Nikolai Berdiaev, who lived there in the West, wrote in 1937 fifteen years after he had emigrated, "The disgraceful staging of the Soviet trials alone, in which everyone confesses just like everyone else, can inspire disgust for the whole system."[4]

Leaders of the foreign communist parties were active collaborators with Stalin and sent hundreds of their Party comrades to the cellars of the NKVD: M. Thorez, P. Togliatti, H. Pollitt, E. Dennis, W. Pieck, W. Ulbricht, B. Bierut, M. Rakoczy, G. Dmitrov, K. Gottwald.

Why did people here in the Soviet Union denounce others and carry on? It seems to us that the primary motivations were baseness and selfishness. We will try to explain.

Let us look briefly at the conditions of power. The authorities need the unanimous support of society, but that is devilishly hard to obtain. There is, however, another way. They can bestow the title of representatives of the people only on those who agree to approve. The rest they can get along without, though they will keep their eyes on them. Let the stubborn ones build the bridges, grow the grain, sing the arias at the opera. The state would not survive without the bridge-builders, or the grain growers, or the singers in any case. But these must not be permitted to be silent on behalf of the people, only for themselves. It is not a problem that the silent number in the millions. Silence is frightening and significant only when it is universal, but in Russia it is covered over by the moving voices of those who do approve; and they are sufficiently plentiful.

Where then was the selfishness? It was most apparent. Those who loudly (we are not discussing sincerity) supported the authorities were reckoned among the elect. They got their share of honors, medals, titles, and material goods. They were permitted to speak for the whole nation, which, of course, flattered their egos and their hunger for recognition. If they were asked for support, they were needed. The Motherland needed them. These simplehearted people easily confused the Motherland with the government, just as the state put them in place of the people. More practically, the massive slaughter cleared the way for careers, removed competitors, freed places at the trough. It was an extremely risky game, and for millions it had a fatal ending; but greed seldom mates with sagacity.

We turn to baseness. Most of the approvers knew that with their signatures they signed death sentences; on behalf of the people they consecrated the axes in the executioners' hands. They took upon themselves the right to predetermine the decisions of these make-believe courts. They usually had no proof whatsoever, as was the case with the officers. This means they sent to their deaths people of whose guilt they were at the very least uncertain. In such cases the fair judge—every normal person—must refrain from carrying out the sentence, especially if the sentence is extreme and irrevocable.

They soothed their consciences with justifications like the following: "Even if the accused are innocent (more often they said, they must be guilty of something; the authorities wouldn't try people who were absolutely innocent), they are nonetheless doomed. The authorities are too powerful and merciless. I cannot change their fate. Better to sign—it is just a formality—and then they will leave me in peace."

Such subterfuges do not alter the case. To protest against repression in such cases was suicide; such at least was the common assumption. That would be heroic; and no one has the right to demand it of another. However, it is the duty of every civilized person to maintain his silent dignity and not to join the armed mob in its attack on a single unarmed individual. Whoever for the sake of personal gain or comfort cheers on the murderers is a villain, an accomplice in the crime, and a criminal himself.

Whatever aims and methods of state revolution were envisioned by the Stalinists, it could not have happened without broad social support. That support gave strength and scope to the repressions. It not only allowed the repression to continue, but gave them the appearance of legality, justified them in the eyes of our people and the whole world. It shut the mouths and bound the hands of Stalin's opponents, stifled their will to resist. They felt their isolation and helplessness not only before Stalin's punitive machine, but before the *people*.

In the final analysis the historical success of Stalin's career is based on the large number of academicians and weavers, novelists and lathe operators, surgeons and farmers, who were ready to serve him in crime. He entangled them in mutual responsibility for mutually spilled blood and bribed them with special rations and fancy apartments, which were all the more attractive against the background of national poverty. He freed their consciences of doubts and responsibility, taking that burden upon his own conscience, but he never possessed a conscience. They followed him and made him their idol, a model to emulate. If they did not resemble their Great Leader in every way, it was not for want of trying, but simply because not everyone was able to rise to such heights of depravity and perfidy. Soon they were bound fast to Stalin's chariot by invisible chains stronger than any metal. Scraps of these chains still whip about the heads and backs of the people.

They beat their own people without pity, drowned them in horror and blood, and at the same time prepared them for a worse fate. Responsibility for the victims and the destruction of the military lie entirely on Stalin and on those who helped him, zealously or reluctantly, silently or with joyous squeals. Those who clapped their bloody hands and gasped in slavish ecstasy at the destruction of all that was best in the Red Army in June 1937 brought on the events June 1941 with the mountains of corpses, the shame of retreat, and the scorched earth of the Motherland.

One need not be a genius to understand that the Army is different from the Party and other political institutions. If the politicians fight and scratch and bite for positions and influence, those are the natural rules of the game. People joined the Party to get power. It was all the same to the country when one ambitious and incompetent secretary or people's commissar replaced another. One was as bad as the other. It is not the same in the Army, which exists to defend the Fatherland; or at least so it is normally supposed. Therefore when the Army, which is not participating in that struggle for power, is attacked, nothing good can come of it.

Justice demands that we note that not everyone did remain silent. It is said that Rudzutak, Eikhe, Ordzhonikidze, Postyshev, and a number of others did protest the massive slaughter of the cadres. Kirov and Kuibyshev had already expressed their disagreement with extreme forms of terror. It is significant that they acted for utilitarian rather than humanitarian reasons. But that belated and puny protest had no effect, primarily because it was kept secret within the ruling circles. They did not have the courage to share their alarm with the country. Nor did they have the moral right. The memory was still vivid of how these same comrades had smashed the oppositionists, pitilessly destroyed the kulaks. Now they had become the oppositionists and would share their natural fate.

The larger part of society did not understand the practical harm of the purges. Having scorned the elementary feelings of justice and compassion, they made speeches, they scoffed at the open graves and danced at the funeral feast of their best defenders. Shame on you, you blind and venal creatures. You signed your servile, cannibalistic letters with the blood of your countrymen. You brought unprecedented sorrow upon Russia.

These people still insisted that they believed: believed in the historical rightness of Stalin, believed in the guilt of his victims. However, faith and sincerity of motives are deeply personal things and are not suitable justification for social behavior. Arkady Belinkov said it beautifully:

> Sincerity has no bearing on what a person does and cannot serve as a justification for it. That Genghis Khan or Hitler sincerely believed in his misanthropic ideas and following them tried to destroy everything he could get his hands on, makes their crime no less. Man must be sincere. But this may not be the only virtue to justify his doubtful or evil acts. Sincerity does not replace other virtues. Sometimes it may replace stupidity. But it must never replace reason.[5]

Along with everything else, what could we say about the mental capacity of those people who for so many years trusted Stalin and accepted without proof everything he told them? What can be said of their consciences?

Chosen to be the pride of the nation, they became its damnation. The justifications of the menials, who have outlived their master, sound vile and false. "We believed. . . . We did not know. . . . They made us. . . ."

Were the brother Academicians Vavilov as trusting in physics and genetics, or did they subject every little fact there to repeated and detailed confirmation? If they did not care to search out every truth in societal matters, why didn't they prefer to remain silent?

Did they not know? Raskolnikov could know, knew and wrote about it. Pilniak wrote about the liquidation of Frunze in 1926. The rest were smart enough and had enough information to understand how the NKVD fabricated cases. If they did not know, it was only because they chose not to know the truth.

"They made us . . ." Another lie. Why, then, so many years later when the cult was dismantled did none of them explain how they were made to act—or why they did not renounce their own denunciations?

Soviet society, the intelligentsia in particular, knew. They had to know, for they took upon themselves the expression of public opinion. They preferred to act otherwise. They licked the bloody hands of the tyrant, and he in his turn admitted them to the trough, awarded them hastily contrived titles and distributed coupons for immortality.

Every educated, intelligent man bears inescapable responsibility. It is not a material debt. It does not come from the duty to repay society for his education. The intelligent man must see farther than others and use his knowledge for the good of mankind. To tell the people the truth, to warn them of impending disaster, to point out their errors and sins, to work to make life better, cleaner, more just—that is the calling and position of the intelligentsia. That is the responsibility of the seeing to the blind, the strong to the infirm, of men to women, adults to children.

Not understanding this responsibility or scorning it—whether from fear, selfishness, or thoughtlessness, it is all the same—one has no right to call himself an intellectual. More than that, such a person is morally and socially defective. No system runs all by itself. Why is it we always have a surfeit of people to carry out various injustices and abominations and so few for good, honest work?

Let the people know the names of their malefactors—not for revenge and abuse, but for all time to learn the terrible lesson.

Epilogue

The Bloody Hangover

They finally won. They defeated themselves and their people.
—Korzhavin

23 Conspiracy Against Peace

Stalin, in his report to the Eighteenth Congress in March 1939, said:

We do not fear the threats of the aggressor and are prepared to answer double blow for blow the instigators of war, who are trying to violate the inviolability of the Soviet borders. We must be careful and not let our country be drawn into conflicts by the warmongers, who are used to stoking the fire with others' arms. . . .

Or, for example, take Germany. They gave her Austria—gave her the Sudetenland, left Czechoslovakia to its own fate, ignoring all obligations, and then began to shout lies in the press about "the weakness of the Russian Army," about the "decay of Russian aviation," about "disorders" in the Soviet Union, pushing the Germans farther east. They promised Germany easy pickings, saying again and again: you just start a war with the Bolsheviks and everything will be just fine . . . that looks a lot like incitement to the aggressor. The noise the Anglo-French and North American press made about the Soviet Union is typical. That suspicious noise seems to have been meant to anger the Soviet Union against Germany, poison the atmosphere, and provoke a conflict with Germany where there was no apparent reason for it. One might think that they gave the Germans parts of Czechoslovakia as payment for starting a war with the Soviet Union, but the Germans are refusing now to pay the IOU, making them concede more.
—Stalin, Report to the Eighteenth Congress, March 1939

The time had come to celebrate their most recent triumphs, but the joy of celebration had a bitter aftertaste. No, the blood they had spilled and the injustices they had done did not keep Stalin and his valiant comrades from enjoying the fruits of their victory. But they were disturbed by conditions in Europe, which in 1938 smelled strongly of a new war.

The NKVD still worked hard at killing the military leadership while the need for a strong army became ever more vital and immediate. Hitler began his conquests. In 1938 Austria and Czechoslovakia fell.

Too late Western leaders recognized the suicidal uselessness of the Munich policy. Taking advantage of their shortsightedness and selfishness, Germany had shaken off the chains of Versailles and broken the ring of little countries that France had taken such pains to erect around her.

France was sure of its military might. England for many years had not seriously prepared for war. While Germany had day by day made ever more brazen overtures toward Poland, the Western Allies had fussed about. Finally appeasement was replaced by intimidation. The guarantees of inviolability, which England and France hastened to give the Poles, were not only a bluff, but also an unwitting provocation. Since they had no borders with Poland, the Allies could not physically come to its aid. Moreover, their armed forces were not prepared to do so. The Polish army was fairly large, but its organization was outdated and it did not have sufficient modern weapons. The Anglo-French coalition was similarly weak. They were also very short of tanks and planes.

Hitler felt tempted to show up the rash acts of the Allies. He understood that so favorable a military situation could not last forever. England was already beginning to modernize its army. Their solid economic and engineering potential would enable them to make up quickly for lost time. Moreover, behind them stood the American colossus. Therefore, the best time to attack Poland was immediately, but only under the condition that Russia did not interfere. Hitler understood that well.

The allies realized it also. They hoped that a renewed Franco-Russian-English alliance would prevent war in Europe. In any case, they thought that if the Soviet Union joined in the guarantees for Poland, Germany would not attack. Therefore in the summer of 1939 the lines of force of European interests came together in Moscow.

The Kremlin was not unaware of this. But at the time the Soviet leadership was entirely comprised of amateurs and parvenus. All of these people were incompetent in international politics and grand strategy. Previously they had all heeded the advice of military specialists and diplomats of the Chicherin-Litvinov school. During the Great Purge, however, the staff of the People's Commissariat of Defense, the General Staff, strategic intelligence, and the diplomatic corps were all destroyed. Commissar of Foreign Affairs M. M. Litvinov, who had survived only by a miracle was in complete isolation. He was a half-dead fish out of water, surrounded by people who all their lives had been busy with intrigues and murders, who had never been abroad, who little understood diplomacy, and who for various good reasons did not even comprehend geography.[1] On May 4, 1939, while policy was in the process of changing, Litvinov was retired.

The new course was worthy of the new leaders of foreign policy. Having come to the center of European attention, they quickly displayed their true nature. They wanted to know what was in it for them. It was explained to them that a war was coming and that Russia would unavoidably become involved, and they thought of the immediate advantages to be gained, first of all through territorial acquisitions. (Here and below when speaking of territorial expansion, we will not discuss ethical aspects or questions of international law. We will be interested only in examining national expediency: how these annexations affected the defense capabilities of the country.)

A. A. Zhdanov, who had risen quickly to power, became the architect of foreign policy. Chairman of the Council of People's Commissars V. M. Molotov, who jointly headed the diplomatic apparatus after Litvinov, took all practical concerns upon himself. Already in the spring of 1939 Zhdanov had expressed the opinion that Germany was a worthy partner and long-term ally. Their political structure, that is, Hitlerism, was an internal German matter, and Zhdanov felt we would be wiser to abandon our one-sided orientation in foreign affairs. Litvinov, who had worked hard for an Anglo-Soviet rapprochement, was opposed to this policy, but there was nothing he could do. He was fortunate not to be denounced as an agent of British imperialism. He had after all lived many years in London and married an English woman.

Zhdanov's idea fell on fertile soil. Stalin had already dropped a few curtseys to Hitler in his speech before the Seventeenth Congress (April 26, 1934): "As everyone knows, during the first imperialist war they also tried to destroy one of the great powers, Germany, and get rich at her expense. And what came of it? They did not destroy Germany, but sowed in Germany such hatred toward the victors, made the soil so fertile for revanche, that to this day they cannot, nor will they soon be able to, swallow the *disgusting gruel* they cooked up there."[2]

So that's what it was all about. World War I was undertaken ("the gruel cooked up") to destroy Germany and get rich at her expense. The trial in Leipzig of G. Dimitrov and his comrades had only recently been completed, on December 23, 1933. The accused, who were Communists, were acquitted for lack of evidence; but in the sentence the Communist Party of Germany was blamed for the burning of the Reichstag.

Stalin did not say a word in his report about that very important trial, while at the same time he agreed with the Nazis' explanation of the cause of the First World War. Another part of the speech proves that the excerpt above is no accidental slip of the tongue or carelessness in the wording:

> Some German politicians [read Nazis] say that the USSR is aligned today with France and Poland, that having been an opponent of the Versailles Treaty, we have become its supporter, and that change is explained by the establishment of the fascist regime in Germany. That is *not true*. Of course, we are far from celebrating the fascist regime in Germany. *But fascism is not the problem* here [we willingly believe I. V.; authors], because *fascism* in Italy, for example, did not prevent the USSR from establishing the *best* of relations with that country. Nor is the problem our *supposed* change of attitude toward the Versailles Treaty. [Listen, listen in Berlin!] It is not for us, who experienced the shame of the Brest peace, to praise the Versailles Treaty. We disapprove only insofar as the world is plunged from that treaty of peace into the abyss of another war.[3]

Thus he let Hitler know: we were not his enemies. Although Hitler had stuck most of the German Communists in jail, the two nations could come to an arrangement. His silence on the Leipzig trial was not accidental. Dimitrov and Tanev had been acquitted by the court, but they were kept in jail while secret negotiations were carried out. On February 15 the Soviet government decided to accept the Bulgarian Communists as Soviet subjects, and on the twenty-seventh the Gestapo flew them in a special plane to Moscow. The first contact with the new German regime had led to constructive results.

In March 1939, at the Eighteenth Congress, Stalin continued the same line. He unambiguously said that Germany and the USSR wanted the English and French ("supporters of nonintervention") to bump heads, and directed the fire of his criticism against them: "I have no intention to moralize about the policy of nonintervention, to speak of treason, of treachery, and so forth. It is naive to tell morals to people who do not recognize human morality. Politics is politics, as the old, arch-bourgeois diplomats say. It is necessary, however, to note that the great and dangerous political game begun by the proponents of the policy of nonintervention might end for them in a serious failure."[4]

Thus in 1939 there loomed the possibility of reestablishing German-Soviet cooperation, which had been fairly successful in the period between Rapallo and Hitler's coming to power. There had been reciprocity in many spheres, including the military. Soviet commanders had studied at the German Academy of the General Staff, and in return the USSR had helped Germany get around the restrictive articles of the Versailles Treaty by letting them use airfields and training grounds on Soviet territory.

All of this would have been unimportant if Soviet-German rapprochement were seen as only one of several avenues for foreign policy. Unfortunately the Kremlin completely misread the situation in Europe. A prisoner of his Marxist phraseology, Stalin could only understand a united front of imperialists. From his point of view Germany and England were the same. They arranged their affairs at the expense of third countries like Czechoslovakia. (This was partly true, but a secret Anglo-German alliance existed only in Stalin's imagination; Stalin, thinking everyone was like himself, suspected everyone of boundless perfidy and treachery.)

Thus, when both sides began to flirt with Moscow, the suspicious Leader immediately smelled a conspiracy. There arose the temptation to make his secret allies bump heads, in the words of official propaganda: "to disrupt the united imperialist front against the USSR." And the desire to move the border of the USSR westward as soon as borders in Europe became unstable was called: "using the contradictions among the imperialist powers." Stalin also wanted to postpone the entrance of the USSR into the war; this had no official name, but was still the greatest foolishness since there was no one to attack: neither England, France, nor Germany had common borders with the Soviet Union, and Poland was not an aggressor. These considerations were not based on a realistic evaluation of the circumstances and poorly agreed with one another.

Greed, incompetence, and a tendency to intrigue had their effect. Stalin accepted Zhdanov's proposed alliance with Hitler, and there was no one in the country to object. The lonely voice of Litvinov, who had personal reasons to attract him to England and national motives to hate fascism, disappeared in the cowardly silence of the People's Commissariat of Defense (Voroshilov), the General Staff (Shaposhnikov), and military intelligence (Golikov). Tukhachevsky was no longer alive, that Tukhachevsky who in 1935 had warned of the German threat and in 1936 had unequivocally told the chief of the French general staff, General Gamelin, that Hitler would eventually collide with the USSR but that he would start with France. If we suppose that Stalin had thought of an alliance with Germany before the summer of 1939, for that reason alone he would have wanted to get rid of Tukhachevsky and his comrades. For them such a course would have been unthinkable and organically unacceptable as pure treason.

There was much to be said for the choice Stalin made: traditional Bolshevik Germanophilia, the similarities of their methods of wielding power, the amazing coincidence in their propaganda apparatuses.[5] In the honeymoon of the alliance there was excellent mutual understanding, not only in economics and politics,[6] but also between the NKVD and the Gestapo.[7] Two other factors were of decisive importance. Hitler was more than glad to agree with Moscow's expansionist designs, while the Western Allies spoke only of how to guarantee the inviolability of the Polish state or how to create a new system of collective security. Second, the repression had seriously undermined the fighting ability of the Red Army. Stalin knew that; he could not help but see. He instinctively feared a real war. It would be much better to have the pushy Hitler as a friend and ally.

Negotiations with the English and French dragged on lethargically and without results. Finally at the end of August, during Ribbentrop's brief visit to Moscow, the Soviet-German nonaggression pact was concluded. Secret articles of the pact included agreed-upon spheres of interest or, more precisely, territorial claims. The partitioning of Poland was the main part of the deal: Hitler got the western regions of the country, Stalin the eastern. Besides that, the USSR recognized German acquisitions in Austria and Czechoslovakia; Germany recognized Soviet claims in the Baltic region. The fate of the *Rzech Pospolyta* and of peace in Europe had been decided.

Hitler was beside himself with joy: "In this way I knocked their weapons out of the hands of the western gentlemen [England and France]. We put Poland in a situation much more favorable for achieving military success. . . . Stalin writes that this policy promises much good for both countries. A gigantic turnabout in European politics."[8]

In September the Wehrmacht began its invasion of Poland.[9] England and France declared war on Germany. The Second World War had begun.

Stalin had every reason to be satisfied. Already by the second half of September, following the disastrous failures of the Polish army, the Soviet Union occupied the Western Ukraine and Western Belorussia. In the winter of 1939–40 they seized the Kola Isthmus from Finland. In the summer and fall of 1940 the three Baltic states, Bessarabia, and Northern Bukovina, taken from Rumania, were added to the USSR. Only the Finnish acquisition required actual military action; this did cost large human sacrifice, but it ended in the victory of the USSR (population 190 million) over Finland (population 4 million). The other large territories were obtained bloodlessly.

There would be no end, it seemed, to their success. By the end of 1940 France had been defeated. Germany and the Soviet Union had become the masters of the European continent. The touching union of these two great powers gave rise to the fondest hopes. In the fall of 1939 Molotov recognized Nazism as the organic ideology of the German people, against which one might polemicize, but which one must not try to combat with force of arms.[10] Brotherly feelings led him even further. "We believe that a strong Germany is a guarantee of peace in Europe," he declared at a session of the Supreme Soviet. Stalin, just to be safe, never did make a public apologia for fascism, but to all appearances he seemed to think that everything was going well.[11] True, England had not yet been brought to her knees, but that was Hitler's problem. The USSR still had normal diplomatic relations with the United Kingdom, all the while carrying on hostile propaganda against the British.

If Stalin and his inner circle had been capable of sober analysis, they would at once have restrained their joy. The territorial gains were significant and had been acquired at no little cost; however, the strategic situation of the USSR had not changed for the better. It had actually worsened. We will discuss the main points.

The Red Army, or to be more accurate, what remained of it, had gone through a serious crisis. The liquidation of practically the entire higher command staff had sown uncertainty and fear among the ranks. Its fighting ability had been terribly weakened. The new command was inferior to the former in many ways—in leadership, education, and combat experience. There were no especially talented men among the new leaders. All of them in one way or another were unprepared to hold the high posts these bloody times had forced upon them. The weakness of the command had already been apparent during the limited operations in the Far East, but they were made painfully obvious in the first serious campaign, that against Finland.

The choice of the time to begin the campaign promised nothing good. The Soviets set out to fight the Finns, who were used to the cold, in the conditions most favorable to the latter—in winter—as if they were dealing with the warmth-loving French or Italians. The strategic plan of the attack was prepared as badly as it could have been. Shaposhnikov's and Shtern's suggestion to attack across the undefended Kandalaksha region was rejected on the grounds that the terrain was too difficult for the troops to negotiate. (How could these neophyte strategists know that in modern warfare traversing difficult terrain gives the attackers a good chance to take the enemy by surprise. The Germans twice proved that with their successful attacks through the Ardennes. The magnificent success of the Belorussian operation of the Soviet Army depended on their striking a blow through a swamp.) Instead the troops were made to storm the heavily defended Mannerheim line.[12] The attackers' battle losses were huge. Tens of thousands who fell casualties to the cold added to the losses.

The confusion was complete. Therefore as soon as the Finnish defenses had been broken, Stalin hastened to end military operations. Since the Finnish army was still able to fight, Stalin had to be content with rather modest acquisitions.

The failure of the campaign led to changes in the Army leadership. Voroshilov was replaced as People's Commissar by S. K. Timoshenko, who was soon given the rank of marshal. Of course, it was easier to pass out marshals' batons than to raise real commanders. If the former cavalryman Timoshenko differed from Voroshilov, it was for the worse. He was even more ignorant; he had no experience in high command, nor did he possess political skills. From the beginning of the Fatherland War even Stalin noticed that.

Another fresh-baked marshal, G. I. Kulik, held the post of chief of ordnance. As a braggart and ignoramus, he was unrivaled, even in these Soviet conditions. His career advanced because Stalin had once seen him command ten smallish guns at Tsaritsyn. Kulik worked hard to destroy the accomplishments of his predecessors Tukhachevsky and Khalepsky. He did not give the troops new types of weapons, because his own knowledge remained at the level of the Civil War. Stalin trusted him completely. Because of Kulik's opposition to it, the т-34 tank, which proved to be the best in the Second World War, almost did not become part of the Army's equipment. The People's Commissar of Combat Supplies, B. L. Vannikov, who actively fought against Kulik, wound up in the Lubianka until the war brought him justice. Vannikov was returned to his former post and earned four Hero's stars, while Kulik in the first months of fighting was demoted first to major general and later to major.

In this shake-up the experienced Shaposhnikov, through no fault of his own, lost his position as chief of General Staff. Stalin explained that although Shaposhnikov's plan had proved to be right, he had to be fired along with Voroshilov to satisfy public opinion. K. A. Meretskov occupied the vacant post. In January 1941, for no particular reason, he was replaced by G. K. Zhukov. In the year preceding the outbreak of the war the General Staff did not have stable leadership.

In the operational-tactical sphere the army was thrown backward twenty years to a linear combat disposition. The theory of deep operations was declared treasonous wrecking. Once again the cavalry dominated the military to the detriment of the armored tank and mechanized troops. In case of war the deployment of ninety-nine [!] cavalry divisions was planned. In 1936 the Germans had two-and-a-half divisions. The cavalry cost the Soviet people more than their entire system of education.

Inclusion of the various new regions in the USSR established a Soviet-German border that stretched for hundreds of kilometers. This was unquestionably a strategic disadvantage. The danger of a surprise attack by Germany increased many times. The aggressor could now at his discretion choose where along the border he would launch an attack; the defender would have to defend the whole length of the border, which required a huge number of forces. Previously, to come into contact with Soviet troops the Germans would have had to cross Poland or the Baltic countries. Under those conditions an attack could not come completely by surprise. The Red Army had a certain amount of time in which to prepare a counterstrike. Possible points for invasion could more or less be predicted.

The acquisition of the extensive security zone, which stretched to three hundred kilometers in places, complicated the Soviets' strategic position.

The position of the Red Army was further weakened by two glaring errors of the political leadership. During the 1930s powerful defensive works, which were in no way inferior to the Maginot Line, were constructed along the old borders. Construction of a new line more nearly suited to the new borders was begun in 1940. It would have taken several years to build. Without waiting for it to be completed, however, Stalin ordered that the bunkers and weapons at the old fortifications be dismantled. The second error was associated with Stalin's fantastic literalism in matters he did not clearly understand. Basing his order on the propagandistic slogan "Do not give the enemy an inch of our land," Stalin ordered that the new defense line follow exactly the configuration of the western border. The extent of the defense line grew catastrophically because of that. Stalin absolutely refused to employ mobile defenses. No use was made of powerful natural boundaries, such as the Neman River in its middle course, the August Canal, or the Bobr River, only because they were a few dozen kilometers from the border. Twelve armies plus detached corps and divisions of the Odessa district defended the Soviet border from the Barents Sea to Bukovina. Two-thirds of the mechanized corps, those already formed and some just completing formation, were thrown in. Nonetheless, these tremendous forces did not suffice for a solid defense.

The territorial seizures of 1939 and 1940 put the Soviet Union's neighbors, which had formerly acted as buffers, into the camp of the potential enemy. This was most true of Romania and Finland. The Germans were indifferent to the annexations of Bukovina, Bessarabia, and the Kola Isthmus, although they were not agreed to in the secret articles of the Molotov-Ribbentrop pact. Now Bucharest and Helsinki became true allies of Berlin in the coming war. Germany got new platforms from which to launch an invasion and additional manpower that it especially needed. The Romanian episode doubtless strengthened German influence in two other Balkan states, Hungary and Bulgaria.

Still Stalin's appetite continued to grow. During Molotov's visit to Berlin, the Germans suggested that the USSR join the trilateral (anti-Comintern) pact. On November 25, 1940, Stalin informed Hitler of his agreement in principle and of the conditions under which the Soviet Union would join. He asked for "the conclusion of five secret protocols":

1. Concerning Finland, with which the USSR wishes to come to an agreement without the use of force [but with the threat of force and German pressure].

2. Concerning Bulgaria, which must [not otherwise] conclude a nonaggression pact with Russia.

3. About the lease of strong points on the Bosporus.

4. Concerning Turkey, which should be required to join the trilateral pact. If Turkey should agree to join, her borders would be guaranteed. If she refused, the diplomatic and military pressure of Germany, Italy, and Russia would be brought to bear. Japan must be made to give up its concession on Sakhalin.

5. Concerning the Russian sphere of influence south of the line Batumi-Baku.[13]

Hitler did not respond to these suggestions. Apparently strengthening the Soviet Union in this way did not enter into his plans. He decided to fight in the East, and less than a month later confirmed plan "Barbarossa."

24 The Blindness

Our state machinery is suited for defense, not for attack. It gives us as much steadfastness as it deprives us of mobility. When we passively defend ourselves, we are stronger than we really are, for we add to our defense forces our inability to understand our powerlessness. That is, our courage is increased so that even if frightened we do not soon run away. On the contrary, attacking we act with only 10 percent of our strength. The rest is expended to get that 10 percent into motion. . . . Strength is action, not potential; when not combined with discipline, it kills itself. We are lower organisms in the international zoology: we continue to move after we have lost our head.
—Kliuchevsky

The last act of the prewar drama began at the moment of the Pyrrhic victory in the Finnish campaign. Having paired with Hitler to get the Second World War started, Stalin quite seriously counted on staying out of the main battles. He amused himself with the thought that while Germany and the West were busy destroying each other, he would snap up the tastiest morsels without risk. If he did get involved, it would be at the end, to participate in cutting up the world pie. All Soviet plans foresaw the possibility of entering the war but not before the end of 1942, when, according to Stalin's calculations, the main battles would already have been fought.

The source of the catastrophe of 1941 must be sought first of all in the absolute incompetence of the Kremlin leadership. Rarely in history has such a collection of selfish, incompetent, and simply ignorant men gathered at the feeding troughs of a great power. What were all these Stalins, Molotovs, Malenkovs, and Berias thinking about? Only about how to solidify and increase their own power. Even in June 1941, a time of mortal danger for the Motherland, they could not behave differently. While the terrified Leader drank heavily in seclusion for two weeks, Beria and Malenkov carried out a quiet coup in their narrow circle. They created the State Committee for Defense headed by the incapacitated Leader, but including only Molotov of the former members of the Politburo.

Even looking at things more calmly, it is impossible not to see that in 1940 and the first half of 1941 the Kremlin leadership was doing the same thing that the Western Allies were in 1938 and 1939: nothing, wasting time. Meanwhile, Hitler's appetite was growing daily. He went hunting through Europe looking for easy pickings and finding them. France fell. England desperately clung to its existence. Greece, Norway, Denmark, and Yugoslavia were seized.

It all meant nothing to Stalin. In Moscow they continued to lull themselves with the idiotic illusion that Germany would not try to fight a two-front war. (That was worth remembering in December 1941 when Hitler, already fighting on two fronts—and what fronts!—nonetheless declared war on the United States.) The incorrigible doctrinaires, the seminary and high school dropouts whose whole intellectual baggage consisted of ten ready formulas, had very firmly absorbed the lesson that war is a continuation of politics by other means, and economic factors play the decisive role in war (and social development). Why would Germany (population 70 million) attack the USSR (population 190 million), while they were still fighting England (population 50 million), behind whom stood the United States (population 150 million) with its huge economic potential? And the Soviet Union's productive relations were more progressive than theirs, not to mention our social structure. They must have learned something from history. Bismarck taught the Germans not to meddle in the East; Zhdanov especially emphasized that. No, under no circumstances would the Germans attack, thought the Russians. They must not. And if they dared (here the voice hardens), they would find their graves in our immense land. Like Napoleon. That they had learned. The Soviets were too busy to remember that Bonaparte had reached Moscow and had spent some time there. They did not want to think the possibility all the way through; but they did let Hitler reach the very walls of the capital—probably so as not to ruin the historical analogy.

A country must prepare for war, and in an orderly, thoughtful fashion. Therefore a plan was approved for putting industry on a war footing. The completion of the project was foreseen in the end of 1942. What was the hurry? Therefore Malenkov did not transmit to the Army's political workers directives for immediate combat readiness. That happened on June 3, 1941: "The document was composed as if war would begin tomorrow. Such an approach is completely unacceptable." Stalin agreed with Malenkov. And Georgi Maksimilianovich proved right—the war did not break out for another nineteen days.

Consequently, nine hours after German troops had attacked in Belorussia, Russian troops still did not have combat orders.

In assessing the possibility of attack by a potential enemy, one cannot study only military strengths. That only asks the question who in the end will win the war. But the aggressor does not always act only when he is sure of success. Otherwise Napoleon, for example, would not have marched into Russia, and the powers of the Triple Entente would not have started the First World War.

It is much more important in analyzing an enemy's intentions to understand the logic and psychology of his strategy. If Stalin had been capable of that realistic sort of thinking, he would almost have had to come to the conclusion that Hitler had little choice but to attack the Soviet Union and to do it soon. Stalin and his comrades only hoped in vain that while Germany fought in the West, they could not start a war against the USSR. Hitler had to think differently. England was not yet broken and Hitler hated and feared England. Behind England stood mighty America, which sooner or later would be drawn into the war. When Molotov visited Berlin in November 1940, he did not respond to the call for the USSR to participate in the war against England. Hitler saw that the Russians were crafty, and that if a good moment presented itself they would fight against Germany. Before he got into the unavoidable clash with America, he wanted to rid himself of the Damocles' sword, Russia,[1] and at the same time to obtain a decisive strategic advantage. As a matter of fact, if the campaign in the East were quick (and he did not think it would be otherwise), Hitler would have huge material and, very likely, almost endless human resources. Then England would have to face an unbelievably strengthened Germany in Europe and in Asia, the Japanese, who were eager to get into the fray. The war would then be settled in favor of the Axis powers. England could not continue the fight and would have to accept German conditions for peace. Even in the case of American intervention, Hitler, as chess players say, would have a stronger position without the Russian colossus at his back.

That sort of thinking might seem farfetched, but, according to the German Chief of Staff, General Franz Halder, that is what Hitler himself had to say about it at a meeting of the Wehrmacht headquarters staff on January 9, 1941:

> The hope that the Russians will intervene encourages the English.
> They will cease to resist when their last hope on the continent is

destroyed. He, the Fuhrer, does not believe that the English are "hopelessly stupid." If they cannot see help coming, they will stop fighting. If they lose, they will never find the moral strength in themselves to preserve the empire. If they can go on and form 30–40 divisions, and if the USA and Russia extend help, that will create a very difficult situation for Germany. We cannot allow that.[2]

Thus for Hitler the continuing war with England was a powerful motivation to attack Russia, just as Stalin saw it as the guarantee of his security.

It is necessary to destroy Russia. Then either England would surrender or Germany would continue the war against England in favorable conditions. The defeat of Russia would also permit Japan to turn their forces against the USA. And that would keep the latter from entering the war. . . . The question of time is especially important for the defeat of Russia. Although the Russian armed forces are a clay colossus without a head, it is impossible to foresee precisely their future development. Inasmuch as it is necessary in any case to defeat Russia, it would be better to do it now while the Russian Army is leaderless and badly prepared. . . . Nonetheless we must not underestimate the Russians now.[3]

Hitler made a fatal error. But that in no way excuses Stalin. He did not foresee the course of events and displayed complete misunderstanding of the aggressor's motives. It is not so, as the official historians say, that the pact of 1939 gave the USSR needed time to strengthen its defenses. On the contrary, it permitted Hitler to take Poland and make preparations to attack the East. In 1939 Germany could not only not have attacked the USSR, but in the absence of the pact would probably not have dared attack Poland for fear of countermeasures taken in concert with England and France.

A great deal of ink and simpleminded effort have been spent to defend Stalin's behavior. In the end there is the elementary conclusion that the Great Leader made a mistake. The country, under the leadership of the Party, prepared to repel aggression; but their timing was off, which put us in a rather bad position early in the war.

This formulation deserves our attention only as an example of shameless disregard for facts and as further proof of the happy certainty of its authors that they would get away with whatever lies they uttered. We will say more later on the preparedness of the USSR for war and on the difficulty of our position. First of all we note that a statesman who makes such mistakes at the very least is not in the right job, and he should find some more suitable and harmless occupation.

Let us try to find some justifications for Stalin's behavior. Maybe he really was a great philanthropist trying to save the country from the horror of war? Any war, even the most just (and who is to be judge of that), brings the people incalculable suffering and causes a loss of human life that is not compensated for by any conquests. The statesman who wisely keeps his country out of war is blessed. But as hard as we try, we will not find those noble intentions in Stalin. He certainly did not want war. He feared war, primarily because he felt his own incapacity as a leader. He also understood that the real military leaders had been destroyed at his personal orders. The fear of war paralyzed Stalin. He sacrificed the country's security for the sake of intrigue that gratified his imperial ambitions. He paralyzed the preparations for defense and too frequently, through ignorance, did things that helped the enemy.

Might we still be underestimating Stalin? Maybe there was some clever plan concealed in his actions. What if he were trying to avoid that catastrophic error of tsarist policy—when Russia got entangled in a war she was unprepared to fight. If Russia had remained neutral as long as possible, both coalitions would have wooed her—as a potential ally or undesired enemy—and the tsar could have chosen the better deal for Russia.

But there resemblance is only apparent. At the end of the 1930s there were not two equally powerful alliances; there was instead a brazen aggressor and the rest of the world, who rather carelessly and then with alarm, but always passively, watched the aggressor. Besides, Stalin's way of keeping Russia out of the war was highly questionable. For someone who was not eager to fight, he certainly was quick to share in the division of the spoils. If Stalin had wanted to wait out the turn of events as a neutral, he ought not to have begun with a secret deal with the aggressor, providing for territorial acquisitions. That should have been the payment, to speak cynically, at the end of the war for the victorious reinforcement of one of the sides. That hurriedly swallowed bit got stuck in his craw.

When he ventured into such a delicate game, Stalin had to understand the intentions and foresee the actions of the contending sides. He had to understand that Hitler would not tolerate the neutrality of Russia for long, for fear that the Russian card would become the decisive trump in the hands of the Western Allies. If Russia did not become Germany's military ally, then according to Hitler's logic Russia would have to be defeated and subjugated. Hitler's decision was made easier by the display of the Red Army's weakness in the war with Finland in 1940.

Anyone who had taken the trouble to study Hitler's strategic behavior would have to expect him to attack after the failure in Karelia. Hitler's strategy was based on hypertrophied aggressiveness. Seeing weakness anywhere, he was certain to attack. But first he would try to further weaken, disorganize, and demoralize the enemy. Signs of all of that were apparent in the USSR after 1937, thanks to Stalin and his stewardship. Hitler, unlike Stalin, valued the element of time. He hurried, understanding that favorable circumstances could change. Finally Hitler clearly understood the confusion and indecision of the Kremlin dictator. Informing his generals of his plan for war with Russia, he assured them that for the present the USSR would not act first: "Smart men are in charge in Moscow."

This undermines the belief that Stalin had a well-thought-through Fabian strategy. Explanations based on Hitler's perfidy, which Soviet propaganda is so quick to use, do not deserve serious discussion. It was irresponsible to take at his word a man who neither in theory nor in practice recognized any treaties except those that were advantageous to him.

There remains one other explanation, which is more believable. Stalin knew without doubt that Russia was unprepared for war and feared it beyond reason. He hypnotized himself and others with a vain hope for a miracle. Therefore he did not want to hear about even the plainest signs that war was approaching. Such information could not help him much. He still did not know what to do. His will was paralyzed. He lost all the chances he had to correct his mistake. A mystical horror reigned in the Kremlin. To moderate the tension of hopelessness, Stalin invented the theory of the peaceloving nature of Hitler, with whom the bloodthirsty generals were pushing us into war. Therefore we were to sit quietly, not to provoke anyone, not to give the Germans an excuse for war. Fear and apathy reached such heights in the Kremlin that had Hitler thought to roar more loudly, Stalin might have thrown himself at his feet.[4]

He had already gone down on one knee when on June 14, 1941, he issued a TASS announcement, which in black and white assured the people and the whole world that despite the fantasies of hostile propaganda (apparently British) the colossal buildup of German troops at the Soviet border was not aimed against the USSR. Only a week later the invasion began. All of the shameful efforts of the Stalin clique were in vain.[5]

History has laughed cynically at Stalin. It was he who turned out to be the ally and accomplice of German fascism, not those defendants at the Moscow trials who went to their deaths branded agents of the Gestapo.

Stalin's comrades were a lot like their leader. With dull fatalism they awaited the enemy attack. It did not occur to them to remove the incapacitated dictator and busy themselves with saving the Motherland. Woe to the country that entrusts its fate to such leaders.

25 Retribution

We do not have a parade, we have a war.
—Pushkin

> As far as decisiveness, enterprise, and willingness to take respon-
> sibility are concerned, the whole system in the Russian Army
> encouraged not the development but the suppression of these
> moral qualities, the most important for war.
>
> Leadership of the troops has long been the weakest side of the
> Russian Army. In its extensive combat experience over the last
> hundred years much bravery has been displayed but precious little
> military skill. Usually Russian commanders do everything they
> can to lose a war, and if nonetheless war is won, success can be
> explained only by the selflessness of the former Russian soldiers
> who atoned for mistakes of the command with their blood, and by
> the weakness of the enemies with whom Russia has had to clash.
>
> Formerly in Russia they did not attribute special significance to
> the mental development of military leaders. In government circles
> until very recently they held firmly to the conviction that brains
> were not especially needed to command troops in peacetime, and
> who knew when war would come.   —E. I. Martynov[1]

The German attack caught us unaware, but it was an unnecessary
surprise. The Army's ears had been plugged, its eyes blindfolded, its
hands tied. Stalin and the leaders of the People's Commissariat of
Defense had done that.

It is impossible to secretly prepare and send into battle an army of
several million men. There were sufficient warnings of the approaching
invasion. Stalin preferred to ignore them. In normal circumstances he
would have been sent before a tribunal for that alone. And beside him
in the defendants' box, if justice were to be served, would be many
others, including especially the People's Commissar of Defense, Semen
Timoshenko, the Chief of the General Staff Georgi Zhukov, and the
Chief of Military Intelligence Filipp Golikov.

One cannot justify the actions of that trio by the political circumstances of those years. They maliciously and consistently violated their soldier's obligation to be ready always to defend the Fatherland. Even if we accept the thesis that the tyrant was blind and ignorant and ran things according to preconceived notions, that does not reduce the guilt of the others. They occupied the highest military posts in the country, but they did not even try to oppose Stalin; they did not dare try to show him the inescapable fatal consequences of his policies. On the contrary, they worked closely with him and suppressed those people in the Army who tried to do anything about the situation that was deteriorating from day to day.

Failures of the Early Period

Soviet propaganda explains the defeats of 1941 by the unexpectedness of the attack, the numerical superiority of the German army, and its superior weaponry. All of this is a deliberate lie.

Unexpectedness. Soviet intelligence first obtained information about preparation of a plan to attack the USSR in July 1940, only a few days after the German general staff began work on it.

Hitler approved plan "Barbarossa" on December 18, 1940. Exactly a week later the Soviet military attaché in Berlin received an anonymous letter informing him that the Germans would attack Russia the following spring. By December 29 Soviet intelligence knew the most important facts of plan Barbarossa—its goals and timetable.

American Deputy Secretary of State S. Wallace warned Soviet Ambassador K. Umansky in January 1941 about Germany's plan to attack the USSR.

The Soviet General Staff got hold of extensive material about plan Barbarossa on March 25.[2]

March 25 the Main Intelligence Administration (GRU) reported that 120 German divisions had been moved up to the Soviet borders.

Stalin received a warning from Churchill through British Ambassador S. Cripps on April 3.

The GRU reported on May 5, "Military preparations are being carried on openly in Poland. German officers and soldiers speak of war as a certainty, to begin after spring field work."[3]

On May 22 the assistant to the military attaché in Berlin, Khlopov, sent a report that the invasion would begin on June 15 or slightly earlier. General Tupikov, the military attaché in Berlin, reported almost daily on the Germans' preparations for war.

June 6. A report of the GRU on the concentration of 4 million German troops on the border. By a strange irony it was on that day that Stalin, as chairman of the Council of People's Commissars, confirmed the plan for putting industry on a war footing by the end of 1942.

With such a quantity of information it is a sin to complain of ignorance or unexpectedness. And we have not yet spoken of Richard Sorge!

He sent his first report of a coming war with Germany on November 18, 1940. On November 28 he informed Moscow about the formation of a new reserve army of forty divisions in Leipzig. Eighty divisions were already stationed along the Soviet-German border, and twenty more were being transferred from France.[4]

On March 5, 1941, Sorge dispatched a photocopy of a telegram from Ribbentrop to Otto, the German ambassador in Tokyo. In it the date for the invasion was set for mid-July.

Sorge's report of April 11 said, "The representative of the General Staff in Japan informs me that immediately after the end of the war in Europe, war with the Soviet Union will commence."

On May 2 Sorge wrote, "Hitler has decided to begin war and to destroy the USSR in order to use the European part of the USSR as a source of raw materials and grain. The most likely times for war to begin: (a) the defeat of Yugoslavia, (b) the end of spring harvest, (c) the end of negotiations with Turkey. Hitler will make the decision about when to begin war in May." On May 4 he reported that war would begin at the end of that month. On May 15 he reported that war would begin between the twentieth and the twenty-second of June. On May 19 he reported, "Nine armies, 150 divisions, are concentrated against the USSR."

Sorge copied a map from the German military attaché in Tokyo on which were marked military objectives in the Soviet Union and indications of the plans of attack. One such objective was to occupy the Ukraine and to use 1 to 2 million prisoners of war as laborers. Between 170 and 190 divisions would be gathered on the borders, and combat operations would be begun without a declaration of war. The Red Army and the Soviet order would be expected to fall in two months. Moscow expressed doubts to Sorge about the reliability of his information on June 12.

The sadly famous TASS announcement that called the threat of Germany going to war against the Soviet Union an invention of hostile propaganda was promulgated in the West on June 13. It appeared in the Soviet press the following day. That same day, after reading the idiotic document, an enraged Sorge radioed, "I repeat: on June 22, nine armies, 150 divisions will invade at dawn."

Thus, as far as unexpectedness is concerned the case is more or less clear. Concerning the other two theses, Soviet authors have created considerable dialectic confusion. It all depends on the context in which the facts are presented. If it is necessary to explain away the failures of the early period, the numbers of German troops are exaggerated and the Soviet troops are said to have had less modern equipment than they did, which fully justifies our temporary setbacks. In those cases when it is necessary to prove that Stalin and his underlings were not dreaming, that they were prepared for war, the tone and content of the speeches change. We learn that our Army was supplied with sufficient amounts of all sorts of the most modern military equipment and that the potential of our military industry surpassed that of Germany by one-and-a-half times. The numbers of our troops and combat units do not change much from report to report.

Numerical Superiority

As we have already said, there is great confusion in numbering the German troops. Moreover, it is very important to know what sort of troops Hitler threw against Russia in June 1941. Some Soviet sources[5] say that a monstrous army of 8.5 million men was thrown into plan Barbarossa. Another assessment says that the 190 divisions comprised 5.5 million men.[6] But alas, these convenient figures do not stand up even under superficial analysis. It turns out that between 1939 and the end of May 1941, 7.4 million were called up into the Wehrmacht.[7] If the losses of the Polish campaign and on the Western Front are subtracted, we find the remainder is around 7 million. We must remember that Germany continued to fight in the West and in Africa and maintained occupation forces over the greater part of the European continent.

In the interests of comparability we will take statistics of only the land forces of both sides. We have to do that because these are the only figures available for the Red Army.

Hitler threw against the Soviet Union land forces numbering 3.3 million.[8] The Red Army then numbered approximately 5 million men, 2.9 million of whom were in the western regions.[9] Besides that, before the war the 16th Army (M. F. Lukin), the 19th Army, and two corps were transferred from the North Caucasus region to the Ukraine. Altogether there were five armies near the western borders. In the European part of the country there were no fewer than 4 million men under arms.

Several works give statistics on the number of divisions: Germany had 152; the USSR in the western regions, 170 divisions and two brigades.[10] Halder gives slightly different figures in his "Diary": 141 and 213 divisions, respectively.[11] We must keep in mind that German divisions were larger than the Soviet.

The conclusion is simple. If the Germans did have more men at the front, their numerical superiority cannot be termed impressive or overwhelming.[12] The defenders should most certainly have been able to put up an organized resistance.

Technical Superiority

Here we encounter not only the simple distortion of facts, but also unsubstantiated, brazen, and blasphemous lies. To tell such things to the Soviet people who had gone hungry and died of starvation during the Five-Year Plan for the sake of creating defensive power—people who make such assertions carelessly, without bothering to explain the reasons, must have armor-plated consciences. Truly, as the Ukrainian saying goes, no conscience, no shame.

It is interesting that they avoided using statistics on this point. If one considers the quality of weapons, then the war showed that in most types of weaponry the USSR surpassed Germany. Our medium tank, the T-34, was undoubtedly the best in Europe; the KV heavy tank was in any case not inferior to its German counterpart. Both of these Soviet tanks were available in significant numbers at the beginning of the war. Our artillery was more powerful and more numerous than the Germans'. Such effective weapons as rocket launchers (Katiusha) were developed long before the war. Only the sluggishness of the leadership (Stalin and Kulik) kept them from being supplied to the troops.

In aviation the picture was not so clear. In numbers of airplanes we were far ahead of the Germans, but many of ours were no longer suited by their technical-tactical characteristics for modern warfare; they were obsolete. It was discovered during the war in Spain that we had been developing our air force improperly. Steps were taken to correct the deficiency. By 1941, new planes had been produced that were as good as what the Germans had—the MIG-3, IAK-1, LA-3. The enemy was not able to build an attack plane to match the IL-2 during the whole war. These new planes were put into mass production, and by the commencement of hostilities more than 3,000 had been given to the air force. Our fleet was more powerful than the Germans' as well.

Where we did lag behind the Germans was in supplying automatic weapons to the troops. Here Kulik, of unhappy memory, with Stalin's protection, had laid his dirty hand.

We will not go into great statistical detail. We hope that these fairly general statistics (table 25.1) will be sufficient. Because of contradictions in the sources on Soviet arms, we will offer several variations.

We will permit ourselves a brief comment on table 25.1. The Germans did not have an advantage in tanks. Assault guns and a fairly large number of obsolete tanks, German, French, and Czechoslovakian, were included in the 2,800 combat vehicles. The Wehrmacht clearly did not have enough new tanks. German industry produced only 2,800 medium tanks in 1940 and the first half of 1941. Heavy tanks appeared only in 1943 and then only 100.[13] The Wehrmacht did not surpass the Red Army in modern medium tanks; in heavy tanks they lagged behind (we had 654 KV tanks in 1941); in light tanks they were far behind.

The enemy's air power was even more questionable. In 1940 and the first half of 1941 German aviation plants produced 10,000 fighter planes, attack planes, and bombers. Losses for that period exceeded 7,500.[14]

We should also remember that in manpower and military economic potential, Germany was far behind Russia (see table 25.2). If you also consider England, the picture looks even worse.[15]

Even if we add in Italy, which had a population of 43 million and a weak economy, and which fought its own war and did not participate in the war against the USSR, the position of the Third Reich looked pretty doubtful even in June 1941—months before the United States entered the war.

But that leaves us with a paradox. It turns out that the Germans were not stronger than we were. But how do we get from there to the fact that in 1941 they dealt the Red Army a series of stinging defeats; captured

Table 25.1 Comparison of German and Soviet Large Armaments, 1940–41.

Wehrmacht, in the East		Red Army		
Type of weapon		VOV[a]	Zhukov[b]	Lototsky[c]
Tanks	2,800 (including assault guns)	Western regions, 1,475[d] (only T-34s and KVs)	7,000 total; Western regions; 1,800 heavy and medium (two-thirds new) and many light	—
Artillery (guns and mortars)	48,000	of .76 caliber or larger, one-half as many as the Germans	92,578 total; Western regions; 35,000	67,335 total (excluding 50 mm mortars); 34,695 in Western regions
Airplanes	4,950 (including 1,000 Romanian and Finnish)	—	17,745 total; 3,719 new models; Western regions; 1,500 new and a larger number of obsolete	—

a *Velikaia otechestvennaia voina Sovetskogo Soiuza, 1941–1945* (Moscow: Voenizdat, 1969), pp. 33, 53.
b G. Zhukov, *Vospominaniia i razmyshleniia* (Moscow: Novosti, 1969), pp. 205, 206, 209.
c S. S. Lototsky, *Istoriia voin i voennogo iskusstva* (Moscow: Voenizdat, 1970), p. 157.
d See *Istoriia Velikoi otechestvennoi voiny Sovetskogo Soiuza, 1941–1945*, edited by P. N. Pospelov, 6 vols. (Moscow: Voenizdat, 1961–65), vol. 1, p. 415.

Belorussia, the Ukraine, and the Baltic region; marched to Moscow; and besieged Leningrad? How could they? Was the German soldier that much superior to the Russian?

Such a suggestion is far from accurate; there are no facts to substantiate it. But if we apply that yardstick to the command staff, the conclusion forces itself upon us. The limits of our book are too narrow for a detailed and exhaustive analysis; but we can reliably conclude that in 1941 the Soviet command, especially the high command, was inferior to Germany's in practically all ways. Our troops' lack of combat experience also had an effect, but it was secondary. The major cause of our early defeats was that the Germans surpassed us in the quality of

Table 25.2   Comparison of Manpower and Military Economic Potential
of Three Countries in 1940–41

Country	Population in millions	Military production in billions of dollars, 1944 prices
USSR	190.6	8.5
England	48.2	6.5
Combined	238.8	15.0
Germany	69.8	6.0

leadership on all levels: in strategic planning, in operations, and even in tactical thinking. The Germans had their problems. They were hampered by ineffective organization of their higher command and by Hitler's inconsistency, wildness, and dilletantism—but to a lesser degree than we were by analogous problems.

The recent destruction of our officer corps played an enormous, possibly decisive, role in our weakness. Who is to blame for that is sufficiently clear. But the top leaders of the Red Army, Timoshenko and Zhukov, must bear a large share of responsibility also. However tattered and disorganized their staff might have been, they were still obliged to do everything humanly possible to keep the enemy from catching us unaware. All the more so, since they had vast human and material resources at their disposal. They neglected much that was their responsibility to do. They shamefully and spinelessly followed the tyrant down the path to national ruin. Here is a far from complete summary of their mistakes.

The mistakes before the war include:

(1) They made an incorrect evaluation of the strength and intentions of the enemy.

(2) There was no plan for strategic deployment in case of war.

(3) Troops of the western regions were not deployed in combat-ready positions but remained in garrisons; the regional commands were not informed that war might soon be upon them.

(4) They neglected border fortifications (the old fortifications were destroyed before the new ones were constructed).

(5) They stopped all precautionary measures usually carried out by the troops.[16]

(6) The carelessness of the leadership extended so far that no spe-

cially equipped command post was built for headquarters in Moscow in case of war.[17]

(7) Most important, Timoshenko and Zhukov did not insist on mobilization, which would not have been too late even at the beginning of June. Such a measure would certainly have disrupted the Germans' plans and might have prevented the invasion altogether.

In the first hours and days of war the leaders of the Peoples' Commissariat of Defense did no better. A few examples include:

(1) When they had learned of the German invasion, Timoshenko and Zhukov squabbled for a long while over who should call Stalin. This happened in the presence of Admiral Kuznetsov.

(2) They lost control of the troops.[18] NKO directive Number One (Order on the Commencement of War) was announced no earlier than 7:15 AM, that is, four hours after the invasion. The order bore the stamp of confusion. It did not say that the USSR and Germany were in a state of war. Our troops were ordered to destroy the invading forces, but were forbidden to cross the Soviet border. It almost sounds like a cruel joke. Aerial reconnaissance was permitted to fly only 100–150 kilometers into enemy territory. They could bomb only Konigsberg and Memel. Flights over Romania and Finland without special permission were forbidden.[19]

(3) They were guided by the fallacious strategy of defending every scrap of land, which was developed in conditions when the initiative was entirely on the side of the enemy.[20] That was like trying to put out a forest fire by piling brushwood in its path. As early as the 1920s, A. A. Svechin had warned of the fatal danger of such a course. We should instead have made a rapid and orderly retreat to lines that we could realistically defend. That would have avoided the senseless losses and demoralization of the troops, and the momentum of the attacking enemy would have been partly absorbed by the distance. But where could Timoshenko and Zhukov have read Svechin! Even with the strategy of Barclay de Tolly and Kutuzov, they were acquainted only by hearsay.

We cannot omit the figure of Golikov, who headed strategic intelligence before the war. That the intelligence organs continuously warned of the danger of an attack would seem to exonerate Golikov of any blame and even put him among those who suffered for the truth. But things were not that simple.

Golikov did not conceal his agents' reports. He delivered them to the

Defense Commissariat, the General Staff, and to Stalin, but in a most unusual way. He put information about the Germans' preparations for war and about the date of the attack in the category of rumors and other unreliable information. When many years later he was asked why he had done this, he replied that he had acted with the best intentions, that Stalin believed in rumors more than anything else. Possibly admirers of paradoxes will accept that admission, but the tedious duties of the historian force us to another conclusion: that Golikov wanted to please the leadership by telling Stalin what he wanted to hear. Golikov and others like him helped to create an atmosphere in higher Soviet circles that Harrison Salisbury has accurately characterized: "The record strongly suggests that Stalin, Zhdanov and his associates were living in a world turned inside out, in which black was assumed to be white, in which danger was seen as security, in which vigilance was assessed as treason and friendly warning as cunning provocation."

Of course that was not all Golikov's doing. That sort of social pathology was characteristic of the Stalinist system: "Unless there is a clear channel from lower to top levels, unless the leadership insists upon honest and objective reporting and is prepared to act upon such reports, regardless of preconceptions, prejudices, past commitments, and personal politics, the best intelligence in the world goes to waste— or, even worse, is turned into an instrument of self-deceit."[21]

Golikov wrote on one of Sorge's last reports that his story was invented by the English, who were eager to draw the USSR into the war. Stalin believed him. It was precisely that formula that was used in the notorious TASS announcement.[22]

However shamefully the intelligence chief conducted himself, he got away with it all. It was much worse for the real heroes of the secret front. A vivid example is the fate of Sorge himself. He was a German who worked many years against Germany and provided invaluable services for the USSR. His reward was distrust. In October and November 1941 he warned of Japan's plans to attack the United States. That removed the Japanese threat to the Soviet Far East for the foreseeable future and permitted the so-called Siberian divisions to be transferred west where they played a decisive role in the defense of Moscow.

Soon after that, Sorge fell into the hands of the Japanese in circumstances that suggest he may have been betrayed. Unbeknownst to him his wife was already in a Soviet camp. He spent almost three years in a Japanese prison. Stalin did not get around to arranging an exchange for him.[23]

Stalin as a Commander

The flattering phrases that were lavished on Stalin's military genius while he was alive do not deserve our attention, all the more so since he wrote the score for the performance. Nonetheless, to this day many people, including many high-ranking military officers, continue to think of Stalin as a great commander. The logic in that is straightforward. The Soviet Union won the war. You know who was at the head of the Army: QED. The venerable memoirists (such as Zhukov, Vasilevsky, Shtemenko) present us with that general conclusion without backing it up with facts, although when they speak of specific incidents in which the Great Leader participated, another conclusion thrusts itself upon the reader. The more one becomes acquainted with military memoirs, the more he is confirmed in the opinion that Stalin's personal decisions concerning the Army and Navy were not only wrong, but that they often worked to the advantage of the enemy.

The proof of that thesis as applied to the prewar period is the whole of our book. As far as the war itself is concerned, we refer the reader to the memoirs of Soviet commanders and invite him to make his own conclusions. Here we will give space to only a few striking facts, picked more or less at random.

(1) Stalin, as tyrants often are, was a coward. News of the invasion therefore made him despondent. Not knowing that fate had prepared for him the laurels of the Greatest Commander of all Times and Peoples, he still hoped against hope that there would be some way to avoid war and come to a friendly agreement with the aggressor. Halder's Diary for June 22 contains the following entry: "*12:00 (2:00 P.M. in Moscow)*. News has arrived that the Russians have resumed international radio communication that was broken off yesterday morning. They have appealed to Japan to represent Russia's interests in the matter of political and economic relations between Russia and Germany and are carrying on lively negotiations by radio with the German minister of foreign affairs."[24]

These urgent, shameful efforts were futile. Hitler preferred to fight. Now Stalin was really stuck. He secluded himself in his Kremlin apartments and got drunk. Stumbling out he uttered for history the pompous phrase, "Lenin's great work has perished. We were unable to defend it."

To resort to alcohol at critical moments was in character for Stalin.

When the tsarist police caught Kamo-Petrosian after the hold-up of the Tiflis bank, Stalin, the main organizer of the raid, conducted himself in a similar manner. He got drunk and shook with fear. (Kamo did not betray him. A grateful Stalin removed him in 1924.) Now it seemed that no miracle would save the erstwhile seminarian. In the June days of 1941, Stalin was more interested in his personal fate than in the outcome of the war. He expected that they would simply take him, the bankrupt adventurer who led the country to the brink of the abyss, and put him against the wall. But time passed, and this did not happen. Finally, on June 29th, the eighth day of the war, several members of the Politburo came to the hermit. They found him dirty and unshaven. Here we go, thought Stalin. But nothing of the sort. The Red courtiers wanted only to ask for a meeting of the TSK and SNK. Stalin relaxed. Then they very gently hinted that he could retire if he chose to. This was the sort of conversation Stalin could comprehend. If they were not planning to kill him, he was certainly not going to give up his power. They somehow managed to make the Great Leader presentable. On July 3 he made a radio address to the Soviet people.

Stalin took heart and once again picked up all the reins of state and military administration. Naming himself Supreme Commander-in-Chief did not, however, fill him with martial valor. He preferred not to visit areas where the fighting was going on. He is known to have visited a front area only once, near Viazma in August 1943; and on that occasion, according to A. I. Eremenko, he did not create an impression of bravery.

(2) Despite his phenomenal memory, Stalin had a very foggy notion about the organization of a modern army. Because of that he was receptive to all sorts of fantastic projects. N. N. Voronov writes, "From time to time completely absurd plans would appear at Headquarters. I was surprised that Stalin took them seriously." For example, late in 1943, he was taken by the idea to unite artillery and tanks into a single arm of the service. The consequences of such an innovation—it was not done—were easy to predict. At the same time he thought to reintroduce the institution of commanders-in-chief of groups of fronts, an idea that had failed spectacularly in 1941.[25]

Still earlier, before the war, Stalin had with one stroke of the pen liquidated the position of commander-in-chief of artillery of the Red Army and had transferred those functions to the Chief Artillery Administration under his favorite, Kulik.[26] When the latter failed so completely in the first days of the war, Stalin wondered; " 'how could it be,' he asked Voronov, 'that our artillery has no commander-in-chief? By whom and when was that decision made?' 'By you, sir!' I wanted to answer. I reminded him in a few words of the meeting in the Kremlin where that question had been decided."[27]

In July 1941, Stalin asked Commander-in-Chief of the Antiaircraft Defense Voronov to take charge of constructing defense works in the Ukraine: Volonov's recollection was that Molotov supported him. "I had to prove that I was not a specialist at such work. I advised them to assign the work of building defense lines to the commander of the Chief Engineering Administration, that that was in the immediate sphere of his responsibilities. They were both surprised: 'We really have such a thing?' 'Of course. Our Chief of Engineering Administration is General Kotliar.' "[28]

We could tell many such anecdotes. Here is one more. In winter 1942 rear services reported to Stalin a shortage of special packings. That was official language for ammunition boxes. Commander of Rear Services A. V. Khrulev suggested that an order be issued making return of used boxes mandatory. The solution was brilliant. Stalin agreed with it and added a note, "if any units do not return ammunition boxes, their supply of ammunition should be immediately cut off, *no matter how the battle is going*." No more, no less. Josef Vissarionovich did not want to seem any less decisive than Alexander the Great.[29]

(3) Stalin was completely incapable of strategic thinking. An obvious illustration is his behavior in early 1942. After Soviet troops had pushed the Germans back from Moscow, the Great Leader was immediately seized with uncontrollable optimism. He was sure that that had been the turning point in the war and that victory was just around the corner. How was he to understand that the German commander-in-chief of land forces had evaluated his situation, found it unfavorable, and had accomplished an orderly strategic retreat to a preselected position? In so doing he had managed to preserve his forces: "The 4th Army and the 3rd Tank Group were not destroyed, and the 2nd Tank Group retained its entire strength."[30] Hitler fired Brauchitsch for that. He, like Stalin, was more impressed by the "butchery strategy," bloody battles for every scrap of land. Nonetheless, the German retreat continued.

What did Stalin do? He instructed the Military Councils of the fronts: "Our task is to give the Germans no chance to catch their breath, to drive them west without stopping, to force them to expend their reserves before spring, when we will have large new reserves but the Germans will have no more reserves, and thus ensure the *complete destruction of Hitler's troops in 1942.*"[31]

That stirring order from the Supreme Commander thoroughly disoriented all of the front commanders. Everywhere they saw the enemy's retreat as panicked flight. Even the careful Vatutin was enchanted by the mood. The behavior of the front commanders is to a certain degree understandable. Each might think that Stalin had based his order on an analysis of the whole strategic situation, that Headquarters had information about the critical situation of the enemy.

The general Soviet attack on all fronts quickly expired. It resulted only in the complete expenditures of reserves, which had been gathered with immense effort. But Stalin did not give up his obsession, to defeat the Germans in 1942. In May he supported Timoshenko's and Khrushchev's lamebrained plan to attack Kharkov. As a result, four Soviet armies wound up encircled by the enemy. Stalin did not permit them to withdraw in time and they were destroyed. The Germans gained decisive superiority on the left wing of our troops and were able to reach the main Caucasus ridge and the Volga. The airborne operation in the Crimea did not accomplish its purposes. Leningrad continued to agonize in blockade. The spring-summer campaign of 1942 was lost by the Soviet command.

The crown, the peak of Stalin's work as a commander is rightfully considered the Berlin operation. Of course, even without it he would have enriched military science. We have already spoken of some of his exploits, but much more has been left out, for example, the very original suggestion to create another Horse Army, put forth in 1942. Only the unconscionable but unanimous opposition of the General Staff kept that thought from being made flesh. But the Berlin operation is a special subject that we cannot avoid.

Strategists of the old school saw their main objective not in winning every individual battle, but in gaining final victory, putting the enemy out of the war. Stalin was a strategist of the new school and did not have the right to act according to old precepts. Already in November 1944 he foresaw that the war would be ended by the taking of Berlin. It was then decided that the capture of the imperial capital would be assigned to Marshal Zhukov, who had remained the Supreme Commander's first deputy. With that end in mind he was appointed commander of the First Belorussian Front. The question of the expediency of the Berlin operation, of how it would be accomplished, was never discussed at Headquarters.

That the war would have to end with the victorious entrance of Soviet troops into Berlin was axiomatic for Stalin. True, in the First World War Germany had been defeated without the enemy's entering German territory. But Stalin was always prone to primitive symbolism, as was Hitler, who gave Stalingrad such mystical importance, who wasted so many troops in the fruitless efforts to take it. We can assume without doubt that in 1945 Germany, hard-pressed from two sides, would not have been able to hold out for long. The last inches of victory could have been had without a dramatic final assault and without the heavy casualties, the last senseless, unneeded casualties, that did inevitably result. But what did Stalin care for the grief and tears of hundreds of thousands of mothers, whose sons did not survive those last days and hours before peace? Still, since it did not come within the purview of the Soviet command, we will leave the strategic foundation of the Berlin operation in peace.

On January 26, 1945, Zhukov's and Konev's troops reached the Oder. Both commanders saw their chance to keep moving into an attack on Berlin and asked permission from Headquarters. Stalin, who had taken upon himself coordination of all efforts in the direction of Berlin,[32] confirmed the plan only a day later. A line was demarcated between the two fronts as Zhukov had recommended. That in itself was artificial and limiting. Stalin did not forget that he had already appointed Zhukov the victor of Berlin. Zhukov himself had no desire to share the laurels with anyone else. Therefore the line they drew did not leave Konev a "window" through which to strike at his objective. There arose a paradoxical situation, which then Deputy Chief of the General Staff Shtemenko has described thus: "The result was an obvious absurdity: on the one hand they confirmed the decision that Marshal Konev would be the right wing in the attack on Berlin, and on the other established a line of demarcation that would not permit him to do it."[33]

The assault on Berlin did not happen in February, however, because at the last moment Zhukov hesitated. He considered the threat of an attack on his flank by the enemy concentrated in Eastern Pomerania too serious. It is hard to say how well-founded his fears were. In any case his subordinate V. I. Chuikov, whose 8th Guard Army stood sixty kilometers from Berlin, held a different opinion, which he maintained even after the war. Chuikov claimed that Berlin was practically defenseless and that he could take it before the Germans could mount a flanking attack. We do not plan to be the judges of that argument. We note only that Zhukov preferred to postpone the storming and to attack without Konev. (Had he attacked with Konev, he could have detached part of his forces to defend his flank.)

By the end of March both fronts, especially Zhukov's, had amassed huge reserves. The capture of Berlin was put back onto the agenda. The plan of the operation was reviewed in the General Staff on March 31 with the participation of Zhukov and Konev. The latter, extremely annoyed by his awkward situation, insisted that the line of demarcation be altered. But who could change Stalin's decision?

The next day the Supreme Commander in Chief decided to accelerate the seizure of Berlin. He feared that the Americans and English might beat him to it.[34] A new meeting was called, this time with Stalin present. From the very beginning, Chief of General Staff A. I. Antonov objected to such a plan of operation. He had already shown Stalin the faults in the plan, but all he had achieved was that Stalin had forbidden him to raise the question. On April 1 Antonov decided nonetheless to try again, understanding fully how risky such insistence was in relation to Stalin. He expressed the opinion that not letting the troops of the 1st Ukrainian Front attack the German capital might make the operation unnecessarily long. Stalin exploded, and capitulated. Without saying a word he walked to the map and erased a sixty-kilometer sector of the demarcation line from Liuben to Berlin. The road to Berlin was open for Konev's troops.

Stalin valued Antonov's courage. After the war, unlike most of the other leaders of the war effort, he was not made a marshal.

The Price

With hindsight it is easy to find mistakes and say what ought to have been done. In real life, when time to think is short and information is always insufficient, mistakes are inevitable. No one can choose to fight only when he is sure of success. Why then stir up the past? Especially since we won.

Still there are two questions we want to ask: (1) who won in the Fatherland war? (2) at what cost was victory gained?

The most general, negative reply to the first question flows logically from all our books: not Stalin. But discussing his role once more is not excessive. Too many of our countrymen know too little of the truth about the war.

Stalin himself touched upon that problem immediately after the victory. He wanted above all to give his own interpretation of events and at the same time to close, to settle, the question, not to give anyone else a chance to explain. On May 24, 1945, he made a toast at a reception honoring the troop commanders of the Red Army. This brief speech is filled with profound political significance: "I would like to raise a toast to the health of our Soviet people and first of all to the Russian people. . . . I drink, first of all, to the health of the Russian people because it is the most outstanding nation of all nations comprising the Soviet Union."[35]

"The most outstanding nation" and further on "the leading force" and "the leading nation." Such a point of view was sensational innovation in the official lexicon. Until then the leading force had always been expressed in terms of class—the working class and its Party. Now the ruler had proclaimed the superiority of one, the main, people over the others. It was new and unexpected. It was an important change with far-reaching consequences.

Stalin had openly declared his solidarity with Nazi doctrine. The "leading nation" is but a translation of the German expression "nation-Fuhrer." The other peoples of the Soviet nation had been pronounced inferior, which encouraged nationalistic prejudice and rubbed salt in recent wounds. The rewriting of history was immediately begun. It was soon discovered that tsarist Russia was not at all the "prison of peoples," as the Bolsheviks had been fond of saying, and that the national minorities—who for so many years had resisted the encroachment of the Russian empire—had in fact joined the empire voluntarily. Even the conquest of the Caucasus, so vividly described by Marlinsky, Lermontov, and L. Tolstoy, was said not to have taken place. Dagestan was presented with a holiday to celebrate its union with Russia; Shamil was discovered to be a Turkish spy. The thesis of superiority of the Russian people also served as a signal for a new anti-Semitic campaign, which was at its worst from 1949 to 1953. The inferior Jews were removed from important positions, driven from scientific, cultural, and ideological institutions, not permitted to enroll in institutes of higher education, slandered as rootless cosmopolitans. The circle closed: the war with fascism, whose banner proclaimed the final solution, ended with the adoption of their anti-Semitic policy in our country.

But that is not all that can be found in the five-minute toast. At the official reception in honor of the victory, Stalin also spoke of recent failures: "Our government made more than a few mistakes. We had our moments of despair in 1941 and 1942 when our Army retreated . . . because there was nothing else we could do." Stalin did not try to analyze his mistakes. He resorted to a standard rhetorical gambit—he set up a straw man and then easily demolished it. "Another people might say to the Government, You have not met our expectations, get thee gone. We will erect another government which will make peace with Germany and give us peace."

The alternative was transparently false; there could not be peace with the aggressor. It was Stalin himself who had played that suicidal game with Hitler and had tried to make a deal even after the Nazi invasion. There was another solution: to put an honest and capable leader at the head of the country. But it was not in the Great Leader's interests to discuss that possibility.

Not long before, Stalin had paid the Russian people a generous compliment: "it has a clear mind, a firm character, and patience." By itself such a characterization is meaningless. It can be said of any nation that it has a dull mind and so forth. This was a cruel and capricious mockery. Here the whole point was in the patience: "But the Russian people did not choose that path, because it believed in the rightness of the policies of its Government and chose the path of sacrifice to ensure the defeat of Germany." The tyrant was flushed with the triumph, and still he could not keep from taunting. The Russian people had taken it all with patience: collectivization, famine, the purges, and the right policies, which had led the country into despair.

The final flourish was easy for Stalin: "And that trust of the Russian people for its Soviet government was the decisive force that gave us the historical victory over the enemy of mankind—over fascism."

Oh, how neat. The victory was gained not by the struggle of the people, not by its desperate efforts, not by its sacrifices (we have yet to speak of its unthinkable enormity), but by its trust in the government, that is, in Stalin. It was clear who had won—Stalin.

Now we will make our own conclusions. The war was won by the peoples of the Soviet Union, the Russians and all the others. Any reference to the exceptional contribution of any one of them is a mockery of the countless graves in which our soldiers and citizens lie without regard to nationality. Our soldiers at the front, our women, the old men, and youths in the rear won the war despite Stalin and his subordinates, whose policies were treason to the Motherland, committed for the most selfish reasons. Our people defended their homes and their land, not Stalin and the yoke of steel he fastened on the necks of the people.

Stalin, Voroshilov, Timoshenko, Zhukov, Golikov, Kulik, Mekhlis, Molotov, Zhdanov, Beria, and the others like them lost their war; in vain they ruined millions of human lives. Although they decorated themselves with splendid trinkets, that was not their just reward for the peoples' victory. Zhukov and Vasilevsky, who stood at the wheel of the Soviet war machine, have given us their memoirs. It is futile, however, to expect from them an honest evaluation of their own actions or of the policies of their Leader. They are bound with the same chain to Stalin. Stalin has taken them into a dirty, vile, and bloody history. They hoped to the last that history could be cleaned up, whitewashed, and lacquered, and that they could remain in it. They found a pair of unattractive features in their Generalissimo, but on the whole they thought of him favorably and respectfully. In him they saw and judged themselves.[36]

We have only a bit more to say, but it is the most horrifying—about our losses. When we speak of the difficulties of the Soviet Union in the early part of the war, we must not let that conceal the fact that Hitler's attack was a mad adventure. He counted on beating the Red Army in six weeks. When that failed—and it could not have succeeded—Hitler was lost. We had important advantages on our side (we will take only those that can be realistically evaluated): (1) enormous territory; (2) greater human and material resources; (3) armaments, which were no worse than Germany's at the start of the war and superior later on; and (4) stronger allies. In a long struggle the weaker enemy would have to capitulate in the end. Consequently, it makes more sense to speak not of the victory itself, which was foreordained by our superiority, but of the cost that we paid for that victory. Only in that way can we make an objective judgment of the quality of the country's leadership during the war.

We might expect that the losses we suffered for victory would at the very worst be equal to the losses of the defeated enemy. We will begin with those. First we will make a brief observation. Usually the statistics of war include as casualties of all those who were somehow lost to the armed forces—killed, wounded, captured, and missing in action. We will be most interested in those who died, who were killed or died

Table 25.3   German War Casualties, September 1, 1939–April 20, 1945

Type of casualty	Eastern Front	Western Front	Total
Killed	1,044,178	156,796	1,201,974
Wounded	4,122,041	557,510	4,679,551
MIA and POW	1,400,646	987,985	2,388,631
All casualties	6,567,465	1,703,291	8,270,756

of wounds, that is, people who were irretrievably lost to the country.

Casualty statistics were well kept in the German army almost to the very end of the war. Table 25.3 details the figures for the period from September 1, 1939, to April 20, 1945.[37] According to table 25.3, the German army lost 1.2 million men killed on both fronts, including more than 1 million on the Eastern Front. But this is not the answer to the question about the numbers killed. Some of the wounded died of their wounds, and some of the MIAs were also killed. In addition, this table does not include information on the last eighteen days of the war, during which the battle for Berlin took place. Almost a million German soldiers took part in that battle.

A complete accounting would bring us close to the figures given in Western sources. The German army lost approximately 3 million men who were killed outright or died of wounds. Losses among the civilian population were also approximately 3 million.

No such detailed Soviet statistics have ever been published. It is said that they simply do not exist. Our sources speak of casualties unwillingly, sparingly, and every time slightly differently. Immediately after the victory it was announced that the USSR's losses in the war totalled 6 million people. A few years later the figure was made a more nearly precise 9 million; somewhat later the count was given at 10 million. In the 1950s a certain colonel of the MGB defected to the West with a secret figure—of 20 million. Official Soviet organs at first disavowed that statistic but soon began to use it themselves. Khrushchev once said it was 22 million. These figures all refer to total deaths for the Army and the civilian population combined. As many civilians seem to have died as soldiers.

Now we are told that the Red Army lost 10 million soldiers and officers. Alas, that is but half the truth. Demographic calculations by a former Soviet professor, Kurganov, based on comparisons

of the censuses of 1939 and 1959, yield even more horrifying figures: total losses, 45 million; in the Army, 22 million.[38]

So, then, 45:6, 22:3, such were the ratios of losses borne by the
Soviet and German people. The difference in population size between
the two countries does not reduce the enormity. Germany sacrificed 8.6
percent of its population on the altar of war; we gave 23 percent,
almost a quarter of the nation. That is the cost of Stalin's genius, of his
policies—inalterably right for all times—the cost of destroying the
Army in peacetime, of unanimous and enthusiastic approval. God,
bless Russia! Spare us from such trials and leaders!

Afterword

Our book has come to its end. We have gathered—fragmentarily and incompletely, but as well as we could—material about the sorrowful fate of the Red Army. As best we could we have told of its fall, which was so tragic for the whole country, which drained its lifeblood, which deprived it of millions of its sons and daughters. We have told you again and again: remember the names of the executioners of the Army, the destroyers of the Motherland. Now we will tell you something else.

It would be the greatest hypocrisy to lay the whole blame for the most enormous bloodbath in the history of Russia and the memory of man on Stalin and Voroshilov, Molotov and Malenkov, Ezhov and Beria, on the yes-men and their inspirers. Such a conclusion would be comforting and would soothe our consciences. The most caustic bleach will not whiten the blackness of the evil done by these people. But it is not the whole truth.

There is something not quite right with ourselves. These evil demons did not come from other countries or worlds. They are our countrymen, our brothers, fathers, uncles, our relations, our twins. Let the modern Russian chauvinists console themselves that all of the problems of Holy Russia are caused by the ubiquitous Jews, the Georgians, the Catholic Poles, Latvian gunmen. That is explanation enough for the spritually empty and the born blind. It is not an answer, however, to the anguishing, soul-devouring question; it is only the twisting of primitive thought.

Let us not feel sorry for ourselves. There is a flaw, a wormhole in our national consciousness. It is hard to describe it in a few words, but primarily it lies in our toleration of evil and our submissiveness to unjust authority. We accept the deliberate and obvious lies. So it has been, so it will be. Taking it all, getting used to the stench of falsehood, we lose faith in the ability of our own reason; we grow deaf to the voice of moral feeling and subordinate our weak wills to the iron decisiveness of the tyrants. Many go further. They find rapture, passion, and ecstasy in the very loss of personality, vision, and reason. It gets so that the people devour themselves following the reckless ventures of the leaders. What would Stalin's cannibalistic thoughts have come to if he had not found millions of assistants, most of whom did not manage to save their own heads. They presented themselves. They came at the first call to do the paranoid's bidding, and dying they blessed him. Hysterically they mourned his death. Despite the unheard of suffering of their country they found cause to boast and swagger. Even after a small part of the truth of Stalin's crimes were revealed, they (we?) remained secret admirers of the fallen Leader.

This tragedy is not simply a page of history, but an open wound in the heart of Russia, the fetters on its soul, the blinders on its eyes. Words of revenge would be out of place. That would not bring back our dead. And on whom do we take revenge when the organizers and inspirers of the slaughter are already in their honored graves? The aged Molotov perhaps, or Malenkov, or hundreds of lesser executioners?

To tell the truth about everything, to hide nothing, to clean nothing up—that is our sacred duty to the memory of the innocent dead, to our children, to the future of the Motherland. The spiritual rebirth of the country is impossible while evil remains hidden away, unjudged, while the triumphant lie paralyzes our will, devours our soul, and lulls our conscience.

June 11, 1977
Moscow

Appendixes

I. Higher Commanders of the RKKA Who Died in the Repressions of 1937–1939, by Rank

These lists, and the list in appendix II, were made primarily by comparing official lists of military promotions published in 1935 and 1940. Because it is impossible at present to conduct a thorough check, it is possible that there is some inaccuracy at the brigade level.

Marshal of the Soviet Union

1. Blucher, V. K.
2. Egorov, A. I.
3. Tukhachevsky, M. N.

Army Commander First Class (General of the Army)

4. Belov, I. P.
5. Uborevich, I. P.
6. Iakir, I. E.

Army Commissar First Class (General of the Army)

7. Gamarnik, Ia. B.

Army Commander Second Class (Colonel General)

8. Alksnis, Ia. I.
9. Vatsetis, I. I.
10. Dubovoi, I. N.
11. Dybenko, P. E.
12. Kashirin, N. D.
13. Kork, A. I.
14. Levandovsky, M. K.
15. Sediakin, A. I.
16. Fedko, I. F.
17. Khalepsky, I. A.

Army Commissar Second Class (Colonel General)

18. Amelin, M. P.
19. Aronshtam, L. N.
20. Bulin, A. S.
21. Beklichev, G. I.
22. Grishin, A. S.
23. Gugin, G. I.
24. Ippo, B. M.
25. Kozhevnikov, S. N.
26. Landa, M. M.
27. Mezis, A. N.
28. Okunev, G. S.
29. Osepian, G. A.
30. Slavin, I. E.
31. Smirnov, P. A.
32. Shifres, A. A.
32a. Khakhanian, G. D.

Corps Commander (Lieutenant General)

33.	Alafuzo, M. I.	58.	Kutiakov, I. S.
34.	Appoga, E. F.	59.	Lavrov, V. K.
35.	Bazilevich, G. D.	60.	Lapin, A. Ia.
36.	Batorsky, M. A.	61.	Levichev, V. N.
37.	Bogomiagkov, S. N.	62.	Lepin, E. D.
38.	Vainer, L. Ia.	63.	Lisovsky, N. V.
39.	Vasilenko, M. I.	64.	Longva, P. V.
40.	Velikanov, M. D.	65.	Mezheninov, S. A.
41.	Gai (Bzhishkian), G. D.	66.	Mulin, V. M.
42.	Gailit, Ia. P.	67.	Petin, N. N.
43.	Garkavyi, I. I.	68.	Primakov, V. M.
44.	Gekker, A. I.	69.	Pugachev, S. A.
45.	Germanovich, M. Ia.	70.	Putna, V. K.
46.	Gittis, V. M.	71.	Sangursky, M. V.
47.	Gorbachev, B. S.	72.	Smolin, I. I.
48.	Gribov, S. E.	73.	Sokolov, V. N.
49.	Griaznov, I. K.	74.	Storozhenko, A. A.
50.	Efimov, N. A.	75.	Stutska, K. A.
51.	Zonberg, Zh. F.	76.	Turovsky, S. A.
52.	Ingaunis, F. A.	77.	Uritsky, S. P.
53.	Kalmykov, M. V.	78.	Feldman, B. M.
54.	Kovtiukh, E. I.	79.	Fesenko, D. S.
55.	Kosogov, I. D.	80.	Khripin, V. V.
56.	Krivoruchko, N. N.	81.	Chaikovsky, K. A.
57.	Kuibyshev, N. V.	82.	Eideman, R. P.

Corps Commissar (Lieutenant General)

83.	Avinovitsky, Ia. L.	95.	Orlov, N. I.
84.	Apse, M. Ia.	96.	Petukhov, I. P.
85.	Artuzov, A. Kh.	97.	Prokovev, A. P.
86.	Berezkin, M. F.	98.	Rodionov, F. E.
87.	Berzin, Ia. K.	99.	Savko, N. A.
88.	Vitte, A. M.	100.	Sidorov, K. G.
89.	Grinberg, I. M.	101.	Troianker, B. U.
90.	Gruber, L. Ia.	102.	Khorosh, M. L.
91.	Ilin, N. I.	103.	Shestakov, V. N.
92.	Karin, F. Ia.	104.	Shteinbriuk, O. O.
93.	Nemerzelli, I. F.	105.	Iartsev, A. P.
94.	Neronov, I. G.	106.	Iastrebov, G. G.

Corps Engineer (Lieutenant General of Engineers)

107.　Siniavsky, M. M.

Corps Intendant (Lieutenant General)

108.	Khiltsov, A. I.	110.	Oshlei, P. M.
109.	Kosich, D. I.		

Corps Physician (Lieutenant General, Medical Services)

111. Baranov, M. I.

Corps Veterinarian (Lieutenant General, Medical Services)

112. Nikolsky, N. M.

Corps Military Jurist (Lieutenant General)

113. Rozovsky, N. P.

Divisional Commander (Major General)

114. Alksnis, Ia. Ia.
115. Andriiashev, L. P.
116. Aplok, Iu. Iu.
117. Artemenko, N. F.
118. Artemev, K. P.
119. Atoian, A. T.
120. Bakshi, M. M.
121. Balakirev, A. F.
122. Belitsky, S. M.
123. Bely, S. O.
124. Berggolts, A. I.
125. Bergstrem, V. K.
126. Blazhevich, I. F.
127. Blomberg, Zh. K.
128. Bobrov, B. I.
129. Bobrov, N. M.
130. Bokis, G. G.
131. Bondar, G. I.
132. Borisenko, A. N.
133. Brianskikh, P. A.
134. Buachidze, F. M.
135. Bukshtynovich, M. F.
136. Burichenkov, G. A.
137. Butyrsky, V. P.
138. Vakulich, P. I.
139. Vasilev, F. V.
140. Ventsov-Krants, S. I.
141. Vizirov, G. M.
142. Volpe, A. M.
143. Garf, V. E.
144. Germonius, V. E.
145. Golovkin, V. G.
146. Gorbunov, M. Iu.
147. Goriachev, E. I.
148. Grigor'ev, P. P.
149. Grushetsky, V. F.

150. Davidovsky, Ia. L.
151. Dannenberg, E. E.
152. Demichev, M. A.
153. Derevtsov, S. I.
154. Dikalov, E. P.
155. Dobrovolsky, V. P.
156. Zamilatsky, G. S.
157. Zinovev, I. Z.
158. Ziuz-Iakovenko, Ia. I.
159. Ivanov, Ia. K.
160. Inno, A. A.
161. Kazansky, E. S.
162. Kakurin, N. E.
163. Kapulovsky, I. D.
164. Karklin, I. I.
165. Karpov, M. P.
166. Kassin, G. I.
167. Kariagin, G. B.
168. Kaufeldt, F. P.
169. Kviatek, K. F.
170. Kilvein, G. Ia.
171. Kniagnitsky, P. E.
172. Kozhevnikov, A. T.
173. Kozitsky, A. D.
174. Kolsheiko, F. A.
175. Korolev, D. K.
176. Kotov, N. Ia.
177. Kokhansky, V. S.
178. Kuk, A. I.
179. Kutateladze, G. N.
180. Kychinsky, D. A.
181. Lazarevich, M. S.
182. Laur, Zh. I.
183. Lopatin, V. N.
184. Maksimov, I. F.
185. Maslov, K. V.

186. Mednikov, M. L.
187. Melik-Shakhnazarov, A. P.
188. Murzin, D. K.
189. Neiman, K. A.
190. Nikitin, S. V.
191. Nikiforov, L. I.
192. Nikonov, A. M.
193. Ovchinnikov, G. I.
194. Olshansky, M. M.
195. Olshevsky, F. I.
196. Pavlov, A. V.
197. Pashkovsky, K. K.
198. Peremytov, A. M.
199. Poga, Zh. Ia.
200. Pogrebnoy, V. S.
201. Pokus, Ia. Z.
202. Rakitin, N. V.
203. Raudmets, I. I.
204. Rink, I. A.
205. Rogalev, F. F.
206. Rogovsky, N. M.
207. Rokhi, V. Iu.
208. Rubinov, Ia. G.
209. Sablin, Iu. V.
210. Savitsky, S. M.
211. Savchenko, S. N.
212. Sazontov, A. Ia.
213. Svechin, A. A.
214. Semenov, N. G.
215. Serdich, D. F.
216. Sergeev, E. N.
217. Sidorenko, V. S.
218. Sokolov-Sokolovsky, P. L.
219. Sollogub, N. V.
220. Stepanov, V. A.
221. Stepanov, M. O.
222. Talkovsky, A. A.
223. Tarasenko, V. V.
224. Tarasov, A. I.
225. Testov, S. V.
226. Tkalun, P. P.
227. Tomashevich, I. A.
228. Tochenov, N. I.
229. Trizna, D. D.
230. Tukhareli, G. A.
231. Uvarov, N. M.

232. Ushakov, K. P.
233. Fedotov, A. V.
234. Firsov, D. S.
235. Florovsky, I. D.
236. Khoroshilov, I. Ia.
237. Chernobrovin, S. A.
238. Shalimo, M. N.
239. Sharskov, I. F.
240. Sheko, Ia. V.
241. Shiroky, I. F.
242. Shmidt, D. A.
243. Shcheglov, N. V.
244. Iushkevich, V. A.
245. Antonov, M. A.
246. Balchenko, R. L.
247. Barger, M. P.
248. Bauzer, F. D.
249. Blaushvili, N. K.
250. Bogdanov, P. P.
251. Boitsov, D. P.
252. Borovich, Ia. A.
253. Bocharov, L. P.
254. Vaineros, I. D.
255. Genin, Ia. F.
256. Gladyshev, N. Ia.
257. Gorin, G. I.
258. Gornostaev, I. M.
259. Zaitsev, V. E.
260. Zeldovich, M. E.
261. Zemskov, S. I.
262. Zilbert, L. I.
263. Zinovev, G. A.
264. Ivanov, S. E.
265. Indrikson, Ia. G.
266. Isaenko, M. G.
267. Kavalers, P. E.
268. Kalpus, B. A.
269. Kamensky, P. G.
270. Kolotilov, V. N.
271. Konovalov, V. F.
272. Kropachev, A. M.
273. Lavrov, M. V.
274. Levenzon, F. Ia.
275. Markov, G. N.
276. Minchuk, A. I.
277. Mirovitsky, P. V.

278. Mustafin, I. A.
279. Nevraev, G. F.
280. Ozol, V. K.
281. Padarin, N. I.
282. Pismanik, G. E.
283. Plau, D. D.
284. Rabinovich, I. Iu.
285. Rabinovich, S. Z.
286. Rittel, G. I.
287. Saakov, O. A.
288. Safronov, I. V.
289. Svinkin, I. A.
290. Serpukhovitin, V. V.
291. Simonov, M. E.
292. Skortsov, S. A.
293. Slavin, M. E.

294. Slavinsky, K. E.
295. Smolensky, Ia. L.
296. Sokolenko, F. N.
297. Suslov, P. V.
298. Tarutinsky, A. V.
299. Udilov, P. S.
300. Usatenko, A. V.
301. Feldman, P. M.
302. Kharitonov, Kh. Kh.
303. Khromenko, A. N.
304. Tsarev, Ia. T.
305. Shimanovsky, G. S.
306. Shchegolev, L. I.
307. Iung, N. A.
308. Iakubovsky, L. G.

Divisional Engineer (Major General-Engineer)

309. Aksenov, A. M.
310. Andreev, E. S.
311. Bandin, A. P.
312. Barkalov, E. A.

313. Bordovsky, S. V.
314. Konnert, V. S.
315. Polischuk, K. E.
316. Potapov, G. Kh.

Divisional Intendant (Major General)

317. Ankudinov, I. Ia.
318. Bakov, P. G.
319. Bekker, S. I.
320. Vanag, A. Ia.
321. Gorshkov, V. S.
322. Gurev, K. P.
323. Dzydza, G. A.
324. Zuev, N. N.
325. Ivanov, B. N.

326. Kniazev, P. G.
327. Kurkov, P. I.
328. Maksimov, S. M.
329. Matson-Krashinsky, O. P.
330. Peterson, R. A.
331. Proshkin, I. G.
332. Sokolov, A. M.
333. Stankovsky, N. V.
334. Fedorov, V. F.

Divisional Physician (Major General, Medical Service)

335. Kiuchariants, A. G.

336. Rainer, B. A.

Divisional Veterinarian (Major General, Medical Service)

337. Vlasov, N. M.

338. Petukhovsky, A. A.

Brigade Commander (Brigadier General)*

339. Agladze, L. M.
340. Alekseev, P. G.
341. Alekhin, E. S.
342. Andrianov, N. G.
343. Androsiuk, N. I.

344. Antonov, P. I.
345. Arsenev, B. N.
346. Ausem-Orlov, V. V.
347. Afonsky, V. L.
348. Bazhanov, N. N.

349. Bazenkov, B. I.
350. Balabin, B. N.
351. Batenin, V. N.
352. Bakhrushin, A. M.
353. Bebris, I. G.
354. Blium, I. E.
355. Blium, N. Ia.
356. Bolotkov, M. I.
357. Bondariuk, G. M.
358. Borisov, A. B.
359. Buzanov, D. I.
360. Biuler, V. A.
361. Vainerkh, D. A.
362. Vasilchenko, N. N.
363. Vasnetsovich, V. K.
364. Varfolomeev, N. E.
365. Vishnerevsky, V. A.
366. Volkov, G. D.
367. Voronokov, V. M.
368. Viazemsky, M. F.
369. Gavrichenko, F. N.
370. Gavriushenko, G. F.
371. Genin, V. M.
372. Glagolev, V. P.
373. Golikov, A. G.
374. Gorev, V. E.
375. Gorshkov, B. N.
376. Goffe, A. I.
377. Gravin, N. M.
378. Grachev, V. G.
379. Grechanik, A. I.
380. Grosberg, I. K.
381. Grudiaev, P. I.
382. Gudkov, D. I.
383. Guskov, N. F.
384. Daniliuk, G. S.
385. Dashichev, I. F.
386. Dobrolezh, A. G.
387. Dotol, F. K.
388. Dragilev, V. G.
389. Drozdov, A. K.
390. Diakov, V. A.
391. Evdokimov, Ia. K.
392. Evseev, N. F.
393. Egorov, N. G.
394. Emelnov, P. V.

395. Zhabin, N. I.
396. Zhivin, N. I.
397. Zhigur, Ia. M.
398. Zhitov, A. A.
399. Zhorkov, V. A.
400. Zaitsev, A. S.
401. Zaks, Ia. E.
402. Zalevsky, A. I.
403. Zaporozhchenko, M. I.
404. Zakhoder, V. N.
405. Zubok, A. E.
406. Zybin, S. P.
407. Ivanov, S. I.
408. Ignatov, N. G.
409. Igneus-Matson, E. G.
410. Ikonostasov, V. M.
411. Kagan, M. A.
412. Kalvan, I. I.
413. Kaptsevich, G. A.
414. Karev, G. S.
415. Karmaliuk, F. F.
416. Kartaev, L. V.
417. Kasinov, S. M.
418. Kevlishvili, P. G.
419. Keiris, R. I.
420. Kirichenko, I. G.
421. Kiselev, M. F.
422. Kit-Vaitenko, I. P.
423. Klein-Burzin, V. A.
424. Klementev, V. G.
425. Klochko, I. G.
426. Kliava, K. Iu.
427. Kovalev, D. M.
428. Kozlovsky, V. N.
429. Kolesnichenko, M. Ia.
430. Koltunov, I. S.
431. Kolchuk, F. S.
432. Konovalov, L. I.
433. Korobov, I. A.
434. Korchits, V. V.
435. Kosiakin, V. V.
436. Kosmatov, A. V.
437. Kruk, I. M.
438. Kuzmmichev, B. I.
439. Kuznetsov, I. I.
440. Kunitsky, I. F.

441. Kushakov, V. A.
442. Labas, A. A.
443. Lavinovskikh, B. Ia.
444. Lakovnikov, P. I.
445. Lapchinsky, A. N.
446. Lakhinsky, K. K.
447. Letsky, G. I.
448. Lunev, D. D.
449. Lunev, P. M.
450. Lukin, E. D.
451. Liubimov, V. V.
452. Mager, M. P.
453. Magon, E. Ia.
454. Malovsky, A. D.
455. Malofeev, V. I.
456. Malyshev, A. K.
457. Malyshenkov, G. F.
458. Malyshkin, V. F.
459. Mamonov, P. D.
460. Markevich, N. L.
461. Martynovsky, S. L.
462. Marchenko, P. G.
463. Matuzenko, A. I.
464. Makhrov, N. S.
465. Medvedev, M. E.
466. Mediansky, M. S.
467. Meier, A. P.
468. Mernov, V. I.
469. Meshkov, A. T.
470. Miliunas, I. A.
471. Mironov, A. M.
472. Mishuk, N. I.
473. Mozolevsky, V. A.
474. Molodtsov, P. P.
475. Mosin, A. N.
476. Muev, D. D.
477. Murtazin, M. L.
478. Nakhichevansky, D. D.
479. Neborak, A. A.
480. Nesterovsky, N. A.
481. Nikulin, I. E.
482. Obysov, S. P.
483. Ogorodnikov, F. E.
484. Orlov, A. G.
485. Ostrovsky, A. I.
486. Pavlov, P. A.

487. Pavlovsky, V. I.
488. Pavlovsky, K. V.
489. Petrenko-Lunev, S. V.
490. Petrov, M. I.
491. Petrov, M. O.
492. Petrusevich, B. V.
493. Podshivalov, V. I.
494. Podshivalov, I. M.
495. Pozniakov, S. V.
496. Polunov, M. L.
497. Poliakov, V. I.
498. Poliakov, N. S.
499. Poliansky, N. A.
500. Potancpko, P. R.
501. Prokopchuk, N. A.
502. Rataush, R. K.
503. Rachinsky, N. I.
504. Reztsov, V. I.
505. Rozynko, A. F.
506. Rosman, I. D.
507. Rudenko, D. M.
508. Rudinsky, N. S.
509. Rulev, P. P.
510. Rybakov, M. A.
511. Rybkin, P. D.
512. Ryzhenkov, M. M.
513. Samoilov, I. Ia.
514. Satin, A. I.
515. Svechnikov, M. S.
516. Selivanov, V. V.
517. Semenov, N. A.
518. Seredin, V. P.
519. Serpokrylov, M. S.
520. Skulachenko, A. E.
521. Smirnov, S. S.
522. Sokolov, A. D.
523. Sokolov, A. N.
524. Sokolov, G. I.
525. Sokolov-Strakhov, K. I.
526. Solomatin, M. D.
527. Sonin, K. A.
528. Sorokin, Ia. V.
529. Stakhansky, N. M.
530. Stoilov, A. G.
531. Suleiman, N. A.
532. Suslov, A. A.

533. Scheskulevich, A. S.
534. Sysoev, P. V.
535. Tantlevsky, E. B.
536. Tarnovsky-Tarletsky, A. M.
537. Titov, A. P.
538. Tikhomirov, E. M.
539. Tikhomirov, P. P.
540. Tishchenko, Z. P.
541. Tkachev, M. L.
542. Tolkachev, F. A.
543. Trifonov, A. P.
544. Trukhanov, N. F.
545. Turchak, V. M.
546. Tyltyn, A. M.
547. Ulasevich, S. A.
548. Ulman, Zh. K.
549. Fedin, A. T.
550. Fedorov, N. F.

551. Fesenko, P. G.
552. Fogel, I. I.
553. Fokin, I. V.
554. Tsiemgal, A. I.
555. Chernov, F. M.
556. Chernozatonsky, L. N.
557. Cherny, I. I.
558. Cherniavsky, M. L.
559. Shafransky, I. O.
560. Shashkin, V. V.
561. Sheideman, E. S.
562. Shipov, V. F.
563. Shmai-Kreitsberg, A. I.
564. Shoshkin, M. A.
565. Shuvalikov, V. V.
566. Iakimov, M. M.
567. Iakimov, M. P.
568. Iakubov, R. A.

Brigade Engineer*

569. Aleksandrov, V. V.
570. Alliluev, P. S.
571. Argentov, A. A.
572. Bruevich, N. G.
573. Venttsel, D. A.
574. Geveling, N. V.
575. Gruzdup, A. Kh.
576. Demianovsky, V. V.
577. Zhelezniakov, Ia. M.
578. Zhukov, L. I.
579. Zhukovsky, I. P.
580. Zhukovsky, N. I.
581. Zemsky, B. M.
582. Isakov, K. V.
583. Iudin, S. D.
584. Kozlov, S. G.
585. Kokadeev, A. N.

586. Lastochkin, A. F.
587. Lilienfeld, A. E.
588. Maksimov, N. A.
589. Mogilevkin, V. N.
590. Novikov, L. V.
591. Ogloblin, A. P.
592. Pavlov, I. S.
593. Petrov, O. D.
594. Sakrier, I. F.
595. Saravaisky, S. A.
596. Sviridov, V. D.
597. Stepanov, Iu. A.
598. Faivush, Ia. A.
599. Fedorov, I. A.
600. Khandrikov, V. P.
601. Kheil, I. G.
602. Shapiro, S. G.

Brigade Intendant*

603. Abol, E. F.
604. Blinov, S. V.
605. Buznikov, A. D.
606. Vitkovsky, P. P.
607. Gludin, I. I.
608. Evtushenko, N. N.
609. Zafran, I. I.

610. Kalinin. S. I.
611. Klatovsky, N.A.
612. Kupriukhin, A. M.
613. Pevzner, I. B.
614. Pertsovsky, Z. D.
615. Petrovich, N. G.
616. Pretter, K. A.

617. Satterup, D. V.

618. Trukhanin, M. Z.

619. Chibar, Ia. A.

620. Shchetinin, P. A.

*There is no such rank in the Soviet Armed forces now. When the new rank nomenclature was introduced in 1940, those brigade commanders who had escaped the repressions received the title of major-general. A few of the brigade commanders who returned from the camps (Isserson, G. S., Tsalkovich, I. M., et al.) were made colonels.

II. Higher Naval Commanders Who Died in the Repressions of 1937–1939

Flagman of the Fleet First Class (Admiral of the Fleet)

1. Viktorov, M. V.
2. Orlov, V. M.

Flagman of the Fleet Second Class (Admiral)

3. Kozhanov, I. K.
4. Muklevich, R. A.

Flagman First Class (Vice Admiral)

5. Dushenov, K. I.
6. Kadatsky-Rudnev, I. N.
7. Kireev, G. P.
8. Ludri, I. M.
9. Pantserzhansky, E. S.

Flagman Second Class (Rear Admiral)

10. Vasilev, A. V.
11. Vasilev, G. V.
12. Vinogradsky, G. G.
13. Galkin, G. P.
14. Isakov, D. P.
15. Ozolin, Ia. I.
16. Samborsky, E. K.
17. Sivkov, A. K.
18. Smirnov, P. I.

Flagman-Engineer Second Class (Rear Admiral, Engineer)

19. Aliakrinsky, N. V.

Flagman-Engineer Third Class*

20. Antsipo-Chikunsky, L. V.
21. Brykin, A. E.
22. Vasilev, V. V.
23. Gorbunov, N. I.
24. Gorshkov, V. A.
25. Messer, P. V.
26. Miroshkin, A. F.
27. Motorny, I. D.
28. Platonov, A. P.
29. Posazhennikov, A. D.
30. Rashevich, F. K.
31. Khait, N. M.

*This corresponds to the brigade level of the land forces. See explanation (*) of these ranks in appendix I.

III. Higher Command Staff Personnel Freed and Rehabilitated After the June Plenum of the TsK of 1957

This list is incomplete. There should be approximately fifteen men in this category, but we were not able to confirm the others.

There was also a large group of commanders, who were repressed but freed before the war and who participated in combat action. Among them were Marshal K. K. Rokossovsky, General of the Army A. V. Gorbatov, Lieutenant Generals L. G. Petrovsky, G. D. Stelmakh, and others; altogether seventy men.

Name	Rank at the time of arrest	Rank after rehabilitation
1. Todorsky, A. I.	Corps commander	Lieutenant-general
2. Govorukhin, T. K.	Corps commissar	Major-general
3. Fishman, Ia. M.	Corps engineer	Major-general, engineer
4. Melkumov, Ia. A.	Division commander	Colonel
5. Kolosov, P. I.	Division commissar	Major-general
6. Isserson, G. S.	Brigade commander	Colonel
7. Iungmeister, V. A.	Brigade commander	Colonel
8. Tsalkovich, I. M.	Brigade engineer	Colonel, engineer

IV

Table 1.   Changes on the Top Level of the People's Commissariat of Defense
of the USSR, June 20, 1934–June 22, 1941

Position	Names and dates	
People's Commissar of Defense	K. E. Voroshilov to May 6, 1940	S. K. Timoshenko from May 6, 1940
First Deputy (from August 1940, Deputy); Chief of the Main Political Directorate	*Ya. B. Gamarnik[1]* to May 31, 1937 L. Z. Mekhlis[2] December 1937– September 1940	P. A. Smirnov July 15–December 1937 A. I. Zaporozhets from October 7, 1940
First Deputy	*M. N. Tukhachevsky[3]* April 9, 1936– May 11, 1937 I. F. Fedko January 25– July 7, 1938	*A. I. Egorov[4]* May 11, 1937– January 21, 1938 S. M. Budenny from August 15, 1940
Deputy; Chief of the General Staff (from 1936)	A. I. Egorov to May 11, 1937 K. A. Meretskov August 15, 1940– February 1941	B. M. Shaposhnikov May 11, 1937– August 15, 1940 G. K. Zhukov from February 1941
Deputy; Chief of Armaments	M. N. Tukhachevsky to April 9, 1936 G. I. Kulik from May 26, 1937	*A. I. Khalepsky[5]* April 9, 1936– April 4, 1937
Deputy	K. A. Meretskov June 7–August 15, 1940; from February 1941	
Deputy	B. M. Shaposhnikov from August 15, 1940	

Table 1.   (continued)

Position	Names and dates	
Deputy, Intelligence; Chief of the Fifth Main Directorate	*I. I. Proskurov*[6] April 14, 1939– July 27, 1940	
Deputy (from January 1937); Chief of the Air Force	*Ya. I. Alksnis* to November 24, 1937	*A. D. Loktionov*[7] November 28, 1937– July 11, 1940
	Ya. V. Smushkevich[8] July 20–August 28, 1940	*P. V. Rychagov* August 28, 1940– April 1941 P. F. Zhigarev from April 1941
Deputy, Cadre	E. A. Shchadenko[9] January 1938– December 6, 1940	
Deputy (from January 1937); Chief of the Naval Forces	*V. M. Orlov* to June 15, 1937	*M. V. Viktorov* August 15– November 1937
People's Commissar of the Navy (from December 30, 1937)	*P. A. Smirnov* to November 1938 N. G. Kuznetsov from March 1939	*M. P. Frinovsky* November 1938–March 1939

Key: Italicized names indicate arrested and perished.

1. By order of the People's Commissar of Defense of May 31, 1937, Gamarnik was "removed from his post, expelled from the Military Council, and discharged from the RKKA as a person having close group links with Yakir, who was recently expelled from the Party for his participation in a fascist military conspiracy." Gamarnik shot himself on the same day.

2. In September 1940 appointed Deputy Chairman of the Council of People's Commissars and People's Commissar of State Control.

3. On May 11, 1937, appointed Commander of the Volga Military District. Arrested on May 26.

4. On January 25, 1938, appointed Commander of the Trans-Caucasus Military District. On February 25 was discharged from the RKKA by the reason of illness. Arrested and perished.

5. Nominally was not a Deputy People's Commissar. On April 4, 1937, was appointed People's Commissar of Communications. Arrested and perished.

6. On September 6, 1940, appointed Deputy Air Force Commander of the Far East Front. From October 23 he was Deputy Chief of the Air Force of the Red Army,

Long-range Bombardment Aviation. Was arrested in January 1941; perished.

7. Appointed Commander of the Baltic Military District. Arrested in January 1941; perished.

8. On August 15, 1940, appointed Inspector General of the Air Force; on December 3, Deputy Chief of the General Staff, Aviation. Arrested in January 1941; perished.

9. Dismissed by the decision of the plenary session of the Central Committee, but reinstated in the same post after the beginning of the war.

Table 2.   Administration of Military Districts and Fleets,
June 20, 1934–June 22, 1941

District and position	Names and dates		
Arkhangelsk Military District (MD) formed in 1940			
1. Commander	N. V. Kurdyumov March–April 1940	V. Ya. Kachalov from June 1940	
2. Head of Political District (member of the District Military Council)	N. N. Vashugin March–April 1940	N. N. Klementiev May–December 1940	
3. Chief of Staff	P. A. Ivanov March–April 1940	P. G. Egorov from June 1940	
Belorussian MD since 1939—Belorussian Special; since 1940—Western Special			
1. Commander	*I. P. Uborevich* to May 11, 1937 D. G. Pavlov from June 1940	*I. P. Belov* June 5, 1937– April 1938	M. P. Kovalev April 1938– April 11, 1940
2. Head of Political District (member of the District Military Council)	P. A. Smirnov to November 29, 1935 I. V. Rogov September 10, 1938–March 25, 1939	A. S. Bulin November 29, 1935–April 15, 1937 I. Z. Susaikov March 27, 1939– February 11, 1940	F. I. Golikov December 30, 1937–September 10, 1938 Ya. A. Fominykh from June 7, 1940
3. Chief of Staff	K. A. Meretskov to December 1934 M. A. Purkaev April 3, 1938– August 31, 1939 V. E. Klimovskikh from July 27, 1940	*B. I. Bobrov* January 23, 1935– May 31, 1937 V. E. Klimovskikh September 27, 1939–March 1940	*A. I. Peremytov* June 28, 1937– March 1938 M. A. Purkaev March 1940– July 26, 1940
Transbaycal MD formed in 1935 from the Far Eastern Red Army			
1. Commander	*I. K. Gryaznov*	*M. D. Velikanov*	M. G. Efremov

Table 2.   (continued)

District and position	Names and dates		
	June 1, 1935– July 1937 Y. F. Yakovlev June 29, 1938– June 22, 1939 L. A. Kurochkin from February 1941	July 9–November 1937 S. K. Remezov June 11, 1940	November 1937– April 29, 1938 I. S. Konev July 22, 1940– February 1941
2. Head of Political District (member of the District Military Council)	*V. N. Shestakov* June 1, 1935– July 1937 *G. A. Vasilyev* February– December 1938 K. N. Zimin from February 1941	A. S. Chcherbakov July 9–October 1937 D. A. Gapanovich December 1938– December 1939	*A. M. Bitte* October 1937– January 28, 1938 D. S. Leonov January 1940– February 1941
3. Chief of Staff	*Ya. G. Rubinov* May 1, 1935– June 16, 1937 E. G. Trotsenko from February 1941	*A. I. Tarasov* January 1940	*P. K. Korytnikov* January 1940– February 1941
Transcaucasus MD formed in 1935 from Caucasus Red Army			
1. Commander	*M. K. Levandovsky* to June 10, 1937 I. V. Tulenev March 8, 1938– September 3, 1940	*N. V. Kuibyshev* June 10, 1937– February 4, 1938 M. G. Efremov September 3, 1940–February 1941	*A. I. Egorov* February 4– February 21, 1938 D. G. Kozlov from February 1941
2. Head of Political District (member of the District Military Council)	*A. P. Yartsev* to August 26, 1937 A. Ya. Doronin June 24, 1938– December 1940	*M. Ya. Apse* September 18, 1937–December 30, 1937 F. A. Shamanin from December 1940	*P. N. Figin* December 30, 1937–June 24, 1938
3. Chief of Staff	*M. I. Alfuzo*[k] to February 11,	*S. M. Savitsky* February 11,	V. N. Lvov July 17, 1937–

Table 2.   (continued)

District and position		Names and dates	
	1935	1935–May 25, 1937	April 17, 1938
	A. A. Khriashchev April 17, 1938– August 2, 1938	F. I. Tolbukhin from August 3, 1938	

Kalininsky MD
formed in 1938; disbanded in 1940

1. Commander	I. V. Boldin August 1938– October 1939	V. F. Yakovlev October 1939– June 1940	
2. Head of Political District (member of the District Military Council)	A. V. Sokolin September 1938– July 1939	A. S. Nikolaiev July 11, 1939– June 1940	I. Z. Susaikov June–July 1940
3. Chief of Staff	E. G. Trotsenko August 1938– December 1939	V. N. Gordov December 1939– June 1940	

Kiev MD
to 1935 Ukrainian; from 1939 Kiev Special District

1. Commander	*I. E. Yakir* to May 11, 1937	*I. F. Fedko*[2] May 26, 1937– January 21, 1938	S. K. Timoshenko January 21, 1938– May 1940
	G. K. Zhukov May 1940– January 1941	M. P. Kirponos from January 1941	
2. Head of Political District (member of the District Military Council)	*N. P. Amelin* to May 11, 1937	E. A. Shchadenko May 22, 1937– January 7, 1938	*A. K. Smirnov* January 7, 1938– April 3, 1938
	M. N. Poliakov April–December 1938	A. S. Nikolaiev December 1938– July 11, 1938	V. N. Borisov July 11– September 16, 1939
	S. K. Kozhevnikov September 16, 1939–August 1940	N. N. Vashugin from November 1940	
3. Chief of Staff	*D. A. Kuchinsky*[3] to May 11, 1936	*V. P. Butyrsky* May 14, 1936– April 25, 1937	N. I. Podchufarov April 25, 1937– July 23, 1937

Table 2.   (continued)

District and position	Names and dates		
	I. G. Zakharkin July 23, 1937– May 27, 1938 M. A. Pukarev from July 26, 1940	I. V. Smorodinov May 27, 1938– October 27, 1938	N. F. Vatutin October 27, 1938– July 26, 1940
Leningrad MD 1. Commander	I. P. Belov to October 17, 1935 M. S. Khozin April 3, 1938– February 13, 1939 M. M. Popov from February 1941	B. M. Shaposhnikov October 29, 1935– May 11, 1937 K. A. Meretskov February 13, 1939–July 3, 1940	*P. E. Dybenko* June 7, 1937– January 6, 1938 M. P. Kirponos July 3, 1940– January 1941
2. Head of Political District (member of the District Military Council)	*I. E. Slavin*[4] to October 17, 1935 N. N. Vashugin October 9, 1938– March 1940	*P. A. Smirnov*[5] December 2, 1935–June 1937 T. F. Shtykov March–November 1940	T. K. Govorukhin[6] June 7, 1937– September 17, 1938 N. N. Klementiev from February 1941
3. Chief of Staff	*Ya. I. Zuz-Yakovenko*[k] to June 1935 N. E. Chibisov June 1, 1938– July 9, 1940	*A. V. Fedotov* October 21, 1935– June 1937 P. G. Ponedelin July 9, 1940– October 1940	M. V. Zakharov July 19, 1937– May 31, 1938
Moscow MD 1. Commander	*A. I. Kork*[7] to September 29, 1935 I. V. Tulenev from August 14, 1940	I. P. Belov September 29, 1935–May 31, 1937	S. M. Budenny June 8, 1937– August 14, 1940
2. Head of Political	*G. I. Veklichev*	L. N. Aronshtam	B. U. Troyanker

Table 2.   (continued)

District and position	Names and dates		
District (member of the District Military Council)	to August 1936	December 13, 1936–May 20, 1937	May 31, 1937– November 20, 1937
	S. E. Kolonin February 26, 1937–February 24, 1938 V. N. Bogatkin from September 24, 1940	L. G. Petrovsky[8] February 24, 1938–March 16, 1938	A. I. Zaporozhets April 16, 1938– September 20, 1940
3. Chief of Staff	A. M. Volpe[9] to May 1935	V. A. Stepanov[k] May 1935–May 20, 1936	A. M. Peremytov May 28, 1936– June 28, 1937
	A. I. Antonov July 5, 1937– April 6, 1938	V. D. Sokolovsky April 17, 1938– February 1941	G. D. Shishenin from February 1941
Odessa MD formed in 1939			
1. Commander	I. V. Boldin October 1939– July 11, 1940	Ya. T. Cherevichenko from July 11, 1940	
2. Head of Political District (member of the District Military Council)	A. F. Kolobiakov from October 1939		
3. Chief of Staff	P. I. Liapin October 1939– July 11, 1940	M. V. Zakharov from July 11, 1940	
Orlov MD formed in 1938			
1. Commander	M. G. Efremov July 1938–June 1940	F. N. Remezov from June 11, 1940	
2. Head of Political District (member of the District Military Council)	I. Z. Susaikov September 2, 1938–March 27, 1939	F. A. Semenovsky from March 27 1939	

Table 2.   (continued)

District and position	Names and dates		
3. Chief of Staff	A. D. Kornev from July 1938		

Baltic MD
formed in 1940

1. Commander	A. D. Loktionov July 11, 1940– December 25, 1940	F. I. Kuznetsov from December 25, 1940	
2. Head of Political District (member of the District Military Council)	I. Z. Susaikov July 13, 1940– December 25, 1940	P. A. Dibrova from February 1941	
3. Chief of Staff	P. S. Klienov from July 11, 1940		

Volga MD

1. Commander	P. E. Dybenko to May 11, 1937	M. N. Tukhachevsky May 11–May 26, 1937	M. G. Efremov June 5–December 1937
	P. A. Brianskikh December 1937– October 1938 V. F. Gerasimenko from July 1940	K. A. Meretskov October 1938– February 1939	T. I. Shevaldin ? February 1939– July 1940
2. Head of Political District (member of the District Military Council)	P. A. Smirnov to February 1934 L. A. Balychenko August 1937– September 1938 S.I. Kolonin from February 1941	A. I. Mezis February 1934– May 11, 1937 A. Ya. Fominykh September 1938– July 22, 1939	L. N. Aronshtam May 11–May 31, 1937 A. S. Zheltov July 1939– February 1941
3. Chief of Staff	N. V. Lisovsky[k] to April 1936 V. N. Gordov from July 1940	N. E. Varfolomeev April 1936– March 1938	P. S. Klenov April 1938– July 1940

Table 2.   (continued)

District and position	Names and dates		
North Caucasus MD			
1. Commander	*N. D. Kashirin*[k] to May 5, 1937	*S. E. Gribov* September 3, 1937–January 9, 1938	V. Ya. Kachalov March 16, 1938– June 11, 1940
	M. G. Efremov June 11, 1940– August 15, 1940 M. A. Reiter from June 1941	F. I. Kuznetsov August 15, 1940– December 25, 1940	I. S. Konev January–June 1941
2. Head of Political District (member of the District Military Council)	*S. N. Kozhevnikov*[k] to August 1936 K. G. Sidorov August–November 1937	*G. I. Veklichev* August 1936– June 1937 K. N. Zimin November 27, 1937–March 21, 1938	*A. P. Prokofiev* June–August 1937 I. P. Sheklanov from March 27, 1938
3. Chief of Staff	*P. I. Vakulich*[k] to June 1, 1936 S. G. Trofimenko August 15, 1940– February 1941	*S. P. Tsvetkov* June 1936– August 1937 V. M. Zlobin from February 1941	D. N. Nikishov August 1937– August 15, 1940
Siberian MD			
1. Commander	*Ya. P. Gailit* to May 11, 1937	M. A. Antoniuk June 25, 1937– June 2, 1938	S. A. Kalinin from July 17, 1938
2. Head of Political District (member of the District Military Council)	*A. P. Prokofiev*[k] to May 31, 1937	*N. A. Yung* August 22– December 1937	P. K. Smirnov from December 30, 1937
3. Chief of Staff	*M. S. Serpokrylov*[k] to January 1935 P. E. Glinsky from January 2, 1940	*I. Z. Zinoviev* January 23, 1935– July 1937	M. F. Lukin January 1938– January 2, 1940

Table 2.   (continued)

District and position	Names and dates		
Central Asian MD			
1. Commander	*M. D. Velikanov* to June 15, 1937	*I. K. Gryaznov* July 3–August 10, 1937	A. D. Loktionov August 20– December 17, 1937
	L. G. Petrovsky December 19, 1937–March 10, 1938	I. R. Apanasenko March 10, 1938– December 31, 1940	S. G. Trofimenko from January 14, 1941
2. Head of Political District (member of the District Military Council)	*G. G. Yastrebov* to May 8, 1937	*D. D. Bauzer* August 20– November 16, 1937	K. L. Pantas January 28– October 8, 1938
	M. S. Petrenko ? October 26, 1938– April 19, 1940	E. P. Rykov April 19, 1940– December 31, 1940	??
3. Chief of Staff	*G. S. Zamilitsky* to May 19, 1937 ??	*A. K. Malyshev* May 23, 1937– March 31, 1938	M. I. Kazakov April 10, 1938– December 31, 1940
Ural MD			
1. Commander	*I. I. Garkavy* to March 1937	*B. S. Gorbachev* March 22–April 17, 1937	*Ya. P. Gailit* May 19–August 1937
	G. P. Sofronov August 11, 1937– July 15, 1938	F. A. Ershakov from July 15, 1938	
2. Head of Political District (member of the District Military Council)	*G. A. Zinoviev* to August 14, 1937	*A. V. Tarutinsky* August 14– December 1937	T. A. Nicolaev December 30, 1937–March 1939
	D. S. Leonov March 19, 1939– December 1940	??	
3. Chief of Staff	V. D. Sokolovsky to April 3, 1938	A. M. Markov ? April 9, 1938– August 19, 1938	G. F. Zakharov from August 19, 1938
Kharkov MD formed in 1935			
1. Commander	*I. N. Dubovoy* July 1935–	S. K. Timoshenko November 1937–	I. K. Smirnov ? April 1938–

Table 2.   (continued)

District and position	Names and dates		
	June 1937 M. P. Kovaliev April 11, 1940– February 1941	February 1938 A. N. Chernikov from February 1941	April 11, 1940
2. Head of Political District (member of the District Military Council)	*M. F. Berezkin*[k] May–September 1935 *K. I. Ozolin* August–November 1937	S. N. Kozhevnikov September 1935– November 1936 T. P. Krugliakov ? January 1938– March 1939	E. A. Shchadenko December 1936– January 1937 T. L. Nikolaiev ?? March 1939–April 1940
3. Chief of Staff	*P. L. Sokolov* July 1935–June 1937 P. G. Zakharkin May 27, 1938– July 1938	K. N. Galitsky August–November 1937 P. I. Tupikov April 28, 1939	I. V. Smorodinov November 1937– May 27, 1938

Detached Red Banner Far Eastern Army
from April 28, 1938 — Far Eastern Red Banner Front; disbanded September 4, 1938

1. Commander	*V. K. Blyukher* to September 4, 1938		
2. Head of Political District (member of the District Military Council)	L. N. Aronshtam to December 13, 1936	*G. D. Khakhanian* February 1, 1937– April 20, 1938	P. I. Mazepov April 20, 1938– September 4, 1938
3. Chief of Staff	*I. V. Sangursky*[10] to December 25, 1934 G. M. Shtern April 3– September 4, 1938	K. A. Meretskov December 25, 1934–March 22, 1936	*S. N. Bogomyagkov* March 22, 1936– February 8, 1938

First Detached Red Banner Army
formed September 4, 1938; disbanded July 1, 1940

1. Commander	G. M. Shtern September 4, 1938–July 1, 1939	M. M. Popov July 1, 1939– July 1, 1940	

Table 2.   (continued)

District and position	Names and dates	
2. Head of Political District (member of the District Military Council)	F. A. Semenovsky September 4, 1938–March 24, 1939	??
3. Chief of Staff	M. M. Popov September 4, 1938–July 1, 1939	G. A. Shelekhov July 1, 1939– July 1, 1940

Second Detached Red Banner Army
formed September 4, 1938; disbanded July 1, 1940

1. Commander	I. S. Konev September 4, 1938–July 1, 1940	
2. Head of Political District (member of the District Military Council)	N. I. Biryukov September 4, 1938–July 22, 1939	A. Ya. Fominykh July 22, 1939– July 1, 1940
3. Chief of Staff	K. S. Melnik	E. G. Trotsenko

Chita Front Group (Khal'Khan Gol)
formed July 5, 1939; disbanded July 1, 1940

1. Commander	*G. M. Shtern*[11] July 5, 1939– October 1939	
2. Head of Political District (member of the District Military Council)	N. I. Biryukov July 5, 1939– July 1, 1940	
3. Chief of Staff	P. G. Kuznetsov July 5, 1939– July 1, 1940	

Far Eastern Front
formed July 1, 1940

1. Commander	??	I. R. Apanasenko from January 1941
2. Head of Political District (member of the District Military Council)	N. I. Biryukov from July 1, 1940	

Table 2.   (continued)

District and position	Names and dates		
3. Chief of Staff	P. G. Kuznetsov from July 1, 1940		
Baltic Fleet			
1. Commander	L. M. Galler	*A. K. Sivkov* to July 1937	I. S. Isakov July 1937– February 1938
	G. I. Levchenko February 1938– May 1939	V. F. Tributs from May 1939	
2. Head of Political District (member of the District Military Council)	*A. S. Grishin* A. T. Muraviev	*Ya. V. Volkov* N. G. Yakovenko	*A. A. Bulyshkin* N. K. Smirnov
3. Chief of Staff	?? Yu. A. Panteleev	I. S. Isakov to July 1937	??
Black Sea Fleet			
1. Commander	*I. K. Kozhanov* F. S. Oktiabr'sky from August 1939	*P. I. Smirnov*	I. S. Yumashev to August 1939
2. Head of Political District (member of the District Military Council)	*G. I. Gugin*[k] S. D. Morosov ?	I. B. Razgon from December 1936 V. A. Nikitin ?	Zemskov ? A. T. Muraviev
3. Chief of Staff	?? I. D. Eliseev	K. I. Dushenov	??
Northern Fleet formed in May 1937 from Northern Flotilla			
1. Commander	*Z. A. Zakupnev*[k] A. G. Golovko	*K. I. Dushenov* to June 1938	V. P. Drozd ? to July 1939
2. Head of Political District (member of the District Military Council)	*P. P. Bairachny* N. M. Kulakov	D. I. Kornienko ? N. K. Smirnov	F. G. Masslaov ? A. A. Nikolaev
3. Chief of Staff	Yu. A. Panteleev	P. S. Smirnov ? since 1935	??

Table 2.   (continued)

District and position	Names and dates		
	I. F. Golubev-Monatkin ?		S. G. Kucherov
Pacific Fleet formed in 1936 from Pacific Flotilla			
1. Commander	*M. V. Viktorov*[12] to June 1937 I. S. Yumashev	G. P. Kireev	N. G. Kuznetsov to March 1939
2. Head of Political District (member of the District Military Council)	G. S. Okunev ?	S. E. Zakharov ?	??
3. Chief of Staff	O. S. Salonnikov ??	??	V. Ya. Bogdenko ?

Key: ? = fate unknown; ?? = no information; italicized name indicates that the person was purged and killed; italicized name with superscript[k] indicates that the person was transferred to an unestablished post, purged, and killed.

Notes:
1. Appointed deputy chief of Main Political Directorate; purged and killed in the fall of 1937.
2. See table 1 in appendix IV.
3. Commandant of the General Staff Academy from July 1936; purged and killed in the summer of 1937.
4. Appointed chief of the Directorate of Military Educational Institutions; purged and killed in the summer of 1937.
5. See table 1 in appendix IV.
6. Purged but survived; in 1957 received rank of major general.
7. Appointed commandant of the Frunze Academy; perished in 1937.
8. Discharged from military service in 1938, returned in 1940; was killed in the hostilities in September 1941.
9. From the end of 1936 editor-in-chief of the journal *Military Thought (Voennaya Mysl)*; purged and killed in 1937.
10. Appointed deputy commander of the Detached Red Banner Far Eastern Army; perished in 1937.
11. Commander of the Eighth Army during the Finnish campaign. He was arrested in March 1940 and shot in October 1941.
12. See table 1 in appendix IV.

V. Naum Ettingon

Information about Naum Iakovlevich Ettingon is laughably scarce. Nonetheless, he was an amazing man. For many years until the end of the 1930s he was the principal organizer of subversive activities for the NKVD in the West.

Of Ettingon's origins we know only that "his father founded a hospital in Leipzig. A street is named after him there. At his death he left his sons 20 million marks."[1] There were two sons.

Mark Ettingon was a psychiatrist, a student of Sigmund Freud, and a friend of Princess Maria Bonaparte. For many years he was the generous patron of Nadezhda Plevitskaia. She said at her trial that "he dressed me from head to foot." He financed the publication of her two autobiographical books.[2] It is unlikely he did so only for the love of Russian music. It is more likely that he acted as messenger and finance agent for his brother Naum.

Naum Ettingon began to work for the Cheka during the Civil War. There is some evidence that he recruited Plevitskaia in the summer of 1919. The singer was then performing in Odessa, where she established close contact with the top local Soviet leadership. Together with the popular vaudeville singer Iza Kremer, she frequently participated in wild parties in the building of the military commandant's office. She bestowed her favors on assistant military commandant Shulga.

In the 1930s Naum Ettingon pulled the strings for many (possibly all) of the NKVD's foreign subversive acts, particularly the kidnappings of General Kutepov, General Miller, and Trotsky's grandson. He lived continuously abroad, where trade in Soviet furs in London served as his cover. Naum Ettingon stood at the helm of the NKVD's diversion machine and pressed its many buttons but managed to remain unnoticed. It is interesting that among the many publications on the activities of Soviet intelligence that appeared in the Russian émigré press, his name is not mentioned. His brother was not quite so lucky. At Plevitskaia's trial it was established that Mark Ettingon had been in Paris in September 1937 and had left on the twentieth, only two days before the kidnapping of General Miller. Skoblin and Plevitskaia accompanied him to the station. He left for Florence and from there to Palestine.

The last of Naum Ettingon's large and famous operations was the murder of L. Trotsky. After that he was recalled to Moscow but, unlike many of his colleagues in the NKVD, not to be killed. Ettingon was taken directly from the station to the Kremlin for an audience with Stalin, at which Beria was present. He was given the Order of Lenin due him, but that was not all. Stalin was exceptionally friendly. He embraced Ettingon and swore that as long as he, Stalin, lived, not a single hair would fall from Ettingon's head.

Ettingon was appointed deputy chief of the Main Intelligence Administration of the General Staff. He remained in that position for more than ten years and continued to work in his specialty—he directed subversion, but now from Moscow. In the late 1940s and early 1950s his superior, General Sudoplatov, received complaints that Ettingon had reverted to old habits, was taking too much on himself, and was acting beyond the limits of his authority. It is quite possible that Ettingon was too independent and did not pick up on new trends in Soviet subversive policy. But it must be remembered that this was a time of active anti-Semitism when many Jews were removed from responsible positions.

Sudoplatov ignored the signals he was getting for as long as he could. He apparently considered Ettingon an expert at his work and trusted him implicitly. Furthermore it would not have been discreet to touch Stalin's protégé. In 1952 Ettingon's enemies reached Stalin and presented Ettingon's activities in an unfavorable light. Stalin ordered that Ettingon be removed from his position but did not say anything more about his further fate. It did not happen like that often, but it did happen.

The MGB, lacking precise instructions, did not risk leaving Ettingon at large, but neither did they dare to lock him up. They stashed him at a special dacha outside Moscow where he lived in complete comfort and strict isolation—no visitors, no papers, no radio.[3]

After Stalin's death Ettingon was not immediately dealt with. There was much else to do. The year 1953 was taken up with the liquidation of Beria and his henchmen, and also with the reorganization of the MVD-MGB. But then it was our hero's turn. The investigator of the Procuracy of the USSR called him in for interrogation. Ettingon tried to pretend that he was just an old, sick man with nothing important to say. When the investigator convinced him that he would not tolerate his playing the fool, Ettingon sadly commented, "Josef Vissarionovich Stalin has died."

"What does Stalin have to do with this?"

"Josef Vissarionovich once promised that while he lived not a hair would fall from my head. The way you talk to me I know that comrade Stalin is no longer among the living." Ettingon was tried and sentenced to twelve years in prison. Apparently they saw some violations of socialist legality in his activities. More likely they got him as a supporter of Beria. That was at the end of 1953 or in the very beginning of 1954.

Ettingon served his twelve years and returned to Moscow. He was met at the station with flowers and champagne by a group of former colleagues. They had prepared a pleasant surprise for him—an order for a room in Moscow.

Not long after, the engaging old man went to work for the publishing house *Mezhdunarodnaia Kniga* (International Book). The new editor knew five or six languages, but he did not write about himself in any of them.

Nothing more is known about the fate of Ettingon.

Notes

Chapter 1

1. I. F. Gornostaev and Ia. M. Bugoslavsky, *Po Moskve i eia okrestnostiam. Putovoditel' — spravochnik dlia turista i moskvicha* (Moscow, 1903), p. 183.
2. Ivan Timofeevich Kokorev, *Moskva sorokovykh godov, ocherki i povesti o Moskve XIX veka* (Moscow: Moskovskii rabochii, 1959), p. 73.
3. *Osoaviakhim* is a syllabic acronym for the Society of the Promotion of Defense and Aero-Chemical Development, a Soviet paramilitary organization established in 1927 to train civilians in skills useful in time of war.
4. *Vsia Moskva v karmane* (Moscow, 1926), p. 63.
5. Andrei Yaniuarevich Vyshinsky played the role of chief prosecutor in the purge trials. See chapters 19 and 20.
6. Apparently they tried to observe a Russian state tradition. This is how Nicholas I dealt with the condemned Decembrists: "The sentence was carried out furtively . . . on the glaçis of the fortress where there was an illusion of justice and under the cover of suddenly gathered troops. . . . Relatives were forbidden to take the bodies of the hanged men: at night they threw them into a pit, covered them with quicklime, and on the next day publicly thanked God that they had spilled their blood." See Mikhail Lunin, *Sochineniia* (New York: Khronika, 1976).

Chapter 2

1. Tukhachevsky, *Novye voprosy voiny*. The 1936 work itself was never published, but three chapters of the 1932 edition were reprinted in *Voprosy strategiia i operativnogo iskusstva v sovetskikh trudakh, 1917–1940* (Moscow: Voennoe izd-vo, 1965), pp. 116–44.
2. Tukhachevsky, *Voennye plany nyneshnei Germanii* (Moscow: Voenizdat, 1935).
3. Norbert Wiener, *The Human Use of Human Beings; Cybernetics and Society* (Boston: Houghton Mifflin, 1950). This was translated into Russian as *Kibernetika i obshchestvo*.
4. Tukhachevsky, "Kharakter prigranichnikh srazhenii." This is an unpublished work.
5. A. I. Todorsky in *Marshal Tukhachevsky* (Moscow: Izd-vo Politicheskoi literatury, 1963), pp. 89–90; G. Isserson, "Zapiski sovremennika o M. N. Tukhachevskom," *Voenno-istoricheskii zhurnal* 4 (1963): 64–78.
6. Hitler never did understand that he had an ally in Poland. On November 10, 1937, a year after the Kremlin war games, he announced at a meeting of the

political and military leaders of Germany, "If Czechoslovakia is destroyed and a border between Germany and Hungary is established, then we can expect that Poland would remain neutral in case we go to war with France. . . . If Germany is unsuccessful, we can expect Poland to move against Eastern Prussia, and maybe against Pomerania and Silesia as well." See *"Sovershenno sekretno! Tol'ko dlia komandovaniia!" Strategiia fashistskoi Germanii v voine protiv SSR. Dokumenty i materialy*, edited by N. G. Pavlenko (Moscow: Nauka, 1967), pp. 58–59.

7. Isserson, "Zapiski sovremennika," pp. 64–78.
8. Ibid.
9. Ibid.

Chapter 4

1. Cited in K. E. Voroshilov, "Stalin i Krasnaia Armiia" *Pravda* December 21, 1929.
2. The authors found this citation in Soviet archives of the Red Army.
3. Voroshilov, "Stalin i Krasnaia Armii."
4. P. N. Krasnov, *Ot dvuglavago orla k krasnomu znameni, 1894–1921* (Berlin, 1921). This was translated into English as *From the Two-Headed Eagle to the Red Flag, 1894–1921* (1923).

Chapter 6

1. *Istoriia grazhdanskoi voiny, 1918–1921*, edited by A. S. Bubnov, S. S. Kamenev, M. N. Tukhachevsky, and R. P. Eideman (Moscow: Gosudarstvennoe izd-vo, 1930), vol. 3, p. 261.
2. Later I. S. Kutiakov, who commanded the 25th "Chapaev" Infantry Division on the Polish Front, together with N. M. Khlebnokov, wrote *Kievskie Kanny*, in which they explained how the 3rd Polish Army escaped encirclement and destruction. Kutiakov showed the book to People's Commissar Voroshilov in 1937. Not long thereafter he was arrested and killed. This manuscript has not been published.
3. This quote has not been verified. Lenin said something very similar at the September 1920 Party Conference. "Our Army's approach to Warsaw irrefutably proved that the center of the whole system of world imperialism, resting on the Versailles Treaty, lies somewhere near to it." *Istoriia grazhdanskoi voiny* (1930), vol. 3, p. 396.
4. Even Stalin admitted this in "K voprosu o strategii i taktike russkikh kommunistov." Despite that, until the Second World War the thesis that the proletariat of countries at war with the Soviet Union would support the Red Army remained a basic part of Soviet military doctrine. It also penetrated deeply into popular consciousness. Stalin's article is available in English as "Concerning the Question of the Strategy and Tactics of the Russian Communists," *Works* (Moscow: Foreign Language Publishing House, 1954), vol. 5, pp. 163–83.
5. See his *Pokhod za Vislu* (Moscow: Voennoe izd-vo, 1923). It does not necessar-

ily follow, however, that had there not been problems in the First Horse, that Warsaw would have been taken and Poland defeated. Our description concerns only operational conditions. A higher analysis would have to consider that the whole military and, especially, economic might of the Entente stood at Poland's back. Lenin openly called the failure of the Polish campaign a political miscalculation. Concerning the purely military aspect of the campaign, he once said, "Who do you know who goes to Warsaw through Lvov . . . ?"

6. According to the authors, this is derived from a 1933 brochure, *Klim Voroshilov*, written by a certain Orlovsky.

7. Ibid.

Chapter 7

1. Official propaganda is not concerned, understandably, with historical accuracy. In the late 1960s a memorial was erected on the site of the battle for Kakhovka, celebrated in song and poetry, a memorial in the form of a machine-gun cart, which immediately brings to mind an image of the First Horse. But at the time of that battle—July 1920—it was fighting on the Polish Front hundreds of versts from Kakhovka. The victory was won by infantry units of the Lettish 3rd, 46th, and 52nd divisions. One might suppose that the machine-gun cart belonged to Makhno's army, but the insurgent army came over to the Reds' side only in October.

2. V. V. Dushenkin, *Vtoraia Konnaia* (Moscow: Voenizdat, 1968).

3. Sergei Starikov and Roy Medvedev, *Philip Mironov and the Russian Civil War*, translated by Guy Daniels (New York: Alfred A. Knopf, 1978).

4. It is usual to trace the lineage of the Cossacks from runaway peasants. L. N. Gumilev thinks, however, that on the Don before that there were settlements of surviving *Khazars*, who along with others lay the foundation stone for the Cossack tribe. After the final conquest of the Don during the reign of Peter I, runaways continued to find refuge there, but they were not taken in by the Cossacks. Thus arose the population of non-Cossacks (*inogorodnie*). Later former serfs of local serf owners joined the non-Cossacks.

5. Mikhail Sholokhov, *And Quiet Flows the Don*, translated by Stephen Garry (New York: Alfred A. Knopf, 1941).

6. The chairman of the Donburo Syrtsov instructed after the Veshensk rebellion had begun, "For every Red Armyman and revolutionary committee member killed, shoot *one hundred* Cossacks. Prepare staging areas to send the *entire male population* from eighteen to fifty-five inclusive to forced labor in *Voronezh guberniia*, Pavlovsk, and other places. Order the convoy guards to shoot *five* for *every* [Cossack] who escapes. Require the Cossacks to watch out for one another by a system of mutual guarantee."

7. During the Civil War 48,409 former officers served in the Red Army. Altogether at the end of the war there were 130,000 commanders in the RKKA. See A. M. Iovlev and D. A. Voropaev, *Bor'ba kommunisticheskoi partii za sozdanie voennykh kadrov* (Moscow: Voenizdat, 1955) p. 18. The overwhelming majority of combat officers from the battalion level on up were tsarist

officers. At headquarters level it goes without saying.

8. Interestingly, when Rosenberg was in Yaroslavl in 1918, he tried to join the Russian Communist Party. He did not succeed because, as a student from a bourgeois family in the Baltic region, he did not know anyone, and he had not shown himself to be a revolutionary. What else would he do but travel to Germany and join another party?

Chapter 8

1. General Aleksei Andreevich Arakcheev (1769–1834), a favorite of Emperor Alexander I, is remembered for his severity of manner and strict discipline.

2. Today the course and the content of the discussion seems a farce. Trotsky and his ally, Bukharin, openly demanded that the unions be turned into a weapon for the repression of the working class, leaving workers no means with which to defend themselves from the state, which was to become the master of all factories and plants. Lenin and Zinovev agreed in principle with this approach (in a resolution offered by Lenin and accepted by the Central Committee the formula "healthy forms of the militarization of labor" was approved), but they insisted on more careful public phraseology ("trade unions are schools of Communism"). The "workers' opposition" decried the unbearably hard conditions of the proletariat and the massive exodus of workers from the Party, and demanded the transfer of all authority in industry to trade union functionaries in the All-Russian Congress of Producers. Among the leaders of the "workers' opposition" the tone was set by former proletarians Shliapnikov, Kutuzov, and Medvedev, together with a daughter of a tsarist general, Aleksandra Kollontai. In the heat of their polemics they insisted on the domination of the intelligentsia in the Party. At times they spoke even more candidly and said Jews. Not surprisingly, the groups headed by Lenin and Trotsky were able to find a common language and put up a common front. Shliapnikov's group earned the epithets "Marxist apostates" and "anarcho-syndicalists." They were routed at the Tenth Congress. All that is left of their venture are the sham workers' councils in Yugoslavia.

3. All of these startling documents are published. See *Direktivy komandovaniia frontov Krasnoi Armii, 1917–1922* (Moscow: Voenizdat, 1974), vol. 3, 508–9. The order referred to in the radio appeal for surrender has not been published. Did it ever exist?

4. See V. V. Maiakovsky, *Sochineniia v trekh tomakh* (Moscow: Khudozhestvennaia Literatura, 1965), vol. 3, 332–33. That section of the poem begins, "The quiet Jew, Pavel Ilich Lavut, told me." Ibid., p. 327.

5. Frunze reported to Lenin and the Central Committee that the Red losses in storming the isthmus were "not less than 10,000 killed."

6. This is the same chivalrous Bela Kun who was named chairman of the Crimean Revolutionary Committee.

7. An outside observer could immediately see that all was not right with the workers' and peasants' power. E. Colombino, a member of an Italian Communist delegation that visited Russia in the summer of 1920, wrote in his book *Three Months in Soviet Russia*, "Many times we were told, repeatedly told, that the

basic principle of the Russian revolution was the dictatorship of the proletariat. But in this case we are dealing, at least a little, with exaggeration. A dictatorship exists, one possibly in the interests of the proletariat, but the proletariat itself, poor thing, has little to say about it. . . . The dictatorship is run by the Communist Party, or more accurately, by a fraction of it. . . . It is undoubtedly a dictatorship of a few. This socialist tsarism is easy to understand, if not to justify, in a country which has behind it centuries of slavery and tsarist dictatorship." *Desiatyi sezd RKP(b). Stenograficheskii otchet* (Moscow, 1933), pp. 884–85.

8. Aleksandr Nikolaevich Slepkov, *Kronshtadtskii miatezh* (Moscow, 1928).

9. S. Uritsky, "Krasnyi Kronshtadt vo vlasti vragov revoliutsii," in *Gradzhdanskaia Voina, 1918–1921*, edited by A. S. Bubov, S. S. Kamenev, and R. P. Eideman (Moscow: Gosizdat, 1928), vol. 1, pp. 358–74.

10. S. Semanov *Likvidatsiia antisovetskogo kronshtadtskogo miatezha 1921 goda* (Moscow Nauka, 1973), p. 185. It would be nice to know the names of the men Semanov claims to have interviewed. The emphases in the quotation are ours.

11. *Antonovshchina. Sbornik Tambovskogo gubkoma RKP*, edited by S. Evgenov and O. Litovsky (Tambov, 1923), p. 14.

12. Vladimir Dokukin, *Pravda o banditakh* (Tambov: Gosizdat, 1921). Emphasis in the original.

13. Ibid. Our emphasis this time.

14. *Antonovshchina*, p. 12.

15. The troops sent against the rebels were not to be laughed at. While the main force of the rebels did not even have a rifle for every man, they had to face the heavily armed shock group of Uborevich: the 14th Cavalry Brigade, with a thousand cavalry troops and two heavy guns, Kotovsky's cavalry brigade, and three armored detachments.

Chapter 9

1. From time to time lower-ranking activists would violate that rule. For example, the "workers' opposition" tried to continue their struggle after the Tenth Party Congress, where they had suffered a crushing defeat. Lenin almost expelled Shliapnikov from the Central Committee for that.

2. We will explain Trotsky's dismissal in detail in the next chapter. Zinoviev was at this time chairman and undisputed leader of the Leningrad Provincial Committee.

3. Concluding words of the Fourteenth Congress. *XIV S"ezd Vsesoiuznoi kommunisticheskoi Partii (b) 18–31 dekabria 1925 g. Stenograficheskii otchet* (Moscow: Gosizdat, 1926), p. 502.

4. The *oprichnina* was a bloody "reform" carried out by Ivan IV (the Terrible) between 1565 and 1572 to weaken the nobility and enhance his own power as autocrat. Approximately four thousand people perished in the *oprichnina*, and many more were dispossessed and displaced.

5. *Glavkontsesskom*: the Main Committee on Concessions. A concession was permission for a foreign firm to operate a factory or business in the Soviet Union. For example, Armand Hammer held several concessions in the 1920s, including a pencil factory in Moscow.

6. This point permitted the Central Committee to apply the extreme measure of expulsion from the Party for violations of discipline or factionalism. The punishment could be extended even to members of the TSK. In that case a plenum of the TSK including all candidate members of the TSK and members of the Control Commission would be convened. Expulsion required a two-thirds vote. Earlier such a measure had been the prerogative of a Party Congress. The draft of the resolution, which was written by Lenin, upset many of the delegates who were slow to be persuaded. Lenin assured them that the provision would never be used and was introduced only as a warning ("aim the machine guns"). The confusion was so great that a roll call vote was required. Only 59 percent of the delegates voted for the resolution. It was decided not to make point 7 public. Only a year later it was used against TSK member A. Shliapnikov, but the vote for expulsion fell three short. (It was Lenin, of course, who asked for his expulsion.) Stalin did not participate in the vote at the Tenth Congress as he had only a deliberative vote, but nonetheless he made good use of this Leninist instrument. It was he, by the way, who first divulged the point during a polemic with the Trotskyites at the Thirteenth Conference in 1923.

7. The majority of those expelled returned to the Party, but several of them, Zinoviev and Kamenev, for example, were expelled repeatedly. These people were excluded from political life and thoroughly demoralized. None of them were fated to survive the Great Purge.

8. Stalin, Molotov, and Voroshilov favored pressing the case. Rykov, Tomsky, and Bukharin were against it. The matter was decided by the votes of Kalinin, Rudzutak, and Kuibyshev, who after brief vacillation joined the Stalinists.

9. Nabokov wrote in the Kadet paper *Rul* on November 18, 1921, "The Communist Party came to power as a small group of highly principled, energetic activists, who had a small number of disciplined workers among the peasants and workers. Then the Party gradually, but relatively slowly, grew while the struggle on several fronts helped maintain iron discipline in the ranks of the Party. Recently a huge number of petit bourgeoisie—clerks, office workers, shop assistants, and others—have flooded the Party. The former muscular organism of the Party that could withstand the hardest blows began to weaken, to get fat. . . . The flow of principled people into the Party ceased. For the most part people seeking various ways to make their lives easier rushed to join. . . . Tests included in examinations on the program of the Communist Party had very negative results. In the great majority of cases, even in the cities, it was impossible to get satisfactory answers. . . ."

10. Arkady Belinkov, "Poet i tolstiak," *Baikal* (1968), nos. 1–2.

11. Malinin and Burin were authors of a widely used arithmetic text in prerevolutionary Russia.

12. Voroshilov, "Stalin i Krasnaia Armiia," *Pravda*, December 21, 1929.

Chapter 10

1. Vladimir Ilich Lenin, "K derevenskoi bednote," *Polnoe sobranie sochinenii*, 5th ed. (Moscow, 1969), vol. 7, p. 170.

2. Lenin, "Voisko i revoliutsii," *PSS*, vol. 12, pp. 113–14.

3. Lenin, "Itogi diskusii o samoopredelenii," *PSS*, vol. 30, pp. 17–58.

4. Lenin, "Dvenadtsat' kratkikh tezisov o zashchite Greilikhom zashchity otechestva," *PSS*, vol. 30, p. 331.

5. These are Marx's words from *The Civil War in France*, quoted by Lenin in "Gosudarstvo i revoliutsii," *PSS*, vol. 33, p. 41.

6. On Dmitri Milyutin's military reforms, see Forrestt A. Miller, *Dmitrii Miliutin and the Reform Era in Russia* (Nashville: Vanderbilt University Press, 1968).

7. See chapter 8, note 1, on Arakcheev. On his work with the military colonies, see Alan Ferguson, "The Russian Military Settlements, 1816–1866" (Ph.D. dissertation, Yale University, 1954).

8. I. Berkhin, *Voennaia reforma v SSSR, 1924–1925 gg.* (Moscow: Voennoe izd-vo, 1958).

9. Lenin, "Rech' v den' krasnogo ofitsera," *PSS*, vol. 37, p. 200.

10. When his opponents allied as the "military opposition" at the Eighth Congress, Trotsky demonstratively departed for the Eastern Front, leaving Lenin to restore order in the Party. Decisively, but not without difficulty, Lenin put down the little mutiny, and the military specialists remained at their posts.

11. Skliansky did not have long to live. A doctor by profession, he was appointed director of the Moscow textile trust (*Mossukno*). In the summer of 1925 he drowned at a foreign resort.

12. These important changes were made not only without Trotsky, but also without the new Chairman of the Council of People's Commissars Rykov, who was also away until April.

13. *Trinadtsatyi s'ezd RKP(b), Mai 1924 goda. Stenograficheskii otchet* (Moscow, 1963), p. 240.

14. This was discussed in the previous chapter.

15. See *Pravda*, November 11, 1925.

16. Ibid.

17. Ibid.

18. Boris Pilnyak, *Povest' nepogashennoi luny* (Sofia, 1927). The story was to have appeared in the journal *Novy Mir*, but at the last minute that whole issue was confiscated. The editorial board admitted that same year, 1926, that it had been a political mistake to accept the story for publication. It was published in Sofia in 1927, but it is still not available to Soviet readers.

19. *Pravda*, November 5, 1925. Our emphasis.

20. This is from Stalin's speech at Dzerzhinsky's funeral on July 22, 1926. It can be found as "F. Dzerzhinsky (In Memory of F. Dzerzhinsky)," *Works* (Moscow: Foreign Language Publishing House, 1954), vol. 8, pp. 203–4.

21. I. A. Teliatnikov quotes Tukhachevsky in his published memoirs and adds that these words later hurt Tukhachevsky's relations with Voroshilov. In Teliatnikov's article, "Vnikaia vo vse," in *Marshal Tukhachevskii: vospominaniia druzei i soratnikov* (Moscow: Voennoe izd-vo, 1965), pp. 162–75, he says Tukhachevsky was friendly with Frunze and Ordzhonikidze and that Frunze and Tukhachevsky criticized Trotsky at the Eleventh Party Congress in March 1922.

22. That same year, 1925, Stalin removed his potential rival Kviring from the Party

apparatus and transferred him to economic work in VSNKh. Later, and until his death in 1937, he worked in Gosplan. In the Ukraine the inveterate Stalinist Kaganovich replaced Kviring.

23. Malicious tongues, for the time being speaking the truth, relate the following episode about Voroshilov's selection. Rukhimovich announced, "We all know Klim well. He's a brave fellow, but why give him the Army to command. A company would be more than enough!" This was Moisei Lvovich Rukhimovich, a Bolshevik since 1913, who served in the Red Army in the Ukraine during the Civil War. He was arrested in 1938 during the purges and died in prison.

24. This citation was taken from an unpublished review of L. Nikulin, *Marshal Tukhachevsky*, by A. I. Todorsky. The authors possess a copy of the review. See also Todorsky, *Marshal Tukhachevsky* (Moscow: Izd-vo politicheskoi literatury, 1963).

25. RVS order #698, November 13, 1925. This document is not published.

26. Of the military men, only the Zinovievite M. Lashevich, the new deputy chairman of the RVS USSR, fought on the side of the "Leningrad opposition" at the Congress. For that he was exiled to the Chinese Eastern Railroad where he died or killed himself in 1928.

Chapter 11

1. See M. V. Frunze, "Edinaia voennaia doktrina i Krasnaia Armiia," in *Voprosy strategii i operativnogo iskusstva v sovetskikh trudakh, 1917–1940* (Moscow: Voennoe izd-vo, 1965), pp. 29–40.

2. L. D. Trotsky, "Voennaia doktrina ili mnimo-voennoe doktrinerstvo," translated as, "Military Doctrine or Pseudo-Military Doctrinairism," in *Military Writings* (New York: Merit Publishers, 1969), pp. 31–69.

3. During a discussion at the editorial offices of *Voenno-istoricheskii Zhurnal* (*Military History Journal*) several historians—M. Angarsky, S. Naida, A. Kadishev, A. Golubev, and others—called for an end to the mythological representation of the campaign of fourteen nations. See *VIZh* (1966), no. 2. The righteous patriotic anger of the leadership knew no bounds; all of the editors of the journal, including the editor-in-chief, were sacked. See N. Pavlenko, "Nekotorye voprosy razvitiia teorii strategii v 20kh godakh," *VIZh* (1966), no. 5: 10–26.

4. See *Grazhdanskaia voina, 1918–1921* (Moscow, 1930), vol. 3, pp. 130–31; also *Malaia Sovetskaia Entsiklopediia* (Moscow, 1930), vol. 3, p. 480.

5. The lone exception is the article by A. V. Golubev in *Voenno-istoricheskii zhurnal*. See Golubev, "Obrashchena li byla v proshloe nasha voennaia teoriia v 20-e gody?" *VIZh* (1965), no. 10: 35–47.

6. Chapaev, by the way, possessed an extraordinarily fine mind. He was made a caricature by filmmakers who must have read Furmanov's book with one bad eye. On the orders of their socialist keepers they created a fantastic image, half a Red St. George the dragon slayer, half a jester. Chapaev was a talented and brave commander and had none of those foolish quirks ascribed to him by the pseudo-brothers Vasiliev. But it cannot be denied that he was poorly educated. It is enough to present Chapaev's request to leave the Academy as he wrote it:

Much-respected comrade Lindov [a member of the 4th Army Revolutionary Military Council]

I request You most humbly to recall me to the headquarters of the 4th Army in any position commander or commissar in any regiment as I the education of the Academy is not doing me any good what they are teaching I have already gone through in pragtic you know that i need my general education qualification which I am not receiving here and am bored for no reason in these walls I disagree this seems a prison and ask humbly that you do not exhaust me in this confinement I want to work and not lie about and if you do not recall me I will go to the doctor which will free me and I will lie around uselessly but I want to work and help you if you want me to help you I will with pleasure be at your service be so kind to get me out of these stone walls.

Respectively yours Chapaev

Lindov's response was "Tell Chapaev that we do not have the right to recall him from the Academy as he was sent there on the orders of comrade Trotsky."

The authors found this in A. Todorsky's review of L. Nikulin, *Marshal Tukhachevsky*, cited above.

7. We list only a few editions: *V vostochnom otriade* (Warsaw, 1908); *Vozdukho-plavanie v Germanii* (St. Petersburg, 1910); *Voina v gorakh* (St. Petersburg, 1906–7); *Strategiia* (Moscow: Gosvoenizd-vo, 1926), 2nd ed. (Moscow: Voen-nyi vestnik, 1927); *Istoriia voennogo iskusstva* (Moscow, 1922–23), 2nd ed. (Moscow, 1925); *Strategiia v trudakh voennykh klassikov* (Moscow, 1924–26); *Evoliutsiia voennogo iskusstva* (Moscow-Leningrad, 1927–28); *Iskusstovo vozh-deniia polka* (Moscow-Leningrad, 1930); *Klauzevits* (Moscow, 1935); *Russko-Iaponskaia Voina, 1904–1905* (Oranienbaum: Ofitserskaia stroevaia shkola, 1910).

8. *Strategiia*, which is difficult to find in this country, has been excerpted in *Voprosy strategii i operativnogo iskusstva*. See note 1 above.

9. Ibid., p. 232.

10. Ibid., p. 243.

11. General Zhilin has written several books on military history and particularly on World War II. See, e.g., *Problemy voennoi istorii* (Moscow: Voenizdat, 1975); *Vazhneishie operatsii Velikoi Otechestvennoi Voiny, 1941–1945; sbornik statei* (Moscow: Voennoe izd-vo, 1956); *Kak fashistskaia Germaniia gotovila napa-denie na Sovetskii Soiuz* (Moscow: Mysl, 1965). This last title has been trans-lated as *They Sealed Their Own Doom*, translated by David Fidlon (Moscow: Progress, 1970).

12. From *Strategiia*, in *Voprosy strategii i operativnogo iskusstva*, p. 245.

13. Frunze's writing is included in *Sobranie sochinenii*, edited by A. S. Bubnov (Moscow: Gosizd-vo, 1926), and in *Voprosy strategii i operativnogo iskusstva*. For this quote, see "Edinaia voennaia doktrina i Krasnaia Armiia," in *Voprosy*, p. 33.

14. Ibid., p. 35.

15. Ibid., p. 36.

16. M. V. Frunze, "O kharaktere operatsii grazhdnaskoi voiny v SSSR i budush-chikh operatsii Sovetskoi armii," in *Voprosy*.
17. Ibid., p. 43.
18. "Front i tyl v voine budushchego," in *Voprosy*, p. 63.
19. Ibid., p. 65.
20. Ibid., p. 68.
21. Ibid.
22. M. N. Tukhachevsky, "Strategiia natsionalnaia i klassovaia," in *Izbrannye proizvedeniia*, compiled by G. I. Oskin and P. P. Chernushkov (Moscow: Voen-noe izd-vo, 1964), pp. 31–50. See esp. p. 32.
23. Ibid.
24. Ibid., p. 47.
25. See *Voprosy vysshego komandovaniia* (Moscow: Gosvoenizdat, 1924); *Voprosy sovremennoi strategii* (Moscow: Voennyi Vestnik, 1926); *Taktika i strategiia*, in *Sbornik Voennoi akademii im. M. V. Frunze* 1 (Moscow, 1926); *Kommentarii k polevomu ustavu 1929 g.*, excerpted in *Voprosy*.
26. See *Voprosy sovremennoi strategii*, in *Izbrannye proizvedeniia*, pp. 244–61.
27. Ibid.

Chapter 12

1. K. E. Voroshilov, "Stalin i Krasnaia Armiia," *Pravda*, December 21, 1929.
2. Ibid.
3. Ibid. This is in a telegram, #00079, from Sverdlov.
4. Voroshilov, "Stalin i Krasnaia Armiia."
5. See chapter 6 of this book on the First Horse Army.
6. Voroshilov, "Stalin i Krasnaia Armiia."
7. In February 1920 Stalin persuaded Budenny and Voroshilov to subordinate themselves to a new commander and called Tukhachevsky "the demon of the Civil War."
8. *Istoriia Grazhdanskoi Voiny, 1918–1921* (1930), p. 271.
9. A. I. Egorov, *Razgrom Denikina, 1919* (Moscow: Gosudarstvennoe voennoe izd-vo, 1931), pp. 3–4.

Chapter 13

1. See Lenin's note to People's Commissar of Justice Kursky on terror, 1921. This and similar documents emphasizing Lenin's role in creating the Cheka and approving and urging the use of terror may be found in Lennard Gerson, *The Secret Police in Lenin's Russia* (Philadelphia: Temple University Press, 1976), and George Leggett, *The Cheka: Lenin's Political Police* (Oxford: Clarendon Press, 1981).
2. *Trianadtsatyi s'ezd RKP(b). Mai 1924 goda. Stenograficheskii otchet* (Moscow, 1963), p. 711.
3. It may be that three hundred years is as long as any significant phenomenon can

last in Russia. Like the Mongol Yoke, like serfdom, the Romanovs outlasted their stay and were chased from the scene.

4. Apparently as every actress has her admirers, every tyrant, however cruel, after his death leaves sighing admirers. Compared to Stalin, Nero was a child, a sissy, but in his time he managed to annoy a fair number of Romans. Seutonius describes the mood of society after the princeps' suicide: "His death caused such rejoicing in society, that people ran all through the city with felt hats on their heads as a symbol of liberation from slavery. Nonetheless there were many others who long after [his death] in spring and summer decorated his grave with flowers; they put images of him on rostra in a wide-bordered toga and with his edicts, just as if he were alive, just as if they expected his imminent return." After that we ought not be surprised that there is a demand for homemade souvenirs with likenesses of Stalin. And not only in Georgia.

5. Nationalization was not the realization of the goals of the proletarian revolution. The Bolshevik program called for workers' control of industry. Nationalization, as Lenin explained, was revenge against the bourgeoisie for their unwillingness to cooperate with the new regime. Of course, for the owners of the nationalized enterprises that distinction was unimportant.

6. Every household was left a small private plot of about 0.20–0.25 hectares. Individuals who remained outside the collective systems received less land than members of kolkhozes. Only in a few regions with particularly favorable conditions, such as Transcaucasia and Central Asia, was this enough land to feed a family.

7. *The Collected Works of Sir Winston Churchill*, vol. 25, *The Second World War*, vol. 4, *The Hinge of Fate* (London: Library of Imperial History, 1975), p. 322.

8. The culture has proved amazingly hardy and has now infected many countries. The carriers have many names. Some see them as freedom fighters, others as terrorists, even as common criminals and murderers.

9. The comparison of Trotsky to Stavrogin made by Aleksei Tolstoy during the Great Purge was a strained interpretation that was meant to be useful, not accurate. It counted on the public's ignorance. That comparsion was made in *Izvestiia*. See chapter 22.

10. It is hard to restrain from offering a long quote: "He had everything right on paper . . . it was espionage. Every member of the society watched one another and was obliged to report. Each belonged to all, and all to every. All were slaves and in their slavery equal. In extreme cases calumny and murder, but the main thing was equality. The first thing was to lower the level of education, science, and talents. A high level of science and talents was attainable by only higher abilities . . . higher abilities were not needed! . . . Slaves must be equal: without despotism there never would have been freedom or equality, but in the herd there must be equality. That is Shigalev's theory." F. M. Dostoevsky, *Polnoe sobranie sochinenii* (Leningrad, 1974), vol. 10, p. 322. This translation is mine, as are those that follow.

11. Ibid., p. 311.

12. Ibid., p. 312.

13. See N. Korzhavin, *Vremena* (Frankfurt: Posev, 1976).

14. A psychiatrist would not find it hard to qualify such escapades as megalomania and exhibitionism. However, as the sad example of Professor Bekhterev shows, it is dangerous to apply professional diagnoses in times of social unrest. More recently the relations between psychiatry and real life have taken a new direction.

15. Dostoevsky, *Polnoe sobranie*, vol. 10, p. 323.

Chapter 14

1. This is from A. I. Todorsky's review of L. Nikulin, *Marshal Tukhachevsky*. See chapter 10, note 24.

2. *Protiv reaktsionnykh teorii na voennonauchnom fronte. Kritika strategicheskikh i voennoistoricheskikh vzgliadov prof. Svechina* (Leningrad, 1931).

3. Ibid.

4. Ibid.

5. These are the words Svechin uses to describe the economic policy of wartime: "We will have to temporarily repeal the eight-hour work day and suspend the operation of the Code of Laws on labor. We will have to increase the intensity of labor and the length of the working day, to reduce real wages. Announcing these demands to the people, dooming them to labor as in penal servitude, depriving them of tolerable conditions of existence will go parallel with the struggle [fought] for these very people. . . . To fight means more than making a demonstration." Unheard of! There was nothing like it in the Fatherland War.

Chapter 15

1. *XVI S"ezd Vsesoiuznoi Kommunisticheskoi Partii (b). Stenograficheskii otchet* (Moscow: Moskovii rabochii, 1934), pp. 282–89.

2. Ibid., pp. 476–89.

3. Ibid., pp. 506–8.

4. Ibid., pp. 632–34. The old cavalryman complained bitterly that he was being made fun of in the press because of his passion for horse breeding—both in words and in caricatures. Budenny was very popular, but the public still enjoyed the ridicule. The stenographic record notes eleven interruptions of laughter, one of general laughter, and another of Homeric laughter, but Budenny stood his ground. Without horse power the national economy would founder. The same was even truer of the Army: "I am not just saying that the horse is enormously important in the country's defense. The defense of the country without horses is unthinkable." Unfortunately, Budenny was not the only one who thought that way.

5. Vladimir Kiriakovich Triandafillov, *Kharakter operatsii sovremennykh armii*, in *Voprosy strategii i operativnogo iskusstva*, pp. 291–345.

6. Ibid. Triandafillov wrote: "at the present time, thinking abstractly, it is easier to establish a stable front on defense than it used to be. The problem with defense is that it is purposely conducted by a small force and cannot always provide a sufficiently strong front for battle formations." Because of this excessive dogmatism, this assertion has proved wrong. One can point to Stalingrad and the Kursk

arc where the exceptional stubbornness of the defense created the conditions for enormously important operational success.

7. Lieutenant-General Dzenit recalls that in 1930 in order to demonstrate to Stalin and members of the Politburo the increasing importance of armored troops "large maneuvers were conducted outside Moscow with the participation of the only mechanized brigade and motorized detachment, which were attached to the Moscow proletarian division. . . . It became impossible to continue to ignore Tukhachevsky's suggestions. A decision was soon made to allocate significant funds for tanks." Stalin probably saw tanks for the first time, and they took his fancy. The quotation above comes from Dzenit, "S vyshki," in *Marshal Tukhachevskii: vospominaiia druzei i soratnikov* (Moscow: Voennoe izd-vo, 1965), pp. 130–34.

8. A rather complete presentation of the state of Soviet military thought of the 1920s and 1930s is given by two recently published anthologies: *Voprosy strategii i operativnogo iskusstva*; and *Voprosy taktiki v sovetskikh voennykh trudakh, 1917–1940* (Moscow, 1970).

9. G. S. Isserson, "Istoricheskie korni novykh form boia" *Voennaia Mysl* (1937), no. 1: 4.

10. Isserson, "Evoliutsiia operativnogo iskusstva," in *Voprosy strategii i operativnogo iskusstva*, pp. 398–99.

11. Ibid.

12. B. H. Liddell Hart, *The Strategy of Indirect Approach* (London: Faber and Faber, 1941). The quote can be found in a more recent edition, *Strategy* (New York: Frederick A. Praeger, 1954), p. 328. This work was translated into Russian as *Strategiia nepriamykh deistvii* (Moscow, 1957). Liddell Hart, who advanced the theory of indirect actions, began his scholarly career at the same time as Svechin. His first work, *Paris, or Future War*, was published in 1925, two years after Svechin's *Strategiia*. The English author is like his Russian colleague in many of his fundamental ideas, although he was not acquainted with Svechin's work.

13. G. Isserson, "Razvitie teorii sovetskogo operativnogo iskusstva v 30-e gody," *Voenno-istoricheskii zhurnal* (1965), no. 1: 36–46.

14. See chapter 2 of this book.

15. Liddell Hart, *Strategy of Indirect Approach*, p. 121.

Chapter 16

1. It would have been better to express these in tons, but in centners they look ten times as impressive.

2. This number is figured on the basis of relative indices from the report at the previous Congress. It would seem that these indices are overstated by 5 percent. If we accept them for the following years, then the proper figure for 1929 would be 754 million centners.

3. We are assuming the given tempo of growth of marketability, 15 percent per year, continued. It was painfully tempting in 1932 or 1933 to reach the level of 1913.

4. Based on the growth of marketability we have assumed.

5. At that time the kolkhozes owned 74 percent of land under grain. *Sovkhozes*, or state farms, had another 11 percent. That left the individual farmers, who were 34 percent of the peasant population, only 15 percent of the land.

6. At the very least Stalin bragged that the marketability of kolkhoz produce, unlike that of the muzhiks', reached 30 to 40 percent. If the collections were at the upper limit, life must have been very hard for the comrade kolkhozniks. The marketability of grain is now approximately 40 percent, but the gross yield is 2.5 times greater, and the rural population has decreased by 50 percent.

7. This is assuming a ratio of harvested grain to seed of 5:1. Generally in these years the area of sown land increased 15 to 20 percent.

8. It is possible (oh, so possible!) that these figures on the gross yield are *inflated*. Later, in the 1950s, Khrushchev revealed a little secret about how the grain problem was solved. Instead of weighing the grain put in granaries, the productivity of selected fields (naturally, rather good fields) was determined, and this figure was multiplied by the area of sown land. Thanks to this rather simple device, grain that was lost during harvesting or transportation, or never produced on poorer land, could be considered *collected*. If Stalin had discovered this un-Euclidian math in the early 1930s, then the peasants' nutrition must have been even worse.

9. If the statistics bore you, please read *Kotlovan* by the magnificent and honest master Andrei Platonov. People in the starving villages feeling the approach of death would lie down in coffins they had prepared beforehand—to make it easier to bury them. Platonov, *The Foundation Pit. Kotlovan*, translated by Thomas A. Whitney (Ann Arbor: Ardis, 1973). This is a bilingual text.

10. Grain was the major source of foreign currency, but not the only source; lumber, furs, bristles, and leather were sent abroad. But all that was not enough, and a real search was begun in the country for currency and gold. The OGPU carried out mass seizures of valuables from the population in 1929–30. During the first Five-Year Plan the hotels and restaurants of Moscow and Leningrad served only foreigners. A huge number of paintings and other valuable artworks from the Hermitage collection and also details of decorations from the ruins of the Christ the Savior Cathedral in Moscow were sold abroad in those years.

11. There were also a small number of *Komsomoltsy*, who later got the credit for building *everything*.

12. There is information that in 1928–29 forty-eight people from the Gosplan staff were shot.

13. *XVI S"ezd Vsesoiuznoi Kommunisticheskoi Partii (b). Stenograficheskii otchet* (Moscow: Moskovskii rabochii, 1934), pp. 482–83.

14. *XVII S"ezd Vsesoiuznoi Kommunisticheskoi Partii (b). 26 ianvaria–10 fevralia 1934 g. Stenograficheskii otchet* (Moscow, 1934), p. 176.

15. Ibid., pp. 263–66.

16. *XVI S"ezd*, p. 487.

17. *XVII S"ezd*, p. 356.

18. Ibid., p. 178. Also, according to Ordzhonikidze, 21.5 billion rubles were spent in heavy industry, while the basic fund grew to 13.6 billion. Apparently he included circulating capital in the final sum.

19. Ibid., pp. 455–64. Piatakov also spoke at the Congress. He had been expelled in 1927 and readmitted in 1929, but he had apparently been long forgiven because his speech was exclusively devoted to questions of heavy industry. He was Ordzhonikidze's first deputy. "Prolonged applause" greeted Piatakov's speech.

20. The Scientific-Technical Administration is in Russian *Nauchno-Tekhnicheskoe upravlenie*. The Main Concessions Committee, *Glavkontsesskom*. *Tsentrosoiuz* was an administrative umbrella organ meant to organize numerous small shops and industries.

21. *XVII S"ezd*, pp. 124–29. The emphasis in this quotation and below is Bukharin's.

22. Dobchinsky and Bobchinsky are characters, famous for lacking any personal opinions, in Gogol's play "Revizor" ("The Inspector General").

23. *XVII S"ezd*, pp. 492–97.

24. Ibid., pp. 516–22.

25. Ibid., pp. 209–12.

26. Ibid., pp. 251–57. Kirov's speech was entitled "Samyi iarkii dokument epokhi."

27. Ibid., pp. 236–39.

28. Ibid., pp. 245–49.

29. That means he must have joined the Party in 1892. The founding of the RSDRP, from which most Bolsheviks count the years, occurred in 1898. Some, including Lenin, began to count from their service in the St. Petersburg "Union of Struggle," which was founded in 1895. It is unclear what this old warrior was counting from.

30. See ibid., p. 641. It is only grain that we still have less of than, say, farmers in the United States. Those who doubt this mystifying information can turn to the stenographic reports published in 1934.

31. Ibid., pp. 464–65.

32. Everyone who needed to knew that Stalin was hostile to Tukhachevsky and all of his proposals. Once when it was necessary to have the Politburo approve an increase in Army manpower, Tukhachevsky and his friend Triandafillov resorted to military cunning. Tukhachevsky cited incorrect figures in his report, not those he desired. Triandafillov objected and introduced the correct figures. Stalin was glad of a chance to spite Tukhachevsky and sided with Triandafillov. The proposal was accepted as Stalin and Triandafillov's.

Chapter 17

1. *XVI S"ezd Vsesiouznoi Kommunisticheskoi Partii (b). Stenograficheskii otchet* (Moscow: Moskovii rabochii, 1934), p. 36. Stalin's emphasis.

2. That same Sergei Ivanovich Syrtsov, who as chairman of the Donburo was notorious for his untiring cruelty in persecuting the Cossacks. See chapter 7 of this book.

3. On August 11, 1936, the TSIK introduced several amendments to the law of December 1: (*a*) open court sessions, (*b*) admission of lawyers, (*c*) seventy-two hours given in which to ask for pardon. The amelioration was timed to precede the infamous trial of 1936 to give hope to the defendants who had been promised

their lives in exchange for certain testimony. In fact, nothing changed. In 1937 the law, which was so easy to manipulate, was toughened again.

4. In the 1920s statements about such things were very unclear. Later they became quite definite. The facts about medical murders are now openly admitted, and the murderers were selected from a suitable circle of people. The deaths of Gorky, Menzhinsky, and Kuibyshev were blamed on their personal secretaries and doctors Levin, Pletnev, and Kazakov. A group of Jewish doctors in the Kremlin were accused of the deaths of Sherbakov and Zhdanov. Stalin's personal physician, Vinogradov, was included in the group to make the case more convincing. He played his part well. In 1938 he signed several falsified documents about their ill-intentioned healing, which sufficed as death sentences for his colleagues.

5. His sister who was at home was apparently the source of this version of the story.

6. That is one of the versions. According to the other, Zinoviev and Kamenev demanded to talk to the Politburo. They were supposedly taken to the Kremlin where they talked with Stalin, Voroshilov, and Ezhov who comprised a special commission of the Politburo. The versions agree that they were promised their lives and the security for their families if they accepted the prosecution's line at the trial.

7. Tomsky shot himself on August 22, 1936, when he received the newspaper account of the trial. Stalin played cat and mouse with Rykov and Bukharin a while longer. A short announcement appeared in the papers on September 10 that investigation in their case had been halted "for absence of any evidence of their criminal activity." In the January trial Radek again pointed a finger at the rightists as conspirators.

8. In the trial of August 1936 there was a whole squad of provocateurs: V. Olberg, F. David, Berman-Iurin, M. Lurie, N. Lurie. There seems to have been only one in the January 1937 trial—Shestov.

9. Again there is a parallel version. It dates this episode to the January trial and associates it with Piatakov. Sergo highly valued his assistant in the People's Commissariat of Heavy Industry and might have dealt with Stalin for his life. It is known that he did visit Piatakov in prison. The nearness of the dates also supports this version: Piatakov was executed at the end of January, Sergo's murder occurred in mid-February.

10. They telegraphed Molotov, Kaganovich, and other members of the Politburo from Sochi on September 25, 1936: "We consider it absolutely necessary and urgent that comrade Ezhov be appointed to the post of People's Commissar of Internal Affairs. Yagoda showed himself to be clearly incapable of uncovering the Trotskyite-Zinovievite bloc. The OGPU is four years behind in this matter." The figure had not been chosen at random. It referred to 1932, to Riutin's case. For the time being, until he was eliminated, Yagoda was appointed People's Commissar of Communications, because of which its former chairman Rykov was removed from the Council of People's Commissars.

Chapter 18

1. See Joseph Stalin, "Address to the Graduates of the Red Army Academies," in *Selected Writings* (Westport, Conn.: Greenwood Press, 1970), pp. 361–65.

The quotes that follow are also from this source.

2. Nothing in history disappears without a trace. The Kremlin command sent the Academy a bill for the broken gate. It has been preserved.

3. Higher military commanders okayed the arrest of their subordinates. Substantial lists signed by Gamarnik, Primakov, Blucher, Uborevich, and many others have been preserved. There are none signed by Yakir or Tukhachevsky.

4. Anastasia Ruban, a worker with the NKVD, told Yakir that the accusation against Sablin, which she had seen, was entirely fabricated. Three days later she shot herself; officially she died of a heart attack.

5. The trial's scriptwriters, particularly Vyshinsky, were uninventive and humorless. The monstrous acts of their drama looked like the escapades of second-rate swindlers. For example, Chairman Zelensky of Tsentrosoiuz gave this testimony at the 1938 trial: "When a person comes to buy things in a store he is overcharged, given false weight or false measure, that is, they name a price higher than the real price of the goods, or give him less than they should or give something of a lesser quality." These are merely the basic principles of our trade; it is shameful to pretend it is unusual wrecking. Zelensky continued: "To illustrate the extent of this wrecking I will say that of 135,000 shops checked by the inspectorate of the trade-cooperative network, incidents of mismeasure and deceit of customers were found in 13,000. Another important form of wrecking, also meant to *cause discontent in the population*, is the freezing of goods, achieved by the incorrect or delayed shipping of goods. For example, there have been cases when *summer goods* were shipped *in the winter*, and vice versa, *winter* goods have arrived in the stores in the *summer*.

VYSHINSKY. That is to say the population has been offered winter boots in the summer, and slippers in the winter?

ZELENSKY. Yes.

V. This was done intentionally, according to your testimony?

Z. Yes.

V. For reasons of provocation?

Z. Yes.

[The emphasis above is ours.]

We hasten to calm the departed souls of comrades Zelensky (posthumously rehabilitated) and Vyshinsky (never prosecuted). Wrecking like that in retail trade, "with the aim of causing dissatisfaction in the population," goes on to this day with undiminished success. The public was fed similar flannel at all the open trials. It is not impossible that the accused prompted the prosecution with the funnier examples in the secret hope they could demonstrate to the people the absurdity of the accusations.

6. The following example demonstrates that Radek was an informer. Blumkin, the left SR who killed German ambassador Mirbach in 1918, was an NKVD worker. Because of his outstanding capabilities. Dzerzhinsky decided to save him. He was taken out of the public's eye and used for special assignments. For example, he was put in a cell with Savinkov, where he became so accustomed to the ways of the illustrious warrior that he was able to compose a document that was passed

off as Savinkov's last letter when his murder was announced as suicide. Even Savinkov's son thought the letter authentic. In 1930 or 1931 Blumkin was abroad on a secret mission and on his own initiative went to see Trotsky on the Prince Islands (Kizil Adalar). Trotsky asked him to carry a letter to Radek. Blumkin carried out his request, but Radek went straight to the OGPU with it. That time Blumkin was not spared.

7. The Red Montesquieu, comrade Vyshinsky, said that for sentence to be passed, *probability* of a guilty verdict was sufficient.

8. *Detstvo v tiur'me; memuary Petra Iakira*, 2nd ed. (London: Macmillan, 1972), pp. 15–17. In English as *A Childhood in Prison* (London: Macmillan, 1972).

9. This comes from *Komandarm Iakir: vospominaniia druzei i soratnikov* (Moscow, 1963).

Chapter 19

1. He had just been appointed chief of the Administration of Cadres of the RKKA on May 23. In the fall of 1937 he was arrested and perished.

2. This version seems neater, which does not, however, increase its authenticity. Gamarnik apparently killed himself after he learned from Bulin that he had been removed from his post as chief of the Political Administration of the RKKA, and that Yakir had been arrested.

3. A. Dunaevsky, *Po sledam Gaia* (Erevan, 1966), pp. 188, 232–33.

4. A. Dunaevsky tells very little about Gai's escape and provides no dates. If the story of his meeting with Putna is true, then that episode took place no earlier than September 1936, that is, a year after his arrest in Minsk. Gai was sent to Iaroslavl again to serve his five-year term, but on December 12, 1937, after a new trial, he was shot.

5. The head of the local Cheka, Liushkov, did not wait for his natural end when Mekhlis and Frinovsky arrived. On June 13 he defected to the Japanese in Manchuria.

6. The fact that the Soviets were not particularly successful in battle is confirmed by the meagerness and restrained tone of articles in the papers. Announced losses were 236 killed and 611 wounded on our side and 600 killed and 2,500 wounded for the Japanese. They are hardly accurate. In any case, the Japanese began an open attack the next year at Kalkhin-Gola.

Chapter 20

1. See *Sudebnyi otchet po delu antisovetskogo "pravo-trotskistskogo bloka"* (Moscow: Iuridicheskoe izdatel'stvo NKIu SSSR, 1938). March 2 was the first day of the trial. G. F. Grinko was a prominent Ukrainian Bolshevik. In the last years before his arrest he served as People's Commissar of Finance of the USSR. Liubchenko, a former chairman of the Council of People's Commissars of the Ukraine, had committed suicide. The full text of the 1938 trial was published in many languages in 1938. In 1965 Robert C. Tucker and Stephen F. Cohen edited the full text and published it with very useful notes and an introduction by

Tucker. *The Great Purge Trial* (New York: Grosset & Dunlap, 1965). This translation is mine.

2. It is easy to believe that no one closely associated with Yakir or Gamarnik was found suitable for his job. They had to find someone in the People's Commissariat of Finance. The absence of Shmidt and Kuzmichev's names is typical.

3. Member of the Politburo and organizational secretary of the TSK in the first years after the Revolution. Prior to his arrest he had been Deputy People's Commissar of Foreign Affairs and Deputy People's Commissar of Foreign Trade.

4. Immediately after the trial in 1937 no one dared to say such nonsense even in private conversations. When an American diplomat asked a Soviet colleague about the marshal's motives, he was told that Tukhachevsky had taken up with a woman who turned out to be a German spy.

5. People's Commissar of Foreign Trade. During the Civil War he was chairman of the tribunal on Trotsky's personal train.

6. B. S. Gorbachev served in the First Horse Army as commander of a Special Cavalry Brigade. He was killed in 1937.

7. The author of the dreadful, pretentious, and thoroughly inaccurate book, *Marshal Tukhachevsky*, the first Soviet biography of Tukhachevsky to appear after the revelations about the cult of Stalin at the Twentieth and Twenty-Second Congresses.

8. Biographies of Skoblin and Plevitskaia may be found in a book by B. Prianishnikov, *Nezrimaia pautina* (*The Invisible Web*), published by the author in 1979. It includes a very thorough picture of the penetration of the NKVD into all corners of the life of the Russian emigration and its organizations throughout the world, and particularly in the ROVS. *Nezrimaia pautina* (Silver Spring, Md., 1979).

9. Very little is known about the evil figure N. Ettingon. We have put the information we have been able to gather in appendix V.

10. V. Aleksandrov's work, *Delo Tukhachevskogo*, first appeared in 1960 in the Roman newspaper *Giornale d'Italia*. For a long while he could not find a publisher. It was immediately noted in the Soviet Union, where Khrushchev ordered it be translated into Russian for a narrow circle of high officials. When Khrushchev spoke at the Twenty-Second Congress of the KPSS of "one foreign source" in connection with the causes of the arrest of Yakir, Tukhachevsky, and others, he certainly had in mind Aleksandrov's publication. As far as we know, the official Soviet verison is still based on Aleksandrov's book. It appeared as a book in French in 1962, *L'affaire Toukhatchevsky* (Paris: Robert Laffont). We have used the American edition, *The Tukhachevsky Affair*, translated from French by John Hewish (Englewood Cliffs, N.J.: Prentice-Hall, 1964).

11. Robert Conquest, *The Great Terror: Stalin's Purge of the Thirties* (New York: Macmillan, 1968). This has been translated into Russian: Robert Konkvest, *Bolshoi Terror*, translated by L. Vladimirov (Florence, 1974).

12. Common sources for both authors. V. Getl (pseudonym, V. Khagen) *Sekretnyi Front*; (W. Hoettle, *The Secret Front* [New York, 1954]); Dzhon Erikson, *Sovetskoe vyschee komandovanie* (John Erickson, *The Soviet High Command* [London, 1962]); U. Cherchill, *Vtoria Mirovaia Voina* (W. Churchill, *The Second World War*, vol. 1 [London, 1948]). Conquest also cited a report by W. Gomulka (*Tribuna Ludu*, November 23, 1961), and a book by the Soviet defector Kri-

vitsky (Krivitsky, *I Was Stalin's Agent* [London, 1940]).

Aleksandrov, in addition to these, made use of Schellenberg's memoirs, Reitlinger's book, *Heydrich and the SS*, Victor Serge's books *Memoirs, Carnets* and *The Tulaev Affair*, the archives of V. L. Burtsev and the Russian Historical Commission in Paris, and the émigré press (particularly the publications of B. I. Nikolaevsky). He claims that he received information from conversations with the Czech secret service agents Volganin and Nemanov, with the Polish General V. Grosz and another anonymous Pole, with Soviet defectors F. Raskolnikov, V. Krivitsky, and A. Barmin, with the German communist E. Wollenberg, with the former French premier E. Daladier, and with journalists L. Nord and J. Tabui. Aleksandrov claims that he was asked in 1936 by a German resident in Athens to deliver a letter to the Czechs, allegedly written by Tukhachevsky, expressing his pro-German sympathies. Aleksandrov refused. Schellenberg's memoirs are Walter Schellenberg, *The Schellenberg Memoirs*, translated by Louis Hagen (London: A. Deutsch, 1956). Gerald Reitlinger has written several books on the Second World War, including *The SS: Alibi of a Nation, 1922–1945* (London: Heineman, 1956). Victor Serge's books are *Memoirs of a Revolutionary, 1901–1941*, translated and edited by Peter Sedgwich (London: Oxford University Press, 1963); *Carnets* (Paris: R. Julliard, 1952); *The Case of Comrade Tulaev*, translated by Willard R. Trask (Garden City, N.Y.: Doubleday, 1950).

13. It is interesting to note that although Conquest used a huge number of sources in his book, which was published in 1968, he did not refer to Aleksandrov. Nor do other authors. A possible explanation is that the book is written with considerable artistic license. It contains a large number of inaccuracies. Nonetheless, we think it unwise to ignore the book entirely.

14. Aleksandrov bases his account of the meeting between Radek and Nikolai on the following sources: (1) a conversation with an anonymous witness to that meeting, (2) information received from General Victor Grosz, director of the information branch of the Polish MID, (3) and notes in the Russian émigré paper *Narodnaia Pravda* (Paris) by the famous historian B. I. Nikolaevsky and a certain Bondar, a former NKVD associate, which do not state the date of the meeting or the names of the participants.

15. The matter is especially complicated by the absence of dates. In any case, Aleksandrov is wrong when he writes that Radek was returned from exile and immediately sent to Poland. In August 1936 Radek published several articles in *Izvestiia* during the Zinoviev-Kamenev trial.

16. Here again there is confusion about the dates. Aleksandrov writes that the day they arrived in Paris was very hot. That is strange because Ezhov's appointment occurred in late November.

17. Aleksandrov depicts Skoblin's conversation with Heydrich very colorfully. Insisting on the necessity of removing Tukhachevsky, Skoblin pointed out not only the Red Marshal's anti-Nazism, but also that he was a twenty-third degree Mason and had Jewish ancestors.

18. Aleksandrov and Conquest refer to his book *Sekretnyi Front*. See note 12.

19. In 1945 Berens was captured by the Allies and turned over to the Yugoslavs as a war criminal (as head of the Gestapo in Serbia). In the course of interrogations

Berens gave a great deal of testimony about "the Tukhachevsky affair." Aleksandrov states that this information was transmitted to Moscow. He also gives to understand that he is familiar with Berens' testimony. Berens was sentenced to die and was hanged.

20. Both authors refer to him.

21. V. Aleksandrov does not say how the NKVD came to know about the preparation of the documents. As we recall, the idea originated with Skoblin who decided to "outplay" his Soviet bosses.

22. This money turned out to be counterfeit. Prianishnikov says this and names the sum of 3 million rubles. "Three German agents spending that money in the USSR were arrested by the NKVD. Heydrich was incensed that the Soviets would pay for forged papers with counterfeit paper." See B. Prianishnikov, *Nezrimaia pautina*, p. 347.

23. Some say that Gamarnik was removed from his post as Deputy People's Commissar but kept on as commander of the Political Administration of the RKKA at the same time; but those reports are hard to believe. In any case, nothing was said about it in the press.

24. One Soviet source says he was deputy troop commander of the LVO until November 1936. But we need not accept that as the date of his arrest. It appears that he too was taken at the end of May. The fact that Primakov was officially removed from the staff of the Leningrad Council on June 6 or 7 as an "unmasked enemy of the people" supports that view.

25. In 1936 Aronshtam was chief of the Political Administration of the Special Far Eastern Red Banner Army under Blucher. He was later transferred to the same position in Moscow district. He was arrested in May 1937.

26. They did not save Beria in 1953. Security organs will always lose in a confrontation with regular forces if the latter resist.

27. Only once in the 1940s did he show his old courage. When the men of the MGB came for his wife, Ekaterina Davidovna, Voroshilov brandished a pistol (maybe it was a Mauser!) and said he would not give her up. And he did not.

28. He had earlier run things in Leningrad where he had a reputation for extreme cruelty in interrogations. Zakovsky bragged that if Karl Marx had fallen into his hands he would soon have confessed to be an agent for Bismarck. In January 1938 he was promoted to Deputy People's Commissar. Beria had him killed not long after.

29. As of January 1, 1937. Therefore our data differ somewhat from those offerd by Todorsky and E. Genri.

30. That is in the official history of World War II, *The Great Patriotic War, 1941–1945* (*Velikaia Otechestvennaia voina Sovetskogo Soiuza 1941–1945*) (Moscow: Voenizdat, 1965), pp. 39–40, 51.

31. Yuri P. Petrov, *Partiinoe stroitel'stvo v Sovetskoi Armii i Flote* (Moscow: Voenizdat, 1964), pp. 298–317, 341.

32. That is why Stalin never dared to accuse Ezhov publicly. Years after the "Iron Commissar" had been killed, even when Stalin spoke of him to close associates, he had to play the fool. This is how aircraft designer A. Yakovlev reports one such talk. (See *Tsel' zhizni* [Moscow, 1969], p. 509): "Once at home over

dinner Stalin spoke about the lack of good workers in all fields. 'Ezhov was a villain! He killed our best cadres. He was a corrupt man. You call him at the Commissariat and they tell you he's gone to the TSK. Call the TSK and they say he's gone to work. Send for him at home, and it turns out he's in bed dead drunk. He killed a lot of innocent people. That's why we shot him.'" Too bad Nikolai Ivanovich shirked his duties. Had he stayed in his office during working hours, he would still be alive and well today.

33.   The Great Purge reached more deeply into the punitive organs than into the other branches of the state apparatus. That is another topic, but one fact is worth mentioning. Of the large number of people who were appointed generals in the NKVD in 1935 only one, S. A. Goglidze, was still at work at the end of the war. And one other, T. Deribas, remained alive—because he had been put in an insane asylum. This must contain some sort of lesson or at least serve as food for thought.

34.   We are not speaking of Stalin's *ober*-executioner V. Ulrikh. He lived out his days in comfort and died after the war.

35.   The marshal supposedly told this story himself to a correspondent of *Komsomol'skaia Pravda* in the brief period of unmasking the cult. Observing how others about him were being arrested, Budenny decided to take care of himself. He took several machine guns to his dacha and set them up in the garret. He set soldiers on guard around the clock. He slept only at the dacha and frequently led the all-around observation from the observation post personally. Once when Chekists came for him, Budenny shouted to them through a megaphone about the machine guns and warned them not to cross a line marked in the yard or he would open fire. He then called Stalin. Stalin, as might be expected, answered that he had nothing to do with it. He told Budenny that he had no more idea what was going on in the NKVD than Budenny did, that they might come for him the next day. Budenny responded that he would open fire, which greatly amused the Great Leader. Go ahead, give it to them, Stalin said, chase them off. That is probably folklore, but composed with much understanding of the affair.

36.   Ezhov's further fate is hard to follow. At first he remained a candidate member of the Politburo and People's Commissar of Water Transport, which position he had held along with his others since the previous summer. In March 1939 he spoke at the Twenty-third Congress of the Bolshevik Party. Apparently not yet understanding the changes that had taken place, he thought to speak of the achievements of the punitive organs under his leadership. Stalin cut him off and called him a fool. Several months later that fallen executioner was taken to his dacha under house arrest. The Chekists assigned to him were ordered not only to guard him but to see to his needs. Ezhov was regularly so drunk he ceased to look human, which was for him natural. At the beginning of December the guards were told to leave the dacha. Other NKVD employees made the arrest. It is said that Ezhov was put through the usual butchery of physical interrogation, forced to sign what he was ordered, and was shot. The reasons: deceiving the party and the people, unjustified repressions, destruction of the cadres, etc. This happened very late in 1939.

37.   See *Velikaia Otechestvennaia Voina Sovetskogo Soiuza* (Moscow, 1967), pp. 39–40.

Chapter 21

1. See chapter 14.
2. It is said that Tukhachevsky, sitting on a saddled horse, could do a pull-up, horse and all.
3. Tukhachevsky, *Strategiia natsional'naia i klassovaia* (Rostov na Donu, 1920).
4. In May 1937 he told his sister, "When I was a boy, father wanted to give me a violin. It's too bad he didn't. I'd have become a violinist."
5. They met in the Second House of the People's Commissariat of Defense, across from the Kremlin—that is, on Army territory. The NKVD guards never came into the hall during such meetings. Brutus and Cassius made better use of their opportunity.

Chapter 22

1. Emphasis here and below is the authors'.
2. In 1957 he told this story to Dr. Nilson: "My wife was pregnant. She cried and pleaded with me to sign the document, but I could not. That day I weighed everything and tried to determine what my chances were of staying alive. I was convinced they would arrest me, that it was my turn. I was ready for that. I was repulsed by all that blood, I couldn't stand it any more. But nothing happened. I was saved, I learned later in some roundabout way, by my colleagues. No one dared tell the higher-ups that I had refused to sign." To report, of course, does take some courage, but apparently one of the literary bigwigs decided to include Pasternak's signature without his knowledge. The motives could have been various. It is possible that there were other similar cases. But no one else has since claimed that to be so, even when there was not a threat. Consequently, the others have taken *that* responsibility on themselves.
3. Daix was clever enough to write in the 1930s, "the camps . . . in the Soviet Union are an achievement, testifying to the complete abolition of the exploitation of man by man." Years later he wrote a sympathetic foreword to the French translation of Solzhenitsyn's novelette *One Day in the Life of Ivan Denisovich*. See Pierre Daix, *Une Journee d'Ivan Denissovitch* (Paris: Julliard, 1969).
4. *Istoki i smysl russkogo kommunizma* (Paris, 1955), p. 121. This is from the Russian edition. English and French editions were published in 1937. See *The Origin of Russian Communism* (London: G. Blas, [1939]).
5. Arkadi Belinkov, "Poet i tolstiak," *Baikal* (1968), nos. 1–2.

Chapter 23

1. M. Djilas describes how in a conversation after the war Stalin said seriously that only Belgium and Luxemburg were members of Benelux, that the Netherlands was not. Molotov, who was present, did not dare correct the Great Leader, who apparently went to his grave believing that was so. See Milovan Djilas, *Conversations with Stalin*, translated by Michael B. Petrovich (New York: Harcourt, Brace & World, 1962), p. 181.

2. *XVII S''ezd Vsesoiuznoi Kommunisticheskoi partii (b). 26 ianvaria–10 fevralia 1934 g. Stenograficheskii otchet* (Moscow, 1934), p. 11.
3. Ibid., pp. 13–14.
4. *Vosem'nadtsatyi S''ezd vsesoiuznoi kommunisticheskoi partii (b). 10–21 marta 1939 g. Stenograficheskii otchet* (Moscow, 1939), p. 14.
5. Mussolini, with whom Stalin, in his own words, had "the very best relations," wrote in October 1939, "Bolshevism in Russia has disappeared and has been replaced by a Slavic form of fascism." Earlier that year a special emissary of the German government, Dr. Shnurre, had emphasized, "There is one thing in common in the ideology of Germany, Italy, and the USSR: opposition to capitalist democracy. Neither we nor Italy have anything in common with the capitalist West. Therefore it would be utterly paradoxical to us if the Soviet Union as a socialist nation would wind up on the side of the western democracies." The foundation for such an evaluation was Molotov's assertion in an official speech on May 31 that the anti-Comintern pact was only camouflage for the union of the Axis powers against the war.
6. The Germans were most interested in the economic side of the pact, and they began with that. The Kremlin, however, made conclusion of the economic agreement conditional upon general political settlement. They agreed that both pacts be prepared in parallel. The trade agreement, Shnurre-Mikoyan, was concluded on August 19, that is, on the eve of the Ribbentrop-Molotov pact. An abundant flow of raw materials (oil) and foodstuffs (wheat) immediately poured into Germany. The German deliveries (machines and equipment) were hopelessly delayed and were never filled. The new agreement of February 11, 1940, was again very favorable for Germany: the term for the Soviet deliveries was eighteen months, for the German, twenty-four months. Besides that, the USSR obligated itself to buy metals for the Reich in third countries to help Germany get around the British blockade. According to Halder, Germany had a monthly shortfall in steel of 600,000 tons. The Germans, on their side, intentionally delayed shipping goods with military significance. If they did give some things, they were defective. Halder recalls the sale to Russia of a heavy cruiser with construction defects. The fools in the Kremlin scrupulously fulfilled all of their obligations on time. In April 1941 they delivered to Germany: 208 million tons of grain, 90,000 tons of oil, 8,300 tons of cotton, 6,400 tons of copper, steel, nickel, and other metals, and 4,000 tons of rubber. A large part of these goods, including the rubber, was obtained in third countries. As a result, on June 22, 1941, German tanks and planes invaded the USSR with Soviet fuel in their tanks. Their crews' bellies were full of Russian bread. The authors used the Russian translation of Halder's diaries: Frants Galder, *Voennyi Dnevnik. Ezhednevnye zapisi nach. Gen. Shtaba sukhoputnykh voisk, 1939–1942 gg* 2 vols. (Moscow, 1968–69). These were first available in English: Franz Halder, *The Halder Diaries: The Private War Journals of Colonel General Franz Halder*, introduction by Trevor N. Dupuy, 2 vols. (Boulder, Colo.: Westview Press, 1976). This is a reprint of the eight-volume work originally published by the Office of Chief Counsel for War Crimes, Office of Military Government for Germany, in Nuremberg in 1946. For the information in this note, see the Westview Press reprint, pp. 101, 158, 174–75.
7. The goon squads got on famously. They looked kindly on the heartfelt agreement

of their masters. At the banquet to celebrate the signing of the pact Stalin proclaimed, "I know how deeply the German people love their great leader [in German, Führer]. Therefore I want to drink to his health." The toast was not provided for by the protocol. For understandable reasons, the text of it did not get into the papers. Recalling the banquet, Ribbentrop said that "in the Kremlin he felt just as if he was among old party comrades." Should we be surprised that the executioners began an intensive exchange of experience and instruments of torture, and also of political prisoners? See Abdurakhman Avtorkhanov, "Zakulisnaia istoriia pakta 'Ribbentrop-Molotov'," *Kontinent* (1975), no. 4: 300–320.

8. *Halder Diaries*, vol. 1, pp. 21–22.

9. It is significant that the German invasion began on September 1, the day after the Soviet-German pact was ratified by Moscow.

10. Here are the words as they appeared in the Soviet press on November 1: "The ideology of Hitlerism, like every other ideological system, can be accepted or rejected. . . . But *everybody* understands that ideology cannot be destroyed by force, cannot be killed by war. Therefore it is not only *senseless* but *criminal* to wage such a war, as a *war to destroy Hitlerism!*" [*Pravda*, November 1, 1939; emphasis is ours]. Hitler and Goebbels could not be at the Nuremburg trials because they were dead. Too bad that for other reasons Stalin and Molotov were not among the defendants.

11. The people were given to understand that the Soviet-German rapprochement was meant to last a long while. *Mein Kampf* was published in Russian and for several hours was actually sold in one of Moscow's bookstores. The ban on Wagner was lifted, and the Bolshoi Theater staged the Führer's favorite operas, *Die Walküre* and *Die Meistersinger*. Richard Strauss's works were begun to be performed. One memoirist tells that "Muscovites jammed the concert halls to hear the 'fascist,' 'Hitlerian' music that had been forbidden just yesterday." Iu. Elagin, *Ukroshchenie iskusstv* (New York: Izd-vo im. Chekhova, 1952), Juri Jelagin, *Taming of the Arts*, translated by Nicholas Wreden (New York: Dutton, 1951), pp. 238–39.

12. Shaposhnikov also suggested storming the Mannerheim line, but while simultaneously striking a diversionary blow through Kandalaksha. In Shtern's plan that blow was the main one. Instead, the disposition of the great strategist Timoshenko, who had just been made commander of the Leningrad region (which soon became the Northwestern Front), was accepted. Timoshenko announced, "Never in history have the most powerful fortifications withstood massive attacks. And in general as comrade Stalin teaches us 'there are no fortresses that Bolsheviks cannot take.'"

13. *Halder Diaries*, vol. 1, pp. 51–53.

Chapter 24

1. Even as it was at that time, the Red Army presented a mortal threat to Germany, which was undefended in the East.

2. The quote is not found in *Halder's Diaries*, but similar information, including some similar wording, is found in vol. 1, p. 751.

3. Ibid.

4. The German diplomat Von Hassel wrote in his diary on June 15, 1941, "A rumor is spreading with astonishing unanimity . . . that a mutual understanding with Russia is inevitable, that Stalin is coming, and so forth." There was a lot of talk in Berlin about a "peaceful capitulation," Stalin's last trump. The rumor had it that in exchange for Germany's agreement to hold back from war he had agreed to let the Germans work the natural resources of the Ukraine and take over the Russian aviation industry. It is highly unlikely, and there is no documentary evidence for it, but how must he have been behaving to give rise to such humiliating rumors. See Ulrich von Hassell, *The von Hassell Diaries, 1938–1944; the Story of the Forces against Hitler Inside Germany, as Recorded by Ambassador Ulrich von Hassell, a Leader of the Movement* (Westport, Conn.: Greenwood Press, 1971), pp. 197–98.

5. When the German Ambassador Von Schulenburg, who not long before had risked his life to warn the Kremlin that an attack was unavoidable, told People's Commissar of Foreign Affairs Molotov on June 22 that war had begun, Molotov cried, "We did not deserve that!" Indeed, Hitler had displayed the basest ingratitude.

Chapter 25

1. E. I. Martynov, *Tsarskaia armiia v fevral'skom perevorote*. (Moscow: NKVM i RVS SSSR, 1927), pp. 20–22. The author was a lieutenant general in the imperial Russian army.

2. See G. Zhukov, *Vospominaniia i razmyshleniia* (Moscow, 1969), p. 239.

3. See Harrison Salisbury, *The 900 Days* (New York: Harper, 1973), p. 60.

4. Ibid.

5. Zhukov, *Vospominaniia*, p. 204; N. Kozlov and A. Zaitsev, *Srazhaiushchaiasia partiia*. (Moscow: Voenizdat, 1975), p. 61; and a large number of equally respectable authors.

6. See, for example, S. Lototsky et al., *Armiia Sovetskaia* (Moscow: Politizdat, 1969), pp. 155–56.

7. See, "*Sovershenno sekretno. Tol'ko dlia komandovaniia*," p. 713; *Promyshlennost' Germanii v period voiny, 1939–1945* (Moscow, 1956), p. 189.

8. See, "*Sovershenno sekretno . . . ,*" p. 658; *Velikaia Otechestvennaia Voina Sovetskogo Soiuza, 1941–1945* (Moscow: Voenizdat, 1967), p. 33; *Dnevnik Gal'dera*, vol. 3, book 1, p. 161.

9. Zhukov, *Vospominaniia*, p. 204.

10. *Velikaia Otechestvennaia*, pp. 33, 53; "*Sovershenno sekretno . . . ,*" p. 88; *Porazhenie germanskogo imperialzma vo vtoroi mirovoi voine* (Moscow, 1961), pp. 582–83.

11. *Dnevnik Gal'dera*, vol. 2, pp. 582–83.

12. Sometimes the troops of satellite countries are counted along with the Germans — twenty-nine divisions, 900,000 men. See *Velikaia Otechestvennaia*, p. 33. We should note, however, that (*a*) these troops were not immediately used and (*b*) their combat effectiveness was not high.

13. "*Sovershenno sekretno . . . ,*" p. 726.

14. Ibid., pp. 730–31.

15. Ibid.

16. German reconnaissance planes freely violated our border. It was forbidden to shoot them down. Pilots who disobeyed that order were court-martialed. F. I. Kuznetsov, the commander of the Pribaltic region, began a blackout of cities and other potential targets. On June 20 N. N. Voronov, the newly appointed commander of the anti-aircraft defenses, asked Zhukov for permission to extend that measure to other regions. "In reply I heard curses and threats directed at Kuznetsov. A short while later the commander of the Pribaltic region was directed to rescind his order." N. Voronov, *Na sluzhbe voennoi* (Moscow: Voenizdat, 1963), p. 173.

17. On June 22 after the German invasion Voroshilov asked I. V. Tiulenev, commander of the Moscow Military District, about that. Tiulenev was embarrassed. They had forgotten about an underground headquarters. Only Admiral N. G. Kuznetsov, the People's Commissar of the Navy, had built such a shelter—on his own responsibility. The leaders of the Navy in general took the threat of war more seriously. As early as March 3, 1941, Kuznetsov, under pressure from the commander of the Baltic Fleet, Admiral Tributs, permitted his men to open fire without warning on German planes violating our airspace. German planes were fired at on March 17 and 18 at Libavaia (Liepaia) and near Odessa. Stalin and Beria chewed Kuznetsov out and forced him to cancel the order. Tributs kept up his pressure on the commissar, and on June 21 the highest state of combat readiness was declared in the Navy. Timoshenko and Zhukov did not do the same for the land forces. The warships of the Baltic Fleet managed to get away into Kronshtadt with few losses. However, the evacuation of the Tallin garrison (50,000 men) was delayed because of Voroshilov. As a result only 12,000 men broke through to safety. See *Voenno-istoricheskii zhurnal*, (1966), no. 10: 19–31.

18. This was immediately noticed by the Germans. Halder wrote on the first day of war, "A number of command levels of the enemy knew nothing of the situation, and therefore on a number of sectors of the front there was practically no leadership of the troops from higher headquarters." *Dnevnik Gal'dera*, vol. 3, book 1, p. 27.

19. We paid dearly for that stupidity. Halder writes: "22 June . . . Border bridges across the Bug and other rivers are seized everywhere by our troops *without a battle and undamaged*. The complete surprise of our attack for the enemy is testified to by the fact that whole units were caught unawares in their barracks, airplanes *stood* at the airfields covered by canvas, and forward units suddenly attacked by our troops asked their commanders *what* they should do." Ibid., p. 25; our emphasis. Commanders who asked for instructions from higher command paid a cruel price. Many of them died in battle, some (including the commander of the Belorussian Military District, Pavlov, and his chief of staff, Klimovskikh) were shot as a lesson to others. Their guilt was to wait as usual for orders from above, for orders that either were long delayed, or were senseless.

20. Halder: "There is no trace of strategic retreat. It is entirely likely that the possibility of organizing such a retreat had been simply excluded. . . . It would

seem that thanks to their sluggishness the Russian command will not be able to organize strategic resistance to our attack in the near future. The Russians were forced to accept battle in the formations they were in when we attacked." Ibid., p. 27.

21. Salisbury, *900 Days*, pp. 129, 107.

22. Sorge's report with Golikov's annotation surfaced in the sixties. Golikov, at that time a marshal and deputy minister of defense, kept his head. He climbed up on a table, tore at his mouth with his fingers, screamed, etc. The old veteran was retired. There was no investigation. Other facts reveal that Golikov was not an honest man. Shtemenko recalls that during the war Front Commander Golikov often sent false reports to headquarters: "In those days of the most critical development of events on the Voronezh front it was impossible to get an objective picture from the reports of F. I. Golikov." S. Shtemenko, *General'nyi shtab v gody voiny* (Moscow: Voenizdat, 1968), p. 109; see also p. 99.

23. Someone named Kindermann in the Federal Republic of Germany has announced very recently that Sorge was freed on exchange. Kindermann claims to have something to do with the deal. According to his version, Sorge was executed in 1949. Out of the frying pan into the fire.

24. *Dnevnik Gal'dera*, vol. 3, book 1, p. 26.

25. Having become Supreme Commander in Chief, Stalin on July 10, 1941, appointed his trusted Horse Army friends to head groups of fronts: Voroshilov (Northwest), Budenny (Southwest), Timoshenko (West). Soon, in August and September the sickly child was laid to rest. As a result of the deplorable results of the experiment the whole troika had to be removed from commanding troops and were not permitted to do so again until the very end of the war. The incompetent strategists were kept on in honorable inactivity at Headquarters and on rare occasions ventured out to inspire the men at the fronts. In 1944 Voroshilov was even removed from the State Defense Committee.

26. The Chief Artillery Administration supplies the troops with artillery and infantry arms but does not direct the combat use of artillery.

27. Voronov, *Na sluzhbe voennoi*, p. 183. Like Raskolnikov yelling at Porfiry, "Who killed anybody!" "You did, Rodion Romanovich, nobody else."

28. Ibid., p. 182.

29. See the memoirs of L. Grachev, "Doroga ot Volkhova," *Druzhba Narodov* (1979), no. 9: 171.

30. Interrogation of Keitel, June 17, 1945 in "*Sovershenno sekretno . . .*," p. 648.

31. Cited in A. Vasilevsky, *Delo vsei zhizhni* (Moscow: Politizdat, 1976), p. 200.

32. Several memoirists including I. S. Konev have said that before that, in 1944, Stalin's petty tutelage over the fronts had noticeably weakened, and commanders received a certain freedom of action. See I. S. Konev, *Zapiski kamanduiushchego frontom, 1943–1944* (Moscow: Nauka, 1972).

33. S. M. Shtemenko, *General'nyi shtab v gody voiny* (Moscow: Voenizdat, 1968–1973); *The Soviet General Staff at War (1941–1945)*, translated by Robert Daglish (Moscow: Progress, 1970).

34. That was another figment of Stalin's imagination. What importance could it have

had after the conferees at Yalta had agreed to four-power control of Berlin? Three-fourths of the city, gained at awful expense by Soviet soldiers, was turned over to the allies.

35. Stalin, *O Velikoi Otechestvennoi voine Sovetskogo Soiuza* (Moscow: Politizdat, 1948), pp. 196, 197. The following quotations are from pp. 413–15.

36. A. Eremenko, I. Bagramian, B. Vannikov, N. Voronov, N. Kuzentsov have written much more truthfully; but the careful reader must find the *first* editions of their memoirs. In later editions careful editors have removed the sharper criticisms with red pencils and scissors. And they were not able to say all that much the first time around.

37. *Voenno-istoricheskii zhurnal* (1965), no. 12: 60. Similar statistics for the period up to March 31, 1945, may be found in "*Sovershenno sekretno . . . ,*" pp. 714–15.

38. This finds unexpected confirmation in an official Soviet textbook, *Kurs demografii*, edited by Boiarskii (Moscow, 1967), p. 347. There mortality for all of the armies in the Second World War is put at 30 million. German deaths are said to have been 6 million. If we subtract losses of the Allies and Japan, we find the losses of our army were approximately 21 million.

Appendix V

1. From the testimony of Leonid Raigorodsky at the trial of Plevitskaia in Paris. B. Prianichnikov, *op. cit.*, p. 353. The family name is spelled Eitingon in this source. Concerning the 20 million marks: even if the witness were right about the sum, the fantastic inflation in Germany in the 1920s would have made the money worth very little.

2. See I. Nestev, *Zvezdy russkoi estrady* (Moscow: Sovetsky kompositor, 1970).

3. So Ezhov had lived in 1939, and Abakumov in 1951–54.

Index

Library of Congress Cataloging-in-Publication Data
Rapoport, Vitaly, 1937–
High treason.
Translated from the Russian.
Includes index.
1. Soviet Union. Raboche-Krest'iânskaiâ Krasnaiâ
Armiiâ—History—Addresses, essays, lectures. 2. Soviet
Union—History, Military—1917–   —Addresses,
essays, lectures. I. Alexeev, Yuri. II. Treml,
Vladimir G. III. Adams, Bruce. IV. Title.
UA772.R34 1985 355'.00947 85-16322
ISBN 0-8223-0647-6

5

WITHDRAWN

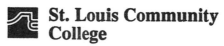

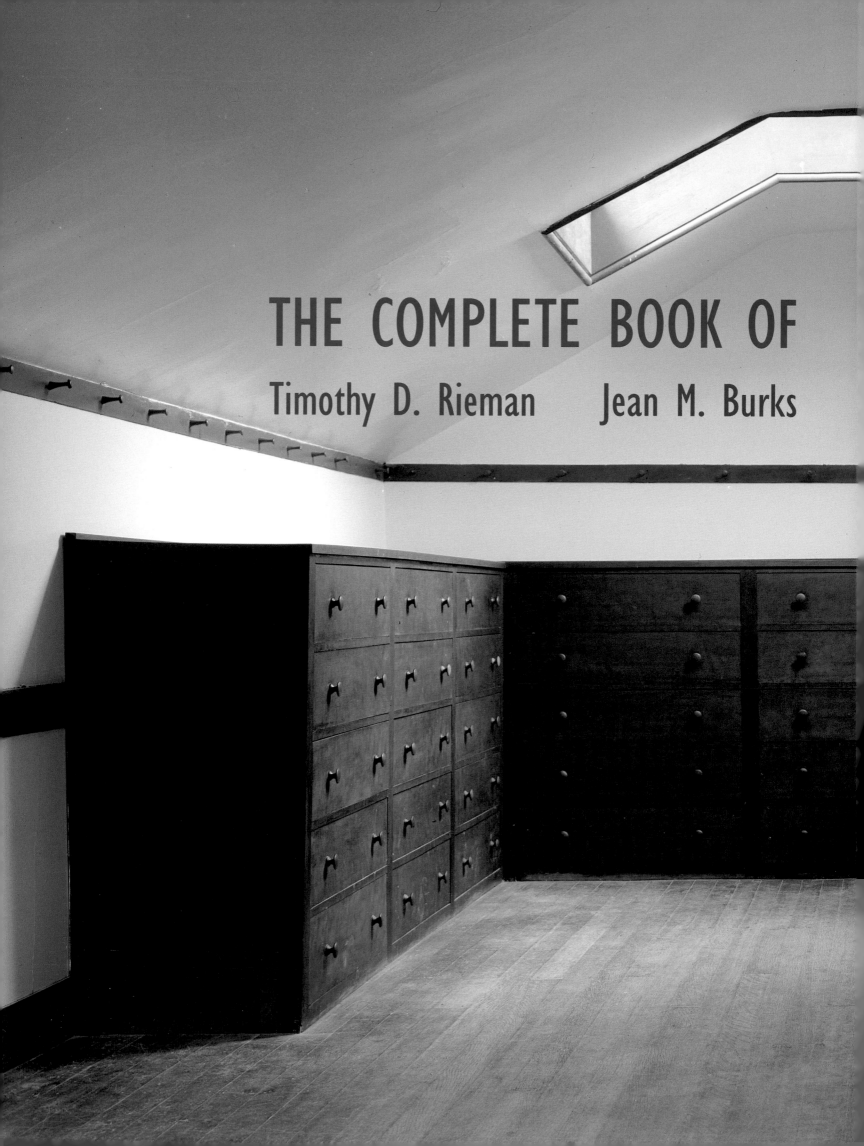

THE COMPLETE BOOK OF

Timothy D. Rieman   Jean M. Burks

Shaker Furniture

Harry N. Abrams, Inc., Publishers

Page 1: Rocker, Harvard, Massachusetts, c. 1830. Curly maple and pine, h 51". Private collection

Page 2: Washstand, Enfield, New Hampshire, c. 1840. Pine, with walnut knobs, chrome yellow paint, and steel slip catch, h 36⅝ w 29⅞ d 17⅞". Private collection

Page 3: Desk, attributed to Delmer Wilson (1873–1961), Sabbathday Lake, Maine, c. 1890. Sycamore and pine, with cast-brass pulls and escutcheons, h 51 w 35⅛ d 23½". Collection of The United Society of Shakers, Sabbathday Lake, Maine. See p. 285, pl. 255 for discussion

Pages 4–5: Built-in Cases of Drawers, Attic, Centre Family Dwelling House, Pleasant Hill, Kentucky, 1824–34. Cherry and poplar, with varnish or shellac, h 49¼ w 114⅝, 112¾, 114⅝ d 24¾". Collection of Shaker Village of Pleasant Hill, Harrodsburg, Kentucky. See p. 325, pl. 285 for discussion

EDITOR: *Lory Frankel*
DESIGNER: *Darilyn Lowe Carnes*

Library of Congress Cataloging-in-Publication Data

Rieman, Timothy D.
   The complete book of Shaker furniture / Timothy D. Rieman, Jean M. Burks.
      p.   cm.
   Includes bibliographical references and index.
   ISBN 0–8109–3841–3
   1. Furniture, Shaker.   I. Burks, Jean M., 1949– .   II. Title.
NK2407.R54   1993
749.213'08'8288—dc20   92–47357
                                                              CIP

Text copyright © 1993 Timothy D. Rieman and Jean M. Burks
Illustrations copyright © 1993 Harry N. Abrams, Inc.

Printed and bound in Japan

Contents

Acknowledgments

This book, the culmination of over ten years of research and over three years of collaboration between the authors, could not have been completed without the generous cooperation of many institutions and individuals. The information presented here could not have been gathered without the support of the following museums, whose directors, curators, librarians, and volunteer staff provided physical access to their collections, generously shared research material, and lent their particular areas of expertise to this project while pursuing their daily responsibilities: Eldress Bertha Lindsay, Scott Swank, Richard Kathmann, Charles "Bud" Thompson, Darryl Thompson, Mary Ann Sanborn, Renée Fox, Leah Gowan, and Sandy Scripture of Canterbury Shaker Village, Inc., New Hampshire; Brother Arnold Hadd, Leonard Brooks, David Richards, Paige Lilly, and Anne Gilbert of Sabbathday Lake, Maine; Maggie Stier, Fruitlands Museums, Harvard, Massachusetts; June Sprigg, Beth Parker Miller, Andy Vadnais, Magda-Gabor Hotchkiss, and Robert F.W. Meader of Hancock Shaker Village, Pittsfield, Massachusetts; John Scherer and Craig Williams of the New York State Museum, Albany; Jack Lindsay of the Philadelphia Museum of Art; Elizabeth Shaver of The Shaker Historical Society, Albany; the late Jean Hudson of the Shaker Historical Society, Shaker Heights, Ohio; Jerry Grant and Virginia McEwen of the Shaker Museum and Library, Old Chatham, New York; Tommy Hines of Shakertown at South Union, Kentucky; Larrie Currie and James Thomas of Shaker Village of Pleasant Hill, Harrodsburg, Kentucky; Mary Payne and Mickey Franer of the Warren County Historical Society, Lebanon, Ohio; Sandy Staebell of The Kentucky Museum, Western Kentucky University, Bowling Green, Kentucky; and Donald Fennimore, Neville Thompson, and E. Richard McKinstry of Winterthur Museum, Delaware. Of these, one person in particular merits special thanks and recognition: Jerry Grant provided support, numerous ideas, and information during the past decade as this book was developed.

We are indebted to the private collectors who invited us into their homes and allowed us to measure, photograph, and examine the furniture which forms the basis of this book.

We also benefited greatly from the knowledge of those individuals who have studied, lectured, and dealt in Shaker furniture: Charles R. Muller, Robert P. Emlen, Wendell Hess, John Ott, Richard Spence, Dale Covington, Sharon Edwards, Leonard Mendelsohn, Fran Kramer, Jane Stokes, Doug Hamel, John Keith Russell, David Schorsch, Bob Hamilton, Richard Rasso, Suzanne Courcier, and Robert W. Wilkins. Many of these authorities are acknowledged for their particular contribution at the beginning of each bishopric chapter.

Our special thanks go to Harry N. Abrams, Inc., for enthusiastically supporting this enterprise, in particular to Julia Moore, who initiated the project; to our editor, Lory Frankel, who saw it through to fruition; and to Darilyn Lowe Carnes, who designed the book.

Our deepest appreciation is extended to our families, Mary Boyle, Kali, and Cooper Rieman and Dan and Charlie Burks, whose patience, encouragement, and support made this endeavor possible.

Desk, Enfield, New Hampshire, c. 1860. Birch and pine, with leather and red and dark brown or black paint, h 39½ w 42 d 30". Hancock Shaker Village, Pittsfield, Massachusetts, #71–239. See page 252, pl. 208, for discussion

Introduction

SINCE THE FIRST books on Shaker life and artifacts appeared in the 1930s, appreciation of Shaker furniture in the United States, Europe, and the Far East has continued to grow at a rapid pace. This enduring and expanding interest has been stimulated by a variety of sources, including several recent television documentaries ("The Shakers: Hands to Work, Hearts to God" 1984, by Ken Burns), magazine articles (Cathy Newman, "The Shakers' Brief Eternity," *National Geographic,* September 1989), and major museum exhibitions—both national and international—devoted exclusively to Shaker design ("Shaker Design," Whitney Museum of American Art, New York, 1986, "Shaker Design: Hancock Shaker Village," Sezon Museum, Tokyo, 1992). Although the public, attracted to the clean lines, natural materials, and fine workmanship, has become familiar with the Shaker aesthetic, there is a need for information of a more technical and scholarly nature on the subject.

A primary goal of *The Complete Book of Shaker Furniture* is to develop useful criteria to help identify Shaker furniture and, when possible, to determine the community of origin, the construction date, and the name of the maker. Among the currently known and available works of Shaker craftsmanship, the authors have examined well over one thousand pieces of furniture. The final selection was based on a number of factors, including the variety of forms represented, the opportunity to present previously unpublished examples along with the familiar classics, and the strength of the documentary evidence. Due to the disappearance of several pieces that had been illustrated in old publications, it was not possible to include every item desired. Aside from small furniture accessories such as steps, racks, stools, and looking glasses, other items that have been omitted include hanging cupboards and wood boxes.

While previous writers have focused on the period of "gospel simplicity" from about 1820 to 1850 and largely ignored furniture made before and after this narrow time frame, this book examines the entire range of furniture forms produced in Shaker communities between the early nineteenth and twentieth centuries. It is our contention that the so-called Victorian era of Shaker design is a valid expression of the Believers' cabinetmaking traditions and provides insight into their material culture. These later pieces form an important part of Shaker artifactual history, and the biases of twentieth-century taste should not lead us to overlook them.

During the evaluation process it was necessary to develop a systematic plan for recording, researching, and evaluating data. Thus, the criteria used to authenticate the furniture included in this book are fourfold. The first and most important consideration was an examination of the objects themselves, including overall form, construction features, ornamental details, design characteristics, use of finish, and presence of makers' marks. While it has often been alleged that very little Shaker furniture is marked, our research indicates that more signed and dated pieces exist than had previously been identified. Using this information as well as primary documents, oral history, United States census records, and reliable secondary sources, we have compiled the names and life dates of over two hundred and fifty craftsmen.

Specific design and construction features that are examined range from wood selection, joinery techniques, profiles of moldings, and locking mechanisms

Counter, Mount Lebanon, New York, c. 1830. Pine, with dark red paint and iron lock and hinges, h 30 w 46 d 22½". Collection David Schorsch

to the style of handwriting and materials (red chalk, pencil, ink, and so on) used to mark parts for accurate assembly. All wood analysis was conducted by visual rather than microscopic examination unless otherwise indicated and is listed in the order of primary, then secondary materials; measurements for height, width, and depth are given in inches to the nearest eighth or sixteenth and represent the largest dimensions in each direction; and, in terms of orientation, each piece is discussed from the viewer's point of view. Unless noted otherwise, the object was photographed by Timothy D. Rieman. New research is presented regarding Shaker shop practices, tools, and technological changes in woodworking machinery as an aid to developing a chronological sequence of Shaker furniture production. We have closely examined the interior woodwork of extant Shaker buildings in order to determine the structural similarities with freestanding furniture. The identification of distinguishing characteristics has provided a data bank with which to compare and contrast Shaker furniture and to attribute related pieces to a specific community or maker.

Our approach makes the basic assumption that numerous consistencies exist within a craftsman's work. Both the repetitious character of woodworking and the conservative nature of traditional apprenticeship arrangements fostered a continuity of style and construction. The resulting craftsmanship of habit can be used to identify not only individual makers but different schools as well.

Schools of cabinetmaking were rarely restricted to individual communities, as there was a great deal of give and take among the Believers in different locations. The Shakers organized their communities into seven bishoprics, which included several villages in close geographic proximity. Each bishopric was governed by a ministry consisting of two elders and two eldresses responsible to the parent society at Mount Lebanon. Because of this structure, close ties developed among nearby communities where bishopric leaders divided their time and individual workers traveled back and forth, literally spreading ideas and techniques. As a result, it makes more sense to discuss styles in Shaker furniture by region rather than by individual community.

There are, of course, external influences that must be considered. For example, how will requirements, such as another member's requests, alter the maker's approach to the construction or design of a particular piece? In what way will an individual cabinetmaker's furniture change over time from his early years of apprenticeship to his work as an elderly Believer? Will another craftsman's influence be felt, given the continual turnover within the Shaker workshops? Is an apprentice's work so similar to his master's that the resulting furniture is indistinguishable? Does the cabinetmaker adapt aspects of worldly style?

A second tool was the examination of primary documents and pictorial sources specifically relating to cabinetmaking, such as diaries, journals, census records, photographs, and oral history regarding provenance. The last resource must be carefully considered, however, because Shaker furniture began to be moved from the time it left the workshop, both within the community of origin as well as to other communities. In the years of decline, some pieces were transferred to new locations with their members as various villages closed or were sold to collectors to supply a growing antiques trade.

The third criterion was a critical appraisal of secondary sources on the subject. In this respect, much of the original research about the Shakers written earlier in the century has been reexamined and reevaluated in light of new information and current research practices.

We also called on our knowledge of furniture prototypes and parallels from other cultures, both high-style and vernacular, since Shaker furniture was not produced in a vacuum. Craftsmen trained in worldly cabinetmaking techniques were familiar with contemporary taste before becoming converts to the Shaker faith. They brought their skills and sensibilities with them into the community, a situation that affected the direction of the Shaker style. Even Believers brought up and trained within the community were aware of stylistic trends in the world.

Finally, for a thorough understanding of the subject, we could not overlook the larger context in which Shaker designs were conceived and executed. An examination of more general Shaker theological writings such as letters, journals, and laws reinforced the assumption that the furniture made by the Shakers was a tangible expression of their religious beliefs. With this in mind, we considered who within the community might have been responsible for legislating Shaker design and how decisions were made that affected the style and construction of the pieces themselves.

We hope this book provides a tool for continuing inquiry into the subject of Shaker furniture and will enable the researcher, collector, and connoisseur to identify new pieces that surface both in the near and distant future as well as prove a constant source of information and visual delight to all who browse through the following pages.

Spirit drawing. 184[8?]. Signed "From Mother Ann to Amy Reed" and dated January 7, 184[8?]. Ink and watercolor, 9¾ x 15¾". Shaker Museum and Library, Old Chatham, New York, #11520

PART ONE: The Background

Shaker Origins

THE ANCESTRAL SPIRIT of Shakerism was born in eighteenth-century France.[1] A small group of persecuted Protestants known as the Camisards, seeking freedom of religious expression, fled to England in 1706. They believed that the Millennium was at hand, an idea that formed the central core of their creed. As they worshiped, they became infused with the Spirit of God; they fell into mystical trances and their bodies shook with violent agitations. In 1747, this band of French enthusiasts arrived in Manchester, where they came across a small group of radical English Quakers, including James and Jane Wardley, who had no formalized doctrine of their own. Inspired by the revivalist teachings of the Camisards, the Wardleys became the first leaders of the new sect. The group that grew around them, which included dissidents from the Anglican Church and Methodist movement, soon came to be called Shaking Quakers in derision of the agitated movement that accompanied their worship.

In 1758, the Wardleys were joined by a young woman called Ann Lees (1736–1784), later shortened to Lee. She was the second of eight children born to a blacksmith living in Manchester during the earliest phases of the Industrial Revolution, with its resulting problems of labor and pollution. The family had been forced from the land into the new slums of the factory city and were both poverty-stricken and illiterate. A contemporary account of Ann Lee's neighborhood in the 1800s described it as "one of the filthiest suburbs of the town, so confined that the winds of heaven could scarcely penetrate it."[2] Ann was variously employed at a cotton mill, a supplier of hatter's fur, and an infirmary, where, as the cook, she witnessed the despair among the poor who were sent there to die.[3] From her youth, she experienced religious impressions and divine manifestations and became convinced that human nature was sinful, particularly in respect to the lusts of the flesh. Despite her beliefs, her parents persuaded her to marry a blacksmith named Abraham Standerin in 1762. Although she agonized between her marital obligations and remorse for sexual sin, she gave birth to four children, all of whom died in infancy. Some believe the traumatic experience of this great personal loss soured her disposition toward marriage and led to her strong views regarding celibacy.

As a Shaking Quaker, Ann zealously practiced her faith and was imprisoned in 1770 for breaking Sabbath laws. While in jail, she was overwhelmed with Christ's presence. The later written accounts of this experience vary greatly: some speak of it as a vision of Christ seen with her eyes, others as a dream of the Fall of man and woman in the Garden of Eden, while another group insists the experience was not "seeing" in the physical sense but rather a transforming consciousness or unifying presence.[4] However, all writers agree that her momentous revelation was the long-awaited Second Coming of Christ. This event became the critical turning point for the first Shakers, who eventually referred to themselves as the United Society of Believers in Christ's First and Second Appearing.[5]

Unlike most Christians, who trust that the original apostles saw Christ, the Shakers actually experienced this reality for themselves. Rather than merely accepting Ann Lee's vision as a given, as she shared her perceptions with them, they were drawn into her unifying experience of Christ and became one with Him and each other. Although Lee was not worshiped as a second Messiah, the Shakers acknowledged that there had been a second revelation of the Gospel first prophesied by Jesus through a woman and realized that she acted as a catalyst by raising their consciousness of the Christ Spirit in them. The idea of a deity with dual aspects, male and female, placed women on equal footing with men. Due to her visionary insight, kindness, and leadership ability, the Shakers recognized Ann Lee as the spiritual mentor of the group and conferred on her the title of Mother. To the Shakers, the Millennium was an ongoing event that began when an individual acknowledged and confessed his or her sin to God before a witness and continued on a daily basis when he or she emulated Christ's pure and humble life on earth.

The Shakers' manner of worship and exercises in public assemblies consisted of spontaneous singing and dancing, shaking and shouting, speaking in tongues and prophesying, and other gifts of the Holy Spirit, which alienated the general public. They suffered fines, beatings, and imprisonment in their homeland, making it impossible to practice their newfound faith without persecution. As a result, Mother Ann led seven of her followers to America. They included her husband, who soon left the group; a brother, William Lee; a weaver named James Whittaker who succeeded Mother Ann for a short time following her death in 1784; and John Hocknell, a man of means who financed the trip.[6] She had a vision that the chosen people in the New World would join the Millennial church and help create an earthly paradise free from the sins of man.

After arriving quietly in New York in 1774, the group dispersed for practical reasons—to earn a living as well as to avoid provoking hostilities from their new neighbors. Some of the party journeyed up the Hudson to look for land while others separated to find work, including Mother Ann, who was employed in a laundry. After a year, they reunited at Niskeyuna, near Albany, New York, now known as Watervliet, where they leased and eventually purchased two hundred acres. For the next four years, Mother Ann and the Shakers plied their trades, planted their crops, and practiced their faith in peace while America was in the throes of the revolution against English rule.

Six years after their arrival in the New World, the Believers emerged into the public eye as a result of external events that made the Shaker community an object of interest. The country was experiencing religious upheavals following the resurgence of the "Great Awakening" several decades earlier. During the first half of the eighteenth century, many Americans, especially New Englanders, complained that organized religion had lost its vitality. The religious leaders throughout the British American colonies were conscious of this spiritual decline and felt the need to renew a deeper interest in Christianity. At this point, an unprecedented evangelical outpouring called the Great Awakening swept over the colonies. During the 1740s and 1750s, many congregations were split between defenders of the new emotional preaching and those who clung to more traditional practices. By the 1780s, the vitality of this movement had abated and many radical Baptists in rural New England and New York who had become disillusioned were searching for a pure religion. To these Americans looking for a new way of life, the Shakers seemed to provide a welcome change. With old norms uncertain, new ideas flourished. It is not surprising that the Shaker philosophy brought a message of hope to a generation of Americans who wanted to participate in the reshaping of the world. This widespread unrest in communities, families, and churches was to prove extremely advantageous to the establishment and rapid spread of America's most successful communal sect.

J. Becker. "The Shakers of New Lebanon—
Religious Exercises in the Meeting-House."
Woodcut engraving. Published in *Frank Leslie's
Illustrated Newspaper*, November 1, 1873. Pri-
vate collection

The Square House at Harvard, Massachusetts, c. 1910. Shaker Museum and Library,
Old Chatham, New York, #3998.23

View of Church Family buildings at Mount Lebanon, New York, c. 1870. Photograph by James Irving, Troy, New York. Shaker Museum and Library, Old Chatham, New York, #11311

It was into this emotionally charged environment that Mother Ann and her followers emerged from seclusion and traveled on missionary trips throughout eastern New York, Massachusetts, and Connecticut from 1781 to 1783. They converted many congregations to their faith and laid the foundation for several Shaker villages that would arise later. However, the spread of Shakerism brought in its wake immediate persecution. With the American Revolution at its height, suspicion immediately focused on these strange English enthusiasts who preached pacifism at a time when most patriots were taking up arms against the crown. Furthermore, the general public was outraged at the concept of celibacy and the idea of full equality of women and men, which threatened to break up families. The Shakers were accused of being British agents and of witchcraft, drunkenness, and a host of other crimes.[7] As a result of frequent beatings, years of deprivation, and strenuous preaching, Mother Ann died in 1784 before the first American Shaker community was officially established. The leadership of the society went briefly to James Whittaker (1751–1787), who called on Believers to gather together and form their own villages apart from their neighbors. He oversaw the building of the first meetinghouse and established the New Lebanon community in 1787, which initiated the communal form of Shaker life.[8]

Shaker orthodoxy called for celibacy, physical separation from the world, and common property holdings, as well as the confession of sins, equality of the sexes, and pacifism. Seventy-five years before the emancipation of the slaves and one hundred and fifty years before women received the vote in America, the Shakers were living in a small society that strove to redress the imbalance in social, sexual, and economic issues. By removing themselves from the imperfect world in order to live a blameless life, the Shakers pursued their mission to live as near as possible to Christ's teachings and make the way of God their own. Purity of mind and body, honesty and integrity, industry and diligence, physical and spiritual order, prudence and economy, plainness and simplicity, and humanity and kindness were the Believers' goals. By following these guiding principles, the Shakers sought to create for themselves a kingdom of heaven on earth, striving for perfection in their work and worship.

Shakerism represented one of hundreds of Utopian experiments that were launched across America in a fever of idealism, including such groups as the Oneidans, the Harmonists, and the Ephratans, to mention a few. The Shakers shared with these other communitarians the dream of a better life outside of society. Rather than trying to change the system from within or to overthrow it, their goal was to create an ideal society that could eventually foster universal reforms. However, the Shakers endured while most other Utopian communities eventually failed. A key ingredient of their success was what they simply called union, which can be defined as similarity of opinion and interest. It was "the cement" or the "golden chain" joining individual souls to the fountain of good, the gospel of pure love. Consequently, the Believers were consolidated in thought, word, and deed, and each member put the needs of the group above self-interest.

The fundamental constituents of Shaker spirituality are rooted in the mystical experience of personal union with Christ through the gift of divine revelation.[9] This ongoing relationship between the spiritual and the temporal, belief and practice, was explained by Harvard cabinetmaker Elijah Myrick, who wrote, "All discoveries, inventions, improvements in the arts and sciences, are so many revelations emanating from the same source as the spiritual."[10] It was part and parcel of the Shakers' philosophy to seek harmony between their spiritual and physical environments. Consequently, one way to analyze Shaker design is to understand their philosophy, which became the force behind their design.

Unfortunately, very little doctrinal material was written down during the formative years of Shaker religion, either during Mother Ann's leadership or when Mother Lucy Wright (1760–1821) and Father Joseph Meacham (1742–1796) assumed its direction and organized the society into his hierarchical governmental structure, called Gospel Order. Joseph Meacham had the greatest impact on the conduct and organization of the United Society after Mother Ann. He established the communitarian system associated with the Shaker movement, structured its administrative organization, and codified the doctrines of the sect.[11] However, the conspicuous absence of primary sources can be attributed to a number of basic factors, including the Believers' continuous struggle for survival, the efforts spent gathering new members, and the time and energy required to establish and build communities throughout the Northeast. At the same time, the leaders deliberately avoided printing rules, which might become too rigid for the essential dynamism inherent in Shakerism or could be used by critics against the faith.[12] Reconstructing the age of the founders has been made very difficult due to this early hostility of the leaders toward written creeds or statements of faith. This opposition stemmed in part from Ann Lee's illiteracy, which fueled her mistrust of the written word, as well as the Shakers' deununciation of established ecclesiastical practices found in formal theological documents.[13] As a result, there were few written regulations up until the early nineteenth century, when an attempt was made to describe the doctrines and the temporal order of the society.

There exist three theological documents written between 1808 and 1823, which present a formal statement of Shaker identity and provide considerable insight into the basic tenets of the Shaker faith. The spiritual progress of Believers envisioned in these sources directly influenced the shape taken by the temporal products of Shaker hands.

The earliest document, the *Testimony of Christ's Second Appearing* by Benjamin Seth Youngs, was first printed in Lebanon, Ohio, in 1808 and reprinted two years later in Albany, New York. An impressive theological work of six hundred pages known as the Shaker Bible, it traced the history of Christianity from the creation to the appearance of the Christ figure and the Second Coming of Christ embodied by Ann Lee. The importance of union, oneness, and harmony with God was emphasized over and over again. As early as 1808, Benjamin Youngs clearly made the connection between the heavenly and earthly spheres and the need to integrate both worlds, stating, "No external exercise can be anything more than an outward expression of an inward spiritual sensation of love and obedience to God."[14]

Particularly for those who joined the faith after Mother Ann's death, the ideals she expressed needed a more concrete form to help new converts feel her presence. It was not until 1816 that Rufus Bishop and Seth Youngs Wells compiled the *Testimonies of the Life, Character, Revelations and Doctrines of Our Ever Blessed Mother Ann Lee*. Sometimes called the "secret book of the Elders," this 405-page volume contains the earliest record of the life, teachings, and precepts of Mother Ann based on the eye- and ear-witness accounts of her spiritual children in the form of personal testimonies. Another book of recollections was published in 1827, and the original 1816 edition was reissued in 1888. Simplicity, cleanliness, order, industry, and perfection—the themes that run throughout the *Testimonies*—reflect Mother Ann's goal to cultivate purity in all things, both in the philosophical foundation of the Believers' life-style and the physical environment in which they lived. A Christian world that fostered the simple life was essential to the realization of her vision. For the same reason, it was important to remove the temptations of the styles and fashions of the world from the Shakers' everyday lives and keep them out. In order to retain a singleness of heart wholly directed to the honor and glory of God, Mother Ann cautioned her followers to eliminate all superfluous objects that feed their vanity, as illustrated in one story from the *Testimonies*:

> Phoebe Spencer, being on a visit to the Church, at Watervliet, asked Mother's council concerning some superfluities which she and her family had gathered, such as gold beads, jewels, silver buckles and other ornaments of the kind. Mother Ann answered, "You may let the moles and bats have them; that is the children of this world; for they set their hearts upon such things; but the people of God do not want them."[15]

The following parable recorded in the chapter "Counsel in Temporal Things" from the *Testimonies* is one of the few of Mother Ann's quotes that relate directly to owning elaborate furniture and material goods:

> While Mother was at Petersham [in 1783], she took an opportunity to instruct some of the heads of families, who were there, concerning their temporal economy; and admonished them against some of their costly and extravagant furniture, and said, "Never put on silver spoons nor table cloths for me; but let your table be clean enough to eat on without table cloths; and if you do not know what to do with them give them to the poor."[16]

Mother Ann specifically preached on the subject of household possessions and urged the importance of temporal economy. Material goods such as furniture were to be functional and humble, not fashionable and grandiose. She implied that to revel in the extravagance of an object not only opened up the heart to pride, vanity, or lust but, by extension, corrupted the natural materials and practical purpose of the piece itself.

Mother Ann's focus on the temporal world was a crucial factor in the spiritual development of each member. By manipulating earthly surroundings, the heavenly progress of each member could be affected in a positive way. The following anecdote taken from the *Testimonies* illustrates the connection between the two spheres: "Lucy Bishop [of the Hancock community] was once scrubbing a room and Mother Ann came in and said: 'Clean your room well; for good spirits will not dwell where there is dirt. There is no dirt in heaven.' "[17] By explicitly relating the two worlds, Mother Ann defined the Believers' goals and directed them to recreate a heaven on earth.

The Believers' focus of creating a heavenly counterpart on earth was of critical importance, for the Shakers believed their duty to God entailed working to support and improve the physical nature of the community. The physical process of designing and building a community of Believers integrated the temporal and spiritual elements within the Shaker religion. Members found that the creation of their environment represented an activity broad enough in scope to accommodate their aspiration to turn the earth into heaven.[18]

Pride in workmanship was one inevitable result of this religious focus on work. Yet the origin of this concept rested not in the earthly sphere but in the heavenly realm. Without pride in their work, the Shakers could never have fashioned objects of such enduring quality and appeal, but excessive pride was frowned upon because the Believers recognized that no achievement could exist without God's help. As members tried to make the work of their hands fit for an earthly heaven, a certain measure of pride was unavoidable.[19] The close connection between work and worship is summed up by the often quoted parable related in the *Testimonies*:

> A certain youth came one day to Mother Ann, with some peach and plum stones in his hand, and asked her if he might plant them. "Yeah," she replied, "do all your work as tho you had a thousand years to live, and as you would if you knew you must die tomorrow."[20]

Patient perfectionism was clearly linked with revivalist urgency. Converts developed into community members whose building skills became legendary.[21] Mother Ann's message to her followers was to devote all their time to pursuing a godly way of life, and work was an important ingredient in the society's recipe for gospel union.

A third Shaker document, *A Summary View of the Millennial Church or United Society of Believers*, 1823, by Calvin Green and Seth Youngs Wells, was composed in response to the request of the Russian consul from New York, who visited the North Family at Mount Lebanon. He wanted an expression of the faith and practice of Believers that he might translate and publish it in Russia.[22] Green and Wells later revised and enlarged the work to the dimensions of the present volume (384 pages). In this document, the beliefs of Mother Ann were further organized and refined as the Shakers attempted to inspire, evangelize, and defend their beliefs against critical apostates and theologians. This exposition of the views of the church provides another basis for understanding the process of Shaker furniture design. *The Millennial Church* explains the connection between the ruling principles of the Believers' lives and the fruits of their labor. In discussing their communities, the authors describe the twelve governing Christian virtues. Among them they emphasize the personal values of honesty, prudence, and simplicity. Believers are warned,

The professor of Christianity who is not honest and sincere, in all his conduct and conversation, who uses any dissimulation, or seeks to cover any of his conduct, in word or deed, under the cloak of deception, who designedly deviates from the truth, in any respect, and does not honestly do good and shun evil, and conduct himself in all things, according to his best light and understanding, transgresses the divine principle of honesty, and sins against God.

The authors praise the prudent individual who "is watchful over all his words and actions; he is careful and discreet in all things. He is industrious and faithful in his duty, both in things spiritual and temporal . . . and makes a wise and temperate use and improvement of all things committed to this charge, according to the best of his understanding and abilities." Finally, simplicity is defined as

A real singleness of heart in all our conversation and conduct. . . . Its thoughts, words and works are plain and simple. . . . It is without ostentation, parade or any vain show, and naturally leads to plainness in all things. In all the objects of its pursuit, in all the exercise of its power, in all its communications of good to others, it is governed solely by the will of God and shows forth its peculiar singleness of heart and mind in all things.[23]

It is not a coincidence that the guiding principles of honesty, prudence, and simplicity were crucial in establishing a particular style of furniture. Consciously and subconsciously these spiritual concepts dictated such material choices as design, color, and even use, both in furniture and architecture. Believers trying to create a heaven on earth as part of their daily routine strived for perfection in all things, which included furniture making. The importance of this virtue is explicitly addressed in the section entitled "A few remarks concerning the true nature of perfection." Wells and Green clearly connect the spiritual concept with temporal objects, then they explain,

Any thing may, with strict propriety, be called perfect, which perfectly answers the purpose for which it was designed. A circle may be called a perfect circle, when it is perfectly round; an apple may be called perfect, when it is perfectly sound, having no defect in it; and so of a thousand other things.[24]

The authors urge all Believers attempting to live a Christian life to improve constantly their ability to attain spiritual perfection in every thought, word, and deed. This philosophy naturally carried over into the Shakers' daily routine and affected the quality of their products in a positive way.[25]

Ann Lee, who died in 1784, was never to see an established Shaker village set apart from the outside world. However, her teachings were put into practice by the first American leaders of the sect, Joseph Meacham and Lucy Wright. In the decade that followed, spiritual visions of a heaven on earth were transformed into a physical reality. While ideas, theology, and divine revelations formed the spiritual basis of this new community, new buildings, expanded farmlands, and small industries constituted the temporal aspect of a new social order. The first meetinghouse built at Mount Lebanon in 1785 and the prototypes that followed at other communities not only provided a physical space for worship but also satisfied a philosophical need to redesign a new and better world and addressed the Shakers' spiritual desire for union or oneness in all matters.

This concept of uniformity in design to be followed in building Shaker communities was addressed for the first time in the early manuscript writings of

Father Joseph Meacham dating from 1790, later compiled by Rufus Bishop in 1850. He focused on the issue of spiritual domination over the earthly sphere and gave instructions to the Shakers concerning temporal matters as well as the establishment of order, duties, and responsibilities.

> All work done, or things made in the Church for their own use ought to be faithfully and well done, but plain and without superfluity. All things ought to be made according to their order and use; and all things kept decent and in good order, according to their order and use. All things made for sale ought to be well done, and suitable for their use. . . . We have a right to improve the inventions of man so far as it is useful and necessary, but not to vain glory or anything superfluous. Plainness and simplicity in both word and deed is becoming the Church and the people of God. Order and conveniency and decency in things temporal.[26]

Father Meacham's mandates represent the first known written regulation of Shaker design. Because of Mother Lucy's fear that a written body of laws might tend to become crystallized and adversely affect the development of the communities or be used by apostates, these regulations governing the society were initially transmitted orally and not widely circulated. Constantly in the process of modification as circumstances required, they were intended only to guide the lead ministry, which was responsible for the development of the autocratic leadership structure. However, soon after the death of Lucy Wright in 1821, the society's leadership took another step toward institutionalization through the codification of these precepts and bylaws as "Orders and Rules of the Church at New Lebanon: Millennial Laws of Gospel Statutes & Ordinances," although they were never published and restricted still to the leadership. While it must be remembered that these "Orders and Rules" were never considered definitive, they greatly illuminate both the government of the order as well as the intimate habits and customs of the people.[27]

The "Millennial Laws" were revised numerous times since they were first implemented. Known copies of 1821, 1845, 1860, and 1887 still exist. Since each version covered a wide variety of issues based on the changing needs of the society, these documents were dynamic rather than static. The bulk of the 1821 "Orders and Rules" deals with spiritual matters such as confession of sin, worship of God, and religious duties, as well as with daily activities, to include the following topics: rules to be observed in going abroad; orders of safety and caution to prevent loss by fire; concerning good order in eating, and so on. Little regarding the products of Shaker hands is discussed, except the general statement, "Members of the church of God . . . are forbidden to make anything for Believers that will have a tendency to feed . . . pride and vanity."[28]

The "Millennial Laws" of 1845 provide an extensive outline of "The General Organization of Society," that is, the community structure of different families and the system of governing by the ministry, elders, and deacons, as originally formulated by Father Joseph Meacham in the 1790s. This document also defined the responsibilities, roles, and duties of various leadership levels within the Shaker community.

According to Father Joseph's organizational structure, supreme authority over the whole United Society of Believers was vested in the central or lead ministry at Mount Lebanon, made up of two elders and two eldresses who received their inspiration directly from Mother Ann. These leaders appointed the branch ministries, consisting in turn of two elders and eldresses serving several outlying

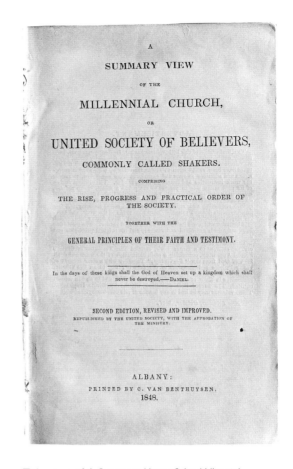

Title page of *A Summary View of the Millennial Church, or United Society of Believers* by Calvin Green and Seth Youngs Wells. Albany: Van Benthuysen, 1848. Private collection

societies, which were usually grouped into bishoprics, determined by geographic proximity. Each community contained several families of up to one hundred individual members who were to "acknowledge and look to their [family] Elders as their lead and protection, in all things." Hence, the government of all spiritual matters was entrusted to the eldership, who received their orders directly from the lead ministry at Mount Lebanon. The temporal affairs of each family was the specific realm of the deacons, generally two of each sex, who took their instructions from the family elders. It was their responsibility to see to "the domestic concerns of the family in which they reside" and manage the daily work of the family. Four trustees were selected to oversee each family's finances and business transactions with the world's people. Believers were instructed to consult the proper authority for the specific tasks. For example, "If sisters desire tools, conveniences, or articles of manufacture which come in the brethren's line of business, and which it would require much time to make, they must apply to the Deaconesses—but if it be small chores, they may apply to either Deacons or Deaconesses for the same."[29] In this way, Gospel Order was maintained throughout the Shaker society and appointments always moved from head to foot, as follows:

CHRIST
Mother Ann
Central Ministry at Mount Lebanon
Bishopric Ministries
Community Church Family Elders/Eldresses
Family Elders/Eldresses
Church Family Deacons and Trustees   Family Deacons and Trustees

The 1845 "Millennial Laws" contain detailed written references regarding the design, construction, and care of furniture—the first in known Shaker documents. For example, the ministry emphasized the need for Believers to use and manufacture only plain and unembellished articles in their communities, for unnecessary adornment was believed to "feed the pride and vanity of man":

> Fancy articles of any kind, or articles which are superfluously finished, trimmed or ornamented, are not suitable for Believers, and may not be used or purchased . . . [such as] brass knobs or handles of any size or kind. . . . Superfluously finished or flowery painted clocks, bureaus and looking glasses. . . .

Decorative woodwork and elaborate finishes were also not allowed, according to the following directive:

> Beadings, mouldings and cornices which are merely for fancy may not be made by Believers. Odd or fanciful styles of architecture, may not be used among Believers, neither should any deviate widely from the common styles of building among Believers, without the union of the Ministry. . . . Varnish, if used in dwelling houses, may be applied only to the moveables therein, as the following, viz., tables, stands, bureaus, cases of drawers, writing desks, or boxes, drawer faces, chests, chairs, etc. etc.[30]

In an effort to promote unity and uniformity on a temporal level, the 1845 "Millennial Laws" outlined the appropriate furnishings for retiring rooms:

> Bedsteads should be painted green. . . . One rocking chair in a room is sufficient, except where the aged reside. One table, one or two stands, a lamp stand may be attached to the woodwork, if desired. One good looking

glass, which ought not to exceed eighteen inches in length, and twelve in width, with a plain frame. A looking glass larger than this, ought never to be purchased by Believers. If necessary a small glass may hang in the closet, and a very small one may be kept in the public cupboard of the room.

Information governing the care of furnishings is also covered with specific directives, such as, "No one should lean back against the wall, bed, or ceiling of dwelling rooms. It is also wrong to sit with the feet on the rounds of chairs. . . . " "All should be careful not to mar or destroy the furniture in their shops or rooms."[31]

Of particular interest are the regulations that outline the absolute control exercised by the lead ministry. Its authority dominated all other levels, because in the Shaker world, spiritual precepts dictated temporal affairs: "No new fashions in manufacture, clothing or wares of any kind, may be introduced into the Church of God without the sanction of the Ministry, thro the medium of the Elders of each family thereof." However, the day-to-day decisions regarding the family's domestic affairs, including matters involving furniture, were the responsibility of the deacons: "It is the duty of the Deacons and Deaconesses to see that suitable furniture for rooms . . . are provided. . . . " "If any person or persons, mar, break or destroy any article or articles of furniture in the retiring rooms, it is such an one's duty, to

Bed, probably Harvard, Massachusetts, c. 1840. Private collection. Photograph: courtesy John Keith Russell Antiques, Inc.

acknowledge the same to the Deacons or Deaconesses, as the case may be and if possible to repair the injury."[32]

Unfortunately, the 1845 "Millennial Laws" are the version most often quoted by writers on the Shakers today. The repeated reference to this document in secondary sources perpetuates the view that it represented the norm for the Believers' daily behavior during the greater part of their history. The reality is that the "Millennial Laws" of 1845 are a product of that era of spiritual ferment and searching in which they were written.[33]

This unique spiritual revival, known as Mother Ann's Work, took hold among the Believers throughout Shakerdom from the late 1830s until about 1850. This period witnessed an influx of manifestations from the spirit world, resulting in thousands of songs, visionary drawings of heaven, and new revelations of God's written word. These gifts and messages were presented by divine inspiration to sensitive members called instruments and shared with the rest of the community. The excitement of Mother's Work was viewed by some devout Believers as a necessary antidote to the insidious spiritual lassitude that had crept into the United Society. One authority feels this spiritual decay was caused by demographic imbalances that had been developing for many years and was evident in the decline of the quality of leadership and the growing proportion of children and young converts who had never experienced a conversion firsthand.[34] In any event, some ministry leaders at Mount Lebanon viewed the revival as an opportunity to purge the church of a certain worldliness. According to one source, the central leadership told Shakers in every community that Mother Ann wanted her children to return to the purity and plainness of her time.[35] From this perspective, the existence of the 1845 laws in stronger language than the previous version indicates that the situations described in the text already existed. These rules were required to purge Believers of temporal excess and to bring them back to orthodoxy. They may have been put in writing to provide guidance for backsliders. There is no evidence that the "Millennial Laws" continued to be seriously observed after the works of spirit manifestation began their decline. There is, on the contrary, much to indicate that they themselves were symbolic indications of the fact that the era of Mother's Work had reached its peak and that the psychic would play an increasingly less important part in the life of Believers.

The decade of the 1850s heralded a steady return to those communal orders from the past that were more deeply rooted both in tradition and common sense.[36] According to the Mount Lebanon ministry, the new written framework was both a revision and reestablishment of the laws previously in effect and culminated in the "Rules and Orders for the Church of Christ's Second Appearing," issued in 1860. However, the most striking aspect of the new rules is the amount and type of information presented in comparison with the 1845 version. The later regulations are more general and provide less specific restrictions regarding furniture construction, design, or use. Rather than including a long, detailed list of all the superfluous articles that Believers may not make or purchase, the orders succinctly state, "The furniture of dwelling rooms, among Believers, should be plain in style, and unembellished by stamps, flowers, paintings and gildings of any kind: and looking glasses ought not to be purchased by Believers, exceeding about 12 by 20 inches."[37]

The question remains how the specific information contained in all the rules and orders were communicated and interpreted to the society's members. It was Father Joseph Meacham who first drew up certain bylaws "forbidding what was wrong and enjoining what was right" in order to ensure internal harmony within the communities through which the religious ideals of the church were finding expression.[38] In the union meetings that he instituted in 1798, the brethren and sisters, according to Edward Deming Andrews (1894–1964), an early scholar of the Shakers, came together for social or religious discourse. There, they often repeated many of these regulations until they became the ingrained tradition of communal procedure.[39] Indoctrination in both spiritual and temporal matters was primarily through an oral rather than written tradition. William J. Haskett, a former Shaker, writing of his experiences in 1828, stated:

> These "orders and gifts" are the articles of the constitution, to which the members must conform. They were never hitherto, written; but committed to memory. In this, as in many other points, they are like the Druids, whose political creed says: "Let no lessons in *writing* be given." "Trust all to *memory*, that Great Gift of heaven." For the instruction of the members, the Elders order every one to repeat the "Gifts" in private meetings. They say them thus. "It is contrary to order for one to do such a thing," and every person both male and female repeats some order. Hence all become acquainted with them. These orders, the Elders declare come from God through the ministry, who every short time, as circumstances may require, introduce some new ones. These are mentioned in meeting by the Elder, who informs the members, as these are the gifts of God from the ministry, to disobey or act contrawise is, unless confessed, punishable with the displeasure of God and probably with his reprobation."[40]

Freegift Wells, a brother and elder from the Watervliet, New York, community, wrote in his journal on November 16, 1817, this "afternoon we read mothers sayings," and on April 5, 1818, "Today we finished reading mothers sayings."[41] A Harvard journal entry dated April 26, 1842, reveals more specifically the content of one such meeting: "Evening reading. Hear a communication from Father James to the Brethren in five parts about temporal things. To be read 4 times a year."[42] This may refer to the public reading of the "Holy Laws of Zion," to remind the brethren to incorporate these temporal regulations into their daily lives.

The issue of union was essential to Shaker communism. Believers were bound together in a united interest, to the effect that the community rather than the individual prevailed. But how was uniformity in temporal matters maintained both within each village as well as among different communities?

The organizational structure of the church, first established by Joseph Meacham in the 1780s, clearly specified the relationship between the spiritual and temporal leaders within the Shaker order. According to this system, appointments moved always from head to foot, as explained in his "Way Marks," a document that linked the heavenly and earthly spheres. Deacons and trustees were to be obeyed in their orders, just as the elders were obeyed in theirs. The elevated status of the leadership is outlined in two references, the first written by a disaffected Believer who eventually left the society, the second by a respected Shaker leader:

> . . . they have *private* meetings consisting only of the first Elder, Eldresses, Deacons and Deaconesses in which, they transact business. These are held in the meeting houses and no members being admitted, they fasten the doors, perhaps only to secure themselves from an interruption of business. The proceedings of these meetings are kept secret.[43]

In 1856, Isaac Newton Youngs reported that "a change was made at the table today in the order of seeting. . . . The Deacons *all* set now at the middle table— family Deacons at the north Side, & John Dean at the [head] West end & the

Office Trustees on the South side."[44] This physical segregation of the deacons suggests a hierarchical relationship in the society's organizational structure.

All leaders were reminded that they should not judge an issue that was out of their domain. Elders were not to meddle in business affairs, and deacons were to keep out of spiritual matters.[45] From the beginning, the deacons were responsible for all temporal activities of the family, a role that is reiterated in the 1821 "Orders and Rules" and the 1845 "Millennial Laws," as previously explained. As early as 1791, it fell to Deacon Jonathan Walker of the Second Family at Mount Lebanon to have the "chief care and oversight relating to the order of buildings, yards and fences." His work was "to lay out the order of the buildings, and to see that the foundations are laid well, that the buildings are not exposed to be damaged by the frost in winter, and to see that the materials for buildings are suitable for their use, according to the order and use of the buildings and that the work is done in due order."[46] A note preceding the section of manuscript entitled "Changes in the Family Deaconship in the former 2nd family of the Church" by Isaac Newton Youngs much later further explains that "Jonathan Walker acted much of the time as a . . . superintendent of Temporal concerns, together with Joseph Bennet [deacon 1788–98] and Richard Spier [deacon 1788–1824] who resided in the first family. Jonathan acted mostly in the line of building while Richard attended principally to providing for the table and common domestic matters assisted by Joseph Bennet."[47]

Meetings between elders and deacons were frequently recorded:

November 30, 1820 This evening there was a meeting at the office comps'd principally of deacons their business was to conclude in what manner to proceed in building a house at the south house &c. . . .

December 27, 1830 The Elders & Deacons have had a meeting to settle matters about building & have agreed to put off building a barn for the office, but have agreed that the second order may put up their waggon house. . . . [48]

June 28, 1842 Elder Freegift submitted the matter of the new Centre house, [at South Union] as to its plan, dimensions &c. &c. to the Elders & Deacons of the Chh., who were authorized to settle upon such a plan as would give the best satisfaction. This evening Daniel Sering, Abner Beadle, James McNemar and Andrew C. Houston were appointed a committee to draft a plan as soon as possible, and present it for consideration. . . .

June 30, 1842 This evening a meeting of the Elders and Deacons of the Church and several others were assembled to examine the draft & plan of the aforesaid house as proposed by said committee. After examination it met with a general & hearty approval.[49]

Another series of journal entries at Harvard illustrates the decision-making process as well as the specific persons involved in matters of temporal interest:

January 10, 1842 Evening the Ministry Elder trustees and Deacons meet together at the office to talk about a new house. . . .

February 1, 1842 The trustees and Family Deacons meet together in union meeting at the office. . . . [50]

July 31, 1845 In the morning the ministry Elders and Deacons meet to agree on some plan for extending the Nursery business. . . .

April 8, 1846 The ministry Elders and Deacons meet together this eve to plan and arrange temporal affairs. . . . [51]

More specifically, "An Extract from the Holy Orders of the Church" of 1841 states, "It will often be necessary to have more than one table in a room, but of this, the Elders and Deacons must be the judges."[52] These writers at several different communities mention a variety of temporal issues, including architecture and gardening. Based on their observations, it is reasonable to assume that the deacons were responsible for decisions regarding furniture construction, design, and use on a regular basis, although no documentation seems to have survived to support this.

Another method of promoting union was through written directives, called circulars, emanating from the central ministry to the outlying communities. Some were dictated by heavenly parents and recorded by human instruments, such as the council "Concerning . . . Spirits, Wine, Cider, Tobacco, Meat, Tea & Coffee" presented by Father William and received by the elders of the First Order on May 18, 1841.[53] The "Circular Concerning the Dress of Believers" written by Giles Avery in 1864 is very specific regarding the need for union among Believers:

> There are very strong reasons in favor of uniformity, both in *style* or *pattern* of dress, and *color* and *quality* of dress fabrics; each one, and all of these subjects, effects, materially, the welfare and prosperity of Believers, both spiritually, socially and financially. Spiritually, because uniformity in style, or pattern in dress, contributes to unanimity of feeling; uniformity of color, and quality have the same effect, and largely so too; because equality of furnish in dress, between members, contributes to peace and union in spirit, inasmuch as the ends of justice are answered, and righteousness and justice are necessary companions. . . . Another subject we should mention in this Circular, is the manifest decline from our standard fashion of uniformity in hats. *Mere fashion* is a cruel tyrant, but consistency is jewel; and *constancy* in consistency, is a diadem of beauty. To the adoption of real improvement, we have no objection; but in this, Zion, should revolutionize *centrifugally* and *not* centripetally; that is, whatever reformations are introduced, should be done in order, and proceed from Zion's centre, outward, and not from her circumference inward.[54]

According to a notation dated October 17, 1865, "Officials of Society of Canterbury meet this evening to hear the dress Circular. Read & see samples of cloths & give their opinion concerning the suggestions of Circular. All full agree in all its sentiments & endorse freely."[55] To summarize, in the words of the Shakers by means of a circular epistle, "It is therefore of essential importance to the maintenance of union & good order, that Believers, in all their labors for new improvements, whether in machinery, dress, manners or customs, should be careful to proceed in union; and by no means to introduce new things into the Society without the consent and approbation of the Ministry & leading authourity of the Church."[56]

It is not known how much authority these temporal leaders delegated to individual craftsmen producing furniture in accordance with Shaker beliefs. Were the cabinetmakers free to interpret the principles of the spoken or written word in their furniture, or were all aspects of their work subject to the scrutiny and approval of the family deacon as well as answerable to a higher authority? An important series of letters between Elder Grove Blanchard at Harvard and the western Massachusetts bishopric leadership provides insight into temporal issues being brought to ministry-level leadership for approval: namely, the time and effort invested in changing the design of chairs. Excerpts from these letters continuously mention the need for union, obtaining a proper pattern, and the importance of approval from the fountainhead:

Enfield, August 15, 1853 Elder Harvey & Others are all pleased with the preliminary steps you have taken in order to secure at the outset a proper pattern of that necessary & convenient article of household furniture. And should circumstances operate favorably you may consider it as pretty much settled for some one or ones to meet you at Lovely Vineyard and pass upon the comelings of the improved pattern. . . .

Watch-Hill, Westerly [Rhode Island], August 25, 1853 If you could consistantly leave home for a few days to take the Sample Chair when done and come to Enfield, where we can all look at it and suggest sutch alterations as may appear adviseable & &. . . .

City of Union, August 31, 1853 Respecting the Chair business, we unite with you in having a sample (as soon as consistant) forwarded to Shaker Village, & have them inspected at Holy Mount, as it appears to be a matter of considerable consequence to get something started right & something which can be owned and blessed at the fountain head, seeing that we are agoing to vary from the old standard among believers. . . .

West Pittsfield, December 2nd 1853 The Ministry at Holy Mount feel considerable interest in the new fashioned chairs & they hope there may be somthing [sic] got up about right which will do for believers to pattern after, & will be an improvement as to chairs.[57]

Their efforts were apparently successful, for on January 2, 1854, Elder Grove Blanchard and Elder William Leonard of Harvard visited Enfield, Connecticut, "with a new style of chair which it was proposed to introduce among Believers."[58] Three days later they traveled to Mount Lebanon with the sample chairs and then to Hancock.

It is not known how frequently this type of exchange occurred, but it is certain that union, or consensus of opinion, was essential in maintaining the spiritual bond of the society as well as in introducing something new in the temporal sphere. It also shows the influence of hierarchy in such design matters.

Insight into how discussions may have proceeded regarding radical changes in furniture design is seen in the following dialogue on the use of varnish. As stated earlier, the 1845 "Millennial Laws" included specific directives on the use of varnish, which was allowed only on "moveable" furnishings and not on "ceilings, casings, or mouldings."[59] In 1865, these limitations were questioned by Brother Orren Haskins (1815–1892), a cabinetmaker at the Church Family, in correspondence between him and Daniel Boler, a member of the lead ministry, regarding the use of varnish on the interior woodwork of their buildings at Mount Lebanon. Elder Daniel's reply addresses the issue of changing rules and practices at the ministry level and illuminates the Shakers' decision-making process. He explained:

Some of the Elders and Deacons at least, may recollect the last general meeting that was held on that subject; and may also recollect the decision of that meeting. . . . At that time was unanimously agreed that Tables, stands, Cases of drawers with Cupboards attached, (& such like wooden furniture which might be termed movable appendages to our dwelling or retiring rooms), might receive a coat of Varnish. . . . It is quite possible that the time has arriven to have another general council held on the same subject. . . . "The world has moved" since that time.[60]

This important discussion implies that the "general meeting" was an oral rather than written procedure for reviewing or changing specific furniture-making practices, but it is not known which community members were allowed to attend. Presumably the ministry leaders, family deacons, and some craftsmen were included in these sessions, but there is no written documentation to substantiate this assumption.

Evidence based on journal entries suggests that individual Shaker craftsmen were influenced by spiritual powers. In his autobiographical writings, David Rowley, a cabinetmaker at Mount Lebanon, described some visionary experiences he had in 1800 that relate directly to his woodworking activities before he became a Shaker:

> While plaining at my bench, my whole soul was enshrouded with a mantle of tribulation; but I kept on at my plaining, & soon it appeared to me that my plain began to go with less physical force or exertion on my part than usual. It moved more & more easily until it seemed that I had to hold on to the tool, in order to keep it from moving itself. I thought perhaps it did not take hold of the wood, & so I watched to see if it thru out shavings. I observed it did, but as it still moved without my aid as it were, I questioned the cause, & turned it over to see if it had not caught some little chip or splinter as plains sometimes do, & thus move without cutting; but to my surprise it was all clear. I then concluded it must be driven by some unseen foreign agency or power.[61]

Forty years later, in 1840, it was reported that Brother David "has been employed for several days in taking out *brass knobs* and putting in their stead wood knobs or buttons, this is because brass ones are considered superfluous through spiritual communication."[62] During the 1830s through the 1850s, the Shakers were experiencing a spiritual revitalization. Some visions were received that dealt directly with temporal matters such as furniture design.

It is apparent that Shaker craftsmen also had strong ideas of their own about design. Thomas Damon, a cabinetmaker from Hancock, wrote in 1846 to George Wilcox at Enfield, Connecticut, to discuss what appears to be a butler's desk that he had made. He completed his description with the observation "for where there is no law there is no transgression."[63] This correspondence not only shows that cabinetmakers shared ideas about design but also indicates an acute awareness of the rules regarding their profession in Shaker communities. Brother Isaac Newton Youngs from the Mount Lebanon community expressed his strong opinions about the use of varnish when he wrote on May 1, 1861, "There is a great proclivity in this, our day, for fixing up matters very nice, & the varnish has to go on to the cupboards, drawers &c & the paint on to floors, everything has to be so slick, that a fly will slip on it!"[64] As late as 1887, Orren Haskins urged his fellow Believers to avoid worldly styles when designing Shaker-made articles:

> Why patronize the out side world or gugaws in our manufactures, when they will say we have enough of them abroad? We want a good plain substantial Shaker article, yea, one that bears credit to our profession & tells who and what we are, true and honest before the world, without hypocrisy or any false covering. The wourld at large can Scarcely keep pace with it self in its stiles and fassions which last but a short time, when something still more worthless or absurd takes its place. Let good enough alone, and take good common sense for our guide in all our persuits, and we are safe within and without.[65]

His words reflected beliefs about his work that he had espoused for more than sixty years, and the furniture he made over the decades embodies those same principles.

Daily Life

THERE WERE SEVERAL important differences between Shaker communities and their worldly neighbors. The primary distinction was size, because at their peak, Shaker communities served the needs of several hundred members living on thousands of acres. With this manpower and expertise, the Believers were able to make large-scale physical improvements to their property which would have been too expensive for the small landowner. For example, the Shakers were more willing to invest in the development of millponds and associated structures to benefit the entire community.

Each Shaker village consisted of a number of often contiguous families, each of which occupied and maintained its own dwelling, workshops, barns, and crops. Families might be located about a half mile apart. This division of the community led to a certain flexibility of production. Every family was expected to develop its own manufacturing and commercial specialties for trade with other families in the community, other Shaker communities, and, increasingly in the course of the nineteenth century, the outside world, out of its own store or Trustees' Office located on a public highway.[1] Some families—the North, South, West, and East—were named for their geographic relation to the central Church Family, where the community's shared meetinghouse stood. Others were called Mill, Brickyard, Hill, Second, for other reasons.

Families also represented different orders or levels of commitment to the Shaker faith. Potential converts who wished to experience Shaker life but were not ready to make a full commitment lived outside the community itself but related closely to the Shakers. Others entered the novitiate or gathering order. Two examples are the North and the Upper and Lower Canaan families at Mount Lebanon. The junior order consisted of those who lived within the community according to the United Society's rules but were not fully committed. After receiving further instruction over time, dedicated members often progessed to the Church order, where they signed the covenant, relinquished their personal property and belongings, and lived fully in the communal setting. Each order could consist of one or several families, the Church Family being the senior order in each village, but otherwise there was no strict uniformity to the system.[2]

Unlike the layout of neighboring towns, where individual houses were often spaced to provide privacy, Shaker structures were arranged closely together according to function. Although there was no universal village plan, the meetinghouse was often placed near the dwelling house, the barns adjacent to the brethren's workshops. However, hierarchical concerns or common sense called for the segregation of certain members. The children brought in by their parents who joined the community as well as the orphans raised by the United Society lived with their caretakers separately from the fully covenanted adult members. In fact, children who had lost one or two parents due to disease or war remained a part of Shaker communities until state and denominational orphan asylums became more numerous. They lived in the Shaker villages until they reached the age of twenty-one, when they could decide whether to become fully covenanted members or to leave. According to Benson Lossing, who visited Mount Lebanon in 1857, "there were children, too, with cheerful faces peering out from their broad hats and deep bonnets, for they were all dressed like old men and women. I marveled at the sight of children in that isolated world of bachelors and maidens, for-

Dining room and hallway, Centre Family Dwelling House, Pleasant Hill, Kentucky

Mount Lebanon, New York, facing north, showing South, Second, Center, Church, and North Family buildings, c. 1906. Shaker Museum and Library, Old Chatham, New York, #8547

getting that it was a refuge for orphans who were unsheltered in the stormy world without."[3] The elderly and infirm were secluded in the infirmary building, where they could recuperate from illness while protecting the rest of the community from contagious disease.[4] The four ministry elders and eldresses occupied their own apartments, dining room, and workshops apart from the family as a whole. This segregation prevented the leaders from mingling with the rank and file members and perhaps developing friendships that might promote favoritism. Neutrality was important for them because the ministry had the final authority in resolving domestic matters.

While Shaker builders had no formal training in environmental planning or architectural design, the communities reflect their commitment to order and efficiency. Secular building forms were dictated by the needs of the specific community and influenced by its geographic location, available raw materials, and skills of the builders. According to Benjamin Seth Youngs, writing from South Union on February 26, 1818:

> It would seem that what is wisdom & prudence with one people in a certain situation, is not always wisdom & prudence with another people in another situation. Countries & climates, people & laws, manners & customs, local situations & circumstances, advantages and disadvantages peculiar to each—all are different—and each requiring a different method of arrangement from the other in the line of outward economy. But generally speaking, perhaps, where there is any particular disadvantage in any country or part of a country in any necessary thing for the comfort and support of life, there is also found some substitute or remedy for this disadvantage. This is much the case with us in regard to building materials— we are much put to it for a little building timber, as it is extremely scarce here, & what little there is, hard to get at and very dear by the time we get it—but good building stone of different kinds & the best kind of materials for brick, we have convenient & in plenty.[5]

However, the general design of the dwelling house in particular reflects the Shakers' commitment to celibacy, equality of the sexes, and communal living. This dormitory-like structure was equipped with dual entrances, halls, and stairways to accommodate the brethren and sisters separately in sleeping or retiring rooms holding two or more Believers. The building also contained kitchens for food

North Family yard, Watervliet, New York, c. 1870. Photograph probably by James Irving, Troy, New York. New York State Museum, Albany, #33.12.107

Church Family Dwelling House kitchen, Hancock, Massachusetts, c. 1900. Collection of The United Society of Shakers, Sabbathday Lake, Maine

J. Becker. "Cutting Bread." Woodcut engraving. Published in *Frank Leslie's Illustrated Newspaper*, September 13, 1873. Private collection

preparation, dining rooms, and space to conduct religious meetings. Over time, as membership requirements increased or decreased and technology improved, the Shakers altered the dwelling houses to suit the community's changing needs. Consequently, room size, storage space, and wall and floor treatments as well as plumbing, heating, and electrical requirements were always subject to change. Just as the Shakers preferred to keep their rules for living fluid, in order to respond to current conditions, they also kept their interiors and furnishings fluid, constantly remodeling to keep up with new ways of living as well as changing needs.

The Shakers' daily routine varied, depending on the time of year, the seasonal tasks at hand, and the skills of the individuals. Diary and journal accounts suggest that if a brother had experience in a certain trade, he devoted the major part of his time to perfecting it and, if qualified, he assumed responsibility for that workshop. In many instances, the brethren were encouraged to master two or more callings, which not only prevented boredom but enabled the community to be less dependent on the contributions of a few key members of the society. For example, in addition to woodworking, Richard McNemar of Union Village was a printer, composer, and preacher, Henry DeWitt of Mount Lebanon was a shoemaker and bookbinder, and Henry Blinn of Canterbury was a dentist, beekeeper, teacher, and historian. The life of Brother Isaac Newton Youngs epitomizes the varied occupations pursued by one individual, which are recorded in his "Biography in Verse":

> I'm overrun with work and chores
> Upon the farm or within doors
> Which every way I turn my eyes;
> Enough to fill me with surprise.
> Of tayl'ring, Join'ring, farming too,
> Almost all kinds that are to do,
> Blacksmithing, Tinkering, mason work,
> When could I find time to shirk?
> Clock work, Jenny work, keeping school
> Enough to puzzle any fool.
> An endless list of chores and notions,
> To keep me in perpetual motion.[6]

The sisters, on the other hand, were involved in a more systematic rotation of labor. They were responsible for traditional women's duties that included monthly turns in the kitchen, bakery, laundry, and housekeeping departments as well as in the dairy, spin shop, and herb house. Both men and women participated in seasonal activities assigned along traditional lines, such as haying, roofing, apple picking, preserving, and making maple sugar, which drew together groups of brothers and sisters in bees of concentrated effort.[7]

Diary and journal references, as well as conversations with present-day Shakers, give clues to their daily routine, which is described by one man in his manuscript entitled "Narrative of Four month's residence among the Shakers at Watervliet":

> . . . the hours for rising were 5 o'clock in the Summer, and half past 5 in the Winter [a half hour earlier in some communities] - the Family all rise at the Toll of the Bell, and in less than ten minutes, vacated the Bed Rooms; - the Sisters, then distributed themselves throughout the Rooms, and made up all the Beds, putting every thing in the most perfect order, before Breakfast; - the Brothers proceeded to their various employments,

Laundry, Church Family, Union Village, Ohio, c. 1910. Shaker Museum and Library, Old Chatham, New York, #15070

Retiring room, Centre Family Dwelling House, Pleasant Hill, Kentucky

and made a commencement for the day; the Cows were milked, and the Horses were fed. At 7 o'clock the Bell rang for Breakfast, but it was ten minutes after, when we went to the Tables. After Breakfast, all proceeded immediately to their respective employments, and continued industriously occupied until ten minutes to twelve o'clock, when the Bell announced dinner. Farmers then left the field, and Mechanics their Shops, all washed their hands, and formed procession again, and marched to Dinner. . . . Immediately after Dinner, they went to work again . . . and continued steady at it until the Bell announced Supper. . . . At eight o'clock all work was ended for the day. . . . [8]

Believers ate their meals in silence at long tables, segregated by sex. Three times a week the sisters and brothers would engage in union meetings. On these occasions, which lasted about an hour, the sexes had an opportunity to socialize in the brethrens' bedrooms, under closely supervised conditions. According to a former member, "when the clock strikes they retire to their bedrooms and hold what they call 'Union Meetings.' Each of these meetings contain about 12 or 14 members of both sexes. They take their seats facing one another. The intention of these meetings is to cement the members into perfect union by pleasant conversation and uninterrupted sociality."[9] The family retired at 9:00 P.M. in the winter and an hour later in the summer.

The Shakers engaged in agriculture, textile-related activities, mechanical arts, and woodworking. They developed an economic system to ensure their self-sufficiency as well as to meet the profitable demands of the world. The Shaker communities began as agricultural settlements dependent on the production of their own food for survival. Farm surpluses brought the Believers their first outside income and acquired for them a reputation for excellence. The kitchen industries produced canned goods, sauces, jellies, dried sweet corn, and apples processed in the form of sauce, cider, and butter. About 1850 they developed a lucrative maple-syrup industry, which lasted for many years. The South Union Shakers were expert horticulturists and specialized in the processing of fruit preserves, which they shipped to worldly markets by train from the nearby railroad station. The garden seed business began about 1795 and continued to the end of the next century. The Shakers were probably the first to package garden seeds for sale in paper envelopes, which were distributed by Shaker peddlers from New England to the South. A wide variety of medicinal herbs were grown, processed, and prepared for home use and eventually sold through pharmaceutical companies. They grew poppies and until the 1830s made most of the opium used in America.[10] They raised broom corn and invented the flat household broom. By 1805 the industry at Mount Lebanon became a major income-producing trade and remained so throughout the century.

In addition to agriculture, the Shakers in the Western societies played an important role in cattle breeding, which earned them recognition in the field of animal husbandry. They purchased purebred bulls from England and Scotland and exchanged them with other Shaker villages to improve the existing herds.[11] Their expertise expanded to include beef and milk cattle, hogs, and sheep, which became a major source of income.

Shaker sisters and brothers supplied the community with many of its textile needs. They spun and wove cloth for seed bags, garments, bed linens, and household items such as carpets, towels, blankets, chair tapes, and shag mats. In fact, P. T. Barnum used to purchase woolen horse blankets for his circus from the Mount Lebanon Shakers.[12] They cultivated flax for linen, an essential fabric for community use, as well as linseed oil to sell to the world. Eventually the Believers created oat, rye, palm leaf, and straw bonnets, baskets, and fans, as well as containers made of strips of woven poplar, for sale to the world. Silkworms were raised in Kentucky and the silk woven into colorful kerchiefs for brothers and sisters at other communities. By the last quarter of the nineteenth century, the New Hampshire communities sold their machine-knit sweaters to colleges throughout New England as well as to the general public. They designed and trademarked the famous "Dorothy" cloak, named after Canterbury Eldress Dorothy Durgin (1825–1898). Constructed of imported French broadcloth, the cloak was practical and stylish enough to appeal to the most discriminating of customers, including Mrs. Grover Cleveland, who wore a gray cloak to her husband's inauguration in 1893.

Skilled Shaker brothers devised new machines to manufacture large quantities of goods of a diverse nature. Tanning was one of the first pursuits, including the manufacture of shoes, saddles, bridles, whips, and bookbinding. The Shaker blacksmiths also produced a wide variety of metal products for their own use, such as kitchenware, agricultural tools, and shop machinery, as well as wrought and cut nails and pen nibs made of steel, brass, and silver for sale to the world. Other trades included the production of clay pipes and hand cards for carding wool, to name a few.

When it came to woodworking, Shaker joiners, carpenters, and cabinetmakers manufactured a wide range of items. Coopering was an active business; there was a steady output of pails, tubs, barrels, measures, and dippers. Sale products offered to the world included baskets, spinning wheels, table swifts for winding yarn, hair and wire sieves, brushes of all kinds (shoe, clothes, scrubbing, dustpan, whisks, and so on), and the first American-made nest of metric mea-

Sisters in the ironing room, North Family, Mount Lebanon, New York, 1880s. From left to right: unknown, unknown, Rosetta Stephens (1860–1948), Elder Daniel Offord (1845–1911), unknown, unknown, Martha or Sarah Burger, Martha Anderson (1844–1897). Photograph by James E. West, "Views of Shakers" series, no. 5. Shaker Museum and Library, Old Chatham, New York, #8130

Sister Martha Burger in the North Family, Mount Lebanon, New York, Store, c. 1890. Photograph by James E. West, "Views of the North Family Shakers" series, no. 14. Shaker Museum and Library, Old Chatham, New York, #7465

sures.[13] Although Believers did not invent the oval storage boxes, they popularized them by refining the construction method and sold them in large quantities throughout the nineteenth century.

The design, marketing, and distribution of chairs represented a major industry for Mount Lebanon, serving as an important source of income for the community. Although the trade was well established before his tenure, Elder Robert M. Wagan (1833–1883) expanded the existing facilities through the use of steam-driven machinery. The chairs were standardized into different sizes, mass-produced, marked with transfer decal labels, and advertised in Shaker catalogues by 1875 (see pp. 142–43 for a more detailed discussion of this trade).

According to Father Joseph Meacham, "We have a right to improve the inventions of man, so far as is useful and necessary, but not to vain glory, or anything superfluous."[14] Throughout their history the Shakers believed in sharing their inventions with the world. These included the flat broom, which proved superior to the round broom then in use, introduced by Theodore Bates of Watervliet in 1798, and what appears to be the first wrinkle-resistant fabric, perfected by the Sabbathday Lake Shakers in the 1840s. According to folk legend, sister Tabitha Babbitt of Harvard devised the circular saw in 1810; however, there is no documentation to substantiate this popular myth.[15] Brother Alonzo Hollister of Mount Lebanon lent his heated, airtight container used in the making of sugar to a visitor named Gail Borden, who conducted experiments in the Shakers' workshops that eventually led to his formula for condensed milk.[16]

Unfortunately, worldly businessmen took advantage of the Shakers' generosity and profited from their ingenuity. In order to protect their own interests, the Believers patented some of their major contributions, such as George O'Donnell's metal ball-and-socket device or tilter for chairs in 1852, Sister Emeline Hart's revolving oven in 1876, and David Parker's water-powered washing machine in 1858 and his sarsaparilla lozenges in 1866.[17] However, the Society was reluctant to invoke government protection, which they regarded as an evil, necessary at best, preferring to rely on the inherent quality in Shaker-made goods to attract consumers. Consequently, the number of Shaker ideas that were patented is small in relation to those that were freely shared.

At the time of the gathering of the church—when the first Shaker communities were established—schools were not very common. As more and more

Mount Lebanon, New York, schoolhouse, c. 1880. Photograph by James Irving, Troy, New York, no. 26. The Mount Lebanon Shaker Collection

children became part of the Shaker communities, the need to set up a formal education program grew pressing. In 1817 a public school in one of the communities was established based on the Lancastrian system—a method that emphasized oral recitation, with the older students instructing the younger ones. The early program focused chiefly on the basic subjects: reading, writing, arithmetic, spelling, and geography. At a later date, music, astronomy, and agricultural chemistry were added to the curriculum.[18] The boys were taught for three months in late fall and winter and the girls for three months in the early spring—terms that were scheduled to free the children when they were most needed in the community work program.[19] Brother Seth Youngs Wells, who had taught in the Albany public schools before joining the Mount Lebanon Shakers, was appointed "General Superintendent of Believers' Literature, Schools, etc." in 1821. From June to October 1823 Wells toured the "Eastern Believers Schools for the purpose of aiding the teachers in educating the scholars."[20] It was not the aim of the Shaker school system to make scholars but rather to give the young people "as much letter learning as may be put to propper use, and fit them for business in the Society of Believers . . . to give proper exercise in their mental faculties, & turn faculties into the propper channel of usefulness for their own benefit & the benefit of their Brethren & Sisters."[21]

Although physical labor was always a major part of Shaker life, the brothers and sisters enjoyed diversions such as popcorn parties, boating, fishing, sleigh rides, and picnics. According to one account of a young Shakeress at Niskeyuna, "Hiding beneath an arcade of the bridge, we would pull off our shoes and stockings and wade knee-deep in the water. Then, loading our palm-leaf bonnets with dandelions, which looked like little white-capped Shakeresses, we would float them down the stream in a race, the boat which won being decorated with buttercups and violets."[22] During the late nineteenth and twentieth centuries, musical instruments were introduced into the society, and singing groups performed regularly both for the community and in concerts for the world's people. The Canterbury sisters also staged religious and mythological plays and pageants of their own composition, called entertainments, for the community and worldly visitors during holiday seasons. Judging from the numerous candid photographs taken by the twentieth-century brothers and sisters, they enjoyed many recreational activities of their own and exhibited quite a sense of humor in their leisure-time pursuits.

A drama presentation by the Beacon Light Club on Washington's Birthday, 1900–25, Sabbathday Lake, Maine. The club, composed of a group of young sisters, met to study the Bible and learn Shaker history. They also published a monthly magazine. Collection of The United Society of Shakers, Sabbathday Lake, Maine, album no. 8, p. 12

The Cultural Setting

Table, Mount Lebanon, New York, c. 1760/ 1825. Inscribed in chalk: 1825. Butternut, mahogany, and pine, with pewter balls, h 26¼ w 32¼ d 22⅝". Private collection

The Shakers took this worldly tea table of about 1760 and changed it to suit their needs: they removed the ogee-shaped portion of the apron and added pieces of wood to extend its depth. They also added a drawer, wood pegs on the side apron, and small pewter balls in the square portion of the leg, presumably to hold a cloth bag.

Built-in closet, Meetinghouse attic, Canterbury, New Hampshire, 1792. Pine, with blue paint and wrought-iron latches and hinges. Canterbury Shaker Village, Inc., Canterbury, New Hampshire

MUCH OF THE serious scholarship on the Shakers has focused on their peculiarity rather than on their continuity with their surrounding cultural environment. Many misconceptions about their products stem directly from this restricted view. Although strongly influenced by their own institutional setting, Shaker designs were not created in a vacuum. Since no one was born a Believer, the earliest converts learned their cabinetmaking skills in the world and brought both the technical skills and stylistic biases of their trade with them when they joined the community. They worked from what they knew, using the ideas, forms, and patterns within their physical and intellectual reach. Most of what was available to them was derived both from the recent and distant past and drew on the accomplishments of their predecessors.

America's origins as a European outpost and its slow evolution toward separateness from the mother country was never fully appreciated in the nationalistic mood that dominated historical studies produced during the late nineteenth century. When culture is transferred to a colonial situation, the old assumptions and traditional attitudes continue to be manifested in the form, structure, and ornamentation of artifacts produced in the new world.[1] The majority of the settlers inhabiting the regions visited by Mother Ann and her followers on their evangelistic missions were religious dissidents of many persuasions from England. Despite political animosity toward the mother country, English tastes in furniture design and craftsmanship prevailed in the colonies.

As the cultural center during the latter part of the eighteenth century, London was the source for fashionable furniture. Here, current designs were influenced in part by numerous pattern books, which were printed and distributed by cabinetmakers for public use. The most significant of these publications included Thomas Chippendale's *The Gentleman & Cabinetmaker's Director* (1754); George Hepplewhite's *The Cabinet-Maker and Upholsterer's Guide* (1788); and Thomas Sheraton's *The Cabinet-Maker and Upholsterer's Drawing Book* (1791). These design books were important sources that provided a continuing reference to the domestic symbols of European culture. However, few cabinetmakers could afford their own copies; only a dozen of Chippendale's *Director*, for example, are now known in America.

In addition to written sources, these new styles were transmitted across the Atlantic primarily by imported English furniture and furniture makers trained in Britain. The ethnic tradition reflected in the native training of immigrant craftsmen was the greatest single means of transferring European material practices to North America. Reflecting their close cultural ties to the mother country, many Americans considered English furniture the most desirable and stylish. American artisans themselves acknowledged this in their advertising, which claimed their products to be "in the latest London fashion" or made by craftsmen "late of London."[2]

Patterns and American price books supporting new trends were also significant in disseminating new ideas from designers and craftsmen to the consumers. They were influential in promoting the prevailing fashions of the day and effective in transmitting the latest forms from English homes to the more well-to-do colonists. However, designs of less fashionable styles and simpler furniture, including plain urban examples and rural pieces, moved most often with the immigration of the craftsmen and their customers to their new homes in America and as they migrated from one region to another within the colonies.

Away from the elite cultural centers, individuals found the opportunity to choose, the independence to combine, and the freedom to introduce new ideas into a system. In a new context, experimentation could flourish, as tradition became less influential. Thus, early America was a combination of two distinct forces: the colonial society as a preserved set of the values of the regional European centers and the colonial society as a changing culture with a slowly developing separate identity.[3]

Between the years 1790 and 1800, the Neoclassical style of furniture introduced by Hepplewhite and Sheraton in England was becoming popular in America. By the nineteenth century, Queen Anne and Chippendale patterns were on the wane, both in London and its American counterparts, the cultural centers of Boston, New York, and Philadelphia. The new furniture took on a very different appearance from previous designs. Even in the rural areas where fashion changed much more slowly, a reactionary swing became noticeable in the move from ornate to simpler forms, curved to straight lines, and three-dimensional applied ornament to flat surface decoration. This preference was reflected in the disappearance of the curved shapes found in the cabriole leg, ogee bracket base, and ball and claw foot of the Chippendale chest. Equally noticeable was the elimination of strong decorative elements such as the carved naturalistic motifs and serpentine, bombé, and block front undulating shapes. Instead, the restrained simplicity, rectilinear lines, and geometric character of the new style appealed to many Americans who, in their new republic, were conscious of their ideological ties to classical Greece and Rome. The furniture seemed to provide high-style designers an opportunity to embody those philosophical ideals through restrained decorations that had allegorical implications, such as symbols of abundance and fertility (cornucopias, baskets of fruit, garlanded putti), elements borrowed from Greek and Roman architecture (urns, fascia, and dentils), and classical figures. More specifically, these new ideas were expressed in the straight, tapering legs, sleek, varnished surfaces, and contrasting veneer work emphasizing the natural grain of the wood. Because of its connection with the developmental period in America's history, the style was called Federal in the new nation. The importance of simplicity and permanence to emerging America is expressed by the statesman Gouverneur Morris, who advised George Washington in 1790, "I think it of very great importance to fix the taste of our country properly, and I think your example will go very far in that respect. It is therefore my wish that everything about you should be *substantiallly good and majestically plain, made to endure*"[4]—ideas in accord with the rational-minded, truth-seeking intellectual movement called the Enlightenment. There are few worldly American designs that embody this philosophy in woodworking more than Federal furniture.

Is it mere coincidence that the Shakers readily incorporated these new, yet basic forms and the ideals they represented in their newly founded communities? The Believers' plain and functional furniture was the inevitable result of two compelling forces—a theology demanding a physical statement of gospel simplicity combined with a worldly cultural environment embracing the new Federal style. The elegance of proportion, verticality of line, and reliance on finish rather than ornament are consistent with fashionable Neoclassical principles of design. Given the fact that the rural vernacular tradition of the western Massachusetts–eastern New York area had already made Queen Anne/Chippendale designs obsolete, it is not surprising that there are very few elements of the older cabriole style reflected within the developing Shaker aesthetic. (Some furniture forms, such as tripod stands with snake feet, tended to remain popular longer in the country than in the more fashion-conscious urban areas.) Furthermore, in the transmission of design, geographic distance between urban high-style centers and rural areas often resulted in a simplification of overall forms and decorative details. Country cabinetmakers tended to produce a more basic, pared-down interpretation of upscale fashions—and these were, for the most part, the craftsmen who brought their talents and tastes into the Shaker population when they converted.

What, then, are the worldly prototypes for certain characteristic Shaker forms? Since written data on the material culture of the Shakers during this formative period are scarce, conclusions must be drawn from an examination and comparison of the existing artifacts themselves. The close relationship between eighteenth- and early-nineteenth-century vernacular and early Shaker woodworking techniques is evident in the architectural details—particularly the interior woodwork, hardware, and trim. The prominent raised-panel work on doors, supported by H-style hand-forged hinges, and the controlled use of painted trim are common to much local New England cabinetwork. The sect's earliest material acquisitions probably would have been supplied by local artisans who learned their trades through an apprenticeship system of training that usually fostered a conservative approach to stylistic and technical innovation. The primary difference between the community's early work and that of neighboring rural areas was simply the minimal use of decorative details.

Most important, the concept of built-in closets, cupboards, and drawers was not a common feature of eighteenth-century interiors. Up until the 1800s,

Built-in cupboards and cases of drawers, fifth floor, Church Family Dwelling House, Enfield, New Hampshire, c. 1840. First Leader Corporation, Enfield, New Hampshire

Chippendale-style case of drawers, New England, late 18th century. Photograph: courtesy Skinner Inc., auctioneers and appraisers

Case of drawers, Mount Lebanon, New York, c. 1840. Pine. Private collection. Photograph: courtesy Suzanne Courcier and Robert W. Wilkins

worldly Americans relied primarily on movable wardrobe units such as the Dutch Kas or German Schrank to store clothing, which suggests that the Shakers were among the first to adopt and institutionalize built-in elements as an integral part of their interiors. By the 1830s, the Shakers had completed a number of large dwelling houses at most of the communities to accommodate their burgeoning membership and equipped each building with impressive storage areas. The 1837 attic at Canterbury was fitted with 6 closets, 14 cupboards, and 101 drawers to house off-season clothing and bedding for the 100 or so Church Family members living there. The Great Stone Dwelling at Enfield, New Hampshire, completed in 1841, featured 860 built-in drawers, which averaged nine apiece for each of the 95 inhabitants. At Hancock the cabinetmakers placed the 100 closet doors, 245 cupboard doors, and 369 drawers throughout the building.

The earliest community structures that remain minimally altered today (see p. 42) are significant because the work was often completed by the same craftsmen making the furniture. Therefore, any similarities in construction features or design details between the built-ins and movable items are revealing. Fixed and freestanding cupboards were constructed with wood-panel doors rather than glazing. Most noteworthy are the broad stiles flanking the cupboard doors; on the surface, this arrangement seems inconsistent with the concept of functionalism, because it makes the space behind it somewhat inaccessible. However, all of these techniques frequently appear as distinguishing characteristics on storage pieces of Germanic origin.[5] It is not known whether this similarity is the result of training on the part of these early Shaker cabinetmakers—although the German population in the New England communities was admittedly small—or rather, a conscious effort to obtain a certain visual effect.

The case of drawers gradually assumed its modern form during the course of the seventeenth century and had superseded the chest by the early eighteenth century. However, these worldly prototypes were symmetrically arranged and typically had a configuration consisting of two short drawers over three to five full-length drawers. They were clearly designed and built to suit the needs of an individual or small household rather than to provide storage requirements for a Shaker retiring room or an entire Shaker family. In comparison, Shaker cases of drawers commonly provided storage space for four to six brothers or sisters living in a single retiring room. Each member was probably assigned the use of two or three drawers, resulting in the need to create a massive case of ten to twelve drawers. Furthermore, the layout tended to be asymmetrical on Shaker units. Curiously, most Shaker case pieces lack dust boards, a common feature of worldly chests.

The majority of storage boxes throughout the Shaker communities are basic six-board chests based on British prototypes, which originated in medieval times. This practical form consists of single, lengthwise planks that have been either nailed together with vertical-grained plank sides with foot cutouts or simply dovetailed on the corners. The absence of paneling, carving, and dovetailing suggests an English rather than Irish, Scottish, or Continental origin.[6]

Counters, as we know them today, first appeared as large pieces of work furniture that the shopkeeper used to display wares. The Shakers greatly enlarged and adapted the form to suit the textile and tailoring needs of the community. Sisters or brothers making clothing for many other members required space to cut out, lay out, and stitch dresses, cloaks, pants, and coats as well as to store related tools and equipment specific to the trade. Consequently, Shaker-made work counters are often on wheels, fitted with an assortment of drawers and cupboards that are accessible from one to four sides. Based on late-nineteenth-century pho-

left

Chippendale-style slant-front desk, New England, 1760–90. Photograph: courtesy Skinner Inc., auctioneers and appraisers

Wardrobe, pl. 85, *The Cabinet-maker and Upholsterer's Guide* by A. Hepplewhite and Co. Cabinet-makers. 3d ed. London: B. T. Batsford, 1897

tographs, it appears that counters were often placed in a large workroom setting (pl. 54).

Desks were produced in many forms at various Shaker communities throughout the nineteenth century. Kneehole (pls. 29, 337), fall-front (pls. 23, 26, 88), slant-front (pls. 27, 184), lift-top (pl. 286), and butler's desks (pl. 24) were all based on worldly prototypes. While various members had occasion to use desks, these types were probably adapted to suit the needs of the trustees, who were responsible for communal record-keeping and other activities that involved writing.

The large, centrally positioned table in monasteries and baronial halls was a medieval tradition in England and the Low Countries. Such trestle tables, which in their medieval setting were intended to be dismantled and stowed away at the end of the meal, were adapted by Believers for communal dining. While retaining the same basic support system and overall length to seat large groups of people, the Shakers usually moved the medial stretcher from its position just above the floor to underneath the top, thus providing the sisters and brothers with more leg room. The Shakers' version was not disassembled but used in a permanent location in the dining room.

In building four-legged, rectangular-topped tables, the Shakers abandoned the curves and carving characteristic of the Chippendale style in favor of square, tapering legs strongly associated with Hepplewhite design or simple turned legs. Some of the communities in Ohio and Kentucky produced tables with round legs and ring turnings reflecting the influence of vernacular prototypes of the Empire period.

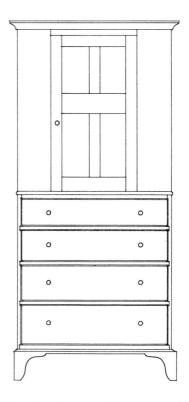

Cupboard and case of drawers, probably Union Village, Ohio, c. 1840

Double drop-leaf table, pl. 62, *The Cabinet-maker and Upholsterer's Guide* by A. Hepplewhite and Co. Cabinet-makers. 3d ed. London: B. T. Batsford, 1897

right

George W. Ro[gers] (working 1809–19), Concord, New Hampshire. Federal-style ladies' secretary. Ex-collection of the late Robert W. Upton, Concord, New Hampshire. Photograph: Frank Kelly, Manchester, New Hampshire

Tilt-top candlestand, Connecticut, c. 1790. Cherry. Photograph: courtesy Skinner Inc., auctioneers and appraisers

The several types of tripod stands produced by Shaker cabinetmakers reflect their strong English connections. Pared-down pedestal tables with simple vase-turned shafts, cabriole legs often flattened in cross section, and snake feet are clearly derived from the Queen Anne style. Another distinctive Shaker stand exhibits arched spider legs adapted from Sheraton prototypes. Some of these examples are also fitted with either underhung or push-pull drawers, suspended beneath the square tops, that slide in and out at either end, perhaps for the convenience of the user.

The production of chairs for both community use and sale to the world represents an important activity within some Shaker workshops. Throughout the years, Shakers made many distinct variations, both with and without arms and rockers, based on the early British prototypes of the ladderback or slat-back style, an important form in the American tradition from the earliest American settlements in New England.[7] Both English regional and Shaker chairs exhibit slats graduated in reverse order from top to bottom, turned posts with distinctive finials, and rush seats. Most significantly, they share one distinctive characteristic in the form of turned stay rails at the top of the posts. More commonly called shawl bars, these rounded top slats, commonly seen in the production Shaker chairs of the 1850s, first appeared in the northwest region of England as early as the mid-eighteenth century.[8] However, the mushroom-shaped post that characterizes Shaker chairs from several communities appears to be derived from eighteenth-century American chairs.

Truckle or trundle beds were small, low children's cots that were fitted with casters to facilitate rolling them underneath another bed for storage. This form was popular in England from the late Middle Ages until the 1750s[9] and was probably the prototype for adult Shaker beds with wooden wheels.

Specialized work furniture such as the sewing desks produced in the Northeastern Shaker communities have no exact counterpart in worldly designs but are somewhat related to the Federal ladies' secretary popular in the New England high-style centers. The decoration has been pared down, however, to suit Shaker taste, and the amount of storage space, with multiple drawers, both above and below, and work surfaces, with pullout slides, was expanded for functional tasks. The more diminutive sewing tables found in Kentucky, which feature splayed legs and shaped tops with surrounding galleries to provide open rather than closed storage, appear to be modeled after worldly worktables produced during the Federal period.

Shaker brothers at Mount Lebanon and Watervliet, New York, produced wall and tall clocks for their own use as well as for the Believers at other communities. Placed primarily in halls, these timepieces ensured the punctuality that was essential to orderly communal living. The brass works are similar to those produced by worldly clockmakers, although the simplified design of the cases reflects the Shakers' religious beliefs. Constructed of local woods and bereft of costly veneers, inlay, and brass embellishments, Shaker timepieces are related in form only to high-style Queen Anne and Chippendale examples, characterized by broken-arched bonnets, ogee bracket feet, and elaborate moldings.

On the whole, Shaker designs were not new but, rather, variations of worldly models based on community ideals, institutional needs, available materials, and the skill of the cabinetmaker. However, while the forms themselves have historical antecedents, their clarity, sharpness, and institutionalization were innovative. As they did not depend on the salability of their products in a traditional competitive marketplace, Shaker craftsmen were able to build unconventional, highly specialized furniture. The interchange of the cabinetmaker's conventions and the client's desires, which is the essence of the worldly furniture-making trade, is much less of a factor in Shaker communities, where furniture embodies and manifests the shared values and experiences of the members rather than the individual experiments of a particular maker and consumers with different sets of needs and expectations.

The plain and simple patterns developed at Mount Lebanon were transmitted to the outlying communities via the ministry. Was it merely coincidence that the leadership at Mount Lebanon sent Benjamin Seth Youngs, who was a woodworker as well as a missionary, to Kentucky in 1805? As a community leader, he brought with him the established standards and regulations in both spiritual and temporal matters.

Within the community, acceptable designs were perpetuated by a traditional apprenticeship program; for example, children growing up in the society were "indentured" to a skilled Shaker craftsman in order to learn the trade. In this way, the concept of appropriate design was passed on from one generation to the next. Given their new communal setting, both cabinetmakers and apprentices were less encumbered with the years of tradition that dominated their worldly counterparts. However, after the United Society's first twenty crucial years, a design interplay from two different directions developed: between those children converts trained as Shaker cabinetmakers by experienced woodworkers in the community and those experienced cabinetmakers coming from the outside world. The continuity in design at Mount Lebanon is due to master-apprentice relationships that evolved over a long period of time. For example, master craftsman David Rowley (1779–1855) trained fifteen-year-old Elisha Blakeman (1819–1900) and later Orren Haskins (1815–1892), who, in turn, took charge of the Church Family Joiners' Shop in 1855 after Brother David's death. Henry Hollister joined the Mount Lebanon community at age three, Orren Haskins at five, Giles Avery at six, Amos Stewart at nine, Elisha Blakeman at eleven, and Samuel Turner at thirteen.[10] This second wave of cabinetmakers who were raised and trained in the community was virtually uncontaminated by worldly influences. It is not coincidental that they were responsible for producing the "classic" Shaker furniture, between 1820 and 1850.

The situation was, however, somewhat different in the outlying communities. While Queen Anne, Chippendale, and early Federal styles were popular during the founding and early growth of the Eastern societies in the eighteenth century, Hepplewhite, Sheraton, and Empire designs prevailed in the West during the nineteenth century, when the Ohio and Kentucky communities were established. Here, worldly converts brought their tastes and training with them into the community and worked within their own cabinetmaking traditions. Consequently, Western Shaker furniture also exhibited the current fashion prevalent in the surrounding geographic area and at times reflected regional preferences more than that produced at the central community. For example, South Union Kentucky sewing tables are small, delicate pieces of furniture that were loosely patterned after Federal-style worktables, with shaped top and fabric storage pouch below. Other forms found only in the Western societies include the press, that is, a one- or two-piece cupboard over case of drawers, and corner cupboards, both of which are based on Southern vernacular prototypes. Western Shaker furniture also used different materials—walnut, cherry, and poplar instead of the maple, birch, and pine found in the Eastern communities.

Shaker design was not static but evolved over time. According to one popular opinion, the "decline" in the furniture produced after the Civil War can be attributed to a breakdown in orthodoxy among the Believers and the loss of the millennial impulse.[11] This view holds that the forsaking of the simple life for worldly display was a result of internal disintegration accelerated by increased contact with the world and a declining enrollment. Instead of paring down worldly fashion, the Shakers masked the fundamental by applying Victorian motifs to simple forms. Perhaps this opinion reflects too closely the twentieth-century biases regarding late Victorian taste and the current preference for modernism in art, architecture, and industrial design. Another, more plausible explanation for this transformation of design recognizes the fact that the Shakers were an extremely progressive sect. For them, this later furniture represented an optimistic revival of spirit, bringing their society into a new era. Several diary and journal references indicate the Shakers themselves were concerned about their image, which felt uncomfortably old-fashioned to them, and, as a result, impeded conversions and complicated business relations. In this light, the Queen Anne revival architectural modifications to the Trustees' Office at Hancock in 1895 (see pl. 98) and Joseph Slingerland's upgrades to the Center House (office building) at Union Village, Ohio, in 1891–92 (see pl. 273), can be viewed as an effort to present a modern environment to the Shakers' business acquaintances and members.

Built-in sink and cupboards, Church Family Trustees' Office, Hancock, Massachusetts, c. 1895. Hancock Shaker Village, Pittsfield, Massachusetts

This concept was ably summarized by Oliver Hampton of Union Village, Ohio, in 1887:

> Forms, fashions, customs, external rules all have to bow to the fiat of evolution and progress toward that which is more perfect. This need not alarm the most conservative Believer. For unless we keep pace with the progress of the universe our individual progress will be an impossibility. We shall be whirled off at some side station and relegated to the limbo of worn out—superannuated and used-up institutions.[12]

The same viewpoint was expressed by an unidentified Believer from Sabbathday Lake, Maine, writing in 1878:

> The style of Building for permanancy, thoroughness and manner of finish, is materially changed, formerly it was to see how plainly if not cheaply the building could be finished. Now particularly upon the inside, with little regard to real comfort and convenience, now, every kind of accomodation for comfort and convenience is studied consistant with Believers principles of prudence and economy.[13]

Elder Otis Sawyer stated in the "Recapitulation of 1883" from the "Alfred Church Record," vol. 2, "The world has moved, change is indellibly impressed on all material things. Decay upon inaction and we find that in our little zion how it requires eternal vigilence and constant effort to keep pace with the progress of the age." Writing in 1904, Anna White of Mount Lebanon articulated the need for flexibility and participation in the world's affairs in order to keep the Shakers in the modern age.

> The Shaker may change his style of coat, may alter the cut of her gown or cease to wear a cap and no harm be done. Vital harm may be done by

retaining either, merely to preserve old forms and customs, when the time is crying out in vain for action; for spontaneous out-reaching sympathy here, aid there, cooperation yonder. FIT Shakerism to humanity today, as the fathers and Mothers of the past fitted it to their age and time.[14]

A more physical expression of this viewpoint is found in Elder Henry Blinn's positive commentary on the upgrades found in various Shaker communities during his 1873 journey from New Hampshire to Kentucky, such as his description of the Trustees' Office at either the Church or North Family at Mount Lebanon:

> It is singular how divergent human beings are. One society is rapidly pushing ahead in one phase of life & perhaps allowing other conditions to drag heavily along. The next society takes up this neglected point & forces itself ahead allowing other equally important points to pass almost unnoticed. Those things which we advocate are as a matter of course, of the first importance. Several changes have been made in the office, which accommodates those who reside here. A small dining room suitable to accommodate three or four persons, has been fitted up in apple pie order, next door to the kitchen. The ceiling is white: the floor is covered with figured oil cloth, of large checks, and the chairs are attractive & easily handled. Portions of the large halls are made into convenient store rooms. Beautifully polished Italian marble sinks, with silver or nickle plated fixings have been placed in the upper & lower halls. While all of these conveniences add to the comfort of life they also add to the burden of life.

Writing from North Union, Ohio, on June 28, Blinn described and approved of their upgrades to the dwelling:

> One part of the house has been repainted & is in striking contrast with that which is left. Some of the doors were grained, others had drab pannels & pink trimmings. Some of the wood work was marbled. The meeting room had a peculiarly neat appearance. The ceiling overhead as well as

Church Family Trustees' Office, Enfield, Connecticut. Published in *Connecticut Quarterly* 3, no. 4 (October–December 1897)

on the sides of the room were painted in colors. It was a new feature &
the Sister attempted to make an apology but it was needless.

The North Family Dwelling House at Enfield, Connecticut, was also decorated
progressively: "The drawers & cupboards are built into the house; the faces are
black walnut & finished with French polish. The remaining part of the woodwork
except the doors is painted white. The doors have white pannels and blut munt-
ings [sic]. This ornamental style of painting in a Shaker house is wholly new to us.
How extensively it has been used we are at present unable to tell."

Elder Henry's evaluation of the dwelling at Pleasant Hill, Kentucky, indicates his acceptance of even embellishments formerly considered superfluous and
tending to feed vanity. He wrote:

> The Brethren's rooms in this dwelling were quite plain & neat. The sisters
> had taken a little more care for the ornamental. A beautifully framed
> chromo of flowers, and a small framed picture of birds hung from the
> walls. In one room the table was so filled with fancy articles, trinkets &
> pictures that we were strongly impressed to regard it as a show case.
> Really we think this is a good way to make an exhibition of this order of
> treasures. Believers are noted for the large number which they possess
> and a free exhibition gives all the pleasure of seeing the many beautiful
> useless things that we hold in possession.[15]

According to Canterbury Church Family journals, upgrades were also
made to interior furnishings and Shaker-made products sold to provide space for
contemporary worldly examples. The Canterbury Shakers owned one of the first
cars in the state of New Hampshire and made electricity available in their own village while the state capital in nearby Concord was still burning gas. In May 1917,
they "Buy of Chas. A. Hoitt Co. Manchester, N.H., Two complete bed room sets.
Each set consisting of two beds with #50 National Springs, dresser, 3 rocking
chairs, 1 straight backed chair, and 1 small writing desk. Also 2 extra Golden Oak
beds and springs and a Chiffonier for the Bath Room. Cost Complete $209.00."
Two months later, they "take out tables and chairs in the Family Dining Room.[16]
Have 7 tables 7 ft. x 3 ft. with Opal glass tops made for us at a cost of $315.00.
Also 56 Brown Leather Seat Oak dining chairs costing $168.00 to take their places.
These bought of Hoitt and Co."[17] This furniture, apparently, did not meet with the
Shakers' approval, as the table surfaces remained cold in the winter months. Con-
sequently, in 1940 they exchanged the unwanted pieces for six maple tables and
twenty-four chairs from Chase & Co., also of Manchester, for a cost of $173.50.[18]

By the early twentieth century, the appearance of the surviving communities had changed dramatically from that of one hundred years earlier. One worldly
visitor to Canterbury about 1917 was unprepared for the contemporary interiors
she encountered: "I remember so well driving up in the big Locomobile limousine;
it didn't look out of place, since they had their own expensive cars. I remember
how surprised Mother was at our guestrooms—no Shaker furniture, just modern
things—probably like Grand Rapids furniture."[19]

It is apparent that the Shaker communities from Maine to Kentucky were
making a conscious effort to modernize their surroundings and to keep pace with
the world according to their "principles of prudence and economy." Clearly the
Believers' later furniture and interiors are as valid a reflection of their belief system
as comparable items produced during the "classic" period. Whether aesthetically
pleasing to the twentieth-century observer or not, the Victorian era of Shaker
design should be viewed as a critical part of the study of their material culture.

Shaker Design

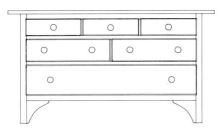

Fig. 1. An example of symmetry: Counter, Mount Lebanon, New York, c. 1830

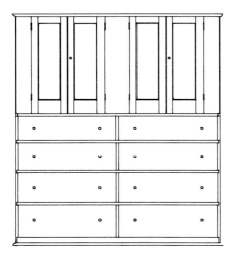

Fig. 2. An example of symmetry: Counter, by Seth Blanchard, Harvard, Massachusetts, 1853 (see pl. 155)

Fig. 3. An example of symmetry: Cupboard and case of drawers, Mount Lebanon, New York, c. 1830 (see pl. 5)

Built-in cupboard and case of drawers, fourth floor, Church Family Dwelling House, Hancock, Massachusetts, 1830. Butternut and pine, with fruitwood and porcelain knobs, chrome yellow paint, red wash, and cast-brass and forged-iron hardware, h 94⅝ w 41¾". Hancock Shaker Village, Pittsfield, Massachusetts

I**N THE PROCESS** of making a piece of furniture, the cabinetmaker or craftsman draws from experience and observation to create a structural, technical, and decorative solution to the problem of design needs. He develops an appropriate approach based on a range of alternatives in his particular cultural and physical environment. These are drawn from his own expectations and abilities, as well as his goal to satisfy the needs of the client. For the Shakers, the client was the community as a whole. While design is often thought of as a creative endeavor, the process is also grounded in reality and involves the craftsman's training, which often has a traditional and conservative bias; the influence of a printed design; the development of new forms from the reorganization of older parts; and the adoption of new materials, tools, and techniques.[1] There are a number of factors, both conscious and unconscious, that affect design. Tradition, function, and specific directives all dictate the way a craftsman might choose to use the design concepts.

Furniture can be appraised in a systematic way by evaluating the form and the nonstructural elements of the object and then observing the effect of the spatial surroundings on each piece. The following principles will be invoked to clarify the concept of Shaker design and identify the diverse elements essential to the evaluation and discussion of Shaker furniture. Although form, construction, and function are inevitably interdependent in a design, it is possible to separate and study the principles under which they operate. By using these concepts, one can identify those artistic elements that characterize Shaker furniture and make it discernible from worldly counterparts as well as recognize forms unique to individual Shaker communities.

An analysis of form draws on the concepts of balance, hierarchy, pattern, proportion, and scale, all of which contribute to the shape of the object. The Shakers were consciously aware of these guiding principles which one Believer verbalized when describing the Great Stone Dwelling at Enfield, New Hampshire. "He supervised the construction of their most splendid edifice—which I have described—with an architectural taste which has introduced to the interior a combination of space, beauty, symmetry and the light and splendor of a summer's day."[2]

Balance entails a state of equilibrium between opposing forces. Symmetry, the distribution of equivalent forms and spaces on either side of a vertical or horizontal axis, is the most commonly used way to achieve balance. Bilateral symmetry, in which the parts on either side of the axis are mirror images of each other, is central to most eighteenth- and nineteenth-century worldly furniture. For example, in a chest of drawers, a sideboard, or a cupboard, the case is divided visually by a vertical axis or center line in which each half mirrors the other. Although some Shaker furniture follows this common pattern, other Shaker cabinetmakers regularly moved away from this rigidly held aesthetic and developed many asymmetrical forms, which can achieve balance by presenting equivalent but nonmatching forms. Presumably, an important motive was to build a functional as well as aesthetically pleasing piece. Unbridled by worldly fashion, customer whim, or the traditionally conservative apprenticeship system, Shaker craftsmen were able to create furniture to suit the community's specific needs, which often involved developing new combinations and layouts.

Counters and sewing desks exemplify the most prominent of asymmetrical arrangements seen in Shaker work furniture. Often built as long horizontal

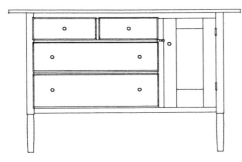

Fig. 4. An example of asymmetry: Counter, attributed to Grove Wright, Hancock, Massachusetts, c. 1830

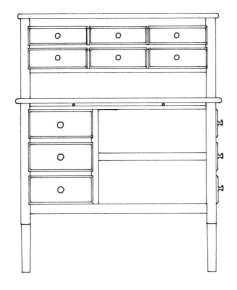

Fig. 5. An example of asymmetry: Sewing desk, Enfield, New Hampshire, c. 1860

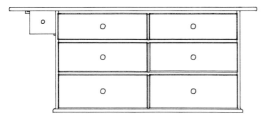

Fig. 6. An example of asymmetry: Counter with underhung drawer, Mount Lebanon, New York, c. 1830

cases, the counters present a highly organized though asymmetrical layout with different shapes placed on either side of the center of the piece. In a counter built by Grove Wright, for example (see fig. 5), a single cupboard door is positioned opposite a much wider bank of drawers. The opposing sections are balanced successfully despite the different horizontal dimensions given to each half. The arrangements of unequal parts are organized around an imaginary visual center line rather than a rigidly placed, geometrically accurate center line.

The sewing desk, in particular, regularly displays an asymmetrical layout. In Benjamin Smith's desks (see pl. 183), the asymmetrically arranged lower storage unit contains three drawers 15 inches long next to four drawers measuring 7½ inches wide. Sometimes one end of a case piece is fitted with a bank of drawers made very accessible by their unusual placement (fig. 5). Tables or counters with overhanging tops will often contain a single underhung drawer (fig. 6). Asymmetry was so well developed in numerous Shaker forms that it has come to be identified with Shaker design.

The arrangement of parts and their importance in terms of function, shape, or size relative to the overall placement defines the hierarchy of a piece. In most Shaker storage units consisting of cupboard over drawers (fig. 7), greater importance is given to the single door by centering it at eye level above a bank of drawers. Considerable prominence is given to the top of the case by means of the wide stiles on either side of the much narrower cupboard. Although the stiles command primary visual importance because of their mass (thereby balancing the stack of drawers below), they are somewhat dysfunctional, as they make the space behind them partially inaccessible. This arrangement, however, is probably the norm within Shaker furniture design. In the Grove Wright counter (fig. 4), more visual prominence is given to the single door than the wider drawers, thus achieving an overall balanced effect. The same is true of the facade of the early Canterbury counter pl. 177, where the smaller cupboard door is more important than the adjacent bank of drawers.

Pattern involves the repetitive use of similar shapes, forms, or spaces to create unity and organization within a design. The most common configuration is found in cases of drawers, with their repetition of similar elements. Here, the expected pattern consists of a bank of graduated drawers. However, the complex counter shown in fig. 8 utilizes two distinct drawer patterns to create an aesthetically pleasing composition. The three drawers increase in size vertically from top to bottom, creating a rhythm typical of worldly furniture. At the same time, drawers decrease in width (38½, 32⅛, 22⁹⁄₁₆, 17, 17, and 17 inches) horizontally across the front of the over-twelve-foot-long case. This results in an unusual yet harmonious design that avoids the monotony of equal-size drawers throughout. In one common pattern each drawer in a single bank is smaller than the one below it (fig. 9). Drawers can also be graduated in sets, or more commonly in pairs, decreasing in size from bottom to top (fig. 10). In other cases, none of the drawers are graduated (fig. 11). The same form may be given different arrangements of drawers, as illustrated in figs. 12–14.

Proportion is determined by the dimensional relationships of the various parts and how they relate to the whole. The measurements for much Shaker furniture lie within the norms established by eighteenth- and nineteenth-century design books. These principles were derived from classical architecture, which emphasized mathematical relationships both in the ratio between the dimensions of the particular parts to the whole and between the parts themselves.[3] "They tend to be the simple proportions of 2 x 3, 3 x 4 and the square. That is, given any

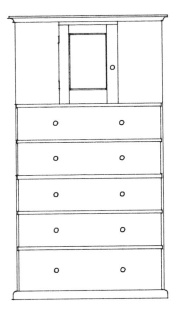

Fig. 7. An example of hierarchy: Cupboard and case of drawers, Mount Lebanon, New York, c. 1820

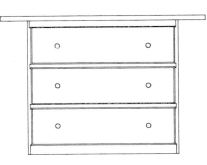

Fig. 8. An example of pattern: Counter with drawers graduated vertically and horizontally, Mount Lebanon, New York, c. 1820

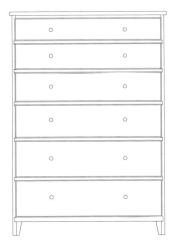

Fig. 9. An example of pattern: Case of drawers with simple graduated drawers, Groveland, New York, c. 1830

Fig. 10. An example of pattern: Case of drawers graduated in sets, Mount Lebanon, New York, c. 1840 (see pl. 19). The top two pairs of drawers are 7 inches in depth, the next four are approximately one inch deeper, and the bottom two are about an inch deeper than the previous tier.

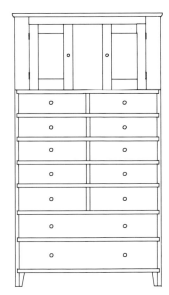

Fig. 11. An example of pattern: Case of drawers, nongraduated, Mount Lebanon, New York, c. 1820

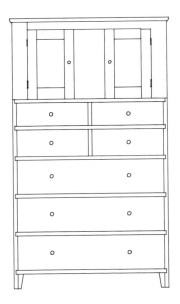

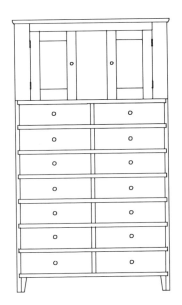

Figs. 12–14. Examples of pattern: Three different groupings of drawers in the same form, cupboard over case of drawers, Mount Lebanon, New York, c. 1840

Figs. 15, 16. An example of scale: A sewing case from Hancock, Massachusetts, c. 1840, 27 inches high and 34 inches wide, compared with multiple cupboards and cases of drawers for communal storage, attic, North Family Dwelling House, Mount Lebanon, New York, c. 1820, approximately 7 feet high by 27 feet long

unit—centimeters, inches, feet, or yards—the proportion 2 x 3 uses two units on one side and three on the other; for 3 x 4, there are three units on one side and four on the other; for a square, each side is of equal length. Combinations of these and other slightly more complex proportions are the fundamental units behind so much of what we prize as beautiful."[4] The goal of this approach was to achieve integration of design, that is, a synthesis of proportion, balance, and hierarchy in a harmonious composition. The importance of these principles lies in the fact that they serve as cornerstones of good design; they direct and determine the way we look at architecture in general and furniture in particular. For example, the case of drawers by a Mount Lebanon cabinetmaker pl. 19 exhibits a masterful handling of proportions due to the relationship between the height and width of the case.

Scale refers to the size of an object relative to its surroundings, which includes other objects, the object's users, and the space it inhabits. In Shaker furniture, the dimensional relationship of a piece to its surrounding space ranges from a diminutive 6-drawer case made at Hancock to the 860 built-in drawers found in the Church Family Dwelling House at Enfield, New Hampshire.[5] Institutional requirements pushed Shaker furniture forms to a scale not seen in worldly design. Trestle tables spanning over twenty feet in length, workbench tops measuring eighteen feet long, and tailoring counters ranging from six to twelve feet long and four feet wide all became commonplace in Shaker communities (see pl. 174).

Extensive storage requirements for the large families, usually consisting of about one hundred members, created the need for whole areas devoted to newly built storage units. At Canterbury, for example (see pl. 168), one entire floor of the 1837 wing in the Church Family Dwelling House was set aside for built-in units placed away from the walls to incorporate the space behind the units into additional off-season clothing storage. The room is lined on both sides with a series of fourteen cupboards above 101 drawers alternating with six closets stretching over forty feet in length. According to surviving journals, David Rowley contributed much of the labor and many of the skills required to build or furnish the North and Church Family residences and shops at Mount Lebanon, where he lived. In January 1837, it was reported, he "has undertaken to make a quantity of cherry tables, to furnish the great house, in the various rooms—has begun 20 tables."[6] It is apparent from Hervey Elkins's description of the Great Stone Dwelling at Enfield, New Hampshire, that the retiring rooms, due to their large size, housed a number of Believers, each with his or her own bed. "In the third and fourth lofts, the corridors, eighteen feet in width, extend longitudinally through the centre, the entire length or one hundred feet. On either side are retiring rooms, all exactly twenty feet square, nine feet high, and of identical furniture and finish, rendering it difficult to determine, but by the number, one room from another."[7]

The surface of an object is determined by its form and function, but its treatment rarely affects either. A surface may be left plain or embellished with ornamentation. Compared to fashionable Federal inlay or Sheraton reeding, Shaker forms were plain and simple. Craftsmen reduced forms to their essence and omitted extraneous detail not necessary to achieve a functional beauty. Although not stripped of all decorative elements, Shaker furniture still made a marked contrast with worldly designs, as many observers have pointed out. Charles Dickens's negative reaction to the Mount Lebanon Shakers following a visit in 1842 was recorded in this familiar quotation:

> We walked into a grim room, where several grim hats were hanging on grim pegs, and the time was grimly told by a grim clock, which uttered every tick with a kind of struggle, as if it broke the grim silence reluctantly and under protest. Ranged against the wall were six or eight stiff high-backed chairs, and they partook so strongly of the general grimness, that one would much rather have sat on the floor than incurred the smallest obligation to any of them.[8]

A comparison of Shaker with rural furniture produced by northern European immigrants in the Hudson River Valley reveals a noticeable absence of both Dutch and German influences. Most early Believers, such as the New Light Baptists and Presbyterians, who joined during the critical early decades of community development, were primarily from England rather than the Continent. Consequently, the decorative work found in storage units such as the Dutch Kas or German Schrank characterized by monumental cornice moldings, bold architectural statements, and vibrantly painted floral surfaces have no counterparts within the broad spectrum of Shaker design. Instead, early and classic Shaker furniture exhibits a restrained use of decorative elaborations on structural forms, such as a rounded table edge or turned chair pommel. It also makes moderate use of moldings, both at midcase and on the cornice, which are relatively small and rather sim-

Desk and cupboard, probably Watervliet, New York, c. 1830. New York State Museum, Albany, #27.7.210

ple, consisting primarily of quarter-round or bull-nose-shaped elements. However, rarely was a piece reduced to its aesthetic minimum. In most cases, Shaker decoration is integrated with the overall form and adds an interesting sense of movement to the piece. For example, the vertical panels forming the sides of sewing desks are structural elements, and at the same time they provide a contrast with the horizontal orientation of the drawer fronts (see pl. 183). The deliberate selection of figured woods for the exposed surfaces of some work furniture reveals the Shaker craftsman's development of a refined functionalism. The lively grain relieves the monotony of the large, bulky form, enhances visual interest, and provides a smooth and aesthetically pleasing working surface.

In the mid- to late nineteenth century, many Shaker cabinetmakers adapted and modified the current Victorian style, among them Henry Blinn (see pls. 186, 187), Thomas Fisher (see pls. 135, 137, 138), Franklin Youngs (see pl. 229), Henry Green (see pls. 248, 249), and Delmer Wilson (see pl. 256). Elder Henry Blinn contributed to the intriguing variations on the ever-broadening style of Shaker design. His sewing desk and secretary desk are characterized by decorative touches such as machine-made molding around drawer faces and white porcelain pulls, in an understated interpretation of Victorian style that reflects not only his acquaintance with but also his acceptance of contemporary worldly fashion.

Whether embellished or left plain, the surface was invariably treated with a protective finish. In a manner generally consistent with worldly practice, the Shakers used paint, stain, and varnish in various combinations on both freestanding furniture and built-in storage units from the late eighteenth through the early twentieth centuries. In selecting paint to finish their work, Shaker craftsmen were continuing the long Anglo-European tradition of using pigment to create a neat and clean appearance and add visual interest to the furniture and its room setting.[9] Color also served either to unify the appearance of a piece of furniture constructed of several different woods or to emphasize certain structural parts.

The selection of a particular color was based on its expense and availability, and in this respect the furniture reflected the taste of the Shakers' rural American neighbors. Due to the low cost, various shades of red served as the traditional paint color for barns and other large-surface exteriors; it also represented the logical choice for Shaker-made freestanding and built-in units. As a result of advances in paint technology, brighter colors became available by the early 1800s, and blue green, ocher, and chrome yellow were frequently employed.[10] The latter, which may have suggested a gilded surface to worldly Americans, often served as a background for decorative "fancy" painting. The Shakers, however, used bright yellow pigment independently as a solid coat of paint. Some authorities theorize that due to the expense, the Shakers reserved dark blue for religious spaces, as this color appears almost exclusively on meetinghouse interiors.[11]

Surviving examples of opaque painted surfaces are found on built-in storage units. These include the dark blue woodwork in the interior of the Sabbathday Lake meetinghouse dating from 1792 and the third floor of the Canterbury meetinghouse, whose woodwork and counter were painted in 1815 (pls. 239, 177). Among the freestanding dated furniture from several communities are a c. 1800 washstand painted yellow (pl. 235); a red case of drawers, c. 1830 (pl. 21); and a box finished with blue-green pigment inscribed 1821 (pl. 156).

By the 1830s, written and physical evidence suggests the Shakers introduced transparent colored stains, which were not as common in American country furniture of the same period.[12] Thinner pigments may have satisfied the same practical and aesthetic needs as opaque paints and simultaneously allowed some of the wood's grain to show through. According to "The order as it respects painting and varnishing," written in 1841, "Ye shall have the stain in your dwelling house, an orange color; and your Shops the same, only a shade darker, your floors in the dwelling house shall be, of a redish yellow; and these at the shops of a yellowish red, not too dark."[13] Surviving evidence for this staining policy is found in William Deming's description of the 1832 Church Family Dwelling House at Hancock. The building contained colorful built-in units consisting of pine cases and 240 pine cupboard doors stained yellow and 369 butternut drawers stained red.[14] The 1837 addition to the Church Family Dwelling House at Canterbury includes a third-floor attic with six walk-in closets, fourteen cupboards, and one hundred drawers, all stained ocher to reveal rather than conceal the grain of the pine beneath (pl. 168). A mixture of paint and stains is found in the 1841 North Shop at Canterbury, which contains a room finished with a mustard wash adjacent to an interior with built-in units painted red. Freestanding furniture also shows this transition in surface treatment. Examples include a c. 1840 counter with chrome yellow paint and red stain (pl. 245) and a c. 1840 case of drawers with a yellow wash (pl. 19).

Information regarding finishes is also documented by several journal references. On January 13, 1835, "Ziba finished the cradle and brought it into the Nurse room where it was stained."[15] According to a sister's journal entry of 1867, she cleaned "the paint off the palm lief shop counter" on September 24 and two days later stainèd it.[16] It is readily apparent from written records and conversations with the twentieth-century Shakers that they regularly refinished both freestanding and built-in furniture during the nineteenth and twentieth centuries, which explains why so few pieces exist with the maker's original surface unchanged.

Dickens's impression of grimness notwithstanding, the Shakers used color to create brilliant living spaces. When considered as part of a room setting, bold colors are used to define specific pieces of furniture or architectural spaces. This is amply illustrated in William Deming's description of the 1832 Church Family Dwelling House: "And I think we may say it is finished from the top to the bottom, handsomely stained inside with a bright orange color. The outer doors are green. The outside of the house is painted with four coats of a beautiful red. The plastering is covered with a coat of hard finish & is a beautiful white."[17] The fourth-floor built-ins still retain their original surface pigment, which consists of drawers stained red surrounded by a case painted chrome yellow. The Centre Family Dwelling House at South Union, Kentucky, presents a dramatic juxtaposition between the ocher-stained peg rail and floor, brick red baseboard, solid white plastered wall, and clear varnished built-ins. The effect is heightened by the addition of movable furniture, which might include mustard yellow side chairs and bottle green painted beds, providing a colorful counterpoint to the interior woodwork and trim. Shaker taste also evolved over time, as the Believers updated interiors to reflect a more contemporary look. By the 1870s, the popular Colonial Revival style became part of the repertoire of prominent worldly architects and is reflected in the Shakers' remodeling efforts. For example, in 1875, Room 10 of the Canterbury Church Family Dwelling House, which was originally stained chrome yellow, was repainted white, a color closely associated with the new style.

Another option besides color, for both Shakers and worldly Americans, was to create a shiny or matte finish. In order to protect the wood and give it a glossy surface, they applied either varnish or shellac over a colored stain or raw wood. It is difficult to distinguish between the two finishes, although references in Shaker journals suggest that varnish was the most common method of treatment.[18] A visitor writing about the interior woodwork of the Great Stone

Case of drawers, Mount Lebanon, New York, c. 1840. Pine, with red wash. Private collection. Photograph: courtesy Suzanne Courcier and Robert W. Wilkins

Dwelling under construction at Enfield, New Hampshire, in 1840 noted that "the paint is very smooth and glossy. Elder Orville says they finished it by dipping the paint brush in boiled oil just as the paint is drying, and brush it over. By this means the oil becomes a varnish which looks elegantly when dry."[19] By the 1860s a common look was that of naturally figured wood with a clear varnish finish.

The issue of applying either a matte or glossy finish was apparently of some concern to the mid-nineteenth-century Believers. The 1845 "Millennial Laws" state, "Varnish, if used in dwelling houses, may be applied only to the moveables therein, as the following, viz., Tables, stands, bureaus, cases of drawers, writing desks or boxes, drawer faces, chests, chairs, etc. etc."[20] Conversely, according to the "Holy Orders of the Church," "These are the things upon which ye shall in no wise use Varnish: The wood work of your dwelling house and Shops; drawers and cupboards . . . chests."[21] By 1861, the more conservative Believers expressed their opposition to the increased use of varnish on surfaces. "There is a great proclivity in this, our day, for fixing up matters very nice, & the varnish has to go on to the cup-boards, drawers &c. & the paint on to floors, everything has to be so slick that a fly will slip on it."[22] Writing in 1865, Daniel Boler in the ministry at Watervliet addressed the same subject in a letter to Orren Haskins at Mount Lebanon.

> In the present case as touching the use of Varnish on the wood work of our dwellings in the Sanctuary at the Mount, we have unitedly decided to have what varnish is used, put into the last coat of paint—Yet some of our members are inclined to feel some like the old Indian who did not want to like much pudding in his rum, and finally concluded he did not care about any—however, on the present occasion, I rather believe I guess we had better have some pudding for union and for example sake."[23]

Entrance of Meetinghouse, Sabbathday Lake, Maine, 1839, with blue paint

Numerous examples from the 1860s survive in the signed and dated sewing desks by Benjamin Smith (see pl. 183) and Eli Kidder (see pl. 181). Emmory Brooks, working at Groveland, New York, also produced distinctive black walnut pieces with a clear finish during the last quarter of the nineteenth century (see pl. 335).

The age of golden oak was made popular in Grand Rapids, Michigan, between about 1890 and 1920. As supplies of dark walnut were depleted, furniture manufacturers created a lighter appearance by finishing oak in layers of shellac. This look was mimicked by the Shakers using varnish on ash and other woods and is evident in the furniture of Amos Stewart at Mount Lebanon, including the drop-front desk dated 1877 (see pl. 29) and that produced by Thomas Fisher at Enfield, Connecticut (see p. 192 and pls. 135, 137).

Throughout the last quarter of the nineteenth century, some documented interiors were further decorated by graining and marbleizing techniques. Graining could be strictly imitative, copying exactly the characteristic features of any wood, or highly fanciful, so that the finished surface was both stylish and economical. In order to achieve the desired result, usually a dark color was applied over a lighter-colored ground with a brush, although rollers, combs, and other graining tools were employed as well (see pls. 209, 246, 251).[24] Henry Blinn's written comments on his 1873 tour of the Shaker villages provides specific information on the treatment of interior woodwork at various societies. At the North Union dwelling he observed, "Some of the doors were grained, others had drab pannels and pink trimmings. Some of the wood work was marbled." At Groveland, Elder Henry noted, "The meeting room at the Meeting house is now painted a light green & the doors are grained like mahogany."[25] When the meeting room in the Church Family Dwelling House at Sabbathday Lake was built in 1884, the doors were grained to match the ash that formed the rest of the woodwork. Jessie Evans of Canterbury recorded in a diary reference of March 22, 1900, "The South dining room of [the] office [building] is being painted by M. Dearborn of Upland. The first ornamental house painting done at the Village. Oak leaf trimming and graining."

In their use of finishes, clearly the Shakers at all the villages were aware of current fashion trends and adopted as well as adapted prevailing practices to suit their changing needs.

Although the placement of a piece of furniture in its site often occurs after its construction, the dynamic relationship between object and setting is usually considered in the initial design stage. For example, the large counter situated in a second-story workroom at Canterbury Shaker Village (pl. 174) measures twelve feet long and four feet wide and was conceived, built, and assembled in place, for the original door openings do not accommodate its removal. This particular design has four usable sides made accessible by the counter's location in the room and the addition of wheels. It contains an assortment of long and short drawers and cupboards to store textile-related materials. This extremely large counter commands primary importance in its surrounding space, which measures only 17 feet ½ inch by 16 feet ¾ inch.

While most dwelling house furniture was probably used against walls, specific freestanding pieces were designed to be used on more than one side. For example, many sewing desks (pls. 183, 185) have, in addition to drawers and work surface in front, storage and pullout slides for extra work space on one or more sides, so more than one Believer could use the desk at the same time. Many counters and worktables were similarly equipped on two or more sides, like the counter pl. 174, which also has wheels for easy mobility. The concept of providing multiple access resulted in a distinctive look for Shaker work furniture.

Molding planes, Canterbury, New Hampshire, stamped ID (James Daniels) and EK (Eli Kidder). From left to right: hollow molding plane, ovolo, quarter-round, quarter-round, ovolo, bead, and bead with cove. Hancock Shaker Village, Pittsfield, Massachusetts, #78-57.1.35, .8, .16, .15, .9, .11, .6

Tools and Technology

OVER THE CENTURIES, a number of different craftsmen with specialized skills have been involved in woodwoorking. Since medieval times, the carpenter was primarily concerned with building construction—either on a large or a small scale—such as timber-framed structures. The joiner, whose craft evolved from carpentry, handled material that was smaller than structural woodwork and produced furniture by fastening wood parts with mortise-and-tenon joints. A projecting tongue or tenon, cut on the end of one member, fit snugly into a rectangular cavity or mortise cut into the adjacent member. This joint would then be secured with a peg.

It was not until the seventeenth century that cabinetmaking techniques evolved. Cabinetmakers were highly skilled makers of furniture who constructed case pieces out of solid boards that were secured with dovetail joints. These craftsmen also used veneering, an elaborate technique introduced into England during the last half of the seventeenth century. Furthermore, they worked with mill-sawn boards, which was a more efficient use of wood than the joiner's use of riven wood. The latter was split from a log in a pie-shaped slice using a mallet and froe. In order to obtain a fairly flat piece of wood, the craftsman had to discard both the thick and thin ends.

In addition to joiners and carpenters who produced furniture, turners specialized in operating a lathe for turning wood. By applying gauges and chisels they could form the shape of balls, rings, vases, and columns. Turners made mostly seating furniture and were known primarily as chair makers. The same types of woodworkers were also found in Shaker communities.[1]

Construction, a major component of furniture design, is influenced by the tools and technology available to the craftsman. Initially, craftsmen relied on hand tools that did not vary much in their design or capabilities over time. However, the nineteenth century saw a dramatic change in tools and technology as the first power tools came into use. The move to a new, more effective power source, combined with innovative developments in woodworking machinery, maximized efficiency by speeding each part of the operation and making standardization possible. One astute writer on the subject defined the difference between "workmanship of risk," which involves using "any kind of technique or apparatus in which the quality of the work is not pre-determined before a single saleable thing is made," and "workmanship of certainty."[2] The element of risk can be replaced by more certainty by using machinery to assist in the production of furniture. Machinery can increase productivity by reducing the required skill and increasing the accuracy of the worker in making the finished product.

In his history of the Shaker Church, Brother Isaac Newton Youngs of Mount Lebanon, New York, recorded the progress in furniture construction in terms of technological innovation and its effect on the finished product:

> There was no essential improvements in this line [of carpenter and joiner work], in a general sense for some years, the people were poor at first, inexperienced, and unable to put up costly and well built houses: their tools and conveniences for work were indifferent and inferior. . . . But after the year 1813 there were some important improvements, particularly the buz saw was introduced for streightening and slitting stuff—also matching works came in use: this greatly relieved the workmen of much

hard labor. Planing machines were introduced since 18- for planing timber and boards, which has been of very great utility. Besides there has been a great increase in the number and quality of tools, and various machines, as mortising, and boring machines, etc. by which work can be done easier, quicker and better.[3]

To fully understand the dramatic transitions Brother Isaac described, it is necessary to examine specific Shaker workshop requirements, the different sources of power utilized, and the developments in woodworking machinery. The materials employed, which were specific to each Shaker community depending on availability, are discussed more fully under each community.

Scattered journal notations provide information regarding Shaker workshop practices. On April 19, 1848, "Orren Haskins moved from the 2nd order to take up his residence here in the first order, and to officiate as woodworkman. This seems to be highly necessary as we have had no one to support that occupation since the absconding of Braman W[icks]." Later, in December 1855, "There has been some changes of late in our shop work - Orren H. has taken charge of the shop formerly occupied by David Rowley, SW room 2 loft-brick shop. William Greaves occupies the old joiners' shop. Horatio Stone has commenced in some degree, to learn the Taylors' trade, and to work some at present with Orren, at woodwork."[4] Although these references reveal the names of several craftsmen assigned to this Mount Lebanon joiners' shop, it tells us little about decision making and working relationships. It is not clear whether or not Orren Haskins, as the "officiating" brother, would make practical decisions regarding the design and form of specific pieces of furniture or if the deacons or ministry were involved as well. Other questions that arise include whether the craftsmen worked together in several large shops or if general joinery and more specific cabinetmaking tasks were performed in different areas. In their journals, Shakers only occasionally explained if each individual completed a project from start to finish or if the brothers pooled their efforts, each performing one step in the overall process.

Information gleaned from journal entries suggests there were different space requirements for the numerous shops within the Shaker communities. Brother Freegift Wells described one small area of the Herb Shop at Watervliet, New York, which he rehabilitated. He had just retired from his responsibilities as an elder within the community and was setting up his work space in this unused area. Between May 20 and December 30, 1857, he partitioned off a small room, installed shelves to hold tools, constructed a writing table, and completed a vise and lathe.[5]

The highly successful chair industry at Mount Lebanon represents the other extreme in workshop requirements. The factory, built under Brother Robert Wagan's direction in 1872, was a thirty-by-sixty-foot two-story frame structure with attic and basement, providing work space for one or two Shakers and about ten non-Shaker employees. The following list of purchases in 1869 indicates new machinery probably acquired for the burgeoning chair industry: "One lathe for turning wood, one planer, one circular saw, one boring machine, one dressing machine."[6] Decades later, when this building fell into disuse, a series of photographs from about 1930 were taken in another chair factory, housed in a Second Family building. These candid images provide a sense of the twentieth-century space—which was far removed from the earlier Shaker workshops partly because the furniture itself, as well as its means of production, had changed. The line shafting crossed overhead to power the machinery, and the floor space was

Workbench, attributed to Franklin Youngs, Enfield, New Hampshire, c. 1880. Canterbury Shaker Village, Inc., Canterbury, New Hampshire, #84.440

covered with heavy cast-iron machinery lining a maze of pathways. The requirements of mass production differed dramatically from those of individual handcrafting, for which the smaller nineteenth-century work spaces of the previous Shakers were adequate.

To visualize accurately the Shaker workshop spaces a century after the fact, some familiarity with the three forms of woodworking shop furniture is helpful. The primary piece of shop furniture was the workbench, which functioned as a specialized worktable. Typical examples measure eight to twelve feet long, the largest known surviving example totaling sixteen feet seven inches. The base usually contains two to four banks of drawers and often a cupboard section with shelving. The heavy frame-and-panel case supported a top that could be as much as four inches thick, which ensured a rigid work surface. An end or tail vise was built into the right end of the bench, which, in conjunction with the bench dogs—a removable and adjustable type of stop—inserted into the square mortised holes along the front, could hold long stock either flat or on edge. Using these devices, the craftsman could plane a board's surface or create a molded edge. Another vise, positioned near the left end of the bench, was used to hold small stock, long boards, or doors on edge with a bench jack supporting the other end. The jack slid on tracks placed on the bottom of the bench and under the top front edge and supported a peg inserted into the hole at the right side to hold the work piece level. Smaller and presumably lighter benches were used on the job site, where a joiner completed the finish carpentry in a new building, such as the stairways, window casing, or trim work. On August 27, 1818, "William & Timothy finished their tables then we carried off our work benches & tools & cleared out the house ready for the sisters to finish painting & staining. . . ."[7]

When storage besides that provided for in the workbench was required, the craftsman might utilize a toolbox, a six-board dovetailed box fitted with interior trays for small tools and space for molding and bench planes. Handles affixed to the ends of these chests facilitated carrying them from the furniture to the joiners' shop or to other temporary work sites.

Extant Shaker tool cupboards are shallow case pieces containing both cupboard and drawer storage space. They were equipped with numerous racks and extra doors designed to hold specific tools, such as a brace and bits, a set of chisels, and crosscut saws, ripsaws, and small and large backsaws.

During the nineteenth century, woodworking tools underwent a number of dramatic changes. An Englishman named Samuel Bentham patented several improvements for woodworking machinery in 1793, including planers, molders, and dovetailers.[8] Few of these designs went into immediate production, however, due to the individual's skills needed to build more complicated machinery or his ability to afford such technological innovations, and did not become more prevalent until the 1820s to 1840s. The other major factor affecting the widespread use of these improvements was the need to develop effective power resources to operate more sophisticated woodworking machinery.

The Shaker joiner or furniture shops were similar to their worldly counterparts during the late eighteenth century in their reliance on hand tools such as planes, saws, chisels, and drills. The gradual transition to power machinery within the Shaker society paralleled the shop practices of craftsmen in the world at large whom they were copying. Although the Shakers are credited with numerous inventions, a critical evaluation of journals and actual machinery suggests that they were probably innovative mechanics rather than inventors in the forefront of woodworking equipment development. The Shaker craftsmen were presumably introduced to new tools and technology through contact with local woodworkers or nearby factories in industrial centers such as Albany, Cincinnati, or Boston. In addition to word-of-mouth recommendations, the Shakers may have read about technological improvements through reference books or one of the numerous trade or scientific journals to which several Shaker communities subscribed. Brother Henry DeWitt of Mount Lebanon, New York, made reference to one such source (currently in the Hancock Shaker Village library with his name in it). He wrote that on "December 9, 1853 . . . I got all the covers on my books today 42 of them [including]. . . . 2 large MECHANICK'S DICTIONARY on machinery for Geo. Wickersham. . . . "[9] Over the years, the Shakers experimented with water, wind, and steam to drive their equipment. Waterpower was first developed within the Shaker community to serve their larger-scale needs, such as sawing lumber for the construction of buildings. Most villages were situated on streams, which allowed for extensive development of waterpower resources. At Watervliet, New York, Brother Freegift Wells was involved in the construction of a waterwheel as early as 1814. On February 5, he recorded, "F went to the 2nd families. Draw a draft for a cogwheel," and on February 11, he "went to Albany with Morrell and got a wheel cast for the Second family's w[e]st mill gears."[10] Despite its successful application over the years, waterpower proved problematic. As the quantity of water in millponds depends on rainfall, so the waterwheel was subject to seasonal flooding and midsummer droughts, as well as freezing, the destruction of dams, and the continual need to maintain the apparatus, all problems frequently recorded in journals.[11]

Given these difficulties, the Shakers eagerly explored other power resources. During the 1820s, Brother Freegift Wells noted that the Watervliet Shakers experimented with windmills to saw stove wood at several locations in the community.[12] However, these, too, depended on the weather, and it was not until the emergence of steam power that these seasonal problems were circumvented. Although Brother Freegift never recorded the use of steam power specifically in the woodworking shops at Watervliet, it was employed there successfully in the new wash house.[13] At Mount Lebanon, on the other hand, a new development was reported in the September 1872 issue of The Shaker: "The South [Family] are building an extensive chair factory . . . with tenant houses attached. A thousand dollar engine from Haskell's Albany works is the drive [for] the machinery."[14] The United States census of manufacturers published just two years prior to the construction of the new chair factory reported its annual output and noted that in 1870 the business operated only nine months out of the year. With the introduction of the new steam power engine the perennial problems of waterpower were overcome, enabling the chair industry to function year-round.

With the introduction of power sources came the development of machinery. By the 1860s many larger furniture shops had circular (buzz) saws, planers, boring machines, and mortisers, which improved the accuracy of many woodworking processes and greatly speeded up the tasks associated with stock preparation and joining parts, such as cutting and planing planks.[15] At the Mount Lebanon factory, the use of power machinery facilitated the mass production of chairs and made possible the standardization of sizes and parts. While the earliest account books designate chair variations as small chair frames, common chair, and large rocker, by the early 1860s the Shakers had changed their terminology to a more precise or uniform system that designated sizes by number from zero (smallest) to seven (largest).[16]

In terms of design, the replacement of hand craftsmanship by machine work is apparent in a number of areas. Designs were changed to facilitate the more

Steam engine, c. 1870. Reproduced from
*Asher & Adams' Pictorial Album of American
Industry,* New York: Asher & Adams, 1876

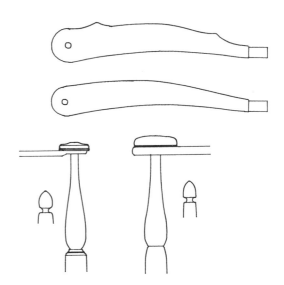

Machine production changed the look of Mount Lebanon chair parts: the arm of 1880–1920 (top), seen from above, became broader than the arm of 1870 (below) and added projections at the wrist and elbow. The front post supporting the arm of c. 1880–1940 (below right) became greatly simplified compared with that of earlier transitional chairs (below left), both in the reduction of vase turnings and the modification of the mushroom-shaped tenon cap. The pommel or finial form became crisper.

Delmer Wilson's shop, Sabbathday Lake, Maine, c. 1923. From left to right: table saw, planer, and shaper, with line shafting above to drive them. Shaker Museum and Library, Old Chatham, New York, #19314

Production wood-turning lathe, c. 1870. Reproduced from *Asher & Adams' Pictorial Album of American Industry*, New York: Asher & Adams, 1876

rapid processing of chair parts with the available machinery. While the top and bottom edges of the back slats of earlier chairs were square, the later production chairs had slats with rounded top and bottom edges that had been cut with a boring or slotting machine and were fitted into corresponding slots. Turnings were also simplified to maximize the use of duplicating lathes. Superfluous detail was eliminated from the vase turnings on the front posts beneath the arms as well as from the pommels, which assumed a crisp acorn shape. Large quantities of stretchers were quickly shaped on production lathes. The back slats, rockers, and arms were consistently made with jigs on a shaper run by a steam engine. The arm style became broad, flat, and uniformly thick, with projections at the wrist and elbow positions. Both the inside and outside edges were identically rounded by a single shaper cutter. The shift to a bent, rather than straight, back post simplified drilling by creating a ninety-degree angle between the side stretchers and the posts. Finally, boring machines mechanically located the holes for the rungs and slots for the back slats, thus eliminating the scribe marks traditionally made by the craftsman while the posts were still on the lathe.

According to Shaker oral tradition, Sister Tabitha Babbitt (1784–1858) of the Harvard community is credited with the invention of the circular saw in 1813, which was in operation by 1817 at least. Constructed "of thin soft sheet iron, six inches in diameter . . . for cutting the hardest steel with the ease of tallow," it was considered too useful a discovery to be monopolized by a patent and was shared by the Shakers freely with the world.[17] *The Manifesto*, a periodical published under various titles by the Believers, stated that "in 1813 a great improvement was accepted by the introduction of a buzz or circular saw. A large amount of work was now done in the mill with a saw running by water power, which was a great relief to the workman who had till now used his hand saw for this same purpose."[18] Initially, the circular saw was used for ripping logs into lumber as well as for cutting the enormous amount of wood required to heat both residential and work spaces. By varying the shape of the teeth and the frame that supported the blade, the saw was adapted for other specialized tasks, such as cutting material for spit boxes, edging dipper hoops, joining shingles, and sawing out chair backs.[19] By the 1820s the saw had become a central piece of equipment for machining rough materials within the furniture makers' shop. A worldly visitor to the Watervliet community noted in 1821,

> The circular saw, so far as I know is a recent invention, and certainly a very useful one. The Shakers, at their village in Watervliet, near Albany, have this invention in very excellent use and great perfection. In a saw mill there, they have a set of machinery on this principle, erected at a very trifling expense, which, for cutting stuff for window sash, grooving floor plank, gaging clap-boards, &c. with one man and a boy to attend it, will perform the labor of thirty men.[20]

The other primary piece of woodworking equipment introduced early in the nineteenth century was the planer. This invention consisted of a rotating spindle with cutters or knives at the periphery. Running at high speeds, the revolving knives shaved the surface of boards being passed under them.[21] It, too, dramatically reduced the time involved in the transformation of rough material into straight, smooth lumber ready for furniture making. An entry in Freegift Wells's journal dated June 16, 1835, reads, "Chauncy and Timothy have been to Albany to pick out plank & take it to the planeing machine."[22] This notation implies that as of that

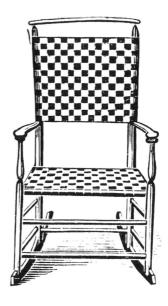

No. 5 production armchair, Mount Lebanon, New York, from *Illustrated Catalogue and Price List of the Shakers' Chairs*, 1876

Buzz saw, c. 1870. Reproduced from *Asher & Adams' Pictorial Album of American Industry*, New York: Asher & Adams, 1876

Shakers and a hired man (left to right: Brother John Pine, Brother John Dorrington, Frank Carpenter, and Brother Hiram Bailey) cutting firewood with a buzz saw, Alfred, Maine, before 1907. Collection of The United Society of Shakers, Sabbathday Lake, Maine

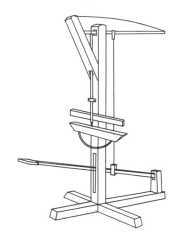

Mortising machine, c. 1835

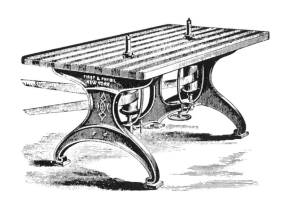

Shaper, c. 1870. Reproduced from *Asher & Adams' Pictorial Album of American Industry*, New York: Asher & Adams, 1876

Metal-turning lathe, c. 1870. Reproduced from *Asher & Adams' Pictorial Album of American Industry*, New York: Asher & Adams, 1876

date, the Watervliet workshops were not yet outfitted with a planer, although they did use one in the area. The situation was somewhat different at Mount Lebanon, where the following journal reference notes the existence of a Daniels-type planer, in use in 1831. "We fixed a little burr in the machine house to try for smoothing boards."[23] The Daniels planer at Mount Lebanon utilized a large cast-iron horizontal disk with small burrs or cutters on its lower surface. The board was fed on a carriage under this rapidly revolving disk, which removed thin shavings, leveling and smoothing the surface. The cutter left shallow, almost imperceptible circular machine marks on the finished wood surface. These marks, visible to the naked eye, provide evidence that this style of planer was used in several communities. The Mount Lebanon mechanics built planing machines for Sodus Bay, New York (later Groveland),[24] Enfield and Canterbury, New Hampshire, and Enfield, Connecticut, between 1833 and 1836.[25]

The mechanization within the workshop progressed beyond the basic mill work operation. Mortising and boring machinery helped supplement the processes previously accomplished by hand tools such as the brace and bit and chisels while improving the accuracy and speed of the craftsman's work. Numerous patents were filed by worldly inventors for mortising machines during the 1830s. A drawing of one such example in *Mechanics Magazine*, vol. 8, no. 1 (July 1836), seems more than coincidentally similar to the one built and used by the Shakers. It consisted of a bench to hold the workpiece and a frame to guide a chisel. The operator depressed a foot lever to force the chisel downward to cut the mortise. Giles Avery revealed in January 1842 that Brother Orren Haskins went to Pittsfield "to see a morticeing machine with the expec[t]ation of making one." According to the same writer, the work was in progress shortly afterward. "The joiners Orren and Joseph are a making a morticeing machine, to mortice the Doors and window sash for the new shop that is to be erected next summer. . . . "[26] Writing eight years later, Brother Isaac Newton Youngs recorded the construction of another mortiser. On April 9, 1850, "Orren Haskins has just finished a mortising machine, that he has had on hand several weeks, it is like to do well. This machine is of great value in joiner work, particularly in making doors. Also a boring machine made an improvement of late years, is of very great benefit to a carpenter. Orren H. is also about having one of these made."[27] At Watervliet, New York, Freegift Wells noted the presence of a mortising machine at the community on February 6, 1861, when he "helped to get the morticing machine from the mill to the shop, took it to pieces & cleaned it all up, and did some morticing &c."[28] For several days following Brother Freegift's entry he recorded mortising chair posts, suggesting that this specialized machine was designed for this purpose.

The boring machine provided mechanical assistance to a simple hand-tool operation and dramatically increased speed and accuracy. The essential elements of this machine included a chuck to hold the drill bit and a mechanism that moved the bit into the board. With it, the craftsman could consistently make holes exactly perpendicular or at any predetermined angle to the piece of stock being worked. This feature was particularly important in the chair-making shop of Brother Freegift Wells. In 1862, he recorded his use of what must have been a rather primitive or simple boring tool: "Brought my old frame for boreing chairs on from the ciderhouse garret, Found it all shackling and entirely unfit for use. Been repairing it, and trying to fit a brace and bit to conform to it."[29] Helpful in the small chair shop, the boring machine, which drilled the chair posts for receiving the rounds, was absolutely essential within the Mount Lebanon factory, which employed mass-production methods and required the exact duplication of parts.

Delmer Wilson in his Sabbathday Lake, Maine, shop, in front of a bandsaw, c. 1910. Collection of The United Society of Shakers, Sabbathday Lake, Maine

The last category of machinery includes the gauge or pattern lathe, shaper, and bandsaw. About 1850 a mechanism was added to the wood-turning lathe, a machine in use for centuries, that permitted the cutter to be fed mechanically as the stock turned in the lathe. A carriage holding the cutter knife or knives was mounted on a bed in front of the work, which was grasped between centers. A pattern cut to the profile of the completed turning was mounted directly below the work. As the screw-feed device advanced the carriage, the cutters followed the pattern, copying each turning detail onto the stock. This improvement allowed the operator to reproduce numerous parts precisely and rapidly—a chair rung could be turned in ten seconds and a chair post in under a minute.

The shaper was used to perform the tasks previously accomplished with molding planes, primarily in the production of decorative details. Each cutter was ground to the contour of a different molding. A variety of shapes could be cut by the machine, employing different cutters, which were driven at high speed on a revolving shaft. Several shapers were employed in the woodworking shops of many communities, including Alfred and Sabbathday Lake, Maine, Enfield and Canterbury, New Hampshire, and Enfield, Connecticut. Later in the century, these tools helped redefine the style of Shaker furniture as it evolved toward Victorian design.

The bandsaw, although patented by the Englishman William Newberry in 1808, was not widely used in the furniture industry due to technical problems until the last quarter of the nineteenth century. As fast and as efficient as the circular saw, the bandsaw featured a continuous, narrow, ribbonlike blade that enabled it to negotiate curved forms. It would have been used for cutting moderate curves such as on the arms, rockers, and back slats of the Shakers' production chairs before they were machined on the shaper.

The metal lathe was mentioned repeatedly in Shaker journals because of its significance in the construction of machinery for the communities' shops. With this piece of equipment a variety of parts as well as entire woodworking machines could be produced within the community itself. On May 28, 1816, Freegift Wells reported, "John Mc Donald has been here to get a main cillinder shaft mended and turned it in our iron lathe."[30]

Despite the dramatic changes brought about by power-generated machinery in the basic preparation of the stock, both Shaker and worldly craftsmen relied on hand tools to complete much of their work. The planes used during the end of the eighteenth and throughout the nineteenth centuries were made of wood. The cutter, or iron, was held in place by a wedge driven into a tapered slot in the body of the plane itself. Adjusting the cutter involved tapping the iron forward until it barely protruded from the throat of the plane, then driving the wedge into place with a mallet, which pinched the iron into position. Anytime the craftsman wanted to change the depth of the cut, he would adjust the iron by loosening the wedge and resetting the iron.

The various types of planes can be divided into several distinct categories according to function. Bench planes, the most basic, served to flatten and smooth the surfaces of the boards that came from the sawmill in the first stages of the furniture-making process. These planes include, in ascending order of size, the smooth, jack, fore, and joiner planes. The smoothing plane was used to level the lumber; the jack, a more general plane, did some smoothing and joinery work; and the fore and joiner planes were employed primarily to level and straighten edges, as in joining the two board edges for a glue joint or table edge. All consist of a flat, smooth sole, with a single or double cutting iron mounted at about forty-five degrees with a large opening for the cutter, the securing wedge, and space for the shavings to escape. Most smoothing planes ranged in size from 7 to 10½ inches and were somewhat boat-shaped or oval as viewed from the top. They did not contain handles; the workman grasped them on the front and rear sections of the body itself. In contrast, the jack (measuring 15 to 18 inches), fore (18 to 24), and joiner (24 to 36 inches) planes were rectangular in shape, and came equipped with handles.

Rabbeting and grooving planes were other essential tools in the Shaker craftsman's workshop. The rabbet plane (also called rabit or rebate) cut a square-edged, flat-bottomed groove along the edge of a board, such as a cupboard door, to help hold the neighboring door closed. The plane varied in width from ¼ inch to possibly 2½ inches and sometimes had a spur on one or both sides to help make a cleaner cut. The fillister plane consisted of a rabbet plane with the simple addition of an adjustable fence to control the width of the cut.

The plow plane, the most elaborate tool in the brothers' tool chest, was employed to cut a narrow groove parallel to, but at some distance from, the edge of a board. For example, it created the groove in a drawer side or front to secure the drawer bottom or made the channel in a door frame to house the panel. The plow plane was equipped with an adjustable fence to control the distance between the groove and the edge of the board and a gauge to determine its depth. The width of the cut could be varied by selecting one of several irons ranging from ¼ to ⅝ inch in size.

Similar in form to the rabbet plane, the dado plane was fitted with a depth stop and a spur cutter placed ahead of the iron to shear the wood fibers. Like the plow plane, it was employed to cut a groove (a dado) across the grain of a board to hold a shelf or drawer support. The skewed angle of the iron assisted in shearing the wood fibers.

Tongue-and-groove or matching planes were produced and sold as a pair, each one performing a specific function. One cut the groove on the edge of a board while the other made a matching tongue on the edge of the board placed

Plow plane, South Union, Kentucky, stamped R. Johns 1824. Museum Collection, Shakertown at South Union, Kentucky, #60-13D

next to it. They were most often employed to make the joints on the horizontal or vertical backboards of cupboards or cases of drawers. Matching planes were available in a number of widths since they were not adjustable for use on stock of variable thicknesses.[31]

The variety of commercially available molding planes was practically endless, as a different plane was required for each style and size of molding made. This type of plane was employed for purely decorative purposes, such as forming applied or integral moldings on case piece cornices or table edges. Although hundreds of profiles could be made from concave or convex curves or a combination of the two, the Shakers incorporated only a small number of the decorative designs possible. Whether made by a brother or purchased commercially, molding planes generally measured just under ten inches long and four inches high, although the width varied according to the size and shape of the specific molding. They worked somewhat differently from the planes previously mentioned, for the iron was shaped to the exact contour of the finished molding and required very careful sharpening to maintain its original profile. The simplest were the hollows used to cut a basic shape such as the edge of a tabletop or drawer front. The round, usually sold as a pair with the hollow, might have been used to cut a cove (concave) molding or a portion of a more complex design. The quarter-round plane was a hollow shape in the form of a simple quarter-arc of a circle, with the addition of a shoulder on each side of the iron, which functioned as a stop. It was used in some communities to produce a lipped drawer. This application offered a visual contrast to the sharp, square edges found on case pieces at other Shaker villages.

The ogee molding consists of an S-shaped symmetrical double curve. Although frequently found in worldly furniture, it is much less common in Shaker designs, occurring occasionally on a bracket base for a blanket box. A bead, sometimes referred to as a quirk bead, is a semicircular shape set off from the rest of the surface of the board by a distinct deep groove or quirk. It can be seen on the door edges or cupboard corners of several Shaker case pieces. On some examples, the plane was used on both the face and side of the case, creating a nearly 270-degree radius on the corner. On some Shaker Victorian-style pieces dating from 1860 through 1920, the decorative bead was used on the sides and backboards of some counters.

Extant furniture indicates the Shakers employed a number of complex molding shapes that could have been executed with either one or two planes. The cove with astragal is composed of a concave curve followed by an astragal consisting of a bead with fillet (or square). It often appears on the cornices of Watervliet case pieces. Another complex curve, the ogee with astragal was less than an inch wide and would have been produced with one plane. This distinctive molding was used to form the midcase band on Canterbury built-in storage units (pl. 168).

Another group of special-purpose shaping tools included the panel-raising, sash, coping, and table planes. The first was used by Shaker brothers during the latter part of the eighteenth and early nineteenth centuries to produce a raised panel on cupboard doors; after about 1810, this was replaced almost exclusively by the flat panel. About fourteen or sixteen inches long and constructed like a wide bench plane, it was equipped with a spur and skewed iron as well as a fence. The primary application of the sash plane was for architectural work on window sashes, although it was also used on freestanding cupboards. Several shapes were commercially available, but it was the quarter-round profile that appeared consistently on the occasional bookcase or glass-door cupboard, where it served to shape the interior edges of the frame and the narrow woodwork (muntins) sup-

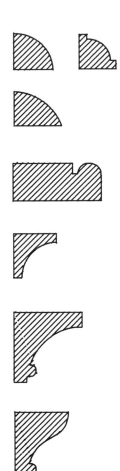

Molding shapes, from top to bottom: quarter-round and quarter-round with fillets; ovolo; bead or bead with fillet; cove; cove with astragal; ogee with astragal.

In a coped mortise-and-tenon joint, the coping plane undercuts the end of the rail (left) to allow the quarter-round molded edge of the stile (right) to fit into it.

porting the multipaned glass. The coping plane was designed for one purpose—to join the two quarter-round edges on the corner of a paneled door. Instead of using a miter joint to connect the molded pieces at a forty-five-degree angle, the craftsman coped or undercut the shoulder of the rail adjacent to the tenon. This allowed the molded edge of the stile to be fitted underneath a portion of the corresponding shoulder of the stile. Whether mitered or coped, the finished joints looked virtually identical, requiring close examination to determine which technique was used. Table planes were available as a pair to form each half of the rule joint used on drop-leaf tables. The convex plane cut the underside of the leaf, allowing it to rest on the convex edge of the fixed top, cut with the matching plane. In this way, the wood of the tabletop, rather than the hinge, supported the inner edge of the leaf.

A complete set of tools required to build the vernacular furniture styles produced by the Shakers would have included the following items:

Workbench

Machines

buzz or table saw
mortiser
lathe

Cutting tools

saws
rip
crosscut
backsaw
bow saw

Measuring and layout tools

marking gauge
tenon gauge
pocket rule
squares
awl

Planes

block
smoothing
fore plane
jointing plane
plow plane
rabbet plane
panel plane
several molding planes

Drilling tools

brace and set of bits
gimblet

Miscellaneous tools

set of chisels
special mortising
  chisels
hammers
set of screwdrivers
clamps
marking dies
tap and dies
hatchet
scrapers
draw knife
rasp
knife

While most of this equipment could have been made by the Shaker craftsmen themselves, they were not averse to purchasing commercial tools and machinery for their shops. Brother Freegift Wells recorded in his "Memorandum of Events" numerous tools purchased over a forty-five-year period, starting on December 11, 1813, when he "spent 7 dollars 3 shillings & 9 p for tools, a plow, back saw, pocket rule, & plain irons." On September 9, 1837, "Freegift has been to Dayton & bought 1 sash saw 12/, 1 rabit plane 8/, 6 firmer gouges 8/, 3 firmer chisels, & 1½ inch screw bit 8/. amounting in all to $4.50." Two decades later, when he was released from his responsibilities as elder, Brother Freegift set up a new shop for himself. On May 26, 1857, he recorded, "The Elder Br. Chauncy & myself sent to Albany & purchaced part of a set of joiners tools for the elders shop," and on July 22, he "went to Albany, bought a bench vise & a number of other tools." The following October he journeyed to Albany again and purchased a "dovetail saw & several other tools."[32]

Several commercial manufacturers of wooden planes, such as Benson & Crannel, J & J Gibson, and Carter, in the Albany-Troy, New York, and Cincinnati areas, were located near Shaker communities. The numerous tools bearing a maker's name and a brother's stamped initials that have been preserved suggest they were used extensively in the Believers' workshops.

Individual craftsmen also made many of their own tools. Between 1814 and 1861 Freegift Wells constructed joiners, fore and rabbet planes, and screw clamps, to name a few.[33] Henry DeWitt, a fellow mechanic, shoemaker, and printer from Mount Lebanon, made numerous tools, including a few for his furniture-making needs, such as chisels and a small square.[34]

Within the Shaker shops, particular needs arose for special tools that were not available commercially. For example, Brother Henry DeWitt noted on April 9, 1822, "I went to the CHH to help Nathan make some tools for putting balls in chair posts." In this case, they required a tool for boring the hollow in the bottom of a rear chair post to hold the tilter. Henry DeWitt worked with Brother David Rowley on March 14, 1844: "I set up a pegging machine. David Rowley made two. I helped some and turned the head block etc."[35] The tools mentioned were probably designed for threading the pins used on the ever-present pegboards. A device of this type is currently in the collection of the Shaker Museum at Old Chatham, New York.

In 1834, Freegift Wells began the construction of a glass-door bookcase over three drawers, which he called a library. In a series of journal entries, which are listed below with a few comments dating from the 1860s added for clarification, the maker discussed his progress on this case piece.[36] This detailed step-by-step description of his work documents each process in the bookcase's construction, which required a broad range of both general-purpose and specialized hand tools.

> January 24, 1834. The Ministry have had a gift for all the Family bring forward their books & pamphletts, have them examined. The work has been going in yesterday and to-day & there is quite a quantity collected. Those that are considered suitable are to be placed in a library under the care of the Elders, for the use of the Family & those that are not considered suitable are to be put away or burned agreeable to the example of the Apostles & our Parents and Elders.

MILL WORK

January 19, 1813: The timber . . . being sufficiently dried was taken out of the kiln.
January 30, 1861: Overhauled my pile of boards & selected stuff. . . . Also made a draught . . . to work by.
January 15, 1864: Worked at . . . boards, taking them out of wind. . . .
January 16, 1864: Finished trueing the boards, so that they are now ready for facing off.
January 21, 1864: Thomas [Almond, his apprentice] has finished facing the . . . boards & I have gauged off one set & took them to the gauge stroke.

LAYOUT

February 14, 1834: F has been buzzing out some stuff for a Library & drawers.
February 15, 1834: F has been rough plaining stuff for the Library.
February 17, 1834: F has plained out the sides of the Library.
February 20, 1834: F has now worked one day and a half at the Library.
February 26, 1834: F has finished the Library except the doors & drawers &c.

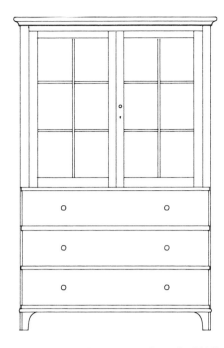

Bookcase, attributed to Freegift Wells, Watervliet, New York, 1834

JOINERY OF DOORS

February 27, 1834: F has put the two Library doors together today.
March 1, 1834: F has hung the library doors & put the lock on &c.

JOINERY OF DRAWERS

June 18, 1861: Slit up some stuff for . . . long draws, tried it out & dressed it out ready for use. Also went to the Mill & got some boards for draw bottoms and tried them out.
June 19, 1861: Finished plaining draw bottoms and glued them together, also laid out my dovetails for the . . . draws, and dadoed the side pieces.
June 20, 1861: Cut out my dovetails.
June 21, 1861: Cut the pins in the front and back end of the drawers, plowed them for the bottom and glued them together. June 22, 1861: Fitted in the draw bottoms and plained them off.
June 23, 1861: Fitted the drawers into their places.
March 27, 1834: F turned some knobs this afternoon for the drawers of the Library.
April 2, 1834: We have moved the library into the house, got the books into it &c.

The work described by Brother Freegift and others has been broken down into several conceptual categories to help define the individual processes, including mill work, layout, joinery of doors and drawers, decorative details, hardware, and finishing. Throughout the bookcase's construction, these arbitrary divisions would be crossed numerous times but they are delineated here to help describe the work processes.

MILL WORK

Brother Freegift was not the sawyer but obtained his lumber already cut at the sawmill in the community. Usually measured in increments such as ¼, ⁵⁄₄, or ⁸⁄₄ inch, these rough stock dimensions allowed for the loss of wood when the planks were planed to a final thickness in order to remove any saw marks or variations in the plank. The planks that came from the sawmill had growth moisture in them and needed to dry out before they could be used. They were either stacked to let the moisture evaporate naturally or dried in the kiln. Numerous journal entries, some

Millwork tools, 19th century. Hancock Shaker Village, Pittsfield, Massachusetts, #78-57.86, .85, .8, #62-62.10, and private collection

as early as 1815, refer to the existence and use of kilns, which reduced drying time considerably.

Brother Freegift then selected the stock, setting aside boards with unusable knots, cracks, or other imperfections, and ripped and crosscut the pieces to the appropriate size with the buzz saw. He went over them with a smoothing plane and fore plane to make one side of the board perfectly flat and straight. A line was scribed with a marking gauge on each edge of the board to indicate its proper thickness. The craftsman then planed the second side of the board to this line and smoothed it in a similar fashion to create a board with consistent thickness and parallel surfaces. Brother Freegift completed the rough mill work for three shelves, the top and bottom of the case, and the door and drawer stock.

Tools for layout of joinery, 19th century. Hancock Shaker Village, Pittsfield, Massachusetts, #62-240A and #78.5.7, and private collection

LAYOUT

Brother Freegift then proceeded with the precise layout of each part. He ripped the sides to width with the buzz saw or handsaw and with a joining plane carefully straightened both the front and rear edges, selecting the best pieces to face the front of the case. He then trimmed the top and bottom square and to length with his fine-tooth crosscut saw. Using adjustable dividers, he scribed out the arc to form the rounded portion of the cut foot on the case side and cut along the lines with a bow saw. On the inside back edge of both sides, Brother Freegift used the fillister plane to cut a rabbet, into which he would later fit the backboards. On each side, he carefully cut several dados with a ⅞-inch dado plane to hold the shelves and drawer guides. He then cut the shelves and the top and bottom of the piece to length, selecting the poorest board for the base, as it would not be seen.

The facing on the case was minimal, consisting of a narrow stile on either side of the doors and five rails located above and below the doors and each of the drawers. Brother Freegift secured each of the rails with small tenons joined into matching mortises in the side of the cupboard and in the stiles beside the doors. With the help of another brother who worked in the shop, the main body of the piece was assembled by nailing the case together where the shelves and sides met and gluing the mortise-and-tenon joints with hot hide glue. He further secured the construction by placing a pin through the mortise-and-tenon joints.

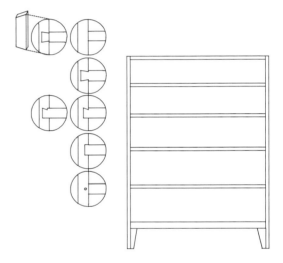

Several different joinery methods for the rail-to-side case joints, top to bottom: dovetail with facing; dovetail; housed half-dovetail and half-dovetail; dado; mortise-and-tenon with peg

LAYOUT OF DOORS

Brother Freegift sorted through the rest of the boards that he had brought to the proper dimensions through the milling process. He grouped and numbered the rails and stiles to be used in each door, measured the overall length, and marked out the mortise-and-tenon joints. Using a rule and a square, he scribed each rail for the tenons and the stiles for the corresponding mortises. He marked the shoulders of the tenon with a try square, adjusted his tenon gauge to the width of the required tenon, and scribed lines on both sides of the rail.

JOINERY OF DOORS

With the door parts already laid out, Freegift used a brace and bit to bore away the excess stock from the mortise in the stile that he had clamped tightly in his bench vise. He worked from both sides of the stile since he was using through tenons. He pared the sides and end of the mortise smooth to the tenon gauge scribe marks with two chisels and a mallet. Working next with the rails, Brother Freegift carefully cut the shoulders and the waste stock from the cheeks of the tenon with a backsaw, and with a rabbet plane shaved the excess wood down to a previously marked line.

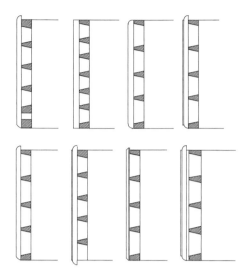

Typical dovetail patterns produced by the joinery of drawers, showing the drawer side (white), with the pins of the joint—their ends marked with a scribe line—shaded. Clockwise from upper left: some pieces from Union Village, Ohio, have an unusual pattern at the bottom, with a square pin rather than a half-dovetail-shaped pin;

dovetail joint with an applied cock bead that covers some of the dovetail itself, found on pieces from Mount Lebanon, New York, Enfield, Connecticut, and South Union, Kentucky. The drawer protrudes in front of the case;

many Mount Lebanon pieces have a rounded, unlipped drawer fitted so the rounded portion is in front of the case. One half-pin on top and bottom;

the most common drawer front found in Shaker communities as well as in worldly furniture is lipped with a thumbnail-edge shaping. One half-pin on top and bottom;

this unusually thick drawer front lipped on top is found on many Groveland, New York, case pieces, particularly those attributed to Brother Emmory Brooks;

beveled, lipped drawer front, found on many Enfield, Connecticut, case pieces, particularly those with tapered drawer sides;

thumbnail-lipped drawer front with the lip on all four edges of the drawer front, and a half-dovetail found only on the top. The drawers of many case pieces from Canterbury, New Hampshire, are constructed this way, except that the half-dovetail is absent on both the top and bottom;

rounded, lipped drawer front with one half-pin on the top and bottom of the joint. This pattern is typical of Mount Lebanon case pieces.

After securing each door rail or stile in his bench vise, Brother Freegift cut a simple but decorative ovolo shape into the inner edge of each piece by carefully guiding the sash plane down the inner edge of the door parts. It took fifteen or twenty passes of the plane to finish the shaping, which gradually emerged as more of the blade made contact with the wood until the final form was complete. Using the sash plane, the decorative edge on the outside face of the door, the ledge for the glass, and the ridge to hold the glazing on the inside of the door were cut in one simple process.

Still with the sash plane, Brother Freegift molded several strips of wood that were to serve as the muntin stock between the six panes of glass on each door. Small tenons were cut on the end of each muntin after they were trimmed to length and fitted into the corresponding mortise on the inside of the stiles and rails. A portion of the ovolo shaping was cut away with a fine backsaw from the section where the door frame rail and stile came together, so the finished joint showed only a tight miter. The fourteen joints on the door were checked by dry fitting each without glue before the whole door was squeezed together with clamps for its final assembly. Another brother helped Freegift in this process, as there were numerous parts to be fitted before the glue began to tack up and dry. The next day he drilled a hole through the door frame joint and pounded a pin into it to provide additional mechanical strength. He trimmed the pin off with his dovetail saw and pared it off cleanly with a chisel, taking care not to scratch the door face.

JOINERY OF DRAWERS

Freegift had previously selected three matching pieces of pine with a similar coloring and grain configuration for the drawer fronts. He cut these boards about ¾ inch longer and ⅜ inch wider than the drawer opening to accommodate the drawer lip. Using an adjustable fillister plane, he cut a rabbet on the top and sides of the drawer front, creating a lip to cover the gap left around the drawer. He rounded the lip with a molding plane cautiously, knowing that there was an increased risk of tearing the wood fibers when working across the grain. After locating the holes for the knobs, he numbered the door fronts and stacked the pieces to allow for the free circulation of air, which prevented warpage of the freshly planed boards. Next he planed stock to a thickness of about 9/16 inch for the drawer sides and backs and glued several additional pieces to make up the drawer bottoms. The sides were ripped to the approximate width with his buzz saw and each edge straightened with the jack and joiner planes to a dimension just under the height of the drawer opening. Brother Freegift needed to allow for some drawer side expansion from humidity during the upcoming New York summer months.

Relying on his years of woodworking experience, Brother Freegift laid out each dovetail by eye rather than measuring each exactly. After cutting the dovetails for the front of the drawer and removing the waste with his chisel and mallet, he repeated the process for the back of the drawer, allowing space for the groove that housed the bottom board in the drawer sides. Using the dovetails on the front and rear of the drawer sides as a guide, he traced the outline of the matching pins onto the end grain of the drawer front and rear. He carefully cut each of the pins with his dovetail saw and chopped out the waste wood with his sharpest chisel.

Using his plow plane, with its 5/16-inch cutter, he proceeded to cut the groove for the drawer bottom. He set the fence to place the groove high enough to prevent the drawer bottom from rubbing against the rail as the drawer was withdrawn from the case and made the ¼-inch-deep groove on the inside of each drawer front and side. Brother Freegift then cut the boards to size and chamfered

three edges of the drawer bottom with a panel-raising plane. He carefully fitted the corresponding drawer parts together, applied hot hide glue to the dovetail joints, squeezed the drawer bottom into place, and drove one nail in the back of the drawer bottom to keep it from moving.

Mortise-and-tenon tools, 19th century. Hancock Shaker Village, Pittsfield, Massachusetts, #80-82.1.9, and private collection

DECORATIVE DETAILS, HARDWARE, AND FINISHING

Brother Freegift's first finishing task was to put hinges on the doors. He used his marking gauge to scribe the location of the back edge of each hinge, which ensured that the door would fit flush with the covered face. After trial-fitting each hinge, he aligned the two doors together so that they overlapped. He had cut a rabbet on one stile of each door so that the right door held the left one shut when the lock bolt was turned. He removed the right door one final time to install the lock. To secure the left door shut Brother Freegift installed a wooden turn latch that engaged a slot on the underside of the middle shelf. He then scribed lines for letting in the lock and cut the wood out with a mallet and chisel. Using a brace and bit he drilled a hole, which he enlarged and shaped for a key.

The case was finished with three decorative moldings. A bull-nose molding was nailed into place covering the joint between the inset cut foot and the base. An identical molding was placed at the top of the case just below the cove with astragal cornice molding.

In order to prepare the wood for a painted finish, Brother Freegift smoothed the surface with a scraper made from a piece of saw blade and sanded it with abrasive paper. Using materials that he had purchased in nearby Albany, he ground some Venetian red pigment, linseed oil, and thinner. To improve the paint's drying qualities, he added some japan. He brushed several coats of his thinned paint over the surface and wiped off the excess to provide a transparent coat. This he covered with several thin coats of his varnish to help protect the red wash underneath.

LOCATION

OF

SHAKER COMMUNITIES

1. Watervliet (Niskeyuna), New York (1787–1938)
2. Mount Lebanon, New York (1787–1947)
3. Hancock, Massachusetts (1790–1960)
4. Harvard, Massachusetts (1791–1918)
5. Tyringham, Massachusetts (1792–1875)
6. Enfield, Connecticut (1792–1917)
7. Canterbury, New Hampshire (1792–1992)
8. Shirley, Massachusetts (1793–1909)
9. Enfield, New Hampshire (1793–1923)
10. Alfred, Maine (1793–1931)
11. Sabbathday Lake, Maine (1794–still active)
12. Union Village, Ohio (1805–1912)
13. Watervliet, Ohio (1806–1900)
14. Pleasant Hill, Kentucky (1806–1910)

15. South Union, Kentucky (1807–1922
16. West Union, Indiana (1810–27)
17. North Union, Ohio (1822–89)
18. White Water, Ohio (1822–1916)
19. Groveland, New York (1836–92)

Short-Lived Villages

Gorham, Maine (1808–19)
Savoy, Massachusetts (1817–25)
Sodus Bay, New York (1826–36)
Narcoossee, Florida (1896–c. 1920)
White Oak, Georgia (1898–1902)

PART TWO: The Bishoprics

ACCORDING TO **I**SAAC Newton Youngs, "by the forepart of 1793 there were four different Bishoprics established in Chh order, similar to that at New Lebanon all having secondary branches."[1] Each bishopric consisted of two or three communities in geographic proximity that were gathered together under a bishopric ministry comprised of two elders and two eldresses. The bishopric leaders, who reported to the lead ministry at Mount Lebanon, traveled a great deal among the villages in their charge. By the 1860s the Shaker communities were organized into the following bishoprics:[2]

> Mount Lebanon: Mount Lebanon, Watervliet, and Groveland, New York
> Hancock: Hancock and Tyringham, Massachusetts, and Enfield, Connecticut
> Harvard: Harvard and Shirley, Massachusetts
> New Hampshire: Canterbury, Enfield
> Maine: Alfred, Sabbathday Lake
> Ohio: Union Village, North Union, Whitewater, Watervliet
> Kentucky: Pleasant Hill, South Union

The villages within these boundaries usually attempted to solve problems themselves before consulting Mount Lebanon, which encouraged a regional closeness of spirit. Considering the normal exchange of ideas between people physically located a few miles apart, it is not surprising that the furniture produced in the same bishopric should be similar. For this reason, it has been possible to trace the origins of various forms of Shaker furniture to a specific bishopric.

While a few special variations remained specific to a bishopric or even a single community, the majority of furniture forms could be found in almost all of the bishoprics. Most of the pieces that survived over the years have been moved many times, and their original use has been inferred through design and construction features, as well as through diary and journal references.

Built-in and freestanding storage units, including cupboards, cases of drawers, and a combination of the two, with infinitely varied configurations of doors and drawers, represent an integral feature of Shaker building interiors. They served a variety of functions and were used to house, among other things, textiles, food, medicine, herbs, and documents. In the Kentucky communities, cupboards over drawers were called presses and could be made as one or two separate units.

A number of bookcases were made to serve the needs of the entire community. Designed as freestanding pieces of furniture of architectural proportions, they were fitted with glazed doors enclosing shelves above cupboards or drawers and, according to oral history, housed books or hymnals.

Counters represent the most diverse form of Shaker work furniture, combining a work surface and storage space in a variety of sizes and configurations. They could be constructed with frame-and-panel or plank sides; with turned legs, casters, or a base that rests flat on the floor; and with overhanging tops or drop leaves. Accessible from two to four sides and fitted both with and without wheels, these versatile pieces were used primarily in the tailoring and textile trades.

Specialized and often personalized workbenches of various sizes, equipped with vises, bench dogs, and bench jacks, served the needs of Shaker woodworkers, both in their shops and on various job sites.

Elder Henry Blinn in his office at Enfield, New Hampshire, c. 1890. Collection Richard Brooker

A variety of styles of writing desks survive, including kneehole, slant-front, lift-top or fall-front, and butler's. However, compared to other types of furniture, few were produced because their use was restricted to those responsible for the spiritual and temporal needs of the community.

Sewing desks, which originated in the New England Shaker communities, contain drawers and doors in various arrangements on one or more sides of the frame and often have an additional slide to extend the work surface. Sewing cases, at Hancock, resemble sewing desks in size and in the use of multiple drawers but few contain doors or the sliding work surface. Some, however, were fitted with rear drop leaves instead. Sewing tables produced at Mount Lebanon, either with or without a gallery section above, had one to three narrow drawers below the work surface, which was not extended by slides or drop leaves. The more diminutive tables found in Kentucky, intended to hold the handwork supplies of a sister seated at a chair nearby, are based on worldly Federal-style worktables. All of these units are workshop pieces designed to assist the sisters in their various textile activities.

Communal trestle tables ranging from short to long were designed exclusively for dining rooms and solved the problem of serving meals to all the members of a large family at once.

The ubiquitous four-legged tables came in many styles and sizes, both with and without drawers, drop leaves, and gatelegs, to fulfill different needs of the community. They were found in kitchens, workshops, retiring rooms, infirmaries, laundries, and dairies, to name a few.

Small tripod stands, with round, square, or rectangular tops and either peg, cabriole, or spider legs, suited a variety of needs in retiring rooms and halls. They might have been used for small sewing projects or for sorting objects such as garden seeds as well as for holding candles.

The washstand was not designed as a specialized piece of furniture until the middle of the eighteenth century, when it appeared in Chippendale's *Director*.[3] The principal variety found in nineteenth-century America was triangular in shape and had three feet, designed to fit into the corner of the room. By comparison, Shaker washstands came in many shapes and layouts—either with four turned legs or resting flat on the floor—but all provide storage space in the form of a cupboard or drawer as well as support for the bowl, and many have a splashboard. They were probably used in a variety of locations, including retiring rooms, infirmaries, and community washhouses.

Similar to their worldly counterparts, six-board lidded chests or boxes with or without drawers served to store textiles or tools.

Shaker-made clocks, both tall case and wall models, were primarily produced at Watervliet, New York, and shipped to other communities, where they were often placed in halls or barns.

Although beds were in short supply during the formative years of the United Society of Believers, as more converts arrived the Believers produced double bedsteads with rope or wooden mattress supports to accommodate two brothers or two sisters. At the peak of the United Society's expansion during the 1840s, the trundle bed came into widespread use as retiring room furniture. In 1850 Elisha Blakeman designed a space-saving sleeping arrangement consisting of "a long bedstead, long enough for 8 boys, side by side & takes up much less room than 4 bedsteads. He has just set it up today and thinks it is fine."[4] According to a journal entry, in December 1869, "Elisha . . . narrowed up nine [double] bedsteads for the boys so they all have single beds but two little boys."[5]

Side chairs and armchairs made for community use might be found in the dining room, at worktables and desks, and in retiring rooms, where they often took the form of rockers. Tilters and swiveling or revolving chairs were other variations. Many communities sold chairs to the public, none on so large a scale as Mount Lebanon.

In the eyes of the ministry, trustees, and deacons, there was a perceived difference between the furniture appropriate for use by the family and that considered acceptable for the areas of the community where business was transacted with the world's people. Writing in 1861, Isaac Newton Youngs summarized a statement that first appeared in the 1845 "Millennial Laws" enjoining Believers "not to employ the world" to make "any tables, stands, chests, drawers, cupboards, or chairs to be used in the habitation of the Church [Family], save at the Outer Court"—that is, at the Trustees' Office.[6] The prohibition implies that the construction of Church Family furniture should be entrusted only to Believers to ensure that the results were pure in design, construction, and, perhaps, materials.

Within the United Society, both physical and written evidence suggests that specific pieces were made for individuals in leadership positions, and many of these pieces clearly exhibit unusual designs or exceptional wood selection. For example, the inscription on one surviving counter signed and dated by Orren Haskins in 1847 reads "made [for] deaconess 2nd Order March 1847" (see pl. 35). It is fitted with an ingenious pullout slide, which presumably provided the family deaconess with a writing surface to assist her in record keeping. Emmory Brooks, who worked at Groveland, is known to have made a walnut bedstead (see pl. 331)

for Eldress Polly Lee in 1869, and it is not unreasonable to speculate that he produced other pieces specifically for the family eldress as well.[7]

Documentation supplies many other instances of specially made furniture,
although the corresponding pieces mentioned have not been identified from the
known pieces still extant. On February 16, 1867, "Giles [Avery] commenced a
writing desk for the Ministry's Shop in this [Mount Lebanon] place"[8] and in 1880 "a
secretary for Eldress Polly."[9] Henry DeWitt "Finished making a counter for the
Deaconesses with 12 drawers took between 3 & 4 weeks work" in March 1841.[10]
Benjamin Lyon and Samuel Turner both made a case of drawers for the elder sisters at Mount Lebanon in 1817 and 1838 respectively, and "David Rowley has
lately [1849] made a case of drawers for the Deaconesses."[11] Working at Watervliet, New York, Freegift Wells recorded he "finished Elder Br. bench" in 1823 and
"finished the Elder Sisters table & they have stained it" in 1834.[12]

The differences among furniture intended for the Church Family, the
ministry, and other members are alluded to in Hervey Elkins's account of his fifteen years at Enfield, New Hampshire, as he described what appears to be the
children's order:

> The house which the boys and girls occupied, was an edifice eighty feet in
> length, and three stories in height. Five large rooms and a meeting hall
> were allotted to the boys. These rooms were furnished in a manner simi-
> lar to those in the stone mansion [Great Stone Dwelling, Church Family]
> devoted for the resident of those over sixteen. The furniture was of
> course not quite so nice.[13]

Given their communal style of life and the openness of their living
arrangements, it may seem contradictory that many pieces of Shaker furniture that
have never left the last two communities at Canterbury, New Hampshire, and Sabbathday Lake, Maine, are fitted with locks. However, an examination of key Shaker
documents reveals that the leadership made a sharp distinction between public
and private possessions and formulated its policy based on the specific contents
under consideration. According to the 1841 "Holy Orders of the Church":

> 1. Ye shall not have, in the dwelling house, any locks and keys, by which ye
> may close any thing, that another may not open it.
> 2. Ye shall not lock nor in any way fasten or cause to be fastened, any cup-
> boards, drawers, chests or writing boxes, belonging to individuals.
> 3. But where publick stores are kept, let the doors, chests, drawers or
> cupboards be secured by *locks and keys*; they shall be kept *locked* and by no
> means carelessly left open or unsecured.[14]

The regulations specifically state that tempting items such as tea, sugar, cider, and
medicines should be secured under lock and key. There were, however, exceptions
to these rules, which directed, "Ye shall not lock your cupboards, chests or tool
boxes, at the shops, except by the counsel of the Elders."[15]

The necessity of using locks was borne out by incidents such as the event
Freegift Wells recorded on November 1, 1822: "Break in some villian or vilans
broke into our office by knocking in 2 panes of glass at the south window & taking
out the fastner shov'd up the lower sash crawled in searched the drawers found a
key to the desk unlock'd the door & took out about 12 dollars & made their
escape before the brethren returned."[16] It is conceivable that certain circumstances arose that required increased reliance on locks for security purposes. One
such influencing factor might have been the annual influx of what Believers called

"winter Shakers"—people who, when cold weather approached, professed a desire to become members "with empty stomachs and empty trunks, and go off with both full as soon as the roses begin to bloom."[17] Locks may have been installed at that time to protect both individual belongings as well as the community's stores from noncovenanted members.

Although the society's written rules discouraged the Shakers from marking their work or their possessions, many pieces carry inscriptions giving the name of the craftsman, the date of manufacture, and/or the user. Perhaps the worldly tradition of signing persisted among some Shaker craftsmen who, as converts, brought their skills, tools, and habits with them into the community. Inscriptions might reveal the identity of the maker or user, clarify the function of a particular piece of furniture, or specify its location. According to the "Holy Orders of the Church," "Ye shall not print your name on anything whatever; that others may hereafter know the work of your hands" (p. 63). However, this rule was apparently not always followed. Cabinetmakers, as well as owners, from many communities often identified themselves in a variety of materials, including pencil, chalk, ink, paper labels, and metal stamps. One Harvard brother wrote, "Thomas Hammond this belongs to his case of draw[er]s" (pl. 148); an elder at the same community marked a case of drawers with the words, "Built by Elder Joseph Myrick 1844. Finished March 8" (pl. 150). Alfred Collier identified his work by signing his name in chalk under a desk lid (pl. 144). Daniel Sering of Union Village, Ohio, marked the back of one drawer in a case in red ink, "Daniel Sering Maker/November 9th 1827" (pl. 264); Benjamin Youngs, Sr., of Watervliet painted his name on the back of several clock faces (pl. 76); and James Smith of Mount Lebanon stamped his name and the date in block letters along the dovetail joints of one of the drawers of a sewing case (pl. 52). These stamped rather than handwritten letters are found on a small group of unrelated Shaker pieces, including chairs made by Freegift Wells of Watervliet, a desk by Thomas Wells from the same community (pl. 87), and a tripod stand by Samuel Turner of Mount Lebanon (pl. 59), as well as on a number of woodworking tools.

On some furniture, a second-hand inscription provides detailed information regarding the original maker or the circumstances surrounding the construction. For example, a paper label affixed to the interior of a Hancock case of drawers explains that "This Case of Drawers were made by/Elder Grove and Brother Thomas and/placed here thursday, January 13th, 1853./It was the day our Ministry expected to/return to the City of Peace, but were detained/on account of the snow storm which/occured on that day" (pl. 103).

The "Holy Orders of the Church" also states, "Brethren shall not stamp their names nor the first letters of their names, upon any thing which they may make, that belongs to the Sisters, such like as shoes, books, rules, or anything of the kind" (pp. 63–64). Based on dated surviving examples, it seems to have become more and more acceptable for Shakers to mark the gifts they made for each other after midcentury. Orren Haskins of Mount Lebanon made a gallery for Sarah Winton's sewing table with the following message: "Our Shaker sister/Worth her weight in gold:/Please accept this little token/Of my approving love;/Altho' tis small it measures more/The half has not been told;/God bless you every every more,/To rest in our clean fold/While on this mortal shore./O.N.H., June 11, 1881, Mount Lebanon,/Columbia Co., N.Y." Brother Eli Kidder at Canterbury wrote on the bottom of a sewing desk drawer, "Made by Br. Eli Kidder at 77 years for Almira Hill at 40 yrs. January 1861 Chh Canterbury N.H./U.S.A." (pl. 181).

Cupboard and case of drawers, Harvard, c. 1800/c. 1840. Pine, h 84 w 31⅜ d 16¹³/₁₆". Private collection

Based on construction evidence, this piece was originally a two-door cupboard with heavy, raised-panel doors and interior shelves. At some point in its history, a Shaker craftsman removed the bottom door, added the sill to extend the depth of the case, and installed the drawers.

Other pieces are inscribed to indicate their purpose or place of use, including a lap desk "Made by Orren Haskins/December 18th 1838./for John Allen & used at the seed/shop upwards of two years./It was then put upon legs by/John Allen & taken into the house/on the first monday in January./1841." Sister Sarah Neale, one of the last Shakers at Mount Lebanon, penciled the following information on the history of a loom: "This loom was made by Henry DeWitt in 1834./It was originally a cloth/loom but in recent years was used to/weave poplar cloth/for baskets./The thread used/for filling was/spun by the Shakers/about 1840./Authority Sister/Sadie Neale/Sept. 13, 1930." Some paper labels indicate where items such as seeds and herbs were stored (pls. 8, 40). One unidentified Shaker sister who was apparently tired of sorting rags pasted her message to the lid of a large bin in the collection of Hancock Shaker Village: "N/B.!! Do be so kind as/to sort your Rags better—Separate the/white & Rip the cotton from the Woolen/In behalf of the public/Menders!"

Perhaps because of the size of Shaker families, members had to devise an efficient system of identifying the location of furnishings in order to maintain order. As a result, some pieces are marked with a specific room or building, such as a "Meetingroom Stand" at South Union, Kentucky (pl. 323) or a counter assigned to the "Meetinghouse" at Mount Lebanon (pl. 39). According to a notation dated November 27, 1817, in his "Memorandum of Events," "Brother Freegift [Wells] has been sorting over & marking chairs. The chairs in the Deacons room are marked 1, the Deaconesses room 2, the Brethern's meeting room 3, the Sisters meeting room 4, the Bretherns front chamber 5, the Sisters front chamber 6, the Brethrens north chamber 7, the Sisters north chamber 8, etc." The use of a numbering system to assign and place chairs to specific rooms appears to have been adopted at other communities, including Canterbury (see pl. 170).

On the other hand, from the beginning, Shaker-made products sold to the outside world, such as spinning wheels and tubs, were routinely marked, often with the initials of one of the community's trustees, such as DM for David Meacham of Mount Lebanon or FW for Francis Winkley of Canterbury. After 1875, chairs produced at the Mount Lebanon factory for sale to the world were identified by a decal. Their 1875 catalogue announced, "All chairs of our make will have a Gold Transfer Trade Mark attached to them and none others are Shakers' Chairs" and warned, "Look for our trademark before purchasing—no chair is genuine without it." Clearly, the Shakers were not reluctant to use their name in the marketplace of the world's people in order to identify and protect the reputation of their products.

A major problem faced by analysts of Shaker furniture is one created by the Shakers themselves. As Isaac Newton Youngs explained, describing changes in the community by 1860, "Not a building remains as it was at the beginning of the present century, all have been rebuilt, reformed or repaired or demolished,"[18] a statement that also applies to many of the original furnishings. After its initial construction, the piece of furniture often underwent one of a number of dramatic changes over the next one hundred and fifty years. As the pieces aged, Shaker cabinetmakers devoted more and more of their time to the repair or modification of existing furniture. According to Henry DeWitt's journal, in 1836 he "put a pair of rockers to a chair for Molly Bennett" and "lowered the upper story to Frederick S[izwer's] Desk & put legs to it." When the Shaker population dropped and many buildings fell into disuse, much of the existing furniture was no longer required, and adaptations were made to the original form to suit changing needs. For example, during March 1854 Henry DeWitt "took off [four drawers from] the end of the Counter that's going to the Washhouse for the Drawer basket business; planed the leaf over &c. &c. Expect to smooth it sometime. . . . I worked fixing a carcass for the 4 drawers I cut of[f] the Counter . . . for the sisters at the Washhouse."[19] On one occasion, the sisters at Hancock removed the excess furniture stored in the attic of the Church Family Dwelling House by throwing a number of beds out the fourth-story window. Some of these original head- and footboards were later reassembled as lawn benches and placed on the grounds of the community.[20] Another large group of furniture was destroyed in the great fires of 1875 at Mount Lebanon, which burned eight buildings in the Church Family and their contents. The five-story dwelling house at the Mill Family, North Union, Ohio, was irretrievably lost in 1890.

What furniture remained intact often was dispersed from the community of origin as villages closed during the twentieth century due to declining membership. Several freight-car loads of furniture were moved to Canterbury between 1919 and 1923 when the remaining members of the Union Village community were relocated from Ohio to New Hampshire. Groveland's furniture underwent an even more complicated itinerary, moving first to Watervliet in 1892, then to Mount Lebanon, and eventually to Hancock, with at least one piece ending up at Canterbury (see pl. 335). At the same time, unneeded furniture was dispersed to the world through public and private sales. A 1922 broadside announcing the auction of household furnishings once used by the Believers at South Union mentioned, among other items, twenty-seven beds, forty cherry chests, and two corner cupboards. At other villages, such as Canterbury and Hancock, the sisters themselves sold pieces to antique dealers as well as private individuals from the 1920s through the 1950s. According to one sister's diary entry of June 30, 1938, "Mr. Magner [Massachusetts antique dealer] . . . arrived with a truck to get antiques. He takes all he can and pays $506.00. We need it to pay the taxes."[21]

It was during this period that the first group of Shaker collectors became fascinated with the sect and began to acquire the products of their culture. Foremost among these were Edward Deming and Faith Andrews, whose intense interest was sparked when they stopped to purchase a loaf of freshly baked bread at Hancock Shaker Village in 1923. They gradually developed a personal relationship with the sisters at Mount Lebanon, Hancock, and Canterbury and became knowledgeable collectors, dealers, and scholars seeking to document in words as well as artifacts the underlying forces behind the Shaker movement. Over the next several decades the Andrews collected, lectured, and wrote numerous books, including *Religion in Wood, Shaker Furniture*, and *The People Called Shakers*, which focused public attention on the Shakers and contributed to a surge of interest in their study. The establishment of several key museum collections in New York State reinforced the growing enthusiasm for things Shaker. With the help of Edward Deming Andrews, the New York State Museum at Albany, under the direction of Charles Adams, formed an impressive collection of Shaker artifacts from the Church Family property at Watervliet.

Another early enthusiast, John Williams, collected tools, machinery, artifacts, and manuscript material from Mount Lebanon and Canterbury and transformed his personal collection into a private museum, which became the Shaker Museum and Library at Old Chatham, New York, founded in 1950. Through his collaboration with pioneer collectors and scholars such as Andrews and Adams, photographer William F. Winter recorded the Believers' culture with his camera at Mount Lebanon, Watervliet, and Hancock. He photographed many scenes, though many were significantly rearranged, to produce influential still life views rather than

Cupboard and case of drawers, Mount Lebanon, Groveland, or Watervliet, New York, c. 1850. Pine, with hardwood knobs and brass latches. Private collection. Photograph: courtesy John Keith Russell Antiques, Inc.

It is extremely difficult to attribute this distinctive piece of furniture to a particular Shaker community. Although the drawer arrangement is identical to several case pieces made by Brother Amos Stewart of Mount Lebanon, the decorative details are quite different. The cornice, consisting of a square with a fillet and cove, is not characteristic of any one community, although the form can be documented to several villages. However, the formulation of the base reveals the craftsman's design independence. The ogee-shaped foot is typical of numerous Canterbury, New Hampshire, pieces, but its combination with the curved or bellied apron is not found elsewhere in Shaker cabinetmaking traditions. The base treatment is applied, as in a small kneehole desk from Groveland (see pl. 337), and several large Watervliet cupboards and cases of drawers (see pl. 79) have wide stiles. Was this unique form produced at Mount Lebanon or Watervliet, New York, by a singularly independent craftsman, or does it represent one of the rare early Groveland pieces produced before the distinctive style of Emmory Brooks emerged in the 1860s? There are numerous clues to assist in the attribution process, but, with no purchase history or markings to help, the accurate determination of a community of origin is not currently possible with the research knowledge presently available.

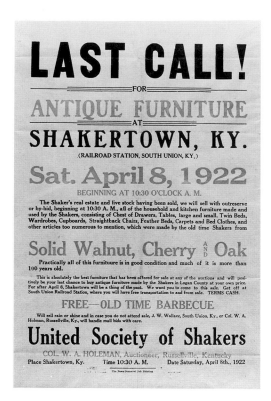

Auction poster, South Union, Kentucky, 1922. Museum Collection, Shakertown at South Union, Kentucky

impromptu room settings that conveyed a reverence for the subject. His photographs, which feature the straight lines of peg rail, the uncluttered surfaces of plain walls and wooden floors, and the balanced arrangement of furniture, create a visual impression of the Shakers' simplicity, purity, and order, which reinforced the Andrews' frozen view of the Believers.[22]

Craftsmen and designers also felt the allure of Shaker furniture. As early as 1880, Gustav Stickley recounted that he borrowed the use of a lathe "and with it blocked out the plainer parts of some very simple chairs made after the 'Shaker' model." He was familiar with Shaker designs as a result of visits to various communities, and the last pieces of furniture he made before his death in 1941 were three Shaker-style rockers for his granddaughter.[23] When the Stickley firm was reorganized by Gustav's four brothers in 1918, the first advertisement that appeared for the company showed "a new line, 'Berkshire' based on Shaker furniture design."[24] More recently, Shaker Workshops, in Concord, Massachusetts, has designed furniture kits based on specific pieces in museums and private collections, making a variety of seating furniture and other accessories available for assembly with common hand tools. The last few decades have witnessed the emergence of many small cabinetmaking workshops that specialize in handmade Shaker furniture, as well as large-scale manufacturers, such as Lane and Ethan Allen, that mass-produce and mass-market a somewhat look-alike Shaker-inspired line.

From a purely visual standpoint, classic Shaker furniture seems to have forecast later modern directions in design. Artist and collector Charles Sheeler, whose work was strongly influenced by Shaker crafts, observed in the 1920s, "It is interesting to note in some of their cabinet work the anticipation by a hundred years or more, of the tendencies of some of our contemporary designers toward economy and what we call the functional in design."[25] The conviction that design should be determined by need and function was fundamental to modernist theory during the 1920s and 1930s. It was clearly expressed in the work of Le Corbusier (1887–1965), the influential architect who was one of the first to appreciate that mass-produced objects exhibited superior merit to handmade items in both beauty as well as utility. He reduced the original prototype to its essential components and redesigned it for factory production in large numbers. The twentieth-century idea that "form follows function" espoused by Louis Sullivan was implicit in the teaching at the Bauhaus (1919–33) under the leadership of Walter Gropius (1883–1969). The aim of the influential German design school was to create "standard types for all the practical commodities of everyday use" that could be easily mass-produced.[26] Marcel Breuer's tubular steel *Cesca* chair, characterized by geometric, constructivist lines, the lack of applied decoration, and a reliance on industrial materials, epitomizes the Bauhaus ideal of purity of form.

A more direct connection can be found in the Shaker-inspired furniture of the Scandinavian Modern designers. The most influential of this distinguished group was the Danish architect Kaare Klint (1888–1954), who made considerable advances in the analysis of the true function of furniture. Through his own professional work as designer for the highly respected furniture-making firm of Rudolf Rasmussen from 1928 as well as his teaching at the Royal Academy of Fine Arts in Copenhagen, he trained an entire generation of young designers and architects and helped establish an independent Danish furniture style. Because Klint respected tradition, he took as his point of departure in the design process the analysis of furniture from other cultures or periods, such as English eighteenth-century styles, Windsor chairs, and Shaker types, whose usefulness had remained largely unchanged through time. Klint's approach to design included a careful study of a chair's form, materials, and construction, as well as its ability to serve the practical and aesthetic needs of the user. In order to understand these concepts more fully, Klint had his pupils prepare measured drawings with the aim of developing new, simple and functional types of furniture. In 1928, when an artist colleague found an interesting chair, Klint instructed one of his students to produce a measured drawing of it. Although captioned "An American rocking chair in the Colonial style—an example of a type which broadly speaking can still be used today,"[27] it was not until the Andrews book *Shaker Furniture* was published in 1937 that the true identity of this icon was revealed. Klint was clearly inspired by the Shaker aesthetic and had the Rasmussen firm produce this prototype as a Kaare Klint design; as late as 1947, he created several additional chairs in the Shaker manner. When a Mount Lebanon rocker is compared to a Klint chair of 1943 that was designed but never put into production, the similarity in the shape of the upright supporting the arm and the use of the mushroom handhold is readily apparent. Chairs designed in 1947 by Børge Morgensen, a student of Klint's, reflect the spindle-back style of the Mount Lebanon revolvers and the Canterbury dining chairs.[28] All of the Danish Modern pieces from the 1930s and 1940s display simple construction, straight lines, visual and physical lightness of shape, and the use of natural materials such as teak, leather, and cloth.

What do contemporary Believers, historians, and designers have to say about Shaker furniture? Sister Mildred Barker (1898–1990) of Sabbathday Lake, Maine, made her attitude very clear in an interview in 1974: "I would like to be remembered as one who had pledged myself to the service of God and had fulfilled that pledge as perfectly as I can—not as a piece of furniture."[29] Ken Ames, material culture historian, looks beyond the visual appeal of popular artifacts and explores their potential as windows to past culture. As a result, he often presents an unromantic view of some of today's most prized antiques, which surprises collectors and scholars alike. According to Ames, "People look at a Shaker chair, praise its simplicity, and create a cultural mythology of the Shaker. But when you see the chair as something people lived with every day, you might see a very static and unfeeling world. The real value of the chair goes beyond its design to its reflection of the men and women who created it and lived with it."[30]

American woodworker George Nakashima was "truly the elder statesman of the American Craft Movement."[31] From the 1930s until his death in 1990, he designed and executed handcrafted furnishings that emphasized vernacular forms with simplified, rectangular lines. In these he combined fundamental joinery techniques, standardized parts, and the use of traditional production technologies as well as materials, such as solid wood. His admiration for New England rustic furniture is evident in pieces that clearly interpret the linear elegance of Windsor designs and others that are suggestive of Shaker seating. He revered this type of generic furniture in which the maker used time and materials most efficiently. In addition, these vernacular prototypes in the native tradition did not depend on sophisticated woodworking skills, and their makers remain mostly anonymous, a quality that appealed to Nakashima.[32] The four-legged, high *Mira* chair of 1951 with turned legs and hand-shaped spindles, 20-inch-high plank seat, and steam-bent crest rail in solid walnut resembles a twentieth-century version of Micajah Tucker's 1834 dining chair of pine stained red (see pl. 193). His daughter Mira Nakashima-Yarnall, who has taken charge of the studio, put it differently, remarking on how "[this little Shaker chair] certainly looks like an early ancestor of our four-legged chair! Many people have mentioned the affinity with both Shaker and Japanese design to Nakashima. Conscious or not, simplicity and material must result in similar design!"[33]

Mount Lebanon Bishopric

THE **MOUNT LEBANON** Bishopric includes the Shaker communities established at Niskeyuna, later called Watervliet (1787–1938), New Lebanon (1787–1947)—renamed Mount Lebanon in 1861—and Groveland (1836–92), relocated from Sodus Bay (1826–36). Due to the geographic distances separating the eastern (Watervliet and Mount Lebanon) and western (Groveland) New York sites, the chronological difference, and the overwhelming significance of Mount Lebanon as the home of the central ministry and leading authority of the Shaker world, each community will be discussed separately.

As the first society to be officially organized, or brought into Gospel Order, the largest eastern colony, and the home of the central ministry for the entire sect, Mount Lebanon assumed primary importance in both spiritual and temporal matters throughout its history. After arriving in New York in 1774, Mother Ann Lee and her small band of seven followers briefly separated in order to earn a living in the New World. Several members journeyed upstate and in 1776 leased and eventually purchased two hundred acres of land near Albany, which was to become the Shakers' base of operations for several years. After reassembling at their new home, originally called Niskeyuna, they quietly pursued their trades and practiced their faith for several years in isolation. As a result of religious revivals among the New Light Baptists at nearby New Lebanon and neighboring towns in 1779 and 1780, the Shaker community became an object of interest. Ann Lee and her followers were forced out of their seclusion and eventually succeeded in converting many to the Shaker religion. It is noteworthy that the opening of the Shaker sect in America resulted from the inquiries of outsiders rather than from initiatives by members of the United Society.[2]

Following Mother Ann's death in 1784, Niskeyuna was replaced by New Lebanon as the center of Shaker spiritual guidance, although its organization as the first official community was a gradual process. It took until 1785 for the New Lebanon meetinghouse to be raised on land donated by David Darrow and others, and until 1795 for the first written covenant drafted by Joseph Meacham (d. 1796) to be adopted. These two events physically symbolized the establishment of the new faith as a visible order. Under the community structure established by Joseph Meacham in 1791, the original community of Mount Lebanon grew to include a total of eight families, including five in the town of New Lebanon, the East Family in Massachusetts, and the Upper and Lower families in the nearby town of Canaan.[3] Each family functioned as an independent, self-supporting entity in spiritual and temporal matters.

At its peak in the 1860s, the Mount Lebanon community consisted of 550 Believers located on six thousand acres in 125 buildings.[4] By the 1920s, membership had declined, and Sisters Sarah and Emma Neale oversaw the selling of furniture to collectors such as Faith and Edward Deming Andrews, who often recorded the oral history associated with their purchases. In 1929–30, Mount Lebanon sold the Church Family grounds to the Lebanon School for Boys—later renamed the Darrow School in honor of George Darrow, an early Shaker convert who had donated his land to accommodate a meetinghouse. In 1930, the Church Family members moved to the North Family, where they lived for the next seventeen years.[5] After maintaining its position as the parent colony and seat of authority for 160 years, Mount Lebanon finally closed in 1947. The remaining six members and

---

1. Cupboard and Case of Drawers
c. 1840
Pine and basswood, with yellow wash, brass latches, and iron hinges
h 81 w 48½ d 20½"
Hancock Shaker Village, Pittsfield, Massachusetts, #62–349

This cupboard, which exhibits beautiful proportions and classical styling, is nearly identical to another piece that was purchased from the North Family at Mount Lebanon.[1] Typical construction features associated with Mount Lebanon design include the plank-sided case, cut feet, ovolo-molded door rail and stiles, unlipped drawer fronts, and threaded knob. Decorative details are found in the extensive use of the beaded edge, which conceals and embellishes the joint between the case face and side and the inner overlapping door edges; the drawers that extend the entire width of the case rather than only the width of the doors; and the use of round surface-mounted brass latches.

their possessions were moved to Hancock, and in 1957 the ministry was transferred to Canterbury, until it was dissolved in 1990 with the death of Eldress Bertha Lindsay.[6]

From the beginning, the Mount Lebanon ministry established a pattern for all the Shaker settlements to follow in the areas of theology, religious practice, and architecture. The Believers' devotional services were conducted in the meetinghouse, which assumed a central importance for each community. The leadership determined that all these structures should have a uniform appearance and selected Moses Johnson (1752–1842), one of the original signers of the Enfield, New Hampshire, covenant and a carpenter by trade, to take charge of framing the building at the center of the Shaker faith. A measure of his competence is indicated in this account of his work in Henry Blinn's "Historical Notes . . . Enfield":

> . . . he visited New Lebanon. The brethren were then cutting timber in the woods, for the Meeting House. Moses accompanied the brethren and they allowed him to fell the trees while other workmen were appointed to line and hew them. After working several days, Moses asked permission to finish one of the timbers. After drawing the line, he began hewing by swinging the axe over his shoulder, to the great astonishment of those looking on. When the stick was finished, it was smooth as though a jack plane had been used on it. So soon as the timber reached the village, Father Joseph Meacham made inquiries to ascertain the name of the workman. On reaching home that evening, Father Joseph thanked Moses and said he need not go to the woods anymore, as his services were needed in the village. The management of the framing and raising of the Meeting House was put in the hands of Moses, to the satisfaction of all. (vol. 1, pp. 301ff.)

With the help of brethren from the Mount Lebanon community, he designed and constructed the first meetinghouse—a two-and-a-half-story building measuring 44 feet wide by 32 feet deep, with gambrel roof, dormers, single shutters, and double doors for the brothers and sisters as well as separate entrances for the four ministry leaders who occupied the second-floor apartments. The gambrel roof with braced ceiling beams derived from English architecture distinguished the meetinghouse from other Shaker buildings, which characteristically had gable roofs. It was painted white and had interior woodwork colored a Prussian blue and yellow-ocher floors. With this building, the style of Shaker religious architecture was established; between 1785 and 1794 Brother Moses reproduced nine and possibly ten other churches after the original pattern, at these locations:

1786 Hancock, Massachusetts
1791 Watervliet, New York
      Enfield, Connecticut
      Harvard, Massachusetts
1792 Canterbury, New Hampshire
      Shirley, Massachusetts
      Tyringham, Massachusetts[7]
1793 Enfield, New Hampshire
1794 Alfred, Maine
      Sabbathday Lake, Maine

A description of the community in the nineteenth century was provided by a visitor during the 1870s, who was impressed by its overall neatness both inside and outside:

Lower Canaan, Mount Lebanon, c. 1880. Courtesy Berkshire Farm Center and Services for Youth

Second Meetinghouse (1824) and first Meetinghouse (right; 1785), Mount Lebanon, c. 1870. Shaker Museum and Library, Old Chatham, New York, #4102

If you are permitted to examine the shops and the dwellings of the family, you will note that the most scrupulous cleanliness is everywhere practised; if there is a stove in the room, a small broom and dust pan hang near it, and a wood-box stands by it; scrapers and mats at the door invite you to make clean your shoes; and if the roads are muddy or snowy, a broom hung up outside the outer door mutely requests you to brush off all the mud and snow. The strips of carpet are easily lifted, and the floor beneath is as clean as though it were a table to be eaten from. The walls are bare of pictures; not only because ornament is wrong, but because frames are

Street view, Second Family, Mount Lebanon, 1881. The chair factory is the second building on the left. Shaker Museum and Library, Old Chatham, New York, #9277

places where dust will lodge. The bedstead is a cot that is easily moved away to allow of dusting and sweeping. Mats meet you at the outer door and at every inner door. The floors of the halls and the dining-room are polished until they shine.[8]

The first Shaker converts brought personal belongings with them, which were shared with other members of the faith. For example, Abigail Hawkins's list of possessions included the following items when she joined in 1789: "One oldish bedstead, two feather beds and beding mixed feathers, 2 oldish chairs, 1 little oldish chair, one Low Case Drawer 13 years old, one midling sized oval Table 13 years old, and one small looking glass."[9] However, the Believers began to produce furniture to suit specific communal needs at an early date. According to the daybook of Brother Joseph Bennet, Jr., on September 25, 1789, "1 Great & 6 Small Chairs" were sold to Brother Elizah Slosson of the Second Family. This transaction illustrates the social and economic independence and interrelatedness of the various families within a Shaker community.[10] An entry in a Mount Lebanon daybook for 1792 includes a table sold for 12 shillings to a Timothy Edwards of Stockbridge; another in 1806 records the payment of 1 pound 14 shillings to John Shapley for a square table; and in 1807 a charge of 1 pound 18 shillings is listed for a table made by Noah Osborn.[11] From these journal entries it is not possible to tell, however, if this furniture was already made and sold because it was unneeded or if it was made specifically to sell to the world's people. Unfortunately, there are very few journal references regarding the design or construction of specific pieces of furniture.

Current documentation for determining the names of active woodworkers at Mount Lebanon rests on three types of sources: extant signed pieces (these names are marked with one square ■); Shaker journal references to joiners and cabinetmakers (these names are marked with two squares ■■); data supplied by the United States census of 1850 unless otherwise specified (these names are marked with three squares ■■■); and oral history information recorded by early collectors such as Faith and Edward Deming Andrews or secondary source material (these names are marked with four squares ■■■■). Some of the craftsmen have extensive documentation, while others are much less solid. Even Isaac Newton Youngs makes the following disclaimer in "A Domestic Journal of Daily Occurrences," which lists the men involved with "Joinering & Carpentering" activities: "There were doubtless several others who worked occasionally at the business, but there are no means to ascertain the particulars. I have not mentioned any out of the 1st order." Considering the size and the 160-year history of the community, the following list must be considered partial; it primarily represents the activities of members of the Church Family.

- AMOS JEWETT (1753–1834), see pl. 63
- SAMUEL ELLIS (1760–1818), in Andrews, *Shaker Furniture*, p. 47
- NOAH OSBORN (1765–1813), in Andrews, *Shaker Furniture*, p. 47
- SAMUEL HUMPHREY TURNER (1775–1842), see pl. 59. Resided in Pleasant Hill 1806–36
- HENRY BENNET (1779–1852), in Youngs, "A Domestic Journal of Daily Occurrences" (hereafter known as "Daily Occurrences"), March 1838
- DAVID ROWLEY (1779–1885), listed as cabinetmaker[12]
- AMOS BISHOP (1780–1857), listed as carpenter
- BENJAMIN LYON (1780–1870), see pl. 36
- PARK AVERY (working 1788?–left 1791), in Youngs, "Daily Occurrences"
- DANIEL HILT (w. 1788?–98), in Youngs, "Daily Occurrences"
- WILLIAM SAFFORD (w. 1788?–died 1813), in Youngs, "Daily Occurrences"
- JOHN LOCKWOOD (1791–1878), listed as carpenter and joiner in 1860 United States census
- DANIEL COPLEY (born 1792), listed as carpenter
- ISAAC NEWTON YOUNGS (1793–1865), see pl. 64[13]
- JAMES WILSON (b. 1794–w. 1848), Canaan Family, listed as carpenter
- HENRY YOUNGS (b. 1794), listed as clockmaker
- RICHARD TREAT (w. 1796–1812), in Youngs, "Daily Occurrences"
- BENJAMIN GOODRICH (l. 1796), in Andrews, *Shaker Furniture*, p. 42
- AMOS STEWART (1802–1884), see pls. 29, 32, 33
- DANIEL BOLER (1804–1892), in "A Register of Incidents and Events," February 27, 1860 "Elder Daniel and Giles [Avery] work at the counter in our shop." Apparently he was visiting Watervliet from Mount Lebanon at the time.
- HENRY DEWITT (1805–1855), see pl. 6
- JOHN SHAPELEY (w. 1806–d. 1812), in Andrews, *Shaker Furniture*, pp. 47, 73
- ERASTUS RUDE (w. 1806), in Andrews, *Religion in Wood*, p. 103[14]
- GEORGE WICKERSHAM (1806–1891), see pl. 18
- JAMES X. SMITH (1806–1888), see pl. 52
- BUSHNELL FITCH (w. 1811–16), in Youngs, "Daily Occurrences"
- JOHN BRUCE (w. 1813?–29), in Youngs, "Daily Occurrences"
- RANSOME GILMAN (1813–1880), in Andrews, *Shaker Furniture*, p. 47
- GIDEON TURNER, SR. (d. 1815), in Andrews, *Shaker Furniture*, p. 47
- GILES AVERY (1815–1890), in Avery, Journals[15]
- ORREN HASKINS (1815–1892), see pl. 35
- JETHRO TURNER (w. 1816–19), in Lyon, Journal, July 26, September 2, 1816, December 3, 1819
- JOHN ALLEN (1816–l. 1846), see pl. 35
- JOHN WILLIAM PORTER (w. 1817), in Lyon, Journal, November 28, 1817
- ANTHONY BREWSTER (w. 1818–37), in Youngs, "Daily Occurrences"[16]
- ELISHA BLAKEMAN (1819–1900), in Blakeman, "Journal of Daily Occurrences"[17]
- JAMES BISHOP (d. 1822), in Andrews, *Shaker Furniture*, p. 47

■■■■ ASA TALCOTT (d. 1822), in Andrews, *Shaker Furniture*, p. 47

■■■ JOHN BROWN (b. 1824), listed as carpenter

■■■ RICHARD NOOCHEON[?] (b. 1828), listed as carpenter

■■■ HENRY SMITH (b. 1829), listed as carpenter

■■■ JOHN CHARLES (b. 1830), listed as carpenter

■ CHARLES WEED (1831–l. 1862), see pl. 36[18]

■■ LUTHER COPLEY (w. 1835), in Youngs, "Daily Occurrences," February 16, 1835

■■ NICHOLAS BENNET (w. 1836), in Youngs, "Daily Occurrences," January 20, 1836

■ ANDREW BARRETT (1836 or 1837–1917), see pl. 53

■■ STEPHEN MUNSON (w. 1838), in Youngs, "Daily Occurrences," March 1838

■ HENRY HOLLISTER (1838–1919), see pl. 30

■ JAMES V. CALVER (1839–l. 1861), see pl. 34

■■ DEROBIGNE BENNET (w. 1840), see Blakeman, "Journal of Daily Occurrences"[19]

■■■■ ABEL KNIGHT (d. 1842), in Andrews, *Shaker Furniture*, p. 47

■■ BRAMAN WICKS (w. 1843–l. 1848), in Youngs, "Daily Occurrences"[20]

■■ EDWARD CHAMBERS (w. 1847), in "A Domestic Journal of Domestic Occurrences" (hereafter referred to as "Domestic Occurrences"), supplement to December 1847

■■ BENJAMIN GATES (w. 1848), in "Domestic Occurrences," July 1848

■■ JUSTUS HARVARD (w. 1848), in "Domestic Occurrences," July 1848

■■ LORIN WICKS (w. 1848), in "Domestic Occurrences," July 1848, and listed as carpenter and joiner in United States census for Watervliet, New York

■■■■ HIRAM RUDE (w. 1851), in Grant and Allen, *Shaker Furniture Makers*, p. 96

■■■■ GIDEON TURNER, JR. (d. 1852), in Andrews, *Shaker Furniture*, p. 47

■■ WILLIAM GREAVES (w. 1855), in "Domestic Occurrences," supplement to April 1855

■■ CALVIN REED (w. 1855), in Youngs, "Daily Occurrences," 1855

■■ ANDREW FORTIER (w. 1859), in "Domestic Occurrences," supplement to November 1859

■■ PETER LONG (w. 1861), in "Domestic Occurrences," supplement to February 1861

■■ SAMUEL WHITE (w. 1868), in Youngs, "Daily Occurrences," July 1868[21]

■■■■ SAMUEL CHAPMAN, in Andrews, *Shaker Furniture*, p. 47

■■■■ EDWARD CHASE, in Andrews, *Shaker Furniture*, p. 47

■■■■ NATHAN KENDAL, in Grant and Allen, *Shaker Furniture Makers*, p. 56

■■■■ CLAWSON MIDDLETON, Canaan Family, in Andrews, *Shaker Furniture*, p. 47

■■■■ THOMAS MUNSON, in Andrews, *Shaker Furniture*, p. 47

■■■■ WILLIAM TRIP, in Andrews, *Shaker Furniture*, p. 47

CHAIR MAKERS

■■■■ GILBERT AVERY (1775–1853), in Andrews, *Shaker Furniture*, p. 46; see pl. 60

■■■■ THOMAS ESTES (b. 1782), in Andrews, *Religion in Wood*, p. 103

■■■ JAMES FARNHAM (1784–1858), listed as chair maker

■■■■ WILLIAM THRASHER (1796–1896), in Andrews, *Religion in Wood*, p. 103

■■■■ JOHN BISHOP (w. 1814), in Muller and Rieman, *Shaker Chair*, p. 136

■■■ GEORGE O. DONNELL (b. 1823–w. 1852), listed as chair maker

■■ ROBERT WAGAN (1833–1883), industry manager, in Blinn, "A Journey to Kentucky" (Summer 1965), pp. 43–44, and Muller and Rieman, *Shaker Chair*, p. 169

■■■■ JESSIE LEWIS (w. 1860), in Muller and Rieman, *Shaker Chair*, p. 169

■■■■ WILLIAM PERKINS (d. 1934), in Muller and Rieman, *Shaker Chair*, p. 208

■■■■ LILLIAN BARLOW (d. 1942), in Muller and Rieman, *Shaker Chair*, p. 225
■■■■ DANIEL HAWKINS, in Andrews, *Religion in Wood*, p. 103[22]
■■■■ GABRIEL HAWKINS, in Andrews, *Religion in Wood*, p. 62

WORLDLY MAKERS

THOMAS BOWMAN, JR. AND SR. (w. 1830), in Grant and Allen, *Shaker Furniture Makers*, pp. 6–7
JOHN, CHARLES, AND WILLIAM SHUMWAY (w. 1867–75), see pl. 28
AUSTIN E. GAGE (w. 1877), see pl. 15

Living within the Shaker community created broad relationships that lasted for decades or even a lifetime. One set of relationships grew out of eating and worshiping together, another by working together. The brethrens' working relationships ranged from the more formal long-term master and apprenticeship training, described below, which continued over the years, to short-term liaisons that were task-related. For example, Henry DeWitt mentioned in his journal on February 1, 1840, "Derobigne and Elisha B[lakeman] has been to work for the convenience of the herb business having been to work for the business for 9 days past put up a number of shelves, and made a counter 8 feet long with seven drawers in it and 2 cupboards: finished all but top boards & doors." Isaac Newton Youngs wrote in "Domestic Occurrences" on July 1, 1848, "Justus Harvard & Lorin Wicks returned home and took with them a company of workmen to assist them there on building a new meeting house [at Watervliet], viz. Isaac N.Y. (the writer), E[lder] Br[other] Amos Stuart [Stewart], & Benjamin Gates, from the Chh. [Church Family] here, to cover the roof with him. Amos Bishop from the 2nd family, & James Wilson from Canaan family for woodworkmen. (they worked together several weeks)."

While many of the initial converts learned their woodworking skills in the outside world and had to put aside superfluous decoration in their work as Shaker cabinetmakers, there is documentation to suggest that the training of the next generation of craftsmen occurred through long-term master-apprenticeship relationships. David Rowley joined the Shakers at age thirty as a skilled cabinetmaker, having learned the trade from Daniel Gay in his hometown of Sharon, Connecticut. As a member, he continued to ply his trade; journal references detail numerous pieces that he made in the Church and North Family shops for over forty years, until his death in 1855.[23] Shortly after fifteen-year-old Elisha Blakeman's arrival at Mount Lebanon in 1834, he went into "the Brick shop to work at joinering with David Rowley" as his apprentice, according to Youngs's "Daily Occurrences." In 1848, Orren Haskins worked with Brother David on a coffin and later took charge of the joiners' shop after the "Master's" death in 1855, suggesting perhaps a teacher-student relationship between the two.[24] Additional information is provided in "A Domestic Journal of Domestic Occurrences" on April 15, 1848: "Orren Haskins moved from the 2nd order to take up his residence here in the first order and to officiate as woodworkman. This seems to be highly necessary as we have had noone to support that occupation since the absconding of Braman W[icks]." The use of the word "officiate" in this context raises a number of questions regarding the organization of the woodworking shops and the role of individual craftsmen. For instance, what kind of responsibility did Orren Haskins or others who were in charge of the woodworking shop have in influencing design for the community? Did other joiners and carpenters report to him? What were their responsibilities? Was there one person either in the ministry or as the cabinetmaker in charge of the shop who approved of particular forms or designs?

Over the years, Benjamin Lyon collaborated with several different wood-workers on a number of projects, including a case of drawers with Anthony Brewster (1817), twenty-eight benches with John William Porter (1817), and a counter with Charles Weed (1860; see pl. 36).[25] According to a journal entry, fifteen-year-old Amos Stewart worked with Brother Benjamin on some panel doors in 1817 and may first have learned cabinetmaking from him.[26] Amos Stewart, whose career spanned sixty years, was assigned twenty-five-year-old Giles Avery as his junior in the elder's lot or group of the Center Family in 1840. For the next nine years Brother Giles continued honing his woodworking skills under the direction of his mentor, with whom he "had some experience at cabinet work."[27]

Consequently, the continuum of training at Mount Lebanon passed from master craftsman to apprentices who joined the sect as children and were raised in the Shaker style. These second-generation craftsmen, uncontaminated by direct worldly influences, were responsible—along with the brothers who had been in the sect for thirty years—for producing the "pure" furniture during the "classic" period of Shaker design from about 1820 to 1850.

Despite the large number of identified joiners and carpenters living within the community, the Mount Lebanon Shakers often needed to hire worldly cabinetmakers to assist them with seasonal projects. In 1829, Thomas Bowman, Sr. and Jr., of Mount Lebanon, were employed by the Church Family to make bedsteads and the following year to make a case of drawers,[28] and again between 1867 and 1875 John and William Shumway produced a case of drawers, bookcase, and secretary for both the North and Canaan families.[29] After the great fires of 1875, which destroyed eight major structures of the Mount Lebanon Church Family, the Shakers needed to engage the services of local craftsmen to help them replace furniture. The name A. E. Gage, a Pittsfield, Massachusetts, house carpenter, is found on one of a number of case pieces made for the Shakers' use in their new 1877 Church Family Dwelling House (see pl. 15).

Far more documented furniture produced at Mount Lebanon survives than from any other Shaker community. This is not unexpected, due to both the long history of the community, which spanned 160 years, and the sheer number of cabinetmakers who were active during this time. Most major types of work and dwelling house furniture are represented in extant examples, including cupboards, cases of drawers, desks, counters, tables, stands, sewing tables with gallery, washstands, blanket boxes, and chairs. While the sampling is large, each of these different forms evolved over time, which makes it difficult to arrive at accurate generalizations regarding community design and construction features for each type of furniture. The problem is compounded by the idiosyncratic styles of individual cabinetmakers, making it even more difficult to characterize specific or standard production styles, as is possible in other communities where, ironically, there is much less data available to the researcher.

For example, some or all of the following characteristic features can be found in one grouping of early Mount Lebanon storage units: a stained pine or poplar case with plank sides and cut feet; midcase dividing rail molding with lamb's-tongue ends and applied bull-nose cornice molding; flat-panel cupboard doors with rails and stiles coped with a beveled edge; and lipped drawers with small peglike knobs tenoned into the face. In contrast, furniture made after 1870 attributed to Amos Stewart is unusual in design and bold in construction. His kneehole desk, fall-front secretary, and counter are made of open-grained butternut, ash, or cherry and feature unlipped drawers and small, housed half-dovetails to join the rails to the frame. Furthermore, the later storage units produced during the Victorian era show the influence of Empire styling, with frame-and-panel construction, ornate cornices, walnut moldings around the drawer faces, wide stiles, and commercially made porcelain knobs and brass catches.

Desks were presumably employed by deacons, trustees, and elders, who were responsible for keeping records for the community. Surviving examples include a variety of forms created over a long period of time to suit the needs of individual leaders. Among them are a unique Shaker-designed double desk; three pieces derived from worldly styles, including a slant-front secretary complete with secret drawer, a fall-front desk, and a butler's desk; a Victorian secretary built by a worldly cabinetmaker who was commissioned by the Shakers; and a model that appears to be inspired by commercial prototypes of the time.

One furniture form probably incorrectly attributed to Harvard on the basis of oral history is the so-called butler's desk, a worldly form that ran across economic lines. Both high-style and pared-down versions survive in public collections today and may have functioned as space-saving furniture, serving simultaneously as desk and sideboard.[30] However, this design with hinged drawer front that drops down to provide a writing surface is rare in Shaker communities; it may have been placed in a retiring room or office rather than a dining room interior.

Counters range in date from about 1800 to 1880 and reveal the versatility of the form as well as the ingenuity of the cabinetmaker. Whether built into a corner, equipped with an opening to hold a basket, or fitted with a marble top, these examples are clearly designed for specific purposes. The layout varies from perfect symmetry to horizontal or vertical asymmetry. Some distinctive construction features relate a group of pieces to a specific cabinetmaker or school of craftsmanship, as discussed in individual entries.

Tables also exhibit a variety of forms. The Mount Lebanon Shakers modified the medieval-style trestle table for communal dining and designed a form that was adopted at all communities. They raised the horizontal stretcher from floor level to a position beneath the top, which provided stability as well as additional leg room for a large quantity of diners. Work furniture for performing a wide variety of specialized tasks, including baking, cutting, sorting, and dairy activities, have a number of customized enhancements, such as a shaped backboard, an additional lower shelf, or drawers on one or more sides. Dwelling house tables might have been gateleg or with single or double drop leaves with butterfly-shaped swing supports.

After the 1850s, when enrollment began to decline, the sisters assumed a greater role in supporting the community financially by producing small hand-sewn items for sale to the world. This successful industry required a new form of sewing table. It rested on square, tapered legs and had either an added-on or an integral gallery fitted with several narrow drawers on the work surface. This design, which provided individualized work and storage space, was apparently reproduced many times to assist the sisters in their needlework.

The design of tripod stands, which might have rodlike peg legs, S-shaped cabriole legs, or arched spider legs, is based on worldly prototypes. While the majority of surviving examples are fitted with round tops, the details of the stem turnings and the shaping of the foot vary considerably from piece to piece. Several of the existing stands bear a stamped name or inscription attributed to the hand of the same maker, suggesting that some candle or lamp holders were special pieces presented to sisters in leadership positions.

A number of tall case and wall clocks designed by Amos Jewett and Isaac Newton Youngs survive from Mount Lebanon. It is not surprising that both men, who worked together briefly at an early date, specialized in wooden works,

South Family chair showroom, Mount Lebanon, c. 1890. Private collection

Lillian Barlow in the Second Family chair factory, Mount Lebanon, c. 1930. Photograph by Baldwin. New York State Museum, Albany, #PTH3.3, neg.462

although the clock cases themselves were frequently made by another Shaker cabinetmaker.

As far as other furniture forms are concerned, a variety of blanket boxes survive that are indistinguishable from worldly examples. Others with cut feet, one or two drawers, and molded breadboard ends on their tops are clearly Shaker in design. Although single and double washstands from Mount Lebanon exhibit no standard door and drawer arrangement, they all share an ogee shaping on the sides of the gallery, which appears to be a preferred composition feature.

However, the Mount Lebanon community specialized in chair making and was, in fact, the only society to manufacture and market seating furniture on a large-scale basis for sale to the world. By midcentury the South Family was in charge of the industry and had issued broadsides to promote their products. Under Deacon Robert Wagan's direction, they built a new factory equipped with mass-production machinery that increased annual output and standardized the products. The following report was issued by Elder Henry Blinn of Canterbury, New Hampshire, who visited the thriving industry in 1873:

> The building erected last year, & the machinery in it has cost some $25,000. All of this was earned by this little family [South] save $2000 which they borrowed of the Second Family. They have an engine of 15 horse power and a boiler of 20 horse power. The whole building is heated by steam. Some ten hands are employed, & it is expected that they will finish two Doz. chairs per day. They are the old fashioned chairs of one hundred years ago. About two thirds are made with rockers. The large chairs with cushions sell for $18.00 each. Without cushions for $9.00. The small chairs with cushions sell for $13.00 without cushions for $7.00. Only two sizes are made. They are all stained in a hot logwood dye, which forces the color into the wood. When varnished they are bright red. Already they have orders for more than they can furnish. The plush for cushions is made in this same building. In one room we found two old men at work in hand looms, slowly weaving this peculiar cloth. Our guide informed us that they were not americans. . . . These men weave from three to four yards each per day, and are paid fifty cents a yard. One of the men informed me that they usually worked ten hours each day. ("A Journey to Kentucky" [Summer 1965], pp. 43–44)

The typical production chair was available in seven sizes and was characterized by acorn-shaped pommels, bent back posts, crescent-shaped arms with applied mushroom-shaped tenon caps, and tapered stretchers. These models became so popular that imitations appeared on the market. To avoid any confusion and authenticate their products, the Shakers affixed a gold transfer trademark on the chairs. Despite the premature death of Robert Wagan in 1883 and the destruction of the factory in 1923, the business continued, although on a much smaller scale, until 1947.

Furniture produced by worldly craftsmen under the direction of the Shakers has been included in the discussion of late-nineteenth-century Mount Lebanon design. After two devastating fires in 1875, the Believers enlisted outside help to replace all the retiring room furniture while they were engaged in building reconstruction. Consequently, many built-in and freestanding storage units, as well as tables, beds, and seating furniture, made outside the community with a more worldly look were brought into the community.

2. Sister Sarah Collins's Room, South Family Dwelling House

c. 1930s
Photograph by William F. Winter (1899–1939)
New York State Museum, Albany, #PTB.5.42

This storage unit situated in a hallway of the South Family Dwelling House dating from about the 1820s or 1830s is one of many case pieces built into the structure. It is fitted with only one tall door, while other units have two doors above the bull-nose midcase molding, and graduated drawers below. As in many of the twentieth-century Shaker living spaces, wallpaper was applied to decorate the interior.

Although there are numerous built-ins in the Canaan, North,[31] and South families, this is not the case with extant Church Family buildings at Mount Lebanon, including the 1876 dwelling house built after the fires of 1875. It is impossible to know how many were installed in the buildings that were destroyed in the blaze, but the marked absence of these common Shaker case pieces is surprising.

Visible through the doorway of Sister Sarah Collins's (1855–1947) retiring room is a three-drawer blanket box in the background. Although probably made in the 1840s, this form of storage furniture clearly was still used by the Shakers during the twentieth century. This particular example is remarkable for the cabinetmaker's use of three rather than one or two drawers, the decorative ogee-shaped molding above the foot, and the wide applied bracket base.

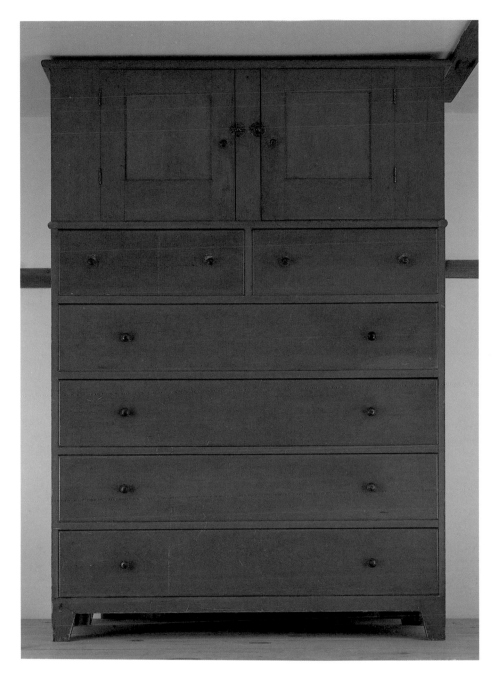

3. Cupboard and Case of Drawers

c. 1840
Pine and basswood, with salmon-color stain, brass latch, and steel hinges
h 68½ w 48¾ d 18⅞"
The Mount Lebanon Shaker Collection

Both the overall and individual proportions of this piece are distinctive. The cupboard section of the case is unusually short relative to the bank of drawers below it. The doors themselves are square rather than rectangular. The lower door rail is particularly wide in relation to the dimensions of the panel directly above. In addition, the exterior stiles are quite wide, forcing a rather narrow central stile to separate the doors.

Other distinctive decorative details include the half-round midcase molding with lamb's-tongue ends, which protrudes beyond the case sides, resulting in a distinct visual separation of the top and bottom sections. The top molding is integral on the front and mitered and applied on the ends to conceal the end grain. The door rail and stiles are coped with an inner beveled edge. On the base, the cut foot and rail are fitted neatly with a miter joint, a shop practice distinctive of some Mount Lebanon community cabinetmakers. One finishing technique characteristic of Mount Lebanon is seen in the rounded drawer edges and the unlipped drawer fronts, which protrude about 5/16 inch beyond the face of the case.

left

4. Cupboard and Case of Drawers
c. 1820
Pine, with fruitwood knobs and chrome yellow
wash on the interior
h 96 w 54 d 14"
Private collection
Photograph: Paul Rocheleau

The craftsman who built this cupboard combined several different design elements to make a case piece unlike any other. The pair of doors on either side of the case creates a tall vertical unit, which is separated by a wide stile and the unique bank of six small drawers. The entire piece is held together visually by the horizontal orientation of the half-width drawers below. Despite its size, the 8-foot-tall case is very shallow—measuring only 14 inches deep.

The internal configuration, consisting of three shelves behind the two upper doors as well as pigeonholes and vertical ledger slots inside the lower left and right cupboards respectively, suggests it had been designed for an office setting. For some unknown reason, the pulls on the half-width drawers, which appear centered, are actually placed above the horizontal center line. This uncommon detail is also found in pl. 6.

5. Cupboard and Case of Drawers
c. 1830
Pine, with dark stain
h 84¾ w 78 d 22½"
The Mount Lebanon Shaker Collection
Photograph: Paul Rocheleau

Measuring 7 feet tall and 6½ feet wide, this large storage unit is perfectly proportioned. The wide stiles surrounding and separating the cupboards above create a vertical thrust that is balanced by the horizontal emphasis of the drawers below. Beaded edges define the front corners of the case and separate each pair of doors. The typical half-round midrail terminates on either end with the lamb's-tongue detail associated with Mount Lebanon design, while the simplest of moldings, a quarter-round, finishes the top and bottom of the case.

6. Cupboard and Case of Drawers
Used or made by Henry DeWitt (1805–1855)
c. 1830
Pine and fruitwood, with yellow wash
h 95½ w 96 d 19"
The Mount Lebanon Shaker Collection

At one time set into a corner of the 1826 Church Family Brethrens' Shop, this piece may have been used by the brothers for tailoring. The stamped numbers marked from 3 feet to 6 feet 6 inches located on the outside between the two sets of doors probably served to measure the height of the Believers to be fitted for clothing. Another cupboard, which was until recently in the Brethrens' Shop, has a similar scale stamped into the case, which includes the names of many Believers.[32] According to a March 7, 1846, entry in Henry DeWitt's "Journal," he "moved out my great cupboard for the accomodation of a closet behind." Originally freestanding, with a small, integral quarter-round cornice molding, the wider molding was added to cover the gap between the top and the ceiling when the unit was moved and made into a built-in cupboard with a closet behind. An unusual feature is the placement

of the drawer knobs above the center line on the bottom two tiers of drawers. This idiosyncratic design element relates this piece to the large case piece pl. 4.

Henry DeWitt served the Shakers in a number of capacities during his life. Originally assigned to the shoemaking trade at the age of seventeen, Brother Henry commented in his journal on other skills, which included bookbinding, printing, and woodworking, in an entry of October 20, 1852:

> This morning I heard the sound of liberty! Liberty from the bondage of old boots and shoes, and after having spent 26 years in the business! I continue at my business which has occupied a portion of my time for the ten last years. Which is the wheel business, & book binding; looms to see to & ok. A new trade is now presented to my charge in addition to the forementioned, which is to do the printing for the garden concerns & the herb business, which will occupy nearly 9 month labor in a year.

Although, according to subsequent journal entries, Henry also built new furniture, most of the joinery work documented by Brother Henry involved repair. On March 7, 1854, for

example, he divided one counter into two for the sisters. He wrote, "I took off [four drawers from] the end of the Counter that's going to the Washhouse for the Drawer basket business; planed the leaf over etc. etc. Expect to smooth it sometime." On March 21, "I worked fixing a carcass for the 4 drawers I cut of[f] the Counter . . . for the sisters at the Washhouse." He also adapted several desks. On August 25, 1836, "I began to make myself a new desk for writing on, out of one I had been using, which was rather inconvenient." On August 27, ". . . I finished said desk about 9 AM . . . I lowered the upper story to Frederick S's desk and put legs to it." According to a journal entry dated April 28, 1837, "I put rockers to a chair for Eliza Ann Taylor; I took the rocker out of a new rocking chair & lowered it about 1½ inches & put them in again."

However, DeWitt's journal records indicate that in the midst of modifying existing pieces, on February 1, 1840, he "made a counter 8 feet long with seven drawers on it & 2 cupboards." Again, on March 20, 1841, he "finished making a counter for the Deaconesses with 12 drawers[;] took between 3 & 4 weeks work."

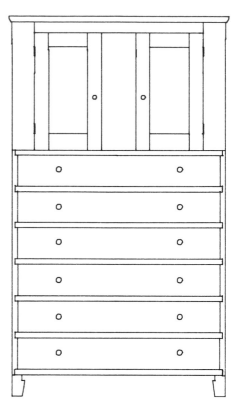

Cupboard and case of drawers, Mount Lebanon, 1817. Written in pencil on case: January 29, 1817. Private collection

7. Cupboard and Case of Drawers
Attributed to Amos Stewart (1802–1884)
1843
Written in red chalk on a drawer bottom: 1843
Pine and basswood, with brass escutcheon and cast-iron hinges
h 78¾ w 42¼ d 21¾"
Private collection

At the age of nine, Amos Stewart was brought to the Mount Lebanon Church Family from Shirley, Massachusetts, by Brother Nathan Kendal, an early Shaker woodworker, who was appointed Amos's guardian on February 11, 1811. It is possible that Brother Nathan introduced his charge to the trade at an early age[33] for, according to Benjamin Lyon's "Journal" of July 2, 1817, "Amos and I begin some panel doars." Based on surviving pieces, Brother Amos produced a variety of furniture over the years, including a counter (pl. 31) and a fall-front secretary (pl. 23), both inscribed 1873, a kneehole desk dated 1877 (pl. 29), a washstand marked 1878 (pl. 32), and a sewing desk (pl. 33). Henry DeWitt mentioned in a journal entry for December 18, 1854, an unusual cabinet to hold printing type: "I was under the necessity of going to the shop on account of meeting William Olford about directions for a type case. Elder

Amos is about making with 16 drawers for type." Unfortunately, this piece is unknown today.

Isaac Newton Youngs reported in "Domestic Occurrences" that in addition to woodworking, Brother Amos served the community in other capacities over the years, including as "a mechanic with a special interest in machinery" (1845) and a "tailor-scribe" (1850). Some of his accomplishments include patenting an "improvement in water-wheels" (1864), building a new planing machine for the Enfield, New Hampshire, Shakers, and, with George Wickersham, completing the interior finishing work on the Watervliet Meetinghouse.[34] He also served in the Mount Lebanon ministry and traveled to other Shaker communities, both East and West.

Made during the period of "gospel simplicity," this freestanding storage unit dated 1843 exhibits basic plank sides, small cut feet, flat-panel cupboard doors, and unlipped drawers. The overall form is closely related to the case piece published in Edward Deming Andrews's *Shaker Furniture* as plate 22 inscribed "December 1830, made by Amos Stewart," which has two pairs of half-width drawers over three full-width drawers. Given the similarity in layout and the use of large red lettering in both pieces, it is probable that Amos Stewart made this case piece as well. Another case signed "Made Feb 1831 Amos Stewart" contains seven tiers of half-width drawers below two cupboards.[35] The various drawer arrangements on all three of these examples create patterns that are not found on worldly furniture. One of the earliest dated Shaker case pieces, dated January 29, 1817, displays very similar layout, materials, and construction details. The appearance of this classical form is well documented here through these two pieces dated twenty-six years apart. The form of the cupboard and case of drawers may have continued for another ten or fifteen years before some basic changes, such as the use of very different woods and finishes, substantially altered its appearance.

The lock with oval brass escutcheon on the cupboard door is contemporary with the piece and suggests that this unit may have contained "public stores" rather than private possessions. According to the 1845 "Millennial Laws" (part 3, section 5) and the 1841 "Holy Orders of the Church," written by Father Joseph, "Where publick stores are kept, let the doors, chests, drawers or cupboards be secured by *locks and keys:* they shall be kept *locked* and by no means carelessly left open or unsecured" (section 14, no. 3).

8. Cupboard and Case of Drawers
c. 1860
Butternut, poplar, and basswood
Printed paper labels on drawer fronts: Slippery Elm. Mug Wort. Hyssop./ Yarrow. Elder Flowers. Lobelia./ Horehound. Sweet Fern. Liver Wort. Summery Savory. Ma[..] & Arsmart.
Written in pencil in script on drawer parts: DB [drawer bottom]; DS [drawer side]
h 66 w 47⅜ d 19¼"
Hancock Shaker Village, Pittsfield, Massachusetts, #62–411

This is one of a pair of distinctive butternut-sill cupboards used in the North Family infirmary to store medicinal herbs.[36] Each drawer is divided and its contents labeled on the outside. Distinctive in form, the drawers, fitted with many glue blocks along the bottom, are set high above the floor—a design rare in Shaker furniture. Smaller design details include the chamfer on the door rails, the bead on the edge of the panel and again on the interior of the door frame, and the plank-sided case without a cut foot.

turned pull. Both have a plank-sided case supported by small cut feet that are narrower than the stile, a feature typical of much larger case pieces, such as pl. 1. The pegs affixed to the right-hand side of the later case—whether original or added later—could have held small brushes or other cleaning utensils.

11. Cupboard and Case of Drawers
c. 1830
Pine, with hardwood knobs and traces of red paint
h 79¾ w 30 d 18½"
Private collection
Photograph: courtesy Suzanne Courcier and Robert W. Wilkins, Richard and Betty Ann Rasso

Several design and construction features suggest that this storage unit is an early Shaker piece: the plank-sided case resting flat on the floor without feet; the bead on the front corner of the stiles that is rabbeted and nailed; the integral rather than applied cornice molding; and the wide, thumbnail-lipped drawer faces. Particularly noteworthy is the tall, two-panel door and the hinged door at the base, which according to oral tradition covered a slot in the floor where dirt could be conveniently swept.

This piece was acquired by John Roberts directly from the Shakers, probably as payment for work he did as a hired man for the community. It formed part of a collection that for years was housed on the site of the Canaan Family, located about two miles from Mount Lebanon.

9. Cupboard
c. 1800
Pine
h 32 w 37⅜ d 17½"
Private collection
Photograph: courtesy John Keith Russell Antiques, Inc.

10. Cupboard
c. 1850
Pine
h 29 w 31 d 17"
Courtesy of the Art Complex Museum, Duxbury, Massachusetts, #29-12

These two small cupboards are representative of the essence of Mount Lebanon design from two different periods. Yet at the same time, they diverge from characteristic Mount Lebanon design in that they function as both table and cupboard simultaneously. The earlier piece, dating from the beginning of the nineteenth century, exhibits a heavy, raised-panel door and arched cut foot. The later example, produced about midcentury, has a flat-panel door, ovolo-edged frame, and small

12. Sisters' Sewing Room
c. 1890
Photograph
Shaker Museum and Library, Old Chatham, New York, #4573

This late-nineteenth-century photograph shows, from left to right, Sisters Augustus Stone, Emma J. Neale (1847–1943), and Mary Hazzard (1811–1899) and an unknown sister in a Mount Lebanon workroom making cloaks and bonnets. The case piece in the background is pl. 13. The sewing desk with gallery is covered with sewing or fancygoods accoutrements, a usage often seen in images of Shakers taken at the end of the century.

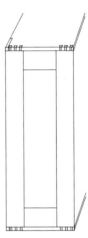

13. Cupboard and Case of Drawers
c. 1840
Pine and poplar, with fruitwood knobs and chrome yellow interior
h 75 w 81½ d 23"
The Mount Lebanon Shaker Collection

This massive—nearly 7 feet wide—but well-designed case piece exhibits several unusual design and construction features. The placement of each door so it is centered directly above the drawer below necessitated the location of a wide panel in the middle of the facade as well as a panel on each end of the case. The drawers are dramatically graduated at 9, 10, 11, and 12 inches deep. Characteristic Mount Lebanon features include the mid-case molding with lamb's-tongue ends and door rails and stiles coped with a beveled edge. The frame-and-panel sides are constructed with stiles (but not rails) that are dovetailed into both the top and bottom of the case. This peculiar joinery detail, as well as the overall form, can also be found in pl. 14, which sugests the same craftsman made both case pieces.[37]

14. Cupboard and Case of Drawers
c. 1870
Pine, with walnut molding, fruitwood knobs, salmon stain under varnish, brass hinges, brass and porcelain slide latch, and chrome yellow interior
h 77½ w 74½ d 23"
The Mount Lebanon Shaker Collection

At first glance this piece appears to have been "modernized." However, on close examination, it is clear that the Empire-style cornice (consisting of a square with a fillet over an ogee with a large astragal) and walnut molding bordering the drawers and side panels are original to the piece, as there is no finish under the molding and no indication of other molding. Related in design and construction to pl. 13, suggesting a common maker, it shares with that cupboard unique, side-to-top dovetail joinery as well as design details such as the particularly wide stiles and the centering of the doors above the banks of drawers. However, distinct differences are seen in the manner in which the craftsman framed around the doors and the commercially made brass slide latches with porcelain knobs, which are used along with inset locks. The interior is finished with a rich chrome yellow wash and the case has an old varnish finish over a salmon-color stain.

15. Cupboard and Case of Drawers

Attributed to Austin E. Gage, house carpenter in Pittsfield, Massachusetts
1877
Ash and poplar, with porcelain knobs, cast-iron latches, and lock
h 65½ w 52 d 22½"
The Mount Lebanon Shaker Collection

Apparently, thirty cases were commissioned from Austin E. Gage, a house carpenter listed in the 1877 Pittsfield city directory. A drawer from an identical but incomplete cupboard and case of drawers carries the penciled inscription "A.E. Gage 1877." Altogether, six or eight of these case pieces are known to have survived.

The movement of this furniture is documented by a series of journal references:

"A thing composed of cupboard & drawers, made at Pittsfield, one for each Brother, now in use" ("Domestic Occurrences," February 23, 1877).
"Arrived, the last of the 30 cases engaged, 17 to Brethren & 13 to Sisters (for the present)" ("Domestic Occurrences," March 1, 1877).
"There have been 17 cases of drawers and cupboards, made in Pittsfield, for Brethrens use, been received into the new house" (March 7, 1877).[38]
"Andrew Fortier, & other teams are drawing new furniture from Pittsfield, for the New Great House, for Sister's rooms" (January 15, 1878).[39]

Even at this late date the classic Shaker form of cupboard over drawers was retained, although it has been altered with the addition of a long door enclosing a space to hang clothing and the dummy drawer front on the bottom right. The latter encloses a space at the bottom, accessible from the inside. The use of a simple quarter-round cornice and base molding keep this piece well within the "plain and simple" regulations still affecting furniture commissioned by the Shakers of "outside contractors."

The Fires of 1875

"Since our form was made up, there has occurred, in the Centre, or Church Family, at Mt. Lebanon - on February 6 - the greatest and most destructive fire ever experienced by Believers. Eight buildings - dwelling-house, Sisters' shop and wood-house combined, ice-house, storehouse, barn, cart-house, cider mill, gas-house and shed entirely consumed. Two other buildings with their contents, damaged. Total loss estimated at $100,000." This account appeared in the official Shaker periodical, *Shaker and Shakeress*, in March 1875 (vol. 1, no. 3, p. 20). There were actually two fires, about a week apart, probably started by an arsonist. Henry Blinn, writing in his "Journal" from New Hampshire during the same year, added, "All Believers have contributed to their aid. Several boxes of goods were sent from this place, - value some $400. Subsequently, several other boxes are sent; in all not less than $1,000 in value. We also learn that Hancock has donated $5,000, Enfield, Conn. $5,000; Harvard $1,000; Shirley $1,000; Alfred $1,000 & Canterbury $3,000." In its account of the fires, an article in *The Berkshire County Eagle* of February 11, 1875 (vol. 46, p. 2), shed light on the function and furnishings of the Church Family Sisters' Shop:

> The building was 80 by 30 feet in size, and in the rooms above the stories of wood; the sisters did their tailoring, dress-making, &c., and there a large number of them were gathered, engaged in their quiet occupations when the alarm was given. The consternation can be imagined. The flames leaped into the upper stories almost simultaneously with the alarm. There was no time to save even the smallest article. One sister was just going through that fascinating exercise, "trying on" a new dress, and a group about her were chirping about the bit to be let out in this place, the seam to be taken in in that place, and the garment was being smoothed about the happy maiden's form, when the cry came, and she was compelled to rush away half nude. The whole building was almost immediately in flames, and there was consumed with it all the paraphernalia of a woman's workshop, a thousand dollars worth of cotton and woolen cloth, stocking yarn, clothes, and six sewing machines, tables, furniture, etc. There was no time to save even a spool of thread or a pair of scissors, but all the contents were utterly destroyed with the building.

The most significant loss was the four-story dwelling house, measuring 60 by 50 feet, from which nothing was saved. In order to replace such a large quantity of furniture while all available brethren were replacing the buildings, the Shakers hired cabinetmakers from the world. Local craftsmen, including the Shumways (see pl. 28) and Austin Gage (see pl. 15), produced storage units, cases of drawers, beds, clocks, and even settees with plywood seats and perforated decorations.[40] According to an entry of November 8, 1876, in "Domestic Occurrences," the Church Family had a "meeting in evening to learn the feeling of those concerned about bedsteads, dining tables, etc. for new house. All prefer stone for tables if not too costly. Bedsteads will probably be engaged outside plain as the times will admit." One clear exception appears to have been chairs, which were supplied by the South Family factory until March 12, 1877, when the Church Family members "received the last of our chairs. Every Br & Sister in the family has one Min[istry] included."

16. Retiring Room, Church Family Dwelling House
August 1895
Photograph
Shaker Museum and Library, Old Chatham, New York, #4009

Although the wall calendar reads August 1895, several of the furnishings in this retiring room date from 1877, acquired as a result of the fire. The case of drawers between the shuttered windows is identical to several purchased from the Darrow School (formerly the New Lebanon School for Boys) on the Mount Lebanon site. Although the drawers are dovetailed, the evidence of machinery in the construction of the case is apparent in the use of the shaper to form the top edge. The choice of ash and the glove drawers on top were features common on commercially available bedroom furniture of the time.

The bed on the right was probably one of many commissioned from an Albany firm to replace those lost in the fire. According to "Domestic Occurrences," "BG with a hired man goes to Albany to get the new bedsteads" (January 2, 1877) "as plain as the times will admit."[41] By March 6, 1877, "there are 18 short bedsteads for Sister's use received home today. There has now been rec'd 25 long steads 6½ ft. & 19 steads 6 ft."[42]

Two rockers, the one on the left from about 1830, the other from about 1890, are decorated with fringe and lace to make them more fitting for a Shaker retiring room of the 1890s. Other Victorian details are evident in the items hung on the wall, the textiles on chairs and tabletops, and the sheer quantity of interior furnishings, which reflect a late-nineteenth-century sensibility.

17. Pedestal Table
1877
Walnut and poplar
h 28½ w 44½ d 38"
The Mount Lebanon Shaker Collection

Until recently, a number of these tables resided within the Church Family buildings at Mount Lebanon, for which they were originally made to replace furniture destroyed by the fires of 1875. Although this particular example is oval, it is otherwise identical to the round tables described in "Domestic Occurrences": March 28, 1877, "Carpenters making round tables for house"; again on April 21, 1877, "The round tables for Brethren's rooms are bro't into the house, not varnished." This design is reminiscent of the tripod candle-stand except that it has a much wider top, which is oval rather than round, a larger pedestal, and the use of four rather than three legs. The shaping of the foot is related to the Mount Lebanon trestle table (see pl. 45), although the scale and proportion has been changed to suit the pedestal-type stand. Several examples, including this one, are fitted with drawers, and at least one other existing table has an oval rather than a round top.[43] The use of walnut is unusual in Mount Lebanon furniture.

One of this group of tables in the Shaker Museum, Old Chatham, New York (acc. no. 274), has a paper label beneath the top with the name E. Cantrell (Elizabeth Cantrell, 1832–1906). Two chairs, one at the Shaker Museum (acc. no. 580), have a similar label indicating her use of the pieces.

18. Bookcase
Attributed to George Wickersham (1806–1891)
c. 1880
Poplar, with walnut and porcelain knobs and brass butt hinges and locks
h 91 w 113½ d 13½"
The Mount Lebanon Shaker Collection

This bookcase was made for the elders' hall, located between two retiring rooms on the first floor of the new (1877) Church Family Dwelling House, and sat in this original location until 1991. Based on its size and placement in the building, the bookcase could have served the needs of the entire Church Family. According to Daniel Crossman's diary for 1880, George Wickersham completed the piece in a period of five months. "January 15, 1880 Office teamster has been to Albany after a load of lumber for library cupboard etc etc etc. . . . " "May 8, 1880 Library cupboard made by Geo. Wickersham & put up in Elder's Hall."[44] Noteworthy design and construction features are found in the use of frame-and-panel sides on the upper section, which, given its narrow width, is unusual; the sill, which is not only part of the upper unit but is 6¾ inches wide and extends considerably beyond the base; and the half-round molding framing the glass.

In addition to this massive piece, Wickersham made a desk for the deaconesses' room, another for the elder brothers' room, and a "case of drawers with cupboards to go into no. 7."[45] According to Henry Blinn of Canterbury, New Hampshire, who visited Mount Lebanon on May 14, 1873, "We now walk

with Br. Geo. Wickersham to the dairy where we inspect a large & beautifully made refrigerator which he made for the sisters. We hardly think it can be excelled for beauty or for convenience" ("A Journey to Kentucky," Summer 1965, p. 53). A signed and dated lap desk bearing the inscription "made by George Wickersham 1841 North Family Phebe Ann Jones" has survived, although its current location is unknown.[46]

Wickersham's interest in woodworking apparently predated his conversion to Shakerism. According to his autobiography, *How I Came to Be a Shaker* (June 1891), his grandmother attempted to entice him away from the Shaker life while he was on a visit home after living within the sect for some time. She "proposed to set me up with a good shop and a full set of tools. She also proposed for me to start by erecting a building for her, which she contemplated having put up for a dwelling" (p. 16). Despite this tempting offer, Brother George was committed to the Shaker life and returned to pursue his talents within the community.

In addition to his abilities as a furniture maker, George Wickersham was a well-respected architect and mechanic. As "Master Workman," or foreman, he directed the framing of the new infirmary in 1858, drafted the plans for the North Family's great stone barn started in 1859, and designed the new dwelling for the Church Family following the fires of 1875.[47] A chest containing a quantity of tools marked with George Wickersham's initials are currently in the collection of the Shaker Museum, Old Chatham, New York.

19. Case of Drawers
c. 1840
Pine and basswood, with fruitwood knobs and
yellow wash
h 73 w 43 d 18½"
Shaker Museum and Library, Old Chatham, New
York, #554

20. Case of Drawers
c. 1840
Pine, with fruitwood knobs and red wash
h 78⅞ w 44¾ d 18¾"
Private collection
Photograph: courtesy Suzanne Courcier and
Robert W. Wilkins

These two beautifully proportioned classic cases of drawers share identical construction details and were probably built by the same craftsman. Both pieces exhibit simple concave cut feet, a bull-nose molding applied to the top, a bold surface color and layout, combining half- and full-width drawers. Furthermore, the rail-to-plank side joint consists of a simple dado, which is reinforced on several of the joints by a large, exposed flat-head wood screw through the side of the case into the rails—a primitive joinery technique for two fine case pieces.

opposite

21. Case of Drawers
c. 1830
Pine, with red paint and bone escutcheon
h 70½ w 63¾ d 20⅜"
Shaker Museum and Library, Old Chatham, New
York, #6970

Although the layout of many Shaker case pieces combines dual columns of half-width drawers, few are as well executed as this one. The case is perfectly symmetrical, with the exception of the top left drawer, which is punctuated by a bone escutcheon. The facade is divided by four vertical rows of drawer pulls but unified by the bold application of red paint. Although the top of the piece has been securely dovetailed, an additional heavy board has been added to help support the span of the dual bank of drawers and prevent it from sagging. These structural elements have been embellished by a bull-nose over a cove molding applied to the top of the case. Simple straight cut feet lift the frame well off the floor.

22. Fall-Front Desk

c. 1830
Pine, with fruitwood knobs and red wash
h 54¼ w 24 d 8½"
Hancock Shaker Village, Pittsfield,
Massachusetts, #65–274

This exceptionally small desk was originally partially built into a wall. Its simple interior allowed for minimal storage of record-keeping materials in the central ledger slot and shelving. A characteristic feature of numerous Mount Lebanon case pieces is the use of stiles of different widths. Here, wider stiles surround the single-panel door above narrower stiles, which frame the double-panel door below. The maker has completely eliminated the stiles beside the fall-front writing surface. The case is softened by the use of cove-shaped front corners, which are interrupted both above and below the fall-front door with two half-round midrails. Because the desk was originally built into the wall about 2 inches deep, the case was made without feet.

opposite above

23. Retiring Room

c. 1930
Photograph
New York State Museum, Albany, #14,093

The fall-front desk pictured in this Victorian retiring room is signed on a drawer bottom "Made 1873 by Amos Stewart."[48] Characteristic features that relate to other documented Amos Stewart pieces include the simple cut foot, unlipped drawers, and dadoed drawer rails reminiscent of much earlier case pieces. The use of ash as one of several primary woods, however, was not common until the 1870s, when this small desk was made. This one piece of furniture therefore presents an interesting mixture of three or four decades of cabinetmaking design and experience.

Although more diminutive in size and made for only one person, the basic format is similar to the double trustees' desk pl. 26, with its bank of drawers below a sill, an interior containing small drawers and shelving, and a fall-front writing surface. The desk, crowded bookshelves, commercially made Victorian stand, and cushioned production rocker of about 1880, as well as the large mirror, photographs on the wall, and carpeting certainly place the interior furnishings well after the turn of the century.

24. Desk

c. 1937
Watercolor, graphite, and colored pencil on paperboard by John Kelleher
h 11 w 9"
National Gallery of Art, Washington, D.C. Index of American Design, #1943.8.10472, Mass-fu-96

Although the origin of the so-called butler's desk is unknown, it was a common nineteenth-century worldly form. However, the appearance of this style of furniture in Shaker communities is rare. A number of examples survive, all with the characteristic fall-front drawer that opens to reveal several interior drawers and pigeonholes combined, and a case with three to nine exterior drawer fronts of either half or full width.

This watercolor was executed at the Mount Lebanon Shaker community. It shows a tall case of drawers made around 1840. With its frame-and-panel sides, cut feet, and rounded, protruding drawer fronts, the desk might be considered typical of Mount Lebanon if it did not have the addition of the fall-front desk drawer. This feature is particularly rare in so large a case; most craftsmen chose to place a fall-front drawer at the top of a smaller four- or five-drawer case piece rather than in the middle of a large case. This creates an unusual pattern on the facade not found on worldly furniture. Elisha Blakeman noted in his journal on March 16, 1849, "E. [Blakeman] remoddles a case of drawers, make a place to write."[49] This raises the question whether this piece was originally made as a case of drawers or a combination desk/case of drawers.

A very similar desk with fall-front drawer and typical Mount Lebanon construction details in the collection of Hancock Shaker Village, Pittsfield, Massachusetts (acc. no. 62–190), was used at the North Family.

25. Desk

c. 1937
Watercolor, graphite and colored pencil on paper by Anne Ger
h 9 w 11"
National Gallery of Art, Washington, D.C. Index of American Design, #1943.8.10468, Mass-fu-58

Although the overall form of this desk of around 1880 is atypical, several design features are common to Mount Lebanon furniture, including the cut foot, flat frame-and-panel case, fall-front writing surface, and creation of more than one functional side. However, the case is unusually wide in relation to its height and is fitted with a large number of interior pigeonholes.

26. Double Trustees' Desk

c. 1840
Pine, with fruitwood knobs
h 84¼ w 48 d 16⅝"
Hancock Shaker Village, Pittsfield,
Massachusetts, #62–7

According to the "Millennial Laws," "All monies, book accounts, deeds, bonds, notes etc. which belong to the Church or family must be kept at the Office unless some other suitable place be provided therefore, by the proper authorities. . . . The Deacons or Trustees should keep all their accounts booked down, regular and exact, and as far as possible avoid controversies with the world."[50] The need to keep accurate business records while conducting affairs with the world required the trustees, deacons, and elders to utilize desks. Unlike the majority of community property, this furniture was designed for office functions and was proba-

bly personalized to meet the needs of individual leaders.

Remarkable for its impressive feeling of height and proportions, this desk is associated by oral tradition with the two trustees of the Center Family.[51] The design provides dual work and storage areas, with two cupboards concealing interior shelves, drop-front writing surfaces with shelves, pigeonholes, and small drawers above two banks of four drawers. Typical construction features associated with Mount Lebanon craftsmanship include the midrail with lamb's-tongue ends, lipped drawers, and rails attached to the case with small housed half-dovetails.

The piece displays a couple of idiosyncratic design details: the two pairs of doors do not align vertically, and the upper cupboards are separated by a stile wider than the one below, which necessitated slightly narrower doors whose inner edges do not correspond to those below them.

27. Slant-Front Desk

c. 1840
Pine, butternut, and cherry, with fruitwood and porcelain knobs, red wash, and brass hinges, escutcheons, and locking mechanism
h 65 w 40½ d 21" (closed), 34" (open)
Private collection

Related to a common worldly style in its overall layout, this one-piece desk represents a very unusual form for the Shakers. It was purchased from the Believers at Hancock, where it had an oral history of originating at Mount Lebanon. This attribution is supported on the basis of the construction details: plank sides, cut feet with mitered corners, bull-nose cornice molding, and doors with beveled inner edges and coped mortise-and-tenon joints. Numerous pegs were placed, nearly randomly, through the mortise-and-tenon joints of the door. The cupboard interior consists of pigeonholes juxtaposed with five tall ledger slots. These specific storage units were presumably designed to suit the record-keeping needs of the family elder or eldress. One noteworthy feature is the small "secret" full-width drawer located directly behind the top drawer in the base. Although this is a design feature commonly built into worldly desks of the eighteenth and nineteenth centuries, it is not often found on Shaker furniture, except, perhaps, on pieces made for ministry use.[52] A Shaker cherry slant-front desk without cupboard doors was owned by Edward Deming and Faith Andrews.[53]

The backboards and top of the desk show evidence of alteration by the Shakers many years ago. The reason for such a change is

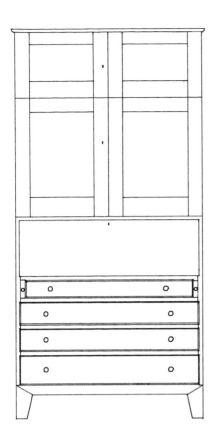

unclear. The desk, which stands 65 inches tall, probably had an additional set of doors above the existing cupboard doors, as is shown in the speculative drawing, or the existing cupboard doors were shortened.

28. Desk

Attributed to William Shumway (working 1867–75)
c. 1875
Written in pencil in script on back of left drawer:
E.J. Neale
Bird's-eye maple, walnut, pine, and poplar, with brass knobs with glass floral inserts
h 56³⁄₈ w 47³⁄₄ d 29⁷⁄₈"
Canterbury Shaker Village, Inc., Canterbury, New Hampshire, #85.234

This Victorian-style writing desk was probably made for the Shakers by William Shumway, a worldly cabinetmaker. The construction of a similar desk in a private collection may have been witnessed by a New Lebanon correspondent of the *Berkshire County Eagle* (March 4, 1875):

> I happened to drop into Wm. Shumway's carpenter shop, where I found he had been making a bookcase and secretary for Thomas Smith, of the Canaan Shakers, which, for artistic taste and durability, far surpasses anything of the kind I ever saw. It

is made of bird's eye maple, butternut and chestnut, and shows more fully what has always been known, that William is one of the best of workmen, and the finest artist in this line we have in town. He has done many complicated jobs for the Shakers, and some which they thought could not be beaten, but William is like cheese, the older he grows the better he is.

As the writer mentioned, this is not the first time that Shumway was hired to do work for the Believers. As early as April 1841 he was employed by the Upper Canaan Shakers after the family moved into their new dwelling "to finish the upper room, with the rest part of the garret, - make the drawers - cupboard doors & stair railing; to the amount of $70.00."[54]

The inscription on this secretary indicates that it was probably used by Eldress Emma J. Neale (1847–1943) of the New Lebanon community. According to Eldress Bertha Lindsay (1897–1990) of Canterbury, this and another identical desk with "plain porcelain

knobs" were probably moved to New Hampshire after the Mount Lebanon community closed.[55] This one remained at Canterbury while the other was sold to a private collector.

In its design, the desk represents the convergence of Shaker functionalism with pared-down elements of Victorian style. The combination of contrasting light and dark woods, the mixture of straight and arched forms, as well as the striking addition of commercially made brass pulls with a blue glass floral insert contributed to a composition that reflects current taste.

This piece may have been located in the Trustees' Office at Canaan, in a setting similar to the 1897 Enfield, Connecticut, office, pictured on p. 52, where the Believers transacted business with the world's people. Aside from purely functional purposes, the secretary symbolically served to inform all visitors of the progressive nature of the community and the members' awareness of current fashion.

29. Desk

Amos Stewart (1802–1884)
1877
Written in pencil on one drawer bottom: made in 1877 by Amos Stewart with one hand age 74
Butternut, cherry, and pine
h 36 w 72 d 36" (approximate)
Private collection

This desk represents a distinctively different form for Shaker furniture. Although the frame-and-panel bases are similar in dimensions and construction to the deep case of drawers pl. 30, the overall layout is derived from a different source. The form of the writing surface supported by two drawer cases is related in concept to commercially available furniture of the time.

This piece is exceptional because it is positively identified as Amos Stewart's work by the inscription, which documents the circumstances under which it was made. He produced this desk after losing his hand in an accident, which is described in the following poignant letter: "On the morning of the 28th of Nov. past, while at work with a Machine plaining boards by poor light & not taking sufficient care, he got his left hand so near the Plainer that the knives caught the fingers of his glove which suddenly brought his hand between the forward roller and Plainer & instantly severed the entire hand from his wrist . . ."[56]

Despite this injury, Elder Amos continued to serve the community in the woodworking shop, making this desk as well as other pieces, including the counter signed "AS 1873" (pl. 31), the desk signed "Made 1873 by Amos Stewart" (pl. 23), and the washstand signed "Amos Stewart March 1878" (pl. 32).

30. Case of Drawers

Henry Hollister (1838–1919)
1861
Written in pencil on bottom of top drawer: No. 6/Henry Hollister/January 61/Tis only he that has no/credit to loose that can/afford to work in this style
Butternut, pine, and walnut
h 30 w 20 d 28"
Courtesy of the Art Complex Museum, Duxbury, Massachusetts, #54–9

The dimensions of this case are atypical, and the purpose it was intended to serve is unknown. The application of a cove molding to the base is also an uncommon feature, not found on other Mount Lebanon furniture. Both the form, consisting of a frame with numerous side panels, and the unusual proportions relate to the pedestal section of the later Amos Stewart kneehole desks (see pl. 29). The cryptic penciled inscription is indicative of Brother Henry's awareness of style.

31. Counter

Attributed to Amos Stewart (1802–1884)
1873
Signed in pencil on inside of right and left rear
panels: AS 1873
Cherry and pine, with cast-iron pulls
h 33½ w 60 d 30"
Collection Collin Becket Richmond
Photograph: Robert F. Kent

The similarity between these initials and those found on Amos Stewart's full signature (see pl. 23) suggests that he made this counter. It is also closely related to an unsigned butternut counter from Mount Lebanon[57] that exhibits the same style of bold maker markings in red chalk, as well as the combination of frame-and-panel construction with a cut-foot base and the use of cleats at either end to fasten the top and prevent warping. The joinery connecting the drawer rails to the frame reveals a common engineering defect in Shaker case pieces. Instead of mortise and tenons or full dovetails, the maker used housed half-dovetails, which on some pieces are not adequately sized to hold the case together. Because these joints lack the necessary strength the sides tend to pull away from the rails.

32. Washstand

Amos Stewart (1802–1884)
1878
Written in pencil on bottom of top large drawer:
Amos Stewart March 1878
Pine, ash, and yellow poplar, with red wash on
frame and sides, clear finish on drawer fronts,
porcelain knobs, and brass hinges
h 38³⁄₁₆ w 35⅞ d 13¾"
Provate collection

Like other Amos Stewart pieces (see pls. 23, 29, 31), this washstand represents an unusual form not found elsewhere in Shaker furniture. Construction features characteristic of his work include the rails attached to the case with housed half-dovetails, the flush-fitting unlipped drawers, and the use of boldly grained hardwoods in combination with porcelain pulls, creating a somewhat worldly look. Noteworthy design features include the striking asymmetry of the front of the case, created by the division of the facade into two unequal banks of drawers; the vertical juxtaposition of a door below drawers; and the unorthodox mixture of woods, combined with the ogee shape of the plank side.

According to oral history, this piece was moved from Mount Lebanon when it closed in 1947 to Canterbury, and it was later purchased directly from the Canterbury Shakers. Interestingly, the washstand was reproduced in 1965 for Sears and Roebuck by the Grays Harbor Chair and Mfg. Co. in Hoquiam, Washington.

33. Sewing Desk

Amos Stewart (1802–1884)
c. 1870
Signed in pencil in script under bottom central
drawer: Amos Stewart
Butternut, yellow poplar, and cherry, with
porcelain knobs and Bennington-type knobs
h 37¼ w 36¼ d 21⁵⁄₁₆"
Private collection

This desk with gallery represents another variation of the sewing table form produced at Mount Lebanon. Furthermore, it is one of several signed pieces by Amos Stewart (see pls. 23, 29, 31, and 32), which exhibits the following characteristic features: the use of frame-and-panel construction, rails affixed to the case with housed half-dovetails, flush-fitting, unlipped drawers, and bold maker's marks in red chalk on the various parts to help facilitate assembly. As is true of so many of Brother Amos's other pieces, the design is both visually and physically distinctive. Although the piece is small, its efficient layout provides for maximum storage space; in this respect the desk is more reminiscent of commercial furniture than workstations designed for individual Shaker sisters. The base has the look of a kneehole desk but the opening is much too small to accommodate a user's knees.

34. Washstand

Attributed to James V. Calver (1839–left 1871)
c. 1860
Pine and poplar, with traces of chrome yellow
color
h 38⅛ w 28 d 18⅜"
Private collection

The craftsman combined two very different design forms that work well together to form a useful washstand. The base is a simple recti-linear case with three graduated drawers and gently rounded drawer faces that stand slightly proud of the case. The overhanging gallery is distinguished by the graceful ogee shaping on the sides, echoed on the back-splash. At least three related stands exist, one of which is marked "Made by/James V. Calver/April 1862."[58] An entry from May 29, 1861, in "Domestic Occurrences" states, "James Calver leaves the gardening & goes into the joiners shop as a joiner & carpenter etc." Judging from the high quality of the stands, it is evident that Brother James had previous experience as a woodworker. The number of these pieces still extant suggests that many may have been produced for insti-tutional use. Perhaps they were assigned to each of the washrooms or hallways in the Church Family where Brother James resided.

35. Counter

Orren Haskins (1815–1892)
1847
Written in pencil on several of the drawers: OH
1847 New Lebanon - March 1847 Made [for?]
deaconess 2nd Order March 1847
Pine and butternut, with maple knobs and red
wash
h 33 w 104 d 32"
The Mount Lebanon Shaker Collection

Orren Haskins's cabinetmaking, which spanned a career of almost fifty years, is richly documented by numerous journal references as well as a group of signed pieces. Brother Orren entered the Children's Order at Mount Lebanon at the age of eight, but there is little information regarding his early training as a carpenter and joiner. According to Isaac Newton Youngs's history of woodworking at Mount Lebanon, he was active in this trade in 1833.[59] Surviving examples of his skill include the following:

1. Red-stained pine cupboard and case of drawers marked "March 27, 1833. Made by Orren H." Location currently unknown. (In Andrews, *Shaker Furniture*, p. 46.)
2. Pine lap desk with pencil inscription "O.H. June 6, 1834." Shaker Museum and Library, Old Chatham, New York.[60]
3. Three-door cupboard or top of a piece—perhaps a desk, table, or counter, now missing—dated and signed "January 6, 1837 O.H." Shaker Museum and Library.[61]
4. Lap or table desk marked "Febuary 6th 1838 by Maker Orren N. Haskins. R.B." Loca-

tion currently unknown. (In Andrews, *Shaker Furniture*, p. 46.)
5. Pine and butternut two-drawer case to which John Allen (1816–left 1846) later added legs. The inscription reads, "Orren Haskins Maker Dec 18th John Allen Made by Orren Haskins December 18th 1831 for John Allen & used at the seed shop upwards of two years. It was then put upon legs by John Allen & taken into the house on the first monday in January. 1841." The Mount Lebanon Shaker Collection.[62]
6. Workbench, signed on two drawer bottoms "OH February 1853" The Mount Lebanon Shaker Collection.[63]
7. Six-drawer gallery added to worktable, signed "Cornelia French May 17, 1874. No 4 OH" Hancock Shaker Village, Pittsfield, Massachusetts.[64]
8. Six-drawer gallery added to worktable, signed "Sarah H. Winton . . . O.N.H. June 11, 1881, Mount Lebanon, Columbia County, N.Y." Hancock Shaker Village.[65]
9. Hanging cupboard with glass doors, The Mount Lebanon Shaker Collection.
10. Hanging cupboard with glass doors, dated 1857. The Mount Lebanon Shaker Collection.

Several of Brother Orren's tools, including a trying plane bearing his OH stamp and dated 1833, a moving fillister, and a rounding plane, are currently in the collection of the Shaker Museum and Library.

The recently discovered signature on this counter places it among Orren Haskins's known production. Although probably designed as a freestanding storage and work unit, it was altered at some later point and

built into the 1877 brick Church Family Dwelling House. The ingenious placement of a pullout writing surface between the top two drawers in the left-hand bank together with the inscription suggests this piece was used for writing as well as for storage. This counter may have assisted the deaconess in keeping records of all business transactions involving the domestic concerns of the family. This is one of the few pieces of furniture with documentation regarding the intended user, in this case, a deaconess of the Second Order.

On most Shaker storage units, the drawers are aligned horizontally, but on a small group of pieces, including counters by Grove Wright (pl. 102), Benjamin Lyon (pl. 37), and this example, the design is made more complicated by the unequal number of drawers in neighboring banks. In this case there are six on the left and three each in the three other banks. The widths of the drawers in the three banks of three are also unequal, increasing on the right, a feature found on only a few pieces of Shaker furniture.

In this example, as well as on some of his other furniture, Brother Orren used a dadoed rail to side joint. Although structurally sound in this application, it is not adequate on some other particularly tall storage units. This counter also exhibits unlipped drawer fronts, which are flush at the drawer edge but actually stand proud of the case because of a subtly beveled drawer face. The same detail is seen on Orren Haskins's workbench[66] and at least one other late workbench, which uses cast-iron drawer pulls, in the collection of the Shaker Museum and Library.

36. Counter
*Benjamin Lyon (1780–1870) and Charles Weed
(1831–left 1862)
1860
Written in pencil on a drawer bottom: made
Feby 1860 by Benjamin Lyon and Charles Weed
h 33½ w 79¼ d 35¾"
Pine, cherry, butternut, and basswood, with
fruitwood pulls and orange-brown stain
The Mount Lebanon Shaker Collection*

37. Counter
*Attributed to Benjamin Lyon (1780–1870)
and/or Charles Weed (1831–left 1862)
c. 1840
Pine, butternut, and basswood, with brass slide
latches, one with porcelain knob
h 37¼ w 122½ d 31⅜"
Shaker Museum and Library, Old Chatham, New
York, #758*

According to Benjamin Lyon's journals of 1816–20, he collaborated with other joiners on a variety of woodworking projects, including a cupboard, case of drawers, dining table, bedstead, and benches. Counter pl. 36 is the only piece of furniture signed by Benjamin Lyon and Charles Weed. It is further documented by a reference in the "Farm Journal," 1858–67, kept by the Second Order of the Church Family. The entry, dated March 1, 1860, states, "Benjamin Lyon and Charles Weed are making a table with two rows of drawers for Hannah Train" (1783–1864).[67]

Two construction features are noteworthy because they point to the clear attribution of counter pl. 37 to either Brothers Benjamin or Charles or both. The first of these idiosyncratic features consists of a flat facing applied to the case stiles, which protrudes beyond the rails about ¼ inch in pl. 36 and 5/16 inch in pl. 37 and stands proud of the side. In addition, the rear edge of the drawer rails, visible when the drawer is removed, is beveled at a 45-degree angle.

The later counter is visually lightened by the pine top with broadly rounded corners and extensive overhang. The earlier counter is striking in its unusual, although symmetrical, arrangement. The facade is organized by four equally sized central drawers between two dramatically graduated banks of five drawers ranging from 3 to 8 inches in depth, flanked by a cupboard at each end. According to oral history preserved in Shaker Museum records, the first condensed milk was made by Gale Bordon on this bench about 1853. When visiting his four motherless children, whom he had sent to Mount Lebanon to live, he noticed the Shakers using a vacuum pan evaporator for making sugar. He borrowed this airtight container and conducted experiments in the Shakers' workshops that led to his formula for condensed milk, patented in 1856.[68]

38. Counter
c. 1880
Pine, poplar, and marble, with porcelain knobs,
cast-iron latch, and brass hinges
h 29⅞ w 45¼ d 30¼"
Private collection

Based on the use of marble for the top, this
counter was presumably built either by or for
the Shakers after the 1875 fires for food
preparation in their new brick dwelling house.
The frame-and-panel case was clearly designed to hold the heavy marble top, as it was
fitted with a subframework with several front
to back stringers placed across the case. A
quarter-round molding surrounds the ends of
the understructure, both to conceal it and
support the top. The porcelain knobs and the
cast-iron latch are identical to those found on
the cupboard and case of drawers made by
Austin E. Gage in 1877 (pl. 15).

39. Counter

c. 1830
Paper label in ink on underside of top printed: EJ
Neale Meetinghouse
Pine, with red wash
h 32¼ w 83¾ d 34¼"
Hancock Shaker Village, Pittsfield,
Massachusetts, #62.488

The most unusual aspect of this classic counter is its documentation as belonging to Eldress Emma J. Neale (1847–1943), one of the few early pieces of Church Family furni-ture to survive the 1875 fires. Miraculously, the Meetinghouse, even though it was adja-cent to the dwelling house and other build-ings that perished in the blazes, escaped the flames. This large work counter was probably housed on the second- or third-floor ministry work and living space. Its overall form and construction is very basic, consisting of a 1¼-inch-thick plank-sided case fitted with six long half-width drawers and a heavy overhanging top. Two slides under the top, accessible from the rear, were pulled out to support a drop leaf, which is now missing.

40. Table

c. 1810
Maple and pine, with iron bails and red wash
h 32¼ w 83½ d 27⅝"
Hancock Shaker Village, Pittsfield,
Massachusetts, #75–140

This six-legged table is difficult to attribute because of its close relationship to vernacular prototypes and the rarity of the usage of the form among Shaker craftsmen. While the stretcher base is not common in Shaker tables, it may have been an early feature adapted by the Believers from worldly style, which is also found in the four-legged table pl. 47. In addition, instead of the more common turned knobs, the drawers are equipped with iron bail pulls and with back plates on both sides of the table. Early examples such as this simply may not have survived into the twentieth century.

Based on proportions, the legs may have originally been longer, as a section of the feet below the stretchers appear to have been cut or worn off.

The table has two push-pull drawers, accessible from either side, one of which is fitted with interior dividers labeled for seeds, such as Horehound, Squash - Summer, Double parsnip, and Peas - English Marrowfat. The herb and garden seed business at Mount Lebanon was one of the community's most successful and stable industries, beginning in 1795 and continuing for another hundred years.[69]

41. Worktable
c. 1830
Birch and pine, with iron knife
h 28³⁄₁₆ w 35¾ d 25⅜"
Hancock Shaker Village, Pittsfield,
Massachusetts, #63–190

42. North Family Bake Room
c. 1882
New York State Museum, Albany[70]

Several of these surviving worktables bear a history from the North and South families at Mount Lebanon. This example, according to Edward Deming Andrews,[71] is from the South Family. It stands on stocky, tapered legs, supporting a single drawer and rail set noticeably back from the more common location flush with the front of the legs. A dovetailed rim surrounds the top on three sides, presumably to control the materials being sliced on the cutting board with the forged knife, which is hinged at the rear of the table.

Several period photographs and graphics, such as this image of the North Family bake room, show the blade on a similar table with round legs being used to cut bread, but it is likely that the table served other functions as well. This table, if it is not the same piece as the example in the collection at the Shaker Museum, Old Chatham, New York (acc. no. 3349), greatly resembles it. The worktable on the left may be the one shown in pl. 44. This space could be compared to the equally specialized institutional stainless steel restaurant kitchens today. It contains brick and forged steel ovens built into the lower level of the North Family Dwelling House.

43. Table
1935–42
Watercolor, graphite, gouache, and colored pencil on paperboard by Lawrence Foster
h 9 w 10⁹/₁₆"
National Gallery of Art, Washington, D.C. Index of American Design, #1943.8.10463, Mass-fu-16

This table, pl. 44, and pl. 41 are all unorthodox in form and function but reveal the variety of work furniture produced at Mount Lebanon to serve a specific purpose.

The watercolor of this unorthodox table was executed for the Index of American Design in the 1930s while the table was in the possession of Faith and Edward Deming Andrews. According to the information accompanying the artwork, the piece was recorded as a "dairy" table produced in the Mount Lebanon Church Family and was signed and dated by Orren Haskins (1815–1892) in 1876. The design relates to no other known Shaker furniture, nor can it be connected to any worldly prototype. Heavily constructed, it appears to be one two-drawer table frame built over another smaller frame. The date recorded leads to the speculation that the table was specifically designed to replace work furniture destroyed in the great fires of 1875. A "dairy" table could have been used either in the newly built barn or the Church Family kitchen.

44. Table
1936
Watercolor, graphite, and colored pencil on paper
h 8¹⁵/₁₆ w 11"
National Gallery of Art, Washington, D.C. Index of American Design, #1948.8.10468, Mass-fu-14

According to the oral history associated with this or a similar table in the Faith and Edward Deming Andrews Collection, this specialized worktable was used in the bake room of the North Family Dwelling House (1818) at Mount Lebanon (see pl. 42). Visually resembling a tall bench with arched ends forming the feet, the table has been fitted with a long, overhanging top to extend the work surface, a rear splashboard to protect the walls, two drawers, and the later addition of a lower shelf, presumably for storage of kitchen utensils and woodenware. Another unusual design feature is the transverse batten with scrolled front edge separating the drawers, which serves to support the front edge of the tabletop in a decorative function. According to a historic photograph by William F. Winter,[72] two semicircular cutouts appear on the rear edge of the end boards, which raises the following questions: Are these a more recent addition to the same table? Did the artist take liberties in the rendition shown here? Or are these two different but closely related tables?

45. Church Family Dining Room
c. 1930
Photograph
Historic American Building Survey, National Park Service, #118352 HABS NY-11 NELEBV 2–5

The Shakers adopted and modified the medieval trestle table form for communal dining. By elevating the lengthwise supporting rail, or stretcher, to fasten beneath the top, it did not obstruct the knees of those seated along each side.

The design that evolved at Mount Lebanon seems to have been the prototype for the dining table for virtually all Shaker communities. Although many details were changed in the various societies, the basic form prevailed. The Mount Lebanon table was built in the following way: A vertical structural member, rectangular in cross section, was tenoned into a smoothly arched foot with rounded toe and held with a bolt from the bottom. The horizontal cross member or cleat was cut to fit in a bridal joint in the upper end of the vertical support. The longitudinal stretcher was secured to the leg assembly with bolts and nuts. The square corners on the vertical support, as well as the underside of the arched leg, were shaped by chamfering, while the top surface on the arch and toe were gently rounded. These tables ranged in length from under 6 feet, presumably for the four ministry members, who ate together, to 22 feet for the rest of the membership.

One humorous incident that took place in the dining room at Mount Lebanon in July 1852, as documented in "Domestic Occurrences," gives insight into the brothers' and sisters' seating arrangements during meals and the continued use of benches for seating into the 1850s:

> This morning at breakfast time we had the read of a letter from our ministry . . . at Union Village. . . . While reading a laughable case occured as we were mostly seating at the tables a rat came running into the room, at which instantly occurred a scene of confusion, not easily described; the rat ran in among the brethren & sprang forward to pitch battle with him, the benches flew round here & there, the sisters were frightened - some did not know what was the matter but some[one] fortunately gave the rat a mortal wound & tost [sic] him out of the window & after becoming a little collected again we finished the reading.

These marble-topped tables made for the Church Family dining room replaced those destroyed in the great fires of 1875. On March 18, 1877, "the marble tables were all put up in the new dining rooms enough room to accomodate 64 people at one sitting. They are very splendid."[73] The day before the mar-

ble tables were set up in the dining room, according to an entry in "Domestic Occurrences" of March 17, 1877, they "receive the last of our chairs, every Br & Sister in the family has one Min[istry] included."

Here the use of marble as a table surface preceded its appearance in a similar application at Union Village, Ohio, in the 1890s. While the use of marble as a tabletop was a distinct innovation, the form of the table remained basically the same as the trestle tables made earlier. The marble-top tables survived in the Darrow School, which occupied the former Mount Lebanon Shaker community, until sometime in the 1970s, when they perished in a fire set by a student which destroyed the school's dining hall.

46. Trestle Table
c. 1830
Pine and birch
h 27⅛ w 240 d 34"
Hancock Shaker Village, Pittsfield,
Massachusetts, #77–3

A twenty-foot table such as this, shown here in the ironing room but originally used in the dining room, could probably seat ten Believers on either side. To eliminate the problem of passing serving dishes on such a large dining table, the Shakers set the tables in squares to accommodate four Believers, two on either side of the table, at each; this table had five squares. Brethren and sisters sat at separate tables and initially ate off pewterware. By the nineteenth century, the Believers were using white, undecorated china such as English ironstone, purchased from the outside world.[74] In 1877 the Mount Lebanon Shakers bought decorated china; examples, along with documentation of their employment, are at the Shaker Museum, Old Chatham, New York.[75] The Shakers ate in silence, according to the "Holy Orders" of 1841, which stated, "There shall be no whispering, laughing, sneezing or blinking be done or carried on at the table."[76]

Although it is not known how the furniture in the dining rooms was physically arranged, it was, apparently, subject to change. Henry DeWitt's "Journal" mentions in passing that on June 20, 1836, they "have the tables turned, that the brethren eat on; East and West & put a short one inbetween which adds 6 more to eat at the first setting." The supplement to "Domestic Occurrences" of May 1857 documented another redecorating effort: "It has been quite a time this month for fixing up matters, painting floors, etc. The dining room floor & overhead has been painted, also the tables & benches & the whole kitchen floor."

left

47. Table

c. 1830
Cherry and birch, with varnish
h 28 w 40 d 30" (extended)
Hancock Shaker Village, Pittsfield,
Massachusetts, #66–200

below

48. Table

c. 1830
Cherry and pine, with fruitwood knob, traces of
red stain, and varnish
h 27½ w 60 d 36"
Collection Bob Hamilton

This small cherry table on the left might be considered a common Hancock form because of its size, materials, and ovolo-molded detail on the apron (see pls. 114, 115). However, the splayed leg, stretcher base, and leaf-support mechanism are distinctive features rare in Shaker work. The craftsman replaced the more common pullout batten with a butterfly-shaped support that is hinged on the apron. Though it differs considerably in size from the table below and does not have the stretcher base, they share the splayed legs and butterfly supports, suggesting a common shop of origin, if not the same maker. The second table might be attributed to Hancock were it not for its strong Mount Lebanon history. It was purchased from Sister Sarah Neale (1849–1948), who documented its mid-twentieth-century use as a dining table by the ministry elders and eldresses.

above

49. Table

c. 1830
Maple and pine, with hardwood knobs
h 37 w 26¾ d 26"
Collection Bob Hamilton

The wide variety in small tables produced at Mount Lebanon is evident in numerous well-designed but vastly different examples. This table, like pl. 50, is fitted with drawers over square, tapered legs, but they could hardly be more different in their proportions.

The orientation of the deep, full-width drawers, one on top of the other, and the extra thickness of the bottom rail, all of which measure half the length of the leg, emphasize the overall storage capacity of the piece.

right

50. Sewing Table

c. 1840
Cherry, pine, and poplar, with red wash
h 25⅞ w 31¾ d 21"
Collection Bob Hamilton

The overall delicacy in the form of this sewing table was achieved by the use of a shallow drawer, the very slender 1¼-inch-square legs, which taper to ¹¹⁄₁₆ inch at the base, and the thin, ⅝-inch-wide top.

Distinctive in its original form, the table was certainly not diminished by the addition of the second drawer. In order to accommodate the placement of a second drawer at a later date, the existing aprons were extended by simply butt-gluing boards to the bottom edge of the apron and toenailing them into the inside of the legs. The need to fit the opening below the original rail resulted in the trapezoidal shape of the lower drawer.

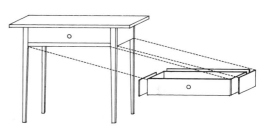

51. Gateleg Table

Probably Mount Lebanon
c. 1840
Cherry and pine
h 26½ w 36 d 28"
Collection Mr. and Mrs. Wm. Brooks

Although gateleg tables are a common worldly form, very few Shaker examples have been identified. This small table and one from Pleasant Hill, Kentucky (see pl. 294), share similar construction characteristics borrowed from worldly cabinetmaking traditions, including the double apron and wooden hinge. A pin inserted into the finger joint at the center of the outer apron allows the two legs to pivot. A half-blind dovetail was used to join the unsupported corner of the table. Other than the hinged leaf-support mechanism, this cherry table fits well within the usual design and construction characteristics associated with Mount Lebanon. Two historic photographs taken by Noel Vicentini for the Index of American Design show a Shaker one-drawer gateleg table made of cherry.[77]

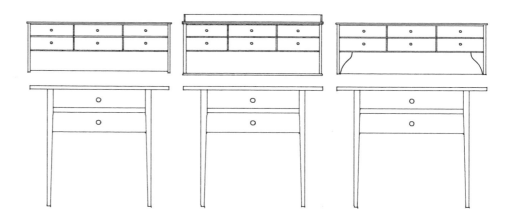

52. Sewing Case of Drawers

James X. Smith (1806–1888)
1843
Stamped along dovetail joint on third drawer
from bottom: 1843
Stamped along dovetail joint on opposite side:
JAS. X. SMITH NEW-LEBANON N.Y.
Cherry, maple, butternut, pine, basswood, and
sycamore
h 28 w 32½ d 23½"
The Metropolitan Museum of Art, New York.
Friends of the American Wing Fund, 1966,
#66.10.18

In 1843, when this piece was completed, James Smith was serving as assistant elder of the Second Family at Mount Lebanon. He was later moved to the Church (1858) and East families before returning to the Church Family in 1860.[78] Several other examples bearing his name exist in private collections, including a potty chair[79] and a number of woodworking tools. Stamped rather than handwritten letters and numbers are found infrequently on Shaker furniture. They appear on two stands by Samuel Turner (pls. 58, 59), a secretary desk and a sewing desk attributed to Henry Blinn (pls. 186, 187), and many of Freegift Wells's chairs. They are also used in the work of a few unidentified craftsmen who marked drawers to delineate their location —a worldly as well as Shaker practice.

This piece is unusual in carrying a 32-inch measuring stick nailed across the front of the overhanging top, possibly to measure material for a specific industry. Decorative details are found in the beading on the rails, around the drawer openings on the front of the case, and under the bottom rail extending to the top of the tapered foot—a rare practice on Shaker furniture.

53. Sewing Table With Add-on

Andrew Barrett (1836 or 1837–1917) (gallery)
c. 1830 (table), 1881 (gallery)
Written on top middle drawer: Made by Andrew
Barrett Feb 1881
Cherry (table); cherry and pine, with porcelain
knobs and brass pins (gallery)
h 41½ w 32½ d 22"
Collection Bob Hamilton

This sewing table seems to be representative of the type commonly in use at Mount Lebanon soon after midcentury. The design consists of either an add-on or integral gallery fitted with several narrow drawers in a variety of layouts, as shown in the drawing, over a base with one to three drawers on square, tapered legs.

The evolution of the sewing table probably resulted from the demographics of the Shaker communities. By the 1860s, many male members had left various societies, and the number of new converts had declined dramatically. As early as 1856, Isaac Newton Youngs confided, "Much depression of spirits has been felt and struggling through dark and gloomy prospects on accounts of apostacies, lifelessness and backsliding of unfaithful members and the scarcity gathering from without."[80] By the last half of the nineteenth century, a major source of income for the community had transferred to the sisters, who were extensively involved in the production of needlework.

This add-on sewing table is noteworthy both for its design and its construction. Unlike the majority of Mount Lebanon examples, the base section contains two half-width shallow drawers over one much deeper full-width drawer rather than one or two full-width drawers. Furthermore, the gallery, which was added later on, is inscribed and dated. Andrew Barrett was admitted to the Church Family at Mount Lebanon in 1850 but left the order in 1851. However, he clearly rejoined sometime prior to 1881, the date of the gallery. Two years later he "removed" to Harvard as an elder, before dying in Hancock in 1917.[81]

Particularly interesting are the small brass pins protruding from the table apron on the sides and back. Most of the sewing tables with galleries and one small table without a gallery have either small brass or bone buttons around the perimeter of the base. One theory regarding their use is that they supported a fabric bag underneath the apron and between the table legs, an idea that was popular during the Federal period in America. This concept was modified by the Shakers with their use of a cloth storage bag mounted on the side of some Hancock sewing chests, as shown in pl. 108. A second theory is that a piece of material was suspended between the pegs to protect the seamstress from winter drafts.[82]

54. Sisters' Sewing Room
c. 1890s
Photograph
Collection Richard Brooker, #8964A

This photograph, while certainly posed, nevertheless provides information on one of the many work spaces and the two types of furniture necessary for one of the Shaker cottage industries. The sisters pictured here are, from left to right, Augusta Stone, Sarah Neale, Emma Neale, Lucy Catherine Wells, Genevieve Kalligan, and Carrie Alice Wade.

A table or counter in the foreground provides the broader surface for the laying out and cutting of material, while the two sewing tables in the background offer more individualized work and storage space. Neither of the sewing tables with gallery shown here corresponds with known extant examples of the form, raising the question as to the number of these pieces actually made. In an unpublished study, one researcher accounted for nine sewing tables.[83]

This photograph helps clarify the use of the sewing desks on a more commercial level in the production of cloaks and smaller fancy-goods as well as for the daily upkeep and manufacture of clothing for community members. A description of the damage caused by the 1875 fires at Mount Lebanon gave an idea of the contents of the sewing room: "The whole building [sisters' shop] was almost immediately in flames, and there was consumed with it all the paraphernalia of a woman's workshop, a thousand dollars worth of cotton and woolen cloth, stocking yarn, clothes, and six sewing machines, tables, furniture, etc."[84]

below

55. Sewing Table
c. 1870
Walnut, cherry, and poplar
h 41⅛ w 32 d 21⅝"
Hancock Shaker Village, Pittsfield,
Massachusetts, #74–75.2

Although retaining the basic form of the previous examples, this sewing table with six-drawer gallery exhibits Victorian decorative details in the curved backboard and turned legs. It is closely related in design to a nearly identical piece in the Shaker Museum, Old Chatham, New York (acc. no. 10626). Both examples also share a gallery affixed to the table with two screws on either side and drawers that are similarly and finely dovetailed throughout, suggesting that both are the work of the same craftsman. The wooden knobs are probably later replacements for the original porcelain pulls, which are still attached to the gallery drawers on the related table. Appropriately exhibited in the remodeled Trustees' Office at Hancock dating from 1895, the desk, along with the flowered wallpaper and the intricately molded woodwork, emphasizes that the later Shakers not only kept abreast of but copied worldly fashion.

56. Tripod Stand
c. 1820
Pine, maple legs, and cherry pedestal
h 25⅜ w 24½ d 16"
Hancock Shaker Village, Pittsfield,
Massachusetts, #62–9

Due to its similarity to worldly prototypes, tripod stands with peg legs may be one of the earliest examples of this form, or they may simply represent a primitive design. One type adjusts in height by means of a threaded peg in the pedestal by which the top can be set at various levels.[85] Both this stand and a closely related example in a private collection are equipped with a rectangular top, underhung drawer fitted in a dovetailed housing attached to the cylindrical post by way of a circular cleat, and a drum-shaped base. The related stand was acquired from the Church Family at Mount Lebanon, where, according to oral tradition, it was used in connection with the garden seed industry.[86]

57. Tripod Stand
c. 1830
Cherry, with varnish and iron plate
h 23½ diameter of top 15³⁄₁₆"
Collection Marc P. Crumpton

This snake-leg stand is a fine representative of one of the major types produced at Mount Lebanon, although the variety of details within this form is extensive. The shaping of each component section differs considerably from stand to stand and visually affects the overall design of each piece. A significant factor is the size of the top and its proportional relation-

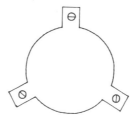

ship to the rest of the stand. The edge of the top may have a dished, beveled, quarter-round, or, as here, only slightly rounded profile. The method of assembly used to reinforce the joint between the top and the pedestal may consist either of a disk-shaped cleat or a rectangular cleat with flat-head screws fastening the cleat to the top. This stand has a threaded joint between the cleat and the stem. The stem ranges from the gradually concave shape shown above to a turning with a much smaller diameter and a straight taper. The snake-leg stands do not display the more bulbous profile of the spider-leg forms. Mount Lebanon examples incorporate a dovetailed joint to fasten the legs to the stem, which is here reinforced by an iron plate. While the profile of most snake legs is usually similar, the foot portion can vary in shape considerably. At one extreme, the foot is quite pointed and supported by a distinctly formed smaller pad; at the other, it is rounded in shape and raised slightly off the floor, as seen here.

Tripod stands from Mount Lebanon: peg leg; spider leg; snake leg. Table edge shapes, clockwise from upper right: square; quarter-round; beveled or chamfered; lipped; bull-nose

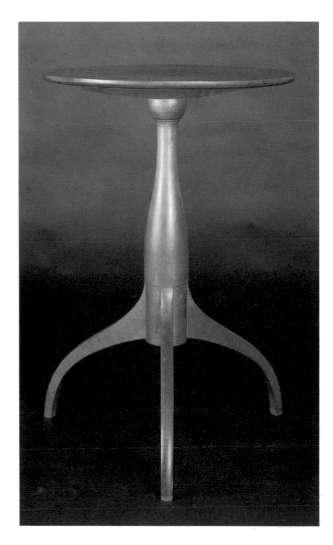

Tripod Stands

The Shakers borrowed from contemporary worldly models for the form of their tripod stands. Peg-leg stands, based on primitive rural eighteenth-century prototypes, may represent the Believers' earliest productions. In these examples, the turned legs were let into holes drilled in the pedestal at a raking angle and secured with glue. The more refined snake-shaped legs are derived from the Queen Anne cabriole style and exhibit the same graceful profile but are generally flat in cross section. On the whole, these S-curved legs were dovetailed into the turned pedestals and further strengthened by the addition of a metal plate screwed into the legs near the base of the stem. A number of stands with arched or spider legs derived from Sheraton styling have been identified as originating at Mount Lebanon. The majority of tripod stands have round tops, although several examples have square or rectangular tops, which are attached to the stem below by means of a tapered, rectangular cleat or a circular disk.

These stands probably held candles initially; the 1845 "Millennial Laws" state that "one or two stands" should be provided for the occupants of every retiring room.[87] By the 1850s however, they may have served to hold lamps, as suggested by a reference of November 5, 1850, in "Domestic Occurrences": "Isaac Y[oungs] has been repairing and fixing a Liverpool lamp to put into the kitchen. We have hitherto used candles altogether in the kitchen and some begin to feel anxious to have lamps." In addition, these small portable pieces of furniture probably found their way to sewing rooms, seed shops, and kitchens.

58. Tripod Stand

Attributed to Samuel Humphrey Turner (1775–1842)
1837
Stamped on underside of cleat: SISTER ASENETH/ELD.S RUTH 1837
Cherry, with varnish
h 25¾ diameter of top 17⅞"
Private collection

Although representative in form of the spider-leg stands produced at Mount Lebanon, this particular example is remarkable for its original finish and documentation. It also has a more robust design than comparable examples, which probably originates from Brother Samuel's experience at the Pleasant Hill, Kentucky, community, where he lived for most of his years as a Shaker.

The stand consists of a circular top with quarter-round molded edges curved slightly inward, a boldly turned pedestal with swelled shaft, and arched tripod base with legs that taper both in section and profile. Particularly noteworthy in terms of construction is the method of assembly. Instead of being planed smooth, the underside of the top is reduced in thickness two-thirds of the distance from the central pedestal connection by a lathe-turned cut. The rectangular cleat, which bears the stamped inscription, is attached to the top with screws and has rounded and chamfered ends to conform with the shaped edges of the top.

Eldress Ruth probably refers to Ruth Landon (1776–1850), who became the first female in the lead ministry after Mother Lucy Wright's death in 1821.[88] Sister Aseneth Clark (1780–1857) was her assistant. This stand was clearly made in 1837 for these two leading figures in the ministry at Mount Lebanon, who as coleaders likely shared a retiring room in the meetinghouse. The style of the stamped inscription and the shape of the stem turning relate this stand to the only known signed and dated piece of furniture by Samuel Turner (see pl. 59). Another tripod stand identical to this one is known, but it provides neither name nor date.

Blanket Boxes

Storage or utility boxes were commonly used by the Shakers, and many are indistinguishable from worldly examples. A great variety of chests survive, ranging from the lidded six-board variety to those containing one to four drawers. Blanket boxes from Mount Lebanon were generally constructed with lids with complex-molded breadboard ends, lipped drawers, and straight feet cut out of the plank sides; some have an applied bracket base. Pine was the material commonly employed because of its availability in wide boards, which were finished with a red or yellow wash. Like their worldly counterparts, many boxes are equipped with small tills on the inside.

opposite above

60. Blanket Box
Attributed to Gilbert Avery (1775–1853)
1837
Written in ink on back of backboard: Made April.1837./Canaan.
Pine, with red paint, iron hinges, bone escutcheons, and steel and brass locks
h 27½ w 41 d 18"
Private collection
Photograph: courtesy David A. Schorsch, Inc.

The inscription indicates that this box was made at the Canaan Family (1813–97), a branch of the North Family Shakers at Mount Lebanon. Although the maker did not sign the piece, it has been attributed by Faith and Edward Deming Andrews to Gilbert Avery, the father of Giles Avery (1815–1890), a cabinetmaker at Mount Lebanon. The chest—and, apparently, the oral history surrounding its origin—was acquired by the Andrews in 1928 directly from the Second Family at Mount Lebanon.[90]

Aside from this written and oral documentation, the box is noteworthy for its original finish, dovetailed construction throughout, and the less common applied base molding, which strangely continues around the back of the case. Furthermore, the interior left end of the case is fitted with a lidded till and an unusual drawer below, which is accessed from the side. The deep molding applied to the ends of the hinged top and the flat shaping of the arched base with convex cutouts relate to other pieces with a Canaan history and may be characteristic of cabinetmaking practices at this family.[91] However, the feet may have been longer originally.

59. Tripod Stand
Samuel Humphrey Turner (1775–1842)
1837
Stamped along right front edge of drawer frame:
SAMUEL. TURNER. TO./RUTH JOHNSON 1837.
Butternut, pine, and cherry
h 25⅜ w 21¼ d 16½"
Collection Bob Hamilton

This tray-top, snake-leg table with drawer—the only signed and dated piece by Samuel Turner—shares similar construction details with the spider-leg stand pl. 58. Most noteworthy are the robust character of the stem turning and the shaping at the top of the post; the style of the metal-stamped inscription, which is executed in block letters; and the fact that both pieces were gifts. Membership records indicate there were two sisters named Ruth Johnson at Mount Lebanon with close ties to the maker, and it is not clear which one was the recipient of this stand. The older Ruth (1765–1854) served as a deaconess until 1837, the year that Brother Samuel dated the stand. The younger Ruth (1779–1862) traveled to Ohio with the maker in 1806 and returned to Mount Lebanon a year before he did, in 1835.[89]

In 1806, Samuel Turner was selected to help organize the Western Shaker communities in Ohio and Kentucky. He was soon appointed to the ministry at the newly gathered society at Pleasant Hill, where he remained for twenty-eight years. After returning to Mount Lebanon, the journal records of Isaac Newton Youngs, "A Domestic Journal of Daily Occurrences," indicate he resumed work as a joiner and in 1837 began a "parcel of round leafed stands for furnishing the great house." Clearly, pl. 58 and perhaps this related example, both dated 1837, were part of this project to make furniture for the Church Family Dwelling House. Although there is no written documentation or surviving evidence of Brother Samuel's woodworking activities while in the west, the exuberant curves, heavier construction, and preference for snake legs rather than spider feet on this example clearly recall Pleasant Hill design (see pl. 298).

61. Blanket Box
c. 1850
Pine and poplar, with walnut knobs, red wash,
varnish, and iron hinges
h 41 w 43 d 21"
Private collection
Photograph: courtesy Suzanne Courcier and
Robert W. Wilkins, Richard and Betty Ann Rasso

This chest probably never left its original site until recently. When the Canaan Family closed in 1897, the property and buildings were purchased by a friend of Eldress Anna White (1831–1910) of the North Family and bought in 1931 by John Roberts, a hired hand of the Shakers, who accumulated a household of furniture from the Shakers at Mount Lebanon—most of it either given to him or as payment for his work.

In addition to this documented history of ownership, several construction features are noteworthy. The box is unusually tall and fitted with drawers dramatically graduated between tiers, as in pl. 62. The applied cut feet are oriented with the grain running diagonally rather than vertically on the front of the case. The cove molding decoratively affixed beneath the breadboard ends combined with the rounded edge of the lid creates a much wider molding than usual.

Construction details of Mount Lebanon boxes: breadboard end with integral cove molding (above left); cut foot with mitered, applied foot (below left); applied bracket base (right).

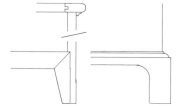

62. Blanket Box

c. 1840
Pine, with fruitwood knobs and chrome yellow wash
h 36⅜ w 42½ d 18¼"
Shaker Museum and Library, Old Chatham, New York, #10526

The drawer proportions on this blanket box do not follow those commonly found on worldly furniture. Rather than graduating the drawer heights, typically, in about 1-inch increments, the maker reduced them dramatically by half from the second to the first tier. Although the craftsman was probably familiar with classical proportions, he was clearly willing to deviate from worldly practices in developing this design.

The flamboyant chrome yellow pigment and atypical proportions contrast with the conservative base treatment, consisting of a cut foot rabbeted to conceal most of the end grain. One construction detail found here and common to many Mount Lebanon blanket boxes is the breadboard end with its integral lip. With its rounded end overlapping the edge of the case, it provides decoration while keeping the top board flat.

The color was probably much brighter when originally applied and would have been visually dominating no matter where it was employed. It is not known whether the pigment was also used as the primary color for a separate clothes room or only on occasional pieces of furniture, as with other similarly finished furniture in a retiring room.

63. Tall Clock

Amos Jewett (1753–1834)
1809
Written on wooden dial: 1809 Amos Jewett,/Lebanon No. [?]0
Poplar, with dark brown stain and varnish, brass hinges and knob
h 89¾ w 16¼ d 7¾"
Private collection
Photograph: courtesy Suzanne Courcier and Robert W. Wilkins, Richard and Betty Ann Rasso

The stark yet pleasing dark poplar case of this 1809 Amos Jewett tall clock speaks to the vernacular as well as the plain Shaker form. Its verticality is exaggerated by the minimal variation in case width, along with the concurrent use of the small cove moldings between the waist, base, and bonnet sections. The case, presumably made by Brother Amos, has little decoration: a base with a simple cut foot, a chamfered waist section with a flush fitted door, and a cornice molding consisting of a square with an ovolo and two fillets. The flat top bonnet, constructed without a door, must be lifted off to reach the thirty-day wooden movement, which strikes on the hour.

According to Isaac Newton Youngs, writing in his "Clock Maker's Journal" in 1815, "I got in to have some privilege in the shop with Amos Jewett who had made wooden clocks, he was very clever to me." The other known examples of Brother Amos's probably extensive clock-making output are a paper-on-wood clock dial inscribed in ink "1789 Amos Jewett New Lebanon No. 12" at the Shaker Museum, Old Chatham, New York (acc. no. 14614); another paper-on-wood dial marked "Amos Jewett/Canaan/No 36," housed in a tall case marked in pencil on the backboard, "Dec 3, 1828 Made by Amos Stewart" in the collection of Hancock Shaker Village, Pittsfield, Massachusetts (acc. no. 89–7); and a clock in a private collection signed "1796 Amos Jewett No. 38."[92] The movement of the clock marked no. 36, not original to the case, is of much later manufacture. If Brother Amos Jewett had already produced thirty-eight clocks by 1796, he may have completed many more during the remainder of his working career.

right

64. Wall Clock

Isaac Newton Youngs (1793–1865)
1840
Painted on dial: 1840
Written in script on back of dial: N° 18/Made by
Isaac N. Youngs/May 12th 1840/O let each one
his moments will improve/To gain abiding bliss in
realms above./I.Y.—
Written on paper label on backboard of case:
Whenever this clock is moved/the weight should
be wound up./To make the clock gain a minute
in a day./turn the screw round once & a half
up./Be careful to keep the doors shut—/I.N.Y.
May 20th 1840
Butternut and pine, with a wood movement and
iron face
Private collection
Photograph: Michael Fredericks; courtesy Richard
and Betty Ann Rasso

Brother Isaac is best known today for his extensive journal writing detailing the history of the Church Family at Mount Lebanon, as well as for his clock-making activities. His interest in this trade began at an early age. He wrote in his "Clock Maker's Journal,"

> When I was a child, I lived with my uncle [Benjamin Youngs], who was a clockmaker—I used to be with him in his shop & watch his motions, learned the parts of a clock, & could put one together perhaps when 6 or 7 years old, & knew the time of day before I could talk plain. I had a relish for clocks & liked to be among them & to handle the tools, but as I left my uncle, the spring before I was 10 years old, I did not arrive to much understanding or judgment in the business. I went to where no such thing was carried on & clocks were scarce—

that is, the Watervliet Shaker community, where he lived with his nephew Seth Youngs Wells until relocating to the Church Family at Mount Lebanon, in 1807.[93]

In his "Journal" Youngs recorded numerous clocks, including a series of six similar to the example shown here. All of the timepieces in this group contain wooden works and are designed to be hung from a wall pegboard. They are fitted with glass on both sides of the case, revealing the interior works, and are signed on the reverse of the face rather than the front, as was the custom of worldly clock makers. Brother Isaac also made furniture and probably constructed the case for this clock, although the floral painting and dial decoration are later embellishments added after the clock had left the community, given to a friend of the Shakers.

Other examples of Youngs's cabinetmaking skills are evident in several long school desks now at Hancock Shaker Village, Pittsfield, Massachusetts. Desks at Shaker Village of Pleasant Hill, Kentucky, were likely con-

structed from his detailed sketches, according to recently discovered correspondence and accompanying sketches.[94] In addition, Brother Isaac mentions on December 7, 1840, and in February 1841 in his journal "Daily Occurrences," that he "began towards two counters or shop boards with drawers for the tayloresses" and several months later "finished a job of work which he has been doing since the 7th of December for the Tayloresses—viz. making two counters with drawers to them."

The Shakers' Web Back Chairs, with Arms and Rockers.
WORSTED LACE SEATS AND BACKS.
Showing a Comparison of Sizes.

| No. 0, | No. 1, | No. 3, | No. 5, | No. 6, | No. 7, |
| $5.00 | $5.50 | $6 50 | $9.50 | $10.50 | $11.00 |

Price per each.

Page from *Illustrated Catalogue and Price List of the Shakers' Chairs*, 1876

Chairs

Throughout its history, the Mount Lebanon Shaker community's craftsmen have specialized in chair making. Entries from the Church Family account book indicate that chairs were sold to Believers at other communities as well as to worldly customers as early as 1789.[95] According to the "Sabbathday Lake (Me.) Church Record and Journal," vol. 4, "August 26, 1895, Elder William Anderson from the South Family Mt. Lebanon arrived to visit us here and also to go to Poland Springs and solicit orders for the Shaker chairs of which he is the manufacturer" (p. 391). The earliest designs are difficult to distinguish from non-Shaker ladderbacks and are characterized by heavy, bulbous rear pommels, nongraduated back slats, and heavy, minimally tapered stretchers. On armchairs the tops of the front posts have integrally turned mushroom caps, crescent-shaped arms, and heavy rockers.

Written documentation confirms that during the nineteenth century, the East, Second, and Canaan families all had chair industries.[96] However, it is difficult to determine if they were producing chairs simultaneously or if chair production moved from one family to another. By the 1840s the style of the Mount Lebanon chair had grown more refined and can be clearly differentiated from worldly prototypes by the following features: slimmer rear posts that taper from the seat up; pointed, oval-shaped pommels with a narrow collar; armchairs with side-scrolled arms terminating in circular handholds tenoned to the top of the front posts; and much lighter rocker blades, measuring about ⅜ inch thick, with concave curves on the top edges.

By 1850, the Second Family had assumed prominence as the leader in the chair business. According to the census of manufacturers in Columbia County, New York, Brother Daniel Hawkins produced two hundred chairs that year, and their marketing was enhanced by the use of a broadside dated 185-, suggesting some standardization in design and construction methods. During this decade the Shaker chair design reached its pinnacle. The finest of these examples are characterized by exquisite proportions, the use of bird's-eye maple, and cane seats. Some carried the metal tilter buttons patented on March 2, 1852, by George O. Donnell, a Mount Lebanon brother. By 1860, the census records indicate that Brother Jesse Lewis was running a small industry that produced six hundred chairs.[97]

Although the output changed very little over the next ten years,[98] the structure of the business underwent a major reorganization that put it into the competitive marketplace. In 1863 the South Family split off from the Second Family and became the primary site of chair manufacture. As the family deacon, Brother Robert Wagan (1833–1883) skillfully managed the chair industry and was responsible for its success. Due to increased demand, the South Family built a new factory in 1872 that accommodated the development of mass-production methods, increased output, and standardization in design. Henry Blinn, who visited the South Family in 1873, described the factory and its enterprising manager in "A Journey to Kentucky":

The building erected last year, & the machinery in it has cost some $25,000. All of this was earned by this little family save $2000 which they borrowed of the Second Family. They have an engine of 15 horse power and a boiler of 20 horse power. The whole building is heated by steam. Some ten hands are employed, & it is expected that they will finish two Doz. chair per day. They are the old fashioned chairs of one hundred years ago. About two thirds are made with rockers. The large chairs with cushions sell for $18.00 each. Without cushions for $9.00. The small chairs with cushions sell for $13.00 without cushions for $7.00. Only two sizes are made. They are all stained in a hot logwood dye, which forces the color into the wood. When varnished they are bright red. Already they have orders for more than they can furnish. The plush for cushions is made in this same building. In one room we found two old men at work in hand looms, slowly weaving this peculiar cloth. Our guide informed us that they were not americans. . . . These men weave from three to four yards each per day, and are paid fifty cents a yard. One of the men informed me that they usually worked ten hours each day.

One of the most singular things connected with this is, that a few years ago they made a small business in making & selling chairs, but never considered it of much importance, till it passed into the hands of the present manager. He enlarged the business and the demand has increased correspondingly. Br. Robert is enterprising. He says anything will sell that is carried into the market. (Summer 1965, pp. 43–44)

By 1874, the catalogues listing chairs by function had been replaced by catalogues designating chairs by numbers, with 0 representing the smallest and 7 the largest. During this period, transitional-style chairs maintained some handcraftsmanship while at the same time introducing machine work. Handwork techniques are evident in the top edges of the back slats, which are slightly beveled, and side-scrolled arms, which are rounded on the inside and beveled on the outside. However, the design of the chairs, the bent back posts, and the absence of scribe marks were clearly influenced by the introduction of production methods.

The standard factory-made chair appears about 1876 and is designed to take advantage of specialized machinery such as jigs, boring machines, and duplicating lathes. Of bolder and heavier proportions than its predecessor, the basic production model has acorn-shaped pommels with simplified turnings, prominently bent rear posts, back slats rounded on both top and bottom edges, arms shaped with two projections on the outside edge, applied mushroom-shaped tenon caps, and tapered stretchers. With the change from a small shop to a mass-production factory, the Shakers were turning out three thousand chairs in 1876, according to the United States census, and as a result of their success, imitations soon entered the market. To distinguish their products from worldly copies, the Shakers introduced a gold transfer trademark, which was applied to the chairs to guarantee authenticity.

According to contemporary catalogue entries, a number of options were available to potential customers. Mahogany was the most common finish, woven wool tapes provided standard seating material, and plush was offered for back and seat cushions or upholstered chairs.

Robert Wagan, who created a nationwide market for Shaker chairs, died prematurely in 1883. As the second century of chair production began at Mount Lebanon, the industry focused on providing the product to major worldly distributors such as Henry A. Turner & Co. of Boston, John Wanamaker of Philadelphia, and Marshall Field of Chicago.[99] In addition to selling by means of catalogues and supplying large retail firms, the Believers operated a retail store on site. After the 1923 fire that destroyed the five-story chair factory, Brother William Perkins (d. 1934) of the Second Family reestablished the business on a smaller scale in one of the neighboring structures. He supervised the manufacture of chair frames while Sister Sarah Collins of the South Family wove the seats. However, the small size and advancing age of the work force and the need to rely on outside manufacturers to supply raw materials resulted in significant design changes after 1923. These chairs are characterized by heavy, straight back posts, long, less shapely turned pommels, large, flat tenon caps, and straight, nontapering stretchers. The death of Lillian Barlow in 1942 finally forced the remaining Shakers to "close up the chair business due to lack of help and not purchase the chair tape due to priorities" in the early 1940s.[100]

66. Side Chair
c. 1800
Maple and cotton tape
h 39⅛ w 19⅜ d 14⅞"
Collection Mr. and Mrs. Richard Hehir

67. Side Chair with Rockers
c. 1800
Maple and splint
h 39½ w 19¼ d 14¾"
Shaker Museum and Library, Old Chatham, New York, #19521

The heavy posts with sausage turnings of the chair on the left and the half-round baluster spindles of the chair with rockers are remnants of worldly design that Shaker chair makers eliminated in later examples. On the other hand, these turn-of-the-century chairs exhibit the early pommel form and basic back slat proportions already in place only one or two decades after the Shaker chair industry began. The rockers were added to the spindle-back chair, which was built originally as a side chair.

65. Armed Rocker
c. 1830
Maple and splint, with red paint
Private collection
Photograph: courtesy Suzanne Courcier and Robert W. Wilkins

This style of rocker was made for a period of thirty years with only slight variations in the overall proportions and in the pommel style. Characteristic details on these examples include simply turned front posts, tapered side-scrolled arms with both beveled and rounded surfaces, and back slats with little or no graduation. The rocker blade style first appeared about 1830 and continued with minor variations through 1875. The pommel with its elliptical shape and slight ridge in the middle of the neck became more sharply defined by the 1850s. The decorative red paint on this chair is much less common than the usual stain and varnish finish.

opposite above left

69. Side Chair with Pewter Tilters

c. 1850
Bird's-eye maple and cane, with pewter tilters
h 42 w 18½ d 14¼"
Private collection
Photograph: courtesy Thomas C. Queen

This unusual chair in figured wood is one of two known examples fitted with pewter tilter buttons and cane seats. The extreme backward tilt is defined by the angle between the side stretchers and the rear posts. They are part of a yet larger group of about fifteen particularly well-made and designed chairs, all with metal tilters, possibly produced by Brother George O. Donnell, whose name appears on the 1850 United States census as a chair maker and on the patent chair pl. 68.

68. Patent Model for Button Joint Tilter

1852
George O. Donnell
Bird's-eye maple and tape, with brass tilters and ferrules
h 15½"
Private collection
Photograph: courtesy David A. Schorsch, Inc.

Listed in the 1850 United States census as a chair maker, George O. Donnell is one of the few Shaker makers whose name appears on his product, painted on the back of the bottom slat. This model—little over a foot high—was submitted to the United States Patent Office in 1852 to support his invention of a "new and improved mode of preventing the wear and tear of carpets and the marring of floors caused by the corners of the back posts of chairs. . . ."[101] Although the wooden tilter is common in Shaker chairs, the metal variation is rare. According to the specifications, this device consists of a separate piece combining a ferrule, ball, and foot. Applied to the back posts, it allows "the chairs [to] take their natural motion of rocking backward and forward, while the metallic feet rest unmoved; flat and square on the floor or carpet. . . ."[102]

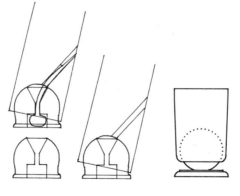

Brass chair tilter, patented by Brother George O. Donnell, 1852

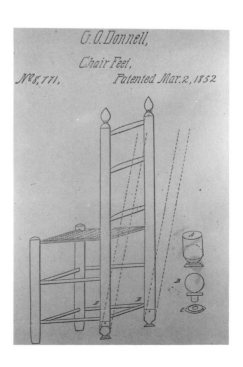

70. Armed Rocker

c. 1860
Maple and tape (not original)
Private collection
Photograph: courtesy John Keith Russell Antiques, Inc.

During the 1860s the South Family at Mount Lebanon made a major decision to increase the size of their chair-making business. Produced during the transitional period, this chair exhibits most of the features adapted by the industry after it became firmly established during the next decade. The front post, tenoned through the arm, required the use of a mushroom-shaped tenon cap to cover the joint. The most striking features of these chairs are the exaggerated design elements, which include the oversize tenon cap with an extra ring on the base, the vase-shaped front post turned to a very small diameter, and the back posts bent to an extreme angle not found on later chairs. The rungs are turned to a very slender diameter, and the arms and back slats are made of particularly thin stock, giving the overall chair a delicate appearance.

71. Production Chairs

c. 1880–1910
Maple and wool and cotton tape
h 23½ w 14¼ d 16½" and h 33 w 18¼ d 23¼"
Hancock Shaker Village, Pittsfield, Massachusetts

These size 0 and size 3 rockers are typical of thousands of examples made in the chair factory built in 1872, which employed about twelve worldly workers under the supervision of the Shakers. The Shakers' commitment to mass production and their selection of several design features created a standard form used for the following half-century. The bent back post, back slats, rockers, and arms were shaped with jigs on machinery run by a steam engine. The rungs, back posts, cushion bars, and vase-shaped front posts were turned in large quantities on production lathes. Due to these techniques, tape-backed (such as these) and upholstered chairs were made available to a much larger market.

72. Armed Rocker
1873
h 40¾ w 24½ d 29"
*Maple, with dark mahogany stain and plush red
and black cushions*
*Shaker Museum and Library, Old Chatham, New
York, #18304 (chair), #6445 A, B (cushions)*

Now quite rare, as the cushions are much more fragile than the chair frame, Shaker chairs with cushions or upholstery were popular when they were first produced, adding comfort and bright color to Victorian households. In the Shaker catalogues, upholstered chairs are priced 50 to 100 percent higher than equivalent slat or tape-back chairs. Elder Henry Blinn recorded the production of the plush material:

> The plush for cushions is made in this same building. In one room we found two old men at work in hand looms, slowly weaving this peculiar cloth. Our guide informed us that they were not americans. . . . These men weave from three to four yards each per day, and are paid fifty cents a yard. One of the men informed me that they usually worked ten hours each day. ("A Journey to Kentucky" [Summer 1965], pp. 43–44)

Chairs with permanent upholstery were also made, as they were illustrated in the Shakers' chair catalogues.[103] Today, many chairs with tape seats have tack holes, evidence that they had previously been upholstered.

This is a number 7 transitional chair, with crescent-shaped arms and slender front and rear posts. It was made with a cushion bar to hold removable cushions, like those bold red and black ones, over a taped seat and back slats.

73. Armchair
c. 1930
Maple and cotton tape
h 51 w 23⅜ d 18½"
*Hancock Shaker Village, Pittsfield,
Massachusetts, #62–807*

After the Shakers' chair factory was destroyed by fire in 1923, new machinery was installed in an adjacent building and production was resumed. Due to the small number of Believers available to work in the industry, they contracted or purchased many chair parts from worldly manufacturers and assembled the final product on site. The chairs produced had the same basic form but many details were changed, making these twentieth-century chairs readily identifiable. Characteristic features found on this example include the straight rather than bent posts, less pronounced pommel and vase turnings, broad crescent-shaped arms without front and rear projections found on production chairs made fifty years earlier, and stretchers made from dowels. This tall, five-slat example, however, is more elegant than most of the Shaker chairs of this period, due to the height of the straight back posts and applied pommels, which were turned separately and doweled into the top of the rear posts.

74. Revolving Stools

c. 1860
Pine, maple, ash, and iron
Left to right: h 20½ diameter of seat 16¼"
New York State Museum, Albany, #40.1.54
h 28¼ w 14¼ d 14¼"
Hancock Shaker Village, Pittsfield,
Massachusetts, #62-155
h 38⅜ w 17¾ d 16¾"
Hancock Shaker Village, Pittsfield,
Massachusetts, #62-475

"They manufacture a new kind of chair, which turns on a pivit screw, every which way different kinds and sizes. . . ."[104] With these words, Elder James Prescott of the North Union, Ohio, community described what was indeed a different product for the Shakers. Two types of revolving stools were made, both with turned and hollowed seats supported by cast-metal yokes mounted on metal screw or swivel shafts. One variation, both with and without a back (center and right), was Windsor in form, with two sets of stretchers mortised into the legs. Many of these chairs, including the two shown above, are not adjustable in height.

The second variation has a spider base made of two wooden arches joined with a half-lap joint at the center. The base supports a tapered cylindrical stem with threaded shaft. The seat above, which is usually adjustable in height, includes a back composed of six to eight spindles supporting a bent, rounded rail. The stool at the left incorporated a wooden pedestal fitted with forged legs with flat, round penny-shaped feet.

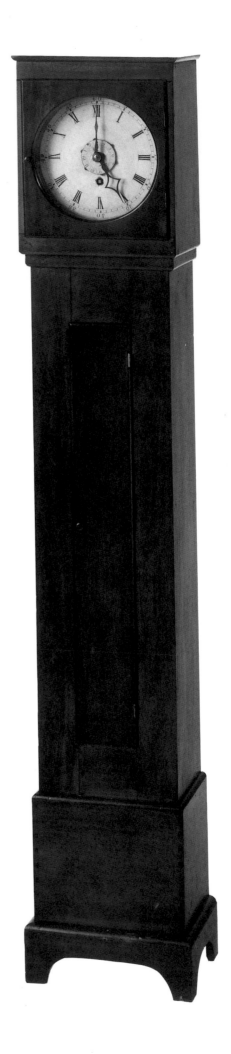

Attributed to Benjamin Youngs, Sr. (1736–1818)
c. 1810
Cherry and pine, with brass movement, knobs,
and hinges
Private collection
Photograph: courtesy Richard and Betty Ann Rasso

This wall clock may be the timepiece pictured in a historic photograph of a North Family sisters' workroom at Mount Lebanon.[1] Two other fine dwarf tall clocks made by Benjamin Youngs survive, in the collections of the Western Reserve Historical Society, Cleveland, Ohio, and the Henry Ford Museum, Dearborn, Michigan.[2]

The wall clocks represent the most severe of all of Brother Benjamin's designs. The flat bonnet was fitted with a very thin bull-nose cornice and a one-piece door, with only a hole cut to receive the glass covering the dial. The base section was either straight or tapered slightly to its minimum width just below the cove molding that supports the bonnet. The case door allowed access to the pendulum for starting or adjusting the movement. The brass timepiece itself was suspended on a movement board affixed to the case behind the enameled wood or metal dial.

76. Dwarf Tall Clock

Benjamin Youngs, Sr. (1736–1818)
1814
Painted on back of face: Watervliet/Made
by/Benjamin Youngs Senr/in the 78th year of his
Age./1814
Stamped on brass works: 1814
Written in ink on paper label below pendulum
inside case: Painted on the back of the
dial/Watervliet/Benjamin Youngs Senr/in the 78
year of his age/1814./Watervliet N.Y. is opposite
Troy, NY./Benjamin Youngs was a shaker in the
colony there.
Cherry and pine, with brass movement with
alarm
h 54 w 10 d 7"
Courtesy of the Art Complex Museum, Duxbury,
Massachusetts, #30-29

Most clock cases were made by a joiner in coordination with the clock maker. Benjamin Youngs made the movement for this clock; his nephew Brother Freegift Wells (1785–1871) may have made the case. Is this the piece that Brother Freegift refers to in a journal notation from his "Memorandum of Events" dated December 12, 1814? He wrote, ". . . finished Mothers clock case except putting in the crystal carried it to the meeting house put the time piece in it and set it going." Except for the addition of the applied bracket base, the clock case greatly resembles that of other Benjamin Youngs wall clocks.

Watervliet Community, New York

A MERICA'S FIRST SHAKER settlement, originally known by its Indian name, Niskeyuna was the first place where Mother Ann and her followers put down roots in this country. In 1775 three of the original Believers, William Lee, James Whittaker, and John Hocknell, leased lands near Albany at "8 Bushells of wheat for every 100 acres" from the Van Rensselaer family,[3] and eventually purchased two hundred acres which formed the basis of this community. Lee found employment in Albany as a blacksmith and Whittaker as a weaver, while Hocknell returned to England to bring his family and that of John Partington back with him. Mother Ann remained in New York City, where she earned a living doing washing and ironing until the group was reunited at Niskeyuna in 1776.[4] During the next three years they drained swamps, tilled the land, and built shelter for present and future needs in isolation from the world. As Mother Ann had prophesied, many visited Niskeyuna to investigate the new religion in 1780, including Joseph Meacham (1742–1796), a Baptist preacher who later became the sect's spiritual leader.

After Mother Ann's death in 1784, the pioneer group at Niskeyuna was no longer the center of Shaker spiritual guidance—the main authority was vested in the central ministry at the newly established Mount Lebanon community. In 1787 Niskeyuna, later Watervliet, became the second Shaker village organized in this country and together with Mount Lebanon and Groveland eventually formed the Mount Lebanon Bishopric. The community grew rapidly as a result of property deeded by Brothers Joseph Bennet in 1788, William Carter between 1803 and 1822, John Partington in 1822, and Benjamin Youngs, Sr., between 1794 and 1826, and eventually encompassed 2,000 acres.[5] By 1840 a peak population of 304 members was living in four separate families—the Church, North, West, and South.[6]

The major occupations that the Shakers engaged in at Watervliet were similar to those found at Mount Lebanon. With Mount Lebanon only about thirty-five miles from Watervliet, a close relationship existed between the two communities, and Believers journeying back and forth traveled through the industrial center of Albany. This city provided an important early market for Shaker goods, a market that eventually extended up and down the Hudson River Valley. Watervliet was the first Shaker community to produce broom corn, and Brother Theodore Bates is credited with inventing the flat broom, which proved superior to the earlier round broom of 1795.[7] According to an interview with Elder Goepper, which appeared in the June 1887 issue of *The Manifesto,*

> [Broom] manufacture is one of their favorite industries, and they have more ways of making it useful than are known to the outside world. They never disgrace it by making it stand behind the door, as if it were responsible for the untidy litter about the house. The Shaker broom is always hung up against the wall when not in use. They put a clean white cotton hood on some of their brooms, and when thus equipped use them to dry-polish their smooth hard wood floors and to remove the last trace of dust from the hard and shining surface.[8]

They also grew and packaged garden seeds, produced clay pipes, and prepared herbal medicines such as Laurus Eye Water.[9] Another important industry during the last half of the nineteenth century was the preserving of vegetables hermetically sealed in tin cans—a progressive idea for its time. According to an 1859

Church Family, Watervliet, c. 1870. The man standing at the right is believed to be Freegift Wells (1785–1871). Photograph by James Irving, Troy, New York. New York State Museum, Albany, #PTA1.114

account book, the peas were first shelled and put through a coarse sieve. After parboiling, they were placed in tins, and the caps, perforated by a small ventilation hole, were soldered onto the cans. These vent holes were also sealed, but after the cans had been boiled for several hours, the holes were reopened to allow the steam to escape. The holes were again resoldered and the cans boiled for two more hours. These specially designed containers were produced at the Shaker tin factory on the road to the Mohawk River farm.[10]

During the twentieth century, the gradual dissolution of the Watervliet property dramatically affected the distribution of the community's furnishings. The West Family property was the first to be sold, in 1915, followed by that of the North Family in 1919, which was subsequently destroyed by fire in 1927. In 1924, the Church Family farm was liquidated and, after many buildings were razed, later became the Ann Lee Home. The South Family complex was closed in 1938 and the remaining three sisters and their possessions moved to Mount Lebanon. At this time, the New York State Museum in Albany actively acquired a number of pieces directly from the Shakers for its collection. It is this group of objects and their associated oral history that forms the basis of many attributions today.

The names of Church Family cabinetmakers and their activities were documented by Freegift Wells (1785–1871) in his "Memorandum of Events Covering the Years 1812–1865." Data from this journal (and others, where specified), indicated by two squares (■■), combined with United States census records for Watervliet (■■■), secondary source information from Andrews's *Religion in Wood* (■■■■), and several pieces of furniture that are either signed or have a strong oral attribution (■), reveal the names of the following craftsmen:

■ BENJAMIN YOUNGS, SR. (1736–1818), see pls. 75, 76, 93, 94

■■■ BENJAMIN WELLS (1770–1851), listed as carpenter and joiner in 1850 United States census

■ CALVIN WELLS (1772–1853), clockmaker, in Gibbs and Meader, *Shaker Clock-makers*, p. 11

■■■ FRANCIS GOODRICH (1774–1859), listed as turner in 1850 census

■■■ BENJAMIN SETH YOUNGS (1774–1855), listed as clockmaker in 1850 census. Lived in South Union, Kentucky, 1805–55

■■ NATHAN SPIER (1775–1827), "July 18, 1816, Nathan Spier & Henry [Bennet] began to make a cupboard to go down to the River house." Henry Bennet (1779–1852) was visiting from Mount Lebanon

■■ WILLIAM YEARSLEY (1776–1846), "August 28, 1818, William and Timothy began to make the benches for the new tables &c."

■■■ DAVID TRAIN (born 1777), listed as carpenter in 1855 census

■■■ JESSE WELLS (1778–1876), listed as carpenter in 1850 census

■ FREEGIFT WELLS (1785–1871), see pl. 96. Lived in Union Village, Ohio, 1836–43

■■■ ISSACHAR BATES, JR. (1790–1875), listed as carpenter and joiner in 1850 census

■■■ JOHN HUGHES (b. 1794), listed as joiner in 1850 census

■■■ JOSEPH LEFUMA (1794–1868), listed as carpenter in 1850 census

■■ TIMOTHY CLEMENT (b. 1798), "May 16, 1815, Timothy built a cupboard for Goodell."

■■■ OLIVER PRENTISS (1798–1885), listed as carpenter in 1850 census

■■ GROVE DOLE (b. 1802), "April 17, 1828, Grove is making a flour chest."

■■ EPHRAIM PRENTISS (1802–1877), "September 10, 1828, Ephraim has been plaining shelves for the milk house."

■■ DANIEL BOLER (1804–1892), in Avery, "A Register of Incidents and Events," February 27, 1860, "Elder Daniel and Giles [Avery] work at the counter in our shop."

■■■ CHARLES J. PRATER (b. 1806), listed as carpenter in 1855 census

■■■ SMITH TAYLOR (b. 1808–left 1855), listed as joiner in 1850 census

■■■ CHANNING PRENTISS (1809–1859), listed as joiner in 1850 census

■■■ GEORGE W. PEAVEY (b. 1811), listed as turner in 1855 census

■■■■ ABRAM ELLIS (1812–1887), in Andrews, *Religion in Wood*, p. 103

■■■ LOREN WICKS (1814–l. 1853), listed as carpenter and joiner in 1850 census. Worked at Mount Lebanon in 1848 according to "Domestic Occurrences," July 1848.

GILES AVERY (1815–1890), of Mount Lebanon, worked at Watervliet in the 1870s and 1880s making counters, cupboards, bureaus, and worktables, according to his pocket diaries

■■■ ROBERT BERNARD (b. 1818), listed as cabinetmaker in 1850 census

■ THOMAS WELLS (1819–l.1854), see pl. 87

■■■ CYRUS BATES (1823–l. 1858), listed as carpenter in 1850 census

■■■ CHARLES SOULE (b. 1827), listed as turner in 1850 census

■■■ DAVID STEPHENS (b. 1828), listed as carpenter in 1850 census

■■ DAVID RICHARDSON (working 1832), "June 7, 1843 David Richardson has finished framing the joiners shop &c."

■■ THOMAS ALMOND (1847–l. 1867), "1858 apr 13: This morning the Elders gave me little Thomas Almond for an apprentice, & a fine boy he is to. I have made him a bench to stand on & set him to turning at my little lathe."

Freegift Wells's "Memorandum of Events," which he kept for most of his life, also describes his daily turning, carpentry, and cabinetmaking activities. During

below

78. Cupboard and Case of Drawers
c. 1830
Pine and poplar, with red paint
h 76½ w 48 d 21"
New York State Museum, Albany, #39.10.18

This majestic case piece derives much of its strength from the distinctive applied bracket base, which is unusually tall and broad. The base stands away from the side of the case due to the addition of a covering cove molding and a spacer board between the case and bracket feet. Raised panels punctuate the doors, a detail unknown on other Shaker pieces. The panels, however, are similar in concept and construction to the raised stiles found on pl. 79, although they are used in a different way. A wide cornice, consisting of a quarter-round, fillet, and cove molding, completes this fine case piece, which has graduated drawers.

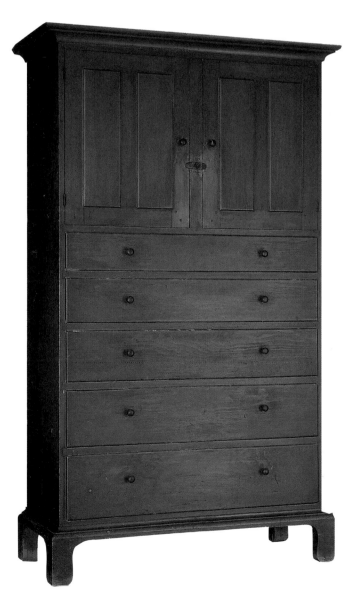

79. Cupboard and Case of Drawers
c. 1840
Pine, with red wash, brass escutcheon and hinges, and iron locks
h 76½ w 48 d 19½"
Private collection

Departing from common shop practice in the world or other Shaker communities, some Watervliet craftsmen built raised stiles shaped like drawer fronts on either side of their cupboard doors. The same distinctive feature is found on two related pieces, one in a mustard color in the collection of Canterbury Shaker Village (acc. no. 84.4266) and another with half-width drawers, frame-and-panel sides, and cut feet in the collection of the Shaker Museum, Old Chatham, New York (acc. no. 14357).

This cupboard is heavily built, with rails dovetailed into very thick pine sides. The unusually thick cornice is molded out of the case top itself. The drawers are graduated in pairs as follows: the bottom two measure a very deep 9¼ inches; the next pair 7 inches; the second tier 6 inches; and a single one at the top a very slender 3¼ inches—presumably built for some specific purpose. Three of the drawers and one of the doors are fitted with locks.

---

80. Cupboard and Case of Drawers

c. 1830
Pine
h 85 w 52½ d 24½"
Collection of the Golden Lamb Inn, Lebanon, Ohio

The craftsman of this great piece of Shaker furniture developed a very strong design by combining several diverse elements, including the wide, built-up cornice molding uniting a quarter-round and cove with fillet, the paired-door configuration, the row of small drawers below, as well as the double arc cutout on the case side with center dropped panel on the front. Furthermore, the small drawers were extended to the side of the case, in contrast to the doors above, which are contained within the wide stiles.

Although the unusual dropped panel is similar to that on an Enfield, New Hampshire, desk in a private collection (pl. 205), there are no other shared construction characteristics to suggest a New England origin. In fact, this piece defies easy classification, but its heavy case construction, similar to that found on pl. 79, and the use of a bead on the case edge and around the small drawers point to Watervliet as the likeliest community of origin.

The internal layout suggests this piece was designed for use in an office. A large lock secures the top doors, each of which covers six pigeonholes and one shelf. Two small drawers are fitted with a secret compartment to the rear. In the lower bank of drawers, a small metal tab embedded in the rail directly above the lock is elevated by the lock bolt and seats into a slot cut into the bottom edge of the upper drawer front.

81. Cupboard

c. 1840
Pine and red wash
h 71½ w 43 d 19⅝"
Shaker Museum and Library, Old Chatham, New York, #400

Very simple, this cupboard is beautifully designed and executed. The wide case stiles and slender double-panel doors create a strong vertical orientation. The case is supported by a simple concave cut foot on both the front and sides. The complex cornice molding, consisting of a quarter-round, fillet with a cove, and astragal, and the beaded edge around both the sides of the case and the edge of one door contribute decorative effects.

82. Bookcase

c. 1830
Pine and poplar or basswood, with brass escutcheons and iron hinges and locks
h 87 w 59 d 17⅜"
Private collection

Traditionally known as a hymnal cupboard, this one-piece bookcase was probably placed in or very near the meeting room at Watervliet. The use of glass in Shaker cupboards such as this seems to have been reserved primarily for the storage of hymnals.

The top of the case is finished with a graceful ovolo with cove cornice molding suitable for a piece that held important music or reference books. The craftsman also made extensive use of the quirk bead on the exterior edge of both the doors and the case frame. A simple concave curve in the bottom rail forms the foot. It is surprising that the maker did not align the door glazing or muntins with the shelves behind, as he left an almost unusable small top shelf.

83. Counter

c. 1840
Pine, with red and black grain painting
h 31 w 74 d 35½"
New York State Museum, Albany, #39.10.7

This Watervliet counter exhibits a number of atypical features. Drop leaves, providing additional work surfaces, are commonly hinged on the back with either crane or pullout supports rather than, as here, hinged on both case ends, supported with pullout slides. The more common plank ends are here replaced by a frame-and-panel structure. Most obvious is the strong painted finish, which was probably applied by the Shakers themselves. While diary and journal entries document the use of grain painting on building interiors,[14] this decorative work is one of the boldest known examples on Shaker freestanding furniture. The provenance is impeccable, as the counter was a gift to the New York State Museum by the Watervliet South Family in 1939.

84. Food Cupboard

c. 1820
Pine, with red paint and porcelain knobs
h 85¼ w 56 d 21"
New York State Museum, Albany, #39.10.14

Known as a food storage cupboard, this large case piece, like the trestle table pl. 91, may more closely reflect Canadian prototypes than influences from Mount Lebanon. This is not surprising, considering the large number of Canadian converts that joined the community, according to the 1850 census rolls. The form, referred to as a "food locker" in *The Early Furniture of French Canada*,[15] incorporates a barred door that provided ventilation for the food stored inside. The overall design is dominated by the unusual arched-slat wooden door and the large built-up cornice molding. The cupboard door on the bottom used to be centrally located and was shifted to the side for some unknown reason by the Shakers. The New York State Museum acquired this piece, with a South Family history, directly from the Watervliet community.

85. Case of Drawers

c. 1840
Pine, with fruitwood knobs, brass escutcheon,
and lock
h 75¼ w 40⅞ d 19¼"
Private collection

While observers of American furniture are accustomed to pieces, whether worldly or Shaker, exhibiting classical proportions and graduated drawers, the Shaker craftsman who constructed this case did not follow traditional practices. Drawer graduation provides a vertical balance that is conspicuously absent in this piece, and the storage unit built into the West Family Dwelling House pl. 77. The shaping and the bulk of both the cornice and base is typical of designs produced at Watervliet. In fact, the current owner acquired this piece from a family in Albany who purchased most of their furnishings directly from the Shaker community there. While the dovetailed base is a construction feature commonly found on high-style worldly furniture, it is less frequently seen on Shaker pieces. Nontraditional construction or design details such as nongraduated drawers and unusual case construction seem prevalent in Watervliet (see pl. 86). It is unclear if these characteristics point to the practices of a shop, a small group of workers, or a single craftsman.

86. Case of Drawers

Attributed to Freegift Wells (1785–1871)
c. 1850
Pine
h 75¼ w 41¼ d 19½"
New York State Museum, Albany, #30.2.110

This case came directly to the museum from the Watervliet Shakers, with an oral attribution to Brother Freegift Wells. The case is not of true frame-and-panel construction, as the maker utilized corner posts without top or bottom rails to complete the case frame, an unusual method of assembly. The tongue-and-groove planks that make up the side panels are primitively nailed to the drawer supports. The flat-faced, threaded knobs of the nongraduated drawers (see pl. 85) reveal a distinct Ohio influence (see pl. 266); Brother Freegift spent the years from 1836 to 1843 at Union Village.

87. Desk

Thomas Wells (1819–left 1854)
1839
Stamped on top of drawer face: T.J. WELLS.
WATERVLIET. APRIL 7. 1839.
Curly maple, cherry, and pine, with walnut
knobs, mother-of-pearl circular escutcheon and
diamond-shaped escutcheons (not original), and
brass interior drawer knobs, pull-up rings, and
side handles (not original)
h 28⅛ w 28 d 18¼"
Private collection
Photograph: courtesy Leigh Keno

The maker's stamps on the top face of one of the drawers identify this very worldly looking desk as the only presently known Thomas Wells piece. As Thomas Wells was nephew and apprentice (from 1830 to 1840, when he left for the world before returning briefly in 1854) of Brother Freegift Wells,[16] the similarity of the case work on his desk and that of his master (see pl. 86) is not surprising. This is evident in the unorthodox frame construction made up of thin, flat lumber without top and bottom rails. Like pl. 86, it gives the appearance of frame-and-panel construction without actually using that method. The hinged top is swung forward to rest on pull-out supports. With the desk in its writing position, the small interior, containing several drawers and pigeonholes, is pulled up into position.

88. Desk

Attributed to Freegift Wells (1785–1871)
c. 1860
Cherry, butternut, pine, and ash, with porcelain
knobs and escutcheon and brass lock
h 40⅝ w 30 d 22⅛"
Collection Fran and Herb Kramer

In its use of several woods, frame-and-panel construction, the size and boxlike form of the case, this fall-front desk resembles the sewing cases attributed to Brother Freegift Wells at the Art Complex Museum, Duxbury, Massachusetts (acc. no. 30–18), and the Shaker Museum, Old Chatham, New York (acc. no. 4231),[17] down to the detail of the small pronounced molding and unusual escutcheons. A movable interior with six butternut drawers and a small compartment beneath an interior trapdoor lid are situated just in front of the writing surface, that is, the open fall-front desk lid, which is hinged so that it stands proud of the case face when closed. When opened, it rests on unique round ash rods fitted with porcelain knobs. The graduated drawers in the case are dovetailed, although the small interior drawers are simply nailed. The case sits on short, minimally turned legs, which were once fitted with casters, like the sewing cases attributed to Freegift Wells.

89. Sewing Desk
Probably Watervliet
c. 1860
Hardwood and pine
Private collection
Photograph: courtesy John Keith Russell Antiques, Inc.

90. "A Mender of Clothing of the Church Family"
1873
Woodcut engraving by J. Becker
Published in Frank Leslie's Illustrated Newspaper, *vol. 37, September 13, 1873, pp. 12–14*

This case piece is unlike any other surviving sewing desk. The mass of the case, which rests flat on the floor, is offset visually by the three vertical panels below the four drawers in the front. Two drawers, accessed from the side, occupy the space behind the panels. The small dimensions of the frame also help to alleviate the bulk created by the absence of feet. The light framework with the look of frame-and-panel construction recalls the work of both Freegift Wells—the case of drawers, pl. 86—and that of his nephew and apprentice Thomas Wells (pl. 87). The gallery with its four drawers and open central section is fastened to the overhanging top by tenons fitted into mortises cut into the surface. Published in a photograph by N. E. Baldwin in *House and Garden* magazine in March 1945, this sewing desk had an additional twelve small drawers fitted into the open central section of the gallery plus eight drawers set below the existing gallery. These were likely a later addition removed since the photograph was taken.

The sewing desk in the print, executed by Joseph Becker, bears some resemblance to this style of case without legs. Here, it is being used in a workroom to hold sewing accessories and what looks like a chalkboard or a mirror while a sister seated in a rocker mends clothing for the Church Family.

91. Trestle Table
c. 1820
Maple and pine
h 29 w 28 d 80"
Private collection

Like the food storage cupboard with barred door (pl. 84), which reflects a Canadian more than Mount Lebanon influence, the Watervliet trestle tables relate more closely to refectory tables from Quebec than to their counterparts at Mount Lebanon.[18] This observation gains support from census material that indicates a small number of converts of French Canadian origin. More specifically, the vertical base member is shaped like a pilaster, rectangular in cross section, with a quarter-round base or capital added to increase the stability where the mortise-and-tenon shoulder is butted to the simply arched foot or the tapered cross member. The craftsman selectively beveled several edges, tenoned the longitudinal stretcher, which is dropped somewhat below the top, all the way through the upright, and fastened it with two heavy dowel pins. Another related form used at Watervliet[19] has a broad, vase-shaped vertical.

Thomas Brown, a onetime member of the Shaker community at Watervliet, wrote the following description of dining room practices in 1812:

> The brethren and sisters generally eat at the same time at two long tables placed in the kitchen, men at one and women at the other; during which time they sit on benches, and are all silent. They go to their meals walking in order, one directly after the other; the head of the family or Elder, takes the lead of the men, and one called Elder Sister takes the lead of the women. Several women are employed in cooking and waiting on the table—they are commonly relieved weekly by others.[20]

92. Blanket Box
c. 1840
Pine
h 57 w 41½ d 18¼"
Collection Mr. and Mrs. Wm. Brooks

Some experts on American furniture speculate that the form of the case of drawers evolved from the lidded blanket chest, with the gradual addition of one, two, then three or more drawers over time.[21] This tall box with drawers represents a mid-nineteenth-century Shaker rendition of the earlier seventeenth- and eighteenth-century prototypes.

This piece is a magnificent storage case, for a number of reasons. With its unusual height, it is probably the tallest of Shaker storage boxes. Its simple rectilinear form is offset by the dovetailed applied bracket with concave shape, the lid molding, and the small pulls. The box has a strong provenance, as Faith and Edward Deming Andrews, early collectors of Shaker furniture who developed a personal relationship with the Shakers, gave this piece in payment for some work to the photographer William F. Winter, whose pictures appear in the Andrews' book on the Shakers *Religion in Wood*.

Benjamin Youngs, Sr. (1736–1818)

Several of the tall clocks of Benjamin Youngs, Sr., for example, those dated 1767, 1797, 1806, 1809, and 1814, show a remarkable development of style, both prior to his joining the Shakers and after becoming a Believer. Although Brother Benjamin may not have personally produced the cases that house his fine brass movements, he was certainly aware of prevailing styles and may have influenced the design of the case. As his father was a clock maker in Connecticut, he was certainly exposed to the more fashionable furniture of the urban New England areas where the Queen Anne and Chippendale forms were in vogue.

An awareness of contemporary worldly design is clearly reflected in Youngs's 1767 clock. The case is fashioned of walnut and adorned with a broken arch bonnet supported by turned columns with cast-brass capitals. The base is supported by an ogee bracket foot with a shaped and applied burl overlay panel. A spectacular brass and silver dial displays the name "B. Yongs." The case mandrels and the elaborately styled engraving and calendar dial place this clock among the best of high-style Albany furniture.

Benjamin's 1797 tall clock was quite obviously made for a different clientele. Marked "Watervt." (Watervliet, New York), the case reflects the rural and simpler tastes of a smaller community. This timepiece was built when Benjamin was living next to the Shakers as a neighbor with his own nuclear family.

The date 1806 is written, probably in the handwriting of his nephew Isaac Newton Youngs (1793–1865), on the cherry tall clock in the Mount Lebanon Shaker Collection (pl. 93), which stood in the 1816 Church Family Dwelling House there until 1991. Built while Benjamin was a member of the Church Family of the Watervliet, New York, community, this case is notably simplified in its design and decoration. The more fashionable elements have been removed so that it fits comfortably with the Shaker community's plain, pared-down furniture style. The base stands on rather delicate cut feet, and the body with beveled corners contains a rather wide rectangular door. A smooth concave molding provides a transition between the waist body and both the base and bonnet sections. The top of the plain, round top bonnet is visually supported by plainly turned columns without the usual brass embellishments. Unlike the two previous examples, characterized by broken arch bonnets, the top here is fully enclosed.

The tall case clock dated 1809 (pl. 94) has a square top bonnet with simple columns enclosing a painted dial with the maker's name enclosed in an oval. Aside from the transitional moldings to separate the base, body,

and bonnet sections, all traces of worldly adornments have been omitted.

One of Benjamin's last timepieces, dated 1814, is a dwarf tall clock standing only 54 inches high (pl. 76). There is very little variation in the width between the base, body, and bonnet sections, making it very rectangular in design. The only round elements are the circular dial and door glass. With this example, Benjamin took to an extreme the overall simplification of these notable cases.

93. Tall Clock

Benjamin Youngs, Sr. (1736–1818)
1806
Cherry, pine, and rosewood, with brass movement
h 83 w 19¼ d 9¼"
The Mount Lebanon Shaker Collection

The case of this clock is virtually identical to an undated, unsigned clock in a private collection. Both clocks share the same basic proportions, although minor variations exist in the case measurements. Rather than eliminating all of the decorative elements on the case, the craftsman reduced them to a minimum, including the arched pediment, simply turned columns, cove-shaped top and bottom waist moldings, beveled waist sides, and cut feet.

94. Tall Clock

Benjamin Youngs, Sr. (1736–1818)
1809
Painted on front of dial: Benjamin Youngs Water Vliet.
Written on back of face: B.Y. Fecit/1809/B.Y. age 72/Oct. 4, 1809
Cherry and pine, with red stain and brass movement with alarm
h 81 w 20 d 9⅞"
Private collection

This and another fine related clock[22] represent rather traditional, although simplified cases. The Shaker influence on Brother Benjamin is found in the painted dial, which, aside from the maker's name and a simple oval surrounding it, is exclusive of typical worldly decoration. Notably absent are any brass embellishments, veneer, inlay, or other superfluous details; only the moldings necessary to provide the transition between the base, body, and bonnet sections remain.

opposite

95. Side Chair

c. 1840
Stamped on front post: SIC
Curly maple and splint, with chrome yellow stain
h 40½ w 16½ d 11½"
Collection Fran and Herb Kramer

Carefully designed and well-crafted elongated pommels, graduated beveled back slats, and sturdy turnings characterize most Watervliet chairs. This fine example retains a warm chrome yellow finish and the abbreviation SIC (for sick) stamped on the front post, which designated its use in the infirmary. Other chairs are stamped PHY and 1840.

96. Armed Rocker

Attributed to Freegift Wells
c. 1840
Maple and tape (not original), with red and
black grain painting
h 41¾ w 19⅝ d 17⅝"
Hancock Shaker Village, Pittsfield,
Massachusetts, #80-72

More than any other cabinetmaker, Freegift Wells provided documentation on the Shaker chair-making process. For example, in his "Memorandum of Events" on May 22, 1819, he noted, "Made 26 chairs this week which is 10 short of a weeks work. It is a comfortable days work to make 6 chairs after posts & rounds are turned and the backs bent. I have done it repeatedly." This armed chair exhibits the pommel forms typical of his work. Brother Freegift's back slats do not have the graduated arrangement of beveled slats more characteristic of Watervliet chairs. As shown here, the maker used much thicker than normal rockers and fastened them into the bottom of the posts with a tenon. Several of his chairs retain a decorative red and black grain painting.

Hancock Bishopric

THE BISHOPRIC LOCATED in western Massachusetts and Connecticut was formed by the communities of Hancock, Massachusetts (1790–1960), Tyringham, Massachusetts (1792–1875), and Enfield, Connecticut (1792–1917). The ministry seat was located at Hancock, which at its peak in 1830 consisted of six families and 338 members, situated on two thousand acres of property.[1] The Enfield society was founded on the homestead of Joseph Meacham (see pp. 19, 23), who succeeded Father James Whittaker as the head of the Shaker ministry in 1787. The community eventually was organized into five families and grew to 113 members by 1830.[2] The small community of Tyringham, with fewer than a hundred members, was the first of the three villages to close.

Sister Rebecca Clark offered a glimpse of community life at Hancock during the eighteenth century in the following recollection, written when she was eighty-five years old:

> In the year 1791, at the age of 21 I was gathered into the Church at Hancock, Mass. . . . There were nearly a hundred in the family where I lived. When the shell was sounded (a token to rise in the morning) we all quickly rose; and we had but fifteen minutes to dress and get ready for meeting. Fourteen of us slept in one room. When we arose, some packed the beds on one another; some swept the room; others got water to wash in. After our morning meeting, we went to our several employments. Some to getting breakfast for the brethren, as they ate first. Our buildings were small and we had to eat and live accordingly. We worked diligently, early and late, and lived sparingly. Our beds, bedding, and clothing that we brought with us, we all divided among the members of the family, as equally as could be. We had but few feather beds, our beds were mostly straw; and we made them on the floor. Many of us slept three on one bed; and when we washed our bedding, we had to dry it the same day, and put it on at night. We were all much engaged to build buildings, and to

97. Tripod Stand

Enfield, Connecticut
c. 1830
Maple and pine
h 24 diameter of top 16¾"
Private collection
Photograph: courtesy David A. Schorsch, Inc.

This unusual stand is noteworthy for its pared-down design and diminutive proportions, evident in the thin top with sharply beveled edge, the minimally turned and tapering pedestal, and the extremely delicate snake legs. The two very finely dovetailed drawers, suspended under a circular rather than a square or rectangular top, may have been added on by the Shakers themselves shortly after the piece was completed. This maple stand has been attributed to Enfield based on the turning detail just above the leg-to-stem joint, which is similar to that on other Enfield, Connecticut, stands.

right
Trustees' Office, Hancock, c. 1895. Private collection

■■ WILLIAM CLARK (1776–1837), in Ely, "Daily Dairy"

■■ SAMUEL CALVIN ELY (1780–1816), joiner, carpenter, and chair maker, in Ely, "Daily Diary"

■■■■ PHILIP BURLINGAME (1794–1866), chair maker, in Andrews, *Religion in Wood*, p. 103

■■■■ RICHARD WILCOX (1815–1884), from Enfield, made chairs for Hancock, in Andrews, *Community Industries*, p. 247

■ THOMAS DAMON (1819–1880), joiner at Enfield and later at Hancock, see pl. 103

■■■■ GEORGE WILCOX (1819–1910), in Andrews, *Shaker Furniture*, p. 48

■■■ THOMAS FISHER (1823–1902), listed as carpenter in 1880 census and see p. 192 and pls. 135, 137–40

■■■■ LORENZO BROOKS (1829–1870), in Andrews, *Shaker Furniture*, p. 48

■■■■ NELSON CHASE (b. 1830), in Andrews, *Shaker Furniture*, p. 48

■■■■ JOHN COPLEY (1841–1908), a maple and butternut deaconesses' desk, pictured in the Women's Auxiliary, *The Shakers: An Exhibition Concerning Their Furniture . . .* , no. 8

■■■ WINT WARNER (b. 1843), listed as carpenter in 1870 census

TYRINGHAM

■■■■ ALBERT BATTLES (d. 1895), in Andrews, *Shaker Furniture*, p. 47

One of the earliest Enfield craftsmen is Calvin Ely, who kept a diary between 1813 and 1816 documenting his activities. During this period he sawed lumber, including walnut, for chair rungs, turned chair posts, and completed a number of different projects, including a sister's workbench, a clock case, and a cherry chest and tables with Brother William (Clark). He was also involved in the "upbuilding" of the Church Family Dwelling House, which involved removing the dormer roof and adding a floor. Between October and December 1815 he and Brother William completed the fifty-seven cupboard doors in the "boddy of the house."[12]

In December 1846 Thomas Damon wrote a letter to George Wilcox that describes an unusual desk the former had made, giving a rare glimpse of Shaker cabinetmakers at work:

> Not having anything of importance to write about, I will proceed to comply with your request respecting the desk although I fear you will hardly obtain 5 cts. worth of information. Length 23 in. Width 21⅛". as wide as the bench would admit. Depth, back side 4½" in. front side 2¾" including lid & bottom. The desk is made precisely as any common desk, and slides in & out exactly like one of the drawers. When it is shoved in, it slides sufficiently far to admit of a false drawer face (about ½ in. in thickness) which is hung with brass butts so as to turn down to admit the desk's sliding out & in freely: this and all the rest that I have said relative to it, would no doubt have occurred to your mind, but as you requested the particulars I have been thus explicit. You will please suit yourself as to size and formation, "For where there is no law there is no transgression."[13]

The location of Elder Thomas's desk described above is unknown, and it is uncertain whether Brother George actually made a similar piece based on this description. However, the letter provides insight into the sharing of ideas on furniture construction among Shaker craftsmen.

Careful examination of handwriting, lettering style, and dovetailing further confirms the connection between several cabinetmakers working at Enfield and

Hancock. A study of signed pieces reveals that Abner Allen and Grove Wright were contemporaries who employed a distinctive joinery technique that likely was passed from one to the other during ministerial trips between the two communities. More specifically, their furniture is characterized by tapered drawer sides, that is, the wood is thicker at the bottom of the drawer side than it is at the top edge. Although both craftsmen died before the Civil War, later cabinetmakers working in the Victorian Shaker tradition, such as Thomas Fisher, carried on this practice at Enfield. While not all furniture produced in the Hancock Bishopric exhibits this peculiar element of drawer construction, the technique has been found in the work of identified (Wright, Allen, and Fisher) and unknown makers and defines a unique shop practice.

Aside from exhibiting distinctive joinery methods, Hancock Bishopric craftsmen used a significant amount of butternut in their furniture, along with a grouping of woods including pine, maple, and cherry. In addition, they showed a preference for highly figured grain. Victorian-era craftsmen, such as Thomas Fisher, expanded the wood selection to include chestnut, oak, ash, and walnut in a variety of combinations. He and other late-nineteenth-century cabinetmakers also adopted a style highly influenced by worldly taste. This is evident in the remodeled Trustees' Office at Hancock Shaker Village. Here the interior woodwork is characterized by a dramatic combination of light and dark woods with a clear finish, a style based on worldly models rather than the earlier Shaker practice of painting or staining; a reliance on applied moldings and cornices and built-up corner columns; and ornamental hardware including commercially made cast-iron or porcelain pulls.

Virtually all of the known furniture from the Hancock Bishopric was produced at either Hancock or Enfield. In 1876, the Mount Lebanon ministry traded the Tyringham property plus other Shaker lands in Wisconsin, Michigan, and New York State to purchase a timber lot in Pennsylvania.[14] The remaining members moved to Hancock and Enfield, presumably with their personal belongings.[15] The distribution of other Believers' furnishings is described in an article that appeared in the New York *Evening Post* twelve years after the closing:

> This whole estate [that is, the Church Family property] passed some years ago into the ownership of Dr. Joseph Jones, a Pennsylvanian, curiously enough of Quaker stock. Dr. Jones has allowed the Lenox people to gratify their fancy for antique furniture, and many treasures have been removed hence, but enough remains to preserve the character of the place.[16]

Although the bishopric organization at Hancock was dissolved in 1893,[17] the two remaining communities continued. Enfield closed in 1917, and its property was acquired by the state of Connecticut for a prison. Several buildings, including the Infirmary and the Trustees' Office and their contents, were destroyed by inmates, and other pieces, considered unneeded, were burned by the prison authorities. The 1876 Church Family Dwelling House became the central cell block, and after it was condemned by the state it was torn down in the mid-1960s.[18] At the time of the closing in 1917, the remaining six members and their possessions joined the Mount Lebanon community.[19] When the headquarters of the United Society of Believers at Mount Lebanon was disbanded in 1947, the remaining six members there relocated to Hancock. Here, the family carried on until 1960, when the Central Ministry, then at Canterbury, decided to close the Hancock community, and the property was sold to become a museum.[20] In order to supplement the community's rapidly declining income and to dispose of

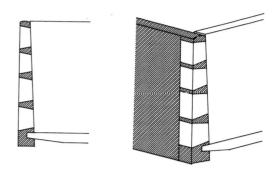

In this representation of the tapered drawer side, the shaded portion is the side of the drawer; the rest represents the back of the drawer and the drawer bottom; the vertical line is a scribe line. The drawing on the left presents the rear view showing a cross section of the tapered drawer side; on the right, a view of the rear corner, showing the dovetail joint pins on the rear.

unneeded furniture during the twentieth century, the Hancock Shakers sold a great deal of furniture to private collectors, many of whom recorded the oral history of their acquisitions. Twentieth-century photographs taken either by the Shakers themselves or by William F. Winter (1899–1939), whose camera preserved interior views, are instrumental in identifying the origins of specific pieces.

Consequently, the surviving pieces that can be documented either by construction, design, or provenance were produced over a long period of time and represent a wide variety of forms. The built-ins throughout the Church Family Dwelling House provide a basis for analyzing Hancock furniture dating from as early as the 1830s. Distinctive features incorporated here include cupboards with slightly convex door panels, cases with beaded edges, drawers with tapered sides, and a color scheme that often juxtaposed chrome yellow and red surface pigment. Perhaps because of the sheer number of these storage units in the brothers' and sisters' retiring rooms in this dwelling, few freestanding chests of drawers were made, which may explain their conspicuous absence today.

Several finely built counters survive today. The design and construction of these large case pieces are associated with Grove Wright or his shop practice; they display drawers with tapered sides and a facade with a deliberate asymmetry. Some feature dramatically figured woods.

One form typically attributed to Hancock, through a historic photograph and oral history, is the diminutive sewing case. Although they share a similar function, these small cases vary considerably in layout. They may contain drawers and/or doors and drop leaves; frame-and-panel, apron, or plank sides; and turned or square, tapered legs.

The double drop-leaf table represents another characteristic Hancock furniture form, of which several examples exist. These cherry pieces are often very small in size, with narrow leaves and one or two drawers. It is possible that they were used in a similar way to the four-legged tables commonly found at other communities but notably unrepresented here.

Similar tripod stands were produced at both Hancock and Enfield, due to the physical proximity and the close working relationship between the two communities. While both circular- and square-topped stands originated in the Hancock Bishopric, those with rectangular surfaces and ovolo corners, baluster-shaped standards over a narrow convex collar, and a leg-to-stem mortise-and-tenon joint, rather than the common dovetail joint, are typical of Hancock.

No chairs have been documented with a clear Hancock origin. As the community was so close to Mount Lebanon, which produced a great number of chairs, it is possible that Hancock members purchased chairs from other communities to suit their needs rather than manufacturing their own. The situation is somewhat different at Enfield, located much further away, where side chairs and rockers with a strong community history exist. Surviving examples exhibit elongated pommels over a sharp concave collar, strongly contoured slats, and a preference for highly figured maple.

This use of dramatically figured maple is particularly associated with known Enfield craftsmanship, although it may represent the work of only one or two craftsmen. Due to the efforts of a private collector, a grouping of furniture that was purchased at Hancock in the 1920s, after the Enfield community closed, was recently returned to Hancock Shaker Village. Many of the pieces, attributed to Abner Allen, exhibit typical construction features associated with his work, including drawers with tapered sides; raised- rather than flat-panel cupboard doors; a flared gallery; and the extensive use of figured maple.

opposite above

98. Built-in Cupboards and Case of Drawers, Trustees' Office

1895
Butternut, maple, and walnut, with porcelain knobs
Hancock Shaker Village, Pittsfield, Massachusetts

This built-in storage unit in the Trustees' Office at Hancock represents the Shakers' late-nineteenth-century efforts to modernize their facilities. Originally built in 1813, the Trustees' Office was enlarged and redesigned several times prior to 1895, when it was transformed into a high Victorian structure complete with tower, Palladian windows, and porches. Worldly interior styling is evident here in the dramatic combination of different woods, elaborate moldings, and decorative porcelain knobs.

A recorded explanation for this ornate remodeling appears in a brief entry in the June 1895 edition of the Shaker magazine *The Manifesto* (p. 138): "It has been decided to enlarge our Trustees' Office on the West or front side. On May 1st, work commenced on the foundation. Carpenters are also at work on the window frames and other work as is to be done in the shop. A description of the addition can be given better at a later date."

According to a catalogue card in the Hancock Shaker Village Library, a Pittsfield contractor named Dillwyn C. Bedell was responsible for the renovation of the building, but it was not recorded if he did the interior work. However, there is no known written documentation to illuminate the rationale behind this work or the details of its execution. With the population of the entire community declining to fewer than fifty members, it is possible that the Shakers' motivation for such drastic changes was an attempt to alter their image. If they could show the world that theirs was an up-to-date, modern community, more people might be encouraged to join.

One can only speculate as to who might have been responsible for creating this new look. The appearance of chamfered edges is a characteristic of the 1890s woodwork in the remodeled Trustees' Office. The use of columns for the case corners appears frequently in the late-nineteenth-century work of Enfield, Connecticut, cabinetmaker Thomas Fisher (see pl. 137). Verbal documentation from Sister Martha Corsin of Hancock suggests the individual most probably involved in supporting the remodeling effort was Joseph Slingerland of Union Village, Ohio (1843–1920; see p. 295). However, factual and logistical data do not corroborate this speculation. Appointed to the ministry at Union Village in 1889, where he remained until 1902, Slingerland was responsible for the massive improvements to the Trustees' Office between 1891 and 1892, adding marble floors and elaborate woodwork. He was also heavily involved in attempting to establish a community in Georgia between 1898 and 1902. Furthermore, he was extremely ill during the summer of 1895, and although brief visits to the Eastern societies in 1894 and 1897 are recorded, there is no current evidence to suggest that he traveled east in 1895 to duplicate his efforts in the Trustees' Office at Hancock.[21]

99. Built-in Corner Cupboard, Church Family Dwelling House Kitchen
1830
Pine, with red stain and cast-brass latches
h 91 w 28 d 32½" across front face
Hancock Shaker Village, Pittsfield, Massachusetts

The two identical corner cupboards on the opposite, or outside wall, seem to be original to the Church Family Dwelling House kitchen, erected in 1830. Although the particular craftsman responsible for them is unknown, several design and construction features relate these units to the other first-floor built-ins (compare with pl. 101). The doors have rounded panels and cast-brass latches, the edges of the cases are decorated with a floor-to-ceiling beading, and the center rail is tenoned into the frame and secured with a single large pin. The interior of the top cupboard is fitted with three fixed shelves.

According to Elder William Deming's letter to Elder Benjamin Seth Youngs, dated January 8, 1832, "The dining room is at the South end [of the ground floor of the Dwelling House] with accommodations for 80 persons to sit down at one time. . . .The victuals is conveyed up into the dining room by means of two sliding cupboards." The dumbwaiter cupboard described here is still located in the far left corner of the room.[22]

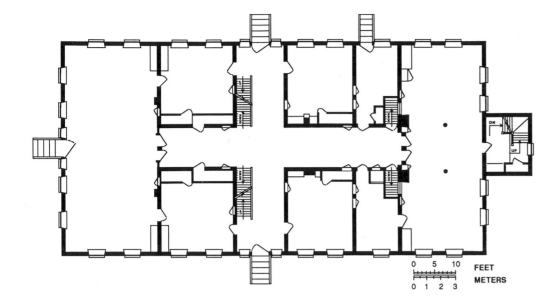

0 5 10 FEET

0 1 2 3 METERS

100. Church Family Dwelling Blueprint

The brick Church Family Dwelling House at Hancock was erected in 1830 to house ninety-four Believers.[23] According to surviving documentation, Elder William Deming (1779–1849) designed the building and executed both the mason and joiner work. In a letter to Elder Benjamin Seth Youngs (1774–1855) dated January 1832, he provided a detailed description of many unique features, such as the built-in units: "There are 100 large doors including outside and closet doors; 240 Cupboard doors—369 drawers— These are placed in the corners of the rooms and by the sides of the chimneys. The drawers are faced with butternut and handsomely stained—they take up little room, and are not to be cleaned under."[24]

The blueprint of the building shown here graphically illustrates some of the many storage units, which Elder William described as follows: "The second loft of garrets is done off with four large rooms. Six large clothes presses with a hall that runs East and West and crosses from North to South and two back rooms that extends the whole length of the house. On the third loft there is ten rooms with closets adjoining each. . . . The second loft has ten rooms with closets. . . ."

It is evident in William Deming's description that he refers to the built-in cupboard and drawer units throughout the building as "presses" and the doors with hanging storage as "closets." The arrangement and placement of these different units vary somewhat from floor to floor (see pl. 101, p. 54).

101. Built-in Cupboard, Case of Drawers, and Closet, Room #7, Church Family Dwelling House
Attributed to Grove Wright (1789–1861)
1830
Pine and butternut, with fruitwood and porcelain knobs, ocher and red stain, and cast-brass and forged-iron latches
case section: h 107 w 43 (drawers); 22"
(cupboard)
Hancock Shaker Village, Pittsfield, Massachusetts

The built-in storage units throughout the first and second floors of the brick dwelling share common design and construction features. These include the combination of a pine case originally stained ocher with butternut drawers and pine cupboard doors stained red, as well as cast-brass "spiral spring catches."[25] Furthermore, the case rails are tenoned and pinned, the pine door panels were slightly rounded with a hand plane, and the outside of the case is defined by a beaded edge. The case is articulated by a small half-round molding, 5/16 inch in diameter, between the cupboard and drawer sections.

The details of the drawer construction—tapered sides, rounded top edges, and chamfered drawer fronts—are identical in the rest of the built-in units on the first and second floors of the Church Family Dwelling House and are associated with Grove Wright (see pl. 103). Drawer parts are numbered in pencil on the inside corners in Grove Wright's typical manner to facilitate assembly.

The overall asymmetrical configuration of drawer unit, cupboard section, and closet varies considerably in different rooms of the dwelling house. Here, in a retiring room designed to house four or more people, the single cupboard over four short and six graduated drawers is distinctly separated from the narrow three-door cupboard by a chimney built into the wall. The closet behind, fitted with three rows of peg rail, is not large enough to accommodate any movable furniture—a storage space very different from the clothes rooms in the Centre Family Dwelling House at Pleasant Hill (see pl. 284). In Meeting Room 4 at Hancock, the format was clearly conceived and executed as a single storage system, with the case of drawers and cupboards built as one. Another distinct arrangement is seen in Room 16, where the facades of the side-by-side units are staggered and are set out from the wall several inches, although there seems to be no structural reason for this atypical layout.

A built-in case of drawers and cupboards on the fourth floor of the same building (see p. 54) shares a similar look, especially with its striking combination of chrome yellow paint and red wash. However, variations in dovetailing and handwriting suggest these units were made by other, unidentified craftsmen.

Grove Wright (1789–1861)

Despite the absence of surviving written records, recently discovered physical evidence has come to light on several signed pieces to help identify a group of furniture produced by Hancock Bishopric cabinetmakers, including Grove Wright. These distinctive construction features include tapered drawer sides with rounded top edges on both sides and back. Although it is not known why these craftsmen assembled drawers in this manner, the technique was probably used to visually lighten the drawers without sacrificing strength. Among the Shakers, this distinctive joinery method is unique to furniture produced at Hancock, Massachusetts, and Enfield, Connecticut. While these idiosyncratic joinery details are readily identifiable, their origins are not yet known. Although existing documentation does not indicate where or when this style of construction

began, at least one important piece of high-style furniture at the Henry Francis du Pont Winterthur Museum with tapered drawer sides, dated 1780–1800, can be traced to the Litchfield County area.[26]

Not all of the furniture makers in the Hancock Bishopric produced furniture with tapered drawer sides. However, although Grove Wright died before the Civil War, Thomas Fisher (1823–1902), a Victorian-era Shaker cabinetmaker at Enfield, seems to have carried on this shop practice.

The distinctive style of handwriting for both letters and numbers is also helpful in attributing pieces to Elder Grove. For example, the drawer parts (excluding the bottom) are marked in pencil in adjacent corners with pairs of numerals to facilitate assembly. Additional corresponding numbers appear on the top of each rail and the back of the drawer fronts to help relocate the drawer in its proper position in the case.

102. Counter

Attributed to Grove Wright (1789–1861)
c. 1830
Curly maple, cherry, and pine, with bone escutcheons
h 33 w 60 d 27⅞"
Collection Suzanne Courcier and Robert W. Wilkins

The quality of construction, the use of dramatically figured curly maple, and masterful proportions that convey grace despite the size of the piece make this counter one of the

masterpieces of Shaker design. The distinctive tapered drawer construction and related handwriting found on this counter strongly suggest the work of Elder Grove (see pl. 103).

The overall design, consisting of frame-and-panel construction with square posts over turned legs, represents an enlarged version of the typical small sewing case made for individual sisters at Hancock (see pl. 107). This and a nearly identical counter made of cherry in the collection of Mr. and Mrs. Jay N. Whipple, Jr.,[27] share the conscious vertical and horizontal asymmetry of three versus four drawers, which respectively occupy one- and two-thirds of the front of the case, and a rear drop leaf that is supported by two wooden sliding supports. A different but conceptually similar asymmetrical layout, with a cupboard door replacing the bank of four short drawers, is seen in the counter on p. 56, fig. 4, also attributed to Grove Wright. The addition of breadboard ends not only helps to keep the top flat but visually serves to obscure the end grain, a sophisticated treatment appropriate for such a distinctive piece of furniture. The overall quality of this tailoring counter raises the question of usage. Was such an exceptional piece of work furniture designed and constructed specifically for the ministry shop for the elders or eldresses working there?

The presence of three bone escutcheons on three drawers indicate that locks were used. Although the "Millennial Laws" forbade the application of locks for private possessions,[28] these locks may have been considered necessary to secure these drawers, which may have held special tools or materials for the tailoring trade.

103. Case of Drawers

Hancock or Enfield, Connecticut
Grove Wright (1789–1861) and Thomas
Damon (1819–1880)
1853
Written in ink on paper label glued to inside of
case: This Case of Drawers were made by/Elder
Grove and Brother Thomas and/placed here
thursday, January 13th, 1853./ It was the day
our Ministry expected to/return to the City of
Peace, but were detained/ on account of the
snow storm which/occured on that day.
Butternut and pine, with walnut knobs
h 84 w 37¹/₄ d 19"
Hancock Shaker Village, Pittsfield,
Massachusetts, #66–244

This signed and dated case of drawers serves as a kind of Rosetta stone in Shaker furniture. The construction features, makers' marks, and handwriting along with the paper label are instrumental in the attribution of an important group of Hancock pieces to Grove Wright, which includes two washstands (pl. 104), three counters (pl. 102), a box (pl. 105), a workbench, and the built-ins on the first two floors of the brick Church Family Dwelling House (pl. 101). From 1816 until his death in 1861, Grove Wright served continuously in the Hancock ministry. While living and working at the three communities in the bishopric (Hancock, Tyringham, and Enfield, Connecticut), he became known as a woodworker producing furniture, pails, and swifts for winding yarn.[29] In 1846, Thomas Damon, a joiner from Enfield, was appointed Elder Grove's assistant in the ministry. This tall case of drawers with detailed label indicates that Brother Thomas and Elder Grove worked together as cabinetmakers as well as sharing leadership responsibilities.

This piece exhibits the characteristic tapered drawer construction, lettering, and numbering system associated with Elder Grove's work. The identical style of writing is found in the twenty built-in cases of drawers on the first two floors of the 1830 Church Family Dwelling House (see pl. 101), which suggests they were made by the same hand.[30] The date 1831, found on one of the built-in drawers in the meeting room, indicates they were made one year after the building was started. Based on the combination of identical drawer construction details, maker's numbering system, and identifiable handwriting on both pieces, an attribution can be made to Grove Wright. More specifically, Elder Grove probably produced the drawers for both the 1831 dwelling house built-in as well as this 1853 freestanding unit, while Brother Thomas assisted on the case. Since Thomas Damon was only twelve years old at the time, it is highly unlikely that he was the master craftsman responsible for the drawers on the built-ins.

Monumental in size, this twelve-drawer case is exceptionally tall for its width. Surviving freestanding cases of drawers are unusual from Hancock, where built-ins were the normal storage form for retiring rooms in the Church Family Dwelling House. However, the configuration of four short drawers over a bank of graduated full-length drawers is consistent in both this freestanding piece and in the dwelling house built-ins. Was this a conscious design decision on the part of the community and the maker?

below

104. Washstand

Attributed to Grove Wright (1789–1861)
c. 1830
Cherry and pine, with bone latch and brass hinges
h 35⁵/₁₆ w 20⅛ d 17½"
Collection Jan and Thomas Pavlovic

Based on its drawer construction and hand-writing characteristics, this cherry washstand is attributed to the work of Grove Wright. The design, however, is unique in the following way. The piece was built as a frame-and-panel case with a gallery. The bottom rail houses a flat panel on each side of the case, and a door is set between side stiles. However, the washstand reveals several details that are unusual in relation to Brother Grove's other work (see pls. 101, 102, 103, and 105). The thumbnail-shaped drawer front is not lipped but stands proud of the case, and the door is primitively hinged to the face of the case rather than to the side of the case and door stile. A bone turn catch is used here.

105. Blanket Box

Attributed to Grove Wright (1789–1861)
c. 1840
Pine and butternut, with grain painting
h 43⅝ w 37 d 17⅛"
Private collection

Although the form—particularly the cut feet—is similar to pieces from Mount Lebanon, the construction details suggest this box was made in the Hancock Bishopric. It is the only known blanket box that relates to the group of furniture attributed to Grove Wright. The distinctive drawer features include tapered sides, pencil numbers on the inside corners, and a chamfer on the interior of the front faces, clearly placing it among furniture made in the Hancock Bishopric.

The most remarkable detail is the finish, which may not be original to the piece, although it probably represents a Shaker refinishing. Certainly the mixture of contrasting colors of finish is not unknown at Hancock; in the Church Family Dwelling House, a red stain is used opposite an ocher coloring in much of the building.

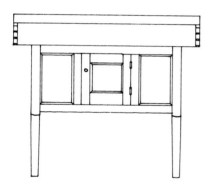

Washstand, Hancock, c. 1830. Hancock Shaker Village, Pittsfield, Massachusetts, #L89-15, on loan from the collection of Bedelia Croly Falls, Salisbury, Connecticut

106. Washstand

c. 1830
Cherry and pine, with red wash
h 34½ w 61¾ d 16"
Private collection
Photograph: courtesy Suzanne Courcier and Robert W. Wilkins

Removed from the South Family at Mount Lebanon several decades ago, this magnificent double washstand was probably produced in the same shop as a much smaller example purchased at Hancock Shaker Village in the 1920s by Mrs. Bedelia Croly Falls, currently on loan to the museum at Hancock Shaker Village (acc. no. L89–15). The latter measures only 36 inches wide, contains a single door, and has a lower gallery without the ogee shaping, although both pieces share the same construction and design elements. In addition, the leg design of this example resembles that of several Hancock counters (see p. 56, fig. 4, and pl. 102). The red wash visually unifies the cherry legs and pine case, door, and panel parts.

opposite

107. Sewing Case

c. 1830
Cherry, butternut, pine, and poplar, with brass knobs and a forged-iron crane
Written in pencil on top of slide: Agnes W. Porter
h 25¾ w 35½ d 14", leaf 14"
Private collection
Photograph: courtesy David A. Schorsch, Inc.

108. Sewing Room, Church Family Dwelling

Photograph by William F. Winter (1899–1939)
c. 1930
New York State Museum, Albany, #14.184

This particular seven-drawer sewing case, constructed with frame-and-panel ends, appears to be identical to the one pictured in the 1930 historic photograph pl. 108, which depicts a portion of the room in the Hancock Church Family Dwelling House with two typical sewing cases in place. Two singular features include the unusual width of the bottom rails and their placement in a position several inches higher than the corresponding front rail. As a result, some of the substructure of the case is revealed rather than concealed. The same design detail is seen in a three-drawer sewing case in the Shaker Museum, Old Chatham, New York (acc. no. 10626).

The forged-iron crane attached to the rear of the backboard swings out to support the drop leaf. The legs taper quickly in comparison to one-drawer tables (see pl. 114), visually giving a heavier weight and proportion to the small case above.

Physical evidence, in the form of dents on the side of the work surface, confirms the fact that fabric bags were clamped in place against the side, as shown in pl. 108, by means of what appear to be metal U-shaped clamps placed over the top. Probably derived from worldly worktables of the Federal period, this device provides accessible storage space for supplies and small sewing projects-in-progress. The pullout slides made of cherry inside a pine housing, probably a twentieth-century addition to the nineteenth-century form, may have been designed to hang additional sewing accoutrements or finished products near the work surface.

The question remains whether this sewing case was originally designed and used for making and maintaining the family's clothing or doing fancywork, as pictured here, or whether it was later adapted for this purpose. The fabric placed on top may have served to protect the work surface or counteract the slipperiness of the varnished finish.

Sewing Cases

This distinctive form represents a scaled-down version of one style of tailoring counter that has been associated with Hancock through oral history and photographic evidence. Most of these small pieces of specialized work furniture share similar construction features, consisting of a varnished cherry case with four posts connected by rails and drawers or doors of various sizes, numbers, and layout. Variations occur in the construction of the ends, which are either frame-and-panel, tablelike deep aprons, or planks. The legs range from a simple square with a taper to a variety of turned shapes. Some sewing cases have drop leaves in back with forged-iron support mechanisms to extend the work surface.

Several different drawer layouts found on sewing cases from Hancock with various leg shapes: square, tapered; turned; turned legs with an ogee-shaped bracket

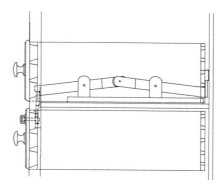

below

110. Sewing Case

c. 1840
Maple and poplar, with fruitwood knobs and varnish
h 27⁷/₁₆ w 35¹³/₁₆ d 15¼", leaf 8³/₁₆"
Hancock Shaker Village, Pittsfield, Massachusetts, #62–157A

Structurally different from other Hancock sewing cases, which exhibit either frame-and-panel or apron-side construction, this example has sides made of a single piece of wood with a simple cutout simultaneously forming the rectangular, tapered legs. It also has a rear drop leaf and a wooden support that could be swiveled on a vertical pin to support the extended work surface. The drawer openings, which measure 2½, 3, 3⅝, and 4⁵/₁₆ inches deep, are unusually shallow.

109. Sewing Case

c. 1840
Cherry, basswood, butternut, and pine, with red wash and iron lock
h 28 w 33⅛ d 22⅞"
Private collection

This piece is representative of a group of three sewing cases with a strong Hancock history. According to oral tradition, this case was used by Fanny Estabrook (1870–1960), the last eldress at Hancock. A similar example in the same private collection has the identical drawer arrangement but, due to the square, tapered legs, a very different look. The sewing case pictured above is also similar in overall form and construction to a related and probably contemporary piece in the collection of Hancock Shaker Village, Pittsfield, Massachusetts, dated January 1846 and initialed D.W.,[31] which is characterized by two half-width drawers over two full drawers, frame-and-panel sides, and turned legs. They also share the unusual feature of long square posts, which extend an extreme 4 inches below the case.

A most noteworthy detail of this piece is the locking mechanism pictured above, which has the whimsical construction quality of a whirligig. When the key in the long drawer is turned, the bolt rises and lifts up the front end of the double fulcrum, which is mounted inside the case behind the second-tier drawer divider. Simultaneously, the rear of the fulcrum pushes up against two vertically oriented wires, which pass into the holes of angle irons affixed to the back of the drawers above, thus locking the entire case at once.

right

111. Sewing Case

c. 1840
Basswood and poplar, with brass knobs, red
wash, and forged-iron crane
h 27 w 34¹⁄₁₆ d 14³⁄₁₆", leaf 18¹⁄₈"
Hancock Shaker Village, Pittsfield, Massachusetts,
#L89.24, on loan from the collection of
Bedelia Croly Falls, Salisbury, Connecticut

With the addition of a rear drop leaf supported by a forged-iron crane (see pl. 107),
this two-drawer table probably functioned as
a sewing case. In comparison with pl. 107, the
sides of the case are formed by an apron with
a fillet with a quarter-round at the bottom
edge. Considering the small size of the piece,
the bottom rail is unusually thick. It is positioned somewhat below rather than at the
same height as the side apron. Especially noteworthy are the legs, which are square and
straight at the top for two inches below the
bottom rail before tapering gradually to the
floor. A similar two-drawer table in cherry
has turned rather than square, tapered legs.[32]

The brass knobs at the side of the case
may have been a later addition to hold miscel-
laneous sewing implements or perhaps a
fabric workbag, as pictured in pl. 108. The
use of basswood as the primary material is
unusual—it was mostly used for drawer bottoms or sides—and may have been chosen
because the piece was to be painted.

112. Sewing Case

c. 1840
Cherry, butternut, and poplar, with red wash and
cast-brass latches, lock, and hinges
h 26¹⁄₈ w 34 d 23³⁄₄"
Private collection

Although similar in function to the previous
examples, this piece of sewing furniture varies
considerably in its form, layout, and proportions. The case consists of a single drawer
over two doors. The absence of a central stile
between the cupboard doors necessitated
the unorthodox positioning of the latches in a
vertical rather than horizontal direction. This
allowed either door to operate independently
of the other. Particularly unusual are the
frame, with large, single-board sides measuring over 18 inches in depth, and the doors,
which are set back ¹⁄₈ inch inside the rails and
posts. In comparison with other sewing cases
produced at Hancock, which are diminutive,
the overall proportions of this one are more
robust: the legs are stockier, the doors have a
broad, almost square panel, and the case is
quite deep. A similar case, with turned rather
than square, tapered legs, appears in a photograph taken for the Index of American
Design, now at the National Gallery of Art,
Washington, D.C.

113. Church Family Dining Room
1925
Photograph
New York State Museum, Albany, #XX9.1984

This cherry trestle table was made for the dining room of the 1830 Church Family Dwelling House at Hancock. It was one of several designed to seat the members of the Church Family, then a total of ninety-four brothers and sisters. The three large, turned standards are related in design to the four cherry columns that support the ceiling of this room. Oral tradition confirms the Hancock Shakers' use of two-slat, low-back chairs for dining room seating. These were probably made at nearby Mount Lebanon.

The medial stretcher placed under the top to provide for greater leg room is fastened to the legs with bolts through either end. The turned pedestal is attached to the cross cleats above and to the highly arched foot with bridle joints. Flat-head screws through the cross cleats secure the top, and an additional metal bracket assists in holding the central support in place. The combination of the turned standards, the curved profile on the cross braces, and the chamfered edges on the feet results in a beautifully integrated design.

DROP-LEAF TABLES

A large group of drop-leaf tables survives both at Hancock Shaker Village and in several private collections. The Hancock attribution of all of them is based primarily on oral history. They also share the following distinctive design characteristics: cherry used as the primary wood and given a clear finish, four turned legs, and wooden pullout leaf supports that terminate in a brass knob or ring. Within these parameters, numerous variations occur. The sizes range from about 22 to 36 inches in length, although one extreme exception is 6 feet long. Most have small drawers set into the front apron, although some examples have no drawers. A small but omnipresent decorative detail is the fillet with ovolo or common thumbnail molding that was cut by the craftsman on the bottom edge of the aprons.

The rarity of small, four-legged tables with a Hancock attribution suggests that perhaps the related drop-leaf form was used here instead. It is not known whether these examples were placed in retiring rooms or work areas, although the former usage seems more likely.

114. Double Drop-Leaf Table
c. 1830
Cherry and maple, with brass knobs
h 26¾ w 34¼ d 14½"
Hancock Shaker Village, Pittsfield, Massachusetts, #62–153

115. Double Drop-Leaf Table
c. 1830
Cherry and pine, with brass knobs and hinges
h 26¼ w 48 d 14", 30" (extended)
Hancock Shaker Village, Pittsfield, Massachusetts, #L89–20, on loan from the collection of Bedelia Croly Falls, Salisbury, Connecticut

The table on the left exhibits the most characteristic simple, rounded transition between the square and turned sections of the posts: a very pleasing spherical turning before the concave shape terminates at the bottom. The smaller table shows a surprisingly small drawer in relation to the oversize top and bottom rails. However, most interesting on this table is the complexity of the transitional leg turning, which incorporates a short cylinder, a ring, then a cove reducing the turning to an extremely delicate slender diameter before the craftsman completed shaping the leg—a degree of complexity highly unusual not only for Hancock but in all Shaker work of its time.

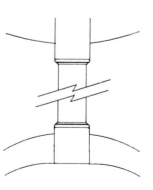

Trestle table, Hancock, c. 1830

116. Box

c. 1830
Pine, with red paint and cast-iron hardware
Written in pen on label attached to box: New
Rugs &/Curtains to/Canopy Top
Car/riage./Laundry.
h 24¼ w 45⅜ d 18"
Private collection
Photograph: courtesy Thomas C. Queen

More often than not, it is difficult to determine the specific use of a piece of furniture at any particular point in its history. According to the paper label attached to the front, this box stored carriage top or side curtains for horse-drawn vehicles during the nineteenth century before the Shakers, like worldly Americans, changed to the automobile. This sturdy, well-constructed chest with dovetailed applied bracket base with simple molded edge was made by a proficient craftsman. The cast-iron handle probably was added several years later. The box was purchased from Hancock in the early 1900s by an early collector of Shaker furniture, which helps support its Hancock Bishopric origin.

117. Tripod Stand

c. 1830
Cherry and pine
h 24¾ diameter of top 16¾"
Hancock Shaker Village, Pittsfield,
Massachusetts, #62–120

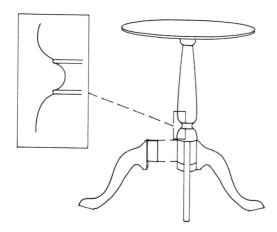

118. Tripod Stand

c. 1830
Cherry and pine
h 25¼ diameter of top 18"
Hancock Shaker Village, Pittsfield, Massachusetts,
#L89–18, on loan from the collection of
Bedelia Croly Falls, Salisbury, Connecticut

These two tables with a solid Hancock history illustrate several characteristic design and construction features strongly associated with the Hancock Shaker community. The stand with spider feet on the right was purchased from the Hancock Shakers in the 1920s and recently was returned to the site. Although not nearly as common as circular-topped stands, those with square-top with ovolo corners are strongly associated with Hancock design. The presence of screw holes in the underside of the top suggests it may originally have had underhung drawers suspended below.

On both examples, the legs are tenoned rather than dovetailed into the pedestal base, which also lacks the usual metal plate typical of other Shaker stands. Most noteable is the shape of the shafts, which consist of a narrow, convex ring beneath the elongated baluster-turned stem. These two features as well as the leg-to-stem tenon joint are critical in identifying tripod stands of Hancock origin.

119. Tripod Stand

c. 1830
Cherry, pine, poplar, maple, and birch, with
fruitwood knobs, traces of red stain, and iron
plates
h 26 w 17⅝ d 21"
Hancock Shaker Village, Pittsfield,
Massachusetts, #62–15

The most outstanding feature of this tripod stand with push-pull drawer is the intricately made yoke. The two vertical members of the U-shaped frame are double-tenoned into the cleat on the underside of the tabletop and dovetailed to the horizontal crosspiece below. The turned stem is tenoned into the horizontal crosspiece. The cleats help prevent the top from warping and provide a hanger for the single, underhung drawer, which is suspended within the yoke. Although all of the woods found on this piece are common in New England, it is unusual to find so many combined in one small piece. Even though the shape of the turned stem and the wide stance of the legs are similar to those of Mount Lebanon stands, the tentative Hancock attribution is made primarily on the basis of the unusual leg-to-stem tenon as opposed to the more common dovetail used in other communities.

120. Built-in Cupboards and Case of Drawers, South Family Dwelling House

c. 1850
Butternut and pine, with walnut knobs, spring latch, and brass hinges
h 120 w 62¼"
Collection the Cybulski family

This midcentury built-in at the South Family Dwelling House resembles many retiring room storage units in the Church Family Dwelling House at Hancock Shaker Village in form, construction details, and materials. While there are fewer half-width drawers and the cupboard doors on the right are smaller than those at Hancock, the most conspicuous difference between the two is the addition of an iron grille built into the lower right-hand corner of the case. This heating grate allowed the warm air radiating from a nearby chimney to flow into each of the rooms—creating in effect a central heating system. A distinctive construction detail is the tapering of the dovetailed drawer sides in thickness from bottom to top. This feature and the use of shallow raised panels on the cupboard doors found in the kitchen and dining area built-ins of the same South Family Dwelling House are characteristic of the work of a group of Enfield craftsmen, including Abner Allen (see p. 190).

Another construction feature peculiar to this built-in is the use of a dovetail, rather than the more common mortise-and-tenon joint, to attach the stile to a rail below the door. In addition, a nonintegral threaded wood tenon was employed to fasten the knobs to the drawers, and numbers were marked with a metal stamp on the drawer sides to ensure the correct placement of the drawers in the case.

121. Cupboard and Case of Drawers

Hancock or Enfield, Connecticut
c. 1840
Walnut and pine, with red stain
h 98½ w 41¾ d 25½"
Collection of Shaker Village of Pleasant Hill, Harrodsburg, Kentucky, #61.4.193

It is not known how or when this massive storage unit was moved from New England to Pleasant Hill, Kentucky. It exhibits several distinct features associated with the Abner Allen-Grove Wright school of craftsmanship, including the overall layout design, rails that are tenoned and pinned with one large peg, a case defined by beaded edges (see pl. 101), tapered drawer sides, and chamfered drawer faces. It is the last detail, as well as the use of beveled moldings on the lipped drawer fronts, the level, rather than rounded drawer sides, and the style of the flat, thick pulls (see pl. 120) that point to an Enfield, Connecticut, attribution. The use of walnut, however, is unusual in Eastern Shaker furniture.

122. Desk

c. 1940
Watercolor by Howard Weld
National Gallery of Art, Washington, D.C. Index of
American Design, #1943.8.10470, Mass FU-91

This desk, now in a private collection, was made about 1870 from butternut, pine, basswood, yellow poplar, and walnut, and has porcelain knobs and iron latches. Its design is unique, although some features—the frame-and-panel construction with cut foot and the placement of doors above the fall front—relate to Shaker case pieces, particularly those from Mount Lebanon. While the lower section is a basic three-drawer case, the cabinetmaker built what appears to be two half-width drawers above. However, the drawer on the right side of the face is only a facade, while the ones on the left face and right end are functional. When opened, the fall front exposes two drawers surrounded by shelves of various sizes and intricate ledger dividers. The tripartite tier of drawers just below the top cupboard doors are uncommon in Shaker design. Beveled edges adorn the drawer lips and case frame edges; beveled moldings appear on the cornice, midcase, and both above and below the one-third-width drawers. Numerous glue blocks were used in the construction of the well-dovetailed drawers and on the bottom of the case.

The artist took some liberties in his rendition of the desk: he chose not to include the ledger dividers, and he drew half-round moldings instead of the beveled moldings actually used on the piece.

123. Trestle Table

c. 1820
Curly maple and ash
h 24⅜ w 50 d 27"
The Metropolitan Museum of Art, New York.
Friends of the American Wing Fund, 1966,
#66.10.3

A photograph of the Enfield dining room in the collection of the New York State Museum, Albany, shows this table or one like it placed against the far wall. Smaller than most trestle tables, it may have been designed for use by the ministry leaders, who ate apart from the family brothers and sisters. The method by which the craftsman achieved the highly unusual shaping of the standards is unknown. It looks as if a piece of wood 5 or 6 inches in diameter was turned on a lathe to create an urn shape with ring turnings above the foot and then cut perfectly straight. The effect is of a slablike piece with very fine shaping on the edges. The slightly arched foot has more in common with Shaker drying racks than with other Shaker trestle tables.

The cleats visible under the tabletop were probably added at a later date to accommodate underhung drawers, now missing. The hole in the stretcher was cut to allow the drawer to slide through.

124. Writing Table and Chair with Hanging Footwarmer on Pegboard
1935–42
Photograph
Index of American Design, © 1992 National Gallery of Art, Washington, D.C., #V33

This fine desk combines two forms, the tripod stand and the lift-top desk. The stand is typical of Enfield, Connecticut, such as pl. 126 and another in a private collection[33] displaying a similarly shaped finely swelled stem turning with V-groove detailing just above the legs. Another desk of a similar form in the collection at Hancock Shaker Village, Pittsfield, Massachusetts (acc. no. 62–191), incorporates a much stockier vase-shaped stem, which may be a Hancock variation of this form, as the turning details more closely resemble those on the tripod stand pl. 117.

The joinery work on all of these pieces is superb. This beautifully dovetailed case is enhanced by the strong curly maple chosen by the craftsman and the bone or ivory escutcheon, seen as well on other Enfield casework.

125. Dining Room, North Family Dwelling House, Mount Lebanon
c. 1930
Photograph
New York State Museum, Albany, #PTB.4.140

This Enfield, Connecticut, table was moved after the community closed to the North Family, Mount Lebanon, dining room, where this photograph was taken. It is closely related to one presently used in the library at Hancock Shaker Village[34] and another at the Art Complex Museum, Duxbury, Massachusetts (acc. no. 31–12). Based on the tapered drawer sides, which are related to other pieces made at Enfield, Connecticut, and the profile of the molded top, which is identical to that of pl. 137, it is attributed to Thomas Fisher (1823–1902). Unusual features on several of these tables include the scalloped bracket supports beneath the tabletop[35] and the boldly shaped legs with both ball and ring turnings. Neither of these details, which represent a pared-down version of Victorian styling, is seen on other Fisher pieces.

A photograph in an 1897 *Connecticut Quarterly*[36] shows these tables in use in the Enfield, Connecticut, Church Family dining room, which is probably the space they were originally intended for.

126. Tripod Stand

c. 1830
Curly maple, cherry, and pine, with red wash
Private collection
Photograph: courtesy John Keith Russell Antiques, Inc.

Traditionally, one- and two-drawer stands have been identified with sewing activities, but their actual nineteenth-century use is unknown. Unlike some stands from nearby Shaker communities, which may have push-pull drawers (see pl. 119), this example can be accessed from one side as only one end of each drawer is finished and fitted with a knob. The center cleat attaches the top to the pedestal and supports the underhung drawers, which are also held by two outer cleat hangers. The gracefully shaped standard increases in diameter at the center; it is further embellished with three shallow ring turnings.

Documentation for such tripod stands is based primarily on design characteristics and oral history. A photograph published in the *Connecticut Quarterly* in 1897[37] helps to confirm this attribution. Typical features include the ring turning just above the legs, the ovolo-cornered square top, and the snake-leg form. This stand is nearly identical to another in a private collection that was used by Eldress Fanny Estabrook (1870–1960) of Hancock, after it was moved there when the Enfield society closed.

127. Tripod Stand

c. 1850
Pine, curly maple, cherry, and butternut, with brass latch and iron base plate
h 21¾ diameter of top 18½"
Private collection
Photograph: courtesy Skinner, Inc., auctioneers and appraisers

This stand represents a Shaker craftsman's interpretation of a worldly eighteenth-century form. The tripod tea table with a top supported and usually hinged by a swiveling device called a bird cage had made a rare appearance in the 1740s but attained its final development in the Chippendale period over twenty years later. Throughout New England, the pedestal table was much less common and simpler in ornament than the version found in Philadelphia, where it represented one of the most popular and elaborate forms.

This rare Shaker design not only omits the characteristic carved and reeded pedestal, piecrust-shaped top, and ball-and-claw feet, it also presents a novel and possibly unique substructure mechanism. Instead of both swiveling and tipping up when not in use, as in high-style examples, the top of this table is fixed in the horizontal position. Circular rotation is made possible in the following unorthodox manner: The top of the post consists of an elongated, round tenon, which passes through the square block of wood

(making up the bottom of the bird cage) and into a round subtop, approximately 12 inches in diameter. Four columns are tenoned into the subtop and through-tenoned and pinned into the floor, forming the bird cage. Screws attach the subtop to the exposed top above. A round metal plate in the center of the subtop, visible only when the top is removed, is screwed into the tenon at the top of the shaft.

This arrangement contrasts markedly with worldly tables, which have a pair of rectangular cleats screwed to the undersurface of the top. Fixed between the cleats is a box—the so-called bird cage—consisting of two square boards connected by four small turned pillars tenoned in place at either end. The sides of one of the top boards extend as dowels that fit into holes in the cleats, forming a hinge by which the top can be tilted. A brass spring latch at the other end holds the top fast in the horizontal position.[38] It is not known how this piece was used by the Shakers. Clearly the maker was familiar with worldly design and adapted it to suit the Believers' specific needs.

The turning of the shaft, with the distinctive swell at the base of the post, is closely related to documented Hancock pieces (see pls. 117, 118), a similarity that is not unexpected in furniture produced in the same bishopric. However, the mixture of many woods and the shape of the stem suggest this stand was produced in Enfield, Connecticut.

128. Washstand
Attributed to Abner Allen (1776–1855)
c. 1830
Curly maple and pine
h 27⅞ w 19 d 16"
Private collection

The characteristic tapered drawer sides and the beveled edges on the top and bottom inner face of the drawers are construction features clearly associated with Brother Abner's work. This stand and one virtually identical to it in a private collection[39] share a common layout, the use of highly figured maple, carefully proportioned turned legs, and a dovetailed gallery with tapered sides and overcut layout markings typical of Brother Abner's work.

129. Case of Drawers
Abner Allen (1776–1855)
1849
Signed in pencil in script on back of drawers:
May 16, 1849. Abner Allen. A.E. age 66.[40]
Butternut and pine
h 27⁹⁄₁₆ w 26 d 18½"
Private collection

Because this small case of drawers is signed and dated by the maker, it is central to the group of pieces attributed to Abner Allen. Details of the drawer construction in particular are distinctive on all examples: the drawer sides taper in thickness from bottom to top; the top of the drawer sides are flat; and the outside back edge of the drawer is heavily chamfered, presumably done with a plane after the drawer was assembled. These same features are evident in the cupboard and case of drawers pl. 131. Furthermore, the bottom rail or apron, which is integral with the front foot, is dovetailed into the side of the case with the grain running in two different directions, which is a very unusual joinery technique, unique among Abner Allen's work and rarely used elsewhere, although it shows up on several stile and rail joints in the South Family built-in pl. 120.

Abner Allen (1776–1855)

Abner Allen was born in 1776 and spent most of his life with the North Family at Enfield, Connecticut. Aside from one reference to his abilities as "a laborious Brother [and] a good mechanic,"[41] little is known about his life beyond several pieces of furniture he made. His ability as a skilled cabinetmaker is documented by two signed and dated cases of drawers and an unusual desk. Unfortunately, Allen's handwriting obscured his actual identity for many years. The tail of the last letter of his surname appears on a small case of drawers to be a *y* rather than an *n*, which has caused him to be known as Abner Alley. However, his name as recorded on Shaker documents is properly spelled Allen.[42] More significant is the presence of a distinctive construction detail on these case pieces: drawer sides that taper in thickness from bottom to top, similar to the way Grove Wright worked. However, three additional details help distinguish Abner Allen's joinery from that of Brother Grove: the top edge of the drawer sides are usually flat rather than rounded, as on Brother Grove's pieces, the outside back edge of the drawers is heavily chamfered, and the lipped drawer fronts have a chamfered edge. Another idiosyncratic feature is his apparent preference for raised- rather than flat-panel doors, an eighteenth-century form found on Brother Abner's pieces produced in the mid-nineteenth-century.

A furniture maker practicing his trade over time evolves certain work habits, consistently repeating these details on many different pieces. Taken together, these construction details form a signature of Abner Allen's work. By carefully analyzing these distinctive features, many other unsigned pieces can be attributed to Abner Allen, including five washstands, a cupboard with drawers, two small chests, and a long worktable.

130. Table
Attributed to Abner Allen (1776–1855)
c. 1840
Curly maple, with brass knobs and varnish
h 29⅜ w 130¾ d 33"
Hancock Shaker Village, Pittsfield, Massachusetts, #65–24

The 11-foot-long, curly maple worktable with two-board top, breadboard ends, and square, tapered legs represents the only known example of this form attributed to Abner Allen. The idiosyncratic drawer construction, including beveled edges on the top and bottom inner drawer face, clearly points to Brother Abner's workmanship. While the two drawers under the long overhanging ends are necessarily different in construction than the three along the table apron, they were probably made at the time the piece was initially constructed by Brother Abner. Its original use is unknown.

Both this worktable and the washstand dated September 18, 1850 (pl. 132), were owned by the artist and early Shaker collector Charles Sheeler (1883–1965). Several of his modernist paintings produced around 1930 portray some of his Shaker furniture, which some experts believe strongly influenced his work.[43]

131. Cupboard and Case of Drawers
Abner Allen (1776–1855)
1830
Pencil inscription on rear of backboards: March 18th 1830 GFM Made by Abner Allen
Pine, with yellow and red wash
h 81½ w 39¼ d 20⅛"
Private collection

The written documentation, oral history, and joinery techniques clearly connect this piece to Abner Allen. Signed by the cabinetmaker and dated 1830, this chest was given to a Miss Davis of Somers, Connecticut, by one of the Enfield sisters in gratitude for nursing care.[44]

Unfortunately, the identity of GFM, initials that may refer to the Shaker for whom Abner Allen made this piece, is unknown.

In addition to construction features such as drawers with tapered sides and chamfered faces and raised-panel cupboard doors, the design vocabulary is also significant. For example, the unusual layout, consisting of cupboards over drawers over cupboards, is found in a built-in unit from the East Family,[45] suggesting a common origin for both pieces.

132. Washstand

Attributed to Abner Allen (1776–1855)
c. 1850
Written in chalk on back: Sept 18, 1850
Curly maple, butternut, and pine
h 37⅝ w 25³⁄₁₆ d 20"
Hancock Shaker Village, Pittsfield, Massachusetts,
#L89-1, on loan from the collection of
Bedelia Croly Falls, Salisbury, Connecticut

133. Washstand

c. 1850
Curly maple and butternut
h 37⅝ w 22¼ d 19¼"
Hancock Shaker Village, Pittsfield,
Massachusetts, #65.296

These two distinctive washstands were purchased from the Hancock Shakers in the 1920s by private collectors. One was acquired by Mrs. Bedelia Croly Falls, who compiled a significant group of Shaker furniture for use in her Connecticut home before returning it to Hancock Shaker Village on loan in 1989. The other washstand was bought by the artist Charles Sheeler (1883–1965).

In addition to the characteristic tapered drawer construction and beveled edges on the top and bottom of the inner face of the drawers, this nearly identical pair of washstands shares the use of curly maple, ogee-shaped gallery sides dovetailed to a chamfered splashboard, and butternut case below. The raised- rather than flat-panel doors are an eighteenth-century form found on Abner Allen pieces produced in the mid-nineteenth-century (see pl. 131). The large, overhanging gallery with curved sides contrasts sharply with the flat, rectangular base, creating an unusual design.

134. Case of Drawers with Gallery

Attributed to Abner Allen (1776–1855)
c. 1850
Curly maple, butternut, and pine
h 31¼ w 27⅞ d 19¼"
Hancock Shaker Village, Pittsfield, Massachusetts,
#L89-2, on loan from the collection of
Bedelia Croly Falls, Salisbury, Connecticut

The tapered drawer sides with flaring gallery, chamfered drawer faces, and the highly figured case of this small piece are typical of Abner Allen's known work. The design demonstrates a careful balance through the drawer layout, bracket feet, and rails dovetailed into plank sides, elements that also appear in the small case of 1849 (pl. 129).

Thomas Fisher (1823–1902)

Listed in the 1880 United States census as a Church Family carpenter by trade, Thomas Fisher carried the Enfield cabinetmaking tradition into the latter part of the nineteenth century. Technically, parts of his work are related to the workshop practices of Brothers Grove Wright and Abner Allen, such as the consistent use of tapered drawer sides on some of his case pieces. However, his furniture exhibits a decidedly different design, characterized by a familiarity with Victorian styling, which he modified to suit the Shaker aesthetic. He combined in his furniture a variety of contrasting light and dark woods, such as oak, ash, cherry, bird's-eye maple, and walnut, and relied on applied moldings and facings, shaped backboards, and complex cornices. Through a combination of design elements such as raised-panel sides, built-up quarter-round case corners, and commercially made cast-iron pulls, he created his own distinctive Victorian style of Shaker furniture.

135. Bookcase
Attributed to Thomas Fisher (1823–1902)
c. 1880
Ash and pine, with porcelain knobs
h 110¾ w 98⅝ d 18¾"
Canterbury Shaker Village, Inc., Canterbury, New Hampshire

Several design and construction features indicate this immense bookcase was produced in Enfield, Connecticut. The combined use of ash and pine, the raised-panel sides and cupboard doors, and the built-up rounded case corners are identical to the five-drawer chest with a strong attribution to Thomas Fisher (see pl. 137). In addition, the applied moldings nailed to the top of the case and the profile of the cupboard top are closely related to those found on the octagonal table of about 1880 (pl. 138). Unfortunately, there are no drawers to examine for evidence of tapered sides, which are characteristic of Thomas Fisher's work (see pl. 137).

However, Jessie Evans (1867–1937) of Canterbury, in a diary entry dated October 2, 1917, confirmed the movement of this piece from Enfield when the community there closed: "Irving Greenwood leaves home [Canterbury] with truck to go to Enfield, CT. He returns late Wed night . . . with a fine large showcase for office hall. . . ." It is not known whether this piece was originally used as a display case, perhaps for handmade Shaker products at Enfield or later in the Canterbury office, where the world's people would have visited, but it still stands in the hall of the Trustees' Office at Canterbury, where it was placed in 1917.

136. Case of Drawers
c. 1860
Butternut, with Bennington-type knobs
h 49¼ w 41½ d 23¼"
Private collection

Construction features such as tapered drawer sides and chamfered drawer fronts verify that this seven-drawer chest originated at Enfield, Connecticut. Additional design details, however, suggest that it may not have been made by either Thomas Fisher or Abner Allen but by another unidentified craftsman who used the distinctive tapered drawer side associated with the Hancock Bishopric. Interesting variations on this piece include the use of frame-and-panel rather than plank-sided construction, a case that rests directly on the floor rather than on legs, and commercially purchased Bennington-type knobs. The breadth and overhang of the nicely beveled top provide a beautiful and unusual lift and flair to what could otherwise be a very plain case.

137. Case of Drawers
Attributed to Thomas Fisher (1823–1902)
c. 1890
Written in pen in script on bottom of fifth drawer: Made in Shaker Village/THOMAS FISHER [pencil caps in different hand]/Enfield, Conn/Sister Lillian Phelps
Written in pencil in script on back of backboards: Mt. Lebanon
Written in pencil on all drawer sides and bottom and on top of corresponding rails: No 1, No 2, No 3, No 4, No 5
Chestnut, cherry, white pine, oak, and ash, with cast-iron pulls
h 42 w 40 d 21⅛"
Canterbury Shaker Village, Inc., Canterbury, New Hampshire, #82.682

This five-drawer chest is one of a group of pieces attributed to Enfield, Connecticut, joiner Thomas Fisher. According to tradition, two chests of drawers, two octagonal tables, and several armchairs (see pls. 135, 138) were removed to Canterbury, New Hampshire, after the sale of the Enfield, Connecticut, property in 1917. Although none of these pieces bears his signature, they have been attributed to Fisher by the twentieth-century Canterbury Shakers. In this case, Sister Lillian Phelps (1876–1973) wrote the inscription on the drawer bottom. The words "Mt. Lebanon" written on the back of the backboards may represent shipping directions, suggesting that this piece was sent to Mount Lebanon at one point in its history—perhaps after the Enfield community closed in 1917. The same type of markings are evident on the backboards of a Union Village, Ohio, case of drawers that was transported from Ohio to New Hampshire (see pl. 266).

Brother Thomas's distinctive style is far removed from gospel simplicity but represents an important development in Shaker design. This five-drawer case and a companion four-drawer piece, both at Canterbury, clearly were designed and built as a pair or at the same time, as the drawers are marked respectively 1–5 and 6–9. They both combine elements of the old, such as raised-panel sides, and the new, including a shaped pine backboard, varnished case surfaces, cherry top with molded edges, and commercial cast-iron pulls. Idiosyncratic features include tapered drawer sides, which are associated with other craftsmen from Enfield (see pl.

132) and Hancock (see pl. 103), built-up corner posts, and a top attached to rails with numerous rectangular blocks supported by iron strips screwed in from below.

A microscopic analysis not only identified the unusual combination of woods used in this chest but revealed a peculiar growth pattern in the white pine backboard. Called compression wood, it is produced in conifers as a reaction to gravity. In trees growing on a slope or in branches that begin growth in a horizontal position, the vascular cambium reacts to this "misalignment" by producing larger growth rings on the underside of the stem or branch. The resulting wood, especially in pine, is usually red in color and was originally termed *rotholz* by early German botanists. Compression wood has a greater density and longitudinal shrinkage and reduced radial and tangential shrinkages than normal wood. These traits tend to manifest themselves in the increased warping and twisting of the boards with changes in relative humidity. Thus, the tensile properties are reduced in compression wood, which makes it vulnerable to breakage under stress.[46]

What is significant is that in the examiner's experience at the Winterthur Museum, Delaware (which comprehends approximately two thousand samples), he did not encounter any examples of compression wood in the furniture there. This raises the question whether the maker consciously selected this material because of its unusual grain and reddish color and whether the same compression pine appears on other Thomas Fisher pieces as a distinguishing characteristic of his cabinetwork.

138. Pedestal Table
Attributed to Thomas Fisher (1823–1902)
c. 1880
Red oak, chestnut, and cherry
h 27 diameter of top 38"
Canterbury Shaker Village, Inc., Canterbury, New Hampshire, #82.687

More innovative than most Shaker attempts at Victorian design, this table with octagonal top, hexagonal pedestal, and exaggerated cabriole legs terminating in modified hooves expresses a novel balance of pomp and plainness.

Tables such as these have been attributed to Thomas Fisher on the basis of oral history and stylistic evidence. The profile of the molded top, consisting of an extended ogee, is identical to that found on both the four- and five-drawer chests (see pl. 137). The top is attached to the frame below by numerous hardwood glue blocks, which have been screwed in from below, in a manner similar to those found on the five-drawer chest. The contour of many parts, including the table edge, legs, and applied facings, was clearly done with the use of a shaper (see p. 73). A recently discovered diary entry confirms that the origin of this unusual group of Victorian furniture was indeed Enfield, Connecticut. According to an entry in Jessie Evans's journal dated October 2, 1917, "Irving Greenwood leaves home [Canterbury] with truck to go to Enfield, CT. He returns late Wed night . . . with a fine large showcase for office hall, a table (octagonal) donated to eldresses front room at shop and a counter placed in A7. The furniture a gift to us from Enfield Shakers." The showcase mentioned is probably the large two-piece unit currently in the entrance hall of the Trustees' Office, at Canterbury (see pl. 135), the location mentioned in the diary notation. The octagonal table pictured here is one of two that are still located in the northeast room of the Church Family Sisters' Shop (Building A) at Canterbury.

It should be noted that what many mistakenly call "walnut" applied decorative pieces in Thomas Fisher's work are actually cutouts of stained cherry, which in this table were applied to the lower section of each leg as well as a shaped one-inch double-cove molding nailed to the base of the apron.

139. Tripod Stand
Attributed to Thomas Fisher (1823–1902)
c. 1880
Ash and maple, with porcelain pulls
h 24"
Private collection
Photograph: courtesy Ed Clerk, reprinted from The Shakers

Probably produced after 1870, this stand and a closely related example that recently sold at auction[47] exhibit the shop practices of craftsmen associated with Thomas Fisher (see p. 192). The attributes of the Shaker Victorian age are found in the unexpected mixture of woods on the top, commercially made porcelain pulls, characteristic molded edge produced by a shaper, and the painting imitative of veneer work around the drawer front. Aside from the application of these decorative details, with its use of cabriole legs, snake feet, turned stem, rectangular top, and underhung drawers, the overall form is identical to earlier stands. Although these small design details are clearly from the Victorian era, the basic form, the cleanly turned stem, and the shaped legs are taken from the traditions of half a century earlier.

140. Sewing Desk
Attributed to Thomas Fisher (1823–1902)
c. 1880
Chestnut, walnut, oak, curly maple, bird's-eye maple, tiger maple, and pine, with porcelain knobs
Written in pencil in script on interior of all long drawer sides and bottoms and on top of each corresponding rail: No 1, No 2, No 3
h 37⅞ w 31 d 19⅝"
Private collection

According to a well-documented family history, this elaborate sewing desk was made at Enfield, Connecticut, and given to Sister Sarah Neale (1849–1948) at Mount Lebanon, New York. She in turn passed it to her nephew in 1936, and his descendants are the present owners. Design details, construction features, and makers' marks strongly place this Victorian piece among those attributed to Thomas Fisher. The use and combination of a variety of figured woods for decorative purposes relates closely to other Fisher pieces, including the chest of drawers of about 1880 (pl. 137). Further evidence is supplied by the tapered drawer sides in the upper gallery, the profile of the molded edge on the work surface, and the built-up, rounded case corners. All of these features represent characteristic techniques associated with this Enfield, Connecticut, craftsman. Particularly significant is the style of handwriting, numbering system, and placement of Arabic numerals on all drawers and corresponding rails, which relates to that found on two documented Fisher chests at Canterbury (see pl. 137).

The case rests on a base molding rather than on the more common turned or tapered legs, and figured maple veneer is used for the small drawers in the gallery. The inside corners of the two drawer sides are cut off at a 45-degree angle beneath the drawer bottom—an important peculiarity.

141. Side Chair
c. 1840
Maple and tape, with green paint
h 41 w 19 d 15"
Courtesy of the Art Complex Museum, Duxbury,
Massachusetts, #30–25

Although exhibiting the elongated pommels, strongly contoured slats, and tall back posts associated with Enfield, Connecticut, the most noteworthy feature of this Enfield chair is the dark green painted pigment.

142. Armed Rocker

c. 1840
Curly maple and rush
h 44½ w 20⅜ d 22"
Private collection

Rocking chairs from Enfield, Connecticut, have a basic simplicity. They are characterized by unusually tall back posts in relationship to the small seat dimensions, elongated oval pommels over a sharp concave collar, minimally shaped front posts with integral mushroom-shaped handholds, and high-arched graduated backslats. The mushroom-shaped front post is derived from eighteenth-century American armchairs. The crescent-shaped arm is tenoned into the post, a construction feature that is rare on Shaker chairs; usually the front post is tenoned into the arm. A noteworthy feature on most of the Enfield, Connecticut, rockers is the absence of a second tier of side stretchers, making a total of five rather than the usual seven stretchers below the seat.

143. Child's Chair

c. 1840
*Bird's-eye maple and hickory, with shellac finish
and rush seat (not original)*
h 39¼ w 16¼ d 12⅝"
Private collection

It is unusual to find children's chairs with such exquisite form and proportions. This example has elongated pommels, graduated slats, and dramatically figured bird's-eye maple throughout. Documentation is provided by a c. 1900 photograph of Sarah Emily Copley (1844–1911) of Enfield, in which two of the four girls with her are seated in small chairs displaying this pommel form.[48] A unique feature shared by a group of these particular chairs is an iron pin that was inserted through the pommels and into the top of the posts to eliminate the risk of snapping the unusually slender pommels.

Harvard Bishopric

144. Desk

Alfred Collier (1823–1884)
c. 1861
Written in white chalk in script under lid: Alfred
Collier
Pine, maple, and chestnut, with green paint,
pressed-brass escutcheon, cast-brass bail pull and
hinge, and iron lock
h 48⅜ w 31 d 25¼"
Private collection

This desk, the only known piece of furniture made by Alfred Collier, may be the piece referred to in several journal entries.[1] On January 31, 1861, he recorded in "A Journal Kept by Alfred Collier for His Own Benefit," "I work in the Shop & Work on a Desk for Elder Grove [Blanchard]." After he interrupted his project for several months, another journal writer asserted on July 4, 1861, "Elder Gr[ove Blanchard] received a new desk from Alfred Collier."[2]

The overall form of this stand-up desk with brass escutcheon and bail handle demonstrates an awareness of worldly design. At the same time, it is a vigorous statement of the Shakers' use of color. Stark and rectilinear, the desk is simply modified by the application of the gently rounded backboard. Although slender, the use of pegged mortise-and-tenon joinery—including three 5⁄16-inch pegs on the front, two on the side and four on the rear posts—and base stretchers has made it quite strong.

This example may have been inspired by worldly designs that Brother Alfred might have seen during his frequent departures from Harvard during the 1850s. Journal entries indicate that after returning to the community, he even produced several pieces for his blood relatives and friends who lived nearby. For example, on November 27, 1857, Alfred noted, "I work in the Shop & blind dovetail a writing desk for my niece in Charlestown."[3]

THE TWO SHAKER communities in eastern Massachusetts comprised Harvard, the bishopric seat, and Shirley, located respectively thirty-five and forty miles west of Boston.[4] In 1781 Mother Ann Lee visited the 1769 Square House in Harvard shortly after the death of Shadrach Ireland, the New Light Baptist preacher, who built it. According to one account, Mother Ann said of Shadrach Ireland's followers, "these are the people and this is the house and place which Mother saw in vision while in England."[5] The Shakers purchased the Square House and used it as Mother Ann's missionary base while she proselytized throughout New England from 1781 to 1783, a year before she died. The community was the fourth to be organized into Gospel Order, in 1791, followed by Shirley in 1793, the latter located on lands donated by Elijah and Ivory Wildes, John Warren, and Nathan Willard.[6] Located on a total of four thousand acres,[7] both villages were relatively small, consisting of about 178 members at Harvard during its peak in 1850 and 84 Believers at Shirley in 1820.[8]

The economic activities at Harvard and Shirley were similar to those undertaken at other Shaker communities. In July 20, 1795, Rev. William Bentley of Salem visited the Harvard Shakers and recorded the earliest account of their trade with the world.

> In the house we found several articles of their own manufacture. We purchased two excellent whips which were made with great ingenuity. We had some stailes [stems] given us for our pipes, & we purchased a specimen of their shoe brushes. They had not a furnace as at Shirley, but they have their Blacksmiths and White smiths & they shewed us a surgeon's instrument made with great exactness.[9]

What became a lucrative packaged seed industry began about 1800. Account books indicate that the Harvard and Shirley Shakers agreed to divide the local selling territory between them to prevent overlap. Harvard sold seeds to the larger cities to the east and south, while Shirley concentrated on the smaller towns to the northwest. Responding to changes in consumer demand in the nineteenth century, the Shakers phased out seed sales in favor of raising and selling fruit trees, which provided a considerable income.[10] A catalogue of nursery stock published about 1845 included twenty-one varieties of apple trees and sixteen kinds of cherry trees.[11] Journals document the sale of peach, pear, and plum trees as well. But the most important industry at Harvard by the 1830s was the herb trade, which thrived under the direction of Elisha Myrick (1825–left 1859). The large herb house, erected in 1849, was 150 feet long and was capable of holding three hundred cords of wood, needed to dry the herbs, with separate workrooms for each of the many steps involved in the drying, pressing, and packaging processes.[12] As they were close to Boston, the Harvard Shakers sold fresh dairy and farm products such as milk, chicken, eggs, and preserved fruit and vegetables directly to city markets. At Shirley, "the main business" was the making of applesauce "of which they sell from five to six tons every year."[13]

As at other societies, worldly visitors to these two communities during the nineteenth century came away with conflicting impressions of Shaker life. Louisa May Alcott's mother, Abigail Alcott, found nothing congenial in the Harvard Believers' life-style and registered the following objections in 1843: "Visited the

- GEORGE WHITING (1827–l. 1858), in "Church Family Journal No. 3," February 10, 1846
- ■ CHARLES W. BABBITT (1833 or 1834–l. 1863), in "A Diary Kept for the Use & Convenience of the Herb Department"
- WILLIAM SPARROW (working 1865), a recently discovered table at Fruitlands Museums, Harvard, Massachusetts, signed "William Sparrow Oct. 1865" in black ink on drawer bottom
- ■■■ DANIEL MILTON (l. 1885), in a letter to Wallace Cathcart, director of the Western Reserve Historical Society, Cleveland, from Eldress Josephine, 1919: "He was an excellent carpenter. A number of his pieces of work was sold when we broke up Harvard."[22]

WORLDLY MAKERS

JOHN A. DAY (w. 1850), listed in 1850 census as "hired carpenter" at North Family

The daybooks and journals kept at Harvard also provide specific information on the type and scope of cabinetmaking activities at the community. The earliest known reference, of September 17, 1801, from the "Account of offering made toward building the meeting house" in "Journal and Manifest Record" describes Luther Lyon's departure from the community with his personal possessions, which included an extensive set of woodworking tools. Among the long list of items returned to him were three joiners (planes), one handsaw, one fine saw, one bitstock and eleven bits, one iron square, two wood squares, and ten molding planes. Although it is not known if Brother Luther made furniture, it is clear he possessed the tools necessary to do so, and he presumably pursued that trade while with the Shakers.

Joseph Hammond, a cabinetmaker at Harvard's South Family, kept a daybook from September 10, 1820, through February 28, 1826, where he recorded the construction of benches for the kitchen, bedsteads, a clock case, a clothespress, and his own workbench. Between February 6 and March 11, 1823, he completed a cupboard with paneled door and several drawers. The successive entries describe its design and fabrication: February 6, "Wrought till 11 o'clock AM planning a cupboard for my chamber. Wrought cutting out stuff for cupboard"; March 3 PM, worked "some at fitting drawer bottoms"; March 5, "Wrought upon pannel door for my cupboard"; March 6, "Wrought upon my cupboard at the brackets"; March 11, "Wrought AM finished cupboard all but trimming been 14½ days making." It is evident from this description that he trimmed this combined paneled cupboard and case of drawers with applied molding and then added a bracket base to the case—two characteristic features of attributed Harvard pieces.

The name Elijah Myrick, along with an unusual political commentary, is inscribed on the back of a built-in two-door cupboard in the Fruitlands Museums collection (acc. no. 1992.32). The inscription reads: "Made by Elijah Myrick March 1869 While reflecting on the improving element in our government telling as it does with irresistible [sic] effect on the whole world. Differing from the past by the alliance of integrity with intelligence in the highest council of the Nation. Massachusetts may well feel a laudible pride in the providential selection to their consideration of her past empire of thy gratified designs possessing the power and ability which integrity and intelligence only can give." While this represents the only surviving piece signed by Brother Elijah, entries from "Journal Containing Some of the Most Important Events" substantiate his extensive woodworking activities. In 1843 he made a sink for the washhouse (February 24), a desk for the office (March 11), and a cupboard for the brethren's room at the Second House (March 23).

George Whiting was another active cabinetmaker whose work is identified through written documentation. The "Church Family Journal No. 3" notes that on March 10, 1846, he completed "tables for the office" and on March 18 "began making a case of drawers for the Brethren's room second house." On February 16, 1846, "George Whiting began to make a large case of drawers for the clothes room in the first house garret, a job that has been in contemplation 10 or 12 years and even begun as long ago. Elder Joseph Hammond, having sent for his cupboard & drawer which set in that clothes room as the cause of making them now." As the latter was assigned to Shirley as elder of the North Family in 1843, it is not surprising that he requested his storage furniture. This account tells us that the Harvard Shakers utilized attic storage in the same manner as their counterparts at other communities (see pls. 168, 285, pp. 4–5) and that they had the right to individual possession of furniture. Apparently, clothes rooms were designed to hold storage furniture while retiring rooms contained beds, tables, and chairs. While it is not clear whether the "clothes room in the first house" contained both built-in and freestanding units, it is apparent that the Harvard Shakers were remodeling this space as late as 1846. It appears that Elder Joseph had the use of his own freestanding cupboard and drawers in the same way that Union Village, Ohio, Believers occupied "Private Bureaus" (see pp. 298–99). This similarity in storage space design and usage at the various villages was probably not coincidental but rather the result of a conscious decision on the part of the Shaker leadership.

In 1862 and 1863, the Harvard carpenter Charles Babbitt, while working in the herb business, kept a diary ("A Diary Kept for the Use & Convenience of the Herb Department by Charles W. Babbitt") of his activities, which ranged from putting a leaf on a table (February 2, 1863) to building, staining, and papering a chest (June 8, 1863).

Aside from several signed and dated pieces, Harvard furniture has traditionally been identified by purchase history or oral tradition. Surviving examples include built-in units, cases of drawers, cupboards with drawers, boxes, desks, trestle tables, tripod stands, and chairs. While few work counters survive, it is certain that the form was produced at Harvard.

A consistent design choice, apparent in many forms, is the preference for curved lines, found on the arched feet of case pieces, trestle tables, and tripod stands as well as the rounded edges of bold midcase moldings and shaped trestle supports. In addition, cupboard doors are often constructed of three panels, oriented with two vertical over one horizontal or vice versa, with a dividing rail wider than the horizontal panel itself. On case pieces, the doors are visually and physically separated from the drawers by a bold bull-nose or half-round molding. Drawers often have very fine dovetail work, faces with rounded lips with a broader profile than the typical thumbnail edge, and bottoms supported by many glue blocks. These recurring construction or design features suggest a conscious school of craftsmanship among Harvard woodworkers.

Cases of drawers are characterized by a dovetailed bracket base, a gracefully arched foot, and, often, a short and shallow underhung drawer added beneath the bracket base, which is unique to Harvard case pieces. An unusual example of what is probably a worldly blanket chest modified by the Shakers with the addition of such a drawer is in the collection of the Fruitlands Museums (acc. no. 1991.48). Harvard trestle tables can be easily distinguished from those produced at other communities by the highly arched foot with pointed toe, the vertical standard that is shaped with a continuous curve through its vertical section and has rounded edges and mortise-and-tenon assembly without the use of bolts. Tripod stands

Cupboard, Harvard, c. 1830. Pine, with iron hinges and bone escutcheon, h 36 w 26 d 8". Private collection. Photograph: courtesy John Keith Russell Antiques, Inc.

exhibit unusual proportions uncharacteristic of Shaker stands, with tall, highly arched spider legs and a relatively short pedestal. They often have small square or rectangular tops rather than the round forms typical of other communities and are supported by a rectangular cleat narrower than the stem itself.

References in existing account books and journals indicate that Harvard Believers produced chairs both for home use and for sale to the world. As early as April 28, 1828, they received six dollars for the sale of "½ Dozen Chairs."[23] The Church Family Trustees' Office was constructed between 1839 and 1841 and would have required extensive furnishings, which explains the following remarks in "An account of chairs made in this family in the years 1841 and 1842" in "Journal Containing Some of the Most Important Events." On January 28, 1843, "There was put to the office 83 common, 3 Rocking chairs with arms, and 6 small ones, 92 in all.... There was carried to the office for sale 1 dozen frames (common) and 1 dozen small frames. Making in all carried to the office 116 chairs. To the Ministry 12 common and 2 small ones, to the 2nd family 7 seated chairs, to North Enfield 1 seated chair, to Shirley 1 small frame."

Surviving Harvard chairs are tall and elegant, with straight back posts terminating in elongated pommels divided by a single scribe line at the center; graduated back slats with a rounded top front edge; front-scrolled arms, reminiscent of those on the Boston or Salem rockers dating from the second quarter of the nineteenth century, which are heavily chamfered on the underside of the handholds; and rockers with a continuous arc on the top edge that are fastened to the posts by rivets and burrs. Three distinctive features differentiate Harvard chairs from those produced at other communities: the single scribe mark on the back posts marking the location of the bottom of each slat; on tilters, the half-spherical balls fastened with leather thongs passing through the center of the posts and secured with tacks at the level of the lowest stretcher; and the consistent use of cane or rush, rather than tape, for seats. An entry from the "Journal Containing Some of the Most Important Events" dated January 21, 1843, states, "Dana White & Elisha Myrick are and have been for some days past seating chairs for the present. They have seated in all this winter 73 chairs." This conclusion is supported by Clara Endicott Sears, who commented in 1916 that "caning chairs occupied many workers."[24]

Surviving documentation suggests the community was also responsible for developing a new style of seating furniture at midcentury. During 1853 and 1854 numerous buildings were erected at Harvard, which created the demand for additional chairs. In correspondence between them, Elder Grove Blanchard of Harvard and the Hancock Bishopric ministry discussed the time and effort expended in redesigning the new chairs. An unsigned letter to Elder Grove, dated August 25, 1853, asked him to "leave home for a few days to take the Sample Chair when done and come to Enfield, where we can all look at it and suggest sutch alterations as may appear adviseable. . . ."[25] A subsequent message to Grove Blanchard from Hancock several months later reported, "The Ministry at Holy Mount [i.e. Mount Lebanon] feel considerable interest in the new fashioned chairs & they hope there may be somthing got up about right which will do for believers to pattern after, & will be an improvement as to chairs."[26] Apparently the prototype met with the approval of the ministry, as the journal of Thomas Damon of Hancock notes that Elders Grove Blanchard and William Leonard of Harvard visited Enfield, Connecticut, on January 2, 1854, "with a new style of chair which it was proposed to introduce among Believers."[27] Although the specific details of this new pattern are unknown, it is noteworthy that the impetus for change originated at Harvard.

145. Built-in Cupboards and Cases of Drawers, Church Family Trustees' Office

1841
Pine, with fruitwood knobs, varnish, and iron latches and locks
h 94 w 115¼"
Private collection

The original Church Family Trustees' Office dating from 1794 was replaced by a much larger building in 1839–41. Still standing today and in use as a private residence, it has forty rooms and dozens of built-ins. This particular wall of built-ins is distinguished by the design and organization of space that is determined by the stairway built between the walls of this and an adjacent room. The layout includes two individual side-by-side cupboards on the right, rather than the more usual single unit found throughout the building. The doors are separated from the drawers below by a bold, horizontal bull-nose molding. The wider central cupboard is set above the chair rail, with a door following the Harvard pattern of one horizontal panel over two vertical panels, or vice versa. The third, and smallest unit, which is square in dimensions, is placed at peg-rail height. Many Harvard built-ins are surrounded by a broad 1-by-3-inch frame, which is rounded on the inner edge. This detail is repeated in some of the interior woodwork around the windows and doors.

146. Built-in Cupboard and Case of Drawers, Church Family Ministry Shop
1847
Pine, with walnut knobs and varnish
h 89½ w 54⅜ d 25"
Private collection

This storage unit, one of several built into the 1847 Church Family Ministry Shop, exemplifies the design and construction features associated with Harvard craftsmanship. The doors, unlike those produced at other Shaker communities, consist of two vertical panels over a horizontal panel, separated by a remarkably wide rail. The layout alternates between graduated half-width and one-third-width drawers, creating a syncopated pattern up the facade of the case. A 3⅜-inch-wide member with quarter-round shaping on the inside edge and mitered corners frames the case, adding decoration and definition, further supplied by the dividing rail that separates the cupboards and drawers with an additional half-round molding that functions as a bold midcase band, a feature often found on Harvard case pieces.

The craftsman's sense of design is clear in the development of the three-two-three drawer configuration on the front of the case. The visual rhythm of the facade is maintained through the unusual expedient of disguising a single full-width drawer in the second to lowest tier to look like two half-width drawers—a rare but not unique feature on Shaker furniture. The drawers are assembled with fine dovetails with a broad, rounded lip, the drawer bottoms supported by numerous glue blocks.

opposite above

147. Built-in Cupboard and Case of Drawers, Church Family Ministry Shop
1847–48
Pine
h 70 w 59¾ d 25"
Private collection

This storage unit was built into the brick Church Family Ministry Shop at Harvard, which served the bishopric leaders as a combination residence and workplace. Grove Blanchard, who was appointed first in the ministry in 1828, was still in office when this building was completed. Typical Harvard features include doors constructed of two vertical panels over one horizontal panel, separated by a wide rail, and drawer lips with broad, rounded edges. The interior is accessed by sliding the cupboard doors to the right or left on a wooden track, an unusual feature that can also be found on several case pieces from Mount Lebanon of about 1860.[28] A wooden slide is also positioned above each bank of drawers to expand the work surface.

148. Case of Drawers

Attributed to Thomas Hammond, Jr.
(1791–1880)
c. 1830
Written in pencil on the base section: Thomas
Hammond this belongs to his case of draw[er]s
Pine, with ocher stain and iron bail handles
h 48¾ w 40½ d 22"
Hancock Shaker Village, Pittsfield,
Massachusetts, #L65–5A

Both Thomas Hammond, Sr. (1744–1824), and Jr. (1791–1881), worked in wood, although there is more written information available regarding the son's extensive chair-making activities (see pl. 161). In addition, several journal entries refer to his other cabinetmaking skills. In the "Church Family Journal No. 3," December 20, 1845, "Thomas works in the shop repairing bedsteads"; on June 27, 1846, "Thomas and Elijah [Myrick] have been making cupboards and shelves for the dining room and bakeroom since the lathing was done." An entry of August 15, 1846, relates that he was involved in an unusual project to build "a cupboard to run vituals from the cellar up to the dining room without the labor of going up and down celler."

According to another reference, on August 25, 1858, "Brother Thomas returned & brot a case of draw[ers] he made at Shirley for his convenience here in the meeting house."[29] Judging from the handles on the side of the case, this may be the same one that he made to carry back and forth between communities, a journey he often made. One of two pieces bearing Thomas Hammonds's inscription (see pl. 162), it exhibits several design and construction features associated with Harvard craftsmanship. These include the overall layout of several full-width drawers surrounded on top and bottom by half-width drawers; an underhung drawer, probably a later addition, placed beneath the finely dovetailed separate bracket base; and the distinctive shallow curve of the foot.

149. Built-in Case of Drawers, South Family Dwelling House

c. 1830
Pine and poplar, with walnut knobs and mustard wash
h 109 w 83 d 14"
Private collection

This unusual storage unit was originally built into the South Family Dwelling House at Harvard, which dates from 1830, and later moved to its current location in the applesauce house. The layout, designed specifically for a space over a stairway, has no known counterpart elsewhere in Shaker cabinetwork. All the drawers are 6 inches high but vary in width by row, from left to right: 13⅛, 13½, 13, 13⅜, and 13⅝ inches. This minor variation in dimensions may have been the result of a hastily built case made by a carpenter. Although the drawers are simply nailed together, a decorative shallow bull-nose molding was used on the drawer rails.

opposite below left

150. Case of Drawers

Joseph Myrick (1804–1849)
1844
Written in pencil on a drawer bottom: Built by
Elder Joseph Myrick 1844. Finished March 8
Pine
h 41½ w 40⅛ d 18⅛"
Fruitlands Museums, Harvard, Massachusetts,
#409.1980

This case of drawers is the only known signed and dated piece by Elder Joseph Myrick. Characteristic Harvard features include the bracket base assembled with more dovetails than are structurally necessary; the graceful shaping of the foot; and drawer lips with rounded edges that have a broader radius and blunter profile than a typical thumbnail edge. Although most cases of drawers are proportioned to be taller than they are wide, this case, with almost equal dimensions of height and width, appears visually balanced.

opposite below right

151. Case of Drawers

c. 1840
Pine, with fruitwood knobs and metal pulls
h 49 w 38 d 17"
Private collection
Photograph: courtesy John Keith Russell Antiques,
Inc.

This case of drawers exhibits a number of features typical of Harvard craftsmanship, including the arched shaping of the dovetailed bracket base and the rounded lip on drawer tops and ends. The shaped backboard, the slide built just above the larger case drawers, and the two small drawers placed on top are not common to Harvard furniture. The drawers, reminiscent of glove boxes on Empire furniture, display the craftsman's familiarity with worldly design. This feature is also found in a related piece in a private collection which has three rather than two small drawers on top of the case.

152. Cupboard and Case of Drawers

c. 1840
Pine, with yellow paint and cast-brass latches
h 78⅝ w 65 d 17¼"
Fruitlands Museums, Harvard, Massachusetts,
#1991.49

Besides its yellow paint, the most striking feature of this storage unit is the drawer configuration. The organization of the facade into decreasing numbers of graduated drawers in successive tiers relates in concept to the signed and dated Seth Blanchard counter (pl. 155). Here, this unusual configuration is as much a statement of pure design on the part of the maker as it might be a response to functional requirements.

An idiosyncracy of the construction is that the drawer dovetails are cut with distinctly wider angles than is characteristic of most other Harvard work. The same angles are found on the sewing table pl. 153. This close similarity of the dovetailing style suggests that both pieces were made by the same craftsman.

opposite

154. Sewing Table

c. 1830/c. 1860
*Pine and poplar, with traces of yellow mustard
wash under red wash, brass escutcheon, and
porcelain pull*
h 40⁹⁄₁₆ w 30¹³⁄₁₆ d 18³⁄₈"
*Fruitlands Museums, Harvard, Massachusetts,
on loan from the estate of Elsie Duncan,
#L.1992.14*
*Photograph: courtesy Skinner, Inc., auctioneers
and appraisers*

Originally a two-drawer table, this example
was altered by the Shakers to accommodate
the community's changing needs. The original
top was removed and reset with spacers
below it to make room for a work slide. Probably at the same time, the new four-drawer
gallery was fastened to the top with brass
angle brackets to provide additional storage
above the work surface. These alterations
were probably executed soon after midcentury to provide the sisters with appropriate
furniture for their sewing activities. The very
fine dovetailing on the original lower drawers
is similar to that in other pieces made at Harvard signed by Joseph Myrick (see pl. 150) and
Thomas Hammond (see pls. 148, 162), supporting a Harvard attribution, even though
there are no other known pieces of similar
design. In addition, this piece was most likely
purchased from the Harvard community in
the 1930s.

153. Sewing Table

c. 1850
Pine, butternut, and basswood, with red wash
h 35⅛ w 34⁵⁄₁₆ d 23¾"
*Photograph: courtesy Skinner, Inc., auctioneers
and appraisers*

There is little information available from written sources or documented pieces to shed
light on the form of Harvard sewing tables.
According to a worldly woman whose
mother was a friend of Sister Josephine Jilson
(1850–1925), one of the last Harvard Shakers,
she recalls "watching them [the sisters] at
work at their sewing tables" about 1915, indicating that this form was used at Harvard.

The writer goes on to describe another
sewing table her mother had been given by
the sisters that "had very small drawers
above, 2 larger ones below and a side cupboard," which in part resembles this piece.[30]

Instead of the Mount Lebanon arrangement of a recessed gallery built above the
tabletop, this Harvard table has two drawers
affixed directly to the rear of the work surface. Rather than being added on later, the
drawer unit appears to be original to the
piece. The drawer dovetail angle, which is
wider than that commonly found on Harvard
furniture, is identical to that in the cupboard
and case of drawers pl. 152, suggesting a common Harvard maker.

155. Counter

Seth Blanchard (1784–1868)
1853
Written in pencil on back of top left drawer:
Seth Blanchard Born/October 21 1784/Erected
this Case April 21 - 1853/Aged 68 years 6
Months.
Walnut, birch, butternut, and pine
h 35⅛ w 66⅜ d 29", leaf 8⅜"
Shaker Museum and Library, Old Chatham, New
York, #14617

Seth Blanchard's only known surviving piece of cabinetwork, this signed and dated counter displays a distinct design and bold construction. He achieved this effect by the frame-and-panel case with large posts, an unusual layout of decreasing tiers of dramatically graduated drawers fitted with large 2½-inch knobs, a novel inset foot, and an unexpected combination of contrasting woods. The horizontal side panels are of different sizes because Brother Seth, presumably for reasons of visual continuity, continued the line of the drawer rails around the side of the case to form the framing members. This counter is fitted with a drop leaf in the rear and a small ironing-board sleeve that pulls out of the left side of the case. Although the combination of idiosyncratic features and the inscription make this a keystone piece of Shaker furniture, it has not been possible to attribute other examples to Brother Seth.

156. Box

Attributed to Ziba Winchester (1800–left 1838)
1821/1824
Painted in red on back: 1821
Written in pencil on back: [illegible]/Winchester
Aged 24 1824/Ziba Winchester of Harvard
Pine, with mahogany and maple knobs, blue-green paint, and iron hinges and lock
h 36⅜ w 39¾ d 20¼"
Hancock Shaker Village, Pittsfield, Massachusetts, #L65–5c

This box is part of a larger group of furniture with underhung drawers, a characteristic design feature associated with Harvard craftsmanship. One of the three related examples in this distinctive style is signed by Thomas Hammond (pl. 148), and a second, in a private collection, is unmarked. The third is a worldly grain-painted, lift-top box with single drawer to which the Shakers added an underhung drawer below the bracket base (Fruitlands Museums, acc. no. 1991.48). It is unclear if the underhung drawer was original to this piece or was added soon after the construction of the case. The blue-green paint is not original but is similar to the pigment underneath.[31] This raises some speculation about the meaning of the two dates. Was the piece finished and painted in 1821 and the drawer added in 1824? Was it made or just painted by Brother Ziba?

157. Trestle Table

c. 1830
Cherry
h 28¼ w 60¾ d 31½"
Private collection
Photograph: courtesy John Keith Russell Antiques, Inc.

Communal dining tables produced at Harvard are distinctively different from their counterparts at other Shaker communities. They are shaped so as to produce one continuous flowing curve from the toe to the end of the horizontal cleat. The trestle assembly includes vertical standards, 1⅛-inches thick, and flat in cross section, with shaped, rounded edges. The vertical member is through-tenoned into the arched foot with pointed toe and tenoned into the cross member above. The standard is supported by a bridle joint into a heavy understructure made up of a 3-by-4-inch longitudinal stretcher with shaped cross cleats screwed into the top from below. Most of these tables required an additional metal brace, added sometime after their construction, to support the inadequate bridle joint.

A glass-plate photograph recently discovered in the archives at Fruitlands Museums shows two sisters seated at a trestle dining table set for a meal with six place settings.

158. Trestle Table
c. 1850
Cherry, pine, and maple, with brass pull
h 27¼ w 28⅞ d 17½"
Fruitlands Museums, Harvard, Massachusetts,
#497.1980

This table has been attributed to the Harvard Shaker community based on design and construction characteristics. Although vastly different in size and proportions from its design prototype, the trestle dining table, they share similar details, including the smoothly arched base with protruding toe, the gracefully shaped upright tenoned into the foot and top cleat, and the absence of bolts to hold the longitudinal stretcher. On the other hand, the base does not display the continuous curve or the rounded edges that make the dining table design so successful. The addition of the very shallow and short underhung drawer lends visual interest to the table and leads to the speculation that its original use may have been as a sewing table, a small desk, or a retiring room table.

159. Armless Rocker
c. 1840
Curly maple and rush
h 48¾ w 18¼ d 14⅛"
Private collection

160. Side Chair
c. 1840
Bird's-eye maple and cane
h 41½ w 18⅛ d 14"
Private collection

The variety of Harvard seating furniture is evident in these two chairs constructed of figured maple. The armless rocker is remarkable for its proportions, incorporating unusually tall rear posts, and for its gracefully arched rockers. The side chair can be compared to Enfield and Canterbury examples in its overall lightness and verticality, which is achieved primarily through the narrow post turnings. The graduation in slat width from bottom to top and the high placement of the seat 19¼ inches off the ground, contribute to its unusual look. It is fitted with tilters that are half of a sphere, unlike those found at many other communities. The balls are fastened with leather thongs that extend straight up through holes drilled in the center of the posts to the level of the lowest stretcher. Additional holes are drilled from the interior of the back posts to the same stretcher holes through which the thongs pass to the exterior, where they are fastened with two tacks.

161. Armed Rocker

c. 1840
Tiger maple and rush (not original)
h 45¾ w 23¼"
Fruitlands Museums, Harvard, Massachusetts,
#389.1980

As early as May 25, 1824, Brother Joseph Hammond recorded in his Day Book, "wrought at the Chh helping Br. Thos. H. stain and put together 12 chairs &c." By 1839, it was noted that "Elder Brother Thomas Hammond has put four new chairs into the Ministry's Kitchen & taken the old ones. He has made all the chairs for many years."[32] According to "An account of chairs made in this family in the Years 1841 and 1842," which appeared in a January 28, 1843, entry of "Journal Containing Some of the Most Important Events," Elder Brother Thomas Hammond was foreman of the chair-making

operation, which produced 339 chairs of all sizes during these two years. "There was put to the office [for sale] 83 common, 3 Rocking chairs with arms, and 6 small ones, 92 in all."

This example may be representative of the typical Harvard chair produced by Brother Thomas. It is characterized by tall, straight back posts turned with elongated pommels, which run in an unbroken curve from their tip to the sharp shoulders; broad, graduated back slats with a slightly rounded top front edge; front-scrolled arms that are heavily chamfered on the underside of the handholds; and rocker blades fastened to the posts by rivets and burrs. Quite distinctive of the Harvard chairs is the single scribe mark on the back posts indicating the position of the bottom of each slat. This feature, not found on other Shaker examples, serves as a highly reliable indicator for chairs produced in the Harvard community.

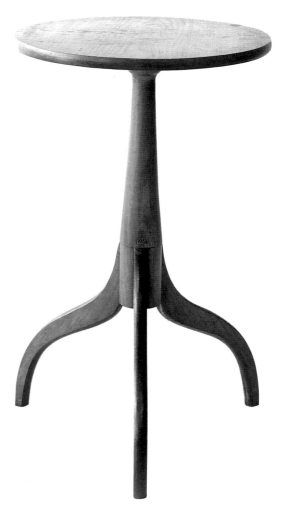

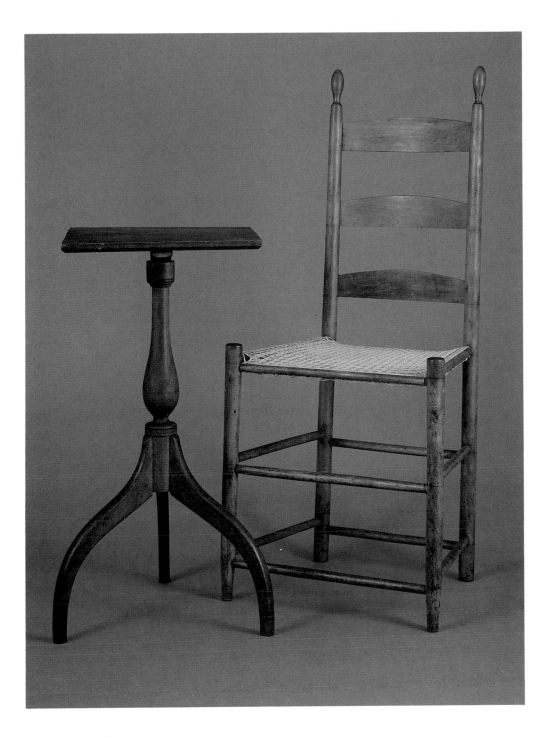

162. Tripod Stand

Thomas Hammond, Jr. (1791–1880)
c. 1830
Written in pencil on the underside of the top:
Made by Thomas Hammond Annie Walker
1883
Cherry and poplar
h 27 diameter of top 16¾"
Private collection

This Federal-style spider-leg stand is note-worthy both for the inscription identifying the maker and the overall design. The relatively high base and shorter pedestal give this stand proportions unlike those found at other Shaker communities. Although the stem turn-ings of Harvard tripod stands vary from a stout simple tapering cylinder, as seen here, to a more elaborate baluster form (see pl. 163), most Harvard examples are decidedly more worldly than "classic" Shaker in spirit. The leg shaping on all Harvard spider-leg stands is distinctly arched and very different than those found on other comparable Shaker examples.

Annie Walker (1847–1912), whose name appears on this stand, was born at the Har-vard community to a Marlboro, Massachu-setts, woman who left her husband to join the Shakers. Annie rose to a position of leader-ship in the community and was probably an eldress in 1883 when she penciled the inscrip-tion on this stand. She was appointed to the ministry in 1905.[33]

163. Tripod Stand

c. 1840
Cherry
h 28¾ w 14¼ d 13¾"
Hancock Shaker Village, Pittsfield,
Massachusetts, #L65-11

164. Side Chair

c. 1845
Maple, birch, and cane
h 41½ w 18 d 14¼"
Hancock Shaker Village, Pittsfield,
Massachusetts, #L65.3A

Many Harvard stands, such as this example, have small rectangular or square tops. Char-acteristic Harvard details include the tall, highly arched feet, short, exuberantly turned short baluster stem, and narrow, rectangular cleat with beveled edge, which is fastened to the top with screws. The more elaborate turning, in sharp contrast with the much sim-pler stems found on most Eastern Shaker tri-pod stands, is more closely related in design to worldly counterparts.

The chair displays several common Har-vard features—a smoothly turned elongated pommel with scribe mark, graduated back slats, cane seat, and, Harvard's most distin-guishing feature, the single scribe line below each slat. The seat is unusually high.

New Hampshire Bishopric

THE **NEW HAMPSHIRE** Bishopric[2] consists of the Canterbury and Enfield Shaker communities, established in 1792 and 1793. For a decade prior to their founding, missionaries from the parent society at Mount Lebanon came regularly to spread the Shaker doctrine among the New Hampshire New Light Baptists. This long period of conversion ensured that the converts had a secure grounding in their new faith and formed a close bond with the Mount Lebanon ministry.

In 1782, Israel Chauncey and Ebeneezer Cooley of Mount Lebanon journeyed to Loudon Center near Canterbury and converted Benjamin and Mary Whitcher and other leading members of the community to the faith. Ten years later, the Shaker community was established on land donated by the Whitcher (Church Family), Wiggin (Second Family), and Sanborn (North Family) families.[3] At the same time, Chauncey and Cooley also visited the Enfield home of James Jewett, a wealthy and influential man in town, who hosted the revival meetings with other prominent residents. Through a combination of buying and swapping land, the United Society of Believers acquired ground on the west side of Mascoma Lake to establish a community in 1793.[4]

Once organized, the new Shaker societies were placed under the charge of Elder Job Bishop (1760–1831), a devoted member of the Mount Lebanon Order who was sent to protect, instruct, and encourage the new Believers in New Hampshire.[5] In addition to his duties as spiritual leader of the newly gathered communities, Father Job may have been a box maker by trade.[6] He may have either personally assisted in the construction of the first New Hampshire buildings or supervised other Shaker joiners and carpenters there, adhering to the standards and the building specifications established by the ministry at Mount Lebanon. According to a series of articles written by Elder Henry Blinn in *The Manifesto* of 1882–83 (vol. 12, nos. 11, 12, 13), "he would show no variation in the style of dress, in the form of the building, in the color of the paint, or in the attachments or capacity of any thing that was manufactured beyond 'the Pattern shown in the Mount' " (p. 102). In his formal role in the New Hampshire ministry, one of his projects was to oversee the framing and construction of the 1792 Meetinghouse at Canterbury, as narrated by Elder Henry Blinn in "A Historical Record of the Society of Believers in Canterbury, N.H.":

> The house was to be built in a plain and substantial manner, without any superfluous embellishments, either on the exterior or interior, as corresponding by more closely with our religious profession. . . . It was to correspond, in every particular size, shape and color, as well as in all the details of finishing, with the one recently built at New Lebanon, or as the Brethren would say, like the pattern in the Mount. . . . The second loft was seven and a half feet. This was to be divided into four rooms and the attic into two rooms. All the wood work on the inside was to be painted dark blue. (vol. 1, pp. 28–29)

No furniture or interior woodwork can be attributed to Elder Job Bishop. Both the Canterbury (1792) and Enfield (1793) meetinghouses were framed by Moses Johnson (1752–1842), originally of Enfield, New Hampshire, who returned to Canterbury after visiting Mount Lebanon. This master craftsman built nine or possibly ten more Shaker meetinghouses based on the Mount Lebanon prototype,

---

165. Counter
Canterbury
c. 1890
Ash and pine, with cast-iron pulls
h 33¾ w 83¼ d 34½"
Canterbury Shaker Village, Inc., Canterbury, New Hampshire

This Victorian work counter shows the Shakers' familiarity with worldly design as well as their willingness to remodel existing interior spaces to suit their changing needs. Built into the 1806 section of the Church Family Laundry Building, this functional and fashionable shop piece blends the old with the new. It is constructed of ash, which has been varnished to reveal rather than conceal the naturally bold, flat-sawn grain of the wood. The drawers are nailed rather than dovetailed together and are fitted with modern, commercially made cast-iron pulls.

To take advantage of all types of light, the Canterbury Shakers strategically set the counter into a corner of the room that they remodeled, surrounding the counter with matching ash tongue-and-groove boards. Natural sunlight streams in from the south window to the left and across the room from the east, while artificial illumination is provided by the lamp hanging above the work surface. (The window above the counter was installed at an earlier date to provide light for the staircase behind.) Electricity was probably added in 1916 or 1917, when this space was used as a schoolroom and lights were suspended over the students' desks, according to former sister Leona Rowell (b. 1905), who was raised by the Shakers but left in 1935.[1]

"Shaker Village, Canterbury, New Hampshire." Engraving. Published in *Balleau's Pictorial Drawing Room Companion*, July 19, 1857, p. 37. Private collection

providing a consistency in layout and design between the parent order and the outlying bishoprics (see p. 94).

Clearly, a large number of skilled craftsmen would have been needed to produce both the built-in and freestanding furniture at Canterbury, which grew to a community of 300 members living in 100 buildings on 3,000 acres by 1850, and Enfield, which peaked in 1845 with 350 members in 70 major buildings on 1,100 acres.[7] However, only a handful of individual cabinetmakers has been identified today, either through signed examples of their work (■), journal records (■■), or oral history and other secondary sources (■■■). At Canterbury, these include:

■■ MICAJAH TUCKER (1764–1848), in Blinn, "Church Record, Canterbury," p. 247, and Blinn, "A Historical Record of . . . Canterbury," p. 83, and see pl. 193

■■ JAMES DANIELS (1767–1851), in Blinn, "Church Record, Canterbury," p. 131: "He was an excellent workman in wood"; and Blinn, "Historical Notes . . . Enfield," obituary record, vols. 1, 2: "In 1788 he was taken to Canterbury [from Enfield], by the advice of Father Job Bishop. James became an excellent workman, and a large number of buildings in Canterbury were made under his direction."

■■ ELIJAH BROWN (1772–1851), in Blinn, "Church Record, Canterbury," p. 129: "He assisted the Enfield Brethren in framing and finishing some buildings."

■■ THOMAS CORBETT (1780–1857), in Blinn, "Church Record, Canterbury," p. 118: "He also made several clocks."

■■ JOSEPH SANBORN (1780–1841), in Irving Greenwood, "Notebook of Information" and Community Building History (private collection): "The backless benches would seat four or five persons and were made by Joseph Sanborn."

■■ ELI KIDDER (1783–1867), see pl. 181

■ JOHN WINKLEY (joined 1792–left 1795), tall case clock signed on dial "John Winkley Canterbury," private collection

■■■ JOSEPH WOODS (1822–1886), listed as cabinetmaker in Andrews, *Shaker Furniture*, p. 48

■ HENRY BLINN (1824–1905), see pl. 186

■ BENJAMIN SMITH (1829–1899), see pls. 183, 185

■■■ WILLIAM STIRLING (1847–l. 1875), in a note written in ink in script on a 3-by-5-inch paper affixed to the bottom of the top left long drawer on a sewing desk currently on loan to Canterbury Shaker Village (acc. no. L82.1): "Sewing Desk/Made by William Stirling/Given to Charles Thompson/by me/Sister Alice Howland [1884–1973]/Canterbury Shakers/Canterbury, N.H."

■■■ WILLIAM BRIGGS (1851–l. 1899), in *The Manifesto*, July 1894, p. 168: "Br. William Briggs is busy with others in the sawing of lumber that is to be used in the manufacture of chairs. A certain quantity is to be furnished each month and the contract holds good during the year."

■■■ EDWARD GROVER, listed as cabinetmaker in Andrews, *Shaker Furniture*, p. 48

■■■ WILLIAM LIBBEY, listed as cabinetmaker in Andrews, *Shaker Furniture*, p. 48

According to Henry Blinn, who wrote "Historical Notes Having Reference to the Believers in Enfield, N.H." in 1897, the absence of data on Enfield was even more pronounced. He prefaced his history of the community with these remarks: "The following pages have been written under very disadvantageous circumstances. Although several years have passed since the work has begun, it has been difficult to obtain the desired information on account of the limited amount of records that have been kept since the organization of the community" (p. 6). Consequently, only nine Enfield craftsmen have been identified, as carpenters, joiners, or mechanics, through one signed piece (■), United States census records and community obituary notices (■■), or oral history (■■■). Surprisingly, only one signed piece of furniture by a documented Enfield craftsman has come to light.

■■ EZEKIAL STEVENS (1744–1830), in Blinn, "Historical Notes . . . Enfield," obituary notices: "Carpenter charged for forming, boarding and shingling a building . . . Ezekial worked on the meeting house at Enfield . . . on the 25th of February 1792 he was moved to Canterbury."

■■ JAMES JOHNSON (1776–1861), in Blinn, "Historical Notes . . . Enfield," obituary notices: "He was a skillful workman at the turning lathe. . . . 1793 James moved to Canterbury."

■■ JAMES JEWETT (1777–1854), in Blinn, "Historical Notes . . . Enfield," obituary notices: "He was a skillful workman in wood."

■ CYRUS JOSEPH JOHNSON (1781–1852), see pl. 223

■■ REUBEN DICKEY (1795–1851), in Blinn, "Historical Notes . . . Enfield," obituary notices: "He was a finished workman on woodwork. . . . He was received from Canterbury and Entered the Society at Enfield in 1808," and listed as carpenter in 1850 census

■■ HARVEY K. ANNIS (1820–1875), in Blinn, "Historical Notes . . . Enfield," obituary notices: "He was a very useful man in all kinds of woodwork. . . . Moved to Canterbury and entered the Church Family Dec 4, 1865."

■■ JOHN CUMINGS (1829–1911), listed as carpenter-joiner in 1860 census

■■ FRANKLIN YOUNGS (1845–1935), in a letter dated January 24, 1923, in the Canterbury Shaker Village Archives (acc. no. 1984.9): "I am pleasantly located to have all my things in place even to my old workbench," and see pl. 229

■■ NELSON CHASE (joined 1855–1898), listed as cabinetmaker in 1850 census and joiner in 1860 census

Surviving interiors date from the late eighteenth through the early twentieth centuries and reveal a dramatic evolution in form and finish. The height of Enfield cabinetmaking in both output and skill was likely reached in the 1830s and 1840s,

drawers adjacent to a panel divided by a horizontal rail, several full-width drawers positioned on the side of the case, a gallery often containing six or eight short drawers in two rows, and a stained red surface.

While known trestle tables from both communities did not survive in any quantity, there are a number of small four-legged tables available for comparative purposes. Examples produced at Canterbury and Enfield are distinguished by their ogee-shaped aprons and large, overhanging rectangular work surfaces. A small number exhibit slender, turned legs and button feet. Those attributed to Enfield tend to be more compact. They generally have square tops fitted with breadboard ends and are attached to the rails with screws reinforced by numerous redundant glue blocks. The drawers are most often unlipped, positioned in the center of the skirt, and fit flush with the top without the use of an upper rail. A small group of these pieces have rimmed work surfaces and galleries with various arrangements of drawers and/or pigeonholes, presumably to store sewing accoutrements.

One furniture form conspicuously absent from both Canterbury and Enfield is the tripod candlestand. It is not known whether these small pedestal tables were not made by the New Hampshire Shakers or whether they simply did not survive with adequate documentation.

The majority of New Hampshire Shaker blanket boxes favor ogee bracket feet. However, a significant group of Canterbury examples have plank sides finished with distinctively shaped bootjack ends, most of them rabbeted and nailed together. Known Enfield boxes, to the contrary, are more frequently joined by dovetails, and some are fitted with a paneled lid—an unusual feature for this form of furniture.

Clocks were produced at Canterbury as early as the 1790s. A tall case clock in a private collection made of pine painted red has a dial inscribed "John Winkley Canterbury."[14] John Winkley, from Kingston, New Hampshire, joined the community in 1792 and left in 1795, which suggests that the timepiece was produced during this period. The vernacular-style case is more closely related to worldly furniture than to examples of the fully developed Shaker aesthetic that unfolded at Watervliet, New York, in the early decades of the nineteenth century.

No Shaker-made beds produced at Canterbury remain at the community, as they were disposed of or sold to the public as membership declined. The situation was very different at Enfield, where Believers owned a shop that produced bedsteads until the mid-nineteenth century. Although they sold the industry to a

Church Family Dwelling House, Canterbury, c. 1880, showing entrance to the chapel (first floor), elders' retiring rooms, shown in pl. 169 (second floor), and attic storage, shown in pl. 168 (third floor). Photograph by W.G.C. Kimball, Concord, New Hampshire. Shaker Museum and Library, Old Chatham, New York, #8981

local manufacturing company in North Enfield (see pl. 229), the Shakers apparently continued to keep abreast of current fashion in the furniture they produced for community use. Surviving examples of late-nineteenth-century beds are elaborate Victorian designs in the midcentury Renaissance Revival style, far removed from earlier prototypes.

A variety of seating furniture was produced in the New Hampshire communities for their use. Canterbury side chairs have bulbous pommels, with or without a small dome turning on top, arched slats with a beveled top edge and convex curved bottom edge, and usually tape seats of either wool or cotton. Rockers exhibit a various number of slats ranging from three to five, drop-scrolled arms, and vase-turned front posts. In 1853, Hervey Elkins described Enfield's production as "plain chairs, bottomed with ratten or rush and light so as to be easily portable" (*Fifteen Years*, p. 25). Surviving examples far surpass this description, illustrating a delicate and beautiful Shaker seating form. Side chairs are noted for their slender posts, backward cant, and elongated elliptical pommels. Rocking chairs have slender, vase-turned front posts, strongly arched back slats, drop-scrolled handholds, and rocker blades with a curve across the top between the posts. Elegant settees with turned spindles, armless benches, and shaped seats are associated with Enfield. Surviving examples of various sizes were built during the last half of the nineteenth century to replace the meetinghouse benches. Specialized seating forms produced by both communities in the New Hampshire Bishopric include low-backed, plank-seated dining room chairs, which were derived from American Windsor chairs.

As membership declined, the South Family at Enfield closed in 1889, followed by the North Family in 1913, and the Church Family in 1918. The dispersal of furniture commenced before five of the oldest sisters moved to Canterbury. An announcement from September 6, 1918, printed in the *Enfield Advocate*, lists some of the contents of the Great Stone Dwelling as it was last furnished by the Enfield Shakers:

> The Church Family Shakers have been having a sale of furniture and other household goods, chairs, tables, chests and drawers of various sizes and quality. They have still many things to dispose of as they contemplate selling the place later on. They have some large pieces like cases of drawers 6 or 8 feet tall, one good roll top desk good as new, two or three tall old style desks or secretaries. Most of these articles were made on the place when there was lumber of a value which we do not have today. Several old clocks quite valuable to one who values old things, and a few more modern clocks. If interested in buying please come and look it over as we shall close the house as the weather gets colder.

At this time, Sisters Mary Jocelyn, Ann Cumings, Elizabeth Estabrook, Mary Darling, and Myra Greene were transferred to Canterbury along with their personal belongings. According to the diary records of Jessie Evans, the schoolteacher at Canterbury (June 14 and 21, July 16 and 23, and September 18, 1918), Elder Irving Greenwood (1876–1939) "took the truck up to Enfield to bring the first load in the transfer of furniture." Between June 14 and September 18 he made no less than six trips to transport the Believers' possessions. It was not until 1923 that Sisters Rosetta Cummings, Fannie Fallon, Mary Batsford, Margaret, Abigail, and Flora Appleton, Ruth Currier, and Brother Franklin Youngs, the last male member of the community, moved to Canterbury, where a great deal of Enfield Shaker furniture still survives.[15] Today, all the extant buildings at Canterbury are from the Church Family and are maintained as a museum by a nonprofit corporation.

166. Built-in Cases of Drawers and Cupboards, Room 10, North Shop, Church Family

1841

Pine, with mustard stain and steel lock plate
h 85½ w 48¼ d 18½"
Canterbury Shaker Village, Inc., Canterbury, New Hampshire

The Church Family North Shop, dating from 1841, was used simultaneously as a woodshed, an herb drying area, and a dry goods storage area for the nearby community kitchen and workrooms.[16] Although the specific purpose of Room 10 is not known, the built-in cupboards and drawers provide an example of Shaker utility cabinetwork, in comparison to the more refined furniture made for a dwelling. The built-ins here, as opposed to those of the 1837 storage attic shown in pl. 168, were clearly designed for a work space. The plain cupboard doors were assembled very simply, with single rather than double pins, and are not embellished with a molding on the interior of the frame, as are the Church Family Dwelling House built-ins of the 1837 storage attic dating from the same period. Drawer sides are constructed of thick, square-edged stock, and the fronts are plain. Assembled with neat but sturdy dovetails, these built-ins suggest the work of a different cabinetmaker from the one who made the dwelling house storage units.

Two cupboards typical of the late eighteenth century, moved from another location, are installed in the left-hand corner of the room. Each 85½ inches high, 36 inches wide, and 13¼ inches deep, they are characterized by raised panels, H hinges, brass escutcheons, and hand-cut brass lock plates. This type of early work remains in scattered examples throughout the Church Family buildings—notably, in the 1816 Laundry, originally converted from the Spin Shop dating from 1795; the East House, built in 1810 as the original Trustees' Office and moved frequently; the Carpenter's Shop, built in 1806; and the Infirmary, built in 1811 as the office and converted in 1849.

167. Case of Drawers
c. 1830
Pine, with cherry or maple knobs and ocher stain
h 74¼ w 40¾ d 18⅛"
Canterbury Shaker Village, Inc., Canterbury, New Hampshire, #82.660

This case of drawers rests on an applied broken ogee-shaped bracket base—a distinct design feature associated with Canterbury blanket chests that is seldom found on free-standing storage units such as this. The eight full-width drawers are graduated into five different sizes, ranging from 6½ to 8 inches deep, all of the bottom four measuring 8 inches. All are fitted with large hardwood knobs with concentric rings.

168. Built-in Storage Room, Attic, Church Family Dwelling House
1837
Pine and basswood, with ocher stain, iron hinges, and cast-iron hardware
Canterbury Shaker Village, Inc., Canterbury, New Hampshire

The ultimate Shaker built-in storage at Canterbury is the "New Attic" of the Dwelling House. Constructed in 1837 as part of a three-story addition to an earlier 1793 building, the 35-foot-long room is equipped with two long undereave storage spaces containing six walk-in closets, fourteen cupboards, and over one hundred drawers. Metal numbers clearly mark individual units used to store off-season bedding, clothing, and crockery.[17]

The new wing is very different in design and construction from the eighteenth-century architecture seen in the Meetinghouse attic (see p. 42). The overall treatment of the woodwork and the placement and contour of the moldings are more refined and sophisticated. Cabinet doors are constructed with flat panels and have an integrally formed, delicate fillet with cove molding on the interior of the door frame. The profile of the 3-inch-wide crown molding running the entire length of the room includes an ogee with a quirk with ogee.

Many Shaker communities employed a horizontal dividing rail between built-in cupboards and drawers, although they used different profiles. The addition of a small complex molding consisting of an attenuated ogee with astragal between the cupboards and the drawers of all of the floor-to-ceiling built-in units appears to be a particular Canterbury feature. Other related examples, but with different profiles, appear on the dwelling house built-ins at Hancock, dating from 1830, probably constructed by Grove Wright (1789–1861) (see pl. 101). Is this placement of moldings on dwelling house storage units simply a coincidence? Is it indicative of a conscious decision on the part of the Shaker leadership to promote uniformity of design in Shaker communities? Or is it the result of traveling craftsmen trading design and construction practices? This distinctive, horizontal molding not only serves to cover the joint between the two sections, the projecting profile also visually organizes the wall into distinct upper and lower units. Each twelve-drawer, two-door unit is further defined and embellished with a quirk bead running down the entire front corner of the case. The doors are hung on butt hinges with cast-iron Norfolk latches instead of the earlier hand-forged hardware. Color is also an important feature in the dwelling house attic. All visible wood surfaces, including drawer fronts, doors, and moldings, are uniformly covered with a transparent ocher stain with no varnish overcoat,

thereby revealing the grain of the pine beneath. This is in marked contrast to the opaque painted surfaces characteristic of the previous century.

Construction features include the single knob on each drawer, which is positioned by a vertical scribe line on the drawer front made with the craftsman's marking gauge on the face. Notable also are the seemingly sloppy horizontal overcuts on the top and bottom of the cupboards' door rails, which resulted while cutting the tenons. These working characteristics may be associated with a particular, as yet unidentified Canterbury cabinetmaker. Finishing out the woodwork in this space are windows equipped with double-hung shutters, which appear to be paneling under the windows when in the open position. This distinct Canterbury design is also found on the Trustees' Office, built six years earlier, in 1831.

169. Built-in Cases of Drawers and Cupboards, Elder Brothers' Retiring Room 18, Church Family Dwelling House
1837
Written in pencil on drawer bottom: Elder Br./No 18
Pine, with white paint over the original chrome yellow wash
Canterbury Shaker Village, Inc., Canterbury, New Hampshire

170. Side Chairs
c. 1840
Stamped on top of left front post of each chair: 18
Maple and cane
h 40⅞ w 18½ d 13¼"
Collection Bob Hamilton

July 1837. We this day raised the L on the North side of the great house which is 52 ft by 43 ft in which is to be the new meeting room in the lower part, in the upper the Elders rooms & 2 rooms for the brethren & sisters. It is said that this is the first building ever raised on friday since the gathering of the Chh not withstanding which we had good luck no one was hurt and matters went well.[18]

The last comment probably refers to a verbal order, which was later reiterated in the 1845 "Millennial Laws": "Father Joseph always taught Believers not to raise buildings, or commence heavy jobs on Friday, or the latter part of the week."[19]

The 1837 addition to the dwelling house provided retiring rooms for the four Church Family elders. In fact, the bottom of one drawer bears the pencil inscription "Elder Br./No 18," indicating that it was made for this specific interior space (Room 18). Specific storage needs also dictated the organization of the built-ins. While they relate very closely in design and construction features to the storage wall in the third-floor attic above, which was made at the same time, probably by the same Shaker cabinetmakers, they show a very different configuration, here, from left to right: cupboard over cupboard; cupboard over drawers; cupboard over drawers over cupboard; and, much less common, a dry sink over cupboard.

Over the next one hundred years, the Canterbury Shakers redecorated and updated this space with the latest functional and fashionable improvements. According to Henry Blinn's Journal, April 1875, "The Elders two retiring rooms, - No's 18 and 19, - were renovated during the season & the woodwork of the walls which had been orange chrome color were now painted white. The floors were repainted, - the long hall leading to said rooms was also repainted." Today, Room 18 shows an intriguing mixture of the past and the present. The original built-ins and Shaker stove of the earlier period contrast with the refinished woodwork in the white colonial revival style, patterned linoleum, an oak crank telephone, and a decorative brass electric light with glass globes overhead. The room still maintains the appearance it had when last used in the 1920s and is furnished with a commercially purchased oak bed and case of drawers, reminiscent of the age of golden oak—a worldly style popular at the end of the nineteenth century, which used light-colored hardwood with a clear finish. Although it is not known when all of these later changes were made, it is clear that the Canterbury Shakers were aware of worldly fashion.

The pair of cane-seated chairs, stamped with their location, Room 18, were probably made for the elder brothers' retiring room. Slender and elegant, they represent two of the finest examples of Canterbury seating furniture used specifically by the Church Family leaders.

171. Case of Drawers
1827
Carved into interior left side of case: 1827
Pine, with birch or maple pulls, ocher stain, iron escutcheon, and steel lock
h 69¾ w 49¼ d 24⅝"
Canterbury Shaker Village, Inc., Canterbury, New Hampshire, #82.211
Photograph: Todd Smith, by courtesy of Canterbury Shaker Village

This six-drawer case of drawers is the earliest known dated Canterbury piece of furniture. Considering the unusually broad proportions of the piece, it has comparatively small knobs, which divide the facade vertically into thirds. The deep moldings nailed to the top and bottom of the case are unusually complex; although presenting a different profile, they relate both in form and color to the built-in storage wall in the 1837 Church Family Dwelling House attic (see pl. 168). Despite its size, the dovetailed case has minimal structural interior framing, consisting only of drawer supports.

    The case piece was found in a small room adjacent to the washroom of the 1816 Laundry Building, the drawers filled with white mesh bags, string, and textile fragments. Considering its size and place of use, this chest may have been originally designed and built to store large, bulky pieces of fabric.

172. Case of Drawers
c. 1830
Painted on the drawer faces, the Arabic numerals from 1 through 11
Pine, with red wash
h 73 w 51⁹⁄₁₆ d 26⅜"
Private collection

This eleven-drawer storage unit was designed and constructed as a utilitarian piece of furniture. The plank-sided case rests flat on the floor rather than on the ogee bracket feet associated with the more sophisticated Canterbury designs such as the case of drawers pl. 173. Furthermore, the maker made no attempt to conceal the nail holes in the crown and base moldings or top and bottom rails, which are joined to the case with housed half-dovetails. Rather than being rabbeted into the case sides, the ends of the horizontal back boards are exposed on either side.

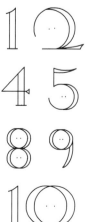

Most interesting are the numbers ranging from one to eleven, which were first scribed with a compass and then painted on the drawer faces. With the exception of the deeper top drawer, measuring 6⁵⁄₁₆ inches, the remaining ten are identical in size, with 5⁵⁄₁₆-inch faces, and fitted with a thumbnail edge on all four sides. This piece was purchased from the Canterbury Shakers by the current owner in the 1950s.

173. Case of Drawers

c. 1840
Pine, with walnut knobs, red paint, and brass escutcheons
h 58¾ w 49¾ d 23¾"
Canterbury Shaker Village, Inc., Canterbury, New Hampshire, #88.498
Photograph: Bill Finney, by courtesy of Canterbury Shaker Village

This chest of drawers, with its unusual grouping of shallow and deep drawers, was found in 1988 in the basement of the Enfield House, Canterbury Shaker Village, where the community's thriving textile industry was located during the twentieth century. Shaker Trustees Emeline Hart (1834–1914) and Lucy Shepard (1836–1926) formed the Hart and Shepard Company sometime during the 1890s and successfully designed, produced, and marketed their famous cloaks and letter sweaters for sale to the world. When acquired by the Canterbury Shaker Village Museum after the death of Sister Mildred Wells in 1987, this chest still contained a large number of paper patterns, cloak fabric, and related materials that were used in the textile business. The shallow drawers are ideally suited to store flat pieces and the deep drawers to hold bonnets, although its original mid-nineteenth-century use is unknown. Additional documentation is provided by a candid Shaker photograph taken about 1920 (Canterbury Shaker Village, Archives, acc. no. 11-P265) that depicts a group of Canterbury sisters celebrating a birthday party in the basement of the Enfield House with the pattern chest in the background.

This case of drawers displays the classic lines and pleasing simplicity of northeastern Shaker furniture. The cabinetmaker used an opaque red pigment for the case that contrasts sharply with the unpainted drawer pulls. Distinctive Canterbury design features include the graceful but sturdy ogee-shaped feet derived from the Queen Anne style set flush into the face of the case and quarter-round lipped edges on both top and bottom of all drawer faces. The double-arched skirt on the ends of the case is also found on several other pieces of Canterbury furniture.

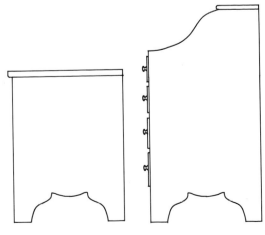

174. Counter

1845

*Written in pencil on bottom of short drawer: Nov
1845*

*Pine, with porcelain pulls, wrought-iron
escutcheons, slip catches, hinges, and internal
locking mechanism, and brass wheels
h 37⅛ w 144¼ d 44¾"
Canterbury Shaker Village, Inc., Canterbury, New
Hampshire, #83.984*

Measuring 12 feet long and almost 4 feet
deep, this Canterbury work counter is the
largest known Shaker example still surviving.
Located on the second floor of the Church
Family Sisters' Shop, a center for community
textile activities, it was most likely assembled
in situ, since the original door openings do
not accommodate its removal. According to
Elder Henry Blinn, writing in 1891 in "A Historical Record of . . . Canterbury," "the north
west room in the second loft [of the sisters'
shop] is used by those who make sisters
dresses" (p. 170) and may have served the
same purpose in 1845 when this specialty
piece of work furniture was constructed.

With the addition of wheels, this counter
is accessible from four sides and offers two
cupboards, sixteen long drawers, and twelve
short drawers to store various fabrics and
related materials, as well as tailoring tools.
Rather than the more frequently seen tongue-
and-groove joint, it has a four-board, spline-fit
top, which is furnished with a brass upholstery button located 21½ inches in from the

end on one side only, perhaps to facilitate the
measuring of specific lengths of cloth. Canterbury details are evident in the drawers lipped
on all four sides and the distinctively turned
knobs. Now stripped, it was originally painted
yellow ocher.

Most interesting is the time-saving locking
mechanism, which enables the user to secure
the bottommost five short drawers by lowering a single wrought-iron latch affixed to the
interior side of the case. It then required only
one key to lock the top drawer, at the same
time fastening the entire bank of drawers
below it. This ingenious device is identical to
that found on a contemporary bank of built-in
drawers in the infirmary attic dating from
1849,[20] which suggests a common Canterbury maker. This unique system has not, to
date, been found on other pieces of documented Shaker furniture. It does, however,
relate in concept to an important Pennsylvania German clothespress, now at the Winterthur Museum, Delaware (acc. no. 58.17.6),
dated 1781. The Hottenstein wardrobe, as it
is called, consists of two cupboards surrounding a central bank of five graduated drawers.
By lowering a wooden lever inside one locking door, all five drawers are secured simultaneously.[21] Although the materials used are
different—wood rather than iron—the principles of the internal locking mechanism are
the same in both designs. Is this an adaptation
of strong Germanic traditions or an independently conceived design?

175. Counter

c. 1840

Pine and beech, with red wash, varnish, and wood wheels

h 35⅝ w 77⅞ d 23½", leaf 12"

Canterbury Shaker Village, Inc., Canterbury, New Hampshire, #85.280

The two square drawers with two central drawers on this counter are unusual in Shaker design. However, the overall arrangement is common in worldly furniture, as an enlarged variation of the early-nineteenth-century Hepplewhite sideboard, characterized by its two narrow central napery drawers, flanked by two deep wine drawers.

The Shakers probably designed this counter with a single pine-board top for tailoring. Two rectangular battens are housed in the rear posts and slide out to support the 12-inch hinged leaf on the rear of the counter. The wheels, fitted into slots in the straight, nontapered legs, enable the table to be easily pulled away from the wall when the drop leaf is raised to a horizontal position. Construction features include the absence of a rail under the top board and the double-pinning of the posts three inches down from the top and two inches above the square to round transition on the leg. Each drawer is equipped with a single large turned knob.

176. Counter

c. 1900

Ash, pine, and marble, with cherry knobs and iron lock

h 31⅝ w 75⅛ d 24⅛"

Shaker Museum and Library, Old Chatham, New York, #13182

A historic photograph of about 1950 from Eldress Bertha Lindsay's (1897–1990) album (Shaker Museum, Old Chatham, New York, acc. no. 6755, photograph no. 61, p. 20) shows this utilitarian post-and-rail work counter in situ at the Church Family Syrup Shop, covered with glass jars—"a day's work of canning," as the handwritten description under the photograph reads. The heavy top and bottom rails, 3-by-4-inch corner posts, and four long bolts spanning the full width and length of the frame are clearly designed to support the 3½-inch-thick marble top. Four tongue-and-groove boards with beaded edges make up the sides of the case. The drawers are simply nailed together, rather than dovetailed, and are fitted with large cherry knobs, features typical of later Shaker design. With their thick necks, these pulls are very unlike the earlier Canterbury examples and relate instead to those found on built-in drawers in the Church Family Brethren's Shop, which was moved to its present site and remodeled in 1884.[22] With the door open, holes through the stiles flanking the door line up with holes in the drawer sides. Inserting a pin into each hole fastens the drawer. When the door is locked with a key, the whole piece is secured.

177. Counter

After 1815
Pine, with birch or maple pulls, dark blue and
salmon-orange paint, and iron hinges
h 39 w 104⅞ d 25⅝"
Shaker Museum and Library, Old Chatham, New
York, #7366

The earliest known documented Canterbury counter was, according to oral tradition and remaining physical evidence, built into the south room on the third floor of the Meeting-house, where the community leaders lived and later worked.[23] After the completion of the building in 1791, Father Job Bishop (1760–1831) moved into the north room in the attic, and Mother Hannah Goodrich (1763–1823) occupied the south room.[24] In 1815, the ministry moved its dwelling rooms onto the floor below, opening up the result-ing space on the third floor for other uses, perhaps for workrooms.

It is probable that this counter was con-structed as part of the general remodeling, since the dark blue paint on the surface matches that on the interior woodwork repainted in 1815.[25] According to Elder Henry Blinn's 1892 description of the alter-ations in the Meetinghouse in his "A Histori-cal Record of . . . Canterbury" (p. 165), "the color was dark blue throughout the whole house. . . . This coating of paint remained without any additional painting until the year 1878 when the meeting room was repainted with a much lighter and brighter shade. . . . The upper rooms of the building still remain as they were when first painted" in 1815. However, it may have been built and posi-tioned into the room a decade or two later. Although blue is prevalent on New England country furniture of the same period, the Shakers seem to have reserved the use of this relatively costly pigment for religious spaces.

In a striking deviation in the color scheme, the interior shelves and the top were painted a salmon color. The use of this uncommon color and the unusual placement of the deep cove molding under the work surface relate this counter to a worktable in the Church Family Laundry Building at Canterbury (see pl. 191). Is the large cove molding on both pieces derived from the Empire style, which was commonplace in the showy veneered furniture popular in the second quarter of the nineteenth century? Perhaps this counter and worktable date from the same period and/or represent the work of the same cabinetmaker.

The broad facade, almost 9 feet wide, is organized as a single cupboard, with flat-panel door, placed off center between two unequal stiles, alongside two wider banks of drawers. Accessible only from the front, the storage layout seems to have been dictated purely by functional requirements, illustrating the asym-metrical arrangement so prominent in Shaker work furniture. This counter was built as a long, horizontal unit, constructed simply with plank sides of pine with the ogee base mold-ing resting flush on the floor. It was removed from the south room of the Meetinghouse attic in 1955 and sold by Canterbury Eldress Emma B. King (1873–1966) to the Shaker Museum in Old Chatham, New York. Today, it is possible to see exactly where the counter stood on the east wall of the attic by the absence of a section of chair rail and base-board molding, a space measuring 100 inches in length, and by the paint history. Further-more, the same salmon-orange color paint of the counter's interior is evident on a strip of wood between the baseboard and the floor, and one of the metal brackets used to secure the piece is still fastened to the remaining chair rail. Since the counter was originally built in, it has no back.

178. Built-in Sink, Church Family Sisters' Shop

1889
Pine and marble, with white paint, chrome- or nickel-plated faucet, and cast-iron and porcelain hardware
h 86 w 32 d 25½"
Canterbury Shaker Village, Inc., Canterbury, New Hampshire

This small room on the south side of the orig-inal 1816 Church Family Sisters' Shop reflects the late-nineteenth-century remodeling ef-forts of the Canterbury Shakers. The two-story building with attic, measuring 32 by 50 feet, underwent a number of interior changes over the years.[26] By 1889, "Rooms have been partitioned and other changes wrought inside—aqueduct pipes inserted, marble wash sinks, etc. etc."[27] The washstand base with ogee feet is an earlier form (c. 1800) that has been adapted into a sink. The ogee shape is echoed in the cabinet side above and reveals the craftsman's attention to design details. A decorative marble top with splashboard, commercially made iron and porcelain pulls, and plated fixtures are domestic improve-ments derived from worldly taste. The same is true of the colonial revival coat of white paint and the patterned linoleum floor. These renovations provide a sharp contrast to the design elements of an earlier era, the three rows of Shaker peg rail in the background.

179. Sewing Desk

c. 1820
Written in pencil in script underneath top board:
platform
White pine and ash, with brass escutcheons
h 36 w 25 d 20"
Courtesy, Winterthur Museum, Delaware,
#62–504

The earliest form of Canterbury sewing desks is somewhat reminiscent of the Chippendale slant-front desk without the lid. The Shakers' pared-down version is a boxlike structure with a lower chest containing several long drawers supported on bracket feet, rimmed "platform" as this Shaker craftsman called the stationary work surface, pullout slide, and scrolled panels supporting a recessed gallery fitted with two or three short drawers. According to oral tradition, this distinctive form evolved at Canterbury—an attribution that is given credence by the following design features, some or all of which appear on this and related pieces: the broken ogee–shaped feet, single knobs with concentric ring turnings, and drawers with lips on all four sides.[28] Particularly noteworthy on this and similar examples is the single pullout loper or slide on one side of the case, suggesting that the desk can be adjusted in the following manner to accommodate two sisters simultaneously. By removing the front slide completely and laying it on top of the drawer and loper on the left side of the case, which have been fully extended, an additional work surface can be created when necessary.[29]

180. Church Family Sisters' Shop

1894 or before
Photograph
Shaker Museum and Library, Old Chatham, New York, #8980

This image[30] depicts the following sisters at work: unknown, Cora Helena Sarle (1867–1956), unknown, Josephine E. Wilson (1860–1942), Jennie Fish (1857–1920), Elizabeth Stirling (b. 1845), Harriet A. Johns (1845–1913), Jane A. Crooker (1834–1916), unknown, Elmira Hillgrove (1835–1916), Mary Louise Wilson (1858–1939), Sarah F. Wilson (1860–1947), unknown. Although engaged in hand-sewing activities, clearly the sisters preferred to work in groups rather than individually. The sewing desk in the foreground functions as an individual workstation and was fitted with sewing accessories to accommodate the sisters' fancywork business.

The quantity and arrangement of furniture and the patterned linoleum floor covering show the Shakers' adaptation of elements of Victorian design. The presence of both the piano and the concertina on the left indicates the usage of this space as workroom and music chamber. According to a comment in Elder Henry Blinn's "Journal" at the end of 1873, "The introduction of the piano into the family is also a great step. Several societies have now introduced musical instruments." He also reported in "A Historical Record of . . . Canterbury," "the large east room is called The Music Room as it has been used since the introduction of musical instruments [i.e. 1873] as a school room for the teaching of vocal and instrumental music" (p. 170).

opposite below

181. Sewing Desk

Eli Kidder (1783–1867)
1861
Written in ink on the underside of the top side drawers: Made by Br. Eli Kidder at 77 years for Almira Hill at 40 yrs. January 1861 Chh Canterbury N.H./U.S.A.
Bird's-eye maple, pine, and poplar
h 38¾ w 25⅝ d 21⅝"
Philadelphia Museum of Art: Given by Mr. and Mrs. Julius Zieget, #63-160-12

Eli Kidder's cabinetmaking work is known through this and another signed sewing desk, which he called work stands, both dated January 1861. The second, at the Shaker Museum, Old Chatham, New York (acc. no. 4838), is marked: "Work Stand Made by Bro. Eli Kidder aged 77 years/ Jan. 1861/Moved into by MEH Jan 18, 1861." MEH was probably Marcia E. Hastings (1811–1891).[31] These two documented sewing desks provide significant links to two other pieces attributed to Kidder, one at Hancock Shaker Village, the other in a private collection.

Eli Kidder was raised as a Canterbury Shaker from childhood and probably learned his woodworking skills from Brother James Daniels (1767–1851). Daniels was taught the house carpenter's trade while at Enfield, New Hampshire, under the direction of master builder Moses Johnson (1752–1842) before joining the Canterbury community in 1792. He was engaged in the framing of nearly every building that was raised at Canterbury during a term of some forty years, although no signed or dated examples of his work are known.[32] Like many Shaker craftsmen, he shared his woodworking skills with other

communities. In 1810 he visited Harvard with Elijah Brown (1772–1851) to raise some of the buildings there and returned to Harvard five years later with Josiah Edgerly (1779–1843) to help complete a dwelling house. In 1811, he and Elijah Brown assisted the Enfield, New Hampshire, brethren in framing and finishing some buildings.[33] Evidently Daniels later gave his planes, marked ID, to Kidder, who may have been his protégé. The initials ID and EK appear together on several planes from a large set, which are now at Hancock Shaker Village and the Shaker Museum at Old Chatham (see pp. 64–65). According to the 1845 "Millennial Laws," part 2, section 12, no. 1, "the initials of a person's name are sufficient mark to put upon any tool, or garment, for the purpose of distinction," and consequently woodworkers were allowed to keep their fine handmade tools apart.

Although the two signed Kidder desks are not identical, they are closely related in design, dimensions, and materials and may have been produced as a pair in 1861 for Sisters Marcia and Almira. Both are of frame-and-panel construction and utilize both the front and sides of the case for maximum storage. The gallery is divided into thirds by a central cupboard surrounded by banks of three drawers on either side. The base contains three long, graduated drawers on the side of the case and a bank of short drawers on the front, asymmetrically placed next to vertical paneling. Both desks have a bird's-eye maple work surface with slide, single knobs on all drawers with concentric rings, and similarly turned feet. The drawers on both pieces are nailed rather than dovetailed together, suggesting that this was a standard construction feature for some craftsmen after about 1860. In addition, this Kidder desk is fitted with an internal locking mechanism that enables the three side drawers to be secured with one key. A rectangular latch is screwed into the rear of the top two rails, which rotates from a horizontal to a vertical position to close each drawer above. By using the latches and locking the bottom drawer, the entire bank could be easily locked.

182. Double Sewing Desk
1839

Written in yellow paint on bottom right drawer: 1839
Written in pencil on bottom right drawer: this desk was newly painted Oct. 19, 1862 by [illeg.]
Pine, with bittersweet red paint over chrome yellow paint and brass escutcheons
h 34½ w 39 d 19¾"
Private collection
Photograph: courtesy Willis Henry Auctions, Inc.

The overall design suggests that this double sewing desk was produced at Canterbury, figuring as a transitional stage in the development of the form. The plank-sided case with ogee-shaped base, sliding work surface, scrolled side panels, and recessed gallery relates closely to the early boxlike structures (see pl. 179), while the overall size of this double unit and the placement of drawers in the side of the case anticipate the paneled sewing desk produced in the 1860s (see pl. 183). Canterbury design features are also found in the single knobs with concentric turnings and drawers with lips on all sides. Three of the eight half-width drawers are fitted with locks.

183. Sewing Desks

Benjamin Smith (1829–1899)
1861
Bird's-eye maple, butternut, and pine, with brass hinges
Written in red ink on interior face of rear rail:
B.F.H. SMITH [S]ept, 1861
h 41¼ w 31¾ d 25¼"
Canterbury Shaker Village, Inc., Canterbury, New Hampshire, #88.736.1 and .2
Photograph: Bill Finney, by courtesy of Canterbury Shaker Village

Benjamin Smith, who signed these two desks placed back-to-back, is one of only a handful of cabinetmakers at Canterbury who have been identified. Between 1860 and the 1890s he served the community in a number of positions and was appointed family elder and trustee. A brief entry in Elder Henry Blinn's "Journal" dated December 31, 1888, refers obliquely to his woodworking activities: "Benjamin H. Smith makes a new saw carriage for the whirl saw." In his obituary notice, in *The Manifesto*, vol. 29, no. 9 (September 1899, p. 134), Canterbury Eldress Josephine Wilson (1866–1946) praised his skills, noting he was "so conscientious that all his handwork should keep close to the perfect pattern of

the Master Workman who drew his affections in early days." Apparently it was not unusual for Shakers to refer to expert craftsmen in this way. For example, in an entry of April 8, 1858 in "The Domestic Journal of Domestic Occurrences," the writer stated, "The timber for the new infirmary was laid out in order for framing. George W[ickersham] Master Workman."

Judging from these rare examples, Benjamin Smith was a skilled artisan in wood. Four signed pieces of his work have been found to date (see pl. 185), matching pieces that are part of a small group of desks that were probably designed to sit together back-to-back to accommodate the group work of the community. Benjamin Smith's desks contain such features as a small cupboard in the gallery; a shallow drawer at the top, perhaps to hold patterns; and an extra space-saving board that pulls out in front to increase the work surface. The remnants of adhesive strips on the work surface suggest that a protective, nonskid material was once used over the highly figured grain.

Visual tension and excitement is created by the rectangular lines of a case balanced atop very slender, delicately turned legs; the straightforward, direct form covered with a surface of dramatically figured woods; and the syncopated drawer arrangement of the case front. The daring asymmetry of three versus four drawers appears here as well as on several other signed and dated sewing desks from Canterbury (see pl. 181). All three examples by Canterbury craftsmen Benjamin Smith and Eli Kidder are dated in the early 1860s, suggesting that this work furniture was produced at the same time to help sisters complete a special commercial project. According to Henry Blinn's two-volume history of the community, "A Historical Record of . . . Canterbury," and "Church Record, Canterbury" the Canterbury Shakers undertook the manufacture of a new line called "Shirt Bosoms" in 1856.[34] This type of garment apparently was fashionable with worldly people; over a ten-year period, the Shakers produced a total of 123,441 units, as follows:

1856	7,167	1861	9,526
1857	33,110	1862	25,272
1858	1,404	1863	3,673
1859	15,692	1865	3,138
1860	22,778	1866	1,684

The demand for this item increased over the years and peaked between the years 1859 and 1862, suggesting the need for additional workstations.

184. Slant-Front Desk

c. 1870
Attributed to Henry Blinn (1824–1905)
Written in ink on a 3-by-5-inch card in upper drawer: This desk was used by Eldress Dorothy Durgin
Chestnut, cherry, and pine, with commercial cast-iron slip catches with porcelain knob and brass lock
Canterbury Shaker Village, Inc., Canterbury, New Hampshire, #82.290

This slant-front desk greatly resembles in design and construction a related example with a strong oral attribution to Henry Blinn. The latter, currently in a private collection,[35] is known as the Manifesto desk. According to oral history, it was made and used by Blinn to store orders for the Shaker periodical *The*

Manifesto, which was printed at Canterbury from 1878 to 1899.[36] While the Manifesto desk has an added two-door cupboard above, it shares with the Dorothy Durgin desk a number of common characteristics on the fall-front writing section and the base. These include closely related frame-and-panel sides, the size and construction of the slant front, the interior layout, the type and combination of woods used, and the shape of the drawer knobs.

Dorothy Durgin (1825–1898), beloved Canterbury eldress for forty-six years, was a strong advocate of the equal division of authority between the brethren and the sisters. She designed a cloak called the Dorothy, which was produced at Canterbury and other Shaker communities.

185. Double Sewing Desk

Benjamin Smith (1829–1899)
1862
Written in pencil on interior rear rail: B.H. Smith
1862, NF 1862
Butternut, birch, cherry, pine, and basswood,
with brass escutcheons
h 44 w 53½ d 26"
Private collection
Photograph: courtesy David A. Schorsch, Inc.

According to Eldress Josephine Wilson's diary entry of Tuesday, October 15, 1935, the Canterbury Shakers sold two double desks at fifty dollars apiece to an antique dealer named Mr. Magner from Hingham, Massachusetts, in October 1935, confirming that several of this unusual form were made.[37] This particular desk was sold by a Boston dealer to a private collector in 1936 who was the second owner after it left the Shakers, suggesting that it may have been one of the two pieces to leave Canterbury in 1935.[38] The form of this double Shaker sewing desk relates to the back-to-back, freestanding pair of desks also signed and dated by Canterbury cabinetmaker Benjamin Smith (see pl. 183). The pencil inscription "B.H. Smith 1862, NF [North Family] 1862" appears on an interior rail and had to be signed before the top was attached.

All three Smith desks share the classic features of Canterbury sewing desks dating from the 1860s. They are characterized by a case of frame-and-panel construction, a gallery combining short drawers (which are nailed rather than dovetailed together) with a cupboard, and a distinctive asymmetrical division of the case. More specifically, the front consists of two banks of four wide drawers alternating with two banks of narrow ones, so that the vertical stiles that separate these drawers do not line up with the stiles that frame the panels on top. Additional Canterbury design and construction features include the single knobs with concentric rings, slides that extend to provide additional work space, and the decorative use of dramatically patterned hardwoods, particularly crotch birch. The upper drawers, like those on the signed and dated Eli Kidder sewing desk (see pl. 181), are equipped with cleat-locking devices consisting of a wooden tab that the user flips up when the drawer below is open. The bottom drawers require keys to secure them.

Instead of turned legs, as expected, this double desk has six ball feet, which creates a lower visual center while providing space for an additional row of four drawers for storage in the bottom of the case. The upper gallery and fixed work surface is flush with the base in front but is 4 inches wider in the back. This rear overhang is supported by two shaped brackets and a horizontal board, suggesting that the double desk was designed as a freestanding workstation for two Shaker sisters.

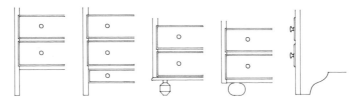

Various base construction features found on Canterbury sewing desks, left to right: plank end; plank end with added drawer beneath the case; case with turned and beveled cylinder foot; case with turned bun-shaped foot; case with drawers on the side and plank front with ogee cut foot

opposite above

186. Sewing Desk

Henry Clay Blinn (1824–1905)
c. 1870
Written on bottom of small drawer in upper gallery: These two Sewing desks were/made from Mother Hannah's Butternut/trees, grown South of Ministries Shop. Were/cared for by her when saplings./Desks made by Elder Henry C. Blinn.
Stamped on inside of drawer faces, Arabic numerals indicating drawer placement
Butternut, bird's-eye maple, pine, and walnut, with porcelain knobs and brass latch
h 42½ w 32 d 25"
Shaker Museum and Library, Old Chatham, New York, #4837

187. Secretary Desk

Attributed to Henry Clay Blinn (1824–1905)
c. 1870
Stamped on inside of drawer faces, Arabic numerals indicating drawer placement
Butternut, walnut, cherry, and basswood, with porcelain and cast-brass knobs and latches
h 82¾ w 37 d 22" (closed); 38" (open)
Shaker Museum and Library, Old Chatham, New York, #7395

Henry Blinn, who made these desks, was a Renaissance man. During his sixty-seven years as a Shaker, he served the Canterbury community in many capacities, including historian, author, printer, beekeeper, tailor, dentist, Church Family leader, ministry elder, and cabinetmaker. Although he never mentions the latter in any of his writings, his woodworking abilities are discussed in a memorial publication: "apartments at the Infirmary were kept at his disposal; though he was never better pleased than when able to spend the day at his carpenter's bench, engaged in light cabinetwork, a favorite occupation."[39] The sewing desk—the only known signed example of Elder Henry's furniture-making skills—follows in the tradition of Eli Kidder (see pl. 181) and Benjamin Smith (see pls. 183, 185), who were working in the 1860s. Characteristic features include frame-and-panel construction, the asymmetrical division of the case into drawers of unequal length, the layout of the gallery, and the combination of dramatically figured woods. The addition of complex, contrasting walnut moldings to the drawer faces and commercially made porcelain pulls reflects a Victorian sensibility on the part of the maker. Mother Hannah referred to in the inscription may be Hannah Goodrich (1763–1820), who served as first eldress of the New Hampshire ministry with Father Job Bishop in 1792.[40]

The two-piece secretary desk was also made by Henry Blinn. The attribution is based on overall design and construction similarities, including the strong directional contrasts found in the vertical movement of the sewing desk sides and secretary top combined with the horizontal orientation of the front of both desks. A significant common detail is the unusual use of metal stamps to mark numbers on the inside of each drawer front to ensure its correct position in the case. This distinctive feature, found on both pieces, is a significant factor in attributing the secretary desk to Elder Henry.

3 1 2 4 8

188. Table
c. 1830
Birch, maple, and pine, with red paint
h 28⅛ w 34¾ d 22⅜"
Canterbury Shaker Village, Inc., Canterbury, New Hampshire, #88.798
Photograph: Bill Finney, by courtesy of Canterbury Shaker Village

189. Picnic at the Mill Pond
1924
Photograph
Canterbury Shaker Village, Inc., Canterbury, New Hampshire, Archives #PN 82

Tables with this deep ogee-shaped apron on all four sides are rare and have been associated by oral tradition with Canterbury. There are many worldly precedents for this design, which appears on rural New England vernacular furniture, such as tea tables.[41] A related Canterbury example, at the Shaker Museum, Old Chatham, New York,[42] exhibits a bracket-shaped apron. More typical Canterbury construction and design characteristics include the drawer with thumbnail edge on all four sides and top with deep overhang (see pl. 190). Additional evidence for this attribution is found in a 1924 photograph of a picnic at the mill pond, which shows Canterbury Sisters Bertha Lindsay (1897–1990) and Miriam Wall (1896–1977) washing dishes on a similar table in a field.

below

190. Table
Canterbury or Enfield
c. 1840
Bird's-eye maple and pine, with fruitwood knobs
h 27½ w 36⅛ d 21³⁄₁₆"
Philadelphia Museum of Art: Gift of Mr. and Mrs. Julius Zieget, #63-160-23
Photograph: A. J. Wyatt

This table was purchased from the Canterbury Shakers in the 1940s. According to oral history, it was used by Sister Zilpha Whitcher (1774–1856) from Canterbury who, accord-

ing to Blinn's "A Historical Record of . . . Canterbury," was a Church Family eldress from 1807 to 1845 (pp. 142, 299). However, it may originally have come from Enfield—an attribution suggested by the presence of the transitional collar joining the square-to-round sections of the leg. The most striking aspect of the piece is the use of dramatically figured bird's-eye maple, which is finished with shellac rather than pigment to reveal the figured wood beneath. This refined example of dwelling house furniture is distinguished by its overall proportions, the dramatic overhang of the top, and the exuberance of the shaping of the legs, which are marked by a single scored line at the point of greatest diameter, a common design feature on turned elements. Another smaller but equally striking bird's-eye table is in the collection of the Shaker Museum, Old Chatham, New York (acc. no. 6054).[43] Here, the craftsman used different proportions and incorporated three drawers to access the space underneath the tabletop.

191. Worktable

Probably Canterbury
c. 1820
Birch and maple, with salmon orange paint and iron lock plate
Painted on sheet-metal label nailed to rail: 4
h 35 w 114 d 41"
Canterbury Shaker Village, Inc., Canterbury, New Hampshire, #82.282

This large, painted worktable is located in the 1816 section of the Laundry Building, where the Canterbury sisters ironed the community's textiles. The height and width of the work surface suggest this specialized table was designed for ironing large sheets, while the empty slots below, which were added at a later date, stored the ironing boards when not in use. The number 4 attached to the rail may refer to the particular room in which the table was used at some point in its history. According to the small pamphlet entitled *Letters and Numbers of Houses* printed in 1883,[44]

Room 4 was the sisters' back room, found on the first floor of the building. However, this small space—10 by 15 feet—seems an unlikely spot either to store or to use such a large nonportable piece of furniture. A more feasible explanation is that the table was assigned to Room 14, the ironing room itself, although there is no clear physical evidence to suggest that the number 1 preceding the 4 on the label is missing.

The unusual salmon color and the 2½-inch-deep cove molding under the top relate it in design to the Meetinghouse counter pl. 177 and suggest a similar construction date. Other noteworthy features include the characteristic Canterbury turned knobs, combined with the distinctive Enfield ring at the junction between the square corner posts and round legs. The large size of the table requires the thickness of the legs at the top, 8 inches in diameter, which, however, have an exceptional taper at the bottom, to 4¾ inches in diameter.

192. Table

c. 1850
Birch and pine, with red stain
h 25⅝ w 32½ d 20¾"
Private collection

This distinctive button-foot table was obtained directly from Canterbury, where it was most recently used as a worktable by Sister Ada Elam (1882–1962) to make lace caps. The style of turning it displays, measuring a slender ⁹⁄₁₆ inch in diameter at the floor, is found on a small number of tables with a Canterbury history. This particular example is larger than most related pieces, which are quite petite in size. Structurally shaped cleats, also present on pl. 225, were employed to secure the top to the base below.

193. Church Family Dining Room

c. 1880
Stereograph
Collection Richard Brooker

Canterbury historian Henry Blinn (1824–1905) documented in his "Church Record, Canterbury" the origin of these distinctive dining room chairs with low backs and boldly beveled pine seats, which Micajah Tucker made for the entire Shaker Family:

> Instead of chairs at the dining table, the first believers used long benches which accomodated some four or five persons each. They were not convenient, especially if one was obliged to leave the table before the others were ready. All were under the necessity of sitting just so far from the table. Elder Br[other] Micajah who was an excellent wood workman has now (1834) furnished the dining hall with chairs very much to the satisfaction of the family generally. At this date (1892) they are all in good repair. (p. 247)

According to a community building history (private collection), these backless benches were originally made by Joseph Sanborn

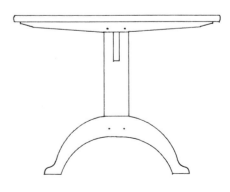

Trestle table, Canterbury, 1846

(1780–1841), who entered the Church Family in 1793. Unfortunately, none of this early seating furniture is known to exist today.

Micajah Tucker served the Canterbury community as Church Family deacon and elder but is perhaps best known as the fine stonecutter who laid most of the granite walks throughout the village. He was also a talented woodworker. According to Blinn ("Historical Record, Canterbury," p. 83), who admired Tucker's ability, "he was of a mechanical turn of mind and skillful in the use of tools. Everything would be done in the best and most substantial manner. The use of all kinds of tools in woodwork, that are usually found in the shop of a carpenter were perfectly familiar to him."

The design of these chairs seems to be derived from eighteenth- and nineteenth-century American Windsors, which are characterized by turned spindles, splayed legs, and plank seats. They are strong, lightweight, and utilitarian while providing support for the lower back. Judging from membership records and dining room capacity, Micajah Tucker probably produced about sixty chairs. The majority of these sturdy chairs was still in service fifty years later, as seen in the stereographic view from about 1880 of the Church Family dining room festooned with holiday decorations.[45]

The interchange of ideas regarding furniture design is evident in the New Hampshire Bishopric. The new dining room of the 1841 Great Stone Dwelling at Enfield (see pl. 218) was equipped with "four long tables, which each seat twenty persons" in low, comb-back, plank-seated chairs.[46] The design and construction of surviving examples in private collections and at the Dartmouth College Museum are similar to Micajah Tucker's 1834 prototype with the following distinctive exceptions. The crest rail is trapezoidal rather than rectangular in shape, the front of the seat appears to flare out more, and the spindles have a greater outward splay.

Some of these chairs have numbers stenciled on the bottom. It is not known if they represent a particular member, seat location in the dining room, or other rooms in which the chairs may have been used.

194. Box
Attributed to Benjamin Smith (1829–1899)
c. 1870
Chestnut and walnut
h 31½ w 34 d 19¼"
Private collection

This box was purchased directly from the Canterbury Shakers, who provided the attribution. In the construction of this two-drawer box, Brother Benjamin Smith combined design concepts from two very different periods. While the ogee-shaped, applied bracket base was a form more commonly used at Canterbury about 1820, Brother Benjamin did not utilize it in the manner of his predecessors but built it flush with the case. The use of this earlier form contrasts with Brother Benjamin's choice of woods, chestnut and walnut, and the addition of the beaded edge, which serve a purely decorative function. Rather than using frame-and-panel construction typical of earlier nineteenth-century boxes, this example is simply nailed together with the decorative elements added to make it look like the more traditional joinery. The overall visual effect parallels the work of contemporary craftsman Elder Henry Blinn, whose furniture is characterized by a combination of Victorian design elements.

195. Box

c. 1840

Written in ink on two paper labels affixed to the top and front: 3
Written in chalk on the till lid: Sisters sock yarn 1865
Pine, with red paint and wrought-iron hinges
h 23¾ w 47 d 18"
Collection Thomas C. Queen

Numerous storage boxes with bootjack ends were produced at Canterbury. Although the specific plank-end cutout is different, conceptually it is similar to the large case piece pl. 173. Many simple Shaker boxes of this type exist that are indistinguishable from their worldly counterparts, which are also assembled with dadoed and nailed front and rear corner joints. This example retains its original red surface pigment and wrought-iron hinges. The lid has molded ovolo edges and similarly shaped cleats positioned under each end of the top to keep it flat. The box has two tills inside. At some point in its history, this storage unit may have been placed in Room 3 of the Church Family Laundry Building to hold wool yarn for the knitting machines.

196. Blanket Box

c. 1830

Pine, with maple or birch pulls and gray-green paint
h 32½ w 49½ d 19"
Canterbury Shaker Village, Inc., Canterbury, New Hampshire, #82.210

The magnificent stature of this box is created by its proportions and overall height, which is unusual for a two-drawer chest. It was sold by the Canterbury sisters to a collector in the 1950s, who returned it to the village in 1981. Characteristic Canterbury construction features include the tall, broken ogee–shaped feet and small, single drawer knobs, which relate in size and shape to those in the 1837 Church Family Dwelling House attic (see pl. 168). The lid has a complex molded edge consisting of a bull-nose above a square with cove, and the base molding is a quirk ogee. Most important, the surface retains its original gray-green finish.

197. Chair Tapes and Tools

c. 1870

Written in ink in script on paper label tacked to box: Utensils for Seating chairs
Butternut(?) (box), metal (tools), and wool (chair tapes)
Box: h 7¼ w 13 d 8½"
Canterbury Shaker Village, Inc., Canterbury, New Hampshire, #88.743.1

This box contains various "Utensils for Seating chairs," including weaving needles to accommodate fabric of various widths, thread for sewing the horsehair-filled fabric supporting the web, and rolls of wool tape. Shakers used rush, cane, and splint for their chair seats, but the most popular material was tape. While tapes were used in the eighteenth and nineteenth centuries for clothing ties and carpet bindings,[47] the idea of weaving cloth strips together to form a seat possibly originated with the Shakers around 1830.[48] They had the advantage of being colorful, comfortable, durable, and easy to install.

Tape production was an important early Shaker activity. The first tapes, like these, were of wool and have homespun, home-dyed threads in a complex pattern. The sisters used two-harness looms to produce plain or checkerboard (tabby) weaves, while four-harness looms may have been used for the more complex herringbone patterns. By 1860, the Shakers purchased commercially produced tapes, most of which consisted of cotton.

These tapes were found at Canterbury neatly rolled in a laundry bag with a handwritten note reading, "Washed and ready for use." This note and conversations with Sister Ethel Hudson (1896–1992) lead to the conclusion that old handmade tapes were removed from chairs, washed, and reused. As recently as 1950, historic photographs show Sister Rebecca Hathaway (1882–1958) using tools such as these to retape old chairs for the community's use.

198. Rocker
c. 1830
Maple and tape, with varnish
Private collection

199. Side Chair
c. 1830
Curly maple and tape, with varnish
Private collection

Broad-back slats and a bulbous pommel with a small dome turning, typical Canterbury features, are common to these chairs. However, they represent very different levels of sophistication. The rockers and back slats of the armless rocker are somewhat crude. Its modest dimensions suggest that it was made for a rather small brother or sister. The side chair, on the other hand, is highly refined, with strongly figured curly maple, carefully turned convex taper on the front post, nicely graduated back slats, and multicolored handwoven cloth tape.

200. Armed Rocker
c. 1830
Maple, with brown stain and varnish
Private collection

The beautifully shaped drop-scrolled arms of this rocker have a clear family resemblance to those made at Enfield. Although this exquisite arm style differs from that used in other Shaker bishoprics, it is found in worldly New England chairs.[49] The subtle difference between the chairs produced in the New Hampshire communities lies primarily in the shaping of the front posts, which at Canterbury is more flowing and less sharp in its detail. Enfield chairs commonly show a collar turning just below the vase form, which is absent here. The Canterbury turners also preferred a more bulbous finial shape. The broad back slats are generally graduated, as also seen in the pair of fine Canterbury side chairs pl. 170.

201. Built-in Cupboards and Cases of Drawers, Church Family Dwelling House
c. 1840
Pine
h 87½ w 95⅜"
First Leader Corporation, Enfield, New Hampshire

---

202. Built-in Cupboards and Case of Drawers, Church Family Dwelling
c. 1840
Pine, with fruitwood knobs
h 103½ w 39"
First Leader Corporation, Enfield, New Hampshire

Built-ins such as these are located in many retiring rooms within the massive stone Church Family residence, or Great Stone Dwelling. Such use of the space in the deep walls of the central corridors, which entirely surround the primary door to the retiring room, for built-in storage seems to be unique to this community. Consistent patterns were developed in the arrangement of the cupboards and drawers flanking the door (pl. 201), which leads to the building's central hall. What visually resembles a pair of doors on the top of many units is actually a false door alongside a functioning cupboard door, identical in construction except it is nailed to the case and not hinged. Decorative elements include an ovolo molding around the overall frame, beaded edges around the cabinet doors, a small bull-nose sill, and applied quirk ovolo moldings around the cupboard door panels.

The tall and narrow case (pl. 202) is set into the wall adjacent to the built-in pl. 201, providing even more storage space for the four to eight community members residing there. The cupboard behind the bottom right door is lined with tin and fitted with a ventilating chimney to hold a chamber pot. The doorway on the right leads to two smaller rooms, probably used for bathing or additional clothing storage, which are similar in concept to the walk-in spaces found in other dwellings, such as those at Hancock, Massachusetts, and Pleasant Hill, Kentucky. Giles Avery's 1843 "Journal of a Trip to the Eastern Societies" describes the retiring rooms:

> Each room is accommodated with a closet which lies between the rooms and each room has one side of it. . . . An offset in the partition is also made to accommodate a case of drawers and cupboard which is attached to the room, of course the room is clear, no cases of drawers, or chimney corners, neither woodboxes to run against. (pp. 42–43)

above

203. Case of Drawers
c. 1840
Birch and pine, with red paint
h 50½ w 43¾ d 23½"
Private collection

Although, with its great mass, this case of drawers is visually most closely related to some of the Pleasant Hill, Kentucky, or Ohio case pieces, it was certainly built in the Enfield community. Here, the combination of a case constructed of mortise-and-tenon joinery, framework enclosing four flat panels on both the sides and back of the piece, and heavy corner posts with turned legs provides more than adequate structural integrity. Small decorative details are evident in the thumbnail-lipped drawer fronts, rails and stiles with ovolo edges, and top molding with a bull-nose edge, which creates a rimmed surface more often found on small worktables (see pl. 220) rather than case pieces.

The location of the piece at Enfield, the four-sided drawer lip construction, and the placement of a single knob on all drawers support the attribution to Enfield even though the overall form is not typical of this community's work. The craftsman's design independence is apparent in the layout of the facade; the unorthodox drawer arrangement is very different from that found on pl. 173, which also originated in the New Hampshire Bishopric. The combination of the various design elements with the quality of joinery resulted in a masterful and unique expression of Enfield Shaker craftsmanship.

204. Case of Drawers
c. 1830
Pine, with hardwood knobs, brown stain, and varnish
h 74 w 37½ d 20⅛"
Private collection

205. Desk
c. 1830
Birch, cherry, and pine, with hardwood knobs and brass latches and hinges
h 76¾ w 41½ d 21"
Private collection
Photograph: Michael Fredericks; courtesy Richard and Betty Ann Rasso

Both of these unusual case pieces have drawn design elements from worldly New Hampshire furniture. More specifically, the central

drop panel on the bottom rail is a distinctive feature that has long been associated with documented work from the Portsmouth, New Hampshire–North Shore of Massachusetts area.[50] In addition, both share the same distinctive side leg shaping and the unusually thick (¾ inch) case side facing, which suggests that they were built by the same Shaker craftsman. The tall chest and desk were acquired at Canterbury or Harvard in the 1940s and 1920s respectively. In addition to the purchase history, the New Hampshire attribution is based on the drop-panel design, the drawers' dovetail construction, and the use of a single knob on the desk drawers. The use of birch in the desk, a wood much more commonly found in Enfield than Canterbury furniture, narrows down the attribution—albeit more tentatively—to Enfield.

206. Desk
c. 1840
Birch and pine, with red wash, varnish, and brass knob
h 27¾ w 26 d 22½" extended
Hancock Shaker Village, Pittsfield, Massachusetts, #66–241

Although similar to a drop-leaf table, this unusually small piece is actually a single drop-leaf desk. The angle of the rule joint between the top and the drop leaf combined with the design of the leaf support position the writing surface at an angle about ten degrees below level. The concept of the slanted leaf that is used as a desk is also found on a two-drawer table/desk, which has two independent pull-out leaf supports. One holds the leaf horizontally, the other at an angle, so the piece can be used either as a table or a desk.[51] It has a strong Enfield history, supporting an attribution of both pieces to the same community. This single drop-leaf desk also contains one full-length drawer, which can be opened from either end, and retains a strong red wash.

207. Sewing Desk

c. 1850
Birch and pine, with hardwood or fruitwood
knobs, red wash, and metal escutcheon
h 35½ w 38¾ d 26¾"
Private collection
Photograph: courtesy John Keith Russell Antiques,
Inc.

By adding the multiple-drawer gallery and the pullout slide, the maker combined the features of two distinct forms: the small work counter and the sewing desk. The double-ogee-shaped gallery sides, the addition of ten gallery drawers—many more than are usual in sewing desks—and the broader proportions of the piece as a whole, including the longer legs, create a design very different from most other Enfield work furniture.

illustrated on page 8

208. Desk

c. 1860
Birch and pine, with leather and red and dark
brown or black paint
h 39½ w 42 d 30"
Hancock Shaker Village, Pittsfield,
Massachusetts, #71–239

This adaptation of the traditional Enfield sewing desk form may be unique in terms of its size, layout, and surface treatment. The case itself is about one-third larger than the usual Shaker sewing desk. Aspects of the desk uncommon in Shaker work are the addition of drawers in the back as well as the front of the gallery and the use of a bank of false drawers, on the right side of the front of the case, to balance the front facade. The finish of dark brown or black pigment, an unusual choice of color for Shaker furniture, in combination with red paint is rare.

A button hidden under the leather top releases the writing surface, which pulls out to expose storage space below. A desk in the collection at Fruitlands Museums[52] exhibits a similar kind of design adaptation to what was otherwise a typical sewing desk with the addition of a large overhanging writing surface. The writing surface was executed as part of the original piece and is clearly not a later alteration. Construction and design characteristics point to Brother Eli Kidder (1783–1867) of the Canterbury Shaker Community as the craftsman of the Fruitlands desk.

209. Sewing Desk

c. 1860
Birch, pine, and butternut, with walnut knobs
and grain painting
h 40⅜ w 31½ d 24"
Private collection
Photograph: courtesy Charles Flint

Although possibly not the original finish, the robust, imitation wood-grain pattern executed in brown over white was evidently applied by the Shakers. Aside from the remarkable surface treatment, this sewing desk displays a form common to other known Enfield work furniture built for sewing activities. This particular example was acquired directly from Shaker descendants, along with a photograph of two Enfield Sisters who used the desk. The customary asymmetrical configuration contains a one-third-width drawer to two-thirds-width panel layout. These narrower drawers are located in the front and a bank of much wider drawers is placed on the side for more convenient access, particularly when the slide is pulled out to provide for additional work surface. The front panel is typically divided by a horizontal rail.

This arrangement can be compared to numerous Canterbury desks, including those attributed to Brother Eli Kidder (1783–1867), in which the facade is divided into two or three vertical panels (see pl. 181). The gallery arrangement shown here is representative, although occasionally eight rather than six drawers are offered. An additional drawer was sometimes installed under the case after the desk was completed to increase the storage capacity.

210. Sister at Sewing Desk
c. 1954
Photograph by Robb Sagendorph
Courtesy Yankee Magazine (July 1954)

This and a nearly identical sewing desk in the Philadelphia Museum of Art (acc. no. 63–160-11) are attributed to Brother Franklin Youngs (1845–1935), according to oral history. This desk, which is now in a private collection, was made about 1870 and measures 39½ inches high, 33¼ inches wide, and 24¼ inches deep. Common to both is the overall drawer configuration with pullout work surface, frame-and-panel construction, and Enfield ring-turned legs—all of these classic elements, dating from the 1860s. However, the contrasting highly figured woods (bird's-eye maple, cherry, walnut, and pine) and applied moldings, complemented by the porcelain pulls and mirrored cupboard-door panel, reveal a strong Victorian influence, as does the bed also attributed to Brother Franklin (see pl. 229). The centrally located mirror was used in place of a small wood panel on the gallery door.

211. Counter
c. 1850
Birch and pine, with red paint
h 30⅞ w 85¾ d 24"
The Museum at Lower Shaker Village, Enfield, New Hampshire, #LSV 978.81

212. Counter
c. 1830
Birch and pine, with varnish
h 28 w 84 d 26¼"
Collection of the Golden Lamb Inn, Lebanon, Ohio
Photograph: John E. Evers

Originally finished in red paint, the 1850 counter shares common characteristics with its earlier counterpart. They both exhibit the same essential proportions, based on a frame that is longer than it is deep, a similar layout, containing two doors separated with wide panels, and post-and-rail construction on turned legs. The 1850 example has a comparatively flat facade, punctuated only by the inset flat-door panels. Clearly with an eye for detail, the craftsman finished the square section of the corner posts with a crisp ovolo molding, which is repeated on the door rails and stiles. The earlier counter borrowed elements from eighteenth-century craftsmanship, including the extensive use of raised-panel work on and between the doors, as well as the ends of the case. Although related in form and probably function, these Enfield case pieces represent the design skills of two very different craftsmen a generation or two apart working within the Shaker tradition.

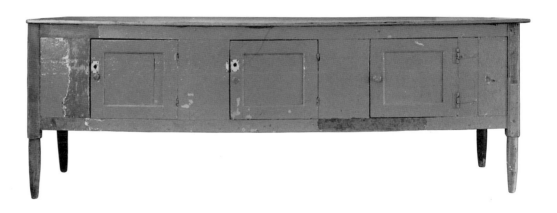

213. Counter

c. 1830
*Birch and pine, with chrome yellow paint and
wrought-iron leaf-support mechanism
h 31¼ w 84 d 28", leaf 28"
Collection of the Golden Lamb Inn, Lebanon,
Ohio*

This counter is unlike any other known example. Instead of the usual door or drawers, it
holds three sliding 23-inch-deep shelves, supported by grooves cut on the interior of the
case—a highly uncharacteristic construction
in any Shaker form. A bracket, probably added

well after the counter was built, houses
another smaller sliding shelf. The rear hinged
leaf, supported by a forged crane affixed on
the case ends and a separate post, doubles
the work surface. The case exhibits a typical
post-and-rail construction, with the addition
of an unusual applied panel set outside rather
than inside the frame. A quirk bead and ovolo
molding give the face of the case finishing
details. The heavy chrome yellow paint was a
second finish applied over varnish. Unfortunately, it is not possible to determine how this
unusual counter was used by the Shakers.

214. Counter
c. 1840
Birch and poplar, with brass hinges and wrought-iron leaf-support mechanism
h 36¾ w 69 d 22⅞"
Canterbury Shaker Village, Inc., Canterbury, New Hampshire, #88.411

215. Sisters' Sewing Room
c. 1880
Photograph
Private collection

This counter with card table–type hinges originated in the Enfield, New Hampshire, Shaker community. The historic photograph clearly shows Sister Fannie Fallon (1856–left 1925) seated in an Enfield sewing room with a pair of sewing desks and this work counter in the background. Construction features that support an Enfield origin include the distinct legs with ring turnings, drawer pulls with short, thick necks that relate to those on the 1850 table by C. Joseph Johnson (see pl. 223), and the use of birch, found most commonly at Enfield. The side facade is deceptive: its two panels set into a frame with two additional "fake" rails give the impression of a four-panel side.

Of special interest is the card table–hinged top with wrought-iron leaf-support mechanism. A device serving the same purpose, although much smaller, is seen on some Shaker tables and cases of drawers, though functioning in a different manner: the forged L-shaped mechanism, similar in design to a fireplace crane, has hinge pins at top and bottom, allowing the horizontal support to swing out parallel to the floor. In this counter, however, the crane is situated differently. A single hinge pin is located at the top of the post, which acts as a central pivot point when the short section of the bracket is swung downward, perpendicular to the floor. The device is made of wrought iron, presumably fashioned by a Shaker blacksmith rather than a commercially purchased piece of hardware. There are two catches integral to the operation of the mechanism: one to keep the crane in its inactive position alongside the side of the case; the other to hold the bracket after it pivots 90 degrees to support the leaf that doubles the work surface. However, with the top in the "open" position, the drawers are functionally unusable, because the extended tabletop swings forward over them.

216. Table
c. 1830
Birch and pine, with red stain and brass knob
h 26½ w 23¾ d 17¾"
Private collection

217. Sewing Room
c. 1910
Shaker Museum and Library, Old Chatham, New York, #4-1-4

This table is identical to one in the collection of Canterbury Shaker Village that has a strong Enfield history. This or a similar table appears in the candid photograph of Sisters Rosetta Cummings (1841–1925) and Henrietta Spooner (b. 1844) in the sewing room at Enfield, New Hampshire. The table pictured could have been brought to Canterbury in 1918 when Elder Irving Greenwood (1876–1939), according to the entry for June 14 in Jessie Evans's diary, "took the truck up to Enfield to bring the first load in the transfer of furniture." Between June 14 and September 18 he made no less than six trips to transport the personal possessions of the Believers at Enfield, New Hampshire, when their community closed and the remaining members were moved to Canterbury. Sister Rosetta herself moved down in 1923 and could have brought the table to Canterbury with her then.[53]

In addition to the typical Enfield leg, these tables share a number of construction characteristics, which suggest a common maker or shop practice. These features include breadboard ends with rounded edges and a top fastened to the apron with screws set into screw pockets and reinforced with at least twelve redundant glue blocks. Because of the absence of a top rail, the upper edge of the drawer with incised bead is set flush with the underside of the tabletop.

opposite above

218. Dining Room, Church Family Dwelling House
c. 1880
Photograph
Private collection

Presently operated as a restaurant, this Church Family dining room survives with most of the cupboards and shutters intact. After a visit to Enfield in 1843, Elder Giles Avery described the space, in the Great Stone Dwelling, in his "Journal of a Trip to the Eastern Societies": "In the dining room there are cupboards and drawers which occupy the whole side of the room, on either side. Drawers under the tables, to put in salt cellars & other things for seasonings; which are not commonly put on the tables" (pp. 42–43). Hervey Elkins, an apostate who left the

219. Double Drop-Leaf Table
c. 1830
h 28 w 37⅜ d 49¾" (extended)
Bird's-eye and curly maple and pine, with hardwood knobs, red wash, and varnish
Private collection, Enfield, New Hampshire

The construction and design of this small drop-leaf table is unorthodox. It has a paneled frame rather than solid aprons and four drawers—two 4-inch-high drawers on each end of the table. More common to the Enfield community is the use of rounded lips on all four edges of the drawer face and the ever-present transitional ring on the turned legs. Two wood pull-out supports hold each drop leaf in position for use. This table was purchased by a previous owner directly from the Enfield Shaker community, where it had been in use on the second floor of the Great Stone Dwelling.

Shakers, described the use of this space in his book *Fifteen Years in the Senior Order of Shakers*:

> In the Senior Order, at the ringing of a large bell, ten minutes before meal time, all may gather into the saloons and retire the ten minutes before the dining hall alarm summons them to the table. All enter four doors and gently arrange themselves at their respective places at the table, then, all, simultaneously, kneel in silent thanks for nearly a minute, then rise and seat themselves almost inaudibly at the table. No talking, laughing, whispering or blinking are allowed while thus partaking of God's blessings. After eating, all rise together at the signal of the first elder, kneel as before, and gently retire to their places of vocation, without stopping in the dining hall, loitering in the corridors and vestibules, or lounging upon the balustrades, doorways and stairs. The tables are long, three feet in width, polished high, without cloth, and furnished with white ware and no tumblers. (pp. 24–25)

The plank-bottom chairs are very similar to those made at Canterbury by Micajah Tucker (see pl. 193) except for a more rounded front edge of the seat.

220. Table

c. 1840
Birch and pine, with hardwood knobs, red wash, and varnish
h 26⅜ w 30¾ d 23½"
Private collection

This table is representative of related examples found at the Hood Museum of Art, Hanover, New Hampshire (acc. no. 46.22.16380) and formerly Collection Karl Mendel.[54] All three two-drawer worktables show proportionally deep aprons, turned legs with the usual Enfield transitional ring, and overhanging tops trimmed with lipped edges. While the other examples are fitted with four- and six-drawer add-on galleries, this piece shows no evidence of ever having had one. These tables have the same basic form as Mount Lebanon sewing tables (see pl. 50).

opposite above

221. Drop-Leaf Table

c. 1850
Birch and pine
h 27 w 30 d 26½" (extended)
Hancock Shaker Village, Pittsfield, Massachusetts, #80–70.3

222. Drop-Leaf Table

c. 1850
Birch
h 26⅞" w 72 d 18½", leaf 9"
Hancock Shaker Village, Pittsfield, Massachusetts, on loan from Mr. and Mrs. Gilbert Lockwood, #L86–2.4

The two drop-leaf tables illustrated here, both of which exhibit the typical Enfield turned leg, display considerable variety within the same form. Extending from 30 to 72 inches in length, these examples also show different styles of turning, ranging from a rather straight leg with minimal taper to a much heavier, more bulbous form. The craftsman who made the smaller table added a single drawer as well as the decorative ovolo with fillet detail on the bottom edge of the apron.

opposite below

223. Table

C. Joseph Johnson (1781–1852)
1850
Written in pencil in script on underside of drawer: C.J. Johnson/March 23, 1850
Birch
h 27 w 56 d 20⅞" (closed)
Canterbury Shaker Village, Inc., Canterbury, New Hampshire, #82.213

Joseph Johnson, as he was called, was born in Enfield and was appointed to the order of the ministry in 1837 with Elder Benjamin Whitcher. He remained in this position until 1852, when he resigned due to ill health and moved to Canterbury.[55] Apparently, his full name was Cyrus Joseph Johnson, according to an entry written by Isaac Newton Youngs in his "Domestic Journal of Domestic Occurrences" in August 1847, which states, "The Canterbury Ministry arrived here. They are C. Joseph Johnson, Abraham Perkins, Harriet Hastings, Hester Ann Abrams." Furthermore, Enfield Membership Records[56] do not include any other Johnsons whose initials correspond with those on this table. Although there is no written evidence of Elder Johnson's skills as a cabinetmaker, it is possible he learned this trade from his famous father, Moses, "a superior workman in wood," as Henry Blinn called him in "A Historical Record of . . . Canterbury." Referring to his hewing a log into a beam with an adz or broad axe, Blinn noted, "His work was nearly as smooth as though trimmed by a Jack Plane" (p. 132).

A distinctive Enfield feature is evident in the plain ring cut at the top of the flared, swelling leg, which echoes the stair balusters in the 1840s Great Stone Dwelling. Each drop leaf is held in the extended position by two supports, which operate in the following manner. When not in use, these two rectangular supports on each side pivot back into the apron, which is grooved to give the user a fingerhold to swing them into position. Although this mechanism is commonly seen on worldly furniture, it appears less frequently on Shaker pieces.

In addition, there are several noteworthy characteristics regarding the drawer construction that deserve further comment. The drawer pulls have an unusually short, thick neck, similar to those found on an Enfield-attributed counter (pl. 214).

224. Worktable
c. 1820
Birch and pine
h 30½ w 72¼ d 30⅞"
Private collection
Photograph: Robert P. Emlen

Wallace Nutting, who first published this table in his classic reference text *Furniture Treasury*,[57] described it as an eighteenth-century worldly kitchen table. However, the overall design as well as the specific turnings, which closely parallel the counter pl. 227, point to a Shaker origin. Features include the addition of an underhung drawer, end-hinged drop leaf, and stretcher-style base. The shelf may have been added later. The slotted apron with ogee shaping may be unique to this unusual Shaker design.

225. Table
c. 1850
Birch and pine, with red paint
h 27 w 84 d 25"
Private collection

This table, purchased directly from the Enfield community in the 1920s, presents a number of unusual features that together add up to a unique design. Several inches below the ogee-shaped apron, distinctive in itself, a turning was cut deeply into the leg, followed by a convex V ring. The leg swells out gracefully and tapers to its minimum diameter a few inches above the floor level, then it flares slightly at the base. The extreme reduction in diameter below the square post, the convex V ring, and the flared profile are rare in Shaker turnings. The only other known example of the convex V ring appears on a much smaller table in a private collection with a leg that exhibits a similar, although less robust shape.

226. Table with Gallery

c. 1860
Birch and pine
h 42⅝ w 28⅞ d 27¼"
The Museum at Lower Shaker Village, Enfield,
New Hampshire, #SM 990.1

Aside from the overall size and proportions, this table is similar to pl. 216, which has a strong Enfield attribution. This example originally had a rimmed top secured to the base with twenty-six glue blocks and a shelf below supported by two rectangular stretchers mortised into the legs. The gallery, however, was added at a later date and represents one of at least ten variations on the add-on. Many, including this example, contain a number of small drawers and pigeonholes, presumably intended to hold sewing tools and accessories.

The gallery case as well as the drawers were carefully dovetailed. The drawer rail edges were rounded and notched where they join the gallery case. The large dome-shaped "boots" on the legs were added to raise the height of the work surface to accommodate different sisters who used it.

227. Counter

c. 1840
Birch and pine, with iron hinges
h 29⅛ w 60½ d 36⅝" (extended)
Hancock Shaker Village, Pittsfield,
Massachusetts, #65–291

Although built strictly as a piece of work furniture, this table was carefully designed. The storage shelf is clearly original to the piece, for the square segment of the post terminates just below the shelf it supports. The leg shows the characteristic ring transition associated with Enfield craftsmanship above the turned section. Two wooden supports for the leaf slide in housings built just outside the table frame. With its generic design, this counter could have been used in the kitchen or many of the community trades.

228. Retiring Room, Church Family Dwelling House
1880
Stereograph by W. G. Kimball, Concord, New Hampshire
Collection of The United Society of Shakers, Sabbathday Lake, Maine

---

229. Bed
Attributed to Franklin Youngs (1845–1935)
c. 1880
Ash, cherry, and walnut
1 67¹/₄ w 42"
Canterbury Shaker Village, Inc., Canterbury, New Hampshire, #82.231

During the last half of the nineteenth century, the Enfield Shakers developed close associations with local businesses. In 1854, they set up a bedstead shop, which after a few years was leased to a manufacturing company in the village of North Enfield. Known variously as Cambridge and Folsom, Cambridge and Huse, and Huse and Berry, the firm enjoyed a substantial trade, at least until 1886.[58] This 1880 stereograph shows a retiring room at the village furnished with an elaborate factory-made bed. It is assumed that the Shakers continued contact with the bedstead factory in town, which certainly influenced their own furniture production.

The bed below is closely related to one made by Franklin Youngs for his own use, which was sold to a worldly friend in 1923.[59] Franklin joined the Enfield Society at the age of seven. He worked as a cabinetmaker, mechanic, and carpenter for the community for many years.[60] The sole surviving brother when Enfield closed, he moved to Canterbury "with most of his things," according to Irving Greenwood in a diary entry of November 2, 1923.[61] In a letter dated January 1924, Franklin Youngs wrote about his new home:

> I am pleasantly located to have all my things in place even to my old workbench. My sitting room is as large as the one at Enfield and much finer. My workshop is only half as large but will do for my needs. I am going to making oval boxes like the ones Mrs. Wells bought of us and had lined.[62]

Clearly, Franklin was still an active woodworker after the move. According to oral tradition, he altered a counter in the Laundry Building and built a small one-drawer table in the Church Family Infirmary for one of the sisters before his death in 1935.[63]

This bed, however, probably dates from his Enfield days. It exhibits the maker's familiarity with the Renaissance Revival style of the 1870s, with its form influenced by Renaissance architecture and applied crests and shields. On the other hand, this bed retains remnants of its Shaker origins in the shape of the turned Enfield leg and the frame-and-panel construction. The division of the surface into horizontal panels of light and dark wood is an extension of the design of the classic Shaker sewing desk of the 1860s (see pls. 181, 183, and 210).

The stereograph shows the varied elements of the Shaker world in the 1880s. This room, fitted with classic built-in storage units and two contemporary side chairs, combined with the later-style stove and patterned linoleum or carpet floor covering, is far removed from the description provided in *Fifteen Years in the Senior Order of Shakers* by Hervey Elkins writing just three decades earlier, in 1853:

> The dwelling rooms are strictly furnished according to the following rules: plain chairs, bottomed with rattan or rush, and light so as to be easily portable; one rocking chair is admissible in each room, but such a luxury is unencouraged; one or two writing tables or desks; one looking glass, not exceeding eighteen inches in length, set in a plain mahogany frame; an elegant but plain stove; two lamps; one candlestick . . . bedsteads painted green; coverlets of a mixed color, blue and white carpets manufactured by themselves, and each containing but three colors. . . . (p. 25)

above

230. Box
c. 1840
Pine and maple, with red paint, steel cleat, and bone or ivory escutcheons
h 26¼ w 40¾ d 21¼"
Canterbury Shaker Village, Inc., Canterbury, New Hampshire, #88.731
Photograph: Bill Finney, by courtesy of Canterbury Shaker Village

The design and construction of this chest remind us that not all Shaker-made furniture is distinctively different from the country furniture of rural America. The chest-over-drawer form, made throughout the eighteenth century in colonial New England, served as a model for this Shaker piece. The dovetailed construction and the use of diamond-shaped escutcheons are clearly borrowed from worldly cabinetmaking techniques. Once the key is turned, the drawer is secured when the bolt catches behind a U-shaped steel cleat driven into the underside of the front board.

Features suggesting an Enfield origin include the size and profile of the ogee-shaped bracket foot, which is closely related to that of the Enfield box pl. 231. Further documentation exists in the recent discovery of another, almost identical piece in a private collection with a handwritten note reading, "blue chest/made by/Enfield, NY./Shakers/same blue as 1st/floor, Canterbury/mtg. House."

231. Box
c. 1830
Pine, with hardwood pulls, red paint, iron hinges and lock, and brass escutcheon
Written in ink on manilla tag tied to key: Key belongs to red Chest. Large
h 29¼ w 49⅝ d 21⅝"
Private collection

Although this chest was purchased from the Canterbury Shakers about 1945, it probably originated in Enfield in the 1830s. A nearly identical chest in another private collection is documented with the following handwritten note from Canterbury Sister Marguerite Frost (1892–1971): "Red blanket chest with two drawers made by Enfield, New Hampshire Shakers owned by Mary Ann Joslyn who gave it to Jessie Evans." Apparently, Sister Mary Ann (1843–1924) brought the related chest from Enfield, New Hampshire, to Canterbury, where she and the few remaining members moved in 1918. Both chests were probably made by the same craftsman. They each have paneled lids—an unusual feature in a storage box—similarly molded edges and turned knobs, and identically shaped ogee feet. The primary difference between the two is size, which explains the tag stating that this particular key belongs to the large (that is, the three-drawer) chest, rather than the smaller, two-drawer companion piece.

232. Settee

c. 1840
Birch and pine, with red stain and varnish
h 32½ w 49 d 16½"
Private collection
Photograph: courtesy John Keith Russell Antiques, Inc.

With their shaped plank seats and tapered comb at the top, Enfield's spindle-back benches resemble Shaker dining chairs (see pl. 218). Both reflect the influence of worldly Windsor models,[64] produced in numerous factories in New Hampshire, except the Shakers modified the Windsor style by omitting both the armrests and the longitudinal stretcher, resulting in an extremely delicate and fragile design. Although no extant journal corroborates the origin of the settee, oral history indicates that the Enfield Shakers built it themselves, for use in the Meetinghouse. According to Dartmouth College student Ashton Willard, visiting the Sunday meeting in 1878, "The Brethren and Sisters sat on benches—without any backs—though the strangers were provided with comfortable settees."[65] This bench, which was originally purchased directly from the Enfield Shakers,[66] is much shorter than other surviving examples, some of which measure up to twelve feet in length.

233. Armed Rocker

c. 1840
Birch and rush, with brown stain and varnish
Private collection

234. Sister in Rocker in Front of a Sewing Desk

Photograph
Courtesy David D. Newell Shaker Literature

Hervey Elkins, in *Fifteen Years in the Senior Order of Shakers*, described Enfield as having "plain chairs, bottomed with ratten or rush, and light so as to be easily portable. . . . " (p. 25). The refinement and elegance of these side and rocking chairs surpass those produced at other Shaker communities. Extremely slender, the posts are turned to their minimum diameter. The elongated candle-flame finials display the ultimate in grace and simplicity. The use of cane on many surviving examples contributes to the lightness referred to by Elkins. By about the 1840s, rattan cane was replacing cattail rush as the primary seating material for these chairs. In the 1870s a sister visiting the community noted that she observed "the shop where sister Sally Ann was bottoming chairs with ratan—partly learned the practice. . . . "[67]

The deeply bent back slats have a quarter-round top edge shape and are noticeably graduated. The arm is very similar to the Canterbury drop-front arm, showing precision shaping, and is supported by a slender, vase-turned front post. The rockers exhibit a gentle curve across the top between the legs.

The historic photograph shows how the armless rockers may have been used—as work seating rather than chairs for leisure, as rockers are envisioned today. Most of the Enfield armless rockers show evidence of sockets cut in the rear posts for tilters. While this may seem to indicate that such chairs had been converted from side chairs to rockers, this was not the case—they were made as rockers originally. The chair maker simply employed back posts already prepared for side chairs, turned, scribed, and drilled—and with sockets cut for tilters. He assembled the chair, then cut slots in the bottom of the posts, thereby producing a rocker.

Maine Bishopric

WHILE THE FLAME of the religious revivals burned throughout the Northeast, Henry Clough, an itinerant preacher from Mount Lebanon, New York, visited the town of Gorham, Maine, in 1780.[1] Here he succeeded in attracting converts through a series of informal meetings held in the kitchens of the local farmers and their families.[2] The following year, John Cotton, a member of the New Light Baptist Church in Alfred, Maine, visited Enfield, New Hampshire, where he met James Jewett, an ardent Believer. He persuaded John to receive the Testimony of Christ's Second Appearing, and John returned home to what would become in 1820 the state of Maine.

Three special ministers—James Jewett of Enfield, Ebenezer Cooley of Mount Lebanon, and Eliphalet Comstock of Hancock—followed him to Alfred (in what was then part of the commonwealth of Massachusetts) to support and strengthen his work. At this time, the headquarters of the Believers was in the home of Benjamin Barnes, one of the first residents to consecrate his property to the church. This land formed the nucleus around which the Alfred community grew.[3]

The first property to form part of what is known today as the Sabbathday Lake community included sections of Thompson's Pond Plantation. The existing Shaker village was annexed to the nearby town of New Gloucester in 1816. At some point during the first half of the nineteenth century, a post office called West Gloucester was established in the Shaker community there. Due to the continuing confusion with West Gloucester, Massachusetts, the name was changed to Sabbathday Lake in 1890, by which it is known today. According to local legend, hunters gathering at the lakeshore every Sunday in the early 1700s called the body of water "Sabbath-Day Pond." More likely the name is based on the word *sabaday*, meaning thoroughfare, in the language of the Abnaki Indians living throughout Maine.[4]

In 1782 Elisha Pote, Nathan Freeman, and Joseph Stone, three Shaker emissaries from Gorham, Maine, visited Thompson's Pond Plantation to preach the gospel of Christ's Second Appearing and succeeded in converting a large group of Free Will Baptists. This dedicated group met at Gowen Wilson's farm, which was situated in what is now the Sabbathday Lake garden field, and converted a number of large households, including the Briggses, Holmeses, Merrills, Wilsons, and Potes. In fact, it was the reception of several generations of large natural families into the church that assured the Shakers' early success in Maine.[5] In 1793, these members were formally organized into a society under the leadership of John Barnes from Alfred. His associates were Robert MacFarland from Gorham and Eldresses Sarah Kendall and Lucy Prescott from Harvard.[6] These four composed the ministry and presided over the United Society of Believers at Alfred, which was formally organized in 1793, and Sabbathday Lake, which was established in 1794. Under the leadership of the Alfred Shakers a community sprang up at Gorham (1807–19), on the farms of Barnabas Bangs, Thomas Banks, and Joseph Bracket, which, for reasons that remain unclear, was later moved to Poland Hill, about one mile north of the existing village at Sabbathday Lake.[7]

The Alfred community consisted of three families situated in 60 buildings on 2,400 acres.[8] At its peak in 1830, it had 158 members. Sabbathday Lake included 136 members by 1840[9] organized into three families in 72 buildings on 2,000 acres.[10] In 1931, the Alfred property was sold to the Brothers of Christian Instruction,[11] and 21 members moved to Sabbathday Lake, which is still active.

---

235. Washstand
Sabbathday Lake
c. 1800
Pine, with hardwood knobs, yellow paint, and iron hinges
h 40 w 37½ d 17½"
Collection of The United Society of Shakers, Sabbathday Lake, Maine

This washstand exhibits several eighteenth-century design features, including a case with ogee-shaped sides that rise to meet the rear backsplash, the wide stiles, and the raised-panel door. Although considerably muted with time, the pigment is still a vibrant yellow—a bold color for a primarily utilitarian piece. It is not known if a washstand such as this occupied retiring rooms or other special-use areas within the family dwelling.

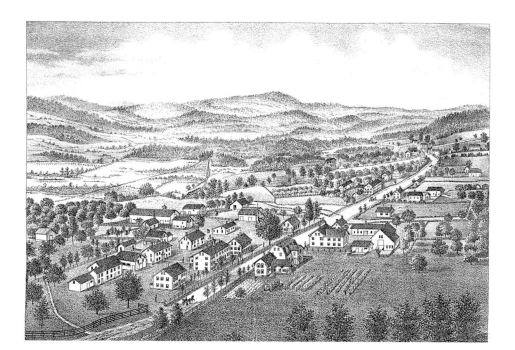

"Shaker Village, Alfred, Maine." Lithograph after a drawing by Phares Fulton Goist, c. 1880. Shaker Museum and Library, Old Chatham, New York, #9746

The Maine societies raised and packaged garden seeds for market and manufactured brooms and brushes at an early date. The Alfred Shakers also produced sieves and woodenware, including dry measures, oval boxes, dippers, tubs, pails, churns, and mortars.[12] At Sabbathday Lake, after the Civil War, the most profitable industry was the manufacture of "oak staves for molasses hogsheads, which are exported to the West Indies."[13] In fact, the machine itself for producing the staves was invented by Brother Hewitt Chandler of Sabbathday Lake in 1873. According to the Metric Bureau in Boston, the first metric dry measures in the United States, ranging in eight sizes from a deciliter to a hectoliter, were made at the Sabbathday Lake mill beginning in 1877.[14] The Sabbathday Lake sisters made poplar boxes, and Brother Granville Merrill invented a planing machine for shaving the wood into thin strands for weaving.[15]

The Alfred Shakers engaged in woodworking activities from an early date. One record states, "Jabez Rickers house was moved up from the mill in 1796," implying that the Shakers acquired this structure and the rights from the Rickers when the latter exchanged property with Eliphaz Ring in Poland Spring. If so, the Shakers very likely ran the mill when the United Society was organized, and they probably milled their own lumber for building and perhaps cabinetmaking purposes.[16] According to research conducted by Brother Ted Johnson (1930–1986) of Sabbathday Lake, "from 1802 to 1817, the Alfred Shakers were selling chairs, tables, stands and candlestands."[17] Although destroyed by fire in 1841, the sawmill was immediately rebuilt and used continuously by the Shakers until 1870, when it was leased to worldly businesses.[18]

Unfortunately, very little information survives in the form of community records to shed light on furniture-making activities at Alfred:

> In 1902, the 1793 meetinghouse and Ministry's house were completely destroyed by . . . fire. It was in this disaster that the Church in Alfred and all Shaker historians suffered an irreparable loss. In the Ministry's house there was housed a complete collection of all Shaker literature from as far back as 1790, including all records and histories of the Alfred Society, which had been collected by Elder Otis Sawyer previous to his death in 1884. Because of this loss, a complete history of Alfred must surely be lacking.[19]

The situation, however, is very different at Sabbathday Lake. Due to that community's continuous history and the survival of community members into the present, it has been possible to attribute by oral tradition beginning in the first generation and handed down to today a large quantity of furniture pieces to a specific community, maker, and, in some cases, original user, as well as provide accurate information regarding the date of construction.

As few signed pieces from Maine have surfaced, individual cabinetmakers have been identified primarily on the basis of oral history (■), scattered journal entries (■■), and undocumented references, presumably from primary sources, in Andrews, *Religion in Wood*, and Grant and Allen, *Shaker Furniture Makers* (■■■).

ALFRED

- ■■■ JOSHUA BUSSELL (1816–1900), in Grant and Allen, *Shaker Furniture Makers*, p. 154
- ■ ISAAC BRACKETT (working 1825), tall case clock currently in hallway of Ministry Shop
- ■ JOSHUA HARDING (w. 1827), in Johnson, "The Least of Mother's Children in the East"
- ■ HENRY GREEN (1844–1931), see pls. 248–50
- ■ FRANKLIN LIBBY (1870–1899), according to his natural sister Eva May Libby (1872–1966), who lived at Sabbathday Lake until her death in 1963, see pl. 253

SABBATHDAY LAKE

- ■ JAMES HOLMES (1771–1856), in a letter of July 23, 1991, from Brother Arnold Hadd (b. 1956).
- ■■■ JOHN COFFIN (1792–1870), in Andrews, *Religion in Wood*, p. 103
- ■ HEWITT CHANDLER (1833–left 1882), in Johnson, "The Least of Mother's Children in the East," and see pl. 251
- ■ GRANVILLE MERRILL (1839–1878), clock that hung on the exterior of the Brethren's Shop that had an automatic bell attached to it, currently at the Shaker Museum, Old Chatham, New York
- ■ DELMER WILSON (1873–1961), see pls. 255 (p. 3) and 256
- ■ GEORGE WASHINGTON JONES (1845–1913), see pl. 248

ALFRED AND SABBATHDAY LAKE

- ■ ELISHA POTE (1764–1845), in Johnson, "The Least of Mother's Children in the East"
- ■ EBENEZER COOLBROTH (1856–1918), according to Brother Arnold, see pl. 254

WORLDLY MAKERS

Fassett and Stevens, George Brock, supervisor, designed 1883–84 Church Family Dwelling House, see pl. 236

Information on the variety of furniture types produced by the Maine Shakers and its use within the community comes by way of surviving examples and scattered journal references. For example, in 1834, Elisha Pote of Alfred wrote to Elder Joseph Bracket at Sabbathday Lake, "the sisters keep me very busy. As soon as I finish one chest or cupboard another is in demand."[20] "A [tripod-based] table was used in the Boys shop. A kerosine lamp stood in the middle of it and the boys studied around it. It was made by Brother Hewitt Chandler. Elder Delmer Wilson could recall having studied around it as a lad." "At Sabbathday Lake Sister Aurelia records in 1872 that for the first time in that year everyone has his or her own bed. To that time there has still been doubling up." In 1873, "Brother Samuel Kendrick went to Alfred to bring back a book case which Brother Henry Green had made for Elder Otis. Some lovely drawers in it." Elder Otis Sawyer of the Maine ministry noted that Deacon James Holmes made six sewing stands.[21]

According to the "No. 1 Ledger Book from Alfred" (Collection of the United Society of Shakers, Sabbathday Lake, Maine), three chairs were "sold to Able Hamilton" for $1.38 as early as December 20, 1834. Shaker chairs from Sabbathday Lake more closely resemble the stocky proportions of the New England slat-back chairs than those from any of the other Shaker villages. The chairs from Alfred are fitted with bulbous pommels adorned with double or triple scribe lines at the midpoint, posts that are abruptly bent just above the seat, and the top graduated slat secured with single or double pins extending through the post. The stretchers taper to a central scribe mark, imitating the bamboo turnings on Windsor chairs—a feature not seen on Shaker chairs produced at other communities. Side-scrolled arms receive the front post tenons well behind the circular part of the handhold. Drop-scrolled arms are similar in shape to the so-called Boston rockers mass-produced by many worldly manufacturers during the last half of the nineteenth century. Both arm types often are heavily chamfered on the bottom edges. The primary chair seating materials in Maine were leather, produced at the Alfred North Family tannery, splint, and woven tapes.

Elder Otis Sawyer of Alfred, who kept the "History, or record of the first seven years of the second degree of travel or second Cycle in the progress of the Church and Society in Alfred," wrote in 1872 that he thought "it may be interesting to make a brief review of the most important and conspicuous repairs and improvements made on buildings together with other more or less expensive additions to furniture and accommodations every one of which has added to the comfort and convenience of the brethren and sisters and serve to make their labor much easier and pleasant and beautiful [for] our Zion home" (p. 7). During the 1870s, the Alfred Shakers made a concerted effort to renovate both existing structures and their interior furnishings. For example, "each room in the Sisters shop is accommodated with a large clothes press . . . the north attic has tiers of Drawers occupying one entire side of the room for storage" (p. 7). The following year, "a large addition was annexed to the office by which five rooms were added. The lower part furnished, kitchen and dining room for workmen and three bedrooms in the second story. A capacious room in the attic for household storage. . . . In the main building the garret was finished lathed & plastered and tiers of drawers line the entire west side numbering fifty of ample depth and length. . . . Six new bedsteads and some number of bedsprings were furnished the visiting rooms" (p. 10). In 1877, "the deaconesses room [in the Sister's Shop] in the north east corner beautifully lighted, a clothes press, cupboard, and a tier of drawers are firnished which are ample for all purposes necessary for their accomodation. The attic is firnished with sixty drawers in which to stow away bedding and clothes[?] &c." (p. 22). It is evident from these excerpts that as late as the 1870s, the Believers were installing additional built-in units to improve storage throughout the village.

In addition to placing "spacious clothes presses and tires [i.e. tiers] of drawers and accomodations in each room" (p. 11) of the ministry's shop during the remodeling of 1874 for functional purposes, the Believers were clearly aware of modern design and both the visual enjoyment and physical comfort it afforded. "The ministrys working room floors are covered with oil cloths carpets and their retiring rooms with carpets of Goodall's manufacture. The liberal mind whose thoughtful care[?] is constantly suggesting the introduction of things needful, supplied the Ministry with conveniences as which are highly appreciated in addition to what has been named. A marble sink adorns as well as benefits the room of the writer & a beautiful secretary, with every necessary convenience for books, paper and for writing" (p. 12).

Unfortunately, Maine Shaker furniture was both consolidated and dispersed from several communities between 1887 and 1972, making attributions to Alfred or Sabbathday Lake very difficult without an accompanying oral history. According to Brother Ted Johnson, the "Sabbathday Lake Church Record and Journal" kept by Eldress Hester Ann Adams for 1887 records that thirty-seven wagon loads of furniture were moved from the North Family at Sabbathday Lake when it consolidated with the Church Family in 1887.[22] Again, in 1918 "the soon closing of the community at Harvard was to occur and the Elders there telegraphed to Elder William Dumont & Eldress Elizabeth Noyes at Sabbathday Lake and said in essence come and take what you want. Elder William and Eldress Elizabeth filled a box car with furnishings from Harvard in 1918." Alfred, too, received items from the Harvard community. Finally, "in 1931 when Alfred closed, 41 truckloads of furniture were brought from Alfred to Sabbathday Lake." Over the years, pieces were sold to collectors visiting the Sabbathday Lake community and a major public auction in 1972 offered counters, desks, and tables for sale.

Much of the surviving Shaker furniture from Alfred and Sabbathday Lake dates from the Victorian period, making generalizations regarding earlier forms difficult. The two Maine communities remained relatively active during the late nineteenth and early twentieth centuries, and this strength is revealed in the large output of furniture reflecting worldly fashion. As Brother Ted summarized in 1969 in his book *Hands to Work and Hearts to God*, "despite the fact that these productions of the late nineteenth century are to most of us less pleasing than are those of the classic era, they are still a valid part of the Shaker story. They are in their way as meaningful a reflection of the evolution of a processual community as are the earlier pieces which accord so much more with contemporary taste."

During this later period, Maine craftsmen began to employ unusual woods, such as sycamore and elm, at the same time placing an increasing emphasis on naturally figured wood with a dramatic grain, such as quarter-sawn oak, bird's-eye maple, fruitwoods, and walnut. In comparison with the other Shaker communities, the Maine Shakers made greater use of pigment, staining as well as painting their pieces colors such as an indigo-based blue, chrome and mustard yellow, and various shades of red. According to oral tradition,[23] Elder Henry Green used the coloring from cochineal bugs as a medium for obtaining the bright red color on his sewing desks. The striking effect of this pigment was often heightened with an extremely glossy finish. The custom of staining drawer fronts and finishing other parts in clear varnish, or vice versa, seems to have been particular to both Alfred and Sabbathday Lake. Veneer, rare in Shaker usage, is found on a desk at Sabbathday Lake made by Brother George Washington Jones (1845–1913), and nonimitative grain painting, which was introduced during this period, appears on several surviving examples (pls. 246, 251, and a four-drawer bureau and grained washstand made by Elder Henry).[24]

The influence of worldly design emerges in startling form in the production of secretary desks ornamented with unusually sawn crests, many with inventive cutouts, elaborately shaped band-sawn feet, and vertical spindles combining both square and round elements. The earlier turned wooden pulls were uniformly replaced by commercially made cast-iron or brass hardware.

236. Built-in Cupboards and Cases of Drawers, Church Family Dwelling House

Sabbathday Lake
1883–84
Ash, varnish, and iron pulls
Collection of The United Society of Shakers,
Sabbathday Lake, Maine

The use of ash, complex wide molding, commercial latches, and widely set iron pulls visually place this built-in many decades after the example on the opposite page. It was, however, constructed less than ten years later as part of the 1883–84 brick Church Family Dwelling House situated just across the road. The Shakers contracted the design work of the structure to the Portland architectural firm of Fassett and Stevens, and it was constructed under the supervision of George Brock of Portland.[25] Were these worldly contractors, who presumably constructed the built-in units as well, partly responsible for the contemporary Victorian look? Or did they build to the design specifications of the Shakers? This storage unit combined the Shaker forms with contemporary decorative elements.

opposite below

237. Shaker Store, Trustees' Office
Sabbathday Lake
After 1911
Photograph by Brother Delmer Wilson
Collection of The United Society of Shakers,
Sabbathday Lake, Maine

Located on a busy road between Portland and the tourist resort at Poland Spring, the Sabbathday Lake community developed several industries to cater to this important seasonal trade. The Trustees' Office housed a store that sold such Shaker-made articles as pincushions, oval carriers, brushes, and Shaker cloaks.

In 1910–11, according to oral history, Brother Ebenezer Coolbroth (1856–1918) renovated the 1816 Trustees' Office. This photograph of the store was taken sometime after 1911 by Brother Delmer Wilson (1873–1961). The built-in store fixtures include glass-door cupboards mounted against the wall and counters that displayed the merchandise. The rear of the counter seen here is lined with rows of drawers decorated with commercially made cast-iron pulls. The display fixtures, although probably similar to other worldly examples, are an extension of other Shaker-made "commercial" work pieces, including counters, tables, and sewing desks. According to oral history (Brother Nelson Chase), the table was not made by the Shakers but purchased.

Brother Eben, as he is still referred to by the family at Sabbathday Lake, was gathered at the Alfred community in 1867 and left in 1886. He married and in 1910 returned to the Believers at Sabbathday Lake with his daughter Eugenia (1898–left 1947).[26]

238. Cupboard and Case of Drawers
Sabbathday Lake
c. 1820
Pine, with hardwood knobs and gray-blue paint
h 70¾ w 40⅜ d 19¼"
Collection of The United Society of Shakers,
Sabbathday Lake, Maine

This cupboard, which incorporates several distinctive features associated with Maine Shaker furniture, may be representative of Maine's freestanding case pieces. Most prominently, the bottom case rail is rabbeted into the sides, resulting in a shallow cut foot fashioned from a horizontal rather than a vertical case member. A similar foot, with identical construction, is found on the painted blanket chest, pl. 244. Furthermore, the drawers are of nailed rather than dovetailed construction, and the faces are lipped on all four sides. The top molding, which combines a square with a double ovolo, is distinctive. The case retains its original gray-blue painted finish. The escutcheon is probably a replacement.

239. Built-in Cupboards, Meetinghouse
Sabbathday Lake
1792
Pine with hardwood knobs, blue paint, wrought-iron hinges, iron lock, and tin escutcheon
h 89⅜ w 29⅛"
Collection of The United Society of Shakers, Sabbathday Lake, Maine

These cupboards are located next to a structural post, which is cased and finished on its right side with a ¾-inch bead. Among the earliest of Shaker furniture, this storage unit is certainly related to many freestanding pieces no longer extant, and can be compared to similar cupboards built into the Meetinghouse at Canterbury as well as to the vernacular furniture of the Northeastern United States in the use of pine, wrought-iron H hinges, heavy raised panels, pegged mortise-and-tenon joints, and the thumbnail edge on the door stiles and rails. All of the built-in units used throughout the three floors of the 1792 Meetinghouse, along with the peg and chair rail and other architectural trim, is painted a deep blue—a color thought to be original to the building's interior.[27]

opposite

240. Built-in Cupboards and Cases of Drawers, Attic, Ministry Shop
Sabbathday Lake
Attributed to Hewitt Chandler (1833–left 1882)
1875
Pine, with hardwood knobs, light blue paint, and iron hinges
h 83 w 137¼"
Collection of The United Society of Shakers, Sabbathday Lake, Maine

This third-floor garret or attic space was created in 1875 in the course of a renovation to correct the 1839 Ministry Shop's original flat roof, which leaked badly in the inclement Maine winters. This storage space housed ministry possessions, off-season clothing, and possibly poplarware, the industry pursued by Eldress Elizabeth Haskell, who resided and worked in the building.[28] Although not immediately apparent, the left bank of drawers is 5 inches wider than those on the right, placing them off-center in relation to the cupboards above. The drawers, most likely made by Brother Hewitt Chandler, are simply nailed together and exhibit a rounded lip found on both Shaker and worldly furniture of this type. The light blue paint, now faded to white, and contrasting stained hardwood knobs appear to be original to this built-in.

242. Table
Alfred
c. 1870
Birch and pine, with gray paint
h 27¼ w 23⅜ d 18¼"
Private collection

This table painted in gray displays the leg turning form seen most often at Alfred. Rather than making an abrupt transition between the square and round sections, the craftsman's lathe tool cut directly but gradually into the square post to form a full round over an inch or two of space. Most worldly tables—and those from other Shaker communities—took only a half-inch to complete the transition from square to round. The Alfred attribution is made on the basis of this design characteristic, although this table has an additional short collar within the transitional area, which places it somewhat outside of the norm.

241. Case of Drawers
Alfred
c. 1820
Pine, with hardwood knobs, tan paint over red paint, and metal casters
h 58⅜ w 50¾ d 28½"
Collection of The United Society of Shakers, Sabbathday Lake, Maine

This deep six-drawer case is situated in the Church Family Sisters' Shop at the Sabbathday Lake community. Unusual construction details include the molding that covers the case sides and drawer rails that protrude beyond the face of the lipped drawers, which are usually flush with the case. The small turned knobs are located noticeably above the center of the drawer faces. The case currently has an old tan paint applied over an earlier, probably original, red paint. This piece, as well as two others in the Sabbathday Lake collection, came from the Trustees' Office at Alfred. In the twentieth century, they were used to store fancy goods, as were the cupboard boxes stacked on top of this case of drawers.

243. Dining Room, Church Family Dwelling House

Sabbathday Lake

The Church Family dining room is located in the lower rear of the 1883–84 brick dwelling. The family ate its first meal in this building, in this new dining room, on Thanksgiving Day in 1884.[29] While the chairs shown in this 1991 photograph are of recent manufacture, the trestle tables were made in 1926 by Brother Delmer Wilson (1873–1961), who copied the earlier 1795 pine prototypes. They are typical in their use of mortise-and-tenon joints for the vertical and two horizontals. The longitudinal stretcher is attached with a bridle joint rather than bolted.

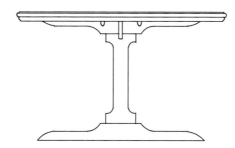

244. Blanket Box
Alfred
c. 1830
Pine, with green paint and iron hinges
h 49 w 39 d 18¼"
Private collection
Photograph: courtesy John Keith Russell Antiques, Inc.

This simply but solidly built box displays a green color not seen on other Shaker furniture. The shaping and construction of the bottom rail, which is rabbeted into the case sides to form a shallow cut foot, is a feature found on other Maine Shaker furniture, including a cupboard/case of drawers (see pl. 238) and a two-drawer, light green blanket box at the Sabbathday Lake community with the penciled inscription of Sister "Hannah Walton Dutton, Poland 1838" written on the lid. The drawers on this blanket box, like those on many Canterbury case pieces, are lipped on all four sides.

245. Counter
Sabbathday Lake
c. 1840
Elm and pine, with chrome yellow paint and red stain
h 34⅝ w 66 d 27⅝"
Collection of The United Society of Shakers, Sabbathday Lake, Maine

The maker of this piece of work furniture deftly exploited the asymmetrical balance and the contrast between the yellow paint and the clear finished posts and knobs to create a wonderful design. The craftsman intensified the contrast of pigment and wood by recessing the drawers and rails slightly behind the square portion of the framing members. The chrome yellow paint on the body of the counter is much more subdued than it was when initially applied to this piece. The vertical members are turned in elm, a wood rarely incorporated in either Shaker or worldly furniture.

246. Counter

Sabbathday Lake
c. 1880
Pine, cherry, ash, and walnut, with grain painting
and porcelain pulls
h 34¾ w 61½ d 26½"
Collection of The United Society of Shakers,
Sabbathday Lake, Maine

The known history of this counter, still in use in the Trustees' Office at the Sabbathday Lake community, goes back to 1910. At this time it was employed in the workroom by Trustee Ada Cummings (1862–1926) for cutting aprons made for sale to the world through the Trustees' Office store (see pl. 237).[30] Although it is impossible to date this counter precisely, the fact that the molded top edge was made with a shaper definitely places it after 1860.

The grained finish, which does not attempt to imitate any particular type of wood, may not be original to the piece, but it was certainly applied before 1900. The cherry drawer fronts offer considerable contrast both in color and texture to the decorative paint on the sides of the case. The full-length pullout slide, providing additional work surface, rests on supports of the form found on worldly fall-front desks.

247. Counter

Alfred
Attributed to Henry Green (1844–1931)
c. 1850
Birch and pine, with red paint
h 32¼ w 52½ d 26"
Collection of The United Society of Shakers,
Sabbathday Lake, Maine

Furniture for the Shaker tailoring or seamstress trades was designed with a variety of drawer arrangements. This example, which is attributed to Henry Green by oral history, exhibits a number of unusual features: the configuration of four over two drawers, the placement of single, small knobs on the top drawers above a pair of widely spaced larger knobs on the bottom drawers, and the proportions of the long legs in relation to the size of the case. For some inexplicable reason, several of the drawers are only 12 inches deep, considerably shorter than the rest. The craftsman's decision to place color only on the drawer faces and the legs above the case rails also lends this counter an unusual aspect.

248. Writing Desk

Alfred
Attributed to Henry Green (1844–1931)
c. 1880
Butternut and pine
h 62 w 32 d 16"
Collection of The United Society of Shakers,
Sabbathday Lake, Maine

An 1883 account written by Elder Otis Sawyer in "Recapitulation for 1883" of the "Alfred Church Record," vol. 2, describes three similar pieces: "Brother Henry Green made three very nice writing desks, two of which were for the Ministry Sisters and [one for] Eldress Eliza Smith. They contain four larger and [inside] two small drawers a folding leaf, partings for paper and on top two shelves for books."

Boasting a wide range of decorative elements, this desk and its companion pieces are visually a world apart from the bookcase and secretary desk that Brother Henry made for the library (see pl. 249), yet they were constructed during the same period. What influenced Henry Green's progressive designs? As business agent for the Shakers for over fifty years,[31] he was undoubtedly exposed to worldly styles on his travels to seaside and mountain resorts selling Shaker fancywork goods. He may also have encountered local woodworkers in the New England area. There are, unfortunately, no records that can ascertain whether he developed his versatility independently or discussed and worked out his ideas openly with other Shaker craftsmen in the community. In any event, the decorative details he employed varied widely, to include elaborately shaped band-sawn feet, vertical spindles incorporating both square and turned elements, and intricately sawn crests with cutout sections. These are in marked contrast to the drawer and fall-front portions of the case, which are constructed according to traditional Shaker design concepts. The comparatively simple interior of the desk contains pigeonholes in a variety of sizes as well as drawers.

An entry of May 13, 1882, in volume 2 of the "Alfred Church Record" states, "During the week *two beautiful Writing Desks* were put into the visiting rooms at the office. They were made by Brother Henry Green of butternut. Shellacked and varnished and they are really splendid" (p. 224). Photographed in the Trustees' Office at Sabbathday Lake, this piece of writing furniture is presently being used in a location comparable to its original placement at Alfred, Maine. It may not be coincidental that a progressive design of this nature was specifically situated in the Trustees' Office, as the journal account affirms. In the office, where worldly people visited, it might visually prove that the Shakers were not an outdated sect but actively kept abreast of contemporary fashion.

Several of these desks are still being used in the Sabbathday Lake community, suggesting that this particular form was made in quantity, with some variations. For example, one desk in the collection that was made by Brother George Washington Jones (1845–1913) is made of walnut and incorporates veneer and an applied raised panel on the desk lid and elaborately carved wooden pulls on the single rather than double drawer below. Others do not have the four-drawer base but rest on a taller case extending all the way to the floor on which the desk top is built.

249. Bookcase
Alfred
Henry Green (1844–1931)
c. 1880
Butternut and walnut
h 87⅜ w 48¾ d 20½"
Collection of The United Society of Shakers,
Sabbathday Lake, Maine

This two-piece butternut bookcase, which Henry Green brought from Alfred to Sabbathday Lake on January 25, 1883, is still in use as it was originally conceived in the Sabbathday Lake community's library.[32] The construction of another, probably similar piece is mentioned in Elder Otis Sawyer's (1815–1884) "History, or record of . . . Alfred." In 1877 Elder Otis described the new "Literary and Social Improvements Library":

> One of the most important improvements of recent date is the establishment of a Public Library. The foundation of which was the liberal contribution of all the Books which Elder John Vance had prudently preserved to which was added what stray[?] books could be found in the Church. Suitable cupboards fronted with glass doors were made by the ingenious hands of Br. Henry Green where the books were deposited. . . . Until now three hundred volumes of the choicest and most judicious selection, consisting of *History, Biography, Scientific, Religious and Miscellaneous* besides Elder John has a necessary number of volumes in his own private Secretary of *Law Books and Medical Works.* (p. 35)

Elder Henry is presently the best known and may have been the most prolific of all the Victorian Shaker cabinetmakers. Although his ornate designs may not be visually appealing to the twentieth-century eye, he was a proficient craftsman. The case exhibits very fine traditional joinery techniques in the dovetailed drawers and mortise-and-tenon work. The use of machinery, in particular the shaper, is evident in the molding surrounding the rounded portions of the glass, where the contour would have been very difficult to achieve with hand tools alone. The decorative walnut trim contrasts with the lighter butternut case, and the beveled molding terminating in a lamb's tongue defines the case corners.

A similar case piece, designed as a three-part desk, in the collection at Sabbathday Lake includes a third central section, replacing the lower half of the upper case with a fall-front desk that when open rests on the sill below. The interior includes a small bank of drawers, pigeonholes, and vertical dividers for ledgers. On both examples, the double doors on the bottom enclose two banks of drawers. Yet another desk is referred to in an undated journal entry from the Alfred Church Record,

vol. 2, 1879–86: "*A splendid secretary* made by the ingenious hands of Brother Henry Green was put into the office for the special accomodation of Brother James Pender."

250. Sewing Desk
Alfred
Attributed to Henry Green (1844–1931)
c. 1860
Birch and pine, with red paint and varnish and porcelain and metal pulls
h 28 w 21 d 20¼"
Private collection
Photograph: courtesy John Keith Russell Antiques, Inc.

The design of this typical 1860s Maine/New Hampshire sewing desk is complemented by the striking original color, which has been remarkably preserved over time. This sewing desk probably would have been used in a sisters' workroom along with up-to-date sewing machines. According to Otis Sawyer's "History, or record of . . . Alfred," "four improved sewing machines will be found in the workrooms adapted to all kinds of work and every sister occupying the house is furnished with an elaborate worktable containing six large and six small drawers" (1872). This brief description of what we call a sewing desk may very well refer to a piece such as this.

According to oral tradition, this piece typifies some of Brother Henry Green's distinctive work furniture. He also made a somewhat smaller matched pair of sewing desks finished in red paint for Eldress Fanny Casey and Sister Mary Walker, currently in the Sabbathday Lake collection.[33] Clearly, as evidenced by his other known output (see pls. 248, 249), he became adept at working in a variety of styles. Henry Green joined the Alfred Shakers at the age of fifteen, when he became a woodworking apprentice to Elder Joshua Bussell,[34] who also made sewing desks of this style. An entry of January 1, 1877, in the "Alfred Church Record," vol. 1, compiled by Otis Sawyer, praises his abilities and describes the specific types of furniture he made:

> Brother Henry Green is Assistant elder, by occupation a Mechanic which embrasses all kinds of jointer work. Assists in making repairs on buildings, repairs waggons and makes waggon bodies, carts, sleds, and all kinds of farming tools. Makes very nice furniture, Secretaries, Tables, Wash stands, Work Tables for Sisters filled with drawers prepaires the boards[?] and frames of boxes for Sisters sale work and in the season of sales disposes of the principal part of it at the mountains and seashore. A very ingenious useful brother.

251. Sewing Desk
Sabbathday Lake
Attributed to Hewitt Chandler (1833–left 1882)
c. 1870
Birch and pine, with grain painting and red paint, porcelain knobs, brass escutcheons, and iron casters
h 49¾ w 36 d 23"
Collection of The United Society of Shakers, Sabbathday Lake, Maine

According to oral tradition, this unusual sewing desk was made by Brother Hewitt Chandler. Constructed very differently from other known Shaker examples, it features a solidly built, dovetailed case that houses the drawers beneath the desk surface and a rear, dovetailed gallery. The exuberant shaping of the crest was created by linking a series of angles and curves in an unorthodox manner to produce an undulating line. Particularly remarkable is the purely decorative rather than imitative grain painting covering the drawer faces, which contrasts sharply with the red paint used to finish the rest of the piece. Two historic photographs in the Sabbathday Lake library collection show Eldress Prudence Stickney in front of this work desk.

Brother Hewitt was apparently a carpenter as well as a furniture maker. He is known to have renovated the Church Family Sisters' Shop in 1878. At this time he also built the reservoir in the west field and conducted the water to the laundry for washing and canning.[35] In the same year he also built a large, round table presently used in the brothers' waiting room in the brick Church Family Dwelling House.[36] For a number of years he was in charge of the community's mill operations, as well as the shop making grain measures.[37]

252. Sewing Desk
Alfred
c. 1820
Pine, with hardwood knobs and traces of yellow
over red wash
h 36¾ w 26 d 17½"
Private collection

This piece was purchased from the Sabbathday Lake community in the 1950s. According
to Sister Mildred Barker (1898–1990), it was
used in the girls' order at Alfred. It is likely
that the form was the earliest used for specialized sewing desks in the Maine communities, although the design details may vary. A
simple four-drawer case with two additional
gallery drawers, the case is rectilinear except
for the nicely curved ogee sides and the simple arched cut foot. The form relates closely
to the washstand pl. 235 and a similar sewing
desk in the collection at Sabbathday Lake.[38]
This desk still at the Sabbathday Lake community differs primarily in its addition of decorative ogee-edged molding applied to the plank
case side.

opposite above

253. Desk
Alfred
Attributed to Franklin Libby (1870–1899)
c. 1890
Butternut and maple, with hardwood and glass
knobs and brass hinges and escutcheon
Collection of The United Society of Shakers,
Sabbathday Lake, Maine

The top section of this desk is reminiscent of
the following example made by Brother
Ebenezer of Sabbathday Lake. The base, however, with a double bank of drawers made of
butternut, is different. Dummy fillers suggestive of pullout, fall-front desk supports
were situated at either side of the top
drawers. Furthermore, several drawers are
glued up from two boards, which is an unusual practice.

An example related in its overall form,
now in the collection of the Shaker Museum,
Old Chatham, New York (acc. no. 6575), has
been attributed to Brother Franklin Libby
through information provided by his natural
sister, Eva May Libby (1872–1966), who lived
at Alfred and later at Sabbathday Lake. This
desk has a similar gallery design, although it
includes more ledger slots and pigeonholes,
and a base with the same construction but
with the parallel banks of drawers separated
to create a kneehole desk form. These design
similarities support the oral attribution of
both desks to Brother Franklin Libby. He
received his training from Elder Henry Green,
and he developed a style that almost mirrored
that of his mentor (see pl. 250).

opposite below

254. Desk
Sabbathday Lake
Attributed to Ebenezer Coolbroth (1856–1918)
c. 1915
Oak, with metal pulls
h 51 w 42 d 22¾"
Collection of The United Society of Shakers,
Sabbathday Lake, Maine

Quarter-sawn oak, a very popular wood at
the turn of the century in the development of
mass-produced Grand Rapids furniture but
rarely used by the Shakers, here provides
spectacular visual surface movement. The
dramatic grain configuration enlivens the
heavy rectangular case, while the scalloped
crest and the semicircular (commercial)
drawer pulls moderate the effect of the busy
pattern by adding visual stability. The shaping
on the top section of the desk relates to
numerous worldly desks and reflects shop
practices within the neighboring Maine rural
communities. Brother Ebenezer Coolbroth
has been identified through oral tradition as
the maker of this piece of furniture (see also
pl. 237).

illustrated on page 3

255. Desk
Sabbathday Lake
Attributed to Delmer Wilson (1873–1961)
c. 1890
Sycamore and pine, with cast-brass pulls and
escutcheons
h 51 w 35⅛ d 23½"
Collection of The United Society of Shakers,
Sabbathday Lake, Maine

This piece, known by oral tradition to have been made by Brother Delmer, must have had special significance to the maker, who kept it in his bedroom and used it as a prop in several photographs, including one with Brother Stephen Gowen (1868–1932) and again in a self-portrait.

Sycamore rarely appears as the primary wood in Shaker furniture, and the form is also unusual. The overall style itself is similar to numerous commercial products, usually made of oak, available to the worldly market. The oval shape on the drawers, often created with inlays on much earlier Federal-style furniture, was probably produced here by punching the wood with a metal tool, following the method used for leather or saddlery work. The source for this motif and the function of the opening between the drawers are unknown. However, the origin of the flowing, organic carved shape on the backboard is closely related to contemporary Art Nouveau designs of the period, which may have been introduced to the Shakers through printed sources.

Brother Delmer came to the community when he was eight with his older brother Harry, who subsequently left. Delmer, at about age fourteen, decided to stay. He became a beekeeper, farmer, and orchardist (the orchard he tended still stands on the hill overlooking the Church Family buildings) as well as a cabinetmaker. Numerous pieces of furniture have been attributed to him, including two desks (see also pl. 256) but in the woodworking field he is best known for his oval boxes, or carriers. He was an avid photographer who created hundreds of glass-plate images chronicling the life of the brothers and sisters at the community, including the self-portrait in his shop with his winter's work of 1,083 carriers (see p. 73).

netry characteristic of early Shaker craftsmen. What makes it distinctive is the decorative design, combining an unusual configuration of two drawers over a pair of cupboard doors, chamfered vertical frame members, turned feet, applied rosettes, and a crest of startling shape. The fall-front section, a common design feature of writing furniture used at Sabbathday Lake, contains small drawers, pigeonholes, and ledger slots.

257. Tripod Stand
Alfred
c. 1830
Birch and pine, with varnish
h 31½ w 17½ d 15½"
Private collection

258. Tripod Stand
Alfred
c. 1840
Birch, with red paint
h 24½ diameter of top 22"
Private collection
Photograph: courtesy John Keith Russell Antiques, Inc.

256. Slant-Front Desk
Sabbathday Lake
Delmer Wilson (1873–1961)
1895
Cherry and pine, with brass pulls, hinges, chain, and lock and iron and wood casters
h 52 w 28 d 16"
Collection of The United Society of Shakers, Sabbathday Lake, Maine

According to the "Sabbathday Lake Church Record and Journal," vol. 4, in an entry dated December 28, 1895, "Delmer is making Sarah and Amanda a writing desk for their room in the Dwelling house." According to oral tradition, Sisters Sarah Fletcher (1853–1923) and Amanda Stickney (1854–1927) took a special interest in Delmer during his younger years. For example, he was allowed to reside in the dwelling house rather than the boys' shop, where most of the young male members were housed, and he apparently felt that he had been the beneficiary of special treatment.[39]

In a marked deviation from earlier Shaker practice, by the end of the nineteenth century, desks were allowed in individual retiring rooms for personal use. While solidly made, this piece does not display the same fine cabi-

The exaggerated shape of the snake leg gives a flamboyant air to these stands and sets them apart from other Shaker or worldly examples. Both the stem and the foot are beautifully elongated, to a point that nearly compromises the strength of the leg. On most Alfred-attributed stands, the top edge of the leg is not flat but ridged. The stand on the right has a graceful swell turning just above the transitional details leading to the straight cylinder section, where the legs are dovetailed into the stem. The large top is secured to the cleat with a threaded joint. A similar red-painted stand in another private collection has a rare rimmed top, known on only a handful of Shaker tripod stands.

The taller example shown on the left, although less graceful in its stem turning, has several uncommon features—unusual height, a square top, and a tilt-top mechanism. It also retains the original painted finish on the underside of the top. Another fine Alfred-attributed tilt-top stand exists in the collection of the Sabbathday Lake, Maine, Shakers.[40]

259. Armchair

Sabbathday Lake
Attributed to Delmer Wilson (1873–1961)
1899
Cherry and pine, with brass rod with knobs,
brown velvet cushion, and casters
h 45 w 24½ d 32"
Collection of The United Society of Shakers,
Sabbathday Lake, Maine

This wonderful example of later Shaker craftsmanship, while one of a kind in comparison with other Shaker chairs, supports the theory that many Believers were interested in change and growth and in staying with or ahead of the world. An entry dated December 6, 1899, in the "Sabbathday Lake (Me.) Church Record and Journal," vol. 5, pointed out Brother Delmer's source of inspiration, the English Arts and Crafts designer William Morris (1834–1899): "Delmer has made a nice chair for his room. It is the form of a Morris chair. Sara [Fletcher] assists him to upolster it today."

This progressive attitude was expressed in a more philosophical manner about fifteen years before this chair was built by Elder Otis Sawyer in "Recapitulation of 1883" from the "Alfred Church Record," vol. 2: "The world moved, change is indelibly impressed on all material things. Decay upon inaction, and we find that in our little zion how it requires eternal vigilance and constant effort to keep pace with the progress of the age."

260. Armed Rocker
Alfred
c. 1820
Birch and leather, with varnish
h 45 w 22¼ d 22¾"
Private collection

The craftsman who made this unique chair combined the traditions of the slat-back and bannister-back chair forms. The scribe lines on the back posts clearly indicate it was laid out to be a four-slat chair, but the maker deviated from his original plan in the following way. The second slat was mortised into the rear post upside down and both it and the top slat were mortised to receive the four vertical spindles which were rounded on the back and flat in front. The remaining design features, typical of Alfred chairs, include bulbous-shaped pommels with scribe lines, front posts with a vase-shaped turning above the seat rails, rungs with centrally located scribe marks, and the simply shaped side-scrolled arm. The leather seat, intact here, survives on only a few chairs.

The attribution to Alfred is supported by Sister Mildred Barker (1898–1990), who lived at Alfred before moving to Sabbathday Lake and documented this chair's use in the "boys house" at Alfred.

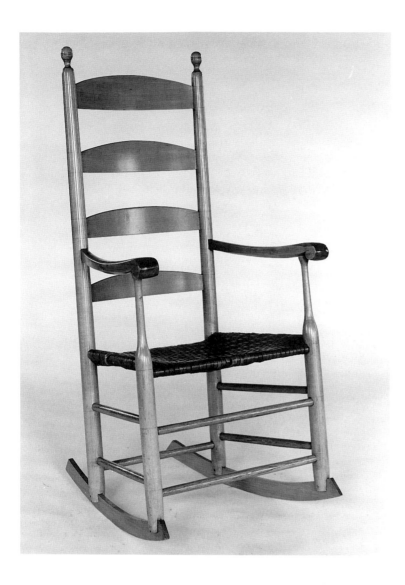

left

261. Armed Rocker
Alfred
c. 1840
Maple and tape
h 40 w 19 d 12½"
Collection of The United Society of Shakers,
Sabbathday Lake, Maine

The drop-scrolled arm typical of many Alfred chairs is similar to the form found on Boston rockers produced by worldly manufacturers during the last quarter of the nineteenth century. The front posts on this and a number of other Alfred rockers in the Sabbathday Lake collection are turned to a very slender diameter between the collar below the arm and the seat.[41] The rocker blades are simple in form and vary from those of uniform width, as shown here, to others with a straight top edge that are much broader at the center than near the ends (see pl. 260).

262. Side Chair
Alfred
c. 1840
Birch and cloth tape
h 40½ w 18 d 13"
Collection of The United Society of Shakers,
Sabbathday Lake, Maine

This fine chair contrasts with the much more primitive typical seating furniture from Sabbathday Lake, which does not show the same finesse in design.[42] The bulbous-shaped pommel has a noticeable scribe mark at its largest diameter and a ridge turning at the shoulder area. The back slats are well formed, with a rounded cross section. Most unusual in a chair of this period—and a distinguishing feature of Alfred seating furniture—is the back post, which is bent just above the seat, while the post above and below is straight. Other details exclusive to Alfred work include the placement of a scribe line in the middle and largest diameter of the rungs, showing the influence of Windsor bamboo chairs, heavy front posts that are tapered above the seat stretcher, and notably graduated back slats pinned on the top slat only.

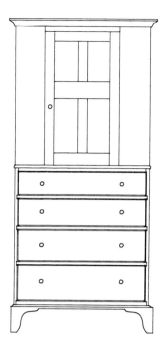

Cupboard and case of drawers, Union Village, c. 1840

---

263. Case of Drawers
Union Village
c. 1840
Curly maple and pine
h 57 w 41⅞ d 21¾"
Courtesy of the Art Complex Museum, Duxbury, Massachusetts, #91-23

Beautifully constructed of heavily figured curly maple, this is one of the finest Western Shaker case pieces extant. A particularly wide 1³⁄₁₆-inch facing covers the case joinery of the frame-and-panel side, and a cove molding finishes both the top and the base of the piece. Widely spaced figured knobs punctuate the drawers, graduated from 5 to 9¾ inches in height. The applied bracket raises the case well above the floor and, like many of the Union Village blanket boxes and cases of drawers, features a single drop just inside the leg itself. However, unlike other Union Village pieces, the bracket base is constructed separately and glued inside the cove molding, creating a light shadow line between the two sections.

The drawing depicts the only known Ohio Shaker example of the classic Shaker cupboard over case of drawers. The craftsman who built this piece about 1840, which stands over 8 feet tall, utilized Ohio design details, particularly in the shaping and use of the bracket base, which closely resembles the one in pl. 263. The Ohio details include a bold cove cornice, which stands above a tall four-panel door, and bull nose midcase molding, unlipped drawers, and a facing to cover the case joinery.

Ohio Bishopric

THE SUCCESS OF the Shaker way in the East, combined with the zeal to convert new members, led to a far-reaching missionary effort on the Western frontier.[1] Mother Ann had once prophesied "the next opening of the gospel will be in the South West but I shall not live to see it."[2] The turn of the nineteenth century was marked by intense evangelical fervor in the Ohio Valley reminiscent of the New Lebanon–Pittsfield revival of 1779. During this earlier period, many radical Baptists in New England and New York, disillusioned with organized religion, were searching for more emotional preaching. A similar movement swept the Ohio area; in 1801 thousands of Presbyterians, Baptists, and Methodists joined in one of the largest revival meetings in history at Cane Ridge, Kentucky, followed by gatherings at Beaver Creek (1803) and Turtle Creek (1805), Ohio.[3] Singing, dancing, praying, and personal confessions took over the crowd as each group struggled to express its point of view. The Presbyterians were divided between orthodox conservatives and those that wished to accept the spirit of revivalism as a means of deliverance from sin. Among the separatists were Richard McNemar, John Dunlavy, and Malcolm Worley. When news reached Mount Lebanon of this tremendous movement in Kentucky, the excitement grew. Mother Lucy of the parent ministry, perhaps convinced the predicted time had come, responded favorably to the groundswell of enthusiasm that arose among her followers.

In 1805, John Meacham (the son of Father Joseph Meacham), Benjamin Youngs, Sr., and Issachar Bates, three of the Shakers' most dynamic leaders, set out on foot on a twelve-hundred-mile journey[4] from Mount Lebanon to locate the organizers of the local revival in Ohio and found the people ready to "suck in our new light as greedily as ever an ox drank water."[5] Richard McNemar, the pastor of the Turtle Creek Presbyterian Church in Warren County, Ohio, and owner of considerable property in the region, was an early convert. His influence as a dynamic speaker and leader was such that most of the members of his congregation followed him into the sect, and together they founded the Shaker Society of Believers at Union Village. Richard McNemar and Malcolm Worley each donated about 160 acres, which became the sites of the Center and East families respectively.[6] Altogether, seven major communities were founded in the Midwest in the early years of the nineteenth century: four in Ohio, two in Kentucky, and one in Indiana.

If the typical Eastern Shaker convert was a millennial revivalistic Baptist, then his counterpart twenty-five years later in the West was a millennial revivalistic Presbyterian. Despite the differences in their theological outlook, the Eastern and Western Shaker leaders agreed on critical matters of faith and practice. One writer who has studied this issue believes that the primary differences between the two groups come down to a matter of emphasis. To the early Eastern Baptist leaders, the operation of the Holy Spirit on the individual's life was far more critical than a textbook understanding of Christianity. In contrast, their Presbyterian counterparts in the West were more biblically oriented and valued an educated ministry far more.

Another religion expert points out that due to the distance between the Ohio Valley and Mount Lebanon, the Western Believers relied more heavily on written communication from ministry to ministry rather than counting solely on personal visitations.[7] The Western missionaries also required materials to instruct new converts in the fundamentals of the faith. Thus, the initiative for the first written statement of Shaker theology came from the Western villages and dates from the publication of the *Testimony of Christ's Second Appearing* (1808) by Benjamin Seth Youngs, *The Kentucky Revival* (1807) by Richard McNemar, and *The Manifesto* (1818) by John Dunlavy. These documents present for the first time the founding principles of Shakerism as expressed in ecclesiastical history and the Bible, thus emphasizing the importance of the Scriptures as the route to salvation.[8] In the East, during the same period, Mother Lucy scrupulously avoided committing the "Millennial Laws" to paper because of her conviction that the "letter killeth but the spirit giveth life." This overriding respect for the Christ Spirit as a source of guidance is in marked contrast to the Western Shaker leaders' overwhelming trust in reason as the biblical basis for the faith.

From the first, Union Village (1805–1912) became the seat of the Western Shaker leadership and the parent of the new Ohio colonies, which consisted of Watervliet (1806–1900), White Water (1822–1916), North Union (1822–89), now Shaker Heights, and West Union, Indiana (1810–27).[9] During its 105-year history, Union Village grew to comprise over two hundred structures, including mills, shops, and dwelling houses. At its peak in the 1830s, the community embraced four thousand acres and six hundred members.[10]

From an early date in their history, the Ohio Shakers used available natural resources to develop a wide variety of industries. White Water developed a stable income source in brooms. The hardwood forests of oak, walnut, maple, and cherry provided lumber for making broom handles, cooperware and woodenware, and wagons—products that formed the income base of the Union Village, Watervliet, and North Union communities. The last also housed a woolen factory, a tannery, and a linseed oil mill. The community's proximity to Cleveland gave it a ready market for milk, cheese, and applesauce. At Union Village, agricultural products

General view of Union Village, with Trustees' Office (known as Center House, later Marble Hall), c. 1900. Shaker Museum and Library, Old Chatham, New York, #4443 9768.47

included wheat and flax for linen—both important crops for home use—and flaxseed oil to sell. As the community grew, the Believers found widespread markets for their garden seeds, medicinal herbs, and broom corn. The land also provided the Shakers with clay and sand for their large-scale brick-making and pottery trades. The carefully bred Shaker sheep produced fine wool, which the sisters manufactured into stocking yarn, blankets, and clothing. For many years the brothers packed pork and beef for sale to the world's people.[11]

Another resource the Ohio Shakers utilized was the ingenuity of their members, who found the most efficient ways to use their labor and materials. At Union Village "Elder JN" designed a horse-powered dough-kneading machine,[12] Abner Bedell and Thomas Tailor invented a silk-reeling device in 1837, and J. Mead and A. B. Kitchell patented an atmospheric steam engine in 1829. At North Union, a power-driven churn, a cream separator, and a miniature railway to transport milk to the cellar were in early use. According to oral history, the common clothespin was invented here.[13] However, it has been suggested that this attribution may have arisen from a confusion over terminology based on a Shaker journal source that calls pegs on peg rails clothes pins, that is, pins to hang clothes on.[14]

Journal references indicate a high level of quality construction carried out by skilled Shaker joiners and carpenters from various communities working together to erect various structures. On January 15, 1820, a number of joiners from Union Village arrived at Watervliet to help finish the new brick dwelling, which was 44 by 50 feet. "The chief part of the business was cutting stone for the house, two courses of foundation stone. door sill and caps. window sill and caps, mantle pieces Door steps &c." Again, in 1822, "The principal business, was working at the house and finishing it off, for which purpose, Samuel Harris and James Voris came from Pleasant Hill—And Robert Johns came from South Union, and the work was kept a going all winter, tho' the weather was pritty cold sometimes."[15] According to Elder David Darrow (1750–1825), who was sent from Mount Lebanon in 1806 to oversee the activities involved in erecting the 1809 Meetinghouse at Union Village and who lived in Union Village until 1826, only seasoned white pine was used for framing; the eave troughs were formed of tall, straight poplar boards; and the interior woodwork consisted of 1½-inch-thick cherry planks with tongue-and-groove joints, which were given an oil finish.[16]

Despite the level of activity, the names of the majority of craftsmen involved in woodworking at the Ohio communities are unknown. The identity of the following woodworkers is known only through the survival of signed pieces (■), scattered journal references (■■), including the "Journal of Visitors Who Stayed Overnight at Union Village Ohio,"[17] and the "History of North Union," kept by James S. Prescott,[18] or secondary source material (■■■).

UNION VILLAGE

- ■ RICHARD McNEMAR (1770–1839), a tool box at Warren County Historical Society, Lebanon, Ohio (acc. no. 264.69.5)
- ■■ FREEGIFT WELLS (1785–1871), from Watervliet, New York, at Union Village 1836–43, in "Wells, Memorandum of Events"
- ■ DANIEL SERING (1792–1870), see pl. 264. Spent at least eight years in White Water (1830–38)
- ■ LEVI McNEMAR (1793–1866), see pl. 266
- ■■■ TIMOTHY BONEL (working 1834), listed as making chairs and wheels in Andrews, Religion in Wood, p. 103
- ■■ WILLIAM COLLIS (w. 1850), listed as carpenter in "Journal of Visitors"

■■ PETER EDWARD (w. 1850), listed as tea tray maker from Lancashire, England, in "Journal of Visitors"

■■ CHARLES FORBES (w. 1850), listed as wood turner in "Journal of Visitors"

■■ ANDREW HOWARD (w. 1850), listed as carpenter in "Journal of Visitors"

■■ WILLIAM LEACH (w. 1850), listed as carpenter in "Journal of Visitors"

■■ LORENZO DOW LITTLETON (w. 1850), listed as carpenter in "Journal of Visitors"

■■ JAMES MORRIS (w. 1850), listed as cabinetmaker in "Journal of Visitors"

■■ JAMES REED (w. 1850), listed as finisher of cabinetware in "Journal of Visitors"

■■ WILLIAM STEVENS (w. 1850), listed as carpenter in "Journal of Visitors"

■■ JOHN WEST (w. 1850), listed as cabinetmaker in "Journal of Visitors"

■■ LOUIS WILKE (w. 1850), listed as cabinetmaker in "Journal of Visitors"

NORTH UNION

■■ RALPH RUSSELL (joined 1822–left 1833), listed as building the first meetinghouse in Piercy, *Valley of God's Pleasure*, pp. 86–87

■■ POMEROY ROOT (j. 1824–1864), listed as furniture maker in Piercy, *Valley of God's Pleasure*, p. 134, and Kliver, *Brother James*, p. 97

■■ JAMES PRESCOTT (j. 1826–1888), listed as furniture maker in Piercy, *Valley of God's Pleasure*, p. 134, and Kliver, *Brother James*, pp. 97–98: "Old James [Prescott] had his workshop there [in the Bee house]. He must have been a carpenter or cabinet-maker. He had a hobby of making little boats. He made a boat one time with a sail on it that went across the pond (Upper Shaker Lake) and then turned around and came back again. It was about five or six feet long, of wood, with a sail. How the blamed thing turned around I don't know."

■■ JAMES McNAMARA, a carpenter by trade who assisted building the Center Family Dwelling House, in Kliver, *Brother James*, p. 78

WATERVLIET

■■ JAMES MEAD (w. 1821), listed as carpenter in MacLean, *Shakers of Ohio*, p. 318

■■ JOSEPH WORLEY, listed as a master mechanic in Piercy, *Valley of God's Pleasure*, p. 95

WHITE WATER

DANIEL SERING (1792–1870), from Union Village, spent at least eight years (1830–38) as second in the ministry under Archibald Meacham, in MacLean, *Shakers of Ohio*, n.p.

The McNemar family is intimately associated with the establishment of Shakerism in the West. Richard, a former Presbyterian minister from Kentucky and Ohio, provided educational and spiritual leadership at Union Village. In addition to his missionary activities, he was an author, printer, bookbinder, songwriter, and cabinetmaker. According to one account,

> In handicraft but few excelled him, as is testified to by much of his labor that still remains. He is just as much at home in the workshop, as in the pulpit, the elder's lot, or with his pen. Besides his manifold duties as a help for the ministry, he found time to exercise his ingenuity as a workman. As a mechanic he could construct a lathe, make a chair, bind a book or weave cloth. From November 15th, 1813, to December, 1817, he manufactured 757 chairs, 20 big wheels, 20 little wheels, 20 reels, besides spools and whirls. Up to April 15th, 1820, he had made 1366 chairs and from that

time until May, 1821, the number was 1403. I own a chair he made for David Darrow. It is strong and honestly made.[19]

The only documented physical evidence of his work survives in a small box that is currently in the collection of the Warren County Historical Society in Lebanon, Ohio (acc. no. 264.69.5). As part of a larger tool chest, it was designed to slide on interior rails to hold his son Benjamin's "little tools."

From 1836 until 1843, Freegift Wells (1785–1871), a skilled craftsman at Watervliet, New York (see pp. 151–52), was sent to Union Village, according to the "Daily Record of Events of the Church Family" of Union Village, "for the purpose of regulating and organizing the society of Believers in that place," which was in a state of disarray and confusion. Although his responsibilities in the West were primarily administrative, Elder Freegift also practiced his trade, producing at least drawers, bedsteads, and chair posts as well as the ubiquitous peg rails. According to a series of entries from the "Daily Record of Events" in 1840, he was engaged in turning pins for the new 1844 brick Church Family Dwelling House:

> May 27. Freegift has put up 114 pins in the new hall, & closerooms at the Center Brick. . . . May 28: F. has got out stuff for 100 more pins, & turned 30 of them. . . . Jun 5: Freegift has turned 320 pins to put up in the new clothers room. . . . Jul 7: Freegift has turned 100 pins for the office.

One person, however, who strongly influenced the physical appearance of the community at the turn of the twentieth century cannot be documented as a cabinetmaker. Joseph Slingerland (1843–1920), a physician in his younger years from Mount Lebanon, came to live at Union Village in 1889. After ascending to leadership positions of trustee and first minister he began making large-scale repairs and improvements to the physical plant, which brought ornamental beauty, substantial utility, and notable comfort to the buildings. The crowning achievement of this reconstruction was the remodeled Trustees' Office, originally known as the Center House, supplied with steam heat, running water, and marble floors, sinks, tables, and tubs. Known today as Marble Hall,[20] it represents the Shakers' conscious efforts to stay in vogue during the late Victorian era. According to the church records of August 22, 1891, "The Ministry are moving from the office to the Meeting House while the former is being renovated & remodelled, in Modern Style."[21]

As an entrepreneur, Slingerland also involved Union Village in a series of financial investments throughout the Midwest and South, including a hotel in Saint Paul and a cemetery in Memphis. However, the most controversial capital venture was the purchase of seven thousand acres of land in Georgia and the construction of a large dwelling house of oak, walnut, and marble to attract new Believers—an experiment that lasted between 1898 and 1902. Unfortunately, all of these enterprises failed, and their accumulated debt of $200,000 ultimately forced Union Village into bankruptcy. Elder Joseph had the support of Mount Lebanon in these endeavors but was greatly opposed in Ohio as a result of his fiscal mismanagement.

Although Slingerland was trained as a carpenter in 1854 while he lived at Mount Lebanon,[22] there is no evidence that he actually designed, sawed, planed, chopped mortises, or otherwise constructed any piece of furniture used in Shaker dwellings.[23] The bulk of the references to his days in the West indicate that he was primarily engaged in overseeing and executing capital improvements and various financial and legal enterprises, coupled with extensive traveling. Apparently, he exercised to the fullest the inherent privileges and responsibilities of his position rather than actively engaging in the carpentry trade.[24]

Church Family Trustees Office (known as Center House, later Marble Hall), Union Village, c. 1910. Shaker Museum and Library, Old Chatham, New York, #6270

Aside from the presence of makers' marks and design and construction features, the provenance or history of specific pieces can help suggest an Ohio Shaker origin. For example, in 1889 when North Union was dissolved and its 1,366 acres of land and some 60 buildings sold to a land developer three years later,[25] the remaining members either moved to Watervliet, Ohio, or Union Village with their possessions, and a public auction was held to dispose of the articles that were left behind.[26] Thus, pieces with a purchase history at the 1889 Shaker sale may well have been made by North Union cabinetmakers. Adding to the potential for confusion, however, was the movement of people and property to Union Village. When Watervliet was dissolved eleven years after the closing of North Union, its members and their belongings were also transferred to Union Village, the last remaining Shaker settlement in Ohio.[27] As a result, the surviving sampling of furniture produced at these two smaller communities has been so mixed together that it is difficult, if not impossible, to identify the exact origin of specific pieces. At White Water, a great deal of furniture belonging to the Center Family was destroyed in the disastrous fire of 1907, and when the community finally closed in 1916 many items presumably were sold to worldly neighbors. The Hodapp family, which purchased the North Family property from the Shakers, dispersed the remaining items from the North Family Dwelling House in a public auction in 1974, making the documentation of surviving White Water pieces extremely difficult.[28]

On the other hand, both the size and longevity of Union Village, together with the documented dispersal of artifacts from the site, make it somewhat easier to identify furniture produced there. When declining membership caused its closing in 1912, the property was sold to the United Brethren Church—now a part of the United Methodist Church—for use as a facility for retired ministers and their families or missionaries, known today as the Otterbein Home Retirement Community. The agreement stipulated that the seventeen remaining Shakers could reside in the Trustees' Office without rent or charge for a period of ten years, from 1913 to 1923. The strong leadership at Canterbury played an instrumental role during this period of transition. In 1919, according to the diary of Sister Jessie Evans, Elder Arthur Bruce (1858–1938) was appointed to the central ministry at Mount Lebanon (May 8, 1919). He and Elder Irving Greenwood (1876–1939), also of Canterbury, made both the business decisions and personal arrangements for the surviving members at Union Village and sent a series of Canterbury sisters there to take charge of the family. On July 2, 1914, Jessie Evans wrote in her diary, "a freight car of furniture from the West arrives in East Concord . . . it was not needed out there owing to the people moving into smaller quarters." More belongings were transported in 1920. This movement of both goods and people from Union Village to Canterbury over the years explains why the collection of the New Hampshire Museum on that Shaker site is so rich in documented Ohio Shaker furniture. However, a great many pieces have remained in the Lebanon, Ohio, area, primarily at the Otterbein Home Retirement Community, the Warren County Historical Society, or the Golden Lamb Inn, where a private collection, started in the 1950s, was assembled by Robert and Virginia Jones.

Ohio Shaker furniture is distinctive in its materials, design, and construction. Union Village cabinetmakers employed their native woods of walnut, cherry, butternut, also called white walnut, poplar, and oak instead of the maple, birch, chestnut, and pine characteristic of the Eastern communities. Rather than using a pigmented paint or stain to conceal the surface of the wood, as was the practice in the East, the Western Shakers on the whole preferred a varnish finish to reveal the natural grain beneath. The resulting look echos that of nineteenth-century worldly furniture.

Perhaps the most significant aspect of Western Shaker furniture is its close relationship to vernacular prototypes. This similarity in form is particularly apparent in freestanding storage units. For example, corner cupboards, which enjoyed tremendous popularity in the urban and rural Midwest, are frequently found in the Ohio and Kentucky Shaker communities. They are distinguished by a cornice with deep cove molding, paneled rather than glazed doors with integral quarter-round edges, and curved bottom rails. Aside from one small hanging example, no full-size freestanding corner cupboards exist in the Eastern communities.

More documented cases of drawers survive than any other furniture form produced at Union Village. With such a large body of material available for examination, a number of generalizations emerge regarding standard visual and structural characteristics. The most striking aspect of Union Village chests is their resemblance to contemporary Hepplewhite-style furniture. This is evident in the consistent use of applied bracket feet with curved skirts, which present a marked contrast to the ogee-shaped feet and straight case sides seen on many Eastern pieces. The base profile, whether it takes the form of a single, double, or scalloped curve, is easily identifiable as a Union Village style.

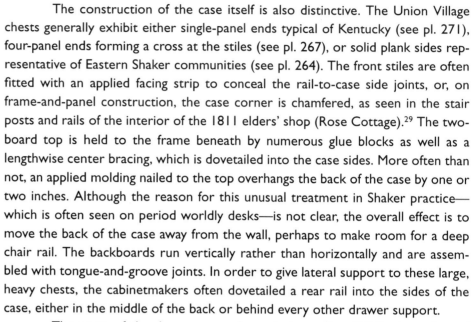

Base details of Ohio cases of drawers, left to right: simple rounded foot; foot with single drop and a single arch centering in the case center; foot with single drop and a double arch in the base; arched cut foot with the arc cut into both the corner post and the bottom case rail

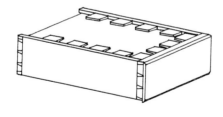

The construction of the case itself is also distinctive. The Union Village chests generally exhibit either single-panel ends typical of Kentucky (see pl. 271), four-panel ends forming a cross at the stiles (see pl. 267), or solid plank sides representative of Eastern Shaker communities (see pl. 264). The front stiles are often fitted with an applied facing strip to conceal the rail-to-case side joints, or, on frame-and-panel construction, the case corner is chamfered, as seen in the stair posts and rails of the interior of the 1811 elders' shop (Rose Cottage).[29] The two-board top is held to the frame beneath by numerous glue blocks as well as a lengthwise center bracing, which is dovetailed into the case sides. More often than not, an applied molding nailed to the top overhangs the back of the case by one or two inches. Although the reason for this unusual treatment in Shaker practice—which is often seen on period worldly desks—is not clear, the overall effect is to move the back of the case away from the wall, perhaps to make room for a deep chair rail. The backboards run vertically rather than horizontally and are assembled with tongue-and-groove joints. In order to give lateral support to these large, heavy chests, the cabinetmakers often dovetailed a rear rail into the sides of the case, either in the middle of the back or behind every other drawer support.

The parts of the drawer were dovetailed together. While the style and quality of the dovetails vary greatly, they were frequently laid out so that the pins are visible on the back, rather than on the sides, of the drawer. The drawer bottom, often pieced together with lumber of varying widths, is set high to reveal the groove cut into the back of the face, and it is supported underneath with numerous wedge-shaped glue blocks. The drawer fronts fit flush and are decorated with a scratch bead around all four edges. They are fitted with either large, flat, wood-threaded or small turned knobs, which are widely spaced across the drawer face and affixed from the inside with flat-head wood screws. The drawers are graduated in an irregular fashion, with the second tier from the top being the deepest. The reason for this may be either the result of a conscious design decision to emulate the proportions of the Empire-style case of drawers with its deep bonnet drawer or simply a matter of convenience. From the user's standpoint, it is certainly easier to access a large drawer at chest rather than ankle level.

The reason for the sheer quantity of Union Village case pieces deserves further comment. While the Eastern Shakers relied heavily on built-in cupboards and drawers, the Ohio Believers preferred freestanding pieces. This may have been an interim measure until permanent living quarters were built, making individual storage forms the norm rather than the exception. According to a letter from the ministry at Union Village to Mount Lebanon dated April 8, 1845, freestanding chests predominated prior to the construction of the brick dwelling house for the Center Family in 1844. This building provided communal closets and space-saving built-in units, which prevailed in the East at a much earlier date, eliminating the need for "private bureaus" such as these.

It has been the custom in the Church for Brethren and Sisters generally to have a chest for their private convenience and a bureau in the room. Is it best to keep up the practice when we move in the new house or not? There will be a large close room in every dwelling room with two large drawers for each person that lives in the room and a large cupboard and ample accomodation in the close room for hanging close. Some have felt as tho this was sufficient accomodation and that the chests and bureaus in the rooms might be dispensed with, as it was quite expensive to keep them up (some have private bureaus). But we would be glad to have the Ministry's counsel, and be as much in union as we can in all things.[30]

Unfortunately, there is no record of Mount Lebanon's response to this inquiry. Other Shaker communities had clothes rooms, although their size and location varied considerably. Each retiring room in the Church Family Dwelling House at Hancock was equipped with a small built-in closet fitted with several rows of peg rail inside (see pl. 101). The situation was very different at Pleasant Hill, where large walk-in closets—many with windows—were accessed from the central hall and had space to hold freestanding cases of drawers and blanket boxes (see pl. 284). At Union Village, the room described above was designed specifically for hanging clothing.

Four documented lidded boxes for blanket storage from Union Village survive in public and private collections. All known examples are constructed of walnut and assembled with half-blind dovetails on both the case and feet and share closely related scrolled bracket bases.

Union Village craftsmen produced a large variety and number of tables to supply the needs of its members. Communal dining tables made there were probably more sturdily built than those from any other Shaker community, East or West. Their construction is distinctive in the layout of the top, which uses several random-width boards, the presence of an added batten between the top and the base to secure the attachment of the two sections, and the placement of the stretcher itself. Unlike their Eastern and Kentucky counterparts, whose stretchers are set directly under the top boards, those from Union Village are located near the floor. In this respect, the Ohio Shaker trestle tables are again more closely related to worldly models. Many of them are also fitted with marble tops—a material frequently found on Victorian furniture, such as parlor tables and cases of drawers dating from the second half of the nineteenth century. Among the smaller four-legged tables, those from Union Village are distinguished from the products of most other communities in the orientation of the drawer in the short rather than the long side of the apron and the shaping of the leg. The latter has several distinct variations, including a slight taper in the round leg from top to bottom; a dramatic narrowing that begins two-thirds of the way down; and a sudden decrease in the diameter of the leg two inches above the floor, where it is turned to a fine point. Another style associated with Union Village is a square ornamentation at the midway point of the leg, which facilitates the attachment of a shelf.

Financial accounts indicate that Richard McNemar was producing chairs as early as 1813.[31] In 1836 he was joined by Freegift Wells, a chairmaker from Watervliet, New York (see pl. 96), who reportedly continued to make chairs in Ohio when he assumed leadership of the ministry. This movement of craftsmen presumably promoted an interchange of chair-making information between the East and West. Ohio produced a style of chair that closely resembles a type made in other communities, characterized by elliptical pommels and strongly arched back slats with rounded top front edges. The slats, which graduate in width from top (widest) to bottom (narrowest), are mortised into the back posts and fastened with pegs from the rear. A second style of Ohio chair exhibits marked regional influences, presenting a dramatic divergence from the traditional Eastern Shaker form. It is distinguished by chamfered back posts, corner-notched slats, and the absence of turned pommels. The form of the rocking chair, like that of storage pieces, was embellished with curves—distinctive S-shaped arms and runners with front-scrolled edges. In sharp contrast to the plain varnish finish uniformly found on Union Village case pieces, a cantaloupe-orange-colored pigment covers the surface of many chairs from the Southwest Ohio communities. Union Village dining room chairs are distinguished by their chamfered back posts and corner-notched slats secured with brads. According to the "Daily Record of Events of the Church Family," on July 13, 1847, "low chairs obtain'd to set on at the dining table instead of benches which had formerly been us'd - an advance in comfort and convenience."[32]

Several major forms are significantly absent from documented Union Village furniture, including counters and sewing desks. When the last Ohio Shakers moved east, there was probably little need for this type of work furniture at Canterbury. The displaced Union Village members were more likely to bring with them cases of drawers. Because of the early closings of the Western communities and the resulting dispersal of property to the noncollecting public, there are few people around today who acquired furnishings directly from the Ohio Shakers. This is in marked contrast to the situation in the East, where early Shaker enthusiasts obtained property directly from the communities during the decades before the Believers left Mount Lebanon in 1947 or Hancock in 1960, for example. The oral history attached to each of these pieces tends to be passed on to future generations of serious collectors when the furniture changes hands today.

The question arises as to why Western Shaker furniture differs so dramatically from its Eastern counterparts. The conventional explanation for the wide variations in style is the physical separation of the Ohio communities from the center of authority and order in New York State, with the geographical distance entailing greater independence and freedom of expression in furniture design. This standard argument, however, does not totally coincide with the facts. During the first half of the nineteenth century, the presence of the parent ministry was strongly felt at Union Village, through the twenty-year leadership of David Darrow, from 1806 to 1826,[33] as well as the seven-year administration of Freegift Wells, from 1836 to 1843, who in addition to his administrative work was an active furniture maker there. Until the 1850s the guiding force of Mount Lebanon also made itself felt through frequent visits by members of the Eastern ministry.[34]

A more logical explanation is the fact that the products of Shaker cabinetmakers mirror the current artistic taste of neighboring rural craftsmen in the world, where they were trained before joining the sect. For example, Queen Anne, Chippendale, and early Federal styles were in vogue during the founding and rapid growth of the Eastern societies in the eighteenth century, while Hepplewhite, Sheraton, and Empire designs prevailed in the West during the nineteenth century, when the Ohio communities were established. These converts were simply working within their own cabinetmaking traditions, training, and abilities to produce Shaker furniture adapted from current styles. However, known Ohio Shaker furniture does not exhibit Victorian-influenced design, which is apparent at Enfield, Connecticut, Canterbury, New Hampshire, and Sabbathday Lake and Alfred, Maine. It is not clear whether these later pieces were sold when the Ohio communities closed and disappeared into the world without a Shaker history or whether few were produced due to declining membership during the last quarter of the nineteenth century.

264. Case of Drawers

Union Village
Daniel Sering (1792–1870)
1827
Written in red ink in script on back of one drawer: Daniel Sering Maker/November 9th 1827
Written in red ink in script on back of another drawer: Daniel Sering/November 9th 1827
Walnut, butternut, and poplar, with varnish
h 51¾ w 43⅝ d 22"
The Warren County Historical Society, Lebanon, Ohio, #805

Daniel Sering joined the fledgling Shaker settlement at Union Village in 1805 and throughout his life served all of the Ohio Shaker communities in a number of capacities. His activities as woodworker, mechanic, and community leader are well documented in contemporary family journals and letters. At Union Village he became Church Family elder in 1826 and deacon in 1841, and he was sent to Whitewater to occupy second place in the ministry there from 1830 to 1838.[35]

In addition to his leadership responsibilities, Sering superintended the woodworking activities for a number of Shaker structures in the Ohio Bishopric. According to the following references from the "Church Journal," on January 22, 1827, he was sent to Whitewater "to put up a large cabin building to make room for an increase of numbers expected from West Union" (the short-lived Indiana community at Busro that closed that year). On June 21, 1849, he journeyed to "North Union to assist them in building their new meeting House." As late as April 2, 1860, he was "at Watervliet [Ohio] for some time directing about their new building at the North House." Writing to Deacons Richard and Stephen on October 12, 1818, David Darrow asserted, "Daniel Sering is the master workman here & he is the greatest mechanic that is in this country among Believers - and he was only a boy of 13 when he came here."[36] At Daniel's death in 1870, a Shaker brother noted, "Daniel was our principal Mechanic for about 50 years. The present meeting house was built by him."[37] Another Believer added, "He was a good mechanic in wood and superintended the building of most of the buildings in Union Village, also a number at Whitewater."[38]

Sering clearly was an active carpenter and joiner, yet this chest of drawers is the only known piece of furniture that he signed and dated. However, it serves to document not only Sering's workmanship but also specific data on design and construction features associated with Ohio workmanship. These include a case top supported underneath with numerous glue blocks and a lengthwise batten dovetailed into the sides; facing strips nailed to the front stiles; vertical tongue-and-groove backboards; and drawers with backs and sides assembled with pins visible on the back of the drawer, and numerous glue blocks underneath. Here, the maker utilized a plank-sided case rather than one of frame-and-panel construction. Both designs were apparently employed at Union Village.

All the drawer faces are decorated with the characteristic scratch-beaded edge and strikingly small, precisely turned original knobs, which are widely spaced and affixed with flat-head screws. The chest has the characteristic cyma-curved bracket base derived from Hepplewhite styling.

opposite above

266. Case of Drawers
Union Village
Levi McNemar (1793–1866)
1841
Cherry and pine, with maple knobs and clear varnish
Written in pencil in script on interior of backboards: March 4th 1841
Written in chalk in script on second-tier drawer rail: L. McNemar
Written in chalk in script on backboards: N.H.
h 53½ w 44¼ d 21⅝"
Canterbury Shaker Village, Inc., Canterbury, New Hampshire, #88.698
Photograph: Bill Finney, by courtesy of Canterbury Shaker Village

Little is known about Levi McNemar, who signed and dated this chest in 1841. According to a letter of 1865 to Elder Freegift Wells from William N. Redman listing the pioneer families and their remaining relatives at Union Village, Levi was the cousin of James (1796–1875) and Vincy (1797–1878), the eldest children of Richard McNemar, one of the original leaders of Union Village.[39] The Record of Deaths for the community implies that Levi was the last of his family when he died in 1866.[40] Levi, who joined the United Society in 1811, was probably the son of Richard's brother Garner (1766–1841).[41] References in journals, logbooks, and census records tell us that Levi served the community in several capacities, as a teamster, farmer, and broom maker.[42] He is also listed as one of a group traveling to Watervliet, Ohio, on August 2, 1841, to help shingle several buildings, indicating he had some knowledge of woodworking.[43] He may have been taught his uncle's trade of cabinetmaker, although no other marked or attributed examples of his work are presently known to exist.

Construction details associated with Union Village workmanship include a top with applied cove moldings and large overhang in back, supported by three lengthwise battens underneath, which are dovetailed to the sides of the case. The two vertical backboards are reinforced by sliding dovetails at midcase to hold a rear subrail. Applied facings are nailed to the stiles. Each of the drawers has many wedge-shaped glue blocks under the bottom, which is set so high that the groove cut into

265. Blanket Box
Union Village
c. 1830
Written in chalk on backboard: ELLEN
Walnut, with cast-brass handles (not original) and varnish
h 20¾ w 40⅜ d 19⅛"
Canterbury Shaker Village, Inc., Canterbury, New Hampshire, #89.267

The name "ELLEN" written in chalk on the backboard confirms the origin and history of this box. According to Jessie Evans's diary, on November 25, 1921, Ellen Ross (1836–1927) was one of three Union Village sisters to move into Enfield House at Canterbury, where this chest was found in 1988. In her entry of August 25, 1927, Jessie Evans wrote that Ellen was born in Covington, Kentucky, in 1836, joined the Union Village Shakers in 1838, and was admitted to Canterbury after her Ohio community closed in 1920.

This blanket box is typical of those produced at Union Village. A closely related example has recently been donated to the Warren County Historical Society in Lebanon, Ohio, by a family whose ancestors originally acquired it from the Shakers. A sim-

ilar box in the Philadelphia Museum of Art (acc. no. 63-160-15) came from a longtime Shaker collector who purchased it at Canterbury from Eldress Emma B. King (1873–1966). According to accession records, Emma traveled to Union Village in 1910 to help with the closing of the community, and she brought that chest back with her to New Hampshire.

Differing dramatically from the rectilinear, painted Eastern boxes (see pl. 62), all three of these examples are constructed of walnut, assembled with half-blind dovetails on the case and feet, and decorated with closely related, if not identical, scrolled base. The fact that the shaping is virtually the same on this blanket box and the signed and dated case of drawers pl. 264 raises the question whether both pieces were made by the same maker, Daniel Sering.

Another similar walnut blanket box in the collection of the Warren County Historical Society (acc. no. 1989.31.H) retains cast-brass handles on each end that show an eagle and the legend "Shakers, Ptd 1872." Patent research to date has not revealed further information.

the back of the drawer front to support the drawer bottom is visible from the side above the bottom half pin. Incised beads run around all drawer faces, which are fitted with distinctive flat-topped, screw-threaded knobs. These original knobs on the full-length drawers contrast sharply with the dome-shaped replacements on the two short drawers above. The straight bracket base is assembled with half-blind dovetails that resemble those found on Ohio blanket boxes (see pl. 265).

The chalk inscription N.H. on the backboards suggests that New Hampshire was the final destination of this Ohio-made case of drawers when the remaining Believers from Union Village and their possessions were moved to Canterbury.

267. Case of Drawers
Union Village
1840
Cherry and poplar, with varnish, bone or ivory escutcheons, and steel lock plate
h 51½ w 45½ d 23⅜"
Canterbury Shaker Village, Inc., Canterbury, New Hampshire, #88.792
Photograph: Bill Finney, by courtesy of Canterbury Shaker Village

This seven-drawer case piece was found at Canterbury in the same building where the last four Union Village sisters lived after relocating to New Hampshire in 1923. Design and construction features are consistent with other documented Ohio Shaker furniture. Particularly noteworthy is the frame-and-panel construction, the stiles and rails on the sides forming the pattern of a cross. This contrasts sharply with the case pieces at Pleasant Hill, Kentucky, which exhibit single-panel sides (see pl. 289). The chamfered edges of the framing members relate directly to architectural details in the interior of the elders' shop (Rose Cottage), dating from 1811 at Union Village, where the stair posts and rails are also chamfered.[44]

The two-board, spline-fit top overhangs slightly in the back. It is secured with two battens running across the depth of the underside, which are both tenoned into the rails at the front and back of the case and screwed from below. The drawer bottoms are fitted with a series of wedge-shaped glue blocks, and the faces have a scratch bead around all four edges. The full-width drawers below the thinner top three drawers are graduated in a manner consistent with Empire cases and measure 9, 7, 8, and 9 inches in depth. Particularly noteworthy is the applied bracket base with elaborately shaped skirt, which relates closely in design to that found on the blanket chest pl. 265, supporting a common Union Village origin.

268. Cupboard

Union Village
c. 1850
Walnut, pine, and poplar, with brass escutcheons
and latch
h 88¾ w 42¾ d 13⅝"
The Warren County Historical Society, Lebanon,
Ohio, #1022, Otterbein Collection

The original use of this four-door cupboard is unknown. Based on physical evidence, including the presence of several quarter-inch holes in both the door and the backboards, the three shelves lining the interior of the top section were added considerably after the construction of the piece. Behind the smaller cupboard doors below is an arrangement of two short over three longer drawers, with a vertical space on either side. Although the drawer unit is probably original to the piece, its specific function has not been determined.

Despite the height of the case, it is relatively shallow, measuring under 14 inches deep, resulting in unusual proportions. The curved bracket base, which corresponds to the style of other Union Village furniture, together with the beaded case edges and rails, the dramatically grained wood cut from flat-sawn walnut boards, and the diamond-shaped escutcheons, offer a decorative contrast to an imposing rectilinear form.

269. Case of Drawers
North Union
c. 1830
Ash or oak and poplar
h 53 w 47½ d 22½"
The Shaker Historical Museum, Shaker Heights, Ohio, #R872

This chest was purchased directly from the North Union community when it closed in 1889 by a former brother and sister who were raised by the Shakers and later married. The plank-sided case and applied bracket base with ogee-shaped foot are features more often associated with Eastern furniture produced during the "classic" period.

Particularly noteworthy is the selection of ash or oak for all visible surfaces; apparently, both native hardwoods were available in abundant supply. A letter dated June 26, 1837, from the Union Village ministry described a visit to North Union: "Their sawmill is superior to any I ever saw. . . . As near as I could assertain they had at that time 13 or 1400 logs on their mill yard, mostly large, straight white-woods, or what they call poplar. In addition to these, they had white oak, red oak, white ash, cherry, basswood and cucumber, all of excellent quality and size except their cherry which was rather small."[45]

270. Case of Drawers
North Union
c. 1840
Walnut, maple, and pine, with traces of red stain
h 44½ w 35½ d 20¾"
The Shaker Historical Museum, Shaker Heights, Ohio, #R490

According to oral history, this case of drawers was purchased at the North Union auction in 1889 by the grandfather of the founder of the Shaker Historical Society and donated to the museum in 1967. Despite its small size, this piece is solidly constructed of frame-and-panel sides and 2-inch-thick square posts. Finishing details include the top with molded edges and ovolo corners and legs with an elongated collar situated between the square post and rounded foot. A variant of this distinctive transitional turning is evident on a blanket box at the Shaker Historical Museum, Shaker Heights, Ohio; it may be a feature of North Union furniture, although the sampling of extant pieces is too small for a definitive conclusion. The unlipped drawer fronts are fitted with the original knobs, featuring a broad top and thick stem with threaded wooden screw. An unusual detail is that the rails and drawer faces are not flush but recessed ⅝ inch from the front face of the posts.

271. Case of Drawers
Union Village
c. 1840
Branded on underside of top drawer support: UV
Cherry, walnut, oak, basswood, and pine, with
brass pulls (not original) and varnish
h 46¼ w 44½ d 21⅜"
Canterbury Shaker Village, Inc., Canterbury, New
Hampshire, #88.2420

At first glance, this decorative case of drawers, with its combination of woods and Empire-style drawer arrangement, looks like a product of worldly craftsmen. However, closer examination reveals the unusual mark on the interior of the case and distinctive construction features that confirm its Shaker origin.

Most significant are the initials UV on the underside of the top drawer support. The fact that they are branded into the surface of the wood, rather than being handwritten or stenciled, suggests that this board with dadoed sides may once have been used as packaging or crate material for other Union Village products sold to the world. The branded drawer support appears to be original, not a later addition or repair, strengthening the theory that the chest was produced by Union Village cabinetmakers. Found in the same dwelling house at Canterbury that was occupied by the last four Ohio Shakers, this chest was probably moved to New Hampshire with the owner when Union Village closed in the early twentieth century.

The use of the branded wood and so many other different secondary woods on interior rails and drawer parts may indicate that the craftsman was using available stock to complete his project. Characteristic construction features associated with Union Village include a top that overhangs the case at the back edge, vertically oriented backboards, three short (2³⁄₁₆ inches high) drawers above full-length drawers, which are graduated in size according to Empire-period fashion (10, 5½, 6⅝, and 7⅝ inches), and the presence of numerous wedge-shaped glue blocks underneath the drawer bottoms.

However, this case of drawers has several distinct construction details that deserve further comment. The top surface has four plugged holes, probably used to hold a mirror frame or glove drawer that has since been removed. Not only are the feet unusually shaped, they are also constructed in an unorthodox manner. The base was formed with triangular pieces of wood fastened to the post and the front and side rails. The foot was then shaped so the arc created by the inserted piece was continued in the leg. Finally, the drawer dovetails are cut inconsistently; they have irregular slopes on the sides and—an important clue in making an attribu-

tion—the bottom two pins are rectangular rather than triangular in shape.

Although this chest cannot be attributed to a documented Shaker craftsman, it shares certain idiosyncratic design and construction features with an almost identical example that has never left the site; it remains in the 1840 dwelling house, now the Otterbein Home Retirement Community. Both pieces have the overall single-panel form, unique foot construction, and distinctive drawer dovetails, which together make up the thumbprint of an unidentified Union Village cabinetmaker.

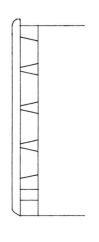

272. Corner Cupboard

Union Village
c. 1840
Walnut and poplar, with varnish
h 72 w 33½ d 19¾"
Collection the Otterbein Home Retirement
Community, Lebanon, Ohio

Freestanding corner cupboards are unknown in the Eastern Shaker communities. The situation is quite different in the Midwest, where the Ohio Shakers adapted this popular regional form for communal use. Surviving examples, such as this, are characterized by paneled rather than glazed doors. The door frame is fitted with ovolo inner edges and a scratch bead around the perimeter. The grain in the wood of the top panels runs horizontally, while that of the bottom panels is vertical. The upper door conceals two interior shelves, while the lower cupboard section has none.

This particular two-door cupboard is extremely small, measuring only 6 feet high compared to other four-door Shaker examples, which are typically at least 7 feet tall. The proportions of both smaller panels on either side of the central panel are unusual. The shallow cove cornice molding is a vernacular form, common on country furniture, and the curved front skirt and shaped legs recall those on many cases of drawers produced at Union Village. In overall design, it represents one of the very finest Western Shaker pieces.

273. Built-in Cupboard, Trustees' Office
Union Village
1891–92
Walnut and poplar, with brass hinges and escutcheon
h 96 w 84½ d 15½"
Collection the Otterbein Home Retirement Community, Lebanon, Ohio

This storage unit was built into the Trustees' Office during the rehabilitation of the building in 1891–92 under the direction of Joseph Slingerland (see p. 295). The building later became known as Marble Hall—a worldly term that came into usage in the late 1930s by the staff and residents at the Otterbein Home, by which it is known today.[46] Although probably not the product of Shaker hands, the updated design reflects the Shakers' concept of the built-in storage unit at the turn of the century. Located between the kitchen and dining room, the cupboard opened into the room on the opposite side of the wall and perhaps provided convenient storage for ceramic tableware. The 5-inch-wide three-part molding (a fillet with ogee, a quarter-round with fillet, and a quarter-round with fillet) around the top of the case, identical to that found on the door frame in Marble Hall, is clearly tied to the overall design of the building. The cabinetmaker also combined elements of the old—raised-panel doors—with the new—complex molding profiles and beaded boards on the side of the case—showing an awareness of contemporary taste.

274. Trestle Table
Union Village
1890–95
Cherry and marble, with varnish
h 28¾ w 104½ d 39½"
Collection the Otterbein Home Retirement Community, Lebanon, Ohio

Union Village trestle tables vary from those produced in other Shaker communities in several distinct ways: the placement of the stretcher, the treatment of the foot, the attachment of the top to the base, and, on some, the use of marble for the surface. Unlike the longitudinal stretchers on their Eastern and Kentucky relatives, placed just beneath the top, those from Union Village are located a foot from the floor. In this respect they are more closely related to worldly models. In addition, the arched foot rises slightly before it joins the vertical support, as opposed to the right angle formed between the two parts on trestle tables from most other communities. Union Village tables are fastened to the base with a cleat screwed both into the top above and into a shaped support below that terminates the upright.

This is in marked contrast to Eastern examples, where the legs are affixed directly into the top.

According to an 1893 journal reference, "Hewitt Horton strained his back by lifting a Marble Table in his room. He is nearly helpless with it."[47] Under the direction of Elder Joseph Slingerland's administration at Union Village, marble was also employed for flooring and sinks during the remodeling of the Trustees' Office in 1891–92.

The Shakers' use of marble on furniture and in interiors is a reflection of worldly Victorian taste. This material is also found in extant pieces of the same period from other Shaker communities, including the trestle table pl. 45 and counter pl. 38 at Mount Lebanon and the counter at Canterbury pl. 176.

above

275. Table

Union Village
c. 1840
Cherry
h 28⅞ w 24⁹⁄₁₆ d 31⁵⁄₁₆"
The Warren County Historical Society, Lebanon, Ohio, # 1989.31.A

In many ways this cherry table is characteristic of Ohio Shaker furniture. The drawer is oriented in the small end of the table, as opposed to Eastern Shaker examples. The shaping of the legs consists of a square upper post with a 90-degree shoulder and a straight turned section that tapers sharply about 4 inches from the floor to form the pointed foot. The square-edged drawer face with characteristic flat knob fits flush to the rails, and the drawer bottom is supported by numerous thin glue blocks. Distinctive features are found in the rimmed shelf below, which is fastened on square sections left at the midpoint of the cylinder section of the turned legs, the line at the transition point between the leg and the tapered foot, and the offset key hole.

A table at Canterbury Shaker Village (acc. no. 88.440), shipped directly from Ohio to New Hampshire when the last Union Village members moved there, shares many construction and design characteristics with this one. It has a similarly shaped leg, with the square upper post and tapered foot, and a drawer bottom supported by numerous glue blocks.

276. Table

Union Village
c. 1830
Cherry and pine, with metal pulls (not original)
h 34 w 72¾ d 35"
Collection the Otterbein Home Retirement Community, Lebanon, Ohio

This worktable exhibits a number of unusual features. The 8-inch-deep front apron is constructed of two rails, one above and below the drawer, which is flanked by a flat panel rather than a stile on either side. The two turned pulls are located 2⅜ inches from the outer edge of the drawer face. The drawer bottom consists of six tongue-and-groove fitted boards. The leg is defined by three half-round turnings beneath the square transition section and is tapered severely to a diameter of ⅞ inch. The work surface, at 34 inches high, is considerably taller than comparable examples, suggesting that this piece was designed for a specific, as yet undetermined, function.

There exist a number of other large Ohio Shaker worktables that are considerably less stylish. They use heavier legs, more related to those on pls. 275 or 277, without the more decorative taper or transitional turnings this table displays. Two have drawers in the short end of the table.[48]

277. Table
Union Village
c. 1830
Walnut, maple, and poplar, with varnish
h 27¹/₁₆ w 28¹/₄ d 20¹/₈"
Collection the Otterbein Home Retirement
Community, Lebanon, Ohio

This small table shares common construction characteristics with other Union Village examples, including the single long drawer that opens on the short side of the frame. The distinctive contrast of the curly maple drawer fronts with the walnut legs, aprons, and top represents a conscious design decision on the part of the craftsman. Particularly noteworthy is the treatment of the legs, which is reminiscent of those of the table pl. 275: below the apron, the square stiles end abruptly with no transition to the round leg, which tapers dramatically several inches above the floor to form the pointed foot.

278. Armed Rocker
Union Village
c. 1830
Maple, ash, and rush (not original), with
cantaloupe orange paint and rug cushion
h 43¼ w 23³⁄₁₆ d 27½"
Collection Ed Clerk

With its vibrant use of color and form, this
rocker is one of the most flamboyant pieces
of Shaker seating furniture. The cantaloupe
orange paint and the exuberantly shaped
arms and rocker blades seem to be unique to
Union Village. Another example in the Warren County Historical Society collection (acc.
no. 807) has a similar arm and rocker form.[49]
However, the craftsman followed the Eastern
Shaker traditions and used a simply contoured back slat and turned finial without the
chamfered and flattened back post typical of
Southern vernacular convention. Four pins
are used to hold each back slat to the rear
posts. The arm is fastened to the rear post
with a screw and to the front with a pin.

279. Tripod Stand
Union Village
c. 1820
Walnut, with varnish
h 23 w 19 d 17"
Collection Mrs. John Murphy

With its bulbous stem turning, this tripod stand is more reminiscent of Kentucky Shaker or vernacular furniture than Eastern or classical Shaker designs. However, it was purchased in the Lebanon, Ohio, area. Carefully designed and constructed, the stand has a plain, nearly square top, which contrasts with the exuberantly formed snake legs and stem turning. The craftsman finished the turning with fine scribe lines on three places on the stem.

280. Side Chair
Union Village
c. 1840
Maple, ash, and rush, with cantaloupe orange
paint
Collection Mrs. John Murphy

281. Side Chair
Union Village
c. 1840
Maple and splint, with varnish
Stamped on front post: 7
h 35⅞ w 18 d 13⅞"
Collection the Otterbein Home Retirement
Community, Lebanon, Ohio, on loan to the
Warren County Historical Society, #1023

According to the "Financial Accounts of the Shaker Community in the Miami Valley, Ohio,"[50] chairs were first sold to the world on May 29, 1813, when "Nathan received $5.25 dollars for chairs." In September, a notation stated "rec'd by the hand of Richard for a set of chairs sold to Isaac Morris senior, $5.25." The same amount was paid to "Richard for one set of chairs" on October 7 and November 6.

Although both of these chairs are typical of Union Village craftsmanship, they are inspired by worldly furniture from different locales. The three-slat example closely resembles those produced at Mount Lebanon. They have tapered posts fitted with finely turned elliptical pommels and arched back slats with rounded front edges. The cantaloupe-colored paint is common on chairs produced at Union Village. The other side chair exhibits the influence of Southern vernacular traditions with the turned and then flattened back posts terminating in a chamfer without a finial. The upper corners of the slats are notched, creating a look very different from the Eastern Shaker chairs. However, most of the Union Village seating furniture has a heavier mass because of the larger diameter turnings at the bottom of the posts, which are reduced below the bottom rung to an abrupt taper to the floor.

282. Trestle Table

Pleasant Hill
c. 1830
Butternut
h 28½ w 70 d 41½"
Collection of Shaker Village of Pleasant Hill,
Harrodsburg, Kentucky, #62.2.3 (table); From
the Collection of the Harrodsburg Historical
Society, Harrodsburg, Kentucky (chairs)

There are two known dining room trestle tables from Pleasant Hill, each with different dimensions, construction features, and assembly techniques, although the leg form is similar. On this example at Shaker Village of Pleasant Hill, the four-board, spline-joined top is supported by two cross cleats with shaped ends, which are screwed into the underside of the top, and by the longitudinal stretcher, which is through-tenoned into the leg assembly. The leg uprights are through-tenoned and double-pinned into the cross members above and the highly arched foot below.

The other known community trestle table, in a private collection, is much longer and consequently required a more elaborate substructure. This consists of two longitudinal stretchers through-tenoned into the leg and connected to each other with a crosswise stub, which is also bolted into the leg. Shaped braces are fastened into the underside of the stretcher to increase stability. The unusually wide top with square, as opposed to shaped, edges, the absence of breadboard ends, and the heavy foot, which is exceptionally broad in cross section, contribute to the visual effect of massiveness characteristic of Pleasant Hill tables. In addition, none of the edges of the leg structure are rounded, which would visually lighten the base. The longer table is inscribed on the stretcher, "Sisters' table, North End [of the dining room], June 1869," providing documentation of its use.

Benches were standard dining room seating for the Pleasant Hill Shakers throughout the first part of the nineteenth century. Records indicate that in 1845, 1856, and 1858 Francis Monfort made dining room benches for the East Family Dwelling House and the Centre Family ("Temporal Journal . . . Book B," p. 7). However, on October 27, 1864, "We introduced chairs instead of benches in our dining rooms" ("Family Journal . . . Book A," p. 282). The chairs pictured here were not made by village craftsmen but purchased from the world and bear the as yet unidentified mark of M & Son painted on the bottom. Other "boughten" chairs have initials such as "W" stenciled under the seat. By midcentury, the male population was in decline, and their work was supplemented by outside labor. Another possible factor in the choice of these chairs may be a decision to replace the benches with more comfortable individual seating.

Pleasant Hill and South Union Communities, Kentucky

WHILE THE ORGANIZED churches in Kentucky at the beginning of the nineteenth century divided sharply into partisan denominations, they were as a whole male-centered and male-administered. The newly opened West required manpower, and a larger family was an important asset for material success. A great deal of the legal structure of this newly formed state (1792) centered around marriage, children, and the descent of property, which reflected the Kentuckians' desire to perpetuate themselves in the land. Into this male-dominated social and religious climate, during the great religious revival that flourished in the early 1800s (see p. 291), came the Eastern Shaker missionaries. Benjamin Seth Youngs, a visiting missionary from Mount Lebanon, and Richard McNemar, Malcolm Worley, and John Dunlavy, newly converted New Light Presbyterian leaders from Ohio, found two men among the local residents, many of whom thought the idea of a female counterpart in Christ anathema, who were willing to listen to the doctrine of Mother Ann Lee.[1] In embracing a faith that had as its base the equality of the sexes, perhaps the area Presbyterians showed that they were more open-minded than the Baptists or Methodists, for a large number of converted Presbyterians made up the Western Shaker societies. Elisha Thomas at Shawnee Run, Mercer County, and Jesse McComb at Gaspar Springs, Logan County, donated their land to form the nucleus of what was to become, respectively, the Pleasant Hill (1806) and South Union (1807) Shaker communities. By their peak, in the 1860s, the Pleasant Hill Shakers had acquired five thousand acres of land and built 266 structures of all kinds,[2] while South Union grew to include over 200 buildings on six thousand acres.[3]

The Pleasant Hill property produced crops of wheat, rye, corn, flax, tobacco, and hemp, which the Shakers processed in various mills and transported to market as far as New Orleans via Shaker-made flatboats. By the mid-nineteenth century the business of packaging and marketing garden seeds to the world had grown to be the most profitable industry in both Kentucky societies.[4] Undoubtedly aware of the fact that mulberry trees thrived throughout the South, the Shakers, as early as 1816, introduced silkworms into the Kentucky communities. By 1832 the South Union sisters had produced enough silk to make themselves new silk kerchiefs measuring 32 by 34 inches hemmed. The following year on New Year's Day they presented the brethren with collar-width silk neckerchiefs that fastened in the back and had a small bow on the front. The vibrant colors ranged from white to blue, pink, and mulberry to dark brown. Some were iridescent, others were checked or had a border of a contrasting color.[5] The South Union sisters also shared their silk with the members of other Shaker communities. According to Elder Henry Blinn of Canterbury, on "January 1, 1856, Every Sister of the Church received a White silk neckerchief for uniform, which was manufactured by the Sisters of South Union, KY."[6] When Elder Henry later traveled to Pleasant Hill, he wrote in "A Journey to Kentucky in the Year 1873" that he was taken to

> . . . visit the house where they are feeding silk worms. Several thousands were laid upon shelves & fed with the leaves of the mulberry. The sister who had charge of them would pick them up & call them "pretty little creatures." They were to be ready in two or three days to begin to spin

thin cocoons. They are raised for the purpose of obtaining sewing silk. It requires one bushel of cocoons to make one pound of silk. Last year they raised ten bushels. We incline to think that the northern sisters would be rather cautious at the handling of silk worms. (Winter 1965, p. 115)

In addition to cultivating the fields, the Shakers at both Kentucky societies also played an important role in the livestock industry, one of the oldest economic activities in Kentucky. Together with the Union Village, Ohio, community, in 1811 they purchased a purebred English shorthorn—the first to be brought to Kentucky—which they named Shaker. On many occasions these Western communities cooperated in the importation of animals and exchanged animals with other Shaker villages, which helped to improve herds. By the 1830s livestock production had become a major source of income and included beef and milk cattle, as well as hogs and sheep. The Shakers devoted a great deal of attention to cattle breeding, which gained them an excellent reputation in the field of animal husbandry.[7]

The South Union Shakers were expert horticulturists who practiced scientific grafting so that some variety of fruit was available year round for sauces and pies. They built preserve and drying houses so that the sisters could process the fruit without disrupting the daily preparation of meals. According to one account book, 3,917 jars of strawberry preserves were made in one day. The finished product was shipped in wooden cases by freight-car load from the railroad station at South Union.[8] In 1869 the South Union Shakers further took advantage of the railroad station by building a tavern that housed a hotel and restaurant for the world's people traveling through. Once the construction was completed, they leased the building to an outside interest for one hundred dollars a month as a business venture. The tavern's architectural features, with its grand columned facade, intricate brickwork, and ornate walnut staircase, all designed to attract the world's people, made a striking contrast with the simplicity of other Shaker interiors.

It is surprising, given the organizational structure among other regional groupings of Shaker communities, that the two Kentucky villages were not united into a single bishopric until membership declined in 1868. A growing lack of capable leaders may have forced the governing ministry of Union Village to consolidate the Kentucky societies—an arrangement that lasted only until 1872. The dissolution of the Kentucky ministry less than four years after it had been formed may have been due to the great distance between the two communities and inadequate travel facilities.[9] Consequently, each community largely developed separately, with different leadership. As a result, the furniture produced at Pleasant Hill and South Union is more closely related to Kentucky vernacular furniture than to each other. After the 1870s, little was produced at either community because the enrollment of the Southern Shaker societies fell off sharply after the Civil War, accounting for a marked absence of Victorian-inspired design.

The Shaker community at Pleasant Hill was officially gathered into Gospel Order in 1806, when forty-four members of legal age signed the covenant. At that time, an inventory was taken of the property and goods of each Believer so that those who had misgivings about their dedication or who could not bear the commitment might withdraw at a later date and have their personal possessions restored. Surviving copies of these inventories list various articles ranging in value from 37½ cents to 150 dollars. However, little furniture is included, except for beds and bedding, which are common to all inventories.[10] In fact, on August 10, 1810, the young converts at Pleasant Hill wrote to the parent ministry at Mount Lebanon: "When we came to Kentucky, it was the gift for us not to bring much property with us; we started with fifty dollars of money, two beds and bedding and

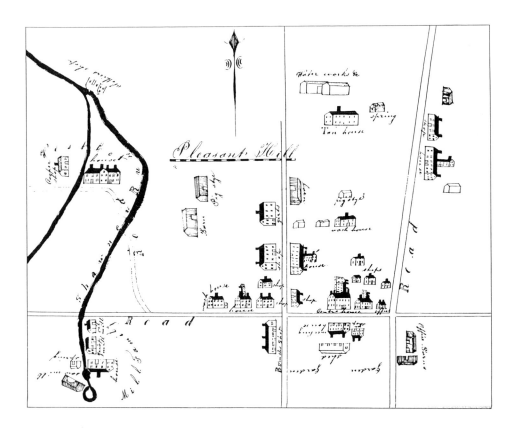

George Kendall, after Isaac Newton Youngs. Map of Pleasant Hill. 1935. Ink and watercolor on paper, 7¾ x 9¾". Copied from Isaac Newton Youngs's journal "Sketches of the Various Societies of Believers in the States of Ohio and Kentucky to which is added a slight sketch of Sodus Bay in the northern part of New York. Also a map containing several of the states on which is laid out the route of Br. Rufus Bishop and Isaac N. Youngs," 1834. Reproduced from an original in the Library of Congress, Washington, D.C. Geography and Map Division

a few smaller things. It was not the faith of the young believers here to bring anything with us."[11]

Therefore, from an early date, Pleasant Hill Shakers were, out of necessity, producing furniture, both for community use and some for sale to the world. The earliest known recorded mention of furniture making there appears on December 18, 1810, in the debit and credit records for the community, which read, "received of Cornelious Banta that he got for a table which he made—$9.00." On March 27, 1811, the Shakers "sold one bureau to Samuel McDowell—$18.00 also 1 sugar chest—$8.00."[12] Brother Maurice Thomas recorded in his journal for Thursday, January 11, 1816, "I got able to begin a table this day." On Monday, January 15, he reported, "I finished my table." As late as 1881, a letter to Brother William in Albany, Indiana, instructs:

> We have a man that has worked at Furniture makeing, he is now at work on a Table for the Hands Dineing room, I want you to go to Belknap or Moss & Simpels and get a pair of Extention Slides for a ten, 10 foot table they wil cost $1.10 cts be Shure to get them as the table will be made and be awaiting for them. We are doing but little in the Shop as there is no job work comeing in.[13]

For a period of at least seventy years, from 1811 to 1881, Kentucky Shaker cabinetmakers were building a variety of furniture types, including tables, bedsteads, bureaus, and school benches, for a diverse clientele.[14]

Fortunately, in addition to four signed and dated pieces by two makers (■), surviving Pleasant Hill journals, accounts, and diaries (■■) provide insight into the types of furniture produced, where it was used, and the names of some of the cabinetmakers themselves. These include:

■■ CORNELIUS BANTA, signed the original covenant in 1806 as well as the one in 1810, in "Daybook," 1810–11[15]

■■ JOHN VORIS, SR. (1758–1845), in unpublished draft of Nickels, "The Shaker Furniture of Pleasant Hill, Kentucky," at Shaker Village of Pleasant Hill, Harrodsburg, Kentucky

■■ SAMUEL HARRIS (1763–1852), in "Temporal Journal . . . Book B," December 18, 1845[16]

■■ STEPHEN MANIER (1771–1850), in "Temporal Journal . . . Book B," January 28, 1847

BENJAMIN SETH YOUNGS (1774–1855), of Watervliet, New York, resided at Pleasant Hill and South Union 1805–55

SAMUEL TURNER (1775–1842), of Mount Lebanon, resided at Pleasant Hill 1806–36

■■ JOHN SHAIN (1779–1872), in Nickels, "The Shaker Furniture of Pleasant Hill, Kentucky," p. 1185

■■ FRANCIS MONFORT (1784–1867), in "Temporal Journal . . . Book B," February 9, 1847

■■ JOHN VORIS, JR. (1789–1856), in "Temporal Journal . . . Book B," April 22, 1854

■■ MAURICE THOMAS (1793–1830), in "Journal of M. Thomas," December 1817

■■ BENJAMIN B. DUNLAVY (1805–1886), in "Temporal Journal . . . Book B," June 12, 1849

■■ STEPHEN LEONIDAS BOISSEAU (1821–1894), in "Temporal Journal . . . Book B," January 26, 1854

■■ JOSEPH CURTIS (1825–expelled 1848), in "Temporal Journal . . . Book B," February 4, 1846

■ LEANDER GETTYS (1832–left 1865), see pls. 292, 293

■■ WILLIAM H. MORSE (b. 1839), in "Temporal Journal . . . Book B," January 10, 1863

■ RICHARD ALEXANDER MILLIGAN (b. 1849), see pl. 301

■■ HENRY DAILY (working 1890), in "Temporal Journal," May 16, 1889–December 2, 1890, entry of November 3, 1890[17]

Samuel Turner and Benjamin Seth Youngs were both sent from Mount Lebanon to help organize the Western communities in Ohio and Kentucky. Samuel Turner arrived at Pleasant Hill in 1806 and remained until 1836.[18] No attributable examples of his cabinetmaking work survive from this time, although he produced one signed stand after he returned to Mount Lebanon in 1836 (see pl. 59), indicating that he probably did some furniture making during his twenty-seven years in Kentucky. Benjamin Seth Youngs, like his brother Isaac and their uncle Benjamin Youngs, Sr. (pls. 75, 76, 93, 94), was a clock maker by trade, who originally joined the Watervliet community in 1794. Although he spent the remainder of his life (1805–1855) at Pleasant Hill and South Union, it is not known whether he produced timepieces during his years in the West. However, according to "Journal A" of the South Union Ministry, Youngs did "put up a new clock (which he took from Enfield, CT last year) at the East House in the South Union community" (December 12, 1828). Clocks are mentioned repeatedly in numerous journal references as "boughten articles" between the years 1829 and 1897. The "Account Book, 1839–1910" for the year 1843 shows that three clocks came to the village from the world, one purchased for twenty-five dollars, the other two, valued at fifty dollars together, taken in trade;[19] on February 29, 1844, they "Paid for a clock 20.00" (p. 76); from the "Account Book, 1825–1833," January 30, 1829, "clock . . . 30.00" (p. 185); from "Temporal Journal . . . Book B," June 6, 1843, "A new brass clock and a grind stone for Francis and the boys" (p. 191); June 12, 1843, "A new clock for the nurses room" (p. 191); July 4, 1848, "2 clocks, one for the brethren's brick shop and the other for the garden house" (p. 194); April 5, 1853, "An eight day

Centre Family Dwelling House, Pleasant Hill, c. 1880. Photograph by Eduard H. Fox, Danville, Kentucky. Shaker Museum and Library, Old Chatham, New York, #12590h

alarm clock" (p. 196); April 7, 1857, "a clock for the Sisters new shop" (p. 199); March 29, 1859, "A clock for the kitchen" (p. 200).

Another key figure in the history of Pleasant Hill was Micajah Burnett (1791–1879), a native of Kentucky who was responsible for the design, layout, and planning of the entire community. According to one Shaker brother who knew him, "he was the principle architect of the village, an accomplished civil engineer . . . a mechanic and machinist of the community first order."[20] His building plan included the East (1817), West (1821), and Centre (1824–34) Family dwelling houses, the Meetinghouse (1820), and the Trustees' Office (1839–40), with its elegant twin spiral staircases, to name a few. With the exception of the clapboard Meetinghouse, all of these structures had either native brick or limestone exteriors, laid in various decorative patterns. Their overall design reveals that he was influenced by the then-popular Federal style of public architecture, which allowed him to provide a maximum amount of space with a minimum amount of internal walls and supports.[21] Under his direction, the village was laid out with a meetinghouse, family houses, craft shops, utility shed, and barns. No documented pieces of furniture have as yet been attributed to him; however, in his journal (January 1, 1816–December 31, 1817, part 2, p. 162), Maurice Thomas recorded that on Wednesday, October 15, 1817, "M Bernett, and my self made some patterns." Could this refer to furniture templates, indicating that he was, indeed, involved in the cabinetmaking trade?

The pieces from Pleasant Hill selected for analysis are either signed by the original maker or have a strong Pleasant Hill provenance. By 1910, the last twelve Shakers deeded the 1,800 remaining acres to Colonel George Bohon, a Harrodsburg resident, with the agreement that he would care for them until the end of their lives. The year after the death of the Shaker doctor, William Pennebaker (1841–1922), an auction was held to dispose of the building contents. Over the next fifty years, the dwellings and shops were sold and/or leased to various tenants, until Shakertown Inc. was formed in 1961 to purchase, preserve, and interpret the remaining 313 structures on site. Therefore, pieces of furniture with a Bohon provenance, either through purchase at public sales or continuous descent in the family, most probably were either made or used by the Pleasant Hill Shakers.

Due to the loss of so many pieces over the years, the sampling available for study is limited. Even in this small group, the variety among related forms can be bewildering. However, from characteristic design and construction features as well as materials, it is possible to make valid generalizations about community origins. In general, Pleasant Hill furniture is constructed of cherry and walnut, with poplar as the secondary wood of choice. Oak, ash, or hickory were occasionally used for the stretchers and slats of chairs because of their superior structural characteristics. As is typical of much Western vernacular case furniture, each piece is solidly constructed, with thick stock for posts, rails, and tops.

Somewhat surprisingly, there appears to be little relationship between the interior architecture and the freestanding furniture. For example, the Centre Family Dwelling House, erected between 1824 and 1834, features raised-panel doors throughout, which is more typical of the eighteenth than the nineteenth century; curved plaster ceilings and arched fanlights; a molded chair rail with complex profile consisting of a bead over a stepped cove and an astragal; and paneled wainscoting with engaged columns. Throughout the dwelling the wood trim retains its original dark blue paint and the baseboards a contrasting brick red. These details are not, for the most part, repeated in the community's furniture.

The items most often mentioned in period manuscripts and most plentiful today are chairs. Francis Monfort, the most prolific maker, produced a wide variety of types, including eighty-seven "common" or side chairs, fourteen armchairs, eight rocking chairs, thirty-five chairs for children, three sweating chairs for the nurses' rooms, and one stool chair.[22] Distinguishing characteristics of Pleasant Hill seating furniture include bulbous or elongated oval pommels, curved slats rounded on the top front edge, seat stretchers pinned to the posts, and handholds that are screwed into the tops of the arms. Neither tenon caps, as on Mount Lebanon chairs (see pl. 71), nor integral mushroom caps typical of some Eastern Shaker examples (see pl. 142), these handholds are placed on the arm in front of the front post.

Pleasant Hill craftsmen made several types of tables, each with recognizable features. Four-legged tables consistently exhibit tops with plain, square edges. These are attached to rails beneath with screws in numerous screw pockets. Particularly noteworthy is the shape of the legs, which feature an abrupt transition between the square stile and the round section. This design appears on two signed examples by Brother Leander Gettys dating from the 1860s (see pls. 292 and 293) and one table in a private collection by Brother Richard Milligan of the 1870s. There is a dramatic difference between this severe leg and the vigorously turned, bulbous, inverted baluster-shaped feet (also placed abruptly below the square stile without transition) found on earlier cases of drawers, which share the complexity if not the detail of the turned stair posts in the Centre Family Dwelling House (1824–34). One possibility for the change in style is that the leg form on the signed pieces may have been introduced after the revivalist period of the 1840s, when the Shakers rededicated themselves to the principles of gospel simplicity, therefore representing a conscious design change on the part of these postreform furniture makers.

Pleasant Hill tripod stands can be recognized by tops tapered to a thin edge, disk-shaped collars, and vase-shaped pedestals. According to contemporary journal entries, they were one of the few furniture forms specifically made for use in halls as well as to be sold commercially to the world.[23]

Trestle tables from Pleasant Hill are massive in proportions and construction and have wide tops with square edges and broad, highly arched feet. The latter show little shaping in cross section and have square rather than rounded edges. These large tables were designed primarily for family dining rooms.

The majority of case pieces, including some built-ins (see pl. 285, pp. 4–5), are characterized by frame-and-panel construction, which appears to be a feature of Kentucky and Ohio Shaker case furniture. More specifically, cases of drawers are built with flush drawers, plain tops without molding and with minimal overhang, and vigorously turned legs. Drawer construction features include knobs that are mortised, rather than screwed, into the faces, multiple rectangular blocks glued underneath the bottoms, and, occasionally, rear drawer dovetails with pins exposed on the back rather than the sides of the drawers.

The freestanding press, or cupboard over case of drawers, is a Shaker furniture form made primarily in the Western communities. According to contemporary Shaker records, it was used to store clothing and textiles. When writing to Benjamin S. Youngs at South Union in 1832, William Deming of Hancock described the brick Church Family Dwelling House there as follows: "The second loft of garrets is done off with four large rooms. Six large clothes presses with a hall that runs East and West and crosses from North to South and two back rooms that extends the whole length of the house." He is probably referring to the many built-in cupboards over cases of drawers found in the attic as presses. Manuscript material and physical evidence reveal that some of the freestanding examples in the Western communities were originally built as one piece, while other cupboard sections were added to existing cases of drawers, or, as the Pleasant Hill Shakers called them, "bureaus," to form two-part storage units. Typically, the Pleasant Hill press exhibits extremely tall, slender proportions. The paneled doors, which often have beveled rather than shiplap edges where they meet, have two unequal panels, comparable to the dimensions of the Centre Family Dwelling House doors and built-ins. The case rails are occasionally decorated with a bead, which echoes that found on the interior woodwork.

Pleasant Hill beds differ significantly from their Eastern counterparts. Whether high, low, or trundle beds, most are characterized by wedge-shaped posts without turned knobs on top and a variety of headboards, ranging from horizontal or vertical slats to curved or scalloped designs, some with applied carving.

The only furniture forms not currently represented in any quantity are counters. Although probably made and used by the Pleasant Hill Shakers, they simply may have been sold from the community, and they have not surfaced in known public or private collections.

Unlike the Eastern communities, the Kentucky Shakers probably did not produce many Victorian-influenced designs. Due to declining enrollment after the Civil War, there was little need to fabricate furniture for additional members. This, coupled with the absence of Western Shaker collectors, accounts for the lack of known surviving Victorian-style pieces with a documented Pleasant Hill history.

While a great deal of information survives regarding the names of specific Pleasant Hill cabinetmakers, there are no known pieces of furniture signed by the maker and little extant written documentation to shed light on the activities of individual craftsmen at South Union. Scattered journal references give the names of men who made chairs and those who worked on specific construction projects, including interior woodwork and boat building, as carpenters. In the South Union Ministry "Journal A" (1807–36), it was announced on October 30, 1826 (■) that "Saml S. Eades, John Smith, David Barrett, William Pearce & Milton Homer Robinson all go to the East House to work and this week laid 8 doors & window sills & brick floors thro all the Kitchen & Dining Room part of the house." On December 17, 1828 (■■), "Today the Brethren, Carpenters commence to do the joiner work of the Great Brick Centre Building, which was covered in, in the month of December 1824. It will doubtless be 4 more years yet before it will be ready to occupy. The carpenters are, to begin with, Robt Johns foreman, Benj'm Good-Hope, Br. Heath N Heriston & L L Martin." On October 12, 1829 (■■■), "Brn. David Smith, Jesse McComb, Lorenzo L Martin, Rhinaldo Martin, Danl M. Whyte, Napoleon Small, Seth Meigs & Jo Morrison started to Clarksville to build a boat 60 X 14 feet for coasting to Orleans. It is to be loaded with cattle, garden seed, brooms, carpeting, etc. for the Southern Market. Robt and Patterson Johns, U.E. Johns also went." It is probable that all or many of these carpenters also produced furniture.

■■■ JESSE McCOMB, SR. (1750–1815)
■ SAMUEL S. EADES (1778–1862)
■■■ DAVID SMITH (1782–1863)
WILLIAM RICE (1783–1863), listed as chair maker in "Journal A," April 4, 1822, and in "Journal B," January 5, 1849
■■ ROBERT JOHNS (1795–1863), listed as chair maker in "Journal A," April 4, 1822, and in "Journal B," January 5, 1849, and described by Elder Benjamin Seth Youngs in "Journal A," December 22, 1834: "Robt Johns, 39 years old today, our leading carpenter and workman." A plow plane with his name and the date 1824 (see p. 74) supplies evidence that he worked as a carpenter
■ DAVID BARRETT (1796–1853)
■■■ URBAN E. JOHNS (1802–1878)
■■■ PATTERSON JOHNS (1804–1863)
■ WILLIAM PEARCE (1805–1835)
HARVEY L. EADES (1807–1892), in "Journal A," November 15, 1830: he "goes to work at the carpenters trade today planing white oak plank for the floor of the Centre House." He was also the community's schoolteacher, tailor, tinsmith, and shoemaker
■■ LORENZO L. MARTIN (working 1812–37)
■ MILTON HOMER ROBINSON (w. 1812–34)
■ JOHN SMITH (w. 1812–48)
■■ BENJAMIN GOODHOPE (d. 1814)
RUEBEN WISE (1818–1893), listed as chair maker in "Journal A," April 4, 1822, and in "Journal B," January 5, 1849
■■■ DANIEL M. WHYTE (w. 1818–29)
■■■ RHINALDO MARTIN (w. 1822–29)
■■■ SETH MEIGS (w. August 11, 1825)
■■■ NAPOLEON SMALL (w. 1827–31)
■■ HEATH N. HERISTON (w. 1828)
■■■ JOE MORRISON (w. 1829)

Without any known signed pieces, South Union furniture has been attributed either through oral tradition or purchase history. Surviving examples either have a history of ownership by the Shakers themselves, or they were found on site, or they were bought at a series of auctions held between 1920 and 1922 after the parent ministry at Mount Lebanon decided that the Society at South Union should be disbanded. Of the nine remaining brothers and sisters, seven elected to accept a ten-thousand-dollar stipend and return to the world and two moved to Mount Lebanon to live out the remainder of their lives as Shakers. All of the community's land, buildings, and furnishings were put up for public sale.

Characteristic South Union construction and design features differ markedly from those found at Pleasant Hill as well as Eastern Shaker furniture. On the whole, the furniture is much more closely related to the interior woodwork and architectural details of the corresponding Shaker buildings. Certain forms, such as four-legged tables, sewing stands, and food cupboards, are visibly derived from vernacular prototypes. In marked contrast to Eastern Shaker furniture, most of the surfaces and structural elements show decorative details in the form of liberal use of scribe lines, applied moldings, and shaping and turning. Native hardwoods of choice include walnut, cherry, and chestnut, with poplar serving as a secondary wood, which were used to construct furniture of massive proportions and heavy stock.

Case pieces (built-ins, presses, and cases of drawers) exhibit frame-and-panel construction, integral quarter-round moldings around the interior edges of the door frames, beaded backboards, and turned legs similar to the stair post supports on each landing. The few original knobs tend to have wide, flat tops.

Tables are associated with worldly prototypes from the mid-Atlantic states, the birthplace of many of the Kentucky converts. The most distinctive feature, which appears repeatedly, is the combination of square and baluster-turned legs with an intermediate lamb's-tongue shoulder, styled in the same manner as the dwelling house attic posts. This profile is also apparent on South Union bedposts, which have identical head and footboards, of various Gothic and Empire-style designs.

Although visually similar to those produced at Pleasant Hill, South Union tripod stands are characterized by uniformly thick tops, long, tapering cleats, and modified vase-shaped standards decorated with numerous incised scribe lines, which have a more distinct horizontal shoulder than the pure vase-shaped standards with sloping shoulders found at Pleasant Hill. They are supported by cabriole legs that are joined with dovetails and metal staples.

Among surviving South Union sewing tables are several that offer a striking contrast with their Eastern counterparts in size and design. Closely modeled after Federal worktables, they feature splayed legs and shaped tops with surrounding galleries to provide open rather than closed storage space for sewing accoutrements.

South Union trestle tables are distinguished by the use of numerous crosswise rather than lengthwise boards, which require an entirely different substructure from the form produced in the East. The typical flat, elongated feet, very different from the arched legs seen at Pleasant Hill, can also be found on ironing tables, drying racks, and a sewing desk with a South Union history.

In contrast to Pleasant Hill, neither chair nor tape production appears to have been a major industry here. Seating furniture was, apparently, produced by craftsmen to supply the needs of the family community only. Design and construction features include egg-shaped pommels with a distinct ring at the base; posts that taper sharply about one inch below the lower stretcher to form the pointed foot, which is found on many Southern vernacular slat-back chairs; and bent back slats, arched on the top edges and concave on the lower ones. The use of hand tools in chamfering the distinct curvature is particularly evident. Judging by traces of pigment, mustard yellow appears to have been the dominant color.

It is surprising that no documented South Union counters survive, considering that Elder Harvey Eades was responsible for printing an illustrated volume on Shaker clothing, *The Tailor's Division System, Founded upon, and Combined with Actual Measurements: Containing Thirty Diagrams and Designs, Reduced to Mathematical Principles* (Union Village, Ohio, 1849). Copies of these rules of measurement were sent to each of the Shaker communities to guide the Believers in the uniform making of clothes. Produced during the 1830s and 1840s, tailoring counters probably were sold from the community long before the twentieth century and consequently were no longer available for the public auction in 1922.

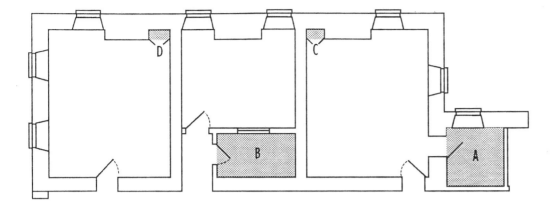

283. Blueprint of Centre Family Dwelling House
1824–34

284. Closet, Centre Family Dwelling House
Collection of Shaker Village of Pleasant Hill, Harrodsburg, Kentucky

The Centre Family Dwelling House, begun in 1824 and completed in 1834, was built of limestone quarried on nearby Shaker land. The front section of the three-story structure measures 55 by 60 feet, to which was appended a 34-by-85-foot dining room and kitchen in the rear. The largest building in the village accommodated over one hundred occupants and was designed to replace the third Centre Family Dwelling House constructed between 1812 and 1815.

Storage space was provided in various places, including the attic (see pl. 285, pp. 4–5), individual retiring rooms, and even the halls. Located on the west side of the building, each of the sisters' rooms was equipped with a built-in three-shelf cupboard over three drawers on the outer walls. The arrangement on the east side of the building was somewhat different. Here the drawer unit was replaced with a one-shelf cupboard (see pl. 299), which suggests that the Shakers recognized the different storage requirements of the male and female members of the family.

The floor plan of part of the Centre Family Dwelling House shows the three retiring rooms to the left of the central hall, which nearly mirror those on the right side of the building. The shaded areas C and D are built-in cupboard-over-drawer case pieces. Areas A and B are walk-in clothing storage areas with either interior or exterior windows. These wardrobe rooms had two or three rows of peg rail and were large enough to accommodate movable chests of drawers or blanket boxes.

illustrated on pages 4–5

285. Built-in Cases of Drawers, Attic, Centre Family Dwelling House
1824–34
Cherry and poplar, with varnish or shellac
h 49¼ w 114⅝, 112¾, 114⅝ d 24¾"
Collection of Shaker Village of Pleasant Hill, Harrodsburg, Kentucky

In order to reduce the risk of fire, the "Millennial Laws" specified, "No one may enter a closet, garret or clothes room or other places not frequented with a lighted lamp or candle, unless it be enclosed in a lantern . . . or go to the chests of clothing, drawers . . . with a lighted candle or pipe."[24] This forty-five-drawer unit was built into the garret or attic of the Centre Family Dwelling House at Pleasant Hill and probably provided off-season storage for both the brethren and the sisters. The architectural skylight, strategically placed overhead, provided adequate illumination, making candles or lamps generally unnecessary. In addition, the lower part of each double-hung window slides up to promote the free circulation of air, ventilate clothing in storage, and eliminate mildew.

Structurally overbuilt considering the size, each bank of drawers exhibits a very heavy frame-and-panel construction, also found on the freestanding furniture, which is the form favored by the Kentucky and Ohio Shakers. This style of construction contrasts sharply with the plank-sided case pieces that were frequently found throughout the Eastern communities until about 1860. The drawers are assembled with the dovetails and pins reversed, compared to the more common arrangement. Here, the pins are exposed on the back rather than on the drawer side, an idiosyncratic method of construction found occasionally on other Pleasant Hill as well as Ohio pieces. Additional characteristic features include the use of many (here, ten) rectangular glue blocks under the drawer bottom, two drawer stops nailed on top of each rail, and knobs that are mortised rather than threaded into the drawer faces.

Particularly noteworthy is the presence of stamped numbers ranging from one through fifteen on the left-hand exterior of each drawer side on all three units. The U-shaped complex was assembled as three separate fifteen-drawer units and then built into the garret area. The placement of the peg rail so close to the top of the built-ins and the continuation of the chair rail and baseboard behind the units raise the question of whether the space was redesigned during the ten-year construction period or if the storage drawers were added as an afterthought following the completion of the attic.

286. Secretary
c. 1840
Cherry and poplar, with fruitwood knobs and brass hardware
h 83¾ w 47 d 22"
Private collection

The form incorporated in the base of this secretary desk has its antecedents in the Eastern Shaker butler's desk, but the construction clearly points to a Western origin. With the desk drawer closed, the piece resembles the furniture form of the press, or cupboard over case of drawers. Western Shaker construction characteristics include the use of cherry as the primary wood, the frame-and-panel case work, and the turned legs. Several specific features are similar to other known Pleasant Hill pieces; for example, the turned leg resembles that in the case piece pl. 290; the cornice that in the press pl. 287; and the case itself with the Centre Family attic built-ins pl. 285, pp. 4–5. The interior of the desk, although simple, echoes worldly examples in the use of the interior drawers over slightly decorated pigeonholes.

287. Press

c. 1830 (case of drawers), c. 1860 (cupboard)
Cherry and poplar
Cupboard: h 57 w 41 d 11⅛"
Case of drawers: h 42½ w 46½ d 22"
Collection of Shaker Village of Pleasant Hill,
Harrodsburg, Kentucky, #70.8.1A, B

The top and bottom parts of some two-piece storage units were not made at the same time, as the entry from "Temporal Journal . . . Book B" of October 29, 1859, suggests: "S.L. Boisseau finished making a cherry press for the Nurses room, to set on a bureau made by him about two years before." Unlike pl. 288, this cupboard and case of drawers are not permanently joined and were likely combined by the Shakers at a later date. According to oral history, this press was used by Mary Settles (1836–1923), the last surviving sister at Pleasant Hill.

The construction and design features that relate this unit to other furniture attributed to Pleasant Hill are the frame-and-panel construction throughout, the panels flat rather than raised; the overall proportions of the narrow doors, which are hinged to the side of the case rather than to the exterior face rails, which have not been used here; and the division of each door into sections of two-thirds and one-third by virtue of the placement of the rail—all features also found on pl. 288. Furthermore, both presses have a deep cove cornice molding and similar midcase molding, consisting of an ogee with a fillet. Although affixed in a different way—here, nailed to the base of the cupboard, which is screwed into the bottom shelf from below, rather than permanently doweled into the upper section, as in pl. 288—the overall effect is that of a tall cupboard set on top of a transitional molding over a case of drawers. The door edge is beveled rather than lapped where they meet, to ensure a secure closure.

Other noteworthy construction characteristics are the unusually thick side panels in the bureau section, which have an 8-inch-long chamfer, seen on the interior of the case, to accommodate insertion into the surrounding frame, and elaborately turned (now truncated) feet, rather than square or tapered legs, suggesting an earlier date of the 1830s.

The knobs are mortised rather than threaded into the drawer fronts and appear to be original, although they are shaped differently from those seen in the attic (see pl. 285) or on the signed and dated table by Leander Gettys (see pl. 293).

288. Press
c. 1860
Cherry and poplar, with brass hinges
h 92½ w 56 d 21"
Private collection

In Pleasant Hill journals, the cupboard over case of drawers is often referred to as a "press on bureau." According to a December 7, 1847, entry in the "Temporal Journal . . . Book B," the East Family "made . . . a cupboard to set on a bureau for Amy and the girls." The freestanding Shaker press is a furniture form made only in the Western communities, based on Southern vernacular prototypes, which was used to store clothes and textiles—although one Hancock writer makes reference to similar built-in units in the 1832 brick Church Family Dwelling House (see p. 174). On June 12, 1849, "A cupboard or press was finished by B. Dunlavy for the Deaconesses to store away clothes and cloth in." Some examples, such as this one, were conceived and executed as one piece. On April 22, 1854, the "Temporal Journal . . . Book B" reported, "two new bureaus [were] made by John Voris, one with a press on it to stand in the lower hall, the other went to the N.E. room, second story."

This example has an impeccable Pleasant Hill provenance and appears in a historic photograph taken in the hall of the Centre Family Dwelling House about 1922. It was then acquired by the Bohons directly from the Shakers (see p. 319) and has descended in the family to the current owners.

The press is remarkable for its overall size. Yet the maker was able to combine successfully the very tall cupboard having exceptionally long panels with the much shorter and simpler base into a balanced whole. The absence of finish between the two sections and the use of screws to secure the units together indicate the top and bottom were clearly conceived and built as one piece.

The facade of the press section is asymmetrical for a number of reasons. The juxtaposition of a single-door cupboard next to a wider double-door cupboard resulted in the off-center placement of one interior stile and the complete absence of exterior stiles. This in turn dictated that the outside door hinges be attached to the side of the case. An applied half-round molding is nailed to only two of the doors and serves to cover the gap when they are closed. The third door is, in turn, secured by an interior wooden latch and exterior lock. The latter has a wooden rather than metal escutcheon that was probably purchased by the Shakers.

The single-door cupboard on the right contains a shelf, supported by three cleats nailed to the interior of the case, above a small peg screwed into the center of the

backboards. Inside the double-door cupboard on the left are three movable shelves, which can be adjusted in a series of notches cut out on either side.

Decorative features similar to those of pl. 287 include the deep cove cornice molding affixed on top of the case, which is further embellished by the addition of two applied rectangular strips running parallel to the cornice, and the similar profile of the midcase molding. However, here the strip is doweled directly into the case. Despite the fact that this press looks significantly earlier, the late construction date of 1860 is also supported

by the use of the commercially available wood rather than metal escutcheons.

Characteristic Pleasant Hill design and construction features are evident in the frame-and-panel assembly for the bureau and the proportions of the long and narrow double- (as opposed to single-) panel doors, which relate to the dimensions of the built-ins and doors in the Centre Family Dwelling House. The base uses simply shaped square-to-round legs, with turnings that reflect the late yet stark design associated with Leander Gettys (see pls. 292, 293), also dating from the 1860s.

289. Case of Drawers
c. 1840
Cherry and poplar, with varnish
h 58½ w 42¼ d 20⅜"
Private collection

This five-drawer case piece exhibits the big, bold proportions typical of Western Shaker furniture. Sold by the last Believers directly to the Bohon family, this case of drawers has an excellent Pleasant Hill history. Construction details that strengthen this attribution include the use of heavy frame-and-panel construction—the stiles are 2¾ inches wide—a square-edged top with minimal overhang, lacking embellishment, and inverted vase-turned feet that do not have a transitional shoulder between the square and turned sections.

Fine, although idiosyncratic workmanship is seen in the drawers, which have an incised bead around the drawer face, rectangular glue blocks underneath the bottoms, stops nailed on top of the rails, and the less common dovetail orientation with the pins visible from the rear.

290. Cupboard and Case of Drawers
c. 1840
Cherry and poplar
h 43⅜ w 46¼ d 29"
Collection of Shaker Village of Pleasant Hill, Harrodsburg, Kentucky, #SP 80.200

The unusual design of this double-hinged cupboard with drawers is attributed to the fact that it was built for a specific person and/or purpose. According to oral tradition, this cabinet was made for William Pennebaker (1841–1922), who came to Pleasant Hill as an orphan and was sent by the Shakers to medical school in Cincinnati. He assumed the position of Pleasant Hill physician in 1876.[25] The distinctive arrangement consisting of narrow graduated drawers alongside two paneled, hinged doors suggests it was laid out to store such things as small implements and large articles of medical equipment.

The oral history associated with this piece is supported by a documented history of ownership. The cabinet descended through the Pennebakers to their housekeeper, Mrs. Letch Mathews Allen (who tended them in the last few years of their lives), and then through her family before being returned to Pleasant Hill in 1980.

291. Cupboard
1856–57
Written in black ink on back of third interior shelf: Began Dec. 1856 finished Jan. 1857
Scratched into central rail of upper door: P. Hill
Poplar, with red stain and iron hinges
h 85¼ w 44 d 21¹⁄₁₆"
Collection of Shaker Village of Pleasant Hill, Harrodsburg, Kentucky, #61.4.365

This cupboard is noteworthy because the design and construction features can be accurately dated. Unlike the interior woodwork of the Centre Family Dwelling House, these doors have flat panels, which on the top door are divided into four equal sections rather than exhibiting the one-to-two relationship seen in pls. 287 and 288. Rounded bull-nose moldings are nailed to the cornice, middle, and bottom of the case, offsetting the cupboard's strong vertical proportions. Particularly striking are the cove-shaped feet, which are cut from the stiles instead of being applied or turned.

Although it is risky to make generalizations based on the evidence of one dated piece, it is possible that these simplified design and construction features characterize Pleasant Hill workmanship of the 1850s, well after the era of gospel simplicity.

292. Table

Leander Gettys (1832–left 1865)
1860
Written in red paint on the interior rear rail: L.
GETTYS, OCT. 4, 1860
Cherry, with blue-gray stain
h 31½ w 97⅛ d 41½
Collection of Shaker Village of Pleasant Hill,
Harrodsburg, Kentucky, #61.4.369

Pleasant Hill cabinetmaker Leander Gettys, a member of the Centre Family, signed and dated this heavy-duty worktable and the dwelling house table pl. 293. Although designed for two entirely different uses, both pieces of furniture share common construction features: an overhanging top attached to rails with numerous screws in screw pockets (here, a total of sixteen) and similarly designed legs with an abrupt or minimal transition between the rectangular and round sections.

Unlike in the dwelling house table, both ends of this four-board top with spline joints are reinforced by two horizontal cleats with ovolo-shaped ends. They extend nearly the entire width of the top and are screwed in from below. These cleats, used primarily to keep the top flat, are often seen in Pennsylvania German vernacular furniture and reflect the origin and training of settlers, including the cabinetmaker Leander Gettys, who migrated southwest to Kentucky. Born in Pittsburgh, Pennsylvania, in 1832, he joined the United Society in 1847, where he was a member of the Church Family, and later taught school for the boys of the Church Family before leaving the community in 1865.[26]

Both tables were produced within a four-month period (October 1860 and January 1861), suggesting that the community had a specific need for additional furniture at this time.

293. Table

Leander Gettys (1832–left 1865)
Written in black paint inside back rail: L.
GETTYS, JAN. 1861
Cherry and poplar, with traces of varnish
h 27¾ w 31½ d 27½"
Collection of Shaker Village of Pleasant Hill,
Harrodsburg, Kentucky, #67.5.7

Only a few pieces of furniture from Pleasant Hill are known to have been signed by the maker. This is one of two surviving tables (see pl. 292) made and signed by Leander Gettys. According to an entry in "Temporal Journal . . . Book B," possibly referring to this piece, it was produced "for the North East room 1st story, East House by Leander Gettys" (p. 88). Unlike those in other Shaker communities, none of the dwelling house rooms at Pleasant Hill are numbered, and compass directions were used to indicate specific spaces. Unfortunately, no other mention of Gettys as a furniture maker appears in surviving journals.

This four-legged table shares several design and construction features with three similar unsigned tables, one at Pleasant Hill (acc. no. 61.3.354) and two in a private collection. One of the last is marked "September 15th, 1868" in black paint on the interior back rail; the other has an unusually narrow top, measuring only 12 inches deep. These atypical dimensions suggest the latter was made for a specific space or use.

All four pieces in this group exhibit variants of the same leg construction, with minimal or no transition from the square to round sections; a wide, overhanging tabletop connected to the side and back with numerous screws and deep pockets; and the absence of a rail above the drawer. The knob of the signed table is turned in a manner similar to those found on the drawers of the built-ins in the Centre Family Dwelling House attic (see pl. 285, pp. 4–5). These details may signify similar shop practices within a group of furniture makers.

below

294. Gateleg Table

c. 1840
Walnut, with red stain and iron hinges
h 28½ w 48 d 54¾" (extended)
Collection of Shaker Village of Pleasant Hill,
Harrodsburg, Kentucky, #C88.7.1

In its apron and gateleg design, this table shares some construction traits with another example from Mount Lebanon (see pl. 51). However, the Pleasant Hill table is distinctive in having six rather than four legs to support the leaves in a horizontal position. Other features characteristic of Pleasant Hill include a top attached to rails with six screws and legs that taper dramatically, from 2³⁄₁₆ inches to 1⅛ inches in diameter, with minimal transitional section between the square post and turned sections.

295. Double Drop-Leaf Table

c. 1860
Cherry and poplar, with brass knobs
h 29 w 36 d 35¾" (extended)
Collection Hazel Hamilton

Although related to a cherry side table with single leaf in the collection of the Shaker Museum, Old Chatham, New York,[27] this is the only known Kentucky Shaker four-legged double drop-leaf table. According to oral tradition, it was used by Mary Settles (1836–1923), the last surviving sister at Pleasant Hill, and descended in her family before being purchased by its present owner. Characterized by stocky rails a full 1¼ inches thick, a square-edged top, and legs with no transition between the rectangular and round sections, this table clearly fits into the Western Shaker tradition of furniture construction. The leaves are supported by two square pullout slides with brass knobs contained inside a wooden housing, which is screwed into the top. Following another Pleasant Hill tradition (see pls. 292–94 and 297), the top is affixed to the rails with screws, here in fourteen large screw pockets. Particularly unusual is the presence of leather washers between each screw and the wood undersurface, all of which appear to be original. These may have allowed for a little more flexibility in the top-to-apron attachment, where some seasonal movement occurs.

296. Table with Hinged Top

c. 1860

Cherry and poplar, with traces of red stain on interior and brass hinges

h 28½ w 28½ d 19"

Collection of Shaker Village of Pleasant Hill, Harrodsburg, Kentucky, #61.4.150

Tables with hinged top are virtually unknown, and it is only possible to speculate on their use. Ed Nickels, the former director of collections at Shaker Village of Pleasant Hill, referred to this piece as a sewing table. However, there are no clamp marks on the underside of the lid, as is often the case with sewing work furniture, to suggest that screwball, or clamp-on, pincushions or other Shaker sewing accessories were used. This form also differs dramatically from the more delicate splay-leg sewing tables found at South Union (see pls. 313–15) and the sewing furniture used in the Eastern Shaker communities that combined work surface with storage unit (see pls. 181, 183, 185), suggesting it may have had another usage. Aside from the singular hinged top, the table displays many construction details, including the ⅞-inch-thick, square-edged cherry stock for the top, 1-inch-thick rails, and square-tapered legs that are double-pinned on the rear posts only, common to other documented Pleasant Hill four-legged tables produced during the 1860s (see pl. 293).

297. Sewing Table

c. 1860

Cherry, butternut, and poplar, with brass knobs and escutcheon

h 28 w 28¼ d 26⅝"

Collection Hazel Hamilton

The presence of several indentations on the underside of the top from clamps to hold pincushions and other accoutrements supports the supposition that this two-drawer table was originally used for sewing. Several unusual features include the overall form, the shape of the top, which is almost square, with rounded corners 1⅝ inch in radius, and the slender top drawer.

The following construction details place this piece within the shop practices of the Pleasant Hill cabinetmakers: a top attached to the rails from below with ten screws through screw pockets, including two cut on the front posts; the absence of a top front rail; and the characteristic square-to-round leg somewhat softened by a minimal transitional section (see pls. 292, 293). Of equal significance is the history of this table, which was purchased by a previous owner from Colonel and Mrs. George Bohon about 1952 (see p. 319).

298. Tripod Stand and Templates
1830–50
Cherry
h 25½ diameter of top 16¾"
Collection of Shaker Village of Pleasant Hill,
Harrodsburg, Kentucky, #61.4.159

Tripod stands such as this were among the first items sold to the world by the Pleasant Hill Shakers. In a letter dated July 25, 1815, Francis Voris wrote to Brother Samuel (probably Samuel Whyte at South Union), "There is a Doctor Joseph McGuffin living in Russellville, who is some in arearage with us for several articles that I deposited with him when he kept store at Nicholasville; the number and what sort of articles I can not perfectly recollect, but I think there was some pipes perhaps 3 or 400; 1 or 2 candlestands, 3 or 4 reeds, and one or two halfbushel Measures. . . . "28

According to the following journal reference, tripod stands were known to be placed in the halls of buildings. On April 4, 1843, according to "Temporal Journal . . . Book B," the Centre Family Dwelling House "received a new candlestand in the second hall made here" (p. 7). Perhaps they served as stationary pieces to hold night lighting or functioned as easily portable stands that could be used in the family meeting room nearby.

The overall form, consisting of a pedestal on three legs, is strongly related to vernacular pieces produced during the eighteenth century in England and the colonies. Several almost identical examples survive in both public and private collections, each with an excellent Pleasant Hill history. Made in six pieces—a round top, disk cleat, turned vase-shaped pedestal, and three cabriole legs—they are very similar in form to South Union stands. However, subtle details of construction create distinctions that point to a Pleasant Hill origin. Particularly noteworthy is the top, which was tapered to a thin edge on a lathe (rather than being chamfered by hand, as on many New England tables, or presenting the same thickness in cross section, as is typical of South Union pieces); the presence of a round "collar" (Shaker term), or disk-shaped cleat, screwed into the top from below (versus the rectangular cleat found at South Union); and the use of a metal plate secured by screws into the base of the pedestal and the legs (rather than the three staples inserted into the pedestal and legs on South Union stands).

Journal entries imply that some stands were made cooperatively by several joiners rather than by a single maker. The "Temporal Journal . . . Book B" lists "1 candlestand stem and collar [made] for Centre Family by Francis M[onfort]" (p. 2), suggesting that, perhaps, the top and legs were the work of another

craftsman. The three templates for the leg of this stand were discovered in the eaves of the community's 1815 carpenter's shop during the restoration of the building. The "Journal of M[aurice] Thomas" records that on Wednesday, October 15, 1817, "M[icajah] Bernett and my self made some patterns" (part 2, p. 162), which could refer to templates for furniture parts such as these.

299. Bed
Unidentified New England community
c. 1840
Maple, with green paint
h 32 l 77¼ w 41½"
Collection of Shaker Village of Pleasant Hill,
Harrodsburg, Kentucky, #61.4.134

300. Bed
Pleasant Hill
c. 1830
Maple, with green paint
h 30¾ l 82 w 40"
Collection of Shaker Village of Pleasant Hill,
Harrodsburg, Kentucky, #61.4.144

Currently located in a first-floor retiring room of the Centre Family Dwelling House at Pleasant Hill, Kentucky (see pl. 283), these two Shaker beds exemplify the similarities and differences between Eastern and Western Shaker design.

Both are narrow, single beds with rope mattress supports, fitted for what the Shakers called wooden rollers, or wheels (now missing), so they could be moved away from a wall to facilitate cleaning underneath. Most signifi-

cant is their color, which complies with the 1845 "Millennial Laws" stating that "bedsteds should be painted green."[29]

Although the shaping of the legs on both examples is similar, the headboards differ significantly. The Eastern bed on the left exhibits a curved headboard and posts that consist of a cylinder over a rectangular section with transitional chamfered shoulder at either end and turned feet. In comparison, the straight Western head rail, composed of longitudinal slats, is tenoned and double-pinned to a square post that tapers on the front edge toward the turned foot. The tapered shaping of the head posts and absence of turned finials can also be found on some vernacular and Ohio Shaker chairs. Variants of this design include beds with tapered foot posts without turned finials and headboards that are either scalloped in shape or flat, vertical slats. Some have applied designs.

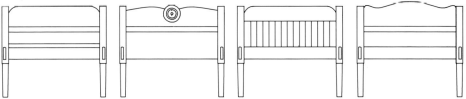

A number of journal entries confirm that several of the Pleasant Hill furniture makers were also involved in the production of bedsteads. For example, "Temporal Journal . . . Book B" states on January 28, 1847, "two bedsteads for East Family [were made] by S. Manire"; on January 26, 1854, "a new high bedstead [was] made by Stephen Boisseau for the North West room, second story"; and in January 1861, Boisseau produced "three bedsteads . . . for the East

House." Perhaps the "high bedstead" mentioned refers to the type of bed pictured above, as opposed to low trundle beds, which were designed to be stored under the high beds and pulled out for use. On March 26, 1863, "two bedsteads, one high, the other low, [were finished] by S.L. Boisseau for the East Family." Another journal entry, dated January 10, 1863, records that "a trundle bedstead [was] made by Wm. Morse for the N.W. room, first story, East House."

301. Desk

Richard Alexander Milligan (born 1849)
1879
Written in ink on bottom of lower drawer on right upper section of desk: Made March 7th/1879/ R.A. Milligan/Pleasant Hill/Mercer Co./Kentucky/for S.L. Boisseau/East Family
Cherry and yellow poplar
h 60 w 43⅞ d 30"
Collection of Shaker Village of Pleasant Hill, Harrodsburg, Kentucky, #65.1.434

This unusual two-part desk, made up of a cupboard over a table, is a rare documented example of Pleasant Hill Victorian design. Richard Alexander Milligan, who made this piece, first joined the Pleasant Hill Society June 26, 1860, and left July 9, 1862. He rejoined the society again in 1868[30] and was made superintendent of the East Family farm

in 1879, a position he held until 1894.[31] It was in the year he took up his farm duties that he constructed this desk for fellow cabinetmaker Stephen Leonidas Boisseau. According to the "Temporal Journal . . . Book B," in addition to beds and presses, Brother Richard made a table for the northwest room in the second story of the East Family Dwelling House (February 1852) and a turning lathe, which was "set up in the brick shop, N.E. room in second story" (June 3, 1847, p. 17).

The narrow hinged door with applied molding on the top section of the desk just beneath the cornice covers nine compartments. The door on the right with oval raised panel conceals four compartments with a drawer beneath, and the matching door on the left covers two compartments and one shelf with a drawer beneath. In addition to the oval insets, other decorative features include vigorously turned legs and drawer fronts veneered with figured cherry and surrounded by bold, projecting moldings.

A newly discovered table with the inscription "Table Made Sept. 28th 1874 RA Milligan" in a private collection shows his interest in figured wood, revealed in the use of crotch-grained cherry as a drawer facing.

302. Box

c. 1840
Cherry, with traces of red paint and steel hinges
h 22¼ w 35½ d 17"
Collection of Shaker Village of Pleasant Hill, Harrodsburg, Kentucky, #SP 66.5

Although it is likely that many boxes were made for storing blankets or clothing, very few still exist that can be attributed to the Pleasant Hill Shakers. This particular example has significant design and construction details that link it to other documented furniture from this community. The four sides are assembled with pegged mortise-and-tenon joints required by the post-and-apron construction rather than with plank sides and dovetailed joinery characteristic of some Eastern Shaker boxes. The 7½-inch-tall legs, like those of the case piece pl. 288, abruptly change from square to round with no transitional shoulder, a characteristic of Pleasant Hill design. The two-board top, secured by a lock, has the addition of breadboard ends with only a slight overhang terminating with a bull-nose edge.

The simple form of this storage box, executed with economy, complies with the 1840 Holy Laws of Zion: "Whatever is fashioned let it be plain and simple and for the good and substantial quality which becomes your calling and profession unembellished by any superfluities, which add nothing to its goodness or durability."[32]

303. Armed Rocker
c. 1840
Maple, hickory, oak, and cane
h 48½ w 21 d 48½"
Collection of Shaker Village of Pleasant Hill,
Harrodsburg, Kentucky, #69.5.5

304. Armed Rocker
c. 1840
Maple, hickory, and rush, with black paint over
traces of earlier red color
h 44¼ w 23¼ d 34¼"
Collection of Shaker Village of Pleasant Hill,
Harrodsburg, Kentucky, #61.4.143

305. Armed Rocker
c. 1840
Hickory, oak, and tape
h 45½ w 22 d 23"
Collection of Shaker Village of Pleasant Hill,
Harrodsburg, Kentucky, #89.4.1

A study of surviving furniture inventories from Pleasant Hill documents that common chairs (see pls. 306, 307) outnumbered rocking chairs by a ratio of seven to one.[33] However, as more interest was expressed in comfortable seating, the Society apparently converted many side chairs made earlier into rockers, as seen in the example on the left. A journal documents one such instance of this alteration: "November 3, 1890 H[enry] D[aily] made & put a new pare of Rockers to his Chair in his shop."[34]

Construction features characteristic of Pleasant Hill armed rockers include bulbous pommels with elongated necks. The deeply bent, graduated slats have a boldly arched contour that flows nearly to a horizontal line before being tenoned into the posts. The upper two slats—rather than just one, as on the common chairs—are pinned through the uprights and have rounded front edges. The front posts have a symmetrical turning, adorned with concentric scribe lines between the seat and the arms. A variation of the more typical side-scrolled arm extends beyond the turned support and is capped with a rounded handhold. In distinct contrast to Eastern Shaker chairs, they do not function as tenon caps to the posts but are attached with screws or wood pegs down into the arms well ahead of the front post. Crescent-shaped rockers extend beyond the front posts. The earliest chairs were bottomed with splint or perhaps Kentucky cane or rolled husks, as seen in one of these examples.[35]

306. Side Chair
c. 1830
*Maple, hickory, oak, and splint (not original),
with green paint over the original red paint*
h 37¾ w 17½ d 14½"
*Collection of Shaker Village of Pleasant Hill,
Harrodsburg, Kentucky, #C90.5.1*

307. Side Chair
c. 1830
*Maple, hickory, oak, and wool tape (not original),
with red paint*
h 39½ w 18¼ d 14½"
*Collection of Shaker Village of Pleasant Hill,
Harrodsburg, Kentucky, #64.3.1*

According to surviving records, the Pleasant Hill Shakers made a variety of chair forms for community use.[36] Francis Monfort (1784–1867) was a most prolific woodworker at the community and produced more chairs than any other furniture form. According to the journals, he made at least eighty-seven side chairs, fourteen armchairs, eight rocking chairs, thirty-five chairs for children, three sweating chairs for the nurses' rooms, and "one stool chair."[37]

What "Temporal Journal . . . Book B" calls "Common Chairs" (February 10, 1849), such as these, possess elongated oval pommels, curved slats rounded on the top front edges, with only the top slat secured by a single wooden pin extending through the posts, and seat stretchers that are often pinned to the posts. Some side chairs bear a stamped letter, such as C, probably referring to Centre Family, in the center of the top slat, while others have numerals stamped on the back of the top or second slat.

The proportions of the chair on the right make it one of the most delicate of all Shaker chairs. Particularly noteworthy is the unequal placement of the slats, which are 6½ and 5½ inches apart. Since two other chairs in the Pleasant Hill collection exhibit this idiosyncrasy, all three examples may have been produced by the same, as yet unidentified, maker.

The seat of the red chair is fitted with wool tape, which was woven and dyed by the Pleasant Hill Shakers as early as 1846, a year in which 285 yards of chair list were produced, according to one journal entry.[38] Although this amount of listing would only seat about ten or twelve chairs, the figure may actually indicate a much larger production of tape at Pleasant Hill. This seat apparently was retaped by the Shakers at some point.

308. Built-in Cupboards and Case of Drawers, Centre Family Dwelling House
1822–33
Cherry and poplar, with porcelain knobs, varnish stain, and brass hinges
h 87½ w 61¾"
Museum Collection, Shakertown at South Union, Kentucky

The brick Centre Family Dwelling House was constructed between 1822 and 1833 from local materials to house ninety covenanted members. The Georgian brick building is four stories high, with forty-two rooms and twin staircases that run top to bottom. Although the built-ins for the male and female members are not identical in layout, two-thirds of the storage units on the brothers' and sisters' sides of the building are placed on the outside east and west walls, respectively, of the dwelling, while the remainder are built into the interior of the room away from the window.

Each of the sisters' units pictured above, on the first floor of the west side of the building, consists of three cupboard doors over a bank of drawers, a single cupboard, and a small door (now missing) to house a chamber pot. This arrangement differs markedly from that found both at Pleasant Hill (see pl. 285, pp. 4–5) and the Eastern communities (see pl. 101).

Inside the built-in unit, two shelves rest in front of beaded backboards that run horizontally. A particularly unusual feature in some similar units is a brick arch (which resembles those found throughout the building) located above the rear wall inside the case, with three rows of peg rail below not visible from the outside. This is a structural part of the building, which incidentally may have served as "wardrobes" for hanging sisters' dresses.

Significant attention was given to the decorative details. The interior edges of the door rails and stiles, as well as the drawer faces, have an incised bead, while the inside of the door frames are shaped with a quarter-round. Furthermore, the top, bottom, and sides of the built-in are surrounded by an applied complex molding consisting of a bead with a stepped cove. The entire unit is surmounted by a deep cornice executed with a large round molding plane or a crown molding plane. Although he left enough space in the corner of the room to finish both ends of the crown molding, the unidentified Shaker furniture maker or finish carpenter mitered only the right end, so it does not match the left-hand edge.

All drawers are dovetailed and adorned with porcelain knobs positioned to form a decorative oval pattern on the facade. These may be replacements for original wood knobs, although none survives in place today. Color also plays an important role in the overall decorative effect within the room, the ocher-stained peg rail, brick red baseboard, and clear varnish finish over the unstained cherry surfaces creating strong contrasts.

left
Stair post in the Centre Family Dwelling House, South Union

309. Press
c. 1830–40
Walnut, cherry, poplar, and maple, with brass knobs
h 56 w 39 d 20"
Museum Collection, Shakertown at South Union, Kentucky, #61–10A,B

The South Union interpretation of this vernacular type is not only much smaller than Shaker counterparts produced at nearby Pleasant Hill but differs notably in its basic form, consisting of a cupboard over single-drawer base rather than full-size case of drawers. In comparison with many Pleasant Hill presses, which have a base that could be used separately, this single-drawer unit could not have functioned independently, suggesting that the top and bottom were constructed together.

This example follows closely the architectural details found in the Centre Family Dwelling House: frame-and-panel construction, use of ovolo with fillet molding on the interior door frames, appearance of a single bead down the sides of the case, and the presence of beaded backboards (see pl. 308). Even the inverted baluster-turned legs and extended button feet show a remarkable resemblance to the stair post supports on each landing of the Centre Family Dwelling House.

Unusual decorative details are seen in the triple-reeded band on the lower edge of the top rail, creating a 3-inch dead space under the cupboard top; the ogee-shaped molding nailed beneath the top as well as to the back and bottom of the side boards, giving the illusion of frame-and-panel construction; and the cock bead around the drawer front. Here, a rabbet has been cut in the drawer face and a strip of maple set in that protrudes beyond the facade. The use of the cock bead is a technique clearly derived from Kentucky vernacular furniture of the Federal period; the cock bead produced a surface with contrasting wood color and depth.[39]

This press has an excellent South Union history. It was purchased at the Shaker public sale in 1922 directly from the Believers and was later returned to the site when it became a museum.

opposite above

310. Case of Drawers
c. 1830
Written in pencil on right side of top right drawer: Bought at Shaker Sale in 1919/by Chas W Jenkins for 50 00/xx/Made in 1814 by Jesse McCoombs/member of the Shaker Colony/ at South Union KY
Cherry and poplar
h 56⅜ w 49 d 22"
Museum Collection, Shakertown at South Union, Kentucky, #70–2

This case of drawers has overall construction features typical of regional vernacular furniture. These similarities include frame-and-panel construction and massive proportions with heavy stock for rails, stiles, and drawer fronts. The shaping of the turned feet contributes to the heavy appearance of this case of drawers. The length of the turned portion is relatively short, given the long lamb's-tongue transition, which leads directly into an inverted quarter-round. The leg is very similar to the base turning of the South Union bed pl. 321 and somewhat related to the table pl.

317. An applied astragal molding along the perimeter of the top decorates the case piece.

This case of drawers has an excellent, although perhaps exaggerated, South Union provenance. Jesse McComb (1750–1815) was a well-known nineteenth-century Shaker involved in the founding of the community in 1809. He donated his home as the first dwelling for the Centre Family and contributed to the joiner work of the Centre Family Dwelling House. Although it is possible that the Shakers were actively producing furniture at this early date, there are several pieces currently in the South Union collection, including a case of drawers and a clock, each with an elaborate inscription such as this, one of which has been proven to be inaccurate.[40] When the community closed and the 1922 auction was held to sell the remaining furniture "made by the old time Shakers from Solid Walnut, Cherry and Oak" (see p. 90) it is probable that the inscriptions were added to attract buyers and to enhance the purchase price.

311. Case of Drawers
c. 1840
Cherry, chestnut, and poplar
h 24½ w 20½ d 13"
Museum Collection, Shakertown at South Union, Kentucky, #61.15

312. Case of Drawers
1852
Written in pencil in script on interior of left panel: March 1852
Walnut and poplar, with cherry knobs
h 43½ w 35¾ d 19"
Museum Collection, Shakertown at South Union, Kentucky, #59.21

Although sharing a common origin (South Union) and a similar construction (frame-and-panel), these two chests of drawers reveal the variety found in one furniture form produced in the same community. Aside from the obvious differences in size, the miniature case of drawers is made of cherry, has an inscribed bead around the drawer fronts (which recalls the decoration on the built-in storage units, pl. 308), and its short, turned peg legs end in button feet. According to oral history, it belonged to Sister Mary Wann, who came to South Union from Scotland in 1850 and was one of the remaining Shakers when South Union disbanded. She went first to Auburn and then to Florida, where she died.[41] In comparison, the full-size piece uses walnut as the primary wood and has plain drawer faces with flat knobs original to the piece, rear dovetail joints assembled with the pin oriented toward the back, and inverted baluster-shaped feet.

313. Sewing Table
1860–70
Cherry and poplar, with dark varnish stain
h 33 w 25 d 19½"
Museum Collection, Shakertown at South Union,
Kentucky, #60–27

314. Sewing Table
1860–70
Cherry and poplar, with walnut knobs
h 27½ w 25⅞ d 21⅛"
Museum Collection, Shakertown at South Union,
Kentucky, #73–2

Western sewing tables, such as these made at South Union, present an entirely different form than their New England counterparts (see pl. 181). The small size, splayed legs, and absence of significant drawer space or surface area suggest they were primarily used by sisters seated nearby holding handwork in their laps. This design contrasts sharply with the substantial case pieces produced in the Maine and New Hampshire communities, which provided both storage and expandable work areas for sisters seated at them.

Western sewing tables were based on the Federal worktable, which enjoyed popularity in East Coast urban centers from about 1785 to 1815. The worldly neoclassical form featured a shaped top, delicate splayed legs, and small storage area below, consisting of either a drawer or a fabric bag.[42] The Shakers' interpretation of this cosmopolitan form is decorative as well as functional.

According to oral history, the Shakers gave the example on the left to Dr. William Burr, their doctor, presumably in gratitude for services rendered to the community. It features an applied rack with single shelf and vertically oriented wire nails, probably added to hold spools of thread; a shallow, underhung drawer attached to the case by a cleat, a system commonly used by the Shakers to suspend drawers beneath trestle tables; and turned, outspread leg, which relates closely to architectural details found elsewhere in the village. More specifically, the transitional lamb's-tongue chamfer between the square and rounded sections is related to the attic posts in the Centre Family Dwelling House (see pl. 309) and is repeated consistently on the bedposts (see pl. 321), and the unusual stretchers with square center section are identical in form to the stair spindles in the community's Laundry Building. A sharp contrast in workmanship is seen in the construction of the carefully dovetailed drawer and the vertically grained gallery, which is attached to the cleat below with exposed flat-head

wood screws. Such a striking disparity in technique suggests that this sewing table may have been the work of two Shaker craftsmen—a furniture maker and a carpenter.

The example on the right, purchased from the South Union Shakers in the 1922 auction, contains a novel vertical drawer for storing spools. It rides in two grooves cut into the surrounding housing and is secured in the upright position by a horizontal wooden catch. The placement of the pullout slide beneath the deep storage drawer indicates that it was probably designed to hold sewing implements while in use rather than to provide an actual extendable work surface, like those found on New England sewing desks. Obvious decorative embellishments are found in the scalloped, serpentine front edge, splayed legs terminating in unusually turned feet, and narrow rim with cyma curve on each end, probably derived from the Federal worktable vocabulary.

315. Sewing Table
c. 1860
Cherry, maple, and poplar, with brass lock plate
h 28¾ w 22⅞ d 15¾"
The Kentucky Museum, Western Kentucky University, Bowling Green, Kentucky, #3902

According to oral history, this small sewing table was made for Sister Angeline Perryman (1818–1909), a teacher at South Union, and probably dates from the Civil War period. Another variation of the worktable form, it was designed specifically with function and decorative effect in mind. The case itself is efficiently assembled with half-lap joints and is nailed rather than dovetailed. In addition to offering a flat work surface and single, underhung drawer, it has a horizontal till across the back of the work platform that provides open storage as well as easy access for small items such as pins via the central cutout. The two thread holders at the rear swivel out to reveal the spools below. The legs are square in section and half-lapped and screwed from the inside into the case and nailed from the outside.

Distinct decorative touches are evident in the baluster-turned spindles encircling the gallery, the sausage-like shaped railing on either side above, and the flat shoe feet with slight taper on either side of the arch. This support system relates in general form to the shape of the legs on surviving South Union trestle tables and towel racks (see pl. 319).

Several later alterations to the original appearance of this sewing table include refinishing; the addition of the two pulls on top of the rear corner posts, and the ogee-shaped foot rest, which shows little wear.

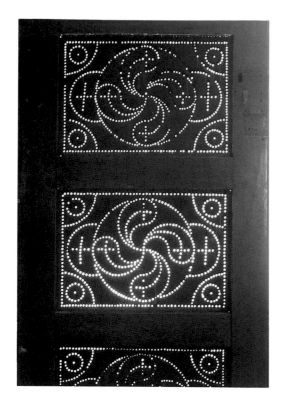

316. Food Cupboard

c. 1840

Walnut and tin, with traces of red paint

h 85½ w 44¼ d 22½"

Museum Collection, Shakertown at South Union, Kentucky, #60–84

Found in one of the buildings at South Union after the sale in 1922, this unusual food cupboard or safe combines elements of both Shaker and worldly furniture. The form itself, based on vernacular prototypes, exhibits a simple cut foot and beveled cornice molding nailed under the overhanging square edge. These basic features, however, contrast with the rounded elements: a quarter-round molding on all interior frame edges, a beaded border surrounding the cupboard doors, and the horizontal beaded backboards—these last three details identical to the building's interior woodwork.

The twenty-four elaborately pierced tins, other than providing ventilation within, are purely decorative. The fluid design of the pierced tinwork has more in common with worldly patterns than the style of artwork found in Shaker inspirational drawings. Several details emerge regarding the size and placement of the tins that raise the following design questions: What was the rationale for irregularly graduating the individual door panels from top to bottom? Why were the rails placed irregularly on the sides and front of the case, which do not line up horizontally?

317. Table
c. 1850
Walnut, with porcelain knob, brass escutcheon,
and steel lock plate
h 27 w 29 d 22½"
Museum Collection, Shakertown at South Union,
Kentucky, #61–21

318. Table
c. 1850
Walnut and poplar
h 29 w 47 d 23½"
Museum Collection, Shakertown at South Union,
Kentucky, #63–22

Not immediately recognizable as Shaker-made, these two South Union tables are closely related to vernacular prototypes. The massive proportions, heavy stock, and relatively elaborate turnings reflect the local cultural background of the Kentucky Believers. This vernacular form is in marked contrast to most worldly furniture models found in the eastern United States, which generally display slender dimensions and square tapering or simply turned legs.

The most distinctive feature of these tables is the almost identical outline of the leg. The square corner posts drop abruptly into a short baluster turning with three central scribe lines over a long rectangular section with lamb's-tongue shoulder. Not only is the profile identical, but the gracefully sloping transitional shoulder is closely related to an architectural element in the attic of the Centre Family Dwelling House and is also repeated on the community's bedposts (see pl. 321). The decorative triple scribe lines appear on a great deal of other South Union pieces, including the pedestals of candlestands (see pls. 322, 323). It is not clear whether this is a shop practice or one individual's preferred work habit.

Although the vigorously turned feet vary, they correlate to forms found elsewhere at South Union. Those on the table on the left can be compared to those on the seven-drawer case piece pl. 310, and the feet on the table on the right are similar to the stair posts in the main hallway of the Centre Family Dwelling House (see pl. 309).

319. Trestle Table
c. 1830
Walnut and ash
h 29 w 59¾ d 37½"
Museum Collection, Shakertown at South Union, Kentucky, #58–10

320. Bench
c. 1830
Walnut
h 16 w 54 d 8½"
Museum Collection, Shakertown at South Union, Kentucky, #60–80

Although trestle tables were produced in the majority of Shaker communities, those from South Union display unique design and construction features, including a top formed of numerous crosswise rather than lengthwise boards and rounded edges without breadboard ends. Particularly noteworthy is the substructure, which is permanently assembled and, unlike those built in the East, cannot be readily dismantled with the simple removal of several bolts and screws. Three longitudinal cleats with ogee-shaped ends are fastened to the top boards with wood screws from below; the two free-floating cross members

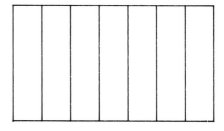

at either end, set an inch below the undersurface of the top, are tenoned into the three cleats. Rather than using a removable bolt at the end of the central trestle, the craftsman cut the latter with a bridle joint to accept both the cross member and the upper end of the leg, which is pinned to the cross member above and to the arched foot below. The foot is flat with an inverted V-shaped cutout in the center, which is in marked contrast to those produced in the Eastern communities.

This table may have been made in 1834, for on May 10, 1834, according to "Journal A" of the South Union Ministry, "new dining room tables [were] put in the Centre House and all old ones removed from dining room to wash house." According to a January 1, 1849, entry in "Journal B," dining room benches such as these were replaced by the one- or two-slat low-back chair: "Brethren on this Blessed New Years Day begin to make chairs for the dining room and so get clear of the benches." These sturdy benches were assembled using cross-lap joints between the legs and medial stretcher. The top is connected to the base with double-wedged through-tenons supported by dado joints on the underside of the top.

321. Bed
c. 1830
Cherry
h 34⅝ l 75¹⁵⁄₁₆ w 41"
Museum Collection, Shakertown at South Union, Kentucky, #89–34A

The Centre Family Dwelling House, built between 1822 and 1833, contains twenty-four retiring rooms and housed ninety Believers. The beds designed for their use reveal distinct South Union construction features. Surviving examples, such as this, are permanently pinned together, unlike beds from Eastern communities, which are easily disassembled with the removal of iron bed bolts. They consistently exhibit cyma-shaped side rails, identical head- and footboards of the same height, and distinctly turned corner posts. These corner posts constitute a virtual compendium of South Union turning styles: the cylindrical turnings under the oval knobs recall those on the stair posts (see pl. 309); the rectangular section with lamb's-tongue transition resemble those on the attic pillars; and the baluster turning and vase-shaped foot echo those on South Union tables and cases of drawers (see pl. 318). Variations in the details of the head- and footboards range from Gothic arch cutouts to sausage-turned rails fixed to the top that are reminiscent of Empire styling.

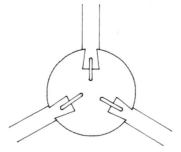

322. Tripod Stand
c. 1840
Walnut
h 28¼ diameter of top 16¼"
Museum Collection, Shakertown at South Union,
Kentucky, #67-4

323. Tripod Stand
c. 1840
Written in pencil in script under top:
Meetingroom Stand
Cherry
h 33¾ diameter of top 17½"
Museum Collection, Shakertown at South Union,
Kentucky, #64-24

Surviving South Union tripod stands share common construction and design features, including thick cherry or walnut tops (here, ⅝- and 1-inch thick) with nontapered edges, vase-shaped standards capped with a cylindrical turning, and the liberal use of incised scribe lines as surface decoration. They differ somewhat from their Eastern Shaker counterparts in their method of assembly. Instead of being threaded or glued, the upper end of the standard has a round stub tenon that passes through a long tapered cleat and is pinned in place. Although the round-edged cabriole legs are dovetailed into the standard, they are not capped with a sheet-iron reinforcing plate common to related tables in the East. Instead, each foot is fitted with a 1¼-inch-long metal staple, which helps secure the legs to the standard.

The unusually tall stand is inscribed "Meetingroom"; according to oral tradition, it was used in the meeting room of the dwelling house as a book support or lectern for family Bible reading.

Another remarkable example of this form with a South Union history is currently in a private collection. This is the only known stand with an oval top, an unusual Shaker design that is clearly related to worldly Sheraton models of the period.

324. Side Chair
c. 1820
Maple, ash, and tape (not original), with yellow paint
h 37 w 14½ d 18"
Museum Collection, Shakertown at South Union, Kentucky, #60-46

325. Armed Rocker
c. 1840
Cherry, maple, and splint
h 46½ w 20½ d 26¼"
Museum Collection, Shakertown at South Union, Kentucky, #91-14

326. Child's Chair
c. 1820
Stamped on front posts: 8
Ash, maple, and cane (not original)
h 24½ w 13¾ d 9½"
Museum Collection, Shakertown at South Union, Kentucky, #80–10-B

327. Side Chair
c. 1830
Stamped on front posts: 12
Ash, maple, and cane (not original)
h 38¾ w 18¼ d 14¼"
Museum Collection, Shakertown at South Union, Kentucky, #91-24

South Union Ministry's "Journal A" states that on April 4, 1822, "the chair shop [was] raised. . . . Called Wm. Rice's Shop [it stands] East of South from Ministrys Shop." Since the building bears his name, William Rice (1783–1863) must have been an early maker, along with Robert Johns (1795–1863) and Rueben Wise (1818–1893), who were producing seating furniture over two decades later in 1849.[43] The available resource material concerning chair making at South Union suggests that production was limited to supplying the needs of the community.

The typical South Union chair is distinguished by oval-shaped pommels, flattened on the top and with a noticeable ridge at the base, the whole resembling an egg in a cup; posts that taper sharply about one inch below the lowest stretcher to form the pointer foot; and back slats often arched on both top and lower edges. The front face of the bent back slats was shaped with a plane or draw knife, creating a somewhat rounded cross section, rather than the more typical rectangular slat. Other noteworthy features of these examples are the armed rocker posts, which are shaped like the pedestal of the "Meetingroom Stand" (see pl. 323), and the stamped numbers on the front posts, suggesting that they were used in Rooms 8 and 12 of the Centre Family Dwelling House.

Groveland Community, New York

This small walnut sewing table at Canterbury Shaker Village and a related example at the Shaker Museum, Old Chatham, New York, with recessed gallery and square, tapered legs (acc. no. 18180),[1] are attributed to Emmory Brooks based on oral tradition. The cabinetmaker's use of walnut, the rounded stiles, and the unusually thick dovetailed drawer fronts with nailed backs, an unusual construction feature, lend support to the attribution. Visually, the layout of half-width drawers echoes that of Brother Emmory's larger case pieces. A historic photograph in a private collection dating from the early twentieth century shows Sister Esther Marion Kate Scott of Watervliet, seated next to this desk.

The design of this sewing desk sets it apart from other furniture attributed to Emmory Brooks. Its bold proprtions, rectilinear orientation, and strong effect seem to foreshadow the furniture of the Arts and Crafts movement, which came to life in western New York within a decade of Brother Emmory's death (see pl. 339). The rounded case and drawer stiles in the gallery and the notched ovolo corners of the work surface soften the overall effect of the stocky construction, and the facade gains character from the highly unusual pulls, uncommon in Brother Emmory's—or any other Shaker craftsman's—work: brass knobs with inset white porcelain stars raised above the drawer surface on a dark walnut pyramid.

ALTHOUGH PART OF the New York Bishopric, the Groveland community occupied a unique role in Shaker history. It was the last village to be established, the only one to be relocated, and, situated midway between the eastern New York and Ohio societies, it combined a little bit of both East and West.

The site of the Groveland Shakers had originally been established at Sodus Bay on the shores of Lake Ontario in Wayne County. In 1824 Joseph and Susanna Pellam, from a nearby hamlet, converted to the faith in Ohio, where Joseph's natural brother Richard Pellam had joined the Union Village community and rapidly risen to a leadership position. After returning to the East, Joseph convinced the central ministry at Mount Lebanon that a new community could be successfully established in western New York. By this time, the United Society had been in America for fifty years, founded eighteen communities in seven states from Maine to Kentucky, and sought expansion in any area receptive to its teachings. Aside from its natural advantages—the lake, fertile farmland, and abundant lumber—the Sodus Bay site provided a midway stopping point for the central ministry at Mount Lebanon on its yearly visits to the Shaker communities in the West. (In fact, Elder Benjamin Youngs and a party visited Sodus in 1827 en route from South Union, Kentucky, to Mount Lebanon, and Richard McNemar stopped on his way back to Ohio in 1829.)[2]

As a result, in 1826, the Shaker leadership purchased 1,331 acres of land for $13,886.45, primarily lent from Canterbury, Enfield, New Hampshire, Shirley, Harvard, and Hancock, and founded the Sodus community.[3] There, the new converts established four families and cut timber and harvested seeds, both for themselves and the world. The Sodus Shakers also sold fruit trees, fished in the bay, and shipped barrels of smoked and salted fish east by canal.[4] Located about twelve miles between Lyons and Clyde, both ports on the Erie Canal, the Shakers were able to ship and receive goods conveniently and inexpensively.

In 1836, the newly organized Sodus Canal Company made an offer to purchase the Shakers' property, which it wanted for the terminus of its contemplated line beginning at Clyde. Having accepted the offer and sold the land and all twenty-three buildings, during 1837 and 1838 the 145 resident Shakers moved to the town of Groveland in Livingston County, about ninety miles southwest. Although the Sodus Canal was never built, the Shakers remained at their new location, where, over the next fifty-six years, they constructed thirty buildings for worship, lodging, and industry. Most of their two-thousand-acre property was fertile farmland, where they planted wheat and other grains that they then ground at their gristmill and sold as flour or meal. They also maintained and expanded their garden seed business, which became a significant source of income. In addition to agricultural products, they raised and sold cattle and meat, as well as lumber cut from their land. Traditional products sold by the Groveland Shakers included palm leaf bonnets and brooms, which they marketed as far away as Chicago and Canada. According to surviving inventories, they made carpet and barn brooms in a variety of sizes and parlor and hearth brushes.[5]

The style of some of the architecture at Groveland was very different from the Shaker prototypes found in the East and West. According to a letter from the ministry at Groveland to the ministry at Mount Lebanon in March 1845, "The [1841] Meetinghouse had more the appearance of a dwelling than a place of wor-

East Family, Groveland, c. 1890. Photograph by S. E. Wright, Mount Morris, New York. New York State Museum, Albany, #PTC1.2

ship."[6] The exterior was painted blue rather than white; the interior had gray walls and doors grained like mahogany instead of Prussian blue woodwork against white plaster walls. The 1858 brick dwelling house was Italianate in style and included a rooftop cupola with rounded arch windows, an entrance flanked with pilasters, and cornices and stone window caps throughout. These ornamental details reflect the current Victorian taste in the region, which was far removed from traditional eighteenth-century Shaker architecture, exemplified by the Eastern structures.

On the whole, little is known about furniture production at either Sodus or Groveland, particularly that built before midcentury. Much of the furniture used at Sodus may have been brought in by the early converts, purchased from the Eastern communities and transported via the Erie Canal, or acquired locally.[7] For example, when Sister Jennie Wells, the last surviving Shaker from Groveland, donated community artifacts to the New York State Museum at Albany in the 1930s, she indicated that Groveland ordered chairs from Mount Lebanon. In addition, an 1869 journal from Groveland refers to furniture purchases in nearby Mount Morris: "Elder C. bought some rocking chairs for the Office."[8]

There is little written documentation to indicate the names of the many woodworkers and cabinetmakers who must have been responsible for constructing the thirty buildings and interior furnishings at Groveland during the community's fifty-six-year history. However, five men have been identified to date as woodworkers or cabinetmakers, through journal references (■), oral history (■■), or United States census records (■■■):

JOHN LOCKWOOD (1791–1878), in Andrews, *Shaker Furniture*, p. 47; originally from Mount Lebanon, he was sent to Groveland in 1826 as an elder[9]

■■ EMMORY BROOKS (1807–1891), credited with making black walnut furniture by oral history, see pls. 328, 332–36, and 339, and listed as carpenter in 1875 census

■■■ JOHN B. CARRINGTON (1823–1866), listed as joiner in 1850 census

■■■ FRANKLIN FRUER (born 1824), listed as joiner in 1850 census

■ ROLIN CRAMER (working 1837–left 1850), in a Groveland diary entry of April 18, 1837: "Rolin Cramer made a table for the Kitchen."[10]

According to several journal references, Groveland and other communities shared both raw materials as well as finished furniture. For example, Sister Ana Buckingham of Watervliet noted in her diary on December 21, 1846, that the walnut "timber for meetinghouse" [benches] "came from Groveland."[11] In 1863, David Parker of Canterbury wrote in a letter to Lydia Dole of Groveland, "My heart is big enough to give every one of the sisters in Groveland, a work table, equal to this one, but it is not in my power to do it. The one now sent was built by one of our workmen, for a person who did not need it, when it was done; and as only one could have it, the lot falls upon Eldress Lydia, in union with Lebanon Ministry, our Ministry and Elders, as well as with your humble writer."[12] According to "A Register of Incidents and Events . . . kept by Giles Avery," on February 18, 1864, "Elder Peter [Long] goes to Lebanon this afternoon [from Watervliet]; he wishes to get some chairs for the New House, at Groveland."

As a result of written records, verbal attributions, and a quantity of extant pieces, more information survives regarding the activities of Emmory Brooks than of any other Groveland cabinetmaker. Twenty-year-old Emmory and his mother, father, three brothers, and sister came from Brutus, Canada, to join the Sodus Bay Shakers in 1827.[13] Although the rest of the Brooks family left the next year, Emmory remained and served in many leadership capacities throughout his life— associate minister from 1838 to 1851; first minister from 1851 to 1859; elder of the gathering order from 1859 to 1861; and first deacon of the West Family from 1861.[14] In addition to these administrative roles, he sold seeds, brooms, and brushes along the Western route as far as Illinois and Michigan, built the community's schoolhouse, and made many pieces of furniture for Groveland between 1860 and 1890.

Although Elder Emmory's signature does not appear on any of the pieces attributed to him, documentation of his cabinetmaking abilities was supplied by Shaker sisters who knew him—Jennie Wells (1878–1956), Polly Lee (1821–1916), and Ella Winship (1857–1941). In 1869, Emmory Brooks wrote from Enfield, Connecticut, to caution Eldress Polly Lee at Groveland: "I am coming home after a while to finish your bedstead so do not let others medle with it or try to have it finished before I return" (see pl. 331).[15] The fact that Elder Emmory was concerned someone else might complete his work suggests that there were others working in wood at Groveland.

When the community closed in 1892 due to financial difficulties, much of the remaining furniture was transferred to the Watervliet society. According to "A Family Journal, Second Family, Watervliet N.Y. 1885," a member brought "from depot a carload of furniture for the Groveland folks. What are left at the North family are moved to the Chh family to make place for the Groveland people (5 sisters 1 brother move)."[16] Several weeks later, on November 15, the Watervliet journalist recorded "three carloads of Household goods arrives from Groveland help draw them home."

In the 1930s the Shakers donated several of Emmory Brooks's pieces to

329. Case of Drawers

c. 1830
Pine, with hardwood knobs, red paint, and metal escutcheon
Written in pencil on several drawer sides: Office; Office sisters
h 62½ w 43 d 18¾"
Private collection

The case of drawers depicted here in a drawing is one of the earliest known Groveland case pieces. Originating as it does in the New York Bishopric, it is not surprising that it displays both Mount Lebanon and Groveland features. The former is seen in the straightforward design with graduated lipped drawers, plank case sides, cut feet, and a painted finish. The clues to its Groveland origin are found in the heavy drawer fronts and unusual drawer construction. The front joints are carefully dovetailed together while the back joints are fastened to the sides with screws instead of the more customary dovetails typical of other communities.

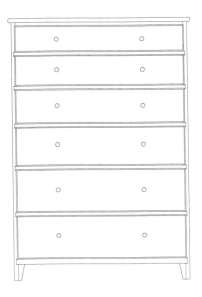

the New York State Museum in Albany, where they remain today (see pls. 334, 336). Later, in 1943, Sister Jennie Wells wrote to Dr. Charles Adams, the museum director, that Emmory Brooks "made all the [Groveland] sisters a black walnut bedstead" (see pl. 332).[17]

Aside from written evidence, Emmory Brooks's work can also be recognized by its physical characteristics: materials, distinctive construction details, and Victorian styling, which also dominated Groveland architecture at midcentury. The most unusual feature of his work is the consistent use of walnut, a native wood that grew abundantly in nearby groves and which he used for furniture during the last quarter of the nineteenth century. His exuberant designs, which resemble more closely the furniture of the Western and Southern Shaker communities than the classic styles of the East, may have been influenced by the worldly furniture he saw during selling trips throughout the Midwest to merchandise Shaker products. More specifically, the massive proportions, frame-and-panel construction, overhanging upper-drawer sections, complex cornice moldings, and rounded stiles are derived from Empire styling. The scalloped bases on some case pieces look like they come from French Provincial designs, which Brother Emmory may have seen during his early years in Canada or when traveling through Ontario en route to Michigan and Illinois. Additional idiosyncrasies found in Emmory Brooks's work are the exceptionally thick—up to 1½ inches—drawer fronts and unusual drawer assembly process, in which the sides are dovetailed to the drawer faces and the drawer backs are nailed or fastened with screws to the sides. The drawer fronts on most of his case pieces do not have molded edges but are flush with the frame. The knobs on some of his furniture are tiered and are either turned in one piece or composed of three separate parts: a two-inch stepped cap, a collar, and a connecting tenon. The latter is glued into the cap, passes through the collar, and is fastened into the drawer front.

Although Emmory Brooks produced at least beds, stands, sewing desks, and tables, more cases of drawers survive than any of the other furniture forms attributed to him. Perhaps like the Union Village Believers (see pp. 298–99) the Groveland Shakers preferred freestanding to built-in storage units. Only a few small built-ins exist in extant structures. Several of his cases of drawers consist of a frame-and-panel case fitted with a double bank of six half-width drawers, each with a single knob. It is not clear why the maker consistently chose this type of storage arrangement, making a lower, wide case rather than the high one more typical of Shaker case pieces. Whether it was for functional reasons, to serve the needs of two Believers simultaneously, or purely for visual effect, this design was a conscious decision on the part of the maker.

A rare surviving letter provides insight into the cabinetmaker's concerns regarding the Shakers' conservative and outmoded attitudes in the late nineteenth century. On January 6, 1869, he wrote to Eldress Polly, "the dust of ages covers some of our organizations and the parchment on which the records of the past work of God are written is become debased and deformed. . . . Our theology wants revising in some important particulars or the light that will be soon reflected on all men will say to us you are weighed in the balance and found wanting."[18] Perhaps Emmory Brooks's ardent plea for change on the spiritual level is reflected in the progressive furniture designs with which he is associated.

330. Cupboard and Case of Drawers
c. 1850
h 67 w 42 d 17"
Pine, with hardwood knobs, yellow paint, and brass hinges
Collection Fran and Herb Kramer
Photograph: Paul Rocheleau by courtesy of The Magazine Antiques

This cupboard over case of drawers is one of three known mid-nineteenth-century pieces that share similar construction and design features distinctive of Groveland craftsmanship. All have doors that extend to the side of the case without added case stiles and incorporate a rather primitive but traditional eighteenth-century method of attaching the doors with hinges that are not let in but screwed directly into the face of the door and case. This is surprising, given the vintage of these pieces, one of which is dated 1853. In addition, the cases are all of painted pine, with plank sides and cut feet—elements attuned to Mount Lebanon design, which is not unexpected, given their bishopric connections. This group of furniture, including pl. 329, is important because it gives some indication of the furniture styles of Groveland at midcentury. These earlier design features, it seems, were not continued by Brother Emmory Brooks, whose extant work presently best represents known Groveland furniture. One of the cases, however, has rounded case stiles, a feature also found in Brother Emmory's work.

331. Retiring Room, South Family Dwelling House, Watervliet

Photograph by William F. Winter (1899–1939) 1930

New York State Museum, Albany, #PTA 252

This 1930 photograph taken by William F. Winter shows Eldress Anna Case's retiring room at Watervliet's South Family Dwelling House. The room features several pieces of furniture that have been attributed to Emmory Brooks by Groveland Sister Jennie Wells. When the community closed in 1892, she moved first to the North Family at Watervliet, then to the South Family in 1915, and finally to Hancock about 1935. The massive storage unit pictured here (currently in the collection of the New York State Museum, acc. no. 30.2.51) was constructed in two pieces; the cupboard top was probably made at a later date and attached to what had originally been only a case of drawers. Design and construction features associated with Brother Emmory's work include the heavy walnut stock used throughout, frame-and-panel construction, cove-shaped cornice molding, rounded case stiles, characteristic double-bank drawer configuration (see pl. 334), and applied molded base.

The bed with walnut frame and paneled footboard is currently in the collection of the Shaker Heritage Society, Albany (acc. no. SHF.124). This may be the one that Brother Emmory described in a letter of January 6, 1869, written from Enfield, Connecticut, to Eldress Polly Lee at Groveland: "I am coming home after a while to finish your bedstead so do not let others medle with it or try to have it finished before I return."[19] In the 1930s, Gertrude Reno Sherburne, who had been raised by the Watervliet Shakers, purchased the bed that she recalled as having belonged to Eldress Polly directly from them.[20] Later, in 1943, Sister Jennie Wells wrote to Dr. Charles Adams, Director of the New York State Museum, confirming the fact that Emmory Brooks "made all the sisters a black walnut bedstead."[21]

In addition to the furniture, the wallpaper, patterned oilcloth under the stove, linoleum, Oriental carpet, fringe on the chair, and artwork also reflect the twentieth-century Shakers' enjoyment of worldly decoration.

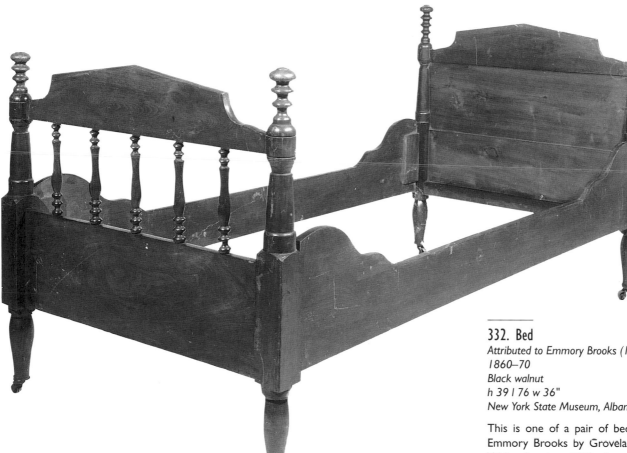

332. Bed
Attributed to Emmory Brooks (1807–1891)
1860–70
Black walnut
h 39 l 76 w 36"
New York State Museum, Albany, #30.2.117

This is one of a pair of beds attributed to Emmory Brooks by Groveland Sister Jennie Wells. Another 1930 photograph taken by William F. Winter (1899–1939) shows the guest room at Watervliet's South Family with the identical bed in place.[22] The inverted baluster-shaped legs are the only visual connection with more common Shaker design. The vigorously turned spindles and corner post finials were widely made by furniture manufacturers in the United States and Canada in the mid-nineteenth century and indicate the acceptance of Victorian elements into the design.[23]

333. Bed
c. 1870
Attributed to Emmory Brooks (1807–1891)
Walnut
h 41¾ l 59⁹⁄₁₆ w 22¼"
Private collection

The mother of the present owner of this bed was raised by Sister Jennie Wells (1878–1956), who presented her charge with this bed when the former left the community at the age of sixteen. The maker of this child's bed not only created a unique three-leg design, he also gave the legs a highly unusual shape, which probably reflects a Canadian influence. Although the design of the bed is quite uncommon, the construction and detailing of the head- and footboards are indentical to Emmory Brooks's work, particularly the arched shaping of the headboard and its top molding, the paneled ends, and the reliance on walnut throughout (see pl. 331).

334. Case of Drawers
Attributed to Emmory Brooks (1807–1891)
1860–70
Walnut and pine, with varnish
h 55 w 59¼ d 23¾"
New York State Museum, Albany, #30.2.109

The overall heavy proportions and thick stock employed for rails, stiles, and drawers lend this case of drawers crafted from walnut a distinctive quality very different from the restrained simplicity of the earlier Eastern Shaker style. During the 1930s, it was donated to the New York State Museum by the Shakers when the Watervliet community closed. In a letter to the museum director in 1943, Sister Jennie Wells, a former Groveland resident, identified Brother Emmory Brooks as the maker, noting, "Brooks is the one I told you made so much of the Groveland black walnut furniture."[24] The frame-and-panel construction, composite cove molding, distinctive three-piece drawer knobs, and drawer assem-bly consisting of sides dovetailed to front faces but nailed to the backs are associated with Brother Emmory's work.

This case of drawers is one of several storage units with a close family resemblance in public and private collections. Another example at the Shaker Museum at Old Chatham, New York (acc. no. 6774), is fitted with two vertical banks of six drawers and has a scalloped base possibly derived from French Provincial designs, as shown below.[25] A third piece, measuring 58 by 53 by 21 inches, has fourteen drawers and exhibits flaring Chinese feet rather than the more usual applied bracket base found here.[26]

The configuration found in all of these storage units attributed to Emmory Brooks consists of two side-by-side banks of six or seven half-width drawers. This layout, whether devised for functional, structural, or purely visual reasons, is probably intentional on the part of the cabinetmaker.

335. Cupboard and Case of Drawers

Attributed to Emmory Brooks (1807–1891)
1860–70
Written in pencil on outside of upper left drawer:
Elders 1L/Sisters/No 20
Written in pencil on rear of lower left drawer: E.J.
Kellam 1915/Foreman for/North Family/Shakers
Typed note found near the bureau at
Canterbury: THIS BUREAU WAS MADE
BY/ELDER EMORY BROOKS FROM BLACK
WALNUT WOOD GROWN/AT GROVELAND
NEW YORK 1860–1870
Walnut and pine, with porcelain knobs and brass
slip catches and hinges
h 46¾ w 50 d 23¼"
Canterbury Shaker Village, Inc., Canterbury, New
Hampshire, #88.676
Photograph: Bill Finney, by courtesy of
Canterbury Shaker Village

The design and construction of this distinctive storage unit are typical of the furniture attributed to Emmory Brooks. Characteristic features include the abundant use of walnut for all visible surfaces and the thick, heavy stock for feet, rails, stiles, and drawer faces. The overhanging drawer section with deep cove molding, rounded top and stiles, and single-panel sides are all worldly elements that have been borrowed from Empire styling. The bracket base with exuberantly scalloped skirt, related in form and feel to French Provincial decoration, may have been the result of Canadian influence from Brother Emmory's frequent travels. An adjustable mirror, now missing, was originally fitted to the top of the case by means of the vertical support. This idea was derived from worldly furniture, since the 1845 "Millennial Laws" recommended keeping looking glasses—very small ones—in the public cupboard of a retiring room.

This cupboard and case of drawers from Groveland is similar in form and construction to a four-drawer, two-door bureau currently at the Shaker Museum, Old Chatham, New York (acc. no. 6448), although it has a cut foot and straight base, rather than bracket foot with scalloped skirt, and square as opposed to rounded stiles.[27]

Although this storage unit's history and use are unknown, the inscriptions suggest that it was used by the senior female leader ("Elder Sister") of the Church Family in the Groveland community and assigned to Room 20 of the large Shaker dwelling house built in 1858. As Emmory Brooks is known to have made a walnut bedstead for Eldress Polly Lee in 1869 (see pl. 331), it is not unreasonable to speculate that he produced a storage cupboard for the family eldress as well. Surviving records indicate that Abigail Crosman was in charge of the family in 1875 and may have used Brother Emmory's bureau at some point in its history.[28]

After the Groveland community closed in 1892, the remaining members and their furniture took over the North Family Dwelling House at Watervliet near Albany, where this case piece was used by a hired hand named E. J. Kellam. Employed as foreman for the Shakers from 1915, he had a somewhat checkered career. According to a journal entry of May 15, 1917, the Watervliet family elders complained to the Mount Lebanon ministry about "The broken down and bankrupt condition the Foreman, Elmer Kellam, left them in at North Family. Stole and broke everything he could lay his hands on."[29] Following the 1919 breakup of the North Family due to financial reasons and the removal of the eight remaining members to the Church Family, all unnecessary furnishings were sold or distributed to other Shaker communities. Perhaps during this transitional period, when Elder Arthur Bruce of Canterbury visited Watervliet to participate in the closing, he arranged to ship excess furniture such as this cupboard and case of drawers back to New Hampshire.[30]

It was at Canterbury, where the Shakers had a practice of recording the name of the craftsman associated with important pieces of furniture, that the typed note attributing Brooks as the maker was found near the cupboard. Clearly, oral tradition credits this craftsmanship to Emmory Brooks.

336. Bookcase
Attributed to Emmory Brooks (1807–1891)
1860–70
Walnut, pine, and glass, with porcelain knobs,
mustard yellow stain, varnish, and escutcheons
h 99 w 72 d 18½"
New York State Museum, Albany, #39.10.5

After the closing of Groveland in 1892, this unusual bookcase or, as it was sometimes called, hymnal cupboard, was moved first to Watervliet and then, in the 1930s, to Mount Lebanon, where it stood in the meeting room of the North Family Dwelling House.

In addition to this solid history of use, the following design and construction features suggest a Groveland origin and Brooks's workmanship: heavy walnut stock, rounded edges on stiles and horizontal surfaces, and a deep composite cornice molding. This piece is distinctive in the repetition of a half-round molding at the top and bottom of the bookcase and along the edges of the doors. The elaborate shaping at the top of the glazed panels, similar in style to the scalloped bases on documented Emmory Brooks pieces (see pl. 335), calls to mind the French Provincial and Gothic Revival styles.[31]

337. Desk
c. 1870
Walnut and pine, with metal locks
h 40½ w 43 d 19¾"
Collection Marian Curtis

This walnut kneehole desk is one of two known examples with a Groveland history. It was given by Sister Jennie Wells to a member of the present owner's family when she left the Watervliet Shakers in the 1920s. The carefully turned gallery sets this late piece apart from other Shaker desks. The sides of the case form a cut foot, while the front has an applied shaped foot, an unusual choice for a desk of this type. All five dovetailed drawers are fitted with locks; the heavily constructed door opens to reveal ledger dividers installed behind.

338. Table with Gallery
c. 1830 (table), c. 1860 (gallery)
Walnut and pine
h 42 w 33 d 22"
Collection Marian Curtis
Photograph: courtesy Rochester Museum and Science Center, Rochester, New York

This basic table with square, tapering legs, which was given by the Watervliet Shakers directly to the present owner's family, may be typical of many that were used throughout the Groveland community for a variety of purposes. Very simple in both form and execution, it expresses its worldly origins as well as its Shaker form in the long overhang of the top. The strong rectilinear lines are broken by the ovolo curvature on the gallery top. The four-drawer gallery built for sewing purposes was likely added after the table was completed and probably dates from the 1860s, when the sisters' fancywork became an important community industry.

339. Table
Attributed to Emmory Brooks (1807–1891)
c. 1880
Walnut
h 28 w 36 d 24¼"
Canterbury Shaker Village, Inc., Canterbury, New Hampshire, #85.1980

Several distinctive features relate this table to the Groveland Shaker community, including the use of heavy walnut stock throughout and the unusual drawer construction, typical of Emmory Brooks's work. These characteristics, also found on the sewing table pl. 328, include relatively thin sides dovetailed to 1-inch-thick drawer faces, drawer backs nailed to the sides, a drawer bottom set high in the sides, and a three-piece knob.

The singular look of this table comes from several decorative touches that, among the known work of Brother Emmory, are, in fact, unique to it: the beading on the outer edges of the posts and on the underside of the top; the two projecting side rails that are accentuated on the front of the frame; and the slightly tapered turned legs with an unexpected reduction in size just above the unusually turned foot.

The thickness of the members, the exposed joinery of the side rails, and the profile of the foot evoke the English Arts and Crafts furniture produced in the 1880s. In particular, the leg treatment found on Emmory Brooks's piece is related to the bobbin foot seen in the work of Arthur Mackmurdo dating from the same period.[32]

From a philosophical viewpoint, some of the socialist ideals espoused in Arts and Crafts workshops resonate with the Shakers' convictions. For example, wealth was held by the community as a whole; work undertaken by men and women was considered to be of equal value; and crafts were nurtured within a secluded community. The preindustrial techniques of the Shakers imported from eighteenth-century England were in many cases the very traditions to which followers of the Arts and Crafts movement were returning.[33] Brother Emmory could have been exposed to Arts and Crafts productions through English publications such as *The Studio* magazine. It is possible that periodicals such as this may have been available to Believers and placed, perhaps, in the magnificent bookcase that Brooks built for the community (see pl. 336). It is impossible to say whether Brooks consciously emulated the ideals of the English movement or simply adapted an aesthetically pleasing style.

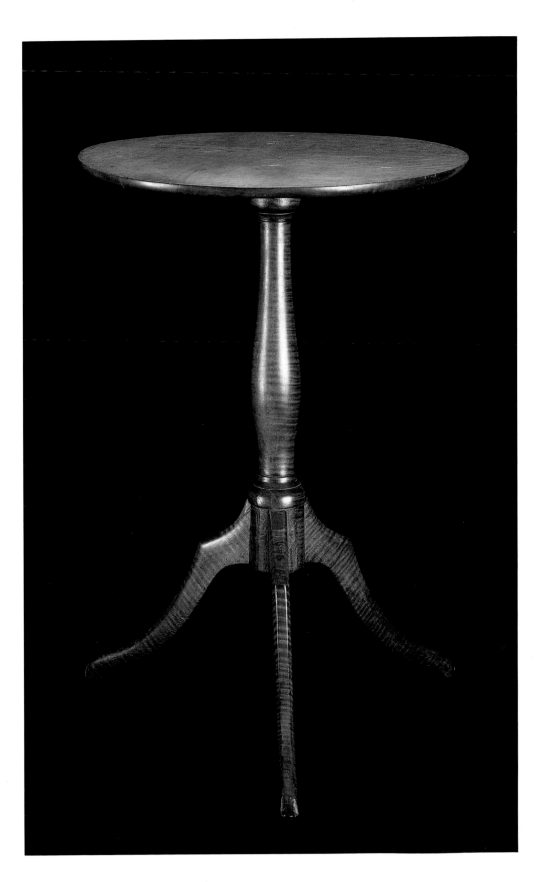

340. Tripod Stand
1830–50
Curly maple
h 28 diameter of top 19"
Collection Mrs. Hugh M. Russ
Photograph: Paul Rocheleau by courtesy of The
Magazine Antiques

This candle stand is one of very few surviving examples representing the work of an unidentified Groveland cabinetmaker working before Emmory Brooks's time, which ranged from about 1860 to 1890. It descended in the family of a man who had been the Groveland Shakers' banker and may have been paid for his financial services with Shaker-made products.[34] Additional support for a Groveland attribution appears in a photograph of a similar stand taken in the 1930s by Edward Deming Andrews. On the back, Andrews wrote: "The joiners' shop at Groveland which usually produced rather heavy [illeg.] walnut furniture turned out a number of graceful candlestands in this wood."[35] The photograph and its inscription, part of the Andrews Shaker Collection at Winterthur Museum, Delaware, may corroborate the making of a quantity of candle stands similar to those produced in the Eastern communities but with a distinctive Groveland touch in the sharp angles at the top of their legs.

Notes

SHAKER ORIGINS

1. See Henry C. Blinn, "A Historical Record of the Society of Believers in Canterbury, N.H. . . . Vol II. [vol. I], East Canterbury, 1892," pp. 1–7, CAN, 763.

2. Nick Apple, "Ann Lee's Toad Lane Changed to Todd Street," *The Shaker Messenger* 3, no. 3 (Spring 1981): 12.

3. See Robley Edward Whitson, ed., *The Shakers: Two Centuries of Spiritual Perfection* (New York: Paulist Press, 1983), 11.

4. Ibid., 11–12.

5. According to Jerry Grant, Shaker Museum and Library, Old Chatham, N.Y., this term was not officially used until the early 1820s and first appears only on the spine title of the fourth edition of *The Testimony of Christ's Second Appearing . . .* by Benjamin Seth Youngs (Albany: Van Benthuysen, 1856), WIN, 462–5.

6. See Flo Morse, *The Shakers and the World's People* (Hanover, N.H.: University Press of New England, 1980), 20.

7. See Whitson, *The Shakers*, 15.

8. The name of New Lebanon was changed in 1861 to Mount Lebanon and will be referred to as such throughout this text to reflect the continuing nature of the United Society into the present.

9. See Whitson, *The Shakers*, 5.

10. Elijah Myrick, *The Shaker* 2, no. 5 (1872): 34–35.

11. See E. Richard McKinstry, comp., *The Edward Deming Andrews Memorial Shaker Collection* (New York: Garland, 1987), xx.

12. See Whitson, *The Shakers*, 18.

13. See Stephen J. Stein, *The Shaker Experience in America* (New Haven: Yale University Press, 1992), 9.

14. Benjamin Seth Youngs, *The Testimony of Christ's Second Appearing, Containing a General Statement of All Things Pertaining to the Faith and Practice of the Church of God in This Latter-day . . .* (Lebanon, Ohio: John M'Clean, Office of the Western Star, 1808), 581; revised and enlarged editions: Albany, 1810; Union Village, Ohio, 1823; Albany, 1856.

15. Rufus Bishop and Seth Youngs Wells, eds., *Testimonies of the Life, Character, Revelations and Doctrines of Our Ever Blessed Mother Ann Lee . . .*, 2d ed., revised by Giles B. Avery (Albany: Weed, Parsons & Co., 1888), 208, no. 11.

16. Ibid., 267–68, no. 15.

17. Ibid., 264–65, no. 6.

18. See Dolores Hayden, *The Architecture of Communitarian Socialism 1790–1975* (Cambridge, Mass.: MIT Press, 1976), 66.

19. See Priscilla J. Brewer, *Shaker Communities, Shaker Lives* (Hanover, N.H.: University Press of New England, 1986), 82.

20. Bishop and Wells, *Testimonies*, 264, no. 4.

21. Hayden, *The Architecture of Communitarian Socialism*, 65.

22. See Anna White and Leila S. Taylor, *Shakerism: Its Meaning and Message* (Columbus, Ohio: Fred J. Heer, 1905), 321.

23. Calvin Green and Seth Youngs Wells, *A Summary View of the Millennial Church, or United Society of Believers . . .* (Albany: Packard & Van Benthuysen, 1823), 296, no. 12; 299, no. 25; 297, no. 17.

24. Ibid., 371–72.

25. See ibid., 373, nos. 7, 8.

26. Joseph Meacham, "Collection of Writings Concerning Church Order and Government, Copied Here by Rufus Bishop in 1850," 1791–96, pp. 42, 45, WRHS, VIIB:59.

27. See Theodore E. Johnson, ed., "The 'Millennial Laws' of 1821," *The Shaker Quarterly* 7, no. 2 (Summer 1967): 35–37.

28. Johnson, "The 'Millennial Laws,'" [Chapter V, 9th]: 52.

29. "Millennial Laws," 1845, pt. I, sec. 3, no. 6; sec 4, no. 2; sec. 4, no. 25, reprinted in Edward Deming Andrews, *The People Called Shakers* (New York: Oxford University Press, 1953), 256, 257, 259.

30. "Millennial Laws," pt. 3, sec. 4, no. 5; sec. 4, nos. 2, 3; sec. 9, nos. 2 and 10, in Andrews, *The People Called Shakers*, 283, 282, 285–86.

31. "Millennial Laws," pt. 2, sec. 10, nos. 2, 3; sec. 18, no. 14; pt. 4, no. 29, in Andrews, *The People Called Shakers*, 271–72, 279, 288.

32. "Millennial Laws," pt. I, sec. 4, no. 3; sec. 4, no. 29; pt. 2, sec. 10, no. 10, in Andrews, *The People Called Shakers*, 257, 260, 272.

33. See Theodore E. Johnson, ed., "Rules and Orders for the Church of Christ's Second Appearing," *The Shaker Quarterly* 11, no. 4 (Winter 1971): 139–40.

34. See Brewer, *Shaker Communities*, 115–16.

35. See Morse, *The Shakers and the World's People*, 174.

36. See Johnson, "Rules and Orders," 141.

37. Johnson, "Rules and Orders," [pt. 2, sec. 7, no. 4] 155.

38. Johnson, "The 'Millennial Laws,'" 35.

39. See Andrews, *The People Called Shakers*, 61.

40. William J. Haskett, *Shakerism Unmasked* (Pittsfield, Mass.: published by the author, 1828), pp. 166–67, WIN, 264.

41. Freegift Wells, "Memorandum of Events," 1812–65, Church Family, Watervliet, N.Y., WRHS, VB:286.

42. "Journal Containing Some of the Most Important Events of the Day," November 1840–June 1843, Harvard, Mass., FM, 2.3.

43. Haskett, *Shakerism Unmasked*, 164.

44. Isaac Newton Youngs, October 22, 1856, "A Domestic Journal of Domestic Occurrences Kept Originally by Joseph Bennet, and then by Isaac Crouch, Nicholas Bennet, Isaac N. Youngs, and John M. Brown," 1788–1877, Church Family, Mount Lebanon, N.Y., WRHS, VB:71.

45. See Brewer, *Shaker Communities*, 50.

46. Joseph Meacham, "Collection of Writings Concerning Church Order and Government, Copied Here by Rufus Bishop in 1850," 1791–96, WRHS, VIIB:59, quoted in Andrews, *The People Called Shakers*, 60.

47. Isaac Newton Youngs, "A Domestic Journal of Daily Occurrences," Church Family, Mount Lebanon, N.Y. NYSL, 13500.

48. Wells, "Memorandum of Events," VB:288, 292.

49. "Daily Record of Events of the Church," 1805–96, Union Village, Ohio, WRHS, VB:230.

50. "Journal Containing Some of the Most Important Events."

51. "Church Family Journal No. 3," July 4, 1845–September 11 1847, Harvard, Mass., FM, 2.4.

52. "An Extract from the Holy Orders of the Church: Written by Father Joseph to the Elders of the Church at New Lebanon and Copied Agreeable to Father Joseph's Word, February 18th, 1841," p. 52, no. 13, WIN, 791.

53. Benjamin Gates, "Counsel Concerning Eating and Drinking," May 18, 1841, Mount Lebanon, N.Y., OC, 12311.

54. Giles Avery, "Circular Concerning the Dress of Believers," 1864, Mount Lebanon, N.Y., OC, 12025.

55. Giles Avery, "A Register of Incidents and Events . . ." October 20, 1859–December 21, 1874, Mount Lebanon, N.Y., p. 257, NYPL-1.

56. "Circular Epistle from the Ministry and Elders New Lebanon," September 1, 1829, WRHS, IVA:35.

57. Letter from Ministry, City of Union and Lovely Vineyard, Enfield, Conn., to Beloved Ministry, August 15, 1853, WRHS, IVA:14; from Watch-Hill, R.I., to Elder Grove Blanchard, August 25, 1853, IVA 26; from Elder Grove, to City of Union, Enfield, Conn., August 31, 1853, IVA:14; from West Pittsfield, Mass., to Elder Grove, December 2 1853, IVA:20.

58. Thomas Damon, "Memoranda, &c Mostly of Eventes and Things Which Have Transpired since the First of Jan 1846," Hancock, Mass., NYSL, quoted in Charles R. Muller and Timothy D. Rieman, The Shaker Chair (Winchester, Ohio: Canal Press, 1984), 65.

59. "Millennial Laws," pt. 3, sec. 9, no. 10, in Andrews, The People Called Shakers, 286.

60. Letter from Daniel Boler at Watervliet, N.Y., to Orren Haskins, Mount Lebanon, N.Y., May 23, 1865, WRHS, IVA:82.

61. David Rowley, quoted in Elisha D. Blakeman, "Religious Experience of David Rowley," 1854, Church Family, Mount Lebanon, N.Y., WRHS, VIB:23.

62. "Domestic Journal of Important Occurrences Kept for the Elder Sisters at New Lebanon" WRHS, VB:60; see also Youngs, "A Domestic Journal of Daily Occurrences," July 4, 1840.

63. Letter from Thomas Damon to George Wilcox, December 23, 1846, WRHS, IVA:19.

64. Youngs, "A Domestic Journal of Domestic Occurrences," May 1, 1861, WRHS, VB:71.

65. Orren Haskins, "Reflections, 1887," WRHS, VIIA:8.

DAILY LIFE

1. See Don Gifford, ed., An Early View of the Shakers: Benson John Lossing and the "Harper's" Article of July 1857 (Hanover, N.H.: University Press of New England, 1989), 49, n. 56; and Edward Deming Andrews, The People Called Shakers (New York: Oxford University Press, 1953), 106–7.

2. See Gifford, An Early View, 47, n. 48, 49; and June Sprigg, Shaker Design (New York: Whitney Museum of American Art, 1986), 14–15.

3. Benson Lossing, "The Shakers," Harper's New Monthly Magazine 15 (July 1857): 164–77.

4. See Robert P. Emlen, Shaker Village Views (Hanover, N.H.: University Press of New England, 1987), 8.

5. Letter from Benjamin S. Youngs, South

Union, Ky., to the ministries at Mount Lebanon and Hancock, February 26, 1818, WRHS, IVA:52(21).

6. Isaac Newton Youngs, [Isaac Youngs's "Biography in Verse"], 1837, pp. 129–34, WIN, 1010.

7. See Andrews, The People Called Shakers, 158–59.

8. "Narrative of Four Month's Residence among the Shakers at Watervliet," Yale University Library, quoted in Edward Deming Andrews and Faith Andrews, Work and Worship (Greenwich, Conn.: New York Graphic Society, 1974), 199.

9. William J. Haskett, Shakerism Unmasked (Pittsfield, Mass.: published by the author, 1828), p. 162, WIN, 264.

10. See Ulysses Prentiss Hedrick, A History of Agriculture in New York State, 1933, quoted in Flo Morse, The Shakers and the World's People (Hanover, N.H.: University Press of New England, 1980), 283.

11. See Thomas D. Clark and F. Gerald Ham, Pleasant Hill and Its Shakers (Harrodsburg, Ky.: Pleasant Hill Press, 1986), 31.

12. See Clifton Johnson, "The Passing of the Shakers," Old-Time New England (October 1934), quoted in Morse, The Shakers and the World's People, 283.

13. See A. D. Emerich and A. H. Benning, eds., Community Industries of the Shakers: A New Look (Albany: Shaker Heritage Society, 1983), 15.

14. Joseph Meacham, quoted in Morse, The Shakers and the World's People, 133.

15. See June Sprigg, By Shaker Hands (New York: Alfred A. Knopf, 1975), 174; and Edward Deming Andrews, The Community Industries of the Shakers (Albany: University of the State of New York, 1933), 42.

16. See Dictionary of American Biography (New York: Charles Scribner's Sons, 1964), 457–58.

17. See Andrews, Work and Worship: The Economic Order of the Shakers, 157–58.

18. Ibid., 183.

19. See Julia Neal, "Children Were Special! in Shaker Villages," The Shaker Messenger 12, no. 2 (Winter 1990): 14.

20. Wendell Hess, The Enfield (N.H.) Shakers: A Brief History. Copyright 1988, Wendell Hess, 26.

21. "Letter to the Elders, Deacons, Brethren & Sisters of the Society in Watervliet, New York, Jany 26th 1832," Andrews MS. no. 64, quoted in Andrews, Community Industries, 221.

22. "Fifteen Years a Shakeress," The Galaxy 13, no. 1 (January 1872): 36, quoted in Andrews, The People Called Shakers, 190.

THE CULTURAL SETTING

1. See Francis J. Puig and Michael Conforti, eds., The American Craftsman and the European Tradition 1620–1820 (Minneapolis: Minneapolis Institute of Arts, 1989), xiii.

2. See Oscar P. Fitzgerald, Three Centuries of American Furniture (New York: Gramercy Publishing, 1982), 62.

3. See Puig and Conforti, The American Craftsman, xiv.

4. Gouverneur Morris, quoted in Charles F. Montgomery and Patricia E. Kane, eds., American Art: 1750–1800 Towards Independence (Boston: New York Graphic Society, 1976).

5. Bill Cotton and Scott Swank, authors, personal interviews with author, May 1990.

6. See Gabriel Olive, "West Country Chests, Coffers and Boxes," Regional Furniture 4 (1990): 49–71.

7. See Howard Pain, The Heritage of Country Furniture (Toronto: Van Nostrand Reinhold, 1978), 42.

8. See Bernard D. Cotton, The English Regional Chair (Woodbridge, Eng.: Antique Collectors' Club, 1990), 312, fig. NW2.

9. See Louise Ade Boger and H. Batterson Boger, Dictionary of Antiques and the Decorative Arts (New York: Charles Scribner's Sons, 1967).

10. See Isaac Newton Youngs, "A Domestic Journal of Daily Occurrences," 1834, Church Family, Mount Lebanon, N.Y., 1834, NYSL, 13500; Jerry V. Grant and Douglas R. Allen, Shaker Furniture Makers (Hanover, N.H.: University Press of New England, 1989), 21; December 1855, "A Domestic Journal of Domestic Occurrences Kept Originally by Joseph Bennet, and then by Isaac Crouch, Nicholas Bennet, Isaac N. Youngs, and John M. Brown," 1788–1877, Church Family, Mount Lebanon, N.Y., WRHS, VB:70; Grant and Allen, Shaker Furniture Makers, 5.

11. See Mary Lyn Ray, "A Reappraisal of Shaker Furniture," in Winterthur Portfolio 8, edited by Ian M.G. Quimby (Charlottesville: University Press of Virginia, 1973), 130.

12. Oliver Hampton, The Manifesto 17, no. 3 (1887): 57–58, quoted in Robley Edward Whitson, ed., The Shakers: Two Centuries of Spiritual Perfection (New York: Paulist Press, 1983), 143.

13. Vol. 1, SDL.

14. Otis Sawyer, "Alfred Church Record," vol. 2, 1879–86, SDL, quoted in Amy Stechler Burns and Ken Burns, The Shakers: Hands to Work Hearts to God

(New York: Portland House, 1987), 118–19.

15. Henry Blinn, "A Journey to Kentucky in the Year 1873," reprinted in *The Shaker Quarterly*: May 10, 1873 (Spring 1965); June 30, 1873 (Winter 1966); May 8, 1873 (Spring 1965); June 4, 1873 (Winter 1965).

16. These are the ones made by Micajah Tucker in 1834, see pl. 6h.

17. "Historical Record of the Church Family, East Canterbury, N.H. . . . 1890–1930," CAN, 33, quoted in Grant and Allen, *Shaker Furniture Makers*, 7, 10.

18. See Eldress Bertha Lindsay, *Seasoned with Grace* (Woodstock, Vt.: Countryman Press, 1987), 68–69.

19. Letter from Mrs. Robert Reed. Madison, Wis., to Ms. Androski, Skinner Inc., auctioneers and appraisers, Bolton, April 15, 1991, courtesy Maggie Stier.

SHAKER DESIGN

1. From Ned Cooke, "The Study of Processing American Furniture," in *Perspectives on American Furniture*, ed. Gerald W. Ward (New York: Norton, 1989), 121–23.

2. Hervey Elkins, *Fifteen Years in the Senior Order of Shakers* (Hanover, N.H.: Dartmouth Press, 1953), 49.

3. See Timothy Philbrick, "Tall Chests: The Art of Proportioning," *Fine Woodworking*, no. 9 (Winter 1977): 39–43.

4. John Kirk, *Early American Furniture* (New York: Alfred A. Knopf, 1970), 29.

5. See June Sprigg, *Shaker: Life, Work, and Art* (New York: Stewart, Tabori & Chang, 1987), 89.

6. Isaac Newton Youngs, "A Domestic Journal of Daily Occurrences," 1834, Church Family, Mount Lebanon, N.Y., NYSL, 13500.

7. Elkins, *Fifteen Years*, 39–40.

8. Charles Dickens, *American Notes for General Circulation* (London: Chapman and Hall, 1842), quoted in Flo Morse, *The Shakers and the World's People* (Hanover, N.H.: University Press of New England, 1980), 184.

9. See June Sprigg, *Shaker: Original Paints & Patinas*, exhib. cat. (Allentown, Pa.: Muhlenberg College for the Arts, 1987), 9.

10. See Dean A. Fales, Jr., *American Painted Furniture 1660–1880* (New York: Dutton, 1972), 162; and Monroe H. Fabian, *The Pennsylvania-German Decorated Chest* (New York: Universe Books, 1978), 55–56.

11. See Sprigg, *Original Paints*, 10.

12. See ibid., 13.

13. "An Extract from the Holy Orders of the Church . . . February 18th, 1841," p. 77, no. 128, WIN, 791.

14. Letter from William Deming, Hancock, to Benjamin S. Youngs, South Union, January 8, 1832, in "Copies of Letters from Different Communities from South Union for the Ministry," WRHS, IVB:35.

15. Thomas Hammond, January 13, 1835, "Journal of Thomas Hammond at the Church Family," [1831–40], Harvard, Mass., copy, WRHS, VB:40.

16. September 24 and 26, 1867, "Journal of Upper Family, Canaan, December 23, 1866–December 31, 1874," LC, 46.

17. Deming to Youngs, January 8, 1832.

18. See Sprigg, *Original Paints*, 14, n. 10. Jerry Grant, assistant director of the Shaker Museum and Library, Old Chatham, N.Y., who has done extensive research on Shaker furniture, recalls only one reference to shellac in his readings in Shaker journals, and that was "varnish with shellac."

19. Henry Cumings, "A Sketch of the Life of Caleb M. Dyer," *Enfield Advocate*, December 30, 1904.

20. "Millennial Laws," in Edward Deming Andrews, *The People Called Shakers* (New York: Oxford University Press, 1953), 286.

21. "An Extract from the Holy Orders," 78.

22. May 1, 1961, "A Domestic Journal of Domestic Occurrences Kept Originally by Joseph Bennet, and then by Isaac Crouch, Nicholas Bennet, Isaac N. Youngs, and John M. Brown," 1788–1877, Church Family, Mount Lebanon, N.Y., WRHS, VB:71.

23. Letter from Daniel Boler, Watervliet, to Orren Haskins, Mount Lebanon, May 23, 1865, WRHS, IVA:82.

24. See Fales, *American Painted Furniture*, 198.

25. Henry Blinn, "A Journey to Kentucky in the Year 1873," reprinted in *The Shaker Quarterly* 6, no. 4 (Winter 1966), 141, 143; see John T. Kirk and Jerry V. Grant, "Forty Untouched Masterpieces of Shaker Design," *The Magazine Antiques* 135, no. 5 (May 1989): 1227.

TOOLS AND TECHNOLOGY

1. See Oscar P. Fitzgerald, *Three Centuries of American Furniture* (New York: Gramercy Publishing, 1982), 4–5.

2. David Pye, *The Nature and Art of Workmanship* (New York: Van Nostrand Reinhold, 1968), 7.

3. Isaac Newton Youngs, "A Concise View of the Church of God and of Christ on Earth . . . New Lebanon," 1856, pp. 236, 455, WIN, 861.

4. "A Domestic Journal of Domestic Occurrences Kept Originally by Joseph Bennet, and then by Isaac Crouch, Nicholas Bennet, Isaac N. Youngs, and John M. Brown," 1788–1877, Church Family, Mount Lebanon, N.Y., WRHS, VB:70.

5. See Freegift Wells, "Memorandum of Events," 1812–65, Church Family, Watervliet, N.Y., WRHS, VB:296.

6. "[Census returns for the chair factory] for the year 1869," WIN, 1123.

7. Wells, "Memorandum of Events."

8. See Michael J. Ettema, "Technological Innovation and Design Economics in Furniture Manufacture," in *Winterthur Portfolio 16*, nos. 2–3 (Chicago: University of Chicago Press, 1981), 206.

9. Henry DeWitt, "Journal," Church Family, Mount Lebanon, N.Y., WRHS, VB:97.

10. Wells, "Memorandum of Events," VB:285.

11. See ibid., March 19, 1832, VB:292; and DeWitt, "Journal," January 13, 1842.

12. See Wells, "Memorandum of Events," March 15, 21, 24, April 1, 1823, VB:289.

13. See ibid., December 1859, VB:296.

14. *The Shaker* 2, no. 9 (September 1872).

15. See Ettema, "Technological Innovation," 204.

16. See Charles R. Muller and Timothy D. Rieman, *The Shaker Chair* (Winchester, Ohio: Canal Press, 1984), 172.

17. Edward Deming Andrews and Faith Andrews, *Work and Worship* (Greenwich, Conn.: New York Graphic Society, 1974), 153.

18. "History of the Church at Mount Lebanon, New York, no. 11 Carpentry," *The Manifesto* 20 (May 1890): 98–100.

19. See Wells, "Memorandum of Events," March 4, 1830, VB:292; January 8, 1816, VB:285; March 5, 1816, VB:286; January 1, 1817, VB:286.

20. *Niles' Weekly Register* (Baltimore), August 25, 1821, p. 405, OC, 1821.8.1. (R-3446).

21. See Ettema, "Technological Innovation," 207.

22. Wells, "Memorandum of Events," VB:293.

23. "Domestic Occurrences," VB:68.

24. See the letter from John Dean, Mount Lebanon, to Elder Jeremiah Lallcott, Sodus Bay, N.Y., February 19, 1833, WRHS, IVA:36.

25. Brother Philemon Stewart and Brother Isaac Newton Youngs, a woodworker himself, have chronicled the building of this machine. On December 1, 1835,

"Amos S(tewart) works at the Machine Shop considerable. I understand he has got to take the oversight of making this plaining and matching machine for the New Enfield Brethren," in *Daily Journal Kept by Philemon Stewart*, Mount Lebanon, N.Y., WRHS, VB:130, and on May 21, 1836, "Amos Stewart has this week been packing a plaining machine in readiness to transport to North Enfield. It was made this winter by Amos & Hiram [Rude] with some assistance," in Isaac Newton Youngs, "A Domestic Journal of Daily Occurrences," Church Family, Mount Lebanon, N.Y., NYSL, 13500.

26. Giles Avery, "A Journal of Domestic Events and Transactions in a Brief & Conclusive Form" [1838–47], supplement for February 1842, WRHS, VB:107.

27. Isaac Newton Youngs, "Domestic Occurrences," VB:71.

28. Wells, "Memorandum of Events," VB:296.

29. Ibid., May 8, 1862, VB:296.

30. Ibid., VB:286.

31. The Shakers are credited with inventing a tongue-and-groove machine used for architectural work on flooring or siding, but it was probably not used for furniture work. See John G. Shea, *The American Shakers and Their Furniture* (New York: Van Nostrand Reinhold, 1971), 71–73.

32. Wells, "Memorandum of Events," VB:285, 294, 296.

33. See ibid., VB:285–96.

34. DeWitt, "Journal," March 8, 1852, May 1, 1834, WRHS, VB:97.

35. Ibid., VB:97.

36. Wells, "Memorandum of Events," VB: 285–96.

THE BISHOPRICS

1. Isaac Newton Youngs, "A Concise View of the Church of God and of Christ on Earth . . . New Lebanon," 1856, p. 43, WIN, 861.

2. The names of these bishoprics have been assigned by the authors and do not necessarily reflect what the Shakers may have called them. Originally called New Lebanon, the name was changed in 1861 to Mount Lebanon, and will be referred to as such throughout this text to reflect the continuing nature of the United Society into the present.

3. See Louise Ade Boger, *The Complete Guide to Furniture Styles* (New York: Charles Scribner's Sons, 1969), 293.

4. December 12, 1850, "A Domestic Journal of Domestic Occurrences Kept Originally by Joseph Bennet, and then by Isaac Crouch, Nicholas Bennet, Isaac N. Youngs, and John M. Brown," 1788–1877, Church Family, Mount Lebanon, N.Y., WRHS, VB:70.

5. Elisha D. Blakeman and James S. Glass, "A Daily Journal or Diary, of Work &c. Performed by the Boys and Their Caretaker, in the First Order, New Lebanon, Columbia Co., N.Y." OC, 7212.

6. Youngs, "A Concise View."

7. See John Scherer, *New York State Furniture at the New York State Museum* (Old Town Alexandria, Va.: Highland House, 1983), 107, no. 105.

8. Giles Avery, "A Register of Incidents and Events . . . Kept by Giles B. Avery," October 20, 1859–December 21, 1874, December 21, p. 137, NYPL-1.

9. Giles Avery, "Pocket Diary for 1880," February and March, WRHS, VB:125.

10. "A Domestic Journal of Domestic Occurrences," VB:71; Henry DeWitt, "Journal," Church Family, Mount Lebanon, N.Y., WRHS, VB:97.

11. Benjamin Lyon, January 24, 1817, "Journal of Benjamin Lyon of Canaan, June 12, 1816–February 8, 1818," LC 43; "Domestic Occurrences," 1838 supplement, VB:69; ibid, February 1849 supplement, VB:70.

12. Freegift Wells, January 14, 1823, and December 4, 1834, "Memorandum of Events," 1812–65, Church Family, Watervliet, N.Y., WRHS, VB:289, 293.

13. Hervey Elkins, *Fifteen Years in the Senior Order of Shakers* (Hanover, N.H.: Dartmouth Press, 1953), 77.

14. "An Extract from the Holy Orders of the Church . . . February 18th, 1841," p. 55, WIN, 791.

15. Ibid., 56.

16. Wells, "Memorandum of Events," VB:288.

17. Charles Nordhoff, *The Communistic Societies of the United States . . .* (New York: Harper & Brothers, 1875), quoted in Flo Morse, *The Shakers and the World's People* (Hanover, N.H.: University Press of New England, 1980), 113.

18. Youngs, "A Concise View," 485.

19. DeWitt, "Journal," 1836, WRHS, VB:97, quoted in Jerry V. Grant and Douglas R. Allen, *Shaker Furniture Makers* (Hanover, N.H.: University Press of New England, 1989), 72; and DeWitt, "Journal," March 7 and 21, 1854.

20. See Grant and Allen, *Shaker Furniture Makers*, 10.

21. Jessie Evans, Diary, June 30, 1938, CAN.

22. See Stephen J. Stein, *The Shaker Experience in America* (New Haven: Yale University Press, 1992), 376.

23. John Crosby Freeman, *Forgotten Rebel* (Watkins Glen, N.Y.: Century House, 1966), 13–14.

24. David Cathers, *Furniture of the American Arts & Crafts Movement* (New York: New American Library, 1981), quoted in Charles R. Muller and Timothy D. Rieman, *The Shaker Chair* (Winchester, Ohio: Canal Press, 1984), App. A, 5.

25. Charles Sheeler, in Constance Rourke, *Charles Sheeler: Artist in the American Tradition* (New York: Harcourt, Brace & World, 1938), quoted in Morse, *The Shakers and The World's People*, 138.

26. Philippe Garner, ed., *The Encyclopedia of the Decorative Arts* (New York: Van Nostrand Reinhold, 1978), 34.

27. *Arkitekten*, October 1930.

28. See Charles R. Muller, *The Shaker Way* (Worthington: Ohio Antiques Review, 1979), 105–6.

29. Mildred Barker in Linda Galway, "Sister Mildred Dies at Sabbathday Lake," *The Shaker Messenger* 12, no. 2 (Winter 1990): 8.

30. Ken Ames in "Chief of History at State Museum Takes Holistic View of 19th-Century Collections," *Antiques and the Arts Weekly*, 1990.

31. Derek Ostergard, *George Nakashima Full Circle* (New York: Weidenfeld & Nicolson, 1989), [1].

32. See ibid., 148.

33. Mira Nakashima-Yarnall, letter to the author, September 8, 1990.

MOUNT LEBANON BISHOPRIC

1. See Sotheby Parke Bernet, New York, *Important Shaker Furniture and Related Decorative Arts: The William L. Lassiter Collection*, sales cat. (November 13, 1981), lot 37.

2. The original name, New Lebanon, was changed in 1861 to Mount Lebanon and will be referred to as such throughout this text to reflect the continuing nature of the United Society into the present; see Stephen J. Stein, *The Shaker Experience in America* (New Haven: Yale University Press, 1992), 11–12.

3. See Franklin Ellis, *History of Columbia County, New York* (Philadelphia: Everts & Ensign, 1878), 308.

4. See Priscilla J. Brewer, *Shaker Communities, Shaker Lives* (Hanover, N.H.: University Press of New England, 1986), 215; Roger Hall, "Mount Lebanon Preservation Funds Granted," *The Shaker Messenger* 11, no. 4 (Summer 1989): 19.

5. See Charles L. Flint, *Mount Lebanon Shaker Collection* (New Lebanon, N.Y.: Mount Lebanon Shaker Village, 1988), ix.

6. See "Shakers Leave Mt. Lebanon, Merge with Hancock Group," [newspaper clipping], December 20, 1947, HAN, 9757 B512.

7. See Wendell Hess, "Moses Johnson: Apostate or True Believer?," *The Shaker Messenger* 10, no. 2 (Winter 1988): 9.

8. Charles Nordhoff, *The Communistic Societies of the United States . . .* (New York: Harper & Brothers, 1875), 136–37.

9. "[Inventory of property the] Widow Abigale Hawkins brought with Her," WRHS, IVA:30.

10. Joseph Bennet, Jr., in Charles R. Muller and Timothy D. Rieman, *The Shaker Chair* (Winchester, Ohio: Canal Press, 1984), 132.

11. See Edward Deming Andrews and Faith Andrews, *Shaker Furniture* (New Haven: Yale University Press, 1937), 73.

12. For biographical information on David Rowley, see Jerry V. Grant and Douglas R. Allen, *Shaker Furniture Makers* (Hanover, N.H.: University Press of New England, 1989), 17–21.

13. For biographical information on Isaac Newton Youngs, see Grant and Allen, *Shaker Furniture Makers*, 35–51.

14. A pine clock case, courtesy of the Shaker Museum and Library, Old Chatham, N.Y., illustrated in James W. Gibbs and Robert W. Meader, *Shaker Clock Makers* (Columbia, Pa.: National Association of Watch and Clock Collectors, n.d.), fig. 10, has been attributed to this maker, but physical examination fails to confirm this statement.

15. For biographical information on Giles Avery, see Grant and Allen, *Shaker Furniture Makers*, 112–15.

16. A case of drawers with the initials AB is illustrated in Grant and Allen, *Shaker Furniture Makers*, 5, fig. 3.

17. For biographical information on Elisha Blakeman, see ibid., 102–9.

18. For biographical information on Charles Weed, see ibid., 52–53.

19. See ibid., 103.

20. See ibid., 92.

21. See ibid., 105.

22. According to auctioneer James Julia, a signed five-drawer case of drawers with bracket base was sold at auction on August 27/28, 1992, in Fairfield, Me.

23. See Grant and Allen, *Shaker Furniture Makers*, 19–20.

24. Quoted in ibid., 21.

25. See ibid., 52.

26. See Benjamin Lyon, "Journal of Benjamin Lyon of Canaan, June 12, 1816–February 8, 1818," LC, 43.

27. Quoted in Grant and Allen, *Shaker Furniture Makers*, 113.

28. New Lebanon Church Family Account Books, according to Grant and Allen, 6.

29. See "A History of the Lower [Canaan] Family Commenced in 1869 and Continued Annually Thereafter," Mount Lebanon, N.Y., WRHS, VB:84; "Lebanon Springs," *Berkshire County Eagle*, March 4, 1875, 3.

30. Philip Zea, curator, Historic Deerfield, Mass., telephone conversation with author, August 1991.

31. See John Kassay, *The Book of Shaker Furniture* (Amherst: University of Massachusetts, 1980), 34; Herbert F. Schiffer, comp., *Shaker Architecture* (Exton, Pa.: Schiffer Publishing, 1979), 56; and Sotheby Parke Bernet, *Important Shaker Furniture*, 41.

32. See Flint, *Mount Lebanon Shaker Collection*, 42.

33. See "A Domestic Journal of Domestic Occurrences Kept Originally by Joseph Bennet, and then by Isaac Crouch, Nicholas Bennet, Isaac N. Youngs, and John M. Brown," 1788–1877, Church Family, Mount Lebanon, N.Y., WRHS, VB:67; and Grant and Allen, *Shaker Furniture Makers*, 56.

34. See Grant and Allen, *Shaker Furniture Makers*, 56, 58.

35. Illustrated in ibid., pl. 34.

36. See Edward Deming Andrews, *Religion in Wood* (Bloomington: Indiana University Press, 1966), 91.

37. The case piece illustrated in Flint, *Mount Lebanon Shaker Collection*, 28–29, has the same joinery detail.

38. "Records Kept by the Order of the Church."

39. Ibid.

40. Journals that mention the purchase of worldly furniture for the new Church Family Dwelling House include "Domestic Occurrences," WRHS, VB:71; Journals and Diaries kept by Giles B. Avery, WRHS, VB:123, 124; and "Records Kept by the Order of the Church at New Lebanon, New York," vol. 4, August 13, 1871–August 31, 1905, OC, 10,343.

41. "Domestic Occurrences," VB:71, quoted in Grant and Allen, *Shaker Furniture Makers*, 7.

42. "Records Kept by the Order of the Church."

43. See Flint, *Mount Lebanon Shaker Collection*, 62.

44. Daniel Crossman, Diary, OC, 19211.

45. Ibid., August 26, 1881; Anna Dodgson and Cornelia French, "A Family Journal Kept by Order of the Deaconesses 1886–92," 1888, OC, 8853; and "Domestic Occurrences," supplement to January 1857, WRHS, VB:71.

46. Illustrated in the Women's Auxiliary of the United Cerebral Palsy Association of Greater Hartford, Hartford, Conn., *The Shakers: An Exhibition Concerning Their Furniture, Artifacts and Religion with Emphasis on Enfield, Connecticut,* exhib. cat. (1975), no. 38.

47. See "Domestic Occurrences," April 8, 1858, VB:71; February 28, 1859, VB:71; and Grant and Allen, *Shaker Furniture Makers*, 116.

48. Illustrated in Grant and Allen, *Shaker Furniture Makers*, 63–64.

49. Elisha Blakeman, "The Boy's Journal of Work," 1844–65, Mount Lebanon, WRHS, VB:137.

50. "Millennial Laws," pt. I, sec. 4, no. 8, reprinted in Edward Deming Andrews, *The People Called Shakers* (New York: Oxford University Press, 1953), 257.

51. See A. D. Emerich and Arlen Benning, *Shaker: Furniture and Objects from the Faith and Edward Deming Andrews Collections* (Washington, D.C.: Smithsonian Institution Press, published for The Renwick Gallery of the National Collections of Fine Arts, 1973), 48.

52. See Kassay, *The Book of Shaker Furniture*, 57, no. 21; see also pl. 80 in "Watervliet Community, New York."

53. Illustrated in Ejner Hanbert, *Shop Drawings of Shaker Furniture and Woodenware*, vol. 2 (Stockbridge, Mass.: Berkshire Traveler Press, 1975), 4–5.

54. "Journal of a Shaker Community at Canaan, 1813–43," Upper Canaan Family, Mount Lebanon, N.Y., LC, 40, quoted in Grant and Allen, *Shaker Furniture Makers*, 6.

55. Bertha Lindsay, personal interview with Mary Boswell, former curator, Canterbury Shaker Village, November 26, 1985.

56. Letter from the ministry, Mount Lebanon, to Elder Peter Long, Groveland, December 19, 1865, WRHS, IVA:25.

57. See Flint, *Mount Lebanon Shaker Collection*, 2–3.

58. See June Sprigg, *Shaker Design* (New York: Whitney Museum of American Art, 1986), 86–87, no. 40.

59. See "Domestic Occurrences," VB:70.

60. Illustrated in Grant and Allen, *Shaker Furniture Makers*, 92, fig. 66.

61. Illustrated in Robert F. W. Meader, *Illustrated Guide to Shaker Furniture* (New York: Dover, 1982), 73, pl. 139.

62. Illustrated in Grant and Allen, *Shaker Furniture Makers*, 93, fig. 67.

63. Illustrated in ibid., 97, fig. 74.

64. Illustrated in ibid., 99, fig. 76.

65. Illustrated in ibid., 101, fig. 79.

66. See ibid., 97.

67. "Farm Journal," 1858–67, [Church

Family Second Order, Mount Lebanon, N.Y.], HAN, 401.

68. See *Dictionary of American Biography* (New York: Charles Scribner's Sons, 1964), 457–58.

69. See Edward Deming Andrews, *Work and Worship* (Greenwich, Conn.: New York Graphic Society, 1974), 53, 60.

70. This photograph was originally published in *New York State Museum Bulletin* 323 (1941): 108.

71. See Edward Deming Andrews and Faith Andrews, *Shaker Furniture* (New Haven: Yale University Press, 1937), 73.

72. Reproduced in Andrews, *Shaker Furniture*, pl. 11.

73 "Records Kept by the Order of the Church."

74. See June Sprigg, *Shaker: Life, Work, and Art* (New York: Stewart, Tabori & Chang, 1987), 72.

75. See "Collections Report," *Shaker Museum Report* 1, no. 1 (May 1990): [3].

76. "Holy Orders of the Church Written by Father Joseph to the Elders of the Church at New Lebanon . . . ," 1841, WIN, 792, quoted in Sprigg, *Life, Work and Art*, 43.

77. See Index of American Design, WPA Federal Art Project, 1935–36, nos. V-128 and V-93. The latter is illustrated in John G. Shea, *The American Shakers and Their Furniture* (New York: Van Nostrand Reinhold, 1971), 85.

78. See Sprigg, *Shaker Design*, 54.

79. Illustrated in Muller and Rieman, *The Shaker Chair*, 157.

80. Isaac Newton Youngs, quoted in Martha Wetherbee and Nathan Taylor, *Shaker Baskets* (Sanbornton, N.H.: Martha Wetherbee Basket Shop, 1988), 88.

81. See Paula Laverty, "The Sewing Tables of the Shaker Sisters at Mount Lebanon, New York," May 10, 1989, OC.

82. See ibid.

83. See ibid.

84. "A Great Fire," OC, 1875.2.9.

85. See Kassay, *The Book of Shaker Furniture*, 191.

86. See Sprigg, *Shaker Design*, pl. 24.

87. "Millennial Laws," pt. 2, sec. 10, no. 3, reprinted in Andrews, *The People Called Shakers*, 272.

88. See Skinner Inc., auctioneers and appraisers, Bolton, Mass., *Americana*, sales cat. (March 25, 1989), lot 118.

89. See Sprigg, *Shaker Design*, pl. 25.

90. For attribution to Gilbert Avery, see Decorative Arts Photographic Collection at Winterthur, acc. no. 69.306; for acquisition history, see *Shaker: A Uniquely American Aesthetic* (New York: David A. Schorsch Incorporated, n.d.), n.p.

91. David Schorsch, telephone conversation with author, July 1991.

92. Illustrated in Gibbs and Meader, *Shaker Clock Makers*, 6.

93. See Grant and Allen, *Shaker Furniture Makers*, 36.

94. See ibid., 38–42.

95. See Muller and Rieman, *The Shaker Chair*, 132.

96. See ibid., 136–37.

97. See ibid., 158, 169.

98. See ibid., 169.

99. See ibid., 211.

100. Letter from Sister Frances Hall, Mount Lebanon, to Margaret Brown, Rye, N.Y., [collection of items relating to Shaker furniture], February 3, 1944, WIN, 1089.

101. United States Patent Office specification, March 2, 1852, no. 8771.

102. Ibid.

103. See Muller and Rieman, *The Shaker Chair*, 189.

104. James Prescott, Diary, October 5, 1860, describing a visit to Mount Lebanon, Collection Ohio Historical Society, quoted in Muller and Rieman, *The Shaker Chair*, 153.

WATERVLIET, NEW YORK

1. Reproduced in Elmer Pearson, Julia Neal, and Walter Muir Whitehill, *The Shaker Image* (Boston: New York Graphic Society, 1974), 98, pl. 72.

2. Illustrated in John Kassay, *The Book of Shaker Furniture* (Amherst: University of Massachusetts, 1980), 130–31.

3. Donald MacDonald, Diaries, 1824, Shaker Museum and Library, Old Chatham, N.Y., quoted in Dorothy M. Filley, *Recapturing Wisdom's Valley: The Watervliet Shaker Heritage 1775–1975* (Colonie, N.Y.: Town of Colonie and Albany Institute of History and Art, 1975), 12.

4. See Edward Deming and Faith Andrews, *Work and Worship* (Greenwich, Conn.: New York Graphic Society, 1974), 14.

5. See Filley, *Recapturing Wisdom's Valley*, 20, 30, 97.

6. See Priscilla J. Brewer, *Shaker Communities, Shaker Lives* (Hanover, N.H.: University Press of New England, 1986), 215.

7. See Edward Deming Andrews, *The Community Industries of the Shakers* (Albany: University of the State of New York, 1932), 49, 130.

8. Elder Goepper, *The Manifesto* (June 1887), quoted in Andrews, *Community Industries*, 130.

9. See Filley, *Recapturing Wisdom's Valley*, 44, 61.

10. See Andrews, *Community Industries*, 77.

11. See Edward Deming Andrews and Faith Andrews, *Shaker Furniture* (New Haven: Yale University Press, 1937), 111.

12. Reproduced in *New York State Museum Bulletin* 323 (1941): 114.

13. The authors wish to thank the Library, Hancock Shaker Village, Inc., Pittsfield, Mass., Robert Meader, and Magda Gabor-Hotchkiss for their assistance with this chart. Glendyne Wergland shared the Youngs family tree from her Master's thesis, "One Shaker Life: Isaac Newton Youngs: 1793–1865," Mount Holyoke College, October 1991, copyright © 1992.

14. See, for example, Jessie Evans, Diaries, 1892–1931, CAN, March 27, 1900: "The south dining room of office is being painted by Mr. Dearborn of Upland. The first ornamental house painting done at the village. Oak leaf trimming and graining."

15. Jean Palardy, *The Early Furniture of French Canada* (Toronto: Macmillan of Canada, 1965), pls. 180–81.

16. See Jerry V. Grant and Douglas R. Allen, *Shaker Furniture Makers* (Hanover, N.H.: University Press of New England, 1989), 2–23.

17. Illustrated in ibid., 28, 30.

18. See Palardy, *The Early Furniture of French Canada*, pl. 376.

19. Illustrated in Edward Deming Andrews, *Religion in Wood* (Bloomington: Indiana University Press, 1966), 81.

20. Thomas Brown, *Account of the People Called Shakers: Their Faith, Doctrines, and Practice* (Troy: Parker and Bliss, 1812), 360.

21. See Helen Comstock, *American Furniture* (Exton, Pa.: Schiffer Publishing, n.d.), 14; and John Fleming and Hugh Honour, *Dictionary of the Decorative Arts* (New York: Harper & Row, 1977), s.v. "Chest of Drawers."

22. See Sotheby Parke Bernet, New York, *Important Shaker Furniture and Related Decorative Arts: The William L. Lassiter Collection*, sales cat. (November 13, 1981), no. 128.

HANCOCK BISHOPRIC

1. See Priscilla J. Brewer, *Shaker Communities, Shaker Lives* (Hanover, N.H.: University Press of New England, 1986), 231; John Harlow Ott, *Hancock Shaker Village: A Guidebook and History*, (Shaker Community, Inc., 1976), 30.

2. See Brewer, *Shaker Communities*, 231; *The Connecticut Quarterly* 3, no. 4 (October–December 1897).

3. Rebecca Clark, quoted in Ott, *Hancock Shaker Village*, 21, 23, 25.

4. Quoted in ibid., 26.

5. Quoted in ibid., 117.
6. Letter from Grove Wright, Hancock, to Grove Blanchard, Harvard, December 26, 1853, WRHS, IVA:10.
7. Letter from Evert A. Duyckinck to his wife, August 1851, in Luther Stearns Mansfield, "Glimpses of Herman Melville's Life in Pittsfield, 1850–1851: Some Unpublished Letters of Evert A. Duyckinck," *American Literature*, March 1937 (Duyckinck was a literary friend of Melville and Hawthorne), quoted in Flo Morse, *The Shakers and the World's People* (Hanover, N.H.: University Press of New England, 1980), 194.
8. See George Albert, "A Flying Visit," *The Manifesto* (December 1876): 94.
9. *Connecticut Quarterly* 3, no. 4 (October–December 1897): 467.
10. George Noyes Miller, "Notes on the Shakers," *The Manifesto* (July 1877): 51.
11. See Ott, *Hancock Shaker Village*, Bibliography, 133–35.
12. Calvin Ely, "Diary Kept by Calvin Ely, 1780–1816," WRHS, VB:11.
13. Letter from Thomas Damon, Hancock, to George Wilcox, Hancock, December 1846, quoted in Jerry V. Grant and Douglas R. Allen, *Shaker Furniture Makers* (Hanover, N.H.: University Press of New England, 1989), 132.
14. See Ott, *Hancock Shaker Village*, 54.
15. See Irving Greenwood, "Notebook of Information . . . " [c. 1782–1939], CAN, 28.
16. "Down in Tyringham. As a New York Correspondent Saw Things," *The Pittsfield Sun*, September 15, 1887, 6, reprinted from the *New York Evening Post*.
17. See Ott, *Hancock Shaker Village*, 56.
18. See Elaine Piraino-Holevoet, "Enfield, Connecticut," HAN, letter from Richard Steinert to Elaine Piraino-Holevoet, August 30, 1977.
19. See "Fine Collection of Shaker Material in Hands of Historical Society," *Springfield Republican*, January 6, 1924.
20. See "Shakers Leave Mt. Lebanon, Merge with Hancock Group," [magazine clipping] HAN, 9757 B512; Ott, *Hancock Shaker Village*, 159.
21. Letter from Dale Covington, Shaker scholar and author, to the author, June 4, 1992.
22. The dumbwaiter is illustrated in June Sprigg, *Shaker: Life, Work, and Art* (New York: Stewart, Tabori & Chang, 1987), 69.
23. See Ott, *Hancock Shaker Village*, 73.
24. Letter from William Deming, Hancock, to Benjamin S. Youngs, South Union, Ky., January 8, 1832, in "Copies of Letters from Different Communities from South Union for the Ministry,"

WRHS, IVB:35, and Ott, *Hancock Shaker Village*, 73–74.
25. Deming to Youngs, January 8, 1832.
26. Chest-on-chest, signed Ruben Beman, 1780–1800, Litchfield County, Connecticut, acc. no. 51.22.
27. Illustrated in June Sprigg, *Shaker Design* (New York: Whitney Museum of American Art, 1986), fig. 12.
28. See "Millennial Laws," pt. 3, sec. 5, reprinted in Edward Deming Andrews, *The People Called Shakers* (New York: Oxford University Press, 1953), 283.
29. See Grant and Allen, *Shaker Furniture Makers*, 83.
30. See Ott, *Hancock Shaker Village*, 77.
31. Illustrated in June Sprigg, "Marked Shaker Furnishings," *The Magazine Antiques*, 115, no. 5 (May 1979): 1053, pl. 9.
32. Illustrated in Edward Deming Andrews and Faith Andrews, *Shaker Furniture* (New Haven: Yale University Press, 1937), pl. 8.
33. Illustrated in John Kassay, *The Book of Shaker Furniture* (Amherst: University of Mass., 1980), 205.
34. Illustrated in Grant and Allen, *Shaker Furniture Makers*, 161.
35. See ibid.
36. *Connecticut Quarterly* 3, no. 4 (October–December 1897): 465.
37. Ibid.
38. See Morrison Heckscher, *American Chippendale Furniture in the Metropolitan Museum of Art* (New York: The Metropolitan Museum of Art and Random House, 1985), 191.
39. Illustrated in *Divine Design: A Shaker Legacy*, exhib. cat. (Philadelphia: The 1991 Philadelphia Antiques Show, 1991), 47.
40. The date on this inscription suggests Brother Abner was born in 1782 or 1783. However, census records confirm his year of birth as 1776.
41. Letter from the ministry, Enfield, Conn., to Grove Blanchard, Harvard, December 20, 1852, WRHS, IVA:10, quoted in Grant and Allen, *Shaker Furniture Makers*, 77.
42. See ibid., 78.
43. See Constance Rourke, *Charles Sheeler: Artist in the American Tradition* (1938; reprint, New York: Kennedy Galleries and Da Capo Press, 1969).
44. See the Women's Auxiliary of the United Cerebral Palsy Association of Greater Hartford, Hartford, Conn., *The Shakers: An Exhibition Concerning Their Furniture, Artifacts and Religion with Emphasis on Enfield, Connecticut*, exhib. cat. (1975), 7.
45. Illustrated in Sprigg, *Shaker Design*, 26–27, pl. 2; also Willis Henry Auctions,

Inc., Marshfield, Mass., *Shaker Auction*, sales cat. (September 22, 1991), no. 105.
46. Letter from Harry Alden, wood researcher, Tallahassee, Fla., to author, December 14, 1989.
47. Willis Henry Auctions, Inc., Marshfield, Mass., *Shaker Auction*, sales cat. (August 5, 1990), fig. 179.
48. Reproduced in Muller and Rieman, *The Shaker Chair*, 79.

HARVARD BISHOPRIC

1. See Jerry V. Grant and Douglas R. Allen, *Shaker Furniture Makers* (Hanover, N.H.: University Press of New England, 1989), 121.
2. July 4, 1861, "Daily Record of Activities both at Harvard and Shirley, Mass.," VB:55. Note that book no. 2 is miscatalogued in WRHS as "Journal Kept by an Unidentified Resident," under Shirley, VB:219, rather than Harvard.
3. "Journal Kept by an Unidentified Resident," 1856–59, Harvard, WRHS, VB:219 (miscatalogued as Shirley).
4. The authors would like to thank Maggie Stier, curator of Fruitlands Museums, for generously sharing research material on the Harvard Shakers and reading this chapter critically.
5. Roxalana Grosvernor, "Circumstances Regarding the Square House as Related by Br. Abel Jewett, Jona. Clark Jr, and Others," 1846, from "Sayings of Mother Ann and the First Elders Gathered from Different Individuals, at Harvard and Shirley Who Were Eye and Ear Witnesses," c. 1846, SDL.
6. See Diana Van Kolken, "A Journey to the Good Ol' Days at Shirley," *The Shaker Messenger* 4, no. 1 (Fall 1981): 10.
7. See Edward R. Horgan, *The Shaker Holy Land* (Harvard: Harvard Common Press, 1982), 70.
8. See Priscilla J. Brewer, *Shaker Communities, Shaker Lives* (Hanover, N.H.: University Press of New England, 1986), 217.
9. Rev. William Bentley, quoted in Russell W. Knight, "Rev. William Bentley Visits the Shakers," *Shaker Quarterly* 4, no. 1 (Spring 1964): 3–12.
10. See Maggie Stier, "'A Good Name Is Better than Riches': The Harvard Shakers' Commerce with the World," *The Shaker Quarterly* 20, no. 2 (Summer 1992): 52–64.
11. *Catalogue of Fruit Trees, Etc. Raised in the Shaker Nursery, Harvard, Mass.* Elijah Myrick, South Groton, Mass. (Boston: Geo. C. Rand & Ayer, n.d.).

12. See Steir, "'A Good Name Is Better than Riches.'"

13. Charles Nordhoff, *The Communistic Societies of the United States . . .* (New York: Harper & Brothers, 1875), 194.

14. Abigail M. Alcott, August 26, 1843, in *Journals of Bronson Alcott*, ed. Odell Shepard (Boston: Little, Brown, 1938), 154.

15. William Dean Howells, "A Shaker Village," *Atlantic Monthly* 37 (June 1876): 699–710.

16. See Horgan, *The Shaker Holy Land*, 149–50.

17. See ibid., 151–52.

18. See Grant and Allen, *Shaker Furniture Makers*, 11.

19. "Journal of Daily Events, Sept. 1910–Jan. 1920," Mount Lebanon, OC, 8851, 9758N5.

20. See Charles R. Muller and Timothy D. Rieman, *The Shaker Chair* (Winchester, Ohio: Canal Press, 1984), 61.

21. See Muller and Rieman, *The Shaker Chair*, 61.

22. Letter from Eldress Josephine Jilson, Harvard, to Wallace Cathcart, Cleveland, 1919, WRHS, IVA:28.

23. "Financial Accounts 1826–1836," Harvard, FM.

24. Clara Endicott Sears, *Gleanings from Old Shaker Journals* (Boston: Houghton Mifflin, 1916), 273.

25. Letter from Watch-Hill, R.I., to Grove Blanchard, August 25, 1853, WRHS, IVA:26.

26. Letter from Hancock, West Pittsfield, Mass., to Grove Blanchard, December 2, 1853, WRHS, IVA:20.

27. Thomas Damon, "Memoranda, &c Mostly of Events and Things Which Have Transpired since the First of Jan 1846," Hancock, Mass., NYSL.

28. See Charles L. Flint, *Mount Lebanon Shaker Collection* (New Lebanon, N.Y.: Mount Lebanon Shaker Village, 1988), 41.

29. "Daily Record of Activities," VB:54.

30. Letter from Mrs. Robert Reed, Madison, Wis., to Ms. Androski, Skinner Inc., auctioneers and appraisers, Bolton, Mass., April 15, 1991.

31. Information based on a paint analysis conducted for Hancock Shaker Village by Williamstown Regional Art Conservation Laboratory, Inc., 1992.

32. Thomas Hammond, "Journal of Thomas Hammond at the Church Family," [1831–40], Harvard, copy, WRHS, VB:40.

33. Maggie Stier, curator, Fruitlands Museums, Harvard, telephone conversation with author, September 11, 1991; and "Record of Succession in the Ministry at Harvard and Shirley, and of the Journeys Undertaken by the Ministry from 1791 to 1880," WRHS, VB:59.

THE NEW HAMPSHIRE BISHOPRIC

1. Leona Rowell, personal interview with author, October 8, 1989.

2. The authors are deeply indebted to Robert Emlen, currently director of the John Nicholas Brown Center, Providence, R.I., for generously sharing his pioneering research on Enfield, New Hampshire, furniture, initiated in 1978. Information from this unpublished manuscript regarding construction similarities between woodwork in the Great Stone Dwelling and Enfield freestanding furniture has been included in this chapter. Wendell Hess, engaged in a long-term study of Enfield, has also been instrumental in providing documentation on Enfield cabinetmakers, through journal references as well as conversations with the last Canterbury Shakers.

3. See Henry C. Blinn, "A Historical Record of the Society of Believers in Canterbury, N.H. . . . vol 2. [vol. 1?] East Canterbury, 1892," pp. 10, 25, 26, CAN, 763.

4. See Wendell Hess, *The Enfield (N.H.) Shakers: A Brief History* (published by Wendell Hess, 1988), 10, 11.

5. See *The Manifesto* 12, nos. 11–13 (1882–83), CAN.

6. There are three boxes that are attributed to Father Job—two at the Philadelphia Museum of Art and one at the United Society of Shakers, Sabbathday Lake, Maine.

7. See Hess, *The Enfield Shakers*, 42, 48.

8. See Robert Emlen, "The Great Stone Dwelling of the Enfield, New Hampshire Shakers," *Old-Time New England* 69, no. 3 (January–June 1979): 69–71.

9. Letter from the ministry at Enfield to the New Lebanon Ministry, November 13, 1839, quoted in Emlen, "The Great Stone Dwelling," 77–78.

10. The authors would like to credit Robert Emlen with this observation.

11. Nancy E. Moore, "Journal of a Trip to the Various Societies, September 1854–October 1854," WRHS, quoted in Emlen, "The Great Stone Dwelling," 78.

12. See Hess, *The Enfield Shakers*, 46.

13. July 4, 1840, "New Lebanon Ministry Sisters' Journal," quoted in Edward Deming Andrews and Faith Andrews, *Shaker Furniture* (New Haven: Yale University Press, 1937), 19.

14. Illustrated in *Canterbury Shaker Village: Guide to the Collection* (Canterbury, N.H.: Shaker Village, Inc., 1983), cover and no. 14.

15. See Hess, *The Enfield Shakers*, 46, 48.

16. Community Building History, Canterbury, private collection.

17. Ibid.

18. Francis Winkley, "Journal," 1784–1845, Canterbury, CAN, 25.

19. "Millennial Laws," pt. 4, no. 22, reprinted in Edward Deming Andrews, *The People Called Shakers* (New York: Oxford University Press, 1953), 288.

20. Community Building History.

21. Illustrated in Scott T. Swank, *Arts of the Pennsylvania Germans* (New York: Norton, 1983), 163, fig. 102.

22. Community Building History.

23. Ibid.

24. See Blinn, "A Historical Record of . . . Canterbury," 29.

25. See Jerry Grant, "Collections Note," *Shaker Museum Report* 1, no. 2 (October 1990).

26. Community Building History.

27. "Dates of Buildings, 1889," Canterbury, CAN, 1984.13, 15.

28. Other examples are illustrated in *Shaker Messenger* 14, no. 1 (Spring 1992): 4, and 8, no. 1 (Fall 1985): inside cover.

29. The authors would like to credit Doug Hamel, antiques dealer, with this observation.

30. The photograph was published in *Granite Monthly* (Concord, N.H.) 16 (May 1894): 324, accompanying the article "A Glimpse into the Inner Circle" by Agatha B.E. Chandler. The authors would like to thank Magda Gabor-Hotchkiss, associate librarian of Hancock Shaker Village and annotator of the forthcoming second edition of *The Shaker Image* (Boston: New York Graphic Society, 1974) for sharing her research on the identity of the sisters pictured here.

31. The name suggested by these initials and the corresponding life dates were acquired from a membership list maintained by the Canterbury Shakers on notecards at the community and now in the archives at the museum.

32. See *The Manifesto* 13, no. 5 (May 1883), 104–6.

33. See Henry C. Blinn, "Church Record, Canterbury, 1784–1879," [vol. 2] pp. 129, 131, CAN, 764.

34. Mary Ann Sanborn at Canterbury Shaker Village, who directed the authors to the information in Blinn, is currently researching this newly discovered industry at Canterbury.

35. Illustrated in the Willis Henry Auctions, Inc., Marshfield, Mass., *Shaker Auction*,

sales cat. (August 4, 1985), no. 109.

36. See Blinn, "Church Record, Canterbury," 220.

37. Josephine E. Wilson, Diaries, 1911–16, 1917–40, Canterbury, CAN, 1985.45–49, 51–74.

38. See Lita Solis-Cohen, "A Double Sewing Desk at Tepper," *Maine Antique Digest,* February 1990: 18-A.

39. *In Memoriam: Elder Henry C. Blinn 1824–1902* (Concord, N.H.: Rumford Printing, 1905).

40. See Blinn, "A Historical Record of ... Canterbury," 30–31.

41. See Joseph Downs, *American Furniture: Queen Anne and Chippendale Periods in the Henry Francis du Pont Winterthur Museum* (New York: Macmillan, 1952).

42. Illustrated in Robert F.W. Meader, *Illustrated Guide to Shaker Furniture* (New York: Dover, 1982), pl. 114.

43. Illustrated in John Kassay, *The Book of Shaker Furniture* (Amherst: University of Massachusetts, 1980), 243, pl. 14.

44. *Letters and Numbers of Houses,* 1883, Canterbury, CAN, 1763.

45. See Charles Robinson, *The Shakers and Their Homes* (East Canterbury, N.H.: Shaker Village, Inc., 1893), 110. According to Irving Greenwood, "Notebook of Information" (CAN, 28), all stereopticon views were taken by Kimball between 1870 and 1880.

46. "The Shakers in 1853: Two Busy Summer Days at the Church Family," *Enfield Advocate,* July 20, 1906.

47. See Beverly Gordon, *Shaker Textile Arts* (Hanover, N.H.: University Press of New England, 1980), 130.

48. See Charles R. Muller and Timothy D. Rieman, *The Shaker Chair* (Winchester, Ohio: Canal Press, 1984), 200.

49. See Muller and Rieman, *The Shaker Chair,* 3.

50. See *Plain & Elegant, Rich & Common Documented New Hampshire Furniture, 1750–1859* (Concord: New Hampshire Historical Society, 1979), 74.

51. Illustrated in *Maine Antique Digest,* March 1982: 19B.

52. Illustrated in June Sprigg, *Shaker: Life, Work, and Art* (New York: Stewart, Tabori & Chang, 1987), 171.

53. See Jessie Evans, Diary, Canterbury, November 3, 1923, CAN, 1985.6–4.3.

54. Illustrated in Willis Henry Auctions, Inc., Marshfield, Mass. *The Karl Mendel Shaker Collection,* sales cat. (September 25, 1988), no. 160.

55. See Blinn, "A Historical Record of ... Canterbury," 132–33.

56. Membership Records, Enfield, N.H., CAN, 156.

57. Wallace Nutting, *Furniture Treasury* (New York: Macmillan, 1954), pl. 976.

58. See Hamilton Child, *Gazetteer of Grafton County* (Syracuse: Syracuse Journal Company, 1886).

59. See Mary Lyn Ray, *True Gospel Simplicity: Shaker Furniture in New Hampshire* (Concord: New Hampshire Historical Society, 1974), no. 3.

60. See Evans, Diary, November 6, 1923.

61. Irving Greenwood, Daily Diaries, 1894–1939, Canterbury, CAN, 270.

62. Letter from Franklin Youngs, January 1924, scrapbook compiled by Nellie Pierce of Enfield, New Hampshire Material, CAN, 1984.9.

63. Eldress Bertha Lindsay (1897–1990), personal interview with author, 1989.

64. See *Plain & Elegant,* pls. 12, 29, 58, 59.

65. Letter from Ashton Willard to the Honorable and Mrs. H. C. Willard, September 23, 1878, Willard Papers, courtesy Vermont Historical Society, Montpelier. Willard's letter and sketch of the bench arrangement is reproduced in Robert Emlen, "Ashton Willard Goes to Meeting," *The Shaker Messenger* 6, no. 2 (Winter 1984): 8–9.

66. Letter from Robert Emlen to the author, September 11, 1992.

67. [Journal of a Trip from Enfield, Connecticut, to Shaker Communities in Maine, New Hampshire, and Massachusetts, c. 1875], WIN, 833.

MAINE BISHOPRIC

1. The authors are grateful to Brother Arnold Hadd, Librarians Anne Gilbert and Paige Lilly, Museum Director Leonard Brooks and Curator David Richards of the United Society of Shakers, Sabbathday Lake, Maine, for their assistance with this chapter. They generously gave their time to share their knowledge, pass on oral history information, and review all the material presented here on the Maine Shakers.

2. See Sister R. Mildred Barker, "History of Union Branch, Gorham, Maine, 1784–1819," *The Shaker Quarterly* 7, no. 2 (Summer 1967): 64.

3. See Sister R. Mildred Barker, *Holy Land: A History of the Alfred Shakers* (Sabbathday Lake, Me.: The Shaker Press, 1986).

4. See Gerard C. Wertkin, *The Four Seasons of Shaker Life* (New York: Simon & Schuster, 1986), 16–19.

5. See ibid., 34.

6. See Sister R. Mildred Barker, *The Sabbathday Lake Shakers: An Introduction to the Shaker Heritage* (Sabbathday Lake, Me.: The Shaker Press, 1978).

7. See Wertkin, *The Four Seasons,* 40; and Barker, "History of Union Branch," 67.

8. See Barker, *Holy Land,* n.p.

9. See Priscilla J. Brewer, *Shaker Communities, Shaker Lives* (Hanover, N.H.: University Press of New England, 1986), 215.

10. Letter from Anne Gilbert, Librarian, the United Society of Shakers, Sabbathday Lake, Me., to the author, June 9, 1992.

11. See Barker, *Holy Land.*

12. See Edward Deming Andrews, *The Community Industries of the Shakers* (Albany: University of the State of New York, 1932), 257.

13. Charles Nordoff, *The Communistic Societies of the United States ...* (New York: Harper & Brothers, 1875), pl. 182.

14. See Edward Deming Andrews and Faith Andrews, *Work and Worship* (Greenwich, Conn.: New York Graphic Society, 1974), 156.

15. See Andrews, *Community Industries,* 257.

16. See Barker, *Holy Land.*

17. Brother Theodore E. Johnson, "The Least of Mother's Children in the East," lecture given at the Metropolitan Museum of Art, New York, March 27, 1982.

18. See Barker, *Holy Land.*

19. See ibid.

20. All quotes in this paragraph are quoted in Johnson, "The Least of Mother's Children."

21. Letter from Brother Arnold Hadd, the United Society of Shakers, Sabbathday Lake, Me., to the author, July 23, 1991.

22. This information and the following quotes come from Johnson, "The Least of Mother's Children."

23. Ibid.

24. The last two items were identified by Brother Arnold Hadd in a letter of July 23, 1991, to the author.

25. See United Society of Shakers, Sabbathday Lake, Me., *Time and Eternity: Maine Shakers in the Industrial Age 1872–1918,* exhib. cat. (1986).

26. Letter from Brother Arnold Hadd and the Shaker Library, the United Society of Shakers, Sabbathday Lake, to the author, October 1991.

27. See Brother Theodore E. Johnson, *Hands to Work and Hearts to God* (Brunswick, Me.: Bowdoin College of Art, 1969), for examples of other built-ins.

28. David Richards, curator, the United Society of Shakers, Sabbathday Lake, personal interview with author, 1991.

29. See United Society of Shakers, *Time and Eternity,* 7.

30. Brother Arnold Hadd, conversation with author, June 1991.

31. See Jerry V. Grant and Douglas R. Allen, *Shaker Furniture Makers* (Hanover, N.H.: University Press of New England, 1989), 154.

32. According to Brother Arnold Hadd.

33. Illustrated in Johnson, *Hands to Work*, pl. 11.

34. See Grant and Allen, *Shaker Furniture Makers*, 154.

35. See Barker, *The Sabbathday Lake Shakers*.

36. See Johnson, "The Least of Mother's Children."

37. David Richards, personal interview with author, 1992.

38. Illustrated in Johnson, *Hands to Work*, pl. 8, and John G. Shea, *The American Shakers and Their Furniture* (New York: Van Nostrand Reinhold, 1971), 186.

39. David Richards, personal interview with author, 1992.

40. Illustrated in Johnson, *Hands to Work*, pl. 29.

41. A chair similar to this appears in a historic photograph of Eldress Mary Walker at Alfred, c. 1910, illustrated in Charles R. Muller and Timothy D. Rieman, *The Shaker Chair* (Winchester, Ohio: Canal Press, 1984), 97.

42. See Muller and Rieman, *The Shaker Chair*, 92–94.

OHIO BISHOPRIC

1. The authors would like to thank the late Jean Hudson, curator, the Shaker Historical Museum, Shaker Heights, Ohio, and Mickie Franer and Mary Payne, directors, the Warren County Historical Society, Lebanon, Ohio, for making their collections available for research; and Dale Covington, Richard Spence, Charles Muller, and Sharon Edwards for generously sharing their expertise with us.

2. "Testimony of Jemima Blanchard," in "Testimonies and Wise Sayings, Counsel and Instruction of Mother Ann and the Elders," comp. Eunice Bathrick, 1859, Harvard, Mass., p. 85, WRHS, VIB:10–13.

3. See John Patterson MacLean, *Shakers of Ohio* (Philadelphia: Porcupine Press, 1975), 194.

4. See Stephen J. Stein, *The Shaker Experience in America* (New Haven: Yale University Press, 1992), 58.

5. Quoted in Gerald F. Ham, "Pleasant Hill: A Century of Kentucky Shakerism 1805–1910" (Master's thesis, University of Kentucky, Lexington, 1955), 3.

6. Letter from Shaker scholar Richard Spence to the author, August 29, 1992.

7. See Michael Taylor, "Theological Differences of Eastern and Western Shakers," *Shaker Messenger* 5, no. 2 (Winter 1983): 13–14.

8. See Stein, *The Shaker Experience*, 66–75.

9. There is quite a discrepancy among the dates given for the active Ohio Shaker communities by Shaker historians— Union Village: 1812–1910 (June Sprigg and Jerry Grant); 1805 (MacLean); 1812 (Stein); 1806–1912 (Brewer); 1805–1912 (Warren County Historical Society); Watervliet: 1806–1910 (Brewer); 1806–1900 (MacLean and Warren County Historical Society); 1813–1900 (June Sprigg and Jerry Grant); White Water: 1824–1907 (Grant and Sprigg), 1822 (Stein); North Union: 1822–89 (Brewer and Stein); 1826–89 (Jerry Grant and June Sprigg); 1828 (MacLean). We have adopted the following dates for each community for the following reasons:
 Union Village: 1805–1912 as 1805 is the year of the conversions of Malcolm Worley and Richard McNemar and the arrival of Elder David Darrow, and 1912 is the sale date between the Shakers and the United Brethren Church. The contract was signed in October 1912 by Joseph Holden, William Funk, and J. Phillippi.
 Watervliet: 1806–1900 as, according to MacLean, *Shakers of Ohio*, p. 198, "Often Shaker Documents affirm Watervliet took its rise in 1806 . . . " and in 1900, according to MacLean, p. 224, Slingerland decided to disband the community and merge its members with Union Village: "The removal took place on October 11, 1900."
 White Water: 1822–1916; in a letter from Richard Spence, August 29, 1992, to the author, he affirmed that in 1822, "The Believers were gathering on a farm about two miles north of the present site of the North family," and 1916 is the date of the final sale of the property and the departure of the Shakers for Mount Lebanon and Hancock.
 North Union: 1822–89, as 1822 is recognized as the community's opening date in "The History of North Union, kept by James S. Prescott," and in 1889, the twenty-seven remaining members were relocated to either Watervliet or Union Village.

10. Richard Spence, "The Layout and Architecture of Union Village," lecture given at Union Village Seminar, October 26, 1989, Warren County Historical Society, Lebanon, Ohio.

11. Sharon Edwards, "Brooms, Looms and Flumes: Union Village Industries, 1805–1870," lecture given at Union Village Seminar, October 26, 1989.

12. See March 10, 1848, "Daily Record of Events of the Church Family," Union Village, Ohio, WRHS, VB:230.

13. See Edward Deming Andrews and Faith Andrews, *Work and Worship* (Greenwich, Conn.: New York Graphic Society, 1974), 154–59.

14. Jerry Grant, lecture given at Collectors' Forum, Hancock Shaker Village, Pittsfield, Mass., May 2, 1992.

15. Quoted in MacLean, *Shakers of Ohio*, 202, 319.

16. See letter from Elder David Darrow to Beloved Brethren, Deacons Richard & Stephen, October 12, 1818, WRHS, IVA:69.

17. "Journal of Visitors Who Stayed Overnight at Union Village, Ohio," 1850–79, LC, 239.

18. James S. Prescott, "The History of North Union," 1822–70, WRHS, VIIB:221, quoted in Caroline B. Piercy, *The Valley of God's Pleasure* (New York: Stratford House, 1951), and Richard D. Klyver, *Brother James* (Shaker Heights, Ohio: Shaker Historical Society, 1992), who mistakenly attribute the quote to "The Prescott Journals."

19. J. P. MacLean, *A Sketch of the Life and Labors of Richard McNemar* (Franklin, Ohio: Franklin Chronicle, 1905).

20. This appears to be a worldly term that came into usage in the late 1930s by the staff and residents at the Otterbein Home Retirement Community, which took over the building. No mention of the name Marble Hall appears in MacLean. The building is always referred to as the Adminstration Building in Otterbein records from 1910 to 1936, when Otterbein officially renamed it Funk Memorial Hall. The official name did not stick long, as Marble Hall crept into the Superintendent's Report in 1939 and appears in the annual Board Meeting minutes in 1942. The present official name for the building is Marble Hall. This information was provided by Richard Spence, in a letter to the author, August 29, 1992.

21. Quoted in Mary Lou Conlin, "A Tour of the Western Societies and Museums," *The Shaker Quarterly*, Summer 1962: 74.

22. "[Collection of apprenticeships]," 1809–95, WIN, 751.

23. Mary Lyn Ray, in "A Reappraisal of Shaker Furniture," in *Winterthur Portfolio* 8, ed. Ian M.G. Quimby (Charlottesville: University Press of Virginia, 1973), 129, refers to a desk made for Eldress Augusta Stone "'after Big fire at Lebanon N.Y. 1875 by Elder Joseph Slingerland,'" fig. 28. However, no other written, oral, or physical documentation is known to support this statement.

24. Information on Slingerland courtesy of Dale Covington, from a lecture entitled "Union Village and the Shaker Colonies in Georgia," given at Union Village Seminar, October 26, 1989, and letters

to the author dated January 16, 1991, and June 4, 1992.

25. See *The Shaker Heritage* (Shaker Heights, Ohio: Shaker Historical Society, 1980), 10.

26. See MacLean, *Shakers of Ohio*, 133.

27. See ibid., 223–24, 269, 328.

28. Letter from Richard Spence to the author, August 29, 1992.

29. Illustrated in Charles R. Muller, *The Shaker Way* (Worthington: Ohio Antique Review, 1979), 35.

30. Letter from the Union Village Ministry to the Mount Lebanon Ministry, April 8, 1845, WRHS, IVA:72.

31. See Charles R. Muller and Timothy D. Rieman, *The Shaker Chair* (Winchester, Ohio: Canal Press, 1984), 99.

32. "Daily Record of Events," WRHS, VB:230.

33. See Hazel Spencer Phillips, "Shakers in the West," *Philadelphia Museum Bulletin* 57 (Spring 1962): 83–88.

34. Leonard Mendelsohn, "Eastern Shakers and Their Western Communities," lecture given at Union Village Seminar, October 27, 1989.

35. See "Daily Record of Events," May 16, 1826, February 21, 1841, and November 11, 1830, WRHS, VB:230.

36. Letter from David Darrow, Union Village, to Deacons Richard and Stephen, October 12, 1818, WRHS, IVA:69.

37. "Church Journal of Current Events at Union Village Kept by William Reynolds," WRHS, VB:259.

38. Ibid., VB:257.

39. Letter from William N. Redman to Elder Freegift Wells, July 24, 1865, WRHS, IVA:74. The authors would like to thank Sharon Edwards for bringing this reference to our attention.

40. Record of Deaths, Ohio Historical Society, Columbus.

41. Sharon Edwards, letter to the author, March 28, 1991.

42. "Register of Deaths at Union Village, Warren Co. Oh.," p. 44, CAN, 169; and United States Census records for 1850 and 1860.

43. See MacLean, *Shakers of Ohio*, 208.

44. See Muller, *The Shaker Way*, 35.

45. Letter from Union Village Ministry to "Dearly Beloved Ministry" June 26, 1837, WRHS, IVB:24.

46. Letter from Richard Spence, with information from Mary Lue Warner, archivist at the Otterbein Home Retirement Community, Lebanon, Ohio, to the author, August 29, 1992.

47. Quoted in Jerry V. Grant and Douglas R. Allen, *Shaker Furniture Makers* (Hanover, N.H.: University Press of New England, 1989), 7.

48. Illustrated in Muller, *The Shaker Way*, 93, fig. 7.

49. Illustrated in Muller and Rieman, *The Shaker Chair*, 98.

50. "Financial Accounts of the Shaker Community in the Miami Valley, Ohio," 1807–15, LC, 152.

PLEASANT HILL AND SOUTH UNION, KENTUCKY

1. See Gerald F. Ham, "Pleasant Hill: A Century of Kentucky Shakerism, 1805–1910" (Master's thesis, University of Kentucky, Lexington, 1955), 9.

2. See Julia Neal, *The Kentucky Shakers* (Lexington: University of Kentucky, 1977), 14.

3. The authors are deeply indebted to Larrie Curry, director of collections at Shaker Village of Pleasant Hill, and her energetic staff, for generously sharing their own research as well as the accumulated notes and unpublished manuscripts of the late Edward Nickels. This invaluable journal material has been included throughout the general information and specific caption data on Pleasant Hill. Sincere thanks are also given to Tommy Hines, director of Shakertown at South Union, who provided much of the background material, both oral and written, on the history of the Centre Family Dwelling House and community furniture. Larrie and Tommy generously gave their time to provide access to the furniture in their collections for examination and analysis.

4. See Ham, "Pleasant Hill," 27–33.

5. See Julia Neal, "Shaker Industries in Kentucky," in *Shaker Tradition and Design*, ed. Milton C. Rose and Emily Mason Rose (New York: Bonanza Books, 1975), 117–18.

6. Henry Clay Blinn, January 1, 1856, "Church Record, Canterbury, 1784–1879," p. 113, CAN, 764.

7. See Ham, "Pleasant Hill," 30–33.

8. See Julia Neal, "Shaker Industries," 116.

9. See Ham, "Pleasant Hill," 235, 237.

10. See Gass vs. Wilhite, Lincoln County court records (November 1, 1830), 35–44.

11. Letter from Pleasant Hill Ministry to Mount Lebanon Ministry, August 10, 1810, WRHS, IVA:52.

12. "Daybook," 1810–11, Pleasant Hill, WRHS, IIB:48 mislabeled as South Union.

13. Letter from Pleasant Hill to Brother William, Albany, Ind., March 13, 1881, PH.

14. See Edward E. Nickels, "The Shaker Furniture of Pleasant Hill, Kentucky," *The Magazine Antiques* 137, no. 5 (May 1990): 1188, n. 23, for a listing of references to furniture made for sale.

15. "Daybook," December 18, 1810.

16. See Nickels, "The Shaker Furniture of Pleasant Hill," where most of this and the following information regarding Pleasant Hill craftsmen first appeared.

17. "Temporal Journal," May 16, 1889–December 2, 1890, Pleasant Hill, FC.

18. See Jerry V. Grant and Douglas R. Allen, *Shaker Furniture Makers* (Hanover, N.H.: University Press of New England, 1989), 110.

19. "Account Book, 1839–1910," South Union, Collection of Shaker Village of Pleasant Hill, Harrodsburg, Ky., on deposit at Margaret I. King Library, University of Kentucky, Lexington, 63.

20. Quoted in James C. Thomas, "Micajah Burnett and the Buildings at Pleasant Hill," *The Magazine Antiques* 98, no. 4 (October 1970): 600.

21. See Ham, "Pleasant Hill," 18.

22. See "Temporal Journal Kept by Order of the Deacons of the East House, January 11, 1843–February 19, 1884, Book B," Pleasant Hill, pp. 7, 10–12, 14, 17–20, 23, 24, 27, 29, 30, 32, 34, 37, 39–42, 45, 48, 51, FC.

23. See "Temporal Journal . . . Book B," April 4, 1843, p. 7.

24. "Millennial Laws," pt. 3, sec. 2, nos. 2, 5, reprinted in Edward Deming Andrews, *The People Called Shakers* (New York: Oxford University Press, 1953), 281.

25. See Ham, "Pleasant Hill," 238–39.

26. See Nickels, "The Shaker Furniture of Pleasant Hill," 1185.

27. Illustrated in Robert F. W. Meader, *Illustrated Guide to Shaker Furniture* (New York: Dover, 1982), pl. 104.

28. Letter from Francis Voris, Pleasant Hill, to Brother Samuel, South Union, July 25, 1815, WRHS, IVA:52.

29. "Millennial Laws," pt. 2, sec. 10, no. 2, reprinted in Andrews, *The People Called Shakers*, 271.

30. See May 9, 1862, March 10, 1868, "Journal of the East Family, January 1, 1856–February 13, 1871," Pleasant Hill, PH.

31. See R. A. Milligan Collection, SC 137, Department of Library Special Collections, WKU.

32. Philemon Stewart, "A General Statement of the Holy Laws of Zion," 1840, Mount Lebanon, N.Y., WIN, 802.

33. See Nickels, "The Shaker Furniture of Pleasant Hill," 1180.

34. "Temporal Journal," May 16, 1889–December 2, 1890.

35. See "Journal of M. Thomas, 1 January

1816–31 December 1817," pp. 95–97, FC, quoted in Nickels, "The Shaker Furniture of Pleasant Hill," 1184.

36. See Charles R. Muller and Timothy D. Rieman, *The Shaker Chair,* 113; and Nickels, "The Shaker Furniture of Pleasant Hill," 1184.

37. "Temporal Journal . . . Book B," pp. 7, 10–12, 14, 17–20, 23, 24, 27, 29, 30, 32, 34, 37, 39–42, 45, 48, 51.

38. See Muller and Rieman, *The Shaker Chair,* 114.

39. See Lois Olcott, "Kentucky Federal Furniture," *The Magazine Antiques* 105, no. 4 (April 1974): 870.

40. Tommy Hines, director of Shakertown at South Union, telephone conversation with author, October 8, 1992.

41. Letter from Tommy Hines to the author, January 3, 1992.

42. See Joseph D. Watson, "Worktables of Early America," *Southern Accents,* July–August 1990: 30–39.

43. See January 5, 1849, "Journal B," 1836–1864, South Union Ministry, SU.

GROVELAND

1. Illustrated in Jerry V. Grant and Douglas R. Allen, *Shaker Furniture Makers* (Hanover, N.H.: University Press of New England, 1989), 138.

2. See "A Record of the Commencement and Progress, of Believers at Sodus—Port Bay . . . " 1826–38, WRHS, VB:21, 22.

3. Record of the purchase of 1,300 acres of land in Sodus from R. C. Nicholas, WRHS, IIB:8–8c.

4. See Fran Kramer, *Simply Shaker: Groveland and the New York Communities,* exhib. cat. (Rochester, N.Y.: Rochester

Museum & Science Center, 1991), 11–12; Herbert A. Wisby, Jr., *The Sodus Shaker Community* (Lyons, N.Y.: Wayne County Historical Society, 1982), 15–16.

5. See Kramer, *Simply Shaker,* 13, 17, 21, 22; and Wisby, *The Sodus Shaker Community,* 25, 27.

6. Letter from the Groveland Ministry to the Mount Lebanon Ministry, March 1845, WRHS, IVA:16.

7. See Wisby, *The Sodus Shaker Community,* 15.

8. Quoted in Kramer, *Simply Shaker,* 23; Wisby, *The Sodus Shaker Community,* 15.

9. See Kramer, *Simply Shaker,* 12.

10. Quoted in ibid., 23.

11. Quoted in Dorothy M. Filley, *Recapturing Wisdom's Valley: The Watervliet Shaker Heritage 1775–1975* (Colonie, N.Y.: Town of Colonie and Albany Institute of History and Art, 1975), 51.

12. Letter from David Parker, Canterbury, to Lydia Dole, Groveland, September 7, 1863, WRHS, IVA:7.

13. See John Scherer, "Groveland's Atypical Shaker," *New York–Pennsylvania Collector,* April 6, 1981.

14. See Kramer, *Simply Shaker,* 23.

15. This correspondence was included in a letter from Jennie Wells, Watervliet, N.Y., to Dr. Charles Adams, director, New York State Museum, Albany, May 22, 1943, NYSL.

16. "A Family Journal, Second Family, Watervliet, N.Y., 1885," October 29, 1892, Shaker Collection, Williams College Archives, Williamstown, Mass., 217.F21.

17. Wells to Adams, May 22, 1943.

18. Letter from Emmory Brooks, Enfield,

Conn., to Eldress Polly Lee, Groveland, January 6, 1869, NYSL.

19. This correspondence was included in a letter from Wells to Adams, May 22, 1943.

20. See Grant and Allen, *Shaker Furniture Makers,* 140.

21. Wells to Adams, May 22, 1943.

22. Illustrated in Grant and Allen, *Shaker Furniture Makers,* 141, pl. 111.

23. See Jean Palardy, *The Early Furniture of French Canada* (Toronto: Macmillan of Canada, 1965), fig. 216.

24. Wells to Adams, May 22, 1943.

25. Illustrated in Kramer, *Simply Shaker,* 82.

26. Illustrated in Willis Henry Auctions, Inc., Marshfield, Mass., *Shaker Auction,* sales cat. (August 4, 1985), no. 216.

27. Illustrated in Kramer, *Simply Shaker,* 78.

28. See Daniel Fraser, *The Divine Afflatus* (Boston: Rand, Avery & Co., 1875; published by the United Society, Shirley, Mass., 1875), WIN, 234.

29. Anna Goepper, "Journal of Watervliet South Family," vol. 3, 1917–18, NYSL.

30. See ibid., August 8, 1917.

31. See Palardy, *The Early Furniture of French Canada,* p. 28 and sec. 1.

32. See Lionel Lambourne, *Utopian Craftsmen* (Salt Lake City: Peregrine Smith, 1980), p. 42, ill. 38. The authors would like to thank Robert Rust for sharing his expertise on the English Arts and Crafts movement.

33. See Steven Adams, *The Arts and Crafts Movement* (Secaucus, N.J.: Chartwell Books, 1987), 25.

34. See Fran Kramer, "Groveland Shakers," *Maine Antique Digest,* May 1991, 32C.

35. Quoted in Kramer, *Simply Shaker,* 73.

Selected Bibliography

ABBREVIATIONS

CAN   Archives, Canterbury Shaker Village, Canterbury, N.H.

FC   Library of the Filson Club, Louisville, Ky.

FM   Fruitlands Museums Library, Harvard, Mass.

HAN   Library, Hancock Shaker Village, Pittsfield, Mass.

LC   Shaker Collection, Library of Congress, Washington, D.C.

NYPL   New York Public Library, Rare Books and Manuscripts Division, New York

NYSL   New York State Library, Shaker Collection, Albany

OC   Emma B. King Library, Shaker Museum and Library, Old Chatham, N.Y.

SDL   Library, The United Society of Shakers, Sabbathday Lake, Me.

SU   Museum at South Union, Ky.

WIN   Andrews Shaker Collection, Winterthur Museum, Winterthur, Del.

WKU   The Kentucky Library, Western Kentucky University, Bowling Green

WRHS   Western Reserve Historical Society, Shaker Collection, Cleveland

SHAKER SOURCES

"Alfred Church Record," vol. 1, 1872–78, vol. 2, 1879–86, compiled by Elder Otis Sawyer to 1884 and Elder John Vance to 1889. SDL.

Avery, Giles. "Journal of a Trip to the Eastern Societies," 1843, Mount Lebanon, N.Y. OC, MS. 12744.

———. "A Register of Incidents and Events . . . Kept by Giles B. Avery." October 20, 1859–December 21, 1874. Mount Lebanon, N.Y. NYPL-1.

———. Series of Journals and Diaries from 1832–47, 1859–69, and 1871–81, Mount Lebanon, N.Y. WRHS, VB:104–7, 109–15, and 117–26, including "Pocket Diary for 1880," VB:125.

Babbitt, Charles W. "A Diary Kept for the Use & Convenience of the Herb Department by Charles W. Babbitt, Commencing February 17th on Monday 1862," Harvard, Mass. SDL.

Barker, Sister R. Mildred. *Holy Land: A History of the Alfred Shakers.* Sabbathday Lake, Me.: The Shaker Press, 1986.

———. *The Sabbathday Lake Shakers: An Introduction to the Shaker Heritage.* Sabbathday Lake, Me.: The Shaker Press, 1978.

Bishop, Rufus, and Seth Youngs Wells, eds. *Testimonies of the Life, Character, Revelations and Doctrines of Our Ever Blessed Mother Ann Lee . . .* Hancock, Mass.: J. Tallcott & J. Deming, June 15, 1816. 2d ed., revised by Giles B. Avery. Albany: Weed, Parsons, 1888.

Blakeman, Elisha D. "Journal of Daily Occurrences," 1834–40, Mount Lebanon, N.Y. WRHS, VB:131.

———. "Religious Experience of David Rowley," 1854, Church Family, Mount Lebanon, N.Y. WRHS, VIB:23.

Blinn, Henry C. "Church Record, Canterbury, 1784–1879," CAN, 764.

———. "Historical Notes Having Reference to the Believers in Enfield, N.H. . . . [vol. 1]," [1782]–1847. CAN, 761.

———. "Historical Notes Having Reference to the Believers in Enfield, N.H. . . . Vol. II," 1847–1902. CAN, 762.

————. "A Historical Record of the Society of Believers in Canterbury, N.H. From the time of its organization in 1792 till the year one thousand eight hundred and forty eight . . . Vol II [vol. 1] East Canterbury, 1892." CAN, 763.

————. "Journal," 1872–89. Continuation of Whitcher, "Brief History," Canterbury, N.H. CAN, 22.

————. "A Journey to Kentucky in the Year 1873." Reprinted in *The Shaker Quarterly* 5–7, no. 1 (Spring 1965–Spring 1967).

Brown, Thomas. *Account of the People Called Shakers: Their Faith, Doctrines, and Practice.* Troy: Parker and Bliss, 1012.

"Church Family Journal No. 3," July 4, 1845–September 11, 1847, Harvard, Mass. FM, 2.4.

Collier, Alfred. "A Journal Kept by Alfred Collier for His Own Benefit," February 1859–July 1861 [subsequent to vol. 219, reel 39, WRHS, miscatalogued as Shirley], Church Family, Harvard, Mass. FM, 2.2.

"Daily Record of Events of the Church," 1805–96, Union Village, Ohio. WRHS, VB:230.

Deming, William. Letter to Elder Benjamin [S. Youngs] and Eldress Polly [Molly? Goodrich], South Union, Ky., January 8, 1832. In "Copies of Letters from Different Communities from South Union for the Ministry." WRHS, IVB:35. [Typescript copy available at HAN 9768.H2 D369.]

DeWitt, Henry. "Journal," 1827–67, Church Family, Mount Lebanon, N.Y. WRHS, VB:97.

"Domestic Journal of Domestic Occurrences Kept Originally by Joseph Bennet, and then by Isaac Crouch, Nicholas Bennet, Isaac N. Youngs, and John M. Brown, A" 1788–1877, Church Family, Mount Lebanon, N.Y. WRHS, VB:63–71.

"Domestic Journal of Important Occurrences Kept for the Elder Sisters at New Lebanon," 1780–1860. WRHS, VB:60–1.

Elkins, Hervey. *Fifteen Years in the Senior Order of Shakers.* Hanover, N.H: Dartmouth Press, 1953.

Ely, Calvin. "Diary Kept by Calvin Ely, 1780–1816," Enfield, Conn. WRHS, VB:11.

Evans, Jessie. Diaries, 1892–1931, Canterbury, N.H. CAN, 1985.6–.43.

"Extract from the Holy Orders of the Church, An: Written by Father Joseph to the Elders of the Church at New Lebanon and Copied Agreeable to Father Joseph's Word, February 18th, 1841." WIN, 791.

"Family Journal Kept by the Deaconesses of the East House, Book A, June 1, 1843–October 19, 1871," Pleasant Hill, Ky. FC.

Green, Calvin, and Seth Youngs Wells. *A Summary View of the Millennial Church or United Society of Believers . . .* Albany: Packard & Van Benthuysen, 1823.

Greenwood, Irving. "Notebook of Information on Machinery, Buildings, Equipment, Property, etc.," [c. 1782–1939, Canterbury]. CAN, 28.

Hammond, Joseph. "Joseph Hammond's Day Book," September 10, 1820–February 28, 1826, Harvard, Mass. FM, 1.10.

Haskett, William J. *Shakerism Unmasked.* Pittsfield, Massachusetts: published by the author, 1828. WIN, 264.

Haskins, Orren. "Reflections, 1887," Mount Lebanon, N.Y. WRHS, VIIA:8.

Johnson, Brother Theodore E. *Hands to Work and Hearts to God.* Brunswick, Me.: Bowdoin College of Art, 1969.

————. "The Least of Mother's Children in the East." Lecture given at the Metropolitan Museum of Art, New York, March 27, 1982. Transcript, SDL.

————, ed. "The 'Millennial Laws' of 1821," *The Shaker Quarterly* 7, no. 2 (Summer 1967): 35–58.

"Journal A," 1807–36, South Union Ministry, Ky. WKU.

"Journal B," 1836–64, South Union Ministry, Ky. SU.

"Journal and Manifest Record," 1791–1806, Harvard, Mass. FM, 1.7.

"Journal Containing Some of the Most Important Events of the Day," November 1840–June 1843, Harvard, Mass. FM, 2.3.

Lyon, Benjamin. "Journal of Benjamin Lyon of Canaan, June 12, 1816–February 8, 1818, concerning Events in the Family of the Second Order," Mount Lebanon, N.Y. LC, 43.

————. "Journal of Benjamin Lyon of Canaan, February 1818–March 1820, Concerning Events in the Family of the Second Order," Mount Lebanon, N.Y. LC, 44.

The Manifesto 1–29, January 1871–December 1899. [East Canterbury, N.H.: United Societies, 1871–99.] Published monthly, in 1871–72 by the Mount Lebanon Bishopric as *The Shaker*; in 1873–75 by the United Society as *Shaker and Shakeress*; in 1876–77 by the Canterbury Shakers, Henry Clay Blinn, editor, as *The Shaker*; in 1878–82 as *The Shaker Manifesto*; in 1883–99 as *The Manifesto*. CAN.

[Meacham, Joseph.] "Collection of Writings Concerning Church Order and Government" [copied here by Rufus Bishop in 1850], 1791- 96. WRHS, VIIB:59.

[————.] "Extract from the Holy Orders of the Church, An: Written by Father Joseph to the Elders of the Church at New Lebanon and Copied Agreeable to Father Joseph's Word, February 18th, 1841." WIN, 791.

"Millennial Laws of Gospel Statutes and Ordinances Adopted to the Day of Christ's Second Appearing, The." Revised and reestablished by the Ministry and Elders, October 1845. Reprinted in Andrews, *The People Called Shakers*, 253–89.

"'Millennial Laws' of 1821, The." Edited and with an introduction by Theodore E. Johnson, *The Shaker Quarterly* 7, no. 2 (Summer 1967): 35–58.

Prescott, James, S. "The History of North Union," 1822–70. WRHS, VIIB:221.

"Sabbathday Lake (Me.) Church Record and Journal." SDL.

Sawyer, Otis. "History, or Record of the First Seven Years of the Second Degree of Travel or Second Cycle in the Progress of the Church and Society in Alfred, York Co., Maine, January 1, 1872–February 25, 1879." SDL.

"Temporal Journal Kept by Order of the Deacons of the East House, January 11, 1843–February 19, 1884, Book B," Pleasant Hill, Ky. FC.

Thomas, M. "Journal of M. Thomas, 1 January 1816–31 December 1817," Pleasant Hill, Ky. FC.

Wells, Freegift. "Memorandum of Events," 1812–65, Church Family, Watervliet, N.Y. WRHS, VB:285–96.

[Wells, Seth Youngs.] *Testimonies Concerning the Character and Ministry of Mother Ann Lee and the First Witnesses of the Gospel of Christ's Second Appearing . . .* Albany: Packard & Van Benthuysen, 1827. WIN, 439.

Western Reserve Historical Society, Shaker Collection. List of Believers at the Various Shaker Communities. WRHS, Microfilm, reel 123.

Whitcher, John. "A Brief History or Record of the Commencement & Progress of the United Society of Believers at Canterbury," vol. 1, 1782–1871. CAN, 21. Vol. 2: see Blinn, "Journal," 1872–89.

White, Anna, and Leila S. Taylor. *Shakerism: Its Meaning and Message*. Columbus, Ohio: Fred Herr, 1904.

[Youngs, Benjamin Seth.] *The Testimony of Christ's Second Appearing, Containing a General Statement of All Things Pertaining to the Faith and Practice of the Church of God in This Latter-day . . .* Lebanon, Ohio: 1808. Rev. and enl. Albany, 1810; Union Village, Ohio: 1823; Albany, 1856. WIN, 462–5.

Youngs, Isaac N. "Clock Maker's Journal with Remarks & Observations. Experiments &c. Beginning in 1815," 1815–35, Church Family, Mount Lebanon, N.Y. WRHS, VB:86.

———. "A Concise View of the Church of God and of Christ on Earth: Having Its Foundation in the Faith of Christ's First and Second Appearing," 1856, Church Family, Mount Lebanon, N.Y. WIN, 861.

———. "A Domestic Journal of Daily Occurrences," Church Family, Mount Lebanon, N.Y. NYSL, 13500.

———. "Journal Kept by Isaac N. Youngs," 1839–58, Church Family, Mount Lebanon, N.Y. WRHS, VB:134.

———. See also "A Domestic Journal of Domestic Occurrences . . . "

BOOKS AND ARTICLES

Andrews, Edward Deming. *The Community Industries of the Shakers.* New York State Museum Handbook, no. 15. Albany: University of the State of New York, 1933.

———. *The People Called Shakers.* New York: Oxford University Press, 1953.

———, and Faith Andrews. *Religion in Wood: A Book of Shaker Furniture.* Bloomington: Indiana University Press, 1966.

———. *Shaker Furniture: The Craftsmanship of an American Communal Sect.* New Haven: Yale University Press, 1937.

———. *Work and Worship: The Economic Order of the Shakers.* Greenwich, Conn.: New York Graphic Society, 1974.

Brewer, Priscilla J. *Shaker Communities, Shaker Lives.* Hanover, N.H.: University Press of New England, 1986.

Burns, Amy Stechler, and Ken Burns. *The Shakers: Hands to Work Hearts to God.* New York: Portland House, 1987.

Carpenter, Mary Grace, and Charles H. Carpenter. "The Shaker Furniture of Elder Henry Green." *The Magazine Antiques* 105, no. 5 (May 1974): 119–25.

Ching, Francis D.K. *Architecture: Form, Space & Order.* New York: Van Nostrand Reinhold, 1979.

Clark, Thomas D., and F. Gerald Ham. *Pleasant Hill and Its Shakers.* Harrodsburg, Ky.: Pleasant Hill Press, 1986.

Emlen, Robert P. *Shaker Village Views: Illustrated Maps and Landscape Drawings by Shaker Artists of the Nineteenth Century.* Hanover, N.H.: University Press of New England, 1987.

Emerich, A. D., and A. H. Benning, eds. *Community Industries of the Shakers: A New Look.* Exhib. cat. Albany: Shaker Heritage Society, 1983.

Emerich, A. D., and Arlen Benning, *Shaker: Furniture and Objects from the Faith and Edward Deming Andrews Collections.* Washington, D.C.: Smithsonian Institution Press, published for The Renwick Gallery of the National Collections of Fine Arts, 1973.

Filley, Dorothy M. *Recapturing Wisdom's Valley: The Watervliet Shaker Heritage 1775–1975.* Colonie, N.Y.: Town of Colonie and Albany Institute of History and Art, 1975.

Flint, Charles L. *Mount Lebanon Shaker Collection*. New Lebanon, N.Y.: Mount Lebanon Shaker Village, 1988.

Gibbs, James W., and Robert W. Meader. *Shaker Clock Makers*. Columbia, Pa.: The National Association of Watch and Clock Collectors.

Gifford, Don, ed. *An Early View of the Shakers: Benson John Lossing and the "Harper's" Article of July 1857*. Hanover, N.H.: University Press of New England, 1989.

Grant, Jerry V., and Douglas R. Allen. *Shaker Furniture Makers*. Hanover, N.H.: University Press of New England, published for Hancock Shaker Village, Inc., Pittsfield, Mass., 1989.

Ham, F. Gerald. "Pleasant Hill: A Century of Kentucky Shakerism 1805–1910." Master's thesis, University of Kentucky, Lexington, 1955.

Hess, Wendell. *The Enfield (N.H.) Shakers: A Brief History*. Published by Wendell Hess, 1980.

Kassay, John. *The Book of Shaker Furniture*. Amherst: University of Massachusetts, 1980.

Klyver, Richard D. *Brother James: The Life and Times of Shaker Elder James Prescott*. Shaker Heights, Ohio: The Shaker Historical Society, 1992.

Kramer, Fran. *Simply Shaker: Groveland and the New York Communities*. Exhib. cat. Rochester, N.Y.: Rochester Museum & Science Center, 1991.

McKinstry, E. Richard, comp. *The Edward Deming Andrews Memorial Shaker Collection*. New York: Garland, 1987.

MacLean, J. P. *Shakers of Ohio: Fugitive Papers Concerning the Shakers of Ohio, with Unpublished Manuscripts*. Philadelphia: Porcupine Press, 1975.

Meader, Robert F.W. *Illustrated Guide to Shaker Furniture*. New York: Dover, 1982.

Morse, Flo. *The Shakers and the World's People*. Hanover, N.H.: University Press of New England, 1987.

Muhlenberg College for the Arts, Allentown, Pa. *Shaker: Original Paints & Patinas*. Exhib. cat. by June Sprigg. 1987.

Muller, Charles R. *The Shaker Way*. Worthington: Ohio Antique Review, 1979.

———, and Timothy D. Rieman. *The Shaker Chair*. Winchester, Ohio: Canal Press, 1984.

Neal, Julia. *By Their Fruits*. Chapel Hill: University of North Carolina Press, 1947.

———. *The Kentucky Shakers*. Lexington: University of Kentucky, 1977.

———. "Regional Characteristics of Western Shaker Furniture." *The Magazine Antiques* 98, no. 4 (October 1970): 611–17.

———. "Shaker Industries in Kentucky." In *Shaker Tradition and Design*, edited by Milton C. Rose and Emily Mason Rose, 110–15. New York: Bonanza Books, 1975.

New Hampshire Historical Society, Concord. *Plain & Elegant Rich & Common Documented New Hampshire Furniture, 1750–1859*. Exhib. cat. Concord: New Hampshire Historical Society, 1979.

———. *True Gospel Simplicity: Shaker Furniture in New Hampshire*. Exhib. cat. by Mary Lyn Ray. 1974.

Newman, Cathy. "The Shakers' Brief Eternity." *National Geographic* 176, no. 3 (September 1989): 303–25.

Nickels, Edward E. "The Shaker Furniture of Pleasant Hill, Kentucky." *The Magazine Antiques* 137, no. 5 (May 1990): 1178–89.

Nordhoff, Charles. *The Communistic Societies of the United States . . .* New York: Harper & Brothers, 1875.

Ott, John Harlow. *Hancock Shaker Village: A Guidebook and History*. Shaker Community, Inc., 1976.

Palardy, Jean. *The Early Furniture of French Canada.* Toronto: Macmillan of Canada, 1965.

Pearson, Elmer R., Julia Neal, and Walter Muir Whitehill. *The Shaker Image.* Boston: New York Graphic Society, in collaboration with Shaker Community, Inc., Hancock, Mass., 1974.

Péladeau, Marius B. "The Shaker Meetinghouses of Moses Johnson." *The Magazine Antiques* 98, no. 4 (October 1970): 594–99.

Piercy, Caroline B. *The Valley of God's Pleasure: A Saga of the North Union Shaker Community.* New York: Stratford House, 1951. Based on the records of Elder James Prescott of North Union, 1822–1888, at WRHS.

Puig, Francis J., and Michael Conforti, eds. *The American Craftsman and the European Tradition 1620–1820.* Minneapolis: The Minneapolis Institute of Arts, 1989.

Ray, Mary Lyn. "A Reappraisal of Shaker Furniture." In *Winterthur Portfolio 8*, edited by Ian M.G. Quimby. Charlottesville: University Press of Virginia, 1973.

Scherer, John L. *New York Furniture at the New York State Museum.* Alexandria, Va.: Highland House, 1984.

The Shaker Heritage: An Annotated Pictorial Guide to the Collection of the Shaker Historical Museum. Shaker Heights, Ohio: The Shaker Historical Society, 1980.

The Shakers: Pure of Spirit, Pure of Mind. Exhib. cat. Duxbury, Mass.: Art Complex Museum, 1983.

The Shakers: Their Arts and Crafts. Philadelphia Museum Bulletin 57 (Spring 1962).

Shea, John G. *The American Shakers and Their Furniture, with Measured Drawings of Museum Classics.* New York: Van Nostrand Reinhold, 1971.

Smith, Nancy A. *Old Furniture: Understanding the Craftsman's Art.* Boston: Little, Brown, 1975.

Sotheby Parke Bernet, New York. *Important Shaker Furniture and Related Decorative Arts: The William L. Lassiter Collection.* Sales cat., November 13, 1981.

Sprigg, June. *By Shaker Hands.* New York: Alfred A. Knopf, 1975.

———. *Inner Light: The Shaker Legacy.* New York: Alfred A. Knopf, 1985.

———. *Shaker: Masterworks of Utilitarian Design Created between 1800 and 1875 by the Master Craftsmen and Craftswomen of America's Foremost Communal Religious Sect.* Exhib. cat. Katonah, N.Y.: Katonah Gallery, 1983.

———. *Shaker Design.* Exhib. cat. New York: Whitney Museum of American Art, 1986.

———, and David Larkin. *Shaker: Life, Work, and Art.* New York: Stewart, Tabori & Chang, 1987.

Starbuck, David R. "Documenting the Canterbury Shakers." *Historical New Hampshire* 43, no. 1 (Spring 1988): 1–21.

Stein, Stephen J. *The Shaker Experience in America.* New Haven: Yale University Press, 1992.

Taylor, Michael. "Theological Differences of Eastern and Western Shakers." *The Shaker Messenger,* Winter 1983: 13–14, 28.

True Gospel Simplicity: Shaker Furniture in New Hampshire. New Hampshire Historical Society, Concord, N.H. July 3–September 30, 1974. Concord, N.H.: New Hampshire Historical Society, 1974.

Van Kolken, Diana. *Introducing the Shakers: An Explanation & Directory.* Bowling Green, Ohio: Gabriel's Horn, 1985.

Wertkin, Gerard C. *The Four Seasons of Shaker Life.* New York: Simon & Schuster, 1986.

Whitson, Robley Edward, ed. *The Shakers: Two Centuries of Spiritual Perfection.* New York: Paulist Press, 1983.

Willis Henry Auctions, Inc., Marshfield, Mass. *Shaker Auction* sales cats., 1982–92.

Wisby, Herbert A., Jr. *The Sodus Shaker Community*. Lyons, N.Y.: Wayne County Historical Society, 1982.

Women's Auxiliary of the United Cerebral Palsy Association of Greater Hartford, Conn. *The Shakers: An Exhibition Concerning Their Furniture, Artifacts and Religion with Emphasis on Enfield, Connecticut.* Exhib. cat. Hartford, Conn.: The Woman's Auxiliary of the United Cerebral Palsy Association of Greater Hartford, 1975.

Glossary of Shaker Terms

Believer A covenanted member of the sect officially named the United Society of Believers in Christ's First and Second Appearing, commonly called the Shakers.

Bishopric An administrative territory encompassing two or three communities in the same geographic area run by a ministry consisting of two elders and two eldresses that reports to the central or lead ministry at Mount Lebanon. By the 1860s there were seven bishoprics, including Maine, New Hampshire, Mount Lebanon, Hancock, Harvard, Kentucky, and Ohio.

Brother/Sister The mode of address of the male and female rank and file members of the Shaker faith.

Covenant The legal document that established a convert's spiritual commitment to the faith and the transfer of his or her private property to the joint interest of the United Society. The first written covenant was signed at Mount Lebanon in 1795.

Deacon/ Deaconess Male and female members appointed by the family ministry leaders to supervise temporal affairs. Each family might have two deacons and two deaconesses to manage the farm, kitchen, garden, orchards, and other areas of daily life.

Dwelling Name of the building in which the brothers and sisters in a Shaker family lived. It contained retiring, dining, and meeting rooms, a bakery and a kitchen.

Elder/Eldress Two male and two female members appointed as leaders at various levels to supervise spiritual matters. In the Shaker hierarchy there were lead ministry elders at Mount Lebanon, bishopric elders, and family elders.

Elder Brother/ Elder Sister Terms used specifically to refer to the senior family leaders, one of each sex.

Family The smallest Shaker social unit, consisting of up to one hundred members. It was governed by a quartet of elders and eldresses. Typically, several families in close geographic proximity comprised a particular Shaker community. Some families—the North, South, West, and East—were named for their geographic relation to the central Church Family. Others were called Mill, Brickyard, Hill, Second, and so on.

Gather To organize a group of converts into a community governed by the Shaker hierarchical structure, for example, to gather into Gospel Order.

Gospel Order The establishment of a community with a ministry under the authority of the lead ministry at Mount Lebanon. All members were governed by the hierarchical structure established by Joseph Meacham between 1787 and 1796.

Lead Ministry The highest level of Shaker leadership, consisting of two elders and two eldresses living at Mount Lebanon, New York. They received their guidance directly from Mother Ann Lee and shared the spiritual responsibility for the entire sect. Also referred to as the central ministry or the Mount or New Lebanon ministry.

Meetinghouse	The building constructed for worship in the Church Family of each community. It most often was a two-and-a-half-story gambrel-roof structure with separate entrances for the male and female members of the sect. The first floor consisted of one large room designed to accommodate the Believers' dances of worship. The four ministry leaders occupied the second-floor apartments.
"Millennial Laws"	A series of regulations assembled in 1821 that dealt primarily with the proper relations between members and with members' duties to leaders. A dynamic rather than static document, it was revised in 1845, 1860, 1887 and 1912 to meet the changing needs of the United Society.
Ministry	The governing body of a bishopric, consisting of two elders and two eldresses appointed by the lead ministry at Mount Lebanon.
New Lebanon	The community established in 1784 and the seat of the governing authority for the entire sect. The name was changed in 1861 to Mount Lebanon, which was used throughout this text.
Order	1) An important goal of Shaker life that means standards of behavior acceptable to the leadership. Also synonymous with rules called orders outlined in the "Millennial Laws" governing items such as appropriate worship, language, and personal conduct as a Believer; 2) Level of commitment to the Shaker faith, such as Gathering Order for those deciding whether to officially join the sect and Senior Order for covenanted members of long standing.
Trustee	Two male and two female members appointed by the elders in each family to oversee business affairs. They often lived apart from the community and resided in the Trustees' Office or Office Building, where financial dealings with the world were transacted.
Union	One of the most important guiding principles of Shaker life, which emphasized the spiritual bond among members of the sect, Mother Ann Lee, and Christ.
United Society	Abbreviated term referring to the Shakers' official title, the United Society of Believers in Christ's First and Second Appearing.
World	Term denoting non-Believers; those living outside of the sect.

Glossary of Technical Terms

Apron	A horizontal rail, either plain or shaped, set directly underneath a tabletop that joins the table legs.
Astragal	A projecting half-round molding, often used with other profiles, such as a cove or an ogee.
Baluster-turned	A shape resembling a teardrop, derived from the vertical members of a balustrade, created by a lathe.
Band saw	A saw with two wheels holding a narrow continuous blade capable of cutting curved patterns.
Bench dog	A rectangular piece of metal used in conjunction with the end vise to clamp wood on the workbench top for planing and other operations.
Bird's-eye	A figured grain appearing in maple resembling birds' eyes.
Bootjack	A cutout shape, found on the bottom of plank-sided boxes and cases of drawers produced in the New Hampshire Shaker communities, whose curving profile resembles a bootjack—the device used to help remove high boots.
Boring machine	A hand or line-shaft-driven machine fitted with a drill bit that rotates under pressure to make holes in wood.
Bracket base	The shaped boards applied to the base of a piece of case furniture to form the feet. It is joined at the corners with a miter or dovetail joint.
Breadboard	The name given to boards fastened to each end of a tabletop perpendicular to the grain of the top boards to restrict warping. It is commonly attached with a tongue-and-groove joint and fastened with screws or nails.
Bridle joint	An all-wood joint used by several Shaker communities on trestle tables. The longitudinal member beneath the table is notched to accept a correspondingly notched crosspiece, which forms the top of the leg standard.
Bull nose	A molding profile consisting of an arc, curved more gently than a half-round shape.
Butler's desk	A dual-purpose piece of furniture serving simultaneously as a desk and a case of drawers.
Butt joint	A joint formed by gluing together the squared edges of two boards.
Cabinetmaker	A highly skilled and specialized woodworker who builds furniture.
Cabriole	A double curved leg with a projecting knee and an incurved ankle, associated with the Queen Anne and Chippendale styles. It terminates in a variety of feet, including ball and claw, pad, scroll, or hoof.
Carpenter	A woodworker who constructs buildings; some specialize in framing and finish work.
Chamfer	A term used for the beveled edge formed by sawing or planing at an angle to the adjacent surfaces of a board. This decorative shaping is occasionally found on Shaker case furniture from Ohio.
Chippendale	A style of furniture popular in eighteenth-century England and

America, characterized by ornate decoration and rococo motifs such as carved shells, c-scrolls, and ball-and-claw feet.

Circular or buzz saw According to Shaker tradition, a machine invented by Sister Tabitha Babbitt of the Harvard community about 1813; it was in use in other communities soon after. It consists of a circular blade with teeth mounted on a revolving shaft and was driven by steam or waterpower.

Cleat A thin wooden board or batten applied across the grain to the underside of a wide surface such as a tabletop. Its primary function was to hold a tabletop flat, to support an underhung drawer, or to fasten the top to its base. On tripod stands the cleat is placed between the top and the stem. It may take the form of a long, flat board, designed to restrain the top from warping, or simply a disk whose function is to fasten the top to the stem.

Close chair A potty or convenience chair.

Cock bead A diminutive half-round projecting molding applied to the edge of a drawer front for decorative purposes. It is a separate piece, often of contrasting wood, fitted into a rabbet and nailed and glued into the drawer front.

Cornice An architectural term referring to the uppermost horizontal section of an entablature, consisting of one or more moldings. In furniture, it applies to the top molding, integral or applied, of case pieces.

Cove A simple concave molding profile, used predominantly on the cornices of case pieces.

Curly maple An unusual wavy grain pattern occurring in hard or soft maple. Also called tiger maple.

Cushion bar The turned bent rail placed on top of the chair posts from which a cushion can be hung.

Cut foot A decorative base cut directly from the plank side or front stiles of a case. It may be straight or take the shape of a variety of more complex rounded forms.

Dado A square groove cut across the grain of a board, as in the side of a cupboard or case of drawers, to hold a shelf or drawer.

Dovetail A strong mechanical joint of interlocking pins and tails on the ends of flat boards used in the construction of boxes, case pieces, and drawers. A through-dovetail is visible on both surfaces. A half-blind dovetail is visible on one side only, for example, the front of most drawers. On the rear corner of most drawers, the pins are situated on the side of the drawer and the tails on the back. In another application, a dovetail joint fastens a drawer rail to a case side. A housed dovetail or half-dovetail, when used in a drawer rail, was completely contained within the case side.

Dowel A short wooden pin about 5/16 inch in diameter used for aligning and joining two pieces of wood together. This joinery method is primarily found in place of mortise-and-tenons in later machine-made furniture and only occasionally was used by Shaker craftsmen.

Drawer guide A horizontal piece of wood placed inside a case piece behind and perpendicular to the drawer rail to support the drawer. An additional piece of wood may be fastened at right angles to the guide's top surface to restrict the drawer's sideways movement if the side of the case is not directly adjacent to the drawer.

Drawer stop	A block of wood set either on top of a drawer rail or inside a case back to stop the drawer face perfectly flush with the front of the case or projecting a specific distance.
Escutcheon	A wood, metal, bone, or ivory plate surrounding a keyhole that protects the surface and adds ornamental detail.
Facing	A narrow strip of wood nailed to the front edge of a case side to conceal the joinery, creating a more sophisticated, finished look.
Federal style	A term applied to the American decorative arts during the period of the establishment of the Federal government from 1789 to about 1830. It is based on the designs of English cabinetmakers such as Hepplewhite and Sheraton and characterized by straight lines, smooth surfaces, and restrained ornamentation.
Fillet	A small v-shaped groove used in conjunction with one or more moldings.
Finial	In Shaker furniture, the decorative turned element used on the upper ends of rear chair posts. Most Shaker communities made chairs with distinctive finial forms. The Shaker chair makers used the term *pommel* rather than *finial*, which has come into common usage in the twentieth century.
Frame-and-panel	A type of construction used for doors or the sides of case pieces consisting of vertical (stiles) and horizontal (rails) members forming the frame into which is set a thin board or panel.
Gallery	1) A raised edge or rim attached to tabletops; 2) a unit of drawers placed above a tabletop, often used as an add-on to Shaker sewing tables.
Gateleg	A drop-leaf table with leaves supported by hinged legs rather than by pullout supports. Also called swingleg.
Glue block	A small piece of wood glued to two surfaces, such as drawer bottoms and sides, or tabletop and apron, to reinforce the joints.
Grain painting	The use of paint on inexpensive woods to imitate the grain of other wood or to create decorative patterns. Generally, a coat of paint applied over a colored undercoat is scratched while still wet to reveal some of the undercoat.
Jig	A device that guides a tool in making parts according to a pattern.
Joiner	A woodworker specialized in finish carpentry or making furniture.
Jointer	A machine designed to prepare boards for joining by planing and straightening their surfaces and edges.
Lamb's-tongue	An ogee-shaped finishing detail resembling a tongue. It provides a decorative transition between the beveled edge and the right angle or a half-round molding.
Miter	The beveled joint of two boards usually placed at right angles to each other.
Molding	A shaped edge of a furniture or structural surface (integral) or a strip of wood placed on a piece of furniture or structure (applied) to conceal joins and/or to add decoration. A molding can use a simple concave or convex profile, or a combination of the two, or additional forms.
Mortise	1) The rectangular cavity cut into a piece of wood to accept the

	corresponding projecting tenon to form a joint; 2) a hole cut into a piece of wood to fit a lock or a hinge.
Muntin	The narrow wooden member that frames the glass panes of windows or cupboard doors; also called *mullion*.
Ogee	An S-shaped molding profile formed by connecting concave and convex curves.
Ovolo	A quarter-round molding surrounded on either side by a fillet, often in the form of an asymmetrical curve rather than a true arc.
Panel	A thin board set between the stiles and rails of a door or case frame.
Peg rail	A functional, yet decorative addition to Shaker interiors, consisting of a narrow board holding turned pins inset at equal intervals affixed to walls six feet above the floor. It was used for hanging clothing, chairs, candlesticks, and cleaning equipment.
Pin	A wooden peg that is driven into a hole to secure a mortise-and-tenon joint.
Planer	A machine used to reduce the thickness or to flatten and smooth the surface of rough lumber.
Plank-side	A flat case side formed by a single board or several boards glued together.
Pommel	See Finial.
Posts	The vertical members of a piece of furniture such as a chair or bed.
Press	A piece of furniture used for clothes or linen storage. 1) The top half only, consisting of a cupboard that rests on top of a previously made piece of furniture, such as a case of drawers. 2) A complete one- or two-part piece of furniture with cupboard above case of drawers.
Primary wood	The type of wood or woods used on the visible surfaces of a piece of furniture.
Queen Anne	A furniture style of eighteenth-century England and America, characterized by curvaceous forms, cabriole legs, and restrained ornament.
Quirk	A groove used on one or both sides of a molding to set it off.
Rabbet	A rectangular channel or groove cut into the edge of a board, also called a rebate.
Rail	1) The horizontal frame member of a door or case frame as opposed to the vertical frame member, the stile. The unit is usually assembled with mortise-and-tenon joints. A panel is fitted into a groove cut into the inside edge of the rails and stiles; 2) the horizontal board located in a case piece between drawers, known as a drawer rail.
Rule joint	A hinged joint that is formed by matching the convex edge of a fixed tabletop with the concave edge on a table leaf. It opens and closes like the action of a pocket rule.
Scratch bead	The simplest form of incised carving, consisting of a single line scratched in the surface of woodwork, such as around drawer fronts.
Screw pocket	A cavity cut with chisels, drills, or gouges inside a table apron or case of drawers to allow for the use of screws to fasten a table apron to the top.

Scribe line	An incised line made with a cutting tool to mark the location where furniture parts are joined together or where a joint is to be cut.
Secondary wood	An inexpensive wood used in the construction of furniture parts such as shelves, drawer interiors, and backboards that are not seen.
Ship lap or half lap	An edge joint formed by cutting rabbets through half the thickness of two adjacent boards to allow them to overlap. Sometimes a bead is cut to decorate or conceal the joint.
Skirt	See Apron.
Slat	The horizontal bent boards of a chair back.
Snake leg	A shaped leg resembling an S curve that appeared frequently in tripod tables during the first quarter of the eighteenth century.
Spindles	Rodlike vertical elements that might form the back of a chair or settee.
Splay	The angling of legs outward from their more common vertical orientation between the tabletop and the floor.
Spline	A thin piece of wood fitted in the grooves cut into the edges of two adjacent boards to form a reinforcing joint.
Stile	The vertical frame member of a door or case frame as opposed to the horizontal frame member, the rail. See also Rail.
Strap hinge	A hinge with leaves that are much longer than wide. Strap hinges were most often used on Shaker boxes.
Tenon	See Mortise.
Thumbnail molding	A quarter-round profile resembling the end of the thumb shape, commonly found on the edge of drawers in the Queen Anne and Chippendale periods and on many Shaker case pieces.
Tilter	A device designed by Shaker chair makers to allow the chair to tilt backward slightly without causing damage to the wood floors. It consisted of a half-sphere inserted into the hollowed rear post of a side chair, secured with a leather thong passing through holes drilled into either side of the post and through the rounded portion of the ball. A metal version was patented by Brother George O. Donnell of Mount Lebanon in 1852.
Tongue-and-groove	A joint usually formed by cutting a groove centrally in the edge of one board with one plane while a matching plane cuts a rabbet on each edge of the other board. The resulting tongue fits into the corresponding groove when the joint is assembled and provides additional glue surface when used on a tabletop. When used on the back of a case piece, the joint is not glued.
Trestle table	A medieval form consisting of a long board supported by a composite leg at each end. The latter consists of a horizontal crosspiece attached to a vertical standard with a mortise-and-tenon joint above an arched foot.
Tripod table	A pedestal table with turned shaft or column and three radiating legs in a variety of forms, including peg, spider, and snake leg.
Trundle bed	A low, moveable bed, often on wheels, that is small enough to be stored beneath another bed when not in use.
Vase-turned	A turning resembling a vase, with an ogee shaped curve. It is the reverse of a baluster form.

Vernacular furniture

Simple but well-constructed furniture, as opposed to high-style, more sophisticated furniture, usually made in urban centers. This term better describes the large quantity of locally made furniture than the more commonly used term *country furniture*.

Worktable

A four-legged table designed for use in numerous trades within the Shaker community, including laundry, tailoring, food preparation, fancy goods, and seed packaging. In some communities, tripod tables also functioned as sewing or work furniture.

Index

NOTE: Illustrations are indicated by page numbers in *italic type*. Individual objects are capitalized, while generic furniture types are lowercased.

Photograph/Illustration Credits

The drawings were created by Timothy D. Rieman especially for this book. Reproduced from *Asher & Adams' Pictorial Album of American Industry,* New York: Asher & Adams, 1876; reprint, New York: Rutledge Press, 1976, pp. 71, 16, 118: pages 69, 70, 71, 72. Blueprint taken from a drawing by E. Ray Pearson, Courtesy Hancock Shaker Village, Pittsfield, Massachusetts: page 174. Paul Rocheleau, photographer: pages 105, 175, 190 above.